W. W. NORTON & DISCOVERY EDUCATION

When you buy *Psychology*, Seventh Edition, by Henry Gleitman, Daniel Reisberg, and James Gross, you get a FREE registration code to online streaming videos from Discovery Education.

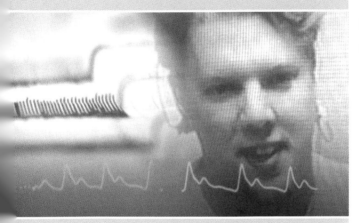

TO ACTIVATE YOUR REGISTRATION CODE:

- Go to wwnorton.com/studyspace and select the **StudySpace** site for *Psychology*, Seventh Edition.

- Select **Discovery Videos** from the menu.

- Click on "Register."

- Enter the registration code printed below. You will be asked to provide an email address. We will send you an initial password. You will be able to change both the email address and the password later.

Discovery Channel and the Discovery Channel logo are trademarks of Discovery Communications, Inc., used under license.

W. W. Norton & Company
500 Fifth Avenue / New York, NY 10110
www.wwnorton.com

WXTB-QKAI

Please visit our technical support Web site at www.wwnorton.com/web/HelpDesk if you have any difficulties or need assistance.

PSYCHOLOGY

SEVENTH EDITION

W · W · NORTON & COMPANY · NEW YORK · LONDON

PSYCHOLOGY

SEVENTH EDITION

HENRY GLEITMAN

DANIEL REISBERG

JAMES GROSS

W. W. Norton & Company has been independent since its founding in 1923, when William Warder Norton and Mary D. Herter Norton first published lectures delivered at the People's Institute, the adult education division of New York City's Cooper Union. The Nortons soon expanded their program beyond the Institute, publishing books by celebrated academics from America and abroad. By mid-century, the two major pillars of Norton's publishing program—trade books and college texts—were firmly established. In the 1950s, the Norton family transferred control of the company to its employees, and today—with a staff of four hundred and a comparable number of trade, college, and professional titles published each year—W. W. Norton & Company stands as the largest and oldest publishing house owned wholly by its employees.

Editor: Jon Durbin
Managing Editor—College: Marian Johnson
Marketing Manager: Ken Barton
Senior Project Editor: Kim Yi
Copy Editors: Alice Vigliani and Abigail Winograd
Editorial Assistant: Rob Haber
Director of Manufacturing—College: Roy Tedoff
Art Director: Antonina Krass
Photo Researcher: Kelly Mitchell
Illustrations: Frank Forney
Composition: TSI Graphics
Manufacturing: Von Hoffmann

Library of Congress Cataloging-in-Publication Data

Gleitman, Henry.
    Psychology/Henry Gleitman, Daniel Reisberg, James Gross.—7th ed.
        p. cm.
    Includes bibliographical references and index.
    ISBN-13: 978-0-393-97768-4
    ISBN-10: 0-393-97768-4
    1. Psychology—Textbooks. I. Reisberg, Daniel. II. Gross, James J., Ph. D. III. Title.

BF121.G58 2007
150—dc22   2006047021

W. W. Norton & Company, Inc., 500 Fifth Avenue, New York, NY 10110
www.wwnorton.com
W. W. Norton & Company Ltd., Castle House, 75/76 Wells Street, London W1T 3QT

1 2 3 4 5 6 7 8 9 0

TO ALL THE PEOPLE WHO HAVE MADE THIS BOOK POSSIBLE—
OUR TEACHERS, OUR COLLEAGUES, OUR FAMILIES, AND OUR STUDENTS.

ABOUT THE AUTHORS

Henry Gleitman is Professor of Psychology and the former chair of the department at the University of Pennsylvania. He is the recipient of the American Psychological Foundation's Distinguished Teaching in Psychology Award (1982) and, from the University of Pennsylvania, the Abrams Award (1988) and the Lindback Award (1977). He has served as President of the APA's Division 1: General Psychology and Division 10: Psychology and the Arts. Most importantly, Professor Gleitman has taught introductory psychology for five decades to over 40,000 students.

Daniel Reisberg, author of the bestselling *Cognition: Exploring the Science of the Mind*, Third Edition (Norton, 2006), is Professor of Psychology and chair of the department at Reed College in Portland, Oregon. Professor Reisberg's research has focused on the nature of mental imagery as well as on people's ability to remember emotionally significant events. He has served on the editorial boards of many of the field's journals, including a recent term as Associate Editor of *Psychological Bulletin*.

James Gross is Associate Professor of Psychology at Stanford University. Professor Gross's research focuses on emotion and emotion regulation processes in healthy and clinical populations. His publications include *The Handbook of Emotion Regulation* (Guilford, 2007), and he has received early career awards from the American Psychological Association, the Western Psychological Association, and the Society for Psychophysiological Research. Professor Gross is also an award-winning teacher, a Bass University Fellow in Undergraduate Education, and the Director of the Stanford Psychology One Teaching Program.

Contents in Brief

PART 1 | FOUNDATIONS 36

PART 2 | KNOWLEDGE AND THOUGHT 192

PART 3 | THE PERSON IN CONTEXT 354

PREFACE

In this text, we will introduce you to the full breadth of psychology—its theories, its evidence, and its methods. We will cover material that addresses long-standing philosophical questions, and also material that is immediately useful in improving our day-to-day lives. We will describe claims that are well established, but we will also highlight the areas of uncertainty, areas where more research is needed.

From one end to the other, psychology is an exciting field, with new ideas and new data emerging at a remarkable pace. This forward progress means that any description of the field—such as the coverage in a textbook—is soon out of date and in need of revision. It is our field's advances, therefore—plus the suggestions offered by students and colleagues who have used this text—that have spurred each of the previous revisions of this text, and they also provide the impetus for this, the seventh edition.

Across all of the editions, though, our main goals for this text have not changed: The field of psychology covers an extraordinary range of topics, and this in turn demands a remarkable diversity of methods and intellectual perspectives. We have therefore done all we can to convey this diversity, so that readers can see the full richness of our field. At the same time, psychology is a coherent intellectual enterprise, with many strands uniting the various types of work that psychologists do and the broad range of issues that psychologists care about. In writing *Psychology*, we have tried to convey this unity, so that readers can understand how the various elements of our field are connected to each other and form a rich, cohesive fabric.

COHESION IN A DIVERSE FIELD

What is it that unites psychology? As we will discuss in Chapter 1, the unity comes in part from the set of questions that are of interest to all psychologists, no matter what specific problem they are working on: Why do we do what we do, and feel what we feel? How did we come to be as we are—either across the millions of years during which humans evolved, or across the few dozen years that constitute our individual lifetimes? How is each of us different from the others around us, and how are we the same? What makes humans different from other species, and how are we like other species? How is each of us influenced by the context in which we live—our immediate social surrounding, and our broader culture?

Psychology is also united by its commitment to science. Some psychologists work in the laboratory; some gather data in the field. Some do studies of existing conditions; some do experiments in which they change conditions in one fashion or another. Some study humans, alone or in groups; others study nonhuman animals. In all cases, though, psychologists are united in having an open-minded but critical attitude; throughout this book, we emphasize how this attitude shapes and strengthens our field, and why it is that psychological data, well established through the methods of science, must be taken seriously.

We should emphasize, though, that this commitment to science does not entail a commitment to a particular set of methods or a particular explanatory framework. Some of psychology's founding figures did propose that our field needed a specific set of methods, so that, for example, Freud and his followers argued that we needed to draw our evidence primarily from the psychoanalyst's case book; the early behaviorists insisted that our clearest data would come from the study of animals in carefully controlled laboratories. In the last half-century, however, psychologists have rejected these claims. We now realize that virtually any topic within psychology can only be understood through diverse perspectives, relying on diverse research strategies. We will see this in Chapter 1, when we consider biological, social, and cultural influences on how, when, and how much people eat. We will see the same theme when we consider sex and romance—again topics shaped by our biology, our social surroundings, our culture, and more. The same theme will emerge when we consider mental illness and discuss how depression, for example, needs to be understood in terms of someone's beliefs, his experiences, his genetic heritage, and his cultural surrounding.

This need for a diversity of methods and frameworks is paralleled by another theme that characterizes modern psychology and thus unites our field—a need to consider multiple factors in our explanations, and, with that, a need to avoid easy dichotomies in thinking about human behavior: Are mental disorders, such as depression or schizophrenia, best thought of as medical problems or mental problems? Are people, at root, really all the same, so that we can meaningfully talk about "human nature," or are people (in different cultures, perhaps, or even within a culture) fundamentally different from each other? Are someone's actions shaped more by who she is, or by factors in her circumstances? When people reach foolish conclusions or do bad things, is the problem in their thinking or in their emotions (so that, somehow, their feelings are pulling their thoughts "off track")? Each of these questions offers a crucial distinction, but, nonetheless, these questions are potentially misleading. That is because, in each question, *both* of the proposals that are offered are correct, and so we need to acknowledge the importance of both poles of each dichotomy. In addition, the two factors named in these dichotomies invariably interact with each other, so that, for example, the way circumstances influence someone depends on who that someone is. Likewise, our thoughts and emotions are not separate forces, each tugging us in one direction or another. Instead, what we think depends heavily on our emotional reactions, and our emotions, in turn, are powerfully guided by our perception and understanding of the world.

In this context, one often-offered dichotomy deserves special attention: Is our behavior shaped more by nature (biology) or nurture (experience)? Here, too, the dichotomy is misleading, because, as we will see, every aspect of our behavior, our feelings, and our thoughts is shaped both by our biology (including the mechanisms within our bodies and our evolutionary past) and by our life experiences. Why does someone have a particular level of intelligence? Why do we find certain people attractive, but not others? How—and how well—do we remember our experiences? In each case, answering these questions will require us to look at the biology of the nervous system, but also to consider how these capacities and behaviors are changed and developed through our day-to-day learning. And here, too, these two influences interact in important ways, so that the way our biological mechanisms operate depends on our experiences, and our experiences are shaped (and, indeed, made possible by) our biology.

Two other themes also link the various elements of our field, and they will arise repeatedly in this text. First, we will see over and over that humans (and other organisms as well) play an enormously active role in shaping their own experience. This is evident in the very earliest stages of perception, in which our sensory systems emphasize some aspects of the input and downplay other aspects. It is evident in our memories, which are heavily shaped by our thoughts and what we have paid attention to. It is evident in the process of child development, in which each child plays a key role in influencing his surroundings, and thus shaping his own experience. It is also evident in the social domain, in which each of us shapes (and is shaped by) the others around us. As we will see again and again, therefore, each of us is, in important ways, the creator of our own world, the creator of our own experiences.

Second, one more theme, evident throughout this book, is the degree to which our thoughts and feelings and actions are shaped by processes outside of our awareness. This will be a crucial theme in our discussion of perception, when we discuss the role of "unconscious inference"; it will be crucial in our discussion of racial prejudice, when we discuss "implicit prejudice"—prejudice that people are unaware they have. The same theme will emerge in our discussion of memory, when we talk about "memory without awareness." Over and over, we will see that our mental and emotional lives are enormously shaped by events going on "backstage," events that can be revealed by careful research but that are utterly invisible in our conscious experience.

These various themes bind together all the corners of psychology, and they also bind together the different topics in this text. In chapter after chapter, we will see psychology's emphasis on science (but its commitment to an eclectic science, with diverse methods). We will repeatedly encounter the need for "multicausal explanations"—explanations in which multiple (and diverse) factors play a role. This will force us to consider both poles of various dichotomies, and it will demand that we not think about these dichotomies in "either/or" terms. We will again and again see evidence for our activity in shaping our own experience, and also the role of unconscious processes. In short, these themes unite our field, and we will highlight them in order to unite our discussion across the many pages of this book.

GENERAL ORGANIZATION

The themes just described allow us to present psychology as an interwoven fabric, and not a mere cataloging of data and hypotheses. In addition, we have done all we can to emphasize the connections within each of our chapters and also between adjacent chapters, so that, in the end, we have tried, throughout the text, to make the book "a good read."

Within each chapter, for example, we consider modern research against the backdrop of major ideas that have provided, and continue to provide, the organizing and unifying framework for contemporary inquiry. Thus, the chapter on the biological roots of behavior showcases Descartes' conception of the organism as a machine;

PART 3: THE PERSON IN CONTEXT

To understand who we are, and why we do what we do, it is important to consider two aspects of the context in which we live: the context provided by life events, as each of us grows from infancy to childhood and then to adulthood, and also the context provided by the other people in our lives. This part of the book examines these two types of context—with two chapters devoted to developmental psychology, and two to social psychology.

Chapter 10 ("Cognitive Development") asks how we gain knowledge and skills across the years of childhood, and then how these skills diminish as we age. The chapter begins with the framework set out many years ago by Jean Piaget, but then it emphasizes more modern approaches to development, including, for the first time in this edition, coverage of dynamic systems theory.

Chapter 11 ("Social Development") has been completely recast for this edition. It now focuses on the processes and continuity that shape a child as she learns about the social world—how to relate to other people, how to be a moral being, and how to express and regulate emotion.

Chapter 12 ("Social Cognition and Emotion") has also been completely recast. It now focuses on how we perceive and understand others and ourselves, how attitudes develop and change over time, and how our emotions influence our behavior. There is also a new section on how we regulate our emotions. Discussions of how culture influences our social behavior are also integrated throughout the chapter, as crucial aspects of our understanding of humans as social beings.

Chapter 13 ("Social Influence and Relationships") also has been substantially reworked in this edition. The chapter now focuses on three major types of social influence (conformity, obedience, and compliance), on how groups influence our thinking and behavior, and on the many types of relationships that make up our social world.

PART 4: INDIVIDUAL DIFFERENCES

This part begins with a chapter on mental testing in general and intelligence testing in particular (Chapter 14) and then continues with a chapter on personality assessment and theory (Chapter 15). It continues by looking at several varieties of psychopathology and asking how they arise (Chapter 16), and concludes by examining various methods of treatment and therapy (Chapter 17).

Chapter 14 ("Intelligence") has been updated in its coverage of the debate over the IQ test's validity, the definition of g, and the genetic roots of IQ. We ask whether it is possible to measure intelligence, and whether our measures are accurate. We also ask whether intelligence is one thing (so that we can speak of people being "smart in general,") or whether intelligence instead involves a set of diverse talents, so that someone might be smart in some ways but not others. Also now covered is work on emotional intelligence, and also stereotype threat, and how this threat may contribute to the observed differences among groups in their IQ scores.

Chapter 15 ("Personality") considers methods of personality assessment and discusses trait theory and social-cognitive theory as theoretical approaches to personality, with particular attention to the trait-situation controversy and to recent attempts to look for biological and genetic bases of personality differences.

Both Chapter 16 ("Psychopathology") and Chapter 17 ("Treatment of Mental Disorders") have been heavily updated to include modern developments. Chapter 16 now has extensive coverage of multicausal models and the biopsychosocial viewpoint. Chapter 17 now contains an extended discussion of evidence-based practice and the current

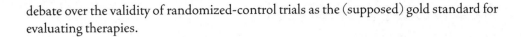

debate over the validity of randomized-control trials as the (supposed) gold standard for evaluating therapies.

THE READER AND THE BOOK

We have, in this Preface, said a great deal about this book's organization—including its structure and its themes. But what about the content itself? It is often said that students in the introductory course want to learn about things that are relevant to their own lives, and, in truth, this seems an entirely sensible view. But it also seems certain that psychology will meet this demand. After all, psychology deals with the nature of human experience and behavior, the hows and whys of what we do, think, and feel. How could an exploration of these topics not be relevant to someone's life? Everyone has perceived, learned, remembered, and forgotten; has been angry and afraid and in love; has given in to group pressure and stood up to it. In short, everyone has experienced most of the phenomena that psychology tries to explain. This being so, psychology cannot fail to be relevant.

But we can easily lose sight of this relevance amid the torrent of facts, theories, and methodological lessons that constitute our field. To keep the relevance in view, therefore, we rely in this text on a liberal use of everyday examples and frequently employ metaphors of one kind or another, providing a succession of bridges between the psychological phenomena we discuss and the reader's own life.

At the same time, though, one can go too far down this path—relying so much on examples and metaphors that the book's main content is lost. In our view, the best shield against this latter danger lies in our respect for the reader: We are convinced that readers (university undergraduates or otherwise) want and deserve a sophisticated treatment of our field, one that conveys the real substance and captures the full range of subtleties and implications. We have therefore tried to ensure throughout that the book is as sophisticated as it is accessible, as deep as it is wide, as intriguing intellectually as it is fun to read.

In this effort, and, indeed, in every aspect of the book, our most important guide has been our own experience as teachers (with a combined total of roughly 100 years in the classroom!). This experience leaves us with no doubt that one of the best ways of learning something is to teach it, because in trying to explain something to others we first have to clarify it for ourselves. This holds for the subject matter of every course we have ever taught, but most especially for the introductory course. Students in an advanced course come at us with tough and searching questions; they want to know about the evidence that bears on a theory of, say, color vision, language acquisition, or the placebo effect, and about how that evidence was obtained. But students in an introductory course ask the toughest questions of all. They ask why anyone would ever want to know about color vision (or language acquisition or the placebo effect) in the first place. And they also ask what any one topic has to do with any other. They ask such questions because they—unlike advanced students—have not yet accepted the premises of the field. They wonder whether the emperor is really wearing any clothes. As a result, they make us ask ourselves again and again what the field of psychology is all about—what the emperor's clothes are really like when you look at them closely.

This edition, as well as its predecessors, reflects our attempts to answer such questions, and to answer them not only to satisfy the students but also to satisfy ourselves.

ACKNOWLEDGMENTS

Finally, there remains the joyful task of thanking the friends and colleagues who helped so greatly in the writing of this book. Some read parts of the manuscript and gave valuable advice and criticism. Others talked to us at length about various issues in the field. We are grateful to them all. The many helpers on the first five editions, and the main areas in which they advised us, are listed first. The names of those who guided us in the production of the two most recent editions follow.

BIOLOGICAL FOUNDATIONS

Elizabeth Adkins-Regan, Cornell University; Norman T. Adler, Yeshiva University; Gregory Ball, Johns Hopkins University; Robert C. Bolles, University of Washington; Brooks Carder; Dorothy Cheney, University of Pennsylvania; John D. Corbit, Brown University; Alan N. Epstein, late of the University of Pennsylvania; Steven Fluharty, University of Pennsylvania; Charles R. Gallistel, University of California, Los Angeles; Harvey J. Grill, University of Pennsylvania; Jerre Levy, University of Chicago; Martha McClintock, University of Chicago; Peter M. Milner, McGill University; Douglas G. Mook, University of Virginia; Allen Parducci, University of California, Los Angeles; Judith Rodin, University of Pennsylvania; Paul Rozin, University of Pennsylvania; Jonathan I. Schull, University of Rochester and Swarthmore College; Robert Seyfarth, University of Pennsylvania; Paul G. Shinkman, University of North Carolina; Peter Shizgall, Concordia University; W. John Smith, University of Pennsylvania; Edward M. Stricker, University of Pittsburgh.

LEARNING

Ruth Colwill, Brown University; Frank Costin, University of Illinois; Richard B. Day, McMaster University; Paula Durlach, McMaster University; Richard C. Gonzales, Bryn Mawr College; Robert Henderson, University of Illinois; Werner Honig, Dalhousie University; Francis W. Irwin, late of the University of Pennsylvania; Nicholas Mackintosh, Cambridge University; Robert Rescorla, University of Pennsylvania; Paul Rozin, University of Pennsylvania; Jonathan I. Schull, University of Rochester and Swarthmore College; Barry Schwartz, Swarthmore College; Richard L. Solomon, late of the University of Pennsylvania; John Staddon, Duke University.

SENSATION AND PERCEPTION

Linda Bartoshuk, Yale University; Michael Gamble, Malaspina College; Bruce Goldstein, University of Pittsburgh; John Henderson, Michigan State University; Julian E. Hochberg, Columbia University; Leo M. Hurvich, University of Pennsylvania; Dorothea Jameson, late of the University of Pennsylvania; R. Duncan Luce, University of California, Irvine; Neil A. MacMillan, Brooklyn College; James L. McClelland, Carnegie Mellon; Jacob Nachmias, University of Pennsylvania; Edward Pugh, University of Pennsylvania; Irwin Rock, late of the University of California, Berkeley; Burton S. Rosner, Oxford University; Robert Steinman, University of Maryland; Denise Varner, University of Washington; Brian Wandell, Stanford University; Jeremy M. Wolfe, Massachussetts Institute of Technology; James L. Zacks, Michigan State University.

COGNITION

Lynn A. Cooper, Columbia University; Robert G. Crowder, Yale University; Kathie Galotti, Carleton College; Lila R. Gleitman, University of Pennsylvania; Douglas Hintzman,

University of Oregon; Francis C. Keil, Cornell University; Deborah Kemler, Swarthmore College; Stephen M. Kosslyn, Harvard University; John Jonides, University of Michigan; Michael McCloskey, Johns Hopkins University; Douglas Medin, University of Illinois; Morris Moscovitch, University of Toronto; Ulric Neisser, Cornell University; Daniel N. Osherson, Massachusetts Institute of Technology; David Premack, Emeritus, University of Pennsylvania; Miriam W. Schustack, University of California, San Diego; Myrna Schwartz, Moss Rehabilitation Hospital; Michael Turvey, University of Connecticut; Rose T. Zacks, Michigan State University.

LANGUAGE

Sharon L. Armstrong, Drake University; Anne Fowler, Bryn Mawr College; John Gilbert, University of British Columbia; Roberta Golinkoff, University of Delaware; Barbara Landau, University of Delaware; Elissa Newport, University of Rochester; Ruth Ostrin, Medical Research Council, Cambridge, England; Ted Suppala, University of Rochester; Kenneth Wexler, Massachusetts Institute of Technology.

SOCIAL PSYCHOLOGY

Emir Andrews, Memorial University of Newfoundland; Solomon E. Asch, late of the University of Pennsylvania; Su Boatright-Horowitz, University of Rhode Island; Joel Cooper, Princeton University; Mary Crawford, West Chester University of Pennsylvania; Phoebe C. Ellsworth, University of Michigan; Frederick J. Evans, Carrier Foundation, Belle Mead, New Jersey; Larry Gross, University of Pennsylvania; Mark Hauser, Harvard University; Michael Lessac; Clark R. McCauley Jr., Bryn Mawr College; Stanley Milgram, late of City College of New York; Martin T. Orne, University of Pennsylvania; Albert Pepitone, University of Pennsylvania; Dennis Regan, Cornell University; Lee Ross, Stanford University; James Russell, University of British Columbia; John Sabini, University of Pennsylvania; Philip R. Shaver, University of California, Davis; R. Lance Shotland, Pennsylvania State University.

DEVELOPMENT

Justin Aronfreed, University of Pennsylvania; Thomas Ayres, Clarkson College of Technology; Renée Baillargeon, University of Illinois; Edwin Boswell, Ardmore, Pennsylvania; Anne L. Brown, University of Illinois; Adele Diamond, Eunice Kennedy Shriver Center, Waltham, Massachusetts; Carol S. Dweck, Columbia University; Margery B. Franklin, Sarah Lawrence College; Rochel Gelman, University of California, Los Angeles; Frederick Gibbons, Iowa State University; Ellen Gleitman, Devon, Pennsylvania; Susan Scanlon Jones, Indiana University; Ed Kako, University of Pennsylvania; Philip J. Kellman, University of California, Los Angeles; Ellen Markman, Stanford University; Elizabeth Spelke, Massachusetts Institute of Technology; Douglas Wallen, Mankato State University; Sheldon White, Harvard University.

INTELLIGENCE

Jonathan Baron, University of Pennsylvania; James F. Crow, University of Wisconsin; Daniel B. Keating, University of Minnesota; Robert Sternberg, Yale University.

PERSONALITY

Hal Bertilson, Saint Joseph's University; Jack Block, Massachusetts Institute of Technology; Nathan Brody, Wesleyan University; Peter Gay, Yale University; Lewis R.

Goldberg, University of Oregon, Eugene; Ruben Gur, University of Pennsylvania; Judith Harackiewicz, Columbia University; John Kihlstrom, University of California, Berkeley; Lester B. Luborsky, University of Pennsylvania; Carl Malmquist, University of Minnesota; James Russell, University of British Columbia; Jerry S. Wiggins, University of British Columbia.

PSYCHOPATHOLOGY

Lyn Y. Abramson, University of Wisconsin; Lauren Alloy, Temple University; Kayla F. Bernheim, Livingston County Counseling Services, Geneseo, New York; John B. Brady, University of Pennsylvania; Gerald C. Davison, University of Southern California; Leonard M. Horowitz, Stanford University; Steven Matthysse, McLean Hospital, Belmont, Massachusetts; Sue Mineka, Northwestern University; Ann James Premack, Somis, California; Rena Repetti, University of California, Los Angeles; Martin E. P. Seligman, University of Pennsylvania; Larry Stein, University of California, Irvine; Hans H. Strupp, Vanderbilt University; Paul L. Wachtel, College of the City University of New York; Ingrid I. Waldron, University of Pennsylvania; Richard Warner, University of Southern California; David R. Williams, University of Pennsylvania; Julius Wishner, late of the University of Pennsylvania; Lisa Zorilla, University of Pennsylvania.

INTELLECTUAL HISTORY

Mark B. Adams, University of Pennsylvania; David DeVries, New York University; Claire E. Gleitman, Ithaca College; Alan C. Kors, University of Pennsylvania; Elisabeth Rozin, Upper Darby, Pennsylvania; John Sabini, University of Pennsylvania; Harris B. Savin, Philadelphia, Pennsylvania.

Other colleagues provided guidance for the sixth edition, and we are grateful for their input: Lori Badura, University of Buffalo; Michael Bailey, Northwestern University; Tara Callaghan, St. Francis Xavier University; Kimberly Cassidy, Bryn Mawr College; Richard Catrambone, Georgia Institute of Technology; Fernanda Ferreira, Michigan State University of Pennsylvania; Vic Ferreira, University of California, San Diego; Don Hoffman, University of California, Irvine; John Hollonquist, University College of the Cariboo; Ken Kotovsky, Carnegie Mellon University; Monica Luciana, University of Minnesota; Al Porterfield, Oberlin College; Michael Renner, West Chester University of Pennsylvania; Leslie Rescorla, Bryn Mawr College; Wendy Rogers, Georgia Institute of Technology; Alex Rothman, University of Minnesota; Avril Thorne, University of California, Santa Cruz; Nancy Woolf, University of California, Los Angeles.

Finally, we are profoundly grateful for the colleagues who advised us for the current edition:

Glen Adams, University of Toronto
Jo-Anne Bachorowski, Vanderbilt University
Jean Burr, Hamilton College
Thomas Capo, University of Maryland
Brian Carpenter, Washington University
Louis Castonquay, Pennsylvania State University
Ted Coons, New York University
Mieke Donk, Vrije Universiteit Amsterdam
Randy Engle, Georgia Tech
Don Ernst, Hillsdale College
Lisa Feldman Barrett, Boston College
Chris Fraley, University of Illinois/Urbana-Champaign
Preston Garraghty, University of Indiana

Caroline Green, University of Aberdeen
Nikki Harre, University of Auckland
Laurie Heatherington, Williams College
Steve Joordens, University of Toronto, Scarborough
Ann Kring, University of California, Berkeley
Alan Lambert, Washington University
Kerri McCarthy, University of Newcastle
Deborah McGann, University of Northumbria
Jesper Mogensen, University of Copenhagen, Amager
Benoit Monin, Stanford University
Peter Monk, Reed College
Al Porterfield, Oberlin College
Matthew Prull, Whitmore College
Dell Rhodes, Reed College
Susan Rivers, Skidmore College
Steve Robbins, Arcadia University
Art Shimamura, University of California, Berkeley
Nichael Siegal, University of Sheffield
Carol Slater, Alma College
Alana Snibbe, Stanford University
Sanjay Srivastava, University of Oregon
James Stringham, University of Georgia
Karl Teigan, University of Oslo
Dick Terry, University of Stirling
Ross Thompson, University of California, Davis
Carlos J. Velez-Blasini, Middlebury College
Jeremy Wolfe, Harvard University

Thanks also to Neil Macmillan, who wrote the original version of "Statistics: The Collection, Organization, and Interpretation of Data," an appendix for *Psychology*, with a fine sense of balance between the twin demands of the subject matter and expositional clarity.

Lila R. Gleitman co-authored Chapter 9, "Language," and we are grateful for her expertise, her clarity, and her humor. She also read virtually every chapter in earlier editions of the book, and the current edition still shows the benefits of her counsel—on the book's substance, its style, and its broadest goals.

Paul Rozin read every chapter of the fourth edition of this book, and his insightful and wide-ranging comments testify to his extraordinary breadth of knowledge and depth of thought, and continue to influence us. He has helped us see many facets of the field in a new way, especially those that involve issues of evolutionary and cultural development.

Further thanks go to the many people at W. W. Norton & Company: Roy Tedoff who skillfully managed the production of the book; Antonina Krass, whose brilliance as a book designer continues to astound us; Frank Forney who executed the fine new drawings and illustrations; Kelly Mitchell and Stephanie Romeo, for leaving no stone unturned in researching new photos for this edition; Neil Hoos, for sensitivity, patience, and good advice in the search for chapter and part opening art; Alice Vigliani and Abigail Winograd for their careful copyediting; Kim Yi for quadruple checking every element of the book, while working diligently with an optimistic spirit to keep the whole project on schedule; Rob Haber, who performed his multifarious duties as editorial assistant with skill and speed; Marian Johnson for steady manuscript supervision; and Denise Shanks who provided invaluable editorial guidance on the ancillary program. Finally, we also thank Ken Barton for his on-going efforts to market successfully the new edition.

We are especially indebted to four indefatigable editors, who, while no longer at Norton, played essential roles in the history of the book. One is Cathy Wick, who provided invaluable advice and continual encouragement, and whose personal contact with many psychology instructors throughout the country was of enormous benefit. The second is Margaret Farley, whose care and skill are evident everywhere and whose patience was unflagging no matter how we taxed her. The third is Jane Carter, a person of superb literary taste and judgement, who combines the skills of a first-rate organizer with those of a fine critic. The fourth is Jaime Marshall, an editor who cared deeply about this text, and whose input reflected both that devotion to our project and his remarkably good taste, and who also played a tireless role as therapist, negotiator, and—when needed—taskmaster. We hope they all know how deeply we appreciated them.

For the most recent edition, we were finally able to work with Jon Durbin from start to finish. We have known Jon for over 15 years now, 12 of which he has spent contributing to this book in various capacities. Jon showed a firm sense of both the book's original purpose and long-term goals and of the evolution of our field and of our readers. Jon is a rare person among college psychology textbook editors; he clearly enjoys and understands our field.

Our final thanks go to Norton's former chairman of the board, Donald Lamm, who was responsible for bringing Henry Gleitman and W. W. Norton together over three decades ago. As Gleitman put it in a previous edition, "Age has not withered nor custom staled his infinite variety. His ideas are brilliant and outrageous as ever; his puns are as bad as ever. And my esteem and affection for him are as great as ever." We all remain greatly indebted to him.

Merion, Pennsylvania
Portland, Oregon
San Francisco, California
July 2006

SUPPLEMENTARY MATERIALS

Psychology, Seventh Edition, comes with a support package that reinforces the book's strengths. The package includes a wide array of student and instructor resources with a focus on research in action.

For Students:

StudySpace—wwnorton.com/studyspace

This innovative online learning tool offers a wealth of resources for study and review. In addition to timelines, vocabulary flashcards, and detailed chapter reviews, the site includes:

- **Diagnostic Quizzes** with smart feedback that allow students to pinpoint strengths and weaknesses
- NEW **Discovery Channel Video Exercises**
- The **Norton Gradebook** feature, which allows students and instructors to track quiz results
- **Interactive Activities and Animations** that clarify difficult psychological concepts
- **Psychology in the News**, a unique section, updated weekly, that gathers relevant news coverage and analysis
- **Psychology in the Arts**, a series of web supplements for every chapter that explore the relationship between psychology and the arts. These join the strong natural-science emphasis throughout the book to help students understand the many links between psychology and the arts.

Study Guide (John Jonides, *University of Michigan*, and Paul Rozin, *University of Pennsylvania*)

Each chapter of this widely used study guide includes learning objectives, programmed exercises, and a self-test. Moreover, for each chapter, the guide provides experiments and observational studies that students can carry out on their own to get firsthand experience with psychology's subject matter.

The Norton Psychology Reader

Gary Marcus, *New York University*
ISBN-10: 0-393-92712-X / ISBN-13: ISBN-10: 978-0-393-92712-X / paper / 375 pages

The Norton Psychology Reader is a diverse collection of edited popular readings to enliven classroom discussion and inform student research. Most of the selections were written in the last decade and are by popular writers like Pinker, Damasio, Gladwell, Angier, and Taylor. The reader is organized to follow the general outline of a typical introductory psychology course. Each reading is approximately ten pages long and is accompanied by a headnote and study questions. Available alone or packaged with *Psychology*, Seventh Edition, this engaging reader highlights some of the exciting ideas in the field today. Contact your local Norton representative for details.

ZAPS: The Norton Psychology Labs

These online labs give students a firm understanding of fundamental psychological concepts by allowing them to take the role of either researcher or participant in diverse experiments and demonstrations. Ideal for introductory courses, *ZAPS* demonstrate the significance of psychological research in a clear, four-part pedagogical structure: introduction, experiment, relevant theory, and further info. This structure helps students understand and retain the fundamental concepts behind each experiment.

A class-results feature allows instructors to collect aggregate *ZAPS* data in real time. *ZAPS* is also integrated with the password-protected Norton Gradebook, where instructors can access student lab results and sort them by section, student name, and date.

ZAPS can be packaged with *Psychology*. Visit **wwnorton.com/zaps** for more information.

Norton Gradebook (wwnorton.com/college/nrl/gradebook)

Students can access the password-protected Gradebook to review their personal results and see how they performed in relation to the class, as well as to all classes using the Gradebook nationally. Registration for the Gradebook is instant and no setup is required.

For Instructors:

The Norton/Discovery Education Psychology DVD (selected by Patrick Carrol, *University of Texas, Austin*). This DVD offers 30 Discovery Education video clips (totaling about 90 minutes) of psychological research being performed. Free to qualified adopters.

Instructor's Website (wwnorton.com/instructors)

The Instructor's Website offers a PDF version of the Instructor's Manual, Lecture PowerPoints with Clicker questions, art from the book in PowerPoint and JPEG formats, a Glossary, and everything you need for WebCT and BlackBoard courses.

Norton Gradebook (wwnorton.com/college/nrl/gradebook)

Norton Gradebook allows instructors and students to store and track online quiz results. Student results from each quiz are uploaded to the password-protected Gradebook, where instructors can access and sort them by section, chapter, book, student name, and date. As mentioned earlier, students can also access the Gradebook to review their personal results. Registration for the Gradebook is instant and no setup is required.

Norton Video Library

A collection of first-rate documentary films focusing on psychological science drawn from the Films for Sciences and Humanities catalog and other fine video collections. Available to qualifying adopters.

Instructor's Manual (Kelly McGonigal, *Stanford University*, Daniel Reisberg, *Reed College*, and Henry and Lila Gleitman, *University of Pennsylvania*)

Carefully revised to correspond to the Seventh Edition, the Instructor's Manual now features advice on integrating *ZAPS*, *The Norton Psychology Reader*, and the Norton/Discovery Channel Psychology DVD in your teaching. This manual also offers specific suggestions for every chapter, including discussion topics, a bibliography, an annotated film and media guide, and classroom demonstrations. Included with the demonstration suggestions are materials for some 30 in-class experiments covering a range of topics, such as the speed of the nervous impulse, perceptual phenomena, reasoning problems, the perception of personality, and gender stereotypes. The demonstrations cover both classic procedures (the Stroop effect) and procedures prominent in more recent studies (the Deese-Roediger-McDermott paradigm for studying memory errors), and also provide powerful evidence for the students that they, too, show the patterns being described in the text (e.g., patterns of perceptual error, or patterns of social judgment). Transparency masters, student worksheets, data summaries, and detailed instructions for the teacher are included. The demonstrations are adapted from those that we and our collaborators, Paul Rozin (of the University of Pennsylvania) and Lila Gleitman, have used in our own teaching.

Test Bank (William Todd Schultz, *Pacific University*)

Revised and expanded for the Seventh Edition, the questions range from factual to conceptual, covering the full breadth of topics in every chapter and the statistics appendix. The Test Bank is available in print format and in easy-to-use ExamView software.

Transparencies of art from the text are available to qualified adopters.

PSYCHOLOGY

SEVENTH EDITION

INTRODUCTION

What is psychology? It is a field often defined as the scientific study of behavior and mental processes. But what does this mean? Psychology is, for a start, concerned with why we do what we do, feel what we feel, and think what we think. It is concerned with what it is that distinguishes humans from other animals, but also with the traits that humans share with other animals. Psychology considers what all humans have in common with each other, but also how each of us differs from the others in our species—in our beliefs, our personalities, and our capabilities. The field is concerned with who each of us is and also how we came to be what and who we are. And psychology is not just concerned with each of us as individuals; it also seeks to understand how we act in groups, including how we perceive each other, treat each other, and feel about each other.

To address all of these issues, psychology needs to include a wide range of topics—including topics that many nonpsychologists don't expect to find within our field! As we will see, some of these topics involve phenomena also studied by biologists; other topics touch on anthropology and sociology; still others provide insights into issues of interest to philosophers, political scientists, computer scientists, or economists. But the simple fact is that we need this diverse coverage if we are to understand the many aspects of our thoughts, actions, and feelings, and, in this text, we will cover all of these points and more.

1.2 *Displays* *(A) Threat display of the male mandrill, a large West African baboon. (B) The human smile.*

These social communications are usually specific to a particular species and have arisen as a consequence of natural selection—the process that is at the heart of biological evolution. They are ways by which individuals inform one another of their status and current intentions. We have just listed communications that serve as mating displays, but other communications serve other functions. Some, for example, are threats ("Back off or else!"; Figure 1.2A). Still others are attempts at appeasement ("Don't hurt me. I mean no harm!").

Do humans rely on such built-in displays? The evidence suggests that we do, and one example is the smile, a response found in all babies, even in those born blind (who could not have learned to smile by imitation). The smile is often considered a biologically rooted signal by which humans tell each other: "Be good to me. I wish you well" (Figure 1.2B).

SOCIAL BEHAVIOR IN HUMANS

In obvious ways, human social interactions—and the signals we give off in the process—are different from those of other animals. One difference is that human interactions are usually more varied than those of other animals. Peacocks have just one way of courting—they spread their tail feathers and hope for the best. Human males and females are more flexible and much more complex, whether in courtship or in any other social interaction. In part, this reflects the fact that much of human social life is based on one person's appraisal of how another will respond to her actions: "If I do this, . . . he will think this, . . . then I will have to do that . . .," and so on. These calculations allow humans to weigh options in selecting their social maneuvers; if one plan fails, they can choose another. Such subtleties are beyond peacocks. If their usual courtship ritual fails, they have no recourse. They will not try to build bowers or buy a dozen roses; all they can do is to fluff their tail feathers again and again.

This description of things makes it sound as if human social behavior is thought-out and sensible—and, in many circumstances, it is. There are other cases, however, in which we seem to act with little thought or reason. This is especially likely when we are in large groups. For example, consider the people who take part in a riot—whether during a political crisis or after a soccer game. The individuals participating in the riot are probably each, on their own, peace-loving, law-abiding, and responsible. But when part of an inflamed group, the individuals are capable of horrible destruction and, in some cases, brutal violence. Why does the crowd act in ways so unlike the individuals that constitute it? For both intellectual and social reasons, this is an important question for psychology.

THE DIVERSITY OF PSYCHOLOGY'S PERSPECTIVES

These various illustrations document the enormous range within the *content* of psychology. But psychology is also diverse in another sense: in the different *approaches* it needs to take. In other words, not only is there diversity (as we have just seen) in *what* psychologists study, there is also diversity in *how* psychologists study the various phenomena of interest to them. Psychology's diverse perspectives are obvious when we consider how the field approaches topics as different from each other as crowd violence and the biological roots of arithmetic. But the need for diverse approaches is evident even when we consider how psychologists approach a single phenomenon. To demonstrate this point, let us focus on just one topic, *eating*.

We eat in order to survive—to gain the nutrients and energy that our bodies need to function. This is true for every human in every culture, just as it is true for every animal. In a real sense, then, eating is required by our biology and, as we will see in a moment, controlled by our biology. But we need to consider far more than biology if we are to understand what, when, and how much each of us eats. This is obvious, for example, in the fact that people in some cultures savor foods that people in another culture find disgusting. It is also obvious when we consider cases in which people choose to eat so little that they put themselves into medical danger, motivated, it would seem, by a bizarre idea of what their bodies should look like. Let's trace these points through, by examining some of the different perspectives we need if we are to understand these, and other aspects, of eating.

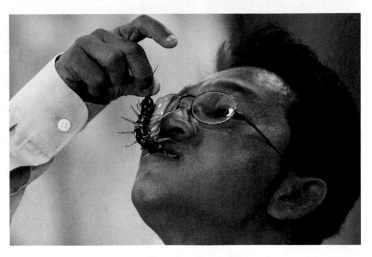

Culture and food preferences   **People in some cultures savor foods that people in another culture find disgusting.**

THE BIOLOGICAL BASIS FOR EATING

The survival of every animal requires an adequate supply of energy and also a number of specific nutrients, all derived from food. An organism insensitive to these needs would have a short life span, and so it is no surprise that all animals have sophisticated internal mechanisms that monitor the availability, within the body, of various nutrients. And, of course, these mechanisms can, when the need arises, cause the animal to seek food.

The success of these mechanisms is evident in the fact that, when food is freely available, animals usually eat just about the right amount to satisfy their needs, while keeping their weight roughly constant. The "right amount" here refers not to the volume of food, but to the number of calories—and hence, the metabolic energy it can provide. This was demonstrated in a study many years ago in which researchers adulterated the caloric levels of rats' food by adding nonnutritive cellulose. The more diluted the food, the more the rats ate, in a quantity that kept the total caloric content roughly constant (Adolph, 1947).

How does the rat (or any other organism) manage this self-regulation? The answer is complex, but one crucial source of information comes from the liver, which controls the major nutrient used for short-term energy: the blood sugar *glucose*. Immediately after a meal, glucose is plentiful. Some is used right away, but much is converted to *glycogen* and various fatty acids, which are stored for later use. When this stored energy is needed, the process is reversed, and the glycogen and fatty acids are turned back into usable glucose.

Thin is beautiful—or is it?   **The Boston organization Boycott Anorexic Marketing is a group of women who believe that the glamorization of ultrathin models in advertising tends to encourage the development of eating disorders in young women. To call attention to this relationship, such groups sometimes annotate the ads of those they see as culprits.**

An obese rat   Photograph of a rat several months after receiving a lesion in the ventromedial region of the hypothalamus.

The liver manages this conversion process and also informs other organs in which direction the metabolic transaction is going, from glucose to glycogen or vice versa. If the balance tips toward storage (supply currently exceeds demand so that the excess can be converted into glycogen), the liver sends a satiety signal and the animal stops eating. If the balance tips toward glucose production (demand exceeds supply so that reserves are being used), the liver sends a hunger signal and the animal eats.

But where do these signals, sent by the liver, end up? Part of the answer lies in a brain structure called the hypothalamus. As we will discuss in Chapter 2, many brain areas play a role in controlling food intake, but one important site is the lateral region of the hypothalamus, which serves as one of the brain areas responsible for the *initiation* of feeding. If this region is damaged, animals do not eat and will starve to death unless force-fed. Another important site is the ventromedial region, which is one of the brain areas that tells the animal when to *stop* feeding. Surgically induced damage here causes rats to eat voraciously, until they finally reach a weight three times as great as before surgery. In humans, tumors in this hypothalamic region have the same effect—leading to enormous obesity (Hoebel & Teitelbaum, 1976; Miller, Bailey, & Stevenson, 1950; Teitelbaum & Epstein, 1962).

CULTURAL INFLUENCES ON EATING

There can be no question that the liver, the hypothalamus, and other biological structures play a crucial role in deciding when and how much we eat. But it is equally clear that other factors are also critical, including the culture in which we live. As one obvious fact, why is it that many Europeans feel hungry for their main meal of the day in the early afternoon, while others on the continent—the French, for example—hunger for their main meal only in the evening? Likewise, why is it that most Americans grow hungry for dinner at 6:00 p.m. or so, while the British are likely to seek food a couple of hours earlier, at tea-time? These questions surely cannot be answered in terms of differences among French, American, or British livers, or geographical variation in how the hypothalamus is wired. Instead, these points remind us, in an obvious way, that the pattern of our feeding is very much shaped by the cultural environment in which we live.

Changing conceptions of the relation between body weight and attractiveness   An underlying cause of many eating disorders in Western women is their belief that being slender is beautiful. And certainly our modern culture does celebrate thinness: compare (A) The Three Graces, painted by the Flemish master Peter Paul Reubens in 1639 with (B) Gisele Bundchen, a contemporary supermodel regarded by many as beautiful, but who is vastly thinner than the women who appeared beautiful at other time periods.

Just as important, culture governs how much we eat. Many of us put considerable effort into controlling our food intake, usually with the aim of achieving a particular body weight or a specific clothing size. And, in most cases, the body weight we aim at is lower than our current weight, leading to enormous popularity for dieting, low-calorie foods, and exercise programs geared toward weight loss. These weight reduction steps are particularly popular with women, who are much more likely than men to believe they are overweight (Fallon & Rozin, 1985).

But what defines the ideal toward which so many people are striving? The answer lies in the cultural setting, and different cultures set quite different standards. The women painted by Rubens, Matisse, and Renoir, for example, were considered beautiful in their day, and all three artists would probably judge today's supermodels to be undernourished and unappealing.

The "ideal" body weight celebrated by each culture is enforced in many ways—including, in modern times, a barrage of media images promoting thinness as an ideal. This makes it immensely difficult for overweight (or even normal weight!) individuals simply to accept themselves as they are. They might understand completely that there is nothing sacred about a society's ideal body weight, but this knowledge is a puny defense against a world of weight-obsessed peers and parents, Hollywood screen idols, and fashion advertisements, all celebrating a level of thinness that is, for many of us, unnatural and unhealthy (for further discussion, see Smith, 1996).

EATING AND THE SOCIAL WORLD

Cultural factors provide a constant backdrop for our thinking, expectations, and perceptions. But we are also influenced by the specific situations that we find ourselves in, and these, too, must be examined if we are to understand when, what, and how much people eat.

As one example, let's note that there are direct social influences on feeding, so that, for example, we are more likely to eat when we are surrounded by others who are eating. The classic demonstration of this comes from an experiment done years ago; it showed that a hen who has had her fill of grain will eagerly resume her meal if joined by other hens that are still hungry (Bayer, 1929). Similar effects can easily be observed with humans.

Social influences are also tied to our earlier comments about people's aspirations (and sometimes unhealthy aspirations) toward thinness. In ways we will discuss later in the book, each of us is powerfully influenced by the people around us, so that how we act—and, indeed, what we think about ourselves—are shaped by how they perceive us and what they expect from us. And the simple fact is that how people perceive us, and what they expect, is shaped by our bodily form—in particular, how heavy or thin we are.

In one study, the research participants were shown pictures of fat and thin women (Bessenoff & Sherman, 2000). Immediately afterwards, the participants were shown strings of letters and had to decide whether each string was a legitimate word or not. Notice that the judgment about the letters did not depend in any way on the pictures, but even so, the judgment was influenced by the pictures: When the participants saw a picture of a fat woman, this automatically triggered thoughts about fat people, and the thoughts tended to be negative. If the letter string that appeared next happened to be a negative label ("ugly"), then the string fit with the mind-set that the picture had created, so that participants were, in effect, already primed for the word. As a result, they were able to respond (signaling that "yes, this is a word in English") relatively quickly. But if, in contrast, the letter string that appeared after a picture of someone fat happened to be a positive label ("clever"), this didn't fit the mind-set that the picture had created, and so participants were not at all primed for the word, and responses were correspondingly slower.

It appears, then, that people automatically associate certain (negative) ideas with being fat, and this will inescapably color their interactions with, and evaluations of, the fat people they meet. As a result, our day-to-day social functioning, and the way other people think about us, will help reinforce our aspirations for a certain body shape or size—and may, in many cases, reinforce aspirations toward a body shape that isn't at all healthy for us.

EATING DISORDERS

Throughout psychology, we must understand those regards in which people are alike, and also the regards in which they differ. Some of the differences among people can be understood as variations within the range that we can consider "healthy" or "normal"; these include differences in personality, in aptitudes, in beliefs, and so on. Other differences, though, unmistakably take us outside of the range that we can call "healthy."

For example, we have mentioned that many people desire to be thinner than they are and take various actions to achieve this goal. But in some cases, the desire to be thin can be so extreme that it leads to eating disorders with serious health implications. One such condition is *anorexia nervosa,* for which the defining feature is a "relentless pursuit of thinness through self-starvation, even unto death" (Bruch, 1973, p. 4; also American Psychiatric Association, 1994). Anorexia afflects up to 1% of young people in Western societies, almost all of them female, although it is a growing concern for young males and for women in their forties and fifties.

Anorexics are intensely and continually preoccupied by the fear of becoming fat. They eat only low-calorie food, if they eat at all. In addition, they may induce vomiting to purge whatever they do eat and may use laxatives to speed weight loss. They often engage in strenuous exercise, sometimes for many hours per day. This regimen leads to drastic weight loss, sometimes reaching body weights that can dwindle to as little as 50% of what could be considered normal. Further symptoms include hyperactivity, sleep disorders, and avoidance of sex.

Anorexia   Our culture powerfully influences our standards of beauty, leading some people to monitor their body dimensions constantly (A), and leading others, such as the fashion model on the right (B), to maintain a body shape that is probably unhealthy.

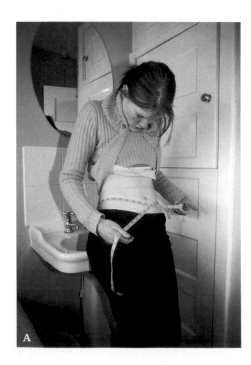

What leads to anorexia nervosa? Some authorities believe that the primary causes are psychological and reflect our culture's modern obsession with slimness (Logue, 1986). In other cases, the main cause may be a fear of sexuality or a defiance of one's parents and a fierce desire to assert some degree of personal autonomy and control (Bruch, 1978). More biologically oriented authors have suggested that a genetic predisposition may be likely. In all cases, though, anorexia nervosa draws attention to the fact that our understanding of feeding and hunger must include efforts toward understanding both the normal and the abnormal, both the ordinary and the extreme.

COGNITIVE CONTROL OVER EATING

One more factor influences our eating, and it is perhaps a surprising factor: It is our memory, because it turns out that whether we eat or not is influenced by what we remember—and, in particular, our memory for what else we have eaten recently.

This point was illustrated by a study of two patients suffering from *clinical amnesia*—a disorder of memory, produced by brain damage, that is so severe that the patient is unable to function in a normal setting and must be cared for in a hospital. The study took place at the normal lunchtime for the patients, and it began with the researcher setting a full meal in front of the patient, with the comment "Here's lunch." When the patient had eaten, the plate was removed, and, after a few minutes of conversation, the patient had completely forgotten that a meal had been delivered and consumed. This is, of course, simply a confirmation of the patient's diagnosis. But then, after a few more minutes, another full meal was provided, with no hint that it was a second lunch and only with the same comment of "Here's lunch" (Rozin, Dow, Moskovitch, & Rajaram, 1998).

One might think that the patients would be able to feel that their bellies were full and would therefore decide not to eat any more. After all, we have all had the experience of turning down a second serving at dinner, or perhaps deciding against dessert, because we already felt full. But things went differently in the experiment, and both of the patients with amnesia readily ate the second full lunch when it was offered—and also, a few minutes later, a third. Apparently, the *memory* that we have just eaten is one of the factors that controls our feeding. When that memory is absent (as it is in these amnesic patients), and so when, in other words, we simply don't remember that we've just eaten, our control over our own eating is impaired, and we are correspondingly more influenced by external cues (such as the sight of available food).

One other aspect of this study with amnesic patients is also important: Immediately after eating their first meal, the patients were asked how hungry they felt, and, despite the fact that they had just eaten, they reported that they were fairly hungry. This is in clear contrast to people with intact memories, who reliably report feeling less hungry right after they finish a meal. It would seem, then, that the feeling of hunger is not just the result of our having an empty stomach (or some other internal cue). Instead, the subjective feeling of hunger is also shaped by memory and, more specifically, by the recollection of how long it has been since our last meal.

THE DEVELOPMENT OF FOOD PREFERENCES

So far we have focused on how, and how much, people eat. But we can also examine *what* people eat—what foods they like, which they dislike, and which they find disgusting. And here, too, we need to consider a wide range of factors. For example, culture obviously plays a role; we mentioned earlier the fact that people in some cultures enjoy foods that seem utterly revolting to people in other cultural settings. Cognitive factors also have an influence. This is clear, for example, in the case of people who decide that

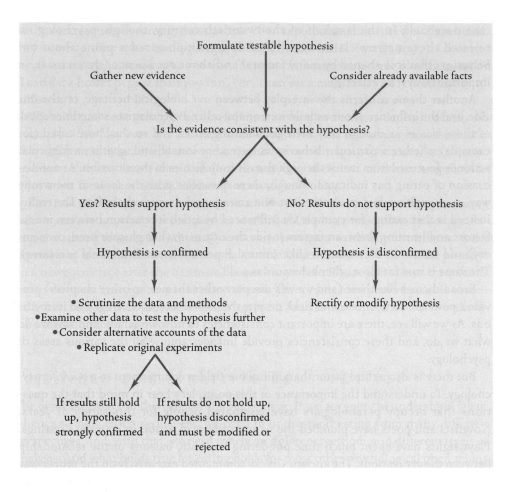

Formulate testable hypothesis

Gather new evidence   Consider already available facts

Is the evidence consistent with the hypothesis?

Yes? Results support hypothesis   No? Results do not support hypothesis

Hypothesis is confirmed   Hypothesis is disconfirmed

• Scrutinize the data and methods   Rectify or modify hypothesis
•Examine other data to test the hypothesis further
• Consider alternative accounts of the data
• Replicate original experiments

If results still hold   If results do not hold up,
up, hypothesis   hypothesis disconfirmed
strongly confirmed   and must be modified or
                             rejected

1.4   The scientific method   *The actual steps a scientist takes in developing and testing a hypothesis vary according to the particulars of the case. However, the basic logic is always the same and follows the flow of steps shown here.*

Science takes a long time   Doing science is a slow process, and any scientific achievement builds on the work of other, earlier scientists.

predictions are then put to the test. Often this means gathering new data, either by observation or by experiment. Sometimes predictions can be checked by using data already available—perhaps the result of some previous study or the data gathered for a country's census. No matter where the data come from, though, there are strict rules regarding how the data should be gathered and evaluated. For example, it is not acceptable for scientists to consider only those facts that favor their hypotheses and ignore those that do not. It is also not acceptable to add new assumptions on the spot to explain away facts that do not support the hypothesis. Scientists should also consider only those facts that were collected in a reliable, objective manner. And, of course, fudging or concocting data for any reason— whether for fame and fortune or because of a sincere belief that claiming a certain result will ultimately benefit society—is anathema to science; indeed, it is fraud and grounds for expulsion from the scientific community.

If the facts are not consistent with the prediction, then the hypothesis is *disconfirmed*. In this case, the scientist is obliged to set the hypothesis aside, turning instead to some new hypothesis. What the scientist cannot do is cling to a hypothesis that has been tested and found wanting.

If, however, the results are consistent with the prediction, then the hypothesis is *confirmed*. Notice, though, that we say *confirmed* and not *proven*. That is, in part, because the process is not yet done: The method used to gather the data and the data themselves must be made accessible to other members of the scientific community; for psychologists, this usually means giving a presentation at a scientific meeting or publishing an article in a professional journal. This allows other investigators to scrutinize the method and data to ensure that the hypothesis was evaluated correctly. It also allows others to *replicate* the study—to run the same procedure with a new group of participants. A successful replication (a repetition of the study that yields the same results) assures us that there was nothing peculiar about the initial study and that the study's results are reliable.

Publication of a study also allows other investigators to run alternative experiments in an attempt to challenge the initial findings. And then, even when the results have survived all of this scrutiny, we still cannot regard the hypothesis as "proven." That is because scientists, in an open-minded fashion, always allow for the possibility that some new facts may become available, challenging the hypothesis or showing that the hypothesis is correct only in certain circumstances. On this basis, no scientific hypothesis, no matter how often it has been confirmed, is regarded as truly "proven." But, of course, if a hypothesis has been confirmed again and again and has withstood a wide range of challenges, scientists regard the hypothesis as extremely likely to be correct, and that they can, at last, confidently build from there.

DESIGNING A PERSUASIVE EXPERIMENT

One important tool that psychologists use (although by no means the only tool) is the testing of hypotheses via an *experiment*. Let's examine how one designs an experiment to make certain that it is scientifically persuasive.

FORMULATING A TESTABLE HYPOTHESIS

As we have already noted, the scientific process requires that we begin with a testable hypothesis—a claim that is specific enough so that we can know with certainty what facts would confirm the hypothesis and what facts would disconfirm it. Said differently, we need to avoid hypotheses that are phrased in a fashion that is so open-ended that virtually any set of circumstances could count as confirmation; for a hypothesis like that, a scientific test is not possible.

For example, imagine an astrologer who, after consulting the stars, announces: "An important public figure will die in the coming year!" (The example is adapted from Gilovich, 1991.) This prediction might make for interesting reading in the supermarket checkout line, but it is too vague to be testable. Who counts as an important public figure? Would the death of Ohio's director of the Department of Motor Vehicles confirm the hypothesis? How about the death of a once-prominent movie star? The astrologer's prediction provides no guidance for making these judgments, and so it is open to debate whether these facts would confirm the prediction or not. As a result, the "test" of this hypothesis depends on each person's opinion about whether, say, the Ohio bureaucrat counts as an "important public figure." And, of course, since the "test" depends on someone's opinion, the test cannot be definitive. This is fine for the astrologer (because, no matter how the facts turn out, he can claim he was correct), but unacceptable for science.

Similarly, consider the superstition that "bad things always come in threes." Chief among the problems here is the unspecified time interval. Three bank robberies occurring within a single week might seem to confirm this claim. But what if two occur within a week and another occurs 6 weeks later? Would this confirm the hypothesis? The hypothesis as stated provides no guidance on this issue, so, again, there is room for debate about whether the data support the hypothesis or not. Therefore this hypothesis, too, cannot be tested in a definitive way: The "test" depends on someone's opinion about what the phrase "come in threes" really means, and a test that depends on opinion is no test at all.

Of course, we can modify these hypotheses to come up with testable predictions. For example, a testable version of "bad things come in threes" would stipulate precisely

"I think you should be more explicit here in step two."

Testable claims *A scientific claim must be specific enough to be testable; vague claims cannot be tested.*

Testable hypotheses? *Astrologers and newspaper tabloids often make predictions about the future, but they usually phrase the predictions in a fashion that is open-ended enough so that the predictions cannot be tested in any rigorous fashion.*

what counts as a "bad thing" and would define "coming in threes." An example might be "If one Oscar-winning actor dies, then two others will die within that same month, followed by a period of at least one month during which no additional Oscar-winning actors die." This prediction is far clumsier than the original platitude, but, unlike the platitude, it is testable!

THE NEED FOR SYSTEMATIC DATA COLLECTION

In addition to a testable hypothesis, science also requires systematically gathered data. To see why, let us consider an example.

Many companies sell audio recordings that contain subliminal messages embedded in background music. The message might be an instruction to give up smoking or to curb overeating, or it might be a message designed to build self-esteem or to overcome shyness. The message is played so softly that you cannot consciously detect it when listening to the recording, but nonetheless it is alleged to provide important benefits—helping you to quit smoking or to stay on a diet, increasing your success in attracting a romantic partner, and so on.

Some *anecdotal evidence*—evidence that has been informally collected and reported—suggests that these subliminal messages can be quite effective. Anecdotal evidence can take many forms: "My next-door neighbor tried the recordings and lost 40 pounds," or "I've heard many people say that the recordings really work." People often offer evidence like this when trying to convince each other in casual conversation, but, in truth, observations like these have no scientific value. Notice, as one problem, that these anecdotes are typically secondhand reports ("It's my neighbor who tried the recordings, but I'm the one talking about it"), and this raises questions about whether the story has grown in the re-telling. Even if the report were firsthand ("I tried the recordings and they just didn't work"), this "evidence" is still of little worth. The key problem here is that the report provides only one person's description of the data, leaving us with no way to determine whether the description is accurate and whether the data were collected in an appropriate manner. (We will say more in later sections about what an "appropriate manner" would be.) As a result, anecdotal evidence is usually dismissed by scientists for roughly the same reasons that hearsay evidence is dismissed by judges in the courtroom.

Note also that anecdotal evidence usually describes just a single case—for example, a case in which subliminal persuasion seemed to have had a powerful effect. In Chapter 8, we will call these "man who" (or "woman who") stories—"I know a man who tried almost everything to give up smoking but finally succeeded by using a subliminal suggestion recording." Even if these cases are well documented, they are still problematic. Perhaps that man is the only one who was helped by such a recording. Or perhaps he would have (at last) given up smoking even without the recording. To evaluate these concerns, scientific studies need data from a broader set of observations.

How can we get beyond these various problems? At the least, we need to collect multiple observations to ensure that we are not being influenced by a small number of (perhaps atypical) cases. It is crucial, though, that this collection of observations be done systematically. For example, imagine that you have heard from several friends who were able to quit smoking after using the subliminal suggestion recordings. Does this mean the recordings are effective? The problem here is that these observations may suffer from a *report bias*—that is, a tendency for some observations to be reported, while other observations are not. After all, a friend who used the subliminal suggestion recordings and kicked the cigarette habit will probably be proud of this achievement and announce it to everyone. But a friend who tried the recordings and made no progress may be embarrassed by this failure and so report it to no one. As a result, you only hear about the successes, and so you end up with a lopsided view of the recordings' effectiveness.

The right method *Scientific data must be collected systematically—and, of course, the method for data collection must be an appropriate one for the specific questions being investigated.*

Report bias can take many forms, but the version just described is referred to as the *file-drawer problem*—a reference to the fact that studies with encouraging results are often published (or, in less formal settings, simply announced), while studies with disappointing results are dumped into a file drawer, never to be seen again. Because of this problem, there is a real chance that data available to you may be biased, with so-called "positive results" being overrepresented in the data and "negative results" underrepresented.

To avoid the file-drawer problem, you would want to collect data from a sample of people who had used the subliminal suggestion recordings *independent of whether the recordings had "worked" for them or not.* One way to do this would be to question everyone who had bought the recordings during, say, a particular week. Assuming that you could do that, how should the data be recorded and evaluated? You might rely on your memory, seeking to recall what these people said about their experiences with the subliminal suggestion recordings. This would give you a general sense of the recordings' success rate, but the accuracy of this approach is far from guaranteed: Memory errors are common, and this could compromise your recall of the evidence (see Chapter 7). Memory can also be selective. In Chapter 8, we will consider a pattern known as *confirmation bias*, which would lead you to recall more of the success stories if you expect the subliminal recordings to be effective or more failures if you expect the opposite.

Of course, report biases and memory errors do not happen all the time, and confirmation bias does not always occur. Let's bear in mind, though, that scientists want to be certain that their data do reflect reality, and, with that, they want to be sure that their hypotheses have been tested in a manner that is not open to challenge. As a result, scientists cannot afford any risk that report bias or memory error has influenced the results, and this is why they regard informal, memory-based reports as inadequate to their needs.

SPECIFYING THE DEPENDENT VARIABLE

To avoid the problems just catalogued, we need to collect all the data (to avoid the file-drawer problem) and to record the data faithfully (so there is no chance of memory error). But how do we do this? Let us pursue this question by continuing with our example. Imagine that an investigator wants to evaluate the subliminal self-help recordings scientifically. She selects for the study a recording advertised as "certain to increase personal attractiveness," and she hypothesizes that the recording will have the advertised effect. How should she run the test? It won't be enough simply to ask people whether the tapes worked for them or not—no matter how carefully and systematically these reports are collected. That is because people who tried the tapes might not be able to assess their own attractiveness, or they might disagree about what "attractiveness" really means. To avoid these concerns, the investigator needs some defensible way of measuring attractiveness; without this measure, she will have no way of knowing whether the subliminal recordings work or not. This attractiveness measure will provide the experiment's *dependent variable*, so called because the investigator wants to find out if this variable depends on some other factor. The *independent variable*, in contrast, is the variable whose effects she wishes to examine. In this example, the independent variable is using or not using the subliminal self-help recording.

Often, a dependent variable is a quantity that can be assessed directly—a percentage of correct answers on some test, or the number of seconds needed to complete a task. But a quality like attractiveness requires a different sort of yardstick. One option is to use a panel of judges who assess the study's participants on the relevant dimension. The investigator could, for example, videotape the participants during an interview and then show the tape to the judges, who would rate each participant's attractiveness on,

Panels of judges   *It is often useful to rely on a panel of judges in making an assessment, and researchers rely on these assessments only if the judges agree with each other to a reasonable extent. This ensures that the judgments are neither arbitrary nor idiosyncratic.*

say, a 7-point scale. Having the judges evaluate all the participants using the same scale would provide a basis for comparison and so for testing the hypothesis.

Why a panel of judges rather than just one judge? For a variable like attractiveness, it is certainly possible that different judges might view things differently, because, after all, what is attractive to one person may not be attractive to someone else. By using a panel of judges and comparing their ratings, the investigator can check on this possibility. If the judges disagree with one another, then no conclusions should be drawn from the study. But if the judges agree to a reasonable extent, then the investigator can be confident that their assessments are not arbitrary or idiosyncratic.

USING A CONTROL GROUP

Using the measurement just described, an investigator might gather data in a straightforward way: She could ask 20 students to listen to the subliminal suggestion recording and then have the judges rate the attractiveness of each student. If all the students turn out to be rated as reasonably attractive, what could she conclude? In truth, she could conclude nothing, because this result would be ambiguous. Perhaps the recordings did help, and that is why the students now seem attractive. But it is also possible that the students were simply attractive to begin with, independent of the recording. With no way to choose between these interpretations, the investigator can draw no conclusions from the study.

To remove this ambiguity, the investigator needs some basis for comparison in her study. There are several ways this comparison might be arranged, but one option is for the investigator to use two separate groups of participants. One group would be interviewed after hearing the recording containing the subliminal message; the other group would be interviewed after hearing something else. Here the first group would be the *experimental group* because it is with these participants that the investigator introduces the *experimental manipulation* (in our example, listening to the recording with the subliminal message). The second group would be the *control group* and would provide a basis for comparison, allowing the investigator to assess the effects of the experimental manipulation.

What should the procedure be for the members of the control group? One possibility is that they would hear no recording at all, whereas those in the experimental group would hear the recording containing the subliminal message embedded in music. If we then find a contrast between the two groups, wouldn't that tell us that the subliminal recordings are effective?

Once again, though, this result would be ambiguous, so that we should draw no conclusions from it. A contrast between the two groups might indicate that the subliminal message has the predicted effect. But, as an alternative, notice that the subliminal message is embedded in music, and so perhaps it is the music, and not the message, that influences the experimental group! (Perhaps the participants find it relaxing to listen to music and thus appear more attractive later on because they are more relaxed.) In this case, it helps to listen to the recording, but the result would be the same if there had been no subliminal message at all.

To avoid this ambiguity, the control group must be matched to the experimental group in all respects except for the experimental manipulation. If the experimental group hears music containing the subliminal message, the control group must hear the identical music without any subliminal message. If, for the experimental group, 10 minutes elapse between hearing the recording and being interviewed, then the same amount of time must elapse for the control group. It is also important for the experimenter to treat the two groups in precisely the same way. If members of the experimental group are told that they are participating in an activity that might increase their attractiveness, then members of the control group should be told the same thing. That

Placebos   *Placebo effects can be quite powerful, and must be controlled for (typically by a double-blind design) to ensure that it is the experimenter's manipulation that is having an effect, and not merely the participants' expectations about that manipulation.*

way, the two groups will have similar expectations about the procedure. This is crucial because participants' expectations can have a profound effect on a study's results. In Chapter 17, for example, we will discuss the role of *placebo effects*—effects caused by someone's beliefs or expectations about a drug or therapy. Numerous studies have shown that placebo effects can be strong. For example, patients report considerable pain relief after taking placebos, be they disguised sugar pills or injections of salt water. Similarly, experimental participants might benefit from listening to the subliminal suggestion recordings simply because they believe the recordings will be effective. In this case, it is their belief about the recording, not the recording itself, that is having an effect.

Another factor to consider is that participants usually want to present themselves in the best possible light, and so they try to perform as well as they can on the experimental task, and they generally try to be helpful to the experimenter. If, therefore, there are cues in the situation signaling that one response is more desirable than another, participants will respond accordingly. Psychologists call such cues the *demand characteristics* of an experiment. Sometimes the demand characteristics derive from the way questions are phrased ("You do brush your teeth every morning, don't you?"). Sometimes they are conveyed more subtly. Perhaps the investigator inadvertently smiles and is more encouraging when the participants answer in one way rather than another, or perhaps the investigator smiles and is encouraging to members of the experimental group but not to members of the control group.

Investigators take several measures to avoid all of these problems. First, they phrase questions and instructions so that no response is identifiable as preferred or "better." In addition, investigators do all they can to make sure that the two groups are treated in the same way (except, of course, for the experimental manipulation). One often-used means of ensuring this identical treatment is a *double-blind design*, in which neither the investigator nor the study's participants know who is in the experimental group and who is in the control group. In our example, the investigator's assistant might be the one who decides which participants hear the recording with the subliminal message and which ones hear the recording without the message. This information would then be revealed to the investigator only after the experiment is completed.

A double-blind design ensures that the participants in the two groups will have identical expectations about the procedure and that the experimenter will treat the two groups of participants in exactly the same way. As a result, any difference observed between the two groups can be attributed to the one factor that distinguishes the groups—the experimental manipulation itself.

A variant on double-blind testing

REMOVING CONFOUNDS

There is an obvious theme running through the last few sections: Over and over, we have noted that a particular procedure, or particular comparison, might yield data that are open to more than one interpretation. Over and over, therefore, we have adjusted the procedure, or added a precaution, to avoid this sort of ambiguity. That way, when we get our result, we won't be stuck in the position of saying that maybe *this* caused the result or maybe *that* caused the result. In other words, we want to set up the experiment from the start so that, if we observe an effect, there will only be one way to explain it. That is the situation in which we will be able to draw conclusions about the impact of our independent variable.

Said differently, it is crucial for investigators to remove from the procedure any *confounds*—uncontrolled factors that could influence the comparison between the experimental and control conditions. For example, if those in the experimental group were interviewed early in the morning and those in the control group were interviewed late in the afternoon, then time of day would be a confound: We would have no way of knowing whether differences between the groups were due to experimental manipulation or to time of day. Similarly, if those in the experimental group received encouraging instructions from the experimenter whereas those in the control group received discouraging or neutral instructions, then the manner of instruction would be a confound.

If confounds are present in an experiment, then the experiment lacks *internal validity*. An experiment is considered internally valid only if it successfully measures what it is intended to measure; for this goal, we must be sure that confounds are removed and that the dependent variable is assessed in an appropriate fashion. Ensuring that the experimental and control groups are treated in exactly the same way (except for the experimental manipulation itself) is therefore a crucial part of ensuring an experiment's validity.

RANDOM ASSIGNMENT

We have now said a lot about the importance of control groups and how the control group should be treated. But one more question is crucial: How do we decide which participants in the study to put in the experimental group, and which in the control group?

The key to this question lies in the fact that the experimental and control groups must be identical to each other at the experiment's start. If the two groups then differ at the end of the experiment, we can obviously conclude that the difference was created during the experiment itself, and this is, of course, what we want.

To see how important this is, imagine a researcher who is extremely curious to know what the data will be from his experimental group, and so he collects data from the participants in this group first. Then, satisfied with this initial round of results, the experimenter proceeds to the next step and collects data from participants in the control group. This sequence of events would actually be unacceptable because it is possible that there is some systematic difference between the "early" and "late" participants, so that the two groups differ from each other for reasons independent of the experiment. For example, imagine that the experimenter recruits participants by telephoning people who have, at some earlier time, indicated a willingness to be in the study. If he calls people with particularly busy lives, he will be able to schedule their participation in the study only with a week or two's lead time; these (busy) participants will therefore end up in the control group. If he calls people with more free time, he will be able to get them into the lab sooner, and so they will end up in the experimental group. As a result, the two groups will be different before the experiment begins— with the control participants being people who are busier and perhaps more harried.

In that case, the experimenter has introduced a confound into the study and will have no way to know whether the results should be explained in terms of the experimental manipulation or in terms of the initial difference between the groups.

As a different example, imagine an experimenter who is concerned that her experimental condition sets a particularly difficult task for participants, while the control condition involves an easier task. If a participant enters the lab looking anxious, the experimenter might decide to spare that participant the burden of the experimental condition, so she will place him in the control group. But this practice, too, would create a confound: If the two groups produce different results, is it because of the experimental manipulation or because the groups differed from the start, with one group filled with anxious people and the other filled with calm people?

How can an experimenter avoid concerns like these? The answer is to assign participants *randomly* to the experimental or control group. Thus, for example, the experimenter might flip a coin just before each participant arrives in the lab and then use the coin toss to determine which group the participant will be in. Given groups of sufficient size, this **random assignment** makes it extremely unlikely that all the busy participants, say, would end up in one group and all the less-harried participants in the other, or that all the anxious participants would end up in one group and all the calm participants in the other. In this fashion, random assignment virtually guarantees that the groups are matched at the outset.

Notice that, even with random assignment, the participants will still vary in how busy or anxious they are; there is no way to avoid that. But the key is that the experimental group will contain both busy and relaxed participants, and so will the control group (and likewise for any other dimension of difference among the participants). Hence the experimental and control groups will start out matched to each other—both containing the same mix of participants—and so, if we find that the groups differ at the *end* of the experiment, it must be because of the experimental manipulations, leaving no doubt about what caused the difference.

WITHIN-SUBJECT COMPARISONS

The psychologist's tool kit includes one other technique for ensuring that the experimental and control groups match each other at the very start of the experiment. This technique involves using the *same people* for the two groups, thus guaranteeing that the two groups are identical in their attitudes, backgrounds, motivations, and so forth. An experiment that uses this technique—comparing participants' behavior in one setting to the same participants' behavior in another setting—is said to use **within-subject comparisons**, in contrast to the other designs we have been considering so far, which use **between-subject comparisons**.

Within-subject comparisons are advantageous—because they remove any doubt about whether the experimental and control groups are matched to each other. But within-subject comparisons also introduce their own complications. Let's say, for example, that participants are first tested in the proper circumstances for the control condition, then tested in the circumstances for the experimental condition. In this case, *test sequence* would be a confound: If we find a difference between the conditions, is it because of the experimental manipulation? Or is it because the experimental condition came second, when, perhaps, participants were more comfortable in the laboratory situation or more familiar with the experiment's requirements?

Fortunately, there are several techniques we can use to remove this sort of confound from a within-subjects design. For example, in the case just sketched, we could run the control condition first for half the participants, and the experimental condition first for the other half. That way, any effects of sequence would have the same impact on both conditions, so they could not influence the comparison between the conditions. With techniques like this, psychologists often can rely on within-subjects designs, and thus they can remove any question about whether the participants in the two conditions are truly comparable to each other!

AN OVERVIEW OF AN EXPERIMENT'S DESIGN

Our discussion has now grown complicated, but the complexities are unavoidable: A scientific experiment will be convincing only if many safeguards ensure that the data provide an unambiguous test of the investigator's hypothesis. The investigator must start with a clear statement of the hypothesis so that there is no question about what evidence would confirm or disconfirm it. The dependent variables must be well defined so that the results of the experiment can be measured accurately and reliably. The data themselves must be unambiguous and faithfully recorded so that there is no issue of misinterpretation or misremembering. In addition, and perhaps most important, we have described the many steps needed to eliminate all influences on the data other than the influence we care about—the independent variable. This includes careful matching of the groups as well as removal of confounds, and only when this is done can we draw any conclusions from the data.

All of these safeguards ensure that our hypothesis receives a definitive test so that, in the end, we know for certain whether the hypothesis is confirmed or not. And, by the way, with these safeguards in place, what about our earlier example? Are recordings containing subliminal suggestions an effective way to give up smoking or to increase your attractiveness? Several carefully designed studies have examined the effects of this type of recording, and the results are clear: Once the investigator controls for placebo effects, the subliminal messages themselves have no effect (Greenwald, Spangenberg, Pratkanis, & Eskenazi, 1991).

EVALUATING EVIDENCE OUTSIDE THE LABORATORY

It is not only scientists who want to draw conclusions from evidence. Jesse always takes a large dose of vitamin C when she feels a cold coming on and has noticed that her colds are usually mild and brief. She concludes that the vitamins help her. Sol reads his horoscope in the paper every morning and believes that the forecast is usually correct: Whenever the stars indicate that he is going to have a day filled with new opportunities, he does! Julie

Evaluating evidence outside the lab **Do vitamins and diet supplements provide a real benefit? Answering everyday questions like this one requires roughly the same logic that scientists use in testing their hypotheses.**

regrets that for months Jacob showed no interest in her. She suspected he was turned off by her shyness, so she tried to act less timid when he was around, and now they are great friends. Julie concludes that her plan was a success. In all of these cases, people are drawing conclusions based on their experiences. Are their conclusions justified?

Notice that Jesse always takes vitamin C. As a result, she has an experimental "group" (herself) that takes vitamin C when coming down with a cold, but no control group (people who take no vitamins). It is possible, therefore, that her colds would be just as mild without the vitamins, and so her conclusion (that the vitamin C helps) is unwarranted.

Sol does have a comparison—days with a certain astrological prediction and days without such a prediction. But there is an obvious confound in this comparison: Sol reads his horoscope in the morning paper, so he starts the day with expectations based on what he has read. Perhaps, therefore, he is more likely to notice his opportunities if the astrological forecast is good. In this case, the pattern Sol has observed indicates only the power of positive expectations and says nothing about the accuracy of astrology.

Julie's comparison (act timid versus act bold) also suffers from a confound. Maybe Jacob is just slow in noticing people, and it wasn't her boldness, but merely the passage of time, that made the difference.

As these examples show, the scientist's concerns also apply to cases of commonsense reasoning. In the laboratory and in life, control groups are needed if we hope to draw convincing conclusions. In both arenas, we need to rule out confounds if we wish to be certain about the factors leading to a particular outcome. In these ways, the logic of scientific investigation turns out to have a use outside of the laboratory, and, by using this logic, we can avoid drawing unwarranted conclusions. As a result, we can end up with a clearer and more accurate understanding of our personal and social environment.

The methods of science can also apply to our daily lives in another fashion: Scientists take evidence very seriously, and they do not continue to maintain beliefs that are contradicted by the evidence. To be sure, scientists are often hesitant about abandoning their theories, and so challenges to their beliefs are scrutinized with care. But when the evidence makes it plain that a particular belief is mistaken, then the belief must be set aside.

The same attitude would serve people well in many of their day-to-day activities. Of course, each of us holds many beliefs that depend on our values, rather than the facts, and these beliefs are not subject to any sort of testing. But many of our beliefs do rest on facts, and, in these cases, it is surely unwise to ignore the facts. As one example, for many years policymakers denied a connection between cigarette smoking and health problems, even though the scientific evidence for the link was utterly compelling; the cost of this refusal to take the evidence seriously is plain. As a different example, there is now overwhelming evidence that human activities are contributing to global warming, but some politicians choose to ignore this evidence, and so they offer policies that are quite likely to damage our planet in irreversible ways. Other examples are easy to find and powerfully remind us of the value of science—both as a source of specific information, and also as a broader model of the steps we need to take (and the honesty we need to display) in order to keep our beliefs in line with the facts. (For other examples of the frequent divergence between public policy and science, see Mooney, 2005.)

Evidence and questions of public policy   In many cases, public policy needs to be guided by the available evidence. The debate over global warming, in contrast, has often been guided more by political convenience than by facts.

OBSERVATIONAL STUDIES

Our focus so far has been on experimental studies—studies in which an investigator randomly assigns participants to one group or another, then deliberately manipulates some variable and observes the results. In many cases, however, experiments are either impossible or inappropriate. For example, an investigator might wish to find out whether short people are treated differently than tall people. In this case, physical stature is the independent variable, but obviously the investigator cannot manipulate it, and he certainly cannot use random assignment to decide which group each participant is in. (Obviously, he can't flip a coin before each participant arrives in the lab and, depending on the coin toss, wave a magic wand that puts the participant into the "short" or "tall" group.) Instead, participants are in one group or another because of who they are prior to the study's start, and it is these preexisting differences that provide the investigator's basis of comparison.

Similarly, an investigator might wish to understand how the thought patterns of depressed patients compare with those of the nondepressed. Here, too, we have an independent variable (presence or absence of depression) that involves differences existing prior to the study's start, and not a variable that can be manipulated by the experimenter.

In other cases, an investigator could in principle manipulate the independent variable but must not do so for ethical reasons. For example, how does physical abuse influence a child's subsequent development? Here an experiment is possible in principle, but it would be ethically repugnant. No investigator would deliberately abuse children to observe the effect, no matter what scientific questions are at stake.

For these reasons, many questions in psychology cannot be pursued through deliberate experimentation. Nonetheless, we can investigate such questions by exploiting differences that already exist. We can compare short individuals with tall ones and in this way ask whether society treats these two groups differently. We can compare depressed individuals with nondepressed. Tragically, many children have been physically abused, and we can compare them with those who have not in order to investigate the effects of this abuse.

In all of these cases, investigators rely on *observational studies* rather than experiments. This terminology reflects the fact that in these studies the investigator observes the key factors, rather than manipulating them directly.

CORRELATIONAL STUDIES AND CAUSAL AMBIGUITY

There are several types of observational studies, but let's focus on *correlational studies* in which the investigator seeks to observe the relationship (or correlation) between two variables—the independent variable (height, level of depression, and so on) and some dependent variable. As in an experiment, the investigator seeks to determine whether the dependent variable depends on the independent variable. Given someone's height, for example, can we predict how that person will be treated by others? Given an individual with depression, can we predict the pattern of his or her thoughts?

In many ways, correlational studies are similar to the experiments we have been discussing. In both, the investigator needs to start out with a clearly stated, testable hypothesis. In both, the dependent variable must be well defined and reliably measured. In both, the data must be systematically recorded and analyzed using appropriate statistics. And in both, we need to be alert to confounds. If the depressed people in our study are observed in their homes and the nondepressed are observed at school, we might wonder whether the observed differences should be attributed to depression or to the setting. If short individuals encounter a warm and encouraging interviewer and tall individuals encounter someone cold and discouraging, the results would be uninterpretable. As in an experiment, care must be taken to isolate the independent variable.

AMBIGUITY ABOUT THE DIRECTION OF CAUSATION

We have listed similarities between correlational studies and experiments, but there is also an important difference: In correlational studies, it is often difficult to determine what is causing what. To illustrate this point, let us say that we do find that the thought patterns of depressed individuals are different from those of people who are not depressed. This might indicate that depression causes a change in how someone thinks. Or it might indicate the opposite—that a tendency to think about the world in certain ways is actually causing the depression.

This sort of ambiguity is a common problem in correlational studies, and it often makes correlations difficult to interpret. In Chapter 16, for example, we will discuss the fact that schizophrenia is more prevalent among the poor than among the wealthy. Is this because poverty increases the risk of schizophrenia? Or is it because of *downward drift*, with schizophrenia leading to poverty? (After all, someone suffering from schizophrenia may have difficulty holding a job, managing expenses, and so on.)

In some cases, this ambiguity can be resolved by collecting further data. For example, it is sometimes possible to determine which factor arrived on the scene first. Was the person depressed before she started showing the distinctive thought patterns, or did she have the distinctive patterns before she became depressed? Here we exploit the simple fact that causes must precede effects, that something cannot be caused by an event that has not yet happened.

Cause and effect   Correlational data are often ambiguous with regard to cause and effect relations. For example, being overweight is correlated with many health problems, but does the excess weight cause the problems? A different possibility is that excess weight is often associated with inactivity, and it may be the inactivity, not the weight, that undermines health. Support for this latter claim comes from studies of people who are overweight but still active, like these sumo wrestlers.

THE THIRD-VARIABLE PROBLEM

It seems, then, that correlational data raise questions about which factor is the *cause* and which is the *effect*—schizophrenia leading to poverty, or poverty leading to schizophrenia; depression leading to a certain style of thinking, or the thinking leading to depression. But there is also another possibility to consider: Perhaps a third factor, different from the dependent and independent variables, is causing both. This is the **third-variable problem**.

For example, students who take Latin in high school often get better-than-average grades in college (Figure 1.5), and one might think that this is a cause-and-effect

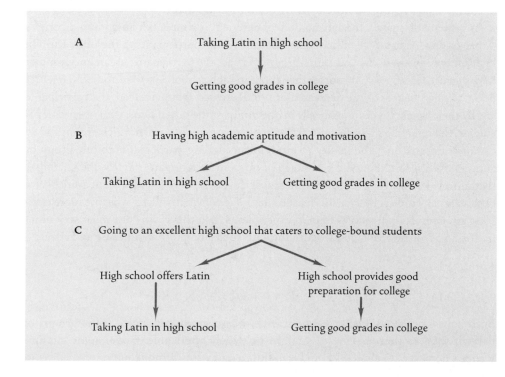

1.5   The third-variable problem   Students who take Latin in high school get better grades on average than do their college classmates who did not take Latin. Is Latin the cause of collegiate success (A) or is there some other underlying factor? (B) Maybe what matters is the type of student who takes Latin. (C) Alternatively, maybe what matters is the type of school where Latin is offered. Any of these possibilities is compatible with the observation that taking Latin and better grades go together; hence the observation is ambiguous, and no conclusions can be drawn from it.

relationship: Background in Latin provides insight into the roots of many modern words, improving someone's vocabulary and thus aiding his college performance. This suggestion certainly seems plausible and is, of course, compatible with the data.

But here is a different way to think about the data: What sorts of students take Latin in high school? In many cases, it is students who are academically ambitious, motivated, and able, and, of course, these same traits are likely to ensure that these students do well in college. Thus, the distinctive characteristics of these students—their motivation and their aptitude—become the "third variable," a variable that leads both to taking Latin and to better college grades. On this basis, taking Latin would be associated with good college grades, but not because one caused the other. Instead, both might be the products of the same underlying cause. (Figure 1.5 also illustrates yet another possibility—with a different notion of what the third variable might be in this example.)

The third-variable problem, like the ambiguity about causal direction, often makes it difficult to interpret correlational data, and this leads psychologists to emphasize that *correlation does not imply causation*. Sometimes correlations do reflect causality: Smoking cigarettes is correlated with, and is a cause of, emphysema, lung cancer, and heart disease. Being depressed is correlated with, and is a cause of, sleep disruption. But often correlations do not imply causes: For example, the number of ashtrays an individual owns is correlated with poor health, but not because owning ashtrays is hazardous. Similarly, there is a correlation between how many tomatoes a family eats in a month and how late the children in the family go to bed. But this is not because tomato eating keeps the kids awake. Instead, tomato eating and late bedtimes are correlated because both are more likely to occur in the summer.

Why is it that these problems (direction of causality and the third-variable problem) are complications for observational studies, but not for experiments? The answer is straightforward: Thanks to random assignment, we know that the groups in an experiment are matched at the outset. This tells us immediately that there is no other dimension on which the comparison groups differ, outside of the experimental conditions, and so there is no third variable to worry about. Likewise, random assignment guarantees that the experimental and control groups start out identical to each other and come to differ only after the experimental manipulation is introduced. This makes it clear which came first (the manipulation) and which second (the contrast between the groups). As a result, there can be no ambiguity about the direction of causation. This is, of course, a powerful advantage of using random assignment.

As we have discussed, though, random assignment is simply not an option in correlational studies. After all, the experimenter doesn't assign participants to the "took Latin in high school" group or the "no Latin" group. Instead, the participants are in one group or the other according to what courses they chose in high school. Likewise, the experimenter doesn't assign people to the depressed or nondepressed group; instead, the participants are, by their own status, automatically in one group or the other. Thus, with observational studies, the researcher has no control over which participants are in which group, and so certainly doesn't have the luxury of randomly assigning participants to one group or another. As a result, the main advantage of random assignment (namely, the guarantee that it provides that the groups are matched at the outset of the study) is not available for observational studies. It is for this reason that issues of what-caused-what are more troubling in observational studies than in experiments, and this is why one must seek other means, in observational studies, of dealing with such ambiguity about cause and effect.

STUDIES OF SINGLE PARTICIPANTS

Both correlational studies and experiments are generally conducted using groups of participants, so that their results might be widely applicable. Under some circumstances, however, psychologists find it useful to study single individuals.

In *case studies*, investigators observe and then describe an individual—one case—in great detail. Historically, case studies have played an enormous role in guiding the development of psychological theory. For example, Sigmund Freud developed most of his ideas based on his detailed observations of individual patients (Chapter 15). Likewise, Jean Piaget's theory was based initially on the study of just three children—his own—although Piaget and his followers went on to test his claims with much larger groups of children (Chapter 10).

In recent years, case studies of patients with brain damage have taught us a great deal about the brain and have illuminated many psychological questions. One example is the case of H.M., whose memory deficits (resulting from neurosurgery for epilepsy) are both severe and intriguing (Chapter 7). H.M. may well be the most studied person in the history of psychology, and the pattern of neuropsychological deficits that he shows has provided numerous insights into how normal memory functions. Similarly, the case of Phineas Gage (Chapter 3) was influential in shaping early conceptions of the functions of the brain's frontal lobes. Other important examples of case studies include those of patients with agnosia (Chapters 3 and 5), aphasia (Chapter 9), and blindsight (Chapter 8).

Case studies obviously differ from other forms of research in the size of the "group" being studied. In most other ways, though, case studies resemble the experiments and observational studies we have already considered. In case studies, just as in any other research, one needs to make sure the hypothesis is testable and that the data are collected in a systematic and appropriate fashion. If the case study involves a dependent variable that is difficult to measure objectively, then, as in any research, one can still rely on a panel of judges to make sure that the assessment is not idiosyncratic or hopelessly variable. In addition, it is also possible to do formal experiments even with a single participant; this is, in effect, the extreme of a within-subjects design (cf. Barlow & Herson, 1984). With these various precautions in place, case studies become a strong and persuasive form of research, and an important part of the psychologist's tool kit.

Jean Piaget and his "test subjects"   **Most of Piaget's initial theorizing was based on careful study of his own three children.**

METHODOLOGICAL ECLECTICISM

We have now discussed three broad categories of research—experiments, observations, and case studies. Each type has its advantages, and none is better than the others.

Case studies are often necessary, such as when an investigator is studying an individual (perhaps someone with brain damage) who truly is unique; in a situation like this, a larger-scale study with multiple participants is just not possible. In many cases, the case study provides insights, or suggests effects, that can then be pursued with a larger group, but, in some cases, the case study is by itself deeply and richly instructive. This is, by the way, not a unique feature of psychology: For example, geologists routinely report "case studies" examining a single volcano; oceanographers study single tsunamis. In both of these disciplines, the investigators understand that they are "merely" describing a single case, but they proceed on the knowledge that the single case can provide powerful insights into more general issues and phenomena.

In a similar vein, experiments are not always possible. As we have mentioned, manipulation of a variable, or random assignment, is sometimes ruled out by practical or logical considerations, and sometimes forbidden by ethical constraints. When random assignment *is* possible, it provides a powerful benefit: It guarantees that the groups being compared were matched to each other at the outset. But this benefit comes with a cost attached: An experiment requires that an investigator be in control of a situation (in order to do the random assignment, or to introduce the experimental manipulation), and that typically requires some artificiality in the setting, in order to gain that control. The artificiality in turn raises questions about whether the experiment accurately mirrors the real-world phenomenon that the investigator hopes to understand.

This concern is usually diminished in observational studies, and this is one of the strengths of these studies. Of course, observational studies can themselves be artificial, limiting the conclusions one can draw. (We pursue this point in the next section.) But observational studies—whether in the laboratory or in the field—at least draw on naturally occurring variations and so avoid much of the artificiality that is often associated with experiments.

How do researchers deal with these various trade-offs, sometimes favoring one method, sometimes favoring another? The decision is made on a case-by-case basis, but, in many circumstances, the preferred path is to use multiple methods, with the hope that the different methods will converge on the same answer. In this way, each of the methods complements the other, and each can remove concerns that might have arisen had just the other methods been used. This provides a powerful means of arguing that our results are not some peculiar byproduct of using this or that research tool, but, instead, are telling us about the world as it truly is.

Generalizing from Research

The previous section draws our attention to one further step that is a crucial part of the overall process of doing scientific research. Once the data are collected and analyzed, and once the hypothesis is evaluated, investigators want to *generalize* from their data. They have studied just a small number of research participants but hope to draw conclusions that apply to a vast number of people. Are such generalizations justified?

The answer to this question depends on the *external validity* of the study in question. A study is considered externally valid if its participants, stimuli, and procedures adequately reflect the world as it is outside of the investigation. To ensure external validity, the study's participants should be representative of the population to which the results are expected to apply, and the study's stimuli should be representative of the stimuli encountered outside of the laboratory.

Selecting Participants

Psychologists usually want their conclusions to apply to a particular *population*: all members of a given group—say, all 3-year-old boys, all patients suffering from schizophrenia, all U.S. voters, and, in some cases, all humans. But, in almost all cases, investigators can study only a *sample*—a subset of the population they are interested in.

Generalizations from a sample are justified only if the sample is representative of the broader population. As an example of how important this is, consider the classic case of a 1936 poll that predicted that Franklin D. Roosevelt would lose the U.S. presidential election. In fact, he won by a landslide. This error was produced by a biased sample: All those polled were selected from telephone directories; but in 1936, having a telephone was much more likely among people of higher socioeconomic status. As a result, the sample was not representative of the voting population as a whole. Since socioeconomic level affected voting preference, the poll was externally invalid, and, as a result, its prediction was false.

Ironically, modern pollsters continue to sample opinion by calling numbers drawn from phone directories, and this may still be a problem: The directories do not include cell-phone numbers, and so the pollsters' samples exclude people whose only phone is a cell phone. How much of a bias this causes in the polls has been a matter of consider-

Sample bias   A 1936 poll predicted incorrectly that Franklin D. Roosevelt (shown here in the car) would lose the presidential election. The poll was misleading because it was based on a biased sample: the people surveyed were all selected from the telephone directory. In 1936, having a telephone was much more likely among people of higher socioeconomic status, so the sample was not representative of the broader population.

able discussion, and this complication may force pollsters to seek new ways of sampling public opinion.

More generally, though, we also need to bear in mind that each individual within the broader population is different from every other individual in that population. Even if we restrict our claims to, say, the population of college students, the fact remains that some students are better readers, some are worse; some are motivated to do well in our study, and some are not. Researchers use several different techniques for dealing with this diversity, but a crucial tool is the use of *random sampling*—a procedure in which every member of the population has an equal chance of being picked for inclusion in the study. With random sampling (especially if the sample is large), the investigators hope to ensure that the diversity in the population is mirrored within their sample, so that the sample really can inform them about the properties of the population at large.

EXTERNAL VALIDITY

External validity obviously depends on the details of an investigation: how the participants were chosen, how the stimuli or responses were selected, and so on. But external validity also depends on what is being investigated. An investigator interested in the

External validity   Can we study college students and draw conclusions about the population at large? For some topics, we can. For example, the visual system in a college student works in just the same way as it does in any other human. In other ways, college students can be rather strange—and not representative of the population as a whole.

visual system can probably study American college students and draw valid conclusions about how vision works in all humans. This is because the properties of the visual system are rooted in the biology of our species, allowing us to generalize widely. This is plainly different from, say, a study of romantic fantasies among college students. In this case, the results might tell us little about the fantasies of anyone other than the particular group studied.

We emphasize, though, that questions of external validity must be resolved through research and not be based on assumptions. For example, one might think that the social behavior of college students would be different from that of nonstudents or of people of other cultures. Yet research indicates that some of the principles of social behavior are shared across cultures (Chapters 12 and 13). This research has obvious implications for how we think about external validity in social psychological studies: In some regards, it is appropriate to generalize from studies of college students; in other regards, it is not.

As a different example, consider the studies of eyewitness memory that ask how well an observer or victim of a crime will recall that crime. Will she remember the sequence of events or the face of the criminal? Many laboratory experiments have tried to address these questions, but do the principles derived from laboratory studies apply to someone who is deeply afraid and involved in an event the way an eyewitness is? This is a matter of ongoing debate. One way to resolve the issue is to combine the laboratory studies with case studies of actual eyewitnesses. The case studies are by themselves sometimes difficult to interpret because (among other concerns) life rarely provides well-designed control groups. But we can nonetheless ask whether the results from a case study are as we would expect, based on the laboratory investigations. If they are, this obviously provides some assurance that our laboratory studies are externally valid. (For examples of the discussion of external validity in eyewitness research, see Kerr & Bray, 2005; Loftus, 1993; Ross, Read, & Toglia, 1994; Shobe & Kihlstrom, 1997.)

Questions about external validity are of great importance in all areas of psychology. Are our categories of mental disorder appropriate only in the context of North America and Western Europe, or do they apply across cultures (Chapter 16)? Does the pattern of cognitive development seen in healthy, middle-class children describe the cognitive development of children from other socioeconomic groups and other nations (Chapter 10)? Does human reasoning inside the laboratory reflect how people reason in their day-to-day lives (Chapter 8)? Each of these questions is the focus of ongoing research.

RESEARCH ETHICS

We are almost finished with our broad tour of how scientific research proceeds. There is, however, one last issue that demands comment. It is not a point concerned with how research is carried out or how findings are interpreted. Instead, it is an issue concerned with what research one can and cannot do.

As we have seen, the external validity of an investigation depends on the relationship between a study and its real-world context. This, in turn, requires us to study real people and real animals. And this fact brings with it a demand that psychological research be conducted ethically, in a fashion that protects the rights and well-being of the research participants.

Psychologists take the issue of research ethics very seriously, and virtually every institution sponsoring research—every college and university, every funding agency—has special committees charged with the task of protecting human and animal participants. In the United States, psychological research with human participants must also follow the guidelines established by the American Psychological Association (1981, 1982), one of psychology's most prominent professional organizations. The U.S. government also has regulations governing how research with human participants must be carried out; institutions that do not follow these regulations are ineligible to receive grants from federal agencies (such as the National Science Foundation, or the National Institutes of Health). Similar guidelines to protect research participants are in place in many other countries. (See Kondro, 1998, for a discussion about protection of research participants in Canada.) And, independent of international boundaries, most of psychology's research journals require that authors make it clear, when publishing research, that the study was done in accordance with all the relevant rules for protecting research participants.

If laboratory animals are used, the investigator must protect their health and ensure the adequacy of their housing and nutrition. Human participants must not only be protected physically; their privacy, autonomy, and dignity must be respected as well. Accordingly, an investigator must guarantee that the data will be collected either anonymously or confidentially and that participants will not be manipulated in a fashion they might find objectionable. Before the study begins, participants must be fully informed about what their task will involve, must be apprised of any risks, and must have the prerogative to leave the study at any time. In short, the investigator must obtain each participant's *informed consent*.

Just as an experiment must begin with informed consent, the experiment must end with a full *debriefing*. If the experiment involved any deception or hidden manipulation, this must be revealed and explained; if the study involved any manipulation of beliefs, mood, or emotion, the investigator must attempt to undo these manipulations. And, ideally, participants should end their participation in a study with some understanding of how it, and their participation in it, may be beneficial to psychological knowledge and human welfare.

It should be noted, though, that these ethical protections—especially the need to obtain informed consent—can produce their own difficulties. In some cases, for example, the validity of a study requires that research participants not be fully informed about the study's design. Participants in a control group, as one illustration, cannot be told they are receiving a placebo, because placebos only work when recipients believe that they are getting "real" medicine. In the same way, subliminal suggestion recordings are alleged to work through unconscious mechanisms. Thus, it may be important that the person hearing the recording not realize exactly what words are spoken on the recording.

Considerations like these indicate that, in many studies, the need for informed consent can conflict with the procedures needed to ensure the study's validity. How can investigators resolve this conflict, ensuring experimental validity while continuing to honor ethical standards? Overall, it seems clear that greater priority must be given to the ethical considerations, and so, in general, investigators must do everything they can to minimize the use of deception, just as they must do everything possible to minimize risks to research participants. If any risk remains, there must be a clear and persuasive argument that the information to be gained from the experiment really does justify that risk. Similarly, if an experiment involves deception, we need to be certain that the scientific value of the experiment justifies that deception.

Decisions about risk or deception are sometimes difficult, and the history of psychology includes many conflicts over the ethical acceptability of psychological studies (e.g., Baumrind, 1964; Hermann & Yoder, 1998; Korn, 1997; Milgram & Murray, 1992; Savin, 1973; Zimbardo, 1973). This is one of the reasons why decisions about ethical acceptability are usually made not by the investigators

WHAT IS IT THAT UNITES PSYCHOLOGY?

- What is it that unites the field of psychology? Part of the answer lies in the *questions* that all psychologists pursue—questions that focus on why we do what we do, feel what we feel, and think what we think. The coherence of psychology is also fostered by the broad themes that apply to many different aspects of our science. One such theme concerns the need to consider the interplay between our biological heritage and the influence of our experiences. Another theme that unites our field is the commitment to the scientific method, a commitment that has allowed psychologists to develop secure and solid claims about the way people act or why they do what they do.

THE SCIENTIFIC METHOD

- Psychologists use the *scientific method* to ensure that their claims are correct and reliable. This requires a *testable hypothesis*, and it also requires that the data be systematically collected and tallied. The scientific method also requires that the *dependent variable* be well defined and easily measured. It is also essential that a study's *experimental group* be matched to the *control group* in all regards except for the experimental manipulation.

- A study is said to be *internally valid* if it successfully evaluates what it purports to evaluate. To ensure validity, all *confounds* must be removed. In an experiment, this usually requires *random assignment* of participants to each group, to ensure that all groups contain the same mix of participants at the start of the experiment.

OBSERVATIONAL STUDIES

- In an *experiment*, the investigator manipulates the *independent variable* and measures the effect of the manipulation on the dependent variable. In an *observational study*, the dependent and independent variables are observed rather than manipulated. One type of observational study is a *correlational study*, in which the investigator seeks to observe the relationship between the dependent and independent variables. Correlational studies often suffer from ambiguity with regard to cause-and-effect relationships, but this ambiguity can generally be resolved by collecting further data or by carrying out a more fine-grained inspection of the evidence.

METHODOLOGICAL ECLECTICISM

- Each of the methods discussed in this chapter has strengths and weaknesses. The best path forward, therefore, is to draw on all of these methods, pooling the advantages of each.

GENERALIZING FROM RESEARCH

- Generalizing from the results of a study is justified only if the study is *externally valid*. However, external validity depends on the particular issue being investigated, and it must be resolved through appropriate research.

RESEARCH ETHICS

- Precautions must be taken to protect the physical well-being of the research participants as well as their privacy, autonomy, and dignity. If these ethical requirements collide with procedures needed to ensure a study's validity, then all risks to the participants must be minimized, and those risks that remain must be fully justified on scientific grounds.

FOUNDATIONS

PART

1

WE ARE, OF COURSE, CREATURES MADE of flesh, blood, and bone, and so all that we do, all that we think or feel, depends on our biological equipment—especially the 3 or 4 pounds of tissue that we call the brain. Therefore, if we are to understand who we are and why we act as we do, we must understand our underlying biology. This in turn requires us to explore several issues: What can psychologists hope to gain from a biological perspective? What can we learn about ourselves by comparing humans to other creatures? What limits might there be on this perspective? And, at the most basic level, how does our biological tissue make possible our thoughts, feelings, and actions?

At the same time, it is no less true that we are creatures massively influenced by experience: We observe. We imitate. We learn. Therefore, if we are to understand human knowledge and all that is shaped by that knowledge, then we must understand the nature of this experience, starting at the most basic level with how we perceive the world around us. How accurate is our perception? How complete and how objective?

These issues—an understanding of the biological basis for our behavior, and an understanding of perception as the root of all experience—can thus be regarded as the foundations on which all psychology must be built, and they are the central issues in the next four chapters.

Evolution and the Biological Roots of Behavior

*H*umans are biological creatures. Each of us has a heart and lungs, just as horses and hyenas do. We have bones and muscles, just like wolves or whales. Our bodies contain trillions of cells, each of which needs glucose and oxygen to survive—just like the cells in your pet dog or the squirrels in the park.

These points of resemblance between humans and other species have been enormously instructive for scientists. We have learned a great deal about physiology, and anatomy, and the effects of various drugs, by studying other animals—simply because their bodies contain many of the same structures, and rely on the same mechanisms, that ours do.

But what about our behavior? Can a biological perspective help us to understand who we are and why we act as we do? In this chapter, we will pursue this broad issue, focusing on topics for which biological influences seem particularly likely, because they are topics directly related to basic needs shared by all animal species. First, all animals need to eat, in order to maintain an adequate supply of nutrients for the body. Hence our initial focus will be on eating, discussing when, how much, and what organisms eat, and we will build directly on our consideration of feeding in Chapter 1. Second, organisms also need to deal with the fact that sometimes threats to their safety arise, and, when they do, the organisms must have a means of responding—by fleeing, or perhaps by fighting back against the threat. Hence we will consider how organisms, humans and others, deal with threat. Third, if a species is to avoid extinction, then it is crucial that individuals reproduce, so that their biological heritage is transmitted to future generations. We will therefore turn to behaviors involving courtship, mate selection, and mating.

Notice, then, that we have a double agenda in this chapter: On the one side, we will be discussing behaviors of considerable importance for us—feeding, fighting, fleeing, and sex. On the other side, we will be exploring in a more general way why psychology needs in part to be a *biological science*, a science that cares deeply about the biological processes that make us who we are. But what exactly does it mean to be a "biological science"? A biological perspective leads us, first, to examine the specific mechanisms within the body that control our behaviors, thoughts, and feelings. What are the underlying processes that make us act as we do? Second, this perspective leads us to ask: How does human behavior compare to that of other species? When we find similarities among species (and we often do), this encourages theorizing cast in terms of the forces in the natural world that apply to all creatures. When we find contrasts (and these, too, will be prominent), this encourages theorizing that emphasizes the role of culture and complex learning in shaping who we are. Third, the biological perspective leads us to ask how various behaviors came to be—how they evolved and what purpose they serve; for this reason, we will spend the early part of the chapter with an explicit focus on evolution.

These various aspects of the biological perspective—a focus on *mechanism*; a *comparative approach*; and an *evolutionary perspective*—will each be useful in our discussion of this chapter's main topics, and perhaps this isn't surprising. After all, the topics are tied to essential survival needs, making it virtually certain that behaviors serving these needs would have been shaped by processes deeply rooted in our biology, and by forces that are likely to apply to other (nonhuman) species as well. Even with these topics, though, we will see that our behavior is also governed by a range of uniquely human factors, hinging on the experiences each of us has during our lifetime. This will lead back to a theme that we encountered in Chapter 1—namely, that it's an error to ask simply whether behavior grows out of biological mechanisms or learning, whether the behavior depends on nature or nurture, and whether it is governed by processes shared with other organisms or processes that are distinctly human. Instead, we need to ask how these pieces all weave together to produce the complex fabric of who we are. ●

THE EVOLUTIONARY ROOTS OF MOTIVATED BEHAVIOR

We humans take pride in being an "advanced" species; sometimes we speak of the contrast between humans and "lower" life-forms. But, in truth, humans have far more in common with other species than most people expect. For example, we often celebrate the human capacity for compassion and caring; we are deeply impressed by acts of heroism or altruism, in which one person sacrifices his or her own well-being for the sake of others. It turns out, though, that many species produce altruistic behaviors, with prairie

Playtime *Humans are, of course, different from other animals, but, even so, we have an enormous amount in common with other species, including an enjoyment of playtime.*

dogs sometimes sacrificing themselves for the sake of their colony, mother grouse putting themselves in danger in order to protect their chicks, and so on. Likewise, certain intellectual traits might initially seem to be uniquely human, but, in fact, they are widely shared across diverse species. For instance, a sense of *curiosity* is found in many species, and so is a sense of *play*.

To be sure, there are capacities that only humans have (e.g., the capacity for language), but there is no question that we share many traits with the other animals that populate this planet. But why should this be? Why is there so much overlap between human thoughts or feelings and the behavior of other, seemingly less-complex creatures? A large part of the answer lies in the basic mechanisms of evolution by natural selection, mechanisms that have shaped who we are no less than they have shaped the characteristics of every other species.

THE BASIC PRINCIPLES OF NATURAL SELECTION

Charles Darwin (1809–1882) published his theory of evolution in 1859 in an extraordinary book, *The Origin of Species*. In the years since then, we have learned a great deal about evolution, and the more recent evidence has provided overwhelming support for Darwin's proposals. Even so, our basic understanding of evolution still follows the outline that Darwin offered more than a century ago.

In Darwin's time, it was well known that the creatures populating the planet were markedly different from those that had been around in earlier epochs; the fossil record made this perfectly clear. But what had produced the change? Darwin's answer to this question was shaped by many factors, including his famous voyage aboard the HMS *Beagle*, a ship surveying the coast of South America for the British Royal Navy. On the *Beagle*, Darwin visited the Galapagos Islands off the coast of Ecuador, and there he was struck by the diversity of creatures on the islands. For example, he noticed that the local finches varied considerably in the sizes and shapes of their beaks. Darwin did not understand the importance of this observation, though, until years later—when he read the works of the English economist Thomas Malthus (1776–1834). Malthus noted that living things reproduce rapidly enough so that populations are always growing—and, crucially, growing more rapidly than the food supply is. As a result, shortages of resources are inevitable,

Charles Darwin (1809–1882)

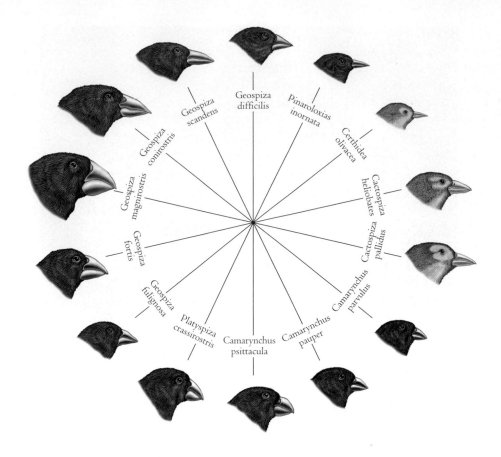

The finches of the Galapagos Islands   The variation among these finch species was an important source of evidence for Darwin's theories about evolution.

with the consequence that some individuals will survive, but others will not. That, for Darwin, was the key.

Which individuals would do well in this competition for resources, and which would do poorly? Darwin realized that the answer was linked to his observations of how individuals in a species differed from each other. A finch with a wide bill might be better able to crack open seeds than its narrow-billed fellow, and so a wide-billed finch would have an advantage in the competition for food. As a result, a wide-billed finch would be more likely to survive and eventually to reproduce. Darwin also knew that offspring tend to resemble their parents in many ways, and so the wide-billed finch was likely to have wide-billed progeny. A narrow-billed finch, on the other hand, might not survive long enough to reproduce, and so obviously would not contribute any narrow-billed descendants to the next generation. The consequence of all this is that the next generation would contain more wide-billed birds, and fewer narrow-billed birds, than the generation before.

Of course, the same logic would also apply to other species. Fish vary in their coloration, and those that are slightly darker in color might be better camouflaged against the river's bottom—and so more likely to escape predators. Again, this would help the darker-colored fish to survive long enough to reproduce, allowing them to leave behind offspring that inherit their coloration. In this way, there would be a greater number of dark-skinned fish in the next generation.

Darwin realized that this process of selection, if repeated generation after generation, could produce large changes in a species. If dark-colored fish are more likely to reproduce in this generation, and the next, and the next after that, then eventually many (and perhaps most) of the surviving fish will be the descendants of dark-colored ancestors and probably will be dark-colored themselves. In this fashion, a survival advantage for a trait will lead, over the generations, to a change in the entire species.

In these examples, variations in a species lead to a reproductive advantage, but not all variations have this effect, and which variations are in fact beneficial depends largely on the organism's environment. If, for example, there are few predators, the light-colored fish may fare as well as the dark ones. Even if the predators are numerous, the dark-colored fish will benefit only if the river bottom is dark. If the river bottom is sandy, then it might be the light-colored fish that are better camouflaged. Notice, then, that we cannot think of evolution as favoring the "better" or "more advanced" organism. Instead, evolution merely favors the organism that is better suited to the environment currently in place—and if the environment changes (e.g., a sandy river bottom becomes muddy), then the pattern of selective advantages will change as well.

GENES

Darwin understood that not all of an adult's traits are passed to its young, but he knew that many traits are passed along. This was evident, for example, in the success that farmers had in developing heavier pigs by methodically breeding larger males and larger females, to obtain larger offspring. It was also evident in the success that horticultural-ists had in developing new strains of plants by carefully arranging cross-pollination. Darwin therefore hypothesized that some mechanism served to pass traits from one generation to the next, and this was, of course, crucial for his theory.

In the years since Darwin, we have learned much more about this particular issue, and it is now clear that this inheritance of characteristics is governed by genes—the complex molecules that provide the basic blueprint for each organism and steer its development from fertilized cell to mature animal or plant. The genes consist of mole-cules of *deoxyribonucleic acid (DNA)*, and the exact structure of each individual's DNA controls the production of other molecules—proteins and enzymes—that serve as the building blocks and regulators of every structure and every process in their bodies.

Genes are stored within the *chromosomes* in the cell's nucleus, with each chromosome holding a thousand or more of these genetic commands. In organisms that reproduce sexually, the chromosomes come in pairs, with one member of each pair contributed by the mother, the other by the father. Scientists have been striving for decades to identify the exact sequence of genes on each chromosome, and they have succeeded for many species. In 2001, they reported a complete draft of the human *genome*—the catalog of all our genes (International Human Genome Sequencing Consortium, 2001; Venter et al., 2001). As a result, we now know that our biological inheritance is specified by a surpris-ingly small number of genes, all contained on the 23 pairs of chromosomes that consti-tute the human genome. According to the draft released in 2001, the human genome contains as few as 30,000 genes; more recent estimates have ranged as high as 70,000 or 80,000 genes. In all cases, though, it is clear that the complexity of our bodies is spec-ified by a smaller number of genes than scientists had anticipated.

In thinking about these counts, however, we must bear in mind that most traits in the body are not specified by single genes. Instead, what matters is the combination of genes (and 70,000 genes allow for a lot of combinations). Thus, species with similar genomes can end up markedly different in their anatomy, physiology, and behavior, because even if the genes are similar, the combinations may not be.

DOMINANT AND RECESSIVE GENES

Scientists are just beginning to understand exactly how genes lead to a particular struc-ture, but we already know a lot about the broad patterns of inheritance. As noted earlier, chromosomes come in pairs, and the same is true for genes: Each gene occupies a spe-cific position within its chromosome, and so, for each gene, there is a partner gene, located at the corresponding position on the other member of the chromosomal pair. The two genes in each pair—one contributed by each parent—may or may not be iden-tical. Consider eye color, which is one of the traits largely controlled by a single gene. If

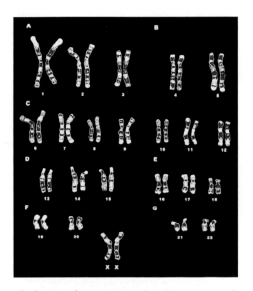

The human chromosome pairs *The 23 pairs of chromosomes provide the full genetic heritage of each human; the 23rd pair (in this case, XX) determines the genetic sex of the individual.*

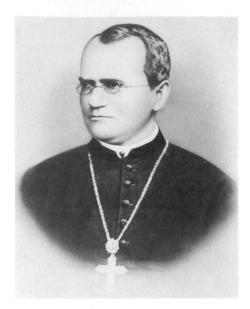

Gregor Mendel (1823–1884)   Much of what we know about inheritance builds on principles uncovered by Mendel.

both genes in the pair specify the same eye color (both coding for blue or both for brown), the eye color will follow suit. But suppose they are different. In humans, the gene for brown eyes is *dominant*; it will exert its effect regardless of whether the other member of the gene pair calls for brown or blue eyes. In contrast, the gene for blue eyes is *recessive*. This recessive gene will lead to blue eyes only if the gene in the corresponding locus of the paired chromosome also calls for blue eyes. Or, to put this differently, the baby's eyes will be blue only if both parents contributed a genetic instruction for blue; if either parent contributed an instruction for brown, the eyes will be brown.

A handful of other human traits are also based on a single gene pair, with one trait dominant and the others recessive. The list includes dark hair, dimples, and thick lips (all dominant), and baldness, red hair, and straight nose (all recessive). A single gene pair also determines red-green color blindness and susceptibility to poison ivy (both recessive).

More often, though, an organism's attributes are influenced by a large number of gene pairs—a pattern known as *polygenic inheritance*. But even for these attributes, the genes come in alternate forms, with one form typically dominant and the other recessive.

GENOTYPE AND PHENOTYPE

Whether a single gene pair or multiple pairs influence a trait, we need to be clear that the genes do not directly control what an organism will look like, or what its anatomical structure will be, or how its physiology will unfold. Instead, what each gene truly controls is just the production of a specific protein or enzyme. These newly produced molecules then regulate specific biochemical processes within the developing organism, and it is these processes that eventually determine the organism's manifest traits.

This sequence—from genes to proteins to complex structures to observable traits—is quite intricate, and such intricacy guarantees that the link between the genetic blueprint—the *genotype*—and the organism's actual characteristics—the *phenotype*—is indirect. Genes guide the biochemical processes that eventually lead to the characteristics we observe in an individual. But other factors also influence the same processes, including factors needed to foster the development (e.g., the presence of nutrients, the temperature, certain forms of stimulation) and also factors that can throw the development off track (e.g., toxins, germs). As a result, genes cannot be understood as rigidly programming the structure of the body; instead, they merely set out the guidelines for its completion. Put differently, the genetic influences on development are profoundly important, but, even so, they are just one of the factors that determine each aspect of the developing organism.

PERSONAL AND GENETIC SURVIVAL

Darwin's theory is usually termed *evolution via natural selection*, on the basis that some individuals are "selected" by the environment as more fit, or better adapted, for their life circumstances. This process is often described with the phrase "survival of the fittest," but, in truth, this phrase is misleading, and our discussion of the genes tells us why. Survival itself is really not what evolution is about. Personal survival matters, of course, but only insofar as that survival leads to reproductive success, so that the organism can pass its genes along to the next generation, so that its offspring, in turn, can pass the genes along to subsequent generations. From an evolutionary perspective, an animal that manages to outlive all its competitors but leaves no offspring has not flourished. An organism whose offspring do not themselves reproduce is also, in evolutionary terms, a failure. Thus, what really matters for evolution is not personal survival, but the survival of one's genes, because it is via one's genes that future generations will be shaped.

This emphasis on genetic survival and, with it, an emphasis on reproductive success, helps us understand some otherwise puzzling facts. For example, the magnificent tail feathers of the peacock are actually cumbersome to drag along and may diminish the peacock's chances of escaping predators. But the tail does contribute to the peacock's evolutionary fitness. This is because the peacock has to compete with his fellow males for access to the peahen; the larger and more magnificent his tail, the more likely it is that she will respond to his sexual overtures. From an evolutionary point of view, the potential gain evidently offsets the possible loss; as a result, long tail feathers eventually flourished in males.

EVOLUTION OF BEHAVIOR

Darwin believed that all of these claims about natural selection applied both to an organism's structural traits (like the finch's bill width, or the fish's coloration) and to its behavioral traits (like being a skilled problem solver, or being a protective parent). Cast in modern terms, his proposal was that if some behavior, mental capacity, or pattern of preferences was shaped by the genes, *and* if that trait produced some reproductive advantage, then natural selection would favor the trait. As a result, the trait would become more common in subsequent generations and might eventually become a trait shared by the entire species.

In fact, a wide range of behaviors have been shaped in this fashion. We know, for example, that many species are extraordinarily skillful in navigating across great distances, even though the individuals in this species have no opportunity to learn or practice this skill; hence the skill must be rooted in their biology. Likewise, the young of many species have an inborn capacity for finding food or building shelters, obviously abilities with great importance for survival. And, similarly, many species have particular behaviors through which they attract mates, and also strong preferences in which mates they choose. These traits, too, have surely been shaped by evolution.

What about human behavior? We know that many aspects of who we are and how we behave are rooted in our genetic heritage. This is reflected, for example, in studies of twins: Identical twins inherit exactly the same genetic pattern, in contrast to other kinds of siblings, who share only half of their genes. And it turns out that this genetic overlap matters: Identical twins usually end up more similar to each other in their personalities and preferences than are other kinds of siblings, even if the twins were raised in separate households thousands of miles apart (Chapters 14 and 15). We also know that many intellectual capacities are influenced by heredity—so that highly verbal parents are likely to have highly verbal children, even if the children have never met the parents and so cannot have learned from their parents in any fashion (Chapter 14).

Do these facts tell us that natural selection favored certain personalities and certain intellectual skills? The answer is actually not clear, because not all traits shaped by the genes are the result of natural selection—some, for example, are just the byproducts of other traits that were, in fact, selected by evolution (cf. Gould & Lewontin, 1979). As a concrete case, genetic influences have been identified for how much TV someone watches (Chapter 15), but surely this does not mean that TV viewing is the product of natural selection. (Natural selection requires many thousands of years to shape a species, and TV has existed for less than a century.) Instead, TV viewing is likely to be a byproduct of other tendencies (such as intraversion) that were shaped by evolution.

To ask whether a trait was shaped by evolution, therefore, we need further evidence. What could the evidence be? Some psychologists believe we should try to reconstruct our ancestors' life pattern during the Pleistocene epoch (a period spanning from roughly 1.8 million years ago until roughly 10,000 years ago), because this was, they claim, the period in which humans evolved into their modern status (e.g., Cosmides & Tooby, 1992; Pinker, 1999a). This was, for example, the period in which

Television viewing and genetics **The tendency to watch a lot of television seems to be inherited—people who have similar genes tend to have similar viewing habits. However, this cannot mean that TV viewing is specifically encoded in the genes. Instead, the tendency to watch TV must be shaped by some other trait that is, in fact, powerfully influenced by the genes.**

Stone Age people learned to use tools, and language first appeared. Moreover, the period since then (the years in which humans became agriculturalists and then developed industrial societies) has been far too short to allow significant evolutionary change. Therefore, with little opportunity for change, our brains now must be pretty similar in their form and function to the brains of our Pleistocene ancestors. Thus, some psychologists claim, if we understand the survival pressures on people during that ancient period, we can figure out how human behaviors must have evolved. (We consider examples of this approach later in the chapter.)

In addition, we can get further insights into the evolution of behavior by comparing human behavior to that of other organisms. If we find parallels between, say, human aggression and aggression in other species, this would bolster the belief that our aggression is fueled (at least in part) by forces that operate on all creatures—including the process of natural selection. Moreover, since other animals are less likely to be affected by cultural factors or complex decision making, finding parallels with other species would suggest a smaller role for these (distinctly human) influences.

As we will see, the outcome of all these inquiries is mixed. In some regards, who we are and how we act are heavily influenced by specific biological mechanisms that are unmistakably the product of natural selection. Hence we cannot ignore evolution in our thinking about psychology. In other regards, though, how we behave is massively influenced by the experiences we have during our lifetimes, and how we reflect on, and react to, these experiences. Hence we will need to place our evolutionary claims within a broader context that acknowledges other influences, and so—here as elsewhere—a biological perspective on our behavior will be important, but it will be just one component of our overall theorizing.

THE ACHIEVEMENT OF HOMEOSTASIS

Even when evolution's influence on us is clear, the influence is indirect. After all, organisms do not eat because they think to themselves, "Natural selection requires that I eat" or because they remember, "My genes demand that I get enough protein." We need to ask, therefore, what the bridge might be between evolutionary pressures, on the one side, and actual behaviors, on the other: What are the immediate triggers for eating (or any other behavior), triggers that were shaped by evolution but that have a direct impact on the animal's moment-by-moment actions? The answer lies in genetically programmed control mechanisms, which can monitor the organism's immediate circumstances and, when necessary, launch an appropriate response.

HOMEOSTASIS

The French physiologist Claude Bernard (1813–1878) was among the first to emphasize that every organism has both an external environment and an internal one. The external environment is obvious, and includes the other creatures that the organism interacts with, and also the physical surrounding—the temperature, the topography, the availability of shelter and water, and so on. But the organism's *internal* environment is just as important, and includes the concentrations of various salts in the body's fluids, the dissolved oxygen levels and pH, and the quantities of nutrients like glucose (the sugar that most organisms use as their body's main fuel).

Moreover, Bernard noted that even with large-scale fluctuations in the outside environment, there is a striking constancy in the organism's internal state. All of the internal conditions we just listed fluctuate only within narrow limits, and, indeed, they must stay within these limits, because otherwise the organism is at severe risk. Apparently, therefore, the organism is capable of making rapid changes in order to compensate for the variations it encounters in the world.

The maintenance of this internal equilibrium involves a process known as *homeostasis* (literally, "equal state"), a process so awe inspiring in its effectiveness that it was said to reflect a "wisdom of the body" (Cannon, 1932). Homeostasis itself involves many mechanisms, including those that rely on *negative feedback*: changes that are produced by an action but which then are used to stop, or even reverse, that action. A simple example is the system that controls most home heating systems. A thermostat turns on the heater when the house's temperature falls below a given setting. The heater then causes the house's temperature to rise, and this rise serves as negative feedback for the thermostat: When the house reaches the preset temperature, the thermostat turns the heater off.

THE AUTONOMIC NERVOUS SYSTEM

Does the body rely on control systems shaped by negative feedback? A clear example showing that it does is provided by thermoregulation, the mechanisms through which organisms control their own body temperatures. All mammals (and all birds) are *endotherms*, organisms that maintain stable body temperatures. (Fish, reptiles, and many other organisms, in contrast, are *ectotherms*; they have a far more variable internal temparture.) Endotherms use many mechanisms to hold their temperatures more or less constant, including large-scale bodily changes such as gaining weight and growing insulating fur in preparation for cold months, and losing both during warm months. They also make behavioral changes (such as moving into an insulated nest when the weather gets cold). But, in addition, endotherms also rely on a number of more immediate changes, controlled by feedback.

Endothermic animals sometimes become too warm and therefore need to lose heat, and sometimes too cold and therefore need to preserve the heat created by their own metabolic activity. These two activities—losing heat and preserving it—are directly controlled by the *autonomic nervous system (ANS)*, a system of nerves, outside of the brain and spinal cord, that send control to the *glands* and to the *smooth muscles* of the internal organs and blood vessels. (The name "smooth muscles" refers to how these muscles look when observed under a microscope; this is in contrast to the skeletal muscles, which look striped.) The ANS has two parts: the *sympathetic branch*, which tends

2.1   The sympathetic and parasympathetic branches of the autonomic nervous system *The parasympathetic system (shown in red) slows the heart and lungs, stimulates digestive functions, permits sexual activity, and so on. In contrast, the sympathetic system (shown in blue) helps ready the organism for emergency: It accelerates the heart and lungs, liberates nutrient fuels for muscular effort, and inhibits digestive and sexual functions. Note that the fibers of the sympathetic system are interconnected through a chain of ganglionic fibers outside of the spinal cord. As a result, sympathetic activation has a diffuse character; any sympathetic excitation tends to affect all of the viscera rather than just some.*

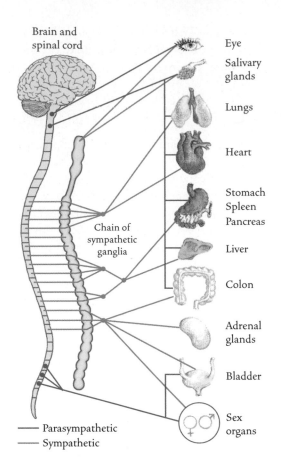

Brain and spinal cord

Chain of sympathetic ganglia

Eye
Salivary glands
Lungs
Heart
Stomach
Spleen
Pancreas
Liver
Colon
Adrenal glands
Bladder
Sex organs

—— Parasympathetic
—— Sympathetic

PARASYMPATHETIC SYSTEM
Constriction of pupil
Secretion of tears
Salivation
Slowing of heart action
Constriction of respiratory passages
Stomach contraction; secretion of digestive fluids
Intestinal peristalsis
Contraction of bladder
Erection

SYMPATHETIC SYSTEM
Dilation of pupil
Inhibition of tear glands
Inhibition of salivation
Acceleration of heart action
Opens respiratory passages
Inhibits stomach contractions and digestive secretion
Inhibits intestinal peristalsis
Relaxes bladder
Inhibits erection

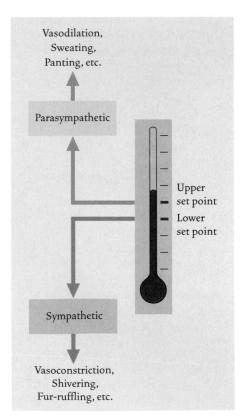

Vasodilation, Sweating, Panting, etc.

Parasympathetic

Upper set point
Lower set point

Sympathetic

Vasoconstriction, Shivering, Fur-ruffling, etc.

2.2   Reflexive temperature regulation in mammals *When the temperature deviates from an internal set point, various reflexive reactions occur to restore the temperature.*

to "rev up" bodily activities in preparation for vigorous action, and the ***parasympathetic branch***, which tends to restore the body's internal activities to normal after the action has been completed (Figure 2.1).

These divisions of the ANS act reciprocally, and so excitation of the sympathetic branch leads to an increased heart rate, while excitation of the parasympathetic branch leads to cardiac slowing. Sympathetic activation produces a slowing down of peristalsis (rhythmic contractions of the intestines) so that we're not using energy for digesting when we're on the run; parasympathetic activation does the opposite—it speeds up peristalsis.

How does this help control temperature? When the body's internal temperature gets too high, this causes activation of the parasympathetic branch of the nervous system, which triggers a series of changes, including sweating (in humans) and panting (in dogs), both of which produce heat loss by evaporation, and also ***vasodilation***, a widening of the skin's capillaries. Vasodilation sends warm blood to the body's surface and results in heat loss by radiation. As the body cools, though, the triggers for these actions are no longer present, so sweating and vasodilation cease—and there is the role for negative feedback (Figure 2.2).

The opposite pattern comes into play when the animal's internal temperature drops too low. Here the sympathetic branch acts to conserve heat: Sweating and panting stop, and ***vasoconstriction*** occurs—a contraction of the capillaries that squeezes blood away from the cold periphery and keeps it instead in the body's warmer core.

What governs the ANS itself? Said differently, where is the body's (version of a) thermostat? A crucial brain region is the ***hypothalamus***, located at the base of the ***forebrain*** (Figure 2.3). This brain structure is only about the size of a pea, but it contains over 20 clusters of neurons that regulate many of the body's internal systems. Among its other functions, the hypothalamus appears to contain a control mechanism that detects

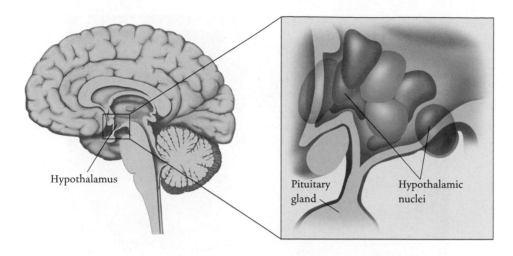

2.3 *The hypothalamus*

when the body is too cold or too hot. This was shown many years ago in an experiment in which researchers implanted an electrode in the anterior hypothalamus of cats. When the electrode was heated gently, the cats panted and vasodilated as though they were too hot and needed to cool themselves, even though their body temperature was well below normal (Magoun, Harrison, Brobeck, & Ranson, 1938).

EATING

Temperature regulation provides a clear example of homeostatic control, and it also provides an example of both the ways in which humans are like other creatures and the ways in which we are different: Humans sweat and vasodilate when they are hot, just like most other mammals, and these actions are controlled by our autonomic nervous system, just as they are in many other creatures. But humans—unlike most species— also have a set of more sophisticated options for maintaining their body temperature: We can, for example, check the weather forecast and adjust our clothing accordingly. Thus, unmistakably, we are shaped by a mix of forces rooted in natural selection and forces rooted in our learning and culture.

What about other motives, like hunger? As we saw in Chapter 1, a broad set of factors governs when and how much we eat—including cultural factors, and social, and cognitive. Is it still useful, therefore, to think of eating in terms of the underlying homeostatic mechanisms, mechanisms shaped by evolution and that we share with other species? Concretely, is there an "appestat" that controls appetite and turns appropriate actions on and off to govern the intake of nutrients, the same way a thermostat controls the body's temperature? The answer turns out to be yes, but only within the context of a complicated, multipart control system.

SET POINTS

Through the process of digestion, nutrients are extracted from food and then converted into energy that supplies body heat, enables the muscles to contract, and, in general, supports all of our life functions. Animals with big brains also devote considerable energy—up to 20% of their total expenditure—to the maintenance of cell activity in the brain.

As we described in Chapter 1, animals seem to take in just the right amount of food to meet their various needs—consuming just the proper number of calories to maintain their functioning and keep their body weight more or less constant (pp. 7–8). If

Peasant Wedding Feast **Painting
by Peter Brueghel the Elder, 1568.**

animals are temporarily deprived of food, they usually eat more later on, to return their bodies to the original weight "set point." If they are force-fed extra food, they later on eat *less*, again returning to the set point. In these ways, animals do act as if they have an internal "appestat," maintaining a relatively steady weight, just as the body's thermostat maintains a relatively constant temperature.

Similar claims apply to humans, with the data indicating that each of us seems to have our own set point—a target weight that our bodies work homeostatically to maintain. These set points are probably genetically determined (Foch & McClearn, 1980), and they help explain why some people end up heavier than others even if they eat no more and exercise no less than their slender neighbors. Evidence for these set points comes from many sources, including the fact that people who go on crash diets return rapidly to their starting weight as soon as they go off their diets. Moreover, dieters do not lose nearly as much weight as we might expect based on their reduced caloric intake. This is probably because the body actually compensates for the caloric loss by reducing its metabolic rate (Guesbeck et al., 2001). In essence, the body gets less food but responds by burning less, defending the already-established set point. The consequence, of course, is that the decreased eating does not lead to the hoped-for weight loss.

THE ROLE OF THE LIVER

What mechanisms serve to maintain someone's body weight at the appropriate set point? The answer has several parts, including (as we've just suggested) some flexibility in each person's metabolic rate. But, of course, a crucial part of the story involves the intake of food, and so we need to ask: What makes an organism eat? What makes the organism feel hungry? How do organisms know when to stop eating? The answers to these questions involve a number of internal signals, including signals that reflect the availability of glucose (again: the sugar that serves as the body's main fuel) in the blood.

As we described in Chapter 1, mechanisms in the liver maintain a roughly constant level of glucose in the bloodstream, and so, if glucose levels increase (as they would right after a meal), much of it is converted to glyogen and fatty acids, and stored for later use. Conversely, if glucose levels start to decrease, then the process is reversed, and glycogen and fatty acids are turned back into glucose.

Given its central role in this process, it is not surprising that some of the control of feeding comes from the liver itself. When cells within the liver detect that excess glucose is available and being converted to glycogen, the liver sends a signal that causes the animal to stop eating (Figure 2.4). When the cells detect that the process is running the other way (so that glycogen is being converted to glucose), the liver sends a hunger signal and the animal eats (Friedman & Stricker, 1976; Russek, 1971).

Notice, though, that this regulatory system must deal with a considerable time lag. Imagine that the liver waited until glucose supplies were low and only then gave the signal to start eating. Since it often takes time to locate food, ingest it, and then digest it, hours might elapse between the moment at which the liver sends a "Need glucose!" signal and the time that the glucose finally arrives. Nutrient supplies would be exhausted, and the animal could die. To avert this calamity, the liver anticipates the body's needs so that the nutrient supplies are replenished well before they are needed.

How does the liver manage to do this? When an organism has not eaten for a while, the level of glucose in the blood begins to drop. Before the level drops too far, the liver takes action, drawing some glycogen out of storage and converting it to glucose. As a result, the blood glucose level bounces back to normal. The result of this sequence of events is an easily identifiable pattern—a gradual drop in blood glucose, usually lasting many minutes, followed by a quick rise, resulting from the liver's compensatory action.

This slow-drop/quick-rise pattern does not indicate that the energy account is empty; it just means that the organism is drawing on its reserves, making it a good time to make a deposit. When this blood glucose pattern occurs in rats, the animals start to eat (Campfield & Smith, 1990a, b). When it occurs in humans, they say they are hungry and want something to eat (Campfield & Rosenbaum, 1992).

OTHER CONTROL SIGNALS FOR FEEDING

The liver, although important, is only one component in regulating food intake. The hypothalamus also contains cells that are sensitive to glucose levels in the blood. Evidence for such **glucoreceptors** comes from studies in which researchers injected the hypothalamus with a chemical that made its cells insensitive to glucose. The result was ravenous eating. This treatment presumably silenced the glucoreceptors; their silence was then interpreted by other brain mechanisms as indicating a fuel deficiency, which in turn led to feeding (Miselis & Epstein, 1970).

Other signals come from the stomach and the duodenum, the first part of the small intestine. The stomach walls, for example, contain receptors sensitive to the nutrients dissolved in the digestive juices, and these receptors can signal the brain that nutrient supplies are on their way; and the result is that the organism stops eating (Deutsch, Puerto, & Wang, 1978). Note, though, that it is the *nutrients*, and not just the presence of bulk, that launches this signal. Thus, animals do not eat until they are full; they eat until they have received the nutrients they need.

Still other signals come from the fatty tissues themselves. To understand the importance of these signals, bear in mind that animals do not eat just for the moment. That is because they cannot be sure that food will be available the next time they need energy, and so they must eat enough both to satisfy their current needs and to create a store of potential nutrients for later. This long-term store is provided by the fat, or *adipose cells*, distributed throughout their body. These cells absorb the fatty acids created by the liver and swell in the process. When the animal's glycogen supplies are exhausted, it must turn to these longer-term reserves. Fatty acids are then drained from the adipose cells into the bloodstream and converted into glucose.

Adipose tissue used to be regarded only as a kind of inert storage, but we now know that it plays a major role in governing hunger. Fat cells, when full, secrete the chemical **leptin** into the bloodstream, where it is sensed by receptors in several places in the brain, including the hypothalamus (Bouret, Draper, & Simerly, 2004; Maffei et al., 1995; McGregor et al., 1996; Pinto et al., 2004). Leptin seems to provide a signal

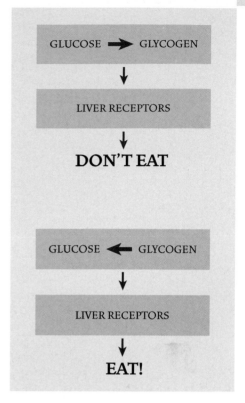

2.4   The relation between the glucose-glycogen balance in the liver and eating.

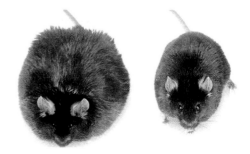

The importance of leptin   Cells in the adipose tissue, when full, secrete the chemical leptin, signaling that there is plenty of fat in storage and no need to add more. The mouse shown on the left is deficient in leptin, and so its brain never receives this feedback signal from the adipose tissue. As a result, the animal eats and eats, with the result shown in the photo.

indicating that there is plenty of fat in storage and no need to add more, and it may be one of the most important factors in governing an organism's food intake over the long term. Leptin appears to work by inhibiting the actions of several other neurochemicals, such as *neuropeptide Y (NPY)*, manufactured in the hypothalamus and the gut. NPY itself turns out to be a powerful appetite stimulant (Gibbs, 1996; Stanley, Magdalin, & Leibowitz, 1989), so leptin secretion seems to be the negative feedback, produced by fat cells already in the body, holding NPY in check.

WHY SO MANY SIGNALS?

We have acknowledged a broad set of signals controlling when an organism starts eating and when it stops, signals from the liver and from glucoreceptors in the brain, signals from the stomach and the duodenum and from the adipose tissue. And, in truth, other signals should be added to this list, including, of course, the sensory qualities of the food itself. Thus, when we see a delicious-looking pastry or smell hot, fresh popcorn, these sensory cues can make us feel hungry and cause us to eat even if we are experiencing no caloric need.

Why do we need so many cues? Why didn't evolution just find one way for organisms to monitor their nutritional state, and let that mechanism control all? Part of the answer lies in the safety provided by backup systems—so that, if one system fails for some reason, the organism is still protected. And part of the answer lies in the fact that different signals monitor different aspects of our nutritional needs—some (such as leptin) keeping tabs on our longer-term needs, and others (cues from the stomach) providing an index of our more immediate status and allowing us to deal with hour-by-hour variations in our energy requirements.

Let us also note that the various cues play different roles within the overall control of feeding. Some cues, for example, directly signal the availability of food in the environment; this is true, of course, for the sensory cues of the food itself. These cues, therefore, can be used to trigger the actual behaviors needed for feeding—reaching out to grab the slice of pizza; picking up the fork to commence eating dinner. Other cues play their main role in creating a motivational state for the organism, so that, broadly put, these cues lead the organism to feel hungry, so that it is motivated to go out and seek food. Finally, some cues *potentiate* other cues—that is, they make the other cues more salient and more persuasive. In one study, for example, researchers recorded activity levels in cells in a waking monkey's hypothalamus (Mora, Rolls, & Burton, 1976; also Rolls, 1978). Those cells were activated when the animal was shown a peanut or banana, but only when the animal was hungry. In this fashion, the cues reflecting the animal's internal state did not directly influence its behavior. Instead, these cues potentiated the sensory cues, so that the animal would be more likely to detect (and respond to) the immediate availability of food when, in fact, it was in need of nutrients.

HYPOTHALAMIC CONTROL CENTERS

We have now talked about many cues that signal an organism's nutritional needs, but what mechanism detects, and responds to, these cues? For many years, the best candidate was the hypothalamus. We have already mentioned that the hypothalamus does its own monitoring of blood sugar levels, but, in addition, the hypothalamus has been proposed as the receiving station for the body's other eating-related cues, so that the hypothalamus becomes, in effect, the main control center for feeding. Specifically, the *dual-center theory* proposed that one part of the hypothalamus—the lateral region—served as the "go" center for eating, while a different part—the ventromedial region—served as the "stop" center.

We considered some of the evidence for this view in Chapter 1. Let us now add, however, that subsequent research has shown that the mechanisms described in this theory are only part of the story of how feeding is controlled. For example, lesions of the ventromedial hypothalamus (the supposed "stop" center) have been found not just to increase appetite (because the "stop" center is no longer functioning), but also to increase the rate of fat storage (Stricker & Zigmond, 1976). In addition, the lateral hypothalamus appears only to be one of the "go" centers for feeding. This is indicated by the fact that the appetite stimulant NPY exerts its strongest effects *outside of* the lateral hypothalamus (Leibowitz, 1991).

These and other results indicate that even though the hypothalamus is critical for the control of eating, other mechanisms are also crucial, some specialized for short-term energy needs, others for long-term storage. As a group, these various sytems provide the organism with an extremely effective safety net.

OBESITY

The mechanisms regulating an organism's food intake work remarkably well—but they do not work perfectly. We see this in the fact that organisms (humans in particular!) can end up with weights that are genuinely unhealthy for them. The most obvious example is obesity, a problem so widespread that the World Health Organization has classified obesity as a global epidemic (Ravussin & Bouchard, 2000).

Obesity is sometimes defined as a body weight that exceeds the average for a given height by 20%. More commonly, though, researchers use a definition cast in terms of the ***Body Mass Index (BMI)***, defined as someone's weight in kilograms divided by the square of his height in meters (Table 2.1). A BMI between 18.5 and 24.9 is considered normal. A BMI between 25 and 30 counts as overweight, and a BMI of 30 or more is considered obese. A BMI over 40 defines ***morbid obesity***—the level of obesity at which someone's health is genuinely at risk. For most people, morbid obesity means a weight roughly 100 pounds (45.3 kg) beyond their ideal.

Current estimates indicate that roughly 30% of U.S. adults are obese; another 35% are merely overweight (Friedman, 2003). Among children and adolescents, the figures are slightly better—with 15% fatter than they should be (Marx, 2003).

TABLE 2.1 CONVERTING HEIGHT AND WEIGHT TO BODY MASS INDEX

HEIGHT	WEIGHT (IN POUNDS)						
	120	130	140	150	160	170	180
5'0"	23.4	25.4	27.3	29.3	31.2	33.2	35.1
5'2"	21.9	23.8	25.6	27.4	29.3	31.1	32.9
5'4"	20.6	22.3	24.0	25.7	27.5	29.2	30.9
5'6"	19.4	21.0	22.6	24.2	25.8	27.4	29.0
5'8"	18.2	19.8	21.3	22.8	24.3	25.8	27.4
5'10"	17.2	18.7	20.1	21.5	23.0	24.4	25.8
6'0"	16.3	17.6	19.0	20.3	21.7	23.1	24.4

NOTE: the green area = normal; the blue area = overweight; the red area = obese.

THE GENETIC ROOTS OF OBESITY

Why do people become obese? The simplest hypothesis is just that some people eat too much, and therefore they become fat. In this view, obesity might be understood as the end result of self-indulgence, or perhaps the consequence of an inability to resist temptation.

This hypothesis makes it sound like people could be blamed for their obesity; the condition is, in essence, their own fault. Such a view of obesity, however, is almost certainly a mistake, because this perspective ignores the powerful forces that can put someone onto the path toward obesity in the first place. Of course, people do have considerable control over what and how much they eat, but, even so, the evidence suggests that some people are strongly predisposed toward obesity, thanks to their individual genetic pattern.

We have already mentioned one point relevant to this claim—namely, that each of us seems to have a genetically determined set point for our body weight, and obese individuals may, in many cases, simply be those who have a particularly high set point. Other evidence for a genetic influence comes from studies of identical twins. As we mentioned earlier, identical twins have the same genes, so they provide a means of examining whether this sharing of genes leads to a shared outcome; if it does, then this finding obviously suggests the genes play an important role in determining that outcome.

One long-term study examined 12 pairs of male identical twins. Each of these men was fed about 1,000 calories per day above the amount required to maintain his initial weight. The activities of each participant were kept as constant as possible, and there was very little exercise. This regimen continued for one 100 days. Needless to say, all 24 men gained weight, but the amounts they gained varied substantially, from about 10 to 30 pounds. Also varying was where on their bodies the weight was deposited. For some participants, it was the abdomen; for others, it was the thighs and buttocks. Crucially, though, the amount each person gained was statistically related to the weight gain of his twin (Figure 2.5). The twins also tended to deposit the weight in the same place. If one developed a prominent paunch, so did his twin; if another deposited the fat in his thighs, his twin did, too (Bouchard, Lykken, McGue, Segal, & Tellegen, 1990; also see Herbert et al. 2006).

It seems, therefore, that the tendency to turn extra calories into fat has a genetic basis. In fact, several mechanisms may be involved in this pattern, so that, in the end, obesity can arise from a variety of causes. For example, some people seem to be less sensitive to leptin and thus are more vulnerable to the effects of appetite stimulants such as NPY (Friedman, 2003). For these people, a tendency to overeat may be driven by powerful biological forces that are genetically rooted. In addition, people differ in the efficiency of their digestive apparatus, with some people simply extracting more calories from any given food. People also differ in their overall metabolic level; if, as a result, less nutrient fuel is burned up, then more is left for fatty storage (Astrup, 2000; also Friedman, 1990a, b; Sims, 1986).

Given these various mechanisms, should we perhaps think about obesity as some sort of genetic *defect*, a biologically rooted condition that leads to substantial health risk? This suggestion is emphatically rejected by proponents of the "thrifty gene" hypothesis. They note that our ancestors lived in times when food supplies were unpredictable and food shortages were common, so natural selection may have favored individuals who had especially inefficient metabolisms and, as a result, stored more fat. These individuals would have been better prepared for lean times and thus may have had a survival advantage. As a result, the genes leading to this fat storage might have been assets, not defects (Friedman, 2003; Fujimoto et al., 1995; Groop & Tuomi, 1997; Ravussin, 1994).

ENVIRONMENTAL FACTORS AND OBESITY

The "thrifty gene" hypothesis draws attention to a crucial theme: No matter what the genetic basis for obesity, we must always recall that genes do not by themselves produce obesity, because, as we have discussed, the genes by themselves do not produce any

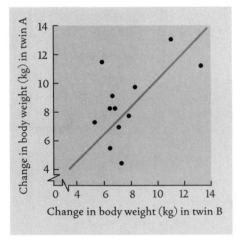

2.5 Similarity of weight gains in identical twins Weight gains for 12 pairs of identical twins after 100 days of the same degree of overfeeding. Each point represents one twin pair, with the weight gain of twin A plotted on the vertical axis and the weight gain of twin B plotted on the horizontal axis. Weight gains are plotted in kilograms (1 kg = 2.2 lbs). The closer the points are to the diagonal line, the more similar the weight gains of the twins are to each other.

trait. Instead, genes only provide guidelines for how an organism will develop; other factors, including stimuli available from the environment, play an equally important role in shaping how things unfold within those guidelines.

In short, we must always understand genetic influences as interacting with environmental factors and life experiences. Thus, "thrifty genes" might have helped our ancestors to maintain a healthy body weight, but our ancestors lived in a time in which food was often scarce. The same genes will have a different outcome in modern times—especially for people living in an affluent culture in which a quick trip to the supermarket provides all the calories one wishes. In this modern context, the "thrifty genes" can lead to levels of obesity that create serious health problems.

As a related point, consider the fact that obesity rates are climbing across the globe. In the United States, roughly 23% of the population in 1991 was obese; the current rate—30%—is appreciably higher (Friedman, 2003). Similar patterns are evident in other countries. Over the last 10 years, for example, the obesity rates in most European countries have increased by at least 10%, and, in some countries, by as much as 40%. These shifts could not possibly be a change in the human genome; genetic changes proceed at a much slower pace. Instead, the increase has to be understood in terms of changes in diet and activity level—with people consuming more calorically dense, high-fat foods and living a lifestyle that causes them to expend relatively few calories in their daily routines.

This increase in obesity rates is troubling, because, as we have noted, obesity is associated with health problems, including heart attack, stroke, Type 2 diabetes, and some types of cancer. There continues to be debate over the severity of these risks for people with moderate levels of obesity—e.g., a BMI between 30 and 40 (Couzin, 2005; Yan et al., 2006). There is no debate, however, about the health risks of so-called morbid obesity (a BMI of 40 or higher), and this makes the worldwide statistics on obesity a serious concern for health professionals.

Overall, then, obesity reminds us that we need to consider multiple factors if we want to understand how much someone eats and what weight she maintains. Let's note in passing that the same message can be drawn from consideration of the eating disorder *anorexia nervosa*, which we described briefly in Chapter 1. In anorexia, the body's homeostatic mechanisms are clearly overruled by other mechanisms, leading to a pattern of behavior that can be truly life-threatening. Like obesity, anorexia has genetic roots (Andreasen & Black, 1996), but it is also becoming more and more common in many countries, a shift that has to be attributed to environmental, not genetic, factors. It is not completely clear what these environmental factors are, but the modern obsession with being slender is surely relevant (Figure 2.6). In any case, anorexia provides yet another reminder of the complexity—and, in some cases, the fragility—of the mechanisms that

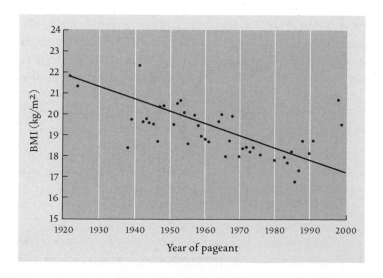

2.6 Changing standards of beauty *For many years, the winners of the Miss America pageant were becoming thinner and thinner, presumably reflecting a change in the aesthetic standards of the judges. Indeed, many of the winners were, by some standards, actually under-nourished. However, this trend seems to have reversed in recent years. This may reflect a change in the judges' aesthetic standards or it may reflect the judges' response to criticisms of the pageant.*

control our food intake. Genetic mechanisms are crucial, but they interact with environ-mental inputs. Our homeostatic mechanisms are effective, but they are not perfect and can sometimes by overwhelmed by other forces.

THREAT AND AGGRESSION

Our emphasis so far has been on motives (hunger and, briefly, thermoregulation) that are primarily regulated by mechanisms that monitor and maintain our internal envi-ronment. As we have seen, though, these motives are not entirely regulated from within. The sight of food can cause us to eat even when we are not hungry; the anticipa-tion of winter can trigger nest building before it gets cold.

Other motives take this emphasis on external triggers one step further, since their primary spurs to action are largely external. An example is our reaction to intense threat. In this case, the instigation is the threatening event or object—the lion about to pounce, or the bully about to strike us down. Despite these differences, though, our dis-cussion of threat will bring us to the same themes that arose in our discussion of hunger: Our bodies make numerous internal adjustments in response to the threat; these adjustments are tightly controlled by complex regulatory mechanisms that have unmistakably been shaped by natural selection, and which seem to function in roughly the same way in humans as they do in other species. Genetic mechanisms are crucial, but—once again—the unfolding of these genetic mechanisms is heavily shaped by events in our environment and in our experience.

THREAT AND THE AUTOMATIC NERVOUS SYSTEM

What biological mechanisms underlie our reactions to threat? We have discussed the fact that the autonomic nervous system is divided into two branches: sympathetic and parasympathetic (pp. 47–48). According to American physiologist Walter B. Cannon (1871–1945), these branches serve two broad and different functions. The parasympa-thetic branch handles the mundane functions of ordinary life: the conservation of bodily resources, reproduction, and the disposal of wastes. In effect, these reflect an organism's operations during times of peace—a low and steady heart rate, peristaltic movements of stomach and intestines, secretions by digestive glands, and the like. In contrast, the sym-pathetic branch has an activating function. It summons the body's resources in times of crisis and gets the organism ready for vigorous action (Cannon, 1929).*

We have mentioned some of the effects of sympathetic excitation, but, in addition, this excitation stimulates the inner core of the adrenal gland, the adrenal medulla, to pour epi-nephrine (adrenaline) and norepinephrine into the bloodstream. These chemicals have effects similar to those of sympathetic stimulation—they accelerate the heart rate, speed up metabolism, and so on. As a result, the sympathetic effects are amplified even further.

THE EMERGENCY REACTION

Cannon argued that intense sympathetic arousal serves as an emergency reaction that mobilizes the organism for a crisis—for "flight or fight," as he described it. Con-sider a grazing zebra, placidly maintaining homeostasis by nibbling at the grass and

---

* Many students have trouble remembering which is the sympathetic branch and which is the parasym-pathetic. It may help, therefore, to bear in mind that the parasympathetic branch prepares us for times of peace, and the sympathetic branch can provide us with a surge of energy.

vasodilatating in the hot African sun. Suddenly it sees a lion closing in for the kill. Escape will require pronounced muscular exertion, with the support of the entire bodily machinery, and this is exactly what intense sympathetic activation provides. Because of this activation, more nutrient fuel is available to the muscles and can be delivered rapidly through wide-open blood vessels. At the same time, waste products are jettisoned and all less-essential organic activities are brought to a halt.

Cannon produced considerable evidence suggesting that a similar autonomic reaction occurs when the pattern is one of attack rather than of flight. A cat about to tangle with a dog shows accelerated heartbeat, piloerection (its hair standing on end, normally a heat-conserving device), and pupillary dilation—all signs of sympathetic arousal, signs that the body is girding itself for violent muscular effort (Figure 2.7).

It turns out, however, that Cannon's "fight or flight" formulation is overly simple, because organisms respond to threat in many different ways. For example, many animals stand perfectly immobile when threatened, so that predators are less likely to notice them. Other animals have more exotic means of self-protection: For example, some species of fish pale when threatened, which makes them harder to spot against the sandy ocean bottom. This effect is produced by the direct action of adrenal epinephrine on various pigments in the animal's skin (Odiorne, 1957). Despite this variety, though, situations involving threat require that the organism be ready for immediate action, and so sympathetic arousal is crucial for all of them.

2.7 *Sympathetic emergency reaction* A cat's *response to a threatening encounter.*

DISRUPTIVE EFFECTS OF AUTONOMIC AROUSAL

The emergency system we have been discussing has undoubted biological value, but strong arousal of the sympathetic branch of the ANS can also be disruptive and even damaging. This is especially clear in humans. In our day-to-day lives, we rarely encounter emergencies that call for violent physical effort, but our biological nature has not changed just because the modern world generally contains no threats from saber-toothed tigers. We are plagued instead by chronic stressors like traffic jams, ornery bosses, and agonizing world crises, and although we often feel impelled to defend ourselves against these threats of the modern world, physical action is frequently inappropriate, ineffective, or illegal. Nonetheless, we are stuck with the same emergency reactions that our ancestors had, and so we keep ourselves armed physiologically against situations we cannot really control. The resulting bodily wear and tear can take a serious toll (e.g., Sapolsky, 1998).

The disruptive effects of threat upon our digestion or sexual responses are common knowledge. During periods of acute anxiety, diarrhea or constipation are widespread, and it is difficult to achieve or maintain sexual arousal. This is hardly surprising since our digestive functions and many aspects of our sexuality (e.g., erections in males and vaginal lubrication in females) are largely controlled by the parasympathetic nervous system, and so they are inhibited by intense sympathetic arousal. The aftereffects of threat can also be disabling, causing disorders such as stomachaches and headaches. If the threat continues, the prolonged stress responses result in chronic suppression of the immune system, which can make us vulnerable to infection by pathogens like bacteria and viruses.

AGGRESSION AND PREDATION

It seems, then, that our biological reaction to threat—by activation of the sympathetic nervous system, with the various effects already described—may not serve us all that well in our modern environment. Nonetheless, this reaction is well rooted in our biology, and it is certainly similar to the reaction pattern easily observed in many other species. It is a reaction pattern that has been shaped by natural selection and that has, over each species' history, contributed to survival by preparing the organism for whatever energetic activities it needs to escape the threat.

But what does the animal do once aroused, once the emergency reaction is under way? Are the subsequent steps also shared across species and shaped by evolution? If so, does this mean, perhaps, that the tendency to fight with enemies might have biological underpinnings? To answer this question, it is helpful to draw on the *comparative method*, studying nonhumans as well as humans to see whether there are commonalities that reflect some shared biological heritage.

As a first and crucial point, though, we need to distinguish two forms of violence that organisms engage in—*aggression* and *predation*. Predators hunt and kill for food, but they do so quite dispassionately. A predator about to pounce on its prey shows none of the signs of anger, and so a dog on the verge of catching a rabbit never growls, nor does it have its ears laid back (Lorenz, 1966). Predatory attack is instead an outgrowth of the hunger motive, and it is controlled by the same brain sites as eating (Hutchinson & Renfrew, 1966). In contrast, aggressive or self-defense behaviors are controlled by their own brain areas, triggered by different situations, and certainly show a different behavioral profile. In our discussion of aggression, therefore, it will be best to hold predatory attack to the side—as part of an animal's food-gathering repertoire, and not part of its response to threat.

MALE AGGRESSION AND HORMONES

Genuine combat is, in fact, widespread among animals, and there is probably no species that has foresworn aggression altogether. Fish chase and nip each other; lizards lunge and push; birds attack with wing, beak, and claw; and on and on. In most cases, the individuals we identify as aggressive are male, because, among vertebrates, the male is by far the more physically aggressive sex. In some mammals, this difference in combativeness is apparent even in childhood play. Young male rhesus monkeys, for instance, engage in much more vigorous rough-and-tumble play than their sisters (Harlow, 1962). Among humans, boys worldwide are more physically aggressive than girls (Geary & Bjorklund, 2000; and see Chapter 13), and as adults, male murderers outnumber females by a ratio of 10:1 (Anderson & Bushman, 2002).

But this gender difference only holds for physical aggression. Human females are also aggressive, but their aggression tends to rely on verbal or social assaults, not physical

Animal combat   Animals in many species often engage in ferocious combat, usually over some resource (such as food, territory, or a potential mate).

violence. Thus, females attack by means of insults or the spreading of rumors; they take steps to isolate someone from friends and allies. If we focus on these sorts of aggression, then it is women, not men, who are the aggressive sex (Oesterman et al., 1998).

Why is physical aggression so much more prevalent in men? Biological factors are clearly relevant, because aggression is partially influenced by hormones, particularly the sex hormone *testosterone*. High testosterone levels in the bloodstream are associated with increased physical aggressiveness in many different species, including fish, lizards, turtles, birds, rats, mice, and monkeys (Davis, 1964; Siegel & Demetrikopoulos, 1993). However, the relationship between testosterone and physical aggression is complex. As one complication, at least some human aggression bears no relationship to testosterone levels, so it must be shaped by other factors (e.g., Book, Starzyk, & Qunisey, 2001). In addition, it would in all cases be inaccurate to say simply that for any species testosterone causes aggression, because in fact it can be both a cause and an effect. Thus, testosterone administered externally can increase subsequent aggressiveness, but successful aggressive encounters can cause increased secretion of testosterone (Dabbs, 1992; Rosenzweig, Leiman, & Breedlove, 1996; Sapolsky, 1998).

TERRITORIALITY

What do nonhuman animals fight about? Their struggles are generally about a scarce resource—a food source, perhaps, or a water hole or a mate. To secure such resources, many animals stake out a *territory*—one that includes or will lead to the desired resource—and then they defend that territory as their exclusive preserve. Thus, for example, in the spring, male songbirds endlessly patrol their little fiefdoms and furiously repel all male intruders who violate their borders. Contrary to the poet's fancy, the male bird who bursts into full-throated song is not giving vent to inexpressible joy, pouring out his "full heart in profuse strains of unpremeditated art" (Shelley, 1821). Instead, his message is prosaic and double-edged. It is a warning to other males: "Don't trespass!" And it is an invitation to unattached females, who on their flybys are appraising his song for tips to his vigor and thus his mateworthiness: "Am fit, have territory, will share."

Fighting to acquire or defend territory is common in many types of birds, fish, and mammals, and the evolutionary roots of this behavior are easy to see, because territoriality promotes reproductive success in an obvious way: A male able to secure a resource-filled territory provides well for his offspring, and likewise for a female who selects a male with ample resources in his domain. In addition, territoriality helps to keep aggressiveness within bounds. Good fences make good neighbors, at least in the sense that they keep the antagonists out of each others' hair (or fins or feathers). One mechanism that accomplishes this is rather simple. Once a territory is established, its owner tends to be courageous on his home ground; if he ventures beyond it, he becomes timid and is readily repulsed (Krebs, 1982). This virtually guarantees an uneven status between intruder and defender, because the former is certain to be less assertive than the latter, with the result that there may be occasional border skirmishes but few actual conflicts.

Do humans show the same patterns? It is true that we stake out territories, but the contrasts between human and animal territoriality are striking. Humans do have a tendency to regard the physical zone surrounding them as "theirs"; they mark this zone in a variety of ways and guard against intrusions into this space. On a train or bus, for example, people carefully choose their seats so as to leave some distance between themselves and their nearest neighbor. The same pattern can be observed when people choose seats in a movie theater or arrange their blankets on the beach (Figure 2.8). Even within the home, individual family members each have their private preserves—their own rooms or corners, their places at the dinner table, and so on.

Social aggression   *In males, aggression is often physical (pushing or punching). In females, aggression usually takes a different form: They may attack each other, for example, by spreading gossip or rumors; they take steps to isolate someone from friends and allies.*

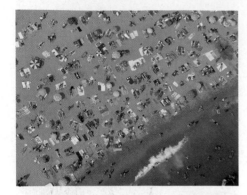

2.8 Personal space *In many public spaces, humans arrange themselves in remarkably uniform spatial patterns, as if each is respecting the territory of the others. This is certainly visible whenever people spread out their blankets on the beach.*

A desire to maintain some minimal personal space seems universal, but the physical dimensions of this space are strongly affected by the standards of each culture. In North America, acquaintances stand 2 to 3 feet apart during a conversation; if one moves closer, the other feels crowded or pushed into unwanted intimacy. For Latin Americans, the acceptable distance is much less. Under the circumstances, misunderstanding is almost inevitable. The North American regards the Latin American as overly intrusive; the Latin American in turn feels that the North American is unfriendly and cold (Hall, 1966).

Human cultures do not just differ in the dimensions of each individual's personal space; cultures also differ in how territories are conceptualized. In some societies, individuals own certain spaces and (just like wolves or songbirds) have control over the resources within that space. In other societies, ownership is communal and resources are shared. Even within Western society, some individuals fiercely protect their real estate, while others are indifferent to the exclusiveness of their surroundings. These differences are difficult to understand in strictly biological terms, for the simple reason that all humans have roughly the same genes and the same evolutionary past. It seems more plausible, therefore, that human territoriality is best understood in terms of learning—as each of us draws from our experiences and culture a sense of the space around us, and our relation to it.

PATTERNS OF HUMAN AGGRESSION

Whatever the source of human territoriality, it is clear that humans, like other species, sometimes engage in aggression to secure resources or to maintain (or obtain) a hold on that which they think is theirs. This is evident in the many wars that have grown out of national disagreements about who owns a particular expanse of territory; on a smaller scale, it is evident when two drivers come to blows over a parking space or—more commonly—two men fight jealously about a woman whom they each claim as "their own."

It's debatable, however, how much we gain by thinking about these cases of human aggression in strictly biological terms. As we have already seen, human territoriality seems in many cases quite different from territoriality in other species, and, indeed, it seems odd to talk about how humans position their blankets on the beach in the same way we talk about a grizzly bear defending its turf. The latter is plainly about the defense of resources, with implications both for immediate survival and, eventually, reproductive success; beach blanket placement, on the other hand, is much more temporary and much less consequential.

Just as important, human aggression is often motivated by forces that have little to do with the direct demands of territoriality or resources. The aggression is instead motivated by complex beliefs—beliefs about historical rights, or prior injuries, or future opportunities. These beliefs, in turn, depend on the sophisticated human capacity for symbolism, a capacity that gives rise to our conceptions of honor, or religion, or tribal (or national) heritage. It is typically insults to these conceptions, rather than palpable threats to our welfare, that give rise to many instances of human aggression (Geen, 2001).

In addition, just as humans vary in their attitudes toward territory, we also vary enormously in how aggressive we are. Some of us do respond to provocation with violence. Some turn the other cheek. Some find nonviolent means of asserting themselves or their privileges. What determines how someone responds? Consistent with the broader themes of this chapter, the answer has many parts. Some factors are biological; other factors are tied to the individual's personality; still others are rooted in the person's culture.

We have already mentioned some biological factors that can predispose a person toward violence—for example, the level of the hormone testosterone in the person's bloodstream. What are the personality traits that lead to violence? For many years, investigators believed that aggression was more likely to come from people with relatively low self-esteem, on the argument that such individuals were particularly vulnerable to insult and also likely to have few other means of responding. More recent work, however, suggests that the opposite is the case, that social provocations are more likely to inspire aggression if the person provoked has unrealistically high self-esteem (Baumeister, 2001; Bushman & Baumeister, 2002; see also Chapter 12). Such a person is particularly likely to perceive the provocation as a grievous assault, challenging his inflated self-image; in many cases, violence will be the result.

Other personality traits are also relevant to aggression. For example, some people are high on measures of *sensation seeking*, which means that, in general, they seek out varied and novel experiences in their daily lives. High levels of sensation seeking are associated with aggressiveness, and so also are high scores on tests designed to measure the personality trait of *impulsivity*, a tendency to act without reflecting on one's actions (Anderson & Bushman, 2002; Joireman, Anderson, & Strathman, 2003).

In addition, whether someone turns to aggression or not is influenced heavily by the culture in which he was raised. Some cultures explicitly eschew violence; this is true, for example, in communities of Quakers. But other cultures prescribe violence, often via rules of chivalry and honor that demand certain responses to certain insults. Gang violence in many U.S. cities can be understood partly in this way, and so can many cases of larger-scale violence (e.g., some of the fighting among the warlords of Somalia). Cultural differences are also evident when we compare different regions within the United States; for example, the homicide rate in the South is reliably higher than in the North, and statistical evidence suggests that this contrast is best attributed to social differences and not to factors like population density, economic conditions, or climate (Nisbett & Cohen, 1996).

These cultural differences also draw our attention to another issue: For obvious reasons, discussions of aggression showcase the evils that aggression can produce, and, sadly, these evils are all too easy to catalog—the devastation of war, the brutality of many crimes, the numerous cases of genocide our species has attempted. But we should note that in some cultures and in some settings, aggression is initiated by motives that are not so dark: the defense of honor, or the wish to defeat an awful enemy. Many people would argue that even in these cases, the aggression is unacceptable and its outcome inevitably tragic—this is, after all, the position of "conscientious objectors" who refuse military service under any circumstances. However one views this moral position, though, the psychological point should be clear: Aggression can arise from a variety of motives, some of which are certainly condemnable, but some of which may not be.

The non-universality of human aggression **Humans vary enormously in how aggressive they are. Some (like His Holiness the Dalai Lama) develop a capacity for loving compassion that makes aggression almost unthinkable; others (like these gang members) participate in violent aggression in almost every day of their lives.**

LEARNING TO BE AGGRESSIVE

We have just suggested that the cultural context can play a considerable role in encouraging or discouraging aggression. But how does culture influence us? The answer, not surprisingly, is *through learning*—with the suggestion that each person, during his or her lifetime, can learn to be aggressive (or not to be). In some cases, this learning involves explicit teaching—when, for example, our parents or teachers tell us not to be aggressive. In other cases, the learning involves our picking up subtle cues that tell us (for example) whether our friends think that aggression is acceptable or not (or repugnant, or cool). In still other cases, the learning is of a different sort—when the people around us model through their own actions how one should handle situations that might provoke aggression.

In addition, learning can proceed on a much larger scale, thanks to the societal influences that we are all exposed to. For example, consider the violence that is

Television violence Prime-time television, on some estimates, displays an average of five violent acts per hour; Saturday-morning children's programming is far worse, as characters constantly punch, shoot at, and sometimes kill each other.

portrayed in the television shows we watch and the movies we see. On some accounts, prime-time television programs contain an average of five violent acts per hour, as characters punch, shoot at, and sometimes murder each other. Saturday-morning children's shows are even worse; overall, investigators estimate that the average American child observes more than 10,000 acts of TV violence every year (e.g., Anderson & Bushman, 2001).

Does this exposure to violence promote violence in the viewer? Some of the pertinent evidence comes from studies of violence levels within a community before and after television was introduced, or before and after the broadcast of particularly gruesome footage of murders or assassinations. These studies consistently show that assault and homicide rates increase after such exposures (Centerwall, 1989; Joy, Kimball, & Zabrack, 1986). Other studies indicate that children who are not particularly aggressive become more so after viewing TV violence (e.g., Huesmann, Lagerspetz, & Eron, 1984; Huesmann & Miller, 1994; for related data showing the effects of playing violent video games, see Carnagey & Anderson, 2005).

These studies leave little doubt that there is a strong correlation, such that those who view violence are likely to be violent themselves. But does this correlation reveal a cause-and-effect relationship, in which the viewing actually causes someone to be more violent? Many investigators believe it does (Anderson & Bushman, 2001, 2002). Indeed, the evidence persuaded six major professional societies (including the American Psychological Association, the American Medical Association, and the American Psychiatric Association) to issue a joint statement noting that studies "point overwhelmingly to a causal connection between media violence and aggressive behavior in some children" (Joint Statement, 2000, p. 1).

Other investigators, however, have urged caution on these points—especially since the most obvious remedy to media violence is some sort of broad censorship, which is itself a troubling prospect for many people. What is the basis for the caution? Some researchers have suggested that, in at least some of the studies, the direction of causality is uncertain. Perhaps people who are inclined toward violence are the ones who seek out violent television, so that being more violent causes one to view more violence, and not the other way around. Another concern comes from the fact that not all studies show a relationship between viewing violence and being violent, and at least some texts suggest that this is because the effect of viewing violence may be short-lived (for a review, see Green, 1998). In light of these concerns, and given the urgency of the issue overall, we can only hope that these points are resolved soon.

IS AGGRESSION INEVITABLE?

Whether spurred by cultural values or testosterone, whether motivated by a wish to defend a territory or a desire to repay an insult, aggression is costly. If we focus just on the biological costs to the combatants, aggression is dangerous and can lead to death or injury. In addition, it distracts the animal from other vital pursuits. The male who is continually fighting with his sexual rivals will have little time (let alone energy) to gather food or to mate with the female after his competitors have fled (Enquist & Leimar, 1990).

For some species, and for some forms of violence, these costs are simply the price animals pay in order to gain certain advantages—for survival or for reproduction (e.g., Pennisi, 2005). Even so, natural selection has consistently favored ways of limiting these costs—so that the price of aggression is kept as low as possible.

Some of the limits on aggression hinge on the fact that animals are keenly sensitive to the strength of their enemies. If the enemy seems much stronger (or more agile or better armed or armored) than oneself, the best bet is to concede defeat quickly, or better yet, never to start the battle at all. Animals therefore use a variety of strategies to proclaim their strength, with a goal of winning the battle before it starts. They roar, they puff themselves up, and they offer all sorts of threats, all with the aim of appearing as powerful as they possibly can (Figure 2.9). Conversely, once an animal determines that it is the weaker one, and likely to lose a battle, it uses a variety of strategies for avoiding a bloody defeat, usually involving specific conciliatory signals, such as crouching or exposing one's belly (Figure 2.10).

Another constraint on aggression, found in many species, is a **dominance hierarchy**, in which each member of the group has an assigned status that determines who has access to mates, who gets first turn at the food supply, who gets the best nest site, and so on. With all of these issues settled by one's place in the hierarchy, fighting over them is much reduced, and thus overall aggression is decreased. (For more on how dominance is established, see Cheney & Seyfarth, 1990; de Waal, 1982; Hrdy & Williams, 1983; Silk, 1986.)

Similar mechanisms are evident in humans. For example, the participants in a bar fight or a schoolyard tussle try to puff themselves up to intimidate their opponents, just as a moose or a mouse would. Likewise, we humans have a range of conciliatory gestures we use to avoid combat—body postures and words of appeasement. All of these mechanisms, however, apply largely to face-to-face combat; sad to say, these biologically based controls have little effect on the long-distance, large-scale aggression that our species often engages in. As a result, battles between nations will probably not be avoided by political leaders roaring or thumping their chests; soldiers operating a missle-launcher cannot see (much less respond to) their targets' conciliatory body posture.

Our best hope for reducing human aggression, therefore, is that the human capacity for moral and intellectual reflection will pull us away from combat, and that a consideration of

2.9 *Threat displays* **(A) Some species threaten by making themselves appear larger and more impressive. (B) Other species threaten by shouting at the top of their lungs, like howler monkeys, who scream at each other for hours on end.**

2.10 *Conciliatory display* **In most species, animal combat ends before either animal suffers a mortal wound. As soon as one of the combatants determines that its defeat is likely, it surrenders and explicitly signals the surrender through a submissive display—such as exposing the belly or the throat.**

the horrors, cruelty, and destruction of violence will lead us to choose other means of reconciling differences. But how optimistic should we be about this point? Is aggression perhaps an inevitable part of our lives? Recent history suggests an encouraging view. True, the daily headlines describe a horrifying succession of bomb blasts, homicides, armed assaults, and so on, but, in fact, careful studies indicate a consistent decline in the number and intensity of armed conflicts in the world, with a 15-year trend showing a 50% reduction in the amount of organized violence on our planet (Marshall & Gurr, 2005; also Easterbrook, 2005). Likewise, the number of people involved in organized fighting has decreased around the world, even though the total population of the planet has grown (Marshall & Gurr, 2005). Within the United States, the Federal Bureau of Investigation reports that the rate of violent crime continues to drop—following a trend that has lasted at least a decade (Federal Bureau of Investigation, 2004).

These data are all relatively recent, and it is possible, of course, that the worldwide trends will reverse and that violence and aggression will once again begin a bloody increase. At least for now, though, the data provide an encouraging signal that our species—whatever our biological heritage—is finding a way to avoid the most destructive and horrifying forms of aggression.

SEX

We have now considered two motives in detail—hunger and the response to threat. In both cases, we have discussed mechanisms that are plainly shared with other creatures (e.g., the homeostatic regulation of blood sugar, the biological response to threat), and in both cases the evolutionary roots of these mechanisms are easy to discern. In addition, we have seen in both domains that genetically rooted mechanisms, as powerful as they are, cannot be our entire story: In Chapter 1 and earlier in this chapter, we discussed influences on our eating that are shaped by learning and culture, rather than by evolution. Likewise, we have discussed important influences on aggression that are unmistakably shaped by the culture in which we live. In short, these two motives are obviously tied to our biology, but our theorizing must also include distinctly human factors such as complex learning, thoughtful reflection, and cultural values.

The same broad themes will emerge in our consideration of one last motive: sex. This motive is unmistakably biological, rooted in our physiology just as thermoregulation, hunger, or the response to threat are. In some ways, however, sex is different: Unlike most of the other biological motives, sex is inherently social, and in humans its pursuit is intertwined with all manner of cultural patterns and attitudes.

Let us start our discussion with the aspects of sexual behavior that are most obviously tied to our biology—mating itself, and, within that, the role of hormones in controlling an organism's behavior. We will then turn to aspects for which the influence of biology, and our evolutionary past in particular, is less clear-cut and has, in fact, been the subject of considerable debate. (We will turn to the related topics of love and romance in a later chapter, when we will be less concerned with the biological perspective on these issues and more concerned with the social issues of how humans relate to each other.)

HORMONES AND ANIMAL SEXUALITY

Sexual behavior in animals is all about arranging for the union of sperm and ova, and this can proceed only after male and female have met, courted, and determined each other to be a suitable mate. At that point, at least for terrestrial mammals and birds, the male generally introduces his sperm cells into the genital tract of the female. The sperm then has to encounter a ready ovum, and finally, the fertilized egg can develop only if it is provided with the appropriate conditions. The sequence of events necessary for all these events requires a complex hormonal control system linking the brain and the reproductive organs, and what's crucial for us is that the hormones govern both internal events and the organism's behavior.

HORMONAL CYCLES

Timing is everything. Most animals are sexually receptive, and both biologically and behaviorally prepared to mate, only at certain points in the year. In mammals, this period of sexual receptivity is known as *estrus*, and how often it occurs depends on the species. Female rats, for example, go through a 15-hour estrus period every four days. At all other times, they will resolutely reject any male's advances. If he nuzzles a female outside of estrus or tries to mount, she will kick and bite him. But during estrus, the female responds quite differently to the male's approach. She first retreats in small hops, then stops to look back and wiggles her ears (McClintock & Adler, 1978). Eventually, she stands still, her back arched, her tail held to the side—a willing sexual partner.

What brings about this change in the female's behavior? The mechanism is an interlocking system of hormonal and neurological controls that involves the pituitary gland, the hypothalamus, and the ovaries. There are three phases. During the first, *follicles* (ova-containing sacs) in the ovary mature under the influence of pituitary secretions. The follicles produce the sex hormone *estrogen*. As the concentration of estrogen in the bloodstream rises, the hypothalamus responds by directing the pituitary to change its secretions. In consequence, follicle growth is accelerated until the follicle ruptures and releases the mature ovum.

This triggers the second phase, during which the animal is in estrus. Estrogen production peaks and stimulates certain structures in the hypothalamus, which make the animal sexually receptive.

The third phase is dominated by the action of another sex hormone, *progesterone*, which is produced by the ruptured follicle. Its secretion leads to a thickening of the uterine lining, a first step in preparing the uterus to receive the embryo. If the ovum is fertilized, there are further steps in preparing the uterus. If it is not, the thickened uterine walls are reabsorbed, and another cycle begins. In humans and some primates, this thickening of the uterine wall involves too much extra tissue to be easily reabsorbed; the thickened uterine lining is therefore sloughed off as *menstrual flow* (Figure 2.11).

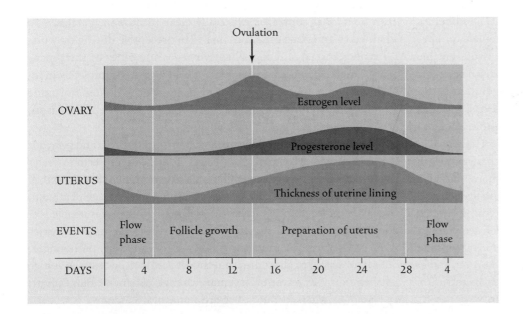

2.11 *The main stages of the human menstrual cycle* **The figure shows estrogen and progesterone levels and thickness of the uterine lining during the human menstrual cycle. The cycle begins with the growth of a follicle, continues through ovulation and a maximum estrogen level, is followed by a phase during which the uterus becomes prepared to receive the embryo, and ends with a flow phase during which the thickened uterine lining is sloughed off.**

HORMONAL CHANGES AND BEHAVIOR

These hormonal changes affect behavior dramatically. When female rats' ovaries are removed, they soon lose all sexual interest and capacity, as do male rats when castrated. But sexual behavior is quickly restored in the male by appropriate injections of testosterone and in the female mainly by estrogen (the female also needs, and secretes, a small amount of testosterone).

Many investigators believe that the behavioral effects of these hormones are mediated by receptors in the hypothalamus. This hypothesis has been tested by injecting tiny quantities of various hormones into different regions of the hypothalamus. Such studies reveal, for example, that a spayed female cat will go into estrus when estrogen is implanted (Harris & Michael, 1964) and that castrated males will resume sexual behavior after receiving doses of the appropriate male hormones (Davidson, 1969; Feder, 1984; McEwen et al., 1982).

Hormones affect behavior, but the effect can also be the other way around. What an animal experiences and what it does can substantially affect it hormonally. In some animals, the female's courtship behavior can trigger the release of testosterone in courting males. In animals such as rodents, the female's sexual receptivity is triggered by chemicals contained in the male's urine. In other cases, copulation itself produces reproductive readiness. For example, the female rat secretes some progesterone during the normal cycle but not enough to permit the implantation of the fertilized ovum in the uterus. The critical dose is secreted only as a reflex response to sexual stimulation. This leaves the sexually aroused male rat with two reproductive functions: supplying sperm, and providing the mechanical stimulation necessary for hormonal secretion. Should he ejaculate too quickly and thus leave the female inadequately stimulated, all is lost, for no pregnancy results (Adler, 1979; Rosenzweig, Leiman, & Breedlove, 1996).

HORMONES AND HUMAN SEXUALITY

Compared to other animals, humans are much less automatic in their sexual activities, much more varied, and much more affected by prior experience. This difference is especially marked when we consider the effects of sex hormones. In rats and cats, sexual behavior is highly dependent upon hormone levels; castrated males and spayed females stop copulating a few months after the removal of their gonads. In humans, on the other hand, sexual activity may persist for years, even decades, after castration or ovariectomy, provided that the operation was performed after puberty (Bermant & Davidson, 1974).

The liberation from hormonal control is especially clear in human females. The female rat or cat is chained to an estrus cycle that makes her receptive during only one period, but human females can respond sexually at virtually all points of their menstrual cycle. This does not mean, however, that human sexual desire is completely independent of hormonal influence: If a man or woman has abnormally low hormone levels, injections of hormones will generally increase his or her sex drive (Davidson, 1986; Rosenzweig et al., 1996).

Hormonal influences are also evident in the fact that women's preferences and behavior change as they move through their menstrual cycle. For example, women seem to prefer more "masculine" faces (with a slightly stronger chin and more prominent brows) if they are tested during the fertile phase of their cycle (Frost, 1994; Johnston, Hagel, Franklin, Fink, & Grammer, 2001; Penton-Voak & Perrett, 2000; for more on the faces people prefer, see p. 68). In addition, some evidence suggests that women's sexual desire increases during the middle of the cycle, when ovulation occurs. This effect is not very pronounced, however, and has not been observed in all studies, and thus it seems to be only the vestige of an estrus cycle, left behind by waves of evolutionary change (Adams, Gold, & Burt, 1978; Bancroft, 1986; Hamburg, Moos, & Yalom, 1968; Spitz, Gold, & Adams, 1975).

SELECTING A MATE

The act of sexual coupling is, of course, an act of enormous biological significance (because it is a prerequisite for reproduction!) and also an act that is under considerable biological control. One might think, though, that other aspects of human mating—finding and choosing a mate, for example—are governed less by biology or by our evolutionary past. After all, we say things like "there's no accounting for taste" or "beauty is in the eye of the beholder." These expressions seem to imply that the selection of romantic or sexual partners is a matter of idiosyncratic preference, shaped by a diverse set of factors lodged in each person's individual experience. But many scholars reject these commonsense ideas and argue instead that there are consistent and powerful forces governing how we seek, find, and select a mate—forces that, in their view, have been directly shaped by natural selection.

In fact, these points play a central role in an approach to psychology called *evolutionary psychology* (e.g., Buss, 2004; Pinker, 1999a, 2002; Symons, 1979; Tooby & Cosmides, 1990). We have already alluded to some of the arguments put forward within this approach—including an emphasis on the survival demands that our ancestors faced during the Pleistocene epoch, based on the idea that this was the period in which natural selection led to many of the traits of modern humanity. Given the evolutionary importance of successful reproduction, though, it is not surprising that some of the central claims of the evolutionary psychologists involve mating. Let's consider some of their arguments. We will begin with some basic facts about attractiveness, and then we will examine how those facts might be explained from an evolutionary perspective.

PHYSICAL ATTRACTIVENESS

How do we select our mates? One obvious factor is physical appearance, so that we are likely to prefer a mate who is attractive over one who looks repulsive. This is true for both men and women (although, as we will see, attractiveness matters more for men when they are choosing a mate than it does for women).

Common sense tells us that physical appearance is important for mating, and formal evidence confirms the point. In one study, for example, freshmen were randomly paired at a dance and later asked how much they liked their partner and whether he or she was someone they might want to date. What mainly determined each person's desirability as a future date was his or her physical attractiveness (Walster, Aronson, Abrahams, & Rottman, 1966). Similar results were found among clients of a commercial video-dating service who selected partners based on files that included a photograph, background information, and details about interests, hobbies, and personal ideals. When it came down to the actual choice, the primary determinant was the photograph (Green, Buchanan, & Heuer, 1984).

Physically attractive individuals also benefit from the common belief that what is beautiful is good, because people tend to associate physical attractiveness with a variety of other positive traits, including intelligence, happiness, and good mental health (e.g., Bessenoff & Sherman, 2000; Dion, Berscheid, & Walster, 1972; Eagly, Ashmore, Makhijani, & Longo, 1991; Feingold, 1992; Jackson, Hunter, & Hodge, 1995; Langlois et al., 2000). This is, in fact, part of a larger pattern sometimes referred to as the "halo effect," a term that refers to our tendency to assume that people who have one good trait are likely to have others (and, conversely, that people with one bad trait are likely to be bad in other regards as well). In some cases, there may be a kernel of truth in this pattern of beliefs, but unmistakably the "halo" extends farther than it should. For example, people seem to make judgments about how *competent* someone is based only on facial appearance, and so, remarkably, judgments about appearance turn out to be powerful predictors of whom people will vote for in U.S. congressional elections (Todorov, Mandisodza, Goren, & Hall, 2005).

WHAT IS PHYSICALLY ATTRACTIVE?

What is it that makes someone physically attractive? Many people regard this as a matter of "personal taste," but, in truth, there is considerable agreement about who is attractive and who is not—including agreement among people of different cultures and different generations (Cunningham, Roberts, Barbee, Druen, & Wu, 1998; Langlois et al., 2000; but also see Hönekopp, 2006). Evidence also indicates that infants prefer to look at faces that adults consider attractive, suggesting that the allure of these faces may be based on innate factors (Langlois et al., 1987).

Who are the attractive people? Across ages, generations, and cultures, attractive people are almost always those with clear skin, shiny hair, and no visible deformities. Faces that are symmetrical are usually considered more attractive than those that are not, and, generally speaking, "average faces" (those of average width, average eye size, and so on) are more attractive than faces that deviate from the average (see, for example, Grammer, Fink, Moller, & Thornhill, 2003; Mealey, Bridgstock, & Townsend, 1999; Rhodes, 2006; Rhodes, Proffitt, Grady, & Sumich, 1998; Rhodes, Sumich, & Byatt, 1999; Thornhill & Gangestad, 1999).

Some departures from the average, though, increase attractiveness, and these departures seem to be ones that exaggerate certain features found in the average face. The average female, for example, has big eyes, full lips, and a small chin. A female face will be more attractive, therefore, if she has slightly larger-than-average eyes, fuller-than-average lips, and so on—in essence, a slight caricature of the average. Similarly, the average male has a strong chin, a large jaw, and prominent brows; a male face will be more attractive if these features are slightly exaggerated (Fink & Penton-Voak, 2002; Rhodes, 2006).

Of course, it is not just faces we find attractive but bodies as well, and there is no question about the fact that the preferred body dimensions vary from culture to culture and from one time period to the next. As we mentioned in Chapter 1, the beautiful women painted by Rubens in the 1600s look quite chunky by today's standards; in contrast, contemporary supermodels would have seemed horribly emaciated in Rubens's time. But even here there may be consistency in the preferred proportions. One line of research has focused on the waist-to-hip ratio, which is simply the waist circumference divided by the hip circumference. Several studies indicate that, in a range of cultures, women are perceived to be more attractive if their ratio is approximately 7:10. Thus, if a particular culture favors slender women, someone with a 24-inch waist and 35-inch hips will be considered attractive. If a culture favors larger women, then someone with a 32-inch waist and 46-inch hips might be the ideal. In both cases, the 7:10 ratio is preserved—a plausible candidate for a universal standard of corporeal female beauty (Furnham, Tan, & McManus, 1997; Henss, 2000; Singh, 1993; Singh & Luis, 1995).

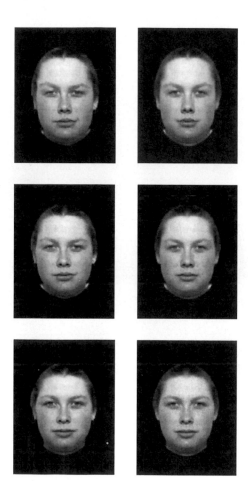

What makes a face attractive? **The faces in the middle row have been altered to make them slightly closer to the average face than those in the top row; the faces in the bottom row have been made even closer to the average. As the faces become more average (i.e., as one moves downward in the figure), do the faces become more attractive? In addition, the faces in the right column are perfectly symmetrical; those in the left column are not. Does symmetry make a face more attractive? Research suggest that the answer is "yes" to both of these questions— more average, and symmetrical faces are generally preferred.**

THE BIOLOGICAL BASIS FOR ATTRACTIVENESS

Why is it that people find average faces attractive and a certain waist-to-hip ratio appealing? Evolutionary psychologists believe the answer lies in our species' ancient past. In their view, a 7:10 waist-to-hip ratio in women is indicative of a mature pelvis and an adequate supply of fat, both showing a readiness for pregnancy and so signaling a fertile partner (Singh, 1993, 1994). Therefore, any of our male ancestors with a preference for this shape would have maximized his chances for reproductive success, and so natural selection would have favored individuals with this preference. If this selection were repeated, generation after generation, eventually this preference would have become widespread in our species—as it indeed appears to be.

What about the preference for average, or symmetrical, faces? This, too, may have evolutionary roots. A wide variety of health problems can lead to asymmetrical faces, or faces that depart widely from the average; thus, facial symmetry and proximity to the average may indicate the absence of these problems. Hence any of our ancestors who were attracted to these features would have been more likely to end up with healthy partners, increasing their chances of healthy offspring (Grammer et al., 2003; Thornhill & Gangestad, 1999). Thus, natural selection would favor an organism that found average and symmetrical faces attractive.

Other scholars, though, are skeptical about these evolutionary claims. The preference for a 7:10 waist-to-hip ratio, for example, is certainly widespread, but is the preference universal? Evidence that it is not comes from many sources, including the judgments of males in an isolated indigenous tribe in Peru; they favored a 9:10 ratio, and one male in the group commented that one of the females with a 7:10 ratio looked like she "had diarrhea a few days ago" (Yu & Shepard, 1998). Likewise, members of a hunter-gatherer population in Tanzania also preferred women who—by Western standards—would be counted as overweight (Marlowe & Wetsman, 2001). Even in the modern West, the 7:10 ratio may not define female beauty. Studies of *Playboy* centerfold models, for example, or winners of beauty pageants, show that these women—presumably selected for their attractiveness—vary considerably in their waist-to-hip ratios (e.g., Freese & Meland, 2002). It seems, therefore, that the 7:10 ratio is *often* preferred but is certainly not the universal standard of female beauty that some authors have proposed.

In addition, a number of studies suggest that the relationship between facial attractiveness and health is actually quite weak; if so, this undermines a key premise of the evolutionary argument for why we prefer average and symmetrical faces (Kalick, Zebrowitz, Langlois, & Johnson, 1998; Weeden & Sabini, 2005; but also see Geary, 2005; Grammer, Fink, Moller, Manning, 2005; Rhodes, 2006). Moreover, it is possible that our preference for average faces derives from an entirely different source—namely, a general aesthetic preference for "average-ness" in all the stimuli we encounter, a preference that not only guides how we think about faces but also leads us to prefer average wristwatches over unusual ones, and average birds over peculiar ones (Halberstadt & Rhodes, 2000; Rhodes, 2006; also see Hosken, 2001).

THE MATCHING HYPOTHESIS

Even with the complications just noted, there is no question that physical attractiveness is a crucial guide in the selection of mates. However, we should also note two limits on the effects of attractiveness.

First, people plainly do not seek out the most attractive of all possible mates. That is because there simply are not enough supermodels to go around, and so, if we all set our sights on only the most beautiful people, the world would soon be depopulated. Obviously, then, people are choosing their partners on some more sensible basis; in particular, they seem to balance their desire for an attractive mate with a down-to-earth perception of their own desirability and attractiveness. As a result, people seek partners who are roughly at the same level of attractiveness that they are. Much evidence favors this **matching hypothesis**, which states, simply, that there will be a strong correlation between the levels of physical attractiveness of the two partners (Berscheid, Dion, Walster, & Walster, 1971; Berscheid & Walster, 1974; Feingold, 1988; White, 1980).

Second, no matter how important physical attractiveness is, it is obviously not the only thing that draws two people together. We also need to consider the aspects of someone's personality or behavior that make him or her likable or not, charismatic or not, charming or not. But here, too, there are a number of simple factors that play a large role in making someone attractive, and one of the most important of these is similarity. That is, not only do people *seek* others similar to themselves (i.e., the matching hypothesis), but they also *prefer* others similar to themselves. Specifically, people usually prefer others who are like themselves on attributes such as race, ethnic origin, social and educational

Evidence for the matching hypothesis
American Gothic *by Grant Wood, 1930.*

level, family background, income, and religion, as well as behavioral patterns like gregariousness and habits related to drinking and smoking (e.g., Burgess & Wallin, 1943; Cate, Levin, & Richmond, 2002).

We will have more to say about this issue in Chapter 12, when we consider some of the bases for attraction other than physical beauty. Our point for now, though, is simply that physical beauty is enormously important in determining how attractive someone is, but our theorizing obviously needs to take other considerations into account as well.

DIFFERENCES BETWEEN THE SEXES IN MATING STRATEGIES

The study of attractiveness considers both what makes a male attractive and what makes a female attractive. In most species, however, the two sexes play very different roles in seeking and selecting a partner. Here, too, the evolutionary psychologists have offered powerful claims—concerning both why and how the sexes differ.

THE COSTS OF MATING

It is usually the female who makes the final choice of whether to mate or not, and the biological reason for this is straightforward: It is the female who shoulders the major costs of reproduction. If she is a bird, she supplies not only the ovum but also the food supply that is stored within the eggshell to nourish the developing embryo. If she is a mammal, she carries the embryo within her body and later provides it with milk. In either case, her biological burden is vastly greater than the male's. This burden can be measured in many ways, including the sheer amount of time that each sex must invest in its offspring. In order for a doe's offspring to survive, for example, she must commit an entire breeding season to carrying her young in her womb and then nursing them. In comparison, the stag's commitment is minimal: He provides a few minutes of his time and some easily replaced sperm, and then he unconcernedly goes on about his business. No wonder, then, that females are choosy in picking their mates. For the female, reproduction is a serious business with heavy biological costs; for the males of most species, reproduction requires relatively little (Bjorklund & Shackelford, 1999; Geary, 2000; Trivers, 1972).

ADVERTISING ONE'S SEX

This contrast between the male and female roles has many implications—including implications for anatomy. Among those species that reproduce sexually, one of the first tasks in reproduction is for the organism to find a potential mate, and this usually requires each animal to advertise his or her availability and also his or her sex (so that the males' availability is noticed by females, and vice versa). Many animals have anatomical structures whose function seems to be nothing other than this sexual advertising, and since it is typically the female who does the choosing, it is usually the male who does the more extravagant self-promotion. Hence, in many species, the male is brightly colored, while the female's fur or plumage is relatively drab; in many species, the male has conspicuous anatomic features (such as striking antlers or an extraordinary tail) that the female lacks (Figure 2.12).

These various structures on the male are crucial for mating. In one species of widow birds, the males have long tail feathers, up to 20 inches long. To study the importance of this trait, an unsympathetic investigator cut the tails on some males and placed feather extensions on others. After a suitable period, the investigator counted the number of nests in each bird's territory. The males whose tails were cosmetically extended had more nests than did the unaltered males, who in turn had more nests than their unfortunate fellows whose tails had been shortened (Andersson, 1982). It evidently pays to advertise.

2.12 Advertising one's sex *The comb and wattle of this barred rock rooster proclaim that he is a male.*

Note, though, that there are some exceptions to this broad pattern in the animal world. One is the phalarope, a species of artic seabird whose eggs are hatched, and whose chicks are fed, by the male. Here the greater biological burden falls on the male, and we should expect a corresponding increase in his sexual choosiness. This is just what happens. Among the phalaropes, the female does the wooing. She is brightly plumaged and aggressively pursues the careful, dull-colored male (Williams, 1966). Another example is the seahorse, whose young are carried in a brood pouch by the male (Figure 2.13). In this animal, the male makes the greater reproductive investment; consistent with this role, he exhibits greater fussiness in his choice of partner than the female.

THE CRITERIA FOR SEXUAL SELECTION AMONG HUMANS

What about our species? Do we also show a difference between males and females in how we select our mates? In most cultures in the modern world, both men and women are selective in choosing their sexual partners, and mating happens only when both partners consent. However, many studies suggest that the sexes differ in the criteria they use in making their choices. According to a number of surveys, the physical attractiveness of the partner seems more important to men than to women. It also appears that men generally prefer younger women, whereas women prefer older men. Yet another difference concerns the social and financial status of the partner, which seems to matter much more to women than it does to men. The data also indicate that these male-female differences are not unique to our own society but are found in countries as diverse as China, India, France, Nigeria, and Iran (Buss, 1989, 1992; Buss & Barnes, 1986). Interestingly, though, the two sexes agree on one point: Across cultures, both men and women value kindness and intelligence in their prospective mates (Buss, 1992).

These results are easily understood in evolutionary terms. An attractive woman, the argument goes, is likely to be healthy and fertile, so a male selecting an attractive partner would increase his chances of reproductive success. Likewise for a woman's age: A younger woman will have more reproductive years ahead of her, so a male choosing a younger partner could plausibly look forward to more offspring. On this logic, natural selection would favor any male selecting his mates based on their youth and beauty, and this would virtually guarantee that these preferences would become widespread among the males of our species.

The female's preferences are also sensible from an evolutionary perspective. Because of her high investment in each child, she is better off having just a few offspring and doing all she can to ensure the survival of each. A wealthy, high-status mate would help her reach this goal, because he would be able to provide the food and other resources her children need. Thus, there would be a reproductive advantage associated with a preference for such a male, and so a gradual evolution toward all females in the species having this preference (Bjorklund & Shackelford, 1999; Buss, 1992).

These arguments are certainly plausible, but the data can also be interpreted in another way: Perhaps human females prefer wealthy, high-status males simply because the females have learned, across their lifetimes, the social and economic advantages they will gain from such a mate. Why is status of mate more important for females than for males? It may be because, in many cultures, women soon learn that their professional and educational opportunities are limited, and so "marrying wealth" is their best strategy for gathering resources for themselves and their young.

If this culture-based account is correct, then mating preferences may well be different in those cultures that provide more opportunities for women. In this case, "marrying wealth" is not a woman's only chance for economic and social security, and, correspondingly, a potential husband's resources become less important in mate selection. Various studies confirm this prediction and show that the priority attached to the male's social and economic status is indeed lower in cultures with more opportunities

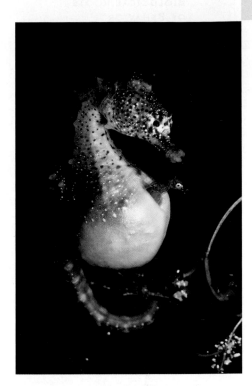

2.13 *Male sea horse "giving birth"*

Mating tendencies **Rather consistently, women prefer mates somewhat older than they are; men prefer mates who are younger. For men, mate selection is powerfully influenced by the woman's appearance; for women, mate selection is influenced by the status and resources of a potential partner. Are these tendencies rooted in our evolutionary past, or the product of culture-based learning?**

for women (Kasser & Sharma, 1999; also see Baumeister & Vohs, 2004; Buller, 2005; Eagly & Wood, 1999; Wood & Eagly, 2002).

In short, there does seem to be considerable consistency in mating preferences and also a contrast between the criteria males and females typically use; this consistency has been documented in many cultures and across several generations. But there are also variations in mate-selection preferences that are clearly attributable to the cultural context. Do these variations indicate that mating preferences are shaped from the start by the cultural context and so of course are dependent on that context? Or do they indicate merely that the cultural context is able, in some settings, to override the biologically rooted pattern? This is a difficult question to resolve. Until the evidence becomes clearer, the issue remains open.

COMMITMENT TO ONE'S MATE

The same evolutionary logic has implications for how the sexes should differ in their sense of *commitment* to an already-established relationship. From the female's point of view, long-term commitment is highly desirable: If the male stays around during her pregnancy and while she is nursing the young, then he can provide resources and protect their shared territory; this will maximize the likelihood that the female's offspring will survive, thereby increasing the chances that her genes will be passed on to the next generation. From the male's point of view, though, things look different: The male can impregnate a female with just a few minutes of copulation, and so it is possible for a male to impregnate many different females in a single season and to provide minimal support for each. This will, of course, put each of his offspring at some risk (because each will be supported by only a single parent), but the odds are good that several of the young will survive even if cared for only by the mother. Thus, whatever risk is created by this male indifference to his young will be balanced by the sheer number of his offspring—even if just a few survive, the male's genes will still be passed on.

This logic seems to suggest that our female ancestors who preferred (and worked toward) long-term relationships would have had an evolutionary advantage (i.e., would have produced more offspring carrying their genes); thus, through the process of natural selection, this female preference for commitment would have become part of our genetic endowment. Our male ancestors who preferred short-term relationships, in contrast, would have had an evolutionary advantage; thus, this tendency, too, would have become part of our biological heritage.

Consistent with these suggestions, studies indicate that males do prefer to have a large number of shorter-term relationships, while females prefer a small number of longer-term commitments (e.g., Buss & Schmitt, 1993). Likewise, several studies have shown that women tend to emphasize commited relationships as the context for sexuality; men are more open to the possibility of sexual relationships independent of any commitment (Baumeister, Catanese, & Vohs, 2001; Peplau, 2003; Regan & Berscheid, 1999). Similarly, if one asks men and women how many sexual partners they would like to have over the next 30 years, men on average express a desire for 7.7 partners in that timespan, while women express a desire for only 2.8 over the same period (Pederson, Miller, Putcha-Bhagavatula, & Yang, 2002).

Other results, however, cloud this picture. For example, alongside the differences between men and women, there are also some points of strong resemblance, including the fact that virtually all men (98.9%) and all women (99.2%) want eventually to settle down in a long-term mutually exclusive sexual relationship, preferably within the next five years (Miller, Putcha-Bhagavatula, & Pederson, 2002). In addition, the findings for how many partners men and women desire may be misleading, because the average for men is driven up by a few males who wish for an enormous number of partners. If we remove these few Lotharios from the data, we again find impressive resemblance

Commitment   According to an evolutionary perspective, women should seek an emotional commitment from their romantic partners. Men, on the other hand, should be less concerned with commitment, but should become jealous if their partners are sexually unfaithful. These broad themes are often reflected in Hollywood's portrayal of men and women, including the characters in the 2004 film, Alfie.

between the sexes—with many men indicating that their ideal number of sexual partners, over the next three decades, would be just one, a desire apparently contrary to the evolutionary logic we have described. (For related data, see Buller, 2005; Buss, Larsen, Westen, & Semmelroth, 2001; DeSteno, Bartlett, & Salovey, 2002; Harris, 2002.)

JEALOUSY

What happens when the commitment is not honored, so that one or the other party is unfaithful? Here, too, the evolutionary perspective has a prediction—about the emotional feeling we call *jealousy*. Jealousy is, of course, found in both men (as in Shakespeare's *Othello*) and women (it's commonly said: "Hell hath no fury like a woman scorned"). But there is some suggestion that the basis for this jealousy is different in men and in women. Men, it is alleged, care more about sexual loyalty than emotional loyalty; it is worse, in their view, if their partner is sleeping with someone else than it is if their partner is merely emotionally engaged with someone else. For women, it is alleged, this pattern reverses, with greater concern about emotional disloyalty than about sexual transgressions.

This pattern is easily understood in evolutionary terms. From that perspective, a woman has little reason to care if her mate has sex with others. For purposes of reproduction, she only needs one of his sperm cells to launch her own pregnancy, and once she is pregnant, it won't matter for her how the male distributes his "surplus" sperm. What the female does need from the male, though, are the resources he provides, and it would therefore be worrisome for her if he starts devoting these resources to other women (and their offspring). To prevent this calamity, what the female wants is an *emotional* commitment from her mate, so that he remains loyal to her and focused on her needs. Hence it is her mate's emotional disloyalty, not his sexual wanderings, that is threatening to the woman's evolutionary self-interest.

What about men? If a man devotes his resources to a woman and her children, he needs to be sure that these children carry his genes—otherwise, he has spent his resources to promote another male's legacy. On this basis, it should be very troubling for a male if his mate is sexually unfaithful; that would create doubts about the paternity of her offspring. But, on the other hand, emotional infidelity is less worrisome: It is okay if his mate loves someone else, provided that her love does not lead her to have sex with that someone else.

Evidence consistent with these evolutionary claims comes from studies in which men and women were asked to imagine themselves in a romantic relationship in which an infidelity takes place. They were then asked to indicate whether they would be more upset if their partner had a sexual relationship with another person or if their partner fell in love with that other person. In several such studies, the results were in line with the evolutionary

Jealousy *Do men and women differ in what makes them jealous? This question, crucial for evolutionary psychologists, provided one of the themes for the 2004 film,* Closer.

hypothesis: Women said that they would be more upset by a mate's emotional infidelity, and men by a mate's sexual infidelity (Buss, Larsen, Westen, & Semmelroth, 2001).

Once again, though, the studies yielding these results have been seriously criticized. One critic pointed out that these studies relied only on hypothetical scenarios. Would the results have been the same if the infidelities were real rather than merely imagined? To find out, the investigator focused on people who had had an actual experience with a mate cheating and asked them how they felt about the infidelity. There was no gender difference whatsoever in the respondent's reactions. Contrary to the evolutionary hypothesis, both men and women were more upset by an emotional than a sexual infidelity (Harris, 2002; for corroborating data, see DeSteno, Bartlett, & Salovey, 2002). In short, then, there may be differences in how men and women *think about* infidelity, in a fashion consistent with evolutionary theorizing. The available evidence, though, suggests that how men and women *react to* infidelity is rather similar. (However, for some other data, apparently favoring the evolutionary perspective on mating and, in particular, on "poaching" on another's mate, see Schmitt & Buss, 2001; for other concerns about the evolutionary perspective, see Miller et al., 2002.)

THE EVOLUTIONARY PERSPECTIVE IN PERSPECTIVE

It is certainly true that men and women have different views of sexuality—including the fact that, on many measures, men seem to show greater sexual desire than women do (Baumeister et al., 2001; Peplau, 2003). As we have seen, many of these differences can easily be explained from an evolutionary perspective, which is one of the reasons why this perspective has caused considerable excitement among psychologists. More, the evolutionary perspective has been a source of many new predictions about human behavior, so this perspective has unquestionably been a productive way to think about who we are and why we act as we do (e.g., Buss, 2004; Pinker, 1999a, 2002; Symons, 1979; Tooby & Cosmides, 1990.)

At the same time, however, the evolutionary psychology perspective has been controversial, and we have seen some of the reasons. In some cases, the data themselves are in dispute (e.g., whether the sexes truly differ with regard to jealousy). In other cases, the interpretation of the data is uncertain (e.g., why average faces are preferred, or why women seek out high-status partners). In addition, some writers have questioned several of the assumptions built into the evolutionary arguments—including assumptions about the degree to which we are influenced by inborn mechanisms. (For glimpses of the sometimes heated debate, see Buller, 2005; Buller, Fodor, & Crume, 2005; Buss &

Haselton, 2005; Cosmides, Tooby, Fiddick, & Bryant, 2005; Daly & Wilson, 2005; Gould, 1991; Gould & Lewontin, 1979.)

Perhaps future research will settle these issues, but perhaps not. After all, evolution does not provide us with control groups, making it difficult to test evolutionary claims in any direct fashion. In addition, the fossil record tells us a lot about our ancestors' anatomy, but little about their *behavior*, and this also makes it hard to test evolutionary hypotheses. Even with these difficulties, though, it is clear that the evolutionary psychologists have introduced new questions, and new data, into our discussions of human sexuality, and, by those measures, they have made a significant contribution to our field. But their research—and the controversy it has provoked—also highlight for us the difficulties involved whenever we try to untangle the influences of our biological past and our social and cultural present.

SOME FINAL THOUGHTS: REFLECTIONS ON THE CONTRIBUTION OF THE BIOLOGICAL PERSPECTIVE

We began this chapter with a broad question of whether we can learn about human behavior (and thoughts, feelings, and motivation) by taking a biological perspective—one that includes attention to underlying mechanisms in the body, comparison to other species, and an exploration of the evolutionary forces that might have shaped our behavior.

It is, in the end, undeniable that we do have much in common with other creatures, and so—for example—we have learned an enormous amount about the control of eating by a close examination of biological mechanisms that are shared with many other species. The same is true for sexuality and our response to threat: Here, too, humans are governed in part by mechanisms essentially identical to those found in many other animals, and so, once again, we must acknowledge the biology and the evolutionary history that we share with other animals.

At the same time, we have seen powerful indicators that our behavior is also shaped by our individual experiences and the circumstances in which each of us lives. To understand obesity, for example, we must understand the interaction between an individual's genes and that person's life situation (including the easy availability of high-calorie foods). Likewise, a full understanding of human mating surely requires that we consider the context of love and romance—considerations that may well be uniquely human and that are surely influenced in mighty ways by the culture in which we live. (We will have more to say about love and romance in Chapter 12.)

Does psychology, therefore, need to be a biological science? The answer is plain: yes, but only in part. We can gain insights from a biological perspective, examining, as we have in this chapter, biological mechanisms underlying behavior, comparisons to other species, and the evolutionary roots of our behavior. But we must not limit our view to these biological considerations; we also need to consider a variety of other factors not easily translated into biological terms. Our science, as we have repeatedly asserted, needs a diversity of methods, a diversity of perspectives.

Finally, we should also acknowledge that our focus in this chapter has been primarily on larger-scale biological processes and mechanisms. We have, for example, talked about the autonomic nervous system and the hypothalamus, and we have considered the function of these bits of biological tissue but said little about how these structures do their jobs. Clearly, though, we have to zoom in for these finer-grained questions. Humans are, in important ways, biological machines; thus, if we are to understand our behavior, we must examine how the machinery functions. We turn to that broad problem in the next chapter.

SUMMARY

Should psychology be (at least in part) a biological science? This would involve focusing on the neural mechanisms that make our thoughts, feelings, and behaviors possible. It would also involve an exploration of how humans are similar to other species, and a consideration of how our thoughts and behaviors might have been shaped by evolution.

THE EVOLUTIONARY ROOTS OF MOTIVATED BEHAVIOR

- Each individual organism differs from the others in its species, and some of these differences increase the likelihood of that individual reproducing—and so passing its genes on to the next generation. This is the essential mechanism of evolution by natural selection. What is passed to each generation, though, is the organism's *genotype*; other factors also play a pivotal role in determining how the organism will develop, and so what its finished traits, or *phenotype*, will be.
- There is ample evidence that human behavior is shaped by genetic influences. There is controversy, however, over whether this means the relevant behaviors were favored by evolution; instead, the behaviors may be the by-products of other traits that were favored by evolution.

THE ACHIEVEMENT OF HOMEOSTATIS

- Evolution provided organisms with *homeostatic mechanisms* that monitor the organism's internal environment and work to maintain stability in that environment. Homeostatic control is evident in many settings, including *thermoregulation*. When an endothermic organism is cold, this activates the *sympathetic branch* of the *autonomic nervous system*, which leads to increased heart rate, *vasodilation*, a slowing down of digestion, and other effects. When the organism is overheated, this triggers the *parasympathetic* branch of the autonomic nervous system, which has the opposite effects.

EATING

- Homeostatic mechanisms also play a crucial role in the control of eating. Each person seems to have a biologically determined set point for his or her weight, and several mechanisms work to maintain that set point. Some of these mechanisms are in the liver; others depend on

glucoreceptors in the hypothalamus; still others rely on signals from the *adipose cells*. When full of fat, these cells release *leptin*, a chemical that causes the organism to stop eating.
- This multiplicity of signals provides safety for the organism, because each signal provides a "backup" system in case the other signals fail. In addition, the various signals play different roles, with some monitoring long-term needs, some providing an index of immediate status, and some signals serving to *potentiate* other signals.
- Some cases of *obesity* are produced by genetically rooted differences in a person's set point; other cases involve changes in metabolic efficiency. Obesity in some people may represent the operation of "thrifty genes" that code for slower metabolisms. These genes were helpful in ancient times when food was scarce, but the same genes now promote unhealthy weights, thanks to the fact that we live in a world in which food is usually always available.

THREAT AND AGGRESSION

- Our response to *threat* is controlled by biological mechanisms centered on the operations of the autonomic nervous system. When we are threatened, the sympathetic branch activates the body by (among other steps) increasing the available metabolic fuel and accelerating the fuel's utilization by increasing heart rate and respiration. This *emergency reaction* was once understood as preparing us for "fight or flight," but actually it gets us ready for a number of different responses.
- Virtually every species shows some sort of aggression, and, in most species, physical aggression is more prevalent in males, perhaps because of the influence of the hormone *testosterone*. In many cases, animals fight in order to gain and maintain a *territory*. Humans also stake out territories, although there is enormous variation in the size of, and how humans think about, their "space."
- Human aggression is commonly triggered by complex beliefs and symbol systems, and, in this regard, it seems different from aggression in other species. Humans also vary in how aggressive they are, with some of the variation due to an individual's personality, and some to the cultural setting.
- Many species have built-in limits on aggression, but these limits are often inapplicable to human aggres-

sion. However, humans do seem to be becoming less violent, although trends in the last decade could easily reverse.

SEX

- Like all motivated behavior, sexual behaviors are shaped by a mix of biological factors and cultural influences. The timing of sexual behavior, for example, is heavily influenced in most species by the *estrus cycle*, but the influence of this cycle is much smaller for humans.
- Humans' selection of a mate is—perhaps surprisingly—heavily influenced by genetic factors, a point that has been emphasized by proponents of a perspective known as *evolutionary psychology*. For example, mate selection is powerfully influenced by physical attractiveness, which in turn is shaped heavily by how "average" someone's appearance is, with faces closer to the average being regarded as more attractive. According to evolutionary psychologists, this is because average faces indicate good health and fertility, and so any of our ancestors preferring average faces would have ended up with a healthy mate.
- In most species, the two sexes play very different roles in selecting a mating partner. Evolutionary psychologists explain this difference in terms of the greater investment that the female (in most species) makes in child rearing; from this base, they provide explanations for how the different sexes select a mate, and how they view commitment to a mate. However, other psychologists have challenged this evolutionary interpretation of the data (and, in some cases, have challenged the data as well).
- Overall, the evolutionary perspective has been a source of new predictions about human behavior, and the success of these predictions leaves no doubt that this is a productive way to think about our species' behavior. At the same time, evolutionary psychology's claims have been controversial, serving to remind us of the considerable difficulties in disentangling the effects of genetics and experience on our behavior. The main message of this debate may be that psychology must in part be a biological science, but it must also heed the effects of culture and experience in determining why we act as we do.

CHAPTER

3

THE BRAIN AND THE NERVOUS SYSTEM

*I*n Chapter 2, we saw powerful reminders that humans are biological organisms, with much in common with the other creatures that populate this planet. This means, among other things, that we need to understand our behavior, thoughts, and feelings in terms of the biological machinery inside each of us, machinery that makes possible all that we do. This machinery, in turn, has been shaped to an enormous extent by the genes we each inherit from our parents, and the genes, finally, are the end-product of thousands of generations of natural selection.

But how exactly are these biological influences actualized? What mechanisms inside the body, in the present time, produce the behaviors that were favored by natural selection long ago? For that matter, what mechanisms in the body make possible *new* behaviors, produced in response to the information that each organism acquires during its lifetime? In this chapter, we tackle these questions by taking a closer look at how the brain, and the nervous system in general, supports all of our capacities, achievements, and behaviors.

In our discussion, we will view the brain essentially as a piece of machinery—akin, perhaps, to the computer that sits on your desk—and, for modern readers, this perspective is hardly new. We live, after all, in a world filled with a variety of sophisticated electronic devices, and so the notion of a machine that thinks is probably surprising to no one. We find it quite natural to think of the brain as a bit of biological machinery to be scrutinized, analyzed, and, if appropriate, adjusted. But, in truth, this is a very modern perspective, and the suggestion that our brain and body could be thought of as parts of a complex machine was long regarded as heretical, a state of affairs that changed only 400 years ago. ●

THE ORGANISM AS A MACHINE

The idea that the brain is really some kind of complicated machine, to be analyzed by taking it apart, seeing how the parts connect, and testing what each of the parts does, was first raised seriously by the French philosopher René Descartes (1596–1650). Prior to Descartes' time, people in the Western world had regarded human behavior as complex and mysterious, but in any case best understood as the result of the soul's directives, and certainly not the product of some mere machinery.

This broad conception of humanity had stood largely unchallenged for roughly 15 centuries. In the 1500s and 1600s, however, intellectuals began shifting to a dramatically different perspective. Part of the impetus for this change came from scientific advances: Kepler and Galileo were developing ideas about the movements of the stars and planets visible in the night sky; their observations were part of the intellectual growth that led to Isaac Newton's formulation of the laws of motion, summarized in 1687 in his extraordinary book *Principia Mathematica*. These new views of the universe suggested that natural phenomena could be understood in terms of relatively straightforward principles of acceleration, inertia, and momentum that could be described with simple mathematical laws. These laws seemed to explain events ranging from the drop of a stone to the motions of planets. The same laws could be seen operating—rigidly, precisely, immutably—in the workings of ingenious mechanical contrivances that were all the rage in the wealthy homes of Europe: cuckoo clocks that sounded on the hour, water-driven gargoyles with nodding heads, statues in the king's garden that bowed to visitors who stepped on hidden springs. The turning of a gear, the release of a spring—these simple mechanisms could cause all kinds of clever effects.

With these intellectual and technical developments in place and with so many complex phenomena explicable in such simple terms, it was only a matter of time before someone asked the crucial question: Could human actions be explained just as mechanically?

René Descartes

3.1   Reflex action as envisaged by Descartes
In this sketch by Descartes, the heat from the fire (A) starts a chain of processes that begins at the affected spot of the skin (B) and continues up the nerve tube until a pore of a cavity (F) is opened. Descartes believed that this opening allowed the animal spirits in the cavity to enter the nerve tube and eventually travel to the muscles that pull the foot from the fire.

DESCARTES AND THE REFLEX CONCEPT

Descartes' view of action—whether the actions of a human or some other animal—was both radical and straightforward. He proposed in essence that every action by an organism is a direct response to some event in the outside world. Something from the outside excites one of the senses; this, in turn, excites a nerve that transmits the excitation to the brain, which then diverts the excitation to a muscle and makes the muscle contract. In effect, the energy from the outside is "reflected" back by the nervous system to the animal's muscles, a conception that gave rise to the term *reflex* (Figure 3.1).

Seen in this light, human and animal actions could be regarded as the doings of a machine. But Descartes also understood that he needed some account of the *flexibility* in our behavior. After all, the sight of food might trigger an action of reaching toward the food if we are hungry, but trigger no action at all if we are not. In Descartes' terms, therefore, it seemed that excitation from the senses could be reflected back to one set of muscles on one occasion and an entirely different set on another, as though the reflex mechanisms included some sort of central switching system, controlling which incoming signal would trigger which outgoing one.

How could Descartes explain this switching system? He was aware that a strictly mechanical explanation would have unsettling theological implications: If all human action was explained in terms of some sort of machinery, what role was left for the soul? In addition, Descartes was prudent—he knew that Galileo was condemned by the Inquisition to life-long imprisonment because his scientific beliefs threatened the doctrines of the Church. Perhaps it is not surprising, therefore, that Descartes proposed that the centralized controller of human behavior was not a machine at all. Many processes within the brain, he argued, did function mechanically, but what truly governed our behavior, what made reason and choice possible, and what distinguished us from other animals, was the soul—operating through the brain, choosing among nervous pathways, and controlling our bodies like a puppeteer pulling the strings on a marionette.

Over the next decades, though, as theology's grip on science loosened, other thinkers went further. They believed that the laws of the physical universe could ultimately explain all action, whether human or animal, so that a scientific account required no further "ghost in the machine"—that is, no reference to the soul. They therefore extended Descartes' logic to all of human functioning, arguing that humans differ from other animals only in being more finely constructed mechanisms.

Of course, the ultimate question of whether humans are just machines (whether machines governed by fluid pressures and gears, as Descartes envisioned, or machines resembling computers, as more modern scholars propose) is as much a question about faith as it is about science. Because no one knows how to test for the existence of an intangible soul, the issue of whether we are machines, or machines with souls, is not something that can be determined by science. What is undeniable, though, is that the strategy of regarding humans as machines, with no mention of a soul in our scientific theorizing, has fostered dramatic breakthroughs in understanding ourselves and our fellow animals.

HOW THE NERVOUS
SYSTEM IS STUDIED

Descartes' views were based largely on conjecture, because in his time scientists knew little about the functioning of the nervous system. Today, roughly 350 years later, we know far more, and our theorizing can be correspondingly more sophisticated. In fact, the data and research tools now available have allowed the development of a new and rapidly growing field called **neuroscience**, a multidisciplinary effort that seeks to understand the nature, function, and origins of the nervous system. Neuroscientists include psychologists, of course, but they also include biologists, computer scientists, physicians, and others, in a research effort that ranges from the attempt to understand the interactions among the molecules inside individual nerve cells, to the investigation of how large tracts of neural tissue give rise to conscious experience.

Let us be clear from the start, though, that the study of the brain is, to say the least, an enormously daunting task. Within the human brain, the total number of **neurons**—the individual cells that act as the main information processors of the nervous system

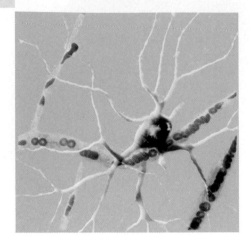

3.2 *Observing the nervous system through a microscope* *A single nerve cell shows as green here; nearby a capillary (pink) contains red blood cells. This nerve cell comes from the retina, the light-sensitive part of the eye.*

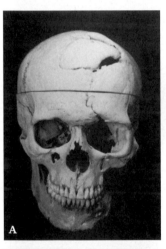

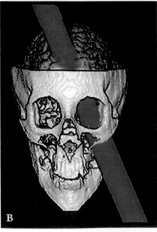

3.3 *Phineas Gage's skull* *(A) A photograph showing the damage to Phineas Gage's skull. (B) A computer reconstruction showing the path of the rod.*

(Figure 3.2)—has been estimated to be as high as 100 billion (approximately the same number as the total count of stars in the Milky Way), with each neuron connecting to as many as 50 thousand others (Nauta & Feirtag, 1986). The brain also contains another type of cell, *glia*, whose function we are just beginning to understand, and glia in some parts of the brain outnumber the neurons by 10 to 1. All of these cells, and all the interconnections among them, are contained within an organ that weighs only 3 to 4 pounds, leading many writers to suggest that the human brain is the most complex known object in the universe. How can we study such a complex object?

CLINICAL OBSERVATION

Probably the first technique used for studying the brain was direct *clinical observation* of patients with brain damage or disease. The goal of this technique is to link physical brain abnormality with observable changes in behavior. For example, consider the grisly case of Phineas Gage, who in 1848 was working as a construction foreman. While he was preparing a site for demolition, some blasting powder misfired and launched a 3-foot iron rod into his cheek, through the front part of his brain, and out the top of his head (Figure 3.3). Gage lived, but not well. As we will discuss later (p. 96), he suffered intellectual and emotional impairments that gave valuable clues about the roles of the brain's frontal lobes (Valenstein, 1986).

In Gage's case, the brain damage was clear, and the task for investigators was to discover the damage's consequences. In other cases, the logic is reversed: The behavioral effects are known, but the brain damage cannot be assessed until after death. The search for the brain regions responsible for speech is one example. They were first isolated during autopsy by examining the brains of adults who had suffered traumatic losses of speech years before (see pp. 95–96 later in this chapter).

NEUROPSYCHOLOGY

Like the clinical method, *neuropsychology* seeks to understand brain function by closely examining individuals who have suffered some form of brain damage. However, neuropsychologists do not rely only on the symptoms associated with the brain injury; instead, they often do fine-grained experiments, to find out exactly what the brain-damaged individual can and cannot do. These experiments are usually combined with the neuroimaging techniques we will describe in a moment, so that a precise picture of the person's brain damage can be matched with an equally precise assessment of her deficits.

As one example of what we can learn from neuropsychology, various cases of brain damage make it clear that our perception of the world around us depends on a number of specialized "modules," with each module responsive to just one aspect of the stimulus information. One module seems specialized for the perception of motion, so damage to this module leaves the person unable to perceive movement; the world appears to such a person as a succession of static snapshots. Another module is concerned with the perception of position; damage here produces an inability to reach toward objects, although the person can still perceive the shape and size of the objects. Each of these cases is interesting on its own, but together these (and related) cases provide crucial insights into how seeing is made possible by the nervous system. (For more on perception, see Chapters 4 and 5.)

EXPERIMENTAL TECHNIQUES

In clinical evidence or neuropsychology, investigators rely on naturally occurring injuries to the brain—including damage caused by medical problems and injuries caused by wounds. These injuries are tragic, and they are also relatively coarse—typically involving large tracts of brain tissue. More fine-grained data come from experiments in which investigators stimulate a particular area of the brain, or disrupt it, and then observe the effects.

Work of this type can be traced to the mid-1800s, when investigators began to study the brain directly by opening the skull and "invading" the brain matter while the subject was alive (hence this research is said to involve *invasive techniques*). In these procedures, investigators can activate brain areas with chemicals, temperature changes, or weak applications of electricity. Tissue can be deactivated in several different ways: The tissue can be removed, or it can be *lesioned* (destroyed in place). If the connecting pathways to that tissue are known, then the tissue can be isolated by cutting—technically, *transecting*—the relevant pathways.

Each of these techniques has been a valuable source of new knowledge, but it should be obvious that the techniques, which involve altering the brain of another living creature, raise a host of ethical questions—especially when the results of a procedure are not known fully in advance, or when the procedures are used with animals (which cannot possibly give their consent). And, sadly, there have unmistakably been some abuses of these procedures, leading in some instances to professional censure or criminal prosecution. Nevertheless, when used wisely, invasive techniques have their place and have yielded both scientific insights and medical advances.

In the last few years, investigators have added another experimental technique to their repertoire, and it is a crucial one because it produces only *temporary* brain dysfunction, which allows investigators to perform experiments that would otherwise not be possible. This technique—*transcranial magnetic stimulation (TMS)*—involves the creation of a series of strong magnetic pulses at a particular location on the scalp. At low intensities, these pulses stimulate the brain region directly underneath this scalp area; at high intensities, the pulses create a temporary disruption in that region.

In effect, TMS allows investigators to "turn off" a brain mechanism for a short period of time and observe the results. This obviously provides an enormous range of experimental options, allowing investigators to examine in detail the function of this or that brain region. However, TMS does have limits as a research tool: It only influences structures near the surface of the brain (i.e., immediately inside the skull). Even so, TMS is a powerful additon to the neuroscientists' toolkit.

There has also been discussion about whether TMS might have potential as a therapy tool, activating otherwise sluggish brain regions or perhaps derailing dysfunctional patterns in the brain. Some researchers believe that TMS may be especially useful as a treatment for depression (Gershon, Dannon, & Grunhaus, 2003), but actual use of TMS in clinical settings is, at best, still years off.

NEUROIMAGING TECHNIQUES

In the last few decades, our understanding of the linkage between brain and behavior has been revolutionized by a number of *neuroimaging techniques*. These provide remarkable views of the brain's anatomy (structure) or its physiology (functioning), with absolutely no invasion of brain tissue and with the brain's owner awake and fully conscious throughout the procedure.

One technique for imaging brain anatomy is the *CT (computerized tomography) scan* (or *CAT scan*, an abbreviation for "computerized axial tomography"), which involves a series of X rays of a brain area taken at different angles and then the use of a computer to construct a detailed composite picture from these X-ray images.

A more widely used neuroimaging technique is *magnetic resonance imaging* (*MRI*; Figure 3.4). MRI scans are safer because they involve no X rays. Instead, MRI scans pass

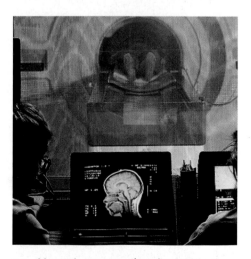

3.4 *Magnetic resonance imaging (MRI)* **A patient goes through the MRI procedure, while a medical specialist watches the image on a screen.**

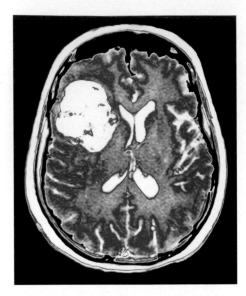

3.5 *Brain cancer* *Magnetic resonance imaging (MRI) scan of a patient's brain showing a cancerous brain tumor (white area, upper left). The front of the brain is at the top.*

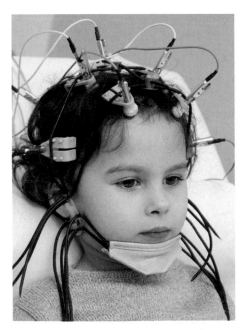

Record brain waves *The overall electricity of the brain can be measured via electrodes placed on the surface of the scalp.*

a magnetic field through the brain to align the spinning of the nuclei of all the atoms that make up the brain tissue; then a brief pulse of electromagnetic energy is used to disrupt these spins. After the disruption, the spins of the nuclei shift back into alignment with the magnetic field, and, as this shift happens, the atoms give off electromagnetic energy. This energy is recorded by a bank of detectors arrayed around the person's head, analyzed by a computer, and assembled into a magnificently detailed three-dimensional representation of the brain that can show both the healthy tissue and also tumors, tissue degeneration, and the blood clots or leaks that may signal strokes (Figure 3.5).

CT and MRI scans allow only anatomical depictions—that is, they can reveal the shape and size of various brain structures, the presence or absence of a tumor, and so on. However, these procedures cannot tell us about the brain's moment-by-moment functioning, including which areas of the brain are particularly active at any point in time and which are less active. To address brain activity, experimenters use other techniques. The earliest developed was *electroencephalography* (*EEG*), which detects the tiny electrical currents generated by the neurons in the brain. This procedure only requires affixing tiny metal electrodes to the top and sides of the head.

EEGs can be richly informative, but they are inexact in specifying where in the brain the measured activity is taking place. For more precise, three-dimensional localization of brain function, investigators can use *positron emission tomography* (*PET*) *scans*. In PET scans, the participant is injected with a safe dose of radioactive sugar that resembles glucose (the only metabolic fuel the brain can use). The brain cells that are more active at any moment will soak up more of this sugar and thus give off more radioactivity, which can be detected and used to derive an image in much the same way as CT and MRI scans. The resulting PET scan can thus tell the physician or researcher which regions within the brain are particularly active at any moment in time.

A newer technique, *functional MRI* (*fMRI*) *scanning* (Figure 3.6), adapts standard MRI procedures to detect relatively fast-changing aspects of brain physiology (mostly blood flow and oxygen use) without using any radioactivity. The end result is a three-dimensional image of the brain at work, showing the parts that are most active at any particular moment.

EEG data, PET scans, and fMRI scans all measure the activity of individual brain areas, but, in interpreting any of these types of data, we should bear in mind that the entire brain is active all of the time. This is because some parts of the brain are constantly involved in the maintenance of basic life functions (like breathing, or circulating the blood); other parts are always at work maintaining our posture and our body position; still other parts are constantly monitoring the senses for incoming information. Even in brain areas that are not working on anything in particular at the moment, there is always a high level of activity; this is because nerve cells actually spend considerable energy just maintaining their baseline state, so that they are ready for action when needed.

What EEG, PET, and fMRI measure, therefore, is a pattern of *increases* beyond this constant state of activity. In other words, the measurement is not "which areas are active when someone is (say) listening to music?" Instead, the measurement is "which areas become more active when someone is listening?" These increases are typically assessed by a process that, in the end, resembles simple subtraction: Researchers measure the brain's activity when someone is engaged in the task that is being investigated, and they subtract from this a measurement of the brain's activity when the person is not engaged in the task. Of course, it is important to design this baseline measurement with care, so that (like any control condition) it is identical to the experimental condition in all ways except the contrast of special interest to the researchers. Thus, careful design of the control condition becomes part of the craft of using any of the neuroimaging techniques.

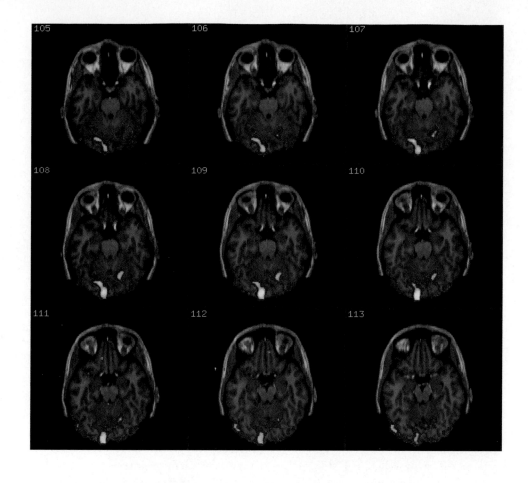

3.6 Functional MRI Using functional magnetic-resonance imaging, researchers can produce precise summaries of brain activity. These images show the brain as viewed from above, with the front of the skull shown at the top of each image; the successive images show horizontal "slices" higher and higher in the brain. The brightly colored areas show regions of greater activity.

CORRELATION AND CAUSATION

Each of the investigative techniques we have described has its strengths and weaknesses. Some techniques examine structures but not activation levels within those structures; some do the reverse. Some are excellent in telling us when a particular bit of activity took place but are imprecise regarding where in the brain the activity was located; others do the reverse: They are precise with regard to locations in the brain, but at the cost of sightly coarser time measurements.

It is not surprising, therefore, that neuroscientists typically base their conclusions on data drawn from multiple techniques—with each technique contributing its own strengths to the overall argument. In addition, a combination of techniques can help us with a crucial interpretive problem: The neuroimaging techniques, as powerful as they are, merely tell us what brain areas are activated during a particular process, but does this mean the brain areas are actually needed for the process? Perhaps the brain activity is a *consequence* of the process, much as sweating is a consequence of (and not a cause) of physical activity. In this case, the brain activity would be *correlated* with a mental process, but it would not play a role in guiding or supporting that process.

To assess this possibility, neuroscientists often combine neuroimagery with studies of brain damage, on the logic that, if damage to a brain site disrupts a function, this is an indication that the site does play a role in supporting the function. Likewise, TMS allows us (temporarily) to "turn off" a particular brain site. If this causes a disruption in some process, this too indicates that the site plays a role in supporting that function. The key, though, is that we rely on a variety of techniques and draw our conclusions only from a convergence of evidence drawn from many paradigms.

Finally, neuroscientists also have another tool in their repertoire, but it is a conceptual tool, a particular form of argument, rather than a bit of technology. To understand the issue that is at stake here, imagine that we find (from lesion data or TMS) that disruption of a certain brain site causes problems in, say, perception but not in memory. Does that mean these two processes—perception and memory—are served by distinct areas in the brain? Perhaps they rely on the same brain areas, but perception is just a bit more complicated as a process, and so more fragile, and so more easily disrupted, than memory is. That hypothesis, too, would fit with the data just sketched.

How could we check on this new possibility? If, in fact, perception is simply more easily disrupted than memory, then that leads to a simple prediction: Any brain damage severe enough to interfere with memory should certainly be strong enough to disrupt the (more fragile) processes of perception. In contrast, if the two processes are supported by distinct brain areas, then we should make a different prediction. We have already supposed that there are forms of brain damage that disrupt perception but spare memory. If memory relies on its own brain supports, then we should also be able to find the complementary case: instances of damage that interfere with the brain areas needed for memory, but not perception. In fact, we can find such instances, confirming that the two processes do indeed depend on different brain circuits. Neuroscientists refer to this crucial form of argument as a *double dissociation*—a pattern of evidence in which we show that X can be disrupted while sparing Y, and also that Y can be disrupted while sparing X. This pattern of data rules out the possibility that one or another process is just more fragile, more easily disrupted, than the other, and it provides powerful confirmation that the two are instead made possible by distinct brain mechanisms.

THE ARCHITECTURE OF THE NERVOUS SYSTEM

Whether based on clinical observation or PET scans, invasive procedures or fMRI images, our investigations have taught us a great deal about the nervous system. One central message, though, emerging from study after study, is that the individual parts of the nervous system are each specialized. This is evident, for example, in the simple fact that the results of brain damage depend powerfully on where the damage occurred. Phineas Gage, with damage to the front of his brain, suffered from a range of intellectual and emotional problems. In 1861, physician Paul Broca noted that damage on the left side of the brain led to disruption of language skills. Damage in still other regions produces profound amnesia. And so on.

These observations make it clear that we need to understand the brain with reference to anatomy—so that we can talk about the function of this part as opposed to the function of that part. Let us start, therefore, with a broad tour of the nervous system. Then, with this framework in place, we can zoom in for a closer look at how the nervous system actually does its work.

THE CENTRAL AND PERIPHERAL NERVOUS SYSTEMS

The nervous system is, at the most general level, subdivided into several parts (Figure 3.7). The *central nervous system* (*CNS*) includes the brain and spinal cord, working as one integrated unit. All nerves in the body are part of the *peripheral nervous system*; this

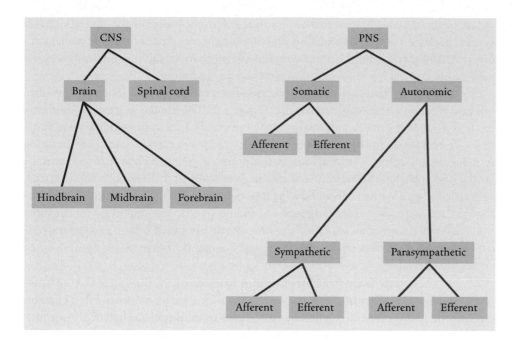

3.7 *Principle parts of the nervous system*

system includes *efferent nerves*, carrying signals *from* the CNS, and also *afferent nerves*, carrying signals from the rest of the body to the CNS.* Virtually all of the nerves in the peripheral nervous system connect to the CNS via the spinal cord, which is part of the reason why damage to the cord is so dangerous, and likewise why the cord is protected by the bones and connective tissue of the spine itself. Of course, the brain, too, is well protected. It is, first, covered in a shell of bone (the skull) and three layers of tough membranes (the meninges). The brain is also floating in a bath of fluid that (among other things) acts as a shock absorber if the head is abruptly moved this way or that.

Twelve pairs of nerves, however, exit the brain directly, without passing through the spinal cord. These are the so-called *cranial nerves*. These nerves control the movements of the head and neck; carry sensations inward from the eyes, the nose, the tongue, and the ears; and also control various secretions in the head (including tears, saliva, and mucus).

The peripheral nervous system itself has two distinguishable parts. The *somatic division* includes all the (efferent) nerves that control the skeletal muscles and also all the (afferent) nerves that carry information from the sense organs to the CNS. The other division—the *autonomic nervous system*—was introduced in Chapter 2. This system includes all the (efferent) nerves that regulate the various body organs (including the heart and lungs, the blood vessels, the digestive system, the sexual organs, and so on) and also the (afferent) nerves that bring the CNS information about these various internal systems. Then, finally, the autonomic itself is subdivided, as we have seen, into the sympathetic and parasympathetic branches.

HINDBRAIN, MIDBRAIN, FOREBRAIN

The peripheral nervous system is of course crucial: Without it, no motion of the body would be possible; no information would be received about the external world; the body would be unable to control its own digestion or blood circulation. But even so, the

---

* To keep track of which nerves are afferent and which are efferent, some students find it helpful to remember that afferent nerves carry the information arriving in the CNS and are the means through which we are affected by incoming information. In contrast, efferent nerves carry information exiting from the CNS and are the means through which we effect changes in the world.

aspect of the nervous system most interesting to psychologists is the central nervous system, because it is here that we find the complex circuitry crucial for perception, memory, and thinking; it is the CNS that contains the mechanisms that define each person's personality, control his or her emotional responses, and more.

The CNS, as we have said, contains the spine and the brain itself. The brain, in turn, can be divided into three large structures (Figure 3.8). The *hindbrain* sits directly on top of the spinal cord and includes many structures crucial for controlling key life functions. The *midbrain* sits on top of the hindbrain and plays a major role in coordinating movements and relaying information from the senses. The *forebrain* is, in humans, by far the largest part of the brain, and is essential for many of the functions that make us, as a species, who we are—including (as just two examples) our capacity for complex thought and our ability to use language. The forebrain is no less important for the functions that make each of us, *as individuals*, who we are, because it is here that our individual beliefs and memories, our coping styles, and our emotional reactions are established and controlled.

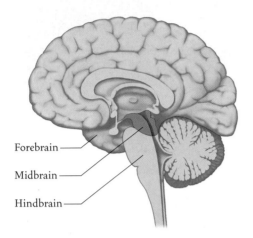

Each of these large-scale structures contains many parts. At the bottom of the hindbrain (Figure 3.9), for example, is the *medulla*, which, among its other roles, controls our breathing and blood circulation and also helps us maintain our balance by controlling head orientation and limb positions with respect to gravity. Above the medulla is the *pons*, which is one of the most important brain areas controlling the brain's overall level of attentiveness and which helps govern the timing of sleep and dreaming.

Forebrain

Midbrain

Hindbrain

3.8   The three main parts of the brain   This drawing shows a brain as if it were split down the middle; the front of the person's head is to the left.

The largest part of the hindbrain is the *cerebellum* (Figure 3.10). For many years, investigators believed the cerebellum's main role was in the coordination of our movements and balance. Recent studies, however, suggest that the cerebellum also has a diverse set of other functions; damage to this organ can cause problems in spatial reasoning, in discriminating sounds, and in integrating the input received from various sensory systems (Bower & Parsons, 2003).

The midbrain is relatively small in mammals and, in humans, serves to a large extent as a relay station directing information to the forebrain, where it is more fully processed and interpreted. But, in addition, the midbrain plays an important part in humans in coordinating our movements, including the precise movements of our eyes as we explore the visual world. Other structures in the midbrain help to regulate our experience of pain.

For many psychological questions, though, the most important brain region is the forebrain. Pictures of the brain (like the one shown in Figure 3.11) show little other than the forebrain, because this structure is large enough in humans to surround and hide from view the entire midbrain and most of the hindbrain. Of course, it is only the outer surface of the forebrain that is visible in such pictures; this is the *cortex* (from the Latin word for "tree bark").

The cortex is just a thin covering on the outer surface of the brain; on average, it is a mere 3 mm thick. Nonetheless, there is a great deal of cortical tissue; by some estimates, the cortex constitutes 80% of the human brain. This considerable volume is made possible by the fact that the cortex, thin as it is, consists of a very large sheet of tissue; if stretched out flat, it would cover roughly 2 square feet. But the cortex isn't stretched flat; instead, it is crumpled up and jammed into the limited space inside the skull. It is this crumpling that produces the brain's most obvious visual feature—the wrinkles, or *convolutions*, that cover the brain's outer surface.

Some of the "valleys" in between the wrinkles are actually deep grooves that anatomically divide the brain into different sections. The deepest groove is the *longitudinal fissure*, running from the front of the brain to the back and dividing the brain into a left half and a right—specifically, the left *cerebral hemisphere* and the right. Other fissures divide the cortex in each hemisphere into four lobes (Figure 3.10), named after the bones that cover them, bones that, as a group, make up the skull. The *frontal lobes* form

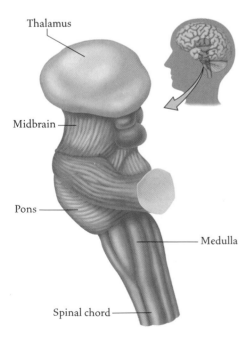

Thalamus

Midbrain

Pons

Medulla

Spinal chord

3.9   The hindbrain

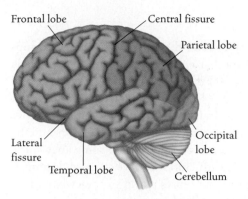

Frontal lobe

Central fissure

Parietal lobe

Lateral fissure

Temporal lobe

Occipital lobe

Cerebellum

3.10 *The cortex of the cerebral hemispheres* *Side-view drawing, showing the brain's convolutions, fissures, and lobes.*

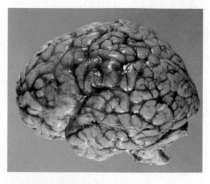

3.11 *The cortex of the cerebral hemispheres* *An actual human brain, shown in side view; the front of the head is towards the left.*

the front of the brain, right behind the forehead. The *central fissure* divides the frontal lobes on each side of the brain from the *parietal lobes*, the brain's topmost part. The bottom edge of the frontal lobes is marked by the *lateral fissure*, and below this are the *temporal lobes*. Finally, at the very back of the brain, connected to the parietal and temporal lobes, are the *occipital lobes*.

As we will see, the cortex of the forebrain controls many crucial functions, and because these functions are so important to what we think, feel, and do, the next section addresses them in detail. Just as important, though, are the structures underneath the cortex—the *subcortical* structures. One of these is the *thalamus*, a brain region that acts as a relay station for nearly all the sensory information going to the cortex. Directly underneath the thalamus is the hypothalamus, crucially involved in the control of motivated behaviors such as eating, drinking, and sexual activity (see Chapter 2). Surrounding the thalamus and hypothalamus is a set of interconnected structures that form the *limbic system* (Figure 3.12). Included here are the *hippocampus* and the *amygdala*. These structures play an essential part in learning and memory, and also in emotional processing.

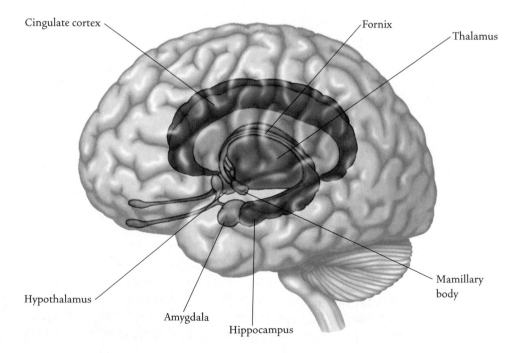

Cingulate cortex

Fornix

Thalamus

Hypothalamus

Amygdala

Hippocampus

Mamillary body

3.12 *The limbic system* *This system is made up of a number of subcortical structures.*

LATERALIZATION

The entire brain is more or less symmetrical around the midline, so there is a hippocampus on the left side of the brain and another on the right, a left-side amygdala and a right-side one. Of course, the same is true for the cortex itself: There is a temporal cortex in the left hemisphere and another in the right, a left occipital cortex and a right one, and so on. In all cases, cortical and subcortical, the left and right structures have roughly the same shape, the same position in their respective sides of the brain, and the same pattern of connections to other brain areas. Even so, there are some anatomical distinctions between the left-side and right-side structures, and we can also document differences in function, with the left-hemisphere structures playing a somewhat different role from that of the corresponding right-hemisphere structures.

The asymmetry in function between the two brain halves is called *lateralization*, and its manifestations influence such diverse phenomena as language, spatial organization, and handedness—that is, the superior dexterity of one hand over the other (Springer & Deutsch, 1998). Let us bear in mind, though, that the two halves of the brain, each performing somewhat different functions, work closely together under almost all circumstances. In other words, the functioning of one side is closely integrated with that of the other side. This integration is made possible by the *commissures*, thick bundles of fibers that carry information back and forth between the two hemispheres. The largest commissure is the *corpus callosum*, but several other structures also ensure that the two brain halves work together as partners in virtually all mental tasks.

In some people, though, the neurological bridge between the hemispheres has been cut for medical reasons. This was, for example, a last-resort treatment for many years in cases of severe epilepsy. The idea was that the epileptic seizure would start in one hemisphere and spread to the other, and this spread was prevented if the two brain halves were disconnected from each other (Bogen, Fisher, & Vogel, 1965; Wilson, Reeves, Gazzaniga, & Culver, 1977). The procedure has largely been abandoned by physicians, who now turn to less drastic surgeries for even the most extreme cases (Woiciechowsky, Vogel, Meyer, & Lehmann, 1997). Nonetheless, this medical procedure produced "split-brain patients" and provided an extraordinary research opportunity—allowing us to examine how the brain halves function when they are not in communication with each other.

This research makes it clear that each hemisphere has its own specialized capacities (Figure 3.13). In the majority of individuals, the left hemisphere has sophisticated language skills and is also capable of sophisticated inferences. The right hemisphere, in contrast, has only limited language skills but outperforms the right hemisphere in a variety of spatial tasks, including facial recognition and tasks involving perception of complex patterns (Gazzaniga, Ivry, & Mangun, 2002; Kingstone, Freisen, & Gazzaniga, 2000).

The differences between the left and right cerebral hemispheres are striking, but they are clearly distinct from many of the conceptions of hemispheric function written for the general public. Some popular authors go so far as to equate left-hemisphere function with Western science and right-hemisphere function with Eastern culture and mysticism. In the same vein, others have argued that Western societies overly encourage rational and analytic "left-brain" functions at the expense of intuitive, artistic, "right-brain" functions.

These popular conceptions do have a kernel of truth, because, as we have said, the two hemispheres are distinct in their modes of functioning. But these often-mentioned conceptions go far beyond the available evidence and in some cases are inconsistent with the evidence (Efron, 1990; Levy, 1985). Worse, these popular conceptions are entirely misleading when they imply that the two cerebral hemispheres, each with its own talents and strategies, endlessly vie for control of our mental life. Instead, each of us has a single brain. Each part of the brain (and not just the cerebral hemispheres) is quite differentiated and so contributes its own specialized abilities to the activity of the whole. But in the end, the complex, sophisticated skills that each of us displays depend on the whole brain and on the coordinated actions of all its components. Our

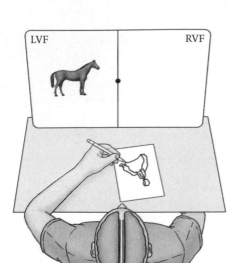

The experimenter asks: "What goes on this?"

The split-brain patient responds: "I don't know."

(but then goes ahead and draws the saddle)

3.13   The split-brain patient   *In this experiment, the horse, shown in the left-visual-field, will be projected to the right hemisphere. If the split-brain patient is then asked, "What goes on this?", the left hemisphere has all the verbal skills it needs for the response, but does not know the answer to the question because the image of the horse never reached this hemisphere. The right hemisphere, in contrast, did see the horse and has enough language skill to understand the question, but not enough language to produce a verbal response. However, the right hemisphere can convey the response nonverbally—if allowed to draw the item rather than name it.*

hemispheres are not cerebral competitors. Instead, they pool their specialized capacities to produce a seamlessly integrated, single mental self.

THE CORTEX

In later chapters, we will have more to say about all the brain areas mentioned here. The hippocampus, for example, is crucial for the establishment of new memories, so we will have more to say about it in Chapter 7; the amygdala plays a pivotal role in triggering and shaping our emotional responses, so we will say more about this structure in Chapter 12. In the interim, though, we need to say more about the brain's largest structure—the forebrain's cortex.

LOCALIZATION OF FUNCTION

The cortex actually serves many different functions, and, indeed, different parts of the cortex each have their own jobs to do. This is, of course, entirely consistent with a broad theme we have already mentioned: The brain is not a homogenous organ but, instead, consists of a large number of separate and highly specialized components. This specialization has set an obvious agenda for researchers—namely, the task of identifying the role of each brain area, a task known as *localization of function*.

Evidence for localization comes from the techniques we mentioned earlier. If damage to a particular brain area—say, the cortex of the occipital lobe—leads to a disruption in vision, then it is evidence that this brain region plays a role in vision. Likewise, if neuroimaging techniques show that a specific structure—say, the amygdala—is highly activated when someone is looking at pictures with emotional content, and that the greater the activation, the greater the chance of *remembering* these pictures later, then this, too, provides a powerful indication of this brain area's function. And, of course, we noted earlier that the strongest evidence for localization comes from a convergence of findings from neuroimaging, lesion data, and more; this provides our best way of asking whether a particular bit of brain tissue actually supports some process, or whether the brain tissue is, as an alternative, merely activated as a consequence of that process.

We should emphasize, though, that most tasks—the ability to read, for example, or the appreciation of music, or the ability to control one's anger—can be disrupted by damage at *many* sites in the brain. Likewise, neuroimaging invariably shows that multiple brain areas are activated for virtually any task a person tries to do. These observations reflect the fact that every site in the brain performs a very narrowly defined function, so that tasks like reading or controlling one's anger are made possibly only by the teamwork of many areas, each responsible for one small part of the overall achievement. As we noted in Chapter 1, it is therefore misleading in most cases to talk about "brain centers"—a "reading center," for example, or an "anger center." Instead, complex achievements like these require many locations, so we will need to consider both the degree of specialization of each brain site and also the question of how the various sites are coordinated with each other to produce the overall performance.

PROJECTION AREAS

Among the earliest discoveries in the study of cortical function was the existence of the primary projection areas. The *primary sensory projection areas* serve as the receiving stations for information arriving from the eyes, ears, and other sense organs. The *primary motor projection area* is the departure point for signals that enter lower parts of the brain and spinal cord, ultimately resulting in muscle movement. The term *projection* is borrowed from map-making, because the sensory and motor primary projection areas seem to form maps in which particular regions of the cortex correspond roughly to the parts of the body they represent or influence.

PRIMARY MOTOR AREA

The discovery of the primary motor projection area dates back to the 1860s, when investigators began to apply mild electric currents to various portions of the cortex of anesthetized animals. The effects were often quite specific. Within the frontal lobe, stimulating one point led to a movement of the forelimb, while stimulating another made the ears prick up. These early studies also provided evidence for the pattern of *contralateral control*: Stimulating the left hemisphere led to movements on the right side of the body; stimulating the right hemisphere caused movements on the left. Contralateral control appears to operate in nearly all nervous systems. It is also evident anatomically because most of the major efferent pathways from the brain cross over to the opposite side within the hindbrain.

Investigators have produced detailed localization "maps" for motor function in the cortex. Canadian neurosurgeon Wilder Penfield, for example, produced such maps from studies using humans who were suffering from severe epilepsy and needed neurosurgery to remove the diseased cells. For these surgeries, Penfield capitalized on the fact that the brain is remarkably insensitive to pain. This allowed Penfield to operate on patients under local anesthesia, leaving them fully awake throughout the experience. In the surgeries, Penfield confirmed that stimulation of the motor area, in the frontal lobe, led to movement of specific parts of the body—much to the surprise of the patients, who had no sense of willing the action or of performing it themselves.

Systematic exploration persuaded Penfield that for each portion of the motor cortex, there was a corresponding part of the body that moved when its cortical counterpart was stimulated. A summary of these findings is often depicted graphically by drawing a "motor homunculus," a schematic picture of the body with each part depicted on the bit of the motor projection area that controls its movement (Figure 3.14).

As Figure 3.14 makes plain, equal-sized areas of the body do not receive equal amounts of cortical space. Instead, parts that we are able to move with the greatest precision (e.g., the fingers, the tongue) receive more cortical space than those over which we have less control (e.g., the shoulder, the abdomen). Evidently, what matters is function, the extent and complexity of use (Penfield & Rasmussen, 1950).

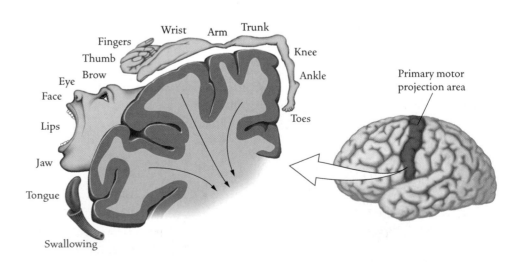

3.14   The primary motor projection area
The primary motor projection area is located at the rearmost edge of the frontal lobe. Each region within the projection area is thought to control the motion of a specific part of the body. The panel on the left shows a cross-sectional slice into the brain, with each body part shown alongside of the brain area that controls its movement.

Methods similar to Penfield's revealed the existence of sensory projection areas. The primary *somatosensory* area is directly behind the primary motor projection area, in the parietal lobe (Figure 3.15). This area is the receiving area for sensory information from the skin senses. Patients stimulated at a particular point in this area usually report tingling somewhere on the opposite side of their bodies. (Less frequently, they report experiences of cold, warmth, or movement.) The somatosensory projection area resembles its motor counterpart in several ways. First, it shows a neat topographic projection, with each part of the body's surface sending its sensory information to a particular part of the cortical somatosensory area. Second, the assignment of cortical space is disproportionate, with the parts of the body that are most sensitive to touch, such as the index finger and the tongue, receiving more cortical space. Finally, sensation—like motor control—is contralateral, with sensory information from each extremity of the body proceeding to the hemisphere on the side opposite to it: the right thumb onto the left hemisphere, the left shoulder onto the right hemisphere, and so on. (Information from the trunk of the body close to the body's midline is represented in both hemispheres.)

Similar primary projection areas exist for vision and for hearing, and they are located in the occipital and temporal lobes, respectively (Figure 3.15). Patients stimulated in the visual projection area report optical experiences, vivid enough but with little form or meaning—flickering lights, streaks of color. Stimulated in the auditory area, patients hear things—clucks, buzzes, booms, and hums.

The visual and auditory areas are, like the somatosensory area, topographically organized. In the occipital lobe (especially the area known as the "visual cortex"), adjacent brain areas represent adjacent locations in visual space. In the temporal lobes, adjacent areas represent similar ranges of pitch. The visual area also respects the principle of contralateral input, so objects seen to the left of a person's line of sight are processed by the right visual area; those seen on the right are processed by the left visual area. The auditory projection area, in contrast, provides one of the few exceptions to the brain's contralateral wiring, because both cerebral hemispheres receive input from both ears.

ASSOCIATION AREAS

The primary projection areas constitute less than one-quarter of the human cortex. What about the rest? These areas were originally referred to as "association areas" because they did not seem to show any kind of fixed sensory mapping and were implicated in such higher mental functions as perceiving, thinking, and speaking.

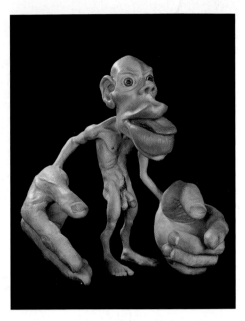

The sensory homunculus   *An artist's rendition of what a man would look like if his appearance were proportional to the area allotted by the somatosensory cortex to his various body parts.*

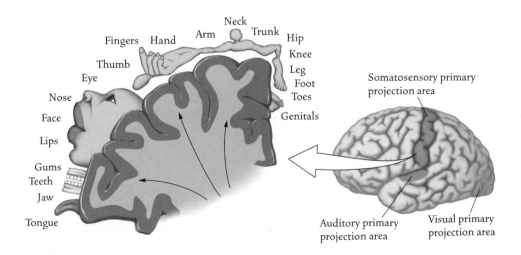

3.15   The primary sensory projection areas The primary sensory projection area for the skin senses is at the forward edge of the parietal lobe. Each region within this area receives input from a specific part of the body; the panel on the left shows a cross-sectional slice into the brain, with each body part shown alongside of the brain area that receives input from this body part. The primary projection areas for vision and hearing are located in the occipital and temporal lobes, respectively. These two are also organized in a systematic fashion. For example, in the visual project area, adjacent areas of the brain receive visual inputs that come from adjacent areas in visual space.

Subsequent research has confirmed that these regions are involved in such higher mental functions, but some of the regions are now known to function as further projection areas, over and above the ones we have just described.

For example, in front of the primary motor projection area are other regions that appear critical to initiating and coordinating complex skilled movements. On the sensory side, each sensory modality may have dozens of secondary projection areas located in the temporal and parietal lobes, with each showing topographical representation and each involved in processing different aspects of sensation. For example, the monkey cortex has at least 25 nonprimary projection areas for vision, each specialized for a different visual quality such as form, color, or movement (Gazzaniga et al., 2002). This is, of course, consistent with our earlier comment about neuropsychological evidence, which shows that one type of brain damage disrupts motion perception, another type disrupts the perception of shapes, and so on—just as we would expect if each type of brain damage is disrupting one of these specialized processing regions.

THE RESULTS OF CORTICAL DAMAGE

As we have now seen several times, specific—and often tragic—problems emerge when someone has suffered damage to a particular region of the brain, whether from a stroke, a tumor, head injury, or some neurological disorder. By scrutinizing these problems, however, we learn a great deal about the brain. Let us look at the rest of the cortex, therefore, through the lens provided by brain damage.

DISORDERS OF ACTION

Some lesions in the cortex of the frontal lobe produce *apraxias*, serious disturbances in the initiation or organization of voluntary action. In some apraxias, the patient is unable to perform well-known actions such as saluting or waving good-bye when asked to do so. In other cases, seemingly simple actions become fragmented and disorganized. When asked to light a cigarette, the patient may strike a match against a matchbox and then strike it again and again after it is already burning; or he may light the match and then put it into his mouth. These deficits are not the result of simple paralysis since the patient can readily perform each part of the action in isolation. His problem is in initiating the sequence or in selecting the right components and fitting them together.

Some apraxias may represent a disconnection between the primary and nonprimary motor areas. Although the primary motor area is responsible for producing the movements of individual muscles, the nonprimary motor areas must first organize and initiate the sequence. Evidence for this distinction came early on from an experiment in which EEG monitoring electrodes were placed on the scalps of participants, who were then asked to press a button in response to various stimuli. The EEG data showed that the neurons in the nonprimary areas fired almost a second before participants actually moved their fingers, suggesting that these areas play a role in preparing that action (Deecke, Scheid, & Kornhuber, 1968). In short, the nonprimary areas seem to be responsible for "Get ready!" and "Get set!" At "Go!" however, the primary motor area takes over (Bear, Connors, & Paradiso, 1996; Roland, Larsen, Lassen, & Skinhøj, 1980).

DISORDERS OF PERCEPTION AND ATTENTION

In other disorders, the patient suffers a disruption in the way she perceives the world, and as we mentioned before, these disorders are usually quite specific. In the *agnosias*, the sufferer cannot identify familiar objects using the affected sensory modality. A patient with visual agnosia, for example, cannot recognize an ordinary fork by looking at it, but she knows what the object is the moment she holds it in her hand. This sort of pattern is typically produced by damage to the occipital cortex or the rearmost part of the parietal cortex—that is, the primary and nonprimary projection areas for vision.

Some patients with visual agnosia can identify the separate details of a picture but are unable to identify the picture as a whole (Farah & Feinberg, 2000; Wapner, Judd, & Gardner, 1978). Similarly, they have difficulties when asked to copy drawings. The individual parts are rendered reasonably well, but they cannot be integrated into a coherent whole (Figure 3.16).

One subtype of agnosia, known as *prosopagnosia*, involves areas in both the temporal and parietal lobes. In prosopagnosia, the main difficulty is in recognizing faces—telling one person from another. In some cases, though, the difficulty may spread beyond faces: A farmer who developed prosopagnosia lost the ability to tell his individual cows apart; a prosopagnosic bird-watcher lost the ability to distinguish different types of warblers (de Renzi, 2000; Farah & Feinberg, 2000). In one remarkable case, a prosopagnosic patient lost the ability to tell cars apart; she could locate her own car in a lot only by reading all the license plates until she found her own (Damasio, Damasio, & Van Hoesen, 1982).

In agnosia, the patient can see (or feel or hear) but is unable to make sense of what his senses tell him. In other disorders, the patient's problem is one of attention, and she systematically ignores certain aspects of the world. A striking example is the *neglect syndrome*, which typically results from damage to certain areas on the right side of the parietal lobe. Its main characteristic is the patient's systematic neglect of the left side: He acts as if it does not exist. When asked to read compound words such as *toothpick* or *baseball*, such a patient will read *pick* and *ball*, ignoring the left half of each word; when asked to draw the face of a clock, he will squeeze all of the numbers onto the clock's right side (Figure 3.17). When eating, he will select and eat food only from the right side of his plate. When dressing, he will ignore the left shirt sleeve and pants leg; when shaving, he will leave the left side of his face unshaven (Awh, Dhaliwal, Christensen, & Matsukura, 2001; Duncan et al., 1999; Rafal & Robertson, 1995; Robertson & Manly, 1999).

DISORDERS OF LANGUAGE

Other lesions in the cortex lead to disruptions of the production or comprehension of speech. Disorders of this kind are called *aphasias*. In right-handers, they are almost always produced by lesions (strokes, typically) in the left hemisphere.

Early studies suggested that aphasias could be divided into two broad types: one that seemed primarily to involve the production of speech, and one that seemed to involve the comprehension of speech. Aphasias of the first sort were often referred to as *nonfluent aphasias* and typically involved lesions in a region of the left frontal lobe called *Broca's area* (after the French physician Pierre-Paul Broca, who in 1861 first noted its relation to speech; see Figure 3.18). The result of this disorder may be mute silence, or speech that resembles a staccato, spoken telegram: "Here . . . head . . . operation . . . here . . . speech . . . none . . . talking . . . what . . . illness" (Luria, 1966, p. 406).

A different pattern is associated with the so-called *fluent aphasias*, cases in which patients seem able to produce speech but do not understand what is said to them, though they usually answer anyway. Unlike patients with nonfluent aphasias, those with fluent aphasias talk freely and rapidly; but while they utter many words, they say very little. The sentences they produce are reasonably grammatical, but they are "word salad," largely composed of the little filler words that provide scant information. A typical example is, "I was over the other one, and then after they had been in the department, I was in this one" (Geschwind, 1970, p. 904). Fluent aphasias are usually associated with a brain site known as *Wernicke's area*, a region that borders on the

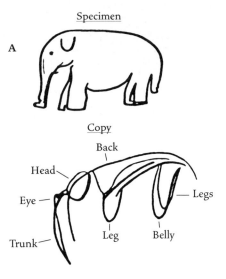

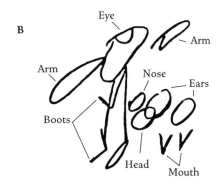

3.16 *Drawings by a patient with visual agnosia* (A) Trying to copy an elephant. (B) Production when asked to draw a man.

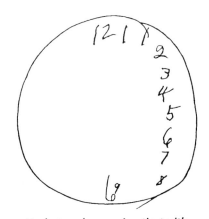

3.17 *Neglect syndrome* A patient with damage to the right parietal cortex was asked to draw a typical clock face. In his drawing the left side was ignored, but the patient still recalled the fact that all twelve numbers had to be displayed; the drawing shows how the patient resolved this dilemma.

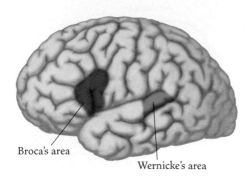

Broca's area

Wernicke's area

3.18 Areas of the brain crucial for language
Many sites in the brain play a key role in the
production and comprehension of language; in
right-handed people, these sites are located in
the left hemisphere, and are generally located
at the lower edge of the frontal lobe and the
upper edge of the temporal lobe. Broca's area
has long been thought to play a central role in
the production of speech (and is alongside of
areas that control the speech muscles—see
Figure 3.14). Wernicke's area plays a central
role in the comprehension of speech (and is
alongside of other areas that play a key part in
audition—see Figure 3.15).

auditory primary projection area; it is named after the nineteenth-century neurologist Carl Wernicke (Figure 3.18).

This distinction—between disorders of production associated with damage to Broca's area and disorders of comprehension associated with damage to Wernicke's area—works as a coarse characterization of aphasia. However, the distinction needs to be refined considerably to capture the real nature, and the full range of types, of aphasia. The reason is simple: Like most mental activities, language use (whether for production or comprehension) involves the coordination of many different steps, many different processes. These include processes needed to "look up" word meanings in one's "mental dictionary," processes needed to figure out the structural relationships within a sentence, processes needed to integrate information gleaned about a sentence's structure with the meanings of the words within the sentence, and so on (Chapter 9). Since each of these processes relies on its own set of brain pathways, damage to those pathways disrupts the process. As a result, the language loss observed in aphasia is often quite specific—with impairment to a particular processing step, followed by a disruption of all subsequent processes that depend on that step. In many cases, this disruption is primarily visible in language production (but not comprehension); in other cases, it is primarily visible in language comprehension (but not production); and in still other cases, the disruption is visible in both activities (see Cabeza & Nyberg, 2000; Demonet, Wise, & Frackowiak, 1993; Habib, Demonet, & Frackowiak, 1996, Kimura & Watson, 1989; Peterson et al., 1988).

DISORDERS OF PLANNING AND SOCIAL COGNITION

Earlier, we referred to the famous case of Phineas Gage. After his head was shot through by the iron rod, Gage could still speak and move fairly normally. But something subtler had changed. As the original medical report on Gage stated:

> He is fitful, irreverent, indulging at times in the grossest profanity (which was not previously his custom), manifesting but little deference for his fellows, impatient of restraint or advice when it conflicts with his desires, at times pertinaciously obstinate, yet capricious and vacillating, devising many plans of future operation, which are no sooner arranged than they are abandoned in turn for others appearing more feasible. Previous to his injury . . . he possessed a well-balanced mind . . . was energetic and persistent in executing all his plans of operation. In this regard his mind was radically changed, so decidedly that his friends and acquaintances said he was "no longer Gage." (Valenstein, 1986, p. 90)

Gage's symptoms fit reasonably well with other things we know about the effect of damage to frontmost part of the frontal lobe—the *prefrontal area* (Bradshaw, 2001; Lichter & Cummings, 2001; Milner & Petrides, 1984). One central manifestation of prefrontal damage is a deficiency in response inhibition. Unable to use rules to control their behavior, patients often break them. This causes many problems for the patients, including difficulties in social interaction and in abiding by the law.

Depending upon the exact site of the injury, patients with prefrontal damage may appear uninvolved, depressed, and apathetic. Alternatively, they may seem like psychopaths, acting flagrantly and crudely, being sexually promiscuous, and perhaps engaging in criminal conduct. In fact, one hypothesis about actual criminal psychopaths suggests that these individuals may suffer from subtle prefrontal damage.

In addition, damage to the orbitofrontal cortex (at the base of the frontal lobe, just above the eyes) seems to impair a person's ability to make decisions—particularly, decisions that involve some degree of risk. According to Antonio Damasio (1994), this is because decision making often relies on "gut feelings"—including our emotional assessment of how we will feel if the decision goes well, and how we will feel if it goes badly. In Damasio's view, this is, in fact, the right way to make decisions, and it is a process that depends on the orbitofrontal cortex. When that brain site is damaged, a person is no longer able to evaluate the emotional impact of his or her decisions, and as a result, the quality of that person's decision making is diminished.

THE ORIGINS OF THE BRAIN

With all of its specialized parts, each connected to—and working with—the others, the brain is unmistakably an organ of extraordinary complexity. How did this magnificent bit of machinery come into being? Not surprisingly, the answer begins with evolution.

THE EVOLUTION OF NERVOUS SYSTEMS

How did the nervous system—and the brain in particular—evolve? Our understanding of this issue has been shaped by many considerations, including a close comparison of the nervous systems of different species. As it turns out, there are important similarities from one species to the next in how the nervous system is organized and how it functions, but there are also important differences, and one of these is in the degree of centralization—whether a species' nervous system relies on regional control (with different control centers in different parts of the body) or one centralized governor.

In general, more complex animals show more central control; in simpler animals, including most invertebrates, regional rule predominates. For example, sea anemones (flowery-looking animals that latch on to the ocean bottom and strain seawater for food) have networks of nerves with no obvious focus of connection. More complex invertebrates like snails, oysters, squids, and octopi have neurons that control individual movements, and these neurons clump together to form **ganglia** (singular, *ganglion*). The ganglia serve primarily to relay messages from the sense organs to the muscles and are usually located near the muscles they control. One mollusk, the sea snail *Aplysia*, has five ganglia that control the animal's entire repertoire of behaviors: sucking food in and out of its siphon, moving its eyes and tentacles, working its sticky foot to enable motion, and managing circulation, gill-breathing, and reproduction (Krasne & Glanzman, 1995; Rosenzweig, Leiman, & Breedlove, 1996).

By clumping their neurons together into ganglia, species like *Aplysia* (and their ancient kin) gained the possibility of coordinating the various neural signals being sent back and forth in their nervous systems, and this in turn allowed them the possibility of coordinating different aspects of their actions. This enabled these creatures to expand their behavioral repertoire and to move into new environments. These changes, in turn, created new challenges and hence new selective pressures on the newly evolved creatures. Part of the response to these pressures was the development of still further complexity in the nervous system, as the initial loose federation of ganglia became increasingly centralized, and some ganglia gradually began to control others. These dominant ganglia tended to be located in the head, and it is not hard to see why: Organisms need information about what lies in front of them as they move; they already know what is at their rear, because they were there just a moment ago. It makes sense, therefore, for receptors for light or chemicals to be located in the animal's head—which is usually the part that leads as the animal moves forward. In addition, for most creatures, starting with the evolutionarily ancient flatworms, the head contains the mouth, and this too makes it useful for the receptors to be located in the head: Taste receptors near the beginning of the digestive tube can be used to signal edibility, allowing an animal to sample its food before deciding to eat it.

To integrate the messages from the various receptors in the head, organisms had to evolve more and more neural machinery. This machinery was best placed close to the receptors, so it, too, needed to be in the head. These ganglionic centers became increasingly complex as organisms evolved and eventually started to coordinate the activity of ganglia elsewhere in the body. Over millions of years of evolution, these centers emerged as the "head" ganglia in status as well as in location. In short, they became the brain.

In this as in all cases, though, we cannot view evolution as moving toward a "superior" design. Instead, evolution merely favors what works in a given environment, and since different organisms occupy different niches, there is a wide variety of designs that "work." This is why the modern world contains complex creatures with centralized nervous systems (e.g., humans), but also other creatures that still rely on regional rule. In fact, while centralization can be advantageous, regional rule has its own virtues. Command hierarchies are slow, and the brains that contain them require a great deal of energy to build and maintain. (Indeed, the human brain, averaging just 2% of our body weight, burns up roughly 18% of the calories we take in.) In contrast, much can get done quickly and economically by avoiding a bureaucratic chain of command. For example, cockroaches have brains, but their brains are tiny and mostly dedicated to their compound eyes. What they lack in brains, however, is made up elsewhere—in a chain of large ganglia spanning nearly the length of their body. One of these ganglia connects to nerve endings in the tail and can trigger quick escape when the tail is stimulated by even the faintest air movement. This decentralized reflex is one reason cockroaches are some of Earth's longest survivors and easily defeat even large-brained mammals who wield both rolled-up newspapers and cans of pesticide.

PHYLOGENY AND ONTOGENY

When we ask how any complex system (including the nervous system) came to be, we need to ask two questions. First, how did the system evolve across many generations? This is a question of *phylogeny*, and it is answered in terms of natural selection. Second, we can ask how the system came to exist in each individual—how, for example, each individual can start with just the pair of cells known as ovum and sperm and then end up, a while later, with a complete and smoothly functioning nervous system. This is a question of *ontogeny*, and it must begin with the detailed specifications contained within an organism's genes, and then describe how the organism develops, guided both by those genes and by environmental circumstances, into mature form.

We have already said a little about the phylogenetic origins of nervous systems. They emerged as various species grew in complexity and developed more sophisticated and more flexible behavioral patterns. This required centralization of control and led, eventually, to nervous systems like those we see in modern creatures. But what about the ontogeny of the nervous system? How, in short, does one grow a brain?

THE DEVELOPING NERVOUS SYSTEM

Soon after an egg is fertilized, genes in the egg turn on and trigger rapid cell reproduction, so that within days there are several dozen identical cells. At that point, other genes turn on and produce chemical signals that induce a process of differentiation among the proliferating cells. Within a week, there are three distinct cell types—those that will later become the nervous system and also the outer skin; those that will form the skeletal system and voluntary muscles; and those that will form the gut and digestive organs. This process of rapid growth and increasing specialization continues, and then, once there is a large enough population of sufficiently differentiated nerve cells in place, other genes turn on and give off chemical signals that serve as "beacons," attracting connections that sprout from other nerve cells. This process of cellular signaling, differentiation, and proliferation is called *neurogenesis*. It happens rapidly, with new nerve cells being generated at a rate of up to 250,000 per minute; in humans, neurogenesis is nearly complete by the fifth month of gestation (Kolb & Whishaw, 2001; Rakic, 1995).

The concentration of nerve cells that will become the brain emerges very early in development (Figure 3.19). In the third week of embryonic life, a thickening starts to develop atop the embryo, running from the head to (nearly) the tail. Within a few days, the left and right edges of this *neural plate* zip together and fuse lengthwise to form the *neural tube*. By one month of embryonic life, the head end of the neural tube develops three identifiable subparts, which will develop into the hindbrain, midbrain, and forebrain. The lower end of the hindbrain marks the beginning of the spinal cord.

In early stages of gestation, the cells that will become the brain show no distinction between neurons and glia—the two types of cells found in the mature brain. As the cells reproduce and differentiate, though, the newly created neurons actually migrate toward their appropriate position, at a rate of up to a millimeter a day. This migration is guided by several factors, including various chemicals that serve as attractants for some types of nerve cells and repellents for other nerve cells (Hatten, 2002). The migration is also guided by glia that act as guidewires, much like beanpoles that guide bean shoots in the garden. The migrating neurons approach the surface of the developing cortex, but the first-arriving neurons stop short of the surface. Later-arriving neurons pass these now-stationary cells, and these in turn are passed by even later arrivals. As a result, the cortex literally develops from the inside out, with layers closer to the surface established later than deeper layers.

Of course, it's not enough that the nerve cells end up in the right places; they also need to end up connected in the right way, so that each nerve cell sends its messages to the right target. (Otherwise, information intended to move the leg might halt digestion instead.) How does each developing nerve cell come to know its eventual target? The answer, of course, begins with the genes. Early in development, genetic specifications lead neurons to form *protomaps*, providing a rough "wiring diagram" for the brain's circuits. The areas mapped in this way seem to attract connections from the appropriate inputs, so that, for example, the protomap in the projection area for vision attracts afferent fibers from the thalamus, with the result that the visual cortex comes to receive the right input signals (e.g., Rakic, 1995; for some complexities, though, see Sur & Rubenstein, 2005).

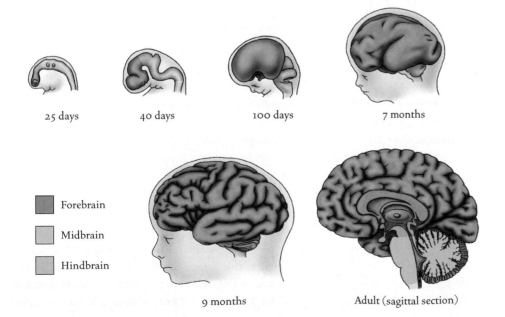

25 days   40 days   100 days   7 months

Forebrain

Midbrain

Hindbrain

9 months   Adult (sagittal section)

3.19 Embryonic-fetal development of the human brain

Inevitably, there are some wiring errors, but there is a safeguard in place to deal with these. It turns out that many more neurons are created than are needed, and each neuron tries to form far more connections than are required. If, therefore, a neuron's connections prove either wrong or redundant, that neuron can withdraw its connections and find better targets, or it can be given a message to die (Kuan, Roth, Flavell, & Rakic, 2000; Rubenstein & Rakic, 1999). In fact, it is normal for between 20 and 80% of neurons to die as the brain develops, depending upon the region of the brain. This decimation primarily occurs early in development—in humans, about 4 to 6 months after conception (Rosenzweig, Leiman, & Breedlove, 1996), but, according to some investigators, it continues at a slower rate for much longer—perhaps even a decade.

In addition, many connections among neurons still remain to be wired at the time of birth. Connections are formed and destroyed at an astounding rate in the infant—up to 100,000 per second, according to one estimate (Rakic, 1995). And many other connections are not formed until much later in life. For example, in humans the connections within Broca's area show dramatic growth around the age of 2, a spurt that coincides with a striking increase in the child's ability to produce spoken language. Yet another example is the wiring of the prefrontal areas, whose connections may not be complete until age 30.

Plainly, then, the ontogenesis of the nervous system is a complex process—with individual neurons migrating to their appropriate positions, then forming connections according to the genetically specified protomap, then attracting more connections (presumably via chemical signals) from the right inputs. Excess or inappropriate connections are then pruned until—at last—the child ends up with a full and normal human nervous system. This entire process is obviously shaped by genetic instructions, but it is also influenced by a range of environmental factors. The biochemical environment in which these processes unfold is crucial, which is one of the reasons why prenatal health care is so important: If the fetus develops inside of a mother who is inadequately nourished or exposed to toxins, or who ingests harmful drugs, this can horribly disrupt the developmental sequence. Also important is the incoming stimulus information—for the fetus and certainly for the young infant. However, before we can discuss the effects of this information input on the developing nervous system, we need to lay some further foundation—discussing at last how the nervous system actually does its work.

THE BUILDING BLOCKS OF THE NERVOUS SYSTEM

So far, most of our discussion about the adult brain has focused on the brain's large-scale design—what the big parts are, and where they are located. We have, in essence, looked under the hood of this extraordinarily complex machine but stayed at the level of identifying its main components (the alternator, the carburetor, and so on). To understand how the brain actually functions, however, we need to zoom in and look at the building blocks of which the nervous system is composed—the individual *neurons* and the *nerve impulses* by which they communicate.

THE NEURON

The neuron is a single cell with three subdivisions: the *dendrites*, the *cell body* (or *soma*), and the *axon* (Figure 3.20). The dendrites, the "input" side of the neuron, receive signals from many other neurons; they are heavily branched and so, for most neurons, resemble a thick and tangled bush. The axon, the "output" side of the neuron, sends

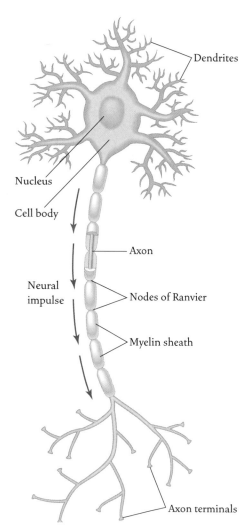

3.20 The neuron *A schematic diagram of the main parts of a motoneuron. Part of the cell is myelinated; that is, its axon is covered with sets of segmented, insulating sheaths formed by encircling glial cells.*

Dendrites

Nucleus

Cell body

Axon

Neural impulse

Nodes of Ranvier

Myelin sheath

Axon terminals

neural impulses to other neurons. The axon usually extends outward from the cell body like a wispy thread, and it may fork into several *axonal branches* at its end.

Neurons actually come in many shapes and sizes, making it difficult to offer claims true for every nerve cell. Neurons' cell bodies vary from 5 to about 100 microns in diameter (1 micron = 1/1,000 millimeter). The average human hair, in contrast, has a diameter of about 100 microns. Dendrites are typically short—say, a few hundred microns. Axons, however, can be much longer. For example, one type of neuron is the motor neuron, or *motoneuron* (Figure 3.20), which provides a pathway that begins within the CNS and transmits a nerve impulse to a muscle fiber. The longest motoneurons in humans run from our spinal cords out through our legs; these are about a meter long. To get a sense of these proportions, this gives the motoneuron a shape that resembles a basketball attached to a thin garden hose almost a mile and a half long.

The motoneuron carries an efferent signal, allowing the brain to control the muscles. Other (afferent) neurons convey information inward, keeping the nervous system informed about both the external world and the body's internal environment. Some of these are neurons attached to specialized receptor cells that respond to external energies such as pressure, chemical changes, light, and so on. These receptor cells translate (more technically, *transduce*) the physical stimuli into electrical changes, which then trigger a nervous impulse in other neurons.

Neurons that convey impulses from receptors toward the rest of the nervous system are called *sensory neurons*. Sometimes the receptor is actually a specialized part of the sensory neuron, but, in most cases, transduction and transmission are separate functions entrusted to different cells. In vision, for example, receptor cells transduce optical stimulation into electrical changes in the cell, which in turn trigger impulses in sensory neurons that then proceed through the nervous system.

So far we have mentioned two broad types of neurons: those that trigger some action (such as the motoneurons), and those that receive information (the sensory neurons). It turns out, though, that the vast majority of nerve cells (roughly 99%!) are neither sensory neurons nor motoneurons. Rather, they are *interneurons*, neurons that are interposed between two or more other neurons.

In most cases, interneurons transmit their message to yet other interneurons, and these send theirs to still other interneurons. Typically, many thousands of such interneurons must interact before the command is finally issued and sent down the path of the efferent nerve fibers. These interneuronal connections form the *microcircuitry* of the central nervous system. The microcircuitry is where the brain conducts most of its information processing, and the bulk of the brain structures we have reviewed consist of just such microcircuitry.

A
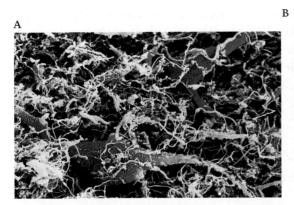

B
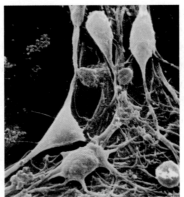

C
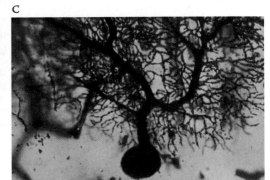

Different kinds of neurons   It is important to remember that while the text discusses the structure of a motoneuron, neurons actually come in a variety of shapes and sizes. Pictured here are neurons from (A) the spinal cord (stained in red), (B) the cerebral cortex, and (C) the cerebellum.

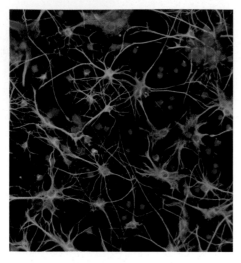

3.21   Glial cells   Glial cells from a rabbit brain.

GLIA

What about the other cells that make up the brain—the glia? In most areas of the brain, the glia are at least as numerous as neurons, and in some regions they outnumber the neurons by a large margin. But for many years, neuroscientists thought the glia served only limited purposes, supporting the neurons and providing the housekeeping for them. Indeed, this second-class status is reflected in the word *glia* itself, which comes from the Greek word for "glue" or "slime."

Despite the derogatory term, glia have many functions. We have noted that during brain development, glia guide migrating neurons to their destinations, and apparently they influence exactly what connections are made among the neurons. Then, once the neurons have established the appropriate connections, chemicals produced by the glia help to shut down the process of neural growth, ensuring a relatively stable pattern of connections (McGee, Yang, Fischer, Daw, & Strittmatter, 2005; Miller, 2005a).

Another function of glial cells is to increase the speed at which neurons can communicate. The specialized glial cells that accomplish this—found only in vertebrates, which move much faster than invertebrates—are mostly made of a fatty substance known as *myelin*. Beginning shortly after birth, cells containing mylein spiral and wrap their fatty tentacles around neurons that have long axons, such as those that proceed from distant sensory organs or travel to distant muscles. Each spiral creates a myelin "wrapper" around a portion of the axon, and soon the entire length of the axon is covered by a succession of these wrappers. As we will see, the uncoated gaps between the wrappers—the **nodes of Ranvier**—are crucial in speeding up the nerve impulses traveling along these myelinated axons (Figure 3.21).

The fact that myelin is white explains why brains are made up of both white and gray matter. What anatomists call **white matter** is the myelinated axons traversing long distances either within the brain or to and from the body (hence the need for speed). Conversely, **gray matter** consists of cell bodies, dendrites, and unmyelinated axons and the interneurons that constitute the nervous system's microcircuitry.

Recent evidence suggests still other functions for the glia. For example, several studies suggest that glia can "talk back" to the neurons, sending signals that help regulate the strength of connections between adjacent neurons In addition, glia may, in some circumstances, release chemicals that increase the reactivity of neurons; this can, unfortunately, sometimes make the neurons too reactive. In the extreme, this may be the source of a horrible medical condition that causes people to suffer extreme pain in response to even a mild touch, and it may also play a role in the development of epilepsy and several other illnesses (Miller, 2005a).

Still other evidence suggests that glial cells may, on their own, constitute a second, slow signaling system within the brain. Glial cells are known to be responsive to various electrical, chemical, and mechanical stimuli. They also form networks that communicate with each other using slow internal voltage changes, with these changes modulating the activities of neurons nearby. The extent to which glial-cell networks interact with neuronal networks in various brain functions has not yet been determined, but it may be considerable (Bullock et al., 2005; Gallo & Chitajallu, 2001; Newman & Zahs, 1998; Verkhratsky, 1998).

COMMUNICATION AMONG NEURONS

There is no question, though, the main signaling within the body is done by the neurons—neurons that bring information from the sensory organs to the brain, and neurons that carry the brain's commands outward to the muscles, and neurons that carry information from one part of the brain to another part. How do neurons perform these functions? And what is it that makes them neurons—different from glia or (for that matter) any of the other cells in the body?

THE ELECTRICAL ACTIVITY OF THE NEURON

The neuron is, in many respects, just a cell. It has a nucleus on the inside and a cell membrane that defines its perimeter. In the middle is a biochemical stew of ions, amino acids, proteins, DNA, and so forth, as well as a collection of smaller structures that provide for the metabolic needs of the cell itself. What makes a neuron distinctive, though, is the peculiarity of its cell membrane. The membrane is irritable. Poke it, stimulate it electrically or chemically, and the neuronal membrane may destabilize, producing a cascade of changes that form the nerve impulse—that is, make the cell fire.

Figure 3.22 shows how the neuron's irritability and its effects can be studied. Two microelectrodes are used, one inserted into a nerve axon and the other contacting its outer surface. In this manner, any electrical activity near the cell membrane can be detected. As it turns out, there is activity even when the cell is not firing, as shown by a voltage difference between the inside and the outside of the fiber. Like a miniature battery with a positive and a negative connection, the inside of the axon is electrically negative with respect to the outside, with the difference measuring about −70 or so millivolts (a standard AA battery, at 1.5 volts, has over 20 times this voltage). Because this small negative voltage occurs when the neuron is stable, it has traditionally been called the neuron's ***resting potential***, although, as we shall see, maintaining this voltage takes work, and in its stable state the neuron is anything but at rest.

What happens when the neuron is irritated and made to fire? To find out, neuroscientists stimulate the surface of the fiber by means of a third microelectrode, which applies a brief electrical pulse. This pulse reduces the voltage difference across the membrane. If the pulse is weak, it may reduce the voltage difference to −65 millivolts or −60.

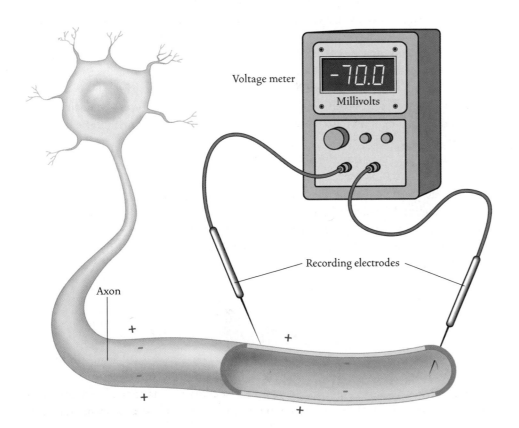

Voltage meter

-70.0

Millivolts

Recording electrodes

Axon

3.22 Recording the voltage within a neuron
A schematic drawing of how the impulse is recorded. One electrode is inserted into the axon; the other records from the axon's outside.

In this case, the neuron's membrane will maintain its integrity and quickly work to restore the resting potential, at −70 millivolts. But if the pulse is strong enough to push the voltage difference past a critical *excitation threshold* (about −55 millivolts in mammals), something dramatic happens. The voltage difference between the inside and outside of the cell abruptly collapses to zero and, in fact, begins to reverse itself. The inside of the membrane no longer shows a negative voltage compared to the outside but instead suddenly swings positive, up to +40 millivolts. This marks the neuron's destabilization, an event that completely disrupts the cell's membrane. Fortunately, the chaos is short-lived; the membrane restabilizes itself within a millisecond or so and returns to its −70 millivolt state. The entire destabilization-restabilization sequence is called the *action potential* (Figure 3.23).

EXPLAINING NEURONAL POTENTIALS

The resting and action potentials are the key to explaining nearly all neuronal communication, and they both derive from movements of ions through the neuron's membrane. Ions are molecules (or single atoms) that have lost or gained electrons and so have a positive or negative charge. In general, the neuron's membrane controls which ions remain inside the neuron and which are kept outside. It does this using biochemical portholes, known as *ion channels*, that let certain ions pass through but block others, as well as *ion pumps* that suck ions in or push them out.

Two kinds of ions are crucial for the resting and action potentials: sodium and potassium. Sodium ions (Na^+) are found mostly outside the neuron and potassium ions (K^+) mostly inside. When the membrane is stable, positively charged sodium ions are continually pumped from the inside of the membrane to the outside and kept there, while potassium ions are free to enter or leave the cell. The result is an excess of positively charged ions on the outside, which accounts for much of the voltage difference in the resting potential—negative on the inside and positive on the outside (Figure 3.24). Maintaining this stable state takes constant work because the membrane is leaky, so the pumps must work constantly to maintain the status quo. Indeed, probably most of the metabolic energy used by the brain is expended on maintaining these so-called resting potentials (Rosenzweig et al., 1996).

When the membrane is sufficiently excited, though (by reducing the voltage difference to the threshold), the sodium channels spring open temporarily. Sodium ions flood in, forcing out some potassium ions a moment later. This short-lived excess of positively charged particles on the inside of the membrane produces the positive voltage swing of the action potential. But immediately afterward, the membrane begins to

3.23 The action potential **Action potential recorded from the squid's giant axon.**

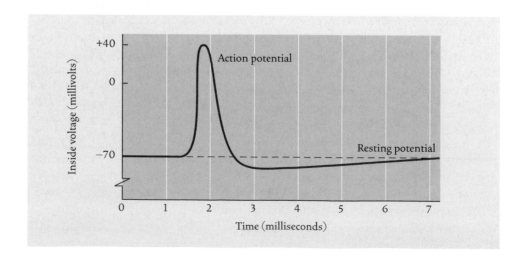

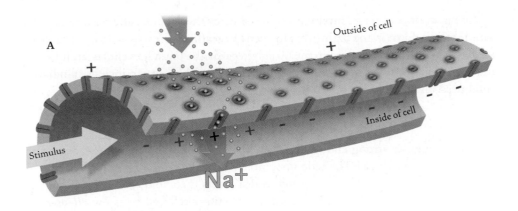

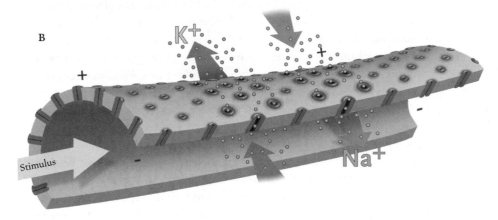

3.24 Ion channels and the action potential
(A) When a stimulus is above threshold, special
ion channels of the membrane open, and
positively charged sodium ions (Na⁺) surge
inside. (B) Immediately thereafter, the gates
that admitted Na⁺ close, and the electrical
balance is restored, because some other
positively charged ions—specifically potassium
ions (K⁺)—are now forced out. The whole
process is repeated at an adjacent point in
the axon.

restore itself to stability. The pumps resume their evacuation of sodium to the outside of the neuron, and the gates slam shut to keep it out; meanwhile, potassium ions begin to seep back into the neuron. The result is the resumption of the membrane's stability and the restoration of the resting potential.

PROPAGATION OF THE ACTION POTENTIAL

These electrochemical events explain what happens at a single region of the membrane. In order to send its signals, though, it is essential that these events "travel" down the length of the axon; what is it that allows this spread of excitation? The answer lies in the fact that the temporarily positive voltage inside the axon induces the opening of ion channels at adjacent regions, which themselves induce more distant channels to open, and so on. The upshot of this domino-like process is that the impulse—the cascade of events that creates the action potential—moves down the entire length of the axon and throughout the rest of the neuron as well. This is known as the *propagation* of the action potential. The whole thing is like a spark traveling along a fuse except that whereas the fuse is consumed by the spark, the ion channels rapidly reclose and the membrane restores itself within milliseconds. As a consequence, the neuron is soon ready to fire again, and if an above-threshold stimulus is still present, then fire it will (Figure 3.25).

At the microscopic level, the chain reaction that produces the propagation of the action potential seems fairly fast, but it actually travels at a rate of only about 1 meter per second—about average walking speed. If this was the fastest that signals could travel, it would be disastrous for most organisms, and fast-paced actions like speaking and jumping would be impossible. Enter the nodes of Ranvier, which, as we mentioned, are the spaces between the glial-cell tentacles that wrap axons with myelin. On these myelinated axons, only the nodes must be destabilized; thus, the changes that produce the action potential can skip from node to node. Myelinated axons can propagate their action potentials at speeds up to 120 meters per second (about 260 miles per hour).

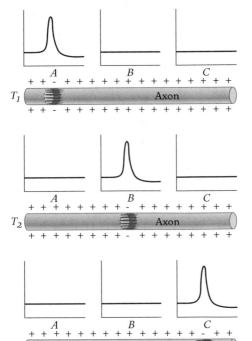

3.25 The action potential as it travels along
the axon **The axon is shown at three different**
moments—T₁, T₂, and T₃—after the
application of a stimulus. The voltage inside the
membrane is shown at three different points
along the axon—A, B, and C.

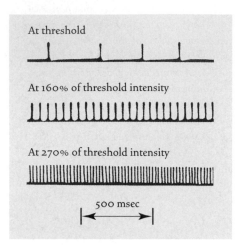

At threshold

At 160% of threshold intensity

At 270% of threshold intensity

500 msec

3.26 *Stimulus intensity and firing frequency
Responses of a crab axon to a continuous
electric current at three levels of current
intensity. The time scale is relatively slow. As a
result, the action potentials show up as single
vertical lines or "spikes." Note that while
increasing the current intensity has no effect on
the height of the spikes (the all-or-none law), it
leads to a marked increase in the frequency of
spikes per second.*

The importance of intact myelin is underscored by the deficits suffered when myelination breaks down in the brain. This happens in *multiple sclerosis* (**MS**), a disease in
which the body's immune system mistakenly regards the brain's myelin as an intruder
and attacks it. The manifestations of MS are highly variable but can include blindness,
numbness, and paralysis.

ALL-OR-NONE LAW

Once a stimulus is strong enough to destabilize the neuronal membrane, an action
potential will be produced. The action potential will be the same size and will be propagated just as rapidly, whether the stimulus just meets threshold or exceeds it by two,
three, or twenty times. This phenomenon is sometimes referred to as the *all-or-none
law*. Just as pounding on a car horn does not make it any louder, a stronger stimulus
does not produce a stronger action potential. A neuron either fires or does not fire. It
knows no in-between.

How can we reconcile the all-or-none law with our everyday experience? The world is
not just black and white, and sounds are not simply on or off. We can obviously see
shades of gray (not to mention colors) and tell the difference between the buzz of a mos-
quito and the roar of a jet engine. How can the nervous system register these differences?

Part of the answer is that more intense stimuli excite greater numbers of neurons.
This is because neurons vary enormously in their excitation thresholds. As a result, a
weak stimulus will only stimulate neurons with relatively low thresholds, while a strong
stimulus will stimulate all of those plus others whose threshold is higher.

The second mechanism applies to individual neurons. When bombarded with a sustained stimulus, most neurons do not just fire once and retire. Instead, they generate a
whole stream, or "volley," of action potentials by means of repeated cycles of destabilization and restabilization. In accordance with the all-or-none principle, the size of
each of the action potentials remains the same; what changes is the impulse frequency—the stronger the stimulus, the more often the axon will fire. This effect holds
until we reach a maximum rate of firing, after which further increases in intensity have
no effect (Figure 3.26). Different neurons have different maximum rates, with the highest in humans on the order of 1,000 impulses per second.

THE SYNAPSE

Propagation of the action potential gets a signal from one end of a neuron (typically,
the dendrites) to the other (typically, the end of the axon). But how is the signal then
passed to the next neuron, so that the message can continue its travel toward its destination? For many years, intellectuals did not realize this was an issue at all. Descartes'
view, for example, was that reflexes were formed from a long and essentially continuous
strand of nervous tissue—in essence, along one neuron. According to this view, the
incoming sensory information triggers a response at one end of this neuron, and then
the response is initiated at the other end of the same neuron. But this view (and a number of variants on it) soon faced a major problem: Various studies showed that the time
it took from sensation to response (roughly one-fifth of a second) was too long for the
route to be direct. The neurons could not be acting like electrical wires because electrical
transmission was nearly instantaneous. By the end of the nineteenth century, therefore,
most observers were convinced that the neurons must be communicating across some
kind of gap. This gap, together with the membranes of the neurons that form it, is called
the *synapse*. Once hypothetical, the synapse was confirmed microscopically in 1888 by
Spanish neurologist Santiago Ramón y Cajal, who observed synapses in the spinal cord
and elsewhere, and called these conjunctions—poetically—"protoplasmic kisses, . . .
the final ecstasy of an epic love story" (Ramón y Cajal, 1937, p. 373).

Other studies, roughly contemporary with Ramón y Cajal's observations, made it clear that the synapse was not just a communications link, conveying signals from one neuron to another, but also an information integrator, collecting inputs from multiple sources. This was evident in the results of studies of reflexes conducted by English physiologist Charles Sherrington (1857–1952). Sherrington had observed that although a reflex response might not be elicited by a single stimulus, several presentations of the same stimulus might trigger the response (e.g., Sherrington, 1906). This process, in which the effects of stimulation accumulate over time, is now called *temporal summation*. Sherrington also found that a reflex response was more likely to be elicited if the animal was stimulated concurrently in several places on its skin rather than in just one, as if the various inputs were somehow adding together in a process we now call *spatial summation*.

How can these observations be explained in terms of synapses? One suggestion—which we now know to be correct—is that neurons communicate via chemical signals (more on this in a moment). A single action potential might not release enough of the chemical to trigger a response in the next neuron, but if the sending neuron fires again and again, this may allow an accumulation of the chemical that eventually does trigger the response—and hence temporal summation. Likewise, we now know that each neuron receives signals from many others. Therefore, the chemical message received from one input may not be enough to trigger a response, but the message received from many may be sufficient. This provides an obvious source of temporal summation.

Sherrington also noted another crucial point: Throughout the body, there are muscle pairs that produce opposite actions (Figure 3.27). For example, in humans the biceps contracts the arm, but the triceps extends it. It would obviously be counterproductive for these muscles to work against each other, and, in fact, it is usually the case that when we contract our biceps, the triceps relaxes automatically, and vice versa. But Sherrington found that stimulation of each muscle in the pair actually made the partner muscle "extra-relaxed"—that is, more relaxed even than when in its normal rest state.

Sherrington realized that this observation, too, could easily be explained in terms of interactions among neurons. All one needs to assume is that there are two types of signals—excitatory and inhibitory. Thus, with appropriate wiring, one could design a system in which the nerves causing one muscle to contract could simultaneously send an inhibitory message to the partner muscle, causing it to "un-contract"—that is, to relax. Sherrington realized that this mechanism of *reciprocal inhibition*—with the excitement of each constituent of the pair causing the inhibition of the other—would aid in the coordination of many processes and could in general provide a means through which one influence could be weakened, neutralized, or even reversed by a negative (inhibitory) one.

THE SYNAPTIC MECHANISM

Sherrington's discoveries were based on behavioral observations; his claims about the synapse were all deduced from these observations. Remarkably, though, his deductions turned out to be essentially correct, and modern research has confirmed his central insight: Neurons communicate with their neighbors via a chemical substance released when the neural impulse reaches the end of the axon.

How exactly does this chemical message work? Let us begin by distinguishing between the *presynaptic neuron*—the cell that sends the message—and the *postsynaptic neuron*—the one that receives it. The actual transmission process begins in the tiny knoblike *axon terminals* of the presynaptic neuron. Within these swellings are numerous tiny sacs, or *synaptic vesicles* ("little vessels"), which are like water balloons filled with *neurotransmitters*, the chemicals that will, when released, influence other neurons.

Sir Charles Sherrington

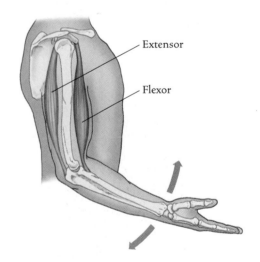

3.27   An example of muscle antagonists
The figure shows how the members of a flexor-extensor pair (biceps and triceps) oppose each other in flexing and extending the forearm. When the flexor contracts (to bend the elbow) the extensor is inhibited, to ensure that it provides no resistance to the flexor. When the extensor contracts (to straighten the elbow) the flexor is inhibited.

When the presynaptic neuron fires, some of the vesicles literally burst and eject their contents through the terminal's membrane into the *synaptic gap* that separates the two cells. The transmitter molecules then diffuse across this gap and impinge upon the *postsynaptic membrane* (Figures 3.28A and B; 3.29). Usually the postsynaptic membrane is part of a dendrite, but it can also be a cell body or even another axon.

Once across the synaptic gap, the transmitters activate specialized molecular receptors in the postsynaptic membrane. When one of these receptors is activated, it opens or closes certain ion channels in the membrane. For example, some neurotransmitters open the channels to sodium ions. As these ions enter the postsynaptic cell, the voltage difference maintained across the membrane is decreased (i.e., it shifts in the direction of zero volts), rendering that part of the membrane less stable (Figure 3.28C and D). As more and more transmitter molecules cross at the synapse, they activate more and more receptors, opening more and more channels, which further reduces the voltage difference. These effects accumulate and spread along the membrane of the postsynaptic neuron. If the voltage difference is reduced enough, the excitation threshold is reached, the action potential is triggered, and the impulse speeds down the postsynaptic cell's axon.

A similar mechanism accounts for inhibition. At some synapses, the presynaptic cell liberates transmitter substances that produce an *increased* voltage difference across the membrane of the postsynaptic neuron. The heightened voltage difference acts to fortify the membrane against other, destabilizing influences. Since most neurons have synaptic connections with neurons that excite them as well as with others that inhibit them, the response of a given postsynaptic cell depends on a final tally of the excitatory and inhibitory "yeas" and "nays" that act upon it. If the net value is excitatory and if this value exceeds the threshold, the cell will fire.

What happens to the transmitter molecules after they have affected the postsynaptic neuron? It would not do just to leave them where they are because they might continue to exert their effects long after the presynaptic neuron had stopped firing, thus making any input permanent. To avoid this problem, some transmitters are inactivated shortly after they have been discharged by special "cleanup" enzymes that break them up into their chemical components. More commonly, though, neurotransmitters are not

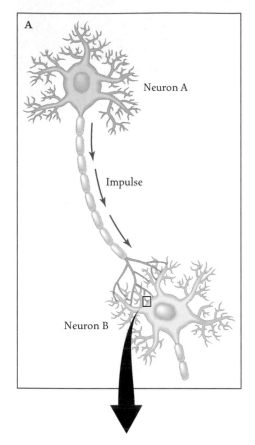

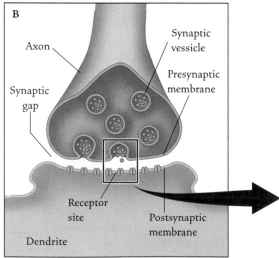

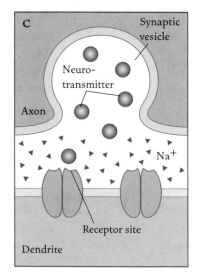

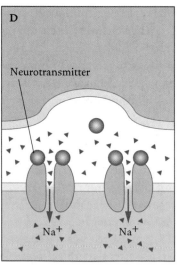

3.28 *Schematic view of synaptic transmission* ***(A) Neuron A transmits a message through synaptic contact with neuron B. (B) The events in the axon knob. (C) The vesicle is released, and neurotransmitter molecules are ejected toward the postsynaptic membrane. (D) Neurotransmitter molecules settle on the receptor site, an ion channel opens, and Na⁺ floods in.***

destroyed but reused. In this process, called *synaptic reuptake*, used neurotransmitter molecules are ejected from the postsynaptic receptors, vacuumed by molecular pumps back into the presynaptic axon terminals, and repackaged into new synaptic vesicles.

These two mechanisms for removing transmitter molecules from the synapse work very quickly. But in some cases, the postsynaptic neuron can be bombarded so rapidly with bursts of neurotransmitter that the mechanisms of enzymatic cleanup and reuptake are momentarily overwhelmed. Such rapid-fire stimulation results in a temporary accumulation of neurotransmitter, and this is, of course, the source of temporal summation—much as Sherrington had proposed almost a century ago.

NEUROTRANSMITTERS

On the face of it, one might think that the nervous system only needs two transmitters: one excitatory, the other inhibitory. But the reality is different, and there are actually a great number of different transmitter substances. About a hundred or so have been isolated thus far, and many more are sure to be discovered.

We will mention just a few of these neurotransmitters here. *Acetylcholine* (*ACh*) is released at many synapses and at the neuromuscular junction (itself a kind of synapse); the release of ACh makes muscle fibers contract. *Serotonin* (*5HT*, after its formula *5-hydroxy-tryptamine*) is a transmitter that is involved in many of the mechanisms of sleep, mood, and arousal. *GABA* (the abbreviation for *gamma-amino butyric acid*) is the most widely distributed inhibitory transmitter of the CNS. Still other transmitters are *norepinephrine* (*NE*) and *dopamine* (*DA*), which will be important later in our discussions of drug effects and certain mental disorders.

Why does the nervous system need this extravagance of signal types? One important reason is that the variety helps the nervous system to keep separate the different types of information being passed back and forth. This separation rests on the fact that individual neurons are very selective in what neurotransmitters they will respond to, so a neuron sensitive to GABA, say, will be oblivious to (and not distracted by) its neighbor's signal conveyed by, say, serotonin.

This selectivity by individual neurons is a consequence of the exact shape and size of the receptors on the postsynaptic neuron, and it is sometimes described in terms of the *lock-and-key model* of transmitter action. This theory proposes that transmitter molecules will only affect the postsynaptic membrane if the molecule's shape fits into certain synaptic receptor molecules, much as a key must fit into a lock. Note, though, that the mere fact that a given molecule fits into the receptor is not enough to qualify it as a transmitter. The key must not just fit into the lock; it must also turn it (Figure 3.30). In the language of neurophysiology, the transmitter molecule must produce the changes in membrane potential that correspond to excitatory and inhibitory processes.

3.29   The synapse   Electron micrograph of the knoblike axon terminals, which contain the synaptic vesicles.

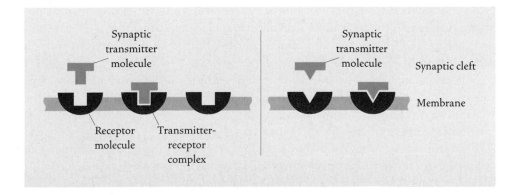

3.30   Lock-and-key model of synaptic transmission   Transmitter molecules will only affect the postsynaptic membrane if their shape fits the shape of certain receptor molecules in that membrane, much as a key has to fit into a lock. The diagram shows two kinds of transmitters and their appropriate receptors.

The lock-and-key model describes many cases of neurotransmission, but, as is often the case, other facts demand complications in the theory. One complication arises from the fact that certain neurotransmitters—the so-called conditional neurotransmitters—work only when other keys have already opened their own locks. More precisely, the conditional neurotransmitters seem to work only in the presence of other neurotransmitters, or if the level of activity is already increased in that neuronal circuit.

As yet another complication, neurons involved in the control of very high-speed acts such as eye movements may circumvent chemical neurotransmission altogether. They may communicate via narrow *electrical synapses*, with the action potential of one neuron directly inducing an action potential in the next (Shepherd, 1994).

Finally, signaling in the nervous system can take still other forms as well. It seems that some neurons signal each other by releasing small quantities of dissolved gases (Navarra, Dello Russo, Mancuso, Preziosi, & Grossman, 2000). Researchers are also increasingly interested in chemical signals sent *within* a neuron. Specifically, neuroscientists now regard the various transmitters released by the presynaptic neuron as the brain's *primary messengers*, responsible for neuron-to-neuron communication. But there are also chemical processes that occur within the postsynaptic neuron after it has been stimulated by a primary messenger and that can render the neuron more or less responsive thereafter. These chemical processes regulate such mechanisms as the creation of receptor sites for specific neurotransmitters and the synthesis of the neuron's own neurotransmitter; they are set in motion by a set of substances known as the neuron's *second messengers* (Shepherd, 1994).

These complexities obviously demand a conception that goes well beyond the simple lock-and-key model. In addition, given the pace of recent discoveries, it seems virtually certain that further signal mechanisms will be found. Clearly, the brain has many other tricks up its metaphorical sleeve. (For a recent catalog of the complexities in how neurons communicate, see Bullock et al., 2005.)

DRUGS AND NEUROTRANSMITTERS

The fact that communication among neurons depends on different neurotransmitter substances (and possibly different processes) has wide implications for both psychology and pharmacology. This is because our knowledge of the brain's neurotransmitters has been crucial to understanding how various drugs—both legal and illegal—exert their effects.

In general, *exogenous agents* (chemicals introduced from the outside) can either enhance or impede the actions of a neurotransmitter. Those that enhance a transmitter's activity are technically called *agonists*, a term borrowed from Greek drama in which the agonist is the name for the hero. Drugs that impede such action are *antagonists*, a term that refers to whoever opposes the hero (so to speak, the villain).

Agonists and antagonists exert their influence in numerous ways at the synapse. Some agonists enhance a transmitter's effect by blocking its synaptic reuptake, thus leaving more transmitter within the synapse. Others act by counteracting the cleanup enzyme or by increasing the availability of some neurotransmitter *precursor* (a substance required for the transmitter's chemical manufacture). Conversely, some antagonists operate by speeding up reuptake, others by augmenting cleanup enzymes, and still others by decreasing available precursors.

Other drugs affect the synaptic receptors. Some are agonists that activate the receptors by mimicking the transmitter's action. Conversely, some antagonists prevent the transmitter effect by binding themselves to the synaptic receptor and blocking off the transmitter, thus serving as a kind of putty in the synaptic lock.

Illustrations of these various mechanisms are easy to find. Amphetamines and cocaine, for example, are agonists; they work by blocking the reuptake of dopamine, norepinephrine, and epinephrine into the presynaptic molecules. The effect is autonomic arousal, restlessness, and, in some cases, euphoria. Many of the antidepression medications work in roughly the same way but specifically block the reupdate of serotin; Prozac, Zoloft, and Paxil all work in roughly this way. Still other drugs are antagonists. Some of the medications used for schizophrenia, for example, block post-synaptic receptors, and they seem effective in helping patients control psychotic thinking and restore normal functioning in their lives.

In many cases, scientists have used what they know about the nervous system to design new drugs; this was the case for Prozac, for example. In other cases, though, the sequence has been the other way around, with scientists using drug effects to illuminate how the brain functions. One celebrated example is the discovery of endorphins—a family of chemicals produced inside the brain that powerfully influence how we perceive and cope with pain (Hughes et al., 1975). These "naturally produced" painkillers influence the brain in much the same way that morphine does, and much of what we know about endorphins comes from parallels with our understanding of how drugs like morphine or heroin influence the body.

Similar logic led to the discovery of a brain receptor for THC (tetrahydrocannabinol), the active ingredient in marijuana. A team of researchers injected a THC-like chemical into the brains of rats and found that it latched on to receptors located especially in the midbrain and in various limbic structures (Devane, Dysarz, Johnson, Melvin, & Howlett, 1988). Research suggests that all vertebrates may have such *cannabinoid (CB) receptors* (Elphick & Egertova, 2001; Van Sickle et al., 2005).

If there are CB receptors in the brain, what function do they serve? Is it possible that the brain produces its own THC-like chemicals, and that these receptors are in place to allow a response to these chemicals? Four years after discovering the first CB receptors, the same research team reported isolating a compound produced by the brain itself with many of THC's properties (Devane et al., 1992). The team named this neurotransmitter *anandamide* (from the Sanskrit word *ananda*, for "bliss") because of the giddy euphoria many marijuana users experience. It is conceivable that anandamide will turn out to be the brain's own marijuana, responsible for our natural euphoric moments.

INTERACTIONS THROUGH THE BLOODSTREAM

We are almost done with our discussion of how signals are transmitted within the body. However, we need to touch briefly on two more topics—both concerned with the interaction between the signaling systems and the bloodstream.

BLOOD CIRCULATION

The cells that make up the central nervous system require considerable energy to function and are thus nutrient gluttons. This makes the circulation of blood—which supplies the brain with oxygen and glucose—particularly crucial. In fact, several different arteries enter the brain separately and join up inside the brain, probably to provide redundancy in the event that any one artery malfunctions.

These cerebral blood vessels do more than ensure that the brain gets enough blood; they also make sure that the blood is pure. The cells making up the nervous system are extremely sensitive to toxins, and so it is essential to protect them. To accomplish this, blood vessels within the brain are surrounded by tightly joined cells that literally act as filters, and together they form the *blood–brain barrier* (Mayhan, 2001). This barrier is remarkably effective; indeed, it sometimes seems too effective to investigators trying to design medicines to help people with brain disorders. For them the task is twofold—to design an effective medicine, and to design one that can outwit the barrier and reach the brain cells.

THE ENDOCRINE SYSTEM

In the brain and throughout the body, the circulation of blood also serves another purpose: It provides a further means of sending signals from one location to another. This other means of internal communication is called the *endocrine system* (Figure 3.31 and Table 3.1). Various *endocrine glands* (such as the *pancreas*, the *adrenal glands*, and the *pituitary*) release chemical secretions—*hormones*—directly into the bloodstream and in this way affect structures that are often far removed from their biochemical birthplace. As an example, take the pituitary gland. One of its components secretes a hormone that tells the kidney to decrease the amount of water excreted in the urine, a useful mechanism when the body is short of water. Another part of the pituitary gland controls the thymus gland in the chest, which in turn produces the T-lymphocyte cells so important in fighting widespread systemic infections (including those from the human immunodeficiency virus, or HIV).

On the face of it, the communication and control provided by the endocrine glands seem very different from that provided by the nervous system. In the nervous system, neurotransmitters are sent to particular addresses through highly specific channels. In contrast, the chemical messengers employed by the endocrine system travel indiscriminately throughout the bloodstream, reaching virtually all parts of the body. Neurotrans-

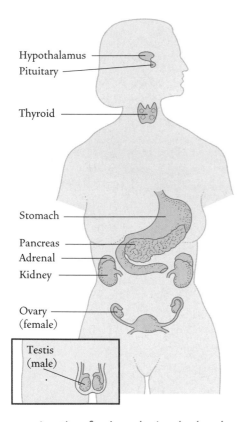

Hypothalamus
Pituitary

Thyroid

Stomach

Pancreas
Adrenal
Kidney

Ovary
(female)

Testis
(male)

3.31   Location of major endocrine glands and hypothalamus

TABLE 3.1   THE MAIN ENDOCRINE GLANDS AND SOME OF THEIR FUNCTIONS

GLAND	FUNCTION(S) OF THE RELEASED HORMONES
Anterior pituitary	Often called the body's master gland because it triggers hormone secretion in many of the other endocrine glands.
Posterior pituitary	Prevents loss of water through kidney.
Thyroid	Affects metabolic rate.
Islet cells in pancreas	Affects utilization of glucose.
Adrenal cortex	Has various effects on metabolism, immunity, and response to stress; has some effects on sexual behavior.
Adrenal medulla	Increases sugar output of liver; stimulates various internal organs in the same direction as the sympathetic branch of the ANS (e.g., accelerates heart rate).
Ovaries	One set of hormones (estrogen) produces female sex characteristics and is relevant to sexual behavior. Another hormone (progesterone) prepares uterus for implantation of embryo.
Testes	Produces male sex characteristics; relevant to sexual arousal.

mitters must only cross the synaptic gap, which is less than 1/10,000 millimeter wide, but the endocrine messengers may have to traverse the entire length of the body.

Despite these differences, the two communication systems have a good deal in common. Obviously, both deliver their messages by the release of chemical substances. In fact, they often use the *same* substances, because a number of chemicals serve both as hormones and as neurotransmitters. Norepinephrine, for example, is one of the hormones secreted by the adrenal gland, and it is also an important neurotransmitter. In addition, the effects produced by norepinephrine as a hormone overlap substantially with the effects produced by activating the neurons that use norepinephrine as their transmitter. Relationships like these suggest that neurons and the cells of the endocrine glands may have evolved from a common origin—an ancestral signaling system from which both our endocrine and nervous systems are derived (LeRoith, Shiloach, & Roth, 1982).

PLASTICITY

During our lifetimes, we learn new facts; we acquire new skills; we gain new perspectives. We are exposed to life's highs and lows, and gradually we adjust to them. Our reactions to the world and, indeed, our entire personalities can change as we acquire some amount of wisdom and maturity.

It is a fundamental assumption of psychology and neuroscience that all these changes correspond to (and are made possible by) changes in the nervous system. Hence the nervous system must somehow be *plastic*—subject to alteration in how it functions. What is the nature of this plasticity?

In our earlier discussion of ontogenesis, we saw that, early in the lifetime of an organism, plasticity is made possible by the proliferation of new neurons and new connections among neurons. Neuronal migration also plays a role, as neurons move into the proper regions, and so does a considerable amount of pruning to eliminate misguided connections. But what form does plasticity take during the remainder of an organism's lifetime?

CHANGES IN NEURONAL CONNECTIONS

Over and over, we have seen that evolution often provides overlapping mechanisms, serving interrelated purposes. In Chapter 2, for example, we discussed that there are multiple signals for hunger and multiple sites in the nervous system where those signals are detected. Earlier in this chapter, we saw that there are multiple neurotransmitters, allowing the nervous system to keep simultaneous messages from leaking into each other. In the same vein, it turns out that the nervous system can make many adjustments in how it functions, and all of these adjustments serve the larger goal of allowing the system to alter its operation so that organisms can gain from experience.

Neurons can, for example, adjust the amount of neurotransmitter they release, as a function of prior experience; this alteration plays an important role in learning, a point we will return to in Chapter 6. Neurons can also change how *sensitive* they are to neurotransmitters, by (among other adjustments) literally gaining new receptors, and this too plays a pivotal role in learning.

Neurons can also create entirely new connections, by adding synapses as a function of experience. The changes in this case seem to take place largely on the dendrites of postsynaptic cells. The dendrites grow new *dendritic spines*, little knobs attached to the surface of the dendrites (Kolb, Gibb, & Robinson, 2003; Moser, 1999; Woolf, 1998). These spines are the "receiving stations" for most synapses, so growing more spines

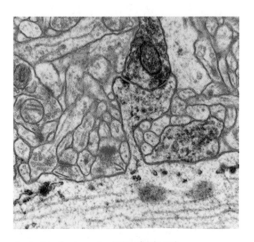

A photomicrograph of dendritic spines.

almost certainly means that, as learning proceeds, the neuron is gaining new synapses, or new lines of communication with its cellular neighbors.

CORTICAL REORGANIZATION

Plasticity does not just involve changes in individual neurons; in addition, an organism's experiences can actually lead to large-scale changes in the brain's architecture. For example, in one study, investigators trained monkeys to respond in one way if they heard a certain musical pitch, and a different way if they heard a slightly different pitch (Recanzone, Schreiner, & Merzenich, 1993). We already know from other evidence that the monkeys' projection areas for sounds are organized in maps—with different regions being responsive to certain frequencies of sound. With training, though, the map was reorganized, so that appreciably more cortical area was devoted to the trained frequencies *after* training than had been the case before training.

Can the same be demonstrated in humans? One research team used neuroimaging to examine the activity levels in somatosensory projection areas for two groups. One group consisted of highly trained musicians who played string instruments; the other group consisted of nonmusicians (Elbert, Pantev, Wienbruch, Rockstroh, & Taub, 1995). The results showed that more cortical area was dedicated to representing input from the fingers of the musicians—with a suggestion that, as a result of their instrumental training, the musicians' brains had been reorganized, devoting more tissue to skills essential for their playing.

NEW NEURONS

One of the long-held doctrines in neuroscience was that, at birth, the brain has all the neurons it will ever have, so plasticity during the organism's lifetime must be due to changes in these neurons. However, neuroscientists have been expressing reservations about this doctrine for years (e.g., Ramón y Cajal, 1913), and it turns out that the reservations were justified: There is growing evidence that neurogenesis continues throughout the organism's lifetime, and that the neurogenesis is promoted specifically by learning and enriched experience. This pattern is particularly striking in the hippocampus, a subcortical structure known to play an essential role in the establishment of new memories (Eriksson et al., 1998).

However, the central nervous system appears unable to grow new neurons for a different purpose: to replace neurons damaged through injury. This is in clear contrast to the peripheral nervous system, where neurons can, for example, regenerate their axons after the original axon has been severed. Why should this limit exist in the central nervous system? The answer may lie in the glial cells, which, we noted earlier, secrete chemicals that inhibit neural growth; the glial cells may also provide a physical barrier to cell growth, because they often form impenetrable scar tissue after brain damage.

In most cases, these limits on neurogenesis are beneficial, because, in the absence of injury, these limitations on new wiring keep the pattern of connections in the nervous system relatively stable. However, limits on neural growth are deeply problematic for anyone who has suffered brain damage through injury or disease—including Parkinson's disease or Alzheimer's disease, both of which involve the destruction of brain tissue. This has led investigators to seek ways to circumvent the brain's limited potential for regeneration—either by implanting new tissue or by seeking external means of encouraging the growth of new neurons.

Some of the most exciting work on this issue involves implanting, into an area of damage, the same sorts of **neural stem cells** that are responsible for building the nervous system in the first place. Stem cells are, in general, cells found in early stages of development that have not begun to specialize or differentiate in any way. These cells, undifferentiated as they are, are enormously pliable, able to develop into virtually any sort of cell found in the body. In this form of therapy, therefore, the nervous system does not actually receive replacement cells for the tissue that is damaged; instead, it receives the precursors of the cells it needs, so that it can, in effect, grow its own replacements.

Preliminary studies suggest that when stem cells are injected into a patch of neurons, the cells are induced to turn into healthy neurons just like their neighbors, taking their shape, producing their neurotransmitters, and filling in for dead neurons (Holm et al., 2001; Isacson, 1999; Philips et al., 2001; Sawamoto et al., 2001). Even brain injury from stroke may respond to stem-cell therapy. That was the conclusion of one study in which rats that had had strokes resulting in profound motor impairments showed near-complete recovery several months after stem cells were implanted (Veizovic, Beech, Stroemer, Watson, & Hodges, 2001). Initial human trials appear promising (Kondziolka et al., 2000).

Such stem-cell studies entail substantial ethical quandaries, because of where the stem cells come from. As part of a fertility treatment, ova are sometimes removed from a woman, fertilized *in vitro* (in a laboratory, outside of the woman's body), and allowed to develop into large masses of cells. One of these masses is then placed back into the woman in hopes that it will implant in the uterus and develop into a normal pregnancy. It is the other masses—the ones not implanted—that have been the main sources for stem cells, and there lies the problem: In principle, these other masses might also have been implanted and might also have developed into a human fetus. On that view, this procedure is a form of abortion, so it is entirely unacceptable to anyone who is an opponent of abortion.

It is no surprise, therefore, that stem-cell research has become controversial. On the one hand, the potential gains from this research are enormous, and stem-cell research could lead to successful therapies for a wide range of diseases and medical problems. The list includes Parkinson's disease, Alzheimer's disease, spinal cord injuries, brain lesions resulting from stroke, and also a list of medical problems external to the nervous system: heart disease, diabetes, burns, osteoarthritis, and perhaps some forms of cancer. On the other hand, this research (at least in its current form) involves procedures that are morally repugnant for some people. With so much at stake on both sides in this debate, the issue may not be resolved anytime soon.

SOME FINAL THOUGHTS: SHOULD ALL PSYCHOLOGICAL QUESTIONS HAVE BIOLOGICAL ANSWERS?

Our examination of the biological basis of behavior—in this chapter and in the last—has brought us enormous fruit: We have learned a great deal both at a microscopic level (e.g., knowledge about individual neurons) and on a larger scale (e.g., knowledge about entire brain areas). The knowledge has allowed sophisticated theorizing, but it has also supported useful applications (e.g., the development of new antidepressants).

Does all of this imply, therefore, that psychology should entirely be a biological science? Will the answers to all psychological questions ultimately be phrased in terms of action potentials and neurotransmitters? The answer is no. Undeniably, many psychological questions do have biological answers, but many do not. To see why, imagine that a journalist or historian wants to know why people voted this way or that in the most recent election. To answer with a paragraph (or a book) about the voters' synaptic connections would be absurd. This neuron-based account might be factually correct, but it would be unilluminating because the question at stake is ultimately a question about reasons, not about neural mechanisms. What is needed is an account phrased in the appropriate terms—the voters' interpretation of the candidates' positions; their own attitudes toward the issues; and so on. Any of these answers might prove inadequate or incomplete, but at least they are aimed at the right level of explanation. In contrast, a statement about neuronal firings in the frontal cortex of each voter seems off the mark. This is not because we do not know enough yet about the nervous system. Even if we could analyze all the neuronal firings in all the voters, this analysis would not provide adequate answers for the journalist or the historian—let alone the ordinary person on the street.

Exactly the same considerations apply to psychologists asking about the mind. When psychologists ask about how humans and animals act, perceive, think, remember, and feel, they often want answers at a level different from that offered by a neurophysiologist. Of course, they are aware that all our actions take place within a framework set by our nervous system. But even so, they believe that many psychological explanations are more appropriately offered in other terms. Just how such psychological explanations are formulated will be the topic of subsequent chapters.

SUMMARY

THE ORGANISM AS A MACHINE

- Many scientists have tried to explain human and animal behavior in mechanistic terms. For Descartes, this involved the reflex concept: A stimulus excites a sense organ that transmits excitation upward to the brain, which in turn relays the excitation downward to a muscle or gland, and so produces action.

HOW THE NERVOUS SYSTEM IS STUDIED

- The techniques for studying the brain include clinical observation and also *neuropsychology*, which typically involves fine-grained experiments exploring how brain damage has compromised a person's functioning. Scientists also study the effects of temporary brain damage, using the technique of *transcranial magnetic stimulation*.
- *Neuroimaging techniques* are used to study the living brain. Some of these techniques (*MRI* and *CT scans*) study the brain's anatomy—the size and location of individual structures. Other techniques, such as *PET* and *fMRI scans*, reveal which brain locations are particularly active at any moment in time. All of these techniques make it clear that most mental activities rely on many brain sites, so that reading (for example) or making decisions are supported by the coordinated functioning of many different parts of the brain.

THE ARCHITECTURE OF THE NERVOUS SYSTEM

- The nervous system is divided into the *central nervous system* (the brain and spinal cord) and the *peripheral nervous system*, which includes both *efferent* and *afferent* nerves. The peripheral nervous system is divided into the *somatic division* and the *autonomic nervous system*.
- In the central nervous system, the *hindbrain* contains structures crucial for controlling life functions. The *midbrain* plays a major role in coordinating movements and also in relaying information from the senses. The *forebrain* is the part of the brain that supports humans' capacity for complex intellectual functions. The *cortex* of the forebrain is a thin covering, but, because of its many folds, it includes a large quantity of tissue. Some of the folds—or *convolutions*—are actually deep grooves that divide the brain into sections, such as the *frontal lobes*, the *parietal lobes*, the *occipital lobes*, and the *temporal lobes*.
- The entire brain is more or less symmetrical around the midline, so that most structures come in pairs—one on the left side, one on the right. The left and right structures are generally similar, but they can be distinguished both anatomically and functionally. Crucially, though, the two halves of the brain work as an integrated whole.

THE CORTEX

- *Localization of function* is the task of determining the function of each brain area. In the cortex, some parts serve as *projection areas*—the first receiving stations for information coming from the sense organs, and also the departure points for signals going to the muscles. Most projection areas have a *contralateral organization*, and each is organized so that (for example) adjacent areas in the motor projection area represent adjacent parts of the body; adjacent areas in the visual projection area represent adjacent regions of space. However, the assignment of cortical space is disproportionate, so that (for example) parts of the body that are most sensitive to touch receive more cortical space.

- Much of what we know about other parts of the cortex comes from cases of brain damage, and damage at identifiable sites can produce *apraxias* (disorders in action), *agnosias* (disorders in perception), or *aphasias* (disorders of language). Still other forms of brain damage produce disorders of planning or social cognition.

THE ORIGINS OF THE BRAIN

- The development of the brain depends on *neurogenesis*, a process through which nerve cells signal each other, differentiate, and attract connections from other nerve cells. More nerve cells are created than are needed, and so a process of pruning is required to leave just the right cells connected in just the right way.

THE BUILDING BLOCKS OF THE NERVOUS SYSTEM

- The basic unit of communication in the nervous system is the *neuron*, and the vast majority of neurons are *interneurons* that typically connect to yet other interneurons, thus forming the *microcircuitry* of the nervous system. The nervous system also contains *glia*, and these cells may constitute a separate, slow signal system.

COMMUNICATION AMONG NEURONS

- When the neuron's membrane is stable, there is an excess of positively charged ions on the outside, resulting in the voltage difference of the *resting potential*. When the membrane is sufficiently irritated, though, ion channels in the membrane spring open, and this allows ion movement that leads to an excess of positively charged particles inside the membrane, producing the positive voltage swing of the *action potential*. The excitation spreads to neighboring regions, and this leads to the *propagation* of the action potential along the axon. The action potential obeys the *all-or-none law*: Once the action potential is launched, further increases in stimulus intensity have no effect on its magnitude.

- Communication between neurons is made possible by the release of *neurotransmitters*. The transmitters cross the *synapse* and trigger a response in a *postsynaptic cell*. Some transmitters are inactivated shortly after they have been discharged by "cleanup" enzymes. More commonly, neurotransmitters are reused by a process of *synaptic reuptake*.

- The *lock-and-key model* proposes that transmitter molecules will only affect the postsynaptic membrane if the molecule's shape fits into certain synaptic receptor molecules. However, drugs called *agonists* can enhance a neurotransmitter's effect; *antagonists* impede its effect. Some agonists enhance a transmitter's effect by blocking its synaptic reuptake; others act by counteracting the cleanup enzyme. Yet other drugs affect the synaptic receptors, by mimicking the transmitter's action.

INTERACTIONS THROUGH THE BLOODSTREAM

- Blood circulation brings energy to the nutrient-hungry brain, but it also aids communication by carrying hormones secreted by the *endocrine* glands to the various target organs throughout the body.

PLASTICITY

- The nervous system is *plastic*—subject to alteration in the way it functions. Some of this plasticity involves changes in how much neurotransmitter a presynaptic neuron releases. Neurons can also change how sensitive they are to neurotransmitters. In addition, neurons can create entirely new connections, by growing new *dendritic spines*.

- Plasticity can also involve larger-scale changes, including changes in the brain's overall architecture. In addition, the central nervous system is able to grow new neurons, although it appears unable to do so in cases of cortical injury. The reason for this may lie in the glial cells, which secrete chemicals that inhibit neural growth. This promotes stability in the brain's connections, but obviously it can be an obstacle to recovery from brain damage.

SENSATION

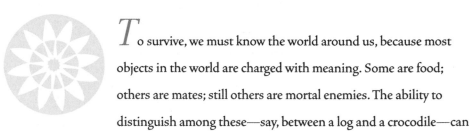*T*o survive, we must know the world around us, because most objects in the world are charged with meaning. Some are food; others are mates; still others are mortal enemies. The ability to distinguish among these—say, between a log and a crocodile—can be a matter of life and death. To make these distinctions, we have to use our senses. We must do our best to see and hear the crocodile so that we can recognize it for what it is before it sees, hears, smells, and (especially) tastes us. But how exactly do our senses function? How accurate and how complete is the sensory information we receive from our eyes, ears, and other sensory organs? And to what extent is our perception of the world *objective*—true to the sensory information we receive, with a minimum of interpretation? Conversely, to what extent is our perception influenced by our biases, our expectations, and perhaps even our hopes? It is to these questions that we now turn.

THE ORIGINS OF KNOWLEDGE

The study of sensory experience grows out of an ancient question, and it is a question closely tied to the broad issues we just mentioned: Where does human knowledge come from? One suggestion is straightforward: Our knowledge comes directly from the world around us, and our eyes, ears and other senses are merely the means of collecting the information the world provides. According to this view, our senses receive and record information much as a camera receives light or a microphone receives sound, and this implies that our perception of the world is a relatively passive affair. After all, a camera does not choose which light beams to receive, nor does it do any interpretation of the light it detects. Instead, it simply records the light available to it. Likewise, a tape recorder does not interpret the speech or appreciate the music; again, in a passive fashion, it simply records. Could this be the way vision and hearing work?

AN EARLY VIEW: THE PASSIVE PERCEIVER

Advocates for the philosophical view known as *empiricism* argue that our senses are passive in this way. One of the earliest proponents of this position was the English philosopher John Locke (1632–1704), who argued that, at birth, the human mind is simply a blank tablet, a *tabula rasa*, on which experience leaves its mark.

> Let us suppose the mind to be, as we say, a white paper void of all characters, without any ideas:—How comes it to be furnished? Whence comes it by that vast store which the busy and boundless fancy of man has painted on it with an almost endless variety? Whence has it all the materials of reason and knowledge? To this I answer, in one word, from experience. In that all our knowledge is founded; and from that it ultimately derives itself. (Locke, 1690)

DISTAL AND PROXIMAL STIMULI

To evaluate Locke's claim, though, we need to be clear about exactly what the information is that the senses receive. Consider what happens, for example, when we look at another person some distance away. We are presumably interested in what the person looks like, who he is, and what he is doing. These are all facts about the *distal stimulus*, the real object (in this case, the person) in the world outside of us. (The distal stimulus is typically at some distance from the perceiver, hence the term *distal*.)

As it turns out, though, we have no direct access to the distal stimulus. Instead, our only information about the distal stimulus lies in the energies that actually reach us— the pattern of light that is reflected off of the person's outer surface, collected by our eyes, and cast as an image on the *retina*, the light-sensitive tissue at the rear of each eyeball. This is the *proximal* (or "nearby") *stimulus*. If there were no proximal stimulus, if the light reflecting off of this person were somehow blocked or interrupted on its way to us, the person would be invisible to us. The same holds for the other senses as well. We can smell a rotten egg (the distal stimulus) only because of the hydrogen sulfide molecules in the air that flows over the sensory cells in our nasal cavities (the proximal stimulus).

The distinction between distal and proximal stimuli raises difficult questions for the empiricist. If the senses are the only portals we have to the outside world, and the proximal stimuli are the only messengers allowed to pass through these gates, then how can we ever know the true qualities of the distal stimulus? To see why this is a problem, consider the concerns raised by another empiricist philosopher, George Berkeley (1685–1753). Berkeley pointed out that a large object, far away from us, can cast the same-size image on our retina as a small object, much closer to us (Figure 4.1). Retinal-image size, therefore, cannot tell us the size of the distal object; how, then, do we tell the large objects in our world from the small? By the same token, since the retina is a two-

John Locke (1632–1704)

Bishop George Berkeley (1685–1753)

dimensional surface, all images—from near objects and far—are cast onto the same plane. Berkeley argued, therefore, that the retinal image cannot directly inform us about the three-dimensional world. Yet, of course, we have little difficulty in moving around the world, avoiding obstacles, grasping the things we want to grasp. How can these achievements be reconciled with the obvious limitations of the proximal stimulus?

THE ROLE OF ASSOCIATION

If, as the empiricists claimed, all knowledge comes from the senses, and if the senses only give us access to the proximal stimulus, how can we know the distal world? According to the empiricists themselves, the answer, in a word, is *learning*. The empiricists argued that prior experience plays a crucial role in shaping our perceptual world, and the key mechanism of this learning is **association**, the process through which one sensory experience is linked to another.

As an example of how this argument unfolds, consider the empiricists' account of how we perceive the three-dimensional layout of the world. They noted that there were a variety of **distance cues** contained within the retinal image, including the cue we call *visual perspective* (Figure 4.2). They argued, though, that our use of this cue depends on learning: We have, in many circumstances, seen the visual cue of perspective and a moment later reached for or walked toward the objects we were viewing. This experience created an association in the mind between the visual cue and the appropriate movement, and because this experience was repeated over and over, the visual cue alone is now able to produce the memory of the movement and thus the experience of depth. (For more on distance cues, see Chapter 5.)

THE ACTIVE PERCEIVER

Other philosophers, however, soon offered a response to the empiricist position, and they argued in particular that the perceiver plays a far more active role than the

4.1 Distal and proximal stimuli   As the person looks out on the world, the retinal image cast by his hand will be roughly the same size as the image of the car. But one of these images obviously represents a much larger object! Clearly then retinal image size (the proximal stimulus) cannot by itself tell us the size of the distant object (the distal stimulus).

4.2 Depth cues in Renaissance painting   This painting by Paris Bordone (1500–1571) shows how distance cues can create a vivid sense of depth on a flat canvas.

empiricists realized. In their view, the perceiver does much more than merely supplement the sensory input with associations. In addition—and more important—the perceiver must categorize and interpret the incoming sensory information.

Many scholars have endorsed this general position, but the view is often attributed to the German philosopher Immanuel Kant (1724–1804). Kant argued that perception is possible only because the mind is able to organize the sensory information into certain preexisting categories. Specifically, Kant claimed that each of us has an innate grasp of certain spatial relationships, so that we understand what it means for one thing to be *next to* or *far from* another thing, and so on. We also have an innate grasp of temporal relationships (and thus what it means for one event to occur *before* another, or *after*), and also of what it means for one event to cause another. These basic understandings provide categories of space, time, and causality that bring order to all of our perception; without these categories, our sensory experience would be chaotic and meaningless: We might detect the individual bits of red or green or heavy or sour, but, without the categories, we would be unable to assemble the bits into a coherent sense of the world.

Notice that, in Kant's view, these categories are what makes perception possible; without the categories, there can be no perception. The categories must be in place, therefore, before any perceptual experience can occur, so they obviously cannot be derived from perceptual experience. Instead, they must be built into the very structure of the mind, as part of our biological heritage, and this is why this philosophical position is known as **nativism**, with a clear emphasis on "native" (i.e., innate) capacities.

Immanuel Kant (1724–1804)

PSYCHOPHYSICS

The dispute between the empiricists and the nativists was a debate among philosophers, with few appeals to scientific evidence of any sort. But, in the broadest terms, it was a debate over the nature, origins, and trustworthiness of all our knowledge. Ultimately, the questions at stake were questions about whether our perceptions of the world reflect reality as it truly is, or reflect reality as it has been interpreted and categorized by us. It is no surprise, therefore, that this dispute focused investigators' attention on the role of the senses and prodded them to explore in a more systematic fashion just how the senses function. In short, this philosophical dispute provided powerful motivation for careful scientific scrutiny of the senses.

At the most fundamental level, this scientific scrutiny must begin with an examination of the exact correspondences between the physical inputs that we receive—the stimuli—and the psychological experiences these stimuli give rise to. This charting of the relationship between physical stimuli and psychological experiences is called **psychophysics**, and it asks such questions as: What changes in our perception of a sound as the frequency of the sound waves changes? What change in the physical attributes of light correspond to the change from perceiving red to perceiving green? Questions like these are quite specific, but they are crucial if we are to understand the basic relationship between our perceptions and the world in which we reside.

MEASURING SENSORY INTENSITY

Psychophysics examines both the *qualities* of a sensory experience (Was the taste sweet or sour? Was the light yellow or blue?) and the *quantity* of the experience (Was the smell intense or mild? Was the sound loud or soft?). Much of the early work, though, was focused just on quantitative issues, and even here there was a problem: It is easy enough to measure the physical stimulus, so we can readily find out how many pounds this bowling ball weighs or how hot this water is in degrees centigrade. But how can we make the corresponding psychological measurements to assess the sensory experience of the subject? How can we quantify how something tastes, sounds, or smells?

Gustav Theodor Fechner (1801–1887), the founder of psychophysics, realized that sensations and the stimuli that produce them belong to two totally different realms— the first belong to the mental world, the second to the physical world. Therefore, they cannot be directly compared to each other. But it is possible, Fechner noted, to make comparisons within each of these realms. Even if sensations cannot be compared to physical stimuli, they can at least be compared to each other, and this can provide a basis for measuring them.

Consider the sensation of visual brightness produced by a patch of light projected onto the eye. We can ask, as a simple question: How much would we have to increase the intensity of this light for the observer to notice the difference? If we increase the intensity by .001%, would he notice the change? Would he notice if we change the intensity by .05%? We can answer these questions with straightforward laboratory procedures and in this fashion define the observer's *difference threshold*—the smallest stimulus change that the observer can reliably detect. If the stimulus is changed by this minimal amount, this creates what psychophysicists call a *just-noticeable difference*, or *jnd*. The jnd is a psychological entity, because it is a direct reflection of an observer's perceptual capacities. But it is expressed in the units of the physical stimulus that produced it. It would seem, therefore, that jnds provide an indirect means of measuring sensory magnitude—by relating *changes* in this magnitude to changes in the physical intensity of the stimulus.

THE WEBER FRACTION AND FECHNER'S LAW

In his thinking about jnds, Fechner was guided by a claim made in 1834 by the German physiologist E. H. Weber (1795–1878). Weber's proposal was that the size of the difference threshold (i.e., the size of a jnd) is a constant fraction of the stimulus we are comparing to. To put this concretely, suppose that an observer can just tell the difference between 100 and 102 candles burning in an otherwise dark room. This does not indicate, Weber argued, that in general we are sensitive to differences of just 2 candles. What matters instead, he suggested, is the proportional difference—in this case, a difference of 2%. Following this logic, we would not be able to distinguish 200 candles from 202 (a 2-candle difference but only a 1% change) or even 203. But we should be able to distinguish 200 candles from 204, or 300 from 306—in each case, a 2% difference.

Fechner referred to this relationship as *Weber's law*, a label by which we still know it. Put algebraically, this law is usually written as

$$\frac{\Delta I}{I} = c$$

I is the intensity of the standard stimulus, the one to which comparisons are being made; ΔI is the amount that must be added to this intensity in order to produce a just-noticeable increase; c is a constant (in our example, it was .02, or 2%). The fraction $\Delta I / I$ is referred to as the *Weber fraction*.

Fechner and his successors performed numerous studies to determine whether Weber's law holds—that is, whether the sensory apparatus is sensitive to percentage changes rather than absolute changes. The evidence suggests that this claim is correct for all of the sensory modalities, across most of the range of intensities to which an organism is sensitive. It does seem, then, that the nervous system is geared to notice percentage differences rather than absolute ones.

Weber's law provides us with several advantages, including the fact that it allows us to compare the sensitivities of different sensory modalities. Suppose we want to know whether the eye is more sensitive than the ear. We cannot compare jnds for brightness and loudness directly; the first is measured in millilamberts, the second in decibels, and there is no way to translate the one into the other. But we can compare the Weber fractions for the two modalities. If the fraction for a specific modality is small, then we know that the sense modality is able to make fine discriminations; put differently, even small percentage changes will be detected by that modality. And, of course, the smaller the Weber fraction, the more sensitive the sense modality. Using these comparisons, we can show that we are much keener at discriminating brightness (we are sensitive to differences of merely 2% or less) than loudness (here we are largely insensitive to differences of less than 10%); the Weber fractions needed for this comparison, and fractions for other sense modalities, are presented in Table 4.1.

Fechner was also able to take this logic one step further. By making a handful of further assumptions, he generalized Weber's finding to express a broad relationship between the psychological intensity of a sensory experience and the physical intensity of a stimulus. The result was *Fechner's law*, which states that the strength of a sensation grows as the logarithm of stimulus intensity:

$$S = k \log I.$$

S stands for psychological (i.e., subjective) magnitude; *I* is the physical intensity of the stimulus; and *k* is a constant whose value depends on the value of the Weber fraction.

In the years since Fechner, we have learned that, in truth, this law does not hold up perfectly in all circumstances. For our purposes, though, the law does hold in a wide range of settings and with a diversity of stimuli, providing a reasonably accurate characterization of the relationship between stimulus intensity and subjective impression.

DETECTION AND DECISION

The measurements that psychophysics provides are a prerequisite for the sorts of scientific testing we must do if we hope to understand the functioning, or the underlying biology, of the various sensory systems. However, there is a substantial complication to be dealt with in making these measurements, because it turns out that the physical characteristics of the stimulus are not the only factors that determine what the research

TABLE 4.1   REPRESENTATIVE (MIDDLE-RANGE) VALUES FOR THE WEBER FRACTION FOR THE DIFFERENT SENSES

SENSORY MODALITY	WEBER FRACTION ($\Delta I / I$)
Vision (brightness, white light)	1/60
Kinesthesis (lifted weights)	1/50
Pain (thermally aroused on skin)	1/30
Audition (tone of middle pitch and moderate loudness)	1/10
Pressure (cutaneous pressure "spot")	1/7
Smell (odor of India rubber)	1/4
Taste (table salt)	1/3

participant does or says in a psychophysical experiment. To see this, imagine a pair of participants, Matt and Fiona. Matt says, "yes, I heard that one," in response to most of the barely audible tones that the experimenter is presenting. Fiona, in contrast, says "yes" to only few of the tones, and she insists that she could not hear anything at all on the remaining test trials.

One interpretation of this pattern is that Matt has more acute hearing than Fiona does; in other words, they differ in their perceptual *sensitivity*. A different possibility, though, is that Matt and Fiona differ only in their *decision criteria*—that is, their rule for when they say yes and when they say no. Specifically, it's possible that Matt is trying to impress the experimenter with how astute he is, and, for this purpose, he wants to make certain he never misses any of the target stimuli. Matt therefore sets himself a rule of "When in doubt, say *yes, I heard that one*." Fiona, on the other hand, might be worried that the experimenter will think she is careless or impulsive if she says yes too often. To avoid this danger, she adopts a more conservative rule: "When in doubt, say *no, I didn't hear that one*." This, too, would explain the difference between Matt's and Fiona's performance: They don't differ in their hearing; they differ only in how they handle uncertainty.

The early psychophysicists hoped that this sort of complication could largely be disregarded. A more recent approach to psychophysics, however, insists that it cannot be, but also provides a way to deal with this extra layer of complexity. The newer approach is *signal-detection theory*, and it has provided a useful way to think about how people make decisions both in the psychophysics laboratory and also in a range of other contexts. Indeed, this approach, developed to study elementary sensations, has been applied to cases as diverse as jury decision making, the memory effects of hypnosis, and the diagnosis of mental disease.

In a signal-detection procedure, the experimenters present a target stimulus on some trials but no stimulus on other trials. This allows them to ask how often the participant gives each of the four possible types of response. One type is a *hit*, with the participant saying, "yes, I detected the target" when there really was one. A second response type is a *false alarm*, with the participant saying, "yes, I detected the target" when there was none. A third response type is a *correct negative*: saying "no target" when this is in fact the correct answer. The final type is a *miss*: saying "no target" even though one was actually presented (Table 4.2).

To see how this information can be used, let's return to the example of Matt and Fiona. We have already said that Matt has a higher *hit* rate than Fiona does, and we have noted that this observation is, by itself, ambiguous: Perhaps Matt has more sensitive hearing than Fiona does, or perhaps he's just more casual in his responding and relies on a relatively loose criterion. Based just on their hit rates, we have no way to tell these possibilities apart. A signal-detection experiment, though, provides other information, and this allows us to figure out what's going on with these two participants. Let's say that, in fact, Matt does have a low criterion, and that's why he usually says yes to each of the faint signals. The same low criterion, though, will encourage Matt to say yes even

TABLE 4.2 THE FOUR POSSIBLE OUTCOMES OF THE DETECTION EXPERIMENT

	STIMULUS PRESENT	STIMULUS ABSENT
RESPONDS YES	Hit	False alarm
RESPONDS NO	Miss	Correct negative

when *no* signal is presented; those trials, too, will often satisfy his rule of "When in doubt, say *yes, I heard that one.*" As a result, Matt will, as we've said, have a high hit rate, but he will also have a relatively high false-alarm rate. His responses, in other words, will tend to be in the top two cells of Table 4.2. In contrast, let's say that Matt's hit rate is high because he does, in truth, have excellent hearing, and this allows him to hear each of the subtle signals. In this case, Matt probably won't be fooled by the stimulus-absent trials; his acute hearing will allow him to realize that these trials contain no stimulus, and so he'll correctly respond no to these trials. Therefore, his false-alarm rate will be low, and his responses overall will accumulate in the top left and bottom right cells of Table 4.2.

This sets the pattern for a signal-detection analysis. In general, if individuals differ in how sensitive they are to the signal, then they will differ in their proportions of correct and incorrect responses—their total number of hits and correct negatives relative to their total number of misses and false alarms. But if they differ in their criterion for responding (e.g., whether they say yes when in doubt, or no), then they will differ in their proportions of yes and no responses. (Of course, it's possible for participants to differ in *both* their sensitivity *and* their criterion, but, with a bit of algebra, we can disentangle these effects from the signal-detection data.) As a result, we can assess individuals' sensitivity to our signals and their criterion for responding by looking at all four types of response and calculating the relative numbers of each; this allows us to specify exactly why they are responding as they are.

EXTENSIONS TO SIGNAL-DETECTION THEORY

In short, signal-detection analyses consider all four types of response—hits and misses, false alarms and correct negatives—and derive from these two quantitative measures: a measure of the participant's *sensitivity* to the input, and a measure of her *criterion*—a measure of how much information the person needs before saying, "yes, I heard it" (or saw it or smelled it or whatever).

This type of analysis turns out to be valuable in many different domains, because the distinction between sensitivity and criterion is relevant whenever someone must decide between two alternatives—and must decide on the basis of imperfect or incomplete information. For example, consider the situation of a juror trying to evaluate the evidence in a criminal trial. Here the decision to be made is between voting "guilty" and voting "not guilty," and the basis for the decision is the evidence presented during the trial. We obviously want the jurors to be as alert to this evidence as possible—and there is the role for sensitivity, the first of signal-detection theory's measurements. In addition, the other measurement—the criterion for responding—plays an equally important role. One juror, for example, might believe that prisons are horrible and inhumane places, with little chance of reforming prisoners. From this perspective, a false alarm (voting "guilty" when the defendant is actually innocent) would have terrible consequences, and so the juror would be determined to avoid this error. As a result, a juror with these beliefs would vote "guilty" only if the quantity of evidence is considerable (a high criterion).

Another juror might see things differently. He might be deeply concerned about cases in which the justice system has set guilty people free, allowing them to break the law again. For this juror, a miss (voting "not guilty" when the defendant is actually guilty) would be an unacceptable prospect; and this would lead him to vote to acquit the defendant only if he were absolutely certain of the defendant's innocence. As a result, the juror is willing to vote "guilty" with a more modest quantity of evidence (a low criterion).

Against this backdrop, we can now ask a variety of questions about the courtroom. For example, in some jurisdictions, the judge gives extra instructions to the jurors, urging them to be cautious about this or that form of evidence. Do these instructions make

Jury decision making   *The logic of signal detection theory can be applied to many cases, including the decision making of a jury. In this case, the "signal" being detected is someone's guilt, and the signal is either present or absent (the defendant is guilty or innocent), and the jury needs to make a judgment about whether the signal is present or absent.*

jurors more sensitive, so that they are better equipped to distinguish truly guilty defendants from truly not-guilty ones? This would surely be a good thing. Or do the instructions instead simply change the jurors' criterion, making them (perhaps) less likely to vote "guilty"? This might or might not be a good thing, depending on one's political views and the particulars of the trial. Plainly, therefore, we would want to ask which of these effects the judge's instructions were having, and signal-detection analysis would allow us to ask this question.

The various applications of signal-detection theory also highlight another crucial point: In virtually all decisions, some errors are inevitable. These errors can either be misses or false alarms, and, for any given test, there is likely to be a trade-off between the two. In order to minimize the number of misses (e.g., to minimize the number of guilty people that we fail to convict), we could lower the cutoff used in our evaluation. (In other words, we could lower how much incriminating evidence we insist on having before voting "guilty.") This would decrease the misses but would also increase the number of false alarms (innocent people whom we found guilty). Conversely, in order to minimize the number of false alarms, we could shift the cutoff in the opposite direction, but this would probably increase the number of misses. Just which trade-off is chosen has to depend on the particulars of the case, as well as the costs and benefits associated with the different errors and correct responses. (For more on how signal detection can be applied to other domains, including medical diagnosis, see, for example, McFall & Treat, 1999; Swets, Dawes, & Monahan, 2000.)

THE FUNCTIONING OF THE SENSES

As we have seen, psychophysics is concerned with the relationship between the physical properties of the stimulus and the sensory experience it gives rise to. To describe this relationship, we need to ask several questions: What is the minimal sensory input that can be detected at all? Answering this question tells us the *detection threshold* for a stimulus. What is the smallest difference between two stimuli that can be detected? This is the measurement of the *difference threshold*. How does the magnitude of the sensory experience grow as the stimulus intensity increases? The equation we call Fechner's Law answers this question.

These questions, however, are only the first step of our inquiry, because we also want to understand the events, step by step, that link the physical stimulus, on the one side, to the conscious experience, on the other. Thus, the study of sensation must begin with the details of light or sound waves, or the physical chemistry of the molecules that give rise to a particular flavor. Research proceeds from there to electrochemistry, in order to examine the means through which these physical inputs trigger events in the nervous system. From there the research moves to the question of how the nervous system analyzes and then recognizes the sights and sounds and smells we encounter. Finally, research moves toward our ultimate target—an explanation of the conscious experience of seeing a beautiful shade of blue, or hearing the guitar's notes, or tasting a rich, smooth chocolate.

Let's note the sheer ambition of this project, rooted in physics but ending in conscious experience, building a bridge from events that are microscopic and physical to events that are large-scale and entirely subjective. But, despite the ambition, this is an arena in which we have made enormous progress, and, in the rest of this chapter, we will survey part of what we have learned, starting with a few comments that apply to all sensory modalities, and then zooming in for a closer look at the two modalities that are unquestionably the most important sources of information for us—namely, hearing and vision.

A

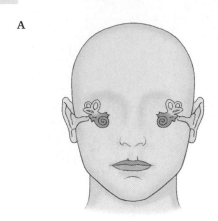

B

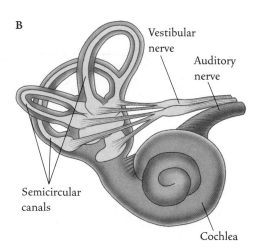

Vestibular
nerve

Auditory
nerve

Semicircular
canals

Cochlea

**4.3   *The vestibular sense*   (A) The location of
the inner ears, which are embedded in bone on
both sides of the skull. The vestibules are indicated in green. The rest of the inner ear is
devoted to the sense of hearing. (B) Close-up of
the vestibular apparatus.**

SENSORY CODING

It is often said that humans have five sense modalities—vision, hearing, touch, taste,
and smell. In truth, though, we have several more than this. To begin with, there is
kinesthesis, a collective term for information that comes from receptors in the muscles,
tendons, and joints and that informs us about our movements and the orientation of
our body in space. Another is the *vestibular sense* (Figure 4.3), whose receptors are in a
cavity within the inner ear and signal movements of the head. Yet another group are the
skin senses. Aristotle believed that all of the senses from the skin could be subsumed
under the broad rubric of *touch*, but we now know that there are at least four different
skin receptors that give rise to the sensations of pressure, warmth, cold, and pain.

Each of these senses is distinct from the others: In some cases (vision, hearing, taste,
and smell), we have specialized organs that collect, concentrate, and amplify the incoming
stimulus information; in other cases (the various skin senses), we simply accept the input,
unamplified, as it arrives. For some senses, the proximal stimulus consists of some form of
energy (a mechanical push against the eardrum in the case of hearing; a photon striking
the back of the eyeball for vision); for other senses, the proximal stimulus is chemical (a
molecule on the tongue or in the nose). Some senses (vision, hearing, smell) can respond
to stimuli that are far away from us; others (touch, taste) respond only to nearby inputs.

Even with these differences, however, the various senses have some crucial features
in common. In all cases, the physical stimulus must be converted into a neural signal;
this is the step of ***transduction***. As we noted in Chapter 3, transduction is usually accomplished by some sort of specialized receptor cells; these pass their signals to neurons
that then transmit the information to other locations for further processing. In the skin
senses, however, there is no separation between transduction and transmission;
instead, the receptor is actually a specialized part of the sensory neurons.

Once the stimulus is transduced, the nervous system needs somehow to represent
the various qualities of the input. At the coarsest level, the nervous system must register
the fact that we saw the porcupine's quills but did not feel them, or that we heard the
approaching car but did not see it. More finely, the nervous system must somehow represent the fact that the flute's note was high, not low, or that the wine was dry, not
sweet, or that the pizza tasted like pizza and not like lemonade. These are issues of
sensory coding. In general, a "code" is a set of rules through which information is transformed from one format into another. An example is the code a fax machine uses to
transform the patterns on a printed page into a sound-based pattern that can be transmitted through a telephone line. In the same way, the nervous system encodes (i.e.,
translates) the various properties of the proximal stimulus into neural impulses so that
these can be transmitted to the brain.

One aspect of sensory coding involves ***psychological intensity***—the difference between
a loud noise and a soft one, or a subtle scent of lavender in contrast to a dense cloud of the
smell. In most cases, the nervous system codes stimulus intensity via the rate of firing by
the neurons in a sensory system: the more intense the stimulus, the greater the rate of firing. Recall that neurons cannot fire more strongly or less strongly; as we discussed in
Chapter 3, either a neuron fires or it does not. But neurons can fire more or less often, and
this seems to be the cue that usually indicates how intense the stimulus was. In addition,
stimulus intensity is also encoded via the sheer number of neurons that are triggered by
the stimulus: the more intense the stimulus, the more neurons it activates, and the greater
the psychological magnitude.

A second aspect of coding is ***sensory quality***—the difference in the neural code that tells
us we are seeing the flower rather than touching or smelling its scent. The sensations of
sight, touch, smell, and so on are obviously produced by very different stimuli, but this is
not what is crucial for the nervous system. What matters, instead, is which nerves are
being stimulated. Stimulation of the optic nerve (whether the stimulation comes from

light or some other source) causes the sense of seeing; this is why strong pressure on the eyeballs leads us to see rings or stars (to the chagrin of boxers and the delight of cartoonists) just as light does. Similarly, stimulation of the auditory nerve (whether the stimulation comes from sound or something else) causes the sense of hearing. This is why people sometimes experience "ringing in their ears" in the absence of any environmental sound—some illness or injury is causing stimulation of the auditory nerve.

These facts are generally summarized in terms of the *doctrine of specific nerve energies*, first formulated in 1826 by Johannes Müller (1801–1858). According to this doctrine, the differences in sensory quality—the difference between seeing and hearing, between hearing and touch, and so on—are not caused by differences in the stimuli themselves but by the different nervous structures that these stimuli excite.

But what about differences *within* a sense modality? For example, blue, green, and red are all visual sensations, but of course they are qualitatively different from each other. Likewise, sweetness and saltiness are both tastes, but plainly distinct for the perceiver. How are differences of these sorts encoded? One hypothesis stays close to Müller's insight, and is often referred to as *specificity theory*. This proposal suggests that different sensory qualities (sweet versus sour, red versus green) are signaled by different neurons, just as the different sense modalities (vision versus pressure) are signaled by different nerves. In this conception, the nervous system acts as if these quality-specific neurons were somehow "labeled" with their quality, so that the nervous system registers the presence of "red" whenever there is an incoming signal in the "red neurons," registers the presence of "hot" whenever there is a signal coming from the "hot neurons," and so on.

The doctrine of specific nerve energies **Stimulation of the optic nerve (whether the stimulation comes from light or some other source) causes the sense of seeing; this is why boxers (whose nerves are stimulated by blows to the head!) sometimes "see stars."**

This proposal turns out to be correct for some cases—for example, the sensation of pain, for which there do seem to be neurons that specifically convey this sensory message. More commonly, though, the data demand a different explanation, usually called *pattern theory*. According to this view, what matters for sensory quality is not which neurons are firing, because virtually all the neurons for a sense modality respond to virtually all inputs. Instead, what identifies the input is the pattern of activation: which neurons are firing more and which less at any given moment.

In the sense of taste, for example, certain neurons in the tongue fire whenever one is tasting "sweet," but they also fire when one is tasting "sour." Obviously, therefore, these neurons do not signal one of these tastes or the other. The neurons do fire more strongly in response to sweet inputs than to sour ones, but, even so, activity in these neurons is ambiguous: If the neurons are firing weakly, is that because the input was sour or because it was sweet and highly diluted? The only way to know is by comparing activity in these neurons to activity in other neurons—including neurons that have the opposite pattern of sensitivities. Thus, the sensory quality is not conveyed by one type of neuron or the other, but is instead identified by the broader pattern of how several different types of neurons are responding.

In short, then, there is no single answer to the question of how sensory coding is achieved. The difference among senses (e.g., taste versus sight, hearing versus smell) is certainly signaled by "labeled lines," so activity in the optic nerve causes the sensation of seeing, activity in the auditory nerve causes the sensation of hearing, and so on. Some qualitative differences within each modality may also be signaled by "labeled lines," but, for most sensory qualities, the nervous system uses a pattern code.

HEARING

Of all the human senses, there is no question that we rely most on hearing and vision. These are the sense modalities that we typically use to communicate with each other and to navigate in the world. We are also more discriminating in these modalities. We can of course smell a wide range of scents, taste a broad array of flavors, and feel the roughness of tree bark or the softness of silk, but these achievements pale alongside of the immense variety of sounds and sights that we can detect, recognize, and appreciate. And, as it turns out, the centrality of hearing and vision is also evident in the brain's organization: These two modalities get appreciably more cortical coverage than any of the other senses. Let us therefore examine how these two modalities function, beginning with our sense of hearing.

THE STIMULUS: SOUND

What is the stimulus for hearing? Outside in the world some physical object is moving—perhaps an animal scurrying through the underbrush or a set of vocal cords vibrating. This movement agitates the air particles that surround the moving object, causing these particles to jostle other particles, which in turn jostle still other particles. The actual movement of these particles is slight (about one-billionth of a centimeter) and short-lived (the particles return to their original position in a few thousandths of a second), but the motion is enough to create a momentary pressure moving outward from the moving object, similar to the ripples set in motion by a stone thrown into a pond.

If the movement continues for even a short time, it will create a series of pressure variations in the air, and when these *sound waves* hit our ears, they initiate a set of further changes that ultimately trigger the auditory receptors. The receptors in turn trigger neural responses, which eventually reach the brain and lead to the experience of hearing.

Sound waves vary in many ways, but, in the simplest case, they take the form shown in Figure 4.4. This is, for example, the pattern that would result if a tuning fork were vibrating back and forth, pushing on the air molecules adjacent to it each time the vibration moved the fork in one direction, and then pulling back on the same air molecules a moment later when the vibration moved the fork in the other direction. That is why the pressure rises and falls as time goes by, in correspondence to the pushes and pulls the tuning fork is creating. (A vibrating guitar string, or a vibrating clarinet reed, would have roughly the same effect, although these instruments would produce a more complex pattern than the one shown in the figure; other movements—like the sound of a voice—would produce still more complex patterns.)

The pattern shown in Figure 4.4, produced by a physical vibration, corresponds exactly to the plot of the trigonometric sine function, so this wave can be accurately

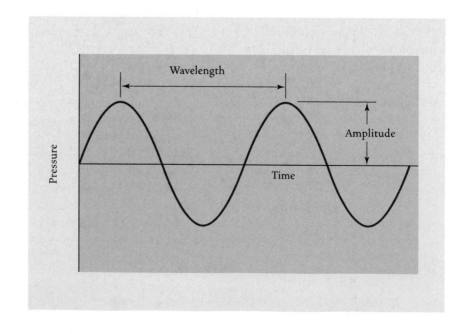

4.4   The stimulus for hearing   A vibrating object creates a series of pressure pulses in the molecules surrounding it; these pulses then spread outward like ripples in a pond into which a stone has been thrown. To describe this pattern, it is useful to measure the air pressure at a single point in space. The pressure of a sound wave waxes and wanes, as shown here. The extent of the pressure determines the height of the wave; the timing between points of maximum pressure determines the wavelength.

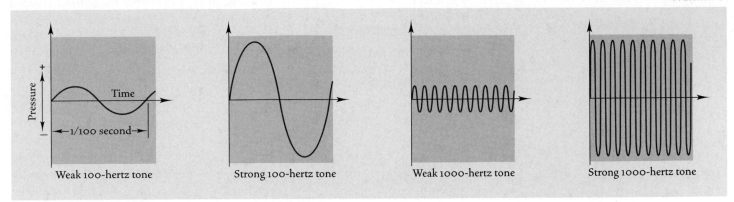

Weak 100-hertz tone	Strong 100-hertz tone	Weak 1000-hertz tone	Strong 1000-hertz tone

4.5 Simple wave forms vary in frequency and amplitude *These curves show the sine waves for a weak and a strong 100-hertz tone (relatively low in pitch) and a weak and a strong 1000 hertz tone (comparatively high in pitch).*

labeled a *sine wave*. To describe the wave more precisely, we need to specify two things. First is the *amplitude*, the amount of pressure exerted by each air particle on the next. As the figure shows, this pressure is constantly changing as the air molecules vibrate toward each other, then away, then toward again; thus, the amplitude we actually measure is the *maximum* pressure achieved, at the crest of the sound wave. Second, we need to specify how widely spaced these pressure crests are. We could do this in terms of *wavelength*, a measurement of how many seconds elapse between one crest and the next. In measuring sounds, however, it is usually more convenient to take the inverse of wavelength; so, instead of measuring seconds-per-crest, we measure crests-per-second, which is the *frequency* of the wave. Thus, our measure is literally a count of how many times in each second the wave reaches its maximum amplitude (Figure 4.5).

Amplitude and frequency are physical dimensions of the sound wave itself, but they correspond reasonably well to the psychological dimensions of loudness and pitch. Roughly speaking, a sound will be heard as louder as its amplitude increases. As it turns out, the range of amplitudes to which humans can respond is enormous, so investigators find it useful to measure these intensities with a logarithmic scale, which compresses the range into a more convenient form. Thus, sound intensities are measured in *decibels* (Table 4.3), and psychologically, perceived loudness doubles each time the intensity of a sound increases by 10 decibels (Stevens, 1955).

TABLE 4.3 INTENSITY LEVELS OF VARIOUS COMMON SOUNDS

SOUND	INTENSITY LEVEL (DECIBELS)
Manned spacecraft launching (from 150 feet)	180
Loudest rock band on record	160
Pain threshold (approximate)	140
Loud thunder; average rock band	120
Shouting	100
Noisy automobile	80
Normal conversation	60
Quiet office	40
Whisper	20
Rustling of leaves	10
Threshold of hearing	0

The frequency of a sound wave is measured in cycles per second, or *hertz* (named after the nineteenth-century German physicist Heinrich Hertz); as frequency increases, the subjective pitch of the sound goes up. Middle C on a piano has a frequency of 256 hertz; the C an octave higher has a frequency of 512 hertz. (In general, a doubling of frequency produces the experienced pitch difference of one octave.) The frequencies associated with other musical tones are shown in Table 4.4. Young adults can hear tones as low as 20 hertz and as high as 20000 hertz, with maximal sensitivity to a middle region in between. As people get older, their sensitivity to sound declines, especially at the higher frequencies. For this reason, there is sometimes little point in a 30- or 40-year-old buying expensive stereo equipment, since what makes the equipment expensive is often its exquisite ability to reproduce high frequencies accurately. In many cases, the middle-aged stereo buyer will be deaf to these frequencies and so probably will not be able to tell the difference between the expensive stereo and a cheaper one!

COMPLEX WAVES

So far, we have been talking only about sine waves, but we rarely encounter sine waves in our day-to-day experience. Instead, the sound waves we usually experience are far more complex; Figure 4.6A, for example, shows the moment-by-moment changes in air pressure produced by a few seconds of music; Figure 4.6B shows the moment-by-moment pressure changes produced by a bit of ordinary speech.

The French mathematician Joseph Fourier (1768–1830) was able to show that these complex waves are actually just the sum of much simpler components—in particular, the sum of a series of sine waves. In essence, then, we can think of sine waves as the "ingredients" from which more complicated sounds are produced. The "recipe" for creating the more complex sound must identify which ingredients are to be used (i.e., which frequencies) and how much of each ingredient is needed (i.e., how much amplitude for each of the frequencies is mixed into the whole). But, with that done, we can use the recipe to create any sound we choose from sine-wave ingredients.

Electronic devices (e.g., keyboards, synthesizers) mix together sine waves to create a variety of complex waves—and so, by adjusting the recipe, they can produce the sound of a flute or an electric guitar, the tolling of a church bell or the hum of a dial tone. The ear performs the opposite operation: It starts with the complex wave and carries out an analysis that allows the auditory system to detect the simpler components within the whole. However, this ability has limits. If the sound is made up of a large enough number of elements, it is perceived as noise, which we can no longer analyze.

TABLE 4.4   SOUND FREQUENCIES OF SOME MUSICAL TONES

SOUND	FREQUENCY (HERTZ)
Top note of grand piano	4244
Top note of piccolo	3951
Top range of soprano voice	1152
Top range of alto voice	640
Middle C	256
Bottom range of baritone voice	96
Bottom range of bass voice	80
Bottom range of contra bassoon	29
Bottom range of grand piano	27
Bottom note of organ*	16

*Can be felt but not heard.

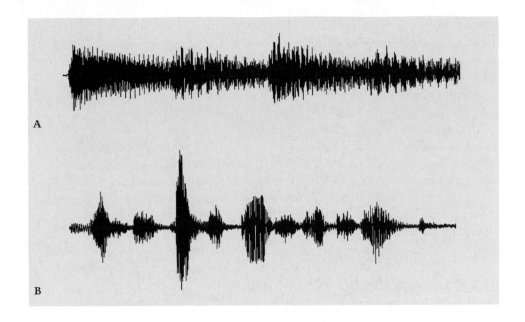

A

B

4.6 *Complex sounds* *(A) Shows the opening few chords of Margie Adam's piano solo, Whimsy Salad. (B) Shows the sound pattern produced when someone utters the words, "This is what speech looks like." Both patterns, complex as they are, can be understood as a composite of simple sine waves and in hearing these sounds, the ear manages to analyze the complex whole and to discover what the ingredient sine waves actually were.*

FROM SOUND WAVES TO HEARING

So far, our discussion has described only the physics of sound waves—the stimulus for hearing. What does our ear, and then our brain, do with this stimulus to produce the sensation of hearing?

GATHERING THE SOUND WAVES

Mammals have their receptors for hearing deep within the ear, in a snail-shaped structure called the *cochlea*. To reach the cochlea, sounds must travel a complicated path. The *outer ear* itself collects the sound waves from the air and directs them toward the *eardrum*, a taut membrane at the end of the *auditory canal*. The sound waves cause the eardrum to vibrate, and these vibrations are then transmitted to the *oval window*, the membrane that separates the *middle ear* from the *inner ear*. This transmission is accomplished by a trio of tiny bones known collectively as the *auditory ossicles*. The vibrations of the eardrum move the first ossicle, which then moves the second, which in turn moves the third, which completes the chain by imparting the vibration pattern to the oval window to which it is attached. The movements of the oval window then give rise to waves in the fluid that fills the cochlea, causing (at last) a response by the receptors (Figure 4.7).

Why do we have this roundabout method of sound transmission? The answer lies in the fact that all of these various components work together to create an entirely

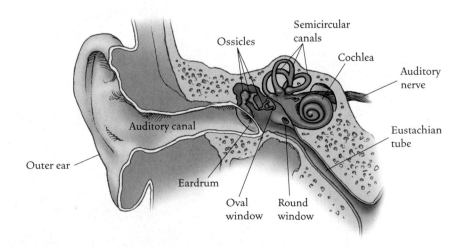

4.7 *The human ear* *Air enters through the outer ear and stimulates the eardrum, which sets the ossicles in the middle ear in motion. These in turn transmit their vibration to the membrane of the oval window, which causes movement of the fluid in the cochlea of the inner ear.*

mechanical—but very high-fidelity—amplifier. The need for amplification derives from the fact that the sound waves reach us through the air, and the proximal stimulus for hearing is made up of minute changes in the air pressure. The inner ear, in contrast, is (like most body parts) filled with fluid—cochlear fluid, to be exact. Therefore, in order for us to hear, the changes in air pressure must cause changes in fluid pressure, and this is a problem, because fluid is harder to set in motion than air is.

To solve this problem, the pressure waves have to be amplified on their way toward the receptors, and this is accomplished by various features of the ear's organization. For example, the outer ear itself is shaped in a fashion that serves as a "sound scoop," funneling the pressure waves toward the auditory canal. Within the middle ear, the ossicles work as levers, using leverage to increase the sound pressure. Finally, the eardrum is about 20 times larger than the portion of the oval window that is moved by the ossicles. As a result, the fairly weak force provided by sound waves acting on the entire eardrum is transformed into a much stronger pressure concentrated on the (smaller) oval window.

TRANSDUCTION IN THE COCHLEA

Throughout most of its length, the cochlea is divided into an upper and lower section by several structures, including the *basilar membrane*. The actual auditory receptors are called *hair cells*, and these cells—some 15,000 of them in each ear—are lodged between the basilar membrane and other membranes above it (Figure 4.8).

Motion of the oval window produces pressure changes in the cochlear fluid that, in turn, lead to vibrations of the basilar membrane. As the basilar membrane vibrates, its deformations bend the hair cells, and it is this physical deformation that triggers the neural response. In general, sound waves arriving at the ear cause the entire basilar membrane to vibrate, but the vibration is not uniform. Some regions of the membrane actually move more than others, and where the motion is greatest depends on the frequency of the incoming sound. For higher frequencies, the region of greatest movement is at the end of the basilar membrane closer to the oval window; for lower frequencies, the region of greatest movement is closer to the cochlear tip.

More than a century ago, these points led Hermann von Helmholtz (1821–1894) to propose the *place theory* of pitch perception. This theory asserts that the nervous system is able to identify a sound's pitch simply by keeping track of where the movement is greatest along the length of the basilar membrane. More specifically, stimulation of hair cells at one end of the membrane leads to the experience of a high tone, while stimulation of hair cells at the other end leads to the sensation of a low tone.

Hermann von Helmholtz (1821–1894)

4.8   Detailed structure of the middle ear and the cochlea   *(A) Movement of the fluid within the cochlea deforms the basilar membrane and stimulates the hair cells that serve as the auditory receptors. (B) Cross section of the cochlea showing the basilar membrane and the hair cell receptors.*

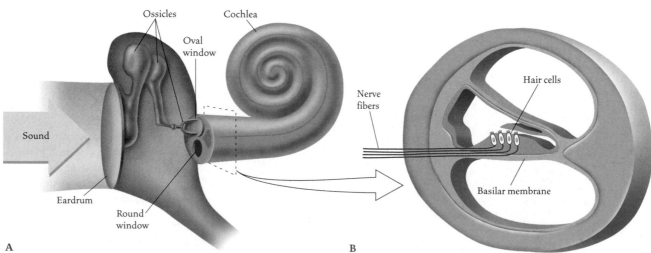

Confirmation for these claims, however, did not come until a half-century later, in a series of classic studies by Georg von Békésy (1899–1972), whose work on auditory function won him a Nobel prize in 1961. Working with preserved specimens of both human and animal cochleas, Békésy was able to remove part of the cochlear wall so that he could observe the basilar membrane through a microscope while the oval window was being vibrated by an electrically powered piston. He found that this stimulation led to a wavelike motion of the basilar membrane (Figure 4.9). As he varied the frequency of the vibrating stimulus, the pattern of the membrane's motion changed, and, in particular, the point of greatest movement shifted in an orderly fashion, just as Helmholtz had proposed (Békésy, 1957).

However, the place theory of pitch faces a major difficulty. As the frequency of the stimulus gets lower and lower, the pattern of movement that it produces on the basilar membrane gets broader and broader. At frequencies below 50 hertz, the movement produced by a sound stimulus deforms the entire membrane just about equally (although, see Hudspeth, 1989; Khanna & Leonard, 1982). Therefore, if we were using the pattern of the basilar's movement as our cue to a sound's frequency, we would be unable to discern these low frequencies. But that is not the case; humans, in fact, can discriminate frequencies as low as 20 hertz. Apparently, then, the nervous system has some means for sensing pitch in addition to basilar location.

This other means for sensing pitch is likely to be tied to the firing frequency of the auditory nerve, a hypothesis referred to as *frequency theory*. For lower frequencies, the frequency of a stimulus seems to be directly translated into the appropriate number of neural impulses per second. This information is then relayed to higher neural centers that interpret this information as pitch.

Consistent with these claims, current evidence indicates that higher frequencies are coded by the place of excitation on the basilar membrane, and lower frequencies by the frequency of the neural impulses. In a middle range of frequencies, between 1000 and 5000 hertz, both mechanisms are operative, and in this range the discrimination of pitches is particularly accurate (Goldstein, 1989; Green, 1976).

FURTHER PROCESSING OF AUDITORY INFORMATION

Neurons carry the auditory signals from the cochlea to the midbrain, and, from there, to the geniculate nucleus in the thalamus, an important subcortical structure in the forebrain (see Chapter 3). Other neurons then carry the signal to the primary projection areas for hearing, in the cortex of the temporal lobe. These and subsequent neurons have much work to do: The auditory signal must be analyzed for its *timbre*—the sound quality that distinguishes a clarinet from an oboe, or one person's voice from another's. The signal must also be tracked across time, in order to evaluate the patterns of pitch change that define a melody, or distinguish an assertion ("I can have it")

4.9   The deformation of the basilar membrane by sound   (A) In this diagram, the membrane is schematically presented as a simple, rectangular sheet. In actuality, of course, it is much thinner and coiled in a spiral shape. **(B)** The relation between sound frequency and the location of the peak of the basilar membrane's deformation. The peak of the deformation is located at varying distances from the stapes (the third ossicle, which sets the membrane in motion by pushing at the oval window). As the figure shows, the higher the frequency of the sound, the closer to the stapes this peak will be.

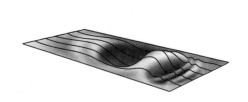

A

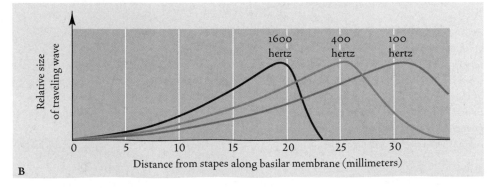

B

from a question ("I can have it??"). The nervous system must also do the analysis that allows us to identify the sounds we hear—so that we know we heard our cell phone and not someone else's, or so that we can recognize the words someone is speaking to us. (For more on the recognition of speech, see Chapter 9.) Finally, the nervous system draws one other type of information from the sound signal: With reasonable accuracy, we can tell where a sound is coming from—whether from the left or the right, for example. This *localization* is made possible by several cues, including a close comparison of the left ear's signal and the right ear's, and also by tracking how the arrival at the two ears changes when we turn our head slightly to the left or right.

Let us continue our focus, though, on the detection of a sound's *pitch*. It turns out that each neuron along the auditory pathway responds to a wide range of pitches, but, even so, each has a "preferred" pitch—a frequency of sound to which that neuron fires more vigorously than it fires to any other frequency. As we mentioned earlier, this makes the activity of any individual neuron impossible to interpret: If, for example, the neuron is firing at a moderate rate, this might mean the neuron is responding to a soft presentation of its preferred pitch, or it might mean the neuron is responding to a louder version of a less-preferred pitch.

To resolve this ambiguity, the nervous system must integrate information from a great many neurons; in other words, the detection of pitch relies on what we earlier called a "pattern code." This integration is facilitated by the fact that, on the cortex, neurons with similar preferred pitches tend to be located close to each other. This pattern is refered to as a **tonotopic map**—a map organized with regard to tone. For example, Figure 4.10 shows the results of a careful mapping of the auditory cortex of the cat, with an obvious ordering of preferred frequencies as we move across the surface of this brain area.

VISION

Important as hearing is, there is one sense still more important, and that is vision. This is reflected, as we mentioned earlier, in the enormous cortical area devoted to vision; it is also evident in the fact that we trust vision more than we trust our other senses. This trust is detectable in some of our common expressions, such as "seeing is believing." It can also be demonstrated more formally in experiments showing that when the senses

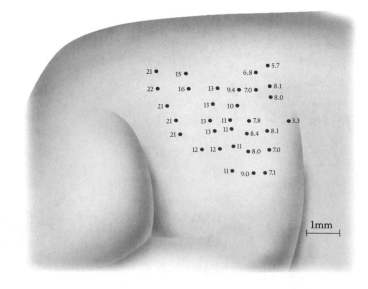

4.10 Tonotopic map *Cells close to each other on the auditory cortex respond to similar auditory frequencies. In this figure, the numbers represent the frequency (in KHz) for which cells at that position are most responsive. Cells positioned on the right are responsive to lower frequencies; as we move to the left, we find cells responsive to higher and higher frequencies.*

provide discrepant information (through some experimenter's trick), we rely on what we see rather than what we hear or feel.

In describing vision, we will focus on three broad issues. First, what are the structures for gathering the stimulus, and how do they work? Second, what is the nature of the transduction process through which the physical energy of the stimulus is converted into a neural signal? Third, what is the nature of the coding processes through which we are able to discriminate the millions of shapes, colors, and patterns of movement that make up our visual world?

THE STIMULUS: LIGHT

Light is produced by many objects in our surroundings—the sun, candles, lamps, and so on—and this light then reflects off of most other objects. It is usually this reflected light—reflected from this book page, for example, or from a friend's face—that launches the processes of vision.

Whether emitted or reflected, though, the stimulus energy we call "light" travels in a wave form that is analogous to the pressure waves that are the stimulus for hearing. To describe these waves, therefore, we need two measurements, just as we did with sound. First, light waves can vary in amplitude, which (just like with sound) is measured as the maximum displacement of the wave away from its baseline; a light wave's amplitude is the major determinant of perceived brightness. Second, light waves can also vary in frequency—how many times per second the wave reaches its maximum amplitude. As it turns out, though, these frequencies are extremely high (because light travels so swiftly), and it is therefore more convenient to describe light waves using the inverse of frequency—*wavelength*, the distance between the crests of two successive waves. Wavelengths are measured in nanometers (millionths of a millimeter) and are the major determinant of perceived color.

The wavelengths to which our visual system is sensitive are only a tiny part of the broader electromagnetic spectrum (Figure 4.11). Light with a wavelength longer than 750 nanometers is invisible to us, although we do feel these longer infrared waves as heat. Likewise, light with a wavelength shorter than 360 nanometers is also invisible to us, although many other organisms—bees, for example—can perceive these ultraviolet wavelengths. Therefore, the light we see consists only of the wavelengths between these two boundaries; this is the *visible spectrum*, with wavelengths close to 400 nanometers usually perceived as violet, wavelengths close to 700 nanometers perceived as red, and the range in between perceived as the rest of the colors in the rainbow.

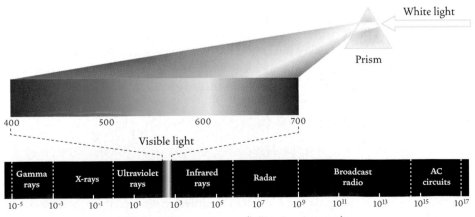

4.11 *The visible spectrum* **The light that we can see is just a tiny portion of the broader electromagnetic spectrum.**

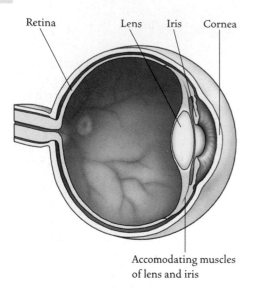

Retina   Lens   Iris   Cornea

Accomodating muscles
of lens and iris

*4.12   The human eye   Light enters the eye
through the cornea, and the cornea and lens
refract the light rays to produce a sharply
focused image on the retina. The iris can open
or close to control the amount of light that
reaches the retina.*

GATHERING THE STIMULUS: THE EYE

Eyes come in many forms. Some invertebrates have simple eyespots sensitive merely to light or dark, while others have complex multicellular organs with crystalline lenses. In vertebrates, the actual detection of light is done by cells called *photoreceptors*, located on the *retina*, a layer of tissue lining the back of the eyeball. Before the light reaches the retina, however, several mechanisms are needed to control the amount of light reaching the photoreceptors and, above all, to ensure a clear and sharply focused *retinal image*.

In the mammalian eye, the *cornea* and the *lens* focus the incoming light, just as a camera lens would (Figure 4.12). The cornea is fixed in its shape, but it begins the process of bending the light rays so that they will end up properly focused. The fine-tuning is then done by the lens, whose shape can be adjusted by a band of muscle that surrounds the lens just like a belt going around your waist. When the muscle tightens, the lens bulges outward, creating the proper shape for focusing images cast by nearby objects; when the muscle relaxes, the lens returns to a flatter shape, allowing the proper focus for objects farther away.

In addition, the eyeball contains another structure that governs the amount of entering light. This is the *iris*, a smooth, circular muscle that surrounds the pupillary opening and contracts or dilates under reflex control as the amount of illumination changes.

THE VISUAL RECEPTORS

Once light reaches the retina, we leave the domain of optics and enter the domain of neurophysiology, because it is at the retina that the physical stimulus energy is transduced into a neural impulse. The retina contains two kinds of receptor cells, the *rods* and the *cones*; the names of these cells reflect their different shapes. The cones are plentiful in the *fovea*, a small, roughly circular region at the center of the retina, but then become less and less prevalent as one moves away from the fovea into the retina's periphery. The opposite is true of the rods; they are completely absent from the fovea but frequent in the periphery. In all, there are some 120 million rods and about 6 million cones in the normal human eye.

The rods and cones do not report to the brain directly. Instead, their message is relayed by several other layers of cells within the retina (Figure 4.13). The receptors stimulate the *bipolar cells*, and these in turn excite the *ganglion cells*. The ganglion cells collect information from all over the retina, and then the axons of these cells converge to form a bundle of fibers that we call the *optic nerve*. Leaving the eyeball, the optic nerve carries information, first, to an important way station in the thalamus, called the *lateral geniculate nucleus*, and then to the cortex. (Note that this path resembles the pathway for auditory signals—which go from the ear to a different section of the geniculate nucleus, and then to the cortex.)

This anatomical arrangement requires that there be a space on the back of each eyeball that serves as the "exit" for the axons of the ganglion cells on their way to the thalamus. This space is entirely filled by these axons, so there is no room left over for rods or cones. As a result, this region literally has no photoreceptors, and so is completely insensitive to light. Appropriately enough, it is called the *blind spot* (Figure 4.14).

THE DUPLEX THEORY OF VISION

The rods and cones differ in structure, number, and placement on the retina; they also differ in function. Roughly a hundred years ago, this distinction led to the *duplex theory of vision*, a theory that has been fully confirmed by more recent research. At its heart, this theory proposes that rods and cones handle different aspects of the visual task. The rods are the receptors for night vision; they operate at low light intensities and lead to

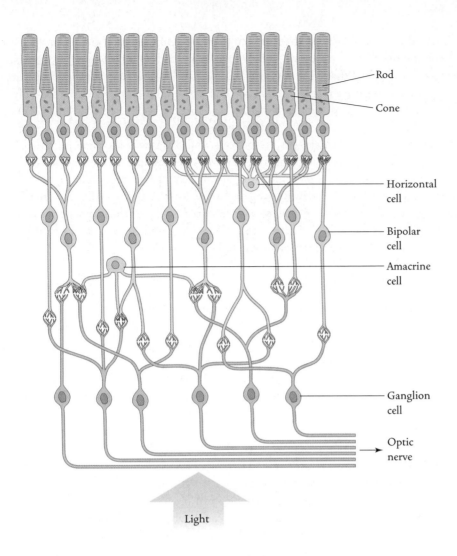

Rod

Cone

Horizontal
cell

Bipolar
cell

Amacrine
cell

Ganglion
cell

Optic
nerve

Light

4.13 The retina *There are three main retinal layers: the rods and cones, which are the photoreceptors; the bipolar cells; and the ganglion cells, whose axons make up the optic nerve. There are also two other kinds of cells, horizontal cells and amacrine cells, that allow for lateral (sideways) interaction. As shown in the diagram, the retina contains an anatomical oddity. As it is constructed, the photoreceptors are at the very back, the bipolar cells are in between, and the ganglion cells are at the top. As a result, light has to pass through the other layers (they are not opaque so this is possible) to reach the rods and cones, whose stimulation starts the visual process.*

achromatic (colorless) sensations. The cones serve day vision; they respond at much higher levels of illumination and are responsible for sensations of color.

The value of this duplex arrangement becomes clear when we consider the enormous range of light intensities encountered by organisms like ourselves that transact their business during both day and night. In humans, the ratio in energy level between the dimmest stimulus we can detect and the brightest we can tolerate is roughly 1:100,000,000,000. Natural selection has allowed for this incredible range by a biological division of labor, with two separate receptor systems responsible for dim-light and bright-light vision.

The enormous sensitivity of the rods, however, comes at a price: The same traits that make the rods sensitive to low levels of light also make them less able to discriminate

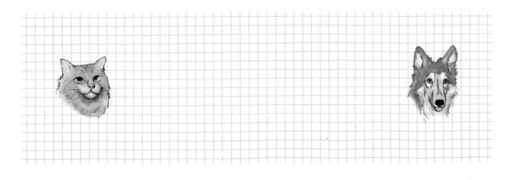

4.14 The blind spot *Close your right eye and stare at the picture of the dog. can you see the cat without moving your eye? Move the book either closer to you or farther. You should be able to find a position (roughly at 7 inches from your face) in which the cat's picture vanishes when you are looking at the dog. That is because, at that distance, the cat's picture is positioned on the retina such that it falls onto the blind spot. Note, though, that the grid pattern seems continuous. With this sort of regular pattern, your visual system is able to "fill in" the gap created by the blind spot.*

fine detail. As a result, *acuity*, the ability to perceive detail, is much greater in the cones. This is the major reason why we point our eyes toward a target whenever we wish to perceive it in detail. What we are actually doing is positioning our eyes so that the image of the target falls onto the fovea, and, as we said earlier, this is the region of the retina in which the cones are most closely packed, and so it is the region with the greatest acuity.

We should note, though, that the differences between rods and cones also create situations in which one wants to rely on the rods, and this is why it's sometimes helpful to look at something "out of the corner of one's eye." For example, sailors and astronomers have known for years that when looking at a barely visible star, it's best not to look directly at the star's location. By looking slightly away from the star, they ensure that the star's image will fall outside of the fovea and onto a region of the retina dense with the more light-sensitive rods. This strategy sacrifices the ability to discern detail but, by relying on the rods, maximizes sensitivity to faint stimuli.

VISUAL PIGMENTS

The rods and cones can be distinguished anatomically (by their shapes) and functionally (by what they do). They can also be distinguished chemically. Inside each photoreceptor is a *photopigment*, a chemical that is sensitive to light, and it is the pigment that allows the transduction of light energy into a neural signal. When light enters the receptor, the light energy changes the chemical form of the photopigment, setting off a chain of events that leads, ultimately, to an electrical signal. In this fashion, the light energy is translated into the language of the nervous system. The pigment itself is then reconstituted by other mechanisms so that it will be ready to react when the next opportunity arises.

Rods and cones contain different photopigments. The pigment inside the rods is *rhodopsin*. There are three different cone pigments, with each cone containing one of the three types. The three cone pigments do not break down as readily as rhodopsin does in response to light; this is part of the reason why the rhodopsin-containing rods are able to function at lower light levels. In addition, the fact that there are three different cone pigments is crucial to the cones' ability to discriminate colors, a topic to which we will turn shortly.

THE IMPORTANCE OF CHANGE: ADAPTATION

The photoreceptors—and the visual system in general—are not just responsive to light, firing more with a bright input and less with a dim one. The photoreceptors are also extremely sensitive to *differences*, so they fire more strongly in response to changes in the incoming stimulation and less strongly in response to an unchanging input. This point can easily be demonstrated in the laboratory, but it can also be shown informally. Stare at the dot in the center of Figure 4.15, trying not to move your eyes at all. After 15 or 20 seconds, the gray haze surrounding the dot will probably appear to shrink and may disappear altogether. (The moment you move your eyes, the haze is restored.)

What is happening in this case? The gray haze is initially a novel stimulus, so it elicits a strong response from the visual system. After a moment or two, this novelty is gone, and, with no change in the input, the response is correspondingly diminished. It is important for this demonstration, though, that the haze has an indistinct edge. While looking at the figure, your eyes will tremble just a bit, so the image of the haze will shift slightly from one retinal position to another. But, because the edge of the haze is blurred, these shifts will produce very little change in the retinal stimulation—hence the haze slowly vanishes from view.

What does the organism gain by this sort of sensory adaptation? Stimuli that have been around for a while have already been inspected; any information they offer has

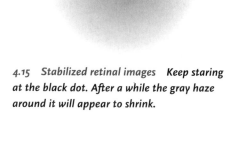

4.15 Stabilized retinal images   Keep staring at the black dot. After a while the gray haze around it will appear to shrink.

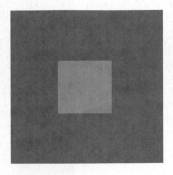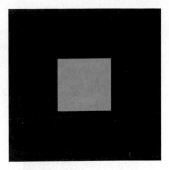

4.16 *Brightness contrast*   *Four (objectively) identical gray squares on different backgrounds. The lighter the background, the darker the gray squares appear.*

already been detected and analyzed. It is sensible, therefore, to give these already-checked inputs less sensory weight. What is important is change, especially sudden change, because this may well signify food to a predator and death to its potential prey. Adaptation is the sensory system's way of ensuring these priorities, by pushing old news off the neurophysiological front page.

INTERACTION IN SPACE: CONTRAST

The visual system is equally sensitive to differences of another sort—the differences between the stimulation in one part of the visual field and the stimulation elsewhere in the field. For example, it has long been known that the identical gray will look much brighter on a black background than it will on a white background—an effect called **brightness contrast** (Figure 4.16). The strength of this effect depends on how great the brightness difference is, and also on the distance between the two contrasting regions—the smaller that distance, the greater the contrast (Figure 4.17).

ACCENTUATING EDGES

Contrast effects give rise to a number of visual illusions and have been used by some artists to create striking effects (Figure 4.18). But these effects also have a practical consequence: They make it easier for us to identify the objects we encounter. This point grows out of the fact that the objects we see are usually viewed against backgrounds that are not at the same brightness level as the objects; hence a change in brightness—from darker to lighter or vice versa—typically marks a visual boundary, a point at which one object stops and some other begins. And, of course, these boundaries are immensely important for the visual system, because they define the object's *shape*, and shape, in turn, is the information we generally use to identify an object.

Perhaps it is not surprising, then, that the visual system does not just detect brightness boundaries, it actually *amplifies* them, allowing us to see the edges between objects more clearly. This exaggeration of brightness differences was noted early on by the physicist

4.17   *The effect of distance between contrasting regions   The white lines in the grid are physically homogenous, but they do not appear to be—each of the "intersections" seems to contain a gray spot. The uneven appearance of the white strips is caused by contrast. Each strip is surrounded by a black square, which contrasts with it and makes it look brighter. But this is not the case at the intersections, which only touch upon the black squares at their corners. As a result, there is little contrast in the middle of the intersections. This accounts for the gray spots seen there.*

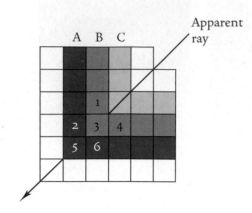

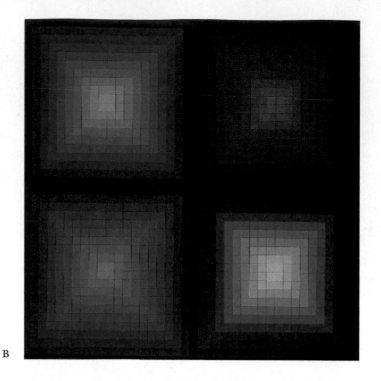

B

4.18   Contrast   (A) *The figure focuses on one of the corners of the painting in (B) to show how the luminous rays are created. Consider squares 1, 3, and 4. Squares 1 and 4 each have an entire side next to the brighter frame C above them. As a result of brightness contrast, they look darker than square 3, which suffers little contrast, for it touches on the brighter frame only at its corner. For the same reason, squares 2 and 6 seem darker than square 5. Since this happens for all the squares at the corners, the observer sees four radiating luminous diagonals. The painting in (B) is* Arcturus *by Victor Vasarely, 1966.*

Ernst Mach (1838–1916) and is illustrated in Figure 4.19A. Each individual strip of gray in this figure is uniform in its brightness. That is, the figure shows a homogenous dark strip, then a uniform slightly lighter strip, then another uniform slightly lighter strip, and so on. This pattern is summarized by Figure 4.19B, in which the actual light intensities for each strip have been plotted against stimulus position.

But the appearance of Figure 4.19A is different from what one might expect based on the pattern shown in Figure 4.19B. At the border between each strip and the neighboring one, there seems to be a band. On the dark side of each juncture, an even darker band is seen; on the bright side of the juncture, a brighter band is visible. This pattern is summarized in Figure 4.19C, which shows *perceived* brightnesses (as opposed to the physical brightnesses, shown in Figure 4.19B).

These illusory bands, called **Mach bands**, are produced by contrast effects similar to the ones we have already described. Specifically, when a light region borders a dark

A

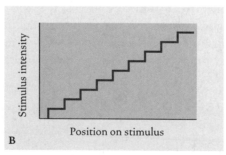

B

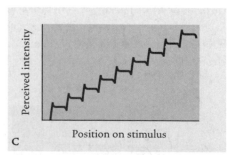

C

4.19   Mach bands   (A) *The series of gray strips is arranged in ascending brightness, from left to right. Physically, each strip is of uniform light intensity, as shown graphically in (B), which plots position against physical light intensity. But the strips do not appear to be uniform. For each strip, contrast makes the left edge (adjacent to its darker neighbor) look brighter than the rest, while the right edge (adjacent to its lighter neighbor) looks darker. The result is an accentuation of the contours that separate one strip from the next. The resulting appearance—the way the figure is perceived—is described graphically in (C).*

region, contrast makes the light region look even lighter; when a dark region borders a light region, contrast makes the dark region look darker still. In both directions, contrast accentuates the difference between the two adjacent regions and in this way highlights the edge where the two regions meet.

LATERAL INHIBITION AND BRIGHTNESS CONTRAST

Edge enhancement is obviously useful for the visual system, making it easier for us to locate the edges that define an object's shape. But what is the physiological mechanism that produces this enhancement?

At many levels in the visual system, activity in one region tends to inhibit responding in the adjacent regions. This tendency is called *lateral inhibition*—it is, in essence, inhibition exerted sideways. This effect is well documented and can be confirmed, for example, by recordings from single cells in the visual system. These recordings clearly show that neighboring regions in the retina tend to inhibit each other. (Similar effects can also be observed at higher levels in the visual system.)

The idea, then, is that the stimulation of a photoreceptor actually has two separate effects. First, the receptor, now excited, transmits its excitation to other cells that will relay this signal to the brain. But, second, a receptor, once excited, also stimulates neurons that extend sideways along the retina. These lateral cells make contact with neighboring cells and inhibit their activation.

To see why this inhibition is important, consider two cells, each receiving stimulation from a brightly lit area (Figure 4.20). One cell (Cell B in the figure) is receiving its stimulation from the middle of the lit area. It is strongly stimulated, but so are its neighbors, so all of the cells in this area are inhibiting each other. As a result, the activity level of Cell B is increased by the stimulation, but it is decreased by the lateral inhibition it is receiving. This combination leads to only a moderate level of activity overall in this cell.

In contrast, another cell (Cell C in the figure) is receiving its stimulation from the edge of the lit area. It is strongly stimulated, and so are its neighbors *on one side*. Therefore, this cell will receive inhibition from one side but not from the other, so it will be less inhibited than Cell B (which is, as we said, receiving inhibition from all sides). So, in short, Cells B and C initially receive the same input, but C is less inhibited than B, so it will end up firing more strongly than B.

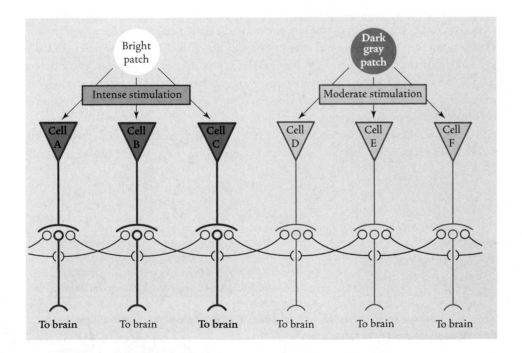

4.20 *Lateral inhibition* **Cells B and C receive the same input. Cell B, however, is inhibited by its neighbors on both sides; Cell C is only inhibited by neighbors on one side. As a result, Cell C will send a stronger signal to the brain, emphasizing the "edge" in the stimulus. Likewise, Cells D and E receive the same input, but Cell D receives more inhibition. This will lead to a weaker signal to the brain, again emphasizing the edge of the dark gray patch.**

As a consequence of all of this, cells detecting the edge of a surface (such as Cell C) will end up producing a stronger response than cells detecting the middle of the surface (such as Cell B). This will, in effect, lead to an exaggerated response along the surface's edges, making these edges easier to detect.

The reverse happens for cells being stimulated by a less-bright patch. Cells D and E both receive the same (weak) input. Cell E is surrounded by cells that are only mildly activated, so it receives only gentle inhibition from its neighbors. Cell D, in contrast, has at least one very excited neighbor (Cell C), so it receives a large dose of inhibition. As a result, Cells D and E both receive the same input, but Cell D (because of the inhibition it receives) ends up firing less strongly than Cell E. Again, this leads to an exaggeration of the edge, with the weakest signal coming from the cell at the edge of the dark patch.

This interaction among cells provides a straightforward account of how the visual system enhances the brightness boundaries it encounters—and, with that, why Mach bands appear as they do. In addition, these mechanisms also illustrate another important point. At the very beginning of this chapter, we asked whether the sensory mechanisms were best thought of as passive recorders of the stimulus input, or whether these mechanisms somehow organize and interpret that input. Our answer to these questions is not yet fully in view, but we are getting some powerful indications of what the answer must be: Thanks to lateral inhibition, the visual system seems to be refining the stimulus information from the very start, emphasizing some aspects of the input (the edges) and understating other aspects (areas that are being uniformly stimulated). Lateral inhibition arises from mechanisms just a synapse or two into the visual system, but, even at this early level, the nervous system is "cleaning up" the input and surely doing far more than merely receiving and recording the incoming stimulus.

COLOR

It is clear, then, that interaction among sensory elements can shape the sensory input and can, in particular, highlight elements such as boundaries and moments of change that are of particular interest to the organism. This pattern of interaction is also evident when we consider a different aspect of vision, namely, the perception of color.

A person with normal color vision can distinguish over 7 million different color shades. These many colors can be classified, though, in terms of just three dimensions. First, *hue* is the attribute that distinguishes blue from green from red, and it is the attribute that is shared by, say, a bright orange, a middle orange, and a dark orange. This term corresponds closely to the way we use the word *color* in everyday life. Hue varies with wavelength (Figure 4.21), so that a wavelength of 465 nanometers is perceived as *unique blue*, a blue that is judged to have no trace of red or green in it; a wavelength of about 500 nanometers is perceived as *unique green* (green with no blue or yellow); a wavelength of 570 nanometers is perceived as *unique yellow* (yellow with no green or red).

Second, *brightness* is the dimension of color that differentiates black (low brightness) from white (high brightness), with various shades of gray in between. Black,

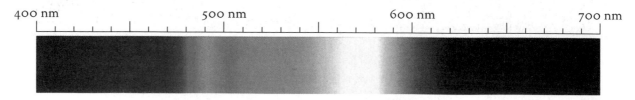

4.21   The visible spectrum and the four unique hues   *The visible spectrum consists of light waves from about 360 to 700 nanometers.*

white, and all of the grays are the *achromatic colors*; these have no hue. But brightness is also a property of the *chromatic colors* (purple, red, yellow, and so forth). Thus, ultramarine blue is darker (i.e., has a lower brightness) than sky blue, just as charcoal gray is darker than pearl gray (Figure 4.22).

Third, *saturation* is the "purity" of a color, the extent to which it is chromatic rather than achromatic. The more gray (or black or white) that is mixed with a color, the less saturation it has. Consider the various blue patches in Figure 4.23. All have the same hue (blue), and all have the same brightness. The patches differ only in one respect: the proportion of blue as opposed to that of gray. The more gray there is, the less saturated the color. When the color is entirely gray, saturation is zero.

THE PHYSIOLOGICAL BASIS OF COLOR VISION

What is the neural basis of color vision? The answer turns out to have two parts—one involving the mechanisms on the retina itself, and the other concerned with how the nervous system handles the information received from the retina.

COLOR RECEPTORS

Normal human color vision depends on three different kinds of cones; thus, our color vision is *trichromatic*. Each of the cone types responds to a broad range of wavelengths in the visible spectrum, but their patterns of sensitivity differ in that one cone type is most sensitive to wavelengths in the short-wave region of the spectrum, the second to wavelengths in the middle-range, and the third to wavelengths in the long range (Bowmaker & Dartnall, 1980; MacNichol, 1986; Figure 4.24).

Since all three cone types respond to a wide range of wavelengths, we cannot discriminate among wavelengths simply by noting which cones are responding—generally all are. Once again, therefore, it appears that the nervous system relies on pattern coding, with the input's wavelength being specified by the relative rates of responding by all three cone types. For an input of 480 nanometers, for example, the "short-preferring" and "middle-preferring" cones will respond equally, and their response will be approximately double the response of the "long-preferring" cones. It is this pattern of response that specifies this particular wavelength; other patterns indicate other wavelengths.

THE YOUNG-HELMHOLTZ THEORY

These observations are broadly consistent with a view proposed in the late nineteenth century by Thomas Young and Hermann von Helmholtz. According to the *Young-Helmholtz theory*, stimulation by red light strongly activates the long-preferring receptors and only weakly activates the other two receptors; the researchers argued that it is this combination that gives rise to the experience of red. Similarly, stimulation by blue light strongly activates the short-preferring receptors and only weakly activates the other two;

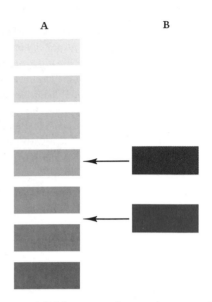

4.22 Brightness *Colors can be arranged according to their brightness. (A) This dimension is most readily recognized when we look at a series of grays, which are totally hueless and vary in brightness only. (B) But chromatic colors can also be classified according to their brightness. The arrows indicate the brightness of the blue and dark green shown here in relation to the series of grays.*

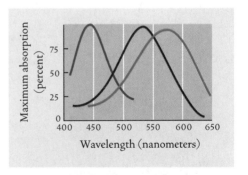

4.24 *Sensitivity curves of three different cones in the primate retina* *The retinas of humans and monkeys contain three different kinds of cones, each with its own photopigment that differs in its sensitivity to different regions of the spectrum. One absorbs more of the shorter wavelengths (and is thus more sensitive to light in this spectral region), a second more of the middle wavelengths, a third more of the longer ones. The resulting sensitivity curves are shown here.*

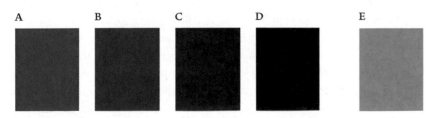

4.23 *Saturation* *The four patches A–D are identical in both hue and brightness. They differ only in saturation, which is greatest for A and decreases from A to D. The gray patch, E, on the far right matches all the other patches in brightness; it was mixed with the blue patch, A, in varying proportions to produce patches B, C, and D.*

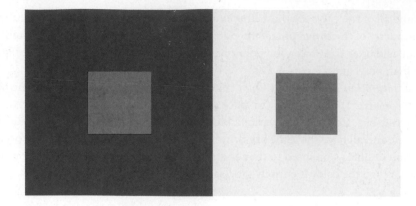

4.25 *Color contrast* *The gray patches on the blue and yellow backgrounds are physically identical. But they do not look that way. To begin with, there is a difference in perceived brightness: The patch on the blue looks brighter than the one on the yellow, a result of brightness contrast. There is also a difference in perceived hue, for the patch on the blue looks somewhat yellowish, while that on the yellow looks bluish. This is color contrast, a demonstration that hues tend to induce their antagonists in neighboring areas.*

this is what gives rise to the perception of blue. Finally, stimulation by green light strongly excites the medium-preferring receptors and only weakly activates the other receptors; this gives rise to the perception of green. All other colors are then derived from mixtures of these three primary experiences.

Young first proposed this view in 1802; Helmholtz's refinements of the theory arrived in 1866. Today, these claims fit reasonably well with what we know about receptor function and the spectral sensitivities of the three cone types. The claims also fit well with some basic facts about color mixing. Artists have known for years that three pigments can be mixed together to produce a wide variety of colors; better still, three different-colored lights can be mixed (in appropriate proportions) to produce any of the colors we can perceive. (This is how a television or computer monitor produces all of the colors that appear on the screen.) These observations strongly suggest a system of color vision based on three basic elements, just as the Young-Helmholtz theory suggests.

COMPLEMENTARY HUES

The trichromatic analysis of color vision allows us to explain why the three so-called primary colors—red, green, and blue—seem to have special status. From the point of view of the theory, this status derives from the fact that each of these colors is the optimal stimulus for one of the receptor types. This fits with the observation that each of these colors looks relatively pure to most observers, in contrast to a color such as purple, say, which looks like a mixture of primary colors (in this case, red and blue).

But other facts seem not to fit with the Young-Helmholtz view. For example, most observers agree that yellow looks like a primary color—that is, it does not look like a mixture. But this fact has no explanation within trichromatic theory, since, in this theory, yellow is not considered a primary color (Bornstein, 1973).

Trichromatic theory also has nothing to say about why colors seem to come in pairs. This pairing is evident, for example, in the phenomenon known as *simultaneous color contrast*, the chromatic counterpart of brightness contrast. *Color contrast* refers to the fact that any chromatic region in the visual field tends to induce a *complementary color* in adjoining areas. For example, a gray patch will tend to look bluish if surrounded by yellow, yellowish if surrounded by blue, and so on (Figure 4.25).

A similar phenomenon involves temporal relationships, rather than spatial ones. Concretely, suppose that we stare at a green patch for a while and then look at a white wall. We will see a *negative afterimage* of the patch, in this case, a reddish spot (Figure 4.26). In the same fashion, staring at a red patch will produce a green afterimage; staring at something blue will produce a yellow afterimage; staring at yellow will produce a blue afterimage. In all cases, the afterimage has the complementary hue of the original stimulus; this again emphasizes the apparent "pairing" of colors, a pairing that trichromatic analyses leave completely unexplained.

The importance of complementary colors is also evident in color mixing, because, if a color is mixed with its complement in appropriate proportions, the result is

4.26 *Negative afterimage* **Stare at the center of the figure for a minute or two, and then look at a white piece of paper. Blink once or twice; the negative afterimage will appear within a few seconds, showing the flower in its correct colors.**

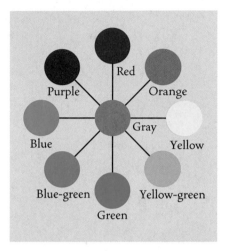

4.27 *Different ways to mix color* *In subtractive color mixing, each constituent (here: each filter) subtracts certain wavelengths from the total light. In additive mixing, each constituent contributes wavelengths. Thus in (A), subtractive mixing on three primaries yields black; in (B), additive mixing yields white.*

achromatic. Thus, if we mix blue and yellow lights, we produce a hue-less white; the same is true if we mix red and green lights. So here, too, it appears that colors are "paired," such that each color has an "opposite" that cancels it—a relationship that, again, has no explanation in trichromatic theory.

As an aside, we should note that these facts about color mixing apply only to the mixing of *lights*—so-called *additive mixing* (Figure 4.27). Things work differently if we mix paints or other pigments. In that case (which involves *subtractive mixing*), a mix of blue and yellow usually produces green, not white. The reason for this lies in the physics: If a blue light is shining on, say, a white surface, then the surface will reflect the wavelengths contained within that blue light. If a yellow light is also shining on the surface, then these, too, will be reflected. Hence the full set of wavelengths reflected will be those from the blue light *plus* those from the yellow—hence "additive" mixture. In contrast, when light shines on a *pigment*, only a certain band of wavelengths is reflected; the rest are absorbed. (In essence, then, the absorbed wavelengths are "subtracted" from the light.) Thus, blue paint reflects the wavelengths between 420 and 520 nanometers, and it absorbs wavelengths outside this range. Yellow paint reflects wavelengths above 480 nanometers, and it absorbs everything else. If the two paints are mixed together, then the only wavelengths reflected by the combination are those not absorbed ("subtracted") from the input) by *either* ingredient. This turns out to be just the wavelengths above 480 nanometers and below 520; this band of wavelengths is seen as green.

Complementary hues *Any hue will yield gray if additively mixed (in the correct proportion) with a hue on the opposite side of the color circle. Such hue pairs are complementaries. Some complementary hues are shown here linked by a line across the circle's center.*

THE OPPONENT-PROCESS THEORY

How should we think about the fact that colors seem to come in pairs? And why is it that yellow seems just as "pure" to observers as red, green, or blue—as though there were four primary colors, and not the three specified by trichromatic theory? The answers lie in the **opponent-process theory**, first suggested by Ewald Hering but then developed by Leo Hurvich and Dorothea Jameson. This theory begins with the

Leo Hurvich and Dorothea Jameson

undeniable fact that we have three cone types, but it argues that the output from these cones is then processed by another layer of neural mechanisms that recode the signal in terms of pairs of colors—red versus green, blue versus yellow, and black versus white. These pairs are said to involve an "opponent process" because the two members of each pair are antagonists: Excitation of one automatically inhibits the other (Figure 4.28). In essence, each of the pairs can be thought of as a balance, and if one arm of the balance goes down, the other necessarily goes up (Hurvich & Jameson, 1957).

According to this conception, the psychological experience of hue depends on two of the opponent-process pairs—red-green and blue-yellow. If, for example, the input tips the red-green balance toward red and the blue-yellow balance toward blue, the perceived hue will be violet. If the input contains neither red nor green (so the red-green pair stays in balance), and the blue-yellow system tips toward blue, we perceive a pure blue. If both hue systems are in balance, there will be no hue at all, and the resulting color will be seen as achromatic (i.e., without hue).

This conception obviously explains the apparent pairing of colors, because the pairing is built into the opponent processes themselves. It also explains why there appear to be four primary colors, even though, without question, our retina has only three cone types. But, in addition, evidence has directly confirmed the claims of the opponent-process theory, by documenting that many of the neurons in the visual system behave exactly as the theory proposes. For example, certain cells increase their firing rate if the retina is stimulated by green light, but they decrease their rate if the retina is stimulated by red light. Other cells show the opposite pattern (increase for red, decrease for green). Still other cells show the appropriate responses for blue and yellow light (Figure 4.29; De Valois, 1965). All of this is exactly what one might expect if these cells embody the mechanisms proposed by the opponent-process theory.

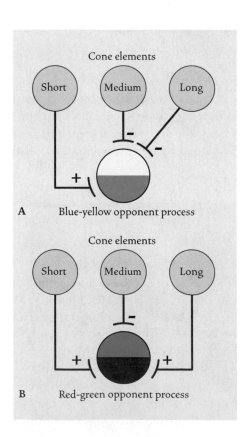

4.28   From receptors to opponent-process pairs   *A simplified presentation of a neural system in which the three receptor elements feed into two color opponent-process pairs. (A) The blue-yellow system is excited by the short-wave receptors and inhibited by the medium- and the long-wave receptors. If excitation outweighs inhibition, the opponent-process signals blue; if inhibition outweighs excitation, it signals yellow; if excitation and inhibition are equal, there is no signal at all and we see gray. (B) The red-green system. This is excited by both the short-wave and the long-wave receptor elements, and is inhibited by the medium-wave elements. If excitation outweighs inhibition, the system signals red; if inhibition outweighs excitation, it signals green; if excitation and inhibition are equal, there is no signal and we see gray.*

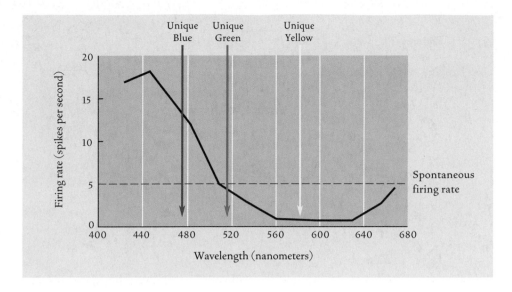

4.29 **Opponent-process cells in the visual system of a monkey** *The figure shows the average firing rate of blue-yellow cells to light of different wavelengths. These cells are excited by shorter wavelengths and inhibited by longer wavelengths, analogous to the cells in the human system that signal the sensation "blue."*

COLOR BLINDNESS

A number of people do not respond to color as the rest of us do, and some form of color-vision defect is found in 8% of all males (but only .03% of females). The deficiencies in color vision come in various forms. Some involve a missing visual pigment, others a defective opponent process, and many involve malfunction at both levels (Hurvich, 1981). Most common is a confusion of reds with greens; least common is total color blindness in which no hues can be distinguished at all. Interestingly, though, most of these problems are rarely noticed in everyday life, and color-blind people can spend many years without even realizing that they are color blind. They call stop signs "red," just as anyone else does, and grass "green." And, presumably, they spend much of their lives believing that others perceive colors just as they do. Their color blindness can be confirmed, therefore, only with special tests, similar to the one shown in Figure 4.30.

How does the world look to someone who is color blind? This question long seemed unanswerable, since most color-blind individuals have no way to compare their experience to that of an individual with normal color vision, and so no way to describe the difference. However, one unusual person (one of the rare women with a color-vision defect) was red-green color blind in one eye but had normal color vision in the other. She was able to describe what she saw with the defective eye by using the color language she had learned to use with her other eye. As she described it, with the color-blind eye she saw only grays, blues, and yellows. Red and green hues were altogether absent, as if one of the opponent-process pairs were missing (Graham & Hsia, 1954).

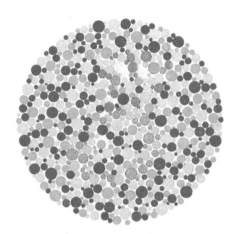

4.30 **Testing for color blindness** *A plate used to test for color blindness. To pick out the number in the plate, an observer has to be able to discriminate certain hues. Those with normal color vision can do it and will see the number 3. Those with red-green color blindness cannot do it.*

PERCEIVING SHAPES

The perception of color is important to us—whether in enhancing our appreciation of art or, more practically, in allowing us to distinguish a ripe fruit from one that is green. But other aspects of vision are far more important. After all, a color-blind individual can live a perfectly normal life. But not so an individual who is unable to discriminate among shapes or forms, or an individual unable to recognize a square or a circle. These individuals (known as *visual agnosics*) are dramatically impaired in their functioning. We need to ask, therefore, how the visual system achieves the perception of shape. This achievement turns out to be quite complex; so while we begin addressing it in this chapter, the issues discussed here will carry over into Chapter 5.

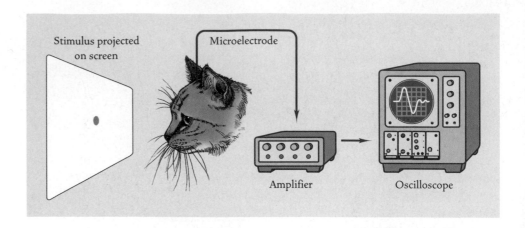

4.31 *Recording from the visual system of a cat* **The experimental setup for recording neural responses from the visual system of a cat. An anesthetized cat has one eye propped open so that visual stimulation can be directed to particular regions of the retina. A microelectrode picks up neural impulses from a single cell in the optic system, amplifies them, and displays them on an oscilloscope.**

FEATURE DETECTORS

Recordings from individual nerve cells have allowed electrophysiologists to examine how particular cells in the visual system respond to certain stimuli. In these studies, a microelectrode is placed into the optic nerve or, in some studies, the brain of an anesthetized animal. (Special care is taken to protect the well-being of the animal, both for ethical reasons and to allow the investigators to assess how neurons function in an intact, healthy organism.) The eye of the animal is then stimulated by visual inputs of varying brightness and different shapes, at different locations (Figure 4.31). In this fashion, the investigator can learn which stimuli evoke a response from that cell.

Results from these studies show that each cell in the visual system has a preferred target, so it responds maximally only to an input that has just the right shape and size, and, for many cells, is at just the right position. These attributes define the *receptive field* for that cell—a region of a particular shape and size within the visual field to which that cell responds (Figure 4.32). In essence, then, the cell seems to act as a "detector," responding strongly just when its preferred target is in view, and the receptive field for that cell identifies what sort of detector it is—a curve detector, an angle detector, and so on.

In many animals, there are just a few types of these specialized detectors, and they are located in the retina itself. Frogs, for example, only need a few bits of information about the world: "Is there a large shape moving toward me? If so, it might be a predator, so a leap to safety would probably be useful." "Is there a small, dark shape, moving around? If so, it might be a fly, so it would be a good idea to flick my tongue in that direction." In light of these limited information needs, it is not surprising that frogs have just a few detector types, on the retina, so that the input is analyzed right from the start into the few components of crucial interest to the frog (Lettvin, Maturan, McCulloch, & Pitts, 1959).

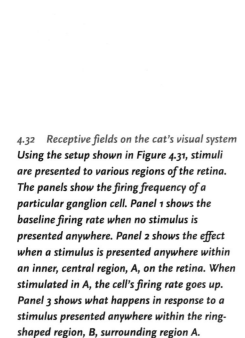

4.32 *Receptive fields on the cat's visual system* **Using the setup shown in Figure 4.31, stimuli are presented to various regions of the retina. The panels show the firing frequency of a particular ganglion cell. Panel 1 shows the baseline firing rate when no stimulus is presented anywhere. Panel 2 shows the effect when a stimulus is presented anywhere within an inner, central region, A, on the retina. When stimulated in A, the cell's firing rate goes up. Panel 3 shows what happens in response to a stimulus presented anywhere within the ring-shaped region, B, surrounding region A. Stimulation in B causes the cell's firing rate to go down. Panel 4 shows what happens when a stimulus is presented outside of either A or B, the regions that together comprise the cell's receptive field. Now there is no significant change from the cell's normal baseline.**

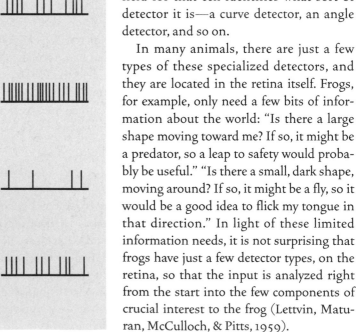

Most higher animals—including the mammals—need more detailed information about the world around them; hence the visual system performs a more complex analysis, supported by a greater variety of detector types located in the cortex, rather than the retina. Most of what we know about this visual analysis derives from the work of David Hubel and Torsten Wiesel, who won a Nobel prize for their research. They found that cells in the cat's visual cortex were each "tuned" for a particular type of stimulus. Some cells, for example, fired maximally only when the visual input was a line or an edge of a specific orientation at a specific retinal position. One such cell might respond to a vertical line at one position in the visual field, while another cell might respond to a line tilted to 45 degrees at the same position; still another cell might respond to a vertical line at some other position. In this fashion, the visual field is blanketed by receptive fields, so that lines of any orientation at any position will be detected by the appropriately tuned cell (Hubel & Wiesel, 1959, 1968).

Other cells in the cat's visual cortex are a bit more sophisticated: They, too, fire only in response to a line or edge of a particular orientation, but they are largely indifferent to the line's specific location within the visual field (Figure 4.33). Cells like these serve as *feature detectors*, detecting certain elements within the visual pattern. Other cells, deeper within the visual system, presumably then assemble these now-detected elements in order to detect larger configurations and more complex patterns.

Consistent with this suggestion, Hubel and Wiesel were able to locate other cells that responded only to more complicated inputs. For example, some cells responded maximally in response to corners, or angles of certain sizes. Other cells responded to movement patterns—firing maximally only when movement of the appropriate velocity, in the appropriate direction, was in view.

DETECTORS FOR COMPLEX FORMS

How does the visual system organize all these features into the countless and highly complex objects that we can recognize? After all, the world we perceive is not filled with swarms of unassembled features; instead, we perceive whole objects—things that look coherent and that are often familiar and meaningful for us. If the visual system begins by detecting simple features—horizontal and vertical lines, bits of curve and color—how are these pieces assembled to create the complex forms that surround us?

In some cases, the answer to this question may be straightforward: There are simply more detectors. For some complex shapes, particularly those that have special significance for a species, there are cells within the visual system with the sole job of detecting this or that particular stimulus. For example, certain cells in a monkey's cortex have been shown to respond to pictures of a monkey's face but not at all to nonface stimuli. Other cells seem to respond almost exclusively to pictures of a monkey's hand, whether the hand appears with an open palm or clenched fist, with the fingers pointed up or pointed down (Desimone, Albright, Gross, & Bruce, 1984).

It seems highly unlikely, though, that such built-in mechanisms could account for all the forms that higher animals—especially humans—perceive and recognize. Simple creatures like frogs are able to recognize only a few patterns, making it plausible that they might have specialized detectors for each one. In contrast, humans easily discriminate among a multitude of patterns, and this simple fact speaks powerfully against the idea that we might have specialized detectors for each of them—triangles, squares, apples, apple pies, champagne bottles, cabbages, kings—the list is endless. We know that the perception of these (and other) forms begins with a feature analysis; this is plain in the functioning of the detector cells. But how are these features glued together to create more complex forms? The answer to this question is surprisingly complex and will be one of our main concerns in Chapter 5.

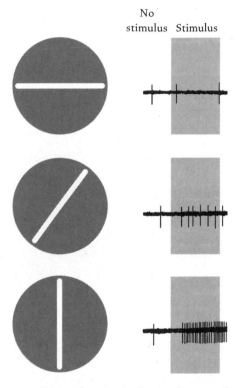

4.33 Feature detectors in the visual system of the cat *The response of a single cortical cell when stimulated by a slit of light in three different orientations. This cell was evidently responsive to the vertical. A horizontal slit led to no response, a tilted slit led to a slight response, while a vertical slit led to a marked increase in firing.*

SOME FINAL THOUGHTS: THE ACTIVE PERCEIVER

We obviously still have more to say about how we come to know the world around us. We have described how sensory systems transduce the proximal stimulus, and how they code the incoming message into the various dimensions of our sensory experience. But we still need to ask how we come to recognize the various objects and events that we encounter every minute of our lives.

Even at this early stage of our discussion, though, we are getting an answer to a question we asked at the very start: In our perception, do we simply open our eyes and receive the information the world provides for us—recording this information faithfully and passively, the way a camera does? Or do we take a more active role, shaping the input and interpreting and organizing it? It should be clear that the evidence favors the latter view: Thanks to mechanisms like lateral inhibition, we do shape the input, accentuating the bits we care about (namely, edges) and de-emphasizing the bits of lesser importance. Likewise, the detectors in our visual systems respond to just those aspects of the input that are likely to be useful. Creatures as simple as frogs need relatively little information from the visual input, so they have a visual system designed to pick out just those few features. As a result, they are essentially blind to any aspects of the input other than those few bits they care about. Our needs are more complicated, but, even so, we have a visual system attuned to an identifiable set of features, so that— inevitably—our subsequent analyses are based on just this featural information. In these and other ways, then, our visual system does shape the visual input from the very start, selecting and emphasizing the aspects of special interest to us.

As we will see in Chapter 5, though, this is just the beginning of the active role we take in our perception of the world. At the earliest levels, our sensory systems are not passive receivers of information, and the level of activity, in shaping and interpreting the input, simply increases as we move more deeply into the processes that make perception possible.

SUMMARY

THE ORIGINS OF KNOWLEDGE

- The study of sensory processes grew out of questions about the origin of human knowledge. John Locke and the other *empiricists* argued that all knowledge comes through stimuli that excite the senses. However, the only way to get information about *distal stimuli* (the objects or events in the world) is through the *proximal stimuli* (the energies that impinge on a sensory surface). How, therefore, do we perceive qualities (e.g., depth, constant size, and shape) not directly given in the proximal stimulus? The empiricists answer by asserting that much of perception is built up through learning by *association*. This view has been challenged by *nativists*, who believe that the sensory input is organized according to a number of *built-in categories*.

PSYCHOPHYSICS

- Research in *psychophysics* seeks to relate the characteristics of the physical stimulus to both the quality and intensity of the sensory experience. One psychophysical measurement is the *difference threshold*—the change in the intensity of a stimulus that is just large enough to be detected, producing a *just-noticeable difference (jnd)*. According to *Weber's law*, the jnd is a constant fraction of the intensity of the comparison stimulus. Building on this principle, *Fechner's law* states that the strength of a sensation grows as the logarithm of stimulus intensity.

- Data in psychophysical procedures are influenced both by a perceiver's sensory *sensitivity* and by her *decision criteria*. These two factors can be assessed separately, though, via a *signal-detection* procedure. An individual's sensitivity to the stimulus is assessed by the proportion of *hits* and *correct negatives* relative to his number of *misses* and *false alarms*. His criterion for responding is measured by the proportions of yes and no responses.

THE FUNCTIONING OF THE SENSES

- *Sensory codes* are the rules by which the nervous system translates the properties of the proximal stimulus into neural impulses. *Psychological intensity* (e.g., loudness or brightness) is usually coded by the rates of firing by the neurons, and also by the sheer number of neurons triggered by the stimulus.
- Other codes are for *sensory quality*. According to the *doctrine of specific nerve energies*, differences in sensory quality (e.g., the difference between seeing and hearing) are not caused by differences in the stimuli themselves but by the different nervous structures that these stimuli excite. In some cases, qualitative differences within a *sensory modality* are best described by specificity theory, which holds that different *sensory qualities* (e.g., red versus green) are signaled by different neurons, just as the different sense modalities are signaled by different nerves. An alternative is *pattern theory*, which holds that certain sensory qualities arise because of different patterns of activation across a whole set of neurons.

HEARING

- *Sound waves* can vary in *amplitude* and *frequency*, and may be simple or complex. These waves set up vibrations in the eardrum that are then transmitted by the *auditory ossicles* to the *oval window*, whose movements create waves in the *cochlea*. Within the cochlea is the *basilar membrane*, which contains the auditory receptors that are stimulated by the membrane's deformation. According to the *place theory*, the experience of pitch is based on the place of the membrane that is most stimulated, each place being especially responsive to a particular frequency and generating a particular pitch sensation. According to the *frequency theory*, the experience of pitch depends on the firing frequency of the auditory nerve. Evidence suggests that both conceptions are correct, with the perception of higher frequencies dependent on the place stimulated on the basilar membrane, and the perception of lower frequencies dependent on firing frequency.

VISION

- Vision is our primary distance sense. Its stimulus is light, which can vary in *intensity* and *wavelength*. Some of the structures of the eye, such as the *lens* and the *iris*, serve to control the amount of light entering the eye and to fashion a proper proximal stimulus, the *retinal image*. Once on the retina, the light stimulus is transduced by the *rods* and *cones*. *Acuity* is greatest in the *fovea*, where the density of the receptors (here, cones) is greatest.
- According to the *duplex theory of vision*, rods and cones differ in function. The rods operate at low light intensities and are insensitive to differences in hue. The cones function at much higher illumination levels and are responsible for sensations of color.
- The various components of the visual system interact constantly, and these interactions actively shape and transform the stimulus input. One kind of interaction—*sensory adaptation*—concerns the relation between the signal a neuron is now receiving and the signal it received a moment ago.
- Interaction also occurs between neighboring regions on the retina. This is shown by *brightness contrast*, which serve to accentuate edges, as in the case of *Mach bands*. The physiological mechanism that underlies this effect is *lateral inhibition*, which provides a clear example of how the visual system refines the stimulus information from the very start, emphasizing some aspects of the input and understating others.
- Visual sensations vary in *color*, and color sensations can be ordered by reference to their *hue*, *brightness*, and *saturation*. Normal human color vision is *trichromatic*, depending on three cone types. However, some facts do not fit with this trichromatic conception, including the fact that colors come in pairs—as shown by the phenomena of *complementary colors*, *simultaneous color contrast*, and *negative afterimages*.
- These latter points are addressed by the *opponent-process theory*. This theory proposes that the output of the cones serves as input for a further layer of mechanisms that recode the signal into three opponent-process pairs: *red-green*, *blue-yellow*, and *black-white*.
- Shape perception depends on specialized *detector cells* that respond to certain characteristics of the stimulus, such as curves and straight edges. The optimal input for each cell—i.e., a stimulus of a certain shape and size at a certain position—defines the cell's *receptive field*. In cats and monkeys, *feature detectors* seem to respond maximally when a line or edge of a specific orientation is in view. Other cells, deeper within the visual system, assemble these elements in order to detect larger configurations and more complex patterns.

CHAPTER

5

PERCEPTION

*I*n the previous chapter, we discussed how the sensory systems detect some of the simpler attributes of sensory experience, such as edges, or red, or high-pitched. The empiricist philosophers thought that these experiences were passively registered by the senses and then glued together, by means of associations, to form more complex perceptions. We have already begun to see, though, that this view is not correct. We have noted that, from the very start, sensory systems actively transform the stimulus input, emphasizing areas of contrast and minimizing areas of uniformity. The level of activity becomes even more striking when we turn to the question of how we apprehend objects and events in the world around us—how we see, not just something bright or something red, but a bright red apple. Let us tackle this issue, turning away from questions of *sensation* (typically understood as the detection of simple stimulus attributes) and turning instead to problems of *perception*—how we organize, integrate, and interpret those sensory elements in order to know the world around us.

One might think that there is nothing simpler than perceiving. You open your eyes and see the world, effortlessly recognizing the objects that are in view. Where, therefore, is the mystery, the complexity, that needs to be explained? But there is complexity here. One problem lies in how we manage to grasp the meaning of the visual input. Having perceived an apple, how do we manage to interpret it as an edible fruit—one that grows on trees, can be used to make pies, and so on? As it turns out, though, these are not the most basic questions for the student of perception. The deeper issue is not why we see a particular kind of object, but rather why we see any object at all. Suppose we show the apple to someone who has never seen this type of fruit before. He will not know what it is or what it is for, but he will certainly see it as some round, red thing of whose tangible existence he has no doubt—in short, he will perceive it as an object.

How do we accomplish this feat? After all, the apple is known to us (at least visually) only through the proximal stimulus it projects onto our retina, and this proximal stimulus is two dimensional and constantly changing. It gets smaller or larger depending on our distance from the apple; it stimulates different regions of the retina each time we move our head or eyes. It reflects much more light to us if we see the apple in bright sunlight than it does if we happen to see it at twilight. How do we get past these continual variations in the proximal stimulus in order to perceive the constant properties of the external object? For that matter, how do we manage to identify the apple's boundaries, treating all of the apple's parts as one unit, separate from those of the banana right beside it? (See p. 167.) How do we compensate for the fact that part of the apple's form is hidden from view by the edge of the fruit bowl? These achievements, simple as they seem, turn out to be impressively complicated, and they are achievements without which perception cannot proceed.

In short, before we can decide whether the object we are looking at is an apple (or, say, a baseball or a human head), we must organize the sensory world into a coherent scene in which there are real objects (such as apples) and real events. Likewise, before we can take a walk down a hallway, we need to perceive the layout of the hallway—which obstacles are nearby and which are far off, whether the people we see are standing still or moving across our path.

The problem of perception **How do we come to perceive the world as it is—to see the flags as smaller than the boat, to see the wall extending continuously behind the people that block some portion of it from view, and so on?**

To accomplish all of this, we have to answer three important questions about whatever it is we see (or hear or feel) in the world outside: Where is it? What is it doing—is it moving or still? And perhaps most important, what is it? Each of these questions is crucial for us, since our very existence demands that we act differently toward a tiger far away rather than one nearby, that we respond appropriately when we see a car streaking toward us, and that we adjust our behavior sensibly when we realize we are standing next to a potential mate rather than a lamppost.

In the next sections, we will consider these three fundamental aspects of perception. Our emphasis initially will be on the sorts of information that we use for these three achievements—the cues that we use for perceiving distance, motion, and form. We will then broaden the focus, considering not just *what* stimulus information people use but also *how* they use this information. All of this will return us squarely to an issue raised in Chapter 4—namely, how active we are in organizing the sensory input we receive. This will in turn demand that we ask, once again: How objective, accurate, and complete is our perception of the world? ●

DISTANCE PERCEPTION: WHERE IS IT?

The retina in each eye is curved, lining the inside surface of the (roughly) spherical eyeball. Even so, the retina is two dimensional: Images on the retina can be closer to the nose or farther from it (i.e., closer to the temples); this corresponds to whether the distal object is more to the left of us or more to the right. Images can also be closer to the forehead or farther from it (i.e., closer to the cheek); this corresponds to whether the distal object is higher in our view or lower. But images on the retina itself cannot be "farther from us" or "closer." Instead, an image of a nearby table falls onto exactly the same surface as the image of the distant horizon, and so, one might think, information about distance is not represented in the proximal stimulus. But this surely must be wrong, because we obviously are able to perceive a three-dimensional world. This capacity is crucial for us—without it, we would be unable to move around in the world. How could we walk if we did not know how far away the various obstacles are? How could we reach for the muffin if we did not know how far it is from us—or whether it is within reach at all? Questions like these have led investigators to a search for *distance cues*, features of the stimulus situation that might indicate how far an object is from the observer, or how far it is from other objects in the world.

BINOCULAR CUES

One important cue for distance comes from the simple fact that our two eyes look out onto the world from slightly different positions; as a result, each eye has a slightly different view. This difference between the two eyes' views is called *binocular disparity*, and it provides important information about distance relationships in the world (Figure 5.1).

Binocular disparity can induce the perception of depth even if no other distance cues are present. For example, the bottom panels of Figure 5.1 show the views that each eye would receive while looking at a pair of nearby objects. If we present each of these views to the appropriate eye (e.g., by drawing the views on two cards and placing one card in front of each eye), we can obtain a striking impression of depth. (The popular child's toy known as the Viewmaster works in the same way, presenting two slightly different pictures to the two eyes; many years ago, the stereopticon viewer used the same principle.)

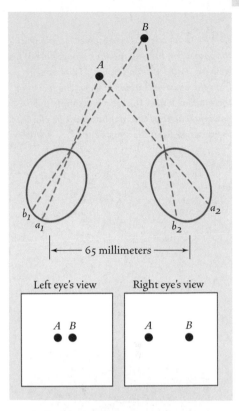

5.1 **Binocular disparity** *Two points, A and B, at different distances from the observer, present somewhat different retinal images. In the left-eye's view, the image cast by A and that cast by B are close together; in the right-eye's view, the images are further apart. This disparity between the views serves as a powerful cue for depth.*

Stereoscope   Invented in 1833, stereoscopes were popular for many years. One picture is presented to the left eye, another to the right, and the disparity between the pictures provides a vivid sense of depth. The View-Master, a popular children's toy, works exactly the same way.

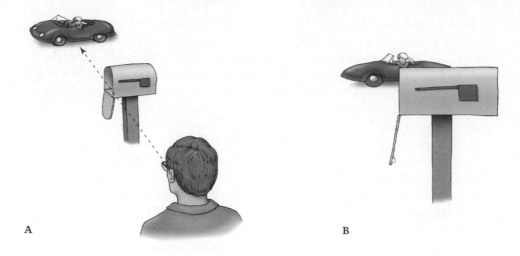

5.2 Pictorial cues *The observer is looking at the sports car, but the mailbox blocks part of his view (A). Panel B shows how this will appear from the observer's point of view. The fact that the mailbox blocks the view is a simple but powerful cue that the mailbox must be closer to the observer than the sports car is.*

A   B

5.3 Interposition with simple displays *Depth cues can also be demonstrated with very simple displays. Because of interposition, the red rectangle in the figure appears to be in front of the blue one.*

MONOCULAR CUES

Binocular disparity is a powerful determinant of perceived depth. But we can also perceive depth with one eye closed, so, clearly, there must be cues for depth that depend only on what each eye sees by itself. These are the ***monocular distance cues***.

Some of the monocular distance cues have been exploited for centuries by artists, in order to create an impression of depth on a flat surface—that is, within a picture, which is why these cues are usually called ***pictorial cues***. In each case, these cues rely on simple principles of physics. For example, imagine a situation in which an observer is trying to admire a sports car, but a mailbox stands between them (Figure 5.2A). In this case, the mailbox will inevitably block the view, for the simple reason that light cannot travel through an opaque object. This is a fact about the physical world, but it also provides a cue that we can use in judging distance, a cue known as ***interposition*** (Figure 5.2B)—the blocking of our view of one object by some other object. In this example, interposition tells the observer that the mailbox is closer than the car; in the case shown in Figure 5.3, it tells us that the red rectangle is closer than the blue.

In the same way, distant objects necessarily produce a smaller retinal image than nearby objects of the same size; this is a fact about optics. But this physical fact again provides us with information we can use; in particular, it provides the basis for the cues of ***linear perspective*** and ***relative size*** (Figures 5.4 and 5.5).

A related sort of pictorial cue is provided by ***texture gradients***. Consider what meets the eye when we look at cobblestones on a street or patterns of sand on a beach. The retinal projection of the sand or the cobblestones shows a pattern of continuous change, with the elements of the texture growing smaller and smaller as they become more distant. This pattern of change by itself can reveal the spatial layout of the relevant surfaces (Figure 5.6); if, in addition, there are discontinuities in these textures, this too can tell us a great deal about how the surfaces are laid out in depth (Figure 5.7; Gibson, 1950, 1966).

THE PERCEPTION OF DEPTH THROUGH MOTION

Whenever we move our heads, the images projected by the objects in our world necessarily move across the retina. For reasons of geometry, the projected images of nearby objects move more than those of distant ones. The *direction* of motion across the retina depends on where we are pointing our eyes. Points closer to us than the target of our gaze appear to be moving in a direction opposite to our own; points farther away appear

5.4   *Linear perspective as a cue for depth*

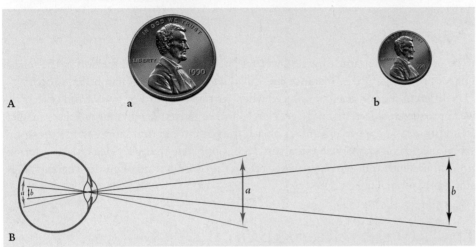

5.5   *Relative size   (A) All other things being equal, the larger of two otherwise identical figures will seem to be closer than the smaller one. This is a consequence of the simple geometry of vision illustrated in (B). Objects a and b are equal in size, but because they are at different distances from the observer, they will project retinal images of different sizes.*

5.6   *Texture gradients as cues for depth Uniformly textured surfaces produce texture gradients that provide information about depth: as the surface recedes, the size of the texture elements decreases, and the density of these elements increases. Such gradients may be produced by sand ripples (A) or stones in a courtyard (B).*

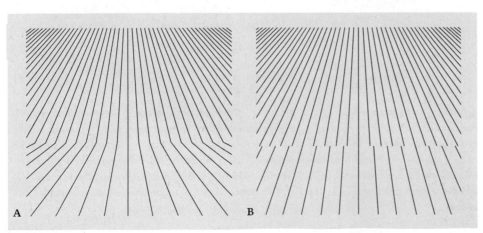

5.7   *The effect of changes in texture gradients Such changes provide important information about spatial arrangements in the world. Examples are (A) an upward tilt at a corner; and (B) a sudden drop.*

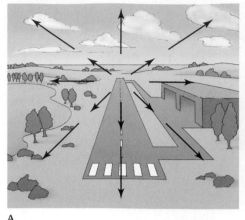 

A   B

5.8 Optic flow (A) The optic flow field as it appears to a pilot landing an airplane. (B) The optic flow field as it appears to a person looking out of the rear window of a railroad car.

to be moving in the same direction we are. This entire pattern of motion in the retinal images provides a further distance cue, called ***motion parallax*** (Helmholtz, 1909).

A different motion cue is produced when we move toward or away from objects. As we approach an object, its image gets larger and larger; as we move away, it gets smaller. In addition, as we move toward an object, the pattern of stimulation across the entire visual field changes, resulting in a pattern of ***optic flow*** that provides crucial information about depth and also plays a large role in the coordination of our movements (Gibson, 1950, 1979; Figure 5.8).

THE ROLE OF REDUNDANCY

The pictorial cues for distance, as already noted, derive from simple facts of geometry and optics. The same is true for the other distance cues. The information we call "binocular disparity," for example, derives in a straightforward fashion from the position of the two eyes and the fact that light travels in a straight path. It is just a fact of our world, therefore, that these cues are available to us as potential indicators of distance.

What is perhaps surprising, however, is that we make use of all these cues (as well as some others we have not described; see Figure 5.9). Our sensitivity to each cue can be

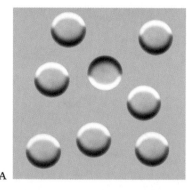 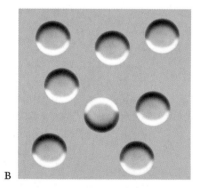

A   B

5.9 Monocular cues to depth: light and shadow   Observers are sensitive to many different depth cues, including depth from shading. (A) Eight circular objects. To most viewers, the one in the middle looks concave, indented, whereas the other seven look as if they are bulging out. (B) The same figure rotated 180 degrees. Now the middle object looks convex, while the other seven seem concave. The reason is the location of the shadows. When the shadow is at the bottom, the object looks convex; when at the top, the object looks concave. This makes sense, since light almost always comes from above.

documented in a straightforward way—by arranging a stimulus situation in which just that single cue is available, and asking whether, in that situation, the person can "read" the information provided by the cue in order to judge how far away something is. In some cases, the experiment requires that the person tell us whether this object is farther or closer than that one, or whether something is bulging forward (toward her) or away (as in Figure 5.9). In other cases, we ask the person for more precise judgments—an estimation, perhaps, of exactly how far away some target is. With any of these procedures, though, the results tell us that people are sensitive to all of the distance cues listed so far, and that people use every one of them as a basis for judging the three-dimensional arrangement of the world around them.

Why did natural selection favor a system influenced by so many cues, especially since the information provided by these cues is often redundant? After all, what we can learn from linear perspective is often the same as what we can learn from motion parallax. Why, then, should we be sensitive to both?

The answer to this question lies in the fact that different distance cues become important in different circumstances. For example, binocular disparity is a powerful cue, but it is informative only for objects relatively close by. (For targets farther than 30 feet away, the two eyes receive virtually the same image.) Likewise, motion parallax tells us a great deal about the spatial layout of our world, but only if objects are moving. Texture gradients are informative only if there is a suitably uniform texture in view. So while these various cues are often redundant, each can provide information in circumstances in which the others cannot. By being sensitive to all, we are able to judge distance in nearly any situation we encounter.

MOTION PERCEPTION: WHAT IS IT DOING?

It is one thing to see someone attractive across a crowded room; it is quite another to see that person smile and walk toward you. Plainly, then, we want to know what an object is and where it is located, but we also want to know what it is doing. Put another way, we want to perceive events as well as objects. And to do this, we must be able to perceive movement.

RETINAL MOTION

One might think that we see things move because they produce an image that moves across the retina. In fact, some cells in the visual cortex do seem responsive to such movements on the retina. These cells are *direction specific*, firing if a stimulus moves across their receptive field from, say, left to right but not if the stimulus moves from right to left. (Other cells, of course, show the reverse pattern.) These cells are therefore well suited to act as *motion detectors* (see, for example, Vaultin & Berkeley, 1977).

APPARENT MOVEMENT

Further evidence makes it clear, however, that retinal motion is only part of the story. Suppose we turn on a light in one location in the visual field, then quickly turn it off, and after an appropriate interval (somewhere between 30 and 200 milliseconds) turn on a second light in a different location. The result is *apparent movement*. The light appears to travel from one point to another, even though there was no motion shown

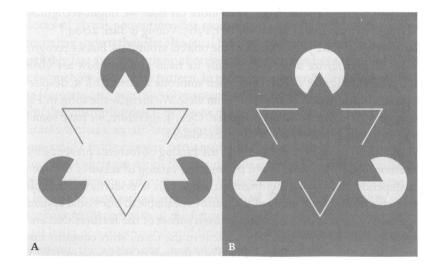

on the features that define the outline of the man's body, telling us that this is, in fact, a picture of a man walking down the street. Likewise, we ignore the outline of the shadow cast by the trees, realizing that the features that make up this outline tell us little about the objects that are in view.

A related point is made by Figure 5.17. Initially, these dark shapes seem to have no meaning, but, after a moment, most people discover the word hidden in the figure. That is, people find a way to reorganize the figure so that the familiar letters come into view. But let us be clear about what this means. At the start, the form seems not to contain the features needed to identify the L, the I, and so on. Once the form is reorganized, though, it does contain these features and the letters are immediately recognized. Apparently, therefore, the analysis of features depends on a prior step in which the form is organized by the viewer, and, with one organization, the key features are absent; with another, they are plainly present. In essence, then, the features are as much "in the eye of the beholder" as they are in the figure itself.

As a different example, you probably have no difficulty reading the word printed in Figure 5.18, although, in truth, most of the features needed for this recognition are absent from the figure. You easily "provide" the missing features though, thanks to the fact that you interpret the black marks in the figure as shadows cast by letters hovering just above the page. Given this interpretation and the extrapolation it requires, you can, with no trouble, "fill in" the missing features, and in this way read a word despite the scant information provided by the stimulus.

As one final example, consider Figure 5.19. Here most people easily perceive two complete triangles, one on the tan background, one on the green. But, again, the features of these triangles are not present on the page, and, specifically, the *sides* of the triangle are not marked in the figure at all. However, the perceiver organizes the overall form in a fashion that fills in the missing sides, and so the triangles, absent from the page, are clearly perceived.

Observations like these were crucial for **Gestalt psychology**, a school of psychology whose adherents believed that *organization* is an essential feature of all mental activity. They insisted that a form is not perceived by somehow taking an inventory of the features or by summing up all the individual components. Instead, they argued that how (or whether) a form is perceived depends on the organization of the entire pattern, a coherent, intact **Gestalt** that is different from the sum of its parts. (The word *Gestalt* is derived from a German word that means "form" or "entire figure.") Thus, in Figures 5.17 and 5.18, the perceiver must take the entire pattern into account, and must organize the pattern appropriately, in order to find anything meaningful. Likewise, the triangles perceived in Figure 5.19 are not indicated by any of the figure's elements. Instead, the

5.17 A hidden figure *Initially, these dark shapes have no meaning, but, after a moment, the hidden figure becomes clearly visible. Notice, therefore, that, at the start, the figure seems not to contain the features needed to identify the various letters. Once the figure is reorganized, however, with the white parts the figure, and not the dark parts, the features are easily detected. Apparently, therefore, the analysis of features depends on a prior step, in which the figure is first organized by the viewer.*

5.18 Missing features *People have no trouble reading this word, despite the fact that most of the features needed for recognition are absent from the stimulus. However, people easily "supply" the missing features, emphasizing once again that the analysis of features depends on a prior step, in which the overall figure is first organized by the viewer.*

5.19 Subjective contours *Subjective contours are a special completion phenomenon in which contours are seen even where none exist. In (A) we see a tan triangle whose vertices lie on top of the three green circles. The three sides of this tan triangle (which looks brighter than the tan background) are clearly visible, even though they don't exist physically. In (B) we see the same effect with green and tan reversed. Here, there is a green triangle (which looks darker than the green background) with subjective green contours.*

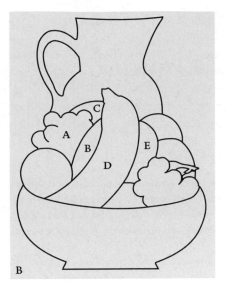

5.20 *Perceptual parsing* (A) *A still life.* (B) *An overlay designating five different segments of the scene shown in (A). To determine what an object is, the perceptual system must first decide what goes with what: Does portion B go with A, with C, D, or E? Or with none of them?*

triangles are perceived because of how the entire pattern is organized and how the pieces seem to fit together. Our sense of the shape, therefore, must derive from the properties of the whole, taken as a coherent unit.

PERCEPTUAL PARSING

What exactly does it mean for a perceiver to find "organization" within a figure? There are actually several parts to this achievement, one of which is *perceptual parsing*. Suppose an observer looks at the still life in Figure 5.20. To make sense of the picture, the perceptual system must somehow group the elements of the scene appropriately. What goes with what? Portion *B* (one half of the apple) must be united with portion *E* (the other half of the apple), even though they are separated by portion *D* (a banana). Portion *B* should not be united with portion *A* (a bunch of grapes), even though they are adjacent and approximately the same color. The bit of the apple hidden from view by the banana must somehow be filled in, so that we perceive an intact apple rather than two apple slices. This whole process is referred to as *parsing*—a process of segregating the scene into its constituent objects—and it is the essential first step in organizing the world that we see.

What cues guides us toward parsing a stimulus pattern one way rather than another? The answer involves both feature information and also information about the larger-scale pattern. For example, we tend to interpret certain features (such as a "T-junction"—Figure 5.21) as indicating that one edge has disappeared behind another; other junctions are interpreted differently. But we are also sensitive to information that involves the entire configuration. For example, we tend to group things together according to a principle of *similarity*, so that, all other things being equal, we group together figures that resemble each other. So in Figure 5.22A, we group blue dots with blue dots, red with red. Because we are also influenced by *proximity*, the closer two figures are to each other, the more they tend to be grouped together perceptually (Figure 5.22B; for more on these principles of perceptual organization, see Palmer, 2002; Wertheimer, 1923).

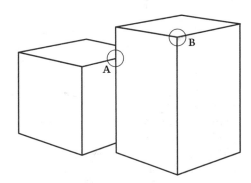

5.21 *Features that guide parsing* We earlier noted that feature analysis depends on a prior step, in which the overall figure is first organized by the viewer. But it turns out that the opposite is also true. How the figure is organized by the viewer depends on the features. For example, a T-intersection (point A) is usually interpreted as one surface dropping from view behind another. A Y-intersection (point B) is usually interpreted as a corner pointing toward the viewer.

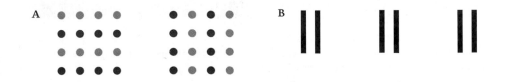

5.22 *Grouping by proximity and similarity* We perceive the dots in (A) as organized into rows on the left and columns on the right, grouping by similarity. We perceive the six lines in (B) as three pairs, grouping the lines by proximity.

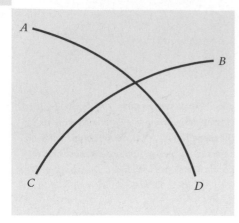

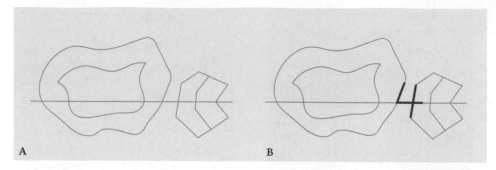

5.24 Good continuation pitted against prior experience   *In (A), virtually all viewers see two complex patterns intersected by a horizontal line. Hardly anyone sees the hidden 4 contained in that figure—and shown in (B)—despite the fact that we have encountered 4s much more often than the two complex patterns, which are probably completely new.*

5.23 Good continuation   *The line segments in the figure will generally be grouped so that the contours continue smoothly. As a result, segment A will be grouped with D and segment C with B, rather than A with B and C with D.*

Our visual system also seems to organize patterns in a fashion that suggests a preference for contours that continue smoothly along their original course (Figure 5.23). This principle of *good continuation* prevails even when pitted against prior experience (Figure 5.24), and it is why camouflage can be an effective means of hiding a creature from view (Figure 5.25). Good continuation may also be relevant to an example we considered earlier (p. 166, Figure 5.19). Some theorists interpret the *subjective contours* visible in this figure as a special case of good continuation. In their view, the contour is seen to continue along its original path, even, if necessary, jumping a gap or two to achieve this continuation (Kellman & Shipley, 1991; Kellman, Garrigan, & Shipley, 2005).

FIGURE AND GROUND

Another crucial part of visual parsing is the separation of the object from its setting, so that the object is seen as a coherent whole, separate from its background. This separation of *figure* and *ground* allows us to recognize (as focal) the familiar shapes of an apple or banana in Figure 5.20A, and it also allows us to ignore the window-shade in the background. But the same process also occurs with figures that have no particular meaning. In Figure 5.26, the white splotch appears as the figure and is typically perceived as closer to the viewer than the blue region (which is seen as the ground). The edge between the blue and white regions is perceived as part of the figure, defining its

5.26 Figure and ground   *The first step in seeing a form is to segregate it from its background. The part seen as figure appears to be more cohesive and sharply delineated. The part seen as ground seems more formless and to extend behind the figure.*

5.25 Camouflage   *The principles of perceptual organization play a key role in explaining why camouflage is effective. Good continuation and similarity help the praying mantis (A) to look like a twig, and the katydid (B) to look like a leaf.*

shape. The same edge does not mark a contour for the blue region but merely marks the point at which this region drops from view (Figure 5.27).

Let us emphasize, though, that this differentiation of figure and ground, like all aspects of parsing, is contributed by the perceiver and is not a property of the stimulus itself. This is most evident when the perceiver discovers that there is more than one way to parse a given stimulus, as there is with Figure 5.18 (in which one figure/ground organization reveals the "hidden" word, but a different organization does not) and also with Figure 5.28, which can be seen either as a white vase or as two blue faces in profile. These *reversible figures* make it clear that the stimulus itself is typically neutral with regard to parsing. What is figure and what is ground is, like many of the form's features, in the eye of the beholder.

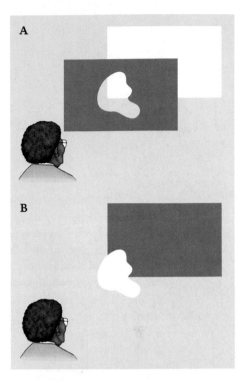

DIFFERENT PERSPECTIVES ON PERCEPTION

How should we think about the data we have discussed so far? We know that the perception of distance involves multiple cues, and this raises a question of how the cues are integrated with, or weighed against, each other. In addition, note that some distance cues rest on assumptions or interpretation: In order to interpret motion parallax, for example, we need to know whether the objects we're looking at are moving or standing still; in order to interpret Figure 5.15, we assume that we're looking at a partially hidden square and not a nearby shape that happens to have a bite taken out of it. How do we arrive at these interpretations?

Likewise, we know that the perception of motion is guided by specialized cells that literally detect motion on the retina, but we also know that this motion must be interpreted, so that we know whether the shift across the retina was caused by a change in our viewing position or by movement in the world. We also know that, when movement is detected, we need to figure out *what* is moving—the moon or the clouds, the dot or the enclosing frame. But what processes make all of this possible?

Similar questions arise for the perception of form. We know that pattern recognition begins with some sort of feature analysis, and we know that the process ends with our being able to recognize shoes and ships, cats and cafés, and a huge number of other familiar objects. In between, we know that the process has to assemble the features into larger wholes, but we also know that the process is impressively sensitive to properties of the entire configuration and uses these overall properties to guide the interpretation of the parts. How should we think about this process? What events get us from the features, at one end of the process, to the recognition of whole objects, at the other end?

In addition, we also need to ask how these elements—distance, motion, and form— are put together, so that we end up with a cohesive view of the world, not just seeing "30 inches away," "still," and "flat," but a pancake at arm's length; not just "far," "moving," and "round," but a baseball flying into left field. How does this integration take place?

These various questions can—and perhaps must be—approached at more than one level. At the most global level—which, for historical reasons, we will call the *classical approach* to perception—we can seek in a general way to describe the broad characteristics of the processes needed for perception. This approach has the advantage of emphasizing the "large-scale picture," so it reveals important traits that apply to many different aspects of perceiving. However, the classical approach tells us relatively little about the step-by-step processes that make perception possible. To describe these processes, we need a second, more finely-grained approach, which we will call the *process-model approach*. This approach provides its own insights and fills in many of the details of how exactly perception proceeds. This approach leaves untouched, however, a separate set of

5.28 *Reversible figure-ground pattern* **The classic example: This figure can be seen as either a pair of silhouetted faces or a white vase.**

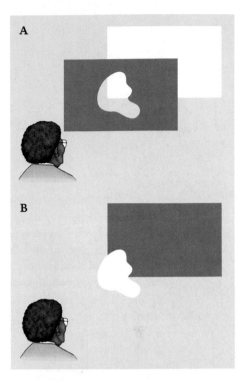

5.27 *Edges belong to the figure* **If we perceive Figure 5.26 as a blue rectangle with a hole in it (A), the edge marks the contour of the hole. The situation is reversed in (B). Now the edge demarcates the white blob, not a break in the blue background. In this sense, the edge belongs to the figure, not the ground.**

issues—namely, how the processes of perception are actually realized within the nervous system. Tackling these issues is central to the ***neuroscience approach*** to perception.

Let us be clear, though, that these three approaches are not in any way competitors with each other, and in fact it is easy to find researchers whose work involves all of these perspectives in combination with each other. Clearly, therefore, none of the approaches should be thought about as the "preferred way" to study perception. Instead, the three approaches merely provide different levels of description of the same achievements, and there is no question that each level has provided valuable insights into how we perceive the world. (For more on the importance of different levels of description in describing perception, see Marr, 1982.)

THE CLASSICAL APPROACH TO PERCEPTION

One approach to perception is relatively global, seeking to characterize the entire set of operations through which we perceive the world. This approach, for example, showcases a point we have several times met—namely, the enormously active role that the perceiver plays in organizing and interpreting the stimulus input. This activity is demanded by the fact that we depend on feature information in a stimulus, but the identity of the features usually depends on how we have organized the stimulus. Likewise, the stimulus information we receive is often ambiguous: Is Figure 5.28 (p. 169) a picture of a vase on a blue background, or a pair of profiles on a white background? Is Figure 5.29A a wire cube aligned with the solid cube shown in Figure 5.29B, or is it aligned with the one shown in Figure 5.29C? These are figures specifically chosen for their ambiguity, and, indeed, either interpretation (vase or profiles, 5.29B or 5.29C) is easily available to most perceivers. But quite ordinary figures can also be ambiguous. For example, does Figure 5.15 (p. 165) show a complete square that is more distant than (and so partly hidden by) the circle? Or does the figure show a square with a "bite" taken out of it, perhaps closer to us than the circle?

Ambiguities of all these sorts are extremely easy to find, but our perception typically resolves the ambiguity so that we easily and quickly perceive the figures as having one organization or another. Apparently, then, our perception routinely goes beyond the information given to us: Figure 5.28 is entirely neutral as to whether it shows a vase or profiles, but our perception adds a layer of interpretation, so that we perceive it as having one organization or another. Likewise, Figure 5.15 is entirely neutral as to whether it shows a complete square, partially hidden behind the circle, or an incomplete square in the same plane as the circle. Again, though, our perception adds a layer of interpretation, and we perceive the form as having a specific, unambiguous, and determinate form.

The perceiver's active contribution is also evident in other ways. Consider Figure 5.30. The second and fifth characters in this pattern are identical, but, influenced by the context, many people do not spot this equivalence and instead fluently read the character as an *H* on the left (and so read the word *THE*) and an *A* on the right (and so *CAT*). This (and other) effects of context draw on the knowledge and expectations that the perceiver brings to a situation, and so again emphasizes the active role of the perceiver.

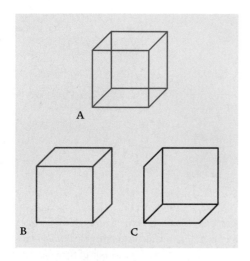

5.29   The Necker cube   The ambiguous Necker cube, shown in (A), can either be perceived as aligned with the cube shown in (B) or the one in (C).

TAE CAT

5.30   The effect of context on letter recognition

PERCEIVING CONSTANCY

The perceiver also has another role to play in interpreting the incoming visual information—namely, the achievement of ***perceptual constancy***. To understand the issue, let us bear in mind that the overall goal of perception is, of course, to provide us with accurate information about the world around us. But there is an important complexity here, since what it means to see the real world is, of course, to see the properties of distal objects—their color, form, size, and location; their movement through space; their permanence or transience. But, as we have noted in other settings, organisms cannot gain experience about the distal stimulus directly. Instead, all information about the external world comes to us only from the proximal stimuli that distal objects project onto our senses. And this creates a problem, because the same distal object can produce many different proximal stimuli. The object's retinal image will get larger or smaller, depending on its distance from us. Its retinal shape will change, depending on its slant relative to our viewing perspective. The amount of light it projects onto our retinas will increase or decrease, depending on the illumination that falls on it.

Somehow, though, we manage to distinguish changes in the proximal stimulus brought about by shifts in our viewing circumstances from changes created by an actual alteration in the world. We manage, in other words, to achieve *perceptual constancy*. Thus, an elephant looks large even at a distance—so, apparently, we achieve *size constancy*, perceiving sizes correctly despite changes in viewing distance. Likewise, a postcard looks rectangular even though its retinal image is a rectangle only when the postcard is viewed head on. Apparently, then, we achieve *shape constancy* (Figure 5.31), perceiving shapes correctly despite changes in our viewing angle. And a crow looks black even in sunlight—an example of *brightness constancy*, in which we perceive brightness accurately despite changes in illumination.

In all of these cases, we transcend the vagaries of the proximal stimulus so that we can react to the world as it truly is. How do we accomplish this feat? We already considered this issue in our discussion of motion. There we noted that each time we move our head or eyes, the pattern of stimulation on the retina changes. But we do not interpret these changes as *motion*; instead, we achieve *position constancy*—perceiving objects as having an unchanging position despite the changes in the proximal stimulus produced by our own movements.

How do we achieve position constancy? As we saw, the answer lies in a process through which we accurately take our own movements into account, and "subtract" the retinal change produced by our own motion from the retinal change that we actually receive. In that way, we compensate quite exactly for changes in the proximal stimulus produced by changes in viewing circumstances.

HIGHER-ORDER INVARIANTS

How do we achieve the other constancies? One explanation was suggested by James J. Gibson (1950, 1966, 1979). He believed that the vital characteristics of an object, including its size, shape, and distance from the observer, are directly signaled by the

James J. Gibson

5.31 Shape constancy When we see a door at various slants from us, it appears rectangular despite the fact that its retinal image is often a trapezoid.

visual stimulus. However, the relevant information is not the size or shape of the retinal image as such; instead, the information that allows constancy is contained in ***higher-order invariants***, unchanging stimulus patterns that involve the relationship between the size (or shape) of the retinal image and other attributes of the stimulus.

The size of the retinal image, for example, necessarily varies as the distal object changes its distance from the observer. But this does not mean that there is no size information in the stimulus that hits the eye. One reason is that objects are usually seen against a background that provides a basis for comparison with the target object. The dog, sitting nearby on the kitchen floor, is half as tall as the chair and hides eight of the kitchen's floor tiles from view. If we take several steps back from the dog, none of these relationships changes, even though the sizes of all the retinal images are reduced (Figure 5.32). Size constancy, therefore, can be achieved by focusing not on the images themselves but on the unchanging relationships, relationships that provide direct, higher-order information about the stable properties of the world.

Evidence suggests that these relationships do contribute to size and shape constancy, so that we are better able to judge size (for example) when comparison objects are in view, or when the target we are judging sits on a surface that has a uniform visual texture (like the floor tiles in our example). But these relationships are not the whole story. Size constancy is found even when the visual scene provides no basis for comparison (if, for example, the object to be judged is the only object that is in view), provided that other cues (such as binocular disparity or motion parallax) signal the distance of the target object. This finding suggests the need for a different theory—in particular, one that makes use of this distance information.

UNCONSCIOUS INFERENCE

How do we achieve constancy when there are no invariant relationships in view to guide our perception? As we just noted, size judgments are usually accurate if cues indicating the distance of the target object are available to the observer (Chevrier & Delorme, 1983; Harvey & Leibowitz, 1967; Holway & Boring, 1947). Likewise, shape judgments tend to be accurate if cues indicating the object's orientation are visible—and, again, this is a matter of distance (because orientation is obviously a function of which parts of the objects are closer to us and which are farther away).

The role of distance cues can also be demonstrated directly: If these cues are manipulated in a fashion that indicates the target object has moved farther away, the perception of size changes. This is true even if the relationship between the target and the background remains constant, a result that simultaneously points to the

*5.32 An invariant relationship that provides information about size   **(A) and (B) show a dog at different distances from the observer. The retinal size of the dog varies with distance, but the ratio between the retinal size of the dog and the retinal size of the textural elements (e.g., the floor tiles) is constant.***

importance of distance information and argues against the view that our perception of a constant world depends only on higher-order relationships in the stimulus input.

How is this distance information used? An influential hypothesis was formulated a century ago by Hermann von Helmholtz. Helmholtz started with the fact that there is a simple inverse relationship between distance and retinal image size. Thus, if an object doubles its distance from the viewer, the size of its image is reduced by half. If an object triples its distance, the size of its image is reduced to a third of its initial size (Figure 5.33).

This relationship is guaranteed to hold true because of the principles of optics, and the relationship makes it possible for perceivers to achieve constancy by means of a simple calculation. First, the perceiver needs to know the size of the image on the retina. Second, the perceiver needs to know how far away the object is (presumably, this information is provided by the distance cues we have already discussed). These two bits of information can then be combined via a process that somehow multiplies the size of the retinal image by the distance of the object from the viewer; it is this calculation that leads to size constancy. Imagine an object that, at a distance of 10 feet, casts an image on the retina that is 4 millimeters across. The same object, at a distance of 20 feet, casts an image of 2 millimeters. In both cases, the product—10 × 4 or 20 × 2— is the same. Of course, Helmholtz knew that we do not make conscious calculations of this sort. But he believed that some such process—or something that produces the same result—is going on outside of our awareness, so he called it **unconscious infer-ence** (Helmholtz, 1909).

At its heart, Helmholtz's proposal is similar to the explanation we offered for position constancy: To perceive objects as holding their position, we take our own movements into account and unconsciously take some steps that have the effect of "subtracting" the result of our own motion from the actual retinal motion. To perceive objects as having a constant size, we take our viewing distance into account and unconsciously take steps that are equivalent to "multiplying" the retinal size by the distance. Likewise, for shape constancy, we somehow take the slant of the surface into account and make appropriate adjustments in our interpretation of the retinal image's shape. In all cases, it does appear that some sort of unconscious inference is drawn by our perceptual system, providing a taking-into-account process that allows us to perceive the constant properties of the visual world.

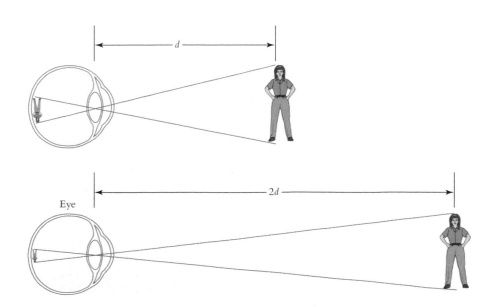

Eye

5.33 The relationship between image size and distance **If an object moves to a new distance, the size of the retinal image cast by that object changes. A doubling of the distance causes the retinal image size to be reduced by half. If the distance is tripled, the retinal image size is cut to one-third of its initial size.**

the system has no information about the first letter. How, then, would it choose among *MAT*, *CAT*, and *RAT*? Suppose that the perceiver has just been shown a series of words, including several names of animals (*dog, mouse, canary*). This experience will activate the detectors for these words, and the activation is likely to spread out to the memory neighbors of these detectors, including (probably) the detectors for *CAT* and *RAT*. (See Chapter 8 for further discussion of memory activation.) Activation of the *CAT* or *RAT* detector, in turn, will cause a knowledge-driven activation of the detectors for the letters in these words, including *C* and *R*.

While all of this is going on, the data-driven analysis is continuing, so that by now the system might have registered the fact that the left edge of the target letter is curved (Figure 5.38B). This bottom-up effect will cause partial activation of the detector for the letter *C*; the partial activation will join up with the activation *C* has already received from *CAT*, so that the *C* detector becomes fully activated. Then, once *C* is activated, this will feed back to the *CAT* detector, activating it still further. (For an example of a model that works in this way, see McClelland, Rumelhart, & Hinton, 1986.)

In effect, then, the initial activation of *CAT* serves as a knowledge-driven "hypothesis," making the visual system more receptive to the relevant "data" from the feature detectors. The arriving data confirm the hypothesis, leading to the suppression of alternative hypotheses. Overall, we are left with a set of processes in which detectors at every level of the hierarchy—from above, below, and both sides—influence each other until a single detector finally wins out.

Cast in different terms, this network achieves what is called ***simultaneous multiple-constraint satisfaction***. This intimidating bit of jargon captures a relatively simple idea. The features detected by the network provide one constraint on the network's output, because the output must be compatible with the information received. The perceiver's expectations provide another constraint: If at all possible, the network's output should be compatible with these expectations. Note, though, that these constraints are not applied one by one, nor are they used as some final step in the process to make sure the output satisfies these requirements. Instead, the constraints are built into the processing itself, with the constraints favoring some detectors and disfavoring others as the detectors do their work. As a result, the network's output is virtually guaranteed to satisfy all of the constraints, or at least to provide the best compromise possible among the various requirements. (For a different example of multiple constraint satisfaction, concerned with how stimulus information interacts with past experience in determining figure-ground assignment, see Peterson & Enns, 2005.)

SENSORY MEMORY

The various processing steps we have described all occur very rapidly—and they need to, so that we can efficiently recognize, and interact with, the objects that fill our world. However, the processing steps do take a measurable amount of time—as much as a fifth of a second in some situations.

This issue of timing is important for several reasons, including the fact that our eyes shift to a new target four or five times each second, making it likely that we sometimes look away from a scene before we have fully registered its contents. Fortunately, though, the visual system has a built-in solution for this problem: The visual system's neural response to a stimulus begins when the stimulus arrives but does not shut off immediately when the stimulus vanishes from view. Instead, the activity, once started, tapers off only gradually, just as the ripples in a pond are started when a stone hits the water but continue for some moments after the stone has sunk to the bottom.

In essence, then, the visual system has a built-in memory—often called a "sensory memory." But this is not a memory in any conventional sense; no snapshot of the input is recorded in any storage spot. Instead, the memory is created simply by the fact that the activity in each processing step takes a fraction of a second to decay, which allows subsequent processing steps to take their input from this continuing activity, even though the stimulus is no longer present.

This sort of sensory memory can be demonstrated in laboratory experiments (e.g., Sperling, 1960) but also is revealed in everyday experience. Imagine that you are focusing your attention on a book when a friend enters the room and says a few words to you. Because you're focused on what you're reading, you don't immediately register your friend's words, so you ask, "What did you say?" But as you're uttering this question, you realize that you *do* know what your friend has said, so your question is superfluous. What has happened here? Your friend's words did trigger activity in your sensory system, but, because your attention was elsewhere, you were slow in comprehending the words, and that is what triggered your request for a repetition. But, thanks to sensory memory, you still have access to the sounds that were uttered, so you can—a moment later—still figure out what the sounds conveyed.

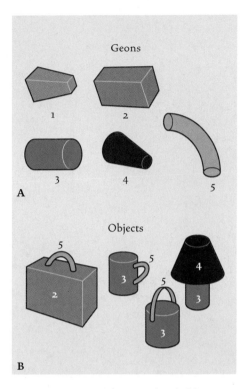

5.39 *Some proposed geometric primitives (A) Some geons. (B) Some objects that can be created from these geons.*

FROM FEATURES TO GEONS TO MEANING

We have now discussed feature nets and how—and how quickly—they can function. Our examples, though, have concerned targets as simple as squares and circles, letters and numerals. But what about the vast variety of three-dimensional objects that surround us? For these, theorists believe that we can still rely on a network of detectors, but we need to add some intermediate levels of analysis.

A model proposed by Irving Biederman, for example, relies on some 30 geometric components that he calls *geons* (short for "geometric ions"). These are three-dimensional figures such as cubes, cylinders, pyramids, and the like. Just about all objects can be analyzed perceptually into some number of these geons. To recognize an object, therefore, we first identify its features and then use these to identify the component geons and their relationships. We then consult our visual memory to see whether there is an object that matches up with what we have detected (Biederman, 1987; Figure 5.39).

Geons and their relationships give us a complete description of an object's geometry in three dimensions. Thus, in Biederman's system, we can describe, say, the structure of a lamp in terms of a certain geon (number 4 in Figure 5.39) on top of another (number 3). But that is not enough to tell the system that the object is a lamp, that it is an object that casts light, can be switched on and off, and so on. For those things, we need some further steps, because, while the geon description does a fine job of representing the object's geometry, it says nothing about the object's meaning.

As with most other aspects of perception, those further steps seem effortless to us most of the time. We see a chair and immediately know what it is, what it is for, and where it probably belongs. But—easy as they seem—these steps are far from trivial, and, remarkably, we can find cases in which the visual system succeeds in achieving an accurate structural description but fails in these last steps—endowing the perceived object with meaning. The cases involve patients who have suffered certain brain lesions, specifically cortical lesions leading to visual agnosia (Farah, 1990). Patients with this disorder can see but cannot recognize what they see (Chapter 3). Some patients can perceive objects well enough to draw recognizable pictures of them but are unable to identify either the objects or their own drawings. One patient, for example, produced the drawings shown in Figure 5.40. When asked to say what these were drawings of, he could not name the key and said that the bird was a tree stump. He evidently had formed adequate structural descriptions of these objects, but his ability to process what he saw stopped there; what he perceived was stripped of its meaning (Farah, 1990, 2004).

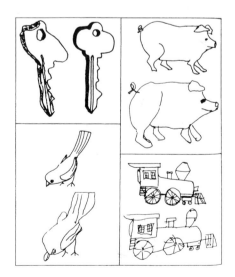

5.40 *Drawings by a patient with associative agnosia   While the patient could see the models well enough to reproduce them fairly accurately, he was unable to recognize these objects.*

THE NEUROSCIENCE APPROACH TO PERCEPTION

We have now discussed two different perspectives that one can take in explaining perception. One perspective seeks to characterize the overall process and emphasizes the traits that broadly characterize how we perceive. A second perspective seeks to characterize the individual steps we take in perceiving. Compared to the first perspective, this approach might tell us less about perception's general characteristics, but it provides a clearer view of the processes that lead to these characteristics.

A third perspective on perception seeks to fill in even more of the details of the processes, by examining how exactly the nervous system makes possible the achievements we have been describing. What has this perspective taught us?

THE VISUAL PATHWAY

As we saw in Chapter 4, the rods and cones pass their signals to the bipolar cells, which relay them to the ganglion cells (Figure 4.13, p. 139). The axons of the ganglion cells form the optic nerve, which leaves the eyeball and begins the journey toward the brain. But even at this early stage, the neurons are specialized in important ways, with different cells being responsible for detecting different aspects of the visual world.

The ganglion cells, for example, can be broadly classified into two categories: the smaller ones are called *parvo cells*, and the larger are called *magno cells*. (The terminology derives from the Latin words for "small" and "large.") Parvo cells, far outnumbering magno cells, blanket the entire retina. Magno cells, in contrast, are found largely in the retina's periphery. Parvo cells appear to be sensitive to color differences (to be more precise, to differences in hue), and they probably play a crucial role in the perception of pattern and form. Magno cells, on the other hand, are color blind but do respond strongly to changes in brightness, and they play a central role in the detection of motion and the perception of depth.

This pattern of neural specialization continues and sharpens as we look more deeply into the nervous system. The relevant evidence comes largely from the single-cell recording technique that we described in Chapter 4, a technique that lets investigators determine which specific stimuli elicit a response from a cell and which do not. This has allowed investigators to explore the visual system cell by cell, and has provided us with a rich understanding of the neural basis for vision.

PARALLEL PROCESSING IN THE VISUAL CORTEX

In Chapter 4, we described cells in the visual cortex that are sensitive to simple characteristics such as the tilt of a line or its position. These cells fire most strongly in response to a line or edge of a specific orientation and position; this "preferred stimulus" for the cell defines the *receptive field* for that cell. Other cells in the visual cortex have different sorts of receptive fields; they are also sensitive to the input's orientation but are less sensitive to its position, so they respond to a stimulus of a particular shape no matter where it appears. Additional cells are sensitive to whether the target is moving or not, and still other cells respond to more complex features, including corners, angles, and notches.

This proliferation of cell types suggests that the visual system relies on a "divide-and-conquer" strategy, with different cells—and, indeed, different areas of the brain—each specializing in a particular kind of analysis. Moreover, these different analyses go on in parallel: Cells analyzing the forms within the visual input do their work at the same time that other cells are analyzing the motion and still others the colors. Using single-cell recording, investigators have been able to map where these various cells are located in the visual cortex and also how they communicate with each other; one such map is shown in Figure 5.41.

Why this heavy reliance on parallel processing? As one advantage, parallel processing allows greater speed, since (for example) brain areas trying to discern the shape of the incoming stimulus do not need to wait until the motion analysis or the color analysis is complete. Instead, all of the analyses can go forward simultaneously, with no waiting time. Another advantage of parallel processing lies in the benefits gained from mutual influence among multiple systems. These benefits derive from the fact that sometimes our understanding of an object's shape depends on our understanding of its motion, while sometimes the reverse is true and our understanding of motion depends on shape. Parallel processing makes both sorts of influence possible, with each type of analysis able to inform the other. Put differently, neither the shape-analyzing system nor the motion-analyzing system gets priority over the other. Instead, the two systems work concurrently and "negotiate" a solution that satisfies both (Van Essen & DeYoe, 1995).

This reliance on mutual influence also provides another benefit. Earlier in the chapter, we emphasized the importance of perceptual organization and argued that the inventory of a pattern's features depends on how the pattern is organized by the perceiver. But let us be clear that the reverse is also true: How you organize the form depends on the form's parts. Thus, no matter how you try, you cannot organize Figure 5.41 so that it looks like a picture of a hippopotamus; the parts you would need for this organization just are not there.

It seems, then, that perception of a pattern's parts depends on organization, but organization depends on the parts. How can we arrange for this two-way relationship? The answer, once again, is parallel processing. The brain areas analyzing a pattern's features do their work at the same time as the brain areas analyzing the pattern's large-scale configuration. More, these two brain areas constantly interact, so that the perception that is achieved is one that makes sense at both the large-scale and fine-grained levels.

Note the parallels between these remarks—describing the functioning of nerve cells—and our earlier discussion of feature nets (p. 177). There we suggested that it

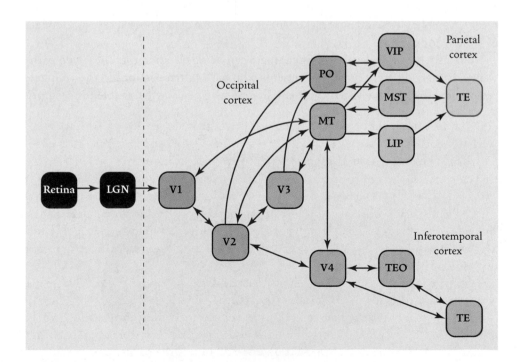

5.41 The visual processing pathways
The visual system relies heavily on parallel processing, with different brain areas engaged in their own specific analyses. Information from the LGN is primarily sent to Area V1, but from there, information is sent along several different pathways.

would be useful if form recognition could depend on a hierarchy of detectors, with each layer of detectors responding to more complex targets than the layer below. This obviously parallels the architecture we are describing in the visual cortex—with cells having receptive fields at different levels of complexity, so that some cells respond to simple features, others to combinations of those features, and others to still more complex shapes. In addition, the parallel processing evident in the visual system provides a biological basis for the process we earlier called "simultaneous multiple-constraint satisfaction" (p. 178). With activity in various parts of the visual system all going on at once, each constraining the others, the brain mechanisms essentially guarantee that vision will end up with the best possible compromise among all the constraints put on it—including what the input's features are, what its overall configuration is, what its pattern of movement is, and its configuration in three dimensions. Overall, then, there is a strong, striking, and intellectually satisfying convergence between the models of perception that have been proposed, based on behavioral data and efforts toward computer simulation of vision, and what we are learning about the actual makeup of the visual system in the brain.

THE "WHAT" AND "WHERE" SYSTEMS

The evidence for specialized neural processes, all operating in parallel, continues as we move beyond the visual cortex. As Figure 5.42 indicates, information from the visual cortex is transmitted to two other important brain areas, in the temporal cortex and the parietal cortex. The pathway that carries information to the temporal cortex is often called the *"what" system*; it plays a major role in the identification of visual objects, telling us whether the object is a cat, an apple, or whatever. The second pathway, which carries information to the parietal cortex, is often called the *"where" system*; it tells us where an object is located—above or below, to our right or left (Ungerleider & Haxby, 1994; Ungerleider & Mishkin, 1982).

There has been some controversy over how exactly we should conceive of these two systems (see, for example, Carey, 2001; Goodale & Milner, 2004; Sereno & Maunsell, 1998). Some theorists, for example, propose that the path to the parietal cortex is primarily involved in the control of our movements, as we reach for, or walk toward, objects in our visual world. In this view, the path to the temporal cortex is more closely associated with our conscious sense of the world around us, including our conscious recognition of objects and our assessment of what these objects look like (e.g., Goodale & Milner, 2004).

No matter how this debate is settled, there can be no question that these two pathways serve very different functions. Patients who have suffered lesions in the occipital-temporal pathway show visual agnosia (Chapter 3). They may be unable to recognize

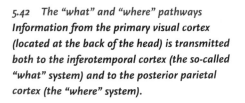

5.42 The "what" and "where" pathways *Information from the primary visual cortex (located at the back of the head) is transmitted both to the inferotemporal cortex (the so-called "what" system) and to the posterior parietal cortex (the "where" system).*

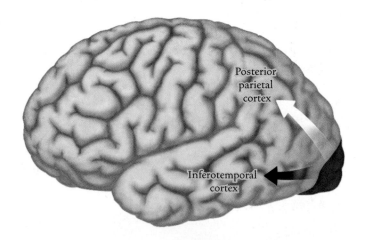

common objects, such as a cup or a pencil, and are often unable to recognize the faces of relatives and friends (although if the relatives speak, the patients recognize them by their voices). On the other hand, these patients show little disorder in visual orientation and reaching. The reverse pattern is observed with patients who have suffered lesions in the occipital-parietal pathway—they have difficulty in reaching but no problem in object identification (A. R. Damasio, Tranel, & Damasio, 1989; Farah, 1990; Goodale, 1995; Newcombe, Ratcliff, & Damasio, 1987).

THE BINDING PROBLEM

It is clear, then, that natural selection has favored a division-of-labor strategy for vision, with the processes of perception made possible by an intricate network of subsystems, each specialized for a particular task and all working together to create the final product: an organized and coherent perception of the world.

We have noted some of the benefits of this design, but the division-of-labor setup also creates a problem for the visual system: If the different aspects of vision—the perception of shape and the perception of color, the perception of movement and the perception of distance—are relegated to different processing modules, then how do we manage to re-integrate these disparate pieces of information into one whole? For example, when we see a ballet dancer in a graceful leap, the leap itself is registered by the magno cells, while the recognition of the ballet dancer depends on parvo cells. How are these pieces put back together? Likewise, when we reach for a coffee cup but stop midway because we see that the cup is empty, the reach itself is guided by the occipital-parietal system (the "where" system); the fact that the cup is empty is perceived by the occipital-temporal system (the "what" system). How are these two streams of processing coordinated?

The same issue can be cast in terms of our subjective impression of the world around us. Our impression, of course, is that we perceive a cohesive and organized world. As we have mentioned in other settings, we do not perceive big and blue and distant; we instead perceive sky. We do not perceive brown and large-shape on top of four shapes and moving; instead, we perceive our pet dog running along. Somehow, therefore, we do manage to re-integrate the separate pieces of visual information. How do we achieve this reunification? Neuroscientists call this the *binding problem*—how the nervous system manages to bind together elements that were initially detected by separate systems.

We are only beginning to understand how the nervous system solves the binding problem, and it is a matter of intense interest to contemporary researchers. The evidence is accumulating, however, that the brain uses a special rhythm to identify which sensory elements belong with which. Specifically, imagine two groups of neurons in the visual cortex. One group of neurons fires maximally whenever a vertical line is in view. Another group of neurons fires maximally whenever a stimulus is in view moving from left to right. Also imagine that, right now, a vertical line is presented, and it is moving to the right. As a result, both groups of neurons are firing strongly. But how does the brain encode the fact that these attributes are bound together, different aspects of a single object? How does the brain differentiate between this stimulus and one in which the features being detected actually belong to different objects—perhaps a static vertical and a moving diagonal?

The visual system seems to encode this difference by means of neural synchrony. If the neurons detecting a vertical line are firing in synchrony with those signaling movement, then these attributes are registered as belonging to the same object. If they are not in synchrony, the features are not bound together. Moreover, the synchrony is made possible by the fact that the neurons are firing at roughly the same rate—about 40 times per second, a rate called a *gamma-band oscillation* (Buzsáki & Draguhn, 2004; Csibra, Davis, Spratling, & Johnson, 2000; Elliott & Müller, 2000; Fries, Reynolds, Rorie, & Desimone, 2001; Gray, Koenig, Engel, & Singer, 1989; Singer, 1996).

The role of neural synchrony is important for many reasons; among them, notice that we may need to broaden our account of how neurons code various aspects of the sensory world. In Chapter 4, we considered coding in terms of which neurons were firing (so that activity in the optic nerve is experienced as seeing, activity in the auditory nerve is experienced as hearing) and also in terms of patterns of activity (so that a particular pattern is experienced as red, another as green, and so on). It now appears that we also need to consider coding in terms of *when* the neurons are firing, with some timing patterns associated with binding (i.e., the experience of coherent objects).

PERCEPTUAL SELECTION: ATTENTION

Synchronized neural firing, therefore, may be the nervous system's way of representing the fact that different attributes are bound together—that is, parts of a single object. But what causes this synchrony? How do the neurons become synchronized in the first place? We do not know yet, but we do know one factor that plays an essential role: attention.

Attention actually plays several different roles in perception. At the least, we are better able to perceive when we are paying attention, and, in some circumstances, we utterly fail to perceive *unless* we are paying attention. Attention also allows us to select some aspects of a scene for consideration while ignoring others. We focus on the figure, not the ground, and if several figures are present, we choose the one to which we will attend. And, as we will see, attention also helps us knit together the sensations we receive to create a unified and coherent perceptual experience.

SELECTION

When a stimulus interests us, we turn our head and eyes to inspect it. Similarly, we actively explore the world with our hands, and we position our ears for better hearing. Other animals do the same, exploring the world with paws or lips or whiskers or even a prehensile tail. These various forms of *orienting* serve to adjust the sensory machinery and to provide one of the most direct means of selecting input—a means through which we focus on the stimuli we care about and disregard those we do not.

In humans, movements of the eyes provide the major means of orienting. Peripheral vision informs us that something is going on, say, in the upper-left section of our field of vision. But our peripheral acuity is not good enough to tell us precisely what it is. To find out, we move our eyes so that the region in which the activity is taking place falls into the visual field of the fovea. In fact, motion in the visual periphery tends to trigger a reflex eye movement, making it difficult not to look toward a moving object.

However, eye movements are not our only means of selecting what we will pay attention to and what we will ignore. The selective control of perception also draws on processes that involve mental adjustments rather than physical ones, and that determine both which inputs we will consider and what we will do with those inputs.

SELECTIVE LOOKING

A widely used method for studying visual attention is the visual search procedure, discussed earlier in this chapter. In this task, a research participant is shown an array of letters, digits, or other visual forms and asked to indicate as quickly as she can whether a particular target is present. As we noted earlier (pp. 164–165), visual search seems almost effortless if the target can be distinguished from the field on the basis of just one feature—for example, searching for a vertical among a field of horizontals, or for a

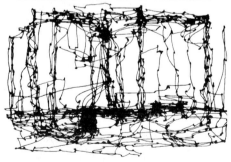

Eye-movement records when looking at pictures **This picture (top) was looked at for 10 minutes. With the picture is the record of the eye movements during this period (bottom). As the records show, most of the eye movements are directed toward the most visually informative regions. As a result, the eye-movement record is a crude mirror of the main contours of the picture.**

green target amidst a group of red distracters. In such cases, the target pops out from the distracter elements, and search time is virtually independent of the number of items in the display.

The situation is different, though, when the target is defined by a combination of features; for example, if the task involves searching for a red *O* among distracters that include green *O*s and red *V*s. Now it is not enough to search for redness or for the *O*'s roundness; instead, the participant must search for a target with both of these features. Under these conditions, the search process is usually serial rather than parallel. Search times are longer and increase with the number of items in the display. (For some exceptions and complications, see Quinlan, 2003; Wolfe, 2003.)

Notice the trade-off that is in place here. When we are searching for just a single feature, our search is remarkably efficient, and we can search through a dozen stimuli just as quickly as we can search through one. When we are searching for a more complex target, our search is much less efficient, and we have to search through the stimuli one by one. But, in return, our attention on a single stimulus reduces our chances for confusion about how the stimulus features within the display are assembled. By focusing a mental spotlight on just a single item, the perceiver avoids any risk of confusion about which elements belong with which stimulus (Figure 5.43).

This view implies that attention plays a central role in solving the binding problem—the problem of figuring out which elements in the stimulus information belong with which. Consistent with this idea, evidence suggests that, in the absence of attention, people often make errors about how features should be combined to make larger wholes. In some studies, for example, people have been shown brief displays while they are thinking about something other than the display. Thus, for example, they might be quickly shown a red *F* and a green *X*, while also trying to remember a short list of numbers they had heard just a moment before. In this situation, participants are likely to have no difficulty perceiving the features in the visual display—so they will know that they saw something red and something green, and they may also know they saw an *F* and an *X* as well. On a fair proportion of trials, though, the participants will be confused about how these various aspects of the display were bundled together, so they may end up reporting *illusory conjunctions*—such as having seen a green *F* and a red *X*. Apparently, then, the combining of features is a separate step from the mere detecting of features, and the combination step seems to require attention.

Related evidence comes from individuals who suffer from severe attention deficits (because of brain damage in the parietal cortex). These individuals are able to do visual search tasks if the target is defined by a single feature, but they are quite impaired if the task requires them to judge how features are conjoined to form complex objects (Cohen & Rafal, 1991; Eglin, Robertson, & Knight, 1989; Robertson, Treisman, Friedman-Hill, & Grabowecky, 1997). Similarly, we earlier suggested that the nervous system identifies how features are bound together through a pattern of synchronized firing, with "bound-together" feature detectors firing in synchrony, at a gamma rhythm. It turns out that this synchronized firing is observed when an animal is attending to a specific

5.43 Searching for feature combinations In (A), it's easy to find the red figure, since it can be distinguished from the background on the basis of a single feature (color). In (B), it's easy to find the O because it too can be distinguished on the basis of a single feature (in this case, shape). In (C), however, it takes some time to locate the red O because now the target is defined in terms of a conjunction of features (color and shape).

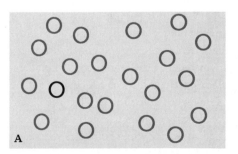

A

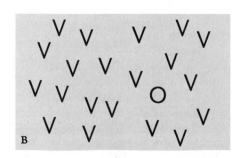

B

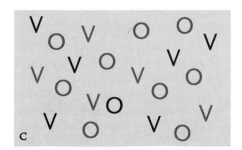

C

stimulus, but it is not observed in neurons activated by an unattended stimulus. This finding obviously strengthens the claim that attention plays a key role in solving the binding problem.

But what exactly does it mean to "focus attention" on a stimulus or to "shine a mental spotlight" on a particular input? How is this selection achieved? The answer is related to a topic we have already discussed—namely, *priming*. If the circumstances lead the perceiver to expect, say, the word *CAT*, then he will prime the appropriate detectors. As a result, when the expected input actually arrives, it will be processed more efficiently: Since the detectors are primed, they need only slight additional activation to trigger a response. Notice, though, that the priming is selective. An individual who expects to see the word *CAT* will be less prepared for anything else. So if the stimulus turns out to be the word *BOG*, for example, it will be processed less efficiently. If the unexpected stimulus is weak (perhaps flashed briefly or only on a dimly lit screen), then it may not trigger a response at all. It is in this fashion that priming can help spare us from distraction—by selectively facilitating the perception of expected stimuli but simultaneously hindering the perception of anything else.

In the example just considered, priming prepared the perceiver for a particular stimulus—the word *CAT*. But priming can also prepare the perceiver for a broad class of stimuli—for example, preparing him for any stimulus that appears in a particular location. In some experiments, participants are asked to point their eyes at a dot on a computer screen. A moment later, an arrow appears for an instant in place of the dot and points either left or right. Then, a fraction of a second later, the stimulus is presented. If it is presented in the location toward which the arrow pointed, the participants respond more quickly than they do without the prime. If the stimulus appears in a different location (so that the prime was actually misleading), participants respond more slowly than they do with no prime at all. Clearly, the prime influences how the participants allocate their processing resources.

This spatial priming is not simply a matter of cuing eye movements. In most studies, the interval between the appearance of the prime and the arrival of the target is too short to permit a voluntary eye movement. But even so (when it is not misleading), the arrow makes the task easier. Evidently, priming affects an internal selection process, as if the mind's eye moves even though the eyes in the head are stationary (Egeth, Jonides, & Wall, 1972; Eriksen & Hoffman, 1972; Gleitman & Jonides, 1976; Jonides, 1980, 1983; Posner, Snyder, & Davidson, 1980).

PERCEPTION IN THE ABSENCE OF ATTENTION

It seems, then, that attention accomplishes several things for us. It orients us toward the stimulus so that we can gain more information. It helps bind the input's features together so that we can perceive a coherent object. And it primes us so that we can perceive more efficiently and so that, to some extent, we are sheltered from unwanted distraction.

If attention is this important, with so many effects, then one might guess that perceiving would be seriously compromised in the absence of attention. Recent studies indicate that this is correct. If research participants are focused on just one aspect of a visual display, they are remarkably insensitive to what is going on in the display outside of the attended elements—that is, to elements they are not paying attention to. For example, in one study, participants watched a video screen in which one group of players, dressed in white shirts, were tossing a ball back and forth. Interspersed with these white-shirted players, and visible on the same video screen, a different group of players, in black shirts, also were tossing a ball. But, when participants were focusing on the white-shirted players, that was all they noticed. They were oblivious to what the black-shirted players were doing, even though they were looking right at them. Indeed, in one remarkable experiment, the participants even failed to notice when someone wearing a (black) gorilla suit strolled right through the middle of the scene (Neisser & Becklen, 1975; Simons & Chabris, 1999).

In a related study, participants were asked to stare at a dot in the middle of a computer screen while trying to make judgments about stimuli presented a bit off their line of view. During the moments in which the to-be-judged stimulus was on the screen, the dot at which the participants were staring changed momentarily to a triangle and then back to a dot. When asked about this a few seconds later, though, the participants insisted that they had seen no change in the dot. When given a choice whether the dot had changed into a triangle, a plus sign, a circle, or a square, they chose randomly. Apparently, with their attention directed elsewhere, the participants were essentially "blind" to a stimulus that had appeared directly in front of their eyes (Mack, 2003; Mack & Rock, 1998; also see Rensink, 2002; Simons, 2000; Vitevitch, 2003).

OTHER MODALITIES

We have almost finished our discussion of perception, but, before we bring the discussion to a close, one last topic remains. Throughout this chapter, we have examined visual perception and how we recognize the things we see. What about the other modalities? How do we hear—and understand—the speech that reaches our ears or the music we listen to? How do we perceive smells and tastes? How do we experience the warmth of the sun or the cold of an icy wind?

As we emphasized in Chapter 4, all of the sense modalities have certain traits in common. All, for example, are influenced by contrast effects, so sugar tastes sweeter after a sip of lemon juice, just as red appears more intense after looking at green. But the senses also differ in important ways. Vision, the dominant sense in humans, can inform us about rich and structured events; this is why vision can tell us about what an object is, where it is, and what it is doing. Smell and taste, on the other hand, do not reveal the events in any direct way, although, of course, these sense modalities can remind us, or lead us to think about, complex events. Vision also encompasses many dimensions of the stimulus—its shape, color, size, and distance—and these must be integrated into a single experience. Smell and taste inform us only about a single dimension of the stimulus.

One sense modality, however, does have much in common with vision: hearing. This is reflected in the fact that many of the phenomena discussed in this chapter have direct parallels in hearing. The recognition of speech sounds, for example, begins with an analysis of the input's (acoustic) features, but it supplements this input with a variety of knowledge-driven effects that draw both on the conversational context and also on our broader knowledge about the world. (For more on speech perception, see Chapter 9.) Likewise, the perception of speech requires a process of parsing, just as vision does: When we hear speech, the sequence of sounds that reaches our ears is essentially unbroken, so it is up to us to decide where one word stops and the next begins. And, in many cases, the sound signal is ambiguous, so that more than one parsing is possible. Thus, the acoustic input that results from someone saying, "Kiss this guy" is virtually identical to the input that results from someone saying, "Kiss the sky." If we receive that input, therefore, we must figure out which parsing is appropriate in that context (Reisberg, Smith, Baxter, and Sonenshine, 1989).

Hearing, like vision, also requires us to group together separate elements in order to hear coherent sequences. This is obvious, for example, in our perception of music, in which we must group together the notes in the melody line, separate from the notes in the harmony, in order to detect the relationships from one note to the next within the melody; otherwise, the melody will be lost to us.

How do you hide a 200-pound gorilla? **In this experiment, subjects were instructed to keep track of the ball players in the white shirts. Intent on their task, the subjects were oblivious to what the black-shirted players were doing, even though they were looking right at them. They also failed to see the person in the (black) gorilla suit, strolling through the scene.**

KNOWLEDGE AND THOUGHT

PART 2

VIRTUALLY EVERYTHING WE DO DEPENDS ON the knowledge we have acquired throughout our lives. What is this knowledge? Where does it come from? How do we store knowledge in our minds, and how do we use it?

In the previous section, we discussed the active role that we take in shaping our perceptual experience, and that same activity will be evident in this section: We do not merely "receive" information from the world, nor is knowledge somehow "stamped into us" by our experience. Instead, we anticipate, we explore, we pay attention, we interpret—and these processes play a crucial role in guiding how, or whether, we learn, and in shaping how, and how well, we think.

These activities make our learning both extraordinarily efficient and remarkably sophisticated, but they sometimes leave us open to error: In anticipating or interpreting, we may occasionally be mistaken, and so, in examining our learning, our memory, and our thoughts, we will need to examine the completeness, the objectivity, and, indeed, the rationality of our cognition.

In this section, we will also need—once again—to consider the interplay between experience and biology. In the section's first chapter, for example, we will consider how learning from experience is, in fact, shaped by our biology. We will then return to this broad theme in the section's last chapter, when we consider a uniquely human form of learning: the learning of language.

LEARNING

*A*s we move through our lives, we are of course responsive to the stimuli around us, but *how* we respond to these stimuli is heavily influenced by learning. It's learning that tells you the object in your hands is a chocolate bar and will taste good if you eat it. It's learning that tells you there is no point in flirting with the man sitting next to you, because he scorned your overtures just yesterday. And it's learning that tells you that spending hours shooting pool the night before an exam is ill-advised and won't improve your academic performance.

But what exactly is learning? We might generally say that learning is an adjustment in our behavior or beliefs, based on past experience, but this definition is fairly coarse and fails to acknowledge some important distinctions among types of learning. After all, some learning does involve changes in behavior or the development of new skills (consider: "She's learning to control her temper" or "He learned how to ski last winter"). But, in other cases, learning centers on the acquisition of new knowledge, without clear implications for behavior ("Physicists hope to learn more about the origins of the universe"). Sometimes learning involves simple associations ("She finally learned that where there's smoke, there's fire"). And sometimes it involves the creation of elaborate belief systems ("He is trying to learn how the Buddhists view the world"). Sometimes the learning is imposed on us by circumstances ("She learned that touching a hot stove is a bad idea"). And sometimes the learning involves ideas or beliefs that we create internally, through our own efforts ("After working on it for hours, he's learned how to derive the Pythagorean formula").

We will consider many of these forms of learning across this chapter and the next three. In this chapter, though, we will focus on relatively simple forms of learning, although—simple or not—these forms of learning are crucial for many aspects of our behavior, and aspects of our emotional lives as well. In addition, it turns out that these simple forms of learning are essential not just for our species but for many of the creatures that populate our planet, and this broad point will allow us to pursue a theme that has emerged in earlier chapters: Humans are of course biological creatures, so it is undeniable that we have much in common with other animals. Other species have a heart and lungs, just as we do; other species must eat, drink, and control their body temperatures, just as we do. It therefore seems likely that we can learn a great deal about humans, and about the role of our biological heritage, by pursuing principles that apply to us just as they apply to many other species. We relied on this theme in exploring key aspects of motivation in Chapter 2, and mechanisms of sensation and perception in Chapters 4 and 5. The theme will be just as important to us in this chapter, in our discussion of learning. ●

THE PERSPECTIVE OF LEARNING THEORY

As we discussed in Chapters 4 and 5, empiricist philosophers like John Locke (1632–1704) and George Berkeley (1685–1753) had offered a simple and straightforward account of learning: Learning, they proposed, involved the creation of *associations*, and the associations, in turn, were the direct result of one's experiences. The perception of seeing the stove was immediately followed by the feeling of heat, and this created an association between this sight and this feeling, and thus you learned: Stoves are hot. The sound of the word *flower* arrives together with the sight and smell of the flower, and thus these ideas become associated. But what about more complicated forms of learning? The answer, according to these philosophers, was easy: More complex learning simply involves more associations, built layer upon layer, so that complicated notions—and whole belief systems—are just the result of creating more and more links among individual ideas.

This proposal has much to recommend it, including the fact that similar conceptions have fared well in other sciences. After all, chemistry teaches us that complex molecules are built up by linking (relatively) simple atoms to each other, and then linking still other atoms to these, and continuing in this way until huge combinations are created, with the whole having properties that are often strikingly different from what one might have expected based on the individual components. Will a similar proposal work as our basic conception of learning?

A large number of researchers, called **learning theorists**, would answer this question with a firm yes, and in their research they are influenced by a striking implication of this view: If all learning depends on essentially the same mechanisms (namely, mechanisms of association), then the same principles, and the same conclusions, should apply to all forms of learning. Therefore, for purposes of doing research, it may not matter very much what forms of learning we choose to study, because the lessons we will draw from our research, the principles we will uncover, should be the same whether we are scrutinizing simple cases of learning or far more complex ones.

In addition, it seems sensible on pragmatic grounds that we would focus, in our experiments, on relatively simple organisms learning relatively simple patterns. This is, of course, a common strategy in all of the sciences: One seeks to understand a process by stripping the process down to its bare essentials, removing the distractions and the complications. Thus, rather than studying learning by examining how a college student, say, learns calculus, perhaps we should examine how less-complicated organisms—rats, for example—learn less-complicated contents.

Is this plausible? Are there uniform principles of learning that will emerge no matter what species, and no matter what instance of learning, we examine? Learning theorists note, after all, that virtually all animal species share a need for learning, and also (as we have noted) that diverse species usually have a great deal in common biologically—in the structure and functioning of their nervous systems, for example, and also in terms of their evolutionary past. It seems reasonable, then, that many species would learn in essentially the same fashion, and this notion led many learning theorists to believe that they would, in fact, be able to identify basic laws of learning that apply equally well to a dog learning to sit on command, a fish learning to navigate its way through a dense growth of algae, or a student learning to play a Mozart sonata.

As we will see, though, this broad argument has met with mixed success. On the one side, we will discuss laws of learning in this chapter that do have amazing generality, applying to many species, situations, and types of behavior. These laws also provide the basis for a number of highly useful techniques, including procedures often used in treating phobias, techniques used to manage prison inmates' behavior, and more. In this sense, then, there are general laws of learning that apply no matter who (or what) is doing the learning, and no matter what is being learned. On the other side, however, some forms of learning seem not to follow the general laws described in this chapter, so our overall account of learning will certainly need to take these distinctive forms of learning into account. Let us turn, therefore, to the data and arguments that underlie these important claims.

HABITUATION

Perhaps the simplest form of learning, and one that is certainly shared across species, is *habituation*. This term refers to the decline in an organism's response to a stimulus once the stimulus has become familiar. To take a concrete case, a sudden noise usually startles us; but the second time the noise is heard, the startle will be diminished, and the third time, it will hardly be evoked. After that, the noise will be ignored altogether: We will have, at this point, become fully habituated to it.

One benefit of habituation is that it narrows the range of stimuli that elicit alarm. Since an unfamiliar stimulus may indicate danger, it makes sense to give our full attention to it. But we do not want to waste our time scrutinizing every stimulus that comes into view; that would distract us away from more important activities. Habituation helps us achieve this goal—by guaranteeing that we will attend to novel inputs but ignore familiar ones.

Habituation requires that the animal somehow compare what it now hears and sees with what it has previously heard and seen. To the extent that the current stimulus matches what is in memory, it is judged to be familiar and not worth attending. "Same noise as before? No need to respond. But what's that movement? That wasn't there before. I'd better check it out." In this fashion, habituation, as simple as it seems, relies on what the organism remembers about its previous experiences and thus surely counts as an example of learning.

Just as important as habituation is *dishabituation*—an *increase* in responsiveness caused by the presentation of something novel. Thus, if an animal hears a loud noise over and over and over, the animal will habituate to the noise and cease responding to it. But if the noise is suddenly a bit louder or changes its position in space, the animal will dishabituate: Detect the change and once again pay full attention to the noise.

The survival value of dishabituation is clear: A change in stimulation often brings the organism important news about its world. If the birds in the nearby trees suddenly stop chirping, is this because they have detected a predator? If so, you want to know about this. If the sound of the brook abruptly grows stronger, could you be threatened by a sudden increase in the water level? This, too, is certainly worth investigating. Thus, dishabituation serves the important function of calling attention to newly arriving information, just as habituation serves the function of helping you ignore old news.

CLASSICAL CONDITIONING

In habituation, an organism learns to recognize an event as familiar but does not learn anything new about that event. Much of our learning, however, does involve new information, and often this information is concerned with the relationship among events or between an event and a particular behavior. Here we see a direct role for the sorts of associations proposed by the empiricist philosophers, with the idea that much learning can be understood as the formation (or strengthening) of associations, or in some cases the weakening of already existing associations. Thus, we learn, for example, to associate thunder with lightning, a smile with friendly behavior, and tigers with danger.

The importance of associations in learning has been emphasized by philosophers for centuries, but the experimental study of these associations did not begin until the end of the late 1800s, with a major contribution coming from the work on conditioning by the Russian physiologist Ivan Petrovich Pavlov (1849–1936).

PAVLOV AND THE CONDITIONED RESPONSE

Pavlov had already earned a Nobel prize for his research on digestion before he began to study conditioning. In that earlier work, Pavlov was exploring the neural control of various digestive reflexes, and many of his laboratory studies focused on the secretion of saliva in dogs.

Pavlov knew from the start that salivation is typically triggered by food (especially dry food) placed in the mouth. In the course of his research, however, a new fact emerged: The salivary reflex could be set off by a range of other stimuli as well, including stimuli that were at first totally neutral. Dogs that had been in the laboratory for a while would salivate not only to the taste and touch of meat in the mouth, but also in response to the mere sight of meat, or the sight of the dish in which the meat was ordinarily placed, or the sight of the person who usually brought the meat, or even the sound of that person's footsteps. Pavlov decided to study these effects in their own right because he recognized that they provided a means through which the reflex concept could embrace learned as well as innate reactions.

Ivan Petrovich Pavlov   Pavlov (center) in his laboratory, with some colleagues and his "best friend."

To study this learning, Pavlov created simple patterns for the animal to detect. For example, he would repeatedly sound a bell and always follow it with food. Later, he observed what happened when the bell was sounded alone, without any food being given (Pavlov, 1927; Figure 6.1).

The result was clear: Repeated pairings of the sound of the bell with food led to salivation when the sound of the bell was presented by itself (i.e., unaccompanied by food). To explain this finding, Pavlov proposed a distinction between *unconditioned* and *conditioned responses*. An unconditioned response (or *UR*), he argued, was a product of the organism's biology and was triggered by a certain stimulus—the *unconditioned stimulus* (or *US*), independent of any learning. Food in the mouth, which unconditionally elicits salivation, would be one example, with food being the unconditioned stimulus and salivation the unconditioned response.

A conditioned response, in contrast, was the product of learning. In this case, the *conditioned stimulus* (or *CS*) is initially a neutral stimulus, and it does not elicit the CR. The CS (in our example so far, the bell) comes to elicit the CR (in our case, salivation) only after some presentations of the CS followed by the US (in this case, food in the

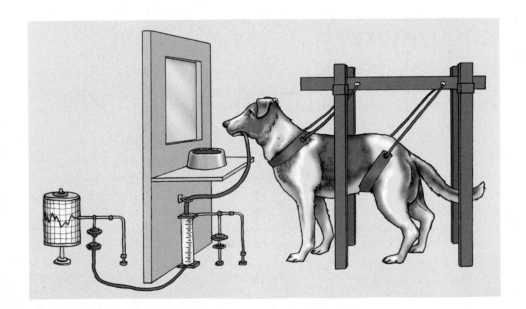

6.1 Apparatus for salivary conditioning The figure shows an early version of Pavlov's apparatus for classical conditioning of the salivary response. The dog was held in a harness; sounds or lights functioned as conditioned stimuli (CS), while meat powder in a dish served as the unconditioned stimulus (US). The conditioned response (CR) was assessed with the aid of a tube connected to an opening in one of the animal's salivary glands.

mouth). These various relationships, which are summarized in Figure 6.2, constitute the basis of what is now known as *classical conditioning*.

Early research on classical conditioning focused on dogs salivating to the sound of bells, to lights, and to the ticking of metronomes, but subsequent research has made it plain that this form of learning, like habituation, occurs in a remarkable range of species and circumstances, so the principles governing classical conditioning do appear to provide general laws of learning with truly wide application. We will say more in a moment about what the relevant principles are, but for now it is worth noting that classical conditioning can be found in species as diverse as ants and anteaters, cats and cockroaches, pigeons and people. Crabs have been conditioned to twitch their tail spines, fish to thrash about, and octopuses to change color, using the appropriate US in each case. Responses conditioned in studies with humans include the galvanic skin response (where the US is typically a loud noise or rap on the knee) and the reflexive eye blink (with the US consisting of a puff of air on the open eye; Kimble, 1961).

Outside of the laboratory, classical conditioning touches many aspects of our everyday lives. We all tend to feel hungry at mealtime and less in between; this probably reflects a conditioning process in which the CS is a particular time of day and the US is the presentation of food (which normally is paired with that time of day). Our emotional responses to certain smells or songs can sometimes be understood in similar terms, with the response likely to be the result of some previous pairing between these stimuli and some emotional experience. Yet another example is sexual arousal, which can often be produced by a special word or gesture the erotic meaning of which is surely learned.

We will say more about these cases and the great breadth of classical conditioning's effects in later sections. For now, we simply note that this is a phenomenon with wide application and of correspondingly great importance.

THE MAJOR PHENOMENA OF CLASSICAL CONDITIONING

Pavlov was able to document many of the central phenomena of classical conditioning, and his findings laid the foundation for subsequent theories in this domain. We begin, therefore, by describing some of Pavlov's basic findings.

6.2 Relationships between CS, US, CR, and UR in classical conditioning

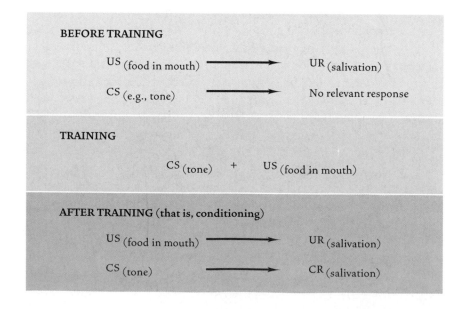

BEFORE TRAINING

US (food in mouth) ⟶ UR (salivation)

CS (e.g., tone) ⟶ No relevant response

TRAINING

CS (tone)   +   US (food in mouth)

AFTER TRAINING (that is, conditioning)

US (food in mouth) ⟶ UR (salivation)

CS (tone) ⟶ CR (salivation)

Initially, the conditioned stimulus (CS) does not elicit the conditioned response (CR). But after several pairings with the unconditioned stimulus (US), the CS (say, the sound of a bell) is able to elicit the CR (salivation). Clearly, then, presenting the US (food) together with (or, more typically, just after) the CS is a critical operation in classical conditioning.

As learning progresses (i.e., as the animal experiences more and more pairings of CS and US), the strength of the CR gradually grows, so that learning typically shows a pattern like the one presented in Figure 6.3. Then, once the CS-US relationship is solidly established, the CS can itself serve to condition yet further stimuli. To give one example, Pavlov first conditioned a dog to salivate to the beat of a metronome, using meat powder as the US. Once this was done, he presented the animal with a black square followed by the metronome beat, but without ever introducing the food. This pairing of black square and metronome beat was repeated several times, and soon the sight of the black square alone was enough to produce salivation. This phenomenon is called *second-order conditioning*. In effect, the black square had become a signal for the beat of the metronome, which in turn signaled the appearance of food.

Second- (and higher-) order conditioning considerably extends the power and importance of classical conditioning. For example, the sight of your dentist might be reliably paired with the discomfort of the dentist's drill; as a result, the sight of the dentist (the CS in this case) might become fearful. But other stimuli are in turn associated with the sight of the dentist—the sight of her office, the sound of her voice, the word *dentist*, and more. Through higher-order conditioning, these stimuli, too, can become fearful—potentially leading to a deep fear of all things related to dentistry. In this way, higher-order conditioning can produce widespread effects and, as in this example, can play a substantial role in shaping key aspects of our emotional lives. (For more on second-order conditioning of fear, see, for example, Gewirtz & Davis, 2000.)

EXTINCTION

Classical conditioning can have considerable adaptive value. Imagine a wolf that has often found many mice to eat at a particular site. It would serve the wolf well to learn about this conjunction of mice and location; that way, the wolf would know where to find a meal the next time it is hungry. But it would be unfortunate if this connection, once established, could never be undone. The mice might leave the area or might all be eaten up, and the wolf would now waste time and energy revisiting this barren spot.

Fortunately, though, classical conditioning can be undone, as Pavlov showed using a procedure not so different from the one that established the conditioning in the first place. To be precise, Pavlov demonstrated that the CR will gradually disappear if the CS is repeatedly presented by itself—that is, without the US. In Pavlov's terms, the CS-US link undergoes *extinction*. Figure 6.4 presents an extinction curve from a salivary extinction experiment, with response strength measured along the *y*-axis, while the *x*-axis indicates the number of extinction trials—that is, trials with a CS, but no US. As the extinction trials proceed, the dog salivates less and less. In effect, the dog has learned that the CS is no longer a signal for food.

But extinction itself can also be undone. One means is through *reconditioning*—that is, by presenting further learning trials. Reconditioning typically proceeds more quickly than the initial conditioning did: The speed of relearning, in other words, is faster than the original speed of learning. This remains true even if the extinction trials were continued until the animal stopped responding to the CS altogether. Apparently, then, extinction does not work by "erasing" the original learning; after extinction, the animal does not return to its original "naive" state. Instead, the animal retains some memory of the learning, and this memory provides it with a head start in the reconditioning trials.

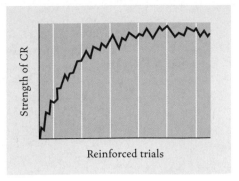

6.3   An idealized learning curve   *Strength of the CR is plotted against the number of reinforced trials. The curve presents the results of many such studies, which by and large show that the strength of the CR rises with increasing number of trials, but each trial adds less strength than the trial just before it.*

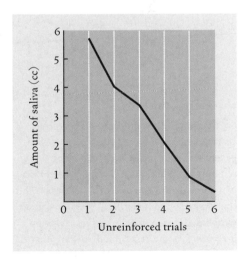

6.4   Extinction of a classically conditioned response   *The figure shows the decrease in the amount of saliva secreted (the CR) with increasing number of extinction trials—that is, trials on which the CS is presented without the US.*

Similar conclusions about extinction can be drawn from the phenomenon of *spontaneous recovery*. This phenomenon is observed in animals that have been through an extinction procedure and then left alone for a rest interval. After this rest period, the CS is again presented, and now the CS will often elicit the CR—even though the CR was fully extinguished earlier.

According to one view of this effect, the extinction trials lead the animal to recognize that a once-informative stimulus is no longer informative. The bell used to signal that food would be coming soon, but now, the animal learns, the bell signals nothing. However, the animal still remembers that the bell was once informative, so when a new experimental session begins, the animal checks to see whether the bell will again be informative in this new setting. Thus, the animal resumes responding to the bell, producing the result we call "spontaneous recovery" (Robbins, 1990).

GENERALIZATION

So far, our discussion has been confined to situations in which the animal is trained with a particular CS—the sound of a bell or metronome, for example—and then later tested with that same stimulus. In the real world, however, things are more complicated than this. The master's voice may always signal food, but his exact intonation will vary from one occasion to another. The sight of an apple tree may well signal the availability of fruit, but apple trees vary in size and shape. These facts demand that animals be able to respond to stimuli that are not identical to the original CS; otherwise, the animals may obtain no benefit from their earlier learning.

It is not surprising, therefore, that animals show a pattern called *stimulus generalization*—that is, they respond to a range of stimuli, provided that these stimuli are sufficiently similar to the original CS. For example, a dog might be conditioned to respond to a yellow light. When tested later on, that dog will respond most strongly if the test light is still yellow. However, the dog will also respond (although a bit less strongly) to an orange light. The dog will probably also respond to a red light, but the response will be weaker still. In general, the greater the difference between the new stimulus and the original CS, the weaker the CR. Figure 6.5 illustrates this pattern, called a *generalization gradient*. The peak of the gradient (the strongest response) is typically found when the test stimulus is identical to the stimulus used in training; the response gets weaker and weaker (so the curve gets lower and lower) as the stimuli become more dissimilar.

DISCRIMINATION

Stimulus generalization is obviously beneficial but can be carried too far. A tiger may be similar to a kitten, but someone who generalizes from one to the other is likely to regret it. What she must do instead is discriminate—and not try to pet the tiger.

The phenomenon of *discrimination* is readily demonstrated in the laboratory. A dog is first conditioned to salivate to a CS—for example, the sight of a black square. After the CR is well established, trials pairing the black square with the US are randomly interspersed with trials with another stimulus—say, the sight of a gray square—and no US. This continues until the animal discriminates perfectly, always salivating to the black square (referred to, generally, as the CS$^+$) and never to the gray (referred to as the CS$^-$). Of course, the dog does not reach this point immediately. During the early trials, it will be confused—or, more precisely, it will generalize rather than discriminate and salivate equally to both the CS$^+$ and the CS$^-$. However, these errors gradually become fewer and fewer until perfect discrimination is achieved.

In understanding this pattern, however, it is important to realize that the animal learns the significance of both the CS$^+$ and the CS$^-$. It learns, of course, that the CS$^+$ signals the approach of the US. What about the CS$^-$? One might think that the animal learns that this stimulus conveys no information—after all, this stimulus is not followed

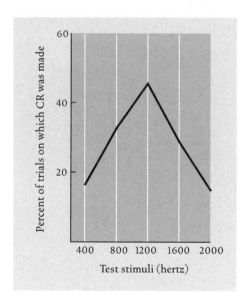

6.5 Generalization gradient of a classically conditioned response *The figure shows the generalization of a conditioned blinking response in rabbits. The CS was a tone of 1200 hertz, and the US was electric shock. After the conditioned response to the original CS was well established, generalization was measured by presenting various test stimuli, ranging from 400 hertz to 2000 hertz and noting the percent of the trials on which the animals gave the CR. The figure shows the results, averaged over several testing sessions.*

by the US. But there *is* information here: The CS⁻ signals a period in which the US is likely not to arrive. If the US is a loud noise, then the CS⁻ signals the start of a period of time that will be noise-free. If the US is food, then the CS⁻ indicates that food is not coming soon.

In essence, then, the CS⁻ takes on a significance opposite to that of the CS⁺. It means "no noise," or "no food," or, in general, "no US." Correspondingly, the animal's response to the CS⁻ tends to be the opposite of its response to the CS⁺. If the US is a noise blast, then the CS⁺ elicits fear and the CS⁻ seems to inhibit fear. If the US is food, then the CS⁺ elicits salivation and the CS⁻ causes the animal to salivate less than it ordinarily would. Thus, the CS⁻ takes on the role of *inhibitor*—it inhibits the response elicited by the CS⁺ in that procedure.

THE CS AS A "SIGNAL"

In describing discrimination, it seems natural to speak about the CS⁺ and CS⁻ as though they were *signals* for the animal, providing information about things to come. And, in fact, this way of thinking about the CS helps us understand several other facts about conditioning, including why the rate at which conditioning develops depends on how the CS and US are related to each other in time.

Conditioning is best when the CS precedes the US by some optimum interval—usually a half-second or so, or perhaps a few seconds at most. If the interval between the CS and US is increased beyond this optimum, the effectiveness of the pairing declines sharply. In addition, presenting the CS and US simultaneously is much less effective in establishing an association, and the backward procedure is even worse (Rescorla, 1988; Figure 6.6).

These facts make perfect sense if we understand the CS as a signal, warning the organism that it should prepare itself for the upcoming US. To see why, imagine a mountain road that contains a dangerous hairpin turn. How should drivers be warned about this turn? The ideal warning would be a "Caution" sign just before the turn (analogous to forward pairing with a short CS-US interval; Figure 6.7). This sign would be informative and would give the driver time to prepare for the relevant maneuver. But it is important that the sign not appear too far in advance of the turn. As an extreme example, imagine a "Caution" sign appearing 100 miles before the turn (analogous to forward pairing with an extremely long CS-US interval). In this case, the driver might

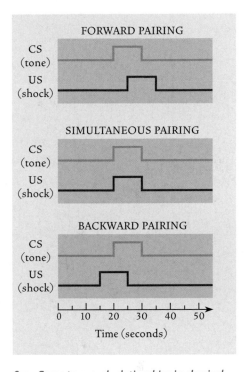

6.7 *Some temporal relationships in classical conditioning*

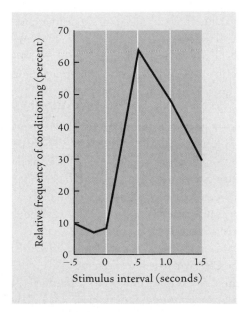

6.6 *The CS-US interval in classical conditioning* **The figure shows the results of a study of the effectiveness of various CS-US intervals in humans. The CR was a finger withdrawal response, the CS a tone, and the US an electric shock. The time between CS and US is plotted on the horizontal axis. Negative intervals mean that the US was presented before the CS (backward pairing), a zero interval means that the two stimuli were presented simultaneously, and a positive interval means that the CS began before the US (forward pairing). The vertical axis indicates the degree of conditioning.**

not connect the sign with what it signifies or, just as bad, might have forgotten about the sign altogether by the time he approaches the curve. Things would be worse still, though, if the sign were prominently displayed right in the middle of the hairpin turn because now the sign's warning comes too late to be of any use (simultaneous pairing). Worst of all, the driver would suspect a degree of malevolence if he discovered the sign placed on the road 100 feet beyond the turn (backward pairing), although he would probably be grateful that he did not find it at the bottom of the ravine.

CONTINGENCY

The CS's role as a signal also has a crucial implication for what it is that *produces* classical conditioning—that is, what the relationship must be between the CS and the US in order for the animal to learn. According to Pavlov, the crucial relationship was *temporal contiguity*—the mere fact that the two events, CS and US, occurred together in time. It turns out, though, that this is not right. Instead, classical conditioning is produced only if the CS is *informative* about things to come.

To see the point, consider a dog in a conditioning experiment. Several times, it has heard a metronome and, a moment later, received some food powder. But many other stimuli were also present. Simultaneous with the metronome, the dog heard some doors slamming and some voices in the background. It saw the laboratory walls and the light fixtures hanging from the ceiling. At that moment, it could also smell a dozen different scents and could feel a similar number of bodily sensations. What, therefore, should the dog learn? If it relies on mere contiguity, then it will learn to associate the food powder with all of these stimuli—metronomes, light fixtures, and everything else that is on the scene. After all, these were all present when the US was introduced.

It should be obvious, though, that many of these stimuli, even if contiguous with the US, are not informative about the US. The light fixtures, for example, were on the scene just before the food power arrived, but they were also on the scene during the many minutes in which no food was on its way. Therefore, "light fixtures visible" cannot signal that food is coming soon, because "light fixtures visible" has just as often conveyed the opposite message. Likewise for the smells and most of the sounds in the laboratory: These were associated with food, but they were also associated with the absence of food. Therefore, none of these stimuli will help the animal if it wants to predict when food is upcoming and when it is not.

If the animal wants to predict the US's arrival, what it needs is some event that reliably occurs when food is about to appear and does not occur otherwise. And, of course, the metronome beat in our example is the stimulus that satisfies these requirements, since it never beats in the intervals between trials when food is not presented. Therefore, if the animal hears the metronome, it is a safe bet that food is on its way. If the animal cares about signaling, it should learn about the metronome and not about these other stimuli, even though they were all contiguous with the target event.

Are animals sensitive to these patterns? Do they notice whether the US is **contingent** on the CS—more likely to occur in its presence than in its absence? In one experiment, rats were exposed to various combinations of a tone (CS) and a shock (US). The tone was never a perfect predictor of shock, but, even so, it was a signal that shock was likely to arrive soon. Specifically, presentation of the tone signaled a 40% chance that a shock was about to arrive.

For some of the rats in this experiment, shocks also arrived 40% of the time without any warning. For these rats, the tone really provided no information; the rats' expectations about things to come should have been the same with the tone or without it. And, in fact, this situation led to no conditioning; the rats learned simply to ignore the tone.

For other rats in the experiment, things were different. For these rats, the tone still signaled a 40% chance of shock, and also as before, shocks still arrived occasionally with no warning. For these animals, though, the likelihood of a shock was smaller (below 40%) when there was no tone than when there was a tone. In this case, the tone was an imperfect predictor of things to come but still provided some information: Shock is more likely following the tone than otherwise. In this situation, the rats did develop a conditioned response and became fearful whenever the tone was sounded.

Because of the way this experiment was set up, both groups of rats experienced the same number of tone-shock pairings, so the degree of contiguity between tone and shock was the same for both groups. What differed between the groups, though, was whether the tone was informative or not; thus, it is the information value, apparently, that matters for conditioning. In addition, notice that the tone was never a perfect predictor of shock: Tones were *not* followed by shock 60% of the time. Even so, conditioning was observed; apparently, an imperfect predictor is better than no predictor at all (Rescorla, 1967, 1988).

THE ABSENCE OF CONTINGENCY

Consider a situation in which the probability of a shock following a tone is equal to the probability of a shock without a tone. One might think that there is nothing to be learned in this setting, because the tone provides no information about things to come. But animals *do* learn something in this situation: They learn that there is danger in this setting, and, crucially, they learn that they can never feel safe.

To see how this works, consider two contrasting situations. In the first, the CS signals that shock is likely to follow. When the CS appears, the animal will become fearful. But when there is no CS, the animal can relax because now shock is less likely. The absence of the CS has become a safety signal, an inhibitor of fear.

In the second situation, no stimulus predicts when shock will occur—there is no CS to elicit fear. But, from the animal's point of view, this makes things worse, not better. Without the CS, there is no safety signal, and, as a result, the animal must be afraid all the time.

The difference between signaled and unsignaled shock may be related to a distinction frequently made between fear and anxiety. According to some theorists, fear is a state elicited by a specific situation or object, whereas anxiety is chronic, is objectless, and occurs in many situations. A number of authors suggest that such unfocused anxiety is in part produced by unpredictability—in essence, by an absence of safety signals (Schwartz, Wasserman, & Robbins, 2002; Seligman, 1975).

THE ROLE OF SURPRISE

It seems clear, then, that animals are influenced by the probabilities inherent in a series of events, but they are obviously not standing by with a calculator, tallying trials on which the CS was followed by a US and dividing this by the number of trials on which the US occurred alone. How, then, do animals learn? And how are they influenced by these probabilities?

Most researchers believe that these questions can be answered in terms of simple mechanisms that serve only to make small trial-by-trial adjustments in the strength of association between CS and US. Thanks to these mechanisms, the animal arrives in each learning trial with certain expectations, based on what it has experienced in the past. If these expectations are correct, then the arrival (or non-arrival) of the US will be no surprise, and, on this basis, there is no reason to adjust the expectations. But if the expectations are wrong, then the US will be a surprise, and it is time to adjust. Specifically, if the US was not expected, and it arrives anyhow, then this will lead to a strengthening of the CS-US association. If the US was expected but does not arrive, then the CS-US association will be weakened. If things continue in this fashion, trial after trial, eventually the expectations will be tuned and retuned until they are in line with reality—including the probabilities that describe the reality (Kamin, 1968; Rescorla & Wagner, 1972; but see also Miller, Barnet, & Grahame, 1995; Pearce & Bouton, 2001).

This view of things implies that *surprise* plays a key role in conditioning—so that learning occurs only when events are not in line with expectations. And, in fact, the role of surprise is easily demonstrated. For example, in a phenomenon called the *blocking effect*, animals are exposed to a three-part procedure. In Stage 1, the animals—rats, for example—hear a hissing noise that is followed by a shock. As one might expect, this noise becomes a CS for conditioned fear. In Stage 2, the shock is preceded by two stimuli presented simultaneously: One is the same hissing noise used in Stage 1; the other is a light. In Stage 3, the light is presented alone to see whether it would also produce a conditioned fear reaction. Results show that it does not. Even though the light has been paired many times with the shock, no learning takes place. Why? Because the light provides only redundant information: The animal already knows that a shock is coming; the hissing noise tells it so. Since no new information is associated with the light, no surprise is evoked by the light, and, therefore, there is no learning. (For more on blocking in humans, see Kruschke & Blair, 2000; for some intriguing complexities in blocking, see Beckers, Miller, De Houwer, & Urushihara, 2006.)

EXTENSIONS OF CLASSICAL CONDITIONING

We have now discussed many aspects of classical conditioning, and the various facts we have reviewed provide classical conditioning with an easily identifiable profile. Classical conditioning, in other words, is a form of learning that reliably shows the features we have described, and this allows us to use these features as a basis for asking whether phenomena outside of the laboratory involve classical conditioning or not. For example, many emotional reactions clearly show this profile, a strong indication that these reactions are, in fact, attributable to classical conditioning. (This is, of course, consistent with our earlier example of higher-order conditioning producing a fear of dentists.) Let us pursue this point, though, by looking more closely at conditioned fear.

CONDITIONED FEAR

In many procedures, the conditioned response involves a single act such as salivating or blinking. Sometimes, though, the CR is more complex. For example, we have mentioned procedures in which the US is an aversive stimulus such as a loud noise. In these procedures, the CS will come to elicit a multifaceted response, including changes in the animal's behavior as well as in its internal state (heart rate, hormone secretions, and so on). In short, the animal will become fearful and will do all the things that animals do when they are afraid.

Many studies have examined these conditioned emotions, especially fear. Often, these studies employ the *conditioned emotional response (CER)* procedure, which relies on the fact that fear tends to disrupt other activities: When you're afraid, you may forget to eat, won't sleep very well, and certainly won't get much work done. This provides us with a means of *measuring* the fear, on the logic that the more afraid you are, the more disruption this will cause in your other activities. Thus, by measuring the disruption, we measure the fear.

Specifically, a rat in a CER procedure is first taught to press a lever for a food reward. After a few training sessions, it learns to press at a steady rate, and this provides the background activity that we will use to measure the fear. We are ready, therefore, to begin the fear conditioning. While the animal is pressing the lever, a CS is presented—perhaps a light or a tone that will stay on for, say, 3 minutes. At the end of that period, the CS stops, and the rat receives a brief electric shock (the US). This causes the rat to freeze and stop its lever pressing for a few seconds. But soon the rat starts pressing again, and, once it does, the CS-US sequence is repeated: another tone and another shock. Again, this causes an interruption in the rat's lever pressing. But after a moment, the rat returns to lever pressing, and the cycle is repeated, with yet another CS-US pairing (Estes & Skinner, 1941; Kamin, 1965).

In this procedure, we measure the fear by asking how much it disrupts the ongoing activity of pressing the lever. Early in training, the animal essentially ignores the CS, so that when the CS is presented, the animal's lever pressing continues almost without interruption. Later on, the animal learns that the CS signals the approach of the US (the shock). At this stage, the CS (and the anticipation of the shock) keeps the animal from its chore of lever pressing, so that it presses less often during the CS (while afraid) than otherwise. By measuring this *response suppression*, we can measure the strength of the conditioning (Figure 6.8).

This technique can be used for many purposes, including the study of inhibitory learning. In one experiment, a tone (the CS⁺) was associated with shock, and a light (the CS⁻) was associated with absence of shock and so signaled a period of relative safety. After some learning, the CS⁺ elicited fear from the animal, but the CS⁻ (the "safety signal") inhibited fear. All of this was evident in the animal's lever pressing: Response rates went down during the CS⁺ (this is the standard pattern of response suppression) but up during the CS⁻. Clearly, then, the CS⁻ had taken on a meaning opposite to that of the CS⁺ and had an opposite effect on the animal's lever pressing (Reberg & Black, 1969).

Can human feelings be conditioned in the same fashion? Our earlier example of fear of dentists implied that they can be; in fact, many studies show that this is correct. We mentioned earlier, for example, that hunger can be triggered by a stimulus (such as time of day) that has been associated with food in the past. Likewise, sexual arousal can be evoked by a stimulus that has merely been associated with sexual activity. Similarly, a preference for a particular stimulus can be created by associating that stimulus with an attractive US. Or, as a different example, many patients who have undergone chemotherapy report that they experience nausea the moment they enter (or even think about) the building in which they received their treatments; here the nausea is the UR produced by the chemotherapy itself, and the response to the building is the CR created by the association between the building and the treatments.

In the case of fear, a frightful experience in a particular room can lead to fear of that room; falling off a bicycle can lead to fear of bike riding. These cases are easily understood in terms of classical conditioning. Some psychologists have also proposed that the irrational fears we call *phobias* can be understood in the same terms (see, for example, Mineka & Zinbarg, 2006). With or without this claim, though, it is clear that classical conditioning can usefully be employed in the treatment of phobias, using a procedure directly modeled after the extinction of a conditioned response. In this procedure, the person is exposed to the phobic stimulus (the snake or the cliff edge, or whatever), but with no dire consequences. This is, in essence, a case in which the CS is presented, but with no US—exactly the procedure for extinction. And, in fact, this procedure is usually an effective means of reducing or elininating the phobia. (For more on phobias and their treatment, see Chapters 16 and 17.)

THE RELATION BETWEEN CR AND UR

The phenomenon of fear conditioning calls attention to an important question: What is the relation between CR and UR? In Pavlov's original studies, the CR and UR seem similar: His dogs salivated both when they heard the CS and when they experienced the US. But, in fact, the CR and UR are rarely identical. When meat is placed in the mouth (the US), a dog's salivation is more copious and much richer in digestive enzymes in comparison to salivation in response to a tone or bell (CS).

The difference between CR and UR is even more pronounced in the case of fear conditioning. When exposed to electric shock, the animal jumps and squeals, and its heart

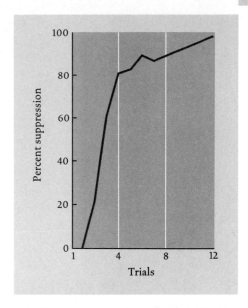

6.8 Response suppression **A rat is trained to press a lever at a steady rate to gain food. The figure plots the extent to which this response is suppressed after successive presentations of a 3-minute light (CS) that is immediately followed by electric shock (US). After 12 such trials, suppression is at 100 percent, and the animal doesn't respond at all during the 3 minutes when the CS is presented.**

beats faster; this is the UR. When the same animal hears or sees a CS that signals the shock, its response (the CR) is different: The animal freezes and tenses its muscles, and its heartbeat slows. This is not an escape-from-shock reaction; it is, instead, a manifestation of fearful anticipation.

All of this makes good biological sense. An animal cannot eat a tone that has been paired with food, and no tissue damage is produced by a light that has been paired with shock. Therefore, it would be pointless for the animal to treat the CS and US in the same fashion. But how, then, should animals respond to the CS? We have already seen that animals seem to interpret the CS as a signal, an indication that the US is about to arrive. That signal is useful precisely because it allows the animals to prepare themselves for the US, so that they can deal with it more easily when it arrives. In this view, the CS essentially serves as a "Get ready!" signal, and the CR is literally the animal's preparation for the US. If the sound of a bell has been reliably followed by food, then the sound now signals that the animal should moisten its mouth, so that it will be ready to eat when the food does arrive. If the sight of a light has been followed by a shock, then it is a signal that the animal should stop moving around and stay at "full alert" so that it will be ready to jump when the shock begins (Domjan, 2005; Holland, 1984; Hollis, 1984). Moreover, the evidence suggests that this preparation for the US is effective—so that (for example) sexual activity is more likely to succeed (e.g., lead to offspring) if some CS announced the imminent arrival of the US (the sights, sounds, and smells of a sexually receptive partner); presumably, this is because the CS allowed the animal to prepare itself for mating (Domjan, 2005). Likewise, digestion is more efficient if a CS announced the imminent arrival of the US (food in the mouth); again, this is presumably because the CS allowed the animal to prepare itself to ingest and digest the food (Domjan, 2005; Woods & Ramsay, 2000).

CONDITIONING AND COMPENSATORY RESPONSES

Preparation for a US can take many forms. Consider, for example, a person who has received many doses of insulin, a hormone that depletes blood sugar. Insulin is normally produced inside the body by the pancreas, and it is essential for the process through which cells absorb energy from sugars. When the body does not produce enough insulin, this hormone must be supplied via injection, which is part of the treatment for diabetes. It turns out, though, that after a number of these injections, the individual begins to respond to the various stimuli that accompany the injections, such as the mere sight of the needle. The response, however, seems peculiar: The insulin injections themselves cause a *decrease* in blood-sugar levels (because the insulin is helping the person to metabolize the sugar, thus removing the sugar from the bloodstream). The sight of the needle, in contrast, or the presentation of any other injection-related stimulus, has exactly the opposite effect, producing an *increase* in blood sugar.

What is going on in this situation? Bear in mind that various mechanisms in the body function to maintain a stable, unchanging internal environment; in Chapter 2, we discussed these as ways of maintaining *homeostasis*. Thus, insulin fosters the metabolism of sugar, which depletes the supply of sugar in the blood. The body then recognizes this depletion as a disruption of the internal stability, because blood-sugar levels are getting lower than they should be. This triggers various homeostatic mechanisms that seek to restore stability by adding sugar to the bloodstream. In essence, then, these mechanisms "repair" the disruption caused by the normal effects of the insulin.

But, of course, *preventing* a problem is usually preferable to repairing the problem after it has occurred. Therefore, rather than waiting until blood-sugar levels get low and then responding, it would be better if the body had a way of dealing with the blood-sugar drop as it happens, so that the blood-sugar level never gets low in the first place. And this is where classical conditioning enters the scene.

Insulin itself is an unconditioned stimulus (US), and the UR is the individual's built-in response to it—that is, the series of metabolic steps that (among other consequences) lead to the decrease in blood sugar. The CS is the set of stimuli (including the sight of the needle) that signal the US is about to arrive. And, as always, the CR is a response that serves to prepare the animal for the upcoming UR. In this case, the CR is a *compensatory response* that can offset (compensate for) the response produced by the drug. Thus, the UR leads to a change in one direction; the CR involves the opposite change, so the two together yield *no change* in blood-sugar level.

Notice that the CR in this case is not blocking the insulin from doing its work. Even with the conditioning, the insulin still helps cells to metabolize glucose, and this still has the effect of using up some of the glucose in the bloodstream. What the CR accomplishes, though, is a simultaneous *adding* of glucose to the bloodstream, so that the blood sugar is replenished as rapidly as it is used, with the highly desirable consequence that the person still receives the benefits of insulin injections, but without this causing dramatic fluctuations in blood-sugar levels.

How do we know that this compensatory response really is produced by classical conditioning? It turns out that the response can be eliminated by a conventional extinction procedure. The response also shows a clear generalization gradient, if we vary the CS. The sight of drug-associated cues (i.e., the CS) can also produce second-order conditioning if these cues are reliably paired with some other stimulus. In short, the learned response to insulin shows all of the effects that constitute the full profile of classical conditioning, strongly suggesting that conditioning is, in fact, the mechanism behind this response.

Moreover, this pattern—with classical conditioning allowing an organism to prepare itself for drug effects—is obviously advantageous for the organism, so it's no surprise that this pattern is not limited to insulin. Similar conditioned responses have been demonstrated for many of the body's hormones and many externally administered drugs, including morphine, caffeine, nicotine, amphetamines, and others (Domjan, 2005; Siegel, 1977, 1983, 1989; Siegel & Allan, 1998; Siegel, Kim, & Sokolwska, 2003; Sokolowska, Siegel, & Kim, 2002). In each case, compensatory mechanisms are activated because of repeated pairings between some CS (e.g., the sight of the needle or the smell of the coffee) and the US (the hormone or the drug). These effects provide powerful confirmation of the importance and widespread applicability of the form of learning that Pavlov documented almost a century ago.

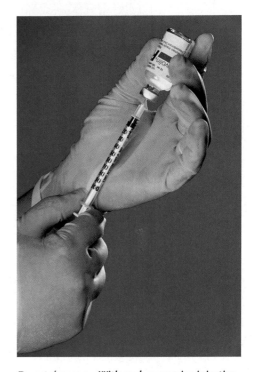

Drug tolerance **With each successive injection, the body becomes more tolerant of the injected drug. Classical conditioning probably plays a considerable role in creating this tolerance, as the text describes.**

INSTRUMENTAL CONDITIONING

Habituation and classical conditioning are two simple forms of learning, each important in its own right. And, as we have seen, each seems to be a *general* form of learning, relevant to many species, many situations, and many different responses—including a variety of overt behaviors, a range of subjective feelings, and a broad set of bodily responses.

However, habituation and classical conditioning are both limited in crucial ways. Habituation, we noted earlier, can decrease an organism's response to a stimulus, but it does not teach the animal anything new about the stimulus. Classical conditioning can produce a wide range of new "reflexes," but, of course, many of our behaviors are not reflexes at all. Many of our behaviors are *voluntary*, not triggered by a stimulus in some automatic fashion, but instead initiated by (and presumably under the control of) the organism itself. For these behaviors, too, we can identify a general form of learning, one known as *instrumental conditioning* (also called *operant conditioning*).

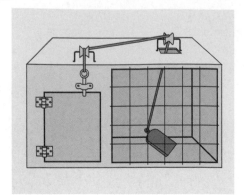

6.9   Puzzle box   *This box is much like those used by Edward Thorndike. The animal steps on a treadle attached to a rope, thereby releasing the latch that locks the door.*

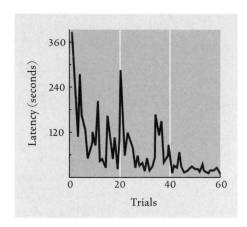

6.10   Learning curve of one of Thorndike's cats   *To get out of the box, the cat had to move a wooden handle from a vertical to a horizontal position. The figure shows the gradual decline in the animal's response latency (the time it takes to get out of the box). Note that the learning curve is by no means smooth but has rather marked fluctuations. This is a common feature of the learning curves of individual subjects. Smooth learning curves are generally produced by averaging the results of many individual subjects.*

THORNDIKE AND THE LAW OF EFFECT

The experimental study of instrumental learning began a century ago as a consequence of the debate over Darwin's theory of evolution by natural selection. Supporters of Darwin's theory emphasized the continuity among species, both living and extinct: Despite their apparent differences, a bird's wing, a whale's fin, and a human arm, for example, all have the same basic bone structure, and this makes it plausible that these diverse organisms all descended, through a series of tiny incremental steps, from common ancestors. But opponents of Darwin's theory pointed to something they perceived as the crucial discontinuity among species: the human ability to think and reason, an ability that animals did not share. Didn't this ability, unique to our species, require some altogether different (non-Darwinian) type of explanation?

In response, Darwin and his colleagues argued that there was, in fact, considerable continuity of mental prowess across the animal kingdom. Yes, humans are smarter in some ways than other species, but the differences might be smaller than they initially seem. In support of this idea, Darwinian naturalists collected stories about the intellectual achievements of various animals (Darwin, 1871). These painted a flattering picture, as in the reports of cunning cats that scattered breadcrumbs on the lawn in order to lure birds into their reach (Romanes, 1882).

In many cases, however, it was unclear whether these reports were genuine or just bits of folklore. If genuine, it was unclear whether the reports had been polished by the loving touch of a proud pet owner. What was needed, therefore, was more systematic, more objective, and better-documented research. That research was made possible by a method described in 1898 by Edward L. Thorndike (1874–1949).

CATS IN A PUZZLE BOX

Thorndike's method was to set up a problem for an animal—in his experiments, usually a hungry cat. The cat was placed inside a box with a door that it could open only by performing some simple action such as pulling a loop of wire or pressing a lever (Figure 6.9). Once outside this ***puzzle box***, the cat was rewarded with a small portion of food. Then it was placed back into the box for another trial so that the procedure could be repeated over and over until the task of escaping the box was mastered.

On the first trial, the typical cat struggled valiantly, meowing, clawing, and biting at the bars. This continued for several minutes until finally, by pure accident, the animal hit upon the correct response. Subsequent trials brought gradual improvement. The moments of struggle grew shorter, and the animal took less and less time to produce the response that unlocked the door. By the time the training sessions were completed, the cat's behavior was almost unrecognizable from what it had been at the start. Placed in the box, it immediately approached the wire loop, yanked it with businesslike dispatch, and hurried through the open door to enjoy the well-deserved reward.

If one merely observed the cat's sophisticated final performance, one might well credit the animal with reason or understanding. But Thorndike argued that the problem was solved in a very different way. For proof, he examined the *learning curves*. He plotted how much time the cat required on each trial to escape from the puzzle box, and he charted how these times changed over the course of learning. Thorndike found that the resulting curves declined quite gradually as the learning proceeded (Figure 6.10). This is not the pattern one would expect if the cats had achieved some understanding of the problem's solution. If they had, their curves would show a sudden drop at some point in the training, when the cats finally got the point. ("Aha!" muttered the insightful cat, "it's the lever that lets me out," and henceforth howled and bit no more.) Instead, these learning curves suggest that the cats learned to escape in small increments, with no evidence at all of understanding and certainly no evidence of any sudden insight into the problem's solution.

In Thorndike's view, the cats' initial responses to this situation were the result of the animals' prior learning, or perhaps some built-in predisposition. As it happened, however, nearly all of these initial responses led to failure. Therefore, as the trials proceeded, the tendency to produce these responses gradually weakened. In contrast, the animals' tendency to produce the correct response was initially weak but, over the trials, gradually grew in strength. In Thorndike's terms, the correct response was gradually "stamped in," while futile ones were correspondingly "stamped out."

What causes this stamping-in or stamping-out? Thorndike's answer was the *law of effect*. Its key proposition is that, if a response is followed by a reward, that response will be strengthened. If a response is followed by no reward (or, worse yet, by punishment), it will be weakened. In general, strength of a response is adjusted according to that response's consequences (Figure 6.11).

In this view, we do not need to postulate any sophisticated intellectual processes to explain the cat's performance. We do not need to assume that the animal noticed a connection between act and consequence or that it was trying to attain some goal. All we need to assert is that, if the animal made a response and reward followed shortly, that response was more likely to be performed later.

Notice that Thorndike's proposal suggests a clear parallel between how an organism learns during its lifetime and how species evolve, thanks to the forces of natural selection. In both cases, variations that "work"—behaviors that lead to successful outcomes, or individuals with successful adaptations—are kept on. In both cases, variations that are less successful are weakened or dropped. And, crucially, in both cases the selection does not involve any guide or supervisor to steer the process forward. Instead, the selection depends only on the consequences of actions or of adaptations and on whether these serve the organism's biological needs or not.

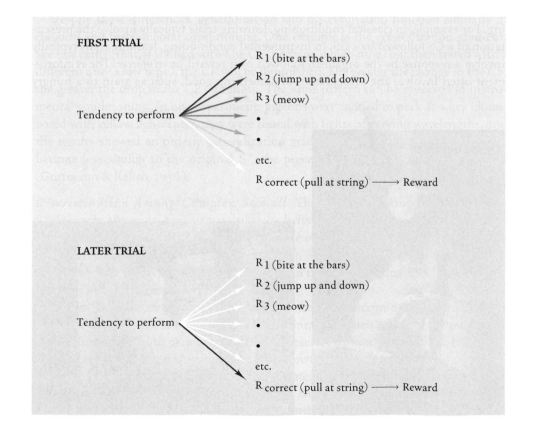

6.11 The law of effect The figure is a schematic presentation of Thorndike's theory of instrumental learning. On the first trial, the tendency to perform various incorrect responses (biting the bars, jumping up and down) is very strong, while the tendency to perform the correct response (pulling the string) is weak or nonexistent. As trials proceed, the strength of these responses changes. The incorrect responses become weaker and weaker, for none of these responses is immediately followed by reward. In contrast, there is a progressive strengthening of the correct response because this is followed more or less immediately by reward.

(Herrnstein, Loveland, & Cable, 1976). Apparently, then, pigeons are capable of discriminating relatively abstract categories, categories not defined in terms of a few simple perceptual features. Similar procedures have shown that pigeons can discriminate between pictures showing trees and pictures not showing trees; thus, for example, they will learn to peck in response to a picture of a leaf-covered tree or a tree bare of leaves, but not to peck in response to a picture of a telephone pole or a picture of a celery stalk. Likewise, pigeons can learn to peck whenever they are shown a picture of a particular human, whether photographed from one angle and close up, or from a very different angle, from far away, and wearing different clothes (Herrnstein, 1979; Lea & Ryan, 1990; for other examples of complex discriminations, see Cook, Cavoto, & Cavoto, 1995; Giurfa et al., 2001; Lazareva, Freiburger, & Wasserman, 2004; Premack, 1976, 1978; Premack & Premack, 1983; Reiss & Marino, 2001; Wasserman, Hugart, & Kirkpatrick-Steger, 1995; Zentall, 2000).

Let us be careful, though, not to overstate the competence revealed by these studies. Pigeons can apparently recognize pictures of water, but do they truly understand the concept *water*? Can they draw conclusions about the concept or use the concept in their reasoning? The answer is probably no; thus, what the pigeons understand about water is a far cry from the sort of understanding humans have for this (or any other) concept. Even so, what the pigeons can do is impressive, and it reminds us of the sophisticated discriminations animals can make in guiding their behavior.

SHAPING

Once a response has been made, reinforcement will act to strengthen it: Once the hypochondriac groans, others can express support, strengthening the response of groaning; once the pigeon pecks the key, food can be delivered, making the next peck more likely. But what causes the animal to perform the desired response in the first place? What leads to the first groan or the first peck? This is no problem for some responses. Pecking, for example, is the sort of thing pigeons do all the time, providing frequent opportunities for a trainer to reinforce (and thus encourage) this response; likewise for rats pressing and manipulating easily reachable objects in their environment.

But what about less-obvious responses? For example, we could place a lever so high that the rat must stretch up on its hind legs to reach it. Now the rat might never press the lever on its own. Nonetheless, it can learn this response if its behavior is suitably *shaped*. This is accomplished by a little "coaching," using the method of *successive approximations*.

How could we train a rat to press the elevated lever? At first, we reinforce the animal merely for walking into the general area where the lever is located. As soon as the rat is there, we deliver food. After a few such trials, the rat will have learned to remain in this neighborhood virtually all the time, allowing us to increase our demand. When the rat is in this neighborhood, sometimes it is facing one way, sometimes another; from this point on, though, the rat is reinforced only if it is in the area and facing the lever. This response also is soon mastered, so that the rat is now facing in the right direction most of the time. Again, therefore, we increase our demand: Sometimes the rat is facing the lever with its nose to the ground; sometimes it is facing the lever with its head elevated. We now reinforce the animal only in the latter situation, and soon this, too, is a well-established response. We continue in this fashion, counting on the fact that, at each step, the rat naturally varies its behavior somewhat, allowing us to reinforce just those variations we prefer. Thus, we can gradually move toward reinforcing the rat only when it stretches up to the lever, then when it actually touches the lever, and so on. Step by step, we move the rat toward the desired response.

By means of this technique, animals have been trained to perform all kinds of complex behavior (Figure 6.14), and closely related techniques have been used outside of the lab with humans. For example, how do parents in Western countries teach their children to

6.14 *Show-business animals* *Nhat is a four-year-old monkey performing with the Hanoi Circus who was trained using techniques closely related to the ones described here—a process of gradual shaping, leading to the desired response.*

eat with knife and fork? At first, the child is rewarded (probably with smiles and praise) merely for holding these implements. This will soon establish a grasp-the-fork operant, and, at that point, the parents can raise the ante: Now the child will be praised just when she touches her food with the fork, and, thanks to this reinforcement, soon this new operant is established. If the parents continue in this fashion, gradually increasing their expectations, the child will soon be eating in the "proper" way.

Similar techniques are often used in therapeutic settings to shape the behavior of the hospitalized mentally ill. Initially, the hospitalized patients might be rewarded merely for getting out of bed. Then, once that behavior is established, the requirement is increased so that, perhaps, the patients have to move around a bit in their room and then, later, to step out of the room and go to breakfast or to get their medicine. In this fashion, the behavior therapist can gradually lead the patients into a fuller, more acceptable level of functioning (see Chapter 17).

WHAT IS A REINFORCER?

We have now said a great deal about what reinforcement can achieve—encouraging some responses, discouraging others, and also (through the process of shaping) creating entirely new responses. But what is it that makes a stimulus serve as a reinforcer?

Some stimuli serve as reinforcers because of their biological significance. These so-called *primary reinforcers* include food, water, escape from the scent of a predator, and so on—all stimuli with obvious biological importance. Other reinforcers are social in nature—for example, the smiles and praise from parents that we mentioned in our example of a child learning to use knife and fork.

Other stimuli are initially neutral in their value but come to act as reinforcers because they have, in the experience of the animal, been repeatedly paired with some other, already established reinforcer. A stimulus in this latter category is called a *conditioned reinforcer*, and it functions just as any other reinforcer would.

Still other reinforcers fall into none of these categories, a point that requires us to broaden our conception of what a reinforcer is. Pigeons, for example, will peck in order to gain *information* about the availability of food (see, for example, Bower, McLean, & Meachem, 1966; Hendry, 1969). Monkeys will work merely to open a small window through which they can see a moving toy train (Butler, 1954). And, in general, animals will respond simply to gain the opportunity to engage in some other, more preferred activity—for instance, press a lever in order to run inside an exercise wheel (Premack, 1965; but also Timberlake & Allison, 1974; Timberlake, 1995).

These (and many other) examples make reinforcement difficult to define; as a consequence, the term *reinforcement* is generally defined only after the fact. Is a glimpse of a toy train reinforcing? We can find out only by asking whether an animal will work to obtain this glimpse. Remarkably, no other more informative definition of a reinforcer is available.

BEHAVIORAL CONTRAST AND INTRINSIC MOTIVATION

Similar complexities arise when we consider the *magnitude* of a reinforcer. It is no surprise that an animal will respond more strongly for a large reward than for a small one. What counts as large or small, however, depends on the context. If a rat is used to getting 60 food pellets for a response, then 16 pellets will seem measly, and the animal will respond only weakly for this puny reward. But if a rat is used to getting only 4 pellets for a response, then 16 pellets will seem like a feast, and the rat's response will be fast and strong (see, for example, Crespi, 1942). Thus, the effectiveness of a reinforcer will depend to a large extent on what other rewards are available (or have recently been available). This pattern is referred to as *behavioral contrast*.

Contrast effects are important for their own sake, but they may also provide a partial explanation for another phenomenon called *intrinsic motivation*. In an early study of

Shaping new behaviors **Parents use the technique of shaping to teach their children to eat with utensils. At first, the child is praised simply for holding the implements. Once that is mastered, the child is praised for using the implements to touch her food. The demands are gradually increased, so that the child's behavior comes more and more to meet the "standard" pattern of using the proper utensils.**

A *variable-interval (VI) schedule* differs from an FI schedule in the same way that a VR schedule differs from an FR schedule. For a VI schedule, reinforcement occurs on average only after some specified interval. However, the actual interval varies unpredictably from trial to trial. An example would be the pattern of rewards available to a predator: If the predator has recently visited a particular part of the forest, then all of the prey animals will probably have fled, so there is no point in continuing to hunt in that area. After a while, though, the prey will return, so a predator's next visit to that area will be rewarded with food. However, the timing of the prey's return will vary—perhaps 24 hours on average, but sometimes less and sometimes more. Hence the predator's return to that part of the forest will be rewarded on a VI schedule.

PUNISHMENT

Our discussion of reinforcement has so far centered on cases of reward, in which responding brings something good. But what about the other side of things, in which a behavior is followed by some bad consequence—perhaps a startling noise for a laboratory rat, or a stern "No!" for a naughty child? How do these consequences affect behavior?

Not surprisingly, punishment is a powerful means of shaping behavior. Specifically, if a response is followed by some aversive event, then that response is less likely to occur in the future. Moreover, more intense punishers (a more painful shock, a louder burst of noise) are more effective in suppressing behavior than less intense punishers. One might conclude, therefore, that, to maximize the effect of punishment, the punishing stimulus should be as intense as possible. Obviously, though, ethical considerations enter the discussion here. An intense punishment might well be judged cruel, even if that punishment is effective in stopping an animal from some destructive behavior. This trade-off between cruelty and effectiveness must be evaluated in any case involving punishment.

Common sense suggests one way to deal with this trade-off, but, in this context, common sense actually leads us astray. Imagine a parent who wishes to stop his child from engaging in some dangerous behavior—perhaps bicycling in traffic without a helmet. To avoid issues of cruelty, the parent might begin with some relatively mild punishment for this behavior, hoping that that is sufficient. If it is not, the parent might slowly escalate the punishment, continuing until he finds the minimal level of punishment (and so the minimal level of cruelty) that will achieve the goal.

Attractive as this strategy might be, the evidence suggests it is ill advised: Punishments that are introduced in mild form and then gradually intensified turn out to be markedly less effective than punishments that are introduced at "full strength" from the start. The hypothetical parent we have just described, therefore, will probably end up delivering more punishment than he might have had he used a strong punishment from the start. (For evidence on this point, see, for example, Azrin & Holz, 1966; Church, 1969. For further discussion of the principles that influence the effectiveness of punishment, and the sometimes complex interplay between the use of punishment and ethical considerations, see Schwartz, Wasserman, & Robbins, 2002.)

CHANGING BEHAVIORS
OR ACQUIRING KNOWLEDGE?

We have almost finished our discussion of instrumental conditioning, but one crucial point remains: What is it exactly that animals learn in an instrumental conditioning procedure? The law of effect implies that the learning is best understood as a change in behavior, with responses either being strengthened or weakened by the mechanical effects of reinforcement. From the earliest days of learning theory, however, there was an alternative view of conditioning, one that asserted that learning is not the change in behavior as such, but is instead the acquisition of new knowledge. One of the most prominent exponents of this view was Edward C. Tolman (1886–1959). As Tolman saw it, the response an animal acquires in the course of a learning experiment is crucial because it provides us with an indication that new knowledge has been gained. But it is the cognition, and not the response, that is the essence of what is learned (Dickinson, 1987).

Powerful evidence for Tolman's position comes from cases of *latent learning*—that is, learning that takes place without any corresponding change in behavior. Latent learning makes no sense if learning is essentially a matter of the strengthening or weakening of responses, but it makes perfect sense if we instead conceive of learning as the acquisition of knowledge that may or may not be expressed in how the animal acts.

Edward C. Tolman

An example of latent learning comes from an experiment in which rats were allowed to explore a maze, without any reward, for 10 days. During these days, there was no detectable change in the rats' behavior, but learning was nonetheless taking place: The rats were learning how to navigate the maze's corridors. This became obvious on the 11th day, when food was placed in the maze's goal box for the first time. The rats learned to run to this goal box, virtually without error, almost immediately. The knowledge they had acquired earlier now took on motivational significance, so the animals swiftly displayed what they already knew (Tolman & Honzik, 1930; also Gleitman, 1963; Tolman, 1948).

This work with rats implies that they can create a *cognitive map* of the world—a mental representation of spatial layout that indicates what is where and what leads to what. Whether the rats will reveal this map, however, depends on other factors—such as whether this knowledge of the world's layout matters for them in some way. In fact, many species rely on such maps—to guide their foraging for food, their navigation to points of safety, and their choice of a path to the watering hole. These maps can be relatively complex and are typically quite accurate. And these maps can also be quickly learned. This is demonstrated, for example, in a study that involved the chimpanzee version of an Easter-egg hunt. In the study, the experimenter carried the animal in his arms while moving around a large enclosure. As they moved along, the experimenter's assistant accompanied them and hid pieces of fruit at various locations. The chimpanzee was not allowed to do anything during this tour, but merely watched as the bits of food were hidden. Nonetheless, the moment the chimp was set down and allowed to move on its own, it dashed from one hiding place to the next, locating and eating the fruit. It had obviously learned—and remembered—the 18 locations after just one trial of passive observation (Menzel, 1973, 1978; for evidence of cognitive maps in other creatures, including invertebrates, see Gallistel, 1994; Gould, 1990).

ACT-OUTCOME REPRESENTATIONS

Cognitive maps are one sort of knowledge animals gain through learning. Animals also acquire knowledge about the specific relationships between their actions and the outcomes of those actions—in other words, they acquire knowledge that can be referred to as an *act-outcome representation* (Tolman, 1932). This knowledge can then be demonstrated in many ways. In one study, rats were trained to make two different responses, each of which produced a different reward. On some days, their experimental chamber contained a lever that projected from one wall. If the animals pressed this lever, they were rewarded with a food pellet. On other days, a chain dangled from the ceiling. If the rats pulled this chain, they were rewarded with a few drops of sugar water.

After a few days of training, the rats were busily lever-pressing and chain-pulling, indicating that instrumental learning had been effective. But what was it that had been learned? One possibility is that the rats had simply acquired a tendency to perform these two responses. Another is that they acquired some knowledge—that lever-pressing leads to food pellets and chain-pulling leads to sugar water.

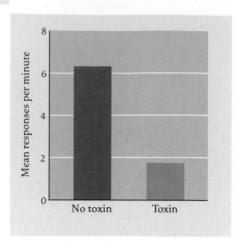

6.15 *Act-outcome cognitions* *The figure shows the results on the final test of an experiment in which two different responses were reinforced by two different food rewards. Once this learned relationship was established, one of the two rewards was paired with a toxin. There was a marked decline in the response leading to the reward that was devalued by the toxin (in green) as compared with the response leading to the reward that was not devalued (red).*

To decide between these alternatives, the experimenters changed the attractiveness of one of the rewards. They allowed the rats to drink some of the sugar water, but then gave them injections of a mild toxin. This created a taste aversion for the sugar (but not for the pellets), so that the rats no longer found the sugar water desirable. (For more on taste aversions, see pp. 222–224.) What effects would this have when the animals were next given the chance to press a lever or pull a chain? The results showed that the rats continued to press the lever to obtain food but no longer pulled the chain. Clearly, the animals had learned which response led to which reward (Colwill & Rescorla, 1985; Rescorla, 1991, 1993a, b; Figure 6.15).

CONTINGENCY IN INSTRUMENTAL CONDITIONING

An organism's cognition is also relevant to instrumental conditioning for another reason. Recall that, in our discussion of classical conditioning, we saw that learning does not depend just on the CS being paired with the US; instead, the CS needs to be *predictive* of the US, telling the animal when the US is more likely, and when less. In the same fashion, instrumental conditioning does not just depend on responses being paired with rewards. Instead, the response needs to be predictive of the reward, so that (for example) the probability of getting a pellet after a lever press is greater than the probability of getting it without the press.

What matters for instrumental conditioning, therefore, is not merely the fact that a reward arrives after the response is made. Instead, what matters is the relationship between responding and getting the reward, and this relationship actually gives the animal some control over the reward: By choosing when to respond, the animal can itself determine when the reward will be delivered. And it turns out that this control is important, because animals can tell when they're in control and when they're not, and they clearly prefer being in control.

One line of evidence comes from a study in which human infants were placed in cribs above which a colorful mobile was suspended. Whenever the infants moved their heads, they closed a switch in their pillows; this activated the overhead mobile, which spun merrily for a second or so. The infants soon learned to shake their heads about, making their mobiles turn. They evidently enjoyed this, smiling and cooing at their mobiles, clearly delighted to see the mobiles move.

A second group of infants was exposed to a similar situation, but with one important difference: Their mobile turned just as often as the mobile for the first group, but it was moved for them, not by them. This turned out to be crucial. After a few days, these infants no longer smiled and cooed at the mobile, nor did they seem particularly interested when it turned. This suggests that what the first group of infants liked about the mobile was not that it moved, but that they made it move. Even a 2-month-old infant wants to be the master of his own fate (Watson, 1967; Figure 6.16).

6.16 *Response control* *Infants who can make a mobile move smile and coo at it, while those who have no control over its motion stop smiling.*

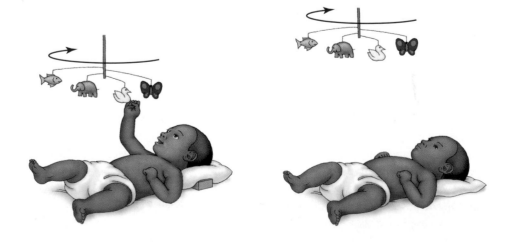

This study with infants illustrates the joy of mastery. Another series of studies demonstrates the despair of no mastery at all. The focus of these studies is on **learned helplessness**, an acquired sense that one has lost control over one's environment, with the sad consequence that one gives up trying (Seligman, 1975).

The classic experiment on learned helplessness used two groups of dogs, A and B, which received strong electric shocks while strapped in a hammock. The dogs in group A were able to exert some control over their situation. They could turn the shock off whenever it began simply by pushing a panel that was placed close to their noses. The dogs in group B had no such power. For them, the shocks were inescapable. But the number and duration of these shocks were the same as for the first group. This was guaranteed by the fact that, for each dog in group A, there was a corresponding animal in group B whose fate was yoked to that of the first dog. Whenever the group A dog was shocked, so was the group B dog. Whenever the group A dog turned off the shock, the shock was turned off for the group B dog. Thus, the physical suffering meted out to both groups was identical; what differed was what the animals could do about it. The dogs in group A were able to exercise some control; those in group B could only endure.

What did the group B dogs learn in this situation? To find out, both groups of dogs were next presented with a task in which they had to learn to jump from one compartment to another to avoid a shock (Figure 6.17). The dogs in group A learned this task easily. During the first few trials, these dogs ran about frantically when the shock began but eventually scrambled over the hurdle into the other compartment. Better still, they quickly learned to jump when they heard a tone signaling that shock was soon to begin, and in this way they learned to avoid the shock entirely. Things were different, though, for the dogs in group B, those who had previously experienced the inescapable shock. Initially, these dogs behaved much like any others, running about, barking, and so on. But they soon became much more passive. They lay down, whined, and simply took whatever shocks were delivered. They neither avoided nor escaped; they just gave up trying. In the first phase of this experiment, they really had been objectively helpless; there truly was nothing they could do. But in the shuttle box, their helplessness was only subjective, for there was now a way in which they could make their lot bearable. But they never discovered it. They had learned to be helpless (Seligman & Maier, 1967).

Martin Seligman (b. 1942), one of the discoverers of the learned-helplessness effect, asserts that a similar mechanism underlies the development of depression in humans. Like the helpless dog, Seligman argues, the depressed patient has come to believe that her acts are uniformly futile. And Seligman maintains that, like the dog, the depressed patient has reached this morbid state because of an exposure to a situation in which she really was helpless. While the dog received inescapable shocks in its hammock, the patient found herself powerless in the face of bereavement, some career failure, or serious illness (Seligman, Klein, & Miller, 1976). In both cases, the outcome is the same—a belief that there is no contingency between acts and outcomes, and so no point in trying. (For more on this theory of depression, see Chapter 16.)*

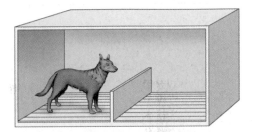

6.17   Shuttle-box avoidance   The animal in this chamber hears a tone, followed by an electric shock. Most animals swiftly learn to escape from the shock by simply hopping over the barrier, onto the other side of the chamber. Better still, most animals soon learn to hop over the barrier the moment they hear the tone—and, in that fashion, they avoid the shock altogether. However, animals who have been through a learned-helplessness procedure seem unable to learn this simple response. Instead, they passively lie down, whine, and suffer through the electric shock.

---

* Before moving on, we should mention that studies of learned helplessness in dogs—like many studies mentioned in this chapter—raise ethical questions. Is it ethically acceptable to deliver electric shock to animals? Is it acceptable given the fact that, in some circumstances, the shock produces a depressionlike state in the animals? These are difficult and worrisome questions, but the link between these studies and human depression may provide an answer. These studies may well help us to understand human depression and lead to more effective forms of treatment for, or even prevention of, depression. These considerations persuade many investigators that the animal work, as troubling as it is, is necessary as a means of working toward the goal of diminishing human suffering.

VARIETIES OF LEARNING

Overall, then, the attempt to find general principles of learning, principles that apply to all species and are independent of what is being learned, has been reasonably successful. Humans are, of course, capable of behaviors and cognitions far more complex than those produced by other animals. But, even so, we seem governed by principles of habituation, classical conditioning, and operant conditioning, no less than other species. On this basis, we have gained insights into human depression by studying helplessness in dogs, and we have increased our understanding of human reactions to drugs thanks to research on classical conditioning in rats.

We must acknowledge, though, that there are also important differences from one species to the next in how learning proceeds. These differences are often best understood by taking a biological perspective on learning, a perspective that highlights the actual *function* of learning in each species' natural environment (see, for example, Bolles & Beecher, 1988; Domjan, 2005; Rozin & Schull, 1988).

BIOLOGICAL INFLUENCES ON LEARNING: BELONGINGNESS

In the early days of learning theory, there was a widespread belief that animals (whether human or not) are capable of connecting any CS to any US (in classical conditioning) and of associating virtually any response with any reinforcer (in instrumental conditioning). A dog could be taught that a tone signaled the approach of food or that a flashing light or a particular smell did. Likewise, a rat could be trained to press a lever to get food, water, or access to a sexually receptive mate.

Much evidence, however, speaks against this idea; instead, each species seems predisposed to form some associations and not others. The predispositions put **biological constraints** on that species' learning, governing what the species can learn easily and what it can learn only with difficulty. These associative predispositions are probably hardwired, a direct product of our evolutionary past, and are helpful for each species in light of the requirements of the environment in which it evolved (Rozin & Kalat, 1971, 1972; Seligman & Hager, 1972).

TASTE-AVERSION LEARNING

From an animal's point of view, some stimuli belong together and some do not. Evidence for this pattern of **belongingness** comes from many sources, including an effect we have already mentioned: **learned taste aversion** (Domjan, 1983, 2005; Garcia & Koelling, 1966).

When a wild rat encounters a novel food, it generally takes only a small bite at first. If the rat suffers no ill effects from this first taste, it will return (perhaps a day or two later) for a second helping and will gradually make the food a part of its regular diet. But what if the food is harmful—either because of some natural toxin, or because it contains poison put there by an exterminator? In that case, the initial taste will make the rat sick, but, because it ate only a little of the food, the rat will probably recover. And, based on this experience, the rat is likely to develop a strong aversion to that particular flavor, so it never returns for a second "dose" of the poison.

Similar effects are easily observed in the laboratory. The subjects, usually rats, are presented with a food or drink that has a novel flavor—perhaps water with some vanilla added. After drinking this flavored water, the rats are exposed to X-ray radiation—not enough to injure them, but enough to make them ill. After they recover, the rats show a strong aversion to the taste of vanilla, and they refuse to drink water flavored in this way.

This sort of learned taste aversion seems to be based on classical conditioning. The CS is a certain flavor (here, vanilla), and the US is the sensation of being sick. In this case, though, the classical conditioning is rapid: One pairing of CS and US is enough to establish the connection between them. Researchers call this *one-trial learning*, a speed of learning much faster than that of ordinary classical conditioning (p. 201). In addition, this conditioning is distinctive in other ways. For example, in most classical conditioning, the CS must be soon followed by the US; if too much time passes between these two stimuli, the likelihood of conditioning is much reduced. In taste-aversion learning, in contrast, conditioning can be observed even if several hours elapse between the CS and the US.

Learned taste aversions are also remarkable for their specificity. In one early study, thirsty rats were allowed to drink sweetened water through a drinking tube. Whenever the rats licked the nozzle of this tube, a bright light flashed and a loud clicking noise sounded. Thus, the sensations of sweetness, bright light, and loud noise were always grouped together; if one was presented, all were presented. Some time later, one group of these rats received an electric shock to the feet. A second group was exposed to a dose of X rays strong enough to produce illness.

Notice, then, that we have two different USs—illness for one group and foot shock for the other. In addition, both groups have received a three-part CS: sweet + bright + noisy. The question is: How will the animals put these pieces together—what will get associated with what?

To find out, the experimenters tested the rats in a new situation. They gave some of the rats water that was saccharin-flavored but unaccompanied by either light or noise. Rats that had received foot shock showed no inclination to avoid this water; apparently, they did not associate foot shock with the sweet flavor. However, rats that had been made ill with X rays refused to drink the sweet water even though the light and noise were absent. They associated their illness with the taste (Table 6.1).

Other rats were tested with plain, unflavored water accompanied by the light and sound cues that were present during training. Now the pattern was reversed. Rats that had become ill showed no objection to this water; they did not associate illness with sights and sounds. Rats that had been shocked refused it; in their minds, pain was associated with bright lights and loud clicks (Garcia & Koelling, 1966).

For the rat, therefore, taste goes with illness, sights and sounds with externally induced pain. And for this species, this pattern makes good biological sense. Illness in wild rats is likely to have been caused by harmful or tainted food, and rats generally select their food largely on the basis of flavor. There is survival value, therefore, in the rats being able to learn quickly about the connection between a particular flavor and illness; this will provide useful information for them as they select their next meal, and it ensures that they do not resample harmful berries or poisoned meat.

TABLE 6.1 BELONGINGNESS IN CLASSICAL CONDITIONING

Training In all groups: CS = saccharine taste + light + sound

US used in training:	Shock		X-ray illness	
Test stimulus:	Saccharine taste	Light + sound	Saccharine taste	Light + sound
Results:	No effect	Aversion	Aversion	No effect

Imitation

Another crucial example is the human capacity for *observational learning*—a process through which we watch how others behave, and we learn from their example. Part of observational learning is *imitation*, a capacity that can be demonstrated in young infants almost from birth. And part of the learning is the capacity to observe which actions in others lead to desirable outcomes and which do not, and then to apply the lessons learned from this to one's own behavior (e.g., Bandura, 1977, 1986).

Without question, other species are also capable of observational learning (e.g., Bugnyar & Kotrschal, 2002; White & Galef, 1998), although the data suggest that this learning is limited to a narrow repertoire of behaviors. In humans, in contrast, observational learning is vastly better—allowing rapid learning of a huge range of responses—and may be a crucial element in how we gain new skills, how we learn to act in social settings, and more.

SIMILARITIES IN WHAT DIFFERENT SPECIES LEARN

Overall, then, we are driven to the perhaps not-surprising claim that there are differences in how species learn, and also similarities. The differences make good biological sense, since, after all, different species live in different environments, need different skills, and thus may need to learn in different ways. But what about the similarities? To put the matter concretely, the rats and pigeons we study in the laboratory do not gather food the way a human does. They do not communicate with their fellows the way a human does. They also have nervous systems that are appreciably simpler than ours. It would not be surprising, therefore, if they learned in different ways than we do. Yet, as we have repeatedly noted, the major phenomena of both classical and instrumental conditioning are found in us just as they are in rats and pigeons (Couvillon & Bitterman, 1980).

How should we think about this point? The answer lies in the fact that various creatures, no matter what their evolutionary history might be, and no matter what ecological niche they inhabit, all share certain needs. Thus, for example, virtually all creatures are better off if they can prepare themselves for upcoming events, and, to do this, they need some means of anticipating what will happen to them in the near future. This anticipation is made possible by the fact that some events are predictable from other events, so it is no wonder that many species have learned to exploit that predictability and are, therefore, capable of classical conditioning.

Similarly, in the world we all inhabit, important outcomes are often influenced by one's behavior, so it pays for all species to repeat actions that have worked well in the past and to abandon actions that have not been successful. Hence we might expect natural selection to favor mechanisms that would allow creatures to learn about the consequences of their actions and to adjust their future acts accordingly. It is these mechanisms that allow instrumental conditioning.

In this fashion, there are straightforward, pragmatic reasons why principles of learning are (and perhaps must be) shared from one species to the next. Thus, our account of learning will include important species differences in how learning proceeds, but it must also include general principles such as those governing classical and instrumental conditioning. Organisms do differ in their learning capacities, but we can also find principles that describe learning in an extraordinary range of species and settings.

THE NEURAL BASIS FOR LEARNING

In short, then, different species all need to learn roughly the same lessons, and this is why we can identify principles of learning that apply with equal force to ants, bats, cows, dolphins, and humans. But, even so, the biological mechanisms that allow this learning may vary considerably from one animal to the next. Evidence suggests, for example, that the mechanisms that allow learning in mammals are different from the mechanisms crucial for reptiles, amphibians, or inverebrates (Macphail, 1996; Woolf, 1998). Indeed, even within a single species, the biological mechanisms needed for learning can vary and seem to depend on the CS, the US, and the procedure (Clark, Manns, & Squire, 2003; Fanselow & Poulos, 2005). Thus, the brain circuits underlying fear conditioning (with electric shock as the US) are centered in the amygdala; the brain circuits underlying eyeblink conditioning (with a puff of air to the eye as the US) are centered in the cerebellum. Conditioning with a long delay between the CS and US typically involves the hippocampus; conditioning with a shorter delay may not require the hippocampus. And so on (Berman & Dudai, 2001; Lattal, Honarvar, & Abel, 2004).

Even with these variations, though, some biological principles do apply to all cases of learning. In all cases, learning depends on *neural plasticity*—the capacity for neurons to change the way they function as a consequence of experience. And this plasticity, in turn, is in general made possible by three types of change. First, learning can produce an increase in the neurotransmitter released by the presynaptic neuron, so that in essence a stronger signal is sent after learning than before. Second, learning can produce an increase in the sensitivity of the postsynaptic neuron, so that the neuron comes to respond to signals that had little impact before learning. And, third, learning can lead to the creation of entirely new synapses, allowing for new lines of communication among neurons.

Evidence for plasticity in presynaptic neurons comes from many sources, including studies of the marine mollusk *Aplysia*. These creatures have simple nervous systems, with a mere 20,000 neurons or so, and are therefore good candidates for detailed scrutiny and analysis. And, crucially, *Aplysia* are also capable of a simple form of associative learning, allowing us to examine the neural changes that support this learning. Studies have revealed that, after conditioning, the *Aplysia*'s sensory neurons—the neurons that received the CS—literally release more neurotransmitter than they did before the conditioning trials; this is why, at the end of learning, these neurons are able to trigger a new response—the CR (e.g., Lisman, 2003; Pittenger & Kandel, 2003).

Other forms of neural plasticity, in other organisms, involve postsynaptic changes—that is, they influence the receiving side of the synapse. A particularly important mechanism in this category is *long-term potentiation (LTP)* (Bliss & Lomo, 1973; Martinez & Derrick, 1996)—"potentiation" because the mechanism involves an increase in the responsiveness of a neuron (an increase in the neuron's potential for firing) and "long term" because this potentiation lasts for days, perhaps even weeks. (A closely related phenomenon is long-term depression, or LTD, which involves a *decrease* in a neuron's responsiveness, caused by experience.)

LTP is produced when one neuron stimulates another over and over and over. The repeated stimulation causes the postsynaptic neuron to become more sensitive to this

- When training an animal using *instrumental* (or *operant*) *conditioning*, a reward or *reinforcement* is only delivered upon performance of the appropriate response. According to Thorndike, learning in this situation is governed by the *law of effect*, which states that the tendency to perform a response is strengthened if it is followed by a reward and weakened if it is not.
- *Operants* are voluntary responses, strengthened by reinforcement, but their acquisition may require some initial *shaping*, through a method of *successive approximations*.
- While some reinforcers are stimuli whose reinforcing power is unlearned, other *conditioned reinforcers* acquire their power from prior presentations with stimuli that already have that capacity. The magnitude of a reinforcer depends on several factors, including the magnitude of other reinforcers that might be available. This is reflected in the phenomenon of *behavioral contrast*, and it may be one source of findings sometimes attributed to *intrinsic motivation*. Some theorists, however, believe that intrinsic motivation involves a separate set of principles, different from those that govern operant conditioning.
- During *partial reinforcement*, the response is reinforced only some of the time. The rule that determines when a reinforcer is given is called a *schedule of reinforcement*. In *ratio schedules*, reinforcement is delivered after a number of responses; the ratio that is used may be fixed or variable. In *interval schedules*, reinforcers are delivered for the first response made after a given interval since the last reinforcement, and this interval, too, can be fixed or variable.
- Learning involves more than a change in behavior; it also involves the acquistion of new knowledge. This is evident in *latent learning*, and also in data that suggest that the animal acquires *act-outcome representations*.
- Operant conditioning results when reinforcement is contingent on a response, and not merely when reinforcement happens to be contiguous with responding. Organisms' sensitivity to contingency can be demonstrated in many ways, including via the phenomenon of *learned helplessness*, in which animals seem to learn that they have no control over the events they are experiencing.

- According to the early *learning theorists*, just about any CS can become associated with any US, and just about any response can be strengthened by any reinforcer. This assertion is challenged by the fact that certain conditioned stimuli are more readily associated with some unconditioned stimuli than with others, as shown by studies of *learned taste aversions*. These studies suggest that animals are biologically prepared to learn certain relations more readily than others. Similar effects occur in instrumental conditioning, with some responses more readily strengthened by some reinforcers than by others.
- According to some investigators, certain forms of learning are *species-specific*; they cite evidence that some animals can readily learn what others cannot. In humans, specialized forms of learning may include our capacity for learning language, and also our remarkable ability to learn by observing others.
- Even though animals vary in how (and what) they learn, there are also striking similarities in diverse species in some aspects of learning. These similarities probably derive from the fact that all organisms live in the same world, and the nature of the world creates a need in many species for the forms of learning we call classical and operant conditioning.

THE NEURAL BASIS FOR LEARNING

- In recent years, investigators have made considerable progress in understanding the neural bases for learning. These bases involve diverse mechanisms, including *presynaptic facilitation*, and also *postsynaptic changes* such as *long-term potentiation* (*LTP*). Still another mechanism involves the creation of new synapses, made possible by the growth of new *dendritic spines*, which act as "receiving stations" for synapses and open new lines of communication between cellular neighbors.

your life—and, with that, your mood and your self-esteem—is dependent on memory.

It is no wonder, then, that psychologists regard the study of memory as a topic of enormous importance, and there are many questions about memory that need to be addressed: How accurate and complete are our memories? Does everything we experience get stored in memory, or is memory somehow selective? Why do we forget? Are there things we can do to help ourselves remember? Let us look at what psychologists have learned about these crucial questions. ●

ACQUISITION, STORAGE, RETRIEVAL

Using memory   Games (like the card game "Memory") obviously depend on what we remember. But memory also matters for a wide range of other functions—including functions that seem, on first inspection, not to depend on remembering at all.

Each of us has a huge number of memories. We can recall what we did yesterday, or last summer. We can remember what the capital of France is, or what the chemical formula is for water. We remember how to ride a bicycle, how to tie our shoes, and how to throw a baseball. It turns out that these various examples—remembering *episodes*, remembering *general facts*, and remembering *skills* or *procedures*—all draw on different memory systems; but it also turns out that these various types of memory all have some things in common, and it will be useful for us to begin with those common elements.

Any act of remembering requires success at three aspects of the memory process. First, in order to remember, you must learn something—that is, you must put some information into your memory. This seems an obvious point, but it deserves emphasis because many failures of memory are, in fact, failures in this initial stage of *acquisition*. For example, imagine meeting someone at a party, being told his name, and moments later realizing that you no longer know it! This common (but embarrassing) experience is probably not the result of ultrarapid forgetting. Instead, it is likely to stem from a failure in acquisition. You were exposed to the name but barely paid attention to it and, as a result, never learned it in the first place.

The next aspect of remembering is **storage**. To be remembered, an experience must leave some record in the nervous system (the *memory trace*); it must be squirreled away and held in some enduring form for later use. One question to be asked here is how *permanent* this storage is: Once information is in storage, does it stay there forever? Or does information in storage gradually fade away? We will tackle these questions later in this chapter.

The final aspect of remembering is *retrieval*, the process through which you draw information from storage and use it in some fashion. Retrieval can actually take many forms. For example, *recall* is a task in which you draw information from memory in response to some cue or question. Trying to answer a question like "What is Sue's boyfriend's name?" or "Can you remember the last time you were in California?" requires recall. A different way to retrieve information is through *recognition*. In this kind of retrieval, you are presented with a name, fact, or situation and are asked if you have encountered it before. "Is this the man you saw at the bank robbery?" or "Was the movie you saw called *Memento*?" are questions requiring recognition. Recognition can also be tested with multiple items: "Which of these pictures is the one you saw earlier?" This latter format obviously resembles a multiple-choice exam, and, in fact, multiple-choice testing in the classroom probes your ability to recognize previously learned material. In contrast, exams that rely on essays or short answers emphasize recall.

ACQUISITION

People commonly speak of "memorizing" new facts or, more broadly, of "learning" new material. However, psychologists prefer the term *memory acquisition*, using it to include cases of deliberate memorization (*intentional learning*) and also cases of *incidental learning*, learning that takes place without any intention to learn and often without the awareness that learning is actually occurring. (You know that grass is green and the sky is blue, and you probably can easily recall what you had for dinner yesterday, but you did not set out to memorize these facts; the learning, therefore, was incidental.)

As we will see, memory acquisition is not a simple matter of "copying" an event or a fact into memory, the way a camera copies an image onto film. Instead, acquisition requires some attention to the to-be-remembered material, and some intellectual engagement with the material—thinking about it in some way. It is the product of this engagement—what you thought about during the to-be-remembered event—that is stored in memory. In a sense, then, memory acquisition involves a translation process, translating the raw input into some intellectual record of the input. Investigators call this process *memory encoding*; thus, we acquire memories by placing encoded information into storage.

THE STAGE THEORY OF MEMORY

How does memory acquisition proceed? The *stage theory of memory*, developed roughly 50 years ago, provides an answer, proposing that, in fact, we have several types of memory, each with different properties, so that memory acquisition is a process of moving memories from one (temporary) store into another (more permanent) resting place (Atkinson & Shiffrin, 1968; Broadbent, 1958; Waugh & Norman, 1965).

Why would we need several kinds of memory? When we are actively working with information, we want the information to be immediately available to us. As an analogy, think about how you spread your notes out on your desktop when you are working on a paper or studying for an exam; that way, the information you need is instantly accessible. The mental equivalent of this is *working memory* (called *short-term memory* in the original theory), a memory that holds onto the information you are working with right now.

But, at the same time, you do not want to put too many things on your desktop. If you did (if, for example, you placed every book you owned out on the desk), then you would start losing track of what's there, and that would destroy the advantage you were seeking—having instant access to the information you are now using. That is why you sensibly leave the books you are not using right now on your bookshelves. In that way, you give up instant access to what's in the books, but you also won't be distracted or overburdened by this extra information, and this allows you to focus on your more immediate tasks. The mental equivalent of your bookshelves is *long-term memory*—the huge repository that contains everything you know, a mostly "dormant" storage for information you are not using right now but may need later.

THE STORAGE CAPACITY OF WORKING AND LONG-TERM MEMORY

Working memory and long-term memory differ in many important ways, including the *storage capacity* of each. The capacity of long-term memory is enormous. The average college student remembers the meanings of 80,000 words, thousands of autobiographical episodes, millions of facts, hundreds of skills, the taste of vanilla, and the smell of lemon. All of this and more are stored in long-term memory.

In contrast, the capacity of working memory is sharply limited. Traditionally, this capacity has been measured by a *memory span* task in which the individual hears a

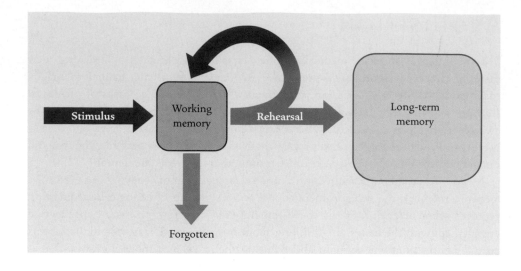

7.1   The relation between working memory and long-term memory as envisaged by stage theory *The figure is a schematic representation of the relation between the two memory systems as stage theorists conceive of them. Information is encoded and enters working memory. To enter the long-term store, it must remain in working memory for a while. The means for maintaining it there is rehearsal.*

series of items and must repeat them, in order, after just one presentation. If the items are randomly chosen letters or digits, adults can repeat seven items or so without error. With longer series, errors are likely. This has led to the assertion that working memory's capacity is seven items, give or take one or two. In fact, many tasks, not just memory span, show this limit of seven plus-or-minus two items, leading psychologists to refer to it as the **magic number** (after Miller, 1956). Given the assumption that a wide range of tasks must rely on working memory, it is perhaps unsurprising that this limit—presumably, a reflection of the small size of this memory—sets a boundary on performance in a variety of settings. (We return to the issue of how working memory's capacity should be measured—with some important updates—in Chapters 8 and 14.)

WORKING MEMORY AS A LOADING PLATFORM

What is the relation between working memory and long-term memory? The stage theory asserts that the road to long-term memory necessarily passes through working memory. Seen in this light, working memory could be regarded as a loading platform, sitting at the entrance to the huge long-term warehouse. But what is it, according to this view, that moves information off of the platform and into more permanent storage? One key factor, according to stage theory, is memory *rehearsal*, a process through which items are kept in working memory for an extended period of time, increasing the likelihood that these items will be transferred to long-term storage (Figure 7.1).

What is rehearsal? It involves several elements, and we will have more to say about it later in this chapter. In many cases, though, rehearsal literally involves saying the to-be-rememembered items over and over, sometimes out loud, but more often silently. This silent rehearsal can be documented in various ways, including PET scans (see Chapter 3) that show considerable activation, when people are silently rehearsing, in brain areas typically involved in the production of speech (e.g., Jonides, 2000).

To see how rehearsal matters, consider how the stage model accounts for some classic results. In these studies, research participants hear a series of unrelated words, one word at a time. At the end of the list, the participants are asked to recall the items in any order they choose (this is why the participants' task is called *free recall*). If the list contains just six or seven items, participants are likely to remember them all. But if the list is longer, the participants will not remember all the words and there is a clear pattern for which ones they recall and which ones they do not: Words presented at the beginning of the list are quite likely to be recalled; this is the **primacy effect**. Likewise, the last few words presented are also likely to be recalled; this is the *recency effect*. The likelihood of recall is appreciably poorer for words in the middle of the list (Figure 7.2).

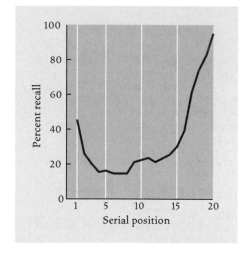

7.2   Primacy and recency effects in free recall *Research participants heard a list of twenty common words presented at a rate of one word per second. Immediately after hearing the list, participants were asked to write down as many of the words on the list as they could recall. The results show that position in the series strongly affected recall: the words at the beginning (primacy effect) and at the end (recency effect) were recalled more frequently than those in the middle.*

What creates this pattern? As the to-be-remembered words are presented, the participant pays attention to them, and this ensures that a representation of each word is placed in working memory. Bear in mind, though, that working memory is limited in size, and so, as participants try to keep up with the list presentation, the newly arriving words will bump the previous words out of this memory. Therefore, as participants proceed through the list, their working memories will at each moment contain just the half-dozen words that arrived most recently.

On this account, the only words that do not get bumped out of working memory are the last few words on the list, because obviously no further input arrives to displace them. Hence when the list presentation ends, these few words are still in working memory and are easily retrieved. This is why participants remember the end of the list so accurately—the pattern we called the recency effect.

The primacy effect comes from a different source. To put this in concrete terms, let us say that the first word on the list is *camera*. When research participants hear this word, they can focus their full attention on it, silently rehearsing "*camera, camera, camera, . . .*" When the second word arrives, they will rehearse that one too, but they will now have to divide their attention between the first word and the second ("*camera, boat, camera, boat, . . .*"). Attention will be divided still further after hearing the third word ("*camera, boat, zebra, camera, boat, zebra, . . .*"), and so on through the list.

Notice, then, that earlier words get more attention than later ones. At the list's start, participants can lavish attention on the few words they have heard so far. But as they hear more and more of the list, they must divide their attention more and more thinly, since they have more words to keep track of. This provides our account of the primacy effect: Earlier words receive more attention than later words and are rehearsed more often; as a result, they are more likely to make it into the long-term warehouse, and so more likely to be recalled later.

Support for these interpretations comes from various manipulations that affect the primacy and recency effects. For example, what happens if we require research participants to do some other task immediately after hearing the words but before recalling them? This other task will briefly require the use of working memory, and this should be enough to displace this memory's current contents. Those contents, of course, are the hypothesized source of the recency effect, and so, according to our hypothesis, this other task, even if it lasts just a few seconds, should disrupt the recency effect. And indeed it does. If participants are required to count backward for just 30 seconds between hearing the words and recalling them, the recency effect is eliminated (Figure 7.3).

Other manipulations produce a different pattern—diminishing the primacy effect but having no effect on recency. For example, if we present the list items more quickly, participants have less time for rehearsal. As a result, there is less transfer to long-term storage. We therefore should expect a reduced primacy effect (since primacy depends on retrieval from long-term memory) but no change in the recency effect (because the recency items are not being retrieved from long-term memory). This is exactly what happens (Figure 7.4).

RECODING TO EXPAND THE CAPACITY OF WORKING MEMORY

As we have seen, working memory has a limited capacity: It can handle only a small number of packages at one time. However, what these packages contain is, to a large extent, up to us. If we can pack the input more efficiently, we can squeeze more information into the same number of memory units.

As an example, consider an individual who tries to recall a series of digits that she heard only once:

149162536496481

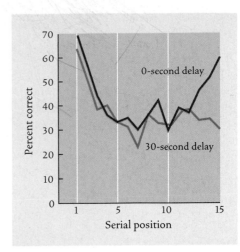

7.3 The recency effect and working memory *Research participants heard several fifteen-word lists. In one condition (red), free recall was tested immediately after they heard the list. In the other condition (green), the recall test was given after a thirty-second delay during which rehearsal was prevented. The delay left the primacy effect unaffected but abolished the recency effect, indicating that this effect is based on retrieval from working memory.*

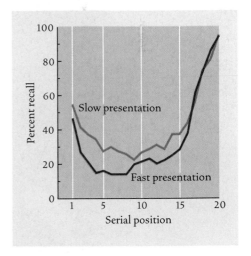

7.4 The primacy effect and long-term storage *The figure compares free-recall performance when item presentation is relatively slow (two seconds per item) and fast (one second per item). Slow presentation enhances the primacy effect but leaves the recency effect unaltered. The additional second per item presumably allows more time for rehearsal, which leads to long-term storage.*

If she treats this as a series of 15 unrelated digits, she will almost surely fail. But if she recognizes that the digits form a pattern, specifically

1 4 9 16 25 36 49 64 81

this task becomes much easier. She only has to remember the underlying relationship, "the squares of the digits from 1 to 9," and the 15 components of the series are easily recreated.

In this example, the person repackages the material to be remembered, recoding the input into larger units that are often called *chunks*. This is important, because, it turns out, working memory's capacity is measured in chunks, rather than in bits of information.

Much of the recoding of memory items, or *chunking*, happens quite automatically. For example, consider memory for sentences. If we have to recall a list of random words (*chair, line, smoke, page,...*), we are unlikely to remember more than six or seven of them. But we can often recall a fairly long sentence after only a single exposure. This fact holds even for sentences that make little sense, such as *The enemy submarine dove into the coffee pot, took fright, and silently flew away.* This dubious bit of naval intelligence consists of 14 words, but it clearly contains fewer than 14 memorial packages: *The enemy submarine* is essentially one unit, *took fright* is another, and so on. (For more on chunking, see Gobet et al., 2001.)

A CHANGED EMPHASIS: ACTIVE MEMORY AND ORGANIZATION

The stage theory describes the architecture of memory in roughly the right way. But, in order to understand how people learn, and how they remember what they have learned, we need to consider more than just the architecture. We also need to consider the learner's activities—his strategies and goals, and the previous knowledge that he brings to the learning situation. This is evident in the process of chunking—in which the person relies on other knowledge (e.g., knowledge about the squares of the digits) to repackage memory's contents. But other evidence makes it clear that the learner's activity plays a far broader role than this.

WORKING MEMORY AS AN ACTIVE PROCESS

Why is it that rehearsal helps to establish material in long-term storage? One possibility is that the transfer of information, from the short-term loading platform into the long-term warehouse, requires some amount of time—perhaps a second or so. If this is right, then rehearsal helps for a very simple reason: It holds the information in working memory, making it possible for the transfer to take place.

It turns out, however, that rehearsal provides much more than this, and that establishing material in long-term memory requires more than the passage of time. This is evident, for example, in studies of *maintenance rehearsal*, a strategy that keeps information in working memory but with little long-term effect. As an everyday example, consider what happens when you look up a telephone number. You need to retain the number long enough to complete the dialing, but you have no need to memorize the number for later use. In this circumstance, you are likely to employ maintenance rehearsal: You mechanically repeat the number to yourself while dialing, barely paying attention to the digits. This strategy is fine if the call goes through, but what if the line is busy? A moment later, you try to dial the number again but realize you have already forgotten it. Maintenance rehearsal kept the number in working memory long enough for you to dial it the first time, but utterly failed to establish it in long-term memory. As a result, the number is forgotten after just a few seconds.

The work in working memory **Working memory is crucial for virtually any task, because it is in this memory that you hold materials or ideas you are working on right now.**

Many studies confirm this observation and make it clear that, in general, you are unlikely to recall stimuli that you thought about only in a mindless, mechanical fashion. Likewise, if a stimulus was in front of your eyes (or presented to your ears) for many seconds, but you paid little attention to the stimulus, you probably will not be able to remember that stimulus later. Even if the stimulus was presented again and again and again, you probably will not be able to recall it unless you actively thought about the stimulus, actively paid attention to it.

As an illustration of these claims, consider people's memory for ordinary coins. Adults in the United States have probably seen pennies, for example, tens of thousands of times; adults in other countries have seen their own coins just as often. If sheer exposure is what counts for memory, then people should remember perfectly what these coins look like. But, of course, most people have little reason to pay attention to the penny. Pennies are a different color and size from the other coins, so they can be identified at a fast glance, with no need for further scrutiny. And, if scrutiny is what matters for memory—or, more broadly, if we remember what we pay attention to and think about—then memory for the coin should be quite poor.

In one study, participants were asked whether Lincoln's profile, shown on the heads side of the penny, faces to the right or to the left. (Which way does it face? Try to decide before looking at Figure 7.5 on p. 240.) Only half of the participants got this question right—exactly what we would expect if they were merely guessing. This result provides striking confirmation of the fact that memory requires mental engagement with a target and not mere exposure (Nickerson & Adams, 1979; Rinck, 1999; for a related demonstration, see Craik & Watkins, 1973).

Active encoding *Placing information into long-term storage requires active attention, and some sort of intellectual engagement with the to-be-remembered material. Passive exposure or rote repetition are largely ineffective in promoting long-term retention. All of this has obvious implications for students hoping to remember the material they learn in their classes!*

PROCESSING AND ORGANIZING: THE ROYAL ROAD INTO MEMORY

It seems, then, that the transfer of information, from working memory into long-term storage, is not automatic. Instead, some sort of work is involved, so that, to put the matter simply, whether you will remember something or not depends on how, and how fully, you encoded that information when you first met it.

Many studies confirm this broad claim, including studies of brain activity during learning. The results from these studies show that greater levels of activity during the initial encoding are reliably associated with greater probabilities of retention later on. This is especially true for brain activity in the hippocampus and regions of the prefrontal cortex (Brewer, Zhao, Desmond, Glover, & Gabrieli, 1998; Wagner, Koutstaal, & Schacter, 1999; Wagner et al., 1998), but it may also include brain activity in the parietal cortex (Wagner, Shannon, Kahn, & Buckner, 2005) (Figure 7.6 on p. 240).

But what exactly is this brain activity accomplishing? One prominent hypothesis, offered 30 years ago, focuses on the "depth" at which the incoming information is processed (Craik & Lockhart, 1972). For verbal materials, *shallow processing* involves encoding that emphasizes the superficial characteristics of a stimulus, such as the font in which a word is printed. In contrast, *deep processing* involves encoding that emphasizes the meaning of the material.

Many experiments confirm that deep processing leads to much better recall. In one study, research participants were told that the researchers were studying perception and speed of reaction and then were shown 48 words. As each word was presented, the participants were asked a question about it. For some words, they were asked about the word's physical appearance ("Is it printed in capital letters?"); this should produce shallow encoding. For others, they were asked about the word's sound ("Does it rhyme with

7.5 An ordinary penny *Despite having seen the U.S. penny thousands and thousands of times, people seem to have little recollection of its layout, including which way Lincoln's profile faces.*

train?"); this should encourage an intermediate level of encoding. For the remainder, they were asked about the word's meaning ("Would it fit into the sentence: The girl placed the _____ on the table?"); this presumably would lead to deep encoding. After the participants had gone through the entire list of words, they were given an unexpected task: They were asked to write down as many of the words as they could remember. The results were in line with the *depth-of-processing hypothesis*. The participants recalled very few of the words that called for shallow processing (typeface); words that required an intermediary level (sound) were recalled a bit better; and words that demanded the deepest level (meaning) were recalled best of all (Craik & Tulving, 1975).

It seems, therefore, that, to create memories, you need to *think about* the to-be-remembered materials in some fashion. This engagement with the materials does not have to involve profound contemplation, and so, for example, merely paying attention to the sound of a word (What does it rhyme with?) is better than, say, a thoughtless echoing of the word's syllables. This is evident, for example, in studies in which participants seem to be engaged in rote memorization. If participants merely repeat the words over and over without thinking about them, then subsequent memory is poor. If, in contrast, participants actually give some thought to the words' sounds as they are repeating them, then memory performance later on is appreciably better. But how do we know which participants are paying attention to the words' sound? This is revealed by fMRI scans (see Chapter 3) while the participants are rehearsing the words: Attention to a word's sound properties is reliably associated with activation in a specific region of the prefrontal cortex, so, if this region is activated during the rehearsal, we know the participant was thinking about the sounds. And, crucially, activation in this area during rote rehearsal is predictive of better memory in subsequent tests (Davachi, Maril, & Wagner, 2001; Poldrak & Wagner, 2004).

Attention to a word's sound, therefore, is better than thoughtless and mechanical rehearsal; but attention to a word's *meaning* is better still, and attention to meaning is almost always associated with a greater likelihood of subsequent recall. And it is not just the *search* for meaning that helps memory. Instead, memory is promoted by *finding* the meaning—that is, by finding an understanding of the to-be-remembered materials. Support for

7.6 Brain activity *Participants in this study were given a succession of words to memorize, and their brain activity was recorded during this initial presentation. These brain scans were then divided into two types—those showing brain activity during the encoding of words that were* remembered *later on in a subsequent test, and those showing activity during encoding of words that were* forgotten *in the test. As the figure shows, activity levels were higher, during encoding, for the later-remembered words than they were for the later-forgotten words. This plainly confirms that whether a word is forgotten or not depends on participants' mental activity when they encountered the word in the first place.*

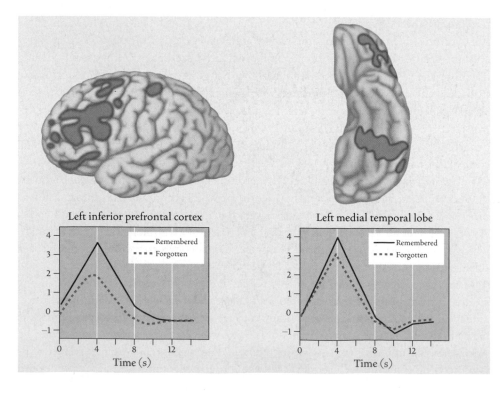

Left inferior prefrontal cortex

Left medial temporal lobe

Time (s)

this claim comes from many sources. In some studies, experimenters gave participants material to read that was difficult to understand, and then, immediately after, they probed the participants to see whether (or how well) they understood the material. Some time later, the experimenters tested the participants' memory for this material. The result was straightforward: the better the understanding, the better the memory later on.

Other studies manipulated whether the to-be-remembered material was understandable or not. For example, in one experiment the following tape-recorded passage was presented:

> The procedure is actually quite simple. First you arrange things into different groups depending on their makeup. Of course, one pile may be sufficient depending on how much there is to do. If you have to go somewhere else due to lack of facilities that is the next step; otherwise you are pretty well set. It is important not to overdo any particular endeavor. That is, it is better to do too few things at once than too many. In the short run this may not seem important, but complications from doing too many can easily arise. A mistake can be expensive as well. The manipulation of the appropriate mechanisms should be self-explanatory, and we need not dwell on it here. At first, the whole procedure will seem complicated. Soon, however, it will become just another facet of life. It is difficult to foresee any end to the necessity for this task in the immediate future, but then one never can tell. (Bransford & Johnson, 1972, p. 722)

Half of the people heard this passage without any further information as to what it was about, and, when tested later, their memory for the passage was poor. The other participants, though, were given a clue that helped them to understand the passage—they were told, "The paragraph you will hear will be about washing clothes." This clue, allowing them to make sense of the material, dramatically improved later recall (Bransford & Johnson, 1972; for a related example, with a nonverbal stimulus, see Figure 7.7).

There is a powerful message here for anyone hoping to remember some body of material—for example, a student trying to learn material for the next quiz. Study techniques that emphasize the meaning of the to-be-remembered material, and that involve efforts toward understanding the material, are likely to pay off with good memory later on. Memory strategies that do not emphasize meaning will provide much more limited effects.

7.7 *Nonverbal stimulus* *In general, we easily remember things that are meaningful but do not remember things that seem to have no meaning. This picture can be used to document this point with a nonverbal stimulus. Initially, the picture looks like a collection of meaningless blotches and as such, is immensely difficult to remember. However, if viewers discover the pattern in the picture, the picture becomes meaningful and then it is effortlessly remembered.*

Let us also note that these data demand some revisions in how we think about working memory. Early theories conceptualized this memory as just a temporary storage spot—the loading platform, we said, for the long-term memory warehouse. But, as we have now seen, working memory is far more dynamic than this description implies. After all, it is in working memory that the memorizer assembles the incoming information into larger memory chunks. Likewise, when someone is trying to understand a story or a picture, this effort is focused on information currently in working memory. For these reasons, working memory seems less like a loading platform and more like an active workbench on which various items of experience can be sorted, manipulated, and organized.

MEMORY CONNECTIONS

We still need to ask, however, why it is that attention to meaning improves memory. What exactly do deep processing and understanding accomplish that promotes retention and subsequent recall? Many investigators believe that the answers lie in the memory connections linking one memory to the next. Their proposal is that, in understanding something—a story, perhaps, or an event—we grasp how each element of the material is linked to the others: We realize that *this* caused *that*, and that *this aspect* is in place despite *that aspect*; *this element* has to balance some others; and so on. In essence, then, we can think of understanding as largely a matter of seeing these connections, and the more connections seen, the deeper the understanding.

When the time comes to recall something, these connections, established during the initial learning, can serve as *retrieval paths*. If, in your understanding of an event, you saw that Jane's smile caused Tarzan to howl, then, later, thinking of Jane's smile will bring Tarzan's howl into your thoughts. The connection you saw early on will lead you from one memory to the other, as if the connection were a pathway along which your thoughts could travel.

There are, to be sure, many questions we need to ask about these connections—what they involve, how they are created, and how exactly they can guide retrieval from one memory to the next. And, in fact, there is considerable disagreement about these issues. According to some researchers, the connections are simply links among ideas (or links among *elements* of ideas), in some ways similar to the associations discussed by Locke and Hume centuries ago (Christiansen, Chater, & Seidenberg, 1999; McClelland & Seidenberg, 2000; Rumelhart, 1997). According to other researchers, the connections are far more complex and, in fact, must have a structure, because otherwise they could not possibly represent our knowledge and our thoughts (Fodor, 1997; Fodor & Pylyshyn 1988; Pinker, 1999).

However the connections are conceptualized, though, psychologists agree that it is useful to think about memory in terms of interconnected ideas. Let us consider some of the evidence for this claim. (For more on memory connections—what they are and how they work—see Reisberg, 2006.)

MNEMONICS

Some of the evidence favoring the idea of memory connections comes from a practical endeavor—the development of techniques for improving memory. These techniques are called **mnemonics**, and, as it turns out, virtually all mnemonics build on the same base: To remember well, it pays to establish memory connections, and, if those connections are established, then remembering is almost guaranteed.

Mnemonics come in many forms. The ancient Greeks were well aware, for example, that it is easier to remember verbal material if it is organized, with each word linked to others within the material being memorized. Verse, with word sequences that maintain a fixed rhythm or rhyme, provides one way to achieve this organization, and

"You simply associate each number with a word, such as 'table' and 3,476,029."

Feats of memory *The Greek poet Homer, who was blind, recited his works from memory—including the book-length poem,* The Iliad. Homer Reciting His Poems *by Thomas Lawrence (1790).*

this is surely why many cultures record their history and their wisdom in verse. Indeed, without the use of verse, preliterate societies might never have transmitted their oral traditions intact from one generation to the next. Even in modern times, verse is still used as an effective mnemonic ("Thirty days hath September, April, June, and November").

Other mnemonics involve the deliberate use of mental imagery. One such technique is the **method of loci**, which requires the learner to visualize each of the items she wants to remember in a different spatial location (locus). In recall, each location is mentally inspected and the item that was placed there in imagination is retrieved.

The effectiveness of this method is easy to demonstrate. In one study, college students had to learn lists of 40 unrelated concrete nouns. Each list was presented once for about 10 minutes, during which the students tried to visualize each of the 40 objects in a specific location on their college campus. Tested immediately, they recalled an average of 38 of the 40 items; tested one day later, they still managed to recall 34 (Bower, 1970, 1972; Higbee, 1977; Roediger, 1980; Ross & Lawrence, 1968). In other studies, participants using the method of loci were able to retain seven times more than their counterparts who learned in a rote manner.

In order for imagery to be helpful, however, the image must link the to-be-remembered materials to each other or to other things the person knows—so here, too, we see the importance of memory connections. To make this point concrete, consider a person who has to learn a list of word pairs and who chooses to use imagery as an aid. He might construct mental pictures that bring the items into some kind of relationship, linking them in some way. For example, to remember the pair *eagle-train*, he might imagine an eagle winging to its nest with a locomotive in its beak. Alternatively, he might only imagine the eagle and the locomotive side by side, not interacting. Evidence indicates that images of the first (interacting) sort produce much better recall than non-unifying images (Wollen, Weber, & Lowry, 1972). A similar effect is found when the test items are pictures, rather than words. Pictures with interacting parts are remembered much more effectively than are pictures with their constituents merely side by side and not interacting (Figure 7.8).

Whether based on imagery or some other system, though, there is no question that mnemonics are enormously useful in memorizing, say, a list of foreign vocabulary words or the names of American presidents. But what about memorizing more meaningful materials, such as a philosopher's argument or a pattern of evidence favoring a particular historical claim? Here it might actually be a mistake to use mnemonics, because the mnemonics, powerful as they are, will not lead to the sort of memory most people want.

Why is this? Part of the reason mnemonics are so effective is that they lead the memorizer to focus on a narrow set of memory links—just the fact that the locomotive is in the eagle's beak, or just the fact that *September* rhymes with *November*. This lavishing of attention on a few links virtually guarantees that the relevant memory connections will end up well established, and thus able to serve as efficient retrieval paths later on.

The problem, though, is that people often want more than a narrow set of links; instead, they want a rich network of connections, tying the to-be-learned material to a range of other beliefs and ideas. Why is this desirable? Seeking this range of connections during learning will place the material into a broader mental context, and this will promote understanding—obviously a good thing. Then, during retrieval, having a range of connections will provide the person with a variety of retrieval paths, all leading to the target material. This will allow the person to recall the material from multiple perspectives and in multiple contexts, which in turn will allow more flexible retrieval, certainly helping the person to use the material she has learned.

These gains, though, all depend on finding multiple memory connections—precisely what mnemonics do not accomplish. Thinking about the eagle with the locomotive in its beak does nothing to draw one's attention to other potential connections—and so does nothing to promote understanding of the fragile ecosystem within which eagles live, or the locomotive's role in moving freight. As a result, when the time comes to remember, the mnemonic will be quite helpful if one is asked, "What word went with *eagle*?" but may be of little value in responding to some other memory cue.

In short, mnemonics are useful for memorizing material that, by itself, has no internal organization. But if the material to be learned is meaningful or already organized, the best approach is to seek an understanding of the material when it is being learned. This will lead to the best memory as well as to flexibility in how the target information can be retrieved.

7.8 Interactive and noninteractive depictions *Research participants shown related elements, such as a doll sitting on a chair and waving a flag (A), are more likely to associate the words doll, flag, and chair than participants who are shown the three objects next to each other but not interacting (B).*

A

B

STORAGE

Once a stimulus is encoded—through deep processing, the use of a mnemonic, or any other means—it must be stored in long-term memory until it is later needed. The "record" in memory, storing the new information, is referred to as the *memory trace* or *engram*; surprisingly, we know relatively little about how exactly engrams are lodged in the brain. At a microscopic level, it seems certain that engrams are created through the forms of neural plasticity described in Chapter 6: Presynaptic neurons can become more effective in sending signals; postsynaptic neurons can become more sensitive to the signals they receive; and new synapses can be created. At a larger-scale level, evidence suggests that the engram for a particular past experience is not recorded in a single location within the brain. Instead, different aspects of an event are likely to be stored in distinct brain regions—one region containing the visual elements of the episode; another containing a record of our emotional reaction; a third area containing a record of our conceptual understanding of the event; and so on (e.g., Damasio & Damasio, 1994). But, within these broad outlines, we know very little about how the information content of a memory is translated into a pattern of neural connections. Thus, to put the matter bluntly, we are many decades away from the science-fiction notion of being able to inspect the wiring of someone's brain in order to discover what he remembers, or being able to "inject" a memory into someone by a suitable rearrangement of her neurons.

One fact about memory storage, however, is well established: Engrams are not created instantly. Instead, a period of time is needed, after each new experience, for the record of that experience to become established in memory. During that time, *memory consolidation* is taking place; this is a process, spread over several hours, in which memories are transformed from a transient and fragile status to a more permanent and robust state (Hasselmo, 1999; McGaugh, 2000, 2003; Meeter & Murre, 2004; Wixted, 2004).

What exactly does consolidation accomplish? The answer is not clear, although the best bet is that this time period allows adjustments in neural connections, creating a pattern of communications among neurons that can represent the newly acquired memory. This process seems to require the creation of new proteins, so it is disrupted by chemical manipulations that block protein synthesis (Davis & Squire, 1984; Santini, Ge, Ren, deOrtiz, & Quirk, 2004; Schafe, Nader, Blair, & LeDoux, 2001).

Some of the clearest evidence for consolidation comes from a type of memory loss sometimes produced by head injuries. Specifically, people who have experienced blows to the head sometimes develop *retrograde amnesia* (*retrograde* means "in a backward direction"), in which they suffer a loss of memory for events prior to the brain injury. This form of amnesia can also be caused by brain tumors, diseases, or strokes (Cipolotti, 2001; Conway & Fthenaki, 1999; Kapur, 1999; Mayes, 1988; Nadel & Moscovitch, 2001).

Retrograde amnesia usually involves *recent* memories. In fact, the older the memory, the less likely it is to be affected by the amnesia, a pattern that is so robust that it is often referred to as Ribot's law, in honor of the nineteenth-century scholar who first discussed it (Ribot, 1882). What produces this pattern? Older memories have presumably had enough time to consolidate, so they are less vulnerable to disruption. Newer memories are not yet consolidated, so they are more liable to disruption (Brown, 2002; Weingartner & Parker, 1984).

There is, however, a complicating factor: Retrograde amnesia sometimes disrupts a person's memory for events that took place months or even years prior to the brain injury. In these cases, interrupted consolidation could not explain the deficit unless one assumes—as some authors do—that consolidation is an exceedingly drawn-out process,

Retrograde amnesia   Soldiers sometimes are unable to remember their experiences in battle—even those that occurred just a day before. This amnesia may be the result of interrupted memory consolidation, with the extreme stress of the battle, exhaustion, and perhaps the effects of wounds, interfering with the biological processes needed to consolidate memories for the experience.

occurring over very long periods (Hasselmo, 1999; McGaugh, 2000; Squire, 1987; Squire & Cohen, 1979, 1982). However, this issue remains a point of debate, making it clear that the last word has not yet been written on how consolidation proceeds.

RETRIEVAL

When we learn, we transfer new information into our long-term store of knowledge, and then we consolidate this newly acquired information. But successful acquisition of a memory is not enough. We must also be able to retrieve the information when we need it, and the success of retrieval is far from guaranteed. This is obvious to anyone who has ever experienced a "block" on a familiar name. We may know the name (we have encoded and stored it) but be unable to retrieve it when trying to introduce an old friend to a new one—an experience that can be quite embarrassing!

Failures to remember something can happen for many reasons, including (as we have already discussed) inadequate encoding. We know that retrieval is the problem, though, in cases in which you initially fail to remember something, but then later on, do remember the desired information, once an adequate *retrieval cue* is provided. A clear illustration of this pattern often arises when someone returns to his hometown after a long absence. This return can unleash a flood of recollection, as the sights and sounds of the place trigger the relevant memories. A word, a smell, a visit from a school friend not seen for years—any of these may summon memories the person thought were utterly lost.

THE RELATION BETWEEN ORIGINAL ENCODING AND RETRIEVAL

What makes a retrieval cue effective? Why do some reminders succeed, while others have no effect? One important factor is whether the cue re-creates the context in which the original learning occurred. For example, if an individual focused on the sounds of words while learning them, then she will be well served by reminders that focus on sound ("Was there a word on the list that rhymes with *log*?"); if she focused on meaning while learning, then the best reminder would be one that again draws her attention toward meaning ("Was one of the words a type of fruit?"; Fisher & Craik, 1977).

Why should this be? Our earlier discussion of memory connections provides the answer. Learning, we suggested, is essentially a process of creating (or strengthening) memory connections that link the to-be-remembered material to other things you already know. When the time comes for retrieval, these same connections serve as retrieval paths, leading you back to the desired information. If, therefore, an individual focused on the sounds of words during learning, this established a corresponding set of memory connections—a connection, for example, between *dog* and *log*. That connection will be useful later if the person is asked the question about rhymes: If she thinks about *log*, the connection will guide her thoughts to the target word, *dog*. But the same connection will play little role in other contexts. If she is asked, "Did any of the words on the list name animals with sharp teeth?" the path from *log* to *dog* is irrelevant; what she needs with this cue is a retrieval path leading from *sharp teeth* to the target.

In this example, the retrieval cue helps someone remember because the cue re-creates a mental context in which the person was thinking about words' sounds, not their meaning. But other forms of *context reinstatement* (a re-creation of the state of mind someone was in during learning) can also help someone to remember. In all cases, though, the logic is the same: If the cues and mental context in place during retrieval match those in place during the initial encoding, then this will help the person to use the connections established earlier.

We have already seen a different example of context reinstatement—the case in which someone returns to his hometown, so that he is re-exposed to the sights and sounds that were present during the to-be-remembered events. As a different example, participants in one study were asked to read an article similar to the ones they routinely read in their college classes; half read the article in a quiet setting, and half read it in a noisy environment. When tested later on, those who read the article in quiet did best if they were tested in quiet; those who read it in a noisy environment did best if tested in a noisy setting (Grant et al., 1998). In both cases, participants showed the benefits of context reinstatement—and, with that, the benefit of being able to use, at time of retrieval, the specific connections established during learning (for another example, see Figure 7.9).

These results make it sound like the physical setting is crucial for memory, but, in truth, the physical setting matters only indirectly: A return to the physical circumstances of learning does help, but only because this return helps re-create the mental context of learning—and it is the mental context that matters. This was evident, for example, in a study in which participants were presented with a long list of words. One day later, the experimenter brought the participants back for an unexpected recall test that took place in either the same room or a different one (one that differed in size, furnishings, and so on, from the context of learning). Not surprisingly, recall was better for those who were tested in the same physical environment, but, crucially, the investigator found a straightforward way of overcoming this context effect. A different group of participants was brought to the new room, but just prior to the test they were asked to think about the room in which they had learned the lists—what it looked like, how it made them feel. By doing so, they mentally re-created the old environment for themselves; on the subsequent recall test, these participants performed just as well as those for whom there was no change of rooms (Smith, 1979; Smith & Vela, 2001). In essence, then, what matters for retrieval is your mental perspective, not what room you are sitting in. If you change the physical context without changing your mental perspective, the physical relocation has no effect.

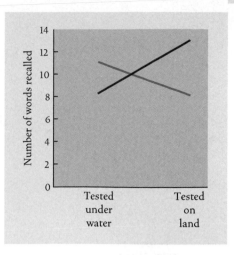

7.9 *The effect of changing the retrieval situation* Scuba divers learned a list of thirty-six unrelated words above water (red) or twenty feet underwater (green) and were then tested above or underwater. The figure shows that retention was better when the retrieval situation was the same as that in which encoding took place.

ENCODING SPECIFICITY

The effectiveness of context reinstatement is important for several reasons, including the fact that it tells us something crucial about how materials are encoded in the first place: When people encounter some stimulus or event, they *think about* this experience in one way or another, and, as we have discussed, this intellectual engagement serves to connect the new experience to other thoughts and other knowledge. We have talked about the fact that these connections can serve as retrieval paths, helping people to recall the target information, but let us note that this is possible only because those connections are themselves part of the memory record. Thus, continuing an earlier example, if people see the word *dog* and think about what it rhymes with, what is stored in memory is not just the word. What is stored is the word plus some record of the connections made to rhyming words, and that is why these connections are available for use during retrieval. Likewise, if people see a picture and think about what it means, what is stored in memory is not just the picture, but a memory of the picture with some record of the connections to other, related ideas.

In short, what is placed in memory is not some neutral transcription of an event. Instead, what is placed in memory is a record of the event as understood from a particular perspective or perceived within a particular context. Psychologists refer to this broad pattern as *encoding specificity*, and this specificity has powerful effects on how—or whether—the past is remembered (Tulving & Osler, 1968; Tulving & Thompson, 1973; also Hintzman, 1990). For example, participants in one study read target words (e.g., *piano*) in either of two contexts: "The man lifted the piano" or "The man tuned the piano." These sentences led the participants to think about the target word in a specific way, and it was this thought that was encoded into memory. Thus, what was recorded in memory was the idea of "piano as something heavy" or "piano as a musical instrument." This difference in memory content became clear when participants were later asked to recall the target words. If they had earlier seen the "lifted" sentence, then they were quite likely to recall the target word if given the hint "something heavy." The hint "something with a nice sound" was much less effective. But if participants had seen the "tuned" sentence, the result reversed: Now the "nice sound" hint was effective, but the "heavy" hint was not (Barcklay, Bransford, Franks, McCarrell, & Nitsch, 1974). In both cases, the memory hint was effective only if it was congruent with what was stored in memory—just as the encoding specificity proposal predicts.

WHEN MEMORY FAILS

All three of the processes we have been discussing—acquisition, storage, and retrieval—usually function extremely well, so that each of us can learn an enormous quantity of information, store that information for long periods of time, and then retrieve the information, when we need it, with relative ease. But of course there are also circumstances in which remembering is less successful. Sometimes we try to remember an episode, but simply draw a blank. Sometimes we recall something, but with no conviction that we are correct: "I think it happened on Tuesday, but I'm not sure." And sometimes our memories fail us in another way: We recall a past episode, but it turns out that our memory is mistaken. Perhaps details of the event were different from the way we recall them; perhaps our memory is altogether wrong, misrepresenting large elements of the original episode. Why, and how often, do these memory failures occur?

Very Bad Memory

INADEQUATE ENCODING

It seems self-evident that we cannot remember something if we never learned it in the first place: If a friend never told you what her middle name is, then obviously you will not be able to recall the name when asked. But, obvious or not, we need to bear in mind that at least some cases of failure to remember are best understood as the result of inadequate learning.

This point can be documented in many ways, including a study we mentioned earlier in the chapter (pp. 239–240). The investigators used fMRI recording to keep track of the moment-by-moment brain activity in participants who were studying a list of words (Wagner et al., 1998; also Brewer et al., 1998). Later, participants were able to remember some of the words they had learned, but not others, allowing the investigators to compare brain activity during encoding for words-later-remembered with the activity during encoding for words-later-forgotten. Figure 7.6 shows the results, with a clear difference, during the initial encoding, between words that were remembered later on and words that were forgotten. The strong implication of this result is that the subsequent "forgetting" was caused by differences that took place during encoding—differences that caused the later-forgotten words to be less well learned in the first place.

FORGETTING

In other cases, though, materials are learned, so that they can (at least for a while) be remembered. Later on, though, those same materials cannot be recalled. What produces this pattern? One clue comes from the fact that it is almost always easier to recall recent events (yesterday's lecture, for example, or this morning's breakfast) than it is to recall more distant events (a lecture or a breakfast 6 months ago). In technical terms, recall decreases, and forgetting increases, as the *retention interval* (the time that elapses between learning and retrieval) grows longer and longer.

This simple fact has been documented in many studies; indeed, the passage of time erodes memory for things as diverse as past hospital stays, our eating or smoking habits in past years, car accidents we experienced, our consumer purchases, and so on (Jobe, Tourangeau, & Smith, 1993). The classic demonstration of this pattern, though, was offered more than a century ago by Hermann Ebbinghaus (1850–1909). Ebbinghaus systematically studied his own memory in a series of careful experiments, examining his ability to retain lists of nonsense syllables, such as *zup* and *rif*. Ebbinghaus plotted a *forgetting curve* by testing himself at various intervals after learning (using different lists for each interval). As expected, he found that memory did decline with the passage of time. However, the decline was uneven, being sharpest soon after the learning and then becoming more gradual (Ebbinghaus, 1885; Figure 7.10).

DECAY

What accounts for the pattern observed by Ebbinghaus? One theory holds that memory traces *decay* as time passes, like mountains that are eroded by wind and water. The erosion of memories is presumably caused by normal metabolic processes that wear down memory traces until they fade and finally disintegrate.

One line of support for this theory exploits the fact that, like most chemical reactions, many metabolic processes increase their rates with increasing temperature. If these metabolic reactions are responsible for memorial decay, then forgetting should increase if body temperature is elevated during the retention interval. This prediction is difficult to test with humans (or any other mammal), because internal mechanisms keep the temperature of our bodies relatively constant (see Chapter 2). However, this prediction was tested with animals such as goldfish whose bodies tend to take on the temperature of their surroundings. By and large, the results are in line with the hypothesis: the higher the temperature of the tank in which the fish were kept during the retention interval, the more forgetting took place (Gleitman & Rozin, as reported in Gleitman, 1971; for more evidence documenting decay, see Altmann & Gray, 2002; Bailey & Chen, 1989).

INTERFERENCE

Other findings, however, make it clear that decay cannot provide the entire explanation of forgetting. As one concern, we will later review evidence for remembering that lasts across many, many years, an observation that is puzzling if the mere passage of time somehow erodes recollection. In addition, several experiments suggest that it is *interference from new learning*, and not the passage of time, that really matters for forgetting. For example, Baddeley & Hitch (1977) asked rugby players to recall the names of the other teams they had played against over the course of a season (Figure 7.11). Not all players made it to all games, because of illness, injuries, or schedule conflicts. These differences allow us to compare players for whom "two games back" means 2 weeks ago, to players for whom "two games back" means 4 weeks ago. Thus, we can look at the effects of retention interval (2 weeks vs. 4) with the number of intervening games held constant. Likewise, we can compare players for whom the game a month ago was "three games back" to players for whom a month ago means "one game back." Now we have the retention interval held constant, and we can look at the effects of intervening events. In

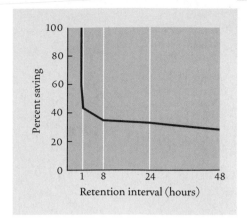

7.10 Forgetting curve *The figure shows retention after various intervals since learning. Retention is here measured in percent saving, that is, the percentage decrease in the number of trials required to relearn the list after an interval of no practice. If the saving is 100 percent, retention is perfect—no trials to relearn are necessary. If the saving is 0 percent, there is no retention at all, for it takes just as many trials to relearn the list as it took to learn it initially.*

7.11 Forgetting from interfering events *Members of a rugby team were asked to recall the names of teams they had played against. Their performance was influenced by the number of games that intervened between the game to be recalled and the attempt to remember. This pattern fits with an interference view of forgetting.*

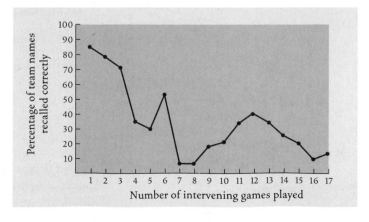

this setting, Baddeley and Hitch report that the mere passage of time accounts for very little; what really matters is the number of intervening events, just as we would expect if interference, and not decay, is the major contributor to forgetting. (For other—classic—data on interference this issue, see Jenkins & Dallenbach, 1924; for a more recent review, see Wixted, 2004.)

Interference can also be easily demonstrated in the laboratory. In a typical study, a control group learns the items on a list (*A*) and then is tested after a specified interval. The experimental group learns the same list (*A*), but, in addition, they must also learn the items on a second list (*B*) during the same retention interval. The result is a marked inferiority in the performance of the experimental group. List *B* seems to interfere with the recall of list *A* (Crowder, 1976; McGeoch & Irion, 1952).

It turns out, though, that not all new learning produces interference; in fact, interference emerges only under certain circumstances. No interference is observed, for example, between dissimilar sorts of material—learning to skate does not interfere with one's memory for irregular French verbs. In addition, interference occurs only if the things to be remembered are essentially incompatible. If the new learning is consistent with the old, no interference is observed; in fact, the subsequent learning helps memory, rather than hindering it. Thus, learning more algebra helps you to remember the algebra you mastered last year; learning more psychology helps you to remember the psychology you have already covered.

RETRIEVAL FAILURE

But why does memory interference occur at all? Why can't newly acquired information peacefully coexist with older memories? One hypothesis is that the forgotten material is neither damaged nor erased; it is simply misplaced. By analogy, consider someone who buys a newspaper each day and then stores it with others in a large pile in the basement. Each newspaper is easy to find when it is still sitting on the breakfast table; it can still be located without difficulty when it is on top of the basement stack. After some days, though, finding the newspaper becomes difficult. It is somewhere in the pile but may not come into view without a great deal of searching. And, of course, the pile grows higher and higher every day; that is why the interference increases as the retention interval grows longer.

If this hypothesis is correct, then forgetting should be reversible. After all, the hypothesis proposes that the "lost" memories are still in storage, even if they are difficult to locate. With a suitable cue or prompt, therefore, these memories might be recovered. And, in fact, we know that this is true for some cases of forgetting, so at least some forgetting can be understood as the result of *retrieval failure*.

We have already seen some of the evidence for this claim. As we have noted, memories can often be triggered by returning to the context in which learning took place. Prior to that return, the target information might not be recalled—an apparent case of forgetting. But then, once the right retrieval cues are available, the memory resurfaces, making it clear that the problem was retrieval failure and not a genuine memory loss.

The idea that forgetting is sometimes produced by retrieval failure also has another implication: It implies that forgetting can be incomplete, so that we might be able to retrieve some aspects of a memory but not others. This pattern is perhaps most clearly evident in the phenomenon psychologists call the *tip-of-the-tongue effect*.

Try to think of the word that means a type of carving done on whalebone, often depicting whaling ships or whales. Try to think of the name of the navigational device used by sailors to determine the positions of stars. Try to think of the name of the Russian sled drawn by three horses. Chances are that, in at least one of these cases, you found yourself in a frustrated state: certain you knew the word but unable to come up with it. The word was, as people say, right on the "tip of the tongue" (TOT).

The tip-of-the-tongue effect **What is the name of the device that sailors use to determine the position of specific stars? What is the name for the type of carving done on whalebone? People trying to answer these questions often are certain that they know the relevant words, and can say what letter the words start with, but cannot remember the words themselves.**

People who are in the so-called TOT state often know correctly that the word is somewhere in their vocabulary, and they often correctly remember what letter the word begins with, how many syllables it has, and approximately what it sounds like (A. Brown, 1991; Brown & McNeill, 1966; Harley & Brown, 1998; James & Burke, 2000; Schwartz, 1999). Thus, a person might remember "It's something like *Sanskrit*" in trying to remember *scrimshaw* (that's the whalebone carving) or might remember "something like *secant*" in trying to remember *sextant* (the navigational device). Similar results have been obtained when people try to recall specific names: Who played the nervous man with the knife in the shower scene in Hitchcock's *Psycho*? What was the name of the Greek orator who taught himself to speak clearly by practicing speeches with pebbles in his mouth? With clues like these, people are often able to recall the number of syllables in the name and the name's initial letter, but not the name itself (Brennen, Baguley, Bright, & Bruce, 1990; Yarmey, 1973; the orator was *Demosthenes*, and *Anthony Perkins* was the nervous man with the knife; the Russian sled is a *troika*).

People in the TOT state cannot recall the target word—and, in that sense, they have forgotten the word. Plainly, though, the word is not absent from their memory. If it were, they would not be able to remember its starting letter or its syllable count. This is, therefore, unmistakably a case of retrieval failure—with information preserved in storage but, for various reasons, inaccessible.

INTRUSIONS AND OVERWRITING

Not all interference effects, however, can be understood in terms of retrieval failure. In some cases, the new learning seems to interfere with memory consolidation for previously learned information. As a result, new learning can actually prevent recent memories from being firmly established in long-term storage (Wixted, 2004). In addition—and perhaps more commonly—new learning can get "mixed up" with older learning, with the consequence that the older episodes can no longer be recalled in their original form.

THE MISINFORMATION EFFECT

Imagine that you witness a crime and see the thief flee in a blue car. The next day, you read a newspaper account of the same crime and learn that another witness reported that the thief fled in a *green* car. How will this experience influence your memory? A number of experiments have examined this issue by exposing participants to an event and then providing some misinformation about the event. In some studies, the misinformation is provided by another person's report ("Here's the way another witness described the event . . ."). In other studies, the misinformation is contained within a leading question: Participants might be asked, for example, "Did you see the children

H.M. has also offered some unsettling comments about his own state:

> Right now, I'm wondering, Have I done or said anything amiss? You see, at this moment everything looks clear to me, but what happened just before? That's what worries me. It's like waking from a dream; I just don't remember. (Milner, 1966)

And on another occasion:

> Every day is alone in itself, whatever enjoyment I've had, and whatever sorrow I've had. (Milner et al., 1968; for more on H.M.'s case, see Hilts, 1995)

WHAT TYPE OF MEMORY IS SPARED IN AMNESIA?

It turns out, however, that patients with anterograde amnesia can acquire some new memories—and this brings us back to the distinction between implicit and explicit memory. Specifically, patients with anterograde amnesia can learn to trace the correct path through a maze, and they get faster each time they redo the same maze. They can also acquire skills such as learning to read print that has been mirror-reversed (Figure 7.15). H.M. plays the piano, and each time he plays a piece, he plays it more skillfully than he did the last time, all the while insisting that he has never seen the music before. In these and many other cases, the patients benefit from practice, so they must have retained something from their previous experience—even though each time they are brought back into the testing situation, they insist that they have never seen the apparatus or the test materials before (Cohen & Squire, 1980; Corkin, 1965; Schacter, 1996; Weiskrantz & Warrington, 1979; for a reverse case, with brain damage disrupting skill acquisition but not memory for episodes, see Gabrieli, Fleischman, Keane, Reminger, & Morrell, 1995).

There is some disagreement among researchers regarding how exactly to characterize the types of memory that are spared in these patients. Some theorists argue that these amnesiacs are still able to acquire new *procedural knowledge*, even though they have lost the capacity to gain new *declarative knowledge*. Procedural knowledge is knowing *how*: how to ride a bicycle or how to read mirror writing. Declarative knowledge, in contrast, is knowing *that*: that there are three outs in an inning, that automobiles run on gasoline, that you had chicken for dinner yesterday, or that you woke up late this morning (e.g., Cohen & Squire, 1980; Squire, 1986).

A clearly related view is that patients with anterograde amnesia are massively disrupted in any task that requires explicit recollection of the past, so they cannot answer a question like "Do you remember . . . ?" or "Do you recognize . . . ?" (at least not if the question pertains to events that occurred after the brain damage). The patients perform normally, however, on tests of implicit memory. To put this in concrete terms, the patients will fail completely if they are shown a number of words and later asked to recall or recognize them. The results are different, though, if the patients are shown a list of words and later tested implicitly—say, with a word-fragment completion task. For example, the patients might be shown __L__P__A__T or B__O__C__S__ and asked to complete these fragments to form English words. This task is quite difficult if the patient has not been primed in any way. But if the patient was previously shown a list containing the words ELEPHANT and BOOKCASE, she is likely to complete the fragments properly. Apparently, the patient does have some memory of seeing these words, and that memory facilitates performance with the word-fragment task (Diamond & Rozin, 1984; Graf, Mandler, & Squire, 1984; Schacter, 1996; Warrington & Weiskrantz, 1978).

Which is the better account? Does anterograde amnesia disrupt declarative knowledge while sparing procedural? Or does it disrupt explicit memory while sparing implicit? It is difficult to say, in part because these distinctions overlap. Procedural

7.15 **An example of what amnesiacs can learn** (A) In mirror drawing, the research participant has to trace a line between two outlines of a figure while looking at her hand in a mirror. Initially, this is very difficult, but after some practice the individual gets very proficient at it. The same is true for amnesiacs. The graphs in (B) show H.M.'s improvement on this task over a period of three days.

knowledge is often implicit; declarative knowledge is generally explicit. In addition, it may turn out that different cases of amnesia require different explanations. Anterograde amnesia is probably not a single disorder, so which conception provides the better account may vary from patient to patient (Squire & Cohen, 1984). With either explanation, though, these cases of brain damage provide powerful reasons for distinguishing at least two types of memory, and continued research on amnesia is certain to sharpen our understanding of this distinction.

EMOTIONAL REMEMBERING

One other distinction among types of memories has been carefully examined by researchers: Some of the events we experience are intensely emotional—because the events made us happy or made us afraid, made us sad or made us angry. How does this emotion influence what we recall? Are emotional memories different from unemotional memories?

REMEMBERING EMOTIONAL EVENTS

Many studies have compared memory for emotional events with memory for similar, but emotionally neutral, events. Some of these studies have examined people's recollection of actual events in their lives; some have examined memory for events witnessed in a laboratory setting. In both sorts of data, though, the pattern of the evidence is clear: Emotional episodes seem to be remembered more vividly, more completely, and more accurately than unemotional events (see Reisberg & Heuer, 2004).

Why should this be? There are several reasons, some of which involve mechanisms we have already described. Emotional events are likely to be interesting to us, guaranteeing that we will pay close attention to them, and we have already seen that attention promotes memory. Emotional events are also likely to be worth thinking about, in the minutes (or hours) after the event, and this mulling-over is tantamount to memory rehearsal. Emotional events are also likely to involve issues or people we care about; this makes it probable that we will readily connect the event to other knowledge (about the issues or the people), and these connections, of course, also promote memory.

In addition, the various biological changes that accompany emotion play a role. Emotional stimuli usually trigger a series of reactions in brain regions centered on the amygdala, and these reactions seem to improve the consolidation of memories. Indeed, in several studies, greater activation in the amygdala (measured by fMRI scans) was reliably associated with greater likelihood of subsequent memory (Buchanan & Adolphs, 2004; Cahill, Babinsky, Markowitsch, & McGaugh, 1996; Canli, Zhao, Brewer, Gabrieli, & Cahill, 2000; Dudai, 2004; Hamann, 2001). Unquestionably, then, these biological effects make the retention of emotional episodes all the more likely.

FLASHBULB MEMORIES

Some emotional memories seem particularly long-lived, so that people claim to remember events from decades past "as if it were yesterday." These especially vivid memories, called *flashbulb memories*, typically concern events that were highly distinctive, unexpected, and strongly emotional (Brown & Kulik, 1977). Sometimes flashbulb memories concern personal events, such as an early-morning telephone call that tells of a parent's death. Others may involve news of national importance; many people have flashbulb memories of the 1995 reading of the verdict in the O. J. Simpson trial, the news of Princess Diana's death in 1997, and the attack on the World Trade Center in 2001.

One striking feature of flashbulb memories is their focus on immediate and personal circumstances. For example, many people remember exactly where they were when they first heard about the attacks on 9/11, what they were doing at the time, who was with

Flashbulb memories   *The classic example of a flashbulb memory is the assassination of John F. Kennedy in November 1963. Virtually any American (and most Europeans) who were at least nine or ten years old on that date still remember the day vividly. The attack on the World Trade Center, on September 11, 2001, is the sort of shocking and highly consequential event that seems very likely to create a flashbulb memory, with the expectation that people will still remember this day clearly even decades from now.*

In addition, it is plausible that memories "recovered" after a period of amnesia are, in some cases, false, fabricated through mechanisms we have already discussed. Thus, for example, we know that the possibility for error is greater in remembering the distant past than it is in remembering recent events. Likewise, we know that close questioning of a witness can create "memories" for entire events that never occurred, particularly if the questions are asked over and over (see, for example, Ceci, Huffman, & Smith, 1994; Hyman, Husband, & Billings, 1995; Loftus, 1997; Ofshe, 1992; Zaragoza & Mitchell, 1996). We also know that false memories, when they occur, can be recalled just as vividly, just as confidently, and, indeed, with just as much distress as memories for actual events.

It is also worth noting that many recovered memories emerge only with the assistance of a therapist who is genuinely convinced that the client's psychological problems stem from childhood abuse. Often, the therapist believes that these problems can be dealt with only if the client faces them squarely and uncovers the buried memories of that abuse (see, for example, Bass & Davis, 1988). To help this process along, the therapist may rely on a variety of techniques aimed at improving memory, including hypnosis, drugs alleged to promote recollection, and guided imagination. In these cases, the therapist's intentions are good, but these techniques actually do little to promote accurate recall, and they substantially increase the risk of false memories.

A therapist who is convinced that abuse took place may also ask suggestive questions that further increase the chances of memory fabrication. Even if the therapist scrupulously avoids leading questions, she can shape the client's memory in other ways—by giving signs of interest or concern if the client hits on the "right" line of exploration, or by spending more time on topics related to the alleged memories than on other issues. In these ways, the climate within the therapeutic session can subtly guide the client toward finding exactly the "memories" the therapist expects to find.

None of this is said to minimize the social and moral problems produced by childhood sexual abuse and incest. These offenses do occur and can have severe consequences for the victim. But here, as in all cases, the veracity of our recollection cannot be taken for granted. We must always be careful in interpreting what seems like a memory of a long-past event, and that caution must be increased if the memory emerged through someone's (e.g., a therapist's) suggestions and hypnosis. (For further discussion of this difficult issue, see Bass & Davis, 1988; Conway, 1997; Freyd, 1996, 1998; Holmes, 1990; Kihlstrom, 1993; Loftus, 1993; Pendergast, 1995; Schacter, 1996.)

SOME FINAL THOUGHTS: DIFFERENT TYPES, BUT COMMON PRINCIPLES

In the end, therefore, we see contrasts, and also common themes, among types of memories. Some principles do apply just to memories of a certain sort—so that, in discussing emotional memories, we need to consider the effects that biological arousal has on consolidation processes; in discussing implicit memories, we need to consider the importance of a stimulus's specific appearance. But other principles apply to memories of many different types, including the crucial contribution that the individual memorizer makes to learning, storage, and retrieval.

What is the individual's contribution? As one way to unpack this point, think about what we would need to ask in order to predict whether a specific person will remember a specific experience. We would need to know whether that individual was paying attention to the event; indeed, we would need to know what aspects of the event he was paying attention to. We would need to know whether the person was thinking about how the event looked or what it meant. We would need to know whether that person brought other knowledge to the situation—knowledge that might help him understand the to-be-remembered event, but also knowledge that might later intrude into his recall of the event. We would also need to know what the person was thinking about when he tried to recall the event—what retrieval cues he was focused on, and whether his mental perspective was the same as the one he had held during learning. This (partial) list reminds us that remembering depends on many factors, and many of them—including the choice of encoding strategy and the influence of other relevant knowledge—depend on the individual person doing the memorizing.

Finally, we also should note a set of themes that link memory on the one hand to perception on the other. Both of these mental capacities need to tell us about reality—the reality available to our sensory organs right now, and the reality we experienced at some point in the past. Both of these capacities, therefore, must begin with certain facts—sensory cues for one, bits provided by genuine recollection for the other, and this allows what, in Chapter 5, we called "bottom-up" processes. But both of these capacities often need to go beyond the available information, so they also rely on "top-down" processes, drawing on other knowledge to fill gaps in what we perceive or recall. And both capacities often seem to involve elements of problem solving and inference, as we try to make sense of the sometimes-partial, sometimes-ambiguous information provided by our senses or our recall. In this sense, both perception and memory are clearly linked to another mental capacity—our capacity for *thinking*, the main topic in the next chapter.

SUMMARY

ACQUISITION, STORAGE, RETRIEVAL

- Any act of remembering begins with *acquisition*, the process of gathering information and placing it into memory. The next aspect of memory is *storage*, the holding of information in some enduring form in the mind for later use. The final phase is *retrieval*, the point at which we draw information from storage and use it in some fashion.

ACQUISITION

- *Memory acquisition* includes cases of intentional learning and also *incidental learning*. In either case, the person must pay attention to the to-be-remembered material in order to achieve *memory encoding*.
- According to the *stage theory of memory*, information is held in *working memory* while one is thinking about it, but lodged in *long-term memory* for storage for longer intervals. This theory is supported by studies of *free recall*. In these studies, *primacy effects* reflect the fact that early

items in a presentation receive more *rehearsal*, and are more likely to be transferred to long-term storage. Recency *effects* reflect the fact that just-heard items can be retrieved directly from working memory.
- *Chunking* is the process through which items are recoded into a smaller number of larger units. The active nature of memory is also evident in the fact that mere *maintenance rehearsal* does little to promote long-term storage. Long-term retention is instead promoted by *elaborative rehearsal*.
- According to the *depth-of-processing hypothesis*, successful remembering depends on the depth at which the incoming information is processed, where *shallow processing* refers to encoding that emphasizes the superficial characteristics of a stimulus, and *deep processing* refers to encoding that emphasizes the meaning of the material. Consistent with this perspective, we remember best material that we have understood, thanks to the memory connections that link one memory to the next. At the time of recall, these connections serve as *retrieval paths*.

- *Mnemonics* help a person form memory connections, and these connections can provide dramatic improvement in memory. Many mnemonics utilize imagery, but imagery is helpful only if the visualized items are imagined in some interaction—linking the items to each other, as one would expect if imagery is a means of promoting memory connections.

STORAGE

- There is debate about how the *memory trace* is actually represented in the brain. However, evidence suggests that different elements of a single memory (what things looked like, how one felt) may be stored in different brain sites.
- The establishment of a long-term memory depends on a *memory consolidation* process, during which new connections are formed among neurons. The need for consolidation is reflected in cases in which this process has been disrupted, resulting in *retrograde amnesia*.

RETRIEVAL

- The retrieval of memories is often promoted by our having an appropriate *retrieval cue*. Whether a cue is useful depends on whether the cue re-creates the context in which the original learning occurred. This *context reinstatement* allows the person to use the connections they formed earlier as retrieval paths.
- What is stored in memory reflects how the person thought about or reacted to the object or event being remembered. This *encoding specificity* is reflected in the fact that remembering is more likely if one thinks about the target information during retrieval in the same fashion that one did during encoding.

WHEN MEMORY FAILS

- Many cases of forgetting can be understood as the result of inadequate encoding. This is reflected in the fact that fMRI data, collected during encoding, show different patterns for later-remembered material and later-forgotten material.
- Forgetting generally increases the longer the *retention interval*, but the causes of forgetting are still a matter of debate. One theory holds that traces gradually decay. Another view argues that the cause of forgetting is *interference* produced by other memories. In some cases, this is because the other memories promote *retrieval failure*—an inability to find information that is nonetheless still in storage. Retrieval failure is evident when some new cue allows us to recall previously forgotten materials, and it is also demonstrated by the *tip-of-the-tongue effect*.

- Interference can also result from the mixing together of memories. These *intrusion errors* are evident in the *misinformation effect*, in which specific episodes are blurred together. In other cases, intrusion errors are the result of *generic memory* intruding into someone's memory of a particular event. This reflects a broader pattern of evidence indicating that events are usually understood (and remembered) with reference to knowledge structures called *scripts* or *schemas*.
- Another source of memory errors is *source confusion*. This mistake is promoted by the fact that *familiarity* and *recollection* are distinct in several ways, including the principles that govern them and also the brain areas that support them during learning and during retrieval.
- Psychologists have searched unsuccessfully for means of distinguishing correct memories from mistaken ones. The *confidence* expressed by the person remembering turns out to be of little value for this discrimination. *Hypnosis* also does nothing to improve memory and can actually increase the risk of memory error.

VARIETIES OF MEMORY

- Researchers find it useful to distinguish several types of memory. *Episodic memories* concern specific episodes; *generic memories* concern broader knowledge, not tied to a particular episode. *Explicit memories* are consciously recalled; *implicit memories* are revealed when there is an effect of some past experience without the person being aware that she is remembering at all—or even that there was a relevant past experience.
- Certain injuries to the brain produce *anterograde amnesia*, in which the patient's ability to fix material in long-term memory is reduced. However, someone with amnesia may still have intact implicit memories or *procedural knowledge*.
- Being emotional at the time of an event seems to promote memory for that event, with several mechanisms contributing to this effect. In the extreme, an emotional event may produce a *flashbulb memory*, which is recalled vividly years after the event. However, flashbulb memories probably do not involve some separate and specialized mechanism, because flashbulb memories can sometimes include errors (just like any other memory), and other memories are also sometimes very long-lived.
- Traumatic events are usually remembered extremely well, but the data pattern is mixed: Some traumatic events seem not to be remembered, and several mechanisms contribute to this forgetting.
- There has been considerable controversy over the status of *repressed memories*. Evidence suggests, though, that enormous caution is required in assessing these memories.

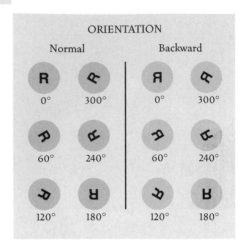

8.1 *Mental rotation   Normal and backward versions of one of the characters used in the mental rotation study, showing the orientations in which it appeared as a test stimulus.*

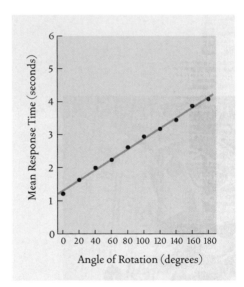

8.2 *Data from a mental rotation experiment Research participants need to imagine a form rotating into an upright position in order to make a judgment about that form. The greater the degree of rotation required, the longer the response time.*

These concerns have led researchers to seek more objective means of studying mental imagery. Their experiments typically ask research participants to do something with the image—to manipulate it in some fashion or to "read off" certain information from the image. And the results of these studies are clear: This turns out to be a case in which introspection leads us in the right direction, because, to a remarkable extent, visual images do function just like mental pictures.

In *mental rotation* experiments, for example, participants are shown a letter or a number, either in its normal version or mirror-reversed (that is, *R* or Я). In addition, the figures are tilted so that participants might encounter an *R* rotated by, say, 180 degrees or an Я rotated by, say, 60 degrees (Figure 8.1). Their task is to press one button if the stimulus is normal, another if it is mirror-reversed.

As the orientation of the letters changes from upright (that is, 0 degree rotation) through 60 degrees to 180 degrees, response times for making this decision steadily increase (Figure 8.2). It seems, therefore, that participants perform this task by imagining the test stimulus rotating into an upright position; only then can they judge it as normal or mirror-reversed. In addition, mental rotation (just like actual movement) takes time: The more the character has to be rotated, the longer it takes (Cooper & Shepard, 1973; Shepard & Cooper, 1982).

Another line of evidence comes from studies on *image scanning*. In a classic study, research participants were first shown the map of a fictitious island containing various objects: a hut, a well, a tree, and so on (Figure 8.3). After memorizing this map, the participants were asked to form a mental image of the entire island. The experimenter then named two objects on the map (e.g., the hut and the tree), and the participants had to imagine a black speck zipping from the first location to the second. The results showed that the time needed for this speck to "travel" from location to location was directly proportional to the distance between the two points. Of course, this is just what one would expect if participants were scanning a physical map with their eyes. That the same holds true when they scan a mental image with the mind's eye highlights the remarkable parallels between mental images and visual stimuli, between imaging and perceiving (Kosslyn, Ball, & Reisser, 1978).

IMAGES AND PICTURES

Clearly, then, visual images do share properties with pictures. Specifically, it seems that the spatial characteristics of a scene or object are directly represented in the image, so

8.3 *Image scanning   Research participants were asked to form a mental image of a map of an island and then to imagine a speck zipping from one location to another.*

that the image truly *depicts* the scene just as a picture does, rather than *describing* it in some symbolic fashion. Thus, if two points are close together in the to-be-represented scene, they will be functionally close together in the image; if they are far apart, they will be functionally far apart in the image. Likewise for the spatial relationship of being "between." If point *B* in the scene is between points *A* and *C*, this relation will be preserved in the image, so one cannot mentally scan from point *A* to point *C* without passing through point *B*.

It is perhaps unsurprising, therefore, that images function just like pictures in many settings. For example, we discussed the role of mnemonic imagery in Chapter 7: Apparently, we can "discover" elements in a mental image and thus be reminded of them, just as we can with a picture. Similarly, mental images can help people solve problems, including problems that require creative solutions (Finke, 1993; Finke, Ward, & Smith, 1992).

In addition, evidence indicates that we use roughly the same brain structures to examine a mental picture or as we do to examine an actual visual stimulus. This is clear, for example, in neuroimaging studies, which show that many of the same brain regions (primarily in the occipital lobe) are active during both visual perception and visual imagery (see the photo on p. 4 of Chapter 1). In fact, the parallels between these two activities are quite precise: When people are asked to imagine movement patterns, for example, high levels of activation are observed in brain areas that are sensitive to motion in ordinary perception. Likewise, for very detailed images, the brain areas that are especially activated tend to be those crucial for the perception of fine detail in an actual stimulus (Behrmann, 2000; Farah, 1988; Goebel, Khorram-Sefat, Muckli, Hacker, & Singer, 1998; Thompson & Kosslyn, 2000).

Evidence also comes from studies of individuals with brain damage. Lesions that disrupt vision also seem to disrupt visual imagery and vice versa, and often these disruptions are quite specific. For example, patients who, because of a stroke, lose the ability to perceive color often seem to lose the ability to imagine scenes in color; patients who lose the ability to perceive fine detail also seem to lose the ability to visualize fine detail (Farah, 1988; Isha & Sagi, 1995; Miyashita, 1995).

Still further evidence comes from a procedure that produces a "temporary lesion" in an otherwise healthy brain. The technique of transcranial magnetic stimulation (TMS) creates a series of strong magnetic pulses at a specific location on the scalp; these pulses cause a short-lived disruption in the brain region directly underneath this scalp area. In this fashion, it is possible to disrupt the primary visual cortex in a normal brain. Not surprisingly, using TMS in this way causes problems in vision. It also causes parallel problems in visual imagery, providing a powerful argument that this brain region is crucial both for the processing of visual information and for the creation and maintenance of visual images (Kosslyn et al., 1999).

All of these findings point to considerable overlap between visualizing and perceiving, and between mental pictures and actual pictures. But alongside this overlap, there are also important contrasts, because, while images are picturelike, they are not actually pictures. Evidence for this point comes from a study in which research participants were shown a figure that they had never seen before. This figure is normally ambiguous: If it is seen as oriented toward the left, it looks like the head of a duck; if oriented toward the right, it looks like the head of a rabbit (Figure 8.4). The picture was then removed, and the participants were asked to form a mental image of it. They were then asked to inspect the mental image and describe what it looked like. All "saw" either a duck or a rabbit with their mind's eye, and some said they saw it very vividly. They were then asked whether their image might look like something else. Not one of the participants came up with a reversal, even after hints and considerable coaxing. The results were very different, though, when, a minute later, they drew the figure and looked at their own drawing. Now everyone came up with the perceptual alternative. These findings seem to indicate that a visual image is not a picture. It is, as we have said, a depiction, and in this regard it

8.4 Images are not pictures *The rabbit-duck figure, first used in 1900 by Joseph Jastrow. (For details see text.)*

is very much like a picture. But, unlike a picture, an image seems to be already organized and interpreted to some extent; as a result, it has lost the potential for easy reinterpretation (Chambers & Reisberg, 1985; also Reisberg & Heuer, 2005).

We should note, though, that, in this last regard, mental images are just like *percepts*, the mental representations of the world around us that are produced during ordinary perceiving. In Chapter 5, we noted that our perception "goes beyond the information given" in the stimulus information, so that our perception of the world contains elements of organization and interpretation that are not present in the sensory input. Apparently, the same is true for mental images. Like pictures, images show us directly what the imaged object or scene looks like (i.e., they *depict* the object or scene). But like percepts, images depict in a fashion that organizes the information and, in the process, removes the ambiguity that is present, say, in the picture shown in Figure 8.4.

SPATIAL THINKING

Mental images, it seems, are clearly a distinctive form of mental representations, and they are immensely useful for storing information about appearances or spatial arrangements. Before moving on, though, we should note that images are not our only way of storing this information. For example, when people are asked to memorize colors, evidence suggests that they often memorize the color's *label* ("dark green," or "mauve," or "like the color of my grandmother's couch") rather than the color's actual appearance. Likewise, when reasoning about spatial arrangements, people often use analogical representations—but not always.

In one study, for example, people were asked questions about geography, such as: "Which is farther to the west—San Diego, California, or Reno, Nevada?" Most participants judged San Diego to be farther west, but this is wrong (Figure 8.5). Similarly, they judged Montreal, Canada, to be farther north than Seattle, Washington, although the reverse is true. These results suggest that they were not basing their answers on mental maps at all. Instead, they seemed to be reasoning in this fashion:

California is west of Nevada.
San Diego is in California.
Reno is in Nevada.
Therefore, San Diego is west of Reno.

8.5 Conceptual mental maps   Research participants tend to judge San Diego to be west of Reno and Montreal to be north of Seattle. But these judgments are in error. (A) A map of California and Nevada with lines of longitude, which show that, in fact, San Diego is east of Reno. (B) A map of the United States and southern Canada with lines of latitude, which show that Seattle is slightly north of Montreal.

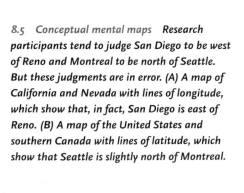

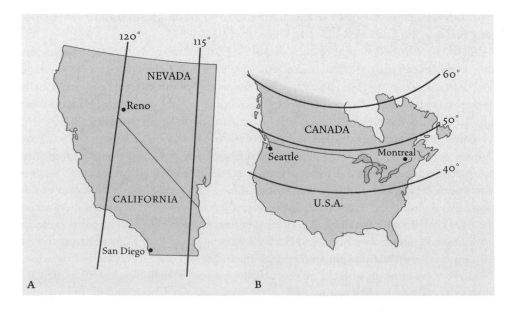

The knowledge being used here ("San Diego is in California") is clearly symbolic, not pictorial. Moreover, these symbolic formulations can (and in this case do) lead to error. Even so, most of us often store spatial information in such a rough-and-ready conceptual way. To the extent that we do store some geographical information under category rubrics, our spatial knowledge is not exclusively—or even largely—picturelike (Stevens & Coupe, 1978).

SYMBOLIC REPRESENTATIONS

Analogical representations (such as images) are plainly important for us, but many theorists would argue that most of our thinking is symbolic, not analogical, in nature. What are the symbols that constitute this form of thinking, and how do these symbols specify what ideas or objects in the world they are symbols of? The attempt to address these questions is relatively recent, at least in psychology. But other disciplines—including philosophy, logic, and linguistics—have wrestled with these issues for many years, and their progress provides crucial groundwork for psychological research in this domain.

SYMBOLIC ELEMENTS

It is important to distinguish two aspects of our symbolic thinking: First, there are concepts, the things we think about, and, second, there are ways of assembling concepts into more complex thoughts and beliefs.

CONCEPTS

The term *concept* describes a mental class or category. An example is *dog*, which includes *poodle*, *beagle*, *dachshund*, and *Alsatian*. Other concepts—such as *length* and *age*—designate qualities or dimensions. Still other concepts are relational, such as *taller than*.

There is disagreement among scholars about how exactly concepts are represented in the mind. Some suggest that the representation is relatively abstract—perhaps a list of features that characterize the concept. Others propose more concrete modes of representation—for example, some memory record of the various individuals within the relevant category, with these records collectively representing the entire concept. Still others argue that concepts are represented only in relationship to each other, so that our mental representation of *airplane*, for example, is intimately connected to our representations of *travel* and of *distance* and so on. We will return to these issues in Chapter 9 (see also Reisberg, 2006). Alongside of these disagreements, though, one point is clear: Concepts are the building blocks of our symbolic knowledge.

PROPOSITIONS

To represent our (sometimes complex) ideas and beliefs, we need a means of combining concepts into more complicated structures. One means of combination is by association, and some scholars argue that a great deal of our thinking can be understood in these terms. Others suggest, though, that associative links may be inadequate as a means of representing the organized regularities of our thoughts; these scholars propose instead that our thoughts take the form of *propositions*—statements that relate a subject (the item about which the statement is being made) and a predicate (what is being asserted about the subject). Propositions can be true or false. For example, "Solomon loves frogs," "Jacob plays lacrosse," and "Squirrels eat burritos" are all propositions. But just the words "Susan" or "is squeamish" are not propositions—the first is a subject without a predicate; the second is a predicate without a subject. (For more on how propositions are structured, and the role they play in our thoughts, see Anderson, 1993, 1996.)

KNOWLEDGE AND MEMORY

When we think, we often form new concepts and formulate new beliefs. But many concepts and beliefs are already stored in memory, where they constitute our accumulated knowledge, the "database" that sustains and informs our thoughts. How is this knowledge organized in memory, and how is it retrieved?

GENERIC MEMORY

In Chapter 7, we said a great deal about how information is stored in, and then retrieved from, memory. Most of the examples we considered in that chapter were concerned with episodic memory, but we also noted the importance of *generic memory*, the memory that contains the knowledge that each of us has—knowledge that is independent of any particular episodes, and certainly independent of where or when we acquired that bit of knowledge. Thus, for example, our generic memories tell us that Paris is the capital of France, that 3 is the square root of 9, and that sugar is an ingredient of most cookies. Rarely, though, do we remember how or when we acquired bits of knowledge like these; if we did, our recollection would be episodic, not generic.

For each person, generic memory contains an extraordinary wealth of knowledge, including countless facts about the world, knowledge of what objects look like, friends' names and the spatial layout of one's hometown, the lyrics for perhaps a hundred songs, the plots from dozens of TV shows, and on and on. Within this huge archive, one of the important components is *semantic memory*, which concerns the meanings of words and concepts. As some authors conceive it, our entire vocabulary is in this store: every word, together with its pronunciation, all of its meanings, its relations to objects in the real world, and the way it is put together with other words to make phrases and sentences.

Given the huge size of generic memory, how do we ever find the information we seek within this vast library? Clearly, there must be some sort of organizational system; otherwise, the hunt for an entry might last for days. But what is that system?

NETWORK MODELS OF GENERIC MEMORY

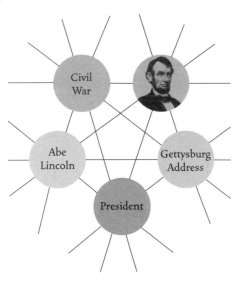

8.6 Associative connections *Many investigators propose that our knowledge is represented through a network of associated ideas, so that the idea of "Lincoln" is linked to "Civil War" and "President," and so on.*

Several investigators have proposed *network models* of generic memory. Within these networks, words or concepts are represented by *nodes*, while the associations between the concepts are indicated by *associative links* (Figure 8.6). As we discussed in Chapter 7, these connections among ideas serve as retrieval paths, but the connections also provide part of the knowledge representation itself—so the link from, say, *Abe Lincoln* to *president* is not just a retrieval path; that link actually represents part of our knowledge about Lincoln.

Links within the network can represent many different kinds of relationships, including relationships based on hierarchical position (as in *canary–bird*) or on similarity of meaning (*apple–orange*) or on well-learned associations (*peanut butter–jelly*). According to some proposals, groups of links can also be organized in a fashion that allows them to represent propositions (Figure 8.7; Anderson, 1993, 1996).

The nodes representing an idea are activated whenever a person is thinking about that idea. This activation then spreads to neighboring nodes, through the associative links, much as electrical current spreads through a network of wires. There are, however, important limits on this spread of activation. First, the spread of activation will be weaker (and will occur more slowly) between nodes that are only weakly associated. Second, the activation will dissipate as it spreads outward, so little or no activation will reach the nodes more distant from the activation's source (Collins & Loftus, 1975).

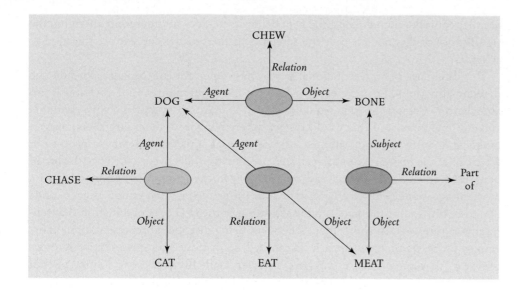

8.7 Propositions One proposal is that your understanding of dogs—what they are, what they are likely to do—is represented by an interconnected network of propositions. In this figure, each proposition is represented by an ellipse, and is the meeting place for the elements that are brought together in the proposition. Thus, this bit of memory network contains the propositions "dogs chew bones," "dogs chase cats," and so on. A complete representation about your knowledge of dogs would include many other propositions as well.

One line of evidence for these claims comes from experiments on **semantic priming**. In a classic study, participants were presented with two strings of letters, one printed above the other (Meyer & Schvaneveldt, 1971). Three examples are:

nurse	*nurse*	*narde*
butter	*doctor*	*doctor*

The participants' job was to press a "yes" button if both sequences were real words (e.g., *nurse–butter* or *nurse–doctor*) and a "no" button if either was not a word (e.g., *narde–doctor*). Our interest is in the two pairs that required a "yes" response. (In these tasks, the "no" items serve only as **catch trials**, ensuring that participants really are doing the task as they were instructed to do.)

Response times in this task were reliably shorter when the two words were related in meaning (as in *nurse–doctor*) than when they were unrelated (*nurse–butter*). This is because the sight of the word *nurse* activated the node for this concept. Once the node was activated, activation spread out from this source to the other nodes nearby. This warmed up these nearby nodes, including the node for *doctor*. If *doctor* was then the next word to be dealt with, the warm-up led to easier activation of its node and thus to a faster response.

CONNECTIONISM

Theorists have offered several different proposals for how a network model might function, and one major difference among these proposals concerns the nature of the representation for individual ideas. According to some theorists, human knowledge is best understood through models relying on **local representations**, in which each concept—say, the concept *fire engine*—is represented by a particular node or set of nodes. When these nodes are activated, one is thinking about fire engines, and when one is thinking about fire engines, these nodes are activated.

Other theorists argue for a different type of model, one relying on **distributed representations**. In these models, each concept is represented, not by a single node, but by a pattern of activation across the entire network. To take a highly simplified case, the concept *fire engine* might be represented by a pattern in which nodes A, D, H, and Q are firing, whereas the concept *ambulance* might be represented by a pattern in which nodes D, F, L, and T are firing. Notice that, in this case, node D is part of the pattern that represents *fire engine* but also part of the patterns that represent *ambulance* and a number of other concepts as well. Thus, the *D* node, by itself, does not represent anything; the significance of this node is only interpretable in the broader context of other nodes' activities.

This difference in representational format has important consequences for how the network functions. Imagine being asked, "What equipment would you find in an ambulance?" Presumably, you would answer this question by starting with thoughts about ambulances, and this would trigger other thoughts—about stretchers, oxygen tanks, and so on. With distributed representations, this must involve a process in which all of the nodes representing *ambulance* manage collectively to activate the broad pattern of nodes representing (say) *oxygen tank*. In the (simplified) terms we used a moment ago, node *D* might trigger node *H* at the same time that node *F* triggers node *Q*, and so on, leading ultimately to the activation of the *H-Q-S-Y* combination that represents *oxygen tank*. In short, then, a network using distributed representations must employ processes that are similarly distributed, so that one widespread activation pattern (e.g., that for *ambulance*) can have broad enough effects to evoke a different (but equally widespread) pattern. Moreover, the steps bringing this about must occur simultaneously—in parallel—with each other, so that one entire representation can smoothly trigger the next entire representation.

It turns out that this reliance on distributed processes brings impressive computational power; in fact, connectionist models have been successfully devised for many cognitive operations, including pattern recognition, memory processes, and aspects of thinking and language (Churchland & Sejnowski, 1992; McClelland & Rumelhart, 1986; Rumelhart, 1997; Seidenberg, 2005). Indeed, proponents of this approach believe that eventually all cognitive operations will be described in these terms. They argue that, in general, the complex phenomena of mental functioning are best understood as the result of many smaller events, much as an avalanche is produced by the movement of many small stones and rocks. Each of these smaller events is computationally simple, but that is okay, since each is responsible only for a fraction of the overall achievement.

These proposals have, however, led to considerable debate, with some researchers strongly advocating connectionist models (see, for example, Christiansen, Chater, & Seidenberg, 1999; Churchland & Sejnowski, 1992; McClelland & Seidenberg, 2000) and others claiming that these models are sharply limited in what they can accomplish (see, for example, Fodor, 1997; Pinker, 1999). How this debate will turn out remains to be seen. This is an exciting area of research, and new advances are coming at a rapid rate.

THE PROCESS OF THINKING: SOLVING PROBLEMS

So far, we have said a lot about the building blocks of thought and knowledge, but what about the more dynamic aspects of thought—the flow of ideas that we move through when we are drawing a conclusion or making a decision? We turn now to these issues, starting with the question of how thought proceeds in a particular area: problem solving.

ORGANIZATION IN PROBLEM SOLVING

How do our thoughts progress when we are trying to figure out how to repair a broken bicycle or, for that matter, a damaged relationship? How do we move forward when searching for a job or for a topic for the term paper due next Friday? In each case, our situation has an *initial state* (we need a paper topic, or the bicycle is not working) and a *goal state* (we have selected a topic, or the bicycle is fine), and our task is to find a path that will bring us from the former to the latter.

In searching for this path forward, we are heavily influenced not just by the problem as it is presented to us, but also by how we understand the problem. At the minimum, this understanding involves knowing what the goal state is, because our thinking about a problem is usually guided both by a sense of where we are right now and by a sense of where we want to get. It turns out, though, that it is often unclear *how* we should think about the goal state. For example, let us say that you want to do something fun next summer. In this case, your understanding of the goal state is rather vague, providing little guidance in your search for a specific plan. Likewise, how should we solve the problem of global warming? Here, too, we do not know exactly what the goal state involves—it might be a situation in which we have found a way to burn less fossil fuel, or one in which we have found a way to remove pollutants already in the atmosphere, or it might take some other form altogether.

Psychologists call problems like these *ill-defined problems*, because, at the start, we do not know exactly what our goal will include, nor do we know what our options might be for reaching the goal. In contrast, a problem like solving an anagram is a *well-defined problem* (e.g., "What English word can be produced by rearranging the letters *subufoal*?"). Here we know from the start that the goal will involve just these eight letters and will be a word in the English language; other examples of well-defined problems are shown in Figure 8.8.

It is no surprise that well-defined problems are easier, because, with them, we know where we are going and we know what possibilities to consider as means of getting there. It is entirely sensible, therefore, that people often try to solve ill-defined problems by first making them well defined—that is, by seeking ways to clarify and specify the goal state. In many cases, this effort involves adding extra constraints or extra assumptions ("Let me assume that my summer of fun will involve spending time near the ocean" or "Let me assume that my summer travel can't cost more than $500"). This will narrow the set of options—and, conceivably, may hide the best options from view—but, for many problems, defining the problem more clearly helps enormously in the search for a solution (Schraw, Dunkle, & Bendixen, 1995).

HIERARCHICAL ORGANIZATION

Having a clear definition of a problem's goal helps the problem solver know which options are worth considering and which are not. Thus, in solving an anagram, you do not waste time in adding extra letters or turning some of the letters into numerals—these steps are incompatible with your goal. (The solution to the earlier example, by the way, is *fabulous*.)

Understanding a problem, though, involves more than just understanding the problem's goal. To see this, consider an often effective problem-solving strategy called *means-end analysis*. To use this strategy, one asks, "What is the difference between my current state and my goal?" Then, with that difference defined, one asks, "What means do I have available for reducing this difference?" Thus, for example: "I want to get to the store. What's the difference between my current state and my goal? One of distance. What changes distance? My automobile. My automobile won't work. What is needed to make it work? A new battery. Where do I get a battery?" And so on (after Newell & Simon, 1972).

A means-end analysis can replace the initial problem (e.g., getting to the store) with a series of subproblems (e.g., getting the car to work, obtaining a new battery), and, with that, the initial goal gets replaced by a series of subgoals. If this process is repeated

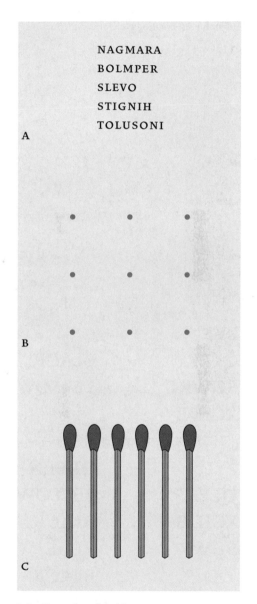

NAGMARA
BOLMPER
SLEVO
STIGNIH
TOLUSONI

A

B

C

8.8 Examples of problems (A) *Anagrams. Rearrange the letters on each line to form a word.* (B) *Nine-dot problem. Nine dots are arranged in a square. Connect them by drawing four continuous straight lines without lifting your pencil from the paper.* (C) *Matchstick problem. Assemble all six matches to form four equilateral triangles, each side of which is equal to the length of one match. (For the solutions to all three problems, see p. 285.)*

8.9 Problems and subproblems   *It is helpful to replace an initial problem with a series of subproblems. By solving these, the initial problem is also solved. Subproblems, in turn, can be broken down into still-smaller subproblems, creating a hierarchical structure.*

Get to the airport

Get on the freeway ── Take freeway to airport exit ── Follow signs to the terminal

etc.   etc.

Go south on 18th Street ── Turn left on Main ── Look for the freeway on-ramp

etc.   etc.

Back out of the driveway ── Go to the corner ── Turn right onto 18th

etc.   etc.

Fasten seatbelt ── Start the engine ── Look in the mirror

(with subproblems being broken down into still smaller subproblems), it can create a hierarchical structure like the one shown in Figure 8.9.

Understanding a problem in terms of this sort of structure has several advantages. First, the subproblems are, by definition, smaller than the initial problem, so they are likely to be easier to solve than the original problem. Second, the subproblems are often quite straightforward. For example, a driver seeking to reach the airport might realize that her best path is the freeway, so the larger problem ("get to the airport") can be replaced with a simpler and more familiar routine ("take the freeway"). This routine in turn is composed of still simpler **subroutines**, such as "go to the on-ramp at Front Street," "accelerate when the light turns green," or even "maneuver through traffic." In this fashion, a series of modular units can be assembled into the larger-scale solution to the initial problem.

AUTOMATICITY

A reliance on subroutines also has another advantage. The modular units are often well practiced, and this allows the problem solver to focus attention on the larger-scale plan, rather than worry about the details of how the plan is to be implemented. In fact, this is one of the reasons why problems that seem impossible for the novice are absurdly easy for the expert: Even when the expert is facing a novel problem, he is likely to rely on a number of familiar subroutines that are already available as "chunks" in memory. Thus, the expert taxi driver gives little thought to maneuvering through traffic and so can focus his thoughts on the more general task of navigation. The novice driver must focus on the maneuvering, and, preoccupied with this, he may miss his exit.

In short, then, it is helpful that subroutines can be executed without much thought; this frees up attention for other aspects of the task. In some circumstances, though, this *automaticity* (the ability to do a task without paying attention to it) can create problems, because automatic actions, once set in motion, are often difficult to turn off or modify.

A striking example is known as the ***Stroop effect***, named after its discoverer (Stroop, 1935). To demonstrate this effect, research participants are asked to name the colors in which groups of letters are printed (Figure 8.10). If the letters are random sequences (*fwis, sgbr*) or irrelevant words (*chair, tape*), this task is rather easy. If, however, the letters form color names (*yellow, red*), the task becomes much harder. Thus, a participant might see *red* printed in green ink, *blue* in brown ink, and so on. Her task, of course, is simply to name

A	B
ZYP	RED
QLEKF	BLACK
SUWRG	YELLOW
XCIDB	BLUE
WOPR	RED
ZYP	GREEN
QLEKF	YELLOW
XCIDB	BLACK
SUWRG	BLUE
WOPR	BLACK

8.10 The Stroop effect   *The two lists, A and B, are printed in five colors—black, red, green, blue, and yellow. To observe the Stroop effect, name the colors (aloud) in which each of the nonsense syllables in list A is printed as fast as you can, continuing downward. Then do the same for list B, calling out the colors in which each of the words of the list is printed, again going from top to bottom. This will very probably be easier for list A than for list B, a demonstration of the Stroop effect.*

the ink color, so she should say "green, brown" in this example. But in this setting, the participant cannot help but read the words, and this produces a strong competing response: She is likely to respond very slowly, because while trying to name the ink colors, she is fighting the tendency to read the words themselves aloud. (For more on automaticity, see Bargh & Ferguson, 2000; Pashler, Johnston, & Ruthruff, 2000; Stolz & Besner, 1999.)

EXPERTS

It seems, then, that well-practiced subroutines can sometimes trap us in habitual responses; that is the point of the Stroop effect. Nonetheless, subroutines are unmistakably part of the toolkit used by expert problem solvers—carpenters figuring out how to construct a cabinet; economists figuring out how to analyze a market trend; students figuring out how to spend their weekend. Indeed, the experts' heavy reliance on subroutines makes it clear that subroutines are genuinely useful for skilled problem solving.

But the use of subroutines is only part of what makes someone an expert, and, in fact, experts have many advantages when compared to those of more modest skill. For example, experts simply know more in their domain of expertise; some theorists have suggested that this is why someone usually needs a full decade to acquire expert status, whether the proficiency is in music, software design, chess, or any other domain. Ten years is presumably the time needed to acquire a large enough knowledge base so that the expert has the necessary facts near at hand and the necessary subroutines well practiced and available (Hayes, 1985). In addition, an expert's knowledge is heavily cross-referenced, so that each bit of information has associations with many other bits. As a result, not only do experts know more, but they also have faster, more effective access to what they know (Bédard & Chi, 1992).

Crucially, though, experts also have a different sort of knowledge than novices do, knowledge focused on higher-order patterns. As a consequence, experts can, in effect, think in larger units, tackling problems in big steps rather than small ones. This is evident, for example, in studies of chess players (Chase & Simon, 1973a, b; de Groot, 1965). Novice chess players think about a game in terms of the position of individual pieces; experts, in contrast, think about the board in terms of pieces organized into broad strategic groupings (e.g., *a king-side attack with pawns*). This is made possible by the fact that the masters have a "chess vocabulary" in which these complex concepts are stored as single memory chunks, each with an associated set of subroutines for how one should respond to that pattern. Some investigators estimate, in fact, that the masters may have as many as 50,000 of these chunks in their memories, each representing a strategic pattern (Chase & Simon, 1973b).

These memory chunks can be detected in many ways, including the way that players recall a game. For example, players of different ranks were shown chess positions for 5 seconds each and then asked to reproduce the positions a few minutes later. Grandmasters and masters did so with hardly an error; lesser players, however, made many errors (Figure 8.11). This difference in performance was not due to the chess masters having better visual memory. When presented with bizarre positions, unlikely ever to arise in the course of a game, they recalled them no better than novices did, and in some cases they remembered the bizarre patterns less accurately than did novices (Gobet & Simon, 1996a, b, but also see Gobet & Simon, 2000; Lassiter, 2000). The superiority of the masters, therefore, was in their conceptual organization of chess, not in their memory for patterns as such.

Experts' sensitivity to a problem's organization can also be demonstrated in other ways. For example, novices in physics tend to group problems in terms of their surface characteristics, so they might group together, say, all the problems involving springs or all the problems involving inclined planes. Experts, in contrast, instantly perceive the deeper structure of each problem, so they group the problems, not according to surface features, but according to the physical principles relevant to each problem's solution. Clearly, then, the experts are more sensitive to the higher-order patterns, and this calls

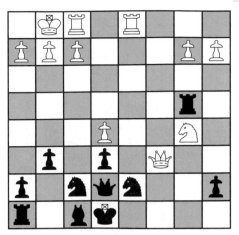

A   Actual position

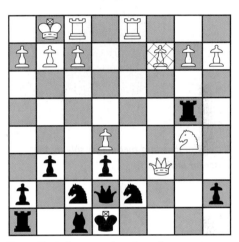

B   Typical master player's performance

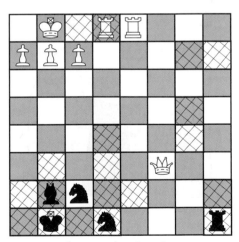

C   Typical average player's performance

8.11 Memory for chess positions in masters and average players (A) An actual chess position that was presented for five seconds after which the positions of the pieces had to be reconstructed. Typical performances by masters and average players are shown in (B) and (C) respectively, with errors indicated in red.

8.15   The water-lily problem   *Water lilies double in area every twenty-four hours. On the first day of summer, there is one water lily, as in (A). On the sixtieth day, the lake is all covered, as in (B). On what day is the lake half-covered?*

it must be half covered on the day before, since lilies double in area every day, which means that the answer is day 59 (after Sternberg & Davidson, 1983; Figure 8.15).

FINDING AN APPROPRIATE ANALOGY

Working backward is an effective strategy when one does not know how to reach a goal or cannot discern a problem's structure. Another important tool for solving difficult problems is to work by analogy, since many problems are similar to each other. A business manager is likely to find that the problem she hears about today reminds her of one she heard a few months back, and her experience with the first can help with the second. Similarly, scientists seeking to understand some new phenomenon often benefit from thinking back to other similar phenomena. In fact, analogies have often played an important role in the history of science, with scientists expanding their knowledge of gases by comparing the molecules to billiard balls or enlarging their understanding of the heart by comparing it to a pump (Gentner & Jeziorski, 1989).

The benefits of analogy are also evident in the laboratory. In one study, research participants were given this problem, devised by Duncker (1945):

> Suppose a patient has an inoperable stomach tumor. There are certain rays that can destroy this tumor if their intensity is great enough. At this intensity, however, the rays will also destroy the healthy tissue that surrounds the tumor (e.g., the stomach walls, the abdominal muscles, and so on). How can the tumor be destroyed without damaging the healthy tissue through which the rays must travel on their way?

The problem is quite difficult, and in this experiment, 90% of the participants failed to solve it. A second group, however, did much better. Before tackling the tumor problem, they read a story about a general who hoped to capture a fortress. He needed a large force of soldiers for this, but all of the roads leading to the fortress were planted with mines. Small groups of soldiers could travel the roads safely, but the mines would be detonated by a larger group. How, therefore, could the general move all the soldiers he would need toward the fortress? He could do this by dividing his army into small groups and sending each group via a different road. When he gave the signal, all the groups marched toward the fortress, where they converged and attacked successfully.

The fortress story is similar in its structure to the tumor problem. In both cases, the solution is to divide the "conquering" force so that it enters from several different directions. Thus, to destroy the tumor, several weak rays can be sent through the body, each from a different angle. The rays converge at the tumor, inflicting their combined effects just as desired (Figure 8.16).

8.16   Solution to the ray-tumor problem   *Several weak rays are sent from various points outside so that they meet at the tumor site. There the radiation of the rays will be intense, for all the effects will summate at this point. But since they are individually weak, the rays will not damage the healthy tissue that surrounds the tumor.*

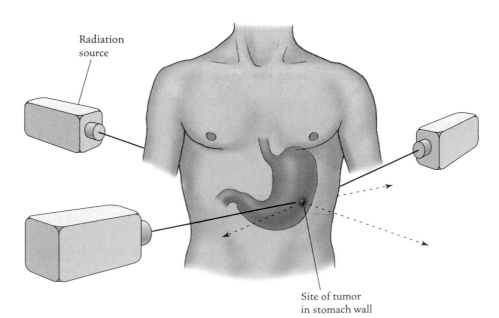

Radiation source

Site of tumor in stomach wall

With no hints, instructions, or analogous cases, only 10% of the participants were able to solve the tumor problem. However, if they were given the fortress story to read and told that it would help them, most (about 80%) did solve it. Obviously, the analogy was massively helpful. But it was not enough merely to know about the fortress story; participants also had to realize that the story is pertinent to the task at hand. And, surprisingly, they often failed to make this discovery. In another condition, participants read the fortress story but were not given any indication that this story was relevant to their task. In this condition, only 30% solved the tumor problem (Gick & Holyoak, 1980, 1983).

Given how beneficial analogies can be, is there anything we can do to encourage their use? Evidence suggests that people are extremely likely to rely on analogies if they see them—and, indeed, the use of analogies may be automatic, once the analogies are detected (e.g., Perrott, Gentner, & Bodenhausen, 2005). The problem lies in getting people to see the analogies in the first place, and there are, in fact, various things we can do to make this detection more likely. For example, people are more likely to use analogies if they are encouraged to focus on the underlying dynamic of the analogies (e.g., the fact that the fortress problem involves converging forces) rather than their more superficial features (e.g., the fact that the problem involves mines). Focusing on the underlying dynamic calls attention to the features shared by the problems, helping people to see the relevance of the analogies and enabling them to map one problem onto another (Blanchette & Dunbar, 2000; Catrambone, 1998; Cummins, 1992; Dunbar & Blanchette, 2001; Needham & Begg, 1991).

RESTRUCTURING

It seems, then, whether a problem is solved or not depends on how the problem was interpreted at the very start. Much depends, for example, on the problem solver's interpretation of the goal (pp. 280–282) and on whether the problem solver perceives the problem's various subgoals (pp. 282–284). A problem solver can also approach the problem with the wrong mental set—i.e., the wrong assumptions about how the problem should be approached (pp. 284–285). The problem solver's interpretation of the problem also influences the prospects for finding a useful analogy: If she understands the problem in terms of its underlying dynamic, she may be led to a helpful analogy and thus to a solution. If she understands the problem in terms of its surface elements, an analogy may not come to mind, making the problem appreciably more difficult.

All of this suggests that, when problem solving *fails*, our best bet may be to change our understanding of the problem—to one that highlights the problem's subgoals or one that suggests an anology. This point certainly seems in line with common experience: Sometimes we are utterly baffled by a problem, but then, later, we find an alternative way to approach the issue and quickly come up with the answer. Sometimes this *restructuring* of the problem is quite abrupt, experienced as a flash of insight with an accompanying exclamation of "Aha!"

It should be said, though, that these flashes of insight, as one moves from one understanding to another, are not uniformly beneficial. Sometimes the (apparent) insights turn out to be false alarms, because the new understanding simply leads to yet another dead end (Metcalfe, 1986; Metcalfe & Weibe, 1987). It seems, therefore, that the "Aha!" experience should not be understood as "I see the solution!" Instead, the experience merely implies, "I've discovered a new approach!" Whether this approach will turn out to be productive can only be decided after the fact. One way or another, though, these changes in the way a problem is defined are often essential for breaking out of an unproductive mental set and moving toward one that may lead to a solution.

CREATIVE THINKING

The restructuring of a problem also plays an important role in those special discoveries we consider creative. In general, scholars call the solution to a problem "creative" if that

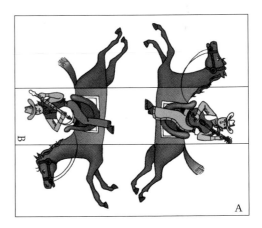

Solution to horse-and-rider problem **Solving the horse-and-rider puzzle (see Figure 8.14, p. 285) requires a change of perceptual set. Part B must be rotated 90 degrees over the middle of A, and then placed as shown here.**

LANGUAGE

By Lila R. Gleitman and Daniel Reisberg

When we consider the social forms and physical artifacts of human societies, we are struck by the diversity of cultures in different times and places. Some humans walk on foot, others travel on camels, and still others ride rockets to the moon. But in all communities and all times, humans are alike in having language. This crucial psychological connection, between *having language* and *being human*, has always intrigued those who are interested in the nature of the human mind. Indeed, to philosophers such as Descartes, language is the mental function that most clearly distinguishes humans from the other beasts, and is "the sole sign and only certain mark of thought hidden and wrapped up in the body." In this chapter, we will provide a general picture of human language and its learning.

THE BASIC UNITS OF LANGUAGE

Languages consist of a hierarchy of building blocks or units, which combine and recombine to form higher and higher level categories. At the bottom are units of **sound** such as *c*, *t*, and *a*, which combine into such **morphemes** and **words** as *cat*, *act*, and *tact*. These words combine in turn into such **phrases** as a *fat cat*, and the phrases then combine into such **sentences** as *A fat cat acts with tact* and *That's the act of a tacky cat*. (Figure 9.1 illustrates this hierarchy of linguistic categories.) Each language gets by with a small inventory of sound units and a limited (though large) inventory of words, but because of the flexibility with which these units combine and recombine, each person can express and understand innumerable new thoughts. We now take up each of these levels of organization in turn.

THE SOUND UNITS

To speak, we force a column of air up from the lungs and out through the mouth, while simultaneously moving the various parts of the vocal apparatus from one position to another (Figure 9.2). Each of these movements shapes the column of moving air and thus changes the sound produced. The human speech apparatus can produce hundreds of different speech sounds clearly and reliably, but each language makes systematic use of only a small number of these units. For example, consider the English word *bus*, which can be pronounced with more or less of a hiss in the *s*. This sound difference, though audible, is irrelevant to the English-language listener, who interprets what was heard to mean "a large vehicle" in either case. But some sound distinctions do matter, for they signal differences in meaning. Thus, neither *but* nor *fuss* will be taken to mean "a large vehicle." This suggests that the distinctions among *s*, *f*, and *t* sounds are relevant to the perception of English, while the difference in hiss magnitude is not. The sound categories that matter in a language are called its

Adam gives names to the animals   *The belief that knowledge of word meanings sets humans above animals goes back to antiquity. An example is the biblical tale (illustrated in this painting by William Blake), which shows Adam assigning names to the animals. According to some ancient legends, this act established Adam's intellectual superiority over all creation, including even the angels.*

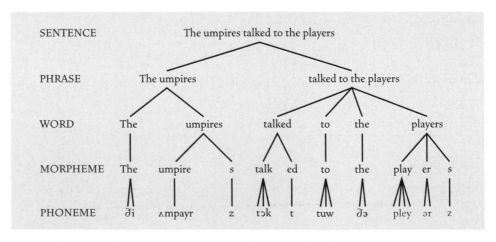

9.1   *The hierarchy of linguistic units*   *Language is hierarchical, with sentences at the top. Sentences are composed of phrases, which in turn are composed of words. Words are made up of morphemes, the smallest units of language that carry meaning. The units of sound that compose morphemes are phonemes. Equivalent gestural units exist for sign languages.*

phonemes. English uses about 40 different phonemes.* Other languages select their own sets. For instance, German uses certain guttural sounds that are never heard in English, and French uses some vowels that are different from the English ones (Ladefoged, 1975).

The phonemes are combined and sequenced to create morphemes and words. However, not every phoneme sequence occurs in every language. Sometimes these gaps are accidental. For instance, it just so happens that there is no English word *pilk.* But other gaps are systematic effects of the language design. As an illustration, could a new breakfast food be called *Pritos?* How about *Glitos* or *Tlitos?* Each of these would be a new sequence in English, and all can be pronounced, but one seems wrong: *Tlitos.* English speakers sense intuitively that English words never start with *tl*, even though this phoneme sequence is perfectly acceptable in the middle of a word (as in *motley* or *battling*). So the new breakfast food will be marketed as tasty, crunchy *Pritos* or *Glitos.* Either of these two names will do, but *Tlitos* is out of the question. The restriction against *tl* beginnings is not a restriction on what human tongues and ears can do. For instance, one Northwest Indian language is named Tlingit, obviously by people who are perfectly willing to have words begin with *tl.* This shows that the restriction is a fact about English specifically. Few of us are conscious of this pattern, but we have learned it and similar patterns exceedingly well, and we honor them in our actual language use.

Languages differ in several other ways at the level of sound (Mehler et al., 1996). There are marked differences in the **rhythm** in which the successive syllables occur, and differences in the use and patterning of **stress** (or accent) and **tone** (or pitch). For instance, in languages such as Mandarin Chinese or Igbo, two words that consist of the same phoneme sequence, but that differ in tone, can mean entirely different things (Cutler, Mehler, Norris, & Segui, 1986; Dupoux et al., 1997; Jusczyk, Cutler, & Redanz, 1993). Languages also differ in how the phonemes can occur together within **syllables**. Some languages, such as Hawaiian and Japanese, regularly alternate a single consonant with a single vowel. Thus, we can recognize words like *Toyota* and *origami* as sounding Japanese when they come into English usage. In contrast, syllables with two or three consonants at the beginning and end are common in English; for example, *flinging* or *strengthen* (Cutler & Otake, 1994; Friederici & Wessels, 1993; Pallier, Christophe, & Mehler, 1997).

* The English alphabet provides only 26 symbols (letters) to write these 40 phonemes, and so often the same symbol is used for more than one phoneme. Thus, for example, the letter *O* stands for two different phonemes in *hot* and *cold*, an "ah" sound and an "oh" sound. This fact—that the written and spoken symbols do not quite match—contributes to the difficulty of learning how to read English.

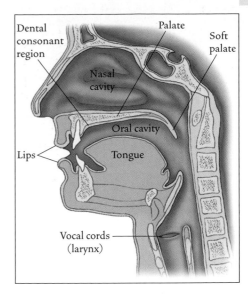

9.2 The human vocal tract *Speech is produced by air flow from the lungs that passes through the larynx (popularly called the voice box) containing the vocal cords and from there through the oral and nasal cavities, which together make up the vocal tract. Different vowels are created by movements of the lips and tongue, which change the size and shape of the vocal cavity. Consonants are produced by various articulatory movements that temporarily obstruct the air flow through the vocal tract.*

The distinctive sound of Hawaiian *The names of these two tropical fish—the* Humuhumunukunu- kapua'a *and the* Hinalea 'Akilolo—*sound foreign to the English listener in part because of the regular alternation between consonant and vowel. English, in contrast, has many words in which two or more consonants occur next to each other—for instance* shrimp, lobster, *and* flounder.

Speech can be understood at rates of up to about 250 words per minute (Foulke & Sticht, 1969). The normal rate is closer to 180 words per minute, which converts to about 14 phonemes per second. These phonemes are usually fired off in a continuous stream, without gaps or silences in between. This is true for phonemes within a single word and also for words within a phrase, so that sometimes it is hard to know whether one is hearing "that great abbey" versus "that gray tabby" or "The sky is falling" versus "This guy is falling" (Liberman, Cooper, Shankweiler, & Studdert-Kennedy, 1967; see Figure 9.3).

MORPHEMES AND WORDS

At the next level of the linguistic hierarchy (Figure 9.1), fixed sequences of phonemes and syllables are joined into morphemes. The *morphemes* are the smallest language units that carry bits of meaning. Examples of morphemes are *talk*, *tree*, and the *ed* morpheme that marks the past tense. Some words consist of a single morpheme, such as *and*, *run*, and *bake*, while others contain more than one, for example, *nightfall* and *downstairs*. Certain morphemes cannot stand alone and must be joined with others to make up a complex word. We mentioned *ed*; other examples are *er* (meaning "one who") and *s* (meaning "more than one"). When these are joined with the morpheme *bake* (meaning "to cook by slow heating") into the complex word *bakers* (bake + er + s), the meaning becomes correspondingly complex ("ones who cook by slow heating").

CONTENT MORPHEMES AND FUNCTION MORPHEMES

Morphemes such as *bake* and *man* that carry the main burden of meaning are called *content morphemes*. The morphemes that not only add details to the meaning but also serve various grammatical purposes (such as the suffixes *-er* and *-ed* and the connecting words *and* and *which*) are called *function morphemes*. This distinction of morpheme type, existing in all languages, is reflected in the sound characteristics of the language, so that content and function morphemes are pronounced somewhat differently (Shi, Morgan, & Allopenna, 1998). Very young children often omit function morphemes in

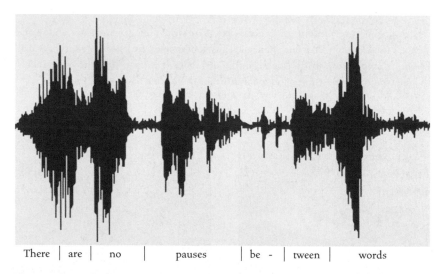

| There | are | no | pauses | be - | tween | words |

9.3 The actual sound pattern of speech   This figure shows the moment-by-moment sound amplitudes produced by a speaker uttering the sentence There are no pauses between words. Notice that there is no gap between the sounds carrying the word are and the sounds carrying no. Nor is there a gap between the sounds carrying between and the sounds carrying words. Therefore listeners must figure out where one word ends and the next begins, a process known as segmentation.

their first primitive English utterances (R. Brown & Bellugi, 1964; Gerken, Landau, & Remez, 1990; L. R. Gleitman & Wanner, 1982). In brain injury, a person's ability to process function morphemes can be compromised while the content words remain intact or close to intact; the reverse condition also sometimes occurs. (See Chapter 3 for a discussion of aphasia.) Recordings of activity in the brain reveal that content and function morphemes are processed in different ways during normal language activities (C. M. Brown, Hagoort, & ter Keurs, 1999).

PHRASES AND SENTENCES

Just as a morpheme is an organized grouping of phonemes and a word is an organized grouping of morphemes, so a **phrase** is an organized grouping of words (*the*, *black*, and *cat* combine to yield the phrase *the black cat*), and a **sentence** is an organized grouping of phrases (*the black cat* and *runs away* combine to yield *The black cat runs away*). Once again, though, there are constraints on the sequences that are allowed. *House the is red* and *Where put you the pepper?* do not sound acceptable (or grammatical) as combinations. One might think that the distinction between grammatical and ungrammatical sentences is just a matter of meaningfulness—whether the combination of words and phrases has yielded a coherent idea or thought. But this is not so. Some nonsentences have meaning (*Me Tarzan; you Jane*). And many grammatical sentences are entirely uninterpretable (*Colorless green ideas sleep furiously*). This sentence makes no sense because ideas have no color and green things are not colorless. But it seems well formed in a way that *Sleep green furiously ideas colorless* does not. Conformance with some rulelike system rather than meaningfulness seems to be behind the notion of grammaticality—regularities of formation like those of the rules of arithmetic or of chess. Much as you cannot (as a competent calculator) add 2 and 2 to yield 5, you cannot say *House the is red* to yield a sentence in English. These constraints on how words and phrases can combine into sentences are called the **rules of syntax**.

The study of syntax has been one of the chief concerns of linguists and psycholinguists, with much of the discussion organized around the theories of Noam Chomsky (Chomsky, 1965, 1981b, 1995). As Chomsky emphasized, this interest in the rules governing word combination is not surprising if one wants to understand the fact that we can say and understand a virtually unlimited number of new things, all of them "in English." To make infinite use of the finite number of words in one's vocabulary, one must understand the patterning that underlies their combination. We put our words together in new sentences to mean new things, but we have to do so systematically or our listeners won't be able to decipher the new combinations.

PHRASE STRUCTURE

Consider the simple sentence *The zebra bit the giraffe*. It consists of two major subparts or phrases, a noun phrase (*the zebra*) and a verb phrase (*bit the giraffe*). Linguists depict this partitioning of the sentence by means of a **tree diagram**, so called because of its branching appearance:

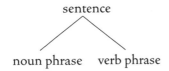

This notation is a useful way of showing that sentences can be thought of as a hierarchy of structures (Figure 9.1, p. 314). Each sentence can be broken down into phrases, and

"Boy, he must think we're pretty stupid to fall for that again."

Noam Chomsky

these phrases into smaller phrases. Thus, our verb phrase redivides as a verb (*bit*) and a noun phrase (*the giraffe*).

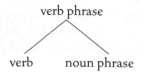

These subphrases in turn break down into the component words and morphemes. The descending branches of the tree correspond to the smaller and smaller units of sentence structure. The whole tree structure is called a ***phrase structure description*** (Figure 9.4).

The phrase structure description is a compact way of describing our implicit knowledge of how sentences are organized. Part of the efficiency is achieved by defining phrases in a way that is independent of where they appear within the sentence. The makeup of an English noun phrase, for example, must always follow the same pattern whether the noun phrase is at the start or the end of a sentence: Articles such as *a* and *the* come first; any adjectives come next; then the noun; and so forth. (Other languages such as Korean choose a different ordering of words inside the phrase, and of phrases inside the sentence, but they do so just as regularly and systematically.)

In essence, then, these rules define groups of words as modules that can be plugged in anywhere that the sentence calls for a phrase of the specified type. Consider the hypothetical sentence *The ball big rolled away*. Anyone who rejects this as a sentence of English is guaranteed also to reject *He chased the ball big* and *The ant was squashed under the ball big*. This is because the phrase *the ball big* does not follow the English-language rules for noun phrases, and so is illegitimate no matter where it occurs in the sentence. By the same token, anyone who accepts *I kissed a girl who is allergic to coconuts* is guaranteed to accept as grammatical *A girl who is allergic to coconuts was chased by a moose*. That is because once the phrase *a girl who is allergic to coconuts* is accepted as a noun phrase, it can be plugged into any position within a sentence that calls for a noun phrase.

The role of phrase structure is evident in many aspects of language use. For example, one investigator asked subjects to memorize strings of nonsense words. Some of the strings had no structure at all, such as *yig wur vum rix hum im jag miv*. Other strings also included various function morphemes, such as *the yigs wur vumly rixing hum im jagest miv*. One might think that sequences of the second type would be harder than the first to memorize, for they are longer. But in fact the opposite is true. The function morphemes in the second version allowed the listeners to organize the sequence as a phrase structure, and these structured sequences were appreciably easier to remember

9.4 *The structure of the sentence* The zebra bit the giraffe   *This tree is called a phrase structure description because it shows how the sentence can be analyzed into phrase units. Notice particularly that there are two noun phrases in this sentence. The first one (the zebra) is the subject of this sentence. The second one (the giraffe) is inside the verb phrase (bit the giraffe). A description of this kind also shows the word class types (e.g., article, noun, verb) of which each phrase consists. Finally, the tree shows the words of the sentence (the bottom row in the tree).*

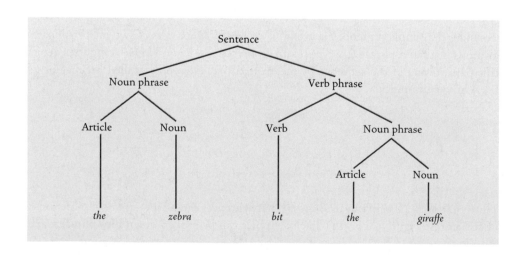

The large tomato	The
made	large tomato made
a satisfying splat	a satisfying
when	splat when it
it hit	hit the
the floor.	floor.

9.5 *Phrase structure organization aids the reader* *The panel on the left (blue) shows a sentence written so that its phrases and major words mostly appear on their own lines of print. This makes reading easier because the sentence has been pre-organized so that the eye can move phrase by phrase down the page. In the panel on the right (green), the sentence has been rewritten so that bits of more than one phrase often appear on a single line. Reading is now slower and may contain more errors because the phrasal organization has been visually disrupted.*

(W. Epstein, 1961; see also Levelt, 1970; for related data, see Chapter 7). Figure 9.5 shows that phrase structure organization aids reading just as it aids listening.

THE REAL COMPLEXITY OF LANGUAGE DESIGN

Most ordinary language users fluently utter, write, and understand many sentences 40, 50, and even 100 morphemes in length. The example below appeared in the "Letters to the Editor" column of a popular TV magazine (quoted in L. R. Gleitman & Wanner, 1982), so we can hardly protest that it was the creation of some linguistic Einstein or literary giant:

> *How Ann Salisbury can claim that Pam Dawber's anger at not receiving her fair share of acclaim for* Mork and Mindy's *success derives from a fragile ego escapes me.*

Leaving aside the peculiar interests of this correspondent, we must be impressed with the intricacy and systematicity with which he put the pieces of this sentence together. For example, the structure signaled by the first word of this sentence (*How*) requires that the 28th word (*escapes*) have an *s* at its end. How does the writer know this? For that matter, how do we readers recognize this same requirement and so conclude that the sentence is grammatical? Surely not by memorizing a table of relations between "all first words of sentences" and "all 28th words of sentences," but rather via appreciating combinatorial regularities of enormous generality and power. Much of this power comes from the fact that the same regularities that apply to the simplest sentences apply in the same way to the complex sentences with just a little tinkering around the edges. The complex sentences are built up by using and reusing the same smallish set of syntax rules that formed the simple sentences, tying them together using function morphemes for the nails and glue (Chomsky 1959; 1981b; Z. Harris, 1951; Jackendoff, 2002; Joshi, 2002).

HOW LANGUAGE CONVEYS MEANING

So far, our survey of language has concentrated attention on the forms of language. Here we turn to the topic of meaning. As we shall see, form and meaning crucially link together in the linguistic organization of thought.

THE MEANINGS OF WORDS

Word meanings are of many different kinds. Some words such as *Madonna* and *Batman* describe individuals in the real and imaginary world; others such as *dog* and *unicorn* are more general and describe categories of things. Yet other words describe substances (*water, Kryptonite*), properties (*green, imaginary*), relations (*similar, uncle*), quantities (*some, zillions*), actions (*run, transform*), states of mind (*knowing, hoping*) or being (*am, seem*), and manners of doing (*carefully, musically*). A moment's thought reveals that the kind of meaning is well correlated with the so-called parts of speech, with things and stuff generally labeled by nouns, acts and states by verbs, properties by adjectives, and manners by adverbs. These correlations between meaning and word class accord with the representation of language in the brain; for example, nouns and verbs are retrieved with different neural systems and can be independently compromised in brain injury (Bates, Chen, Tzeng, Li, & Opie, 1991; Caramazza & Hillis, 1991; Luzzatti et al., 2001).

THE DEFINITIONAL THEORY OF WORD MEANING

At first glance, the words of a language seem to be like little atoms of meaning, each distinct from all the others. But several theories of word meaning assert that only a handful of words in a language describe elementary, "simple" ideas or concepts. The rest are more like molecules: They are composites of more elementary atoms of meaning. Thus, words like *yellow* and *round* might indeed name simple ideas or concepts, but other words seem more complex: For example, the words *canary, yolk,* and *banana* all seem to involve the atom of *yellowness,* but they involve other elements as well (Hume, 1739; Jackendoff, 2002; Katz & Fodor, 1963; Locke, 1690).

These observations are central to a **definitional theory of word meaning**, which states that words are organized in our minds much as they are in standard dictionaries (though not in alphabetical order!). According to this theory, each word can be understood as a bundle of meaning atoms, or **semantic features**. Words that share features are to that extent similar in meaning (*wicked-evil*); words with single opposed features are antonyms (*wicked-good*); words that share no features (*wicked-turqoise*) are unrelated in meaning. The feature similarities also allow us to identify clusters of words—for example, *bachelor, uncle, brother, gander,* and *stallion*—all words that share the feature of [maleness].*

Summarizing, on this definitional view, the full meaning of each word is a set of features that are essential for membership in the class named by the word. Thus, *bachelor* is composed of the set of features [single], [human], [adult], and [male]. These features are **necessary** for bachelorhood, and so, if some creature is missing any one of these features (e.g., if the creature is married, or is an adult male duck), it could not correctly be called "a bachelor." And this set of features is also **sufficient** for bachelorhood—some man might be tall or short, flirtatious or shy, English or Greek, but none of this affects his status as a bachelor. These semantic features constitute the definition of each word, and according to this theory, we carry such definitions in our heads for each of the words in our vocabulary.

Can a white rose be red? *The Queen had ordered the gardeners to plant a red rose bush, but they planted a white one by mistake. They are now trying to repair their error by painting the white roses red. On the definitional theory of meaning, this seems reasonable enough. For the expressions* red rose bush *and* white rose bush *differ by only a single feature—*red *versus* white. *But if so, why are the gardeners so terrified that the Queen will discover what they did? (From Lewis Carroll's,* Alice in Wonderland)

---

* It is important to distinguish between the word and its semantic features. Thus, [male] may be a semantic feature or atom that constitutes part of the meaning of such words as *stallion* and *brother*. But there is also a word *male*. It is the kind of word that consists of only the single semantic feature [male]. At a lower level of language, a related phenomenon exists. The English indefinite article *a* is a word (the one that appears in the phrase *a cat*), but it is also a phoneme. That is, *a* is the rare case of a word that, at the level of sound, contains only one phoneme rather than a sequence of phonemes. In the same sense, *male* is the relatively rare case, according to definitional theory, of a word that contains only a single semantic feature, [male].

THE PROTOTYPE THEORY OF MEANING

The definitional theory faces several problems. For one thing, once we have gone beyond such relatively formal words as *bachelor*, it is surprisingly hard to come up with definitions that cover all the uses of a word or do it justice at all. For instance, consider the (proposed) definition of *bird* in Figure 9.6. This definition seems promising, but, in fact, not all birds are covered with feathers (neither baby birds nor plucked birds have feathers, yet they are birds all the same). The author of the definition in the figure seems to acknowledge this problem by hedging on the feathers issue, writing "more or less covered with feathers." And the picture helps in some ways, filling in what the words miss, but notice that the picture is far too particular to describe the range of real birds; it hardly seems appropriate for the emus or the albatrosses (Armstrong, Gleitman, & Gleitman, 1983; Fodor, 1983; Murphy, 2002; Prinz, 2002; Rey, 1996).

A related problem for definitional theory is that some members of a meaning category appear to exemplify that category better than others do. Thus, a German Shepherd seems to be a more typical dog than a Pekinese, and an armchair seems to be a better example of the concept of furniture than a reading lamp. This seems to be at odds with the analysis we have described thus far, whose aim was to specify the necessary and sufficient attributes that define a concept. When a dictionary says that a bachelor is *an adult human male who has never been married*, it claims to have said it all. Whatever fits under this definitional feature list is a bachelor. Whatever does not, is not. But if so, how can one bachelor be more bachelor-like (or one dog more doglike) than another?

Observations like these have led some investigators to argue for an alternative view, called *prototype theory* (Medin, Goldstone, & Gentner, 1993; Rosch, 1973b; Rosch & Mervis, 1975; E. E. Smith & Medin, 1981; E. E. Smith, Oshershon, Rips, & Kean, 1988). The facts that prototype theory tries to account for can easily be illustrated. Consider again the category *bird*. Are there features that characterize all birds and that characterize birds only? One might think that being able to fly is a feature of all birds, but it is not. (Ostriches can't fly.) One might suppose that having feathers is a feature of all birds, but as we have noted, neither baby birds nor plucked birds have feathers. And not everything that lays eggs (turtles), or flies (airplanes, helicopters), or has feathers (hats, quilts, quill pens) is a bird. With all these failures of the definition in mind, perhaps it is wrong to suppose that we can ever find a set of necessary and sufficient features for the concept of *bird*. But if not, then the definitional theory is not correct.

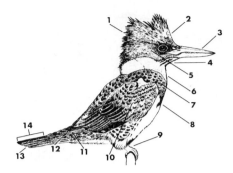

9.6 Is this the entry for bird *in your mental dictionary?* "bird . . . n. . . . [ME, fr. OE bridd] . . . 2: Any of a class (Aves) of warm-blooded vertebrates distinguished by having the body more or less completely covered with feathers and the forelimbs modified as wings. . . . "bird 2 (kingfisher): 1 crest, 2 crown, 3 bill, 4 throat, 5 auricular region, 6 breast, 7 scapulars, 8 abdomen, 9 tarsus, 10 upper wing coverts, 11 primaries, 12 secondaries, 13 rectrix, 14 tail" (Merriam-Webster's Collegiate Dictionary, 10th Ed.)

Diversity within categories **The enormous diversity of instances within categories is one reason why categories are difficult to define. These creatures differ in many regards (e.g., whether they fly or swim, how large they are, the shapes and colors of their feathers, and so forth), but all are instances of the category** bird.

9.7 *The Smith brothers and their family resemblance* **The Smith brothers are related through family resemblance, though no two brothers share all features. The one who has the greatest number of the family attributes is the most prototypical. In the example, it is Brother 9 who has all the family features: brown hair, large ears, large nose, moustache, and eyeglasses.**

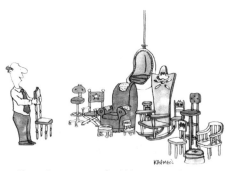

"Attention, everyone! I'd like to introduce the newest member of our family."

According to prototype theory, the meaning of many words is still described as a set of features, but not a necessary and sufficient set of them. Instead, the concept is held together in a *family resemblance structure* (Wittgenstein, 1953). Consider the ways that members of a family resemble each other. Joe may look like his father to the extent that he has his eyes; he may look like his mother by virtue of his prominent chin. His sister Sue may look like her father to the extent that she has his nose, and she may smile just like her mother. But Joe and Sue may have no feature in common (he has his grandfather's nose and she has Aunt Fanny's eyes), and so the two of them do not look alike at all. Even so, they are both easily recognized as members of the family, for they each bear some resemblance to their parents (Figure 9.7). Some members of the family may have more of these features than others do. Accordingly, some members of a category seem more typical or central than others. Thus, a German Shepherd seems "doggy-er" than a Pekinese, presumably because the Shepherd has more of the features associated with the dog family.

How is knowledge about a family resemblance structure represented in the mind? According to some psychologists, we carry in memory a mental *prototype* for each of our concepts—a prototypical bird, a prototypical chair, and so on (Barselou, 1985; Gentner, 1983; Goldstone, Lippa, & Shiffrin, 2001; Rosch, 1973b; Rosch & Mervis, 1975; E. E. Smith & Medin, 1981; Tversky, 1977). These prototypes are generally derived from our experiences, so that each prototype provides something like a mental average of all the examples of the concept that we have encountered. In the case of birds, people in the mainland United States have seen far more robins than penguins. As a result, something that resembles a robin will be stored in their memory system and will then be associated with the word *bird*. When the person later sees a new object, she will judge it to be a bird to the extent that it resembles the prototype in some way. A sparrow resembles it in many ways and so is judged to be a "good" bird; a penguin resembles it just a little and hence is a "marginal" bird; a rowboat resembles it not at all and hence is judged to be no bird.

Support for this view comes from numerous studies. For example, when people are asked to come up with examples of some category, they generally first produce instances that are close to the prototype (e.g., robins rather than ostriches); this is presumably because they start their memory search with the prototype and work outwards from there. A related result concerns the time required to verify category membership. Participants respond yes more quickly to the sentence *A robin is a bird* than to *An ostrich is a bird*. This is perfectly sensible. A robin resembles the bird prototype and so the similarity is readily discerned, allowing a fast response. For an ostrich, one must spend a moment searching for its relatively few birdy features, so verification is correspondingly slower (Rosch, 1978).

COMBINING DEFINITIONAL AND PROTOTYPE THEORIES

The prototype view helps us to understand why robins are perceived to be more typical birds than ostriches. But the definitional theory explains why an ostrich is nevertheless recognized as a bird. The prototype view helps us understand why a trout is fishier than a sea horse, but the definitional theory seems important if we are to explain why a sea horse is far fishier than a whale (which, of course, is not a fish at all, though it has some suspiciously fishy properties). Perhaps we can combine both views of meaning rather than choosing between them.

Consider the word *grandmother*. For this term, there are necessary and sufficient features, so here the definitional theory seems just right: A grandmother is a female parent of a parent. But there may also be a prototype: A grandmotherly grandmother is a person who is old and gray, has a kindly twinkle in her eye, and bakes cookies. When we say that someone is *grandmotherly*, we are surely referring to the prototypical attributes of

*Prototypes and definitions   Tyler Perry playing
the role of Madea might resemble the typical
grandmother, but as a male, he is surely not a
real grandmother. In contrast, Goldie Hawn is
far from the prototype but is, in reality, a grandmother.*

grandmothers, not to genealogy. And, in many circumstances, we use this prototype, rather than the definition. For example, we are likely to rely on our grandmother proto-type for picking a grandmother out of a crowd, for predicting what someone's grand-mother will be like, and so on. But in other circumstances, we rely on the definition: If we know some kindly lady who is gray and twinkly but never had a child, we may think of her as grandmotherly but not as a grandmother.

It appears, therefore, that people may have two partly independent mental representations of *grandmother*, and the same may be true for most other words as well.

WORD MEANINGS IN "FOLK THEORIES" OF THE WORLD

Our understanding of words is embedded in a web of beliefs that is broader than either the theory of definitions or the theory of prototypes can describe (Atran, 1998; Medin, Atran, Cox, Coley, & Proffitt, 2006). We seem to have well-developed ideas (sometimes called "folk theories") of why objects or properties are the way they are, and therefore how they could and could not change without becoming something altogether different (Carey, 1985; Keil, 1989; Locke, 1690; MacNamara, 1982). For instance, lawnmowers that are now made out of steel and plastics might one day be constructed from the kinds of exotic metals that today are only used in spacecraft, but they would still be legitimately called lawnmowers all the same. But some materials such as shaving cream or ice could never be considered for lawnmowers because they could not support the essential function (something capable of cutting grass) of such a device. We therefore confidently say "a lawnmower cannot be made of ice." Notice, though, that such asser-tions are not merely summaries of our experience. It is not merely that we have never seen a (failed) lawnmower made of ice. Rather, we hold a nonconscious "theory" of what makes a lawnmower a lawnmower, and this theory guides us in many aspects of our thinking about lawnmowers (for further examples, see Figure 9.8).

THE MEANINGS OF SENTENCES

Sentences have meanings too, over and above the meanings of the words they contain. This is obvious from the fact that two sentences can be composed of all the same words and yet be meaningfully distinct. For example, *The giraffe bit the zebra* and *The zebra bit the giraffe* describe different events, a meaning difference of some importance, at least to the zebra and the giraffe.

The typical sentence introduces some topic (the **subject** of the sentence) and then makes some comment, or offers some information, about that topic (the **predicate** of the

---

*1. Alfred is an unmarried adult male,
but he has been living with his girlfriend for
the last twenty-three years. Their
relationship is happy and stable. Is Alfred a
bachelor?*

*2. Bernard is an unmarried adult male,
and he does not have a partner. Bernard is a
monk living in a monastery. Is Bernard a
bachelor?*

*3. Charles is a married adult male, but
he has not seen his wife for many years.
Charles is earnestly dating, hoping to find a
new partner. Is Charles a bachelor?*

*4. Donald is a married adult male, but
he lives in a culture that encourages men to
take two wives. Donald is earnestly dating,
hoping to find a new partner. Is Donald a
bachelor?*

*9.8 Word meanings are "theories"   Your
answers to the questions shown here—and
with that, your understanding of* bachelor—
*depends on a web of beliefs about who is
marriageable and who is not.*

HOW WE UNDERSTAND

We have just seen a bit of the true complexity of everyday speech. This makes something of a mystery of how we actually manage to understand each other. How do listeners decipher the drama of who-did-what-to-whom from the myriad sentence forms in which this drama can be expressed? Part of the answer lies in the various function morphemes that speakers helpfully supply, marking the boundaries between propositions and also the roles of various words within the proposition. For instance, when we reorder the phrases in a so-called passive-voice sentence, the telltale morphemes (-*en*, *by*) cue the fact that the done-to rather than the do-er has become the subject of the sequence. But, in addition, listeners also home in on several clues that go beyond syntax to discern the real intents of speakers.

THE FREQUENCY WITH WHICH THINGS HAPPEN

Often a listener's interpretation of a sentence is guided by background knowledge, knowledge that indicates the wild implausibility of one interpretation of an otherwise ambiguous sentence. For example, no sane reader is in doubt over the punishment meted out to the perpetrator after seeing the headline *Drunk Gets Six Months in Violin Case*. But in less extreme cases, the correct interpretation is not immediately obvious. Most of us have had the experience of being partway through a sentence and realizing that somewhere we went wrong; then our eyes whip back so that we can start afresh. For example, we may make a word-grouping error, as in reading a sentence that begins *The fat people eat* . . . The natural inclination is to take *the fat people* as the subject noun phrase and *eat* as the beginning of the verb phrase (Bever, 1970). But suppose the sentence continues:

The fat people eat accumulates on their hips and thighs.

Now one must go back and reread. (Notice that this sentence would have been much easier if, as is certainly allowed in English, the author had placed the function word *that* before the word *people: The fat that people eat accumulates on their hips and thighs.*) The partial misreading (or "mishearing" in the case of spoken language) is termed a **garden path** (in honor of the cliché phrase). Because of the misleading content or structure at the beginning of the sentence, the reader is led toward one interpretation, but he must then retrace his mental footsteps to find a grammatical and understandable alternative.

Psycholinguists have various ways of detecting when people are experiencing a garden path during reading. One is to use a device that records the motion of the reader's eyes as they move across a page of print. Slowdowns and visible regressions of these eye movements tell us where and when the reader has gone wrong and is rereading the passage (MacDonald, Perlmutter, & Seidenberg, 1994; Rayner, Carlson, & Frazier, 1983; Trueswell, Tanenhaus, & Garnsey, 1994). Using this technique, one group of investigators looked at the effects of plausibility on readers' expectations of the structure they were encountering. Suppose that the first three words of a test sentence are

The detectives examined . . .

Participants who read these words typically assume that *The detectives* is the subject of the sentence and that *examined* is the main verb. They therefore expect the sentence to end with some noun phrase—for example: *the evidence*. As a result, they are thrown off track when they dart their eyes forward and instead read that the sentence continues

. . . by the reporter . . .

The readers' puzzlement is evident in their eye movements: They pause and look back at the previous words, obviously realizing that they need to revise their notion that *examined* was the main verb. After this recalculation, they continue on, putting all of the pieces together in a new way, and so grasp the entire sentence:

> *The detectives examined by the reporter revealed the truth about the robbery.*

The initial pause at *by the reporter* showed that readers had been led down the garden path and now had to rethink what they were reading. But what was it exactly that led the participants off course with this sentence? Was the difficulty just that passive-voice sentences are less frequent than active-voice sentences? To find out, the experimenters also presented sentences that began

> *The evidence examined by the reporter . . .*

Now the participants experienced little or no difficulty, and read blithely on as the sentence ended as it had before (. . . *revealed the truth about the robbery*). Why? After all, this sentence has exactly the same structure as the one starting *The detectives . . .* and so, apparently, the problem is not in the structure itself. Instead, the difficulty seems to depend on the plausible semantic relations among the words. The noun *detectives* is a "good subject" of verbs like *examined* because detectives often do examine things—such as footprints in the garden, spots of blood on the snow, and so on. Therefore, plausibility helps the reader to believe that the detectives in the test sentence did the examining—thus leading the reader to the wrong interpretation. Things go differently, though, when the sentence begins *The evidence*, because evidence, of course, is not capable of examining anything. Instead, evidence is a likely *object* of someone's examination, and so a participant who has read *The evidence examined . . .* is not a bit surprised that the next word that comes up is *by*. This is the function morpheme that signals that a passive-voice verb form is on its way—just what the reader expected given the meanings of the first three words of the sentence.

It seems, then, that the process of understanding makes use of word meanings and sentence structuring as mutual guides. We use the meaning of each word (*detectives* versus *evidence*) to guide us toward the intended structure, and we use the expected structure (active versus passive) to guess at the intended meanings of the words.

WHAT IS HAPPENING RIGHT NOW?

Humans often talk about the future, the past, and the altogether imaginary. We devour books on antebellum societies that are now gone with the wind, and tales that speak of

Interpreting two complex sentences **(A) With the sentence** The detectives examined by the reporter revealed the truth about the robbery, *we see that the reporter is examining (interviewing) the detectives to find out about the crime.* **(B) With the sentence** The evidence examined by the reporter revealed the truth about the robbery, *we see that the reporter himself examines the tell-tale evidence (ladder, footsteps, drops of blood) to find out about the crime.*

A

B

9.11 *Understanding a sentence in its situational context* **As soon as the subject hears** Now I want you to eat . . . **his eyes turn toward the only edible thing in sight: the cake.**

9.12 *The observed world influences the interpretation of an ambiguous sentence* **Study participants are asked to follow the instruction to** Put the frog on the napkin in the box, **but the start of this sentence can be understood in two ways. Those who see the array containing a frog sitting on a napkin and a horse (Panel A) initially interpret** on the napkin **as the required destination of the frog and so first peek at the other (empty) napkin. Those who see the array containing two frogs (Panel B) interpret** on the napkin **as specifying a particular frog (the frog that is on a napkin). They immediately look at and pick up this particular frog without a garden-path peek at the empty napkin.**

a Darth Vader galaxy that we hope never to experience. But much of our conversation is focused on more immediate concerns, and in these cases the listener can often see what is being referred to and can witness the actions being described in words. This sets up a two-way influence—with the language we hear guiding how we perceive our surroundings, and the surroundings in turn shaping how we interpret the heard speech.

For example, in one experiment, on viewing the array of four objects pictured in Figure 9.11, participants listening to the sentence *Now I want you to eat some cake* turned their eyes toward the cake as soon as they heard the verb *eat* (Altmann & Kamide, 1999) and before hearing *cake*. After all, it was unlikely that the experimenter would be requesting the participants to ingest the toy train. In this case, the meaning of the verb *eat* focused listeners' attention on only certain aspects of the world in view—the edible aspects!

Just as powerful are the reverse phenomena: effects of the visually observed world on how we interpret a sentence. Consider the array of toy objects in Figure 9.12A (Altmann & Steedman, 1988; Crain & Steedman, 1985; Tanenhaus, Spivey-Knowlton, Eberhard, & Sedivy, 1995; Trueswell, Sekerina, Hill, & Logrip, 1999). These include a little frog sitting on a napkin and another napkin that has no toy on it. When study participants look at such scenes and hear the instruction *Put the frog on the napkin into the box*, most of them experience a garden path, thinking (when they hear the first six words) that *on the napkin* is where a frog should be put, and only realizing (three words later) that this phrase tells them something more specific to help identify the frog itself, with the real destination being the box. This reaction is evident in the participants' eye movements: On hearing *napkin*, participants look to the empty napkin, as if this were the destination of the *put* instruction, but then they look around in confusion when they hear *into the box*. Of course, participants rapidly recover from this momentary confusion, and they go on to execute the instruction correctly, picking up the frog and putting it in the box.

But now consider the array of objects in Figure 9.12B. It differs from Figure 9.12A because now there are two frogs, only one of which is on a napkin. This has a noticeable effect on participants' eye movements. Now, on hearing the same instruction, most of them immediately look to the frog on the napkin when they hear *napkin*, and they show no subsequent confusion on hearing *into the box*.

What caused the difference in reaction? In the array of 9.12A, with only one frog, a listener does not expect the speaker to identify it further by saying *the green frog* or *the frog to the left* or *the frog on the napkin*, for there would be no point in doing so. Though such descriptions are true of that particular frog, there is no need to say that much—it is entirely obvious which frog is being discussed, because only one is in view. When the listener hears *on the napkin*, therefore, she assumes (falsely) that this is a destination, not a further specification of the frog.

Things are different, though, with the array shown in Figure 9.12B. Now there is a risk of confusion about which frog to move, and so listeners expect explicit verbal clues;

"Put the frog <u>on the napkin</u> in the box."

A   B

they expect to be informed that it is either the frog on the napkin or the frog on the plate that is being discussed. In this situation, therefore, the listener correctly assumes that *on the napkin* is the needed cue to the uniquely intended frog, and he does not wander down the mental garden path (Grice, 1975).

CONVERSATIONAL INFERENCE: FILLING IN THE BLANKS

The actual words that pass back and forth between people are merely hints about the thoughts that are being conveyed. In fact, talking would take just about forever if speakers literally had to say all, only, and exactly what they meant. It is crucial, therefore, that the communicating pair take the utterance and its context as the basis for making a series of complicated inferences about the meaning and intent of the conversation (P. Brown & Dell, 1987; Grice, 1975; Lockridge & Brennan, 2002; Papafragou, Massey, & Gleitman, 2006). For example, consider this exchange:

A: Do you own a Cadillac?
B: I wouldn't own *any* American car.

Interpreted literally, Speaker B is refusing to answer Speaker A's yes/no question. But Speaker A will probably understand the response more naturally, supplying a series of plausible inferences that would explain how her query might have prompted B's retort. Speaker A's interpretation might go something like this: "Speaker B knows that I know that a Cadillac is an American car. He's therefore telling me that he does not own a Cadillac in a way that both responds to my question with a *no* and also tells me something else: that he dislikes all American cars."

Such leaps from a speaker's utterance to a listener's interpretation are commonplace. Listeners do not usually wait for everything to be said explicitly. On the contrary, they often supply a chain of inferred causes and effects that were not actually contained in what the speaker said, but that nonetheless capture what the speaker intended (Grice, 1975; Sperber & Wilson, 1986).

In sum, listeners are richly guided by factors external to language itself: by their broad knowledge of likelihoods and plausibilities in the world, and by the immediate circumstances in which speech occurs. These influences are easily demonstrated in the laboratory, and they point to how we understand each other despite the massive vagueness and ambiguity of speech itself. When we hear *These missionaries are ready to eat* or *Smoking volcanoes can be dangerous*, it is only our common sense and language skill that save us from perpetual confusion.

HOW COMPREHENSION WORKS

We have seen that the process of language comprehension is marvelously complex, influenced by syntax, semantics, the extralinguistic context, and inferential activity, all guided by a spirit of communicative cooperation. But how are all these factors integrated "on line" as the speaker fires 14 phonemes a second toward our ear? One hypothesis is that the listener first (during the first few hundred milliseconds) uses the syntax to uncover the structure. This yields an initial hypothesis about the sentence, which is subsequently checked against other sources of information (Frasier & Fodor, 1978). The alternative hypothesis is that all of these sources of information interact from the very start, with the listener using every clue "incrementally" and "immediately" as soon as the words become available during the saying of a sentence. This issue has been a matter of considerable debate, but evidence is accumulating to support the position that these factors interact from the start (Altmann & Steedman, 1988; Carlson & Tanenhaus, 1988; Carpenter, Miyake, & Just, 1995; MacDonald, Pearlmutter, & Seidenberg, 1994; Marslen-Wilson, 1975; Stowe, 1987; Trueswell &

Tanenhaus, 1994). No matter how this debate is resolved, it is clear that several kinds of cues work together to ensure that the listener is not drowned in confusion by the pervasive ambiguity of word, phrase, and sentence structure.

THE GROWTH OF LANGUAGE IN THE CHILD

Our survey of language has revealed it to be of such startling complexity that one might doubt whether mere children could acquire it. But as we will see now, not only can infants acquire language, but they are vastly better at doing so than even the wisest and most knowledgeable adults. From the very first moments after birth, infants' ears and minds are open to detect the sounds of language and to organize them into words. They recognize many words before they can even walk. The rate of word learning rapidly accelerates to about 3 a day in toddlers, to 5 or 8 or so a day in the preschool years, and to 10 to 15 words a day throughout childhood and early adolescence (P. Bloom, 2000; Carey, 1978). The upshot is a vocabulary of about 10,000 words by age 5 and 75,000 or so by adulthood.

Late in the second year of life, toddlers start to put the words together into little sentences—"Throw ball!" "No mommy eat!"—and soon are eagerly acquiring the rules of grammar that, in later school life, we all came to dread. In sum, whatever their circumstances—intelligent or dull, otherwise motivated or apathetic, encouraged by their parents or ignored, exposed to Hindi or to English—children learn the language of their environment in a few short years, with virtuoso syntax a common occurrence by age 4 to 5. An example of this proficiency—and of how well the child can shape language to achieve his social and material goals—is a telephone query from a 5-year-old boy (of course, to his doting grandmother): "Remember that toy that you told me on the phone last night that you would buy me?" How is this rapid, ornate learning possible?

Language is learned in ordinary social interactions

THE SOCIAL ORIGINS OF LANGUAGE LEARNING

Prelinguistic children have nonverbal ways of making contact with the minds, emotions, and social behaviors of others. Neonates' heart rate quickens or slows according to whether they hear a human speaking in a tone that is excited or soothing, or disapproving versus approving. For the most part, babies do not have to learn these emotive qualities of language any more than a puppy has to learn solely by experience which barks or growls from adult dogs are playful and which are threatening. This was shown by recording German mothers talking to their infants and then replaying the audiotape to babies who had heard only English or French up until then. The recording was presented while the baby was playing with a novel toy. When infants hear an approving German sentence with its high notes and mellow cadences, they go right on playing; but on hearing the sharp and low-toned sounds of disapproval, though in a totally unfamiliar language, they drop the toy like a hot potato (Fernald, 1992). Thus, language appears to be social and interpersonal in its very origins. In order to learn to speak and understand, the infant begins with an implicit understanding that "the other" is a fellow human being who lives in the same, mutually perceived world (Bates, 1976; Mandler, 2000; Tomsello, 1991; 1992).

Particularly interesting in this regard are findings about word learning. Suppose that a child is shown a fascinating new toy and allowed to explore it. Suppose at this very moment the child's mother says excitedly, "That's a blicket! Wow, a blicket!" Will the child by a process of automatic association now think that the name for this new toy is "blicket"? The answer is no. First, the child appears to seek evidence that the speaker was attending to the toy too. One investigator put mothers and their 18-month-old children in exactly this situation. When the children heard the mother saying, "That's a blicket!" they immediately turned and glanced into the mother's eyes (just as an adult would). Following the direction of the mother's gaze, these infants evidently set out to determine if the mother herself was looking at the toy in the child's hands (and thus, probably, referring to it and not something else when she said "blicket"). If the mother was looking at this toy, then, when tested later on, the children showed that they had learned the blicket label for the new toy. But if the mother had been looking elsewhere—say, into a bucket whose contents were not visible to the child—the children did not assign this new word as the toy's name. In short, even children under 2 years of age use social context as a critical guide in language learning. They do not form word-to-meaning associations if the social context of language use does not guide them to do so (Baldwin, 1991; see also P. Bloom, 2002; Meltzoff, 1995).

Armed with this social understanding, babies find their way into the world of linguistic communication. Even as they learn to build castles out of alphabet blocks and to stack up colorful rings on a stake, so they search out and organize the building blocks of the human language that they hear spoken around them and to them.

DISCOVERING THE BUILDING BLOCKS OF LANGUAGE

Recent neuroscientific findings show that infants are ready for language learning at birth or almost immediately thereafter (Dehaene-Lambertz, Dehaene, & Hertz-Pannier, 2002; Mehler & Nespor, 2004; Mehler et al., 1988). One group of investigators recorded changes in the blood flow in 2-day-old babies' brains in the presence of linguistic stimulation. Half of the time the babies were hearing recordings of normal human speech, and the other half of the time they were hearing that speech played backward. Blood flow in the babies' left hemisphere increased for the normal speech but not for the backward speech (Peña et al., 2003). Because the left hemisphere of the brain is the major site for linguistic activity in humans, this evidence suggests that the special responsiveness to language-like signals is already happening close to the moment of birth.

THE RHYTHMIC FOUNDATIONS OF LANGUAGE LEARNING

Recall that languages vary in their significant sounds (phonemes and syllables), tones, rhythms, and melodies, enough so that most of us can guess whether a speaker is uttering Japanese or German or French speech even if we do not understand a word of any of these languages. The amazing fact is that newborn infants can do almost as well. Babies' responsiveness can be measured by an ingenious method that takes advantage of the fact that, while newborns can do very few things voluntarily, one of their earliest talents—and pleasures—is sucking at a nipple. In one study, a nonnutritive nipple (or "pacifier") was connected to a recording device such that every time the baby sucked, a bit of French speech was heard coming from a nearby loudspeaker. The 4-day-old French babies rapidly discovered that they had the power to elicit this speech just by sucking, and they sucked faster and faster to hear more of it. After a few minutes, however, they apparently got bored (or habituated to the stimulus—see Chapter 6), and therefore the sucking rate decreased. Now the experimenter switched the speech coming from the microphone from French to English. Did the infants notice? The answer is yes. When the switch was made, the infants' interest was reawakened, and they began sucking faster and faster again (they *dis*habituated). To perfect the experimental proof, the same recordings were flown to the United States, and the experiment was repeated

Detecting phonetic distinctions **This 2½-month-old baby's head is covered with a geodesic sensor net, which picks up signals from the brain. The baby, seated in a carrier on the mother's lap, faces a loudspeaker emitting meaningless syllables, and watches a video of moving colored objects. When repeated spoken syllables were changed to new, different ones, there were significant changes in the event-related potential signals (ERP's), showing that the baby had noticed the change.**

forms such as *ran*, *came*, and *ate*. By the age of 4 or 5, however, the same children start to treat the irregular verbs as though they were regular. Thus, they sometimes say "runned," "bringed," and "holded" (Marcus et al., 1992; Pinker & Ullman, 2002; Prasada & Pinker, 1993a). And these are not simply errors of carelessness or slips of the tongue, as can be seen in the following exchange:

> CHILD: My teacher holded the baby rabbits and we patted them.
> MOTHER: Did you say your teacher *held* the baby rabbits?
> CHILD: Yes.
> MOTHER: What did you say she did?
> CHILD: She holded the baby rabbits and we patted them.
> MOTHER: Did you say she held them tightly?
> CHILD: No, she holded them loosely. (Bellugi, 1971)

This kind of error offers evidence that children do not learn language solely, or even mostly, by imitation. Few adults would say "holded" or "eated," and the mother in the quoted exchange repeatedly offers the correct form of the verb for imitation. In fact, parents are often aghast at these errors. A half-year earlier, their child was speaking correctly but now is making errors. Apparently, he is regressing! So parents often try to correct these errors, but to no avail: The child holds firm, despite the correction.

But if not the result of imitation, then what is it that leads children to produce "errors" where there was correctness before? Many investigators argue that the young child starts out by memorizing the past tense of each verb, learning that the past tense of *want* is *wanted*, the past tense of *climb* is *climbed*, and so on. But this is a highly inefficient strategy. It is far more efficient to detect the pattern: Simply add the *-ed* suffix to a verb every time you are speaking of the past. But once the child detects this pattern, it is apparently quite easy to get carried away, and so **overregularization errors** are produced. The errors will drop out only when the child takes the further step of realizing that, while there is a pattern, there are also exceptions to the pattern. (For an alternative model of this process, see McClelland & Patterson, 2002.)

LANGUAGE LEARNING IN CHANGED ENVIRONMENTS

Under normal conditions, language seems to emerge in much the same way in virtually all children. They progress from babbling to one-word speech, advance to two-word sentences, and eventually graduate to complex sentence forms and meanings. This progression can be observed in children in Beijing learning to speak Chinese, as well as in children in Athens learning to speak Greek. This uniformity from one child to the next, from one language to the next, is certainly consistent with the claim that language development is rooted in our shared biological heritage. But is this pattern truly universal? What happens when children grow up in environments radically different from those in which language growth usually proceeds? Examining these cases may help us to understand the biological roots of human language and will also allow us to ask which aspects of the early environment are essential for language learning.

WILD CHILDREN

In 1920, Indian villagers discovered a wolf mother in her den together with four cubs. Two were baby wolves, but the other two were human children, subsequently named

Kamala and Amala. No one knows how they got there or why the wolf adopted them. Brown (1958) tells us what these children were like:

> Kamala was about eight years old and Amala was only one and one-half. They were thoroughly wolfish in appearance and behavior: Hard callus had developed on their knees and palms from going on all fours. Their teeth were sharp edged. They moved their nostrils sniffing food. Eating and drinking were accomplished by lowering their mouths to the plate. They ate raw meat.... At night they prowled and sometimes howled. They shunned other children but followed the dog and cat. They slept rolled up together on the floor.... Amala died within a year but Kamala lived to be eighteen.... In time, Kamala learned to walk erect, to wear clothing, and even to speak a few words. (p. 100)

The outcome was much the same for the 30 or so other wild children about whom we have reports. When found, they were all shockingly animal-like. None of them could be rehabilitated to use language normally, though some, including Kamala, learned to speak a few words (Figure 9.19).

ISOLATED CHILDREN

The data from these wild children are difficult to interpret, in part because we do not know why the children were abandoned by their parents in the first place. It is even possible that the children were mentally deficient at the start, and this is why their parents left them. If so, then we have no way to tell which of the children's difficulties stem from their retardation, and which from their unusual upbringing. Clearer data come from the (unfortunately many) cases of children who were raised by humans but under conditions that were hideously inhumane, for their parents were either vicious or deranged. Sometimes such parents will deprive a baby of all human contact. For example, "Isabelle" (a code name used to protect the child's privacy) was hidden away, apparently from early infancy, and given only the minimal attention necessary to sustain her life. No one spoke to her (the mother was deaf and also emotionally indifferent).

At the age of 6, Isabelle was discovered by other adults and brought into a normal environment. Of course, she had no language, and her cognitive development was below that of a normal 2-year-old. But within a year she learned to speak, her tested intelligence was normal, and she took her place in an ordinary school (R. Brown, 1958;

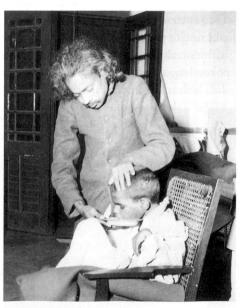

9.19 A modern wild boy *Ramu, a young boy discovered in India in 1976, appears to have been reared by wolves. He was deformed, apparently from lying in cramped positions, as in a den. He could not walk, and drank by lapping with his tongue. His favorite food was raw meat, which he seemed to be able to smell at a distance. After he was found, he lived at the home for destitute children run by Mother Theresa in Lucknow, Utter Pradesh. He learned to bathe and dress himself but never learned to speak. He continued to prefer raw meat and would often sneak out to prey upon fowl in the neighbor's chicken coop. Ramu died at the age of about 10 in February 1985.*

combine together to enlarge the number of messages that can be conveyed. Humans link their words in ever new and structured ways so as to express new thoughts that listeners easily comprehend (that's why there can be "news" in the newspaper, which we can understand even if we dislike or disagree with what it says). This creative kind of communication appears to be closed even to our closest primate cousins. For instance, monkeys have no way to differentiate by language: *Beware! Monkeys-eating-snakes* versus *Beware! Snakes-eating-monkeys*.

Perhaps, though, animal communication in the wild understates what animals are capable of. Perhaps, with just the right training, animals can master communication skills that truly deserve the term *language*. Many researchers have pursued these possibilities, trying to teach language-like systems to animals, using a variety of communication media in which hand gestures, or bits of colored plastic, or symbols on a computer screen, stand for words. Researchers have also tried to train a range of species, including chimpanzees, dolphins, gorillas, parrots, and pygmy chimps (bonobos). These animals have made impressive progress—dramatically increasing their "vocabulary" sizes (to roughly 500 "words" in the case of the bonobo Kanzi), and in some cases, stringing the vocabulary items together (to produce utterances such as "water bird"), and, in a handful of cases, then teaching others in their species what they have learned from their human trainers.

However, the results of these training efforts have all been rather limited and so utterly fail to support the extravangant descriptions of these "linguistic creatures" in the popular media. Their utterances are rarely more than two words long; when longer, they tend to involve repetitions (*Give orange me give eat orange me eat orange give me orange give me you*). Their utterances are typically imitations or expansions of the utterance they just observed in their human trainers, and their mastery of syntax is sharply limited. For example, no nonhuman has mastered the distinction between plural and singular nouns, or verb tense, or any means of marking words for their grammatical class, while every human child of normal mentality does so by the age of 3 or 4, without explicit training. (For reviews, see Kako, 1999; Petitto, 1988; Pinker, 1994; Tomasello, 1994, 2003; although also see Herman & Uyeyama, 1999; Pepperberg, 1999; Savage-Rumbaugh & Fields, 2000.)

LANGUAGE AND THOUGHT

We have seen that the forms and contents of language are very much bound up with the organization of the human brain and with the ways that humans think and perceive the world. Languages are alike insofar as they are the central means for transmitting beliefs,

Testing the limits of animal communication **Psychologist Dr. Sue Savage-Rumbaugh is shown here attempting to teach communicative gestures to a chimpanzee.**

desires, and ideas from one human to another. To accomplish these human communicative goals, each language must have phonemes, morphemes, phrases, and sentences, and tens of thousands of different meaningful words. But within these bounds, languages also differ from one another in various ways. And these differences are not only with the sounds of the words—that the word meaning "dog" is pronounced "dog," "chien," "perro," and so on in different communities. Some languages will simply lack a word that another language has, or refer to the same thing in quite different ways. As one example, we speak of a certain tool as a *screwdriver*, literally alluding to the fact that it is used to push screws in; German uses the term *Schraubenzieher*, which translates as "a screw puller"; and French uses the word *tournevis* ("screw turner") for the same tool, thus referring to both the tool's pushing and pulling functions (Kay, 1996). As we have also mentioned, sometimes the structures differ, as with fixed word-order languages like English and Mandarin Chinese versus those with a quite free word order such as Finnish and Russian. Further differences are at the social level. For example, such languages as Italian and French have different pronouns for use when referring to relative strangers (e.g., French *vous*) or to intimates (*tu*). Finally, languages differ in the idioms and metaphors with which they characteristically refer to the world. Witness English, where your new car can be a *lemon* even though it is inedible, your former friend can be a *snake in the grass*, and your future visit to an underground cave can be *up in the air* until its date is settled.

Do these differences matter? Certainly we would not think that Germans and Americans use different tools for inserting and extracting screws and that only the French have a single tool for both jobs. At the other extreme, having a linguistically built-in way to refer differentially to dear friends and total strangers just might reflect—or even cause—deep distinctions in the social organization of a culture. So here we consider the possibility that the particulars of one's language might influence thought. But before beginning, we have to clarify the question that is being raised.

HOW LANGUAGE CONNECTS TO THOUGHT

In one sense it is totally obvious that language influences thought. Otherwise we would not use it at all. When one person yells "FIRE!" in a crowded room, all of those who hear him rapidly walk, run, or otherwise proceed to the nearest exit. In this case, language influenced the listeners to think, "There's a fire; fire is dangerous; I'd better get out of here FAST." Language use also influences our thought in other ways. It is a convenient way of coding, or chunking, information, with important consequences for memory (see Chapter 7). The way information is framed when we talk or write can also influence our decisions, so that a patient is more likely to choose a medical treatment if she is told it has a 50% chance of success than if she is told it has a 50% chance of failure (see Chapter 8). Finally, language can influence our attitudes (see Chapter 12), a fact well known to advertisers and propagandists: "Eat crunchy Pritos!" "Remember Pearl Harbor!"

In all these examples, the choice of words and sentences affects our thinking. Of course, language is not the only way to influence thought and action. Observing the flames is at least as powerful a motivator to flee as is hearing the cry "FIRE!" Still, language is an enormously effective conveyer of information, emotions, and attitudes. This much ought to be obvious. Why would we ever listen to a lecture or read a poem or a newspaper if we did not believe that language was a means of getting useful or aesthetically pleasing information? But when we speak of language differences influencing thought, it is in quite a different sense from this. In this latter case, we are asking whether the very forms and contents that a language can express change the nature of perception and cognition for its speakers.

Lewis Carroll's poignant tale of how an animal's mind would be different if it had language Alice came to a forest where nothing had a name. She met a fawn that walked trustingly by her side: "So they walked together through the wood, Alice with her arms clasped lovingly around the soft neck of the Fawn, till they came out into another open field [where things had names]. And here the Fawn gave a sudden bound into the air, and shook itself free of Alice's arm. 'I'm a Fawn!' it cried out in a voice of delight. 'And dear me! You're a human child!' A sudden look of alarm came into his beautiful brown eyes, and in another moment it had darted away at full speed." (From Lewis Carroll's, Alice in Wonderland)

DO PEOPLE WHO TALK DIFFERENTLY COME TO UNDERSTAND THE WORLD DIFFERENTLY?

The idea that "we dissect nature along lines laid down by our native languages" was forcefully presented by a linguistic anthropologist, Benjamin Whorf, who studied several native languages of the Americas. Whorf noticed many distinctions of language and culture between native American and European societies, and he argued that often the language differences themselves led to the cultural differences. In his words, "language is not merely a reproducing instrument for voicing ideas but rather is itself the shaper of ideas, the program and guide for the individual's mental activity" (Whorf, 1956, pp. 212–213). So influential have Whorf's ideas become that the general position that language affects thought has come to be identified with his name, as the ***Whorfian hypothesis***.

One frequently mentioned example that Whorf discussed concerns the number of terms for snow in Inuit or Aleut (sometimes called "Eskimo" languages) compared to English. This number in Inuit is sometimes claimed to be as large as 300, with different terms for naming types of snow such as *powder, slush, ice, falling snow* versus *fallen snow*, and so forth. Whorf claimed that speakers of such languages are influenced by this extravagance of vocabulary and so end up able to make much finer distinctions among snow types than are speakers of other languages.

But this example is flawed in several ways. The initial claim about vocabulary size is actually false; English turns out to have more snow-related terms than does Inuit (Martin, 1986; Pullam, 1991). And even if it were true that Inuit had more words for snow, would that explain why its speakers are more sensitive to snow distinctions (if they are) than, say, English-speaking residents of South Carolina or Hawaii? A plausible alternative is that the Inuits' day-to-day activities create a functional need for these discriminations, and this leads both to the larger vocabulary and to the greater skill in picking out different types of snow. On this view, language does not shape perception. On the contrary, language and perception are both shaped by environment and culture.

HOW CAN WE STUDY LANGUAGE AND THOUGHT?

Although, as we have just seen, the Inuit snow case does not really hold water (perhaps we should say it does not hold ice), there are many other aspects in which language distinctions can be and have been more profitably studied.

COLOR TERMS AND COLOR PERCEPTION

Some languages have a rich and subtle vocabulary of color words (e.g., English *puce, mauve, tea, crimson*), while other languages have only a few color terms (Berlin & Kay, 1969). As an extreme case, the Dani people of New Guinea have only two terms for color, one meaning (roughly) "dark" and the other meaning "light" (Heider, 1972). Still, there are strong similarities in how speakers of English and speakers of Dani perceive color, with the named color categories in both cultures based on "favored percepts selected from restricted regions of color space," and with striking agreement, across the cultures, in which are "best examples" of each color (Regier, Kay, & Cook, 2005). Within these limits, however, recent evidence suggests that the different color labeling practices adopted in different languages can influence nonlinguistic categorization (Roberson et al., 2005). The picture we see for the case of color, then, is one of universal samenesses among peoples who are linguistically and culturally diverse, but at the same time—and within the constraints imposed by perception—an influence of language on just how the colors are categorized for nonlinguistic thought (Kay & Regier, 2006).

THE LANGUAGE OF SPATIAL POSITION AND DIRECTION

Another area in which we can examine the interaction of language and thought is in descriptions of space, because there are considerable differences in how various languages describe spatial position. For instance, English speakers would say that "the fruit is in the bowl" and also that "the CD is in the player," using the same preposition (*in*) in both cases. Korean speakers would use two different words in these cases, with one word conveying the idea of fitting in loosely (as "the fruit is in the bowl") and the other describing things that fit in tightly ("the CD is in the player") (Figure 9.26; Choi & Bowerman, 1991). As another example, English distinguishes between vertical contact (*on*) and vertical noncontact (*above*), while both Japanese and Korean use a single word to convey both *on* and *above*.

Despite these linguistic differences, Japanese, Korean, and English speakers all seem to think about spatial position in very similar ways. In one study, participants were shown pictures of objects located at various positions with respect to a reference object. A short time later, they were shown another picture and asked if it depicted the same scene or a slightly different one. In some cases, this new picture was altered slightly, but it preserved the relationship (of *on* or *above*) shown in the original picture. (The first picture, for example, might have shown a cup on a table; the second, a cup still on a table but shifted slightly to the right.) In other cases, the new picture depicted a change in this relationship (with the original picture showing the cup on the table and the test picture showing the cup above the table). If English sensitizes us to the contrast between *on* and *above*, then English speakers should detect alterations that change these relationships more easily than Koreans or Japanese do. But the data show no such effect, and the memory performance of all groups was the same (Landau & Munnich, 1998; also see Hayward & Tarr, 1995; Xu, 2002).

As another example, speakers of Tzeltal (a Mayan language) who live in Tenejapa, a rural region of Chiapas, Mexico, have no terms for "to the left of" or "to the right of," expressions that are obviously available (and often used) in, for example, English, Dutch, Japanese, and even the Spanish-speaking areas of Chiapas. Rather, these Tenejapens speak of things being roughly "to the east," "to the south," and so on. Of course, English speakers too can sensibly use terms like *east*, but in fact we rarely use these terms to refer to very nearby things. For instance, "Hand me the spoon that's to the east of your teacup" sounds quite unnatural.

This terminological distinction could be crucial, because words like *east* and *left* function differently: If you turn 180 degrees, what was previously to your east will

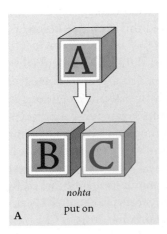

nohta
put on

A

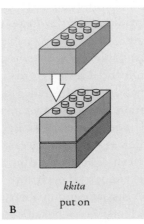

kkita
put on

B

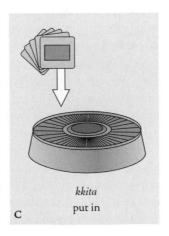

kkita
put in

C

9.26 Spatial words in English and Korean *The three panels show items being put into spatial positions relative to each other. Panel A shows a block being put on other blocks. Panel B shows a Lego being put on other Legos. Panel C shows a photo being put into a carousel. In English we use the same phrase (put on) to express the action in (A) and (B), and a different phrase (put in) for action (C). In contrast, Korean uses one term (nohta) to describe the act in (A), because it consists of putting something on something else loosely, and uses a different term (kkita) to describe the acts in (B) and (C), because both involve bringing the objects into a tight fit.*

9.27   What is "the same" after rotation?
(A) Subjects memorize the order and facing-direction (west; right) of three toy animals while they are seated at the stimulus table. (B) After a brief delay, the subject is turned around to face a different, blank, table (the recall table) and handed the animals to set up again so that the array is "the same as before." (C) The "absolute" response: The subject sets up the animals so they are still facing west (but now face the subject's left rather than her right). (D) The "relative" response: The subject sets up the animals so they are still facing her right (but now are pointing to the east).

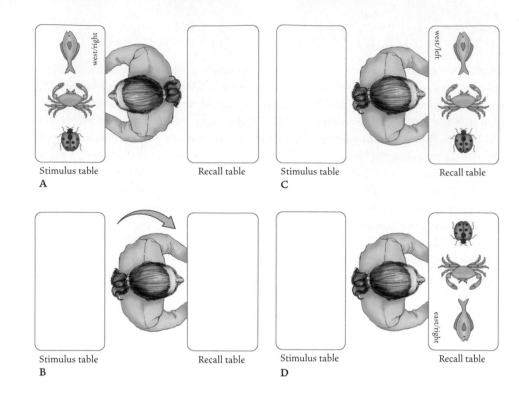

Stimulus table   Recall table
A

Stimulus table   Recall table
C

Stimulus table   Recall table
B

Stimulus table   Recall table
D

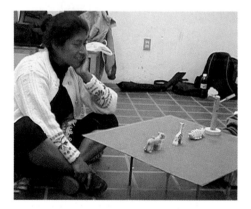

The language of spatial position   The Mayan language, Tzeltal, has no terms for "left" and "right." Instead, position is described in terms of compass directions (north, east, south, west). In contrast, the language of Tsotsil does have terms for "left" and "right." Does this difference in language cause a corresponding difference in how Tsotsil and Tzeltal speakers think about spatial relations? Evidence suggests that it does not. Speakers of these two different languages seem to understand space in the same way.

still be to your east, but what was previously to your left will now be to your right. This is because *east* and *west* have to do with position relative to an outside landmark (where the sun rises), whereas *left* and *right* have to do with position relative to one's own body. This suggests the possibility that spatial reasoning might be different in languages that favor the *left-right* distinction versus those that favor the *east-west* distinction.

Do speakers of Tzeltal actually think about space differently than English or Dutch speakers do? In one study, speakers of these different languages were asked to memorize the positions of toy animals lined up on a table (Figure 9.27, panel A). Then the animals were removed, and the participants were rotated 180 degrees to a new table (Figure 9.27, panel B). The participants were handed the animals and asked to "set them up on this new table so that it is the same as before." Notice that there are two ways to do so (Figure 9.27, panels C and D): The animals can be set up so that they are still going to the right or still going to the west. And, in fact, the terminology used by the subjects in their native tongue predicted the way they solved this problem (Levinson, 2003; Pederson et al., 1998).

This experiment makes a strong initial case that ways of thinking (here, thinking about space) may be directly influenced by the words in use in a specific language. But other investigators argue that these results reflect only the specific conditions of testing. To evaluate this suggestion, these later investigators created test conditions for English speakers like those under which the Tzeltal group had been studied, for example, providing strong landmarks visible to the east and west of the testing area. Under these conditions, American college students behaved much as the Tzeltal speakers (who had been tested outdoors in their own community) had behaved in this task (Li & Gleitman, 2002). The same group of investigators next studied speakers of another Mayan language, Tsotsil, also spoken in certain rural areas of Chiapas.

This language, though very similar to Tzeltal in many ways, does have terms for "left" and "right." Moreover, Tsotsil forms a good comparison case because its speakers are culturally very close to the Tenejapen Tzeltal speakers. Both communities are rural, with farming being the major occupation, and with many community members being semi-literate and isolated from the surrounding communities of Spanish speakers. Testing Tsotsil speakers in the animals-in-a-row task thus allows us to ask whether cultural similarity/difference (Tsotsil/Tzeltal speakers in Chiapas compared to urban-Amsterdam Dutch and Philadelphia English speakers) or language difference in the relevant regard (*east-west* terminology or *left-right* terminology) accounts for how this spatial task is solved. The answers were clear-cut. The culturally similar but linguistically different Mayan groups solved the spatial problem in the same way, rather than the Tsotsil speakers solving it like the Dutch/English speakers with whom they shared the linguistic property in question. In this case, then, cultural-environmental similarity rather than language similarity seems to be what drives spatial reasoning preferences in these populations (Gleitman, Li, Papafragou, Gallistel, & Abarbinell, 2005).

SOME FINAL THOUGHTS: LANGUAGE AND COGNITION

Overall, then, there is no compelling evidence in favor of the strongest form of Whorf's theory. When these claims are put to a direct test, there seem to be only limited relationships between specifics of our language and how we perceive or conceive of the world. These relationships are probably not caused by the language; instead they usually derive from aspects of the culture or environment in which people and societies exist, or, they are general context effects that apply in much the same way inside and outside of language ("I just feel like a different person when I'm speaking French or wearing my Parisian beret").

In fact, there is little reason to have expected that the words and structures of our language would change or restrict our thought patterns in rigid and immutable ways. If they did, it would be very hard to account for how a second—and sometimes third, fourth, and fifth—language could possibly be learned. In addition, there is no doubt that forms of thought are often independent of language. For instance, infants who know no language seem able to think relatively complex thoughts (Chapter 10), and some of our adult thought takes the form of nonlinguistic mental images (Chapter 8). Moreover, creatures such as digger wasps and migrating birds are able to find their way from place to place across great distances without the benefit of words like *north* and *left* (see Gallistel, 1990). Finally, throughout this chapter, we have emphasized the rather impressive sameness of languages in their units and hierarchical structure; in many aspects of their syntax, semantics, and pragmatics; and in the processes involved in their acquisition. This linguistic sameness, in turn, is the reflection of sameness of mentality across the human species. The use of language influences us and guides us, and surely this is no surprise: This is one of the essential functions of communication. But this is quite different from Whorf's suggestion that language acts as a kind of mental straightjacket limiting *how* we can think or *what* we can think. The bulk of the evidence seems to point the other way: Language is a bright, transparent medium through which thoughts flow, relatively undistorted, from one mind to another.

SUMMARY

THE BASIC UNITS OF LANGUAGE

- Languages consist of a *hierarchy of building blocks* that combine and recombine to form higher-level categories. At the bottom are units of *sound*, which combine into *words*.
- The sound categories that matter in a language are called its *phonemes*. English uses about 40 different phonemes. Other languages have their own sets.
- The smallest language units that carry meaning are *morphemes*. *Content morphemes* carry the main burden of meaning. *Function morphemes* add details to the meaning and also serve various grammatical purposes.
- A *phrase* is an organized grouping of words, and a *sentence* is an organized grouping of phrases. Some sequences of words in a language are allowed, but others are not, in accord with the *rules of syntax*. These rules also describe the *phrase structure* of a *sentence*, which can be depicted by means of a *tree diagram*.

HOW LANGUAGE CONVEYS MEANING

- According to the *definitional theory of word meaning*, bundles of *semantic features* constitute the definition of each word. Various observations, however, have led researchers to an alternative proposal—namely, that the meaning of most words is represented by an ideal (or *prototype*) case, and membership in the category depends on resemblance to this prototype.
- Sentences express *propositions*, in which some comment, or *predicate*, is made about a topic (the *subject* of the sentence). A proposition can be regarded as a miniature drama in which the verb is the action and the nouns are the performers, each of which plays a different *semantic role*.
- To understand the particular structure of a sentence and avoid *garden paths*, listeners and readers consider plausible *semantic relations* among the words, and also various aspects of the sentence structure (i.e., whether the sentence is active or passive). They also integrate the sentence with what they can see in the visually observed world. In conversation, a further source of information comes from the fact that speakers and listeners continually fill in the blanks in what is uttered, using inference to help them interpret the full meaning of what is said.

THE GROWTH OF LANGUAGE IN THE CHILD

- From the very first moments after birth, infants' ears and minds are open to detect the sounds of language, and also to organize these sounds into words. Initially, infants respond to just about all sound distinctions made in any language, but by 12 months of age they are more sensitive to sound contrasts in their own language than to those in other languages.
- Eventually, infants learn to identify the boundaries between morphemes and words. One important cue that helps them do this seems to involve a keen sensitivity by the infant to the frequencies with which specific syllables occur right next to each other.
- Word learning is heavily influenced by the ways the child is disposed to categorize objects and events, as reflected in the fact that young children acquire the *basic-level words* for whole objects (*dog*) before learning the *superordinates* (*animal*) or *subordinates* (*Chihuahua*).
- Children also use the *structure* of the language as a way of guiding their word learning. Remarkably, some understanding of syntax, and the way it links up with meaning, is found in children about 17 months of age, even though these children themselves speak only in single-word utterances.
- Children's speech progresses very rapidly by the beginning of the third year of life, with the start of little sentences and the use of function words. *Overregularization errors* (e.g., *holded* for *held*) are clear evidence that children do not learn language by imitation; they suggest instead that young children learn rules that govern how the language is structured.

LANGUAGE LEARNING IN CHANGED ENVIRONMENTS

- Under normal conditions, language emerges in much the same way in virtually all children. They progress from babbling to one-word speech, advance to two-word sentences, and eventually graduate to complex sentence forms and meanings. This progression is consistent with the claim that language development is rooted in our shared biological heritage. But what happens when children grow up in radically different environments? Data from *isolated children*, those deprived of ordinary human contact for many years, suggest that normal language development may take place as long as language learning begins during some *critical period*, which may end roughly at the age of puberty.

- Many persons born deaf learn *sign language*. These gestural systems have hand shapes and positions that combine to form individual words (analogous to the phonemes of spoken language), and they have morphemes and grammatical principles for combining words into sentences that are similar to those of spoken language. Babies born to deaf users of sign language go through the same steps on the way to adult knowledge as do hearing children learning English. Thus, language does not depend on the auditory-vocal channel.

- Blind children learn language as rapidly and as well as sighted children. Here too, language emerges in all of its complexity and on schedule despite a dramatic shift away from the standard circumstances of language learning.

LANGUAGE LEARNING WITH CHANGED ENDOWMENTS

- Since language learning and use are determined by brain function, changing the brain should have strong effects. This is confirmed by many sorts of evidence, including cases of *aphasia*, as well as cases of persons with an apparently inherited syndrome known as *specific language impairment (SLI)*. In addition, as the brain matures, *a critical period for language learning* draws to a close, so that later learning (both of a first language and of later languages) becomes more difficult.

- It appears that even our nearest animal relative, the chimpanzee, cannot come close to attaining human language. For now, the evidence suggests that chimpanzees can learn words and that they do show evidence of *propositional* thought. But there is little evidence that they can create (or understand) the sorts of syntactic structures that humans use routinely.

LANGUAGE AND THOUGHT

- According to the *Whorfian hypothesis*, the language one speaks determines the way one thinks. Language obviously conveys information, and this influences thought; language can also be used to draw our attention to some content, and, again, this influences thought. However, the suggestion that language governs how we can think, or what we can think, lacks a firm basis.

THE PERSON
IN CONTEXT

PART 3

PSYCHOLOGICAL QUESTIONS OFTEN DEMAND A CONSIDERATION of two types of context. First, there is a context of growth and development, so that we need to understand who we are, and what we do now, with reference to who we once were, and what we once knew and did: How do children gain the knowledge they need to understand the world around them? How do they gain the skills they need to interact with others? These will be central concerns for us in the first half of this section, and we will consider the combined influences of biology, culture, and the individual's experience as we examine how each of us grows from infancy to childhood, through adolescence into adulthood, and eventually into old age.

Second, and equally important, there is the context provided by the social world, so that who we are, and how we act, both influence and are influenced by the others around us. This demands its own questions: How do we perceive other people, and how do they perceive us? How are we shaped by the situations we find ourselves in? These issues will be central in the second half of this section. In those chapters, we will ask which of our behaviors or feelings are guided "from within" (by our own beliefs and motivations) and which are guided "from without" (by factors in our social situation). The answers to these questions will confirm the wisdom in John Donne's famous sermon that "no man is an island, entire of itself."

CHAPTER

10

COGNITIVE DEVELOPMENT

A human newborn is tiny, helpless, barely able to control her own movements, and capable of only the most limited interactions with others. A few years later, the child is virtually a different person: Her body is obviously larger and more mature, and she is now capable of a wide variety of skilled movements, including movements (like talking or walking) that require the intricate coordination of many different muscles. The child has also surely gained a broad range of knowledge and intellectual skills, and has learned a great deal about how to get along with others.

Psychologists study all of these forms of development—physical development (changes in the body), motor development (changes in the ability to move), cognitive development (growth in knowledge and intellectual skills), and social development (growth in the skills needed to perceive, understand, and get along with others). And, of course, each of these forms of development continues through the lifespan—so that the skills of a toddler are different from those of a 5-year-old, which are in turn different from those of an adolescent, or an adult. Even in adulthood, development continues, as each of us continues to gain wisdom and new skills, and also has to cope with the many changes associated with aging.

How do these various aspects of development proceed? Does our genetic heritage play a large role—so that our account of development needs (at least in part) to be cast in biological terms? What role does experience play? And how should we think about that experience—for example, how much does the young child (or, for that matter, an *infant*) understand about his experience? And what is the nature of the experience: Does the child learn merely by observing the world, or does he need to "experiment" to find out which actions or strategies achieve his goals, and which do not? And to what extent are the experiences of each child like those of others (perhaps children in the same culture, perhaps those in different cultures), and to what extent do children have different experiences?

We will pursue all these questions in this chapter and the next. In this chapter, we will examine the topics of physical and cognitive development, examining how our bodies grow and also how our knowledge and skills develop. We will tackle the broad topic of social development in Chapter 11. ●

PHYSICAL DEVELOPMENT

Among all the different aspects of development, perhaps the most obvious is physical growth, as the individual changes from fertilized egg to embryo, then into a fetus, then a neonate, and then, eventually, into its adult form. This process can take years, but it certainly takes far longer in humans than in any other species. Humans need 16 or 17 years to reach their full height, and the maturation of our brains needs roughly the same span. What is it that shapes this physical growth, and why, in humans, is it so slow?

GROWTH BEFORE BIRTH

The voyage toward becoming a human being begins at conception, when a sperm and egg cell unite to form the fertilized egg. This egg divides and redivides repeatedly, producing a cellular mass that attaches itself to the wall of the uterus. Two weeks after conception, the mass of cells (now called an *embryo*) begins to differentiate into separate cell layers. Two months after conception, the mass of cells has grown to about 1 inch in length and is now called a *fetus*. In the next month, the fetus grows to about 3 inches in length and begins to resemble a miniature baby, with some functioning organ systems and a number of early reflexes, including sucking movements when the lips are touched. In another 4 months—that is, 7 months after conception—the fetus has grown to 16 inches, has a fully developed reflex pattern, can cry, breathe, and swallow, and has a good chance of survival if it should be delivered at this time.

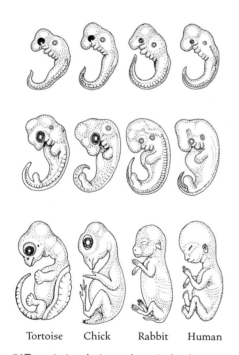

Tortoise Chick Rabbit Human

Differentiation during embryonic development The figure shows three stages in the embryonic development of four different vertebrates— tortoise, chick, rabbit, and human. At the first stage, all of the embryos are very similar to each other. As development proceeds, they diverge more and more. By the third stage, each embryo has taken on some of the distinctive characteristics of its own species.

GROWTH AFTER BIRTH

Nine months after conception, the human fetus is ready to leave the uterus to enter the outer world. *Ready*, however, is a relative term. Most other animals can walk shortly after birth and can take care of themselves almost immediately. Humans, in contrast, are extraordinarily helpless at birth and remain utterly dependent on others and remain so for for many months.

The immaturity of the human infant is easily seen if we examine the brain itself. As we described in Chapter 3, the infant's neurons begin to mature in the later stages of prenatal growth, and their axons and dendrites form increasingly complex interconnections with other nerve cells. But the brain is far from mature at birth. Figure 10.1 shows sections of the human cortex in a newborn, a 3-month-old, and a 15-month-old child (Conel, 1939, 1947, 1955). As the figure clearly shows, there is tremendous growth across this period in the number of neural interconnections. If one simply counts the number of synapses per cortical neuron, this number is 10 times greater for a 1-year-old than it is for a newborn (Huttenlocher, 1979).

The child's growth—in brain size and complexity, and also overall physical growth—continues for many years. This growth is not continuous; rather, it comes in spurts, with each period of accelerated growth lasting only a few months. This is obvious for growth of the body (Figure 10.2), but it is also true for the child's brain. It, too, grows in fits and starts, with the spurts beginning around ages 2, 6, 10, and 14 and continuing for about 2 years each (Epstein, 1978). Each of these spurts leaves the brain up to 10% heavier than it was when the spurt began (Kolb & Whishaw, 1996).

Why is human development so slow? Lions (as just one example) chase their male cubs away from the pride by age 2 or 3. Human parents, in contrast, are burdened with decades of childcare, and one might think that this would be a great disadvantage for our species. It turns out, though, that this long period of dependency is ideal for a creature whose major specialization is its capacity for learning and whose basic invention is culture—the ways of coping with the world that each generation hands on to the next. Human infants, in other words, have a great deal to learn and a huge capacity for learning. Under these circumstances, there is much to be gained by a decade (or two) of living at home—even if it is sometimes inconvenient for child and parent alike.

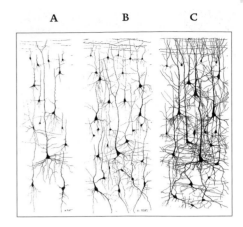

10.1 Growth of neural interconnections Sections of the human cortex in (A) a newborn, (B) a 3-month-old, and (C) a 15-month-old.

THE NEWBORN'S SENSORIMOTOR CAPACITIES

Initially, infants have little ability to control their body movements. They thrash around awkwardly and cannot even hold up their heads. But they also have a number of important reflexes that help them through this period of helplessness. One example is the grasp reflex—when an object touches an infant's palm, she closes her fist tightly around it. If the object is lifted up, the infant hangs on and is lifted along with it, supporting her whole weight for a minute or more. Reflexes of this sort are likely to be a primitive heritage from our primate ancestors, whose infants had to cling to their mothers' furry bodies.

Other infantile reflexes pertain to feeding—for example, the *rooting reflex*. When his cheek is lightly touched, a baby's head turns toward the source of stimulation, his mouth opens, and his head continues to turn until the stimulus (usually a finger or nipple) is in his mouth. When this point is reached, sucking begins.

Many infantile reflexes disappear after a few months, and, in many cases, the reflex is replaced by a more directed response. Thus, infants stop reflexive grasping when they are about 3 or 4 months old, but this does not mean that they never grasp again. Of course they will. But when they do (at about 5 months), they do so because they want to—their grasp has become voluntary rather than reflexive. This voluntary response is more sophisticated and more skilled than the reflex, but it can enter the child's repertoire only after various parts of the brain have matured sufficiently. Until that point, infantile reflexes serve as a temporary substitute.

In contrast to newborns' rather limited motor capacities, their sensory channels function well from the start. Infants can discriminate between tones of different pitch and loudness and, as it turns out, also show an early preference for their mother's voice

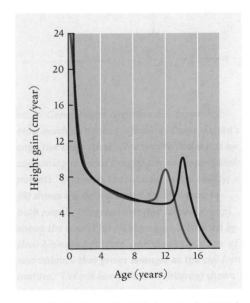

10.2 Physical growth Height gains for British boys (red) and girls (green) from birth until 19 years of age. Physical growth continues for almost 20 years after birth with a special spurt at adolescence.

ENVIRONMENTAL EFFECTS

The data illustrated in Figure 10.4 reveal a powerful role for genetics in shaping a child's abilities, but we must always keep in mind that the genes do not operate in a vacuum, and so the environment also has a crucial part to play in the child's development. But what exactly is the "environment"?

THE ENVIRONMENT BEFORE BIRTH

Children are exposed to many different environmental influences—nutrients or toxins that they ingest; physical events that they can observe; language that they can hear; activities that they can participate in. Importantly, though, the nature of these environmental influences changes as the child matures. For example, consider the earliest stages of embryonic development. Some of the cells in the embryo will eventually become the organism's brain; others will become the gallbladder or the bones of the foot. But every cell in the embryo has the same genes, and so presumably all receive the same genetic instructions. How, therefore, does each cell manage to develop appropriately?

In part, the fate of each cell is determined by its cellular neighbors—the cells that literally form its physical environment. Evidence comes from studies of salamander embryos. Early in their development, salamanders have an outer layer of tissue that gradually differentiates. Cells in this layer will become teeth if they make contact with certain other cells in the embryo's mouth region. Without this contact, cells in this layer instead become skin. This is demonstrated by surgically rearranging cells in the embryo's outer layer. If these cells had stayed in their initial position, they would have developed into skin cells. Transplanted into the embryo's mouth region, these cells became teeth (Spemann, 1967).

In the earliest stages of development, then, each cell's environment consists of its cellular neighbors. Somewhat later, development is affected by another kind of environment—the organism's own bodily fluids, especially its blood. Moreover, the bloodstream of mammalian embryos is intimately connected to the mother's blood supply, and so this too becomes part of the embryo's environment.

An example of the influence exerted through the bloodstream is the development of sexual structures and behavior. What determines whether an individual is biologically male or female? As we mentioned earlier, someone is genetically male if he is chromosomally XY and genetically female if she is XX. But the full story is more complicated than that. At about 6 weeks of gestation, the human embryo has primordial **gonads** that are not yet differentiated as male or female. A week or so later, though, the differentiation begins: In a genetic male, the XY chromosome pair leads to the formation of testes. Once formed, these produce **androgens** (male sex hormones) such as testosterone, and it is the presence of these hormones in the bloodstream that steers fetal development to produce a male—including, of course, the formation of the external genitalia.

The pattern is different for females. The formation of the female's external genitals depends on hormones only indirectly. As long as no androgens circulate in the bloodstream, the fetus will develop the appropriate female organs. Thus, the basic genetic plan for humans, shared by both sexes, seems to call for the building of a female. If it is left undisturbed (i.e., if no androgens are present), the plan runs its course. To build a male, the developmental path has to be diverted by the appropriate hormones. It would seem that biologically—if not biblically—speaking, Adam was created from Eve (Money, 1980; Money & Ehrhardt, 1972).

THE ENVIRONMENT AFTER BIRTH

After birth, the range of environmental events affecting development broadens appreciably and now includes many aspects of the surrounding physical, social, and cognitive

Genetic effects on behavior

The creation of Eve *According to the Bible, Eve was created after Adam. But biologically, the order is reversed. (Panel from the Sistine Chapel ceiling, by Michelangelo, 1508–1512.)*

worlds. We will have much more to say about specific environmental influences later in this chapter, but for now let us simply note that here, too, the role of various environmental factors depends on the child's age. As a simple illustration, imagine a 3-month-old who hears his parents shout, "Surprise!" as they show him a new toy. In all likelihood, the baby will cry in fear, because all he hears is a loud noise. At the age of 3 years, the same shout will probably produce joyous squeals of anticipation, because now the sound has a meaning that is vastly more important than its acoustic intensity.

SENSITIVE PERIODS

It seems, therefore, that a child's reaction to an environmental influence (before or after birth) depends on the child's age. Some developmental theorists, however, believe this idea should be framed in much stronger terms. They argue that there are *critical periods* in development during which certain events will have an enormous impact; outside of these critical periods, the same events will have little or no influence.

The idea of critical periods was derived from embryology, where it refers to the development of tissue differentiation. For example, we previously saw that parts of a salamander embryo's outer tissue, if transplanted early in development, may become skin or teeth, depending on what cells they are adjacent to. But at a later time, this flexibility is gone. If the cells destined to be teeth are transplanted at this point, they still become teeth. For these cells, the critical period has passed, and the path of their development is already set (Spemann, 1967).

Many psychologists believe that similar critical periods exist for key developments after birth, but the boundaries of these periods are not as rigidly fixed as are the critical periods in embryological development. As a result, these windows of opportunity are called *sensitive periods*, to indicate that this is a time in which the organism is especially sensitive to a particular influence. An example is the attachment of the young of many species to their mother, an attachment that is much more readily formed at an early age (see Chapter 11). In humans, a related example is the acquisition of language, which, as we have seen, is easier at younger ages (see Chapter 9).

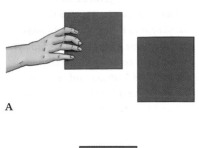

A

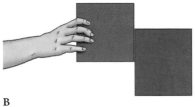

B

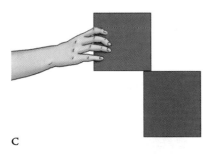

C

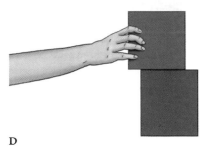

D

10.12 Developing a sense of support **Even very young infants seem to know a lot about the physical world, but they also have much to learn. At the age of 3 months, infants act as if they believe that any physical contact will provide support—and so the red block in (B) will hold its position even if the hand lets go. By roughly 5 months, infants have learned that a support has to be underneath the supported object. Therefore, they act as if the red block in (B) will fall if let go, but not the red block in (C). By roughly 6 months, infants have learned that the support has to be appropriately positioned, and so they expect the red block in (B) or (C) to fall when let go, but not the red block in (D).**

returned. It's no wonder, then, that adults regard this as a puzzling state of affairs, and suspect the experimenter has somehow tricked them.

Do infants react to these events in the same way? The answer is yes. The 4-month-olds evidently found the second condition more surprising (and, presumably, more puzzling) than the first condition, just as adults would. This was revealed by the fact that they spent much more time looking at the stage in the second condition than they did in the first. Apparently, these young infants had some notion of object permanence and continued to believe in the box's existence (and its ability to block the motion of other objects) even when it was entirely hidden from view. In addition, young infants evidently do have some notion of the principles that govern objects in space, including the fact that two objects (here, the screen and the box) cannot occupy the same space at the same time.

INFANTS' UNDERSTANDING OF *SUPPORT*

Infants clearly know more about the world than Piaget gave them credit for. At the same time, though, there are also limits on what infants know, and, correspondingly, there is much intellectual growth during the first year of life. The various situations depicted in Figure 10.12 demonstrate some of these limits. In each case, what will happen if the hand lets go of the red block? According to most adults, the block will drop in the first three situations; only in situation D will the red block maintain its position once it is let go.

Infants believe otherwise. In one study, infants were shown events similar to the ones depicted in Figure 10.12. In some cases, the red block, once it lost its support, fell to the tabletop. In other cases, the experimenters had secretly arranged for a hidden support for the block, and so, when let go, it simply held its position. The question is, which of these outcomes will be surprising to the infant, and which outcomes will simply show the event unfolding as (the infant believes) it should? Surprise in this case is again measured by looking time, on the assumption (supported in many other studies) that infants will look for a longer time at events they find surprising or puzzling, and will look only briefly at events they find ordinary.

The results show a clear developmental trajectory. At the age of 3 months, infants act as if they believe that any physical contact will provide support. They therefore are surprised if the red block does *not* fall in situation A, but they are surprised if it *does* fall in situation B.

By roughly 5 months, infants have learned that contact is not by itself enough to provide support. They now know that the support has to be underneath the target object. Therefore, they expect the red block to fall in situation B, but not in situation C.

By roughly 6 months, infants have learned that the support has to be underneath the target and appropriately positioned, and now their reaction to these displays is similar to that of adults: They expect all the red blocks to fall except for the one in situation D (Baillargeon, 1994; for related data, see, for example, Baillargeon, 2004; Baillargeon & Wang, 2002; Hespos & Baillargeon, 2001a, 2001b; for a broad review of infants' object knowledge, see Mareschal, 2000).

Thus, we see once again that infants begin to understand the physical world at ages far earlier than Piaget claimed. Even so, infants still have much to learn, and one crucial task for developmental psychologists is to explore how the relevant knowledge is acquired.

OBJECT PERMANENCE AND THE SEARCH PROCESS

These (and other) results suggest that, by the time the infant is 8 or 9 months old, he has a reasonable grasp of how the physical world works and, with that, an adequate understanding of what a solid object is. But, in this case, how can we explain Piaget's own findings, findings that led him to conclude that infants lack a concept of object permanence? How, in particular, can we explain the fact that an 8- or 9- month-old consistently fails in retrieving objects that are out of sight?

Most modern investigators suggest that—contrary to Piaget—infants do believe that objects continue to exist even when hidden from view. At the same time, though, infants are exceedingly inept at searching for these objects, and that is why Piaget observed the peculiar failures that he did.

To illustrate this, we can use the A-not-B effect, which (as we have discussed) refers to the infant's tendency to search at a place where she previously found a toy rather than at a place where she has just seen the toy hidden. What accounts for this effect? If the infant has just reached toward *A* several times, then the reaching-toward-*A* response is well primed. To reach toward *B*, therefore, the infant must override this newly acquired habit, and that is the problem. The infant does know where the toy is, but she is unable to inhibit the momentarily potent reach-toward-*A* response. In line with this hypothesis is the fact that many infants look at *B* at the same time that they reach for *A*, as if they knew where the object was but could not tell their arms what they had learned with their eyes (Figure 10.13; Baillargeon & Graber, 1987).

Some investigators believe that the ability to override a dominant action depends on the maturation of certain areas in the prefrontal cortex, a region just in front of the motor projection area. Evidence comes from studies on monkeys with lesions in this area; they show a pattern very similar to the A-not-B error shown by human infants (A. Diamond, 1988, 1989; A. Diamond & Goldman-Rakic, 1989; also see Zelazo & Frye, 1998; for more on the A-not-B error, see pp. 388–389).

In short, Piaget was almost certainly mistaken about infants' understanding of object permanence. Young infants do understand that there are objects out in the world and that these objects (and their parts) continue to exist even when out of view. What infants lack is a full understanding of how to deal with those objects—for example, how to find them when they are hidden.

NUMBER IN INFANCY

Infants also have unexpected competence in other domains. For example, Piaget argued that children younger than 6 years have little understanding of number. After all, children do not conserve number until then, and so might say (for example) that a row of four buttons, all spread out, has more buttons in it than a row of four bunched closely together. This certainly sounds like they have failed to grasp the concept of numbers.

But more recent experiments have shown that very young children do have some numerical ability. In one study, infants only 6 months old were shown a series of slides that displayed different sets of objects. The specific items shown varied from one slide to the next, but each slide contained exactly three objects. One slide, for example, might show a comb, a fork, and a sponge; another might show a bottle, a brush, and a toy drum; and so on. Each slide also differed in the spatial arrangement of the items. They might be set up with two on top and one below, or in a vertical column, or with one above and two below.

With all these variables, would the infants be able to detect the one property shared by all the slides—the fact that all contained three items? To find out, the experimenters used the habituation technique. They presented these sets of threes until the infants became bored and stopped looking. Then they presented a series of new slides in which some of the slides showed two items, while others continued to show three. The infants spent more time looking at the slides that displayed two items rather than three. Evidently, the infants were able to step back from all the particulars of the various slides and detect the one property that all the slides had in common. In this regard, at least,

A

B

C

10.13 A dissociation between what the infant knows and what the infant does
(A) A 7-month-old looks at a toy that has just been placed in B, one of the two wells. (B) He continues to look at well B after both wells are covered. (C) When finally allowed to reach for the toy, he uncovers well A, in which he found the toy on a previous trial, rather than well B, in which he saw the toy being placed. In this particular sequence, he actually still looks at B while uncovering A, suggesting a dissociation between what the infant knows and what he does.

NUMERICAL SKILLS IN PRESCHOOLERS

We have seen that infants can abstract the properties of twoness and threeness, and we have suggested that this provides the starting point for the development of numerical abilities. What happens in the years following infancy?

COUNTING

Some precursors of the skill of counting appear as early as 2½ years. At this age, children may not know the conventional sequence of number terms, but they have grasped the idea of what the counting process is all about. Thus, one 2-year-old counted "1, 2, 6," and another said "1, 13, 19." But what is important is that they used these series consistently and realized that each of these number tags has to be applied to just one object in the to-be-counted set. They also realized that the tags must always be used in the same order and that the last number applied is the number of items in the set. Thus, the child who counted "1, 13, 19" confidently asserted that there were 13 items when she counted a two-item set, and 19 items when she counted a three-item set. This child is obviously not using the adult's terms but does seem to have mastered some of the key ideas on which counting rests (Gallistel & Gelman, 2000; Gelman & Gallistel, 1978; Lipton & Spelke, 2006).

NUMERICAL REASONING

A child who can count has taken a big step, but there is more to numerical understanding than counting. The child must also grasp some principles of numerical reasoning—the ideas of "more than" and "less than," simple principles of arithmetic, and so on. Preschoolers gradually acquire these conceptual basics. When comparing two sets of items, for example, if the number of items is small enough, 3- and 4-year-olds can correctly point to the set that is smaller or larger (Gelman, 1982; Gelman & Gallistel, 1978).

If preschool children have these skills, then why do they fail the Piagetian tests for conservation of number? We have already described the standard Piagetian finding: When preschoolers are asked to compare two rows, each containing, say, four toy ducks, they often say that the longer row contains more ducks, in an apparent confusion of length and number. How can we reconcile this with the demonstrations of the preschooler's numerical competence?

In part, the problem may lie in how the children were questioned in Piaget's studies. In these procedures, the child is typically questioned twice. First, the two rows of items are presented in an evenly spaced manner, so that both rows are the same length. When asked, "Which row has more, or do they both have the same?" the child quickly answers "The same!" Now the experimenter changes the length of one of the rows—perhaps spreading the items out a bit more or pushing them more closely together—and asks again, "Which row has more, or do they both have the same?"

Why is the same question being asked again? From the point of view of the child, this may imply that the experimenter did not like his first answer and so, as adults often do, is providing him the opportunity to try again. This would obviously suggest to the child that his first answer must have been wrong, and so he changes it.

Of course, this misinterpretation is possible only because the child is not totally sure of his answer, and so he is easily swayed by this subtle hint from the experimenter. In other words, Piaget was correct in noting the limits of the preschool child's knowledge: The child's grasp of numerical concepts is tentative enough so that even a slight miscue can draw him off track. But this does not mean the child has no understanding of numbers or counting, and, in fact, if we question the child carefully, provide no misleading hints, and simplify the task just a little (by using smaller numbers of items), preschool children reliably succeed in the conservation task (Siegal, 1997).

It seems, therefore, that the achievements of later periods are built on foundations established much earlier. In this fashion, there is far more continuity in development than Piaget asserted, and the steps of cognitive development are not as all-or-none as the changes from tadpole to frog (let alone from frog to prince).

SOCIAL COGNITION IN PRESCHOOLERS: DEVELOPING A THEORY OF MIND

Similar conclusions emerge when we consider other aspects of early development, including the development of a child's understanding of the social world.

Much of the recent discussion has focused on what theorists call the child's *theory of mind*—the set of beliefs that someone employs whenever she tries to make sense of her own behavior or that of others (Leslie, 1992; D. Premack & Woodruff, 1978; Wellman, 1990). In adults, the theory of mind has many elements: Each of us knows that other people have beliefs, that their beliefs may be true or false, and that their beliefs may differ from our own, which may also be true or false. We know that other people have desires and that these desires may also differ from our own. We also know that other people sometimes know things that we do not, and that we sometimes know things that they do not.

These notions may not sound complex or profound, but they are an essential resource for us all, providing a crucial knowledge base that we rely on in virtually all of our day-to-day social functioning. It is these beliefs that allow us to understand the behavior of other people and, within certain limits, to predict how people will behave in the future. Without these beliefs—that is, without a theory of mind—we would be bewildered by much of the action going on around us and incapable of acting appropriately in most social situations.

THE ROOTS OF THEORY OF MIND

If tested in the right way, even very young children reveal the beginnings of a theory of mind—a rudimentary understanding of the actions and thoughts of other people. For example, if 2-year-old Joey is told that Lisa wants a cookie, then he will correctly predict that Lisa will look for a cookie and that she will be happy if she finds one (see, for example, Wellman & Wooley, 1990). These are hardly earth-shaking insights into Lisa's actions, but they do indicate that the toddler is beginning to understand why other people do the things they do and feel the things they feel.

In the same fashion, in one study 18-month-olds watched as experimenters made "yuk" faces after tasting one food and smiled broadly after tasting another. The experimenters then made a general request to these toddlers for food, and the children responded appropriately—offering the food that the experimenter preferred, even if the children themselves preferred the other food. Here, too, we see indications that young children understand both the relationship between desires and actions and the crucial fact that other people have desires different from their own (Repacholi & Gopnik, 1997, Rieffe, Terwogt, Koops, Stegge, & Oomen, 2001; for more on the child's theory of mind, see Gopnik & Meltzoff, 1997).

TRUE AND FALSE BELIEFS

The child's task becomes more difficult when it comes to beliefs. Suppose you tell 3-year-old Susie that Johnny wants to play with his puppy. You also tell her that Johnny thinks the puppy is under the piano. If Susie is now asked where Johnny will look, she will sensibly say that he will look under the piano (Wellman & Bartsch, 1988). Like an adult, a 3-year-old understands that a person's actions depend not just on what she sees and desires, but also on what she believes.

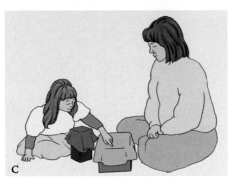

10.17 *The false-belief test* *(A) The child watches as the experimenter makes the teddy bear "hide" the ball in the red box. (B) While the teddy bear is gone, the experimenter and the child move the ball to the green box. (C) When the child is now asked, "Where does the teddy bear think the ball is?" she points to the green box.*

But does the 3-year-old truly understand the concept of belief? In fact, the child's understanding may be quite limited—so that, for example, they seem not to understand how beliefs come to be. As an illustration, if asked what color an object is, 3-year-olds claim that they can find out just as easily by touching an object as they can by looking at it (O'Neill, Astington, & Flavell, 1992). Likewise, 4-year-olds will confidently assert that they have always known something even if they first learned it from the experimenter just moments earlier (Taylor, Esbensen, & Bennett, 1994).

Another apparent limitation concerns the child's understanding of false beliefs. According to many authors, a 3-year-old does not understand the simple facts that beliefs can be true or false and that different people can have different beliefs. This suggests that there is something seriously lacking in the 3-year-old's theory of mind.

Evidence for this claim comes from studies using false-belief tests (Wimmer & Perner, 1983; also Lang & Perner, 2002). In a typical study of this kind, a child and a teddy bear sit in front of two boxes, one red and the other green. The experimenter opens the red box and puts some candy in it. He then opens the green box and shows the child—and the teddy—that this box is empty. The teddy bear is now taken out of the room (to play for a while), and the experimenter and the child move the candy from the red box into the green one. Next comes the crucial step: The teddy bear is brought back into the room, and the child is asked, "Where will the teddy look for the candy?" Virtually all 3-year-olds and some 4-year-olds will answer, "In the green box." If you ask them why, they will answer, "Because that's where it is." It would appear, then, that these children do not really understand the nature of belief. They seem to assume that their beliefs are inevitably shared by others, and likewise, they seem not to appreciate that others might have beliefs that are false (Figure 10.17).

However, by age 4½ or so, children get the idea. Now if they are asked, "Where will the teddy look for the candy?" they will answer, "He'll look in the red box because that's where he thinks the candy is" (Wellman & Lagattuta, 2000; Wellman et al., 2001). The children seem now to have learned that not all knowledge is shared, that different individuals have different beliefs, and that which beliefs one will have depends on appropriate access to the relevant information.

OTHER DOMAINS OF COMPETENCE

Apparently, even young children know something about the beliefs and desires of other people, and older children (e.g., 5-year-olds) know more. But is it sensible to speak of these young children as having a "theory" of mind? Many authors believe it is. A scientist uses a theory to account for evidence and to predict new findings. The child's theory does the same. In a scientist's theory, the various claims are all interrelated, and this, too, is a trait of the child's theory of mind: The child cannot understand how belief influences action unless she also understands what belief is; she cannot truly understand what a belief is without realizing that false beliefs are possible; and so on. Finally, the scientist's theory has a specific domain of application: Einstein's theory of relativity tells us a great deal about space and time but reveals nothing about how to make a really good pizza. Likewise for the child's theory: A theory of mind helps the child understand the behavior of others but is of little use in helping her solve an arithmetic problem or finding her way through the mall.

These parallels do seem to justify using the term *theory* when describing the child's theory of mind. But, in addition, the notion of a theory's limited domain invites a question: Do young children have theories that help them make sense of other aspects of their experience? The evidence suggests that they do. For example, children seem to have a set of interrelated beliefs about biological functioning that provide the basis for their thinking about sickness and health, birth and death (Gelman & Raman, 2002; Inagaki & Hatano, 2004; Wellman & Gelman, 1992). The same beliefs also guide children's thinking about more mundane topics, such as parental instructions concerning good nutrition ("Eat your spinach").

Even though children have several different theories (about life functioning, about the physical world, and so on), the child's theory of mind may have a special status: As our species evolved, it would have been advantageous for our ancestors to be able to predict the actions of other people and, in some settings, to direct the actions of others. On this basis, natural selection would have favored anyone with these capacities, and this may have produced what some theorists describe as a "social cognition module" in our brains—a brain area specialized for thinking about, interpreting, and predicting the actions of other people (Byrne & Whiten, 1988; Cosmides & Tooby, 1992; Hughes & Cutting, 1999; for a broad review, see Gopnik, 1999).

Several pieces of evidence fit well with this proposal, including the fact that specific regions of the brain are reliably more activated whenever someone is thinking about the beliefs, desires, and emotions of others (e.g,. Gallagher & Frith, 2003; Saxe, Carey, & Kanwisher, 2004). In addition, certain forms of brain damage seem to cause impairments specifically to someone's theory of mind, again suggesting a biological specialization for this sort of thinking (see, for example, Happé, Brownell, & Winner, 1999; but also see Frith & Frith, 1999; Frye, Zelazo, & Burack, 1998; Hughes & Cutting, 1999; Perner & Lang, 1999; Rowe, Bullock, Polkey, & Morris, 2001).

Perhaps, therefore, our brains do contain a "social cognition module," specified by our genetics and shaped by our evolutionary past. If so, then what information does this module contain? Here it is important to note that a person's theory of mind depends on his culture, because people in different parts of the world have different views about why people do what they do and feel what they feel (Lillard, 1997, 1998; also Greenfield, Keller, Fuligni, & Maynard, 2003). Therefore, if we are born with a social cognition module, it cannot specify particular beliefs. (If it did, these beliefs would presumably be shared by all in our species.) Perhaps instead the module consists of a sophisticated set of learning strategies, cognitive tools that allow children at a very young age to construct a theory of mind appropriate for the culture in which they are raised. In this way, the module would resemble the innate capacity for language learning (see Chapter 9), a capacity that is shared by all humans but that allows each of us to learn the specific dialect spoken in the community in which we grow up.

SEQUENCE OR STAGES?

Overall, then, the evidence does not reveal the neat, cleanly demarcated stages that Piaget proposed. In Piaget's view, development involves sharp discontinuities, with the skills and capacities of, say, the preoperational child being distinctly different from those of a sensorimotor child. But over and over, we have seen indications of developmental continuity—with later achievements growing out of earlier precursors.

Does this mean that Piaget's developmental milestones have no psychological reality? Certainly not. Consider the difference between a preschool child and a 7-year-old. The younger child can tell the difference between two and three buttons regardless of how they are spaced on the table, and in this fashion seems to be conserving number. But her comprehension is quite fragile, and so, as we have seen, she will fail to conserve if the test is made slightly harder, or if she is pulled off track by subtle hints that (misleadingly) suggest her first answer was mistaken.

The picture is obviously different, though, for a 7-year-old. He can count higher, but that is not the issue. He knows that there is no need to count, because he is confidently aware of the fact that a change in the buttons' arrangement will not change their number. Likewise, he is immune to hints, because he knows securely and confidently what the proper answer is to the experimenter's questions.

Stages?   Even if Piaget's conception is wrong, there are still considerable differences between a pre-school child and a 7-year-old.

Likewise for theory of mind: Here, too, young children will pass our tests if we simplify things appropriately. Thus, for example, 15-month-olds can pass a simple version of the false-belief test—even though the ordinary version of the test (pp. 377–378) baffles most 4-year-olds (Onishi & Baillargeon, 2005; but also see Perner & Ruffman, 2005). We can, therefore, celebrate the achievements of the 15-month-olds, but we must also acknowledge their limits: They pass the false-belief test only with suitable simplifications. The older child, in contrast, needs no simplifications, because, for her, it is utterly clear that other people have their own beliefs, and these beliefs may be false. As a result, the older child can use this understanding in a broad range of circumstances, and the understanding can be revealed in a wide variety of experimental tests.

Thus, there are both similarities and differences between younger children and older ones. Young children have skills that are similar to—and the foundation of—those of older children, and so, as a result, development does not involve the abrupt arrival of wholly new ways of dealing with the world. But the younger child's skills are primitive and fragile, mere precursors of the sophisticated and fluent capacities the child will display just a short time later.

Hand in hand with this, there are both continuities and discontinuities in child development. On the one side, the similarity between younger and older children in their skills, and the fact that new capacities gradually emerge from old ones, indicate that development is far more continuous than Piaget suggested. But, even so, Piaget was correct in noting that there are times in a child's life when she seems to take a giant cognitive leap forward. What produces these leaps? In domain after domain, the child's skills and understanding grow slowly and steadily, but this gradual growth eventually leads to a breakthrough—a point at which (at last!) the child can apply her skills spontaneously (without adult hints or support) and broadly (to a wide range of new problems). At that point the child's performance will become suddenly and markedly better than it was just a few weeks earlier. In this fashion, a gradual increase in skill may produce abrupt improvements in performance.

When do these intellectual breakthroughs occur? They seem to be at age 2 (more or less), and also at age 4 or 5, and then again at age 8 or 9. These are, of course, the ages that Piaget identified as crucial transitions in the life of the child, and so Piaget may have been right in highlighting the importance of these ages, even if his emphasis on qualitative change was not the right way to characterize these transitions.

THE CAUSES OF COGNITIVE GROWTH

We have now said a lot to describe cognitive development as the child proceeds from early infancy into the school years. But what explains these changes? Piaget's account gives us some indications, but it also leaves out some crucial factors. Let us take a closer look at what it is that drives the cognitive changes we have been discussing.

THE ROLE OF BIOLOGICAL INHERITANCE

Piaget—and many scholars who came after him—emphasized the role of the child's experiences, including both what the child sees and what the child does. Evidence collected in the last 25 years, however, makes it clear that we also need to consider the role of biological inheritance, so that, in the end, our accounts of cognitive development will need to describe the rich interplay between the child's experience and her innate capacities.

In fact, we have seen three lines of evidence supporting this claim in our discussion so far. First, we have seen that genetic factors play a large role in shaping one's abilities, so that, for example, people who resemble each other genetically are likely to end up resembling each other in their verbal skills (p. 361, also see Chapter 14). This is, of course, a powerful argument that the development of our intellectual capacities is shaped by our inherited biology.

Second, we have also mentioned the fact that certain cognitive capacities seem tied to particular neural structures, and so damage to those structures causes specific cognitive deficits. These points were prominent in our discussion of language (see Chapter 9) and came up again in our discussion of the child's theory of mind. This, too, strongly indicates that the functioning and development of our cognitive skills must be understood with reference to the relevant aspects of the nervous system.

Third, we have seen indications of cognitive skills in place very early in the child's life, and, in these cases, it is simply implausible that the child has had enough time or experience to learn these skills. It would seem, then, that these capacities are not derived from experience, and so must be innate.

What are the candidates for these innate capacities? This is a matter of debate (see, for example, Hespos & Baillargeon, 2001a; Newcombe, 2002; Spelke, 1994; Spelke & Newport, 1998). Even so, we do have some plausible candidates: For example, we have mentioned that our biological heritage seems to include a sophisticated capacity for learning language, and also a capacity for rapidly acquiring a theory of mind. Notice, therefore, that the genome does not specify a particular content (e.g., the DNA does not transmit certain vocabulary words to the child, nor does it encode particular beliefs about why people act the way they do). Instead, what is inherited is a set of specialized *learning mechanisms*, so that each individual can rapidly develop the skills he needs to gain.

In other cases, though, the genes provide more than learning capacities, and they actually do seem to set up specific processing paths, so that information is, from the start, interpreted one way rather than another. For example, the very young infant seems guided, in her perception of the world, by certain assumptions that are not derived from perceptual experience, but that instead *precede* perceptual experience, and so must be innate (e.g., Spelke, 2003). These assumptions include an assumption of continuity (roughly: that objects do not blink in and out of existence, nor do they abruptly disappear at one location and suddenly reappear at some other location), and also an assumption of cohesion (roughly: that objects connected to each other are likely to stay connected as they shift position, and if different parts of the visual field do move in unison, this probably means they are parts of a single object).

What other assumptions or capacities are innate—providing the child with a basis for understanding number, perhaps, or social interactions, or the physical world in which the child resides? This remains to be seen, but, even with this uncertainty, future theories will certainly have more to say about the interactions between innate capacities and the child's ongoing experience. (For some of the complexities attached to this theorizing, though, see Scerif & Karmiloff-Smith, 2005.)

THE CULTURAL CONTEXT OF COGNITIVE DEVELOPMENT

Another crucial factor for development turns out to be the cultural environment in which a child grows up. We ignored this factor in our discussion of Piaget, because Piaget intended his theory to apply to all children in all settings. But is this right? Is the pattern of development the same in all cultures or all social groups? Related, what role does the social and cultural environment play in shaping development? Our discussion so far has focused largely on the child himself—what he did, what he knew, what he learned. Will our view of development change if we focus instead on the child *together with* the other people (peers and adults) who provide his social surroundings?

DIFFERENCES IN COMPETENCE?

In many regards, mental growth does seem rather similar in children of different cultures and nationalities. The age at which various abilities emerge varies somewhat from culture to culture, so that, for example, children in some cultures may pass the false-belief test at a slightly earlier age; children in other cultures pass the test only at a slightly later age (Greenfield et al., 2003; but also Callaghan et al., 2005). Even with these variations, however, children in diverse cultures all seem to pass the major developmental landmarks we have discussed in essentially the same order, and they make the same errors en route to these landmarks (Greenfield, 1966; Hyde, 1959; Nyiti, 1976).

In other regards, though, cultures differ in their patterns of cognitive development. In the West, for example, most adolescents pass through the stage of concrete operations and into the stage of formal operations. But in some cultures (e.g., that of Australian aborigines and of New Guinea tribesfolk), many adults fail the standard tests of formal operations. In fact, evidence of formal operations (using the standard tests) is rare in cultures in which there is no explicit schooling (Hollos & Richards, 1993; Segall, Dasen, Berry, & Poortinga, 1999). In such cultures, most adults seem unable to deal with certain abstract problems, including problems of syllogistic reasoning. Thus, a sample of unschooled Kpelle farmers in Liberia were informed that "all Kpelle men are rice farmers. Mr. Smith is not a rice farmer." When asked, "Is Mr. Smith a Kpelle man?" they typically failed to give the simple syllogistic "no." Instead, they were noncommittal: "If I know him in person, I can answer that question, but since I do not know him in person, I cannot answer that question" (Scribner, 1975, p. 175).

However, other evidence makes it clear that the same preliterate peoples are capable of complex, sophisticated reasoning within the context of their own lives. One example comes from the !Kung San hunter-gatherers of the Kalahari desert, who perform remarkable feats of inference while hunting game: weighing the chances of tracking down a wounded giraffe against the cost of a drawn-out search, searching for clues in the pattern of crushed grasses, judging whether blood fell on a twig before or after the twig was bent, and evaluating the various interpretations to decide on a course of action (Blurton-Jones & Konner, 1976). Other examples reveal similar sophistication.

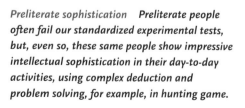

Preliterate sophistication **Preliterate people often fail our standardized experimental tests, but, even so, these same people show impressive intellectual sophistication in their day-to-day activities, using complex deduction and problem solving, for example, in hunting game.**

The data just described create a dilemma. According to our tests, unschooled, preliterate people are incapable of formal reasoning. Yet, when we consider what these people do routinely in their daily lives, it is clear that they are capable of sophisticated reasoning. How can we reconcile these observations?

One possibility is that our tests, designed for Western participants, are simply inappropriate in these other cultures. A test can be inappropriate, for example, if it relies on knowledge or vocabulary not available to the person being tested, and, indeed, this is crucial whether we are testing children in remote areas of the Sahara or in a poor inner-city neighborhood in the United States. (For more on this point, see Chapter 14.)

A test can also be inappropriate for other reasons, including the assumptions often built into the test about what things are important and what are not. For example, one investigator asked unschooled Kpelle participants to sort a collection of objects into groups. Some of the objects were tools and others were foods. Western participants generally use these semantic categories as the basis for their grouping. However, the Kpelle participants sorted the objects by function—a knife with an orange, a hoe with a potato, and so on. Asked why they sorted the objects as they did, they replied, "That is the way a wise man would do it." When the experimenter asked, "How would a fool do it?" he received the response that he had originally looked for—food in one pile and tools in another (Glick, 1975). Thus, the participants obviously were capable of grouping by categories; this simply was not the grouping scheme they deemed most useful.

In addition, it is important to consider what our tests and experiments look like from the point of view of the people being tested. In many tests, it is clear that the investigator already knows the answers to her own questions but is asking the questions anyhow to find out what the person being tested knows. This is a familiar situation for any Western schoolchild—one re-created whenever a teacher gives a test. For people in other cultures, though, this may be an unusual and puzzling situation. The Wolof people of coastal Senegal, for example, rarely ask each other questions to which they already know the answer; when this kind of questioning does occur, it is likely to be understood as "an aggressive challenge, or a riddle with a trick answer" (Irvine, 1978, p. 309). This would obviously put the Wolof at a disadvantage in our tests. (For related discussion, see Rogoff, 1998; Rogoff, Paradise, Arauz, Correa-Chávez, & Angelillo, 2003.)

Navigation skill **Master navigator Mau Piailug teaches navigation to his son and grandson with the help of a star compass consisting of a ring of stones, each stone representing a star or a constellation when it rises or sets on the horizon. The pieces of palm leaf represent the swells which travel from set directions, and so provide further navigational information.**

SOCIAL AND CULTURAL INFLUENCES ON DEVELOPMENT

Clearly, therefore, we must be alert to the cultural backdrop whenever we design our studies and when we are trying to interpret the available evidence. Many investigators, however, believe that our consideration of the sociocultural context needs to go much further than this. Culture is not merely a "filter," coloring how a research participant understands our experimental procedures. Far more important, culture is an active and powerful influence on development, shaping what and how the child learns.

Some cultural influences on development are obvious. In ancient Rome, educated children learned to represent numbers with Roman numerals; modern children in the West, in contrast, learn to represent numbers with Arabic numerals. Modern children in the Oksapmim culture (in New Guinea) learn yet a different system, counting using parts of the body rather than a number system (Saxe, 1981). In each case, this culturally provided tool guides (and in some cases, limits) how the children think about and work with numerical quantities.

COGNITIVE DEVELOPMENT IN OLD AGE

We have now said a great deal about how children develop—in the uterus, during the months of infancy, through the preschool and school years. But development does not cease when the child reaches adulthood. Each of us continues to grow and change across our entire lifetime, a pattern of change often studied under the rubric of *life-span development*. Much of this change involves our emotional and social existence, and we will turn to these points in Chapter 11. But some of the change also involves our cognitive capacities. Let us close the chapter with a brief look at these changes late in life.

AGING AND INTELLIGENCE

New skills, new knowledge   Fluid intelligence declines across the life span, but crystallized intelligence—including new skills and new knowledge—continues to grow with each new experience.

To understand how intellectual functioning changes across the life span, we must distinguish between *fluid* and *crystallized intelligence* (see Chapter 14). *Fluid intelligence* refers to the efficiency and speed of intellectual functioning, usually in arenas that are new to the individual and so require some strategy choice, some decisions about how to proceed, and so on. *Crystallized intelligence* refers to a person's accumulated knowledge, including his vocabulary, the facts he knows, and the strategies he has learned.

Crystallized intelligence remains relatively stable across the life span and, in some studies, seems to grow as the individual gains more and more life experience. Fluid intelligence shows a very different pattern, starting to decline when the person is in his twenties, and with the decline continuing as the years go by (Figure 10.19). However, the decline is far from precipitous, and many individuals maintain much of their intellectual capacity into their sixties and seventies (Craik & Salthouse, 2000; Salthouse, 2000, 2004; Schaie, 1996; Verhaeghen & Salthouse, 1997).

Figure 10.19 suggests that the decline in mental capacities proceeds steadily across the life span. Why, therefore, do we notice the decline primarily in the elderly? Why do people often lament the loss of cognitive capacities between ages 60 and 80, but not comment on the similar drop-off between ages 20 and 40? One reason is that gains in crystallized intelligence, as one matures, often compensate for declines in fluid intelligence. Thus, as the years pass, people master more and more strategies that help them

10.19   Aging and intellectual performance   As they age, people gradually decline in their intellectual performance; the decline can be documented in a range of different tests. However, the opposite pattern—an improvement with age—emerges when we consider vocabulary size, which is a reflection of crystallized, not fluid, intelligence. This figure casts these trends in terms of z-scores, which measure performance relative to the average. (Performance at the average yields a z-score of zero.)

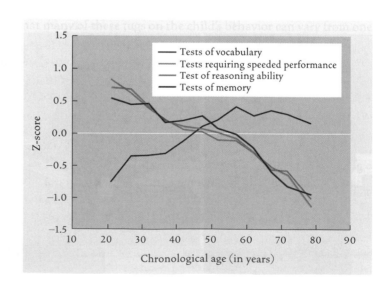

in their daily functioning, and this balances out the fact that their thinking is not as nimble as it used to be. In addition, 30- or 40-year-olds might be less able than 20-year-olds, but we do not detect the decline because the 30- or 40-year-olds still have enough capacity to manage the not-very-demanding routine tasks that fill much of their daily routine. We detect their decline only later, when the gradual drop-off in their mental skills eventually leaves them with insufficient capacity to handle their daily chores (cf. Salthouse, 2004).

Common sense suggests that people differ markedly in how they age—with some people showing a dramatic drop in mental capacities, but others holding on to their abilities with very little loss. This may be an instance, however, in which common sense overstates the facts: If we focus on individuals who are still reasonably active, and who describe themselves as being in "good to excellent health," then we find impressive consistency, from one individual to the next, in how they are affected by the passing years (Salthouse, 2004). Put differently, the drop-off we see in Figure 10.19 is not the result of a few unfortunate individuals who rapidly lose their abilities and so pull down the average. Instead, the drop-off evident in the figure seems to affect most people, and it seems to affect them all to roughly the same degree.

The fact remains, though, that some people do show striking drop-offs in their mental abilities as they age. Why is this? Some investigators propose biological explanations, cast in terms of age-related changes in blood flow or neuroanatomy, or the gradual death of neurons across the life span (but see Stern & Carstensen, 2000; for more on the cognitive neuroscience of aging, see Reuter-Lorenz, 2002). Others focus on educational level or the degree of stimulation in the individual's life (see, for example, Schaie & Willis, 1996), on the notion that those who are less educated or less stimulated will be more vulnerable to the effects of aging. Still others have suggested that the key lies in an age-related decline in working memory or the capacity for paying attention; this claim is sometimes cast in terms of a decline in the mind's "executive function," although the exact meaning of that term, and the role of "executive functioning" in aging, are themselves a matter of debate (Craik & Bialystok, 2006). In addition, let us highlight the fact that these hypotheses may all be correct, and each may describe one of the factors that govern how an individual ages.

How someone ages is also influenced by a variety of medical factors. This reflects the fact that the cells making up the central nervous system can function well only if they receive an ample supply of oxygen and glucose. (In fact, we mentioned in Chapter 3 that the brain consumes almost 20% of the body's metabolic energy, even though it accounts for only about 2% of the overall body weight.) As a result, brain functioning can be impaired by a wide range of bodily changes that diminish the availability of these resources. For example, a decline in kidney function will have an impact throughout the body, but, because of the brain's metabolic needs, the kidney problem may lead to a loss in mental functioning that is detected well before other symptoms appear. Likewise, circulatory problems (including problems with the heart itself or arteriosclerosis) will obviously diminish the quantity and quality of the brain's blood supply, and so can contribute to a cognitive decline (see, for example, Albert et al., 1995). This is one of the reasons why a program of physical exercise can, in many cases, help preserve mental functioning in the elderly, although fitness programs are surely not a cure-all for the effects of aging (see, for example, Cotman & Neeper, 1996; Kramer & Willis, 2002). Finally, cognitive functioning in the elderly is also affected by a number of age-related diseases, including *Alzheimer's disease*, a disorder characterized by a progressive and widespread loss of nerve cells, leading to memory problems, disorientation, and, eventually, total helplessness. Evidence has made it clear that genetic factors can put someone at increased risk for Alzheimer's disease (see, for example, Vickers, Dickson, Adlard, & Saunders, 2000), but the exact causes of the disease remain uncertain.

Some of the goals of socialization are similar all over the world and probably were so throughout human history. No matter if the child is an African bushman or a resident of urban America, she still must learn to control her bodily functions and also how to live with others whose desires take precedence over her own. But other aspects of socialization depend on the social and cultural setting. For example, in cultures based on agriculture, parents generally encourage compliance and conformity in their children, essentially preparing the children for the adult roles they will eventually assume: the patient, cooperative life of a farmer who must plow his soil or milk his cows at specified times. In contrast, hunting and fishing societies generally encourage self-reliance and initiative in their children—reasonable values for people who have to wrest their food from nature in day-to-day encounters (Barry, Child, & Bacon, 1959). Social and economic factors also lead to differences in how boys and girls are raised—with girls in many traditional cultures encouraged to be nurturing and docile, preparing them for lives as homemakers and mothers, and boys encouraged to be more assertive and ambitious, preparing them for roles as wage-earners.

Socialization   *A traditional hunter with his son alongside him, learning to hunt.*

There is, of course, a powerful trade-off here. On the one side, it is beneficial for both the individual and the culture if each person is suitably prepared for the roles he or she will take on in later life; no one benefits if the farmer is too much of a risk-taker or the hunter is too cautious. On the other side, these socialization patterns are harmful if they limit each person's options—forcing people into a specific life path, or, perhaps, keeping a particular social group "in their place." Finding the proper balance between these considerations—providing a child with appropriate preparation for life, but not limiting the child's options—is a considerable challenge for both a society and each pair of parents.

PARENTING STYLES

"They never pushed me. If I wanted to retrieve, shake hands, or roll over, it was entirely up to me."

Apparently, then, parents differ in *what* they teach their children. They also differ in *how* they go about this teaching, and, more broadly, in how they raise their children. This point is obvious to anyone who has watched parents interacting with their children—with some parents being strict, others less so; some parents being anxious and others not; some parents explaining their instructions ("Go to bed, so that you feel better tomorrow") and others just asserting their authority ("Go to bed!"). Across this diversity, though, researchers propose that parenting styles can be largely described in terms of just two dimensions (Maccoby & Martin, 1983). First, parents differ in how accepting they are to their children, and, with that, how responsive they are to the child's actions or needs. Second, parents differ in how demanding or controlling they are of their children's behavior. Putting these two dimensions together, we can think about parenting styles as being divided into four broad types, as shown in Figure 11.6.

These four styles have been described in detail by Diana Baumrind (1967, 1971). *Authoritarian parents* adhere to strict standards about how children should and should not speak and act, and attempt to mold their children's behavior accordingly. Such parents set down firm rules and greet any infractions with stern and sometimes severe punishment. Authoritarian parents do not believe it is necessary to explain the rules to their children, but expect their children to submit to them by virtue of parental authority: "It's because I say so; that's why."

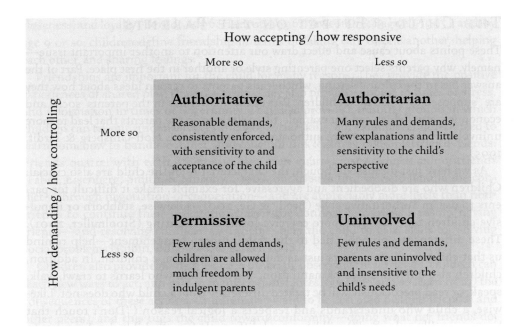

How accepting / how responsive

More so — Less so

Authoritative

Reasonable demands, consistently enforced, with sensitivity to and acceptance of the child

Authoritarian

Many rules and demands, few explanations and little sensitivity to the child's perspective

Permissive

Few rules and demands, children are allowed much freedom by indulgent parents

Uninvolved

Few rules and demands, parents are uninvolved and insensitive to the child's needs

How demanding / how controlling — More so / Less so

11.6 Parenting styles

At the opposite extreme are the *permissive parents*, who set few explicit do's and don'ts for their children. These parents try not to assert their authority, impose few restrictions and controls, tend not to have set schedules (for, say, bedtime or watching TV), and rarely use punishment. They also make few demands on their children—such as putting toys away, doing schoolwork, or helping with chores.

Authoritarian parents brandish parental power; permissive parents abdicate it. A third approach lies between these extremes: *Authoritative parents* exercise their power, but also accept the reciprocal obligation to respond to their children's opinions and reasonable demands. These parents set down rules of conduct and enforce them, assign chores, and expect mature behavior. But they also spend a good deal of time teaching their children how to act appropriately, encourage independence, and allow a good deal of verbal give and take.

Finally, a fourth type of pattern is referred to as *uninvolved parenting*. This is a lax and undemanding approach shown by parents who are so overwhelmed by their own concerns that they have little time for child rearing. They provide few rules and demands, and are also relatively insensitive to their children's needs.

Do these different parenting styles make any difference in the children? Evidence suggests that children of authoritative parents tend to be more cheerful, more responsible, and more cooperative—both with adults and with their peers (Baumrind, 1967). These advantages continue into adolescence: Teenagers raised by authoritative parents seem more confident and more socially skilled (Baumrind, 1991). This parental pattern is also associated with better grades and better SAT scores as well as better social adjustment (Dornbusch, Ritter, Liederman, Roberts, & Fraleigh, 1987; Steinberg, Elkman, & Mounts, 1989; Weiss & Schwartz, 1996).

These results seem to offer a ringing endorsement of the authoritative parenting style, but once again we confront an ambiguity about cause and effect. It is possible, for example, that authoritarian parenting produces sullen, defiant children, but it is also possible that parents faced with sullen, defiant children resort to authoritarian parenting as their only recourse. Similarly, parents of independent, responsible children may develop more peerlike, reciprocal relations early on with their children. Thus, the data do seem to indicate powerful advantages associated with authoritative parenting, but, in light of these ambiguities about what causes what, we need to be cautious in interpreting the data. (For a glimpse of some of the tools we can use in dealing with these ambiguities, though, see Collins, Maccoby, Steinberg, Hetherington, & Bornstein, 2000.)

PROSOCIAL BEHAVIORS AND EMPATHY

Children's capacity for empathy is essential for many aspects of their moral development, but especially so for the development of *prosocial* behavior—behavior that seeks to help and comfort others. Of course, one could take the view that prosocial behavior is actually motivated by self-interest: Parents and teachers constantly hector children about the importance of sharing, so perhaps children share their toys in order to obtain these adults' approval. Likewise, perhaps children learn to share and help others in order to preserve the esteem and support of their friends. Various considerations, however, argue against these claims, and suggest instead that children's prosocial behavior is, in fact, rooted in the child's empathy with other people.

Simple forms of empathy can be found even in very young infants. On hearing another newborn's cry, for example, 1-day-old infants cry, too, and their hearts beat faster (Sagi & Hoffman, 1976; Simner, 1971). Infants are less likely to cry in response to nonhuman noises of comparable loudness, including a computer simulation of another infant's crying.

A child's empathy for others obviously grows as the child matures, and this empathy is unmistakably an important spur to action. For example, some studies have asked teachers to rate how empathic individual children are, or have monitored children's facial expressions of emotion to assess how responsive the children were to others' distress. By either measure, more empathic children are more likely to engage in prosocial behavior (Chapman, Zahn-Waxler, Cooperman, & Iannotti, 1987; Eisenberg et al., 1990). However, this link between empathy and action is weaker for young children; often empathy does not lead to helping. Why not? Part of the problem lies in the fact that young children often detect another person's distress, but cannot figure out what caused the distress. Thus, empathy becomes a stronger influence on behavior only after children have learned to understand others' points of view (Eisenberg, Gershoff, et al., 2001).

In addition, children need to learn *how* to help others. Consider a 2-year-old who sees an adult in pain—say, his mother has cut her finger. The child may become distressed himself, but what will his empathic distress make him do? A number of anecdotes suggest that he will give his mother whatever he finds most comforting himself—for example, his teddy bear. While appreciating his kindly sentiments, the mother would probably have preferred a Band-Aid. But the child at this age is too young to take Mommy's perspective and realize that his mother's needs are not the same as his own (Hoffman, 1977a, 1979, 1984).

It seems, then, that there are many prerequisites to helping others: We need to feel empathy, and understand why we are feeling as we are. We need to understand why other people are feeling as they are. We need to know how to help. For these and other reasons, empathy does not by any means guarantee altruism. Nonetheless, it is a powerful force propelling us toward helping others, and it provides an important part of our explanation for why children do not just avoid moral transgressions but also give to others, share their toys, and comfort friends who are sad.

INDIVIDUAL DIFFERENCES IN PROSOCIAL BEHAVIOR

One last point about prosocial behavior should also be mentioned: Children vary enormously in their prosocial behaviors, with some children being remarkably sensitive, caring and helpful, and others being unhelpful and uncooperative. What accounts for these differences?

Part of the answer is biological, and identical twins tend to be more similar in their prosocial behaviors than fraternal twins or other siblings (Matthews, Batson, Horn, & Rosenman, 1981). These genetic effects may be caused by differences in temperament,

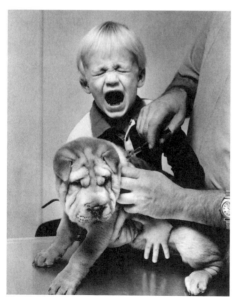

Early empathy   *Even very young infants cry in response to the sound of another infant crying. The same infants do not cry in response to other loud sounds, including a computer simulation of an infant's crying.*

Feeling distress at the distress of another   *The young boy cries as the veterinarian gives an injection to his puppy.*

and, in particular, how emotionally responsive a child is. Children who tend to experience emotion without getting overwhelmed by it are the ones most likely to experience empathy (Eisenberg, Fabes, et al., 1996; Eisenberg & Fabes, 1998). Children who are temperamentally inclined toward positive emotions also tend to be more prosocial (Eisenberg, 2000).

But the environment also matters, and children often imitate other people's helping and sharing (Eisenberg & Fabes, 1998); they are especially likely to imitate adults with whom they have a strong positive relationship (Hart & Fegley, 1995). This helps us understand why parents and children tend to resemble each other in their levels of prosocial behavior (Eisenberg, Fabes, Schaller, Carlo, & Miller, 1991). Parenting style also plays a role: Parents who are supportive in their parenting tend to have children who show more prosocial behavior; parents who are unsympathetic and punishing usually have children who show little prosocial behavior (Miller, Eisenberg, Fabes, & Shell, 1989).

These various considerations lead us once again to a theme that has been in view at many junctures in this chapter: Prosocial behaviors, like most aspects of development, are influenced by many factors, including the child's biology, the child's relationship with parents, and the style of parenting in the child's household. We are complex creatures, and we are sensitive to a correspondingly complex set of influences.

SEXUAL DEVELOPMENT

As they grow, part of what children must learn involves general principles—rules of right and wrong, for example, that apply to all people in virtually all situations. But part of their learning involves differentiation—as the children learn how people are different from each other, and also how they themselves are different from other people. This learning leads the child to a clearer conception of her own "self" and her own personality—what she is really like, in her own eyes and in others' eyes as well.

Seen in this light, social development goes hand in hand with the development of personal identity, and one essential part of this identity is one's sex. Biologically, sex can refer either to *genetic sex*, possessing XX or XY chromosome pairs, or to *morphological* (i.e., structural) *sex*, the possession of a vagina and ovaries or a penis and testes. Psychologically, though, sexuality involves far more than body parts. It also embraces three psychological issues. One is *gender role*—a whole host of behavior patterns that a given culture deems appropriate for each sex. Fundamental to gender roles is the second issue, *gender identity*—our inner sense that we are male or female. A third issue is *sexual orientation*—our inclination toward a sexual partner of the same or opposite sex. Gender role, gender identity, and sexual orientation are surely crucial aspects of a person's experience; how do they come about?

GENDER ROLES

The induction into a male or female role roles begins with the first question typically asked of new parents: "Is it a boy or a girl?" As soon as the answer is supplied—which, thanks to fetal ultrasound, may be months before birth—the process of gender typing begins, and the infant is ushered onto one of two quite different social trajectories. Many of the patterns of gender typing have changed in the wake of modern feminism, but powerful differences in child rearing persist. In our culture, infants are still dressed in either pink or blue; children play with either dolls or toy airplanes.

Besides this inculcation, children can easily observe gender roles in the adult world and discern further clues about how boys and girls are "supposed" to act. While these gender roles are now blurred a bit, children are still likely to observe that adult women

Learning gender roles   *Some of the cues signaling a child's gender roles are subtle; others are far from it.*

(like Mom) often work at home as unpaid housekeepers, cooks, and childcare workers, while adult men (like Dad) go out into the workplace and bring home a paycheck. If both parents work outside the home, children will observe that men and women generally have different kinds of jobs: Mom is unlikely to be a truck driver, or Dad a secretary. Children may observe, too, that society has different expectations about how the two sexes should act. Typically, men are expected to be tough, aggressive, and stoical. In contrast, women are expected to be submissive, emotionally expressive, and more feeling toward others (Good & Sherrod, 2001).

These gender stereotypes are maintained by many forces, including the fact that parents talk to their male and female children differently (Crowley, Callanan, Tenenbaum, & Allen, 2001; M. E. Lamb, 1997), and also treat them differently. In an early study, mothers were introduced to a 6-month-old baby, little "Joey" or "Janie," and asked to play with him or her for a few minutes. In fact, the same 6-month-old was used in both roles, and dressed up either as a boy or as a girl. Even so, the mothers' behavior depended on whether they thought they were playing with "Joey" or "Janie." To "Joey" the mothers offered toys such as hammers or rattles, while "Janie" was invariably given a doll. They also handled "Joey" and "Janie" differently: They often bounced "Joey" about, thus stimulating the whole body. In contrast, their response to "Janie" was gentler and less vigorous (C. Smith & Lloyd, 1978).

Parents and other adults also shape gender roles directly. For example, when young children play with toys that are deemed inappropriate—as when a boy plays with a dollhouse, or a girl with a toy electric drill—their parents are likely to express disapproval (Fagot, 1995; Leaper, Anderson, & Sanders, 1998). This is especially so for fathers, who sternly object to any female-typical behavior in their sons. By and large, girls are allowed more latitude. A girl can be a "tomboy" and be seen as well adjusted; a boy who is a "sissy" is mocked, taunted, or marginalized (Langlois & Downs, 1980; McCreary, 1994).

With all of these influences, it is unsurprising that children start conforming to gender roles at an early age. Well before they are 2 years old, boys show a preference for playing with trucks and cars; girls prefer playing with dolls and soft toys (Smith & Dalish, 1977). Likewise, 3-year-olds in one study were shown a male doll ("Michael") and a female doll ("Lisa"), and asked a variety of questions about each. The children confidently asserted that the boy doll was likely to play with cars and say things such as "I can hit you." The girl doll, they said, was more likely to talk a lot, never hit, and likely to help her mother with cooking (Kuhn, Nash, & Brucken, 1978). Older children add to their beliefs certain expectations for men's and women's personalities: Fourth- and fifth-graders, for example, assert that women are generally weak and emotional, while men are ambitious and assertive (Best et al., 1977; Williams, Satterwhite, & Best, 1999). Similarly, in a different study, grade-school children said they could be friends with a girl who plays football, for example, but were quite condemning of a boy who wears lipstick (Blakemore, 2003; Levy, Taylor, & Gelman, 1995).

SOURCES OF GENDER-ROLE DIFFERENCES

We have mentioned some of the social forces that support these gender-role differences—including differences in how adults play with little boys or little girls, the direct instructions that adults give to children, the way children are treated by their peers, and more. These social forces, in turn, are rooted in our culture, and, in particular, the widely shared ideas that people have about how boys and girls are "supposed" to behave. But these culture-based assumptions are neither universal nor inevitable, a point often illustrated with data collected by anthropologist Margaret Mead. Mead (1928) studied tribal societies in New Guinea, and among the Arapesh, she reported, both males and females were cooperative, nonaggressive, and sensitive to others' needs. Among the Mundugumor, she claimed, both men and women were expected to be assertive, aggressive, and emotionally unresponsive. It surely seems, then, that different cultures have different ideas about what it means to be "male" or "female."

More recent anthropologists, however, have challenged Mead's evidence, with the suggestion that she may have been misled by some of her informants (Freeman, 1983; also see D. E. Brown, 1991). It turns out, though, that we do not need to immerse ourselves in the debate over Mead's data, because other, less exotic data make the same general point: We know that gender roles in Europe and America have changed considerably in the last century—with the differences between men and women (in their behavior, their life trajectories, or their professional options) being much less distinct than they were a few generations back. Obviously, then, cultural ideas about gender are not immutable.

As is usually the case, though, biological influences also play a part. Our biology obviously influences the many anatomical differences between men and women—in their genitals, their body shapes, and so on. Biological forces are also the reason that girls tend to mature more quickly than boys, a difference between the sexes that shows up in a range of measures that include speaking, toilet training, developing fine-motor skills (such as drawing), getting permanent teeth, and the age at which they achieve puberty (Eaton & Yu, 1989; J. A. Martin, King, Maccoby, & Jacklin, 1984; Tanner, 1990).

But biology also matters for the behaviors that constitute each gender's stereotypical role. This is is reflected in several lines of evidence, including studies of *androgenized females*—children who are genetically female but who have been exposed to high levels of the male hormone androgen. This pattern can arise for several reasons, including a (genetically rooted) condition known as *congenital adrenal hyperplasia (CAH)*, in which the girl's adrenal glands produce high levels of androgen. Children with CAH are born with ovaries and a uterus, but with external genitals that resemble a male's (e.g., an enlarged clitoris that looks like a penis).

In many cases, these children receive cosmetic surgery shortly after birth so that their outward appearance matches their internal organs, and they are then raised normally as girls. Nonetheless, the effects of the androgen show up in many ways (Money & Ehrhardt, 1972; also Berenbaum, 2002; Ehrhardt & Baker, 1974; Hines, 2004): These girls often end up as "tomboys" and prefer playing with trucks, rather than dolls. They tend to begin dating later than other girls, and they feel that their careers should take priority over romance. And, impressively, the extent of these effects depends on the amount of androgen exposure: Girls with more severe cases of CAH are the ones who show the strongest interest in traditionally masculine toys and careers (Servin, Nordenstrom, Larsson, & Bohlin, 2003).

GENDER DIFFERENCES IN ABILITY

For a mix of social, cultural, and biological reasons, then, men and women do differ in some personality traits and in some behaviors. They also differ in their intellectual abilities. Before we turn to the evidence on this issue, though, let us highlight two essential points of caution. First, almost all of the differences between the sexes (including the differences in personality and in ability) are relatively small in magnitude; in fact, men and women are much more alike than they are different (despite the cultural mythology to the contrary). Second, when there are differences between the sexes, these are differences in the *averages*. It is true, for example, that the average 3-year-old girl is more dependent than her male counterpart—more likely to cling, to ask for help, and to seek affection (Emmerich, 1966). But this generalization does not apply to every boy and girl, because there are certainly many 3-year-old girls who are less dependent, or more physically aggressive, than many 3-year-old boys. Thus, we must be careful not to overstate the sex differences. There is variability within almost any group, and so findings that describe the average of an entire group cannot be used to characterize any individual within the group.

With that said, how do men and women compare in their intellectual abilities? Overall, neither sex is more intelligent than the other, and there is no reliable difference between the sexes in overall IQ scores (Held, Alderton, Foley, & Segall, 1993; Lynn, 1994). Where the sexes do differ is on more specific tests. On average, boys and men do better on some tests of spatial and mathematical ability, while girls and women do better on some verbal tasks (Halpern, 1992, 2000; Hines, 1990; Levine, Huttenlocher, Taylor, & Langrock, 1999; Maccoby & Jacklin, 1974, 1980; Masters & Sanders, 1993; J. Stanley, 1993). These differences, however, are quite fine-grained, so that it would be a mistake to claim, for example, that women are in general less skilled in math than boys. In fact, girls actually do *better* than boys on some mathematical tests (e.g., those that emphasize computation). Likewise, evidence indicates that men and women take equally demanding math classes in high school, and it is the women who get better grades (Gallagher & Kaufman, 2005). In college, men and women get equal math grades (Bridgeman & Lewis, 1996), even when we match their math classes for difficulty.

Nonetheless, males do out-perform women on many measures of math ability, especially on tests that showcase word problems or geometry (Crawford & Chaffin, 1997; Geary, 1998; Hyde, 2005). What are the skills that give males this edge? A number of theorists have focused on males' apparent superiority in certain visualization tasks, including tasks requiring mental rotation (imagining what a shape would look like if it were rotated into a different position; see Chapter 8, Figures 8.1 and 8.2). It seems plausible that many branches of mathematics rely on this (and related types of) visualization skill, and so do some branches of science and engineering; therefore, this specific capacity might be the source of the male advantage in these fields (Burnett, Lane, & Dratt, 1979; Halpern, 1992; E. Hunt, 1985a; but also see Byrnes, 2005; Spelke, 2005).

Some authors argue that this male advantage is rooted in our biology; to support this position, they point to a study that compared the SAT scores of 40,000 high-school students. The study showed that men (on average) did better than women on the math portion of the test, even when the investigators limited their comparison to men and women who had taken the exact same high-school math courses and had expressed the same degree of interest in mathematics (Benbow, 1988; Benbow, Lubinski, Shea, & Eftekhari-Sanjani, 2000; Benbow & Stanley, 1983; Hedges & Nowell, 1995; Stumpf & Stanley, 1998). Arguably, this eliminates any differences between the sexes in terms of training or motivation; the remaining difference in performance, therefore, must, according to many authors, be understood in biological terms.

This biological claim, however, has been quite controversial. Consistent with the claim, several studies have suggested a relationship between math abilities and the male sex hormone testosterone. In one study, males who produced abnormally low levels of testosterone showed impairments in spatial reasoning (Hier & Crowley, 1982); in another study, older males (age 60–75) showed dramatic improvements in spatial reasoning after receiving testosterone supplements (Cherrier et al., 2001; Janowsky, Oviatt, & Orwoll, 1994). But, on the opposite side, several studies have failed to confirm testosterone's effects on visualization; therefore any conclusions about this point must be tentative (e.g., Hines, 2004; also Collaer & Hines, 1995; also see Spelke, 2005).

In addition, a social or cultural explanation of the sex difference is certainly plausible. After all, many people believe that women are ill suited for math, and expect women not to do well in this domain (Halpern, 1992). Parents expect their sons to do better in math than their daughters (Frome & Eccles, 1998) and often attribute their sons' success in math to ability, while attributing their daughters' success in math to hard work (Parsons, Adler, & Kaczala, 1982).

Do these expectations and interpretations influence women? Evidence that they do comes from studies showing that women perform less well on tests of mathematical ability if they are asked, at the start of the test, simply to record their gender on the test form. Presumably, this serves to prime the relevant stereotype and thus undermines performance (Ambady, Shih, Kim, & Pittinsky, 2001; for more on this sort of "stereotype threat," see Chapter 14). Similarly, sex differences in test scores are clearly influenced by small changes in instructions or context, confirming the role of the expectations and attitudes that are shaped by these situational factors (see, for example, R. P. Brown & Josephs, 1999; Crawford & Chaffin, 1997).

In short, the cognitive differences between sexes are small and specialized—so that men do better on some sorts of verbal tasks; women do better on other sorts; men do better on some sorts of math tests; women do better on other sorts. The suggestion that these differences arise from biological factors is plausible, but so far only weakly supported by evidence. In contrast, women are certainly exposed to cultural stereotypes that discourage math achievement, and they are plainly influenced by these stereotypes. We can therefore hope the stereotypes are gradually weakened, so that we do not, as one author put it, "waste a most valuable resource: the abilities and efforts of more than half the world's population" (Shaffer, 2004, p. 237).

GENDER IDENTITY

What about gender identity—each person's sense of being a male or female? Children start to understand this point at an early age, and, by about the age of 3, most children can report accurately who is male and who is female, and they also know their own sex (Fagot, Leinbach, & Hagen, 1986). But initially their classifications are flexible. For example, when shown a picture of a girl, even 4-year-olds say that she could be a boy if she wanted to or if she wore a boy's haircut or wore a boy's clothes (D. E. Marcus & Overton, 1978). It takes children until the age of 5 or so to achieve the concept of *gender constancy*—the recognition that being male or female is irrevocable and not dependent on what one wears or does.

When children do gain an understanding of their sexual identity, they are clearly influenced by social cues. After all, they have been explicitly and repeatedly told that they are boys or girls, and they have been treated in a fashion that confirms this explicit message. But this turns out not to be the entire story of gender identity, because here, too, biology plays a powerful role. For example, girls whose bodies produce excess androgen (p. 423) are appreciably less likely to say that they are content to be girls, and often express the wish to be boys (Ehrhardt, Epstein, & Money, 1968; Hines, Brook, & Conway, 2004). Conversely, a number of genetic males (i.e., children with an XY chromosomal pattern) are born with a condition called *cloacal exstrophy*, lacking normal male genitals. Often, families decide their best path is to raise these children as girls, but, despite this social influence, and despite the evidence of their own (female) appearance, these children nonetheless tend to think of themselves as males. In one study, 25 out of 25 cases reported that they felt like "boys trapped in girls' bodies" and also showed male-specific patterns of behavior (such as active and sometimes aggressive play; Reiner, 2004; also see Meyer-Bahlburg et al., 1996; Zucker et al., 1996).

In addition, consider the remarkable case of Bruce Reimer, born in 1963 as a genetic XY male with normal genitals, but whose penis was burned beyond repair during minor surgery. The doctors urged Bruce's parents to allow sex reassignment, and at the age of 17 months, he had "corrective" surgery, and his parents, doctors, and teachers all accepted him (now "her") as a girl, giving her a life of dolls, dresses, and "girl things." Bruce was renamed Brenda.

The first report of this case described the reassignment as a success (Money & Ehrhardt, 1972), and the story was widely quoted as showing the power of socialization over biology in determining gender identity. But Bruce/Brenda's life as a girl was far from happy. Her mother reports that from the start Brenda tore off her dresses and, when her brother refused to share his toys, saved her allowance to buy her own toy truck. As she neared puberty, Brenda was given the sex hormone estrogen to help her appear more feminine, but she nonetheless came to believe that she was a boy and kept

11.9 John/Joan *To protect his privacy, David Reimer's name was kept a secret when his case was first described; he was instead called "John/Joan." As an adult, though, Reimer revealed his identity and discussed his life story with the media.*

A lesbian couple *Ellen DeGeneres (on right) and her partner, Portia DeRossi.*

trying to urinate standing up. By age 14, Brenda was depressed and suicidal. She finally revealed her suspicions to her endocrinologist, and—without being apprised of her unique history—she agreed to plastic surgery to construct a penis, along with treatments of male hormones. At this point, Brenda took on the name David, and only after the surgery did her (now his) father finally reveal—to an upset and bewildered son—the original accident and surgery (Colapinto, 2000).

David became an attractive male interested romantically in women, and he married at the age of 25 and adopted his wife's children from her previous marriage. In 2000, he was persuaded to reveal his true identity and to discuss his life story with the media (Figure 11.9), motivated in large part by a concern that no one else have to go through what he went through (Colapinto, 2000; M. Diamond & Sigmundson, 1997; also see Bradley, Oliver, Chernick, & Zucker, 1998). But his story ends sadly: David committed suicide in May 2004.

This tragic story illustrates the power of biology in shaping sexual identity, and it seems likely that David's developing brain was somehow "masculinized" by circulating hormones—with powerful effects on his subsequent behavior and sexual identity. Let us remind ourselves, though, that (here as always!) biology is not destiny. We see this in the numerous reports of individuals who are one gender by virtue of both their biology and their upbringing, but who nonetheless choose to change to the opposite gender. In some cases, this merely involves changes in behavior and clothing. In other cases, individuals choose to have surgery and hormone treatments to alter their body shape. In all instances, though, it is plain that biology and early experience are crucial for sexual identity—but clearly are not the entire story.

SEXUAL ORIENTATION

Let us turn, finally, to the third aspect of sexuality: Alongside of gender roles and gender identity, each person also has a sexual orientation—as a heterosexual, a homosexual, or bisexual. Most men and women are heterosexuals, but the other orientations are not rare. A half-century ago, Alfred Kinsey and his associates reported that 4% of American men described themselves as exclusively homosexual (Kinsey, Pomeroy, & Martin, 1948); the prevalence of homosexuality reported by women was lower—about 2% (Kinsey, Pomeroy, Martin, & Gebhard, 1953). A substantially larger group (13% of American men and 7% of women) described themselves as predominantly homosexual but had also had some heterosexual experience. More recent surveys confirm Kinsey's estimates, both in the United States and in other Western cultures (see, for example, ACSF Investigators, 1992; A. M. Johnson, Wadsworth, Wellings, Bradshaw, & Field, 1992; for some complications, though, see Savin-Williams, 2006).

Thus, a substantial number of men and women are erotically and romantically oriented toward partners of their own sex. And this orientation persists despite the considerable social forces that endorse heterosexuality and often stigmatize homosexuality. Until recently, in fact, homosexual acts—even among consenting adults—were outlawed in nearly half of the United States, and these acts are still illegal in 70 countries, where they are punished by prison, beatings, and executions (Kitzinger, 2001).

We should mention, however, that the cultural taboo against homosexual behavior is by no means universal. According to one cross-cultural survey, two-thirds of the world's societies regard homosexuality as normal and acceptable, at least for some people or for some age groups (Ford & Beach, 1951). In certain historical periods, the practice was extolled, as in classical Greece, where men commonly had young same-sex lovers. Pericles, the great Athenian statesman, was considered odd because he was not attracted to beautiful boys.

It is also important to realize that much of the sexual behavior of gays and lesbians revolves around feelings of romance and love, just as does that of heterosexual people. In other words, dating and love and (often) long-lasting relationships occur within the homosexual community in a manner virtually identical to that observed in the heterosexual community. The only difference, of course, is the obvious one—the gender of the romantic "other" (G. D. Green & Clunis, 1988; Mattison & McWhirter, 1987).

ORIGINS OF HOMOSEXUALITY

There has been much discussion of *why* some people become homosexuals, but, in some ways, this is the wrong question to ask. Instead, we need to ask why people become sexual beings of any sort—why and how romance develops; why people find certain individuals attractive but not others; how people decide to make commitments; and so on. Not surprisingly, the answers to these questions are partly biological (Chapter 2) and partly social (Chapter 13), but, without question, they are partly developmental.

Many young children engage in some form of sexual experimentation, including masturbation and touching other children. The first real sexual attraction, however, usually begins at age 10 or so (Herdt & McClintock, 2000). Sexuality then blossoms (in children's thinking, their interest in others, and their behavior) as they enter puberty and the hormonal changes that come with it. The hormone storms, however, merely trigger the sexual feelings; they do not direct the feelings toward any particular target. This allows us to rule out one hypothesis about homosexuality—that it is the result of some sort of hormonal imbalance. Some of the evidence on this point comes from a study of the effects of testosterone administration on gay men. The injections did make the men more sexually active (just as they would for heterosexual men), but the injections had no impact on the gay men's sexual orientation—their augmented sexual desire was directed toward other men, just as before (Kinsey, Pomeroy, & Martin, 1948; for further discussion of the relation between sexual orientation and hormones, see Gladue, Green, & Hellman, 1984).

So what does lead an individual to seek out men as romantic and sexual partners, or to seek out women? Part of the answer is genetic, because it turns out that if a man's identical twin is gay, then the chances that he will also be gay are 52%; if the gay twin is fraternal, the chances drop to 22% (Bailey & Pillard, 1991). Likewise, a woman's chance of having a homosexual orientation is 48% if she has a lesbian identical twin. If her gay twin is fraternal, the chances drop to 16% (Bailey, Pillard, Neale, & Agyei, 1993). Clearly, then, the greater the similarity in genetic makeup, the greater the likelihood of having the same sexual orientation, powerfully suggesting that one's genotype carries a predisposition toward homosexuality.

How do genes influence sexual orientation? The mechanism probably involves the levels of prenatal hormones, and especially the male hormone androgen. For example, we earlier discussed cases of androgenized females—those who were exposed in the uterus to high androgen levels; it turns out that a large proportion of these women (37%) end up describing themselves as homosexuals or bisexuals. In these women, the high androgen levels are produced by a specific genetic defect, but the same hormonal patterns can be produced by many other factors (including routine genetic variation, with no defect involved). In all cases, though, these shifts in hormone levels during prenatal development seem to influence sexual orientation (Dittmann, Kappes, & Kappes, 1992; Ellis & Ames, 1987; Hines, 2004; Zucker, 2001).

In addition, there are several anatomical and physiological differences between gay and straight men; these provide further indication that homosexuality has biological origins. For example, gay men are more likely than heterosexuals to be left-handed, and also show a specific acoustic response in their inner ear; both of these characteristics are likely to be the result of high levels of certain prenatal hormones (Lalumiere, Blanchard, & Zucker, 2000). Other investigators have reported differences in brain structure between heterosexual and homosexual males. For example, we have known for a long time that certain structures in the hypothalamus affect sexual behavior in animals, and these structures are much larger in the brains of men than they are in the brains of

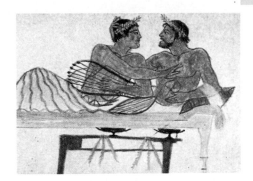

Homosexual behavior in antiquity   Among the ancient Greeks homosexual relations between men were widely practiced and accepted, as the mural from the Tomb of the Diver *(c. 480 B.C.–470 B.C.), found in what was a Greek settlement in southern Italy, suggests.*

The debate over homosexuality   A substantial number of men and women are erotically and romantically oriented toward partners of the same sex—despite the considerable forces that endorse heterosexuality and stigmatize homosexuality. These forces have been in full view during the (often heated) debate over same-sex marriage.

women (Allen, Hines, Shryne, & Gorski, 1989). It turns out that in the brains of gay men, this structure is roughly the size typical for heterosexual women, and therefore only half that typical for heterosexual men (LeVay, 1991).

Let us note, though, that these are again correlational findings, so there is room for debate over whether smaller structures in the hypothalamus lead to homosexuality, or whether this diminished size is a *result* of homosexuality. In addition, even if we take these results at face value, it is clear that biology—and genetic influences in particular— cannot be the whole story. Indeed, if genetics were the only thing that mattered, then identical twins (with 100% overlap in their genes) would show 100% resemblance in their sexual orientation; instead, the concordance rate is just 52%. Obviously, therefore, factors other than the genes matter, but, in truth, no one is sure what these other factors are. Many hypotheses have been offered, but most of these are plainly wrong. For example, there is no evidence that especially strong fathers, or especially weak fathers, are more likely to have homosexual offspring. There is also no evidence that homosexuality derives from some sort of imitation: Children who grow up with gay or lesbian parents are no more likely to end up homosexuals themselves (Bailey & Zucker, 1995; Golombok & Tasker, 1996). Likewise, many people seem to believe that homosexuality results when a boy is "seduced" by an older man or a girl by an older woman, but there is no evidence at all to support this "seduction" proposal.

What we do know is that the main predictor of eventual homosexuality is the way people felt about sexuality when they were younger. Feelings of attraction toward same-sex individuals usually emerge before biological puberty, sometimes as early as age 3 or 4, and they clearly precede any actual homosexual encounters (A. P. Bell, Weinberg, & Hammersmith, 1981). Indeed, many individuals report that "I've been that way all my life" (Saghir & Robins, 1973), and just as future heterosexuals imagine star-struck romances with members of the opposite sex, so do those who will become homosexual imagine same-sex love and romance (R. Green 1979; Zuger, 1984).

In sum, we remain ignorant about what it is that makes someone homosexual, just as we actually do not know what it is that makes someone heterosexual. Genes are relevant, but not the whole story, and we do not yet know what the rest of the story involves. Having said this, though, one last point needs to be emphasized: Whatever the origins of a homosexual (or bisexual) orientation, such an orientation is not in any fashion a psychological disorder or defect. These orientations are "abnormal" only in the limited sense of being unusual, different from the orientation of the majority. But many other traits are "abnormal" in exactly the same sense—being left-handed, for example. Gays, lesbians, and bisexuals are surely neither better nor worse than heterosexuals, and the factors that matter for their relationship quality and stability seem to be exactly the same as those that matter for heterosexual couples (Kurdek, 2005). Their number includes great painters (Leonardo da Vinci), athletes (Martina Navratilova), musicians (Aaron Copland), writers (Oscar Wilde, Gertrude Stein), mathematicians and scientists (Alan Turing, Alfred Kinsey himself), philosophers (Wittgenstein), and warriors (Alexander the Great), but the great majority are ordinary people with ordinary lives. The same no doubt holds for left-handers—and for heterosexuals.

DEVELOPMENT AFTER CHILDHOOD

We have now covered many—but by no means all—topics in social development, but our focus has been on events that take place in childhood. This emphasis reflects the orientation of the major figures in the history of developmental psychology, including Piaget, whose work we met in Chapter 10, and Freud, whose work we will consider in

Chapter 15. In recent years, however, a number of authors have argued that this interpretation of development is too narrow. In their view, humans continue to change throughout their lives: The problems faced by adolescents are not the same as those of young adults about to get married or become parents, let alone those of the middle aged at the peak of parenthood or their careers, or the elderly at the sunset of their lives. And just as the problems change, so do the strategies, responses, and resources used in dealing with these problems. It thus seems reasonable to ask how individuals continue to develop, in adolescence and throughout the life span.

Are there any regularities to development over the life span? On this issue, many investigators have been strongly influenced by the psychoanalyst Erik Erikson's "eight ages of man" (Table 11.2). According to Erikson (1963), all human beings endure a series of major crises as they go through the life cycle. At each stage, there is a critical confrontation between the self the individual has achieved thus far and the various

Erik Erikson **A pioneer in the study of development after childhood.**

TABLE 11.2   ERIKSON'S EIGHT AGES OF MAN

APPROXIMATE AGE	DEVELOPMENTAL TASK OF THAT STAGE	PSYCHOSOCIAL CRISIS OF THAT STAGE
0–1½ years	Attachment to mother, which lays foundation for later trust in others	Trust versus mistrust
1½–3 years	Gaining some basic control of self and environment (e.g., toilet training, exploration)	Autonomy versus shame and doubt
3–6 years	Becoming purposeful and directive	Initiative versus guilt
6 years–puberty	Developing social, physical, and school skills	Competence versus inferiority
Adolescence	Making transition from childhood to adulthood; developing a sense of identity	Identity versus role confusion
Early adulthood	Establishing intimate bonds of love and friendship	Intimacy versus isolation
Middle age	Fulfilling life goals that involve family, career, and society; developing concerns that embrace future generations	Productivity versus stagnation
Later years	Looking back over one's life and accepting its meaning	Integrity versus despair

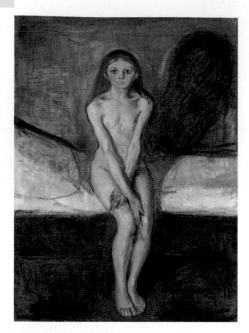

Puberty   *By Edward Munch, 1895.*

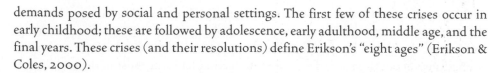

demands posed by social and personal settings. The first few of these crises occur in early childhood; these are followed by adolescence, early adulthood, middle age, and the final years. These crises (and their resolutions) define Erikson's "eight ages" (Erikson & Coles, 2000).

This developmental scheme has influenced many investigators of adult development. We will continue to refer to Erikson's organization as we briefly discuss some issues in the study of adolescence and adulthood.

ADOLESCENCE

Adolescence is is a period of transition in which children become adults. There are biological changes: a growth spurt, a change in bodily proportions, and the attainment of sexual maturity. There is also an enormously important socioeconomic transition: from dependence on one's family, to a legally and morally sanctioned independence. And, of course, there are the numerous psychological changes as well, including those associated with the emergence of romantic and sexual attachments (Figure 11.10).

Traditionally, adolescence has been considered a period of great emotional stress, and it is not difficult to see why this might be so: In adolescent years, children break away from parental control and seek to make their own choices about their activities, diet, schedule, and more. At the same time, adolescents are shifting the focus of their social worlds, so that they spend more time with, and gain much more emotional support from, peers rather than family members. Adolescents are also able to explore a variety of new-found freedoms, including many activities away from adult supervision.

With all of these changes, the stage seems to be set for considerable tension between adolescents and their parents, so it is no surprise that, across the centuries, literature (and, more recently, movies) has featured youths in desperate conflict with an over-controlling adult world. But, in fact, a number of studies suggest that emotional turbulence is by no means universal among adolescents. There are conflicts, of course, and the nature of the conflict changes over the course of adolescence (Laursen, Coy, & Collins, 1998). But, even so, many investigators find that, for most adolescents, "development . . . is slow, gradual, and unremarkable" (Josselson, 1980, p. 189; also see Arnett, 1999).

There is no question, however, that adolescence does pose a number of serious challenges as young adults prepare to become autonomous individuals. And sometimes the process does not go well: Some adolescents engage in highly risky forms of recreation. Some end up with unplanned (and undesired) pregnancies. Some become criminals. Some become drug users. Indeed, statistics show that all of these behaviors (including theft, murder, reckless driving, unprotected sex, and use of illegal drugs) are more likely during adolescence than at any other time of life (Arnett, 1995, 1999).

11.10 Initiation rites *Societies set up a variety of special occasions to mark the transition from youth into adulthood. In western countries we have not one initiation rite but many (none of which would be regarded as especially severe) such as (A) bar (or bat) mitzvahs, (B) puberty rites, such as this Apache ceremony, or (C) quinceaneras.*

Why are risky and unhealthy behaviors so common among adolescents? Not surprisingly, several factors contribute. For example, it seems that, in many settings, adolescents simply do not think about, or take seriously, the dangers and potential consequences associated with their behaviors; they act instead as if they believe they are somehow invulnerable to harm or disease (Elkind, 1978). In addition, evidence suggests that adolescents are especially motivated to seek out new and exciting experiences, and this *sensation seeking* regularly exposes them to risk (Arnett, 1995).

A third hypothesis focuses on the adolescent's brain. It is clear that many areas of the brain are continuing to develop across the teenage years, and the maturation is particularly evident in the prefrontal cortex (Keating, 2004; Kuhn, 2006). This is a brain area critically involved in self-regulation and in the inhibition of habits and impulses. It is possible, therefore, that at least some adolescent risk-taking is attributable to the immaturity of key brain areas.

A final hypothesis about adolescent risk-taking brings us back to Erikson's proposal—namely, that a major goal for adolescents is to discover who and what they really are, as they go through what Erikson called an *identity crisis*. As part of this effort toward discovery, adolescents try on many different roles, to see which ones fit best—which vocation, which ideology, which group membership. In many cases, this means trying on roles that will allow the adolescents to mark the clear distinctions between them and their parents. If their parents prefer safe behaviors, this will tempt the adolescents toward dangerous activities. If their parents prefer slow-paced recreation, the adolescents will seek excitement (Harris, 1995, 1998).

Hand in hand with this, adolescents seek more and more to identify with their own generation. With this, their actions are increasingly influenced by their friends—especially since, in adolescence, people care more and more about being *accepted* by their friends (Bigelow & LaGaipa, 1975). They are also influenced by other peers, including the circle of individuals they interact with every day, and also the "crowd" they identify with—the "brains" or the "jocks" or the "druggies" (Brown, Moray, & Kinney, 1994). And, of course, if their friends engage in risky activities, so will they (Bernt & Keefe, 1995; Reed & Roundtree, 1997).

We need to be careful, though, not to overstate the problems caused by peer influence. In fact, most teenagers report that their friends are more likely to discourage bad behaviors than to encourage them (Brown, Clasen, & Eicher, 1986). And, more generally, most peer influence is aimed neither at good behaviors nor at bad; it is aimed instead at behaviors that are simply *different* from those of the previous generation. This is evident in all of the external trappings that adolescents adopt—the new styles of clothing, the new hair styles, and the new speech idioms (Figure 11.11; B. B. Brown, 1990; Dunphy, 1963). Of course, these styles change with bewildering rapidity, thanks in large part to the fact that adolescent fads diffuse rapidly into the broader social world and become adult fashions. When this happens, new adolescent fads quickly spring up to maintain the differentiation.

Adolescent risk taking

11.11 Adolescent fads *New adolescent fads spring up to maintain the differentiation between the adolescents' own world and that of the adults around them. They then disappear rather quickly to be replaced by yet newer fads.*

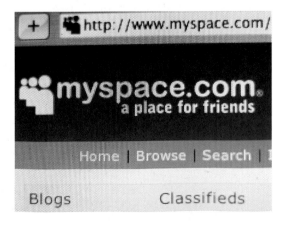

ADULTHOOD

The *start* of adolescence is typically defined by the onset of puberty. The *end* of adolescence, in contrast, and the entry into adulthood, are not well marked. This is evident, for example, in the bewildering variety of ages that different countries (and different states) use for deciding when someone is eligible for "adult privileges" such as buying tobacco products or alcohol, voting, marriage, or serving in a nation's armed forces. Each "privilege" arrives at a different age, highlighting our uncertainty about when "adulthood" begins.

Eventually, though, all of these hurdles are cleared, and one surely then is an "adult." But even then development is not done. Young adults need to develop a capacity for closeness and intimacy through love. In many cases, they must prepare for the commitments of marriage, and then the joys and burdens of parenting. They must learn how to manage the social and financial obligations of adulthood, and must settle into their careers. They may have to cope with a time in which they are responsible both for their children and for their aging and ailing parents. And, eventually, they themselves become old and must come to terms with their own lives, accepting them with a sense of integrity rather than despair. Erikson (1963) eloquently sums up this final reckoning: "It is the acceptance of one's own and only life cycle as something that had to be and that, by necessity, permitted of no substitutes.... Healthy children will not fear life if their elders have integrity enough not to fear death" (pp. 268–269).

Within this flow of events, one stage of adult development has received considerable attention from both Erikson and later authors: the **midlife transition** (which sometimes amounts to the "midlife crisis"). This is the point in adult life at which individuals reappraise what they have done with their lives thus far and may reevaluate their marriage and career (Wethington, 2000; Willis & Reid, 1999). It is a period when individuals begin to see physical changes that show that the summer of life is over and its autumn has begun, a recognition that may occur earlier in women than in men (in part, because of the psychological and physiological impact of menopause). There is a shift in the way one thinks about time, from "How long have I lived?" to "How much time do I have left?"

Evidence suggests that the midlife transition is an important life step for many people, as are all the steps of adult development. But is this developmental trajectory (as Erikson proposed) universal—shared by all people in all cultures? The answer is mixed. On the one side, many of the milestones in adult life are clearly biological and surely inevitable. In all cultures, humans reach a point in life at which they are granted adult privileges, then reach a later point at which they can mate and have children. In all cultures, humans must endure the discomfitures and diseases of old age, and finally die.

But, on the other side, there are also important variations in adult development—from one person to the next, and also from one culture to the next. For example, in Chapter 15, we will discuss some of the ways in which adults cope with life's challenges, and, as we will see, adults differ markedly in their strategies for coping. In addition, there is no question that the specific crises that confront people during their adult years depend on the society in which they live.

Consider, for example, the transition into old age. A century ago in the United States, different generations often lived close together as part of an extended family, and there was much less segregation by age. Nursing homes and retirement communities were unheard of. Older people contributed to the family even when they were too old to work outside the home: They cared for the children, helped with the housekeeping, and so on. Older people were also sought out for advice on matters of child rearing and housekeeping. But today, the elderly have no such recognized family role. They usually live apart, are effectively segregated from the rest of society, are excluded from the workforce, and have lost their role as esteemed advisers. Given these changes, it follows that the transition into senescence is quite different from what it was 100 years ago. People

The changing role of the elderly

still age as they did then—although many more people than ever now live into their seventies, eighties, and even their nineties—but they view aging differently and face different life circumstances (Hareven, 1978).

SOME FINAL THOUGHTS: THE NEED FOR MULTIPLE PERSPECTIVES

Just a few decades back, the study of social development was dominated by a handful of strongly articulated theoretical perspectives, each claiming that it offered the "correct" view of development. One perspective drew on the claims we discussed in Chapter 6, and emphasized the role of the rewards and punishments the child encountered. The idea, roughly, was that these inputs taught the children how to behave—how to interact with others, how to express themselves, and so on. A second perspective was guided by the theorizing of Sigmund Freud (Chapter 15), and argued that emotional events early in the child's life—especially events involving the child's relationship to his mother—created a pattern of beliefs and reactions that colored virtually all of the child's subsequent thoughts, and created a mental framework that powerfully shaped the child's relationships throughout life. A third perspective emphasized the child's biological inheritance, including each child's innate tendency to be cautious or bold in her explorations of the world. These biological tendencies would themselves influence how the child responded in social interactions, and therefore have strong effects in shaping further development. A final perspective was heavily influenced by Jean Piaget's ideas (Chapter 10), and stressed the child's role in constructing his own knowledge and skills, guided in large part by experiences in interacting with others.

As we have now seen—and as is often the case—it turns out that each of these perspectives contributes to our understanding of social development. The child is influenced by rewards and punishments, but the child's early relationships are also enormously important, creating a framework that guides later development. The child's biology does matter, but so does the child's ability to draw inferences and conclusions about the social world, based on her experiences. Our theorizing about social development, therefore, must be theoretically eclectic—and, in this regard, it resembles theorizing in most other areas of psychology.

In addition, it is important to reiterate that our theorizing about social development must find a balance between two demands. On the one side, we need to explain aspects of social development that seem to be universal for our species, observable in all cultures. On the other side, we will certainly need some principles that are tuned to each cultural setting. Even within a culture, we need to explain some data patterns that apply to all children and all parents, and also data patterns that emphasize the differences from one individual to the next. We have seen these differences in newborns (e.g., differences in temperament), in toddlers (e.g., differences in attachment), and in families (e.g., differences in parenting style). Clearly, then, our theorizing needs to explain how we are all alike, and how each of us is different from the others.

SUMMARY

THE PATH TO ATTACHMENT

- From a very early age, infants are keenly interested in face-to-face interaction, strongly prefer moving faces over still ones, and also prefer faces that are responsive to their own movements and expressions.
- Between 7 and 9 months, infants begin to crawl, creating the first conflicts between infants and caregivers (if the infant crawls into a dangerous or inappropriate situation), and also creating the need for *social referencing*, one of the earlier indications of *intersubjectivity*.

ATTACHMENT

- Infants of many species have a need for *contact comfort*, which, according to Bowlby, provides the infant with a *secure base*. For many species, attachment is created by a specialized form of learning called *imprinting*.

THE DIFFERENCES AMONG CHILDREN

- From birth (and perhaps before), infants differ in *temperament*; some infants adapt quickly to new situations, and others are irritable and try to withdraw from new situations.
- Infants differ in their early experience, in part because of differences in temperament, and in part because caregivers differ in how sensitive or responsive they are to the infant's needs. Based on these different experiences, infants form different beliefs about the social world, and this is evident in the different patterns of *attachment*.
- Attachment is usually assessed by observing the behavior of children in the *Strange Situation*. In this situation, some children are classified as *securely attached*, others show *anxious/resistant* or *anxious/avoidant* attachment, and others show a *disorganized* pattern of attachment. Styles of attachment seem relatively stable, but they can change if the child's circumstances change. The style of attachment is also predictive of many subsequent events in the child's social and emotional development, so that securely attached children are more likely to be "leaders" in their nursery schools and more likely to have friends as teenagers. However, there is room for debate over the mechanisms behind these correlational findings.
- Infants form attachments to both mothers and fathers, and this attachment seems not to be disrupted by long hours of childcare, especially if the childcare is of high quality. However, social development may be disrupted by divorce or separation of the parents, although the problems may derive from the prior family conflict rather than from the separation itself. Development is more severely disrupted if there is no attachment at all, as reflected in the tragic evidence from Romanian orphanages.

PARENTING

- The process of *socialization* continues with child rearing by the parents. Some important differences in the way children are reared depend on the dominant values of their culture. In addition, different parents choose different parenting styles, whether *authoritarian, permissive, authoritative,* or *uninvolved*. The selection of this style depends partly on the parents and partly on the child's own characteristics. Evidence suggests that authoritative parenting is preferable, but this conclusion must be viewed with caution because the key data are correlational.

PEER RELATIONSHIPS

- Friendships are important for many reasons, including the support they provide for a child, and also the various skills and knowledge a child can gain from friendships. For example, children learn how to handle conflict by quarreling—and then making up—with their friends.
- Children with friends seem better able to handle many stresses, including major life transitions. Conversely, *rejected* children tend to be more aggressive and, in some cases, more anxious.

EMOTIONAL DEVELOPMENT

- Children need to learn many skills, including how to understand the feelings of the people around them. Much of this learning depends on conversations with others about feelings.
- Children also need to learn to *regulate* their emotions. This includes learning how to express their emotions in accordance with their culture's *display rules*. It also includes self-control of emotions, a skill that becomes reasonably developed by age 4 or 5.

MORAL DEVELOPMENT

- The study of moral development has been strongly affected by Kohlberg's analysis of progressive stages in *moral reasoning*. There may, however, also be sex differences in moral orientation, and also differences among cultural groups.
- A person's moral reasoning is clearly tied to his moral behavior, but other factors also matter for moral behavior, including the person's sense of *conscience*. The development of a conscience seems not to depend on a child's being punished for bad behavior. Instead, the conscience seems to depend on the child's relationship with his parents, and his wish to preserve that relationship. Also crucial for the development of conscience is the child's growing sense of *empathy*. Empathy by itself, however, is not enough to produce moral or *prosocial* behavior; also needed are an ability to understand one's own empathic responses, and knowledge about how to help others.
- There are considerable differences among individuals in their prosocial behavior, with these behaviors particularly likely among children who experience emotion without getting overwhelmed by it.

SEXUAL DEVELOPMENT

- Children learn their appropriate *gender role* at an early age; this learning is supported by the adult behaviors the child observes, and also by the way adults interact with, and talk to, the child. However, biology also matters, as can be seen in the gender roles shown in *androgenized females*.
- There are differences between men and women in their intellectual abilities, but these differences are small in comparison to the variation within either gender. The gender differences that do exist seem to be relatively specialized, such as an advantage for males in some aspects of visualization skill.
- Children's *gender identity* is obviously influenced by what children are told about being a boy or a girl, but here too biology matters, as can be seen in evidence from androgenized females. *Sexual orientation*, whether as heterosexual or homosexual, is also influenced heavily by genes, probably because of the effects of prenatal hormones. Some common beliefs about homosexuality—such as the idea that it results from an early "seduction" of the child—are surely false.

DEVELOPMENT AFTER CHILDHOOD

- Development continues after childhood. Some theorists, notably Erikson, have tried to map later stages of development. One such stage is *adolescence*, which marks the transition into adulthood. While adolescence is sometimes turbulent, it is not always so. Adolescence is also often characterized by risk-taking behaviors; these are in turn the result of adolescents' failing to take dangers seriously, and also immaturity in the adolescents' prefrontal cortex.
- Erikson and other theorists proposed that the stages of adulthood are universal. Whether this is true, however, remains a subject of debate.

SOCIAL COGNITION AND EMOTION

*L*ike ants, chimpanzees, and many other social animals, we humans are surrounded by other members of our species, and spend most of our days interacting with them. Even when we are not directly mingling with other people, we are often thinking about them, making plans involving them, and maybe even fantasizing about them—not to mention obeying (or breaking) their laws, using their products, reading their books, singing their songs, and speaking their languages. In other words, most of our thoughts, feelings, and behaviors are shaped by the social world.

Social psychology is the study of how we think about, feel about, and behave toward other people (both real and imagined), as well as how the thoughts, feelings, and behaviors of other people influence us (Allport, 1968). It is concerned with questions such as these: How does culture shape the way we think about others? Do we perceive ourselves accurately? How can we decrease prejudice? Why do people have the attitudes they have? What role does emotion play in social interaction? Can we control our emotions? In this chapter, we tackle all of these questions, by examining the twin sources of our social behavior: our thoughts and beliefs about other people, on the one side, and then, on the other side, our feelings about other people—our emotional reactions to, and emotional communications with, the others who surround us. In Chapter 13, we turn to a different aspect of social psychology, and there consider how other people influence us, how people behave differently in groups, and how we form relationships. ●

PERCEIVING AND UNDERSTANDING OTHERS

In the course of ordinary life we encounter many other people. The vast majority of them are anonymous extras in our private dramas. But many others have bigger roles, as bit players (a traffic cop whom we ask for directions), supporting cast (a casual acquaintance), and costars (friends, lovers, bosses, enemies). We cannot help but try to understand these people, as they, in turn, try to understand us. This effort toward understanding is not just an intellectual exercise, because much of the plot of our own dramas (and theirs) depends on how we perceive and think about each other, processes that social psychologists refer to as *social cognition*.

ATTRIBUTION

Regardless of their culture, people everywhere spend a lot of time, thought, and talk on the same three questions: Why did she do that? Why did he do that? And why did they do that? Social psychologists call the process by which people answer these questions *causal attribution*, and the study of how people form attributions is one of social psychology's central concerns (see, for example, Heider, 1958; Jones & Nisbett, 1972; Kelley, 1967; Kelley & Michela, 1980).

For example, if Mary smiles at us, is it a sign of affection? Or was she merely in a good mood? Or is she generally polite, smiling at everyone? Our conclusions about Mary—and our actions toward her in the future—will be very different depending on which of these interpretations we choose. Similar ambiguities arise in interpreting a friend's remark, a shove in the subway, or a candidate's warm handshake. In each case, we observe a behavior, but the conclusions we draw and the actions we take depend on what we think caused the behavior.

ATTRIBUTION AS LAY SCIENCE

How do people interpret the behaviors of others? How do they arrive at causal attributions? According to Harold H. Kelley, one of the first investigators in this area, people make attributions in roughly the same way that scientists track down the causes of physical events (1967). For a scientist, an effect (such as an increase in gas pressure) is attributed to a particular condition (such as a rise in temperature) if the effect occurs when the condition is present but does not occur when the condition is absent. In other words, the scientist needs to know whether the cause and the effect **covary** (or correlate). Kelley believed that when people try to explain the behavior of others, they use a similar covariation principle.

This means that, to answer the question Why did Mary smile? we have to consider when Mary smiles. Does she smile consistently whenever we walk into the room? Does she refrain from smiling when others arrive? If the answer to both of these

"I've heard that outside working hours he's really a rather decent sort."

Causal attribution *We often try to explain the behavior of others, such as an acquaintance's smile. The causal attributions we make can have a profound impact on how we respond to others.*

Challenges to attribution **In deciding why someone is behaving as he is, we need to decide whether his behavior is shaped primarily by the circumstances or primarily by who he is. Was Jesse Ventura a wild and aggressive fellow in the wrestling ring because that is what he is really like or because that is the sort of behavior appropriate for (and elicited by) the wrestling ring?**

questions is yes, then her smile does covary with our arrival, and so is probably best understood as a result of her feelings about us. If it turns out, though, that Mary smiles just as broadly when greeting others, then we have to come up with a different explanation (Heider, 1958; Kelley, 1967).

Causal attributions are often concerned with whether a behavior should be understood in terms of a situation (e.g., Mary smiled because the situation demanded that she be polite) or in terms of a person's disposition (e.g., Mary smiled because she is friendly, or because she likes us). In general, *situational attributions* involve factors external to a person, such as other people's expectations, the presence of rewards or punishments, or even the weather. *Dispositional attributions*, on the other hand, focus on factors that are internal to the person, such as a person's traits, preferences, and other internal qualities.

CULTURE AND ATTRIBUTION

How do people choose an attribution for any particular behavior that they observe? Kelley's proposal was that people are sensitive to the data, just as a scientist would be, and draw their conclusions according to the evidence. It turns out, however, that this is not quite right, because people have strong biases in the way they interpret the behavior of others. These biases come from many sources, including the culture in which someone lives.

Every person is a part of many cultures, not just those defined by race, nationality, and ethnicity, but also those defined by gender, socioeconomic status, sexual preference, urbanicity (e.g., city dwelling or rural dwelling), economy (e.g., hunter-gatherer, agricultural, or industrial), and historical cohort (e.g., baby boomer, or gen Xer). This diversity means that cultures differ on many dimensions, but there is reason to believe that one dimension is especially important—whether each culture is more individualistic or more collectivistic (Triandis, 1989, 1994).

As the name suggests, *individualistic cultures* cater to the rights, needs, and preferences of the individual. The majority cultures (e.g., middle-class, of European heritage) of the United States, western Europe, Canada, and Australia are individualistic. In these cultures, people tend to view themselves and others as independent—that is, as fundamentally separate from others and their environment. They also generally think that people behave according to their internal thoughts, feelings, needs, and preferences (Fiske, Kitayama, Markus, & Nisbett, 1998; Markus & Kitayama, 1991), and not according to outside influences, such as other people's expectations or the demands of a situation. To emphasize their independence and distinctiveness, people in individualistic cultures often strive to stand out by achieving personal goals. They still feel obligated to their families and communities, but regularly override these social obligations in order to pursue their own paths.

Individualistic cultures **Members of individualistic cultures tend to view themselves and others as independent, and seek to stand out by achieving personal goals.**

Collectivistic cultures *Members of collectivistic cultures tend to view themselves and others as interdependent, and seek to behave in accordance with situational demands and the expectations of others.*

Collectivistic cultures, on the other hand, stress the importance of maintaining the norms, standards, and traditions of families and other social groups. Most of the world's cultures are collectivistic, including many of those of Latin America, Asia, and Africa. In collectivistic cultures, people tend to view themselves and others as interdependent— that is, as fundamentally connected to the people in their immediate community and to their environment. They usually think that people behave according to the demands of a situation or the expectations of others, and not according to their personal preferences or proclivities. They still have their own dreams, desires, and life plans, of course, but they are more likely to create those plans according to the wishes and expectations of others, and to change them when the situation demands.

It bears emphasizing that not everyone in collectivistic cultures has an interdependent notion of the person, just as not everyone in individualistic cultures has an independent notion. Instead, these terms describe what is typical, as well as what each culture's traditions, laws, schools, and media encourage.

THE FUNDAMENTAL ATTRIBUTION ERROR

For most of its history, social psychology has thrived primarily in individualistic cultures, where experimenters with an independent view of the person have studied participants who shared this view. From these studies, social psychologists concluded that people routinely ascribe others' behavior to dispositions and not to situations—even when there is ample reason to believe that situations are, in fact, playing a crucial role. North Americans of European heritage would judge welfare mothers to be lazy (a dispositional attribution), for example, rather than to be struggling in an economy with high unemployment and few entry-level positions (a situational attribution). Likewise, members of these cultures would view a poor performance on a test as a sign of low intelligence (disposition) rather than as a result of an overly difficult exam (situation). This bias was thought to be so pervasive that it was called the *fundamental attribution error* (Ross, 1977; for a current interpretation, see Sabini, Siepmann, & Stein, 2001).

An American study that dramatized this error had college students participate in a simulated TV quiz show. Students were run in pairs and drew cards to decide who would be the "quizmaster" and who the "contestant." The quizmaster had to make up questions, drawn from any area in which she had some expertise; the contestant had to try to answer these questions. The quiz game then proceeded, and, inevitably, some of the quizmasters' questions were extremely difficult (e.g., "What do the initials *W. H.* stand for in the poet W. H. Auden's name?"). It is unsurprising, therefore, that the contestants' score for correct answers was quite low, averaging only 40 percent.*

This sequence of events was witnessed by a student audience, and, when later asked to rate the two participants, the observers judged the quizmasters to be considerably more knowledgeable than the contestants. After all, the quizmasters seemed to have a wealth of factual knowledge, allowing them to generate challenging questions. The contestants, on the other hand, failed to answer the questions. Obviously, therefore, they did not know facts that the quizmasters knew, and so they were judged to be less knowledgeable.

Of course, the comparison was patently unfair, because the quizmasters could choose any question, any topic, that they wished. Hence, if a quizmaster had some obscure knowledge of just one topic, he could focus all his questions on that topic, avoiding the fact that he had little knowledge in other domains. The contestants, on the other hand, were at the mercy of whatever questions their quizmaster posed. And, in fact, it would have been an impressive coincidence if the area of expertise selected by the quizmaster were also a contestant's area of expertise. No wonder, then, that the contestants did so poorly.

This was, in short, a situation plainly set up to favor the quizmasters, and so any interpretation of the quizmasters' "superiority" needed to take the situational advan-

---

* The answer, by the way, is Wystan Hugh.

Fundamental attribution error **We make the fundamental attribution error when we think a quiz-show host has superior intelligence because he knows answers to questions his contestants find difficult.**

tage into account. But the observers consistently failed to do this. They knew that the roles in the setting—who was quizmaster, who was contestant—had been determined by chance, for they had witnessed the entire procedure. Even so, they could not help regarding the quizmasters as more knowledgeable than the contestants—a tribute to the power of the fundamental attribution error (Ross, Amabile, & Steinmetz, 1977).

This attributional bias is powerful in individualistic cultures, but entirely absent in collectivistic cultures. In one study, for example, Hindu Indians and European Americans were asked to discuss other people's actions. Consistent with other research, the European Americans' comments included twice as many dispositional explanations as situational explanations. The Hindu Indians showed exactly the opposite pattern: They gave twice as many situational explanations as dispositional explanations. As an illustration, one of the vignettes used in the study described a motorcycle accident in which the driver had done less than he might have to help another person. Overall, the Americans typically described the driver as "obviously irresponsible" or "in a state of shock," whereas the Indians typically explained that it was the driver's duty to be at work or that the other person's injury must not have looked serious (Miller, 1984; see also; Fiske et al., 1998; Maass, Karasawa, Politi, & Suga, 2006; Smith & Bond, 1993).

Another study examined newspaper accounts of two murders. The accounts in American newspapers were prominently about personal qualities: The murderer was mentally unstable, or had a "very bad temper" or a "psychological problem." In Chinese newspapers, in contrast, the murders were blamed on the availability of guns, or social isolation, or interpersonal rivalry (Morris & Peng, 1994).

As we mentioned earlier, though, these cultural differences in ways of explaining behavior are not absolutes: People in even the most collectivistic cultures use personal traits and dispositions to talk about behavior, just as those in the most individualistic cultures cite situational causes. Thus, the cultural differences lie in how much attention people pay to situations versus dispositions. For members of collectivistic cultures, the focus is usually on an interlocking relational and historical matrix, in which the actions of any one person reflect the actions of many others. But for members of individualistic cultures, actions tend to be seen as an outgrowth of an individual's dispositions, so there is little need to look further (Fiske et al., 1998; for further discussion of how culture influences our perception, both in the social world and more broadly, see Nisbett & Miyamoto, 2005; Nisbett, Peng, Choir, & Norenzayan, 2001).

COGNITION, PERCEPTION, AND ATTRIBUTION

Among members of individualistic cultures, the tendency to underrate the importance of situational factors occurs primarily when we try to understand the behaviors of others.

The results are quite different when we ourselves are the actors rather than the observers; in that case, the pattern of bias reverses, and the causes seem less in us and more in the external situation (E. E. Jones and Nisbett, 1972). These contrasts illustrate the *actor-observer difference* in attribution.

This difference may arise from the fact that each of us knows how we have acted in situations similar to the one we are in now, and this knowledge may call our attention to the differences in how we have acted on those occasions, potentially sensitizing us to the role of the situation in shaping our behavior; this focus would, of course, draw us away from the fundamental attribution error. A different possibility is perceptual: When we watch another person, our attention is on her and what she is doing, and this vantage point may encourage an interpretation of her behavior in terms of her specific qualities. But when we ourselves are the actors, our own actions are not central to our view. Instead, what are in view are the various constituents of the situation—the place, other people, and so on. This perspective may encourage an interpretation of our own behavior in terms of the situational elements (Heider, 1958).

The importance of these differing vantage points was shown in a study in which two people were videotaped while they were conversing. When the videotape was replayed to the participants later, only one of the conversationalists was visible on the screen (under the pretense that the other's camera had malfunctioned). As a result, half the participants saw just what they had seen before: their fellow conversationalist. But the other half saw something different: themselves. When asked to describe their own behavior, participants who saw the videotape of their partner gave the usual pattern of attribution: They said that their own actions were shaped by a variety of factors in the situation. For the participants who saw themselves, though, the new perspective led to a reversal of the usual actor-observer difference. After watching themselves, they described their own behavior dispositionally (Storms, 1973; Figure 12.1 shows a related result).

PERSON PERCEPTION AND COGNITIVE SCHEMAS

Whenever we make causal attributions, we go beyond the information available to our senses, filling in the blanks with our expectations. This is evident in the fact that different people often make different attributions for the same behavior, each interpreting the evidence in his own way. This variation from one observer to the next makes it plain that the attribution is, indeed, in the eye of the beholder, and not drawn directly from the behaviors we observe.

*12.1 The actor-observer difference **A** schematic figure of a study of the effect of visual perspective on the actor-observer difference. Two actors (actually confederates) were engaged in a conversation and observed from three vantage points: from behind Actor A, from behind Actor B, and from midway between them. The results showed that the observer who watched from behind Actor A believed that B controlled the conversation, and the observer behind Actor B thought the reverse. The observer who watched from midway between the two believed that both were equally influential.*

The same points arise when we consider the broad process through which, to put it simply, we try to make sense of another person—that is, whenever we ask ourselves, "What kind of person is she?" Sometimes we ask this broad question because we are trying to get a general sense of what some person is like—perhaps because we are evaluating the person as a potential roommate, or as a possible friend or employee. But we can also ask the broad question as part of the attributional process (e.g., "Why was he clumsy today? Is he clumsy in general?"). In all cases, however, we make these general assessments in a fashion that, once again, takes us far beyond the information actually available, forcing us to rely, in our interpretations, on all manner of shortcuts and rules of thumb.

Imagine, for example, that we read a description of a person that includes the word *extroverted*. We are quite likely to remember her as spirited and boisterous, even if these words were not used in the description. And if we read that a person is introverted, we may likewise falsely remember seeing words like *shy* and *reserved* in the description (N. Cantor & Mischel, 1979). In this way, social cognition works much like cognition in general. Suppose we briefly looked in a toolbox and then, an hour later, were asked which tools we had seen. We would be likely to remember having seen pliers and a screwdriver even if neither was in view; this is because our toolbox "schema" leads us to expect these things, and the expectation is so powerful that it can influence both our memory and our perception itself (see Chapter 7). In exactly the same way, our schema for an extrovert includes attributes like spirited and boisterous. So in this case, just as in the case of the toolbox, we use the schema to fill in the blanks about what the person is like.

Schemas about people are sometimes called **implicit theories of personality** (Bruner & Tagiuri, 1954; D. J. Schneider, 1973), and they seem to influence how we remember other people, how we perceive them, and how we interpret their actions. The implicit theories bring together a cluster of beliefs, linking one trait (such as extroverted) to others (such as boisterous), but also linking traits to behaviors—so that we have expectations for what sort of husband the extrovert will be, and what sorts of sports he is likely to enjoy, and more.

These implicit theories, however, are another point on which cultures differ. People in individualistic cultures, where the self is understood to be stable across time and situations, tend to view personality as fixed. On the other hand, people in collectivistic cultures, where the self is understood as changing according to relationships and situations, tend to view personality as malleable. One consequence of these different views is that people who believe personality to be fixed—called *entity theorists*—are more likely to go beyond the information given and make more global judgments about others' personalities. In contrast, people who believe personality to be changeable—*incremental theorists*—make more cautious and more specific generalizations about other people's personalities (Dweck, Hong, & Chiu, 1993; Hong, Chiu, & Dweck, 1997; Hong, Chiu, Dweck, & Sacks, 1997).

Implicit theories of personality are enormously helpful. Thanks to these schemas, we do not have to scrutinize every aspect of every situation we encounter; we can instead rely on what we have learned in past encounters. Likewise, a reliance on schematic knowledge means we do not have to recall every detail of every encounter we have had with another person; instead, we can draw on the broad summary provided by our schema for that type of person. These are not small advantages, and, indeed, without schema use every one of our social interactions, however incidental, would leave us buried in thought. Without the ability to make relatively efficient social judgments, we would be unable to make any sense of our social world.

However, while schemas provide shortcuts that are quick and efficient, they also leave us vulnerable to error, with our perception (or recollection) of another person ending up more in line with our preconceptions than with the facts. In many cases this is a small price to pay for the benefits of using schemas, and, for that matter, the errors produced are often easily corrected. But schemas can also lead to more serious errors.

STEREOTYPES

The hazard of schematic thinking is particularly clear in the case of social *stereotypes*, schemas about the characteristics of whole groups, so that we talk about Greeks, Jews, or African Americans (or women, the elderly, or liberals and conservatives) as if we know all of them. These stereotypes are, on their own, worrisome enough, because they can lead us to serious errors when we think about the various individuals we meet. Worse, though, stereotypes can lead to deeper problems, including (at the extreme) the wars, genocides, and "ethnic cleansings" that plague modern life. These larger calamities, however, are not fueled by stereotypes alone. Instead, these horrors grow out of a combination of factors sometimes referred to as the ABCs of prejudice: an *affective* (emotional) component, which leads us to view the other group as "bad," a *behavioral* component, which includes our tendencies to discriminate against other groups, and a cognitive component (the stereotype itself). In combination, these three components can lead to horrific cruelties and injustices, making the study of intergroup bias in general, and stereotypes in particular, a topic of some urgency.

WHERE STEREOTYPES COME FROM

Stereotypes often have deep historical roots and are transmitted to each new generation both explicitly ("Never trust a _____") and implicitly (via jokes, caricatures, portrayals in movies, and the like). Thus, in Western cultures, we hear over and over about athletic blacks, academic Asians, moody women, and lazy Latinos, and, like it or not, these associations eventually sink in and are likely to affect our behavior—regardless of whether we believe that the association has any factual basis.

Other factors also foster the creation and maintenance of stereotypes. Consider, for example, the mere fact that most of us have a lot of exposure to people in our own group, and, as a result, we have ample opportunity to learn about this group, helping us to see that the group is made up of diverse and unique individuals. We generally have much less exposure to other groups, though, and so, with little opportunity for learning, we are likely to perceive the group as merely a mass of more or less similar people. This so-called **out-group homogeneity effect** is reflected in such statements as "All Asians are alike" or "All Germans are alike." The first statement is almost invariably made by a non-Asian; the second, by a non-German.

Stereotypes are also sustained by a powerful tendency called **confirmation bias** (see Chapter 8), a bias that affects our perception, our attention, and our memory. Thanks to confirmation bias, we end up much more sensitive to information that confirms our view (and, in this context, confirms our stereotypes) than to information that might challenge our view. For example, let us assume that we hold the common view that the English are reserved, and suppose we now meet two Englishwomen: Anne, who is reserved, and Elyse, who is gregarious. Other things being equal, we are more likely to recall that Anne is English than Elyse, because Anne fits our schema but Elyse does not. As a result, our stereotype is reinforced, and we may continue to see a correlation where actually there is none, or overestimate a correlation that is in fact quite low (an **illusory correlation**). Various laboratory studies support this conclusion, showing both a "noticing bias" toward cases that confirm our view (see Hamilton & Rose, 1980), and a perception of illusory correlations based on this biased treatment of the evidence.

THE EFFECTS OF STEREOTYPES

Just a few decades ago, many people were perfectly comfortable feeling, expressing, and acting upon their prejudices. They did not hesitate to make derogatory comments about blacks, or women, or Jews in public settings. Indeed, people were often applauded for their racist or sexist actions, and the actions were deemed entirely appropriate. The times have changed, however, and, over the past few decades, stereotyping, prejudice, and discrimination have become socially unacceptable in most quarters of life. As a result, people are now much less likely to endorse explicitly racist or sexist statements than they were in the recent past. Does this mean stereotypes no longer matter? Unfortunately not. Stereotypes still influence people's behavior, but, perniciously, the effects are quite subtle, often happening automatically, outside our awareness (Bargh, Chen, & Burrows, 1996, but see also Cesario, Plaks, & Higgins, 2006).

In one demonstration of the automatic effects of stereotype activation, participants were asked to create grammatical sentences from scrambled word sequences as quickly as they could. In one condition, some of the sentences included words related to the elderly stereotype, such as *old* and *retired*. In another condition, the sentences were unrelated to the elderly stereotype. Once the participants had completed the scrambled sentence test, they were told that they could leave. The experiment was not yet over, however, because the researchers carefully timed how long it took the participants to walk to the elevator. Amazingly, participants who had been primed with an elderly stereotype walked more slowly than those who had not been so primed. Despite the participants' lack of awareness that a stereotype had even been activated, they still acted in a manner consistent with the stereotype (walking slowly, as an elderly person might).

Old age

Whether implicit or explicit, stereotypes have multiple effects: They influence what we believe about another person; they also shape how we act toward that person. Perhaps worst of all, our stereotypes influence how the targets of our stereotypes act—so that, specifically, the stereotype leads the targeted group member to behave in such a way that the target confirms the stereotype. In this way, stereotypes create *self-fulfilling prophecies*.

In a classic demonstration of self-fulfilling prophecies, Robert Rosenthal and Lenore Jacobson (1968) told a group of elementary-school teachers that some of their students were "bloomers," and could be expected to show substantial increases in IQ. Although these "bloomers" were randomly chosen, they in fact showed substantial increases in their test scores over the course of the next year, an effect apparently produced by the teachers' expectations. Several factors probably contributed to this effect, including the greater warmth and encouragement the teachers offered, the individualized feedback they provided, and the increased number of opportunities they gave the children they expected would do well (Harris & Rosenthal, 1985; for a cautionary note about the reliability of these effects, see Rosenthal, 1991, 2002).

Self-fulfilling prophecies   A teacher's expectations can shape a student's performance.

Similar effects can be demonstrated outside a school setting. In one study, male and female college students who did not know one another reported to separate rooms for a study on social interaction. The experimenter gave each of the men a photograph that supposedly showed the woman he would be talking to, but, in truth, the photograph showed someone else. Some of the men were shown a photograph of a woman who had previously been judged highly attractive; the other men were shown a photograph of a less attractive woman. The two participants then talked for a few minutes by telephone. Their conversation was tape-recorded, and, afterward, the researcher erased everything the man had said, played the tape to another group of students, and asked them to rate the warmth and poise of the woman who was speaking.

The data showed that the men talked differently when they thought they were interacting with an attractive woman, and, crucially, this difference on the men's side changed the way the women themselves acted. A woman who talked with a man who thought she was highly attractive ended up warmer and more poised than a woman who talked with a man who thought she was less attractive. This evidence seems to be a powerful testament to the way in which we are shaped by the others around us: If they believe we are attractive, we end up sounding more attractive. Sadly, if they believe we are less attractive, we act in a way that confirms this belief (Snyder, Tanke, & Berscheid, 1977).

How does all of this apply to stereotypes? Here, too, it turns out that people are heavily influenced by others' expectations—although, in this case, we are considering

includes our beliefs about our own traits, and also our knowledge about our own gen-der, physical characteristics, and values. This schema also includes information about what sort of person in general each of us thinks we are, and this information shapes both our behaviors and our emotions. For example, a person might have a schema of himself as a smart person who does well at school. This self-schema will help organize his responses to the world, and will make certain situations (such as achievement tests) more important and more relevant than others (such as quilting contests).

The self-schema is important for all of us, but the *content* of the schema surely varies from individual to individual, and, it seems, from one culture to the next. In the inter-dependent culture of Puerto Rico, for example, people are less likely to use trait labels when describing themselves than are European Americans (Hart, Lucca-Irizarry, & Damon, 1986). Similarly, when asked to complete the statement "I am . . .", Japanese students are more likely to mention social roles like "a sister" or "a student," whereas American students are more likely to mention traits like "smart" or "athletic" (Cousins, 1989). This finding does not mean, though, that Japanese people never think about themselves in terms of traits. When asked to describe themselves in specific situations, such as at home, at school, or with friends, Japanese students do make frequent use of trait terms. Apparently, people in interdependent, collectivistic cultures view them-selves as having certain traits, but only in specific situations, once again highlighting the importance of the situation in their view. In contrast, people in independent, indi-vidualistic cultures view themselves as made up of relatively stable internal traits, traits that apply in all settings. (For more on a cultural perspective on the self, see Ellemers, Spears, & Dossje, 2002; see also Chapter 15.)

In addition, people have schemas not only for who they are now, but also for who they may be in the future. Like other self-schemas, these ***possible selves*** (Markus & Nurius, 1986) help guide our responses to the world around us. Two particularly important types of possible selves are the *ideal self*—the self one would ideally like to be—and the ***ought self***—the self one thinks one should be (E. T. Higgins, 1997). According to E. Tory Higgins, when we compare our actual self to our ideal self, we become motivated to narrow the distance between the two, and develop what he calls a ***promotion focus***. When we have this sort of focus, we actively pursue valued goals—a pursuit that results in pleasure. In contrast, when we compare our actual self to our ought self, we become motivated to avoid doing harm, and develop what Higgins calls a ***prevention focus***. This kind of focus is associated with feelings of relief.

Notice, therefore, that schemas are not just dispassionate observations about our-selves; instead, they often have powerful emotions attached to them and can be a com-pelling source of motivation. This is why the schemas are typically thought of as an aspect of *"hot" cognition* (emotional and motivational) rather than *"cold" cognition* (dis-passionate and analytical).

SELF-ESTEEM AND SELF-ENHANCEMENT

The "hot" nature of self-schemas is evident in another way, because people not only seek to understand who they are but also make judgments about whether they are good or bad. These judgments are the basis for ***self-esteem***, which refers to the relative bal-ance of positive and negative judgments about oneself. Researchers interested in self-esteem distinguish between ***trait self-esteem***, which refers to one's typical self-esteem, and ***state self-esteem***, which can vary from moment to moment depending on what is happening in one's life and the aspects of oneself to which one is attending.

For several decades, social psychologists were interested in self-esteem as a cause of good outcomes. Based on early studies that showed correlations between self-esteem and school performance, popularity, and other positive outcomes, researchers con-cluded that boosting people's self-esteem could heal a range of individual and social

problems, from poor grades, depression, and bullying to sluggish economies, criminality, and pollution. A recent review of these studies, however, suggests that self-esteem is more an *effect* of good things than a *cause* of them. In other words, being popular, earning good grades, and working productively are sources of self-esteem; the self-esteem, then, is not the *cause* of the popularity and the success (Baumeister, Campbell, Krueger, & Vohs, 2003). In addition, and perhaps surprisingly, high self-esteem seems to be the cause of a number of less desirable outcomes, including criminal behavior, aggression, and teenage experimentation with drugs, alcohol, and sex.

These conclusions suggest perhaps that self-esteem is best understood as a sort of internal readout of how one is faring socially (Leary, Tambor, Terdal, & Downs, 1995). On this view, it is unsurprising that successes in one's life (like getting good grades or being popular) lead to a more positive reading. To test this theory more directly, though, Sanjay Srivastava and Jennifer Beer (2005) had initially unacquainted research participants interact with one another in small groups on four occasions. In each of these sessions, the participants engaged in a number of tasks, and then each participant rated his self-esteem as well as how much he liked the other group members. The key finding of this study was that participants who were well liked by their fellow group members at one session had higher self-esteem at the next session.

Once again, though, there are cultural differences in self-esteem that need to be explained. For example, people hailing from the interdependent cultures of Asia, Africa, and the Indian subcontinent tend to have markedly lower self-esteem than do independent, individualistic westerners (Dhawan, Roseman, Naidu, & Rettek, 1995). How should we think about this finding? In individualistic cultures, people seek to distinguish themselves through personal achievement and other forms of self-promotion, with the result of increased self-esteem. In collectivistic cultures, on the other hand, any form of self-promotion threatens the relational and situational bonds that glue the society together. Indeed, to be a "good" person in these cultures, one should seek to be quite ordinary—a strategy that results in social harmony and meeting collective goals, not increased self-esteem (Kitayama, Markus, Matsumoto, & Norasakkunkit, 1997; Pyszczynski, Greenberg, Solomon, Arndt, & Schimel, 2004).

THE ABOVE-AVERAGE EFFECT

Clearly, then, people with an independent notion of the self are motivated to feel good about themselves and their unique traits. This motivation often leads them to view themselves as different from and superior to other people—even in the face of evidence to the contrary. In contrast, people with a more interdependent notion of the self seem less likely to undertake *self-enhancement* (Heine, 2005; Markus & Kitayama, 1991)

These patterns are easily documented. For example, when Americans compare themselves with others on favorable characteristics, the vast majority judge themselves to be above average—in stark defiance of all statistical logic (see Harter, 1990). Thus, in 1976–77 the College Board asked 1 million high-school students to rate themselves against their peers on leadership ability. In response, 70% said they were above average, and only 2% thought they were below. Similar findings have been obtained in people's judgments of talents ranging from managerial skills to driving ability (see Dunning, Meyerowitz, & Holzberg, 1989). And it is not just high-school students who show these effects. One study of university professors found that 94% believed they were better than their colleagues at their jobs (Gilovich, 1991).

What is going on here? Part of the cause lies in the way we search our memories in order to decide whether we have been good leaders or bad, good drivers or poor ones. Evidence suggests that this memory search is often selective, showcasing the occasions in the past on which we have behaved well and neglecting the occasions on which we have done badly. This is probably because each of us starts with the hypothesis that we have in fact behaved well; we then search our memories for episodes that would confirm this obviously self-serving hypothesis (Kunda, 1990; Kunda, Fong, Sanitioso, & Reber, 1993; for more on this sort of confirmation bias, see Chapter 8).

In addition, people seem to capitalize on the fact that the meanings of these traits—effective leader, good at getting along with others—are often ambiguous. This ambiguity allows each of us to interpret a trait, and thus to interpret the evidence, in a fashion that puts us in the best possible light. Take driving ability. Suppose Henry is a slow, careful driver. He will tend to think that he's better than average precisely because he's slow and careful. But suppose Jane, on the other hand, is a fast driver who prides herself on her ability to whiz through traffic and hang tight on hairpin turns. She will also think that she's better than average because of the way she's defined driving skill. As a result, both Henry and Jane (and, indeed, most drivers) end up considering themselves above average. By appropriately redefining success or excellence, we can each conclude that we are the ones who are successful (Dunning and Cohen, 1992; Dunning et al., 1989).

The findings are quite different, though, for members of collectivistic cultures. For them, self-aggrandizement brings disharmony, which is too great a price to pay. Evidence for this conclusion comes from a study in which American and Japanese college students were asked to rank their abilities in areas ranging from math and memory to warmheartedness and athletic skill. The American students showed the usual result: Across all the questions, 70% rated themselves above average on each trait. But among the Japanese students, only 50% rated themselves above average, indicating no self-serving bias, and perhaps pointing instead to a self-harmonizing one (Markus and Kitayama, 1991; Takata, 1987).

THE SELF-SERVING ATTRIBUTIONAL BIAS

The individualistic tendency toward a flattering view of oneself is also evident in how people make attributions about their own behaviors. We saw earlier in this chapter that people in the West tend to make dispositional attributions for others' behaviors, and situational attributions for their own behaviors. We need to refine this claim, though, because the exact pattern depends on what the behavior is. Specifically, people tend to offer dispositional attributions for their own successes ("I did well on the test because I'm smart"), but situational attributions for their failures ("My company is losing money because of the downturn in the economy"; "I lost the match because the sun was in my eyes").

This *self-serving attributional bias* has been documented in many Western cultures (Bradley, 1978). In most studies, participants perform various tasks—ranging from alleged measures of motor skills to tests of social sensitivity—and then receive fake feedback on whether they had achieved some criterion of success (see, for example, Luginbuhl, Crowe, & Kahan, 1975; D. T. Miller, 1976; Sicoly & Ross, 1977; M. L. Snyder, Stephan, & Rosenfield, 1976; Stevens & Jones, 1976). The overall pattern of results is always the same: By and large, the participants attribute their successes to internal factors (they were pretty good at such tasks, and they worked hard) and their failures to external factors (the task was too difficult, and they were unlucky).

The same pattern is easily documented outside the laboratory. One study analyzed the comments of football and baseball players following important games, as published in newspapers. Of the statements made by the winners, 80% were internal attributions: "Our team was great," "Our star player did it all," and so on. In contrast, only 53% of the losers gave internal attributions, and they often explained the outcomes by referring to external, situational factors: "I think we hit the ball all right. But I think we're unlucky" (Lau & Russell, 1980, p. 32).

These attributions are offered, of course, after an event—after the team has won or lost, or after the business has succeeded or failed. But a related pattern arises *before* an event, allowing people to protect themselves against failure and disappointment. One

Attribution **Players on winning teams typically make internal attributions.**

such strategy is known as *self-handicapping*, in which one arranges an obstacle to one's own performance. This way, if failure occurs, it will be attributed to the obstacle and not to one's own limitations (Higgins, Snyder, & Berglas, 1990; Jones & Berglas, 1978). Thus, if Julie is afraid of failing next week's biology exam, she might spend more time than usual watching television. Then, if she fails the exam, it will look as if she did not study hard enough rather than that she is stupid.

Not surprisingly, though, all these forms of self-protection are less likely in collectivistic cultures—that is, among people who are not motivated to view themselves as different from and better than others. But there is some subtlety to the cultural patterning: A recent analysis of the self-serving bias found that the Japanese and Pacific Islanders showed no self-serving biases, Indians displayed a moderate bias, and Chinese and Koreans showed large self-serving biases. It is not clear why these differences arose, and explaining this point is a fruitful area for future research. In the meantime, though, this analysis reminds us of the important point that not all Asian cultures are the same; there is a great deal of heterogeneity within collectivistic, interdependent cultures.

SOCIAL IDENTITIES AND GROUP ENHANCEMENT

People derive their self-concepts and self-esteem not only from their own personal accomplishments, but also from the status and accomplishments of the various groups to which they belong (Turner, Brown, & Tajfel, 1979), an issue that is explored by *social-identity theory*.

The seeds of social-identity theory were planted in the early 1970s, when Henri Tajfel and his colleagues captured a peculiar phenomenon in their laboratory (Tajfel & Billig, 1974; Tajfel, Billig, Bundy, & Flament, 1971). Employing the *minimal groups paradigm*, Tajfel and his colleagues divided participants into two obviously arbitrary groups. Participants then chose from several different schemes for allotting points to members of their own group (i.e., *in-group members*) and members of the other group (i.e., *out-group members*). The researchers found that the participants showed a pattern of *in-group favoritism*, consistently choosing allocation schemes that maximized what their own group received relative to what the out-group received. Later studies have shown the link between this pattern and various emotional reactions. Specifically, evidence

fashion consistent with their strong attitudes than in a fashion consistent with their weak ones (Bassili, 1993, 1995; Kraus, 1995). Also crucial is how specifically the attitude is defined (Armitage & Conner, 2001). The more specific one's definition, the more likely it is to predict a particular bit of behavior. This was evident, for example, in a study of women's attitudes toward birth control. There was no correlation between the women's attitudes toward birth control in general and their likelihood of using oral contraceptives. But there was a strong correlation between their attitudes toward using birth-control pills in particular and their actual use of this method of contraception (Davidson & Jaccard, 1979).

In addition, one further—and perhaps surprising—factor sometimes disrupts the relationship between our attitudes and our behavior: We often take an action (or fail to) without pausing to reflect on whether it is consistent with our values and priorities. As a result, our behaviors are often not guided by (and so are not consistent with) our attitudes. Evidence for this point comes from studies that increase participants' self-consciousness. For example, in one study, participants were presented with two tasks, one highly appealing and one not, and asked to assign one task to themselves and one to a second participant (Batson, Kobrynowicz, Dinnerstein, Kampf, & Wilson, 1997; Batson & Thompson, 2001; Batson, Thompson, & Chen, 2002). Participants overwhelmingly agreed that assigning themselves the positive task was not the right thing to do, but most did so anyhow. But a simple intervention changed the outcome: When the researchers put a mirror in the room, they found that only 50% of participants gave the attractive task to themselves (Batson, Thompson, Seuferling, Whitney, & Strongman, 1999). This study—and others like it—suggest that increasing self-consciousness can bring behavior into line with attitudes.

ATTITUDE FORMATION

How do attitudes—whether explicit or implicit—arise? Some of our attitudes, of course, are based on our consideration of the facts. We carefully weigh the pros and cons of an argument, and make up our minds about whether we should endorse it or not. In many other cases, however, our attitudes have sources that are not quite so rational.

We acquire many of our attitudes from our parents, friends, and surrounding culture through a variety of learning mechanisms. In some cases, what is crucial is some form of associative learning (akin to *classical conditioning*; see Chapter 6). For example, we might repeatedly see a brand of cigarettes paired with an appealing person or a cool cartoon character, and wind up associating the two, leaving us with a positive attitude toward that brand

Advertisements and attitude change Advertisers try hard to shape our attitudes towards particular brands.

of cigarettes (Cacioppo, Marshall-Goodell, Tassinary, & Petty, 1992). In other cases, attitudes can be formed via a process akin to *operant conditioning*. For example, parents try to reward behavior they would like to encourage, such as hard work at school and good table manners. The end result of this training, in many cases, is a favorable attitude toward certain work habits and certain forms of etiquette. In still other cases, attitudes emerge from a sort of *observational learning*: We see a respected peer who endorses a particular attitude, or we observe someone gaining some benefit from an attitude. In either case, we may be led to endorse the attitude ourselves.

ATTITUDE CHANGE:
BEING PERSUADED BY OTHERS

What happens once we form an attitude? In many cases, we are bombarded by messages exhorting us to change our attitudes, and sometimes these messages are effective and sometimes not. Sometimes a TV commercial persuades us to switch our brand of toothpaste, but other times we maintain our loyalty to our usual brand. Sometimes a politician persuades us to change our vote, but other times we hold our ground. Examples like these lead us to ask, When do attitudes change, and when do they stay the same?

To answer this question, we need to make a crucial distinction, because there are actually two routes to persuasion (Cialdini, Petty, & Cacioppo, 1981; McGuire, 1985). There is the *central route to persuasion*, in which we track the information we receive with some care and mentally elaborate its arguments with yet further considerations of our own. We take this route if an issue is one that matters to us and if we are not diverted by other concerns. In this case, we are keenly sensitive to the credibility and trustworthiness of the message's source (Aronson, Turner, & Carlsmith, 1963; Hovland and Weiss, 1952; Walster, Aronson, & Abrahams, 1966). We also pay close attention to the content of the persuasive message, and so—sensibly—strong arguments will be more effective in changing our mind than weak ones.

The situation is quite different, though, if a persuasive message comes by way of what Richard Petty and John Cacioppo call the *peripheral route to persuasion*. We will be induced to take this route if we do not care much about an issue, or if the message is not clearly heard because of background noise, or if we are otherwise distracted. In such circumstances, content and arguments matter little. What counts instead is how or by whom or in what surroundings the message is presented (Petty & Cacioppo, 1985; Petty, Wegener, & Fabrigar, 1997; for a closely related view, see Chaiken, Liberman, & Eagly, 1989; Eagly and Chaiken, 1993). Similarly, we might be more inclined to be persuaded by the good looks of an attractive spokesperson if we are not paying much attention to the content of the message itself (Shavitt, Swan, Lowrey, & Wanke, 1994).

ATTITUDE CHANGE:
BEING PERSUADED BY OURSELVES

Whether it is through the central or the peripheral route, attitudes can (and often do) change as a result of others' efforts. But there is another route to attitude change, and that is through our own behavior. At first, this may sound odd, because common sense argues that attitudes cause behavior, and not the other way around. But sometimes things are the other way around—with our own behaviors causing us to change our views of the world.

The classic work on this problem was provided by Leon Festinger, who argued that people put a high value on being consistent with themselves, and so any perceived inconsistency (among their beliefs, feelings, and behavior) is highly aversive (1957, 1962). Festinger used the term *cognitive dissonance* to refer to this state of perceived inconsistency, and argued that people try to reduce this dissonance whenever possible (1957).

Self-perception and attribution **In the movie Donnie Brasco, *an undercover FBI agent infiltrates the mob. As his involvement deepens, he grows uncertain of his own allegiances. (Johnny Depp and Al Pacino appear in the 1997 film.)***

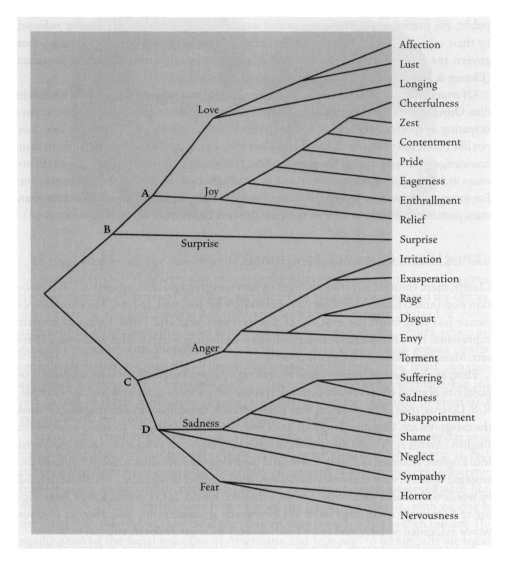

Affection
Lust
Longing
Cheerfulness
Zest
Contentment
Pride
Eagerness
Enthrallment
Relief
Surprise
Irritation
Exasperation
Rage
Disgust
Envy
Torment
Suffering
Sadness
Disappointment
Shame
Neglect
Sympathy
Horror
Nervousness

12.8 Families of emotion words *The words people use to describe their emotional experiences cluster into small groups of similiar words.*

leave untouched many questions about emotional experience. For example, do people in different cultures feel the same emotions? We have already mentioned that cultures differ in their display rules for emotion, and it turns out that cultures also differ markedly in the vocabulary that they use for emotions. Thus, for example, the people who live on the Pacific Island of Ifalik lack a word for "surprise," and the Tahitians lack a word for "sadness." Other cultures have words that describe common emotions for which we have no special terms. The Ifalik sometimes feel an emotion they call *fago*, which involves a complex mixture of compassion, love, and sadness experienced in relationships in which one person is dependent on the other (Lutz, 1986, 1988). And the Japanese report a common emotion called *amae*, which is a desire to be dependent and cared for (Doi, 1973; Morsbach & Tyler, 1986). The German language reserves the word *Schadenfreude* for the special pleasure derived from another's misfortune.

How should we interpret these differences in vocabulary? Should we conclude that cultures differ in the emotional experiences themselves? These are difficult questions, but issues we considered earlier in this chapter may bear on the matter: Recall the contrast between individualistic and collectivistic cultures both in the social roles of their members and in the way their members explain the behavior of others. Given these dramatic differences, some observers question whether emotional experience could ever be identical across cultures, especially for more complex emotions (such as shame, or pride) that seem tied to elaborate (and culture-based) ideas about why we have acted as we have. For example, can someone feel Western-style guilt—an emotion associated

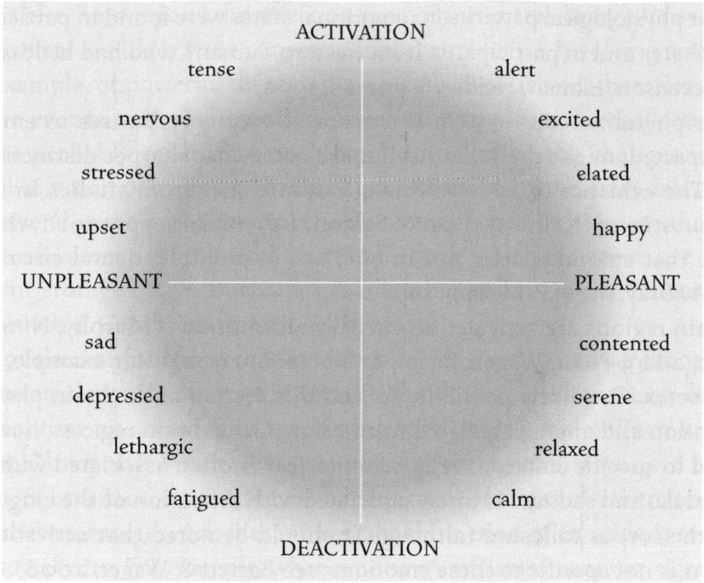

ACTIVATION

tense   alert

nervous   excited

stressed   elated

upset   happy

UNPLEASANT ——————————— PLEASANT

sad   contented

depressed   serene

lethargic   relaxed

fatigued   calm

DEACTIVATION

12.9 *Dimensions of emotional experience*
The two major dimensions of emotional experience are pleasantness and activation.

with individual responsibility—if she believes that a situation determined her actions? Can someone feel Eastern-style shame—a socially focused emotion—if he believes that he is ultimately beholden to no one? These questions raise the possibility that, in diverse cultures, emotions not only may have different names but also may feel different (see Schweder, 1994). On this issue, the jury is still out.

PHYSIOLOGICAL ASPECTS OF EMOTION

As we have discussed, Cannon argued that various emotions tend to produce similar reactions in the body—an elevated heartbeat, a tightened stomach, and so on. Despite his assertions, though, the bodily reactions associated with emotion certainly *feel* different from one another (Levenson, 1994). That is, not only do the emotions differ in how they feel inside our "head," but they also differ in how they feel in the rest of the body: The sick stomach and wrinkled nose of disgust, for example, feel decidedly different from the squared shoulders and puffed chest of pride. And anger's hot head and coiled muscles seem opposite fear's cold feet and faint heart.

Over the past fifty years, researchers have tried to understand how the body produces these reactions during emotional experiences. One of the most interesting findings from this research is that Cannon may have been close to the truth—our perceptions of bodily differences among the emotions may actually be illusions, compelling experiences that are not well grounded in reality (Cacioppo, Berntson; & Klein, 1992). In one classic study, for example, Albert Ax (1953) induced fear among some of his research participants by leading them to believe that the increasing shocks to their fingers were due to a short circuit. Among other participants, he induced anger by having their incompetent "polygraph operator" insult them with rude comments. Ax found that the two emotional states that he had painstakingly created differed in only a subset of the physiological measures he obtained, such as diastolic blood pressure, which increased more for anger, and respiration rate, which increased more for fear.

Ax's findings are more than a half century old, but more recent work has not challenged his central claims. To this day, only a few bodily distinctions among emotions have been documented, such as the finding of greater heart rates in response to anger, fear, and sadness than in response to disgust (Cacioppo, Berntson, Larsen, Poehlmann, & Ito, 2000; Levenson, 1992, 2003; Zajonc & McIntosh, 1992). It bears noting, however, that these relatively modest physiological differences may be reliable across cultures.

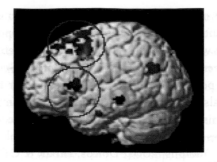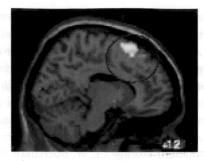

The neural bases of reappraisal **Results from a functional magnetic resonance imaging study in which participants were asked to use reappraisal to change their emotional responses to negative emotion-eliciting slides. Findings indicated that reappraisal was associated with increased activation in the lateral and medial prefrontal cortex.**

experiment were asked about material presented while they were trying to suppress their emotions, they made more errors than they did when they were not suppressing their emotions (Richards & Gross, 2000). Indeed, when asked to suppress their emotions, participants performed as badly on later memory tasks as participants who had been told not to pay attention at all to the material that was being presented (Richards & Gross, 2006).

In contrast, reappraisal dampens experienced emotions without exacting cognitive or physiological costs (Gross, 1998a). For example, researchers showed participants neutral or negative emotion-eliciting slides during a functional magnetic resonance imaging (fMRI) study (Ochsner et al., 2004). In the critical conditions, participants were asked either to view the negative emotion-eliciting slides or to reappraise them by altering their meaning. For example, a participant might see a picture of women crying in front of a church. Instead of thinking of a funeral scene, the participant might try to think of it as a wedding scene and the tears as tears of joy. The reappraisal had many effects: Participants reported feeling less negative emotion when reappraising than they did when just watching the negative slides. Reappraisal also activated the prefrontal regions in the brain, which are associated with self-regulation, and decreased activation in the amygdala and other brain regions associated with negative emotion.

The key message from these studies is that different forms of emotion regulation have quite different consequences. This is not to say one should always reappraise or never suppress. Both processes have their place. But it is becoming clear that compared with keeping a stiff upper lip by means of suppression, reappraisal has a generally more adaptive profile of consequences.

SOME FINAL THOUGHTS: COGNITION, EMOTION, AND SOCIAL PROCESSES

One major theme of this chapter is that we spend an astonishing amount of time trying to figure out others. We ask: Who are they really? What do they want? Why do they do what they do? As is the case whenever we try to make sense of something that is complicated, we rely heavily on cognitive schemas. These cognitive schemas are vital for us as we navigate our social world, and they help us organize and make sense of what would otherwise be an overwhelming amount of information. At the same time, some social schemas—such as stereotypes—can be terribly destructive. By categorizing others, we can miss their unique features and create self-fulfilling prophecies that undermine our own and other people's potential.

In addition, it seems that, in a strange reversal of the golden rule, we do unto ourselves what we do unto others. That is, we use the same kinds of schemas to make sense of our own thoughts, behaviors, and even feelings that we use to make sense of the thoughts, behaviors, and feelings of other people. We of course often give ourselves a privileged place in the social universe. For example, we are more likely to make situational attributions for ourselves than for others, and we are more likely to remember information that is pertinent to us than information that is not. At the same time, though, we work as hard to make sense of our own behavior as we work to make sense of that of others, as when we feel cognitive dissonance and so alter our attitudes to accord better with our actions.

Another major theme that runs through this chapter is that we process and respond to social information in two quite different ways. The first type of processing is automatic, and relatively effortless. This is the kind of processing that is triggered when stereotypes are primed, when implicit attitudes govern our behaviors toward out-group members, when we respond to persuasive communications via the peripheral route, when we make the fundamental attribution error, or when we automatically appraise a threatening stimulus and generate a fear response. All of these responses—and many others like them—have the great advantage that they are quick and relatively effortless, and therefore do not unduly tax our cognitive resources. The second type of processing, in contrast, is controlled, and relatively effortful. This is the kind of processing that is triggered when we focus on individuating information in an effort to combat stereotypes, when we respond to persuasive communications via the central route, when we deliberately correct our initial dispositional attributions by making reference to situational factors, or when we effortfully reappraise our situation so as to decrease the negative emotion that we feel.

The notion that we respond to social information in two such different ways challenges several of our most cherished assumptions. We like to see ourselves as unified selves, but instead we are constantly operating on two tracks. We like to see ourselves as rational, and yet again and again we find that our emotions shape our thoughts and actions, as when we distort reality in order to protect a favorable impression of ourselves. We like to see ourselves as exerting control over our lives, and of course we often do. But at other times, and perhaps more of the time than we care to think, we are influenced by situational factors that operate outside our awareness. Difficult as it may be, we need to accept that we are governed by both automatic and relatively controlled processes in many of the most important domains of our lives. And what is the lasting benefit of this shift in understanding? A clearer conception of who we (and others) really are.

SUMMARY

PERCEIVING AND UNDERSTANDING OTHERS

- How we understand someone's behavior depends on the attribution we choose for the behavior. *Situational attributions* involve factors external to the person we are observing; *dispositional attributions* focus on factors internal to the person.
- People in *collectivistic cultures* emphasize the ways in which people are interdependent and tend to make situational attributions. People in *individualistic cultures* view themselves and others as independent and tend to make dispositional attributions; this tendency is so powerful that it is referred to as the *fundamental attribution error*. This trend reverses, however, when people are interpreting their own behaviors; then people in individualistic cultures tend to make situational attributions for their own behaviors. This *actor-observer difference* may arise

from the knowledge each person has of himself; it may also depend on the difference between what the actor perceives and what observers perceive.

- We rely on *implicit theories of personality* when we think about or remember other individuals. These theories help us understand the situations we encounter, but also leave us vulnerable to error. These errors are obvious when we rely on social *stereotypes*, which are transmitted to each generation both explicitly and implicitly. Stereotypes are also sustained by *confirmation bias*, which can, in some cases, give rise to an *illusory correlation*.
- Stereotypes can influence people's behavior implicitly: By priming a person's stereotype, the person's behavior can be influenced in an unconscious and automatic fashion. Stereotypes can also create *self-fulfilling prophecies*, leading the person we are interacting with to behave in a fashion consistent with the stereotype. A related case involves

The participant in a social pressure experiment (A) The true participant (left) listens to the instructions. (B) On hearing the unanimous verdict of the others, he leans forward to look at the cards more carefully. (C) After 12 such trials, he explains that "I have to call them as I see them."

others, and if that is not an option, then they can try to gain information by comparing their own reactions to those of others (Festinger, 1954; Suls & Miller, 1977). This pattern of relying on others in the face of uncertainty can also be observed in young children, and even in infants. Infants who confront a scary situation and do not know whether to advance or retreat will glance toward their caretaker's face. If she smiles, the infant will tend to advance; if she frowns, he will tend to withdraw and return to her (Chapter 11). This early phenomenon of *social referencing* may be the prototype for what happens all our lives, a general process of validating our reactions by checking on how others are behaving.

Another reason for going along with the crowd is not so much cognitive as motivational. Consider the original Asch study in which a unanimous majority made a grossly incorrect judgment. In this context, the participant likely saw the world much as it is, but he had every reason to believe that the others saw it differently. If he now said what he believed, he could not help but be embarrassed; the others would probably think that he was a fool and might laugh at him. Under the circumstances, the participant would prefer to disguise what he really believed and go along, preferring to be "normal" rather than correct.

Direct evidence for the role of embarrassment comes from a variant of the Asch experiment in which the participant entered the room while the experiment was already in progress. The experimenter told her that since she arrived late, it would be simpler for her to write her answers down in private rather than to announce them out loud. Under these circumstances, there was little yielding. The lines being judged were of the original unambiguous sort (e.g., 8 inches vs. 6 inches in height), so that there was no informational pressure toward conformity. And since the judgments were made in private, there was no (or little) motivational pressure either. As a result, there was a great deal of independence (Asch, 1952).

CULTURE AND CONFORMITY

Conformity   One type of conformity is dressing like our friends.

Asch's studies of conformity and most others like it were conducted on participants from an individualistic society, the United States. Many of these participants did conform but experienced enormous discomfort as a result, plainly suffering from the contrast between their own perceptions and the perceptions of others. The pattern is different in collectivistic cultures. Here individuals are less distressed about conforming even when it means being wrong. Over two dozen Asch-type conformity studies have now been conducted in collectivistic cultures, and they support such a conclusion (Bond & Smith, 1996).

Members of collectivistic and individualistic societies tend to differ in other ways too. Consider the group pressure itself, the pressure that presumably led to the conformity observed in Asch's experiments. On the face of it, one might expect collectivists to

Social comparison *The two museum visitors do not seem quite sure what to make of Marisol's sculpture* The Family *and compare reactions.*

be more sensitive to this pressure, and so to endorse the group's judgments more often than do individualists. But it turns out that this depends on the nature of the group. Collectivists are more likely to conform with members of a group to which they are tied by traditional bonds—their family (including second cousins and great-aunts and so on), classmates, close friends, and fellow workers. But, in contrast, they are less affected than are individualists by people with whom they do not share close interpersonal bonds (Moghaddam, 1998).

There are also cultural differences in how people think about the opposite of conformity: uniqueness (Jetten, Postmes, & McAuliffe, 2002). In one study with both European American and East Asian participants, the participants were invited to choose one of five pens. Four of the pens were of the same color, while the fifth pen was a unique color, different from the other four. European American participants were much more likely to choose the unique pen, while East Asian participants, preferring not to stick out in any way, were much less likely to choose the unique pen (Kim & Markus, 1999). These results underscore that one culture's "uniqueness" is another culture's "deviance," just as one culture's "conformity" can be another culture's "harmony."

MINORITY INFLUENCE

Asch's studies tell us that a unanimous majority exerts a powerful effect, an effect that makes it difficult for any individual to stray from the majority's position. What happens, though, when the individual is no longer alone? An answer to this question comes, once again, from Asch's studies of conformity. In one variation of his experiment, Asch had one of the confederates act as the participant's ally; all of the other confederates gave wrong answers while the ally's judgments were correct. Under these conditions, the pressure to conform largely evaporated, and the participant yielded rarely and was not particularly upset by the odd judgment offered by (the majority of) the confederates.

Note, however, that this study is ambiguous. Was the pressure to conform reduced because the participant had an ally, sharing his views? Or was the pressure reduced merely because the consensus was broken, so that the participant was no longer alone in questioning the majority view? To find out, another variation of the study was conducted in which the confederate again deviated from the majority, but did not do so by giving the correct answer. On the contrary, she gave an answer that was even further from the truth than the group's. Thus, on a trial in which the correct answer was 6¼ inches and the majority answer was 6¾ inches, the confederate's answer might be 8 inches. This

The effect of a consistent minority *A steadfast minority can gradually create genuine changes in what people think and feel, as in the case of the American civil rights movement. A scene from the 1965 march from Selma to Montgomery.*

response was obviously not arrayed on the side of the participant (or of the truth!), but it helped to liberate him even so. The participant now yielded very much less than when he was confronted by a unanimous majority. What evidently mattered was the group's unanimity; once this was broken, the participant felt that he could speak up without fear of embarrassment (Asch, 1952). Similar studies have been performed in other laboratories with similar results (Allen, 1975; Allen & Levine, 1971; Nemeth & Chiles, 1988). Totalitarian systems thus have good reason to stifle dissent of any kind. The moment one voice is raised in dissent, the unanimity is broken, and then others may (and often do) find the courage to express their own dissent, whatever its form.

OBEDIENCE

Conformity, then, is one of the ways that other people influence us, with the effect governed by both cognitive and motivational factors. But there is also another way that others influence our behavior: They instruct us, or even command us, and in many circumstances we obey those commands.

A certain degree of obedience is a necessary ingredient of social life. After all, in any society some individuals need to have authority over others, at least within a limited sphere. Someone needs to direct traffic; someone needs to tell people when they should put their garbage out at the curb for collection; someone needs to instruct children and get them to do their homework. In each of these cases, it is entirely appropriate that the relevant persons be granted authority, and that people obey their instructions.

But obedience can also lead people to violate their own principles and do things they previously felt they should not do. The atrocities of the last century—the Nazi death camps, the Soviet "purges," the Cambodian massacres, the so-called ethnic cleansing in Bosnia, the Rwandan and Sudanese genocides—give terrible proof that this disposition to obedience can become a corrosive poison, and, unquestionably, these atrocities could not have been committed without the obedience of tens or hundreds of thousands and the acquiescence of many more.

How could such obedience have come about? Psychologists who try to answer this question have adopted two different approaches. One approach is based on the intuitively appealing notion that some individuals are more obedient than others, and it is these individuals who are the primary culprits. The second approach emphasizes the social situation in which the obedient person finds herself.

PERSONALITY AND OBEDIENCE

An influential version of the person-centered hypothesis was proposed shortly after World War II by investigators who believed they had discovered a personality type predisposed toward blind obedience. Specifically, people with so-called *authoritarian personalities*, it was proposed, tend to be highly obedient, and they also show a cluster of traits related to this obedience: They are prejudiced against various minority groups and hold certain sentiments about authority, including a general belief that the world is best governed by a system of power and dominance in which each of us must submit to those above us and show harshness to those below. These authoritarian attitudes can be revealed (and measured) by a tendency to agree with statements such as "Obedience and respect for authority are the most important virtues children should learn" and "People can be divided into two distinct classes: the weak and the strong" (Adorno et al., 1950).

Contemporary researchers have broadened the conception of the authoritarian personality by analyzing the motivational basis for conservative ideology (Jost, Glaser, Kruglanski, & Sulloway, 2003), building on the supposition that this ideology—like any belief system—serves the psychological needs of the people who hold these beliefs.

Obedience *The commandant of a concentration camp in Germany stands amid some of his prisoners who were burned or shot as the American army approached the camp during the last days of World War II. Most Nazis who held such positions insisted that they were "just following orders."*

In particular, the *motivated social cognition* perspective maintains that people respond to threat and uncertainty by expressing beliefs that help them to manage their concerns. Evidence supporting this perspective has come from studies showing that political conservatism is positively related to a concern with societal instability and death, a need for order and structure, and intolerance of ambiguity (e.g., Jost et al., 2003).

SITUATIONS AND OBEDIENCE

Can the notion of the authoritarian personality, or, for that matter, any proposal focused on individual personalities, explain the atrocities of recent times? Are the perpetrators of genocide simply a different breed—perhaps people who are, by their nature, all too ready to obey? Or might they be different from the rest of us in some other way—perhaps as moral monsters or similarly deranged? Although some of them probably are (Dicks, 1972), the frightening fact is that many seem to be quite ordinary people.

In a well-known account of the trial of Adolf Eichmann, the man who oversaw the execution of 6 million Jews and other minorities in the Nazi gas chambers, historian Hannah Arendt noted a certain "banality of evil": "The trouble with Eichmann was precisely that so many were like him, and that the many were neither perverted nor sadistic, that they were, and still are, terribly and terrifyingly normal" (Arendt, 1965, p. 276).

The banality of evil   Hannah Arendt found Nazi war criminal Adolf Eichmann "terrifyingly normal."

What would lead normal people to commit hideous crimes? The obvious answer is the situation in which they find themselves, and, under some social systems—Hitler's Germany, Stalin's Russia, Afghanistan under the Taliban—the conditions for obedience may well be extraordinarily powerful.

But what is it that makes a situation influential? And how coercive does a situation have to be in order to elicit monstrous acts? These questions were explored by Stanley Milgram in a series of experiments that are perhaps the best-known studies in all of social psychology (Milgram, 1963; see Blass, 2000, for an examination of the studies' substantial impact). In these studies, Milgram drew his participants not from a group of violent felons, but from a local newspaper advertisement offering $4.50 per hour to persons willing to participate in a study of memory. The respondents, who represented a broad range of incomes and educations, arrived at a laboratory control room where a white-coated experimenter told them that they would be participating in a study of how punishment affected human learning.

The participants were run in pairs and drew lots to determine who within each pair would be the "teacher" and who the "learner." The task of the learner was to master a list of associations. The task of the teacher was to read out the cue word for each association, to record the learner's spoken answer, and—most important—to administer punishment whenever the learner answered incorrectly. The learner was led to a cubicle, where the experimenter strapped him in a chair, to "prevent excess movement," and attached shock electrodes to his wrist—all in full view of the teacher. After the learner was securely strapped in place, the teacher returned to the control room and was seated in front of an imposing-looking shock generator that had 30 switches on it, each labeled with a voltage ranging from 15 volts for the leftmost switch to 450 volts at the opposite end. Below each of the levers there were ominous labels that ranged from "Slight Shock" to "Danger: Severe Shock" to a final, undefined "XXX" (Figure 13.2).

The procedure then began. The teacher presented the cue words, and if, on a given trial, the learner answered correctly, the teacher simply moved on to the next trial. But if the learner made a mistake, the teacher had to give the learner a shock before proceeding. The first shock given was the lowest voltage on the scale, but with each successive error the teacher was required to increase the punishment by one step, proceeding (if needed) through the entire range of available punishments. To ensure that the teacher understood what the learner was experiencing, the teacher was also administered a

13.2 *The obedience experiment* **(A) The "shock generator" used in the experiment. (B) The learner is strapped into his chair and electrodes are attached to his wrist. (C) The teacher receives a sample shock. (D) The teacher breaks off the experiment. It is important to note that most participants did not break off the experiment.**

sample shock that gave him an unpleasant jolt—and it was only 45 volts, just the third step in the 30-step punishment series.

Needless to say, the shock generator never delivered any shocks (except for the test jolt given to the teacher). To make sure the teacher did not discover this, the learner was kept out of sight in a separate cubicle, and all communication between teacher and learner was conducted over an intercom. The initial drawing, deciding who was teacher and who was learner, was also rigged so that the learner was always a confederate, played by a mild-mannered, middle-aged actor. The point of the experiment, then, was not to study punishment and learning at all; that was just a cover story. It was actually to determine how far the participants would go in obeying the experimenter's instructions.

Within the procedure, the learner made a fair number of (scripted) errors, and so the shocks that were to be delivered to the learner kept getting stronger and stronger. By the time 120 volts was reached, the victim shouted that the shocks were becoming too painful. At 150 volts, he demanded that he be let out of the experiment. At 180 volts, he cried out that he could no longer stand the pain, sometimes yelling, "My heart, my heart!" At 300 volts, he screamed, "Get me out of here!" and said he would not answer any more. On the next few shocks, there were agonized screams. After 330 volts, there was unbroken silence.

The learner's responses—from complaints to tormented cries—were all predetermined and well rehearsed. But the real participants—the teachers—did not know that, so they had to decide what to do. When the victim cried out in pain or refused to go on, the participants usually turned to the experimenter for instructions, a tragic form of social referencing (Chapter 11). In response, the experimenter told the participants that the experiment had to go on, indicated that he took full responsibility, and pointed out that "the shocks may be painful but there is no permanent tissue damage."

How far did subjects go in obeying the experimenter? The results were astounding: About 65% of Milgram's subjects—both males and females—continued to obey the experimenter to the bitter end. This proportion was unaffected even when the learner complained of a heart condition. This is not to say that the obedient participants had no moral qualms—quite the contrary. Many of them were seriously upset. They bit their lips, twisted their hands, sweated profusely, and laughed nervously—but obeyed even so. Similar results were obtained when the study was repeated with participants from other countries such as Australia, Germany, and Jordan (Kilham & Mann, 1974; Mantell & Panzarella, 1976; Shanab & Yahya, 1977).

These are striking data—suggesting that it takes remarkably little within a situation to produce truly monstrous acts. But we should also note the profound ethical questions raised by this study: Milgram's participants were of course fully debriefed at the study's end, and so they knew they had done no damage to the "learner" and had inflicted no pain. But the participants also knew that they had obeyed the researcher and had (apparently) been willing to hurt another human—perhaps quite seriously. We therefore need to ask whether the scientific gain from this study is worth the cost—including the horrible self-knowledge the study brought to the participants, or the stress they experienced. This question has been hotly debated, and, in truth, contemporary standards would probably forbid any replication of the Milgram procedure. None of this, however, takes anything away from the main message of the data—namely, how little it takes to pull people toward obedience with extreme and seemingly inhuman commands.

Why were Milgram's participants so obedient? Part of the answer may lie in how each of us thinks about commands and obedience. In essence, when we are following other people's orders, we feel that it is they, and not we, who are in control; they, and not we, who are responsible. The soldier following a general's order and the employee following the boss's command may see themselves merely as the agents who execute another's will: the hammer that strikes the nail, not the carpenter who wields it. As such, they are absolved of responsibility—or, if the actions are bad ones, absolved of guilt.

This feeling of being another person's instrument, with little or no sense of personal responsibility, can be promoted in various ways. One way is by increasing the *psychological distance* between one's own actions and their end result. To explore this possibility, Milgram ran a variation of his procedure in which two "teachers" were involved: one a confederate who administered the shocks, and the other—actually, the real participant—who had to perform subsidiary tasks such as reading the words over a microphone and recording the learner's responses. In this new role, the participant was still an essential part of the experiment, because if he stopped, the victim would receive no further shocks. In this variation, though, the participant was more removed from the impact of his actions, like a minor cog in a bureaucratic machine. After all, he did not do the actual shocking! Under these conditions, over 90% of the participants went to the limit, continuing with the procedure even at the highest level of shock (Milgram, 1963, 1965; see also Kilham & Mann, 1974).

If obedience is increased by decreasing an individual's sense of personal responsibility, does the opposite hold as well? To answer this question, Milgram decreased the psychological distance between what the teacher did and its effect on the victim. Rather than being out of sight in an experimental cubicle, the victim was now seated directly adjacent to the teacher. Instead of merely pressing a lever, the teacher also had to press the victim's hand down on a shock electrode, by force if necessary. (The teacher's own hand was encased in an insulating glove "to protect it from the shock"; Figure 13.3). Now compliance dropped considerably, in analogy to the fact that it is easier to drop bombs on an unseen enemy than to plunge a knife into his body when he looks you in the eye. Even so, 30% of the subjects still obeyed to the end. (For further discussion of this and related issues, see Miller, 1986.)

13.3 *Obedient teacher pressing the learner's hand upon the "shock electrode"*

In addition to emphasizing his role as merely another's instrument, the obedient person has other ways to reinterpret the situation, to diminish any sense of culpability. One of the most common approaches is to put on psychic blinders and try to ignore the fact that the victim is a living, suffering fellow being. According to one of Milgram's participants, "You really begin to forget that there's a guy out there, even though you can hear him. For a long time I just concentrated on pressing the switches and reading the words" (Milgram, 1974, p. 38). This *dehumanization of the victim* allows the participant to think of the victim as an object, not a person, reducing (and perhaps eliminating) any sense of guilt at harming another individual. (Bernard, Ottenberg, & Redl, 1965).

The dehumanization of the victim in Milgram's study has a clear parallel outside of the laboratory: Enemies in war and victims of atrocities are rarely described as people, but instead are referred to as bodies, objects, pests, and numbers. This dehumanization is propped up by euphemistic jargon. The Nazis used terms such as *final solution* (for the mass murder of 6 million people) and *special treatment* (for death by gassing); the nuclear age contributed *fallout problem* and *preemptive attack*; the Vietnam War gave us *free-fire zone* and *body count*; other wars gave *ethnic cleansing* and *collateral damage*—all dry, official phrases that are admirably suited to keep the thoughts of blood and human suffering at a psychologically safe distance.

Thus, people can rely on two different strategies to let themselves off the moral hook—a cognitive reorientation through which the person feels that another person, and not she herself, is responsible for her actions, and also a shift in how the victim is perceived—as an object, not as a person. It is important to realize, however, that neither of these intellectual adjustments is achieved in an instant. Instead, inculcation is gradual, making it important that the initial act of obedience be relatively mild and not seriously clash with the person's own moral outlook. But then, with that step taken, each successive step can be slightly different from the one before. This, of course, was the pattern in Milgram's study, which created a *slippery slope* that participants slid down unawares. A similar program of progressive escalation was used in the indoctrination of death-camp guards in Nazi Germany and prison-camp guards in Somalia. The same is

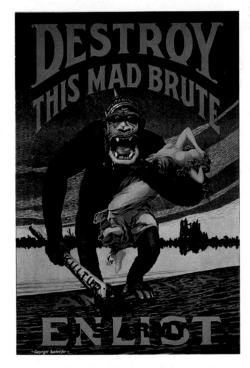

Dehumanizing the opponent **In wartime, propaganda posters routinely dehumanize the opponent, as this World War I poster turns the German enemy into a gorilla savaging the innocent maiden. This dehumanization helps motivate the populace in support of the war effort and also diminishes any sense of guilt about acts of aggression conducted against the enemy.**

true for the military training of soldiers everywhere. Draftees go through "basic train-ing," in part to learn various military skills, but much more importantly, to acquire the habit of instant obedience. Raw recruits are rarely asked to point their guns at another person and shoot. It's not only that they don't know how; it's that most of them proba-bly wouldn't do it.

MILGRAM'S STUDY, THE PERSON, AND THE SITUATION

Milgram's results are a pointed reminder that the situation in which people find them-selves is a powerful determinant of what they do, perhaps more important than the sort of people they are. Everyone knows that this is true for many situations of everyday life; virtually everyone waits their turn in the grocery check-out line, even if they are gener-ally rebellious; almost everyone obeys when the doctor says, "cough," even if they do not respect authorities.

But it is a sobering surprise that a situation such as Milgram's would lead two-thirds of his participants to impose serious pain and harm on another person. And, in fact, it is a surprise to experts just as much as it is to ordinary people. Before Milgram pub-lished his results, he described his study to several groups of experts, including a group of 40 psychiatrists. All of them predicted that he would encounter a great deal of defi-ance. In their view, only a pathological fringe of at most 2% of the participants would go to the maximum shock intensity.

As we now know, the experts' predictions were far off the mark. Clearly, Milgram's results highlight the role of the situation in determining what people do, and so argue against an extreme version of the person-centered view apparently held by these experts—and also expressed by the investigators who studied authoritarianism (see pp. 484–485). But let us be careful not to over-state these points: Situational factors are plainly crucial in governing how we behave, but this should not blind us to the fact that personal factors also matter. The fact that two-thirds of Milgram's participants obeyed to the bitter end is surprising and deeply disturbing. But it is no less true that another third did not obey. Obviously, therefore, the situation shapes people's behavior, but the situation does not influence every single person in the same way. It seems, then, that our account of behavior will have to include both the situation's role *and* the role played by the values, habits, and priorities that each of us brings to the situation. (We return to this issue in Chapter 15.)

COMPLIANCE

When we conform or obey, we change our behaviors because of pressure from groups or commands from authority. But often we alter the way we act for a much milder, more mundane reason: Someone asks us to do so. And so compliance with a request is a third route through which other people bring about changes in our behavior.

According to Robert Cialdini, we often feel most compelled to comply with a request when the requester has done something for us in the past (Cialdini, 1993; Cialdini & Goldstein, 2004). This is because the **norm of reciprocity** is a powerful engine of behav-ior, not only in humans, but also in many other species as well. Cialdini argues that accepting a favor necessarily leads to a sense of indebtedness. We feel that we must repay a donor, even if we did not want his gift in the first place. For example, Cialdini cites the experience of the American Disabled Veterans organization, which uses mail appeals for donations. For a regular appeal, the response rate is 18%. But when the appeal letter comes with a "gift" (address labels), the response rate doubles. Even peo-ple who have no use at all for address labels feel obligated to reciprocate and do so by donating. Another context in which the reciprocity rule is operative is bargaining. The seller states her price. The potential buyer says no. Now the seller makes a concession by offering the item (the house, the car, or whatever) at a lower price. This exerts pressure on the buyer to increase his offer; since the seller offered a concession, he feels that he ought to give a little too.

This pattern is well known to many salespeople but can also be demonstrated experimentally. In one study, an experimenter approached people walking on a university campus and first made a very large request—asking them to work as unpaid volunteer counselors in a juvenile detention center for 2 hours a week over a 2-year period. Not a single person agreed. Using the *door-in-the-face technique*, the experimenter then made a much smaller request: that they accompany a group of boys or girls from the juvenile detention center on a single 2-hour trip to the zoo. When this smaller request came on the heels of the large request that had been refused, 50% of the people consented. In contrast, only 17% of the people acceded to the smaller request when it was not preceded by the larger demand. Apparently, the experimenter's concession (abandoning her large request and moving to the smaller one) made the people feel that they should make a concession of their own, saying yes even though they were initially inclined to say no (Cialdini et al., 1975).

A variant of this technique is the *that's-not-all technique*. Here, however, compliance is not produced by decreasing an initially outrageous request. Instead, compliance is produced by improving an initially rather modest deal, and in this way pulling for reciprocation. This technique is well known from late-night commercials promising that, say, for $19.99 one will receive a dozen steak knives and—that's not all—one will also receive a free knife sharpener. One study demonstrated the power of this technique during a bake sale in which some customers were told that for 75 cents they could buy a cupcake and then were told—after a pause—that for this price the seller would also include a small bag of cookies. Compared to customers who were presented with the cupcake and cookies at the same time, those exposed to the that's-not-all technique were nearly twice as likely to purchase cupcakes (Burger, 1986; see also Burger, Reed, DeCesare, Rauner, & Rozolis, 1999).

These techniques, based on reciprocity, are clearly powerful, and part of their power (and that of other compliance techniques as well) stems from their covert operation. Our reaction to indebtedness is fast, almost automatic, and that is why salespeople (and donation-seekers and many others) rely on these procedures. As Cialdini (1993) suggests, this is one reason why it is so important to learn about these techniques—awareness is the first step in resisting them.

"That's-not-all" technique *Advertisers often make use of this technique.*

LEADERSHIP

While ordinary people are subject to and use conformity, obedience, and compliance every day, leaders use them to much greater effect. After all, leaders have greater power to shape the norms to which people are conforming, have more authority to require obedience, and have more resources with which to request compliance. And so leadership becomes an important fourth lever of social influence.

GREAT PEOPLE AND GREAT SITUATIONS

Where do leaders come from? From one perspective, the great events that play out on the world stage transpire because of exceptional individuals who, for better or worse, determine the course of human events. In the nineteenth century, the proponents of this *great-person theory* often cited the case of Napoléon Bonaparte—a political and military genius, they argued, whose brilliant mind and unyielding will overcame all opposition for over two decades (see, for example, Carlyle, 1841).

A

Leadership—person or situation *(A) Some historians focus on the personality of the individual leader. To them, Napoléon was a military and political genius who shaped history. (B) Others see the leader in the context of the total situation in which he finds himself. To them, instead of history being made by Napoléon, Napoléon was the creation of history. (Napoléon on the Battlefield of Eylau, February 9, 1807, 1808, by Jean-Antoine Gros, Louvre, Paris)*

B

Bill Gates   Would today's software look like it does without Bill Gates or Steve Jobs?

From another perspective, however, the success or failure of individuals like Napoléon is determined by the times in which they lived. Thus, in the view of the great Russian novelist Leo Tolstoy, Napoléon's initial successes were caused by circumstance: the ineptitude of the opposing generals, the zeal of the French soldiers, the huge armies under his command. When Napoléon finally failed, it was not because his genius deserted him, but because of the ferocious Russian winter, the long supply lines, and so on (Tolstoy, 1868).

The same controversy has arisen in analyses of many other historical events. Would there have been a Bolshevik Revolution if Vladimir Lenin had remained exiled from Russia? Would American women have gotten the vote by 1920 without the efforts of Susan B. Anthony? Would the civil rights movement in the United States have captured the people's imagination without the participation of Martin Luther King Jr.? Would the terrorism of September 11, 2001, have been averted if Osama Bin Laden had been killed earlier? The controversy also occurs when we consider intellectual and cultural leadership. Would the theory of natural selection have gained prominence in nineteenth-century biology without Darwin? Would the human genome project have been undertaken without Watson and Crick's labors a half century earlier? Would today's software look like it does without Bill Gates or Steve Jobs? The two poles of the argument, one stressing the genius of the great leader and the other stressing the social context, have surfaced again and again (Burns, 1978; Hook, 1955; Jennings, 1972; Weisberg, 1986).

This debate among historians has its counterpart in an issue we considered in our discussion of obedience: Do we (and should we) attribute a person's actions to his dispositional qualities or to the situation? To be sure, most behaviors studied in the social psychologist's laboratory do not have the momentous quality of those performed by history's leaders. But the underlying questions are quite similar. Do we attribute the participant's changing report of his perceptions to something within him (e.g., he's gullible) or to something in the situation (e.g., everyone else favors a particular answer)? Similarly for issues in history: Do we attribute Napoléon's defeat to something within him (e.g., his genius finally flagged) or to something in the situation (e.g., the fact that the combined armies of England, Russia, and Prussia were too powerful)?

One way to pursue this issue is by asking whether all—or most—successful leaders share any personal characteristics. The great-person theory would predict that they do, that a Napoléon would in all likelihood have achieved leadership even if he had never entered the military. The alternative view, in contrast, implies that there are no special qualities that identify a leader. Napoléon, in effect, just happened to be in the right place at the right time; if someone else with very different qualities had been in his role, the outcome would have been the same. What evidence can social psychology offer in choosing between these positions? Are there identifiable "leadership qualities"?

STUDIES OF LEADERSHIP

What qualities might make for a great leader? To find out, in an early study of leadership, Kurt Lewin (1939) randomly assigned 10-year-old boys to attend one of three after-school activity groups. Each group was led by an adult, and Lewin instructed the adults to adopt one of three *leadership styles*. One was a *laissez-faire* leadership style, in which the adult simply let the boys do as they wished. A second leadership style was the *autocratic* style, in which the adult made all of the decisions about the boys' activities. The third leadership style was a *democratic* style, in which the adult encouraged the boys to decide among themselves what activities to pursue.

Lewin found that the laissez-faire style neither was satisfying for the boys nor led to a large number of completed projects. The other two leadership styles, however, had competing strengths. The autocratic style was the most efficient and led to the greatest number of completed projects, but the boys seemed less involved in the activities, and the crafts that they made were judged to be of inferior quality. The democratic style, by contrast, led to greater satisfaction and less aggression among the boys, but it was less efficient in terms of crafts produced than the autocratic style.

Since Lewin's classic study, research on effective leadership styles has been a central concern of psychologists seeking ways to make organizations such as businesses and universities more efficient. One message from this research is that we cannot focus just on the leader herself, because the situation the leader confronts may be just as important as the leader's own personal characteristics (Bass, 1981; Gerstner & Day, 1994; Hollander, 1985). For example, E. van de Vliert (2006) analyzed survey responses from managers in 61 cultures and found that autocratic (as opposed to democratic) leadership was seen as more effective in resource-poor countries, but less effective in resource-rich countries.

Even within a single country, the situation itself matters, and so the person who is an effective leader of one group may not be effective with some other group. This should not be surprising, since, for example, the qualities that make for leadership on a corporate board of directors are surely different from those that make for leadership in a seminary, Scout troop, or research laboratory (Fiedler, 1978). Can we say anything, though, about the "match" that is needed between a leader's qualities and the nature of a situation? One key lies in the fact that, in some settings, the top priority is to get a certain task done; in other settings, what really matters is a nurturing of relationships among group members, so that (among other benefits) they will be able to work well together in the future. Leaders clearly differ in how they balance these goals against each other, and so this becomes one crucial regard in which the leader will be effective only if he has the qualities needed for a particular setting (Peterson & Behfar, 2005; P. B. Smith et al., 1989).

Even with all these variations, though, the fact remains that there are certain traits that most leaders seem to have: People who are seen as leaders tend to be more outgoing and more dominant than those not considered leaders (see, for example, Kenny & Zaccaro, 1983; Lord, DeVader, & Alliger, 1986). Leaders also tend to be more intelligent, although practical and creative intelligence seem much more involved than traditional IQ measures of intelligence (Riggio & Murphy, 2002; see also Chapter 14).

As it turns out, there are also certain situations that help to make a leader effective. Relatively favorable situations are those in which the leader has considerable authority, the task to be performed is clear cut, and the group members get along with each other and with the leader. To the extent that any of these conditions do not apply, the situation is unfavorable. It seems, then, that both the personal characteristics of would-be leaders and the situations they confront determine how effective they will be.

GROUP DYNAMICS

So far in this chapter, we have described social interaction as though the influence were a "one-way street": A leader directs his followers. The group presses you toward conformity. A salesperson leads you toward a concession. But, of course, social interactions often involve mutual influence—with each person in the group having an impact on every other person in the group. The study of this sort of interaction is the study of *group dynamics*, and it is this aspect of social psychology to which we now turn, first considering how people behave in groups, then how they think in groups, and finally, when (and whether) members of a group help one another.

BEHAVING IN GROUPS

To set the context for how group members influence each other, we first turn to one of the earliest observations of the effects of others—termed *mere presence effects* because these effects seem to arise simply because other people are present.

MERE PRESENCE EFFECTS

More than a century ago, Norman Triplett noticed that cyclists performed better when they competed against others than when they competed against the clock (Triplett, 1898). This observation inspired him to conduct one of social psychology's first experiments, in which he told children to turn a fishing reel as quickly as they could either alone or with another child. Triplett found that children turned the reel more quickly when they were with others than when they were alone.

This initial finding was subsequently replicated many times, and initial results suggested that the social effect is beneficial. When with others who are engaged in the same task, people learn simple mazes more quickly and perform more multiplication problems in the same period of time. Such effects have been grouped under the general

Mere presence effects   Performance is often better in a group setting.

heading *social facilitation* (Allport, 1920). Other studies, however, soon began to accumulate showing that the presence of others can sometimes hinder rather than help. While college students are faster at solving simple mazes when working with others, they are considerably slower when the mazes are more complex (Hunt & Hillery, 1973; Zajonc, 1965, 1980). An audience can evidently lead to *social inhibition* as well as social facilitation. How can such divergent results be reconciled?

Robert Zajonc (1965) argued that the presence of other people increases our arousal, which strengthens the tendency to perform highly dominant responses—the ones that seem to come automatically. When the dominant response is also the correct one, as in performing simple motor skills or learning simple mazes, social presence should help. But when the task gets harder, as in the case of complex mazes, then the dominant response is often incorrect. As a result, performance gets worse when others watch, for in that case the dominant response (enhanced by increased arousal) inhibits the less dominant but correct reaction.

Evidence supporting this view comes from an incredibly wide array of studies. In one study, for example, researchers observed pool players in a college union building. When good players were watched by an audience of four others, their accuracy rose from 71 to 80%. But when poor players were observed, their accuracy became even worse than it was before, dropping from 35 to 25% (Michaels, Bloomel, Brocato, Linkous, & Rowe, 1982). Remarkably, similar effects can be observed even in organisms very different from humans. For example, in one study, cockroaches learned to escape from a bright light by running down a simple alley or by learning a maze. Some performed alone; others were run in pairs. When in the alley, the cockroaches performed better in pairs than alone—for this simple task, the dominant response was appropriate. The reverse was true for the maze—for this more complex task, the dominant response was incorrect and inappropriate (Zajonc, Heingertner, & Herman, 1969).

Recently, Zajonc's long-dominant account of the mere presence effect has been challenged by researchers who have suggested that changes in attention—rather than arousal per se—may be critical to mere presence effects. In one study, Pascal Huguet and colleagues (1999) examined the specific role of attentional factors by presenting participants with the Stroop task (Stroop, 1935). Recall from Chapter 8 that in this task, participants are asked to report the color in which words or symbols are presented. This is an easy task except when color words (e.g., *red*) are presented in font colors that do not match the meaning of the word (e.g., *red* is presented in blue). In such cases, participants are noticeably slower to respond, because the automatic response is to identify the word, and not the color of the font. Huguet reasoned that if the dominant-response view were correct, social presence should compromise performance. By contrast, if social presence narrowed attention, participants should find it easier—not harder—to focus on the aspect of the word that was task relevant, namely, the color of the font. Huguet found that social presence decreased the Stroop effect, in line with an attentional account.

SOCIAL LOAFING

Mere-presence studies are, in essence, concerned with how the presence of an audience affects an individual's performance. But, in many circumstances, there is no distinction between the performer and the audience. Consider, for example, a committee working on an administrative project, or a management team. In cases like these, everyone is a performer and everyone is audience, because every member of the group is contributing to the overall product and, likewise, everyone is able to view, and perhaps to evaluate, the others' contributions. How do group members influence each other in this setting?

Social loafing   *In a tug-of-war, each person seems to pull as hard as he can, but the total force exerted by the group tends to be less than would be the sum of the members' solo efforts.*

In 1913, a French engineer named Max Ringelmann explored this question; he found, for example, that when a group of men pulled on a rope, each pulled less vigorously than if he were pulling alone (Ringelmann, 1913; see also Aronson, Wilson, & Akert, 2005). To describe this phenomenon, Bibb Latané (1981) coined the term *social loafing*, and showed that when individuals work as a group on a common task, all doing the same thing, they often generate less total effort than they would if they each worked alone. In a variant of Ringelmann's original study, Latané and colleagues found that one man working alone pulled with an average force of 139 pounds, while groups of eight pulling together averaged 546 pounds—only about 68 pounds per person. In another study, students were asked to clap and cheer as loudly as they could, sometimes alone, sometimes in groups of two, four, or six. Here, too, the results showed social loafing: Each person cheered and clapped less vigorously the greater the number of others she was with (Latané, Williams, & Harkins, 1979). This general finding that individuals work less hard in groups has now been replicated many times in the United States, India, and China (Karau & Williams, 1993).

Why do individuals work less hard when they are in groups? One reason is that they may feel less accountable, and therefore are less motivated to try as hard as they can. Another reason is that they may think that their contribution is not crucial to group success (Harkins & Szymanski, 1989). There is an old adage: "Many hands make light work." The trouble is that they do not always make it as light as they could.

DEINDIVIDUATION

Under some circumstances, the presence of others does not just inhibit or facilitate behaviors. Instead, it dramatically changes how we act, with people in crowds behaving very differently from the way they do when alone. In a riot or lynch mob, for example, people express aggression with a viciousness that would be inconceivable if they acted in isolation. In a tightly packed auditorium, they become fearful and frantic when someone shouts "Fire!" In a crowd that gathers to watch some disturbed person on a ledge atop a tall building, they often taunt the would-be suicide, urging him to jump. What does the crowd do to its members to make them act so differently from their everyday selves?

One perspective on these questions describes crowd behavior as a kind of mass madness. This view was first offered by Gustav Le Bon (1841–1931), a French writer who contended that people in crowds become wild, stupid, and irrational, and give vent to primitive impulses. Their emotion spreads by a sort of contagion, rising to an ever-higher pitch as more and more crowd members become affected. Thus, fear becomes terror, hostility turns into murderous rage, and each crowd member becomes a barbarian—"a grain of sand among other grains of sand, which the wind stirs up at will" (Le Bon, 1895).

Le Bon's views were plainly shaped by his political prejudices, but even so, many modern psychologists believe that Le Bon's claims contain an important truth. To them, the key to crowd behavior is *deindividuation*, a state in which an individual in a group loses awareness of herself as a separate individual. This state is more likely to occur when there is a high level of arousal and anonymity—just as it would be in a large and angry crowd, or a large and fearful gathering. Deindividuation tends to release impulsive actions that are normally under restraint, and what the impulses are depends on the group and the situation. In a carnival, the (masked) revelers may join in wild orgies; in a lynch mob, the group members may torture or kill (Diener, 1979; Festinger, Pepitone, & Newcomb, 1952; Zimbardo, 1969).

To study deindividuation, one investigation had college students wear identical robes and hoods that made it impossible to identify them. Once in these hoods—which, not coincidentally, looked just like Ku Klux Klan robes—the students were asked to deliver an electric shock to another person; they delivered twice as much shock as those not wearing the robes (Zimbardo, 1970). In these robes, it seemed, the students felt free to "play the part"—and, in this case, the result was ugly. Other studies, though, reveal the good that can be produced by deindividuation. In a different experiment, students were asked to wear nurses' uniforms, rather than KKK costumes; dressed in this way, students delivered less shock than a group without costume (Johnson & Downing, 1979). Thus, deindividuation is not by itself bad—it simply makes it easy for us to give in to the impulses cued by the situation, and the nature of those impulses depends on the circumstances.

Notice, then, that deindividuation can be produced in several different ways. Being in a large crowd produces deindividuation; this is part of why mobs act as they do. Wearing a mask can also produce deindividuation, largely because of the anonymity the mask provides. But deindividuation can also result merely from someone's wearing a uniform and having an assigned role—in essence, he "becomes" the role. This was plainly revealed in a classic demonstration in which Philip Zimbardo transformed the basement of Stanford University's psychology department into a mock prison and randomly assigned undergraduates to the role of either guards or prisoners (Haney, Banks, & Zimbardo, 1973; Zimbardo, 1973; see also Haney & Zimbardo, 1998). Guards and prisoners wore uniforms appropriate to their roles, and prisoners were given prisoner numbers, which were used in interacting with them. The experimenter gave the participants few instructions, and few constraints were placed on their behavior. What rapidly evolved, however, was a set of behaviors remarkably similar to those observed in actual prisons—with cruelty, inhumane treatment, and massive disrespect evident in all the participants. The behaviors observed were sufficiently awful that Zimbardo terminated the *Stanford Prison Study* earlier than intended, before things got really out of hand.

Sadly, the powerful effects of deindividuation and stepping into a role extend well beyond the confines of the laboratory setting. One now-infamous real-world example is the abusive behavior exhibited by military guards in 2004 at Abu Ghraib prison in Iraq near Baghdad. American soldiers made prisoners strip, stacked them in pyramids, and humiliated them. They also hooded them and attached wires to them, leading them to believe they would be shocked or even killed. Worldwide condemnation of this abuse was swift, and Americans struggled to understand how their own countrymen and countrywomen could behave in such an unconscionable fashion. Mindful of the lessons of the Stanford Prison Study, though, Zimbardo and other social psychologists have argued that powerful social forces were at work here that included—among others—the power of deindividuation through reducing people to

Deindividuation   (A) Some deindividuation effects are harmless. (B) Others represent a menace to a humane, democratic society.

FAIRNESS

It should not be surprising that we need to distinguish among these relationship types, because, after all, someone's relationship with her boss is different from her relationship with her best friend, each following its own rules, each having its own character. Her relationships with her next-door neighbor or with a waitress in a restaurant have their own distinctive features. Thus, it would be appropriate to express gratitude to the waitress by leaving a tip at the end of the meal; it would be an offense to do the same at the end of dinner at a friend's house. It would be appropriate to ask one's neighbor for a favor ("As long as you're going to the store, could you buy me a quart of milk?"); it would be quite awkward to make the same request to one's boss.

It seems clear, then, that we need some taxonomy of relationships in order to describe and explain these various differences; that is why the framework just discussed, with its four types of relationships, seems so important. In addition, this cataloguing of relationship types also helps us with some further questions. For example, several times in this chapter we have highlighted the importance of *reciprocity*, but why is reciprocity so important? One answer is cast in terms of self-interest: "I do things for you because I know that you will therefore do things for me, and so I give you a gift, or I do you a favor, because that way I will get something in return." A different answer, though, is cast in terms of *fairness*: "It's not fair if you take more than you give back, or receive more favors than you grant." From this point of view, reciprocity is just a means of ensuring parity, and therefore fairness.

Which view is right? Is reciprocity, at its heart, a matter of self-interested tit-for-tat? Or is it a means of achieving parity and so preserving fairness? The answer depends on the relationship type. If your best friend does some extra work on a shared project, you might regard that as unfair, and so you do a little extra yourself to restore balance. If, however, you are negotiating a purchase price for a used car, you probably will not worry about being fair to the salesperson; if you make a concession, it is in hopes of getting a better deal.

Do people really care about fairness? To find out, researchers have employed the **ultimatum task**. The task involves two people who are told that they are going to share a cash prize, but the two have to figure out for themselves how they will share it. One of the people in the pair—let us call him the "divider"—is asked to decide how the prize should be divided, and so he can, if he wishes, decide on a 50-50 split, a 90-10 split, or any other split he chooses. But then it is the other player's turn. The second person— call her the "decider"—cannot alter the divider's proposal. What she can do is to either accept the proposal (in which case, the money is divided as the divider proposed) or reject the proposal altogether (in which case, neither player gets anything). Notice, then, that the divider offers the decider a strict, "take-it-or-leave-it" proposal; this is how the ultimatum task gets its name.

From a standpoint of crass economic self-interest, what should the players do? The divider should presumably make an offer that leaves him with most of the money, and offer the decider just a few pennies. And the decider should accept this offer, on the simple logic that she is better off with a few pennies than with nothing—and nothing is what she will get if she turns the offer down.

In truth, though, players in this situation usually do not act in this self-interested fashion. Those in the divider's role typically offer a fair division of the cash, even though they could logically get away with keeping more and giving away less. In short, the dividers tend to prize *fairness* over *self-interest*. The same is true for the deciders: They tend to reject offers that are not fair, apparently preferring nothing over the prospect of a small pittance based on an inequitable division (Bazerman, 1998; Guth, Schmittberger, & Schwarze, 1982; Medin, Schwartz, Blok, & Birnbaum, 1999).

Why do people act this way? As we have proposed, the answer, in large part, lies in the nature of the relationship. This is evident in the fact that, if the instructions for the ultimatum task are changed slightly, altering the type of relationship between the players, then people do behave in a fashion guided more by self-interest than by fairness (Medin &

The ultimatum task *Participants in the ultimatum task are told they must figure out how to divide a cash prize. When participants are given an unfair offer, they frequently reject it, even though this means that neither they nor the divider receive any money. Why do they do this? One answer is that their behavior is guided by fairness. Consistent with this interpretation, when participants reject an unfair offer, they report feeling satisfaction, and they show increased levels of activation in brain regions associated with reward processing.*

Bazerman, 1999). And, strikingly, when participants are guided by a sense of fairness, their behaviors seem to be influenced by emotional responses as much as by carefully reasoned intellectual principles. Evidence for this point comes from a neuroimaging study demonstrating that when participants show increased levels of activation in brain regions associated with negative emotion, they are more likely to reject the unfair offer (Sanfey, Rilling, Aronson, Nystrom, & Cohen, 2003). Likewise, when participants in the ultimatum task reject a patently unfair offer, they report feeling satisfaction; indeed, a neuroimaging study shows that such rejections are associated with increased levels of activation in brain regions associated with reward processing (de Quervain et al., 2004; Knutson, 2004).

ATTRACTION

As we have seen, some relationships have a frankly economic basis; some are rooted in fairness. Some relationships are based on pragmatic needs, but others are grounded in the affection one partner feels for another. But this last point—about "affection"—itself demands several new questions: What is it that draws people together? To whom are we attracted? How might we win their affections? We first addressed these questions in Chapter 2, when considering the biological roots of mate selection. We will now flesh out the story by considering these issues from the vantage point of social psychology.

PROXIMITY

As we saw earlier (Chapter 2), one important determinant of interpersonal attraction is physical appearance. This of course accords with common sense—we naturally prefer a partner whom we find physically attractive to a partner we find physically repulsive. But as we also saw in Chapter 2, there is much more to attraction than physical attractiveness. Another important factor is sheer proximity.

By now, dozens of studies have shown that if you want to predict who will make friends with whom, the first thing to ask is who is nearby. Students who live next to each other in a dormitory or sit next to each other in classes develop stronger relations than those who live or sit only a bit farther away. Similarly, members of a bomber crew become much friendlier toward fellow crew members who work right next to them than toward others only a few feet away (Berscheid, 1985; Berscheid & Walster, 1978).

What holds for friendship also holds for mate selection. The statistics are rather impressive. For example, of all the couples who took out marriage licenses in Columbus, Ohio, during the summer of 1949, more than half were people who lived within 16 blocks of each other when they went out on their first date (Clarke, 1952). Much the same holds for the probability that an engagement will ultimately lead to marriage; the farther apart the two live, the greater the chance that the engagement will be broken off (Berscheid & Walster, 1978).

Why should proximity be so important? Part of the answer simply involves logistics rather than psychology, because you cannot like someone you have never met, and the chances of meeting that someone are much greater if he is nearby. But, in addition, it turns out that getting to know someone makes him more *familiar* to you, and familiarity in turn is itself a source of attraction.

In fact, there is a good deal of evidence that people tend to like what is familiar. This seems to hold for just about any stimulus, whether it is a word in a foreign language, a melody, or the name of a commercial product—the more often it is seen or heard, the better it will be liked (Brickman & D'Amato, 1975; Moreland & Zajonc, 1982; Zajonc, 1968). Familiarity probably plays an important role in determining what we feel about other people as well. The hero of the musical *My Fair Lady* explains his affection for the heroine by singing, "I've grown accustomed to her face." In a more prosaic vein, the laboratory provides evidence that photographs of strangers' faces are judged to be more likable the more often they have been seen (Jorgensen & Cervone, 1978). Another study

"Do you really love me, Anthony, or is it just because I live on the thirty-eighth floor?"

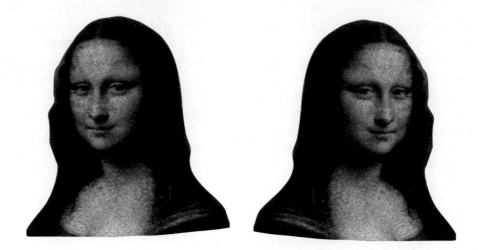

13.7 Familiarity and liking *The figure shows two versions of a rather well-known lady. Which do you like better—the one on the right or the one on the left?* *(Please turn to p. 508.)*

applied this general idea to the comparison of faces and their mirror images. Which will be better liked? If familiarity is the critical variable, then our friends should prefer a photograph of our face to one of its mirror image, since they have seen the first much more often than the second. But we ourselves should prefer the mirror image, which for us is by far the more familiar. The results were as predicted by the familiarity hypothesis (Mita, Dermer, & Knight, 1977; Figure 13.7).

SIMILARITY

Another important factor that influences attractiveness is *similarity*, but in which direction does the effect run? Do people like others who are similar to themselves, or do they prefer those who are very different? To put it differently, which bit of folk wisdom is more accurate: "Birds of a feather flock together" or—perhaps in analogy with magnets— "Opposites attract"? It appears that birds have more to teach us in this matter than magnets do, for the evidence suggests that, in general, people tend to like others who are similar to themselves. For example, elementary school students prefer other children who perform about as well as they do in academics, sports, and music (Tesser, Campbell, & Smith, 1984), and best friends in high school resemble each other in age, race, year in school, and high-school grades (Kandel, 1978).

Often people who attract each other do differ in important personality characteristics— and so an introvert might find an extrovert attractive; an unaggressive person might be attracted to someone relatively aggressive. On other dimensions, though, similarity is crucial. For example, there is no doubt that attributes such as race, ethnic origin, social and educational level, family background, income, and religion do affect attraction in general

Social interaction   Our social interactions depend on many aspects of the relationship between who we are, and who the person is with whom we are interacting. As one small part of this relationship, if the other person is too different from us, we may not be able to communicate. If the person is too similar to us, we may not be able to sustain the relationship.

and marital choice in particular. Also relevant are behavioral patterns such as the degree of gregariousness and drinking and smoking habits. One widely cited study showed that engaged couples in the United States are generally similar along all of these dimensions (Burgess & Wallin, 1943), a pattern that provides evidence for *homogamy*—a powerful tendency for like to select like.

Another study showed that homogamy also plays a role in determining a couple's stability: Couples who remained together after 2½ years were more similar than those who had broken up (Hill, Rubin, & Peplau, 1976). Married couples also tend to be similar on nearly all personality dimensions (Caspi & Herbener, 1990). However, this association may in part be a function of the longevity of the relationship, given that couples may become more alike over time by virtue of their continual interaction; indeed, some evidence suggests that they grow more similar in their verbal skills, degree of open-mindedness, and even their physical appearance (Gruber-Baldini, Schaie, & Willis, 1995; Zajonc, Adelmann, Murphy, & Niedenthal, 1987).

What produces the homogamy pattern? One possibility is that similarity really does lead to mutual liking, so that homogamy can be taken at face value. A different possibility, though, is that similarity does not matter on its own; instead, the apparent effects of similarity are just a by-product of proximity, of the fact that "few of us have an opportunity to meet, interact with, become attracted to, and marry a person markedly dissimilar from ourselves" (Berscheid & Walster, 1978, p. 87). In truth, the answer is uncertain, but, in either case, the end product is the same: Like pairs with like, and few heiresses ever marry the butler except in the movies. We are not really surprised to discover that when a princess kisses a frog he turns into a prince. But we would be surprised to see the frog turn into a peasant, and then see the princess marry him anyway.

Similarity and attraction **The relationship between Democratic strategist James Carville and Republican strategist Mary Matalin might seem to suggest that opposites attract. Even in this case, however, it is important to note how many dimensions of similarity there actually are.**

LOVE

Attraction tends to bring people closer together. If they are close enough, their relationship may be more than friendship, and in Chapter 2, we discussed the ways animals (including humans) select their mates. What we have not yet done, however, is to consider the emotional relationship between the two members of a mating pair.

Many animals show lasting bonds with their mates, but for humans this bonding often takes on a special meaning and importance, something we celebrate with the term *love*. In fact, love involves many elements: a feeling, a physiological upheaval, a desire for sexual union, a set of living and parenting arrangements, a sharing of resources (from bank accounts to friends), a mutual defense and caretaking pact, a merging of extended families, and more. So complex is human loving that, according to some authorities, psychologists might have been "wise to have abdicated responsibility for analysis of this term and left it to poets" (Reber, 1985, p. 409). Wise or not, psychologists have tried to say some things about this strange state of mind that has puzzled both sages and poets throughout the ages.

Psychologists have tried to distinguish among different kinds of love, and some of the resulting classification systems are rather complex. One scheme tries to analyze love relationships according to the presence or absence of three main components: *intimacy* (feelings of being close), *passion* (sexual attraction), and *commitment* (a decision to stay with one's partner) (Sternberg, 1986, 1988). Other psychologists propose that there are two broad categories of love. One is romantic—or passionate—love, the kind of love that one "falls into," that one is "in." The other is companionate love, a less turbulent state that emphasizes companionship, mutual trust, and care (Hatfield, 1988).

ROMANTIC LOVE

Romantic love has been described as essentially passionate: "a wildly emotional state [in which] tender and sexual feelings, elation and pain, anxiety and relief, altruism and

Romantic love **A passionate form of love characterized by tumultuous emotions and an intense focus on the beloved.**

Revisiting Figure 13.7 The familiarity-leads-to-liking hypothesis would predict a preference for the left panel—a retouched photograph of the Mona Lisa (see p. 506). The panel on the right is a mirror image of that photograph, which is presumably the less familiar of the two.

jealousy coexist in a confusion of feelings" (Berscheid & Walster, 1978). The extent to which the lovers feel that they are in the grip of an emotion they cannot control is indicated by the very language in which they describe their love: They "fall in love," "are swept off their feet," and "can't stop themselves." Perhaps surprisingly, men tend to fall in love more often and more quickly than women do, and women tend to fall out of love more easily than men do (Hill, Rubin, & Peplau, 1976).

The tumultuous emotions of romantic love are sharply focused on the beloved, who is almost always seen through a rosy glow (Averill, 1985). The lover constantly thinks about the beloved and continually wants to be in his or her company, sometimes to the point of near obsession. Given this giddy mixture of erotic, irrational, obsessive passions and idealized fantasy, it is understandable why Shakespeare felt that lovers have much in common with both madmen and poets. They are a bit mad because their emotions are so turbulent and their thoughts and actions so obsessive; they are a bit poetic because they do not see their beloved as he or she really is but as an idealized fabrication of their own desires and imaginings.

According to some authors, romantic love involves two distinguishable elements: a state of physiological arousal, and a set of beliefs and attitudes that leads the person to interpret this arousal as passion. What leads to the arousal itself? One obvious source is erotic excitement, but other forms of stimulation may have the same effect. Fear, pain, and anxiety can all heighten general arousal and so can, in fact, lend fuel to romantic passion. One demonstration of this comes from a widely cited experiment in which men were approached by an attractive young woman who asked them to fill out a questionnaire (allegedly to help her with a class project); she then gave them her telephone number so they could call her later if they wanted to know more about the project. The study was conducted in Capilano Park, just north of Vancouver, British Columbia. The park is famous for its narrow, wobbly suspension bridge, precariously suspended over a shallow rapids 230 feet below. Some of the men in the study were approached while they were on the bridge itself. Others were approached after they had already crossed the bridge and were back on safe and solid ground.

Did the men actually call the young woman later (ostensibly to discuss the experiment, but really to ask her for a date)? The likelihood of their making this call depended on whether they were approached while they were on the bridge or later, after they had crossed it. If they filled out the questionnaire while crossing the bridge—at which point

Arousal and romantic love   Men who interacted with an attractive female experimenter on a bridge like this one were more likely to show interest in her later than men who interacted with the same experimenter on solid ground.

they might well have felt some fear and excitement—the chances were almost one in three that the men would call. If they met the young woman when they were back on safe ground, the chances of their doing so were very much lower (Dutton & Aron, 1974; but see also Kenrick & Cialdini, 1977; Kenrick, Cialdini, & Linder, 1979).

What is going on here? One way to think about it is to call to mind the Schachter-Singer theory of emotion (Chapter 12). Being on the bridge would make almost anyone feel a little jittery—it would, in other words, cause a state of arousal. The men who were approached while on the bridge detected this arousal, but they seem to have misinterpreted their own feelings, attributing their elevated heart rate and sweaty palms not to fear, but to their interest in the woman. Then, having misread their own state in this fashion, they followed through in a sensible way, telephoning a woman whom they believed had excited them.

This sequence of events may help us understand why romantic love seems to thrive on obstacles. Shakespeare tells us that the "course of true love never did run smooth," but if it had, the resulting love probably would have been lacking in ardor. The fervor of a wartime romance or an illicit affair is probably fed in part by danger and frustration, and many a lover's passion becomes all the more intense for being unrequited. In all these cases, there is increased arousal, whether through fear, frustration, or anxiety. This arousal continues to be interpreted as love, a cognitive appraisal that fits in perfectly with our ideas about romantic love, since, after all, these ideas include both the rapture of love and the agony.

An interesting demonstration of this phenomenon is the so-called *Romeo-and-Juliet effect* (named after Shakespeare's doomed couple, whose parents violently opposed their love). This term describes the fact that parental opposition tends to intensify the couple's romantic passion rather than to diminish it. In one study, couples were asked whether their parents interfered with their relationship. The greater this interference, the more deeply the couples fell in love (Driscoll, Davis, & Lipetz, 1972). The moral is that if parents want to break up a romance, their best bet is to ignore it. If the feuding Montagues and Capulets had simply looked the other way, Romeo and Juliet might well have become bored with each other by the end of the second act.

The Romeo and Juliet effect   Parental opposition tends to intensify rather than diminish a couple's romantic passion.

COMPANIONATE LOVE

It is widely agreed that romantic love tends to be a short-lived bloom. That wild and tumultuous state, with its intense emotional ups and downs, with its obsessions, fantasies, and idealizations, rarely, if ever, lasts forever. Eventually there are no further surprises and no further obstacles, except those posed by the inevitable problems of ordinary life. The adventure is over, and romantic love ebbs. Sometimes it turns into indifference or active dislike. Other times (and hopefully more often) it transforms into a related but gentler state of affairs—*companionate love.* This type of love is sometimes defined as the "affection we feel for those with whom our lives are deeply intertwined" (Berscheid & Hatfield, 1978, p. 176). In companionate love, the similarity of outlook, mutual caring, and trust that develop through day-to-day living become more important than the fantasies and idealization of romantic love, as the two partners try to live as happily ever after as it is possible to do in the real world. This is not to say that the earlier passion does not flare up occasionally. But it no longer has the obsessive quality that it once had, in which the lover is unable to think of anything but the beloved (Caspi & Herbener, 1990; Hatfield, 1988; Neimeyer, 1984).

CULTURE AND LOVE

It will come as no surprise that Western conceptions of love are—like the many other conceptions that feature so prominently in our interactions with others—a cultural product. Western cultural notions of what love is and what falling in love feels like have been fashioned by a historical heritage that goes back to Greek and Roman times (with

Companionate love   This type of love is based upon the affection we feel for those with whom our lives are intertwined.

tales of lovers hit by Cupid's arrows), were revived during the Middle Ages (with knights in armor slaying dragons to win a lady's favor), and were finally mass-produced by the Hollywood entertainment machine (with a final fade-out in which boy and girl embrace to live happily ever after). This complex set of ideas about what love is, together with an appropriate potential love object—one who is attractive, of the right age, the right sex, more or less available, and so on—constitutes the context that may lead us to interpret physiological arousal as love.

Similar ideas about romantic love are found in many other cultures: Hindu myths and Chinese love songs, for example, celebrate this form of love, and, indeed, a review of the anthropological research revealed that romantic love was in evidence in 147 of 166 cultures (Jankowiak & Fischer, 1992). Even so, it seems unlikely that any other culture has emphasized romantic love over companionate love to the extent that ours does (e.g., De Rougemont, 1940; Grant, 1976). This is reflected in many ways, including the fact that popular American love songs are only half as likely as popular Chinese love songs to refer to loyalty, commitment, and enduring friendship, all features of companionate love (Rothbaum & Tsang, 1998).

Why do cultures differ in these ways? One proposal derives from a point we have met in many other contexts: the contrast between individualistic and collectivistic cultures. Collectivistic cultures emphasize connection to one's group, and this makes it unsurprising that (collectivistic) China would showcase songs emphasizing loyalty—a focus on the relationship, rather than on each individual's feelings. To put this point differently, note that romantic love often places a high premium on pursuing personal fulfillment (even, and perhaps especially, when it conflicts with other duties). On this basis, it is perhaps unsurprising that romantic love is more likely to be seen as important for marriage in individualistic as compared to collectivistic cultures (Dion & Dion, 1996).

Culture and love **Similar ideas about romantic love are found in many different cultural contexts, including Western, Indian, and Chinese cultures. However, individualistic cultures have tended to emphasize romantic love to a greater degree than collectivistic cultures.**

SOME FINAL THOUGHTS: SITUATIONS, CONSTRUALS, AND HUMAN NATURE

One of the principal lessons of social psychology is that we are not the autonomous, self-driven individuals we conceive ourselves to be. Instead, we are intertwined within a complex web of social and cultural influences that shapes how we feel and behave, how we think and interact in groups, whom we help, and the relationships we form. As we have seen, simply having another person pay attention to us changes our behavior. Far more substantial changes in our behavior arise as we conform to others' expectations, or when we are directly instructed or asked by others to act a certain way. Despite the pervasive impact of these social influences, we frequently fail to appreciate just how powerful they are. As we saw in the context of the Milgram studies, even trained professionals miserably underestimated the power of direct instructions to shock another person.

But if our analysis were to stop here, we would have missed our mark. This is because social psychology also teaches that each of us is far from a passive and helpless player on the social stage. We actively try to make sense of the world around us, and so we work hard to understand what others are doing and thinking, and through our construals we create the realities with which we contend. At the same time, we also make frequent efforts to act directly on our social worlds. Sometimes these efforts have small effects. At other times, as we have seen in our discussion of minority influence, leadership, and relationships, our impact on others can be breathtaking.

A third lesson is that the social forces we have discussed are complicated and can vary across time, place, and culture. Yet there is much commonality, too: Such diverse political theorists as Aristotle, Hobbes, and Confucius are still read despite the fact that they lived many centuries ago and under very different political systems than our own; they wrote about human social behavior that we can recognize even today. History provides many other examples of enduring social reactions. There are records of panics in Roman amphitheaters when the stands collapsed and of riots during sporting events in Byzantium. And the Great Wall of China, the pyramids of South and Central America, and the cathedrals of Europe all testify to the ability of large groups of people to work together and to take direction from a leader. Some of the ancients even used certain propaganda devices that are familiar in modern times. When the city of Pompeii was destroyed by a volcano in A.D. 79, it was evidently in the midst of a municipal election. Modern archeologists have found some of the election slogans on the excavated walls: "Vote for Vatius, all the whoremasters vote for him" and "Vote for Vatius, all the wife-beaters vote for him." While the techniques of the anti-Vatius faction may be a bit crude for our modern taste, they certainly prove that the psychology of the smear campaign has a venerable history (Raven & Rubin, 1976). Phenomena of this sort suggest that people's social nature can produce similar practices, understandings, and products in different times and places.

SUMMARY

SOCIAL INFLUENCE

- *Conformity*, *obedience*, and *compliance* are often denigrated, but these three forms of social influence are necessary for the smooth functioning of any social group.
- In studies by Sherif and by Asch, people's perception of the world was shaped by the way others reported what they perceived. One reason for this conformity was *informational influence*—people's desire to be right. Another reason was *normative influence*—people's desire not to appear foolish. The informational influence is increased when the situation is genuinely ambiguous; this leads to increased *social referencing*. The normative influence is eliminated if people make their responses in private. Conformity is also much reduced if there is any break in the group's unanimity.
- In collectivistic cultures, people appear to be less distressed about conforming than people in individualistic cultures. People in collectivistic cultures are also more likely to conform—but only if they are tied to the group by traditional bonds.
- Some researchers propose that people with *authoritarian personalities* are more inclined to obedience. While there is some support for this claim, there is more powerful evidence for the influence of situations in producing obedience, as reflected in Milgram's famous studies of obedience, in which participants obeyed instructions even if these seemed to lead to injury to another person.
- Obedience is more likely if the individual believes he is not ultimately responsible for the actions, and it is also increased either by a sense of *psychological distance* between one's actions and the result of those actions, or by *dehumanizing the victim*. These adjustments, however, are usually achieved gradually, as the person slides down a *slippery slope* toward total obedience.
- Compliance with requests is often compelled by the *norm of reciprocity*. This is evident in the success of the *door-in-the-face* or the *that's-not-all* techniques.
- Some theorists propose that certain people have specific traits that make them great leaders, and, in fact, certain *leadership styles* do seem particularly effective. However, the success of a leadership style depends on the context (e.g., whether there are ample resources available). In addition, in some settings, an effective leader is one who gets a certain job done; in other settings, an effective leader is one who fosters good relations among the group members.

GROUP DYNAMICS

- In *mere presence effects*, how people behave is influenced by the presence of an audience, although the audience can produce either *social facilitation* or *social inhibition*. This mixed data pattern is often explained by claiming that the audience increases an actor's arousal, and this strengthens the tendency to perform highly dominant responses.
- When people work as a team, often the contribution produced by each team member is less than the work she would have done if she were on her own—an effect known as *social loafing*.
- The presence of other people can cause *deindividuation*, a state in which the individual gives in to the impulses suggested by the situation. Deindividuation can lead to riotous behavior in large groups of people, but it can also lead to increased good behaviors if the situation happens to produce impulses promoting those behaviors. Deindividuation can be produced by anonymity, or by just having an assigned role, as was shown in the *Stanford Prison Study*.
- *Group polarization* refers to a tendency for decisions made by groups to be more extreme than the decisions that would have been made by any of the group members working on his own. This effect arises from several influences, including confirmation bias operating during group discussion, and also from each member of the group trying to take a position at the group's leading edge.
- Group decision making sometimes reveals *groupthink*, in which the group members do all they can to promote group cohesion; as a result, they downplay any doubts or disagreements, and they overestimate the likelihood of success.
- People in groups also seem less likely to help others, and several mechanisms contribute to this *bystander effect* of apathy. One factor is ambiguity in the situation, with many individuals convincing themselves that help is not needed. Another factor is *pluralistic ignorance*, with each individual turning to the others to find out if help is needed; but, with all doing this, each is convinced by the others' inaction that no help is needed. Yet another factor is *diffusion of responsibility*, with each group member able to think that others will be the ones who should help.
- People often choose not to help because they are concerned about the time needed or the risks involved. With all of these points acknowledged, though, the fact remains that people sometimes do engage in altruistic acts of helping—even if doing so puts them in considerable danger.

- In describing the wide diversity of social relationships, psychologists distinguish various *equality matching relationships*, *market pricing relationships*, *communal sharing relationships*, and *authority ranking relationships*.
- These types of relationships differ in many ways, including the role of *reciprocity* within the relationships. In some relationships, reciprocity is fueled by self-interest; in others, it derives from a sense of fairness. People's sensitivity to fairness is well documented in the *ultimatum task*.
- Many relationships are grounded in affection. Affection, in turn, is shaped by many factors, including physical attractiveness, proximity, familiarity, and similarity. Thus, for example, best friends in high school generally resemble each other in age, race, year in school, and grades; this broad tendency for like to select like is called *homogamy*.
- The relationship of *love* involves many elements, including *intimacy*, *passion*, and *commitment*. In addition, psychologists often distinguish two types of love—romantic love and companionate love. *Romantic love* is often tumultuous, and it involves a state of physiological arousal and a set of beliefs that leads the person to interpret this arousal as passion. *Companionate love* involves a similarity of outlook, mutual caring, and trust that develop through day-to-day living together.
- Ideas about romantic love are found in many cultures, but romantic love plays a larger role in individualistic cultures than in collectivistic cultures, plausibly because collectivist cultures emphasize connection and loyalty to one's group, rather than the personal fulfillment often associated with romantic love.

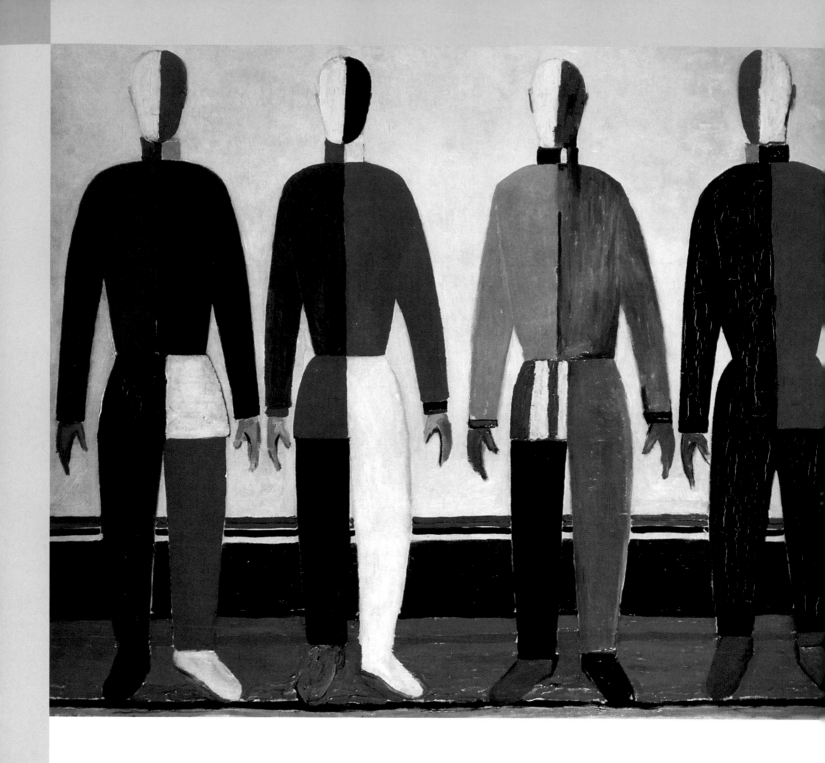

INDIVIDUAL
DIFFERENCES

PART 4

PEOPLE DIFFER FROM ONE ANOTHER IN their height, weight, and eye color. They also vary along many psychological dimensions: Some are proud; others are humble. Some are adventurous; others timid. Some are clever; others slow.

How should we think about these differences from one person to the next? Is there some meaningful way to categorize the various differences, or does the unique nature of each individual defy categorization? Are there ways to measure the differences among us, so that we can decide which person is truly "smarter" than the others, or "more helpful," or "more depressed"? And, above all, where do these various differences come from? This is, of course, a question of why each person is as he or she is: What gives us our intelligence, or our personalities? What role does biology play, and what is the role for our experience—during childhood and across the lifespan?

In tackling these issues, we will begin with the ways in which humans differ in their mental abilities. We will turn next to differences among people in their personalities. Then, in the section's last two chapters, we will consider the more extreme variations that carry some of us outside the "normal" range and into the domain of mental disorder.

someone who is "smart" will be able to conquer all intellectual challenges? Or are there, perhaps, different types of intelligence, so that someone might, for example, have the right sort of intelligence for mathematics but not for studying literature, or the right sort for literature but not the right sort for the world of business?

These questions are interesting for their own sake, but they are also tied to important real-world concerns, because consequential decisions are often shaped by assessments of intelligence. Whether someone gets into a desirable college, for example, or gets a scholarship, is often decided on the basis of a test of her abilities. The same is true for decisions about who gets professional training: Business schools, law schools, medical schools, almost always require an aptitude test as part of the admissions process. Likewise for employment, because many employers use tests to decide whether an applicant writes well, or can learn new tasks quickly. The stakes are high in decisions like these—decisions about who gets the best educational or employment opportunities, or who gets any opportunity at all. These conditions obviously demand that we ask whether the tests are fair and measuring what they are supposed to measure. For both theoretical and pragmatic reasons, therefore, let us examine the relevant science. ●

MENTAL TESTS

Mental tests—measurements of mental abilities—come in many varieties. Some are used to assess *achievement*: They measure what an individual has learned and what skills he has mastered. These tests, therefore, tell us about the test taker's current status, and their results will change as soon as the test taker learns something more.

Other tests are used to assess *aptitude*: They are designed to predict what an individual will be able to do, given the proper training and the right motivation. An example is a test of mechanical aptitude devised to determine the likelihood that an individual will do well as an engineer after an appropriate education. Likewise, the main part of the Scholastic Aptitude Test (SAT), as the name implies, is designed to predict someone's performance in educational settings after high school. (In contrast, the SAT Subject Tests, or "SAT II," are measures of achievement.)

Should we take these tests seriously? Do they measure what they are designed to measure? In order to tackle these issues, we first need to know a bit about how psychologists evaluate measurements using the concepts and vocabulary of statistics.

THE STUDY OF VARIATION

Two hundred years ago, the term *statistics* referred largely to the systematic collection of various state records, such as birth and death rates. In poring over such figures, the Belgian scientist Lambert Adolphe Jacques Quételet (1796–1874) began to see patterns in these numbers, and this realization led him to chart the *frequency distribution* of various observations—that is, how often individual cases fall into different categories, with those categories systematically subdividing the full range of measurements.

For example, Table 14.1 lists the (fictional) height of 50 women. In this format it is difficult to see any pattern at all. The pattern becomes obvious, however, if we summarize these data in terms of a frequency distribution (Table 14.2) and then graph the distribution (Figure 14.1). Now we easily see that the women in this group range in height from 54 inches to 79 inches, but most have a height close to 65 inches. Eight women are in the narrow category that includes this height, and as we move further and further from this middle value, the number of women at each height interval gradually drops.

TABLE 14.1 HEIGHT (IN INCHES) FOR A GROUP OF 50 WOMEN

NAME	HEIGHT (IN INCHES)	NAME	HEIGHT (IN INCHES)
Ann	54.00	Tracey	65.50
Michelle	55.50	Jenny	65.75
Abigail	57.00	Rachel	66.00
Patricia	57.50	Brianna	66.25
Marie	58.25	Amanda	66.75
Erica	58.50	Enriqueta	67.00
Kathryn	59.25	Gretchen	67.00
Angela	60.25	Jeanette	67.25
Allison	60.50	Jessica	67.75
Dina	60.75	Elena	68.00
Jane	61.00	Lynn	68.25
Kelly	61.00	Anna	69.50
Joanna	61.25	Sylvia	69.50
Gena	62.50	Kristina	69.75
Sarah	62.75	Kirsten	70.00
Ingrid	63.00	Chris	70.75
Heather	63.50	Alicia	71.25
Lynn	63.75	Laura	71.50
Deborah	64.00	Eve	71.50
Caitlin	64.00	Jennifer	72.25
Alisha	64.50	Britney	73.50
Elizabeth	64.75	Susan	74.75
Melanie	65.00	Carolyn	76.00
Muriel	65.00	Miriam	77.50
Lois	65.25	Chelsea	79.00

TABLE 14.2 FREQUENCY DISTRIBUTION OF HEIGHTS IN TABLE 14.1

CATEGORY	NUMBER OF CASES
0–54	1
54.25–56.00	1
56.25–58.00	2
58.25–60.00	3
60.25–62.00	6
62.25–64.00	7
64.25–66.00	8
66.25–68.00	7
68.25–70.00	5
70.25–72.00	4
72.25–74.00	2
74.25–76.00	2
76.25–78.00	1
78.25–80.00	1

AVERAGES AND VARIABILITY

Quételet made graphs of frequency distributions for many human attributes—height, weight, waist size, and so on—and realized that, if the sample was large enough, most of these distributions were bell shaped, like the curve in Figure 14.1. To describe such bell-shaped curves, it is usually sufficient to specify just two attributes. First, we must locate the curve's center. This gives us a measure of the "average case"—in Figure 14.1, the average height for women in this group. The most common way of determining this average is to add up all the scores and then divide the sum by the number of scores; this process yields the *mean*. But there are other ways of determining the average as well. For example, it is sometimes convenient to refer to the *median*, which is the score that separates the top 50 percent of the scores from the bottom 50 percent. (In Figure 14.1, the mean and the median are the same, but often this is not the case.)

The second attribute of a bell-shaped curve is its *variability*, or the degree to which individual cases differ from one to the next. A highly variable group will have a frequency distribution that is wide and relatively flat, like the one in Figure 14.2A; a group with little variability will have a frequency distribution that is narrow and steep, like the one in Figure 14.2B.

As one example of why variability is so important, consider the fact that men, on average, earn higher scores than women on some tests of mathematical ability. As we discussed in

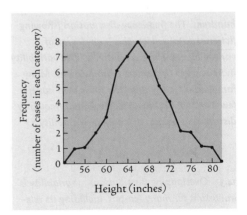

14.1 Graphic display of a frequency distribution *This figure shows the data from Table 14.2 in graphic form. In this format the pattern is easily visible: Most women in this sample have a height close to 65 inches. Values further and further from this middle value are less and less frequent. Each dot represents the frequency of each height (i.e., a row in Table 14.2).*

As we mentioned in Chapter 1, correlations provide a useful measure of the degree to which two variables are related, but they also have an important limitation: They cannot, by themselves, tell us whether there is any cause-and-effect relationship between the variables. Sometimes there is: There is a negative correlation between the number of cigarettes smoked per day and life expectancy (the more cigarettes smoked, the shorter the life expectancy), and the causal link here is well known. But sometimes correlations exist even without a causal connection. For example, there is also a negative correlation between life expectancy and the number of ashtrays an individual owns, but this is not because owning ashtrays is bad for your health. Instead, owning ashtrays is itself associated with cigarette smoking, and smoking is the health risk.

EVALUATING MENTAL TESTS

Galton and his students developed measures of correlation to pursue certain hypotheses (e.g., hypotheses about resemblance between parents and their offspring). It turns out, though, that correlations are also useful for many other purposes, and, in particular, are crucial for a question we posed early on: whether our mental tests measure what they are designed to measure. Specifically, correlations play an essential role in evaluating the *reliability* of these tests, and also their *validity*.

RELIABILITY

One criterion of a test's adequacy is its **reliability**—that is, the consistency with which it measures what it measures. Consider a bathroom scale. Imagine that you step on to the scale, and it shows your weight to be 120 pounds. You step off the scale, surprised by the good news. But then you ask, "Could this be? What about the large pizza I had yesterday?" You step back on to the scale, and it reports your weight as 115 pounds. Puzzled by this change, you step off the scale and quickly back on, and now the scale says you weigh 125 pounds. You would surely conclude that it is time to buy a new scale—this one is not reliable.

This example suggests that one way to assess reliability of a measurement is by administering a test more than once. If we get the same result each time, this indicates that our test is, in fact, reliable. How do we put this logic into practice? We can, as one option, test a group of people twice, allowing some time (perhaps a few weeks) to pass between the first and second test. If the results show that the scores from the first test are correlated with the scores from the second, we can conclude that the test has adequate **test-retest reliability**.

Sometimes, however, we need to assess reliability in a different fashion. To see why, consider a questionnaire designed to measure someone's level of fatigue. This questionnaire is likely to show considerable change from one occasion to the next, and so it would fail any assessment of test-retest reliability. But the problem here is not in the test itself. Instead, the simple fact is that people's level of fatigue changes, and that is why the scores on our test today might not be correlated with the scores from a week ago. Even in this case, though, there is a way to check on reliability: Rather than checking consistency from one test occasion to another, we can check consistency from one question within the test to some other question. Thus, for example, we could ask whether someone's score on the odd-numbered questions on a test is correlated with his score on the even-numbered questions. If a test passes this assessment of **split-half reliability**, we know that the test is consistent in what it measures.

VALIDITY

Reliability tells us whether a test is consistent in its measurements—from one test item to another, or from one occasion to another. But even more important is a test's **validity**,

Thinking about correlations   In thinking about correlations, it may be useful to know that the correlation between height *and* gender *is roughly +.40. This correlation is strong enough that the relationship between these two variables is easy to spot—most people know that men are, on average, taller than women. In other words, most people have, on their own, detected the correlation. But, at the same time, this correlation is weak enough that it is easy to find exceptions to the pattern (tall women, or short men). With stronger correlations (greater than .40), the pattern would be even clearer, and the exceptions fewer.*

defined simply as the extent to which the test measures what it is supposed to measure. Imagine a psychology professor who assigns grades in a course based largely on students' handwriting on the exams. This assessment procedure might be reliable (assuming the professor is consistent in how she evaluates handwriting), but it is surely not valid, since handwriting has nothing to do with mastery of a course's content.

There are actually several ways to evaluate a test's validity. One is *face validity*: whether it makes sense, on reflection, that the test is measuring what it is designed to measure. For example, imagine two intelligence tests: One asks how quickly you can run 100 meters; the other evaluates your performance on a series of word problems. It seems clear that the second test has greater face validity; running quickly does not seem to be the sort of thing to pay attention to if we hope to measure someone's intelligence.

Also helpful is an assessment called *convergent validity*. Imagine that someone's performance on our series of word problems, designed to assess his intelligence, is correlated with his IQ score. In this case, we observe agreement (or convergence) between two measures of intelligence, and this agreement would increase our confidence that the word problems measure what they are supposed to measure.

One might worry, though, that performance on the word problems is correlated with IQ scores for some reason that is separate from intelligence. One possibility, perhaps, is that both tests are heavily influenced by someone's reading speed, so that people who read quickly will do well on both tests; people who read more slowly will do poorly. In that case, performance on the word problems would end up being correlated with IQ score, even if neither test measured what we intended it to measure.

To check on this concern, we might examine the correlation between someone's score on the word problems and some direct measure of reading speed. (We could, for example, give the person a 200-word essay to evaluate, and time how long she needed to read the essay.) A *low* correlation (i.e., a correlation near 0) would indicate *discriminant validity*. It would tell us that our word problems depend on skills that are different from the skill of reading fast, and that information would bolster our argument that success with the word problems depends on what we think it depends on—namely, intelligence.

A last—and extremely important—assessment is a test's *predictive validity*, that is, its ability to predict future performance. If a test claims, for example, to measure scholastic aptitude, then we would probably expect that students who do well on the test will do well in school later on. Similarly, a test of vocational aptitude ought to predict how well people will do on the job. One index of a test's validity, therefore, is its ability to make such predictions.

INTELLIGENCE TESTING

With the concepts of reliability and validity now in place, we are ready (at last) to turn to the form of testing that is our main concern in this chapter: the testing of mental abilities, and the testing of intelligence in particular. First, though, *what is intelligence?* We all have some notion of what this term refers to, and our vocabularies are filled with words that describe different levels and types of intellectual functioning: *smart*, *bright*, and *clever*; *slow*, *stupid*, and *dim-witted*. But it is difficult to say exactly what is meant by any of these terms, and attempts at specification often lead to disagreements.

Experts do offer a definition of intelligence, but it is a definition with many parts: "the ability to reason, plan, solve problems, think abstractly, comprehend complex ideas, learn quickly and learn from experience" (Gottfredson, 1997, p. 13). The definition continues, making the distinction between intelligence and "book learning . . . or

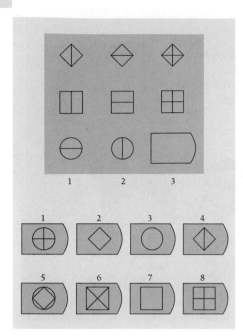

14.7 A sample item from the Raven's Progressive Matrices *The task is to select the alternative that fits into the empty slot above.*

TABLE 14.3 THE RELATION BETWEEN IQ AND HIGHWAY DEATHS	
IQ	DEATH RATE PER 10,000 DRIVERS
>115	51.3
100–115	51.5
85–99	92.2
80–84	146.7

NOTE: In a study of Australian auto accidents, there was a clear link between IQ and outcome; presumably the same would be true in other nations.

were a perfect measurement of intelligence, other factors (e.g., motivation, or physical health) matter for school performance, and this guarantees that there will not be a perfect correspondence between IQ and grades. Nonetheless, there is a strong enough correlation between the two so that we have assurance that the IQ test is measuring what it is supposed to measure.

IQ scores are also good predictors of performance outside the academic world. Indeed, one survey examined many studies collected across a span of 85 years, and, across all of these studies, tests of general mental ability were among the strongest predictors of success in the workplace (Schmidt & Hunter, 1998, 2004). Importantly, though, IQ matters more for some jobs than for others. Jobs of low complexity require relatively little intelligence, so, not surprisingly, the correlation between IQ and job performance is small (although still positive) for such jobs. As jobs become more complex, intelligence matters more, and, sensibly, the correlation between IQ and performance gets stronger as job complexity increases.

Still other results also confirm the importance of IQ scores, documenting the fact that, if we measure someone's intelligence at a relatively early age, we can, from this basis, predict many aspects of her life to come. For example, people with higher IQ scores tend, overall, to achieve higher socioeconomic status (SES), to earn more money during their lifetime, to end up in higher-prestige careers, and even to live longer. Likewise, higher-IQ individuals are less likely to end up in jail, less likely to die in automobile accidents (Table 14.3), less likely to have difficulty following a doctor's instructions. (For a glimpse of this broad data pattern, see Deary & Derr, 2005; Gottfredson, 2004; Kuncel, Hezlett, & Ones, 2004; Lubinski, 2004; Murray, 1998.)

These data leave no doubt about whether IQ tests are measuring something interesting and consequential. We again emphasize, however, that all of these correlations are only moderate in size, so that (for example) some low-IQ individuals do end up in great jobs, and some high-IQ individuals do end up in jail. As before, these points simply remind us that many other factors, in addition to intelligence, count for all these outcomes, so it is inevitable that intelligence accounts for only part of the overall data pattern. But this does not change the fact that intelligence *does* account for a significant part of the data, so that, simply put, if we know someone's IQ, we know a lot about what's likely for him in the years to come. On this basis, the IQ test must be taken seriously.

WHAT IS INTELLIGENCE? THE PSYCHOMETRIC APPROACH

It certainly seems, then, that intelligence tests are measuring something important—something that helps people to do better in both academic and work settings, something that helps them lead healthier, wealthier, and more productive lives. But what exactly is this something?

More than a century ago, Binet assumed that intelligence was a singular ability, applicable to virtually any content. On this view, someone who is intelligent would have an advantage on virtually any mental task—whether it is solving a puzzle, writing a paper, or learning a new mathematical technique. An alternative view, though, is that there really is no such thing as being intelligent in a general sort of way. Instead, perhaps each of us has our own collection of talents, with each talent relevant to some mental tasks but not to others. On this view, we probably should not expect to find people who are successful in every sort of intellectual endeavor, or (conversely) people who are inept in every mental task. Instead, each of us would be strong on some tasks (for which we have the talents) and somewhat weaker on others (that rely on talents we lack)—our own individualized profile of strengths and weaknesses. How can we choose between these proposals?

THE LOGIC OF PSYCHOMETRICS

One option for examining the nature of intelligence is to zoom in for a closer look at the IQ tests themselves, which is what the *psychometric approach* to intelligence attempts to do. This approach does not begin with theory or definitions. Instead, it begins with the actual scores on the tests, and proceeds on the belief that the patterns within these scores may be our best guide in deciding what the tests measure, and what intelligence is. To see how this works, let us begin with a hypothetical example.

Imagine, as a concrete case, that we give a group of individuals three tests, X, Y, and Z. One hypothesis is that all three tests measure the same underlying ability, and so, if a person has a lot of this ability, she has what she needs for all three tests, and will do well on all of them. Conversely, if a person lacks this ability, then she's not well prepared for any of these tests, and so will do poorly on all of them. This obviously implies that, on this hypothesis, a person's score on one of these tests should be similar to her score on the other tests, because, whatever the person's level of ability, it's the *same* ability that matters for all three tests. This hypothesis leads directly to a prediction that there will be a strong correlation between each person's score on test X and her score on test Y, and the same for X and Z or for Y and Z.

A different hypothesis is that each of tests X, Y, and Z measures a different ability, and so it is possible for a person to have the ability needed for X, but not the abilities needed for Y or Z. It is also possible for a person to have the abilities needed for both Y and Z, but not those needed for X. It is possible for a person to have all of these abilities, or none of them. In short, *all* combinations are possible, because we are talking about three separate abilities, and so a person can have any of the three independent of the others. On this view, there is no reason to expect a link between someone's X score and his Y score, or between his Y score and his Z score, just as there is no reason to expect a link between, say, someone's ability to knit well and the size of his vocabulary. Knitting and knowing a lot of words are simply independent capacities, and so you can be good

The logic of psychometrics **The arguments used in psychometrics are complex and mathematical, but the basic idea is quite simple. Imagine someone who observes these serpentlike parts moving across a lake. Is there one serpent here, or two? In other words: how are the visible pieces linked to each other (under the water)? This question is akin to asking how different tests are linked to each other—with the test scores visible, but the links (i.e., the overlap in the capacities needed for each test) not immediately visible. In both cases, we would ask whether the visible bits rise and fall together. If the rising and falling of, say, the second loop were independent of the movements of the first, this would suggest that the loops are not linked, as shown in the observer's second hypothesis. But if the second loop always rose when the first loop rose, and vice versa, this would suggest a link, as in the first hypothesis. In the same way, we can ask how test scores are linked to each other, based on the idea that tests that are linked (i.e., that draw on the same capacities) will rise or fall together, and tests that are not linked will yield scores independent of each other.**

at one, or the other, or both, or neither. Hence there should be no correlation between knitting skill and vocabulary size, and, by the same logic, there should, on this hypothesis, be no correlations among someone's X, Y, and Z scores.

We could also imagine many intermediary hypotheses: Perhaps X and Y tap into the same ability, but Z taps into some other ability. Perhaps Y and Z overlap in the abilities relevant for each, but the overlap is only partial. Throughout, though, the logic is the same: The more two tests overlap in the abilities they require, the greater the correlation will be between the scores on the two tests. And if all tests are correlated with all other tests, this will imply that all the tests overlap in the abilities they require, and this implication would be crucial for us, because it would indicate that there is some ability that is useful for all the tests, and so, apparently, an ability that is truly general in its application.

SPEARMAN AND THE CONCEPT OF GENERAL INTELLIGENCE

What do we find when we apply this logic to real test data? The WAIS-Revised, or WAIS-R, for example, is one of the most widely used intelligence tests; it includes 11 subtests, probing such things as information, or general knowledge; comprehension; arithmetic skill; and vocabulary. As it turns out, the scores on each of these subtests are highly correlated with the scores on the other subtests. The correlation between the knowledge test and comprehension is .70, that between knowledge and arithmetic is .66, and so on. These results are presented in the form of a *correlation matrix* in Table 14.4.

This pattern certainly indicates a high level of consistency in how people perform on the various parts of this test: Individuals who do well generally do so across the board; people who do poorly are usually consistent in their poor performance. This suggests that the tests all overlap with each other in the skills they require; otherwise, we have no explanation for the consistency. Said differently, the tests all draw on roughly the same basic ability, so that individuals who are well endowed with this ability do well on all the tests; individuals with less of the ability do poorly no matter what the test.

It turns out, however, that the correlations summarized in Table 14.4 are not the best way to reveal the consistency in each person's performance. This is because the correlations measure only the relationships among pairs of scores, comparing someone's

---

TABLE 14.4   CORRELATION MATRIX OF FOUR SUBTESTS ON THE WECHSLER ADULT INTELLIGENCE SCALE

	I	C	A	V
I (Information)	—	.70	.66	.81
C (Comprehension)		—	.49	.73
A (Arithmetic)			—	.59
V (Vocabulary)				—

NOTE: The matrix shows the correlation of each subtest with each of the other three. The left-to-right diagonal (which is here indicated by the dashes) cannot have any entries because it is made up of the cells that describe the correlation of each subtest with itself. The cells below the dashes are left blank because they would be redundant.

performance on, say, the knowledge test to her performance on arithmetic problems, or comparing her performance on arithmetic problems with her performance on a vocabulary test. To summarize the overall pattern of the data, what we need is a means of looking not just at pairs of scores, but at all of the scores simultaneously, and, for that purpose, psychologists rely on a statistical technique known as *factor analysis*. This analysis was developed by Charles Spearman (1863–1945), and factor analyses of intelligence scores clearly confirm the claim we have been discussing: There is indeed a common element shared by all the components of the IQ test. Spearman argued that this common element is best described as *general intelligence*, or *g*. He proposed that *g* is a mental attribute called on for any intellectual task, and so individuals with a lot of *g* have an advantage in every intellectual endeavor. If *g* is in short supply, the individual will do poorly on a wide range of tasks.

A HIERARCHICAL MODEL OF INTELLIGENCE

Spearman realized, however, that *g* is not the sole determinant of test performance. If it were, then all tests would, in essence, be tapping into the same skill, and so the correlations between any two subtests should be perfect (i.e., *r* = 1.00). But the correlations, while strongly positive, fall short of this. Eighty years ago, this finding suggested to Spearman that each subtest depends both on *g* and on some other ability that is specific to that particular subtest. Thus, performance on an arithmetic subtest depends on *g* and numerical skills; performance on vocabulary tests depends on *g* and its own specialized (verbal) skill. Moreover, Spearman argued, people differ from each other both in general intelligence and in these different specialized skills, and this difference is why the correlations among different subtests are not perfect (1927).

More recent studies have supported Spearman's claim, and have led researchers to propose a *hierarchical conception* of intelligence (Figure 14.8). At the top of the hierarchy is *g*, contributing to virtually all tasks. At the next level down are several broad categories of tasks. In one often-cited version of the hierarchy, there are three categories: tasks requiring verbal or linguistic ability, tasks requiring quantitative or numerical ability, and tasks requiring spatial or mechanical ability. Then, at the next level down are a large number of more specific capacities, each useful for a narrow and specialized set of tasks (J. B. Carroll, 1993; R. E. Snow, 1994, 1996).

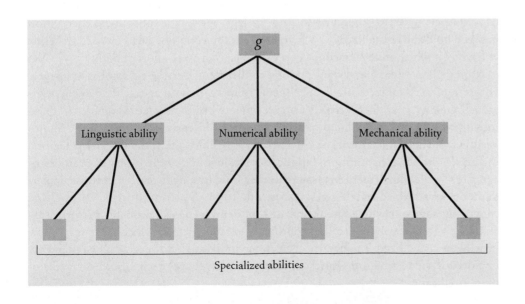

14.8 Hierarchical conception of intelligence *According to many modern theories, intelligence has many components. At the highest level is g, a form of intelligence that applies to virtually any mental task. In addition, each person also has a number of more specialized talents—so that performance on a verbal task depends both on g and on linguistic ability; performance on a mathematical task depends both on g and on numerical ability. Finally, each person also has a much larger number of more specialized abilities—and so performance on a particular verbal task is also influenced by skills directly applicable to just that task; performance on a particular mechanical task is also influenced by skills applicable to just that sort of task, and so on.*

Why should we take this proposal seriously? Once again, the psychometric approach offers an answer rooted in the correlations among test scores. Specifically, if we choose tasks from two different categories—say, a verbal task and a task requiring arithmetic—we find a correlation in performance on the tasks: People who do well on one tend to do well on the other. This is our evidence for *g*, a factor that contributes to all tasks. But if we choose tasks from *within* a category—say, two verbal tasks, or two quantitative tasks—we find *higher* correlations, suggesting that these tasks are more closely related, and overlap more in the abilities they require, than tasks drawn from different categories. This finding is what tells us that the categories are important.

Earlier, we offered two conceptions of intelligence: According to one, there is just one type of intelligence, useful for all endeavors; according to the other, there are multiple forms of intelligence, each useful for a particular type of task. We now can see that both suggestions are correct: Each person has some amount of *g*, and he draws on that capacity in virtually everything he does. But mental tasks also draw on more specialized capacities, and each person has each of these to some extent. This is why each person has his own profile of strengths and weaknesses, his own pattern of things he does relatively well and things he does less well. Thus, a person with a lot of *g* will do well on all intellectual tasks, but, because of his more specific talents, he will do better on some than others. A person with little *g* will do poorly on most tasks, but, again, because of his more specific talents, will do better on some than others.

FLUID AND CRYSTALLIZED *G*

It seems, therefore, that IQ scores are important—that is, they are associated with a number of significant life outcomes. In turn, IQ scores depend to a large extent on *g*, a mental capacity or skill that contributes to performance in many domains. But what is this capacity? What is *g*?

We will need several pages to answer this question fully, but, as a start, it is important to distinguish two aspects of intelligence, often referred to as **fluid *g*** and **crystallized *g***. Fluid *g* refers to the ability to deal with new and unusual problems; it is an ability heavily influenced by mental speed and flexibility. Crystallized *g*, on the other hand, refers to the individual's repertoire of previously acquired skills and information, a repertoire that is useful for dealing with problems that are similar to those already encountered (Cattell, 1963, 1971; J. L. Horn, 1985).

Fluid and crystallized intelligence are linked in an obvious way: Someone with a high level of fluid *g* is likely to be a fast learner, and so will easily acquire the skills and knowledge that crystallized *g* comprises. And, in fact, there is a substantial correlation between fluid and crystallized *g* ($r = +.70$), so that someone who has a lot of one is likely to have a lot of the other; someone short of one is likely to be short of both.

Nonetheless, there are several reasons to distinguish these types of intelligence. For example, crystallized intelligence seems to increase with age, as long as the individual remains in an intellectually stimulating environment (see Chapter 10). Fluid intelligence, on the other hand, reaches its height in early adulthood and declines steadily with age (J. L. Horn, 1985; J. L. Horn & Noll, 1994). Similarly, many factors, including alcohol consumption, fatigue, depression, and some forms of brain damage, cause more impairment in tasks requiring fluid intelligence than in those dependent on crystallized intelligence (Duncan, 1994; E. Hunt, 1995). To put this concretely, someone who is tired (or drunk, or depressed) will probably perform adequately on tests involving familiar routines and familiar facts, since these tests draw heavily on crystallized intelligence. That same individual, however, may be markedly impaired if the test requires quick thinking or a novel approach—both earmarks of fluid intelligence.

THE INFORMATION-PROCESSING APPROACH

What are the capacities or skills that give someone a high level of fluid *g*? To address this question, researchers have turned to a different approach to the study of intelligence, one based on a close analysis of the cognitive operations needed for intellectual performance. To pursue this approach, we still need to consider test scores—because those, ultimately, are what we want to explain. But we can supplement these data with other evidence, including someone's performance on a range of laboratory tasks, as we seek to understand what processes in the mind contribute to someone's being "intelligent."

MENTAL SPEED

Intelligence tests require complex mental processes: The test taker has to detect complicated patterns, work her way through multiple-step plans, and so on. Each of these processes takes some time, and this invites the proposal that the people we consider intelligent may just be those who are especially fast in these processes. This speed would allow them to perform intellectual tasks more quickly; it also would allow them time for *more* steps in comparison with those of us who are not so quick.

One version of this hypothesis proposes that high-IQ people are faster in all mental steps—perhaps because their neurons are in fact more efficient in their information transmission (Eysenck, 1986; Vernon, 1987). A related hypothesis proposes that high-IQ people are faster, not in all mental processes, but in just those needed for intelligent performance (E. Hunt, 1976, 1985b). In either case, what could be the basis for this speed? One possibility is a greater degree of myelination in high-IQ people (E. M. Miller, 1994; see Chapter 3). Alternatively, high-IQ people may have a greater availability of metabolic "fuel" for the neurons (Rae, Digney, McEwan, & Bates, 2003). But, in any of these cases, what is the evidence linking intelligence scores to measures of *speed*?

A number of studies have measured ***simple reaction time***, in which the participant merely responds as quickly as he can when a stimulus appears. Others have measured ***choice reaction time***, in which the participant must again respond as quickly as possible but now has to choose among several responses, depending on the stimulus presented. In such tasks, reaction times are correlated with intelligence scores (with *lower* times—indicating greater speed—correlated with *higher* IQ; see, for example, Jensen, 1987).

Other studies have focused on measures of ***inspection time***—the time someone needs to make a simple discrimination between two stimuli (which of two lines is longer, or which of two tones is higher). These measures correlate around −.50 with intelligence scores (see, for example, T. C. Bates & Shieles, 2003; Danthiir, Roberts, Schulze, & Wilhelm, 2005; Deary & Stough, 1996; Grudnik & Kranzler, 2001; Lohman, 2000; Petrill, Luo, Thompson, & Detterman, 2001; again, the correlation is negative because lower response times go with higher scores on intelligence tests).

WORKING MEMORY AND ATTENTION

The data just cited are certainly consistent with the claim that (at least part of) what it means to be smart is literally to be faster in mental processing. However, this cannot be the entire story. Among other considerations, note that there are plenty of mental tasks that are beyond the reach of lower-IQ individuals, even if they are given all the time in the world to work on these tasks. Clearly, therefore, we need more theory to explain the contrast between high- and low-IQ individuals.

One prominent proposal hinges on the role of working memory and attention in intelligence (see Chapters 7 and 8). To understand this idea, think about what mental tasks demand from you. Many tasks involve multiple bits of information, and you need to keep track of them as you proceed. Many tasks involve multiple steps, and these demand that you shift your focus from one moment to the next—thinking about your overall goal for a moment, in order to figure out what to do next; then focusing on that next step, to deal with its specific demands; then focusing once again on your goal, to choose the *next* step; and so on.

Cast in these terms, it surely sounds as if mental tasks—and certainly tasks that require intelligence—put a heavy demand on working memory, and also on our ability to control our own attention: focusing first here, then there, and not getting lured off track by distractions. Perhaps, therefore, intelligence is, at its heart, the ability to hold things in working memory, and the ability to focus one's attention, and the capacity to coordinate one's goals and priorities in an appropriate fashion. If someone has these abilities, she does well on intelligence tests, and we call her "smart." If she does not have these abilities, she does less well, and we perceive her to lack talent (see, for example, Engle, Tuholski, Laughlin, & Conway, 1999).

To test this proposal, we need some way to measure someone's working memory, in order to ask whether people with a larger working-memory capacity are, in fact, more intelligent. For this purpose, investigators often use measures of **operation span**. We first met these measures in Chapter 8, when we introduced them as a means of asking whether people differ in how well they can control their own mental processes. In the same spirit, we can use these measures to assess the efficiency of working memory when it is actually doing some work: balancing various tasks, inter-coordinating various goals, and so on. There are several ways to do this, but, in one common procedure, participants are asked to read aloud a brief series of sentences, such as

> *Due to his gross inadequacies, his position as director was terminated abruptly.*
> *It is possible, of course, that life did not arise on the Earth at all.*

Immediately after reading the sentences, the participant is asked to recall the final word in each one—in this case, *abruptly* and *all*. If the participant can do this successfully with two sentences, he is asked to do the same task with a group of three sentences, then four, and so on, until the limit of his performance is located.

As we acknowledged in Chapter 8, this task might seem peculiar, but look at what it involves: storing some material (the final words of sentences) for later use in the recall test, while simultaneously working with other material (the full sentences). This juggling of processes, as we move from one part of the task to the next, is exactly what working memory and attention must achieve in their functioning in day-to-day life, and so performance on this test is likely to reflect the efficiency with which working memory will operate in more natural settings. And if, as hypothesized, this efficiency, and the skill it reflects, is essential for intelligent performance, then measurements of operation span should be correlated with intelligence.

The data confirm this prediction. People with a larger working-memory capacity (WMC), measured by the operation span, do have an advantage on many other tests. For example, people with a larger WMC do better on the verbal SAT, on tests of reasoning, on measures of reading comprehension, and on several versions of the IQ test (Ackerman, Beier, & Boyle, 2002; J. Cantor & Engle, 1993; A. R. Conway et al., 2005; Gathercole & Pickering, 2000; J. R. Gray, Chabris, & Braver, 2003; Hannon & Daneman, 2001; Kyllonen & Christal, 1990; Lépine, Barrouillet, & Camos, 2005; for debate about these claims, however, see Ackerman, Beier, & Boyle, 2005; N. Friedman et al., 2006; Kane, Hambrick, & Conway, 2005; Oberauer, Schulze, Oliver, & Süss, 2005).

We also know that certain regions of the brain—particularly the lateral prefrontal cortex—are crucially involved in working-memory tasks, and we know in addition that this brain area is especially activated when people are trying to solve problems on the Raven's Progressive Matrices, a test that offers an excellent measure of fluid intelligence (Duncan, 1995; Duncan et al., 2000; Kane, 2005). This obviously adds to the argument that working memory contributes heavily to intelligence, although we still do not know what variations in this brain area might make some people more intelligent than others.

OTHER CONTRIBUTIONS TO INTELLECTUAL FUNCTIONING

What is it, therefore, that makes someone "intelligent"? Part of the answer seems to be greater mental speed; part seems to be a larger working-memory capacity (and, with it, an ability to stay focused on a goal even in the face of interference or distraction). But there is more to the story than this (and, for some alternative perspectives, see Deary, 2000; Lohman, 2000; Sternberg, 2000). Intelligent performance also depends (as we have discussed) on crystallized intelligence, the knowledge and strategies a person uses for solving problems, learning, and remembering (see, for example, Ackerman & Beier, 2005; Hambrick, 2005). Other relevant factors include attributes that we might not think of as intellectual capacities, but which are nonetheless pertinent to performance on intellectual tasks. These include someone's motivation, her attitude toward testing, her level of anxiety about the test, and her willingness to persevere when a problem becomes frustratingly difficult (see pp. 547–548).

Overall, then, it is plain that a diverse set of attributes contributes to being "intelligent," and, in that sense, intelligence has several constituents. At the same time, these constituents are all correlated with one another, and so can be described or measured with just a single number. Thus, fluid g is different from crystallized g, but someone who has a lot of one is likely also to have a lot of the other, and so a single score (namely, IQ) can be used to summarize both attributes. Likewise, mental speed is different from WMC, but, again, people well endowed with one are likely to be well off on the other, so that both are captured by a single score.

If, therefore, our intention is simply to *measure* intelligence, and then to use that measurement for making predictions about someone's future, then the IQ test, and the score it provides, will be adequate for our needs. But if we wish to understand intelligence, and, more important, if we want to find ways to *improve* someone's intelligence, then we need to look past this single measurement, in order to examine the many components that are apparently contributing to that score.

WHAT IS INTELLIGENCE? BEYOND IQ

We have now made good progress in filling in our portrait of intelligence: We know that we can speak of intelligence in general; the psychometric data tell us that. We also know how to distinguish some more specific forms of intelligence (verbal versus spatial; fluid versus crystallized). And, finally, we know some of the elements that give someone a higher or lower g, elements that include mental speed, working-memory capacity, and the ability to use various strategies.

We might still ask, though, whether there are aspects of intelligence not included in this portrait, aspects that are somehow separate from the capacities we measure with our conventional intelligence tests. Consider, for example, the fact that most of us know people who are "street-smart" or "savvy," but not "school-smart." Such people seem to

The Nutty Professor *Common sense suggests that there are different types of intelligence. This is clearly implied by the popular stereotype of the brilliant scientist or inventor who nonetheless has little practical sense, or little ability to understand social relationships. The stereotype is perhaps applicable to Doc Brown, in the* Back to the Future *movies.*

lack the sort of analytic skill required for strong performance in the classroom, but they are sophisticated and astute in dealing with the practical world. A related aptitude is social competence: the ability to persuade others and to judge their moods and desires. Shrewd salespeople have this ability, as do successful politicians, quite independent of whether they are smart according to IQ tests or not.

In fact, it is easy to confirm these casual observations. For example, one study focused on experienced racetrack handicappers, and asked them to predict the outcomes and payoffs in upcoming horse races. This is a tricky mental task that involves highly complex reasoning. Factors like track records, jockeys, and track conditions all have to be remembered and weighed against one another. On the face of it, the ability to perform such mental calculations is just what intelligence tests should measure. But the results proved otherwise, and the handicappers' success turned out to be completely unrelated to their IQs (Ceci & Liker, 1986). These (and other) findings have persuaded researchers that we need to broaden our conception of intelligence, and consider forms of intelligence that simply are not measured by the IQ test.

PRACTICAL INTELLIGENCE

A number of investigators, particularly Robert Sternberg, have emphasized the importance of *practical intelligence*. In fact, Sternberg argues that there are three types of intelligence: practical intelligence, *analytic intelligence* (the sort of intelligence typically measured by intelligence tests), and *creative intelligence* (Sternberg, 1985; also see P. J. Henry, Sternberg, & Grigorenko, 2005; Sternberg & Kaufman, 1998; Sternberg, R. K. Wagner, Williams, & Horvath, 1995; R. K. Wagner, 2000).

In one study of practical intelligence, business executives were asked to rate the relative importance of various skills needed to head a company department, such as the ability to delegate authority or to promote communication. It turned out that the skills the executives rated most important were excellent predictors of business success: Those who had these skills tended to perform particularly well and to earn the highest salaries. Interestingly, there was virtually no correlation, in this study, between these measures of business success and IQ (Sternberg & Wagner, 1993; R. K. Wagner, 1987; R. K. Wagner & Sternberg, 1987).

What sorts of tasks require practical intelligence? Problems demanding this form of intelligence tend to be poorly defined initially and usually require some amount of information gathering before they can be tackled. Problems requiring analytic intelligence, in contrast, typically have neither of these properties (Neisser, Boodoo, Bouchard, & Boykin, 1996). Sternberg and his colleagues (1995) have also argued that practical intelligence relies heavily on what they call *tacit knowledge*—practical know-how gleaned

Practical intelligence *Bettors at a racetrack rely on sophisticated and complex strategies in deciding which horses will win, but these strategies seem to depend on a form of intelligence separate from that which is assessed by the IQ test.*

from everyday experience. This knowledge is in some cases quite sophisticated (think about those racetrack handicappers), but is, in any case, knowledge that is specialized for use in a particular domain. The business executive acquires tacit knowledge about running a company, which is not pertinent to navigating a ship or handicapping horses. The highly talented handicapper has no advantage in tasks away from the racetrack. Again, all of this is different from analytic intelligence, which seems less dependent on the learning of specific knowledge, and also more general in its application.

EMOTIONAL INTELLIGENCE

A different effort toward broadening the concept of intelligence involves claims about *emotional intelligence*—the ability to understand one's own emotions and others', and also the ability to control one's emotions when appropriate. The term *emotional intelligence* might seem an oxymoron, on the widely held view that emotions often *undermine* our ability to think clearly, and so work against our being intelligent. Many psychologists, however, would reject this claim, and argue instead that emotion plays an important role in guiding our problem solving and decision making (see, for example, Bechara, Damasio, & Damasio, 2000; Damasio, 1994); emotion also plays a role in guiding our attention and shaping what we remember (Reisberg & Hertel, 2004). In these ways, it is probably wrong to claim a strict separation between emotion and cognition. (For more on emotion, see Chapter 12.)

But what is emotional intelligence? One theory suggests that this form of intelligence has four parts: an ability to perceive emotions accurately, an ability to use emotions to facilitate thinking and reasoning, an ability to understand emotions (including the use of language to describe emotions), and an ability to manage emotions in oneself and others (Salovey & Mayer, 1990).

Researchers have developed a number of measures of emotional intelligence, including the Mayer-Salovey-Caruso Emotional Intelligence Test (MSCEIT; Bracket & Mayer, 2003; Mayer, Salovey, Caruso, & Sitarenios, 2003; Figure 14.9). This measure does appear to have predictive validity, so that, for example, people who score higher on the MSCEIT seem to be more successful in social settings. They have fewer conflicts with their peers, are judged to create a more positive atmosphere in the workplace, are more tolerant of stress, and are judged to have more leadership potential (Lopes, Salovey, Côté, & Beers, 2005; Grewal & Salovey, 2005). Likewise, college students with higher MSCEIT scores are rated by their friends as more caring and more supportive, and less likely to experience conflict with their peers (Brackett & Mayer, 2003).

The idea of emotional intelligence has received much attention in the media and popular literature, and, as a result, a number of claims have been offered that are not supported by evidence. (For a glimpse of the relation between the science and the mythology here, and also some concerns about the idea of emotional intelligence, see Matthews, Zeidner, & Roberts, 2003, 2005.) Nonetheless, emotional intelligence does seem to matter for many aspects of day-to-day functioning, can be measured, and is one more way in which people differ from one another in their broad intellectual competence.

THE NOTION OF MULTIPLE INTELLIGENCES

It seems, then, that our measures of *g*—so-called general intelligence—may not be as general as we thought. The capacities measured by *g* are surely important; we see that in the fact that IQ-test performance is predictive of many major life outcomes. But other aspects of intelligence are also important, including practical intelligence, and emotional intelligence, and, according to some authors, *social intelligence* (see, for example, Kihlstrom & Cantor, 2000). Other authors would extend this list still further: In his theory of *multiple*

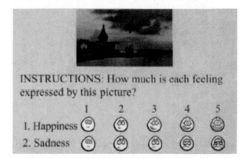

14.9 The Mayer-Salovey-Caruso Emotional Intelligence Test *Shown here are two items similar to the items used on the MSCEIT.*

14.10 Drawing ability in a retarded savant *A work by Nadia, a child with severe retardation and remarkable drawing ability. Nadia was 4 years old when she drew this horse.*

14.11 Unusual numerical achievements in an autistic savant *A scene from the 1988 film* Rain Man, *which depicts an autistic person whose extraordinary numerical gifts enable him to note the exact number of matches remaining in a matchbox after the box has been dropped and some of the matches have been spilled on the floor, to keep track of all the cards in a casino blackjack game, and so forth. (A scene from* Rain Man, *with Dustin Hoffman and Tom Cruise.)*

intelligences, Howard Gardner argued for eight types of intelligence (Gardner, 1983): Three of these are incorporated in most standard intelligence tests: *linguistic intelligence*, *logical-mathematical intelligence*, and *spatial intelligence*. But Gardner also argued that we should acknowledge *musical intelligence*, *bodily-kinesthetic intelligence* (the ability to learn and create complex patterns of movement), *interpersonal intelligence* (the ability to understand other people), *intrapersonal intelligence* (the ability to understand ourselves), and *naturalistic intelligence* (the ability to understand patterns in nature).

Gardner based his argument on several lines of evidence, including studies of patients with brain lesions that devastate some abilities while sparing others. Thus, certain lesions will make a person unable to recognize drawings (a disruption of spatial intelligence), while others will make him unable to perform a sequence of movements (bodily-kinesthetic intelligence) or will devastate musical ability (musical intelligence). Gardner concluded from these cases that each of these capacities is served by a separate part of the brain (and so is disrupted when that part of the brain is damaged), and therefore each is distinct from the others.

Another argument for Gardner's theory comes from the study of people with so-called **savant syndrome**. These individuals have a single extraordinary talent, even though they are otherwise developmentally disabled (either autistic or mentally retarded) to a profound degree. Some display unusual artistic talent (Figure 14.10). Others are "calendar calculators," able to answer immediately (and correctly!) when asked questions such as "What day of the week was March 17 in the year 1682?" (Figure 14.11). Still others have unusual mechanical talents or unusual musical skills—for example, they can effortlessly memorize lengthy and complex musical works (A. L. Hill, 1978; L. K. Miller, 1999).

Gardner's claims have been controversial, in part because some of the data he cites are open to other interpretations (see, for example, L. K. Miller, 1999; Nettelbeck & Young, 1996). Perhaps more important, there is room for disagreement about his basic conceptualization: There is no question that some individuals—whether savants or otherwise—have special talents and that these talents are immensely impressive. However, is it appropriate to think of these talents as forms of intelligence? Or might we be better served by a distinction between *intelligence* and *talent*? It does seem peculiar to use the same term, *intelligence*, to describe both the capacity that Albert Einstein displayed in developing his theories and the capacity that Payton Manning displays on the football field. Similarly, we might celebrate the vocal talent of Whitney Houston, but is hers the same type of talent—and, therefore, sensibly described by the same term, *intelligence*—that a skilled debater relies on in rapidly thinking through the implications of an argument?

Whatever the ultimate verdict on Gardner's theory, though, he has undoubtedly performed a valuable service by drawing our attention to a set of abilities that is often

There are some aptitudes for which no tests have been developed thus far.

"Son, your mother is a remarkable woman."

ignored and undervalued. Gardner is surely correct in noting that we tend to focus too much on the skills and capacities that help people succeed in school, and do too little to celebrate the talents displayed by an artist at her canvas, a skilled dancer in the ballet, or a clergyman's empathy in a hospital room. Whether these other abilities should be counted as forms of intelligence or not, they are surely talents to be highly esteemed and, as much as possible, nurtured and developed.

THE CULTURAL CONTEXT OF INTELLIGENCE

We have now seen several reasons to think that we must broaden our conception of intelligence. Our standard measures (e.g., IQ tests) tell us a lot about someone's mental capacities, but they do not tell us everything. A deeper challenge to our intelligence tests, though, comes from a different source: the question of whether our tests truly measure *intelligence*, or whether they merely measure what is *called* intelligence in our culture.

Different cultures certainly have different conceptions of what intelligence is. For example, some parts of the intelligence test put a premium on quick and decisive responses. But not all cultures share our Western preoccupation with speed. Indians (of southern Asia) and Native Americans, for example, place a higher value on being deliberate; in effect, they would rather be right than quick. In addition, they prefer to qualify, or to say "I don't know" or "I'm not sure," unless they are absolutely certain of their answer. Such deliberation and hedging will not help their test scores; on standard intelligence tests, we get more points if we guess (Sinha, 1983; Triandis, 1989). Similarly, Taiwanese Chinese seem to conceive of intelligence in a way that emphasizes how one relates to others, including when not to show one's intelligence (Yang & Sternberg, 1997; also Nisbett, 2003; for other cultural differences in how intelligence is defined, see Serpell, 2000; Sternberg, 2004).

These cultural differences guarantee that an intelligence test that seems appropriate in one cultural setting may be entirely inappropriate in other cultural settings. In addition, the right procedure to use for measuring intelligence also depends on the cultural setting. This is because people in many countries fail to solve problems that are presented abstractly, or without a familiar context, but do perfectly well with identical problems presented in more meaningful terms. For example, consider the response of an unschooled Russian peasant who was asked, "From Shakhimardan to Vuadil it takes three hours on foot, while to Fergana it is six hours. How much time does it take to go on foot from Vuadil to Fergana?" The reply was "No, it's six hours from Vuadil to Shakhimardan. You're wrong. . . . It's far and you wouldn't get there in three hours" (Luria, 1976, quoted in Sternberg, 1990, p. 229). If this had been a question on a standard intelligence test, the poor peasant would have scored poorly—not because he was unintelligent, but because he did not regard the question as a test of arithmetical reasoning. It turned out that he was quite able to perform the relevant calculation but could not accept the form in which the question was presented.

In light of these concerns, we might well ask whether it is possible to measure intelligence in a fashion that is "culture free"—fair to all cultures, biased against none. The Raven's Progressive Matrices (p. 526) are often claimed to be culture free, because the test is nonverbal and does rely on any sort of specific knowledge. But the very idea of organizing items in rows and columns, an idea that is essential for this test, is unfamiliar in some settings, putting test takers in those settings at a disadvantage with this form of testing.

To put the worry somewhat differently, we could, if we wished, use a standard intelligence test to assess people living in, say, rural Zambia, and the test results probably would allow us to predict whether they will do well in Western schools, or in a Western-style workplace. But this form of testing would tell us nothing about whether these

"You can't build a hut, you don't know how to find edible roots, and you know nothing about predicting the weather. In other words, you do *terribly* on our I.Q. test."

Zambians have the intellectual skills they need to flourish in their own cultural setting. Just as bad, our test would probably give us an absurd understatement of the Zambians' intellectual competence, because our test is simply in the wrong form to reveal that competence.

Against this backdrop, it is important to emphasize that some mental capacities can be found in all cultures —including (as just one example) the core knowledge needed to understand some aspects of mathematics (see, for example, Dehaene, Izard, Pica, & Spelke, 2006). But it is also clear that cultures differ in the skills they need, the skills they value, and the way in which they respond to seemingly straightforward test procedures. As a result, we need to be extremely careful in how we interpret or use our measures of intelligence. Intelligence tests do capture important aspects of intellectual functioning, but they do not capture all aspects or all abilities. These tests are useful instruments for predicting success in Western cultures, but they do much less well in other settings. In the end, therefore, it seems that intelligence tests do measure something of enormous interest, but the meaning and utility of the tests has to be understood in the appropriate cultural context. (For further discussion, see Greenfield, 1997; Serpell, 2000; Sternberg, 2004.)

NATURE, NURTURE, AND INTELLIGENCE

Whatever their strengths or limitations, it is undeniable that scores on intelligence tests are widely used—by educators deciding whom to admit to a program and by employers deciding whom to hire. Perhaps it is no surprise, therefore, that these test scores have been the focus of fierce debate, with important political and social implications. A large part of that debate has focused on a single issue: the role of *genetics* in shaping intelligence.

SOME POLITICAL ISSUES

Intelligence testing has been mired in political controversy from the very beginning. Recall that Binet intended his test as a means of identifying schoolchildren who would benefit from extra training. In the early years of the twentieth century, however, a number of people—scientists and politicians—put the test to a different use. They noted the fact (still true today) that there was a correlation between IQ and SES: People with lower IQ scores usually end up with lower-paid, lower-status jobs; they are also more likely to end up as criminals than are people with higher IQs. Why, therefore, should we try to educate low-IQ individuals? Why waste educational resources, the politicians asked, on people who, because of their low IQ, will never amount to anything anyway?

In contrast, advocates for the disadvantaged took a different view. To begin with, they often disparaged the tests themselves, arguing that they were biased to favor some cultures and some intellectual styles over others. In addition, they argued that the connection between IQ and SES was far from inevitable. Good education, they suggested, can lift the status of almost anyone, and perhaps lift their IQ scores as well. Therefore, spending educational resources on the poor is far from a waste of time; instead, it may be the poor who need and benefit from these resources the most.

These contrasting views obviously lead to different prescriptions for social policy, and for many years, those biased toward the first of these positions dominated the debate. An example is the rationale behind the U.S. immigration policy between World Wars I and II. The immigration act of 1924 (the National Origins Act) set rigid quotas to minimize

Anti-immigration sentiment in the United States **"Immigration Restriction. Prop Wanted."** *A cartoon that appeared in the* **January 23, 1903, issue of the** Philadelphia Inquirer, *calling for more restrictive immigration laws.*

the influx of what were thought to be biologically "weaker stocks," specifically, those from southern and eastern Europe, Asia, and Africa. To "prove" the genetic intellectual inferiority of these immigrants, a congressional committee pointed to the scores by members of these groups on the U.S. Army's intelligence test, which were indeed substantially below those attained by Americans of northern European ancestry.

In fact, these differences were primarily related to the length of time that the immigrants had been in the United States prior to taking the test. When they first arrived, the immigrants lacked fluency in English, as well as knowledge of certain cultural facts important for doing well on the tests; it is no surprise, then, that their test scores were low. After some years of residence in the United States, their cultural knowledge and language skills improved, and their scores became indistinguishable from those of native-born Americans. This observation plainly undermined the hypothesis of a hereditary difference in intelligence between, say, northern and eastern Europeans, but the proponents of immigration quotas did not analyze the results so closely. They had their own reasons for restricting immigration, such as fears of competition from cheap labor. The theory that the excluded groups were innately inferior provided a convenient justification for their policies (Kamin, 1974).

A more contemporary example of the relation between psychological theory and social policy is the argument over differences between Americans of European ancestry and those of African ancestry in their intelligence-test scores. A highly controversial book by Richard J. Herrnstein and Charles Murray (1994) argued that these differences must be taken seriously and noted a number of policy implications that follow from their view, including a reevaluation of many special-education programs, such as Head Start, designed to improve the scholastic performance of disadvantaged preschool children.

Herrnstein and Murray's claims have been criticized on many counts. There has been considerable debate, for example, about their interpretation of the test scores and even about whether race is a meaningful biological category. We will return to these points later in the chapter; for now, we will simply highlight the fact that these questions have profound political importance, making it imperative that we ensure that policy debates are informed by good science.

GENETIC FACTORS

Plainly, people differ from one another in their intelligence and their talents. But what causes these differences? Is it mostly their heredity or mostly their environment? And, in either case, are these differences something that can be altered? Specifically, can people with low intelligence be helped by education or other remediation, or is their intelligence immune to any intervention?

GENETIC TRANSMISSION

Before we tackle these issues, it may be useful to review a few points about the nature of genetic transmission (see also Chapter 2). Each person's genes specify only her *genotype*—something we can think of as the initial blueprint guiding that person's development. For most purposes, though, we are more interested in a person's *phenotype*—the observable traits a person ends up with at the end of development. Of course, the genotype plays an important part in determining the phenotype, but other factors also play a role. Thus, for example, our genes heavily influenced the hair color we were born with (and so two black-haired parents are very unlikely to have a blond child), but obviously hair color can be changed: With a bottle of hair dye, a person can end up with a (phenotypic) hair color rather different from the one specified in his genes.

In the case of hair color, a genetically specified pattern emerges, and can then be altered after the fact. In most other cases, environmental circumstances can shape how

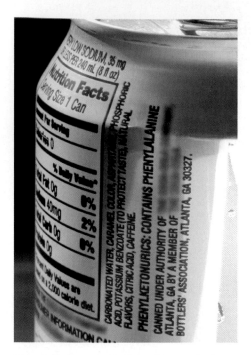

Phenylalanine   *Many diet sodas contain the warning shown here—a warning that is irrelevant to most in the population, but crucial for anyone suffering from phenylketonuria.*

(or whether) the genetically specified pattern is expressed in the first place. This is because—as we have noted in other contexts—genes do not operate in a vacuum. They are instructions to the developing organism specifying how and when certain processes should unfold. But these instructions will be followed only within a given range of environmental conditions—with certain temperatures, nutrient levels, patterns of stimulation, and so on. Moreover, various factors in the environment (e.g., toxins) can knock the development off course. As a result, it makes no sense to talk about a trait being a result of either heredity or environment alone. All traits depend on both. There can be no organism without a genotype, and this genotype cannot express itself independently of the environment.

As an example of how genes and environment interact, consider the medical condition known as *phenylketonuria*, or *PKU*. This condition is caused by a problem with a single gene, a gene that ordinarily governs the production of an enzyme needed to digest phenylalanine, an amino acid that is commonly part of our diet. A defect in this gene, however, derails this process, with the result that phenylalanine is instead converted into a toxic agent. If an infant is born with PKU, therefore, the toxin accumulates in the infant's bloodstream and damages her developing nervous system, leading to profound mental retardation.

PKU is unmistakably of genetic origin, but it can be dealt with by a simple environmental intervention: a special diet that contains very little phenylalanine. If this diet is introduced at an early enough age, retardation can be minimized or avoided altogether. In this case, the genotype for PKU is present but with no phenotypic expression. Notice, therefore, that heredity does not in any way imply immutability: In the case of PKU, we know how to alter the environment in a fashion that renders the genetic problem largely irrelevant (McClearn & DeFries, 1973). Put differently, having the *genotype* for PKU may or may not lead to the phenotype, reminding us that genetic factors are important, but do not set someone's destiny.

GENETICS AND IQ

Even with these complications, the fact remains that some traits (e.g., height, hair and eye color) are heavily influenced by genetics. What about IQ? One way to pursue this issue is to examine the similarities among relatives, and it turns out that the correlation between the IQs of children and the IQs of their parents is about +.40; the correlation between the IQs of siblings is roughly the same. These correlations reveal a relatively strong level of resemblance, and this might suggest inheritance of mental ability, since family members are highly similar genetically. But parents and children also live in similar social and financial circumstances, and they are likely to receive a similar education. So their similar IQs might be attributable to the effects of their shared environment, rather than their overlapping sets of genes.

Apparently, we need better evidence if we are to disentangle the hereditary and environmental contributions to intelligence, and some of the best evidence comes from the study of twins. As we have mentioned in other chapters, there are two types of twins: *Identical*, or *monozygotic (MZ)*, *twins* originate from a single fertilized egg. Early in development, that egg splits into two exact replicas, which develop into two genetically identical individuals. In contrast, *fraternal*, or *dizygotic (DZ)*, *twins* arise from two different eggs, each fertilized by a different sperm cell. As a result, fraternal twins share only 50% of their genetic material, just as ordinary (nontwin) siblings do.

Identical twins, therefore, resemble each other genetically more than fraternal twins do, and this fact makes it striking that identical twins resemble each other in their IQs more than fraternal twins do. In an early summary of the data, the correlation for identical twins was .86; the correlation for fraternal twins was strongly positive, but considerably lower, around .60 (Bouchard & McGue, 1981); other, more recent data confirm this pattern (Figure 14.12, especially the 5th and 6th columns of data). This certainly suggests a strong genetic component in the determination of IQ, with greater genetic similarity (as in identical twins) leading to greater IQ similarity.

The impact of genetic factors is even clearer when we consider results obtained for identical twins who were separated soon after birth, adopted by different families, and reared in different households. The data show a correlation for these twins of about .75, which is not substantially less than the correlation for identical twins reared together (Bouchard, Lykken, McGue, Segal, & Tellegen, 1990; McGue, Bouchard, Iacono, & Lykken, 1993; Plomin & Spinath, 2004). It appears, then, that identical genotypes lead to highly similar IQs even when the individuals grow up in markedly different environments.

Similar conclusions derive from a study we first mentioned in Chapter 10, drawing its data from the Colorado Adoption Project (CAP). The CAP has been tracking 245 adopted children, with a variety of measures available for the children themselves, their adoptive parents, and their biological mothers (Plomin, Fulker, Corley, & DeFries, 1997). The study's results show a strong resemblance between the intelligence scores of each adopted child and the scores of his biological parents, a resemblance that is almost certainly the product of genetic factors (because the adopted children do share 50% of their genetic material with their biological parents), and not the product of environmental influences (because the biological parents were not the adults who raised these children). In contrast, the intelligence scores of the adopted children turn out *not* to resemble the scores of their adoptive parents, again confirming the role of genetics: In this case, there is no sharing of genetic material, and so, despite the shared environment, we find no pattern of resemblance between the IQs of the children and those of the adults who raised them.

What is especially striking about the CAP data, though, is that the resemblance between children and their biological parents *increases* as the years go by: When the children are 4 years old, for example, there's roughly a .10 correlation between the children's intelligence scores and their biological parents' scores. By the time the children are 12, this correlation is almost .20. By the time the children are 16 years old, this correlation is

14.12 Genetics and Intelligence *Evidence powerfully suggests a strong genetic influence on intelligence scores. Monozygotic twins share 100% of their genetic material and tend to resemble each other closely in their intelligence. This is true whether the twins were raised in the same household or (because of adoption) raised apart. In contrast, there is only a low level of resemblance between the intelligence scores of children and their adopted siblings (second bar) or children who have been adopted and their (adoptive) parents (first bar).*

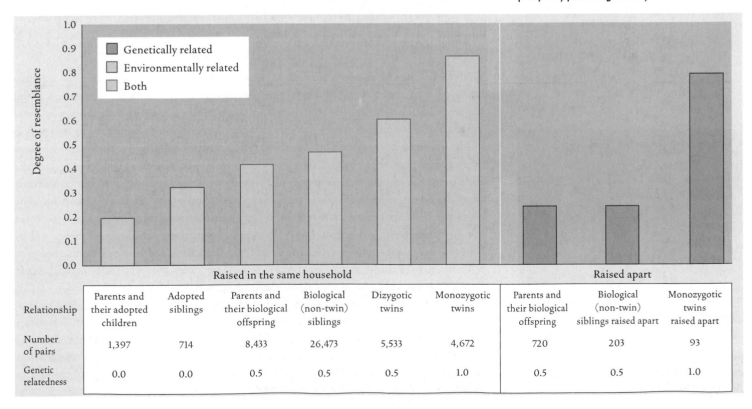

Relationship	Parents and their adopted children	Adopted siblings	Parents and their biological offspring	Biological (non-twin) siblings	Dizygotic twins	Monozygotic twins	Parents and their biological offspring	Biological (non-twin) siblings raised apart	Monozygotic twins raised apart
Number of pairs	1,397	714	8,433	26,473	5,533	4,672	720	203	93
Genetic relatedness	0.0	0.0	0.5	0.5	0.5	1.0	0.5	0.5	1.0

almost .40, despite the fact that, by that point, it has been more than a dozen years since the children and their biological parents have seen each other!

How should we think about this odd result? One possibility is that what is inherited via the genes is a *learning capacity*, and so, in early childhood, a child's *potential* might resemble that of her biological parents, but potentials are not easily visible. On this ground, the resemblance comes into view only after the child has had enough experience in the world, and so enough opportunity to *use* the learning capacity she inherited. That is why the resemblance between parents and their biological offspring grows as the children move through childhood into adolescence (cf. Plomin & DeFries, 1985; Plomin & Spinath, 2004).

ENVIRONMENTAL FACTORS

Clearly, then, genetic influences play a powerful role in shaping someone's intellectual capacities. As we have repeatedly noted, though, genetic effects always unfold within an environmental context, and so—not surprisingly—environmental factors also shape the development of our intellect. Evidence for this point comes from many sources, including studies of the impact of poverty. As we will see, impoverished environments erode intelligence; moving someone into an enriched environment improves his intelligence. In both cases, we see that the IQ score someone ends up with depends on both her genes and the surroundings in which she grew up.

Before considering the data, though, we should deal with one preliminary: We said earlier that IQ scores are remarkably stable across the lifespan, so that someone's IQ at, say, age 11 is a good predictor of what his IQ will be decades later. This does not mean, however, that someone's IQ score can never change. Everyone's IQ varies a bit during her lifetime, although people with a relatively high IQ at an early age are likely to have a high IQ throughout life; people with a relatively low IQ as children will probably always have a low IQ. It is this consistency that leads to the high test-retest reliability for IQ tests. But it is also true that a significant change in someone's life circumstances can lead to a correspondingly large change in his IQ, and, as we will see, this is why we must conclude that IQ scores are influenced by life experiences just as much as they are by genetics.

THE EFFECTS OF CHANGING THE ENVIRONMENT

We have known for many years that impoverished environments can impede intellectual development. For example, researchers studied children who worked on canal boats in England during the 1920s and rarely attended school, and children who lived in rural mountainous Kentucky, where little or no schooling was available. These certainly seem like poor conditions for the development of intellectual skills, and it seems likely that exposure to these conditions would have a cumulative effect: The longer the child remains in such an environment, the lower his IQ should be. This is precisely what the data show. There was a sizable negative correlation between IQ and age. The older the child (the longer she had been in the impoverished environment), the lower her IQ (Asher, 1935; Gordon, 1923). Related results come from communities where schools have closed. These closings typically lead to a decline in intelligence-test scores—in one study, a drop of about 6 points for every year of school missed (R. L. Green, Hoffman, Morse, Hayes, & Morgan, 1964; see also Neisser et al., 1996).

Similarly, a number of studies tell us that *improving* the environment can, in fact, increase IQ. Classic data on this point come from a community in eastern Tennessee that was quite isolated from the U.S. mainstream in 1930 but became less and less so during the following decade, with the introduction of schools, roads, and radios. Between 1930 and 1940, the average IQ of individuals in this community rose by 10 points, from 82 to 92 (L. R. Wheeler, 1942).

IQ and poverty   *IQ is clearly influenced by both genes and environment, and the longer a child lives under conditions of poverty, the lower her IQ will be.*

More recent data focus on the effects of explicit training: The Venezuelan Intelligence Project has provided underprivileged adolescents in Venezuela with extensive training in various thinking skills (Herrnstein, Nickerson, de Sanchez, & Swets, 1986). Assessments after training showed substantial benefits on a wide range of tests. A similar benefit was observed for American preschool children in the Carolina Abecedarian Project (F. A. Campbell & Ramey, 1994). These programs leave no doubt that suitable enrichment and education can provide substantial improvement in intelligence-test scores. (For still other evidence that schooling lifts intelligence scores, see Ceci & Williams, 1997; Grotzer & Perkins, 2000; Perkins & Grotzer, 1997.)

Another line of evidence focuses more directly on SES, and examines statistically the interplay among genetic influences, SES, and IQ (Turkheimer, Haley, Waldron, D'Onofrio, & Gottesman, 2003). The logic here resembles that of the studies we have already considered, and, among higher-SES families, we find the same pattern we have already seen: Genetic resemblance is crucial (and so we observe greater IQ similarity between identical twins than between fraternal twins); influences from the environment are considerably less important. Among lower-SES families, though, the pattern reverses: In this group, environmental influences seem crucial for determining IQ, and genetic factors seem to have little impact.

How should we think about all of these findings? One perspective builds on a suggestion we have already discussed (pp. 541–542): Our biology, it seems, provides each of us with a genetically defined set of intellectual capacities, but these capacities will emerge only if we receive good schooling and health care, as well as adequate stimulation. This is why the genetic influences become more prominent as we mature: As the years go by, our experiences are allowing the potential to show itself. If a child grows up in an impoverished environment, however, it does not matter so much whether he has a fine potential; the environment does not allow the potential to emerge. Hence, in impoverished environments, genetic factors (the source of the potential) count for relatively little. This same logic, of course, also explains why IQ scores are improved when someone escapes poverty, and why genetic factors matter more for high-SES children than for low-SES children.

WORLDWIDE IMPROVEMENT IN IQ SCORES

These various results make it clear that the environment does matter in shaping a child's IQ. The same conclusion also flows from another fact—namely, that the scores on intelligence tests have been gradually increasing over the last few decades, at a rate of approximately 3 points per decade. This pattern is generally known as the *Flynn effect*, after James R. Flynn (1984, 1987, 1999; see also Daley, Whaley, Sigman, Espinosa, & Neumann, 2003; Kanaya, Scullin, & Ceci, 2003), one of the first researchers to document this effect systematically. This improvement seems to be occurring worldwide, with clear IQ gains documented in both the West and many third world countries.

This effect cannot be explained genetically. While the human genome does change gradually (a prerequisite, of course, for human evolution), it does not change at a pace commensurate with the Flynn effect. So how should the effect be explained? Some observers have proposed that this worldwide improvement reflects the increasing complexity and sophistication of our shared culture: Each of us is exposed to more information and a wider set of perspectives than were our grandparents, and this exposure may lead to an improvement in intelligence-test scores. A different possibility is that the Flynn effect is attributable to widespread improvements in nutrition (for a broad discussion, see Dickens & Flynn, 2001; Neisser, 1997, 1998). Whatever the explanation, though, this effect is a compelling reminder that intelligence can be measurably improved by suitable environmental conditions.

HERITABILITY

Overall, then, it is clear that both genetic and environmental factors play a part in determining intelligence. The twins evidence, for example, is an undeniable indication that genetics are important; the Flynn effect is an equally compelling indication that the environment is crucial. What is not clear, though, is the relative weight exerted by each of these factors.

To address this question, investigators usually refer to a technical expression developed by geneticists, the *heritability ratio* (H). For any trait, this ratio begins with an assessment of the total phenotypic variability: How much do individuals differ from each other in their phenotype? We then seek to ask what proportion of this variability can be attributed to genetic variation.

Researchers estimate that the value of H for IQ falls between .40 and .70; often a figure of .50 is quoted (Neisser et al., 1996). This can be understood as the assertion that, of the variability we observe in IQ, approximately 50% is attributable to variations in genetic material. (And, since the other 50% is attributable to factors other than genetics, this means that genes and environment have roughly equal weight in determining IQ.) Let us be clear, though, that by definition, heritability is a measure that applies only to trait variations within a population; it does not apply to individuals. Thus, it would be a mistake (for example) to read this heritability estimate as implying that half of an individual's IQ points come from her genes, and half from her environment. Instead, as we have emphasized throughout, the influence of genes and environment is, for any individual, fully intertwined and interdependent, with both shaping all aspects of whatever the person becomes.

Moreover, heritability is not a fixed number, and heritability estimates can change as circumstances change. In fact, we have seen three examples of this point: First, we mentioned that genetic factors seem to matter more as people move from childhood into adulthood; thus the overall heritability for IQ in children may be .50, but the heritability for adults may be as high as .80 (Plomin & Spinath, 2004). Second, we have mentioned that genetic factors seem to matter more for IQs in high-SES children than for low-SES children; indeed, the heritability ratio may be near 0 for children growing up in a low-SES environment. Third, we mentioned early on the mental retardation caused by PKU. Many years ago, we had no way to remedy this condition, and so the heritability was extremely high: The phenotypic variation (whether someone did or did not have this type of retardation) was almost entirely attributable to whether or not he had the relevant genetic pattern. But we now know that a simple environmental manipulation can minimize the impact of PKU, and, as a result, the heritability estimate for PKU is currently quite low. Whether retardation is observed depends largely on the individual's diet, and so most of the phenotypic variation we observe is due to this environmental factor, not to genes.

In short, then, heritability estimates are a convenient summary of the available data, but they are also quite fluid, providing yet another reminder that genes and environment interact in important ways, so that how (and how much) the genes influence development depends on the circumstances. Thus, the overall heritability of intelligence seems now to be roughly .50, but this estimate could change dramatically if the environment were to change in some relevant fashion (as it did in the case of PKU). Similarly, a very high heritability estimate tells us little about the prospects for changing a trait. Even if a trait's heritability is 1.00, we may be able to alter that trait enormously, once a suitable intervention is found.

Heritability of hair color *The heritability of hair color regularly rises and falls as a function of changes in fashion. The genetic contribution to hair color does not change, of course, but the relative importance of the genes—and so the heritability—drops whenever dying one's hair is in style (because then the phenotype may bear little resemblance to the color specified in the genotype). Heritability rises again when the style changes such that people return to a preference for their "natural" color. This cyclic rise and fall underscores the way in which heritability is fluid, and reflects a particular setting at a particular time.*

GROUP DIFFERENCES IN IQ

So far, we have focused on the intelligence scores of specific individuals—comparing, for example, the IQ scores of particular twins, or comparing a specific child's IQ with the IQ of her biological parents. These person-by-person comparisons, however, are not the focus of the real controversy over the roots of intelligence. The real fury is over another issue: the differences in average IQ that are found between groups, specifically, the difference between American whites and American blacks.

Numerous studies have shown that the average score of American blacks is 10 to 15 IQ points below the average score of the American white population (Jensen, 1985; Loehlin, Lindzey, & Spuhler, 1975; Reynolds, Chastain, Kaufman, & McLean, 1987). The fact that this difference exists is not in dispute. What is at issue is what the difference means and how it came about.

Before proceeding, though, we must emphasize that these differences are between averages. The scores of European American test takers vary enormously, as do the scores of African-American test takers; indeed, these within-group variations are much greater than the between-group variations, and as a consequence, there is huge overlap among these populations. We therefore learn relatively little about any individual's IQ simply by knowing his group membership. Nonetheless, the average differences between groups remain. How should we think about these differences?

BETWEEN-GROUP AND WITHIN-GROUP DIFFERENCES

In addressing this issue, we first need to confront—and remove—a confusion that often muddies discussion of the race difference. The confusion begins with two points that are, in fact, correct: We know that there are genetic differences between white Americans and African Americans; this is evident in such characteristics as skin color and pattern of hair growth. We also know that genetic factors matter a lot for IQ; we have already reviewed the evidence favoring this point. The confusion, though, lies in combining these two points, and thus drawing the conclusion that the race difference in intelligence must be understood in genetic terms. This conclusion is simply an error, and rests on a failure to distinguish *within-group* and *between-group* comparisons (see, for example, Layzer, 1972).

The data we have discussed so far all involve within-group comparisons: In the twin studies, for example, we are comparing white fraternal twins with white identical twins; in the Flynn-effect data, we are comparing Norwegians of one generation with Norwegians of another generation. In sharp contrast, the difference between American whites and American blacks is a *between-group* comparison. And, crucially, between-group differences are often caused by different factors than within-group differences, so we cannot draw conclusions about between-group differences based on within-group data (and vice versa). Hence the data considered so far simply tell us nothing about the race difference in IQ scores.

To make this point concrete, many scholars rely on a straightforward example. Imagine a bag of grass seed that contains several genetically different varieties. Let us say that these seeds are planted in barren soil, and given inadequate care. As a result, the plants are likely to grow poorly, but some will surely do better than others—they will be healthier, grow a bit taller, and so on. These differences from one plant to the next cannot be attributed to environmental factors because, in this setting, all of the seeds are in the same environment: They all get the same low levels of nutrition; they all get the same bad care. If, therefore, some plants do better than others, this must be attributed entirely to genetic factors, with some seeds genetically better prepared for these poor conditions.

But now let us imagine another batch of seeds drawn from the same bag. These seeds are planted in rich soil, and given excellent care. These plants will grow well, but again, some will grow taller than others. As before, these variations from one plant to the next cannot be explained in terms of the environment, because all of these seeds are growing in the same uniform environment. Hence we cannot say that some plants grew taller because they got more water, or more light, because all got the same amount of water

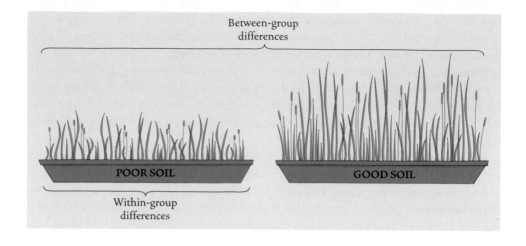

14.13 Between-group and within-group differences *Between-group differences and within-group differences may be caused by very different factors. Here, the between-group difference reflects an environmental factor (soil), while the within-group difference reflects genetic variation (seed).*

and light. Instead, the observed variation must be attributed entirely to genetic sources, with some seeds better prepared to flourish in this rich environment.

Notice where all of this leaves us. In the first environment, the within-group differences (comparisons among the various seeds growing in barren soil) are all produced by genetics. The same is true in the second environment: Here, too, the within-group differences are produced by genetics. But it should be obvious that the contrast between the two groups is attributable entirely to the environment. All the plants growing in rich soil came from the same bag of seeds as all the plants growing in poor soil; hence the variation in genes is probably the same in the two groups. But the two groups obviously differ in the quality of their care, and this difference is why one group flourishes while the other does not (after Lewontin, 1976; Figure 14.13). Plainly, therefore, this between-group difference comes from a very different source from the within-group differences, and that is the point: It is easy to find examples, like this one, in which between-group variations and within-group variations are produced by different factors. Therefore, even if we know a lot about within-group variation (and, specifically, if we know that this variation depends on the genes), we can draw no conclusions about what it is that produces between-group variation. Maybe it is the genes, but maybe not. Sometimes between-group variations come from the same source as within-group variations, and sometimes they do not. Knowing a lot about one type of variation therefore tells us nothing about the other.

ENVIRONMENTAL EFFECTS

It seems, then, that we simply need more data if we are to understand the between-group differences in IQ; we certainly cannot extrapolate from what we know about within-group heritability. But what data should we turn to? One proposal begins with the fact that—as we have noted—IQ scores are influenced by poverty and poor schooling. Let us now add that, undeniably, blacks in the United States tend (on average) to have lower incomes than whites, and are more likely to live in poverty. As a result, a higher proportion of blacks than whites are exposed to poor nutrition, lower-quality educational resources, and poorer health care. Could these socioeconomic factors be the source of the race difference in IQ scores?

To address this question, let us focus our comparison just on blacks and whites with similar backgrounds—so that, for example, we compare working-class blacks with working-class whites, or educated black professionals with educated white professionals. In this way, we can ask if race matters when we remove socioeconomic differences from the picture. And, in fact, studies using this logic find a much-reduced racial difference (see, for example, Loehlin et al., 1975), suggesting that race has only a small effect once we control for these other variables.

A different line of evidence makes a similar point: Rather than trying to match environments, we can ask what happens when the environment is changed. A widely cited example is a study of black children who were adopted at an early age by white middle-class parents, most of whom were college educated (Scarr & Weinberg, 1976). After adoption, the mean IQ of these children was 110, a value exceeding the national average for black children by about 25 points. (For further discussion, see Scarr & Carter-Saltzman, 1982; Scarr & Weinberg, 1983.)

Clearly, then, environmental factors—including factors associated with poverty—play a large part here. But note that equalizing the socioeconomic variables *diminishes* the black-white difference, but does not abolish it. Thus, we need to ask what other factors contribute to the contrast between the races.

STEREOTYPE THREAT

In the previous section, we asked whether blacks' and whites' IQ scores would be the same if we could match their environments. If the answer is yes, then this obviously points toward an environmental explanation of the race difference. But to tackle this question in a thorough manner, it may not be enough to match factors like parental education, income, and occupational level. This is because, even with these steps, black children and white children grow up in different environments. After all, black children grow up knowing that they are black; white children, that they are white. Moreover, each group is treated differently by the people in their social environment because of the color of their skin. In these ways, then, their environments and experiences are not matched—even if the parents have similar jobs and similar income levels.

Do these social experiences matter for intelligence scores? As one indication that they do, consider studies of *stereotype threat*, a term that describes the impact that social stereotypes have on task performance. Concretely, imagine an African American taking an intelligence test. That person might well become anxious, because she believes this is a test on which she is expected to do poorly, and the anxiety might then be compounded by the thought that her poor performance will only serve to confirm others' prejudices. This anxiety, of course, could easily erode performance, by making it more difficult to pay attention and to do her best work. Moreover, given the discouraging thought that poor performance is inevitable, the person might well decide not to expend enormous effort—if she is likely to do poorly, why struggle against the tide?

Evidence for these effects comes from a variety of studies, including some in which two groups of African Americans are given the exact same test. One group is told, at the start, that the test is designed to assess their intelligence; the other group is led to believe that the test is simply composed of challenges and is not designed to assess them in any way. The first group, for which the instructions trigger stereotype threat, does markedly worse (Steele, 1998; Steele & Aronson, 1995).

Related results have been shown in many other circumstances—and have been demonstrated with children as well as adults. Similar data have been reported for other groups (Asians, women) as well as African Americans (Ambady, Shih, Kim, & Pittinsky, 2001; Blascovich, Spencer, Quinn, & Steele, 2001; Cheryan & Bodenhausen, 2000). For example, reminding test takers of their gender just before they take a math test seems to encourage women to think about the stereotype that women cannot do math, and this seems to undermine their test performance—with thoughts about the stereotype increasing the women's anxiety about the test, and cutting into the likelihood that they will work as hard as they can, and persevere if the test grows frustrating.

These results draw our attention back to our earlier comments about what intelligence is, and what performance on "intellectual tasks" requires. One requirement, of course, is a set of cognitive skills and capacities (e.g., mental speed, or working memory). A different

brother and sister grow up in the same household, but with different social expectations for how they will behave, different types of interaction with their friends, and so on. This—combined with the biological differences between the sexes (Chapter 2)—helps us understand why women score higher on the "agreeableness" dimension of the Big Five, and why women are less likely to be sensation-seekers (Zuckerman, 1994). The sexes also differ in their vulnerability to some forms of psychopathology, with women in most cultural groups, for example, being far more vulnerable to depression than men (Chapter 16). In this context, though, we should also note that many of the popularized gender differences in personality are probably overstated; in fact, women and men appear remarkably similar, on average, on many aspects of personality (Feingold, 1994; Hyde, 2005; also see Chapter 11).

CONTRIBUTIONS OF THE TRAIT APPROACH

People differ from one another in a huge number of ways, and one of the major contributions of the trait approach has been to systematize the many ways in which we differ, and to reduce the apparently large number of these differences to manageable size. The emergence of the broad Big Five framework has enabled researchers working within very different traditions to use agreed-upon measures, to communicate effectively, and to share the data they collect with others. As a result, progress on determining the genetic bases and brain correlates of personality differences has accelerated dramatically. It is undeniable, then, that this approach to personality has contributed substantially to our understanding. But it is also undeniable that we must draw on other perspectives as well as if we are to understand what a "personality" is, and how it comes to be.

THE PSYCHODYNAMIC APPROACH: PROBING THE DEPTHS

The comic theatre of the classical and Renaissance ages presented personality as a neatly divisible, finite set of stable types. Once a character entered, the audience knew what to expect of him. If the actor wore the mask of the cowardly soldier, he would brag and run away; if he wore the mask of the miserly old man, he would jealously guard his money.

As we have seen, the trait approach has amended this view in two important ways. First, it has replaced a few stock character types with a number of continuous personality dimensions on which people can vary in almost infinite ways. Second, it has offered a richer notion of how personality and situations jointly shape behavior.

These are important revisions, but according to the *psychodynamic perspective*, these steps are far too timid. What is needed is a much more radical revision of our understanding of personality—an understanding that parallels a more modern approach to drama, in which nothing is quite what it seems. In playing a character, a modern actor often pays attention to the subtext, the unspoken thoughts that go through the character's head while she speaks her lines. And many actors are interested in a still deeper subtext, the thoughts and wishes of which the character is unaware. According to the psychodynamic approach, this most basic subtext is the wellspring of all human personality.

Adherents of the psychodynamic approach do not deny that some people are more sociable than others, or that some are more impulsive or emotionally unstable. But they contend that it is superficial to explain such tendencies as either the expression of a personality trait or the product of situational factors. In their view, what people do and say—and even what they consciously think—is only the tip of the iceberg. As they see it, human acts and thoughts are just the outer expression of a whole host of motives and desires that are often derived from early childhood experiences, that are generally pitted against each other, and that are for the most part unknown to the person himself. They believe that to understand a person is to understand these hidden psychological forces (often called *dynamics*) that make the person an individual divided against himself.

THE ORIGINS OF PSYCHOANALYTIC THOUGHT: FROM HYPNOSIS TO THE TALKING CURE

The founder of psychoanalysis, Sigmund Freud (1856–1939), was a physician by training. During his medical school years, Freud was greatly influenced by Ernst Brucke, who argued that human behavior and mental processes were the result of physiological processes that could be analyzed using the scientific methods that were being so successfully applied in the natural sciences at that time (Gay, 1988). This general outlook left a lasting impression on Freud, and it provided a foundation for his lifelong ambition to expose the inner workings of the mind.

After a stint as a medical researcher, financial pressures led Freud to open a neurology practice in which he found that many of his patients were suffering from a disorder then called *hysteria* (now called *conversion disorder*). The symptoms of hysteria presented an apparently helter-skelter catalog of physical and mental complaints—total or partial blindness or deafness, paralysis or anesthesia of various parts of the body, uncontrollable trembling or convulsive attacks, and gaps in memory. Was there any underlying cause that could make sense of this confusing array of symptoms?

Freud came to suspect that the hysterical symptoms were *psychogenic*—the results of some unknown psychological cause—rather than the product of organic damage to the nervous system. His hypothesis grew out of the work of Jean Charcot (1825–1893), a French neurologist who noticed that many of the bodily symptoms of hysteria made no anatomical sense. For example, some patients who suffered from anesthesia (i.e., lack of feeling) of the hand still had feeling above the wrist. This *glove anesthesia* (so called because of the shape of the affected region) could not possibly be caused by any nerve injury, since an injury to any of the relevant nerve trunks would also affect a portion of the arm above the wrist (Figure 15.2). This ruled out a simple physical cause and suggested that glove anesthesia had some psychological basis.

In collaboration with another physician, Josef Breuer (1842–1925), Freud came to believe that hysterical symptoms were a disguised way to keep certain emotionally charged memories under mental lock and key (S. Freud & Breuer, 1895). The idea, in brief, was that the patients carried some very troubling memory that they needed both to express (because it held such a grip on their thoughts) but also to hide (because thinking about it was so painful). The patients' "compromise," in Freud's view, was to express the memory in a veiled form, and this was the source of their physical symptoms.

To support this hypothesis, Freud needed to find out both what a patient's painful memory was and why she (almost all of Freud's patients were women) found directly expressing her memory to be unacceptable. He therefore needed some method of revealing the memories. At first, Freud and Breuer tried to uncover patients' memories while they were in a hypnotic trance, but Freud eventually abandoned this method, in part because not all patients were readily hypnotized. He decided that crucial memories could instead be recovered in the normal, waking state through the method of *free association*. In this method, his patients were told to say anything that entered their mind, no matter how trivial it seemed, or how embarrassing, disagreeable, or indiscreet. Since Freud assumed that all ideas were linked by association, he concluded that the emotionally charged "forgotten" memories would be mentioned sooner or later.

Sigmund Freud (1856–1939)

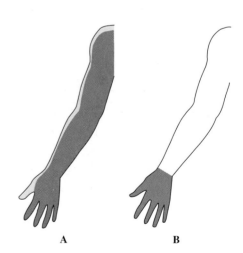

15.2 Glove anesthesia (A) Areas of the arm's skin that send sensory information to the brain by way of different nerves. (B) A typical region of anesthesia in a patient with hysteria. If there were a nerve injury (in the spinal cord), the anesthesia would extend over the length of the arm, following the nerve distribution shown in (A).

But a difficulty arose: Patients did not readily comply with Freud's request. There was a *resistance* of which the patient was often unaware.

> The patient attempts to escape ... by every possible means. First he says nothing comes into his head, then that so much comes into his head that he can't grasp any of it. Then we observe that ... he is giving in to his critical objections, first to this, then to that; he betrays it by the long pauses which occur in his talk. At last he admits that he really cannot say something, he is ashamed to.... Or else, he has thought of something but it concerns someone else and not himself.... Or else, what he has just thought of is really too unimportant, too stupid, and too absurd.... So it goes on, with untold variations, to which one continually replies that telling everything really means telling everything. (S. Freud, 1917, p. 289)

In Freud's view, resistance arose because certain experiences in the patient's life—certain acts, impulses, thoughts, or memories—were especially painful or anxiety-provoking, and, as an act of self-protection, these experiences had been forcefully pushed out of consciousness, or, in Freud's term, *repressed*. The resistance Freud observed in his clinic, he supposed, came from the same source: Just as the patients had originally defended themselves by expelling these thoughts from consciousness, they now, in talking to the psychoanalyst, mobilized the same forces to block the reemergence of these painful experiences.

Freud concluded, therefore, that his patients would not (and perhaps could not) reveal their painful memories directly. He thus set himself the task of developing *indirect* methods of analysis (as he called it, **psychoanalysis**) that he thought would uncover these ideas and memories, and the conflicts that gave rise to them. Freud was convinced that these conflicts were at the root of most symptoms of psychopathology, and so, by revealing the conflicts, he could diminish the symptoms. But Freud also believed that the same mechanisms operate in normal persons, so he viewed his proposals as contributions not only to psychopathology, but also to a general theory of human personality.

MODELS OF MIND

Freud assumed that all psychological phenomena, such as thoughts, feelings, and behaviors, are determined by simple cause-and-effect laws similar to those that govern physical phenomena, such as the law of gravitation or the laws of motion. And when Freud said all psychological phenomena were subject to these laws, he really meant all, including not just the routine behaviors we plan and intend, but also the odd things we do, such as mixing up a friend's name or dreaming we are falling into a bottomless pit.

Of course, we are often not aware of what really causes our behaviors. The mix-up in the friend's name, for example, seems to be just something that happened entirely by accident because we were not paying attention. The dream, we claim, is just the result of a chance association. However, Freud strenuously denied these commonsense proposals and argued that the causes for these events were simply invisible to us, and that is why these events "feel" more or less random.

What did "invisible" mean to Freud? Freud tried to explain mental activity in terms of three levels of mental processes. The first level is the *conscious level*, which refers to thoughts and feelings of which one is currently aware. The second level is the *preconscious level*, which refers to mental processes that are not currently in focal awareness, but that could easily be brought to awareness. Where you slept last night, what you ate for breakfast today, and the pressure of your clothes against your body all were probably at the preconscious level until you read this, at which point they moved to the conscious level of awareness, from which they will (hopefully) soon recede.

But it was the third level, the *unconscious level*, that was the most interesting and provocative. It is this level that Freud emphasized most heavily in his explanations of his patients' symptoms (and also in his explanations of many everyday feelings, thoughts, and behaviors). The unconscious level refers to mental processes that are not—and cannot easily become—the object of focal awareness. But how can we know about this level if its contents cannot become conscious? Much as a black hole is inferred from its distorting influence on the objects around it, so too are unconscious processes usually inferred, rather than directly observed, through an examination of dreams, patterns of resistance, and everyday slips of the tongue. Before we can understand how these inferences proceed, though, and thus how we come to understand the unconscious mind, we need to lay out a bit more of Freud's theory.

Much of Freud's theorizing—and certainly most of his thinking about the unconscious mind—hinges on the conflicts that, in his view, characterize much of the dynamic that shapes each of us. But conflict among whom? When conflict is external, the antagonists are easily identified: David and Goliath, for example, or Dorothy and the Wicked Witch of the West. But what, according to Freud, are the warring forces when the conflict is within the individual?

In essence, the warring factions, in Freud's view, are different wishes or motives, such as a patient's desire to go out dancing versus her guilt over at leaving an ailing father at home. Freud eventually devised a concept of personality that encapsulated these conflicting forces within three distinct subsystems: the *id*, the *ego*, and the *superego*. In some of his writings, Freud treated these three mental systems as if they were separate persons inhabiting the mind. But this is only a metaphor, which must not be taken literally; id, ego, and superego are just the names he gave to three sets of very different reaction patterns, and not persons in their own right (S. Freud, 1923).

The *id* is the most primitive portion of the personality, the portion from which the other two emerge. It consists of all of the basic biological urges, which Freud ultimately grouped into two broad classes: the *life instincts*, concerned with eating, drinking, and the like, as well as with sex; and the *death instincts*, which serve as a motive force for aggression, war, and suicide (S. Freud, 1933). (Note that Freud privileges the same classes of motives that were our focus in Chapter 2—namely, eating, sex, and aggression.) The id seeks constantly to reduce the tensions generated by all these biological urges, and it abides entirely by the *pleasure principle*—satisfaction now and not later, regardless of the circumstances and whatever the cost.

At birth, the infant is all id. But the id's heated striving is soon met by cold reality, because some gratifications take time. Food and drink, for example, are not always present; the infant or young child has to cry to get them. These confrontations between desire and reality lead to a whole set of new reactions that are meant to reconcile the two. Sometimes the result is appropriate action (e.g., saying "please"), and sometimes the result is suppressing a forbidden impulse (e.g., not eating food from someone else's plate). All of these reconciliations become organized into a new subsystem of the personality—the *ego*. The ego obeys a new principle, the *reality principle*. It tries to satisfy the id (i.e., to gain pleasure), but it does so pragmatically, finding strategies that work but also accord with the real world and its real demands.

Initially, the ego only has to worry about the outer world. If the ego inhibits some id-inspired action, it is for some immediate reason—for example, the prospect of punishment. But, as the child gets older, forbidden acts may be suppressed even when there is no chance of being caught and punished. This change occurs because the child starts to act and think as if he himself were the parent who administers praise and reproof. This self-reproach is, in essence, the voice of a new mental agency—the *superego*, which represents the internalized rules and admonitions of the parents, and, through them, of society. If the ego lives up to the superego's dictates, then pride is the reward. But if one of the superego's rules is broken, the superego metes out punishment—feelings of guilt or shame—just as the parents scolded or spanked or withdrew their love.

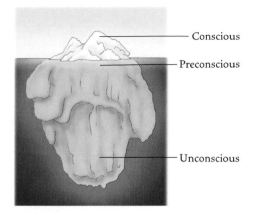

Levels of mental processes **Freud explained mental activity in terms of three levels of processes: conscious, preconscious, and unconscious.**

Inner conflicts as envisaged by Plato **The Greek philosopher Plato anticipated Freud's tripartite division of the mind by over 2,000 years. In one of his dialogues, he likened the soul to a chariot with two horses that often pull in opposed directions. The chariot's driver is Reason, the two horses are Spirit (our nobler emotions) and Appetite. This Renaissance medallion depicts Plato's image of the internal conflict.**

CONFLICT AND DEFENSE

Freud's threefold division of the personality was just a way of saying that our thoughts and actions are determined by the interplay of three major factors: our biological drives (the id), the commands and prohibitions of society (the superego), and the various ways we have learned to satisfy the former while respecting the latter (the ego).

Obviously, though, these three forces will sometimes pull us in different directions—for example, when we want to do something but know we cannot or should not—and this guarantees that there will often be conflict among the competing forces. What is the nature of this conflict? Imagine that a child performs some forbidden act and is then scolded or disciplined by his parents. The parents may resort to physical punishment, or they may merely register their disapproval with a reprimand; in either case, the child feels threatened with the loss of his parents' love and becomes anxious about this. This anxiety leaves its mark, and the next time the child is about to perform the same act—say, touch his penis or pinch his baby brother—he will feel a twinge of *anxiety*, an internal reminder of the prospect that his parents may castigate him and that he will be abandoned and alone.

Since anxiety is very unpleasant, the child will do everything he can to remove it or to ward it off. If the cause of the anxiety is a real-world event or object, the child can simply run away and remove himself from it. But how can he cope with a danger lurking within—a threatening fantasy, a forbidden wish? To quell this anxiety, the child must suppress the thoughts that triggered it, pushing the thoughts from conscious view. In short, the thought must be repressed.

Notice, then, that Freud viewed *repression* as applying to the thought no less than the deed. Almost everyone (both before Freud and after) believes that, say, a 4-year-old boy who is punished for pinching his brother will refrain from such combative acts in the future. What is crucial for Freud, though, is that the boy not only stops performing these acts; he will probably also stop thinking about them and even fail to remember he has done them in the past! In this fashion, the inhibition applies not just to overt action, but to related thoughts, memories, and wishes as well.

Repression serves as the primary *defense mechanism* that protects the individual from anxiety. But repression is often incomplete. The thoughts and urges that were pushed underground may refuse to stay buried and resurface instead. But as they do, so does the anxiety with which they are associated. As a result, various further mechanisms of defense are brought into play to reinforce the original dam against the forbidden impulses.

One such mechanism is *displacement*—a process in which repressed urges find new and often disguised outlets, outlets that are more acceptable to the ego and superego. An example is a child who is disciplined by her parents and who then vents her anger on a doll.

In displacement, the forbidden impulse is rechanneled into a safer course. Other defense mechanisms are attempts to supplement the original repression by blocking the impulse altogether. An example is *reaction formation*, in which the repressed wish is warded off by its diametrical opposite. A young boy who hates his sister and is punished for calling her names may turn his feelings into the very opposite; he now bombards her with exaggerated love and tenderness, a desperate bulwark against aggressive wishes that he cannot accept.

In other defense mechanisms, the repressed thoughts do break through but are reinterpreted or unacknowledged. One example of this is *rationalization*, in which the person interprets her own feelings or actions in more acceptable terms. The cruel father beats his child mercilessly but is sure that he does so "for the child's own good." Another defense mechanism in which cognitive reorganization plays a major role is *projection*. Here the forbidden urges well up and are recognized as such. But the person does not realize that these wishes are his own; instead, he attributes them to others. "I desire you" becomes

Rationalization *The expression* sour grapes *comes from a fable by Aesop, which tells of a fox who desperately desired some grapes that hung overhead. When the fox discovered that the grapes were so high that he could not reach them, he said that he never really wanted them, for they were much too sour.*

"You desire me," and "I hate you" becomes "You hate me"—desperate defenses against repressed sexual or hostile wishes that can no longer be banished from consciousness (S. Freud, 1911; and see Lewis, Bates, & Lawrence, 1994; Schul & Vinokur, 2000).

THE DEVELOPING MIND

Freud (1905) believed that the unconscious conflicts he uncovered derived from events in early childhood. Many of these events were, in his view, remarkably similar from person to person, and give rise to a general set of stages through which we all pass. Because many of these formative events center around our emerging sexual impulses, Freud called these the stages of psychosexual development. Although Freud believed the stages were universal, just how the conflicts at each stage were handled differed from person to person, and it was these differences, in Freud's view, that gave rise both to normal variation in personality, and to psychopathology.

PSYCHOSEXUAL DEVELOPMENT

In Freud's view, the child starts life as a bundle of instincts to seek pleasure, with the pleasure readily found in the stimulation of certain sensitive zones of the body: the mouth, the anus, and the genitals. Initially, most of the child's pleasure seeking is through the mouth, a period of life that Freud termed the *oral stage*. As the infant attains bowel control, the emphasis shifts to the anus (the *anal stage*). Still later, the child shows increased interest in pleasure from genital stimulation (the *phallic stage*). The culmination of psychosexual development is attained in adult sexuality when pleasure involves not just one's own gratification but also the social and bodily satisfaction brought to another person (the *genital stage*).

   The child's progression from one stage to the next is partly a matter of physical maturation. For example, bowel control is simply impossible at birth, because the infant lacks the necessary neuromuscular readiness. But there is another element. As the child's body matures, there is an inevitable change in what the parents allow, prohibit, or demand. Initially, the child nurses but then must be weaned and taught to drink from a cup. She is diapered at first and then toilet trained and expected to retain her feces until she reaches the toilet. When she is old enough, she learns about her "private parts" and is told that they are to be touched only in private, if at all. At each stage, the child is expected to give up her major pleasure and supplant it by the next one in the developmental sequence.

THE ORIGIN OF INDIVIDUAL DIFFERENCES

As Freud saw it, shifting from stage to stage within this sequence is usually frustrating to the infant, as she is asked to give up first one pleasure and then another, and how the infant (and later, the young child) handles the frustration lays the groundwork for the personality traits she will develop as she matures. An example is the adult personality pattern that Freud called the *oral character*, which he believed was grounded in an oral fixation, or being mentally stuck in the oral phase. During the oral stage, Freud argued, the infant feels warm, well fed, and protected, leading an idyllic existence in which all is given and nothing is asked for in return. According to Freud and his student Karl Abraham, fixation at this stage can lead the adult to relate to others as he once did the breast, usually as passive dependency. Thus, the adult "Please love me" derives from the infantile "Feed me" (Abraham, 1927).

   Freud and Abraham also proposed an *anal character*, which derives from severe conflicts during toilet training. One way a child may handle this conflict is to inhibit rather than relax his bowels (Abraham, 1927; S. Freud, 1908). This refusal to defecate then broadens. The child becomes compulsively clean and orderly ("I must not go in my

Anal personality **Ebenezer Scrooge (a character in Charles Dickens's A Christmas Carol) exemplifies what Freud envisioned as an anal personality.**

"Why can't you be more like Oedipus?"

pants" becomes "I shouldn't make a mess"). Another effect is obstinacy and defiance. The child asserts himself by holding back on the potty ("You can't make me go if I don't want to"), a stubbornness that may soon become a more generalized defiant "no." Other characteristics are stinginess and hoarding, which, for Freud, were nothing but symbolic withholding (the infantile "I will never defecate" becomes the adult "I'm keeping this all for myself").

Although he considered the conflicts of the oral and anal stages important in shaping adult personality, Freud believed that their influence paled compared to how the child handled the frustration associated with the phallic stage. Freud called this pivotal point in the child's psychosexual development the *Oedipus complex*, after the Theban king of classical Greek literature who unwittingly committed two awful crimes—killing his father and marrying his mother. According to Freud, an analogous family drama is reenacted in the childhoods of all men and women. Because Freud (1905) came to believe that the sequence of steps is somewhat different in the two sexes, we will take them up separately.

At about the age of 3 or 4 years, the phallic stage begins for the young boy. At this time, he becomes increasingly interested in his penis, and he seeks an external object for his sexual urges. The inevitable choice, in Freud's view, is the most important woman in the boy's young life—his mother. But there is an obstacle—the boy's father. The little boy wants to have his mother all to himself, as a comforter as well as an erotic partner, but this sexual utopia is out of the question. His father is a rival, and he is bigger. The little boy wants his father to go away and not come back—in short, to die.

At this point, a new element enters into the family drama. The little boy begins to fear the father he is jealous of. According to Freud, this is because the boy is certain that the father knows of his son's hostility and will surely answer hate with hate. With childish logic, the little boy becomes convinced the punishment his father will mete out will be catastrophic. This leads to intolerable anxiety, and so the boy tries to push his hostile feelings out of consciousness, but they refuse to stay underground. They return, and the only defense left is projection—"I hate father because father hates me." This naturally increases the boy's fear, which increases his hostility, which is again pushed out of consciousness, resurges, and leads to further projection. The process snowballs, until the father is seen as an overwhelming ogre who threatens to annihilate his little son.

As the little boy grows, so does his rivalry with his father and its accompanying terror. Eventually, though, he hits on a solution. He throws in the towel, relinquishes his mother as an erotic object, identifies with his father, and renounces genital pleasure, at least for a while.

Freud believed that, once this resolution has been achieved, the tumult of the Oedipal conflict dies down, and the boy enters a period of comparative sexual quiescence that lasts until the age of 12 years. This is the latency period during which boys play only with boys and want nothing to do with the opposite sex. But as hormone levels rise and the sex organs mature, the repressed sexual impulses can no longer be denied. As these impulses surge to the fore, parts of the Oedipal family skeleton come out as well, dragging along many of the fears and conflicts that had been comfortably hidden away for all these years. This ushers in the genital stage, as the child becomes an adult.

What about girls? In Freud's view, females go through essentially identical oral and anal phases as do males. And in many ways, the development of her phallic interests (Freud used the same term for both sexes) corresponds to the male's. As he focuses his erotic interests on the mother, so she focuses hers on the father. As he resents and eventually fears his father, so does she her mother. In short, there is a female version of the Oedipus complex (sometimes called the *Electra complex*, after the Greek tragic heroine who goaded her brother into slaying their mother).

Like young boys, young girls' first attachment is to their mother. It is the mother, after all, who nurses the infant (and so provides pleasure during the oral phase). It is likewise the mother who, for most infants, is the primary caregiver. So why, according to Freud, does a girl switch love objects and come to desire her father? To answer this question, Freud elaborated a scheme that is widely regarded as one of the weakest aspects of his whole theory. He proposed that the shift of attachment begins as the little girl discovers that she does not have a penis. According to Freud, she regards this lack as a catastrophe, considers herself unworthy, and develops *penis envy*. One consequence is that she withdraws her love from the mother, whom she regards as equally unworthy. Freud argued that, painfully, she turns to her father, who has the desirable organ and who she believes can help her obtain a penis substitute—a child. (Why child-equals-penis requires even more elaborate arguments.) From here on, the rest of the process unfolds more or less like its counterpart in the boy: love of father, jealousy of mother, increasing fear of mother, eventual repression of the entire complex, and identification with the mother (S. Freud, 1925, 1933; LaFarge, 1993).

WINDOWS INTO THE UNCONSCIOUS

Many people regard this theory as incredibly far-fetched, but Freud believed firmly that his conception was demanded by the evidence he collected. We have already sketched the broad outlines of this evidence: Freud believed that painful beliefs and ideas were repressed, but that the repression was never complete. Therefore, these anxiety-producing ideas would still come to the surface—but (thanks to other defense mechanisms) only in disguised form. The goal of the analyst, therefore, and the source of evidence for Freud's theory, came from a process of interpretation that allowed Freud to penetrate the disguise, and thus to reveal the crucial underlying psychological dynamics. In Freud's view, this analysis was properly focused on thoughts or behaviors for which the disguise, produced by the defense mechanisms, was particularly thin.

For example, Freud continually drew attention to what he called the "psychopathology of everyday life." For example, we might forget a name that reminds us of an embarrassing moment, or suffer a slip of the tongue that unwittingly reveals an underlying motive, or "absent-mindedly" not finish something we did not want to do anyway (see S. Freud, 1901). Freud certainly understood that some slips or lapses do not reveal unconscious motives. The husband who calls a female coworker by his wife's name may not be having unconscious adulterous urges; instead, he may simply be speaking out of habit. But some slips, Freud argued, were revealing, and, if properly interpreted in the context of other evidence, they could provide important insights into an individual's unconscious thoughts and fears.

Freud also believed that we could learn much about an individual through the interpretation of dreams (Fosshage, 1983; S. Freud, 1900), because, in Freud's view, all dreams are at bottom attempts at wish fulfillment. While one is awake, a wish is usually not acted on right away, for there are considerations of both reality (the ego) and morality (the superego) that must be taken into account: Is it possible? Is it allowed? But during sleep these restraining forces are drastically weakened, and the wish then leads to immediate thoughts and images of gratification. In some cases the wish fulfillment is simple and direct. Starving explorers dream of sumptuous meals; people stranded in the desert dream of cool mountain streams. According to a Hungarian proverb quoted by Freud, "Pigs dream of acorns, and geese dream of maize."

What about our more fantastic dreams, the ones with illogical plots, bizarre characters, and opaque symbolism? These are also attempts at wish fulfillment, Freud believed, but with a key difference: They touch on forbidden, anxiety-laden ideas that cannot be entertained directly. As a result, various mechanisms of defense prohibit the literal expression of the idea but allow it to slip through in disguised, symbolic form (e.g., a penis may be symbolized as a sword, a vagina as a cave). Because of this

"Good morning, beheaded—uh, I mean beloved."

Jacob's Ladder by Nicholas Dipre (1495–1523)

disguise, the dreamer may never experience the underlying *latent content* of the dream—the actual wishes and concerns that the dream is constructed to express. What he experiences instead is the carefully laundered version that emerges after the defense mechanisms have done their work—the dream's *manifest content*. This self-protection takes mental effort, but, according to Freud, the alternative—facing our impulses unadulterated—would let very few of us sleep for long.

Yet another form of evidence that Freud pointed to are the myths, legends, and fairy tales shared within a culture. He contended that just as dreams are a window into the individual's unconscious, these (often unwritten) forms of literature allow us a glimpse into the hidden concerns shared by whole cultural groups, if not all of humanity. Indeed, one of Freud's earliest colleagues, the Swiss psychiatrist Carl Jung (1875–1961), argued for a *collective unconscious* consisting of primordial stories and images—he called these *archetypes*—that shape our perceptions and desires just as much as Freud's psychodynamics (Jung, 1964).

Psychoanalysts who have delved into such tales have found, for example, an ample supply of Oedipal themes. There are numerous ogres, dragons, and monsters to be slain before the prize can be won. The villain is often a cruel stepparent—a fairly transparent symbol, in their view, of Oedipal hostilities.

As an illustration of a psychoanalytic interpretation of a fairy tale, consider "Snow White and the Seven Dwarfs" (J. F. Brown, 1940). Snow White is a child princess who is persecuted by her stepmother, the wicked queen. The queen is envious of Snow White's beauty and tries to have her killed. The child escapes and lives with seven dwarfs who work in an underground mine. The queen finally discovers Snow White and persuades her to eat part of a poisoned apple. Snow White falls as if dead. The dwarfs place her in a beautiful casket in which she lies motionless for seven years. At this point, a handsome prince appears, opens the casket with his sword, awakens Snow White from her long sleep, and the two live happily ever after.

According to psychoanalytic authors, this fairy tale is a veiled allegory of the Oedipal sequence (Bettelheim, 1975). The wicked queen is the mother on whom the child projects her own hate and sexual jealousy. The Oedipal—or more precisely, Electra—conflict is temporarily resolved as the child's erotic urges go underground and remain dormant for the seven years of the latency period, symbolized both by Snow White's long sleep and by the seven dwarfs. At the end of this period, her sexuality is reawakened in adult form by the young prince. (The meaning of the sword is left as an exercise for the reader.)

Freud and mythology   Many myths, legends, and stories can be interpreted in psychoanalytic terms.

CRITICISMS AND CRITIQUES

In the early part of the twentieth century, the lay public—especially in the United States—was fascinated by the bearded Viennese doctor who spoke so frankly about sex. Scholars in the social sciences, literature, and the arts flocked to read his writings because they were so far-reaching in scope, so profound in their implications. Freud's theories offered nothing less than a new way to understand human nature, and Freudian insights are still influential in many academic pursuits (e.g., the interpretation of literature) and in popular culture. A century later, however, many psychologists are deeply skeptical about most of Freud's proposals. What are their concerns?

FREUD'S THEORY OF REPRESSION

One of the cornerstones of psychoanalytic thought is repression. Yet results of empirical studies of repression have been mixed. Some studies have yielded data consistent with Freud's view, showing that people are somewhat less likely to recall materials associated with anxiety (Jacobs, 1955). Other studies have shown that participants are more likely to recall events that put them in a good light, in comparison to those that are less flattering (Erdelyi & Goldberg, 1979; Kunda, 1990). Still other studies have indicated that, when we wish to, we can make ourselves less likely to remember certain things, a result that obviously points in the same direction as Freud's claims about repression (Anderson et al., 2004; Joslyn & Oakes 2005). But, alongside of these studies, other research, aimed more specifically at uncovering evidence of repression, has yielded no evidence for the mechanisms Freud proposed (Holmes, 1990), and at least some of the studies allegedly showing repression have been roundly criticized by other researchers (Kihlstrom, 2002).

Even if we take seriously the favorable studies, there is no reason they must be cast in Freudian terms. As we saw in Chapter 7, information will become established in memory only if it is suitably rehearsed, and a person may simply elect not to mull over unpleasant experiences, making her less likely to remember them later. Likewise, memory retrieval is a process that requires both effort and strategy; for unpleasant memories, someone might choose neither to spend the effort nor to engage an effective strategy. In these ways, we can explain a self-serving bias in memory with no appeal to the sort of imperious censor envisioned by Freud. In addition, the self-serving bias in memory is certainly not strong, and people often remember episodes in which they were anxious, or embarrassed, or suffered some loss (see, for example, Gilovich, 1991)—results seemingly in conflict with the proposal of repression.

Even in cases involving genuine trauma, the data provide little indication of repression. A few studies do show poor memory for traumas, but a variety of problems makes these studies difficult to interpret (see, for example, L. Williams, 1994; and then, for critiques, McNally, 2003; Shobe & Kihlstrom, 1997). More typically, the results indicate the opposite of repression—with people fully able to remember, in vivid and horrifying detail, the horrible traumas they have endured. Women who have been raped, for example, are typically plagued by too many memories about their violators and the setting of their violation; children who have witnessed violent crimes are often long haunted by nightmares about them; survivors of Nazi death camps can recall minutiae about the death chambers, the killings, and the carnage fully half a century later; and so on (see, for example, Terr, 1991, 1994). In all such cases, these deeply painful memories would surely be eligible for repression—and for the victims, repression would be merciful. The fact that these memories are not repressed creates a serious problem for Freud's conception. (For further discussion, see Kihlstrom, 1997; McNally, 2003; Nadel & Jacobs, 1998; D. L. Schacter, 1996; Shobe & Kihlstrom, 1997; see also Chapter 7.)

One other line of evidence, sometimes cited as a demonstration of repression, is at best ambiguous. This evidence comes from cases in which people have "recovered"

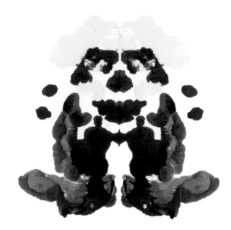

15.4 *An inkblot of the type used in the Rorschach test*   *Because familiarity with the cards makes it difficult to evaluate a person's first reaction, most psychologists prefer not to print the actual inkblots used in the test. Five of the actual cards are in black and white; five others are colored.*

Another popular projective test has the participant describe what he sees in an inkblot (**Rorschach Inkblot Test**: Rorschach, 1921). Ten cards are presented, one at a time, with each card showing a symmetrical inkblot, some colored and some black and white. For each card, the examinee is asked what he sees (see Figure 15.4 for an example of a card similar to those used in the test). After all 10 cards have been presented, the examiner questions the examinee about each response to find out which part of the blot was used and which of its attributes were most important (Exner, 1974, 1978, 1993; Klopfer, Ainsworth, Klopfer, & Holt, 1954). The responses are scored according to various categories, such as the portion of the blot that is used in the response (e.g., the whole blot, a large detail, a small detail), the attributes of the stimulus that are the basis of the response (e.g., form, shading, color), and the content of the response (e.g., human figures, parts of human figures, animals or parts of animals, inanimate objects, blood). Rorschach experts stipulate that the interpretation of a Rorschach record is not a simple cookbook affair, but rather relies on the interrelations among all of the response's features. Nonetheless, Rorschach interpreters do use some general guidelines. For example, using the white space as the foreground of a response is supposed to imply rebelliousness and negativism, and responses that are dominated by color suggest emotionality and impulsivity.

Unfortunately, there is little evidence for the validity of these projective tests (Garb, Wood, Lilienfeld, & Nezworski, 2002; Hunsley & Bailey, 1999). Thus, for example, conclusions drawn from these tests are rarely confirmed (and often contradicted) by evidence from other sources. It would seem, therefore, that instruments such as the Rorschach and the TAT do not provide a more secure foundation for psychodynamic theorizing than did Freud's initial case reports.

PSYCHODYNAMIC FORMULATIONS AFTER FREUD

Throughout his long career, Freud stood firmly at the center of the psychoanalytic movement that he had launched. However, the complexity of Freud's theoretical edifice ensured that even in his lifetime, there were many who developed their own extensions and elaborations of his theorizing, much to Freud's chagrin. Two notable examples were Alfred Adler (1870–1937), who argued that a well-adjusted life requires involvement in one's social community, and Carl Jung (1875–1961), who believed in a collective unconscious that represented the experiences of the ages and expressed itself in universal symbols, or *archetypes*. This led to a splintering of the psychoanalytic movement that only accelerated after Freud's death, producing a welter of schools and camps, all of which are subsumed under the general label "psychodynamic approaches."

EGO PSYCHOLOGY AND MECHANISMS OF DEFENSE

One major theme among those who carried forward the torch of psychoanalytic theory was that Freud had not sufficiently emphasized the skills and adaptive capacities of the ego. Writers of this persuasion, loosely grouped under the heading of *ego psychology*, sought to extend and complete Freud's theorizing. Some of the major figures in the group are Heinz Hartmann (1894–1970), Erik Erikson (1902–1994), and Robert White (1904–2001).

One of the scholars who concentrated on the ego's capabilities was Freud's daughter, Anna Freud (1895–1982). Anna was psychoanalyzed by her father, and throughout her long and distinguished career she delicately balanced the often-inconsistent goals of remaining loyal to her father's thinking while also expressing her own unique vision. In one of her important contributions, Anna Freud systematized and extended what her father had written regarding the types of defenses used to manage the anxieties engendered in the ego by the world, the superego, or the id's impulses that pressed for expression (A. Freud, 1946).

Sigmund and Anna Freud   *This photo of the two was taken in 1913 while they were on a holiday in the Dolomites, Italy.*

Other theorists have refined and extended Anna Freud's thinking about the ego's defense mechanisms (Brenner, 1982). These more contemporary theorists agree with Freud's original contention that unconscious conflict is found in the well adjusted as well as in people with disabling mental disorders; their emphasis, though, is on how those conflicts can be resolved in a fashion that is appropriate, pragmatic, and, ultimately, healthy. Adherents of this position stress the positive aspects of the self as it tries to cope with the world—to deal with reality as it is rather than to distort it or hide from it. Seen in this light, the ego is not just an arbiter between id and superego, but a clever strategist with intrinsic competencies (A. Freud, 1946; Hartmann, 1964).

Building from this perspective, a number of investigators have explored how coping patterns evolve over the course of the life span, and some of the data derive from longitudinal studies covering a span of 20 to 30 years (J. Block & J. H. Block, 2006). An example is George Vaillant's analysis of the case reports of 94 male Harvard College graduates studied at different points in their life span. They were extensively interviewed at age 19, then again at 31, and yet again at 47. Vaillant studied the predominant patterns of defense—that is, ways of coping—each man used at these three ages. He classified the coping patterns according to their level of psychological maturity. At the bottom of the hierarchy were mechanisms that are often found in early childhood and during serious mental disorder, such as denial or gross distortions of external reality. Further up the ladder were patterns often seen in adolescence and in disturbed adults, such as projection, hypochondria, and irrational, emotional outbursts. Still higher were the mechanisms studied by Freud and seen in many adults—repression, reaction formation, and the like. At the top of the hierarchy were coping patterns that Vaillant considered healthy (in adolescents and adults)—such as humor, suppression (a conscious effort to push anxiety-provoking thoughts out of mind, at least for the time being, as opposed to repression, which is an unconscious process), and altruism (in which one tries to give to others what one might wish to receive oneself).

Vaillant's findings indicated considerable continuity. Men with more adaptive coping patterns at age 19 were more likely to have mature patterns in their forties, and these in turn predicted the results on various objective indices that personality psychologists refer to as *life data*, such as satisfaction in marriage, rewarding friendships, gratifying jobs, and good physical health (Figure 15.5). As is so often the case, it is by no means clear just what in those men's lives was cause and what was effect, but regardless of whether the mature coping defenses produced success in marriage and career or vice versa, it is worth knowing that the two tend to be correlated (Vaillant, 1974, 1976, 1977, 1994). And this correlation is not restricted to Harvard males; it was also observed in a study of 131 inner-city males interviewed in junior high school and then surveyed 30 years later (G. E. Vaillant, Bond, & Vaillant, 1986).

OBJECT RELATIONS AND ATTACHMENT THEORY

Many who followed Freud believed he had insufficiently emphasized the real (as opposed to fantasized) relations an individual had with others. Some of the most prominent of these theorists were Melanie Klein (1882–1960), Margaret Mahler (1897–1985), D.W. Winnicott (1896–1971), and Heinz Kohut (1913–1981). Despite their many differences, these *object relations* theorists held that relationships with important others constitute a powerful and relatively neglected motive underlying human behavior. Arguably, the object relations theorist with the broadest and most enduring impact was John Bowlby (1907–1990). As described in Chapter 11, Bowlby was a British psychiatrist who believed people were powerfully motivated by the desire for connection and closeness with others. In particular, Bowlby was concerned with the attachment between infants or young children and their caregivers.

Bowlby believed that a child was powerfully shaped by her experiences with her *primary attachment figure* (typically, but not always, her mother), and emerged from childhood

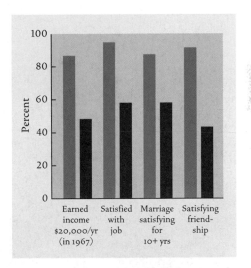

15.5 Maturity of defense mechanisms and life adjustment **Adult success at work and love, as shown by men with predominantly mature (green) and immature (red) adaptive styles.**

with a set of foundational beliefs about both herself (as essentially good and loveable or not) and others (as essentially good and loving or not). These mental representations of self and other are referred to as *working models*.

Bowlby emphasized that different children develop different working models, but it was Mary Ainsworth (1913–1999) who created an experimental procedure designed to probe these differences, and, in particular, to assess what type of attachment a child had formed with his caregiver (Ainsworth, Blehar, Waters, & Wall, 1978). As we discussed in Chapter 11, this Strange Situation test can be used to categorize children as *securely attached*, *anxious/avoidant* in their attachment, *anxious/resistant*, or *disorganized* in their attachment. These attachment patterns, in turn, can then be used as predictors for a number of subsequent measures—including the child's personality in the next years, and the quality of the child's social relations.

Atttachment theory has been a significant source of inspiration for researchers in personality, who have found that the attachment patterns established in early childhood seem to have considerable staying power (Bartholomew & Horowitz, 1991; Brennan, Clark, & Shaver, 1998; Mikulincer & Shaver, 2005). For example, Shaver and Clark (1994) found that compared to secure adults, anxious/avoidant adults are less interested in romantic relationships and seem less upset when they end. In contrast, anxious/resistant adults are highly focused on their relationships, and they fret and fume about them to a much greater extent than secure individuals.

Does all of this mean that one is simply out of luck if one has not developed the "right" working model in childhood? Happily, the answer appears to be no. Working models of self and other seem to be at least somewhat malleable and context dependent, and new experiences (whether with friends, dating partners, or a therapist) seem to have the power to refashion a person's early ideas about self and other. Even so, the ability to predict adult outcomes, based on childhood patterns, does lend support to at least one part of Freud's perspective—namely, the claim that the early years do play a critical role in shaping adult behaviors, expectations, and personality.

CONTRIBUTIONS OF THE PSYCHODYNAMIC APPROACH

Freud's belief that we are creatures riddled by internal conflicts of which we are often oblivious is perhaps his most enduring contribution to the study of personality. Of course, Freud was far from the first to recognize that we are often torn psychologically and do not really know what we want and why (Ellenberger, 1970; Sulloway, 1979). Yet he was the first to make this insight the cornerstone of an entire theory. Freud saw clearly that we do not know ourselves and that we are often not masters of our own psyches.

A second major contribution made by Freud lies in his drawing our attention to a set of ideas whose freshness and relevance today belie the century or more that has passed since he started articulating his views (Westen, 1998). These ideas include the notion that many important psychological processes—especially affective and motivational processes—operate outside of awareness, and also the idea that our motives and impulses are often at odds with one another. Contemporary psychologists would still endorse Freud's claim that people's thoughts, feelings, and behaviors are strongly influenced by their mental representations of important people in their lives, as well as his claim that among other things, development revolves around finding socially acceptable ways of managing sexual and aggressive impulses. Admittedly, many of

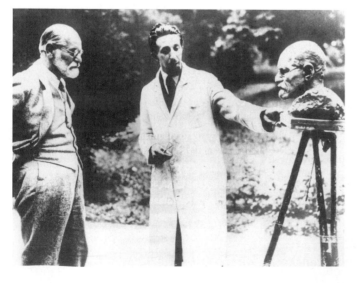

Reflecting on Freud   Freud looking at a bust of himself sculpted for his 75th birthday.

these ideas have their origins in theories predating Freud. It is also true that the modern conception of these ideas is, in important ways, different from Freud's specific proposals, and that these ideas, in the modern era, often have a less central position than they had in Freud's theorizing. Nonetheless, Freud undeniably deserves credit for putting these essential ideas onto center stage for many modern theories of personality.

An additional contribution made by the psychodynamic approach is that it offered a view of human nature that was virtually all-embracing. Whether the view is correct or not, it at least tried to encompass both rational thought and emotional urges. It conceived of psychological ailments as a consequence of the same forces that operate in everyday life. It saw humans as biological organisms as well as social beings, as creatures whose present is rooted in their past. The range of psychological phenomena that Freud encompassed within his theory is staggering—symptoms of mental disorder, personality patterns, social groupings, family relations, humor, slips of the tongue, dreams, artistic production, religious sentiment. While Freud's theory has many and profound faults, it showed us the kinds of questions we must answer before we can claim to have a full theory of human personality.

THE HUMANISTIC APPROACH: APPRECIATING OUR POTENTIAL

Half a century ago, a new perspective on human motivation and personality—the *humanistic approach*—gained prominence. According to its adherents, both trait theorists and psychodynamic theorists have lost sight of what is truly human about human beings. Healthy humans, the humanists argue, want to feel free to choose and determine their own lives rather than to exist as mere pawns driven by demons from within or pushed around by stimuli from without. They seek more than food and sex, and strive for more than mere adjustment—they want to grow and develop their potential.

THE MAJOR FEATURES OF THE HUMANISTIC MOVEMENT

A major feature of humanistic psychology is its conception of human motivation. As Abraham Maslow (1908–1970) noted early on, other approaches to personality conceive of human beings as engaged in a never-ending struggle to remove some internal tension or make up for some deficit. Seen in this light, people always want to get away from something (e.g., anxiety, sexual tension) rather than to gain something positive.

But as Maslow pointed out, release from anxiety and tension does not account for everything we strive for. We sometimes seek things for their own sake, as positive goals in themselves. There is, for example, the satisfaction of solving a difficult problem, the exhilaration of riding a roller coaster or dancing, the ecstasy of fulfilled love, the quiet rapture in contemplating a beautiful sunrise, the grandeur of Beethoven's Ninth Symphony. Maslow (1968, 1996) insisted that to understand what is truly human, psychologists must consider all our motives, including ones that transcend mere deficiency needs that arise from physical requirements such as those for food, water, and the like.

These concerns led Maslow to propose a *hierarchy of needs* in which the lower-order physiological needs are at the bottom, safety needs are further up, the need for attachment and love is still higher, and the desire for esteem is higher yet. Higher

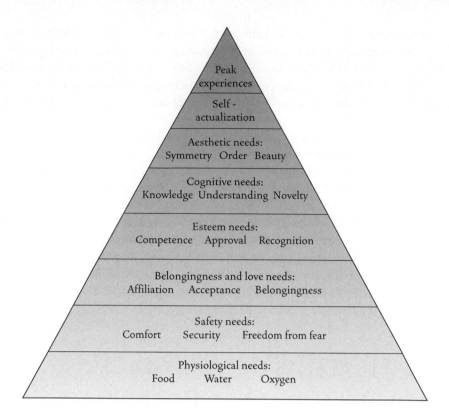

15.6 Maslow's hierarchy of needs *People will strive for higher-order needs (such as esteem or artistic achievement) generally after lower-order needs (hunger, safety) have been satisfied.*

still, toward the top of the hierarchy, is the striving for *self-actualization*—the desire to realize oneself to the fullest (of which more later) (Figure 15.6).

Maslow believed that people will only strive for higher-order needs (e.g., self-esteem or artistic achievement) when lower-order needs (e.g., hunger) are satisfied. By and large this is plausible enough; the urge to write poetry generally takes a back seat if one has not eaten for days. But as Maslow pointed out, there are exceptions. Some artists starve rather than give up their poetry or their painting, and some martyrs proclaim their faith regardless of pain or suffering. But to the extent that Maslow's assumption holds, a motive toward the top of his hierarchy—such as the drive toward self-actualization—will become primary only when all other needs beneath it are satisfied.

THE SELF IN HUMANISTIC PSYCHOLOGY

Before trying to describe what Maslow and other humanistic psychologists mean by self-actualization, we should say a word about the self that is (or is not) being actualized. To humanistic psychologists, the self is enormously important, because one of their primary concerns is with subjective experience—with what the individual thinks and feels right here and now. According to Carl Rogers (1902–1987), a major figure in the humanistic movement, a crucial facet of this subjective experience is the self or *self-concept*. This self-concept develops in early childhood and eventually comes to include one's sense of oneself—the "I"—as an agent who takes (or does not take) actions and makes (or does not make) decisions. It also includes one's sense of oneself as a kind of object—the "me"—that is seen and thought about, liked or disliked (Rogers, 1959, 1961). Ideally, one will develop an abiding, positive sense of self-worth; according to Rogers, this requires that, as a child, the person experience *unconditional positive regard*—the sense of being accepted and loved without condition or reservation.

Carl Rogers

SELF-ACTUALIZATION

Given a reasonable sense of self-worth and the satisfaction of the lower-level needs, the stage is set for the motive at the top of Maslow's hierarchy of needs, the desire for self-actualization. Maslow (1968, 1970) and other humanistic psychologists describe this as the desire to realize one's potential, to fulfill oneself, to become what one can become. But exactly what does this mean?

Maslow gave some examples by presenting case histories of a number of people whom he and his collaborators regarded as self-actualized. Some of them were individuals he had personally interviewed; others were historical figures (e.g., Thomas Jefferson and Eleanor Roosevelt) whose lives were studied by means of historical documents. As Maslow (1968, 1970, 1996) saw it, these self-actualizers were all realistically oriented, accepted themselves and others, were spontaneous, cared more about the problems they were working on than about themselves, had intimate relationships with a few people rather than superficial relationships with many, and had democratic values —all in all, an admirable list of human qualities.

These traits, and the roll call of self-actualized individuals, might make self-actualization sound as though it were only for the few and the powerful. Not so. One of the major themes of humanistic psychology is that we each have within us the impulse to self-actualize. Indeed, Rogers regarded this as our one basic motive, and he argued that we often manage to self-actualize against extraordinary odds, much as a plant does, improbably pushing itself through a crack in a concrete-covered playground (Rogers, 1951, 1961). But Rogers was no Pollyanna. He knew that there were many failures in self-actualization, and he regarded this fact as a testament to the many forces that work against self-actualization in our families and in the larger society, rather than as a sign that self-actualization is not a fundamental motive.

POSITIVE PSYCHOLOGY

Maslow, Rogers, and other humanists all enjoined psychologists not to cast their work in terms of deficiency and pathology, because doing so leads us to ignore our higher-level needs and leaves us with a myopic view of human nature. Many of the same themes underlie a recent movement called *positive psychology*.

Self-actualizers   According to Maslow, Thomas Jefferson, Abraham Lincoln, and Eleanor Roosevelt are clear examples of people who self-actualized.

Advocates of positive psychology note just how many scientifically oriented psychology books, courses, and research programs focus on "fixing" what is wrong with the individual, her brain, her hormones, or her social adjustment, and how few focus on defining *well-being* and saying how it is attained. The positive-psychology movement is an attempt to redress this deficiency by defining the "good life" and discerning methods for promoting it. Unlike the humanistic psychology of Maslow and Rogers, however, positive psychology is intended to move past biographical studies and philosophizing about the human condition, to experiments that determine what defines and engenders optimal human functioning (Seligman & Csikszentmihalyi, 2000). It asks such questions as "What is it that makes people healthy?" (see, for example, Salovey, Rothman, Detweiler, & Steward, 2000) and "What is it that makes us happy?" (see Kahneman, Diener, & Schwarz, 1999) and seeks to understand positive experiences, positive individual traits, and positive institutions (Peterson & Seligman, 2004). In so doing, it broadens our understanding of what it is to be human by considering not just how we can free ourselves from misery, but also how we can attain positive health (Ryff & Singer, 1998).

What are the ingredients of happiness, well-being, and positive health? Various research efforts now under way point to the importance of unvarnished optimism, as well as religious faith, close personal relationships, and a sense of self-determination. These qualities appear to influence not only one's mental life but also one's physical health (Salovey et al., 2000). For example, evidence indicates that people who are generally optimistic also have a better-functioning immune system, with potential consequences for their physical health (Segerstrom, 2000). Cross-cultural research suggests that some predictors of well-being—such as satisfaction with friends and satisfaction with family—are consistent across cultures (Diener, Shigehiro, & Lucas, 2003; Peterson & Seligman, 2004). Other predictors of well-being, though, vary by culture. For example, in individualistic cultures, satisfaction with self is closely tied to overall well-being. However, in collectivistic cultures, satisfaction with self is appreciably less important. (For more on this contrast between individualistic and collectivistic cultures, see Chapter 12.)

Across many settings, though, one factor that is crucial in determining someone's happiness is the phenomenon of *adaptation*—the fact that humans quickly grow accustomed to (and cease paying attention to) any stimulus or state to which they are continually exposed. One remarkable demonstration of this point comes from a study that compared the sense of well-being among a group of people who had won the lottery and a group of paraplegics (Brickman, Coates, & Janoff-Bullman, 1978). Not surprisingly, the two groups were quite different soon after the winning of the lottery or the loss of the use of their limbs. When surveyed a few months after these events, however, the two groups were extremely similar in their sense of contentment with their lives—an extraordinary testimony to the power of adaptation and to the human capacity for adjusting to extreme circumstances.

The capacity for adaptation *Lottery winners are initially thrilled by their good fortune, but soon adapt to their new status and end up no happier than other people.*

Adaptation obviously allows us to cope with life's troubles, but there is a downside to adaptation, because we also adapt to life's gains. Thus, winning the lottery might make us happy for a short while, but then we adapt and so no longer take pleasure from our winnings. Getting a new job, or launching a new romance, might likewise make us happy for a while, but, again, we adapt and so treat our new circumstances merely as "normal," with no gain in well-being.

Fortunately, though, adaptation to positive events is not inevitable. In one study, participants were randomly assigned either to a control condition (in which they wrote about their early memories every night for a week) or to one of several interventions, which included tasks such as writing down three good things that happened each day for a week (Seligman, Steen, Park, & Peterson, 2005). The data showed that, 6 months later, participants in the intervention groups demonstrated greater well-being (and lesser depression). These findings suggest that it indeed may be possible to create interventions that increase longer-term happiness.

CONTRIBUTIONS OF THE HUMANISTIC APPROACH

How should we evaluate the humanistic approach to personality? We certainly need to be cautious in evaluating the conceptual claims offered by Maslow, Rogers, and their contemporaries. After all, just what is meant by *self-actualization*, or by *letting yourself go* and *being yourself*, or by *unconditional positive regard*? Since these terms are only vaguely defined, it is difficult to know how to evaluate any assertions about them.

Similar questions may be raised about many of Maslow's or Rogers's empirical assertions. How do we know that self-actualizers are in fact as Maslow described them—for example, realistically oriented, accepting of themselves and others, spontaneous, problem centered, democratic, and so on? As yet, there is no real evidence that would allow us to draw such conclusions. Consider Maslow's study of self-actualizers. He picked some examples of people who fulfilled their potential and "actualized" themselves, including (as we mentioned earlier) historical figures such as Thomas Jefferson and Eleanor Roosevelt. These were, of course, admirable individuals, but why can't the term *self-actualizer* also be applied to many other individuals who are far less admirable and may, in fact, be veritable monsters? What about Joseph Stalin or Adolf Hitler? Why shouldn't we regard them as self-actualized? Rogers and Maslow both believed that human growth has an inherent tendency toward good rather than evil, and so they would presumably exclude—by definition—such moral monsters. But this line of reasoning obviously begs the question.

In light of these concerns, some critics contend that, despite their noble aspirations, the humanists' concepts are too vague and their assertions too unproven (and maybe too unprovable) to count as serious scientific accomplishments (see, for example, M. B. Smith, 1950). In these critics' view, the humanists serve as moral advocates rather than dispassionate scientists. They tell us what personality should be rather than what it is. Nonetheless, the humanists have made one certain accomplishment. They have reminded us of many phenomena that other approaches to the study of personality have largely bypassed. People do strive for more than food and sex and prestige; they read poetry, listen to music, fall in love, and try to better themselves.

Whether the humanistic psychologists have really helped us understand these phenomena is debatable, but the value of their perspective becomes clear when we consider the contribution of the more modern investigators within the positive-psychology tradition. These researchers are using the powerful tools of science to address questions that have long been neglected by psychology, questions hinging on what it is that makes us happy and healthy, what makes us content with our lives and our relationships. Thus, among other specific issues, researchers are asking—and beginning to answer—questions about how creativity is stimulated, how wisdom is acquired, and how the intellectually gifted can be nourished (Baltes & Staudinger, 2000; Lubinsky & Benbow, 2000; Simonton, 2000; Winner, 2000). Clearly, positive psychology has led researchers in new directions, and it certainly carries on Maslow's vision of a psychology concerned not only with what is basic about human nature, but also with what is good and admirable about us.

"I'm quite fulfilled. I always wanted to be a chicken."

THE SOCIAL-COGNITIVE APPROACH: SEEING THE POWER OF CONSTRUAL

Each of the perspectives we have considered has drawn our attention to a different aspect of the personality puzzle. Trait theorists remind us that people do have stable, internal predispositions—that is, traits—and that an emphasis on these traits allows us to explore a number of crucial issues, such as the biological underpinnings of personality. Psychodynamic theorists remind us of the importance of unconscious motivations and conflicts, and the need to dig beneath the surface in our understanding of who each of us is. Humanistic theorists, in turn, remind us that humans have positive motivations as well as negative—goals we hope to achieve, and not just hardships or tensions we want to avoid or reduce.

Another approach to personality endorses all of these claims, but notes that we have still omitted one essential part of the puzzle—namely, the power of *construal*, or the way people make sense of and interpret the world around them. It is this emphasis that characterizes the social-cognitive approach to personality, to which we now turn.

ORIGINS OF THE SOCIAL-COGNITIVE APPROACH

Social-cognitive theories vary in their specifics, but all derive from two long-standing traditions. The first is the behavioral tradition, set in the vocabulary of reward, punishment, instrumental responses, and observational learning (see Chapter 6). The second is the cognitive view, which places emphasis on the individual as a thinking being.

BEHAVIORAL ROOTS OF SOCIAL-COGNITIVE THEORIES

Central to the behavioral tradition is a worldview that, in its extreme form, asserts that virtually anyone can become anything given proper training. This American "can-do" view was distilled in a well-known pronouncement by the founder of American behaviorism, John B. Watson (1925):

John B. Watson

> Give me a dozen healthy infants, well-formed, and my own specified world to bring them up in and I'll guarantee to take any one at random and train him to become any type of specialist I might select—doctor, lawyer, artist, merchant-chief, and, yes even beggarman and thief, regardless of his talents, penchants, tendencies, abilities, vocations, and race of his ancestors. (p. 82)

Watson's version of behaviorism was relatively primitive, but elements of his view are still visible in more recent theorizing within the social-cognitive perspective. For example, Albert Bandura (like Watson) places a heavy emphasis on the role of experience and learning, and the potential each of us has for developing in a variety of ways, depending on that experience. But Bandura's view of personality goes considerably beyond Watson's and emphasizes the role we play as agents in fashioning our own lives. According to Bandura (2001), we observe relationships between certain actions (whether ours or others') and their real-world consequences (rewards or punishments), and, based on these observations, we develop a set of internalized *outcome expectations*, which then come to govern our actions. In addition, we gradually become aware of ourselves as agents able to produce certain outcomes, marking the emergence of a "self," one with a sense of *self-efficacy*. Once these elements are in place, our actions depend increasingly on a totally internalized system of self-rewards and self-punishments—our values and moral sensibilities—and less on the immediate environment. This reliance on internal standards makes our behavior more consistent than if we were guided simply by the exigencies of the moment, and this consistency is what we know as personality. As seen from this view, personality is not just a reflection of who the individual is, with a substantial contribution from biology. Instead, in Bandura's perspective, personality is a reflection of the situations the person has been exposed to in the past, and the expectations that have been gleaned from those situations.

A related tradition underlying social-cognitive theories of personality is the cognitive view, first detailed by George Kelly (1955). Kelly believed that most personality theories had people either being pushed around by internal forces (trait theories, or "pitchfork theories" in Kelly's words) or being pulled around by external ones (situational and behavioral theories, which Kelly called "carrot theories"). He argued instead that people are always moving on their own accord and do not need to be pushed or pulled. He held that how they move depends on the situation, but, crucially, it depends on their *interpretations* of the situation, which Kelly called their *construals*. According to Kelly, therefore, we will not understand personality unless we consider both the behavior and the construals that explain it.

Kelly's influence is clearly visible in the work of his former student, Walter Mischel—the same Mischel who (as we saw earlier) challenged the very foundations of the trait approach. For Mischel, the study of personality must consider neither fixed traits nor static situations, but should focus instead on how people dynamically process various aspects of their ever-changing world. Like Kelly, Mischel contends that the qualities that form personality are essentially cognitive: different ways of seeing the world, thinking about it, and interacting with it, all acquired over the course of an individual's life.

But how should we conceptualize this cognition, and, with it, the interaction between the individual and the setting? Mischel's answer is framed in terms of each individual's cognitive-affective personality system (CAPS), which consists of five key cognitive qualities on which people can differ. The first is the individual's *encodings*, the set of construals by which he interprets inner and outer experiences. Second, individuals also develop *expectancies and beliefs* about the world, which include the outcome expectations and sense of self-efficacy stressed by Bandura. Third, people differ in their *affects*—that is, their emotional responses to situations. Fourth, they differ in their *goals and values*, the set of outcomes that are considered desirable. Finally, CAPS includes the individual's *competencies and self-regulatory plans*, the way an individual regulates her own behavior by various self-imposed goals and strategies (Mischel, 1973, 1984, 2004; Mischel & Shoda, 1995, 1998, 2000).

Construal *People's responses to a situation (such as watching a sad film) depend on their construals of a situation.*

KEY SOCIAL-COGNITIVE CONCEPTS

Social-cognitive theorists differ in focus and emphasis, but across theorists, three concepts play a crucial role. These are *control*, *attributional style* (which refers to how we typically explain the things that happen in our lives), and *self-control*. We take up each of these in turn.

CONTROL

There is a great deal of evidence that people desire control over the circumstances of their life and benefit from feeling that they have such control (Peterson, 1999; Rodin, 1990; also see Chapter 6).

A widely cited illustration involves elderly people in a nursing home. Patients on one floor of the nursing home were given small houseplants to care for, and they were also asked to choose the time at which they wanted to participate in some of the nursing-home activities (e.g., visiting friends, watching television, planning social events). Patients on another floor were also given plants but with the understanding that the plants would be tended by the staff. They participated in the same activities as the first group of patients, but at times chosen by the staff. The results were clear-cut. According to both nurses' and the patients' own reports, the patients who tended their own houseplants and scheduled their own activities were more active and felt better than the patients who lacked this control, a difference that was still apparent a year later (Langer & Rodin, 1976; Rodin & Langer, 1977).

Control *A person's well-being as she ages may be strongly influenced by the degree of control she has over her routine and her environment.*

Related to our desire for control is our belief that we can make things go our way, which Bandura calls our sense of *self-efficacy* (2001). Researchers have repeatedly found this belief to be associated with better social relationships, work, and health outcomes (Bandura, 1997; 2001; Maddux, 1995; Schwarzer, 1992). Likewise, self-efficacy beliefs about a particular task ("I'm sure I can do this!") are associated with success in that task. This attitude leads to more persistence and a greater tolerance of frustration, both of which contribute to better performance (Schunk, 1984, 1985; also see Chapter 14).

ATTRIBUTIONAL STYLE

Attributional style *A. A. Milne's Eeyore personifies a negative attributional style.*

Objectively, some people have less control over their lives, and some have more. In addition to these objective differences, though, people also differ in their *beliefs* about control, with these beliefs being linked to a fairly stable predisposition known as *attributional style*. This style can be measured by a specially constructed *attributional-style questionnaire (ASQ)* in which a participant is asked to imagine himself in a number of situations (e.g., failing a test) and to indicate what would have caused those events if they had happened to him (Dykema, Bergbower, Doctora, & Peterson, 1996; C. Peterson & Park, 1998; C. Peterson et al., 1982). His responses on the ASQ reveal how he explains his failure. He may think he did not study enough (an internal cause) or that the teacher misled him about what to study (an external cause). He may think he is generally stupid (a global explanation) or is stupid on just that test material (a specific explanation). Finally, he may believe he is always bound to fail (a stable explanation) or that with a little extra studying he can recover nicely (an unstable explanation).

Differences in attributional style matter. Such differences predict important outcomes ranging from performance in insurance sales (Seligman & Schulman, 1986) and competitive sports (Seligman, Nolen-Hoeksema, Thornton, & Thornton, 1990) to HIV progression (Milam, Richardson, Marks, Kerupa, & McCutchan, 2004) and chronic disease (de Ridder, Schreurs, & Bensing, 2000). Importantly, variation in attributional style has also been shown to predict the onset of psychopathology, such as whether a person is likely to suffer from depression (for a description of depression, see Chapter 16). Specifically, being prone to depression is correlated with a particular attributional style—a tendency to attribute unfortunate events to causes that are internal, global, and stable. Thus, a person who is prone to depression is likely to attribute life events to causes related to something within her that applies to many other situations and will continue indefinitely (Buchanan & Seligman, 1995; C. Peterson & Seligman, 1984; C. Peterson & Vaidya, 2001; Seligman & Gillham, 2000).

SELF-CONTROL

So far we have considered each person's control over his life circumstances, and also each person's interpretation of events in his life. Just as important for the social-cognitive theorists, though, is the degree of control each person has over himself and his own actions. Surely people differ in this regard, and these differences in *self-control* are visible in various ways. People differ in their ability to overcome internal forces and obstacles; they also differ in how successfully they can refrain from doing what they want to do but should not. People also differ from each other in their capacity to do things they dislike in order to get what they want eventually.

Examples of self-control (and lack thereof) abound in everyday life. Self-control is manifested whenever we get out of bed in the morning, because we know we should, even though we are still quite sleepy. It is also evident when we eat an extra helping of dessert when we're dieting (or don't), or quit smoking (or don't). In each case, the ability to control oneself is tied to what people often call *will power*, and, according to popular wisdom, some people have more will power than others. But do they really? That is, is "having a lot of will power" a trait that is consistent over time and across situations?

W Miller

Self-control?

Delay of Gratification in Young Children Walter Mischel (1974, 1984) and his associates (Mischel, Shoda, & Rodriguez, 1992) studied this issue in children and showed that self-control, as he measured it, is a stable trait and is related to a number of personality attributes in later life. The participants in his studies were children between 4 and 5 years of age who were shown two snacks, one preferable to the other (e.g., two marshmallows or pretzels versus one). To obtain the snack they preferred, they had to wait about 15 minutes. If they did not want to wait, or grew tired of waiting, they immediately received the less desirable treat but had to forgo the more desirable one.

Whether the children could manage the wait was powerfully influenced by what the children did and thought about while they waited. If they looked at the marshmallow, or worse, thought about eating it, they usually succumbed and grabbed the lesser reward. But they were able to wait for the preferred snack if they found (or were shown) some way of distracting their attention from it, for example, by thinking of something fun, such as Mommy pushing them on a swing. They could also wait for the preferred snack if they thought about the snack in some way other than eating it, for example, by focusing on the pretzels' shape and color rather than on their crunchiness and taste. By mentally transforming their goals, the children managed ultimately to have their cake (or pretzel) and eat it too (Mischel, 1984; Mischel & Baker, 1975; Mischel & Mischel, 1983; Mischel & Moore, 1980; Rodriguez, Mischel, & Shoda, 1989).

Delay of Gratification and Adolescent Competence These various findings show that whether a child delays gratification depends in part on how she construes the situation. But it apparently also depends on some qualities of the child herself. The best evidence comes from follow-up studies that show remarkable correlations between children's ability to delay gratification at the age of 4 years (e.g., the ability to wait for the two pretzels) and some of their personality characteristics a full decade later. Being able to tolerate lengthy delays of gratification in early childhood predicts both academic and social competence in adolescence (as rated by the child's parents), and also general coping ability. When compared to the children who could not delay gratification, those who could were judged (as young teenagers) to be more articulate, attentive, self-reliant, able to plan and think ahead, academically competent, and resilient under stress (Eigsti et al., 2006; Mischel, Shoda, & Peake, 1988; Shoda, Mischel, & Peake, 1990; Figure 15.7).

Why should a 4-year-old's ability to wait 15 minutes to get two pretzels rather than one predict such important qualities as academic and social competence 10 years later? The answer probably lies in the fact that the cognitive processes that underlie this deceptively simple waiting task in childhood are the same ones needed for success in adolescence and adulthood. After all, success in school often requires that short-term goals (e.g., partying during the week) be subordinated to long-term purposes (e.g., getting good grades). The same holds for social relations, because someone who gives in to every momentary impulse will be hard-pressed to keep friends, sustain commitments, or participate in team sports. In both academic and social domains, reaching any long-term goal inevitably means renouncing lesser goals that beckon in the interim. (For more on the processes of "executive control," and their link to a wide range of mental achievements, see Chapter 14.)

If there is some general capacity for delaying gratification, useful for child and adult alike, where does it originate? As we saw in Chapter 14, there appears to be a heritable component to the executive control processes that guide many of our thought processes and that may well be a prerequisite for delaying gratification. It seems likely, however, that there is also a large learned component. Children may acquire certain cognitive skills (e.g., self-distraction, reevaluating rewards, and sustaining attention to distant goals) that they continue to apply and improve upon as they get older. However they originate, though, these attention-diverting strategies appear to emerge in the first 2 years of life and can be seen in the child's attachment behavior with the mother. In one study, toddlers were observed during a brief separation from their mothers, using a

Delay of gratification **A child's ability to delay gratification is powerfully influenced by what she pays attention to and how she thinks about the desired object.**

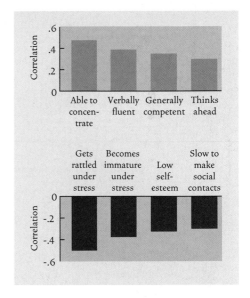

15.7 Childhood delay and adolescent competence **The figure indicates the relation between the ability to delay gratification at age 4 or 5 and personality traits at about age 16; it depicts correlations between various personality traits of adolescents as rated by their parents and the length of time they delayed gratification as preschoolers. Bars in green show positive correlations; bars in red show negative correlations.**

variant of the Strange Situation task already discussed. Some of the toddlers showed immediate distress, while others distracted themselves with other activities. Those who engaged in self-distraction as toddlers were able to delay gratification longer when they reached the age of 5 (Sethi, Mischel, Aber, Shoda, & Rodriguez, 2000).

CONTRIBUTIONS OF THE SOCIAL-COGNITIVE APPROACH

Like the trait approach, social-cognitive theorists have taken a considerable interest in relatively stable personality traits, as revealed by studies of attributional style and delay of gratification. How, then, do they differ from trait theorists? There are two answers. One has to do with the role of the situation. By now, theorists from all perspectives agree that both traits and situations matter, but even so, social-cognitive theorists are more likely than trait theorists to stress the role of the situation and how the individual understands and deals with it. Thus, Mischel found that delay of gratification is an index of a surprisingly stable personal attribute, but he was quick to point out that this index is strongly affected by the way the situation was set up (was the reward visible?) and how it was construed (did the child think about eating the reward?). The second answer concerns the origins of personality. Unlike trait theorists, who are generally inclined to believe that the major personality traits have a built-in, genetic basis, social-cognitive theorists are more likely to assume that these dispositions are learned.

Like the psychodynamic approach, social-cognitive theorists want to dig deeper than the surface of personality in order to understand the psychological processes that support behavior and mental processes. In doing so, social-cognitive theorists are often addressing problems such as delay of gratification that come straight out of Freud's playbook, and the psychological processes that these two types of theorists are interested in overlap considerably, particularly if we include the ego psychologists, with their emphasis on an adaptive, agentic ego, and the object relations theorists' emphasis on social reinforcement. Note, however, the differences. Theorists from these two approaches go about their work using starkly different languages and methods, and holding up quite different views of the role of conscious processes. Social-cognitive theorists emphasize cognitive processes such as construal and beliefs, and prioritize tightly controlled experiments. In contrast, psychodynamic theorists emphasize impulses and defenses, and rely on insights drawn from clinical work with patients.

The parallels between the social-cognitive approach and the humanistic approach are similarly instructive. The positive outlook of the humanistic psychologist Carl Rogers resonates richly with social-cognitive theorists such as Bandura. Both are optimistic about the individual's capacity to overcome difficult circumstances and to show extraordinary resilience in the face of trying times. This optimism hinges for both schools of thought on the conviction that we are not just passively shaped by the swirl of life around us, but also actively seek to shape our world. But, despite this shared optimism about the human capacity for growth and change, the traditions differ: The humanistic theorist describes the growth in terms of a self that is actualized to varying degrees, while the social-cognitive theorist draws attention to a malleable set of processes that guide how the individual acts, and, ultimately, who he is.

SOME FINAL THOUGHTS: THE NEED FOR MULTIPLE APPROACHES

We come to the end of our tour of the major approaches to studying personality. Each of these approaches focuses on a different part of the puzzle of who we are, and each privileges a somewhat different combination of the various types of data used by personality psychologists, including self-report data, informant data, behavioral data, physiological data, and life data.

Today, there are relatively few theorists who would espouse any of these approaches in their most extreme form, or would deny that any of the other approaches have some merit in understanding personality. Most adherents of the trait perspective, for example, appreciate the power of situations that are construed in different ways by different people. Most psychodynamic theorists see unconscious defenses and conscious coping mechanisms as parts of a continuum, and they recognize the extent to which each individual is richly embedded in a social network. Most humanistically oriented theorists grant that what people do depends on both traits and situations, as well as the motive to self-actualize.

Even so, some important differences in approach clearly remain. This is actually fortunate, because these orientations offer different perspectives on the same subject matter. Some aspects of personality have clear temperamental origins (trait theory); others are learned, and they derive from how we think about ourselves and the world (social-cognitive theory); some reflect conflicts of which we are not aware (psychodynamic theory); still others reveal the need for self-actualization (the humanistic approach). We cannot envision what a complete theory of personality will ultimately look like, but it will surely have to describe all of these aspects of human functioning.

SUMMARY

THE TRAIT APPROACH: DEFINING OUR DIFFERENCES

- *Traits* define a person's predominant thoughts, feelings, and behaviors. One of the first aims of trait theory is to find an appropriate *taxonomy* for personality attributes. *Factor analysis* of how people use trait labels suggests that personality can be described in terms of five dimensions, the so-called *Big Five*—extraversion, neuroticism, agreeableness, conscientiousness, and openness to experience. There has been debate, however, over whether the Big Five dimensions are useful for describing personalities in other cultures.

- A challenge to the trait concept is *situationism*—the claim that human behavior is largely determined by the situation in which the individual finds herself. Support for this challenge comes from inconsistency in how people behave as they move from one situation to the next, and also from inconsistency between how people behave and how they respond on personality tests.

- Most theorists now believe that both personality and situations matter, usually in complex interaction. This leads some theorists to describe personalities in terms of an *if . . . then . . .* pattern: "If in this setting, then act in this fashion; if in that setting, then act in that fashion." In

addition, some people are more consistent in their behaviors than others—with this consistency measured by the *Self-Monitoring Scale*.

- Traits grow to some extent out of the individual's *temperament*, a characteristic emotional or behavioral pattern that is largely genetically determined. Twin studies of the Big Five dimensions confirm a high heritability, especially for extraversion and neuroticism. This biological influence may depend on each individual's level of central nervous system reactivity, with introverts more reactive than extraverts. A similar logic has been used to explain *sensation seeking* and *inhibited temperament*.

- Studies of *national character* underline the importance of cultural differences in personality, with these differences in part traceable to how a particular group of people sustains itself. Also important are family effects, but these reflect differences within families (e.g., contrasts between first-borns and second-borns) rather than differences between families. Evidence comes from the fact that the correlation between the personality traits of adopted children and their adoptive siblings is essentially zero, and that the correlations between the traits of identical twins reared together are comparable to those of identical twins reared apart.

CHAPTER

16

PSYCHOPATHOLOGY

We have now discussed some of the ways in which people differ from one another, both in their abilities (Chapter 14) and in their personalities (Chapter 15). We have considered desirable qualities (like being emotionally sensitive or helpful) and also less desirable ones (like being callous or aggressive), but, even so, the attributes we have considered all fall within the range that most people consider acceptable or normal. In this chapter, in contrast, we consider differences that are outside that range—differences that carry us into the realm of mental illness. The study of such conditions is the province of *psychopathology*, or, as it is sometimes called, *abnormal psychology*.

We should say at the start, though, that there is debate about how psychopathology should be defined. The label "abnormal psychology" suggests that we should start with some conception of normalcy, and then define mental illness as variations that are not normal. Thus, we might acknowledge that everyone is sad or frightened at various points in his life, but we might worry about (and try to treat) someone who is far sadder than a normal person is, or far more frightened. However, this perspective invites problems, because something can be an illness even if it is a normal occurrence. (For example, almost everyone gets cavities in her teeth, so, in a statistical sense, it is normal to have cavities. However, this does not change the fact that having cavities is a health problem.) Likewise, many things are "abnormal" without being illnesses. (Pink is not a normal hair color, but this does not mean that someone who dyes his hair pink is sick.) It seems clear, therefore, that we cannot equate being "ill" with being "abnormal."

How, therefore, should we define mental disorders? The commonly accepted definition is the one provided by the American Psychiatric Association (1994) in its manual for categorizing such conditions, the **Diagnostic and Statistical Manual for Mental Disorders** (now in its fourth edition and hence known as the **DSM-IV**). The *DSM-IV* states that

> Each of the mental disorders is conceptualized as a clinically significant behavioral or psychological syndrome or pattern that occurs in a person and that is associated with present distress (a painful symptom) or disability (impairment in one or more important areas of functioning) or with a significantly increased risk of suffering death, pain, disability, or an important loss of freedom. (p. xxi)

Notice that this definition makes no reference to normality—although, in truth, mental disorders often do involve abnormality. The disordered person may, for example, suffer from severe mood swings or behave in ways that are clearly different from the feelings and behavior of "ordinary" people. Thus, deviation from a statistical norm is often found in psychopathology—even if it does not define psychopathology (Wakefield, 1992).

Amid these definitional subtleties, though, let us not lose track of the key point: Mental disorders, no matter how we define them, can be a source of enormous anguish—both for the person who has the disorder and for others around her. Mental illness can also lead to further problems: poor health care, abuse of family members, drug problems, and more. Hence there is clearly tragedy associated with the issues we will be discussing. But—as we will see—we also know how to treat many forms of mental illness, so that this is a part of psychology in which our science can be used rather directly to improve the lives of millions of people.

In this chapter and the next, we will survey what is known about mental illness, focusing first on the diagnosis of mental illness and its causes, and then (in Chapter 17) turning to issues of treatment. We will not try in these chapters to cover all forms of mental illness, because, in truth, mental illness comes in a wide range of types and levels of severity. Instead, we will focus on forms of mental illness that afflict a large number of people, and are particularly disruptive for these individuals' lives. ●

DIFFERENT CONCEPTIONS OF MENTAL DISORDER

Mental illness is surely not a modern problem; it is instead a problem that has plagued humanity since ancient times. One of the earliest-known medical documents, the Ebers papyrus (written about 1550 B.C.), refers to such mental disorders as depression (Okasha & Okasha, 2000). Other ancient cases include King Saul of Judaea, who alternated between bouts of homicidal frenzy and bouts of suicidal depression, and the

An early example of mental disorder   King Nebuchadnezzar as depicted by William Blake (1795).

Babylonian king Nebuchadnezzar, who walked on all fours in the belief that he was a wolf. Across the millennia, though, people have had very different conceptions of what it is that causes these disorders.

EARLY VIEWS OF PSYCHOPATHOLOGY

One of the earliest theories held that the afflicted person was possessed by evil spirits, and various strategies were tried to deal with this problem. In some cases, large holes were cut into someone's skull, so that the demons could be driven out through this "exit" (T. D. Stewart, 1957; Figure 16.1). Other treatments sought to calm the unruly demons with music, to chase them away with prayers, or to purge them with potions that induced vomiting. A different approach was to make the evil spirits so uncomfortable in the patient's body that they would be induced to flee. Accordingly, patients were variously starved, flogged, or immersed in boiling water. Not surprisingly, none of these treatments was effective, and, in fact, these approaches often made patients worse.

By the Middle Ages, though, a more sophisticated conception was available—namely, that mental illness is a type of disease, to be understood in the same way as other illnesses (Allderidge, 1979; Neugebauer, 1979). But this conception did not lead to more humane treatment of the afflicted. The diseased "madmen" were treated with little sympathy, and the interests of society were deemed best served by "putting them away."

Beginning in the sixteenth century, therefore, a number of special hospitals were established throughout Europe. Most of these institutions, however, were hospitals in name only. Their real function was to confine all kinds of social undesirables and isolate them from the rest of humanity. Criminals, beggars, epileptics, incurables of all sorts, were institutionalized and treated the same way as the mentally disturbed (Rosen, 1966). And the treatments were barbaric. One author described conditions in the major mental hospital for Parisian women at the end of the 1700s: "Madwomen seized by fits of violence are chained like dogs at their cell doors, and separated from keepers and visitors alike by a long corridor protected by an iron grille; through this grille is passed their food and the straw on which they sleep; by means of rakes, part of the filth that surrounds them is cleaned out" (Foucault, 1965, p. 72).

At the time, this treatment seemed only natural. After all, "madmen" were like dangerous animals and had to be caged. But since caged animals are interesting to watch,

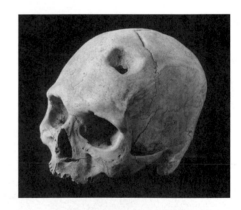

16.1   Trephining   The ancient practice of trephining involved the cutting of holes in the skull, through which demons could be driven out. This photo shows a trephined prehistoric skull found in Peru. The patient apparently survived the operation for a while, for there is some evidence of bone healing.

16.2   *The mentally disturbed on exhibit*
An eighteenth-century depiction of a tour of
Bethlehem asylum. (The Rake's Progress: The
Rake in Bedlam, *1735, by William Hogarth)*

some of the hospitals took on another function—they became zoos. At London's Bethlehem Hospital (known as Bedlam, as it sounds when pronounced with a Cockney accent), the patients were exhibited to anyone curious enough to pay the required penny per visit. In 1814, there were 96,000 such visits (Figure 16.2).

A number of reformers gradually succeeded in eliminating the worst of these practices. The French physician Philippe Pinel (1745–1826), for example, was put in charge of the Parisian hospital system in 1793, when the French Revolution was at its height. Pinel wanted to remove the inmates' chains and fetters and give them exercise and fresh air; the government gave its permission only grudgingly. One official argued with Pinel, "Citizen, are you mad yourself that you want to unchain these animals?" (Zilboorg & Henry, 1941, p. 322; Figure 16.3).

MENTAL DISORDER AS AN ORGANIC ILLNESS

Pinel and other reformers sounded one clear theme: Madness is a disease, and the inmates were patients needing treatment rather than animals deserving confinement. But if the patients had a disease, then what was the cause? Proponents of the *somatogenic hypothesis* (from the Greek *soma*, meaning "body") argued that mental illness, like other forms of illness, could be traced to some injury or infection, and this position gained considerable credibility in the late nineteenth century, thanks to discoveries about *general paresis*. This disorder is characterized by a broad decline in physical and psychological functions, culminating in marked personality aberrations that may include grandiose delusions ("I am the king of England") or profound hypochondriacal depressions ("My heart has stopped beating"). Without treatment, the deterioration progresses, paralysis ensues, and death occurs within a few years (Dale, 1975).

The breakthrough in understanding paresis came in 1897, when the Viennese physician Richard von Krafft-Ebing (1840–1902) found that it was actually a consequence of infection

16.3   *Pinel ordering the removal of the inmates' fetters*

with syphilis. And, once the cause of the disease was known, the path to a successful treatment was straightforward: Antibiotics cure the infection, and, if the drugs are given early enough, the symptoms of paresis can be avoided altogether.

MENTAL DISORDER AS A PSYCHOLOGICAL ILLNESS

It seems, then, that general paresis can be understood and treated just like any other medical problem. Should other forms of mental illness be understood in the same fashion—as the result of some infection, or perhaps some injury? This view gained many supporters in the late 1800s, including Emil Kraepelin (1856–1926), whose 1883 textbook, *Lehrbuch der Psychiatrie*, emphasized the importance of brain pathology in producing mental disorders.

It soon became clear, however, that the somatogenic approach could not explain the full spectrum of mental disorders. For example, this view provided no account of the disorder then known as *hysteria*, which we encountered in our discussion of psycho-analysis (see Chapter 15). Patients with hysteria typically showed odd symptoms that seemed to be neurological, but with other indications that made it plain there was no neurological damage. For example, some patients would report that their limbs were paralyzed, but under hypnosis these same patients could move their limbs perfectly well, indicating that the nerves and muscles were fully functional. For Sigmund Freud and his followers, therefore, the patient's symptoms could not be understood as the result of some sort of bodily injury; instead, the disease had to be understood in psychological terms.

Emil Kraepelin **The major figure in psychiatric classification, Kraepelin distinguished two groups of severe mental disorders, schizophrenia and manic-depressive psychosis (now called bipolar disorder).**

THE MODERN CONCEPTION OF MENTAL DISORDER

The obvious suggestion, therefore, is that some mental disorders (such as paresis) can be understood as the result of a specific biomedical problem, while other disorders (such as hysteria) demand a different sort of explanation. For example, Freud's followers offered *psychodynamic models*, in which mental disorders are thought to be the manifestations of unconscious psychological conflicts, originating in one's childhood experiences. Other theorists, though, have proposed different conceptions. For example, some have offered *learning models*, building on the mechanisms we discussed in Chapter 6. In this view, many mental disorders result from maladaptive learning, and are best corrected with remedial learning.

Each of these approaches builds on a kernel of truth: Biomedical factors do play a critical role in producing some forms of psychopathology; childhood experiences and maladaptive learning unmistakably contribute as well. Even so, each of these approaches is by itself too narrow, and it would probably be a mistake to point to any of these factors as "the cause" of any disorder. To understand why, let us examine the notion of *cause* in this domain, looking at a concrete case.

DIATHESIS-STRESS MODELS

Imagine someone who goes through a sad experience—perhaps the breakup of a long-term relationship—and subsequently becomes depressed. We might be tempted to say that the breakup caused the depression, but this would not be quite right, because it turns out the breakup was not the only force in play here. We know this because many people experience breakups without becoming depressed; this tells us that a breakup

Depression

will cause depression only if other factors are on the scene. What are those other factors? Part of the answer lies in a person's biology, because, as we will see, some people have a genetically rooted tendency toward depression (cf. p. 616). This biological tendency remains unexpressed (and so the person suffers no depression) until the person experiences a particularly stressful event. But then, when that stressful event arrives, the combination of the event plus the biological tendency will likely lead to depression.

A different—but also crucial—factor lies in how someone *thinks* about the events he experiences—and, in particular, whether he thinks that he himself caused the events, and so is open to blame (see pp. 616–618). But, again, this style of thinking, by itself, is not the cause for depression. Instead, the style of thinking only creates a *risk* or a danger of depression; if someone has this problematic thinking style but never experiences a truly sad event, then he may never develop depression.

These considerations suggest that we need a two-part theory of depression, and the same is true for virtually every other form of psychopathology as well. This two-part conception is referred to as a ***diathesis-stress model*** (Zubin & Spring, 1977), with one set of factors (the *diathesis*) creating a predisposition or risk for the disorder, and then a different set of factors (the *stress*) providing the trigger that turns the potential into the actual disorder. Notice that, in this conception, neither the diathesis nor the stress by itself causes the disorder; instead, the disorder emerges only if both sets of factors are present.

MULTICAUSAL MODELS

The diathesis-stress model suggests that we need to consider two separate causes of each mental illness—one that creates the risk, and one that turns the risk into the diagnosable problem. But even this conception is too simple, because often there are *multiple* factors creating the diathesis, and multiple factors creating the stress.

For example, we have mentioned two aspects of the diathesis for depression: a particular thinking style and also a genetically based tendency. But there are other ***risk factors*** as well. One factor is *gender*, because depression is, in most populations, much more common among women than among men (see, for example, Culbertson, 1997). Why is this? Part of the answer is again likely to be biological (e.g., hormone fluctuations in women), but part is cultural, including the differences in how a culture teaches men and women to deal with the stresses of their lives: Most Western cultures are appreciably more tolerant of men's drinking than women's. Therefore, men who face life's difficulties often turn to alcohol, while women facing similar problems become depressed. (And, consistent with this suggestion, alcohol abuse is appreciably more common in men than in women.)

It seems clear, then, that the factors that contribute to depression are diverse—we have now mentioned a thinking style, hormonal factors, the presence (or absence) of other outlets for dealing with stress, and more. In addition, depression is also influenced by a further set of factors, called ***protective factors***, that have the opposite effect of the diathesis. Factors in the home environment, or the support of friends, or an optimistic outlook can *diminish* someone's risk of depression, and make her more resilient if she encounters some source of stress. If we are to explain what causes depression (or any other form of psychopathology), then these, too, must be accounted for.

These points should make it clear why modern investigators insist on a ***multicausal model*** of depression, a model that acknowledges from the start that many different factors contribute to the disorder's emergence. Similar considerations apply to other mental disorders, so that these also require a multicausal model. In addition, to emphasize the *diversity* of factors contributing to each illness, most investigators urge that we take a ***biopsychosocial viewpoint***, one that includes biological factors (like genetics or hormonal influences), psychological factors (like a style of thinking), and social factors (like the presence of social support). This leaves us with a conception of psychopathology that is surely more complex than the straightforward psychogenic and somatogenic accounts offered a century ago—but the complexity is demanded by the available evidence.

CLASSIFYING MENTAL DISORDERS

In the remainder of this chapter, we will examine what is known about various mental disorders, focusing on the mix of factors that seems to cause each disorder. Before we press on, though, we need to say a bit about how individuals are diagnosed as having one disorder or another.

ASSESSMENT

Every case of depression is unique, affecting a different individual in a different set of circumstances. The same is true for every person who suffers from schizophrenia or anxiety. Each is different from the others, and, if we want to understand each case fully, we need to attend to its unique features. Nonetheless, there is a considerable gain from putting mental disorders into categories: If we know that Steven suffers from the same disorder as Mark, then our experience in treating Mark can guide us when we try to help Steven. If we know that Alice suffers from the same disorder as Lindsay, then we can use what we know about Lindsay's recovery as a way of forecasting how Alice will do. And, above all, if Larry, Paul, and José all have the same problem, we can ask what they have in common as a means of asking what factors caused the problem in the first place. In all these regards, psychopathology is just like any other branch of science or medicine: A valid classification scheme helps us develop new knowledge, and helps us apply what we have learned to new cases.

How does this classification proceed? How do we decide what Steven's problem is, or Alice's or Paul's? Mental-health professionals use the term *assessment* to refer to the broad set of procedures used to gather information about an individual. An assessment may or may not lead to a *diagnosis*—a claim that an individual has a specific form of mental illness; if it does, the assessment may also indicate the severity of his problems.

Assessments usually begin with a clinical interview, in which the clinician asks the client to describe her problems and concerns. Some aspects of the interview will be open-ended and flexible, as the clinician explores the client's status and history. But, in addition, the clinician may rely on a *structured interview*, in which specific questions are asked in a specific sequence, with attention to certain types of content. For example, the clinician might rely on the *Structured Clinical Interview for DSM Diagnosis (SCID)*, designed to ask questions directly pertinent to certain diagnostic categories.

Throughout the interview the clinician will pay careful attention to the patient's set of complaints, or *symptoms*. Patients who say, "I hear voices," "I feel nervous all the time," and "I feel hopeless" are reporting symptoms. The clinician also looks for any *signs* that might accompany these symptoms. If the same patients, respectively, turn toward a stapler as though it were speaking, shake visibly, and look teary eyed, these would be signs that parallel the patients' symptoms. Sometimes, though, symptoms do not correspond to signs, and such discrepancies are also important. In some disorders, for example, a patient might state, "My head hurts so bad it's like a buzz saw running through my brain," but the patient seems to be calm and unconcerned while saying it, and this discrepancy, too, is informative.

Assessment   *A clinical assessment usually begins with an interview, in which the clinician asks the client to describe his or her problems and concerns.*

In medical diagnosis, a single symptom like "I feel tired," or a single sign like a fever is rarely sufficient to reach a conclusion about what ails the patient; instead, diagnosis usually depends on a combination of multiple symptoms and multiple signs. The same holds for psychopathology, and so the mental-health practitioner looks for patterns of signs and symptoms that tend to go together. These patterns are called *syndromes*. An example is a pattern of signs like disorganized speech, altered gait, and subdued facial expressions, together with symptoms like restlessness, persecutory beliefs, and hallucinations. This syndrome is characteristic of one kind of schizophrenia.

The practitioner also attempts to obtain other information during the interview with the patient and, if possible, from family and friends. When did the problems start (when was the onset of the illness)? Has the patient's everyday functioning stayed the same, improved, worsened, or been irregular, with good spells and bad spells (what has been the course of the illness)? Has anything extraordinary happened recently in the person's life? Has the person been abusing drugs or alcohol? Does the patient have other medical conditions that might exacerbate or mimic a mental disorder? The clinician will also observe the patient's grooming, mannerisms, style and content of speech, and overall mood, and may ask the patient to engage in brief tasks to assess attention, memory, and judgment. Finally, laboratory tests such as neuroimaging (see Chapter 3) or blood analysis can inform the practitioner about relevant aspects of a patient's physical well-being—for example, whether the patient has suffered a stroke or taken a mood-altering drug.

TABLE 16.1   SOME MMPI SCALES WITH REPRESENTATIVE EXAMPLE ITEMS*

SCALE	CRITERION GROUP	EXAMPLE ITEMS
Depression	Patients with intense unhappiness and feelings of guilt and hopelessness	"I often feel that life is not worth the trouble."
Paranoia	Patients with an unusual degree of suspiciousness, together with feelings of persecution and delusions of grandeur	"Several people are following me everywhere."
Schizophrenia	Patients with a diagnosis of schizophrenia, characterized by bizarre or highly unusual thoughts or behavior, withdrawal, and in many cases delusions and hallucinations	"I seem to hear things that other people cannot hear."
Psychopathic deviance	Patients with marked difficulties in social adjustment, and with histories of delinquency and other antisocial behavior	"I often was in trouble in school, although I do not understand for what reasons."

*In the example items shown here, the response appropriate to the scale is "true." For many other items, the reverse is true. Thus, answering "false" to the item "I liked school" would contribute to the person's score on the Psychopathic Deviance scale.

The full pattern of the patient's signs and symptoms, taken together with their onset and course, will usually allow the practitioner to render an opinion as to the specific disorder(s). This diagnosis is not set in stone, however, but serves as the practitioner's best judgment about the patient's current state. The diagnosis may well be revised as the clinician gains new information, including information about how the patient responds to a particular form of treatment.

THE MMPI

In some clinical assessments, a clinician will also seek to gain information about someone by administering a broad personality test, such as the *Minnesota Multiphasic Personality Inventory*, or *MMPI*. This test was developed in 1940, but was redesigned in 1989; the current version is the MMPI-2 (Butcher, Dahlstrom, Graham, Tellegen, & Kaemmer, 2001; Butcher et al., 1992).

To construct the MMPI, its authors began with a large pool of test questions and administered them to patients known to have a variety of different mental disorders, as well as to a group of nonpatients. The next step was to compare the patients' responses to those of the nonpatients. If the responses for a particular question tended to be the same for all groups, then that question was deemed uninformative, and was removed from the test. A question was kept on the test only if one of the patient groups tended to answer it differently from the nonpatient group. The result, of course, was a test specifically designed to differentiate among these groups.

The MMPI includes items like "I often feel that life is not worth the trouble," or "I seem to hear things that other people cannot hear" (Table 16.1). The person taking the test agrees or disagrees with each item, and the full set of responses is collated and tallied to provide 10 scores. Each score indicates how the examinee's answers compare with those of the relevant comparison group. For example, items on the Paranoia scale are the ones endorsed by paranoid patients but not by nonpatients, and so a person's score on this scale reflects how closely he resembles the paranoid patients. Likewise for the Depression scale, the Introversion scale, and so on. In interpreting the MMPI, however, it is important not to look at the scales individually. Instead, a clinician inspects the score profiles, which graph the examinee's scores (Figure 16.4). For example, a clinician may find that a person has a high score on the Depression scale, but a low score on the Introversion scale. This might lead the clinician to conclude that the patient is depressed, but that the depression is not accompanied by excessive shyness or social withdrawal.

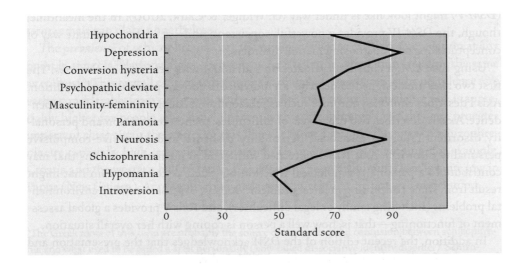

16.4 *MMPI profile   The profile is of an adult male seeking help in a community mental-health center. The scales are those described in Table 16.1. The scores are based on the performance of the standardization group. Scores above 70 will occur in about 2.5% of the cases; scores above 80 in about 0.1%. The profile strongly suggests considerable depression and anxiety.*

The Genain quadruplets   All four of these identical twins, born in 1930, suffer from schizophrenia. (The name Genain is fictitious, and used to preserve their anonymity.)

HEREDITY

It has long been known that schizophrenia runs in families. For example, if a person has a sibling with schizophrenia, then the likelihood that he has (or will get) the disease himself is four times greater than the likelihood of schizophrenia in the general population—8%, compared with 1 or 2% in the broad population (Andreasen & Black, 1996; D. Rosenthal, 1970). This fact, by itself, however, does not prove a genetic contribution. (After all, the increased risk among siblings might reflect some factor in the home or family environment.) Better evidence comes from studies of twins, and it turns out that if one sibling in a set of twins suffers from schizophrenia, then the other twin is much more likely to have the disease as well. The probability of this event, technically called *concordance*, is between 25 and 50% if the twins are identical, compared with 10 or 15% if they are fraternal (Gottesman, 1991).

Separate evidence comes from adoption studies. Consider a child who is born to a mother with schizophrenia and placed in a foster home (with foster parents who are not schizophrenic) within a week or so after birth. The odds are about 8% that this child will develop schizophrenia, the same percentage as for children who remain with a biological parent who has the disease (Kendler & Gruenberg, 1984; Kety, 1988; Tsuang, Gilbertson, & Faraone, 1991). All of these findings suggest a substantial genetic contribution to the development of schizophrenia.

PRENATAL ENVIRONMENT

If genes were the whole story for schizophrenia, then the concordance rate for identical twins would be 100%, and obviously it is not. We need to ask, therefore, what other (nongenetic) factors play a role.

In recent years, attention has focused on prenatal factors—both in the uterus and during delivery. Evidence suggests that a diverse set of birth complications is associated with schizophrenia, and what these complications have in common seems to be a period of diminished oxygen supply to the newborn. This by itself is not enough to produce the disease, but may interfere with the newborn's brain development in a fashion that increases the likelihood that a genetic predisposition will eventually be expressed as schizophrenia (Cannon et al., 2000; Zorilla & Cannon, 1995).

Other evidence implicates an infectious agent in some cases of schizophrenia, probably a virus. The influenza virus has attracted special attention based on the finding that when mothers are in the second trimester of pregnancy during an influenza epidemic, their children are more likely to develop schizophrenia (Brown, Cohen, Harkavy-Friedman, & Babulas, 2001; Mednick, Huttunen, & Macho'n, 1994; Sham et al., 1992). Presumably, the virus crosses the placental barrier and damages vulnerable fetal brain cells and neuronal connections.

Further evidence for an infectious agent comes from epidemiology, because children who develop schizophrenia are disproportionately likely to have been born during the winter (the months of January to March in the Northern Hemisphere, July to September in the Southern Hemisphere), the season during which people stay inside more and thus share more viral infections. In geographic areas where there are no seasons—that is, in areas near the equator—there is no link between schizophrenia and someone's birth month (Battle, Martin, Dorfman, & Miller, 1999; McGrath, Welham, & Pemberton, 1995; Parker, Mehendran, Koh, & Machin, 2000).

The possibility of viral involvement also helps explain another fact about schizophrenia and identical twins. It turns out that there are actually two kinds of identical twins. For about two thirds of identical twins, only one placenta develops, and thus the twins share one prenatal blood supply. In the other third of identical twins, each twin has its own placenta and so its own blood supply from the mother. These two types of twins are difficult to distinguish—they are, after all, both identical twins (that is, identical in their genes)—but they can be told apart on the basis of various biological markers.

If genes were the only prebirth factor that mattered for schizophrenia, then this distinction, separating the two types of twins, would be irrelevant. But the prediction is different when we consider the effect of viruses. A mother's virus is carried to her fetus via the blood supply, and so, if twins share a blood supply, then the odds are good that if one gets the virus, the other will too. If the twins do not share a blood supply, then it is possible that one will get the virus, but the other will not. This difference, then, explains why the concordance rate for schizophrenia is substantially higher for single-placenta twins than it is for two-placenta twins—60% versus 11%. This difference in concordance rates is a powerful argument that some factor in the blood supply matters for producing the disease, and viral infection is our best candidate (J. O. Davis & Phelps, 1995; J. O. Davis, Phelps, & Bracha, 1995).

In short, then, the evidence does seem persuasive that both genetics and prenatal conditions contribute to schizophrenia, and this finding has led some investigators to argue that schizophrenia is a ***neurodevelopmental disorder*** (Sawa & Snyder, 2002; Waddington, Torrey, Crow, & Hirsch, 1991), with the child's brain (in its structure and its chemistry) failing to develop as it should from a fairly early age. One line of evidence for this view comes from the fact that many cases of schizophrenia do show preludes in childhood. Affected children are less active and less "cuddly," and also show delayed motor behavior; by adolescence, they have a host of subtle cognitive and perceptual deficits (Marcus et al., 1993). Additionally, children who will later develop the negative symptoms of schizophrenia tend to be socially unresponsive and to seek isolation, whereas those who will later develop the positive symptoms tend to be irritable, distractible, and aggressive (T. D. Cannon, Mednick, & Parnas, 1990; Parnas & Jorgensen, 1989).

Evidence for these precursors of schizophrenia comes from many sources, including the examination of home movies showing childhood events of individuals who, years later, were diagnosed with schizophrenia (Walker, Grimes, Davis, & Smith, 1993; Walker, Kestler, Bollini, & Hochman, 2004; Walker, Savoie, & Davis, 1994). Careful ratings of these movies shows that the "preschizophrenic children" showed less positive emotion in their facial expressions, and more negative facial emotion, compared with their siblings who did not later develop schizophrenia. The preschizophrenic children also showed unusual motor patterns, including odd hand movements. And in some cases, these differences were visible at a very early age—as young as 2 years old. Clearly, then, schizophrenia does not emerge abruptly in young adulthood; instead, the disease starts influencing the person in early childhood, even if the full disruption caused by the illness is detected only later.

SOCIAL AND PSYCHOLOGICAL ENVIRONMENT

What about stressors later in life? It turns out that these, too, contribute to schizophrenia, in line with the claim that genetic and neurodevelopmental abnormalities create a

Precursors of illness *Individuals who will develop schizophrenia start showing precursors of the disease at an early age. This has been detected by examining the childhood videos of people who later developed schizophrenia.*

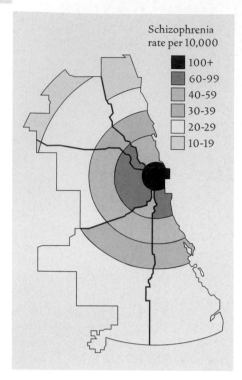

Schizophrenia
rate per 10,000

■ 100+
▨ 60-99
▨ 40-59
▨ 30-39
□ 20-29
□ 10-19

16.6 *The prevalence of schizophrenia in different regions of a city* **A map of Chicago (1922–34) is represented by a series of concentric zones. The center zone is the business and amusement area, which is without residents except for some transients and vagabonds. Surrounding this center is a slum region inhabited largely by unskilled laborers. Further out are more stable regions: a zone largely populated by skilled workers, followed by zones of middle- and upper-middle-class apartment dwellers, and, furthest out, the upper-middle-class commuters. The map shows clearly that the incidence of schizophrenia increases the closer one gets to the city's center.**

substantial risk for the development of schizophrenia, but do not by themselves precipitate the disease.

Almost a century ago, epidemiological studies revealed a link between schizophrenia and socioeconomic status, or SES (Faris & Dunham, 1939). In fact, one study suggested that low-SES individuals are nine times more likely to develop schizophrenia than are high-SES individuals (Hollingshead & Redlich, 1958). The same point can be made geographically, since the prevalence of schizophrenia is highest in the poorest and most dilapidated areas of a city and diminishes as one progresses toward higher-income regions (Figure 16.6; M. L. Kohn, 1968).

What produces this relationship? Part of the answer is, sadly, daily stress, because poverty, inferior status, and low occupational rank are all stressful, and so can help trigger schizophrenia in someone who is (for biological reasons) already vulnerable (Goldberg & Morrison, 1963). But, in addition, there is another reason why schizophrenia is associated with poverty: Someone who suffers from schizophrenia is less likely to do well in school, less likely to get or hold a good job. As a result, people with schizophrenia suffer from *downward drift*, with their disease producing problems that, in turn, put them into a lower social class (Dohrenwend et al., 1992; Jones et al., 1993). Notice, then, that cause and effect run in both directions here: Poverty is a risk factor for schizophrenia, making the disease more likely, but schizophrenia is itself a risk factor for poverty, making poverty more likely.

What about someone's more immediate environment—for example, her family? Some investigators have looked to the personality of a person's parents as a potential source of schizophrenia (Arieti, 1959). Others have focused on the pattern of communication in the family (Bateson, 1959, 1960). There is little evidence, however, in favor of either of these claims. Often there are disturbances in families that include someone with schizophrenia, but this situation is likely to be a consequence of the disease rather than its cause. After all, having a family member who suffers from schizophrenia can be tragic for the family. Parents often blame themselves for their disturbed child, and are also likely to become frustrated and despondent in their attempts to reach their child (Mishler & Waxler, 1968; Torrey, 1983).

In addition, children with schizophrenia may have difficult parents for another reason: Given the link between schizophrenia and genetics, a child with schizophrenia is likely to have at least one parent with the same pathological genes that resulted in the child's disorder. Thus, the parents may have a muted (or perhaps just an undiagnosed) version of the disease, contributing to the family's problems (Holtzman et al., 1988; Reveley, Reveley, & Clifford, 1982; Tsuang et al., 1991).

In short, then, there is no reason to believe that poor familial relations cause a patient's illness. But the family context surely does matter in other ways, including how well a person with schizophrenia copes with the disorder. This role is reflected in the fact that patients, once treated and released from a hospital, are rehospitalized more often if their parents are hostile and critical toward them (Hooley, 1985; see also Hooley, 2004). This makes sense. Such reactions by family members are likely to impede the patient's adjustment to his illness, and may make the hospital look inviting by comparison.

WHAT CAUSES THE SYMPTOMS?

We have been discussing the roots of schizophrenia, but what is it that produces the symptoms? If genetic factors play a role, what do these factors change, inside a person, to produce delusions or hallucinations or any of the other symptoms?

MALFUNCTIONING NEUROTRANSMITTER SYSTEMS

As we discussed in Chapter 3, neurons communicate with one another mainly via the chemicals called *neurotransmitters*, and different circuits in the brain are responsive to different neurotransmitters. According to the **dopamine hypothesis**, the main cause of schizophrenia is an abnormally high level of activity in the brain circuits sensitive to the neurotransmitter dopamine.

The strongest line of evidence for this hypothesis comes from the effects of a number of medications known as *classical antipsychotics*, medications that include the drugs Thorazine and Haldol. These drugs block receptors for dopamine (Figure 16.7), and, as the dopamine hypothesis predicts, they produce relief from many of the symptoms associated with schizophrenia. In addition, some kinds of antipsychotics are more effective than others in producing this blockade, and the stronger the blockade, the more therapeutic the drug (S. H. Snyder, 1976).

Other evidence comes from people who do *not* have schizophrenia, but who have taken overdoses of amphetamines. Amphetamines are stimulants whose effects include the enhancement of dopamine activity, and, when taken in large enough doses, produce a temporary psychosis that is in many ways similar to schizophrenia (Angrist, Sathananthan, Wilk, & Gershon, 1974). As the dopamine hypothesis would predict, medications that block dopamine activity at the synapse also reduce the psychotic symptoms that follow amphetamine abuse.

The dopamine hypothesis has much to recommend it, but in recent years investigators have realized that it is incomplete. For example, people with schizophrenia also may have a dysfunction in glutamate transmission in their brains (either because they have insufficient glutamate, or are relatively insensitive to it). Several pieces of evidence point in this direction, including the fact that the illicit drug phencyclidine (more commonly known as PCP or angel dust) blocks glutamate receptors, and induces symptoms similar to those seen in schizophrenia (Gorelick & Balster, 1995). In addition, drugs that increase glutamate activity alleviate both positive and negative symptoms of schizophrenia (Goff & Coyle, 2001). Let us note, though, that we probably should not think of the dopamine and glutamate proposals as competitors; both might capture part of the truth. Indeed, this reflects one of the messages emerging from recent research on schizophrenia: Multiple neurotransmitters seem to be involved, affecting multiple brain areas, under the control of multiple genes. It seems certain that our explanation of schizophrenia is likely to be complex (cf. Javitt & Coyle, 2004; Sawa & Snyder, 2002).

STRUCTURAL DEFECTS

In addition to the neurochemical disruptions in schizophrenia, research indicates that patients with this disorder also suffer from structural abnormalities in their brains. MRI scans (see Chapter 3) indicate that a certain proportion of people with schizophrenia—males, especially—show an enlargement of the ventricles, the fluid-filled cavities in the brain. The ventricles enlarge because, simply put, there is not enough brain to fill the skull. This indicates that in many cases of schizophrenia, there is either a dramatic loss of brain tissue or a deficiency that existed from the start (Andreasen et al., 1986; Chua & McKenna, 1995; Lawrie & Abukmeil, 1998; Nopoulos, Flaum, & Andreasen, 1997).

Abnormalities associated with schizophrenia have also been reported in other areas of the brain, including parts of the basal ganglia and cerebellum (Heckers, 1997; L. K. Jacobsen et al., 1997). But the most persuasive findings involve the frontal and temporal lobes (Black & Andreasen, 1994; Martin & Albers, 1995). When these areas are examined during autopsy, individuals with schizophrenia show various irregularities, including missing or abnormally sized neurons. These neuronal defects would obviously affect brain function, and, indeed, neuroimaging procedures indicate atypical functioning in patients with schizophrenia in just these areas (F. E. Bloom, 1993; Carter, Mintun, Nichols, & Cohen, 1997; Chua & McKenna, 1995; Woodruff et al., 1997).

COGNITIVE DEFICITS

How are these biological abnormalities linked to the specific symptoms of schizophrenia? The link may lie in the cognitive deficits associated with this disorder, and many

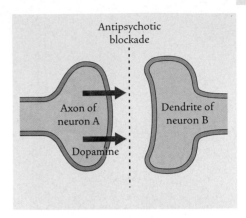

16.7 The dopamine-blockade hypothesis of classical antipsychotic action *According to the dopamine hypothesis, people with schizophrenia suffer from overactivity in the brain circuits that rely on the neurotransmitter dopamine. Consistent with this view, symptoms diminish if dopamine's actions are blocked.*

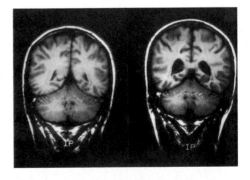

MRI scans of the brains of twins *MRI scans of the brains of 28-year-old identical twins. One (right) is hospitalized for schizophrenia; the other (left) is well. The twin with schizophrenia has enlarged cerebral ventricles. The fact that just one twin has schizophrenia shows that heredity is not the only factor in producing this disorder; the slightly different prenatal environments of the twins, as well as birth complications, may be involved.*

researchers believe these deficits are at the heart of the disease; the various other problems may derive from the underlying cognitive problems (Green, Kern, Braff, & Mintz, 2000).

Several aspects of cognition are disrupted in schizophrenia, starting with the earliest stages of sensory processing (Walker et al., 2004). Recent research, however, has focused on the so-called executive functions, supported by the brain's frontal lobes (Green et al., 2000). These functions include the ability to reason or to plan, the capacity to hold a goal in mind while working on a problem, and the ability, when needed, to inhibit a habitual thought or response. Research has also focused on working memory, the ability to hold ideas in mind in order to develop, integrate, or scrutinize them (Barch, 2003).

These various problems all combine in producing the various symptoms of schizophrenia. The inability to inhibit thoughts and actions, for example, contributes directly to the disrupted speech and behavior associated with the disorder. The difficulties in executive function interfere with the ability to reason, and so foster the delusions.

SCHIZOPHRENIA: A SUMMARY AND A PROGNOSIS

Schizophrenia is devastating in its impact—for the person afflicted and for her family. It is no wonder, therefore, that this disease has been the focus of intense research scrutiny, but the pace of progress has been limited by the nature of the disease itself: Genetic factors are crucial, but, as we have already indicated, many different genes are implicated—perhaps acting in concert, or perhaps providing multiple, independent, paths to the disease (cf. Plomin & McGuffin, 2003). Structural changes in the brain are certainly involved, but these changes are distributed throughout the brain, so that we certainly cannot point to any particular change as *the* problem in schizophrenia. The same is true for the neurotransmitter abnormalities and the cognitive disorders: In each case, schizophrenia does not seem to involve a specific or unique problem, but, instead, seems to be a composite of many different problems.

These facts have led some investigators to wonder whether we need a new approach to the study of schizophrenia—perhaps dividing the illness into subcategories. One proposal is that we seek one explanation for the positive symptoms (like the delusions or the hallucinations) and a different explanation for the negative symptoms (like the absence of emotion; Crow, 1982, 1985). Another proposal divides schizophrenia into three diseases—one that leads to the negative symptoms, one that produces the psychotic symptoms (like the hallucinations), and one that produces the various signs of disorganization (such as the incoherent speech or bizarre behavior; Andreasen, Arndt, Alliger, Miller, & Flaum, 1995; Arndt, Andreasen, Flaum, Miller, & Nopoulos, 1995; Lieberman, 1995). Still other investigators are skeptical about these proposals, but still endorse the distinctions made by the *DSM*, essentially identifying subtypes of a single disease.

This somewhat fractured state of affairs reflects the simple fact that schizophrenia varies from one case to the next—in the specific signs or symptoms shown, and in the severity of the symptoms. Cases also vary in how they respond to treatment, with some people with schizophrenia strongly improved by medication, but others not. Cases vary further in their *prognosis*—the forecast of how they will improve (or fail to). One study tracked down 200 people who had been diagnosed with schizophrenia some 30 years previously. Of these patients, 20% were doing well at the time of the follow-up, while 45% were incapacitated. Two thirds had never married, and 58% had never worked (Andreasen & Black, 1996; Cutting, 1986).

In light of these grim statistics, we can only hope that the odds will improve as researchers converge on the etiology of the disease and perfect new treatments. Indeed, some new treatments for schizophrenia provide grounds for optimism, as we will discuss in the next chapter. In the meantime, schizophrenia may well count as the most serious—and the least understood—of the commonly diagnosed forms of mental illness.

MOOD DISORDERS

In schizophrenia the primary symptoms involve disorders in thinking. In the *mood disorders*, in contrast, the predominant disturbances lie in mood and motivation. These disorders (sometimes called *affective disorders*) are characterized by emotional and energetic extremes—the maelstrom of mania, the despair of depression, or both.

BIPOLAR AND UNIPOLAR SYNDROMES

The *DSM* distinguishes between **bipolar disorder** (formerly called manic-depressive illness) and *major depression*. In bipolar disorder the patient endures episodes at manic and depressive extremes (with normal periods interspersed). These manic and depressive episodes may be as short as a few hours or as long as several months, and they need not alternate: Some patients with bipolar disorder suffer mainly from mania and have few depressions, or vice versa. Moreover, although depression and mania were once regarded as opposite and mutually exclusive, they are now known to co-occur. In such **mixed states**, patients exhibit signs of both (e.g., tearfulness and pessimism combined with grandiosity and racing thoughts).

Bipolar disorder occurs in about 0.5 to 1% of the population. Much more frequent are cases of major depression (sometimes called **unipolar depression**, since the mood extreme is of one kind only). According to several estimates, about 13% of all men and 21% of all women in the United States will suffer from a major depressive episode at some time during their lives (Kessler et al., 1994).

MANIA

In their milder form, manic states are often hard to distinguish from buoyant spirits. At this point the person is said to show **hypomania**. He seems to have shifted into high gear. He is infectiously happy, utterly self-confident, and indefatigable. It is hard to see that something is amiss unless one notices that he jumps from one plan to another, seems unable to sit still for a moment, and quickly shifts from unbounded elation to brittle irritation if he meets even the smallest frustration. Kay Redfield Jamison, an expert on bipolar disorder—and a sufferer of it as well—provided a lyrical and frank account of the ecstatic allure of hypomania:

> When you're high it's tremendous. The ideas and feelings are fast and frequent like shooting stars, and you follow them until you find better and brighter ones. Shyness goes, the right words and gestures are suddenly there, the power to captivate others a felt certainty. There are interests found in uninteresting people. Sensuality is pervasive and the desire to seduce and be seduced irresistible. Feelings of ease, intensity, power, well-being, financial omnipotence, and euphoria pervade one's marrow. (1995, p. 67)

Kay Redfield Jamison

Hypomania sounds like a positive enough state. The real problem emerges, though, when hypomania gives way to full-blown **mania**. Now the motor is racing and all brakes are off, and in her perceived invincibility the sufferer will likely quit all her antimanic medication. She may begin to stay up all night, or engage in an endless stream of talk that runs from one topic to another and knows no inhibitions of social or personal propriety.

These feelings of omnipotence are short-lived, however. They recede as acute or psychotic mania sets in, and invincibility is replaced by terror as the patient loses his grip on reality:

> The fast ideas are too fast, and there are far too many; overwhelming confusion replaces clarity. Memory goes. Humor and absorption on friends' faces are replaced by fear and concern. Everything previously moving with the grain is now against—you are irritable, angry, frightened, uncontrollable, and enmeshed totally in the blackest caves of the mind. (Jamison, 1995, p. 67)

Patients in the acute manic state may burst into shouts of song, smash furniture, exercise endlessly, sleep only rarely, engage in reckless sexual escapades, spend all their money on gambling, conceive grandiose plans for redirecting the nation's foreign policy or making millions in the stock market, and go on drinking or drug-abuse bouts (nearly 60% of people with bipolar disorder are alcohol or drug abusers; Feinman & Dunner, 1996). Jamison described this chaotic state:

> I kept on with my life at a frightening pace. I worked ridiculously long hours and slept next to not at all. When I went home at night it was a place of increasing chaos: Books, many of them newly purchased, were strewn everywhere. . . . There were hundreds of scraps of paper as well. . . . One scrap contained an incoherent and rambling poem; I found it weeks later, apparently triggered by my spice collection, which, needless to say, had grown by leaps and bounds during my mania. I had titled it, for reasons that I am sure made sense at the time, "God is an Herbivore." (1995, p. 79)

This torrent of activity can continue over many days and sleepless nights and will eventually sap the patient's health (and that of those around her) if the disorder goes untreated. Although we have focused only on adults, children can also have bipolar disorder, and over 90% of these children will be plagued by it throughout adulthood (Kessler, Avenevoli, & Ries Merikangas, 2001).

DEPRESSION

Depression is the opposite of mania, and centers on feelings of sadness, hopelessness, and broad apathy about life; the depressed person loses interest in eating, hobbies, sex, and, for that matter, almost everything. Of course, everyone has these feelings at one point or another, especially after some bad event in his life (such as sickness or the death of a friend, the end of a relationship, a significant career failure, and so on). And, in fact, these feelings can sometimes be *good* for us. A period of grieving, for example, after the death of a loved one can help us to deal with, and adjust to, the loss. But diagnosable depression is different, distinguished both by the severity and the duration of its feelings. In fact, the *DSM* suggests a diagnosis of depression only if the feelings of sadness have lasted at least 2 weeks, and are accompanied by other symptoms such as insomnia and feelings of worthlessness.

The novelist William Styron (1925–2006) provided a portrait of depression, written in the depths of his own despair:

> All sense of hope vanished, along with the idea of a futurity; my brain, in thrall to its outlaw hormones, had become less an organ of thought than an instrument registering, minute by minute, varying degrees of its own suffering. The mornings themselves were becoming bad now as I wandered about lethargic . . . but afternoons were still the worst, when I'd feel the horror, like some poisonous fogbank, roll in upon my mind, forcing me into bed. There I would lie for as long as six hours, stuporous and virtually paralyzed, gazing at the ceiling and waiting for that moment of evening when, mysteriously, the crucifixion would ease up just enough to allow me to force down some food and then, like an automaton, seek an hour or two of sleep again. (1990, pp. 58–59)

Depression   *In his book* Darkness Visible, *the writer William Styron (1925–2006) described his battles with depression.*

Many people with depression also experience considerable anxiety, and about 20% also suffer from psychosis; that is, the depression is accompanied by delusions or hallucinations. Some of these are variations on the theme of worthlessness: "It would be better if I had not been born. . . . I am the most inferior person in the world" (Beck, 1967, p. 38). Other delusions concern guilt about some unspeakable, unpardonable sin, and patients report hearing the devil tell them that they will surely burn in hell for eternity (Andreasen & Black, 1996). Whatever the manifestation, depressions with psychotic features are more severe, less responsive to treatment, and more likely to recur (Coryell, 1996).

Specific cognitive deficits, including disrupted attention and working memory, also accompany severe depression. Moreover, depressed patients often exhibit various physical manifestations that can include a loss of appetite and weight loss, weakness, fatigue, poor bowel functioning, sleep disorders, and loss of interest in sex. It is as if both bodily and psychic batteries have run down completely.

Depression is not tied to any particular age or life stage. It is most common in the years starting with adolescence and continuing through middle adulthood, but depression can also emerge in the elderly and in children (Garber & Horowitz, 2002; Kessler, Keller, & Wittchen, 2001). Depressed adolescents show most of the symptoms we have described, but, in addition, some of their symptoms come in distinctly teenage form: Their despair often leads them to substance abuse; their apathy about life shows up in the number of classes they miss; their irritability emerges as belligerence and defiance. To be sure, each of these traits can occur without depression, but the full set of traits, together with other symptoms of depression, can be an indication of profound emotional problems. In younger children, depression takes other forms and often masquerades as "school phobia" ("I hate school"), aggressive outbursts, and bodily complaints like frequent stomachaches (Lamarine, 1995).

DEPRESSION AND SUICIDE

Given the depressed individual's bottomless despair, it is not surprising that suicide is a very real risk. Here is Kay Jamison's description of an episode of depression:

> Each day I awoke deeply tired, a feeling as foreign to my natural self as being bored or indifferent to life. Those were next. Then a gray, bleak preoccupation with death, dying, decaying, that everything was born but to die, best to die now and save the pain while waiting. (1995, p. 38)

Both those with major depression and those in a depressive phase of bipolar disorder can become suicidal. Some actually attempt suicide, and more than a few succeed. The risk of suicide is greater among those with bipolar disorder than among those with major depression. In fact, up to 20% of individuals with bipolar disorder commit suicide. As might be expected, people with bipolar disorder rarely commit suicide during manic episodes (Andreasen & Black, 1996), but surprisingly, suicide risk is also relatively low for those in the depths of depression. At that point, gloom is deepest, but so is inertia, and although the patient may have decided to kill herself, she will have neither the energy nor the tenacity to complete the act. She will be more likely to follow through on her resolution as she begins to recover from depression and emerges from closely supervised care. Times of greatest risk, therefore, include weekend leaves from a hospital and the period immediately after discharge (Beck, 1967).

Women are three times as likely to attempt suicide as men, but when men make the attempt, they are much more likely to succeed; in fact, four times as many men as women kill themselves. One reason for the difference is in the choice of methods. Women are more likely than men to cut their wrists or swallow a bottle of sleeping pills, methods for which there is some prospect of rescue. Men, in contrast, tend to use methods that are irreversible, such as shooting themselves or jumping off a rooftop (Fremouw, Perczel, & Ellis, 1990).

THE ROOTS OF MOOD DISORDERS

What produces mood disorders? Like schizophrenia, depression is thought to result from multiple contributing factors, factors that include genetic, neurochemical, and psychological influences.

Hamlet on depression **Probably no patient in real life has described his preoccupation with death, suicide, and dissolution as eloquently as that greatest depressive in all of English literature, Prince Hamlet:**
"O that this too too sullied flesh would melt,
Thaw, and resolve itself into a dew,
Or that the Everlasting had not fixed
His canon 'gainst self-slaughter! O God, O God,
How weary, stale, flat, and unprofitable
Seem to me all the uses of this world!
Fie on't, ah fie, fie! 'Tis an unweeded garden
That grows to seed;."
(Hamlet, I: ii, photograph from a 2004 Royal Shakespeare Company production of the play starring Toby Sephens.)

HEREDITY

The mood disorders have important hereditary components, reflected in the fact that, overall, concordance rates for depression are roughly two times higher in identical twins than in fraternal twins (Sullivan, Neale, & Kendler, 2002). The pattern is even clearer for bipolar disorder: If someone's identical twin has the disorder, there is a 60% chance that he, too, will have the disorder; the concordance rate for fraternal twins is much lower, 12% (Kelsoe, 1997).

Adoption studies point to the same conclusion, and the biological relatives of adopted children with depression are themselves at high risk for depression (Wender, Kety, Rosenthal, Schulsinger, & Ortmann, 1986). Likewise, the risk of suicide is much higher among the biological relatives of depressed adoptees than it is in the biological kin of nondepressed adoptees (Wallace, Schneider, & McGuffin, 2002).

Importantly, though, the genetic evidence indicates a clear distinction between unipolar depression and bipolar disorder. The two disorders overlap in their symptoms (i.e., clinical depression resembles the depressed phase of bipolar disorder), but they probably arise from different sources. This is evident, for example, in the fact that people with one of these disorders tend to have relatives with the one condition but not the other. Apparently, then, there are separate inheritance pathways for each, making it likely that they are largely separate disorders (Gershon, Nurnberger, Berrettini, & Golding, 1985; Torgersen, 1986; Wender et al., 1986; for more on the genetics of depression, see Caspi et al., 2003; Moffitt, Caspi, & Rutter, 2006).

NEUROCHEMICAL MALFUNCTIONS

Symptom relief for depression is often provided by drugs that influence the effects of various neurotransmitters, and this suggests that the depression arose in the first place because of some disorder in neurotransmission. Three neurotransmitters seem critical: norepinephrine, dopamine, and serotonin, and many of the antidepressant medications work by increasing the availability of these chemicals at the synapse (Schildkraut, 1965).

How these neurochemical abnormalities lead to depression is uncertain, but it is clear that depression involves more than a simple neurotransmitter shortage. This is evident, for example, in the fact that antidepressant drugs work almost immediately to increase the availability of neurotransmitters, but their clinical effects usually do not appear until a few weeks later. Thus, neurotransmitter problems are involved in depression (because otherwise the drugs would not work at all), but the nature of those problems remains to be specified. (For some recent insights into this issue, though, see Jacobs, 2004; Santarelli et al., 2003.)

What of bipolar disorder? Many of the same neurotransmitter systems involved in major depression are also disturbed in bipolar disorder (Baumann & Bogerts, 2001). The mystery here, though, lies in explaining the cycling between manic and depressive episodes, especially since, in some patients, this cycling is quite rapid and seemingly divorced from external circumstances. Some investigators believe the cycling is related to some dysfunction in neuronal membranes, with the consequence that the membranes mismanage fluctuations in the level of various neurotransmitters (Hirschfeld & Goodwin, 1988; Meltzer, 1986). Others believe that bipolar disorder represents a mitochondrial dysfunction (the mitochondria are involved in cellular energy production), especially given findings that bipolar patients often show abnormalities in mitochondrial DNA (Kato & Kato, 2000). Resolving these issues awaits more research.

PSYCHOLOGICAL RISK FACTORS

Our account of the mood disorders also needs to take someone's life experiences into account. This is evident, for example, in the fact that unipolar depression is often

Depression and despair   Edward Adamson, a professional artist, founded a studio in a British mental hospital for the use of the institutionalized patients. Many of their works forcefully express their depression and despair, as in the case of this painting, titled Cri de Coeur, *or* Cry from the Heart. *(Cri de Coeur by Martha Smith)*

precipitated by an identifiable life crisis, whether it involves marital or professional difficulties, serious physical illness, or a death in the family (Monroe & Hadjiyannakis, 2002).

As we mentioned early on, though, life crises do not, by themselves, cause depression. Almost everyone becomes sad (and perhaps profoundly so) if a friend dies, or if she loses her job. But most people recover from the sadness after a while, and so do not end up depressed. What we need to ask, therefore, is why some people seem unable to bounce back after a hard blow, and why, instead of recovering from a tragedy, they spiral downward into depression.

Part of the explanation turns out to be situational, so that, for example, severe stress is less likely to lead to depression if a person has good social support (Brown & Harris, 1978; Joiner, 1997). But a different—and crucial—factor is concerned with the person's mental set, and, specifically, how he thinks about the stressful event when it arrives.

BECK'S COGNITIVE THEORY OF DEPRESSION

Many depressed individuals believe that both they and the world are hopeless and wretched. It seems plausible that these beliefs are produced by the patient's mood, but, according to the psychiatrist Aaron Beck, the opposite is the case: The beliefs come first, and produce the depression (see, for example, Beck, 1967, 1976). Specifically, Beck argues that depression stems from a set of intensely negative and irrational beliefs that some people hold: the beliefs that they are worthless, that their future is bleak, and that whatever happens around them is sure to turn out for the worst. These beliefs form the core of a *negative cognitive schema* by which a person interprets whatever happens to her, and leaves her mood nowhere to go but down.

Beck argues that these beliefs develop during childhood and adolescence, but then may have little effect for years. The beliefs are activated, though, if the person encounters some significant life stress, and, at that point, the stress—interpreted through the cognitive schema—leads to depression.

Consistent with Beck's view, depressed patients are, in fact, more negative in their thinking overall, and certainly in their thinking about themselves (see, for example, Clark & Beck, 1999). And, crucially, several studies suggest that these negative beliefs can be detected in someone years before the depression begins, just as Beck would argue (see, for example, Lewinsohn, Joiner, & Rohde, 2001). Moreover, Beck's conception has led to an effective treatment for depression—called *cognitive therapy*—during which patients confront their defeatist beliefs and replace them with more positive ones (Beck, 1967; Beck, Rush, Shaw, & Emery, 1979; see also Chapter 17).

Nonetheless, there are several reasons to be cautious about Beck's view. First, most depressions subside by themselves without treatment in 3 to 4 months—but does the person's way of thinking spontaneously change this fast, when cognitive therapy usually takes much longer? Second, Beck's theory easily explains why someone with negative beliefs ends up sad (or even despondent), but can the theory explain depression's other symptoms, including the insomnia, the loss of appetite, the broken concentration? This point is far from clear. In fact, many people with depression do not feel sad at all; instead, their primary affect is one of total apathy, and it is not clear how to explain this within Beck's conception. As a result, it seems likely that Beck's view may explain some cases of depression (or may explain some symptoms in a specific patient), but cannot be our entire conception.

HELPLESSNESS AND HOPELESSNESS

Beck's cognitive theory grew out of clinical work with depressed patients. A related account, proposed by Martin Seligman, began instead with studies of animal learning. We first met this line of research in Chapter 6, and it is a line that led to the *learned helplessness theory* of depression (Seligman, 1975).

Depression and social support   *Three students comfort each other during a prayer vigil for the shooting victims of Columbine high school, April 21, 1999. Three thousand people showed up for a gathering in response to the shooting deaths of 15 people at Columbine high school on April 20.*

As we discussed in Chapter 6, learned helplessness was first observed in dogs. The dogs were initially exposed to a situation in which they received a series of electric shocks about which they could do absolutely nothing. They were, in other words, objectively helpless in this situation, and all they could do was endure the shocks. Later on, the same dogs were placed in a situation in which they could escape the shock through a simple response. However, they consistently failed to learn the response. Instead, they gave every indication that they had essentially given up: They lay down, whimpered, and passively accepted their fate. Having once been made helpless, they seemed to have learned that they were helpless in general and so, accordingly, did nothing (Seligman, Maier, & Solomon, 1971).

Seligman argued that this pattern of learned helplessness is similar to depression in humans, and indeed depressed humans and helpless animals respond to the same medications: The helplessness disappears, and the animals behave much like normal (nonhelpless) animals (Porsolt, LePichon, & Jalfre, 1977).

A crucial problem for this conception, though, lies in a point we have already mentioned: Not everyone who has experienced helplessness—not every cancer victim, not every widower—becomes depressed. Some additional factor must be involved, and Seligman and his colleagues soon added a further claim to their theory to describe what this factor might be: Perhaps bad events are not by themselves what makes us depressed; in addition, it matters how we think about these events, and how we try to explain them. Do we think that a bad event happened because of something we did, so that, in some direct way, we caused the event? Do we believe that similar bad events will arise in other aspects of our lives? And do we think that bad events will continue to happen to us, perhaps for the rest of our lives? Seligman proposes that much depends on how we answer these questions, and, moreover, he suggests that each of us has a consistent style for how we tend to answer such questions—what he and his collaborators call an *explanatory style*. In their view, someone is vulnerable to depression if her explanatory style tends to be internal ("I, and not some external factor, caused the event"), global ("This sort of event will also happen in other areas of my life"), and stable ("This is going to keep happening"). With this explanatory style, a person is very likely to end up depressed if something bad happens to him (Abramson, Seligman, & Teasdale, 1978).

Evidence suggests that this pessimistic explanatory style is indeed characteristic of depressed persons (C. Peterson & Seligman, 1984). In addition, it appears that the explanatory style usually predates the depression, with the clear implication that this way of interpreting the world is not caused by depression, but instead (as Seligman and his colleagues propose) constitutes a factor predisposing an individual toward depression (Abramson et al., 2002; Alloy, Abramson, & Francis, 1999).

The Social and Cultural Context of Depression

It seems, then, that there are biochemical and cognitive contributors to depression. As we mentioned earlier, though, depression is also influenced by the social setting. This is evident, for example, in the fact that depression is less likely among individuals who have friends or family who provide a strong social network. The importance of the social surroundings is also visible in another way: the role of culture in shaping the likelihood that depression will emerge, or the form that the disorder takes.

Depression occurs in all cultures, and, in fact, the World Health Organization ranked depression fourth among all causes of disability worldwide (Miller, 2006b). However, the prevalence varies widely from one country to the next. For example, depression is—not surprisingly—more common in countries such as Afghanistan that have been torn

Depression around the world   War has many horrid effects—including an increase in the rate of mental disease. Depression rates are, for example, high in countries like Afghanistan that have been torn apart by war, with many people displaced from their homes and living in poverty in refugee camps like this one.

apart by war (Bolton & Betancourt, 2004); the difficulties in such countries also lead to other disorders, including anxiety (pp. 620–625) and post-traumatic stress disorder (p. 625–626). In contrast, depression is much less commonly diagnosed in China, Taiwan, and Japan than in the West. When the disorder is detected in these Asian countries, the symptoms are less often psychological (such as sadness or apathy) and more often bodily (such as sleep disturbance, weight loss, or, in China, heart pain; Kleinman, 1986; Miller, 2006a; Tsai & Chentsova-Dutton, 2002). Why should this be? There are several possibilities, starting with the fact that cultures differ in their *expression rules*— that is, in how emotion is expressed—and this will obviously influence the presentation and diagnosis of almost any mental disorder. In addition, people in these Asian countries may differ in how they understand and perhaps even experience their own symptoms, and this, too, can influence diagnosis.

Even within a single country, though, the risk of mood disorders varies. Depression, for example, is more common among lower socioeconomic groups (Dohrenwend, 2000; Monroe & Hadjiyannakis, 2002), perhaps because these groups are exposed to more stress. In contrast, bipolar disorder is more common among *higher* socioeconomic groups (Goodwin & Jamison, 1990), conceivably because the behaviors produced during someone's hypomanic phases may lead to increased accomplishment.

In addition, we have already mentioned that depression is more likely to occur in women than in men, with several factors contributing to this difference. For one, evidence suggests that the susceptibility genes for affective disorders may lie on the X chromosome, and women, of course, have two X chromosomes; men have only one. This may double the risk for women. A different explanation is hormonal. Women must cope with cyclic hormonal changes, such as significant drops in estrogen and progesterone levels during the premenstrual period, the postpartum period, and menopause, which are themselves associated with depressed moods (Seeman, 1997).

Cultures also provide different coping mechanisms for women and men, and these may be especially crucial in the early (prediagnosis) stages of depression. For example, women who are depressed often dwell on their despondency, mulling over their problems, and this activity may actually foster the depression. Men, in contrast, often try to distract themselves by fixating on their work or exercising unrelentingly, thus "acting out" their distress rather than manifesting it in depression (Nolen-Hoeksema, 1987). However, this escapist strategy is hardly trouble free, because a major way in which men act out distress is through alcohol

Women and alcohol   Alcohol consumption by women seems to be on the rise. This is worrisome but may lead to a corresponding drop in depression rates in women.

and drug consumption; when depressed, they are much more likely to get drunk or get high than get therapy. There is some suggestion, though, that this pattern is changing, with alcohol consumption by women on the rise as a coping mechanism; whether this change will lead to a corresponding drop in depression rates remains to be seen.

MOOD DISORDERS AND MULTICAUSALITY

At the start of this chapter, we argued that we should not seek single causes for mental disease. Instead, we must acknowledge that multiple factors create a diathesis (an inclination or risk) for an illness, and other factors create a stress (the trigger). Still other factors seem to shelter someone from illness, and so provide, in essence, an anti-diathesis. These broad claims certainly fit well with our descriptions of schizophrenia and the mood disorders. Depression, for example, seems to result from some mixture of a susceptible genotype, psychosocial misfortunes, various neurotransmitter anomalies, and a pessimistic explanatory style. Moreover, these factors interact with one another, so that (for example) negative cognitions and learned helplessness may help to produce the neurotransmitter anomalies, and these same anomalies in the nervous system may help to perpetuate the negative cognitions. Fortunately, though, all this complexity has not prevented the development of ways to treat affective disorders. Many can be treated quickly and effectively, as we discuss in Chapter 17.

ANXIETY DISORDERS

In the affective disorders, a primary symptom is a profoundly altered mood: the highs of mania, the lows of depression. In the *anxiety disorders*, the main problem is still one of mood, but the primary symptoms include both an intense experience of anxiety and a series of efforts (sometimes disruptive, and often unsuccessful) to deal with the anxiety. A patient with one of these disorders is chronically apprehensive, always fears the worst, and must guard vigilantly against anticipated disasters. Although we all experience anxiety in normal life, we are not usually disabled by it; it is only when there is some serious disruption of normal life that the diagnosis of anxiety disorder is warranted.

Anxiety disorders are relatively common, affecting more than 20 million people each year in the United States alone (Greenberg et al., 1999). They are, in fact, the most common type of clinical diagnosis (Kessler et al., 2005), and are found in both sexes, although more commonly in women than in men (Breslau, Chilcoat, Kessler, & Davis, 1999; Graaf, Bijl, Smit, Vollebergh, & Spijker, 2002).

PHOBIAS

Phobias are characterized by an intense and irrational fear, coupled with great efforts to avoid the feared object or situation. Notice the inclusion here of the word *irrational*. Someone living in the middle of a swamp and constantly worried about snakes is not manifesting a phobia; instead, her fear is perfectly reasonable. However, someone living in a San Francisco apartment and incapacitated by the same fear probably does have a phobia. And it does not help that the person with the phobia probably knows that the fear is groundless; for someone with a phobia, this knowledge does not in any way diminish the fear.

SOCIAL PHOBIA

There are several types of phobias, including *specific phobias*, directed at a particular object (like snakes or blood), and *social phobia*, in which the problem is fear of embarrassment or humiliation in front of others (Juster & Heimberg, 1995; Rapaport, Paniccia, & Judd, 1995). Social phobia typically emerges in adolescence, but is also found in children. People with this phobia will desperately try to avoid situations in which they must expose themselves to public scrutiny. They will avoid public speaking or performing because they think others will think they are stupid, they will not eat in restaurants for fear they will choke on their food, and they will not go to parties or professional meetings because they may stutter and stammer when trying to make small talk. When forced into situations of this sort, they may try to "fortify" themselves with alcohol or drugs, making substance abuse or dependence a constant risk (Pollack, 2001).

SPECIFIC PHOBIAS

Unlike the pervasive fear seen in social phobia, the specific phobias concern particular objects or events. During the nineteenth century, many of these irrational fears were cataloged and assigned exotic-sounding Greek or Latin names. Examples are fear of high places (acrophobia), enclosed places (claustrophobia), crowds (ochlophobia), germs (mysophobia), cats (ailurophobia), and even the number 13 (triskaidekaphobia)—the list is long.

Some of these phobias seem quirky and curious, but others can be life changing, because the person suffering from a phobia almost always develops strategies (and sometimes elaborate strategies) for avoiding the phobic object. Thus, people with claustrophobia will insist on climbing many flights of stairs rather than step into an elevator. Likewise, an executive with a fear of heights may choose to quit his job rather than accept a promotion that gives him an office with a glorious view from a 20th-story window. And these phobias will often expand in scope, so that a fear of leopards, say, can grow to become a fear of the place where a zoo is located, of all cats and things catlike, of all spotted objects, and so on.

Among the specific phobias, one is unique: the blood-injection-injury phobia. This phobia often is experienced as a feeling of *disgust* rather than *fear*, and involves a distinctive bodily reaction. For most phobias, an encounter with the phobic stimulus produces panic responses: quick pulse, elevated blood pressure, sweating, and tremor. These are all emergency reactions produced by the sympathetic branch of the autonomic nervous system (Lang, Davis, & Öhman, 2000; see Chapter 3). For the blood-injection-injury phobia, in contrast, the reaction is essentially the opposite: The pulse slows, the blood pressure drops, the muscles go slack, and the person can fall to the ground in a dead faint. In addition, the treatment for blood-injection-injury phobias runs exactly opposite of that for other phobias. For most phobias, the treatment involves teaching the phobic person to relax. For a blood-injection-injury phobia, the sufferer must keep up her blood pressure, and so must learn, on cue, to become tense (Hellstrom, Fellenius, & Ost, 1996).

The Conditioning Account of Specific Phobias What is the mechanism that creates and maintains the specific phobias? One notion goes back to John Locke (1690), who believed that such fears were produced by the chance association of ideas, as when a child is told stories about goblins that come by night and is forever after terrified of the dark. Several modern authors express much the same idea in the language of conditioning theory (see Chapter 6). In their view, phobias result from classical conditioning: The person who suffers from the phobia has experienced some painful, frightening, or embarrassing event, and this is the unconditioned stimulus. The conditioned stimulus, in turn, was linked to the event, and so now has become fearful itself, in much the same way that a bell paired with food delivery becomes a signal that the food will soon arrive. In the case of phobias, though, the conditioned response is fear—including all of the psychological and bodily manifestations of that emotion (cf. Wolpe, 1958).

Specific phobias   Phobias relating to spiders and snakes are very common, even though other objects in our world pose a much greater threat. Falls in bathtubs, for example, are more frequent than snakebites, but this fact seems not to give rise to bathtub phobias.

This account of phobias seems plausible, and, in fact, many phobias can be traced to some traumatic experience that seems to have precipitated the disorder, just as a conditioning account requires (see, for example, Hackmann, Clark, & McManus, 2000). But we need more theory than this if we are to account for the basic facts about phobias. For example, phobias can sometimes emerge without a history of conditioning—so that, for example, someone can develop a snake phobia even if he has never been close to a snake, much less had a frightening encounter with one. How should we think about this? In addition, a simple conditioning account provides no explanation for why some phobias seem rare while others are quite common. For example, automobiles, bathtubs, and hammers are all (statistically) rather dangerous, and frequently associated with painful accidents. In contrast, rather few people have been bitten by a snake or a spider. Therefore, if it is associations with pain or trauma that produce phobias, then we would expect to see many hammer phobias and bathtub phobias, but relatively few snake or spider phobias. But the opposite is the case.

These puzzles are, however, easily solved. A century ago, Ivan Pavlov argued that classical conditioning was necessarily rooted in an organism's own experiences, but more recent studies have demonstrated *vicarious conditioning*, in which a person (or, in some studies, a monkey) can acquire a conditioned response merely by observing the fear demonstrated by someone else (see, for example, Mineka & Ben Hamida, 1998). In addition, in Chapter 6 we discussed the fact that organisms seem "prepared" to learn certain associations (and so learn them quickly), but "unprepared" for other associations (and so learn them more slowly if at all), and, in each case, this preparedness is usually understandable in evolutionary terms. How does this proposal apply to phobias? Snakes and spiders were relatively common dangers for our primate ancestors; natural selection may therefore have favored animals who were innately predisposed (i.e., prepared) to learn to fear these stimuli very quickly, after just one or two experiences with the fearful object (Öhman & Mineka, 2001; Seligman, 1971). On this basis, it is not a problem if painful encounters with these stimuli are rare; the limited experience might still be enough to create and sustain a substantial number of phobias.

With these relatively small modifications, then, we can preserve the claim that, in virtually all cases, phobias are the product of learning—and, in particular, the product of classical conditioning (Mineka & Zinbarg, 2006). Let us add, though, that phobias are also influenced by factors that seem to be separate from someone's life experiences; there is, for example, some evidence for a genetic predisposition toward developing phobias (Kendler, Karkowski, & Prescott, 1999). But perhaps here, too, we can explain things in terms of learning—with the idea that the genetic mechanism may be affecting the speed of conditioning, and thus the ease with which phobias are established.

PANIC DISORDER AND AGORAPHOBIA

A different type of anxiety disorder is the *panic disorder*, characterized by the occurrence of unexpected *panic attacks*—sudden episodes of terrifying bodily symptoms, such as labored breathing, choking, dizziness, tingling in the hands and feet, sweating, trembling, heart palpitations, and chest pain. In many cases, the person becomes convinced that she is having a heart attack, and is near death. It is no surprise, therefore, that panic attacks usually include feelings of intense terror, and a sense of impending doom.

Panic attacks occur in almost all anxiety disorders, so that, for example, a snake-phobia sufferer may have one at the sight of a snake. But the hallmark of panic disorder is that the panic attacks seem to come out of the blue. As a result, the patient often has an intense experience of unreality and fears that he is losing control or going insane. Panic disorder is diagnosed when there are recurrent unexpected attacks and when either behavioral or psychological troubles follow the attacks. Based on that criterion, it is found in about 5% of women and 2% of men (see, for example, Barlow, 2002).

Panic Hoy, 1988, by Rufino Tamayo

Panic attacks can be frightening enough when they occur, but in addition, the mere anticipation of the attacks can be awful. Indeed, people with panic disorder sometimes develop a profound fear of having an attack, especially in public places, where an attack might be embarrassing, or in circumstances such as driving, where the attack could be truly dangerous. As a result, people with panic disorder often develop a powerful tendency not to venture outside their designated "safe" places—their houses or even just their bedrooms. This is why panic disorder is often accompanied by *agoraphobia*, generally defined as a fear of open spaces, but better understood in this context as a fear of being alone and outside the home, especially in a public place. Agoraphobia can itself be quite paralyzing, and so someone with this disorder might refuse to leave her home for days (or even weeks) at a time.

What accounts for panic disorder? Many theorists stress its neurobiological underpinnings and suggest that the main problem is one of instability in the autonomic nervous system (Andreasen & Black, 1996; Wilhelm, Trabert, & Roth, 2001). Other researchers highlight the role that cognition may play. They believe that panic disorder is produced by a vicious cycle that begins with an overreaction to one's own normal bodily responses to threat, such as quicker heartbeats and faster and shallower breathing. The person with the panic disorder believes that these reactions indicate an impending heart attack. This makes him afraid, which intensifies the bodily reactions, which encourages the worry, which amplifies the bodily reaction—a sequence that can spiral upward toward a full-blown panic (D. M. Clark, 1986).

Notice that both of these accounts may be correct: Someone with panic disorder may be overreactive to begin with, perhaps because of genetic factors, and also likely to interpret her reactions as indications of an impending bodily catastrophe. This style of interpretation, in turn, may be a result of both inherited factors and learning. Like most mental disorders, panic disorder is unlikely to be explained in simple terms.

GENERALIZED ANXIETY DISORDER

Both phobias and panic attacks are a source of enormous suffering, and can be horribly disruptive to someone's life. But both are limited in an important sense: In the absence of the phobic stimulus, someone with phobias will feel all right. In between attacks, someone with panic disorder can function more or less normally. These limits are not in place, however, for someone who suffers from *generalized anxiety disorder* (*GAD*). For

The Scream   1893, by Edvard Munch

this person, the anxiety is not related to anything in particular; instead, it is continuous and all-pervasive. Patients with this disorder are visibly worried almost all the time. They feel inadequate, are oversensitive, cannot concentrate, and suffer from insomnia. They have enormous difficulty making decisions, and worry afterward about whether each decision was a mistake. This state of affairs is generally accompanied by any number of physiological concomitants: rapid heart rate, irregular breathing, excessive sweating, and chronic diarrhea (Rickels & Rynn, 2001).

GAD is relatively common, occurring in roughly 3% of the U.S. population in any one year (Kessler et al., 1994). However, there is uncertainty about its cause. Some researchers have suggested that there may be genetic roots, but the evidence for this point is not firm. We do know that GAD involves neurochemical abnormalities (e.g., in norepinephrine and serotonin systems, and especially in the secretion of the neurotransmitter gamma-aminobutric acid, or GABA), but it is unclear whether these abnormalities are the cause of the disorder or one of its effects (Nutt, 2001).

OBSESSIVE-COMPULSIVE DISORDER

In *obsessive-compulsive disorder (OCD)*, the main symptoms are (as the label implies) obsessions (recurrent unwanted and disturbing thoughts) and a series of compulsions intended in large part to deal with the obsessions. The obsessions come in many varieties, but common ones involve concerns about dirt and contamination, fears of harming someone, and an extraordinary need for balance and symmetry. Thus, for example, a salesperson might worry constantly about infection, and so refuse to shake hands with his customers; an otherwise loving parent may have recurrent thoughts of strangling her children; and a seemingly normal businessman may be deeply troubled about disorder in his apartment, and so spend hours each night straightening each of the paintings on the walls. Impressively, these same themes characterize OCD not just in North America, but across a variety of cultures (Craske, 1999).

Obsessive thoughts can produce considerable anxiety, and many compulsions may be understood as attempts to counteract this anxiety. An obsession with dirt may lead to compulsions like ritualistic cleaning or continual hand washing; in severe cases, someone with OCD will wash her hands so often, to ward off germs, that she will end up with open and bleeding sores on her skin. An obsession with forgetting things might lead to checking and rechecking—to make sure that the alarm clock is really turned on, or that the door is really locked. And here, too, the compulsion can become crippling: Someone with OCD may check and recheck the stove so many times, making certain it is really turned off, that he needs hours to leave the house for even the simplest errand. And, in most cases, the sufferers know that their behavior is irrational, and that they are washing or checking far more than they need to. However, they are helpless to stop their thoughts and urges, and so are all the more tormented by them.

OCD often begins in childhood, typically before age 10, and, overall, afflicts as much as 2 to 3% of the population sometime in their lives (March, Leonard, & Swedo, 1995). It is also quite serious: If untreated, most cases worsen over time and are accompanied by recurrent bouts of major depression (Barlow, 1988).

As with many other disorders, there are several factors that predispose an individual to develop OCD, although the evidence is accumulating that biology plays more of a role in this disorder than in any of the other anxiety disorders. There is, for example, a clear genetic influence, as shown by the fact that the concordance rate for OCD is appreciably higher for identical twins than for fraternal twins (Black & Noyes, 1990; S. A. Rasmussen, 1993). In fact, different aspects of OCD (e.g., cleaning or hoarding compulsions) may have separate inheritance paths (Leckman, Zhang, Alsobrook, & Pauls, 2001). In addition, evidence suggests that OCD may be linked to overactivity in three

Compulsive hand washing in literature   A scene from a production of Macbeth. It shows Lady Macbeth walking in her sleep and scrubbing imaginary blood off her hands as she relives the night on which she and her husband murdered the king.

specific brain areas—the orbitofrontal cortex, the caudate nucleus, and the anterior cingulate—although it is unclear whether this activity is the cause of the disease or one of its consequences (Micallef & Blin, 2001). And as with major depression, the neurological substrate for this disorder can be influenced by increasing serotonin in the synapses, with portions of the basal ganglia and frontal cortex implicated the most (Dougherty, Rauch, & Jenike, 2002; Piccinelli, Pini, Bellantuono, & Wilkinson, 1995; Rauch & Savage, 2000; Saxena et al., 1999; Swedo et al., 1992).

THE STRESS DISORDERS

One final category of anxiety disorders includes the two *stress disorders*, triggered abruptly and horribly by an identifiable and horrific event. For women, the most common such devastation is rape or physical assault; for men, it is military combat. Other calamities can also bring humans to this extreme—being in a serious automobile accident, witnessing a homicide, or encountering the carnage following a natural disaster or terrorist attack (Andreasen & Black, 1996; Wolf & Mosnaim, 1990).

For regardless of what the traumatic event is, though, the psychological effects are usually the same: Immediately after the trauma, there is generally a period of numbness, during which the sufferer feels wholly estranged, socially unresponsive, and oddly unaffected by the event, a reaction technically known as *dissociation*. With this *acute stress disorder*, there are often recurrent nightmares and waking flashbacks of the traumatic event. These can be so intense and intrusive that the sufferer may momentarily believe that she is back in the situation, reliving the battle, or being attacked once again by the rapist.

For many individuals the reactions to such traumas are enduring, and if they persist for 1 month after the stressor, the diagnosis technically becomes one of *post-traumatic stress disorder (PTSD)*. Gradually, the psychological numbness subsides, but other consequences remain, including sleep disturbances, outbursts of anger, difficulties in concentration, and exaggerated responses to being startled. Still another effect may be "survival guilt" if friends or relatives were harmed or killed by the same traumatic event (M. J. Friedman & Marsella, 1996).

In all cases it is obvious that a horrific event—a rape, a terrorist attack, a battlefield experience—precipitated the PTSD. Nonetheless, we cannot claim that this event caused the disorder, because not everyone who experiences a trauma develops PTSD. Indeed, according to one estimate, more than 90% of the U.S. population has experienced a trauma at some point, but only 5 to 12% develop PTSD (Lee & Young, 2001). Why is this? Part of the answer lies in the severity of the trauma, and unsurprisingly, more severe trauma is more likely to produce the disorder (see, for example, Sutker, Allain, & Winstead, 1993; E. Jones & Wessely, 2001; but see also McNally, 2003). The individual's level of social support is also relevant, with more and better support after a trauma associated with a decreased likelihood of later developing PTSD (Ozer & Weiss, 2004). Yet another factor is genetic, because evidence suggests that PTSD runs in families: The odds of developing PTSD increase fivefold if a parent has had it (Radant, Tsuang, Peskind, McFall, & Raskind, 2001; True et al., 1993). Studies also suggest that early adverse experiences, such as child abuse or neglect, may predispose an individual to PTSD as an adult

September 11, 2001   The attack on the World Trade Center is likely to produce many long-lasting cases of post-traumatic stress disorder.

(Bremner, Southwick, Johnson, Yehuda, & Charney, 1993; McCranie, Hyer, Boudewyns, & Woods, 1992; Zaidi & Foy, 1994).

How might genes or early life events create a vulnerability to PTSD? Some investigators believe that the key lies in someone's physiological response to stress, with either the genetic contribution or the early trauma making her oversensitive to stress for the remainder of her life. This is consistent with the fact that sufferers of PTSD show abnormally low levels of *cortisol*, a substance secreted by the adrenal glands during stress. These low cortisol levels may be a marker of both early adversity and later vulnerability (Heim, Owens, Plotsky, & Nemeroff, 1997; Ozer & Weiss, 2004; Yehuda, 1997).

DISSOCIATIVE DISORDERS

In the acute and post-traumatic stress disorders, people often try to protect themselves by *dissociating*—essentially distancing themselves psychologically from ongoing events. They establish this distance by saying things like "This can't be happening," or "This is all a dream," or "This isn't happening to me." With these defenses in place, people may, during a calamity, even experience themselves as eerily calm, floating outside their own bodies as they watch themselves react.

These adjustments are often adaptive, a way of coping with horrific events. But such adjustments can go too far and, in their extreme form, are the defining feature of the *dissociative disorders*. In some cases, for example, a person develops *dissociative amnesia*, and is suddenly unable to remember some period of his life, or even his entire past, including his own identity. Such episodes usually last less than 1 week (Kihlstrom & Schacter, 2000; Maldonado, Butler, & Spiegel, 2002). In other cases, the dissociation produces *dissociative fugue*, in which the person wanders away from home and then, days or even months thereafter, suddenly realizes that she is in a strange place, does not know how she got there, and has total amnesia for the entire period.

Far more controversial is the diagnosis of *dissociative identity disorder (DID)*, a condition formerly known as multiple personality disorder. Here the dissociation is said to be so massive that it results in two or more distinct personalities, each with its own style, its own habits, and its own beliefs. The personalities often differ in their interests, their age, their sexual orientation, and their morals.

In one case, for example, a patient named Julie mentioned, during therapy, that she wanted to introduce someone to the therapist. She closed her eyes, frowned, and then opened her eyes slowly, asserting that she was Jerrie, not Julie. Roughly 1 hour later, in the same way, she introduced Jenny, a third personality in the same body. These three women were different in many ways: Julie and Jenny were heterosexuals; Jerrie was a lesbian. Jenny was frightened and insecure; Julie was a sophisticated and caring mother; Jerrie was accomplished and proficient in the business world, and hated the fact that Julie was a heavy smoker (Davis & Osherson, 1977).

Until 20 years ago, cases like this were very rare, with fewer than 200 cases reported before 1975. Now cases number in the thousands; the large majority are women (Kluft, 1987; Ross, 1999). The number of personalities reported in each case has also increased dramatically: A review of the early cases indicated that most people with DID had only 2 or 3 separate identities (Taylor & Martin, 1944); a more recent survey indicates that the average number of identities reported by patients is 15, with some cases reporting far more than this (C. A. Ross, 1997).

These massive increases are one of the reasons this disorder has been a focus of so much debate, with some critics arguing that the flood of diagnoses may reflect a fad among therapists who inadvertently lead their suggestible patients to develop the signs

---

---

and symptoms of the syndrome (Lalonde, Hudson, Gigante, & Pope, 2001; Lilienfeld et al., 1999; Spanos, 1996; for a very different view, though, see Lewis, Yeager, Swica, Pincus, & Lewis, 1997). Contributing to this trend, the critics claim, are the books and movies about DID, including the movies *Sybil* and *The Three Faces of Eve*.

What should we make of this debate? It does seem likely that some cases of DID are faked or inadvertently created by therapists. But it also seems likely that many cases are genuine, and debate continues about the nature of this illness, its causes, and the best way to treat it (cf. Lilienfeld et al., 1999; Ross, 1999).

FACTORS UNDERLYING DISSOCIATIVE DISORDERS

Let us step away from the controversy over DID, and return to the broader category of dissociative disorders. What produces dissociative amnesia or fugue? What factors or events lead someone to these disorders? Here, too, some investigators propose a genetic basis, but research on this point has yielded mixed results (Jang, Paris, Zweig-Frank, & Livesley, 1998; Waller & Ross, 1997). One thing we do know, however, is that people naturally seem to differ in how much, and under what circumstances, they dissociate. Some of the relevant evidence comes from a measure known as the **Dissociative Experiences Scale**, which asks people directly how often they have experienced various perceptions or behaviors characteristic of dissociation (Carlson & Putnam, 1993). Other evidence comes from work on hypnosis, which some investigators regard as a form of guided dissociation (Hilgard, 1986). People differ enormously in how readily or how deeply they can be hypnotized (Ganaway, 1989), and this opens an interesting possibility: Perhaps some people were, as children, particularly adept at self-hypnosis, and learned to use this skill as a defense—putting themselves into a self-induced hypnotic trance as a form of escape from the stresses (or perhaps traumas) in their lives (Bliss, 1980). This skill may then create a preexisting readiness to dissociate in everyday life, perhaps predisposing these individuals to develop dissociative disorder.

Thus, a skill in (or habit of) dissociation may create the diathesis for a dissociative disorder. To precipitate the full-fledged disorder, however, there also has to be some unusual stress, and, in fact, most cases of dissociative amnesia occur after the same kinds of cataclysmic events that may lead to post-traumatic stress disorder. The same holds for dissociative fugues, which can also develop suddenly after personal misfortunes or financial pressures (Andreasen & Black, 1996). The same may be true as well for dissociative identity disorder: In a large percentage of DID case histories, there are terrifying stories of brutal physical or sexual abuse in childhood, often including incest (Putnam, Guroff, Silberman, Barban, & Post, 1986).

We need to be cautious, however, in interpreting these findings, because the link between trauma and dissociative disorders often relies on patients' uncorroborated memories of their childhood, and it is unclear how much faith we can place in these reports (Frankel, 1993; also see Chapter 7). In addition, individuals who are likely to dissociate also may be more prone to developing false memories (Hyman & Billings, 1998; Porter, Birt, Yuille, & Lehman, 2000). Hence, if dissociative symptoms and memories of childhood abuse go together, this may indicate that the incidents of abuse lead to dissociation, or the cause-effect relationship may be the reverse: Dissociation may predispose someone to generate (false) memories of childhood abuse. Because of ambiguities like these, conclusions about abuse in early childhood and dissociative disorders cannot yet be drawn with confidence. Once more, then, we are reminded of the controversial status of the dissociative disorders, and the difficulty of doing persuasive research in this important but contentious domain.

Dissociative identity disorder **According to some critics, the huge increase in DID diagnoses is the result of a diagnostic fad among therapists, or perhaps a result of people imitating famous cases of DID—including the case depicted in the 1958 movie, The Three Faces of Eve.**

DEVELOPMENTAL DISORDERS

We have now considered many—although by no means all—of the diagnostic categories included on the *DSM*'s Axis I. One further category is worth a brief discussion—a category that covers *disorders usually first diagnosed in infancy, childhood, or adolescence.*

Of course, many disorders emerge in children or adolescents. We have mentioned, for example, that depression is often diagnosed at a young age, and that precursors of schizophrenia can be detected in childhood, years before the disease is diagnosed. Various phobias are also common among children. But, in all these cases, the child's development itself seems more or less normal: The child still acquires the knowledge and cognitive capacities that we described in Chapters 10 and 11. However, development is not normal in the disorders encompassed by this last broad category of problems; these include mental retardation, various learning disorders, and also communication disorders. Let us explore this diagnostic category by focusing on just two of its subcategories: *autism*, and the *attention-deficit and disruptive-behavior disorders*.

AUTISM

Autism involves a wide range of developmental problems, including language and motor problems, and also problems in the social sphere. Autism is not common (affecting less than 0.1% of the world's population), but is far more frequent among boys than girls (Volkmar, Szatmari, & Sparrow, 1993). The disorder is usually diagnosed at a very young age—before a child is 3 years old—and may be suspected even earlier.

Children with autism show a range of symptoms. They tend to have little interest in other people—and so they are not cuddly as infants or interested in playmates later on. When they do interact with others, they seem to have little understanding of the others' intentions, beliefs, or goals; they seem unable to join cooperative activities and fail to form friendships. They also seem to lack emotional intelligence (Chapter 14), and so, for example, seem unable to understand others' expressions of emotions or to use their own faces and gestures to convey emotion (Charman et al., 1998).

Children with autism also show marked deficits in language—often not speaking, and typically showing neither skill nor interest in communicating with others. In many cases, they produce high-pitched birdlike noises instead of speech, or show a pattern of simply echoing speech they have heard—perhaps just a moment ago, or perhaps a few days earlier. Often, they have trouble with pronouns—reversing *I* and *you*, and referring to themselves by their own name, rather than saying "I" (Lee, Hobson, & Chiat, 1994).

Autistic children also show peculiar movement patterns—spinning around and around for long periods of time, or rocking back and forth for hours. They also seem

Autism   Children with autism often have little interest in others or can become completely attached to a single toy—although they usually do not play in the ordinary way with the toy.

insistent on sameness, and so become deeply upset—and may throw severe tantrums—if the furniture in their house is rearranged, or their parents vary the household routine in some small way. They become completely attached to one single toy, carrying it around constantly (but often not playing with it in the obvious or ordinary manner).

Finally, children with autism are often mentally retarded, but here there is an odd twist: In many cases, they show islands of preserved (and, indeed, enhanced) skill, so that a child with autism might turn out to be an extraordinary musician, or unbelievably fast in arithmetic calculations.

What produces this broad range of symptoms? The answer is not at all clear, but most accounts of autism emphasize some form of biological dysfunction, with a variety of proposals about what we should count as the "core problem." One hypothesis is that children with autism have some problem in the functioning of their amygdala, a brain structure that plays an essential role in emotion and motivation (Fein, 2001). A different hypothesis points to abnormalities in the cerebellum (Courchesne, Townsend, & Saitoh, 1994). Yet another hypothesis is that the problem lies in a brain structure that functions specifically to help the child learn about, and understand, other people's thoughts and intentions (Scott & Baron-Cohen, 1996).

Whatever the causes of autism, the treatment typically focuses on modifying the behavior of the child with autism. Various medications for autism have been considered, but none seems particularly effective. Instead, behavior-modification techniques are often used successfully—building on the principles of shaping and reinforcement that we described in Chapter 6. These efforts seem to improve both social and intellectual functioning, and can produce appreciable long-term benefits for the child.

ATTENTION-DEFICIT/HYPERACTIVITY DISORDER

Attention-deficit/hyperactivity disorder (ADHD) is characterized by a number of behavioral problems. Children with this disorder are impulsive and constantly fidgeting; they have difficulty keeping their attention focused on a task. They have trouble organizing or completing projects, and are usually perceived to be intrusive and immature, and their school performance tends to be low.

The symptoms of ADHD are quite common, but far more frequent in boys than in girls. The symptoms are most often observed at a young age (e.g., before age 8), and become less intense as the child ages. However, some symptoms can persist throughout the life span.

Research increasingly points to a biological basis for ADHD, with genetic factors playing a large role (Biederman et al., 1995; Burt, Krueger, McGue, & Iacono, 2001; Tannock, 1998). How the genes produce the disorder, however, is not clear. One promising account suggests that the problem lies in an absence of inhibitory circuits in the brain, circuits that ordinarily function to keep a child from following every stray thought, every cue in the environment, wherever it may lead (see, for example, Barkley, 1997, although see also Castellanos, Sonuga-Barke, Milham, & Tannock, 2006). When these circuits are working normally, they protect the child from distractions and momentary impulses; when the circuits are dysfunctional, the result is the pattern of scattered thoughts and actions that characterize the ADHD disorder.

One can describe someone with ADHD as being too active, too energetic, and this might make it puzzling that one of the common treatments is the medication Ritalin, a stimulant. However, the medication is clearly effective in the vast majority of children with ADHD (DuPaul & Barkley, 1998), presumably because it activates the inhibitory circuits within the brain, helping the child to guard against his wayward impulses.

ADHD *ADHD is a real disorder, but there is concern that it is being over-diagnosed. In particular, it may be the label that is given to any child who is just particularly active.*

PERSONALITY DISORDERS

We are almost finished with our tour of the diagnostic categories that guide both the research in psychopathology and also the judgment of working clinicians as they seek to understand the results of any individual assessment. Before we move on, though, we should say a brief word about the so-called *personality disorders*.

DIAGNOSING PERSONALITY DISORDERS

All of the disorders we have considered so far are included on Axis I of the *DSM*. Each involves a specific syndrome with a well-defined set of signs and symptoms. The Axis II diagnoses, in contrast, are characterized by much broader patterns of behavior. These diagnoses are concerned with traits or habits that characterize almost everything a person does. In other words, these diagnoses are concerned with someone's personality.

Of course, people differ widely in their personalities (cf. Chapter 15), and, because of these variations, some people are easier to be with than others, and some have a smoother path through life than others. In some cases, though, a person's personality is maladaptive enough that it creates considerable distress both for that person and for the others around her, and also produces impairment in the person's day-to-day functioning. Someone with this pattern may well be diagnosed as having one or another of the *personality disorders*.

The *DSM* recognizes a wide variety of personality disorders, including the *paranoid personality* (in which a person shows widespread suspiciousness and mistrust of others); the *narcissistic personality* (in which a person is preoccupied with self-promotion and receiving attention); the *antisocial personality* (characterized by a lack of moral constraint); and the *avoidant personality* (in which a person shows extreme shyness and social insecurity). Each of these disorders, however, and indeed all of the Axis II disorders, are difficult to diagnose, and disagreements about diagnosis are common (L. A. Clark & Harrison, 2001; Livesley, 2001). Part of the difficulty here is that the definitions of these disorders tell us, in essence, what a clear-cut and "pure" case of the disorder might look like. In reality, though, an individual's traits are likely only to approximate this prototype, and, indeed, many people have traits that leave them resembling more than one of the prototypes (Shea, 1995). This obviously makes diagnosis complicated. In addition, each of these disorders can be thought of as merely the extreme of some ordinary pattern (Livesley, 2001; Widiger & Sanderson, 1995). Many people, for example, are vain, and it is therefore a judgment call whether someone's vanity is so powerful that it justifies the diagnosis of the narcissistic personality disorder. Likewise, many people are shy, and it is sometimes difficult to decide whether someone's shyness has reached a point that justifies labeling him with the avoidant personality disorder. Clinicians often disagree in these judgments, increasing the uncertainty of the Axis II diagnoses.

These diagnostic problems have in turn been a difficulty for researchers, because it is obviously hard to study a group that cannot be accurately identified (see, for example, Clark & Harrison, 2001). In addition, research in this area typically focuses on people who have already been diagnosed; as a result, it is often difficult to decide which of their traits should be understood as causes of the disorder, and which, instead, are consequences of the disorder.

Even with these limitations, investigators have made impressive progress in understanding several of the personality disorders. And, on some fronts, this research has been quite *useful*. For example, the diagnosis of antisocial personality disorder (and also the closely related diagnosis of psychopathy) is a powerful predictor of whether someone will slide into crime again after a period of imprisonment (Hare, Cooke, & Hart, 1999; Hemphill, Hare, & Wong, 1998), and so can be an important source of information in making parole decisions about a specific prisoner.

Psychotic personality? **In the movie The Departed,** *Jack Nicholson plays Frank Costello, a crime boss who is violent, sadistic, narcissistic, and occasionally crazed. Should he be diagnosed as having a personality disorder?*

The Axis II diagnoses raise a further question for us, and it is a question that we met at the very start of this chapter: What is psychopathology? As we have noted, each of the Axis II disorders can be regarded as the extreme of a continuum, so that, in essence, many people "almost" have the disorder. Should these people be diagnosed and treated? If not, we risk ignoring people who are, in fact, in need of help, even if their condition does not quite reach the level specified by our diagnostic manual. But if we do diagnose them, we risk sliding down a slippery slope in which, eventually, less and less extreme cases are brought under the umbrella of psychopathology. In the end, the term *mental disorder* might be stretched so far that it loses meaning, and is applied to virtually any form of human behavior that causes social harm or personal unhappiness.

It seems clear, then, that we need to find some balance, broadening our diagnostic categories so that we do not neglect people who, in truth, could benefit from our help, but not broadening the categories so far that they lose meaning. Where this balance point lies, however, is surely a matter open to debate.

In fact, this same worry arises for the Axis I disorders. It seems clear that someone who has one of these disorders suffers considerable disruption in her life, and, in most cases, also suffers considerable emotional distress—whether it is the deep sadness of depression, the paralyzing fears associated with the phobias, or the emotional flattening common in schizophrenia. In each case, therefore, it seems appropriate to offer a "diagnosis," and to seek treatment for the afflicted person, trying to bring him back to a normal life. But what about people who have a **subsyndromal case** of a disorder—so that they do show symptoms, but not at the level that would justify a formal diagnosis? This would include people who are sad and not sleeping well, but not quite at the level of severity or for the duration required for a diagnosis of depression. It would also include people who worry about whether they really did turn off the gas, and so check and re-check their stoves so often that it becomes an inconvenience—but, again, not often enough to justify a diagnosis of OCD.

Here, too, we might ask whether we might broaden our diagnostic categories to include these cases, or whether (instead) we should exclude them, in accord with the clear-cut boundaries set by the *DSM*. These are difficult questions, to be settled perhaps by trying to determine what life problems (if any) are associated with subsyndromal pathology, or by asking how readily we can treat these subsyndromal cases. In addition, we again need to worry about whether a broadening of our diagnostic categories will stretch the term *mental disorder* too far, potentially including milder and milder cases, so that the term loses all meaning. These are complex issues, and we will return to them in Chapter 17.

SOME FINAL THOUGHTS: PSYCHOPATHOLOGY AND PHYSICAL MEDICINE

We have now examined many mental disorders, and we wish we could present some kind of simplifying framework for this diverse set of problems. Just a century ago, psychologists would have offered a clean distinction between somatogenic and psychogenic disorders, but that distinction is in many ways misleading. Among other concerns, we have seen over and over that multiple factors contribute to virtually every disorder, with some of the factors best understood in biological terms and some best understood in terms of the person's beliefs or life experiences. Some of these factors seem to create a risk for the disorder (and so constitute the diathesis), and some seem to be the trigger that turns the risk into full-blown symptoms (and so constitute the stress).

BIOMEDICAL THERAPIES

In many cases, treatment for mental disorders relies on the standard tools of the physician's trade: the administration of some drug, or perhaps surgery or some other medical intervention. One might suppose that these procedures are focused on cases in which there is an identifiable biological dysfunction—an overreactive stress response, for example, or a shortage of some neurotransmitter. In such cases, it makes sense that the treatment would focus on repairing these biological problems. This view of things, however, is too simple, because, as we discussed in Chapter 16, mental disorders usually involve a cluster of causes, some biological, and some lodged in a person's circumstances. Thus, even if the immediate trigger for a mental illness is in a person's situation (e.g., a case of depression triggered by the death of a loved one), biological factors will still be involved, and so we might seek biomedical treatment.

Let us note right at the start, therefore, that there may not be a direct correspondence between the immediate triggers of a disorder (a specific biomedical dysfunction, or some problem in the situation) and the nature of the treatment. Some problems arising from a difficult situation are best treated medically; other problems, arising from a biological dysfunction, are best treated with psychotherapy. In choosing a form of therapy, therefore, we should focus on what works, rather than focusing exclusively on how the disorder arose in the first place.

The biomedical approach to treatment has a long history. In Chapter 16, we mentioned, for example, a prehistoric surgical procedure called trephination, in which pieces of the skull are removed in order to provide an escape path for the spirits or demons that were supposedly causing the affliction. Other early procedures involved bloodlettings or purgatives, both intended somehow to restore harmony among the bodily humors. Later developments were hardly milder. For example, Benjamin Rush (1745–1813), one of the signers of the Declaration of Independence and the acknowledged father of American psychiatry, submersed patients in hot or cold water until they were just short of drowning, or twirled them on special devices at speeds that rendered them unconscious (Figure 17.1). Such methods were said to reestablish balance between bodily and mental functions. They almost certainly had no such salutary effects, although they were probably welcomed by hospital attendants, since they undoubtedly terrified the inmates and so helped to "keep order" (Mora, 1975).

PHARMACOTHERAPIES

In the last 100 years or so, biological therapies have become much more sophisticated— and much more effective. A major step forward came with the conquest of the disabling

17.1   Early methods for treating mental disorders *(A) A crib for violent patients; (B) a centrifugal-force bed; (C) a swinging device.*

A

B

C

syndrome of general paresis, which was accomplished by attacking the syphilitic infection that caused it (see Chapter 16). But more dramatic advances have come during the last 50 years or so, with the development of a number of *psychotropic drugs*, medications that seem to control, or at least moderate, the manifestations of mental disorders. These medications have had an enormous impact on mental-health care, and have allowed patients with many different disorders to be treated successfully, often without hospitalization (Olfson & Klerman, 1993).

DRUG TREATMENT OF SCHIZOPHRENIA: ANTIPSYCHOTICS

The development of psychotropic drugs has gone hand in hand with advances in our understanding of mental illness. As we have learned more about causes, this has often pointed the way toward new drug treatments, and—conversely—new drug treatments have often allowed us to test claims about what the causes might be. For example, we saw in the last chapter that a major argument for a neurochemical abnormality in schizophrenia was the effectiveness of certain drugs called antipsychotics. The classical antipsychotics reduce the major positive symptoms of schizophrenia (such as thought disorder and hallucination; see Chapter 16), apparently by blocking dopamine receptors in key brain pathways. The most common classical antipsychotics include Thorazine, Haldol, and Stelazine. Unfortunately, though, these drugs are ineffective in patients with negative symptoms.

This shortcoming was remedied by a newer set of medications, the so-called atypical antipsychotics, such as Clozaril, Risperdal, Zyprexa, and Seroquel. These medications revolutionized the treatment of schizophrenia, because not only do they reduce the major positive symptoms (such as delusions and hallucinations), but they reduce the major negative symptoms as well (Glick, Murray, Vasudevan, Marder, & Hu, 2001). Like the classical antipsychotics, the atypical antipsychotics block the neurotransmission of dopamine, but their enhanced benefits, especially with negative symptoms, are probably due to other mechanisms. These may include alterations in serotonin neurotransmission or a more selective effect on particular subsets of dopamine neurons (Bantick, Deakin, & Grasby, 2001; S. Kapur & Remington, 2001; Tandon & Kane, 1993; Wirshing, Marder, Van Putten, & Ames, 1995).

Other medications are also being developed, including medications that modulate glutamate activity. Development of these drugs has been slow, however, partly because glutamate has such widespread effects in the brain. As a result, there is a risk that any drug influencing glutamate levels might have a far broader impact than was intended. The solution to this difficulty may lie in the fact that glutamate interacts with several different receptor sites on the neuron, and, by focusing on the receptor sites, pharmacologists may be able to design drugs that have a more finely targeted effect (see, for example, Holden, 2003). In roughly the same spirit, some investigators have proposed that we should cease seeking drugs that are designed to cure (or treat) an entire disease; instead, we should perhaps dissect a disease into its component mechanisms, and look for drugs that treat these mechanisms one by one (Hyman & Fenton, 2003). In all cases, we can hope that the future holds medications that are both more effective and more likely to benefit more individuals with the disorder.

The Social Reality of Treating Schizophrenia The development of medications for schizophrenia lent impetus in the United States to a movement called *deinstitutionalization*, which was intended to allow for better and less expensive care for patients in their own communities, at local community mental-health centers rather than at large centralized hospitals. To some extent, this movement worked. In the 1950s, mental hospitals housed about 600,000 patients, but by the 1990s the number had dropped to 100,000 (Narrow, Regier, Rae, Manderscheid, & Locke, 1993). Medications have also made it possible to discharge patients with schizophrenia more quickly than ever. Prior

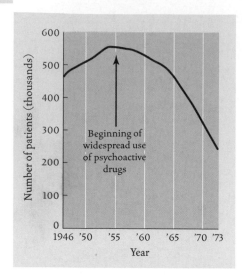

17.2   *The number of residents in state and local government mental hospitals in the United States, 1946–73*

Some adverse effects of deinstitutionalization Some of the homeless in American cities are people who have been discharged from mental hospitals and are unable to adjust to the world outside.

to the introduction of the antipsychotic medications, 2 out of 3 patients with schizophrenia spent most of their lives in a state asylum. In the 1980s, the average stay was about 2 months (J. M. Davis, 1985a; Lamb, 1984; Lamb & Bachrach, 2001; Figure 17.2).

Overall, though, the deinstitutionalization movement has been only a partial success. One concern is that, although the medications for schizophrenia do diminish symptoms, they do not cure the disease or alter its progress. Moreover, the antipsychotics—especially the classical antipsychotics—have potent side effects, which include dramatic weight gain (sometimes 20 to 30 pounds), sedation, blurred vision, cardiac irregularities, tremors and muscle spasms, restlessness, and a curiously inexpressive, masklike face. In light of these side effects, many patients stop taking their medication, leading to flare-ups of their problems and causing repeated hospitalizations—they become "revolving-door patients." Even when they do take their medication regularly, 30 to 50% of patients have recurrent outbreaks of the illness and need further hospitalization or a change in the type of medication (Andreasen & Black, 1996). As a consequence, although fewer patients with schizophrenia remain in psychiatric hospitals (J. M. Davis, 1985a; Lamb, 1984), the number of times they are readmitted for short stays has increased by 80% since the 1960s (Rosenstein, Milazzo-Sayre, & Manderscheid, 1989).

What do these patients do when they are discharged from the hospital? Many live in less-than-ideal board-and-care homes, while still others become drifters and join the swelling ranks of the homeless. According to one report, some 40% of New York City's homeless people suffer persistent mental disorders or have a history of mental illness (Golden, 1990). It is thus clear that while the antipsychotic drugs help to alleviate the symptoms of schizophrenia, they do not provide a cure. Given the current inadequacy—and, in many cases, the complete lack—of appropriate community services, this represents, at least for now, a failure to achieve the intentions of deinstitutionalization (R. E. Jones, 1983; Lamb, 1984, 1998; Westermeyer, 1987; also p. 657).

DRUG TREATMENT OF DEPRESSION: ANTIDEPRESSANTS

Shortly after the introduction of antipsychotics as a treatment for schizophrenia, other drugs were found that seemed to act specifically on depression. These *antidepressants* were of two major classes, the monoamine oxidase (MAO) inhibitors, such as Nardil, and the tricyclic antidepressants (so called because of their chemical structure), such as Tofranil. Of these, the tricyclics became the more widely used, mostly because patients taking MAO inhibitors must conform to difficult dietary restrictions (Burke & Preskhorn, 1995).

Both the MAO inhibitors and the tricyclics appear to work in part by increasing the amount of norepinephrine and serotonin available for synaptic transmission (Blier & Abbott, 2001). These two classes of drugs accomplish this mission in different ways (for details, see Figure 17.3), but both seem effective in counteracting depression, producing marked improvement in up to 65% of the patients who take them (Hollister & Csernansky, 1990). The drugs are not interchangeable, however, because some patients do far better with one than with another (Hollon, Thase, & Markowitz, 2002), presumably because different patients suffer from somewhat different neurochemical deficits.

These early drug treatments for depression were quite successful, but, even so, the use of medication for treating depression changed dramatically in 1988 with the introduction of the first "designer drug" for depression, Prozac (Kramer, 1993). Prozac was engineered in a laboratory to act minimally on norepinephrine and dopamine and maximally on serotonin, thus marking a new class of antidepressants, known as *selective serotonin reuptake inhibitors (SSRIs)*. For most patients, Prozac and the other SSRIs (such as Zoloft, Paxil, Celexa, and Lexapro) ameliorate depression as effectively and as completely as their predecessors (Mulrow et al., 2000), but they have fewer side effects and are thus safer to prescribe—so safe that most are now prescribed not only by psychiatrists but also by primary-care physicians (Olfson & Klerman, 1993). Still, while these antidepressants have been touted by some as panaceas, like all medications, they, too, have their limitations. First, the beneficial effects of the drug emerge only after the medication is taken for a month or so. Second, the SSRIs do have some side effects, including weight gain, nausea, diarrhea, and—in upward of 30% of patients—insomnia, as well as a loss of sexual desire or response (Clayton, 2001; Ferguson, 2001; Gursky & Krahn, 2000; E. Hollander & McCarley, 1992; Jacobsen, 1992; Montgomery, 1995). There has also been some concern that these drugs may be addictive, although the evidence supporting this claim is regarded by many as unpersuasive (see, for example, Haddad, 1999).

For patients who are plagued by undue side effects from SSRIs and cannot take the tricyclics or MAO inhibitors, a separate array of antidepressants is available. These *atypical antidepressants* work in various ways on serotonin, norepinephrine, and dopamine systems, and include Wellbutrin, Effexor, and Serzone. Of these, Wellbutrin is of special interest. It seems to have little effect on serotonin and probably operates on the dopamine and norepinephrine systems instead. However it works, Wellbutrin has no negative sexual side effects, and many patients report heightened sexual interest and response. It is also generally stimulating, and in addition to curbing nicotine cravings (for which it is sold as Zyban), it finds wide use as a treatment for adults with attention deficit disorder.

There have been some concerns, however, that the antidepressants are perhaps being overprescribed (see, for example, Kramer, 1993). This worry is magnified by the fact that these drugs are increasingly used to treat depression in children and adolescents, even though we know less about their side effects in children than in adults. Questions have also been raised in particular about whether the SSRIs may increase the risk of suicide in some young people, but this point is hotly debated, with some investigators claiming that, in truth, the opposite is the case, and that SSRIs, by alleviating depression, *decrease* suicide risk (see, for example, Bachtold, 2003; Couzin, 2004). Until these questions are resolved, it seems clear that clinicians must carefully weigh the benefits and risks when prescribing antidepressants for younger patients.

DRUG TREATMENT OF BIPOLAR DISORDER: ANTIMANICS

Medications are also available to treat bipolar disorder, and these are called *antimanics*, even though they also help forestall the depressive episodes in the disorder. The first medication used specifically for its antimanic action was lithium carbonate (one example is Eskalith), and patients who begin taking lithium can generally expect that their manic episodes will subside within 5 to 10 days.

Despite lithium's effectiveness, it works in only 60 to 80% of patients with bipolar disorder (Calabrese & Woyshville, 1995). Taking it is also problematic for many patients, most of whom must endure unpleasant side effects, such as weight gain, dry mouth, and tremors. Moreover, the fact that lithium is toxic at higher doses means that patients must have their blood tested frequently and makes it a risky treatment for patients who are potentially suicidal and might overdose. Nor can lithium be taken during pregnancy or when a patient has kidney disease. In addition, many patients with bipolar disorder choose not to take their medication because they do not want to give up either the pleasures or the productivity often associated with the manic state; they may decide that these elements outweigh the (sometimes enormous) disruption and distress that the disorder also produces.

Fortunately, though, other drugs are now available that achieve some of lithium's gains but without many of its drawbacks, leading to higher rates of compliance with the medical treatment. The main contenders are Tegretol, Depakote, and Topamax, which were once used strictly as anticonvulsants to treat epilepsy. Like lithium, they also have side effects (some potentially serious), but they are better tolerated by many patients. In most cases, they are just as effective as lithium and may even be superior when the patient's mood cycles are frequent and rapid (Keck & McElroy, 2002).

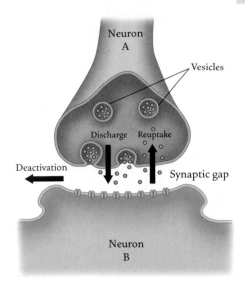

17.3 *A schematic presentation of two ways in which a drug may increase the available supply of a neurotransmitter* A neurotransmitter, norepinephrine (NE), is discharged by Neuron A into the synaptic gap and diffuses across the gap to stimulate Neuron B. The more NE accumulates at the membrane of Neuron B, the more often that neuron will fire. NE at the synapse can be diminished through reuptake, in which NE is pumped back into Neuron A, or through deactivation, whereby certain enzymes (such as MAO) break down the neurotransmitter and render it ineffective. Tricyclics (like Tofranil) and MAO inhibitors (like Nardil) increase the amount of available NE (and serotonin) at the synaptic junction, but in different ways. Tricyclics interfere with neurotransmitter reuptake; MAO inhibitors prevent MAO from breaking down the transmitters. Second-generation antidepressants like the SSRIs (such as Prozac) block reuptake but act selectively on serotonin neurons.

What accounts for the antimanic effects of lithium and the anticonvulsants? According to one hypothesis, lithium carbonate may reregulate neurotransmission by stabilizing the influence of calcium on neuronal membranes (Meltzer, 1986; Wood & Goodwin, 1987). Some evidence also suggests that, like depression, mania may involve a serotonin deficit, and that both lithium and the anticonvulsants augment neurotransmission of serotonin (Shiah & Yatham, 2000).

DRUG TREATMENT OF ANXIETY: ANXIOLYTICS

When patients suffer from disabling anxiety, they are often treated with medications that are popularly called tranquilizers and technically known as *anxiolytics*. Most anxiolytics apparently work by increasing neurotransmission at synapses containing the neurotransmitter gamma-aminobutric acid (GABA; Brailowsky & Garcia, 1999; Shader & Greenblatt, 1995). Probably the most commonly used anxiolytic is alcohol. Many people, patients or otherwise, medicate themselves for their anxiety as part of their lifestyle, inviting the risk of alcohol abuse.

Physicians treat some of the anxiety disorders (e.g., social phobia) by prescribing a *beta-blocker*, a medication intended to control autonomic arousal. For the symptom of anxiety itself, they often prescribe one of the *benzodiazepines*. Some of these medications, such as Valium or Xanax, are prescribed so often that their names have become household words. They are useful as short-term treatments (usually taking effect in 30 or 40 minutes) for generalized anxiety disorder, panic disorder, post-traumatic stress disorder, alcohol withdrawal, insomnia, muscle spasms, tension headaches, and various other stress-related disorders. They are rarely used for long-term treatment because, unlike the medications we have reviewed so far, they are highly addictive and interact dangerously with alcohol, and like alcohol, can cause profound fetal damage if a patient is pregnant. There are also concerns that the benzodiazepines can produce a "rebound" effect, so that, once a person ceases taking the medication, she may end up more anxious than she was prior to taking the drug (Chouinard, 2004). These are, of course, not small concerns, and so researchers continue to seek new anxiolytic medications. Happily, some of the newer drugs, such as BuSpar, are not addictive and are becoming popular substitutes for the older medications, especially for patients who are prone to alcohol or drug abuse or have to take the medication over a long period of time (Lydiard, Brawman-Mintzer, & Ballenger, 1996; Schweitzer, Rickels, & Uhlenhuth, 1995).

THE EFFICACY OF DRUG TREATMENT

Overall, drug therapies do seem to be extremely effective, providing considerable symptom relief for people with a wide range of mental disorders. Indeed, these drugs have lifted many people out of misery and distress and returned them to a reasonably normal life. The drugs have allowed many patients to remain in a family or community setting when they would otherwise have been relegated to long-term hospital stays. As a result, the modern mental hospital can function more as a therapeutic center than as a warehouse. It can provide important social and psychological services, including vocational counseling and psychotherapy, all of which would have been unthinkable in former times. These are, by any measure, enormous gains.

At the same time, though, drug therapy for mental disorders is not an unqualified success. For some disorders (e.g., schizophrenia) the available drugs do not help many patients, and provide only partial relief for others. Moreover, these drugs do not cure the disorder; instead, they do an excellent job of containing it, and, in many cases, if the person stops taking his pills, he quickly relapses into his full set of symptoms.

We have also highlighted the fact that many of these drugs have unpleasant (or even dangerous) side effects. These side effects are bad enough on their own, but, in addition, they often lead people to cease taking their medication, in which case (obviously)

Is the medication effective? Many steps are needed to find out if a medication has the desired effect, and, if it does, whether it is more effective than a mere placebo or other medications already in use.

the drugs can bring no benefit. Thus, a college student might refuse to take her antidepressant because she is concerned about the associated weight gain, even though, without the drug, her bulimia may cause long-term health problems. Likewise, someone might refuse to take medication because of a fear that it will disrupt sexual functioning, even though, without it, his depression is causing immense disruption in his life.

Finally, it is often tricky to get the *doses* correct for many of these drugs, because individuals differ in both their drug reactions and also in how rapidly they metabolize the medication. There are also some group differences, so that many African Americans, for example, metabolize antidepressant medications more slowly than whites (U.S. Department of Health and Human Services, 2001). This means that a clinician prescribing one of these medications often needs to allow for some amount of trial and error in order to find the right drug at the right dose.

These are not small limitations, motivating us to seek other forms of treatment, or newer drugs. Even with this point acknowledged, however, there is no question that modern drug therapies are a major step forward—and have been an enormous boon to many who suffer from a variety of forms of mental illness.

PSYCHOSURGERY

Until the advent of the major psychotropic drugs, physicians relied on several other biological therapies. Some of these consisted of *psychosurgery*, or brain surgery, to alter thinking or behavior. In a prefrontal lobotomy, for example, the neurological connections between the thalamus and the frontal lobes are severed, in whole or in part. This operation was originally meant to liberate a patient's thoughts from the pathological influence of her emotions, on the ill-informed assumption that thought and emotion were localized in the frontal lobes and the thalamus, respectively. In the 1940s and 1950s, many patients were subjected to a lobotomy, and early reports on this procedure were quite enthusiastic. It soon became clear, however, that the surgery had powerful side effects, including a disruption of many cognitive functions, and the procedure is now rarely used (Maher, 1966; Robbin, 1958; Tierney, 2000; Valenstein, 1986).

Recently, psychosurgery has reemerged as a useful technique, but has been refined considerably, both in the procedures used and in the patients judged suitable for them (Hurley, Black, Stip, & Taber, 2000; Rappaport, 1992). In some cases, the surgery is aimed at removing a tumor that had been disrupting brain function, and thus has produced one of the mental disorders. In other cases, the surgery serves to relieve fluid pressures in the brain (e.g., by draining a buildup of cerebrospinal fluid), and this, too, can bring relief from some mental disorders. In still other cases, neurosurgeons do manipulate the nervous system directly, but they do so by creating very precise lesions in specific brain areas instead of disconnecting or destroying whole lobes or regions. In these cases, the surgery is reserved for patients who are severely disabled and show no improvement after all other treatment alternatives have been exhausted. This surgery as last resort has been used in patients with intractable depression and epilepsy, severe obsessive-compulsive disorder, and chronic pain, and it is often beneficial. There are clearly inherent risks, but the risks may be acceptable compared with the severe level of the patients' ongoing disability (Baer et al., 1995; Bridges, 1987; Davies & Weeks, 1993; Hay et al., 1993; Jenike, 2001; Mahli & Bartlett, 2000).

ELECTROCONVULSIVE THERAPY

Another form of biological therapy is *electroconvulsive therapy (ECT)*, sometimes colloquially called shock treatment. For about half a second, a current of moderate intensity

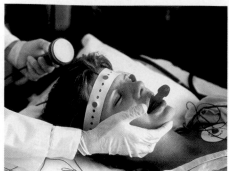

17.4 *Patient about to undergo ECT*

is passed between two electrodes attached to the patient's head. The result is a 30- to 60-second convulsive seizure similar to that seen in epilepsy (Figure 17.4), with the usual course of ECT consisting of six to ten treatments over a period of 1 or 2 weeks.

When ECT first came into use, patients were conscious and thrashed about during their convulsions, often suffering serious bruises or bone fractures. In contrast, modern ECT looks relatively tame. Patients are given short-acting anesthetics to render them temporarily unconscious and muscle relaxants to reduce the manifestations of the seizure to a few slight twitches (Andreasen & Black, 1996).

ECT was originally meant as a treatment for schizophrenia but was soon established as particularly effective for depression. Here, its efficacy is considerable. It works for as many as 70 to 80% of patients who have not responded to any antidepressant medication (Andreasen & Black, 1996; Janicak et al., 1985) or who cannot take such medications because of overdose potential or other medical problems. In addition, ECT acts more quickly than antidepressant medications (R. D. Weiner, 1984b, 1985). ECT also seems quite effective in treating acute mania as well as various psychotic states associated with drug intoxication (Gitlin, 2001; Sackeim, Devanand, & Nobler, 1995).

Despite these advantages, the use of ECT remains controversial, partly because in many cases it can produce memory impairment (Rami-Gonzalez et al., 2001; Squire, 1977). These cognitive side effects are diminished if the ECT is delivered to just one side of the brain, but, unfortunately, this **unilateral ECT** is less effective than **bilateral ECT** (which, again, does produce the cognitive side effects; Sackeim et al., 1993). Under the circumstances, ECT is generally reserved for use only after medication has failed or when there seems to be a serious chance of suicide. In the latter case, the fast-acting quality of ECT may be an overriding advantage (Andreasen & Black, 1996).

PSYCHOTHERAPIES

Early forms of therapy? **This nineteenth-century painting shows David playing the harp before Saul.**

Biomedical therapies are unmistakably effective—providing symptom relief for many patients with many different disorders. But these treatments are also limited, because, as we have repeatedly noted, they often have strong side effects, and usually do not effect a long-term cure. For these (and other) reasons, then, we are certainly motivated to seek alternative forms of treatment, and the obvious alternative is *psychotherapy*, an effort to change a patient's thinking and behavior directly, usually by means of some form of discussion, instruction, or training. In some cases, the therapy is itself intended to deal with the distress. In many other cases, the therapy is offered in conjunction with drug treatment, with the idea that the drug provides immediate relief for the person's problems, and this relief opens up the capacity for the psychotherapy, which is aimed at a longer-term solution to the person's difficulties.

In the minds of many people, psychotherapy involves a patient lying on a couch, talking about his distant childhood, and a therapist quietly drawing conclusions about unconscious fears or desires. This image, however, fails to do justice to the fact that therapy comes in many forms. (Indeed, the form of therapy implied in this commonsense image is relatively rare.) The various forms, or *modes*, of therapy differ markedly in how they conceive of psychopathology, and how the therapy is practiced. Some approaches are based on psychoanalysis (Chapter 15), and these approaches are close to the popular image, emphasizing unconscious conflicts and encouraging introspection and insight. Other modes grow out of the humanistic tradition (Chapter 15), and focus on questions of growth and realizing one's potential. Still others rely on behavioral findings from animal and human experimentation (Chapter 6); these seek to identify maladaptive responses and then promote the learning of new responses. Others take a cognitive approach, focusing on the disabling role of faulty thinking, while teaching more rational thought.

In what follows, we will discuss some of the more common modes of individual psychotherapy (therapy conducted with a single patient) that have grown out of these approaches. Later in this chapter we discuss extensions of psychotherapy that treat families and other groups.

CLASSICAL PSYCHOANALYSIS

Classical psychoanalysis is the method Sigmund Freud developed at the beginning of the twentieth century, and according to many writers, it is the ancestor of virtually all modern modes of psychotherapy. Freud's basic assumption was that a patient's ills (in Freud's terms, his neuroses) stemmed from unconscious conflicts that date back to early childhood (see Chapter 15). By adulthood, the patient has developed a range of defenses designed to deal with these conflicts, but these defenses also shield him from seeing clearly both the outer world and his own inner world. This leads to a range of problems that become manifest as psychological symptoms.

Freud believed that for a patient to overcome her neurosis, she must gain insight into her own buried thoughts and wishes. Importantly, though, this insight cannot be just an intellectual matter. Freud argued that the person must "work through" the conflict, in order to have control over her passions, and not just intellectualize them. If this working through is successful, the person will come to integrate her thoughts and memories in a coherent way, and so will at last be able to step away from the maladaptive patterns that grew out of the unresolved conflicts.

TRANSFERENCE

What does it mean to "work through" a conflict? For Freud, the process involved many elements, but one crucial aspect of the process is *transference*, the patient's tendency to respond to the analyst in ways that re-create her responses to the major figures in her own life. Thus, the patient ends up loving or hating the analyst just as she loved or hated her mother, father, and siblings and, more recently, her lovers and friends. All of these feelings are "transferred" to the analyst, as a kind of repetition of the unresolved problems of the patient's childhood.

Freud argued that the transference-charged relationship with the analyst could be a powerful therapeutic tool. It lets the analyst hold up a mirror to the patient to show her

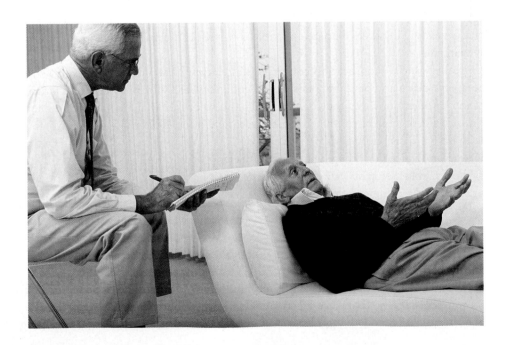

Psychoanalysis   In classic psychoanalysis, the patient lies down, to be fully relaxed, and the analyst stays out of the patient's line of vision, to avoid distracting or influencing the patient.

how she really feels and acts toward the important people in her life. For example, take a person who expresses violent anger at his psychoanalyst and then is immediately seized by unspeakable terror. How would his analyst interpret this? Perhaps the patient has equated the analyst with his own tyrannical father, and having acted with flagrant disrespect, is now expecting some horrible retribution. Needless to say, the analyst will not act like Daddy, but instead might say something mildly reassuring, such as "That was hard to get out, wasn't it?" The analyst might then point out how the patient's traumatic memories of Daddy (and, more generally, the pattern of the patient's past relationships) is being imposed on—and distorting—his current relationships.

Through many such experiences, the patient's anxieties gradually abate. The determinedly neutral analyst allows herself temporarily to stand in for the significant characters in the patient's early family drama but will not let herself be drawn into the play. She lets the patient say the same old lines and go through the same old motions, but she will not respond to them as the cast of characters from childhood did. Her job is to let the patient see what he is really doing, and to help the patient see that old patterns need not be repeated. The effect of all this emotional reeducation is to create a new life script with better lines and a more acceptable ending.

PSYCHODYNAMIC THERAPY

Many present-day psychotherapists still use techniques that bear Freud's imprint, but they have modified the treatment in various ways. Most have stepped away from the intensity of Freud's own procedures (Freud insisted on at least three sessions per week), and have also abandoned the familiar icon of Freud's practice—the analyst's couch (which, in Freud's office, allowed the patient to relax while Freud sat in a position out of the patient's sight). These more modern practitioners—known variously as object-relations, ego-analytic, or psychodynamic therapists—subscribe to neo-Freudian views or to related approaches, such as ego psychology. They endorse many of Freud's claims, but, unlike Freud, emphasize current interpersonal and cultural factors rather than the psychological traumas of early childhood. If early development is discussed in these modern therapies, it is not to discover decades-past episodes but, instead, to identify how the patterns of interaction in one's childhood influence current choices (Eagle & Wolitsky, 1992; Liff, 1992). In these therapies, conscious thoughts receive as much scrutiny as unconscious conflicts, and therapist and patient work together to help the patient develop a coherent and complete sense of self, and to find ways of relating to others that are undistorted by past conflicts or maladaptive defense mechanisms.

Another crucial modification concerns the relation between what goes on in the therapist's office and what happens in the patient's "real" life. For Freud, the crucial theater of operations was the analysis itself, and to ensure that the patient's unconscious conflicts could be contained there, the patient's outside life had to remain stable. He therefore insisted that his patients make no major life decisions, such as getting married or divorced or changing careers, while they were in analysis. In contrast, later psychodynamic therapists came to regard the sessions as a microcosm of the patient's entire life and recommend that the patient actively attempt to apply the lessons learned in therapy to her life outside therapy (Alexander & French, 1946).

INTERPERSONAL THERAPY

In Chapter 15, we discussed some of the neo-Freudian traditions (such as *object relations* and *attachment theory*) that place their main emphasis on an individual's social relationships. These more modern approaches have led to several forms of therapy, including *interpersonal therapy (IPT)*. This approach builds on the claim that mental disorders are often created by a social isolation that cuts a person off from the emotional sustenance provided by healthy relationships (Klerman & Weissman, 1993; Weissman & Markowitz, 1994).

IPT is often used as a treatment for depression, and so a course of IPT might begin with an assessment of what factors changed in the person's life at the time depression arose. For example, one class of factors involves interpersonal role transitions, such as graduation from college, beginning a new love affair, or getting married. For someone distressed over these transitions, the therapist will help him learn to act the new part and fill the expectations of the other people involved in the newly entered social setting. (Thus, for example, a single man must learn what it means to be a husband.) The therapist will also help the patient understand the advantages and disadvantages of both the old and the new roles. In these ways, the therapy helps the patient gain an understanding of how he interacts with others, and then helps him learn new and more beneficial ways of interacting and communicating.

HUMANISTIC-EXPERIENTIAL THERAPIES

Freud played a pivotal role in launching the endeavor that we now call psychotherapy; indeed, the idea of a "talking cure" (the notion that someone could deal with her mental distress through conversation or instruction) was essentially unknown before Freud's work. Nonetheless, most modern psychotherapists employ methods very different from Freud's, and base their therapies on conceptions that explicitly reject many of Freud's ideas.

As we discussed in Chapter 15, psychologists in the humanistic tradition regarded psychoanalysis as being too mechanistic in focus and too concerned with basic urges (like sex and aggression), and, correspondingly, not concerned enough with the search for higher truths and meanings. This orientation led them to propose several different types of therapy: *Client-centered therapy* seeks to help a person accept himself as he is, and to be himself with no pretense or self-imposed limits. In therapy, the therapist listens to the patient attentively and acceptingly. The therapist is not there to question or to direct, but to create an atmosphere in which the patient feels valued and understood (Rogers, 1951, 1959). In *existential therapy*, in contrast, a main focus is on the alienation and depersonalization felt

Alienation in the modern world   **Government Bureau, *1956, by George Tooker***

by many people in modern society. The therapist emphasizes the importance of being aware of one's own existence, and will challenge the patient with questions about the meaning of her life. In *gestalt therapy*, the emphasis is on the unity of mind and body, and a main goal is to increase self-awareness and self-acceptance (Perls, 1967, 1969).

In modern versions of these therapies—often referred to collectively as the ***experiential therapies***—these various approaches are integrated, seeking to create a genuinely empathic and accepting atmosphere in therapy, but also challenging the patient in a more active fashion with the aim of deepening his experience (Elliott, Greenberg & Lietaer, 2004; Folette & Greenberg, 2005). The patient and, indeed, all humans are viewed as oriented toward growth and full development of their potential.

Experiential therapies are also said to be *person centered*. This focus involves genuine concern and respect for the person, with an emphasis on all her qualities, and not just those symptoms that led to a particular diagnosis. The person's subjective experience is also showcased, and the therapist seeks to be as empathic as possible, in order to understand that experience. Moreover, experiential therapists reject Freud's notion of transference; in their view, the relationship between patient and therapist is a genuine human connection, one that provides the patient with an opportunity for a new, emotionally validating experience (Elliot et al., 2004).

BEHAVIOR THERAPY

Like the experiential therapies, behavior therapies emerged in part as a reaction to the Freudian tradition of psychoanalysis. But, while the humanists regarded psychoanalysis as too mechanical, the behavior theorists regarded it as too loose and unscientific. Moreover, in their view, the various conditions Freud called neuroses are simply the result of learning—albeit learning that led the person to undesired or undesirable behaviors. The remedy, therefore, involves new learning, in order to replace the old habits, with the therapeutic procedures drawing on the principles of conditioning discovered in the laboratories of Pavlov, Thorndike, and Skinner (see Chapter 6). Behavior therapists emphasize overt, observable behavior rather than unconscious thoughts and wishes, which they regard as hard to define and impossible to observe. They focus, therefore, on what a person does that causes his distress, but these behaviors are not regarded as "symptoms" through which one can identify and then cure the underlying illness. Instead, the maladaptive behaviors themselves are the problem, and it is they that must be removed.

EXPOSURE TECHNIQUES

As an example of how behavior therapy proceeds, consider the treatment for specific phobias (Emmelkamp, 2004; Wolpe & Plaud, 1997). According to behavior therapists, the irrational fears that characterize these phobias are simply classically conditioned responses, evoked by stimuli that, in the past, have been associated with some truly fearful stimulus (see Chapters 6 and 16). The way to treat these phobias, therefore, is to break the connection between the phobic stimuli and the associated fears, using a technique akin to the *extinction* procedures that, in the laboratory, are effective in diminishing other conditioned responses.

In therapy, this logic leads to *exposure techniques*, including the technique known as *systematic desensitization*, which was developed by the psychiatrist Joseph Wolpe (1958, 1996). Here, the therapist seeks not only to break the connection between the phobic stimulus and the fear response; she simultaneously seeks to create a new connection between this stimulus and a different response, one that is incompatible with fear and will therefore displace it. The competing response is usually deep muscular relaxation, and the patient is taught a relaxation technique, typically through meditation-like exercises, before the formal therapy begins. Then, once the patient can relax deeply on cue, the goal is to condition this relaxation response to the stimuli that have been evoking fear (Figure 17.5).

In Wolpe's technique, the fear-evoking stimulus is usually not physically present in the clinic room during the therapy sessions. Instead, the patient is asked to imagine the fearful stimulus as vividly as possible—to imagine standing next to a snake, or standing on the roof of a very tall building. It turns out that these imagined situations have enough reality to allow most patients to evoke a reasonable amount of anxiety (Wolpe & Lazarus, 1966). However, it is important that the therapist not ask the patient to imagine the scary situations at the very start of the therapy. Instead, the therapist works his way toward these situations very gradually, one small step at a time.

To make this possible, the patient is asked, at the very start of therapy, to construct an *anxiety hierarchy*, in which feared situations are arranged from least to most anxiety provoking, and this hierarchy is then used to set the sequence for therapy. The patient

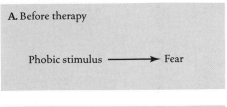

A. Before therapy

Phobic stimulus ⟶ Fear

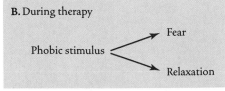

B. During therapy

Phobic stimulus ⟶ Fear
Phobic stimulus ⟶ Relaxation

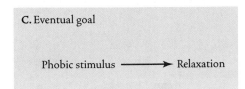

C. Eventual goal

Phobic stimulus ⟶ Relaxation

17.5 Systematic desensitization *(A) The state of affairs in phobia: Various phobic stimuli arouse fear. (B) These stimuli are conditioned to relaxation. As this connection becomes stronger, the connection between the stimuli and the fear is weakened. (C) The outcome when counterconditioning is complete: Relaxation has completely displaced fear.*

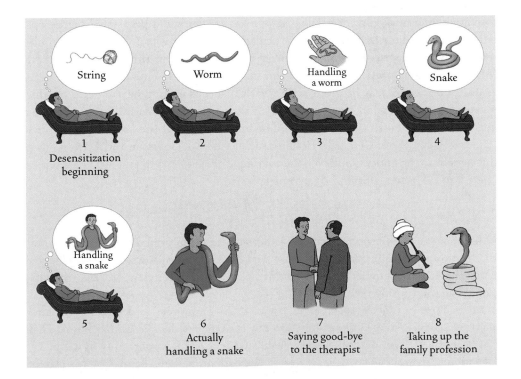

String | Worm | Handling a worm | Snake

1 Desensitization beginning | 2 | 3 | 4

Handling a snake

5 | 6 Actually handling a snake | 7 Saying good-bye to the therapist | 8 Taking up the family profession

Desensitization

In vivo desensitization

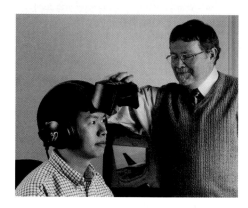

High-tech therapy *A common way to combat anxiety is to expose patients gradually to the anxiety-provoking stimulus. Virtual-reality displays are sometimes used to make the exposures more and more realistic as the therapy progresses, as, for example, in this case, in which a virtual-reality display helps someone overcome a fear of flying.*

starts out by imagining the first scene in the hierarchy (e.g., being on the first floor of a tall building) while in a state of deep relaxation. She will stay with this scene—imagining and relaxing—until she no longer feels any qualms. After this, the next scene is imagined (perhaps looking out a fourth-floor window in the building), and this scene, too, is thoroughly counterconditioned. The process continues, climbing up the anxiety hierarchy until the patient finally can imagine the most frightening scene of all (leaning over the railing of the building's observation tower, more than 100 floors above the ground) and still be able to relax.

Sometimes this imagined exposure is sufficient to treat the phobia, but often patients need to extend the graduated exposure to instances in the real world—for example, actually visiting a tall building, rather than merely thinking about one. This process is called *in vivo desensitization*, whether with the therapist present or by using guided homework assignments (Craske, 1999; Goldfried & Davison, 1994). In addition, real-time computer graphics now provide yet another option: exposing the patient to a virtual-reality version of the frightening stimulus, which seems to be another way to extend and strengthen the desensitization procedure (see, for example, Emmelkamp et al., 2002).

AVERSION THERAPY

Another behavior-therapy technique, *aversion therapy*, uses a different strategy. It attempts to eliminate problematic behavior by attaching negative feelings to it. For example, an individual who wants to quit drinking would, during therapy, be made nauseous with a special medication, such as Antabuse. He is then asked to smell, taste, and swallow his favorite alcoholic beverages, all the while desperately wanting to vomit. After a few such exposures, the person will come to associate the nausea with the alcoholic beverage and should, as a result, be far less likely to reach for or accept a drink (for more on learned taste aversions, see Chapter 6). Several studies have reported the effectiveness of aversive treatment in producing abstinence for at least 1 year in about two thirds of alcoholic patients studied (Elkins, 1991; Wiens & Menustik, 1983; Wilson, 1991, although see also Fuller & Hiller-Sturmhofel, 1999).

This technique has been applied to behaviors that range from overeating and cigarette smoking to certain sexual deviations, such as exhibitionism. But perhaps the most common—and most controversial—use of aversion therapy is with the developmentally disabled and mentally retarded, particularly individuals who are sexually disinhibited or frankly aggressive, or who bite themselves or bang their head repeatedly (Matson & Sevin, 1994). For example, an individual who habitually bangs her head against a brick wall may be given brief electrical shocks every time she performs this self-destructive behavior. In obvious ways, this treatment seems inhumane, but this must be weighed against the likelihood of brain damage if the behavior continues (Duker & Seys, 1996; Gerhardt, Holmes, Alessandri, & Goodman, 1991). Even given this benefit to the patient, however, the technique presents moral and legal quandaries (Herr, 1990; Matson & Sevin, 1994; Mulick, 1990).

OPERANT TECHNIQUES

A different set of behavioral therapies is derived from the principles of instrumental conditioning and emphasizes the relation between acts and consequences (see Chapter 6). Its theme is the same as that which underlies the entire operant approach—the control of behavior through reinforcement.

An example of this approach is the use of token economies in hospital psychiatric wards. In these settings, tokens function much as money does in our economy: They can be exchanged for desirable items, such as snacks or the opportunity to watch TV. Like money, the tokens must be earned by the patient, perhaps by making his bed, or being neatly dressed, or performing various ward chores. In this fashion, the patient can be systematically rewarded for producing desirable behaviors and will not be rewarded for producing undesirable ones.

As in the learning laboratory, the reinforcement contingencies can then be gradually adjusted, using the process known as shaping. Early on, the patient might be reinforced merely for getting out of bed; later on, tokens might be delivered only for getting out of bed and walking to the dining hall. In this fashion, the patient can be led, step-by-step, to a fuller, more acceptable level of functioning. The overall effects of this technique are that the patients become less apathetic and the general ward atmosphere is much improved (Ayllon & Azrin, 1968; for a different use of token economies, see Higgins, Williams, & McLaughlin, 2001).

Other reinforcement procedures can be useful in individual behavior therapy as part of *contingency management*. In contingency management, the person learns that certain behaviors will be followed by strict consequences (Craighead, Craighead, Kazdin, & Mahoney, 1994). For example, a child who is oppositional and defiant can be presented with a menu of "good behaviors" and "bad behaviors," with an associated reward and penalty for each. Being a "good listener" can earn the child the chance to watch a video, cleaning up her room every day can get her a dessert after dinner, and so forth, whereas talking back to Mom or making a mess may result in an early bedtime or a time-out in her room. The idea is ultimately not to bribe or coerce the child but to show her that her actions can change the way in which people react to her. Ideally, her changed behavior will result in a more positive social environment, one that can supplant the "goodies" that initially established the change.

MODELING

One last (and powerful) tool for the behavior therapist is *modeling*, in which someone learns new skills, or changes his behavior, by imitating another person. In some cases, the person who serves as the model is the therapist, but this need not be the case: Therapy with children, for example, sometimes draws on young "assistants" (children at roughly the same age as the child in therapy) who work with the therapist and model the desired behaviors or skills.

Modeling is not limited to overt behaviors; a therapist can also model a thought process or a decision-making strategy. In some forms of therapy, the therapist "thinks out loud" about mundane decisions or situations, in this way providing a model for how the patient should think when in similar settings (Kendall, 1990; Kendall & Braswell, 1985). Likewise, modeling can be used for emotional responses, so that, for example, the therapist can model fearlessness in the presence of some phobic stimulus, and in this fashion diminish the phobia (Bandura, 1969, 2001).

The use of modeling can also be supported by *vicarious reinforcement*, a procedure in which the model experiences some good outcome after exhibiting the desired behavior or emotional reaction. Like other forms of reinforcement (Chapter 6), vicarious reinforcement seems to increase the likelihood that the person in therapy will later produce the same behavior or reaction.

Modeling **In some cases, behavior therapists use young "assistants" who model the desired behaviors or skills.**

COGNITIVE THERAPY

In its early versions, behavior therapy focused on overt behaviors, regarding someone's inner thoughts and feelings as unimportant, and, in any case, not something that could be studied or influenced directly. Roughly 30 years ago, however, behavior therapists started to soften this view, realizing both that thoughts and perceptions do matter and that some of the techniques they had already developed could be applied to these mental events in much the same way they are applied to behaviors. This is obvious in the case of modeling, for example, but is no less true for operant techniques, which can be used to encourage more positive self-evaluations and various adaptive strategies.

In addition, *cognitive therapists* (sometimes called *cognitive-behavior therapists*) rely on other techniques for changing someone's beliefs or habits of interpreting the world. These techniques include outright efforts at persuasion, and also, in some cases, an effort to confront a patient with her maladaptive beliefs. In other cases, patients are also taught strategies for keeping certain thoughts readily available, to be applied instead of more destructive or distressing interpretations of life's events. In short, there is no single list of techniques that are used in cognitive therapy, but, in all cases, the effort is toward changing both a person's behaviors *and* how she thinks about the world.

The desirability of cognitive therapy seems obvious in some cases—especially cases in which a patient's difficulties do not involve clear-cut responses or specific behavioral problems. Suppose a sufferer of obsessive-compulsive disorder is crippled by anxiety because of a constant obsession that he has poisoned his children. He finds temporary peace of mind only by counting his children over and over again, reassuring himself that each one is indeed well. The critical features of this case seem to be internal thoughts and feelings rather than public actions or visible reactions.

Likewise, we argued in Chapter 16 that major depression seems to involve a set of cognitive problems linked to how a person perceives herself and her world: She believes that she is worthless, and her future is bleak. If bad things occur in her life, they are her fault, and indications of widespread patterns of upcoming difficulties. There is room for debate over whether these beliefs are what produced the depression in the first place, but there is no question that these beliefs foster and sustain the depression—and so, to help the patient, it is important to work toward changing the beliefs.

What does therapy for these problems involve? One type of cognitive therapy includes specific training that prepares people to cope with the stresses they will experience in their day-to-day life. This *stress-inoculation therapy* includes specific forms of "self-talk" that the person will engage in during stressful times: "This will be over soon," and "I know I can handle this" (Meichenbaum, 1985, 1993, 1996; see also Foa et al., 1999).

A different form of cognitive therapy is based on Aaron Beck's view of depression (Beck, 1967; see also Chapter 16), although this therapeutic procedure is now applied to disorders as diverse as anxiety, obesity, and chronic pain (Beck, 1976, 1985; Cooper & Fairburn, 2001; Hollon & Beck, 2004; Hollon, Stewart, & Strunk, 2006). In this procedure, patients are taught to identify their own automatic reactions, such as a tendency to say to themselves "It's all my fault," or "If no one loves me, I'm worthless." Once these reactions—and the beliefs behind them—have been identified, the therapist helps the patient see that the reactions are usually illogical and certainly self-destructive.

For example, consider a patient who felt a wave of anxiety when he saw an old friend across the street; what was it that triggered this anxiety? With close attention to his own thinking, the patient may identify the thought that provoked this emotion:

> The anxiety seemed incomprehensible until [the patient] "played back" his thoughts: "If I greet Bob, he may not remember me. He may snub me, it has been so long, he may not know who I am." (Ellis, 1962, quoted in Beck, 1985, p. 1436)

With the source of the anxiety identified ("He may snub me"), the next task for therapist and patient is to reveal the thought's irrationality. After all, Bob may remember the patient, and so the anxiety is completely groundless. And even if Bob does not remember the patient, maybe it is because Bob's memory is faulty or he is preoccupied at the moment with his own problems. Here, the cognitive therapist takes the role of a sympathetic Socrates who asks one question after another until the truth is attained. In other words, the therapist is not an instructor or a persuader; instead, she works to help the patient himself find better ways of thinking about life's events.

And what if the patient's original thought was right—and, in fact, Bob never did like him in the first place? Once again, the therapist's questions will be aimed at helping the patient put this information into perspective: Would Bob's dislike be the end of the world? Is it really necessary to be liked by everybody? With questions like these, the irrationality of the patient's reaction is gradually exposed, helping the patient to substitute more rational thoughts, and thus to feel and function better.

SOME COMMON THEMES

We have now described the major modes of psychotherapy, and, in our description, we have emphasized how each of these forms of therapy is distinct from the others—in its conceptual grounding and in its actual practices. Some modes of therapy focus on overt behaviors; some focus on thoughts and patterns of interpretation that the patient can see within himself; others focus on beliefs or memories that are entirely unconscious. In some modes of therapy, the therapist actively gives instructions or directions; in others, the therapist merely asks questions; in still others, the therapist is a quiet listener.

Even with this diversity, though, the various forms of therapy have certain elements in common. These shared elements will be crucial for us when we ask how—or whether—psychotherapy works in helping people deal with their problems and feel better about their lives.

Relationship Effects Several benefits of therapy are nonspecific—that is, not due to any specific therapeutic techniques; instead, these benefits grow out of the broad relationship that the patient establishes with the therapist. One of these benefits lies simply in the fact that the patient gains an ally against her problems; this *therapeutic alliance* helps most patients believe that they really can conquer their difficulties and achieve better lives (Barber, Connolly, Crits-Christoph, Gladis, & Siqueland, 2000; Horvath & Luborsky, 1993). In fact, some researchers believe that the therapeutic alliance is the most important single ingredient in the effectiveness of psychotherapy and is indispensable even when medication is the primary treatment (Krupnick et al., 1996). A related benefit is that being in therapy fuels the patient's hope that he will finally get better, and this hope can itself promote successes in the outside world. Finally, therapy provides the patient with an intimate, confiding relationship with another person, a kind of secular confessional. This relationship alone may be a boon to some people who have no close bonds to anyone and for whom psychotherapy may amount to "the purchase of friendship" (Schofield, 1964).

Interpersonal Learning The interactions between patient and therapist also provide an important opportunity for learning: These interactions show the patient how she generally reacts to others, and provide a testing ground for trying new and better ways of reacting. These concerns are, of course, center stage in interpersonal therapy, but they are visible in all the other therapies as well.

Emotional Defusing People usually enter psychotherapy with many anxieties: "What's wrong with me?" "Am I normal?" They are often worried that their problems are weird or shameful and either too trivial to warrant therapy or so severe that no treatment will work. They may hope for, and dread, the opportunity to reveal things they have kept secret, often for years. All psychotherapists, regardless of their approach, spend a great deal of time in therapy hearing these concerns and secrets, and responding to them in an accepting and nonjudgmental manner. With some reassurance and a little education, patients let go of their anxieties as they learn that their problems are understandable, rather common, not shameful, and quite treatable.

The advantages of talk *Even with their differences, the various modes of therapy overlap in some important ways. One common feature is the presence of serious, sympathetic, earnest talk helping someone work through a problem. Of course, this sort of helpful talk can also happen outside therapy, but that does not remove the fact that this talk, in therapy, is likely to be part of the reason therapy is helpful.*

Self-Knowledge Most psychotherapists try to help their patients achieve greater self-knowledge, although the various therapeutic schools differ in what kind of self-knowledge they try to bring about. For psychoanalysts, the crucial emotional insights the patient must acquire refer to the patient's past; for behavior therapists, the relevant self-understanding is the patient's correct identification of the eliciting stimuli or consequences that maintain problematic behavior; for interpersonal therapists, the most important insights concern how one has mismanaged—but can now manage—social relationships. In each case, patients can use this self-knowledge to guide their future actions and interactions.

Overlapping Techniques In addition to these elements, which all psychotherapies have in common, the various therapies also resemble each other for another reason: In recent years, therapists from each tradition have begun to borrow ideas and techniques from other traditions, so that there is increasing overlap among the approaches, and, conversely, the distinctions among them have become less and less clear-cut. Thus, some psychoanalytically oriented practitioners have come to use techniques that were formerly the province of behavior therapists, such as modeling and homework assignments (Wachtel, 1977, 1982). From the opposite vantage point, many behavior therapists have come to realize that the client-therapist relationship is a crucial part of treatment, and that something like Freud's transference comes into play even in conditioning therapies such as desensitization (Lazarus, 1971, 1981).

In addition to blending the various forms of psychotherapy, many therapists unite therapy with some form of medication. Indeed, one survey indicates that more than half the patients being treated for mental disorders receive both drugs and psychotherapy (Pincus et al., 1999). Thus, for example, patients suffering from depression are often treated with the combination of an antidepressant and cognitive therapy, with the plausible aim that the drugs will deal immediately with the distress, but that the therapy may provide longer-lasting effects (Hollon & Fawcett, 1995). On similar logic, patients suffering from anxiety disorders usually receive an anxiolytic medication plus therapy.

In light of all this integration across techniques, many psychotherapists advocate what is sometimes called *technical eclecticism*, or *multimodal therapy*—a deliberate weaving together of the various traditions (Beitman, Goldfried, & Norcross, 1989; Castonguay, Reid, & Halperin, in press; Lazarus, 1981; Norcross & Freedheim, 1992). This eclecticism obviously allows the therapist considerable flexibility—and, in particular, it allows the therapist to pursue lines of discussion or specific interventions that seem to be working, and to back off from interventions that seem ineffective. In addition, multimodal therapy makes sense theoretically: In Chapter 16, we argued that mental disorders rarely have a single cause; instead, they emerge from a complex set of factors creating the diathesis, factors creating the more immediate stressors, and also factors that might (if present) serve to protect the patient from distress. It seems sensible, therefore, that the treatment for a disorder might need to work on several of these fronts, and that is, of course, precisely what multimodal therapy is designed to do. On all of these grounds, then, these integrative approaches to therapy seem quite promising. To put the matter differently, we have, in our exposition so far, tried to highlight the differences among modes of therapy in order to distinguish the various traditions. The reality, however, is that these streams often flow together to produce a more flexible and (one hopes) more effective form of combined treatment.

EXTENSIONS OF PSYCHOTHERAPY

We are almost done with our overview of the various forms of psychotherapy. Before moving on, though, we should mention another relatively recent development in therapy—a remarkable broadening, over the last three or four decades, in who receives therapy, who delivers the therapy, and how the therapy proceeds.

In Freud's time, psychotherapy was considered an arcane art, practiced by a few initiates (mostly physicians) and available only to a select group of well-educated adult patients. Since then, psychotherapy has been extended to cover increasingly wider terrain. The individuals now receiving therapy include children, the developmentally disabled, sociopaths, and substance abusers. This broadening of the definition of who can be a patient has been accelerated by the advent of psychotherapy and counseling sessions over the Internet—a development that poses unprecedented challenges to the practice and evaluation of therapy, and tests the limits of therapist-patient communication and confidentiality (see Huang & Alessi, 1996).

THERAPY WITH CHILDREN

As we discussed in Chapter 16, many disorders first emerge in childhood—the list includes autism, attention-deficit disorder, and more. Other disorders, such as anxiety or mood disorders, can emerge at almost any age, including childhood and adolescence. For these reasons, there is an obvious need for therapeutic interventions aimed at children, and, in fact, many children are seen by psychotherapists. The most common concern is one or another *externalizing disorder*—usually a disruptive behavioral problem, such as aggression or antisocial behavior (Kazdin, 2003).

Treatment with children takes many of the same forms as treatment with adults: Medication is often used, especially for the mood disorders (Birmaher & Brent, 1998). Behavior therapy is also common, especially modeling, for cases that include phobias, autism, and various learning disorders (Ollendick & King, 1994). Cognitive therapy is also used, especially for various mood disorders (see for example, P. J. Graham, 1998).

GROUP AND RELATIONSHIP THERAPIES

Another important extension of psychotherapy has been a shift from the original one therapist—one patient formula to various modes of group therapy that feature all conceivable permutations: one therapist and several patients, several therapists and several patients, several patients and no therapist, and so on. Treating patients in groups has an obvious pragmatic advantage, because more patients can be accommodated by a limited number of therapists. But group treatment is appealing for other reasons as well, including the fact that it allows therapists to observe and work with problems that emerge more readily in group settings.

Shared-Problem Groups One approach to therapy is to gather together people all of whom have the same problem. They may all be alcoholics, or abuse victims, or ex-convicts. The members meet, share relevant advice and information, help newcomers along, and exhort and support one another in their resolve to overcome their difficulties. The classic example is Alcoholics Anonymous (AA), which provides the alcoholic with a sense that she is not alone and helps her weather crises without suffering a relapse. Another is Toastmasters, a social club for people with public-speaking phobias. In these "we are all in the same boat" groups, the primary aim is to manage the problem that all the members share. Relatively little attention is paid to emotional problems that are unique to any one individual.

Therapy Groups The rules of the game are very different in groups explicitly organized for the purpose of group therapy. Here, a group of selected patients, usually around 8 to 10, is treated together under the guidance of a trained therapist. The techniques used by the therapist, however, vary considerably: In some groups, the therapist encourages psychoanalytically oriented insights; in others, the therapist may use behavioral or cognitive procedures. No matter what the technique, though, the treatment of

Therapy with children **Therapy with children takes many forms. Here a play therapist is using a doll and play therapy to explain to a sick child how injections are given.**

"When Jud accuses Zack, here, of hostility toward his daughter, like he seems to every session, why, it's plain to me he's only rationalizing his own lack of gumption in standing up to a stepson who's usurping the loyalty of his second wife. The way he lit into him just now shows he's got this here guilt identification with Zack's present family constellation. Calling Zack egotistical ain't nothing but a disguise mechanism for concealing his secret envy of Zack's grit and all-around starch, and shows mighty poor ego boundaries of his own, it appears to me."

A group therapy session

each group member really begins as he realizes that he is not all that different from the others. He learns that there are other people who are painfully afraid of rejection, are desperately lonely, have hostile fantasies about their parents, or whatever. Further benefits come from a sense of group belongingness, of support, and of encouragement. Most important of all is the fact that the group provides a ready-made laboratory in interpersonal relations. The patient can discover just what he does that rubs others the wrong way, how he can relate to certain kinds of people more effectively, and so on (Sadock, 1975).

Couples Therapy and Family Therapy   In the therapy groups we have considered so far, the members are almost always strangers before the sessions begin. This is in marked contrast to what happens in couples and family therapy. Here, the people seeking help know one another very well (sometimes all too well) before they enter therapy.

Couples therapy (including marriage counseling) and family therapy have become major therapeutic movements (Kerr & Bowen, 1988; Minuchin, 1974; Satir, 1967; Snyder, Castellani, & Whisman, 2006). It is probably no coincidence that this growth has occurred during a time of turmoil in American families, evidenced by spiraling divorce rates and reports of child and spousal abuse, and by the increasing number of single-parent households.

Family and couples therapists generally regard the family as an emotional system, so that the feelings and functioning of each individual are heavily influenced by interactions within the system. Thus, one person in the family may be depressed, or one member of a married couple may be aggressive, but the difficulty does not lie just in that person alone. Instead, she is merely the "identified patient" within the system, and her symptoms may reflect some broader problem within the family or the couple (Dadds, 1995). Likewise, one person in the couple or family may have a specific problem, but this problem then ricochets throughout the family and affects all its members (Dadds, 1995). The situation is rather like the joints of the body: A sprained ankle causes an immediate limp, but the sufferer must maintain an imbalance in posture while healing, and this imbalance can cause back strain, headaches, and pain in the other leg. Many couples and family therapists believe that their task is like that of the orthopedist who is treating the sprained ankle: to restore full function to the ankle and to all the affected parts as well.

EXTENDING THE GOALS OF PSYCHOTHERAPY

Treatment with children and the various forms of group therapy all broaden the definition of psychotherapy. But there is another important sense in which psychotherapy has been broadened—in the set of problems therapists treat.

As we discussed in Chapter 16, there has been a tendency in recent years to group more and more behavior patterns under the broad rubric of "mental disorder" and thus make them fodder for psychotherapy. We have reached the point where people who buy too many lottery tickets are called gambling addicts and urged to join a self-help program and women who have had several unrewarding relationships are diagnosed as suffering from an excessive need to love and are referred to groups for "women who love too much," and so on.

Even with this expansion, some observers have suggested that mental-health professionals are still too conservative in diagnosing even the standard set of disorders (i.e., the disorders cataloged in the *DSM-IV*). They argue that many individuals fall just short of the criteria for formal diagnosis, yet they are still hobbled by "shadow syndromes"—mild versions of mental disorders (Ratey & Johnson, 1997). For example, take the man who worries constantly about whether his car's engine needs work and takes his car to the repair shop at least once a week to make sure that everything is OK. Is he just showing an everyday kind of eccentricity, or is he in fact suffering from a mild form of obsessive-compulsive disorder that should be treated?

Some evidence suggests that these shadow syndromes are a genuine concern. For example, one study surveyed over 2,000 individuals for the presence of major depression. Based on their signs and symptoms, these individuals were classified into three groups: normal, diagnosable for major depression, or having *subsyndromal depression*—that is, they had some of the signs and symptoms of major depression but not enough to be diagnosed as having the disorder. Compared with the "normal" subjects, the individuals with both subsyndromal depression and fully diagnosable depression had suffered more financial losses, had poorer health, spent more days in bed because they felt unable to go to work, showed impaired functioning on the job, and reported more stress in the home. On most measures, in fact, the people with subsyndromal and major depression were equally impaired (Judd, Paulus, Wells, & Rapaport, 1996; also Rapaport & Judd, 1998).

Given such evidence, should people with subsyndromal conditions be treated—either with medication or with therapy? Some critics believe that they should, but

Extensions of psychotherapy **Even pets can benefit from a good therapist.**

others argue that this would be a first step down a dangerous path, one in which people take pills or seek therapy to adjust their personalities just as they now seek nose jobs, liposuction, and face-lifts to adjust their body shapes. Indeed, this view might lead to a world in which nearly any human eccentricity is regarded as problematic and a candidate for treatment, with the term *normal* reserved for the relatively few who are sufficiently bland to survive labeling. Moreover, such indiscriminate diagnosis might also lead people to use their subsyndromal conditions to excuse bad social conduct or poor job performance (see Olson, 1997; J. Q. Wilson, 1997). There are obvious dangers here, but let us note as well that diagnostic criteria that are too stringent and rigid may exclude from treatment people who might benefit from it.

EXTENDING PSYCHOTHERAPY TO OTHER GROUPS

Subsyndromal cases represent one important way in which psychotherapy is being broadened—and is reaching out to a set of people who do not suffer from clearly defined mental disorders. But there is another way in which psychotherapy has been—and needs to be—broadened: in its reaching out to people in other socioeconomic and cultural contexts. The need for this broadening is easy to see: According to the World Health Organization, roughly 450 million people worldwide suffer from various mental disorders, and the clear majority live in developing countries; 90% of these people have no access to treatment (Miller, 2006). Even within the United States, many who need mental-health help are not receiving it: We know, for example, that many forms of mental disorder are more common among the poor, and yet the poor have considerably less access to help than the wealthy.

Reaching out to these other groups is not just a matter of opening new clinics, or training new therapists in the procedures we have discussed. The problem is more complex because the standard practices of psychotherapy may be inappropriate for patients from other cultures or backgrounds. Indeed, many authors have argued that we need to train therapists in a fashion that develops *cultural competence*—an understanding of how a patient's beliefs, values, and expectations for therapy are shaped by his cultural background (Sue, 1998). A culturally competent therapist can then modify the goals of therapy so as to conform to the values appropriate for that patient.

For example, many Asian cultures place considerable emphasis on formality in all their affairs. Social roles within these cultures are often clearly defined and tend to be structured largely by age and sex, with a father's authority rarely challenged within the family (Sue & Kirk, 1973). Growing up in such a culture may play an important part in

Therapy and cultural values   Different cultural groups differ in their views of family roles, in their views of the elderly, and also in their views of what causes our behavior in the first place. A therapist who is not sensitive to these cultural differences could easily do more harm to a client than good.

shaping the values a patient brings to therapy. A therapist insensitive to these values risks offending the patient and endangering the therapy. Similarly, a therapy that emphasizes individual autonomy over family loyalties might inadvertently run afoul of the patient's cultural traditions and so be counterproductive.

Likewise, therapists who expect their patients to take responsibility for making changes in their lives may be ineffective with clients whose cultural worldview stipulates that important events are due to situational factors such as fate, chance, or powerful others (Pedersen, Fukuyama, & Heath, 1989). And therapies that solely emphasize personal growth and self-exploration may create rather than reduce a patient's problems of daily living if the individual happens to belong to a group that is regularly discriminated against (Wohl, 1989). Finally, practitioners who consider psychotherapy a secular endeavor would do well to remember that, for non-Western cultures and many Western ones, any kind of healing must fully acknowledge the patient's spirituality.

However, it would be a mistake to assume that "cultural competence" merely involves finding a way to deliver Western-style treatment to a broader and broader audience. In fact, the Western developed world can probably take a few lessons from the cultures in developing countries. For example, the long-term prognosis for schizophrenia is considerably better in developing countries than it is in the United States (Ganev, Onchev, & Ivanov, 1998; Thara, 2004), with patients with schizophrenia in India (as one illustration) showing far more remission of symptoms and fewer relapses, and often recovering enough to hold a full-time job, marry, and otherwise lead reasonably normal lives. Why is this? Some authors suggest that physicians in the United States rely too much on medication in treating schizophrenia and far too little on interventions that emphasize job training and a supportive social network. The opposite is the case in India, where medication is often not available, and institutionalization is usually not an option. Indeed, it is estimated that roughly 99% of individuals with schizophrenia live with their families in India, compared with 15 to 25% in the United States (Thara, 2004). Of course, the style of treatment in the United States is encouraged by many factors, including families that often want to distance themselves from the patient, and insurance companies that are willing to reimburse patients for psychotropic drugs but hesitant to pay for social programs.

It seems, then, that cultural competence needs to be understood broadly: It includes the need for Western-style practitioners to be alert to the cultural background (and so to the assumptions, beliefs, and values) of their patients. But it also includes an openness to the possibility that the style of treating mental illness in other cultures may, for some disorders, actually be preferable to the conventional methods used in the developed West.

EVALUATING THERAPEUTIC OUTCOME

We have now said a great deal about what the various forms of therapy involve, but we obviously need to tackle a crucial and central question: Do these various forms of therapy actually work? Do they help people to feel better and to function better?

These appear to be straightforward questions, and, at one level, they are easily answered: Therapy does help people. However, there are several complications here—especially when we seek to ask *why* therapy works, and also when we seek to compare the various forms of therapy with one another. Let us begin, therefore, by looking briefly at the overall pattern of data, and then zoom in for a closer look at the evidence, asking in particular how any form of treatment (biomedical or psychotherapeutic) should be evaluated.

DOES PSYCHOTHERAPY WORK?

To put things simply, therapy does work—improving the lives of people who suffer from a range of psychological, addictive, and health problems (see, for example, Barlow, 2004; Nathan & Gorman, 2002; Roth & Fonagy, 2004; Wampold et al., 1997). Therapy also helps children at various ages (Kazdin & Weisz, 2003; Weisz, Hawley, & Doss, 2004; Weisz, Doss, & Hawley, 2005). Psychotherapy surely has fewer side effects than medication, and, in many cases, its effects seem to be longer lasting than those of medication (see, for example, Hollon et al., 2006).

Not surprisingly, though, therapy is more effective in some cases than in others. For many years, researchers thought that therapy was most likely to be successful with patients who were young, attractive, high in verbal ability, intelligent, and successful in other domains; however, these turn out *not* to be the key factors (Nathan, Stuart, & Dolan, 2000). Instead, therapy is most effective when the patients feel they have a strong sense of alliance with their therapist (J. P. Barber et al., 2000; Martin, Garske, & Davis, 2000), and also when the patients are fully motivated and optimistic about their chances of recovery (Mussell et al., 2000). Improvement is also more likely with more therapy sessions rather than fewer (Lambert et al., 2001; Seligman, 1995, 1998). And some disorders are more responsive to psychotherapy than others (phobias, for example, are quite responsive to psychotherapy; schizophrenia is not).

In addition, many studies have looked at the effects of specific modes of therapy. Thus, for example, behavior therapy seems effective in treating anxiety disorders, especially the phobias (P. E. Nathan & Gorman, 2002), but is rarely used for, say, personality disorders. Cognitive therapy is effective in treating mood disorders (Hollon et al., 2002), and may be just as effective as drug treatment (but with longer-lasting impact and without the side effects); it is also useful for other diagnoses, such as panic disorder (Hollon & Beck, in press; Shear, Pilkonis, Cloitre, & Leon, 1994) and bulimia (Wilson & Fairburn, 2002). Evidence also suggests that the experiential therapies can alleviate depression and anxiety disorders (Elliott et al., 2004). Ironically, the evidence is least compelling for the form of therapy that historically came first—Freud's psychoanalytic technique. However, the psychodynamic therapies derived from Freud's procedure—especially interpersonal therapy—do seem to be effective, especially for depression (Frank & Spanier, 1995; Hollon et al., 2002).

It should also be noted, though, that therapy does not work for every individual, and, in fact, a certain proportion of patients—between 5 and 10%—actually get *worse* as a result of therapy (Lambert & Bergin, 1994; M. L. Smith, Glass, & Miller, 1980). What produces these deterioration effects? In many cases, the problem seems to be a bad therapist-patient relationship; in other cases, the problem may be outright incompetence in the therapist (Hadley & Strupp, 1976; M. L. Smith, Glass, & Miller, 1980). Still other cases of deterioration may have a subtler cause. Psychotherapy sometimes disrupts what is stable in the patient's life yet provides no substitute (Hadley & Strupp, 1976; Lambert & Bergin, 1994). For example, the therapy may lead a patient to regard her marriage as unsatisfactory, but as she takes steps toward separation or divorce, she may become severely depressed at the prospect of being alone. Good psychotherapists are alert to such dangers and attempt to avert such deterioration whenever possible.

HOW SHOULD THERAPY BE EVALUATED?

The findings just cataloged are rather encouraging: As we said earlier, psychotherapy does produce beneficial results. However, we need to take a closer look at the evidence that lies behind this claim, because there are several complications that we must address, and some controversy that we must acknowledge.

EVIDENCE-BASED PRACTICE

Clinical psychologists have always understood the need to validate their procedures—whether the procedures involve psychotherapy, a biomedical treatment, or some combination—in order to ensure that they are providing benefits and doing no harm. The issue of validation has become more urgent in the last few years, however, fueled by a worldwide movement toward what is called *evidence-based practice (EBP)*—the notion that clinical practice must be based on solid research. This movement was initially aimed at the broad practice of medicine (Sackett, Straus, Richardson, Rosenberg, & Haynes, 2000; Sox & Woolf, 1993), but has led to a similar movement within psychology (American Psychological Association Presidential Task Force on Evidence-Based Practice, 2006).

Many factors have contributed to this movement toward EBP in psychology. One consideration lies in a number of prominent critiques of psychotherapy challenging the effectiveness of the clinicians' work. One of the earliest of these attacks was launched by the British psychologist Hans Eysenck, and was particularly concerned with the efficacy of psychoanalysis and similar "insight" therapies (Eysenck, 1961). Eysenck surveyed some 24 articles that reported the number of patients who improved or failed to improve after psychotherapy. Overall, about 60% improved, a result that might be considered fairly encouraging. But, according to Eysenck's analysis, the number of patents who got better with no treatment at all was, if anything, even higher, about 70%. If that is so, psychotherapy apparently has no curative effects.

In retrospect, it appears that Eysenck's attack was unduly harsh, and today his study is widely discredited (Nathan et al., 2000). Nonetheless, his paper fed into the broader movement demanding that psychotherapy be validated empirically. (For later critiques of psychotherapy, see Dawes, 1994; Torrey, 1992.)

The EBP movement has also been encouraged by the development of the drug treatments we reviewed earlier in this chapter. These medications, as we have seen, often have unfortunate side effects, making it crucial that we use them only with the patients and the disorders for which they are clearly effective. In addition, the availability of these medications invites questions about the value of nonmedical treatment—namely, psychotherapy. Is it possible that hours of therapy might be replaced by the simple taking of a pill? This notion obviously demands a careful evaluation of whether psychotherapy works or not.

One last factor fueling the EBP movement involves the *cost* of therapy. Many of the medications for mental disorders are quite expensive. Psychotherapy requires hours with a trained professional and is therefore also often costly. In many cases, the expenses are covered by insurance policies (making so-called third-party payments), but, as health expenses have risen, insurance companies have grown more concerned about making certain that the treatments they are paying for are worthwhile (see, for example, Zarkin, Grabowski, Mauskopf, Bannerman, & Weisler, 1995).

THE LOGIC OF OUTCOME RESEARCH

How can we find out whether a medication or a form of psychotherapy really works—whether it truly provides relief for someone with a particular disorder? As a way of tackling this issue, let us suppose that we want to find out whether a given drug—say, Wellbutrin—reduces the manifestations of depression. For a first step, we could administer Wellbutrin to a group of patients diagnosed with depression, and assess the patients' status before and after receiving the medication. This assessment would provide useful information, but a little reflection shows that relying only on this procedure would be a mistake.

One problem with the before-and-after assessment is that it ignores the possibility of *spontaneous improvement*: For some disorders, many patients get better on their own,

TABLE 17.1 ELEMENTS OF A RANDOMIZED CONTROL TRIAL (RCT)

1. Need for a comparison group, to control for spontaneous improvement.
2. Groups matched via random assignment.
3. Groups uniform in their diagnosis.
4. Placebo for control group.
5. For therapy: Need uniform treatment, and so "manualized therapy."

whether they receive treatment or not. Therefore, if patients are indeed better off after taking Wellbutrin than they were before, their improvement might reflect the drug's effects, or it might not: It might instead reflect spontaneous improvement and have nothing to do with the medication. In addition, even without spontaneous improvement, most disorders fluctuate in their severity, and it seems likely that patients will seek treatment when they are feeling particularly bad. If so, then the odds are good that the normal ups and downs of the disorder will make them look better a few weeks (or months) later. If they have been receiving drugs during those weeks, we might be fooled into thinking that the drugs had caused the improvement when, in fact, the medication had nothing to do with the change.

To control for these factors, we need to compare two groups of patients, with one group receiving Wellbutrin for, say, 6 weeks, while the other group receives no treatment. We would also need to make certain that these two groups were matched at the start of the study—with similar symptoms, similar backgrounds, and so on. As we discussed in Chapter 1, our best means of achieving this matching would be *via random assignment*—with a coin toss (or the equivalent) determining whether each participant in the study ends up in our treatment group or the no-treatment group. Then, if the participants in the two groups differ at the end of the procedure, we can be sure that the difference arose *during* the study—presumably as a result of our treatment.

In addition, we would want to ensure that the participants in our study are reasonably uniform in their disorder. Thus, to ask whether Wellbutrin works for depression, we would want to make certain that all of the participants in the study were truly depressed, and that their depression was not complicated by other problems that might mask the effects of the treatment. Likewise, we would probably want to make sure the participants were all similar to one another in the duration and severity of their depression. Otherwise, variations from one participant to the next might add so much noise to our data that we would not be able to detect the therapy's effects.

PLACEBO EFFECTS

We have now described most of the elements of a *randomized clinical trial (RCT)*, so called because of the random assignment of participants to groups. In most ways an RCT would be run in the same fashion for evaluating a new medication as for evaluating a specific type of therapy. There are, however, a few differences between RCTs for drugs and RCTs for therapy.

In evaluating any treatment, we need to be alert to the possibility of *placebo effects*. This term refers to the influence of some medically neutral substance (the placebo) that is administered to a patient. Placebos often diminish symptoms, but this effect cannot be understood in terms of the placebo's biomedical impact; that is because placebos are, as we have said, substances that are medically neutral. The placebo's effects therefore have to be understood in terms of the patient's own beliefs and expectations: The patient believes in the pill's powers, and it is his faith in the medication, not the medication itself, that brings the benefits.

In the broad practice of medicine, the evidence is mixed regarding how powerful placebos are. In some studies, placebos seem to produce real improvement (Benson & Friedman, 1996); in other studies, placebo effects are weak or nonexistent (Hrobjartsson & Gotzsche, 2001). One way or another, though, we need to take placebo effects seriously in the study of mental disorders, because it is surely plausible that a patient's distress might be alleviated by her belief in the cure, rather than by the cure itself.

In studies of a medication, therefore, we give the medication we are interested in—Wellbutrin, in our example—to one group of patients, and a placebo to the remaining patients. This second group will receive the same attention from the treatment staff as the Wellbutrin group, and they will be told exactly the same things about their treatment. They will also be given the same number of pills as the patients in the true-drug group, and on the same schedule. In this fashion, we ensure that the two groups have the same expectations and the same beliefs about the treatment. If we find, therefore, that the groups differ at the end of the study, the difference cannot be explained in terms of the patients' beliefs. Instead, the difference must be attributed to the one element that distinguished the two groups—the fact that the patients in one group actually took a medication, while those in the other took pills containing inert materials.

The same logic applies to a study of psychotherapy: Here, too, we should control for placebo effects. However, it is not clear what the placebo would be in this case. Would we want the placebo group to work with a therapist who listens, but without warmth? A therapist who expresses warmth, but provides no counsel? A therapist who offers counsel irrelevant to the patient's problems? The choice between these (or other) options is not clear, making this one source of ambiguity in interpreting RCT data for psychotherapy (Nathan et al., 2000).

MANUALIZED THERAPY

There is one other way in which RCT procedures differ for medications and psychotherapy: When we are testing a medicine, it is easy to ensure that each patient gets the same number of pills, and that the chemical constituents of the pills are the same for everyone in the study. These points are guaranteed, in essence, by quality control in the pharmaceutical factory that provides the medication. But how can we ensure, in a study of therapy, that each patient gets the same treatment—with the same constituents and the same "dose"?

This point is usually addressed by developing a treatment manual that tells the therapists exactly how to proceed during the study—what steps to take in therapy, what instructions to offer, and so on. This *manualized therapy* denies the therapist the option of improvising or adjusting procedures midstream, and plausibly this may sometimes undermine the quality of the therapy. (For more on this point, see Addis & Krasnow, 2000; Wilson, 1998.) However, this standardization seems essential if we are to ask whether a particular therapy accomplishes what it is said to accomplish.

Let us acknowledge, therefore, that there are clear trade-offs associated with the use of manualized therapy: On the positive side, this procedure seems our best hope for learning whether a particular type of treatment works or not. On the negative side, we have already noted that most clinicians adopt an eclectic approach in their work, drawing on many traditions. A related point is that clinicians often adjust their approach as the therapy proceeds and they learn which steps seem promising and which do not. On this basis, RCT data may provide information only about a "pure" form of therapy that is rather different from the therapy ordinarily delivered in a clinic, and so may not give us the information we want if we are to ask whether "ordinary" therapy is effective.

EFFICACY VERSUS UTILITY

Our account of how one assesses therapy (whether biomedical therapy or psychotherapy) is growing somewhat complex: We have identified several elements needed for an

RCT, but we have also highlighted some concerns about RCT procedures—ambiguities about how to design a placebo group when evaluating psychotherapy, and concerns about the use of manualized therapies. Nonetheless, RCT data are extremely useful for us, and allow us to identify certain therapies as "empirically validated." (For catalogs of some of the "validated" psychotherapies, see, for example, Chambless et al., 1998; Nathan & Gorman, 2002; Roth & Fonagy, 2004.)

Some authors, however, are skeptical about the reliance on RCT data (Nathan et al., 2000; Westen & Bradley, 2005; Westen, Novotny, & Thompson-Brenner, 2004; Zimmerman, Mattia, & Posternack, 2002). Specifically, they argue that an RCT might inform us about a therapy's *efficacy* (whether it works in carefully designed tests), but might not tell us about its *clinical utility* (whether it works in more typical circumstances; APA Presidential Task Force on Evidence-Based Practice, 2006).

We have already met one of the bases for this concern—the reliance on manualized therapy. A different concern hinges on the patient groups used in many RCT studies. We earlier discussed the need for reasonably uniform patient groups in an RCT— people who unmistakably suffer from depression and not from some other disorder, or people who suffer from schizophrenia uncomplicated by other problems. This uniformity allows us to ask whether our therapy works for people in a well-defined group, but, again, it undermines the realism of our study: Many of the people who seek out therapy do not have a clear diagnosis, and, indeed, if they do, the diagnosis may be complex. That is because many forms of mental disorder have high rates of *comorbidity*—that is, they occur together with some other disorder. Thus, for example, there is considerable comorbidity between anxiety and depression disorders: Someone who has one often suffers from the other as well. As a result, we are once more led to a concern about the generalizability of the RCT data. They may tell us what happens in therapy with "pure" cases, but not what happens in the (much more common) mixed cases encountered in most clinics.

For these and other reasons, we should be cautious about a reliance on RCT as our sole source of evidence in evaluating any form of therapy. The RCT procedure is undeniably valuable, but it is also limited in some ways, and those limits suggest that we must combine RCT data with other sorts of data, including studies of ordinary clinical practice, case studies, studies of the actual process of change within psychotherapy, and more (APA Presidential Task Force on Evidence-Based Practice, 2006; Shadish et al., 1997). This broader package of evidence will help us understand whether therapy as it is usually practiced, with more typical patients, has the desired effects; it will also tell us whether the worries about manualized therapy are justified.

META-ANALYSES OF THERAPY OUTCOME

The points just raised highlight a new question for us: Apparently, our evaluation of therapy needs to depend on diverse lines of evidence drawn from many different studies. How should we put together all the evidence? What will be the best way to integrate and summarize all the available data? For many investigators, the answer lies in a statistical technique called *meta-analysis*, by means of which the results of many different studies can be combined.

In one of the earliest analyses of this kind, 475 studies comprising 25,000 patients in all were reviewed (M. L. Smith et al., 1980). In each of these studies, patients who received some kind of psychotherapy were compared with a similar group of patients who did not receive any. The studies included in this analysis differed in many respects: One factor that varied was the kind of psychotherapy used—whether psychodynamic, humanistic, behavioral, or cognitive. Another factor that varied was the criterion of improvement. In some cases, the criterion was the level of a symptom: the amount of avoidance that a person with snake phobias eventually showed toward snakes, the number of washing episodes shown by a patient who washed compulsively, and so on. In others, it was based on an improvement in functioning, such as a rise in the grade-point average (GPA) of a student who was disturbed. In still others, such as studies of patients with depression, it was an improvement in mood as rated by scales completed by the patient himself or by knowledgeable outsiders, such as his spouse and children. Given all these differences among the studies, combining the results seems problematic, but meta-analysis provides a method.

Consider two hypothetical studies, *A* and *B*. Let us say that Study *A* shows that, after treatment, the average patient with snake phobia can move closer to a snake than the average patient who received no treatment. Let us also assume that Study *B* found that students with depression who received psychotherapy show a greater increase in GPA than do equivalent students in an untreated control group. On the face of it, there is no way to average the results of the two studies because they use completely different units. In the first case, the average effect of therapy—that is, the difference between the group that received treatment and the one that did not—is measured in feet (how near the snake the patient will go); in the second, it is counted in GPA points. But here is the trick provided by meta-analysis. Let us suppose we find that in Study *A*, 85% of the treated patients are able to move closer to the snake than the average untreated patient. Let us further suppose that in Study *B*, 75% of the students who received psychotherapy earn a GPA higher than the average GPA of the untreated students. Now we can average the scores. To be sure, feet and GPA points are like apples and oranges and cannot be compared. But the percentage relationships—in our case, 85 and 75—are comparable. Since this is so, they can be averaged across different studies.

The conclusion drawn by averaging across the 475 studies that were reviewed was that the "average person who receives therapy is better off at the end of it than 80% of the persons who do not" (M. L. Smith et al., 1980, p. 87). Later meta-analyses have used different criteria in selecting studies for inclusion, but yield similar results (see, for example, Wampold et al., 1997). Other studies showed that these improvements are still found when patients are studied months or years after treatment (Nicholson & Berman, 1983).

COMPARING THERAPIES

It seems, then, that we are moving toward some rather positive claims: Meta-analyses indicate that both drug therapy and psychotherapy are effective for many mental disorders. More focused studies provide a similarly encouraging message: Specific drugs, and specific modes of therapy, considered one by one, also provide help—so that people who receive treatment end up better off than those who do not. But there is one more question we need to tackle: How do the various forms of therapy compare with one another? Are some therapies more effective (faster, or more complete, or more successful, in reaching their aims) than others? These are important questions to ask if we want our therapies to be efficient; they are also important if we consider (as we must) the *cost* of therapy (in time, in emotional energy, and, of course, in dollars).

The answer to these questions is perhaps surprising: Many studies indicate that the various psychotherapies, when compared with one another, are all equally effective. There are some exceptions to this pattern (i.e., studies showing an advantage for one form of therapy over the others), but, in general, the data support a conclusion often referred to as the ***dodo bird verdict***, after the dodo bird in *Alice in Wonderland*, who organized a race among various Wonderland creatures and concluded, "Everyone has won and all must have prizes" (Elkin et al., 1989; Luborsky, Singer, & Luborsky, 1975; Shear et al., 1994; Sloane, Staples, Cristol, Yorkston, & Whipple, 1975; M. L. Smith et al., 1980; Wampold et al., 1997).

The dodo bird verdict has been controversial (see, for example, Crits-Christoph, 1997; Howard, Krause, Saunders, & Kopta, 1997), but, even so, it still seems to offer a

"Everyone has won and all must have prizes."
(From Lewis Carroll's, Alice in Wonderland.**)**

plausible summary of the available evidence (cf. Nathan et al., 2000). Thus, for example, the data suggest that cognitive therapy, drug therapy, some combination of cognitive therapy and drug therapy, and interpersonal therapy are each effective as treatments for depression (although the data do suggest that, within this set, the benefits of some therapies are longer lasting than others). This is, in some ways, a remarkable finding, because, as we have discussed, the various forms of therapy differ enormously in how they proceed. How, therefore, could they all end up roughly equivalent in their effectiveness?

Several factors contribute. One, simply, is a placebo effect. According to this view, the patients get better because they expect to get better, and so what really matters in therapy is the simple fact that patients believe the treatment will help them. This belief, plausibly, can be nurtured by any form of therapy—and hence the dodo bird outcome.

However, placebo effects are surely not the whole story here (Andrews & Harvey, 1981; Robinson, Berman, & Neimeyer, 1990; M. L. Smith et al., 1980). Instead, the therapy itself really does help—but the *reasons* it helps may be shared among diverse forms of therapy. As we discussed earlier, therapies differ in many ways, but they also have some key elements in common: the gaining of an ally, the opportunity to defuse emotional situations, the chance for new interpersonal learning, and so on (pp. 651–652). To the extent that these elements are indeed beneficial and also common to the various modes of therapy, we would again expect all the modes to be effective.

Another contributor to the dodo bird outcome grows out of a central theme of Chapter 16: that mental disorders usually do not have just one cause. Instead, disorders are produced by a mix of factors, some constituting the diathesis, and some the more immediate trigger. If all these factors are relevant, then *removing* any of them should be helpful in preventing or treating the disorder. Thus, depression, for example, is more likely if a person has a particular style of thinking about the world, and so it might be alleviated by shifting this style of thought (as in cognitive therapy). But depression is also more likely if the person does not have the support of an adequate social network, and so might be alleviated by taking steps that will improve this support (as in interpersonal therapy). This logic suggests that either form of therapy might be helpful—

although for different reasons—and this, too, helps us understand the dodo bird result.

On all these grounds, the dodo bird conclusion may be less puzzling than it at first seems. We should say again, though, that the dodo bird claim continues to be controversial: Several meta-analyses confirm it, but some questions have been raised about the analyses; in addition, some RCT data suggest that there may, in fact, be considerable differences in how effective the various forms of psychotherapy are (Nathan et al., 2000). These points highlight, once again, the need for continued research in understanding whether, when, and why psychotherapy is effective.

SOME FINAL THOUGHTS:
FAR, BUT NOT YET FAR ENOUGH

Where does all of this leave us? It has been more than 100 years since Krafft-Ebing's discovery that general paresis is caused by syphilis and since Freud and Breuer's classic studies of hysteria. What can we say today about the treatment of mental disorders?

All in all, there has been considerable progress. Let us begin with the biological therapies, because the progress on this front has been striking. Antipsychotic medications control some of the worst manifestations of schizophrenia. The antidepressants and antimanic medications (and, where appropriate, ECT) are remarkably effective in treating the mood swings of depression and mania, and the anxiolytics do the same for disabling anxiety. Yet these advances are far from what one might wish: We have mentioned that the medicines do not cure; they just keep symptoms in check. We have also discussed the sometimes-substantial side effects associated with various medications. Nonetheless, there can be no question that the biomedical treatments for mental disorders are an extraordinarily powerful tool in diminishing many forms of human suffering.

How about psychotherapy? There is no doubt that therapy does produce benefits; we see this in both the RCT data and the meta-analyses. Moreover, these benefits may be longer lasting than those of the drug treatments, and, of course, psychotherapy does not raise concerns about side effects. But here, too, large questions remain, including questions about what it is that produces these benefits. One factor is certainly the relationship that therapy affords between the patient and the therapist. This relationship helps people by providing someone in whom they can confide, someone who offers advice about troubling matters, who listens to them, and who instills hope that they will get better.

A skeptic might respond to these points by arguing that these benefits do not really involve *therapy*. Instead, the same benefits might as easily have been provided by a wise aunt, the understanding family doctor, or the local clergy. However, this argument is probably not well founded. The RCT data tell us that the specific effects of therapy (the particular procedures used, the particular training delivered) also play a role, highlighting the advantage of a skilled therapist over a wise aunt. To be sure, there is debate over what these specific effects involve, and this is one of the many topics for which more research is needed. Even so, it seems clear that the specific (and beneficial) effects of therapy include the changes in associations among stimuli brought about by behavioral therapy and the changes in beliefs brought about by cognitive therapy. These—plus some amount of emotional defusing, interpersonal learning, and insight—are all acquired within the therapeutic situation and somehow transferred to the patient's life beyond.

Let us acknowledge, however, that there is a kernel of truth in the skeptic's argument: Some of the benefits of therapy do grow out of the fact that a therapist is an understanding and compassionate listener, an ally, a source of hope—and so, in these regards, provides the same function as the wise aunt or the family doctor. But is this a bad thing? Wise aunts are often in short supply, and the family doctor is largely a thing of the past, replaced by an often-harried primary-care physician at the local HMO. Nor do many people today have a member of the clergy as a lifelong confidant. All of this suggests that psychotherapy has come to fill a social vacuum. Some of its effects may well depend on a relationship that has value for reasons not showcased by Freud, or the behavior therapists, or the cognitive therapists, but that takes away nothing from the value of this relationship.

Overall, then, we have certainly come far from where we started more than a century ago. This is especially clear when we look back and compare current practices with those at the time of the American Revolution, when Benjamin Rush dunked his patients into ice-cold water or whirled them around until they were unconscious. Good treatments are now available for a number of mental disorders, and they enable many people to rebound from complete disability and return to normal functioning. Although we have much further to go, there is much to celebrate.

SUMMARY

BIOMEDICAL THERAPIES

- Many mental disorders are treated with drugs. For example, classical *antipsychotics* are helpful in holding in check the major *positive symptoms* of schizophrenia, and new antipsychotics show promise in treating *negative symptoms* as well.

- Drug treatments have allowed a movement toward *deinstitutionalization* of individuals with mental disorders. However, this movement has been only a partial success, in part because of a lack of support services outside mental hospitals.

- Classical *antidepressants* such as the *MAO inhibitors* and *tricyclics* counteract depression. However, these antidepressants all have many undesirable side effects, which have led to a search for better medications. The last few decades have seen the advent of the so-called designer drugs, engineered specifically to enhance—or inhibit—certain neurotransmitters but not others. Of these the best known is *Prozac*, which belongs to the group of *selective serotonin reuptake inhibitors (SSRIs)*. The newer drugs have fewer side effects and are as effective as the older ones in treating depression and obsessive-compulsive disorder.

- *Lithium carbonate* is useful in cases of bipolar disorder, especially in forestalling or reducing the intensity of manic episodes. In addition, *anxiolytics* have proved effective for the treatment of anxiety disorders.

- Other biological therapies include *psychosurgery* and *electroconvulsive therapy (ECT)*, which is markedly effective in cases of severe and potentially suicidal depression.

PSYCHOTHERAPIES

- A different approach to the treatment of mental disorder, *psychotherapy*, relies on efforts to change the patient's thinking and behavior directly, usually by some form of discussion, instruction, or training.

- *Classical psychoanalysis* seeks to help a patient gain insight into his own hidden conflicts and wishes. The person must "work through" the conflicts, so that the insights are not merely intellectual, and this working through depends crucially on the process of *transference*. *Psychodynamic therapy* still preserves many insights from psychoanalysis, but puts as much emphasis on conscious thoughts as on unconscious conflicts, and emphasizes the ways in which a patient's pattern of interaction in childhood can influence (and distort) current social relationships.

- *Interpersonal therapy (IPT)* places its emphasis squarely on social relationships, and seeks to help a patient learn new and more beneficial ways of interacting and communicating. *Humanistic-experiential therapy* seeks to create a genuinely empathic and accepting atmosphere in therapy, but also seeks to deepen the patient's experience.

- *Behavior therapy* seeks to change a patient's behavior directly, drawing on principles of classical and instrumental conditioning. One example is *systematic desensitization*; another is *aversion therapy*, in which undesirable behaviors, thoughts, and desires are coupled with unpleasant stimuli. Therapies based on principles of operant conditioning include the use of *token economies*, in which patients are systematically reinforced for showing desirable behaviors. Yet another behavioral technique is *modeling*.

- *Cognitive therapy* seeks to change a person's beliefs and mode of thinking. One example is *stress-inoculation therapy*, which seeks to prepare people to deal with the stresses they encounter in everyday life. A different example is Aaron Beck's therapy for depression, which tries to help patients identify their automatic thoughts and reactions, and to substitute more beneficial reactions.

- Although these therapies differ in many regards, they all benefit from *relationship effects*, including the *therapeutic alliance*. Other shared benefits include *interpersonal learning*, *emotional defusing*, and a prospect for gaining *self-knowledge*. In addition, the distinctions among therapies are being blurred by the broad trend toward *multimodal therapy*, in which therapists draw on several of the traditions we have named, and combine psychotherapy with drug treatment.

- The last few decades have seen an enormous extension of psychotherapy. One such extension involves the increasing use of therapy with children. Another concerns *group therapy*, in which patients are treated in groups rather than individually. Yet another example is *family* (and *couples*) *therapy*, whose practitioners believe that family distress is not in the pathology of any one individual, but in the relationships within the family system. Practitioners therefore try to rectify these faulty relationships.

- Another extension concerns the therapeutic goals. While the original purpose of psychotherapy was to cure pathology, some practitioners have gradually broadened this goal to include treatment for individuals with *subsyndromal problems*.

- Therapy is also being broadened to reach out to other groups, including members of different cultures and different socioeconomic classes. This broadening requires *cultural competence*, and also an openness to the possibility that Western ways of dealing with mental disorder may not be optimal.

EVALUATING THERAPEUTIC OUTCOME

- There is no question that psychotherapy works in many cases, although more so with some individuals, and some diagnoses, than with others. Therapy appears to be particularly effective when patients feel they have a strong sense of alliance with their therapists, and also when patients are optimistic about their chances of recovery. An increasing emphasis on *evidence-based practice* (*EBP*), however, has called for closer scrutiny of whether, when, and why therapy is effective.

- If people are better off after therapy than before, this might be the result of *spontaneous improvement*. To address this concern, a group receiving therapy should be compared with a matched group that receives no therapy, and the two groups should be uniform in their disorder at the start of therapy. When testing a new drug, it is also crucial to control for *placebo effects*. It is not clear, however, how to control for such effects when testing a form of psychotherapy.

- *Randomized clinical trials* (*RCTs*) are often used to assess the *efficacy* of therapy, but the conditions of these trials are often different from those in actual clinical practice. One difference lies in the use of *manualized therapy*; another lies in the focus on patients with a single diagnosis and no *comorbidity*. For these reasons, it is important to combine data from randomized clinical trials with other forms of data collection.

- One assessment of psychotherapy relies on a statistical technique called *meta-analysis*, by means of which the results of many different studies can be combined. The results of such analyses indicate that the various psychotherapies are effective, but—surprisingly—the meta-analyses also suggest that very different forms of therapy can be equally effective, a result often referred to as the *dodo bird verdict*.

Statistics: The Description, Organization, and Interpretation of Data

In Chapter 1, we considered how psychologists gather data—how they design a study or an experiment, how they ensure external and internal validity, and so on. But what do they do once the data are gathered? In this appendix, we will focus on the statistical methods investigators use to organize and interpret numerical data.

Let us begin with an example. Suppose some investigators want to find out whether three-year-old boys are more physically aggressive than three-year-old girls. To find out, the investigators will first have to come up with some appropriate measure of physical aggression. They will then have to select the participants for the study. Since the investigators presumably want to say something about three-year-olds in general, not just the particular three-year-olds in their study, they must select their participants appropriately. Even more important, they must select boys and girls who are well matched to each other in all regards except gender, so that the investigators can be reasonably sure that any differences between the two groups are attributable to the difference in sex rather than to other factors (such as intellectual development, social class, and so on).

We discussed in Chapter 1 how investigators design studies and collect data. So we'll start here with what investigators do once their data have been collected. Their first task is to organize these data in a meaningful way. Suppose the study used two groups of 50 boys and 50 girls, each observed on 10 separate occasions. This means that the investigators will end up with at least 1,000 separate numerical entries, 500 for the boys and 500 for the girls. Something has to be done to reduce this mass of numbers into some manageable form. This is usually accomplished by some process of averaging scores.

The next step involves statistical interpretation. Suppose the investigators find that the average score for physical aggression is greater for the boys than for the girls. (It probably will be.) How should this fact be interpreted? Should it be taken seriously, or might it just be a fluke, some sort of accident? For it is just about certain that the data contain *variability*: the children within each group will not perform identically to each other; furthermore, the same child may very well behave differently on one occasion than on another. Thus, the number of aggressive acts for the boys might be, say, 5.8 on average, but might vary from a low of 1.3 (the score from completely calm Calvin) to a high of 11.4 (the score from awfully aggressive Albert). The average number of aggressive acts for the girls might be 3.9 (and so lower than the boys' average), but this derives from a range of scores that include 0 (from serene Sarah) and 6.2 (from aggressive Agnes).

Is it possible that this difference between boys and girls is just a matter of chance, an accidental by-product of this variability? For example, what if boys and girls are, in fact, rather similar in their levels of aggression, but—just by chance—the study happened to include four or five extremely aggressive boys and a comparable number of extremely unaggressive girls? After all, we know that our results would have been different if Albert had been absent on the day of our testing; the boys' average, without his contribution, would have been lower. Likewise, Agnes's twin sister was not included in our test group because of the random process through which we selected our research participants. If she had been included, and if she was as aggressive as her twin, then the girls' average would have been higher. Is it possible that accidents like these are the real source of the apparent difference between the groups? If so, then another study, without these same accidents, might yield a different result. One of the main reasons for using statistical methods is to deal with questions of this sort, to help us draw useful conclusions about behavior despite the unavoidable variability, and, specifically, allowing us to ask in a systematic way whether our data pattern is reliable (and so would emerge in subsequent studies) or just the product of accidents.

DESCRIBING THE DATA

In the example above, we assumed that the investigators would be collecting numerical data. We made this assumption because much of the power of statistics results from the fact that numbers can be manipulated using the rules of arithmetic, unlike open-ended responses in an interview, videotapes of social interactions, or lists of words recalled in a memory experiment. (How could you average together one participant's response of "Yes, I like them" with another's response of "Only on weekends"?) As a result, scientists prefer to use numerical response measures whenever possible. Consider our hypothetical study of physical aggression. The investigators who watched the research participants might rate their physical aggression in various situations from 1 to 5, with 1 being "extremely docile" and 5 being "extremely aggressive," or they might count the number of aggressive acts (say, hitting or kicking another child). This operation of assigning numbers to observed events is called *scaling*.

There are several types of scales that will concern us. They differ by the arithmetical operations that can be performed on them.

CATEGORICAL AND ORDINAL SCALES

Sometimes the scores assigned to individuals are merely *categorical* (also called *nominal*). For example, when respondents to a poll are asked to name the television channel they watch most frequently, they might respond "4," "2," or "13." These numbers serve only to group the responses into categories. They can obviously not be subjected to any arithmetic operations. (If a respondent watches channels 2 and 4 equally often, we can't summarize this by claiming that, on average, she watches channel 3!)

Ordinal scales convey more information, in that the relative magnitude of each number is meaningful—not arbitrary, as in the case of categorical scales. If individuals are asked to list the ten people they most admire, the number 1 can be assigned to the most admired person, 2 to the runner-up, and so on. The smaller the number assigned, the more the person is admired. Notice that no such statement can be made of television channels: channel 4 is not more anything than channel 2, just different from it.

Scores that are ordinally scaled cannot, however, be added or subtracted. The first two persons on the most-admired list differ in admirability by 1; so do the last two. Yet the individual who has done the ranking may admire the first person far more than the other nine, all of whom might be very similar in admirability. Imagine, for example, a child who, given this task, lists his mother first, followed by the starting lineup of the Chicago Cubs. In this case, the difference between rank 1 and rank 2 is enormous; the difference between rank 2 and rank 3 (or any other pair of adjacent ranks) is appreciably smaller. Or, to put it another way, the difference of eight between person 2 and person 10 probably represents a smaller difference in judged admirability than the difference of one obtained between persons 1 and 2 (at least so the mother hopes).

INTERVAL SCALES

Scales in which equal differences between scores, or intervals, can be treated as equal units are called *interval scales*. Response time is a common psychological variable that is usually treated as an interval scale. In some memory experiments, for example, the participant must respond as quickly as possible to each of several words, some of which she has seen earlier in the experiment; the task is to indicate, by pressing the appropriate button, whether each word had appeared earlier or not.

Suppose that someone requires an average of 2 seconds to respond to nouns, 3 seconds to verbs, and 4 seconds to adjectives. The difference in decision time between verbs and nouns ($3 - 2 = 1$ second) is the same as the difference in decision time between adjectives and verbs ($4 - 3 = 1$ second). We can make this statement—which in turn suggests various hypotheses about the factors that underlie such differences—precisely because response time can be regarded as an interval scale.

RATIO SCALES

Scores based on an interval scale allow subtraction and addition. But they do not allow multiplication and division. Consider the Celsius scale of temperature. The difference between 10 and 20 degrees Celsius is equal to that between 30 and 40 degrees Celsius. But can one say that 20 degrees Celsius is twice as high a temperature as 10 degrees Celsius? The answer is no, for the Celsius scale of temperature is only an interval scale. It is not a *ratio scale*, which allows statements such as 10 feet is one-fifth as long as 50 feet, or 15 pounds is three times as heavy as 5 pounds. To make such statements, one needs a true zero point. Such a ratio scale with a zero point does exist for temperature—the Kelvin absolute temperature scale, whose zero point (*absolute zero* to chemists and physicists) is about −273 degrees Celsius.

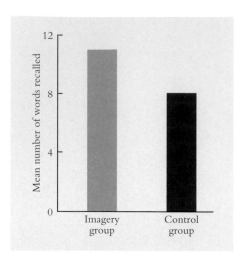

A.2 *The results of an experiment on memorizing* *Participants in the imagery group, who were asked to form visual images of the words they were to memorize, recalled an average of 11 words. Participants in the control group, who received no special instructions, recalled an average of 8 words.*

The third measure of central tendency, the mean (M), is the familiar arithmetic average. If N stands for the number of scores, then

$$M = \frac{\text{sum of scores}}{N}$$

$$= \frac{5+5+6+7+8+9+9+9+11+11}{10} = \frac{80}{10} = 8.0$$

The mean is the measure of central tendency most commonly used by psychologists, in part because a number of further calculations can be based on this measure. It is common, therefore, for the results of experiments like our imagery example to be displayed as shown in Figure A.2. The values of the independent variable (in this case, getting imagery instructions) are indicated on the x-axis, and the values of the dependent variable (mean number of words recalled) on the y-axis.

Despite the common use of the mean, each of these measures of central tendency has its own advantages. The mode is used relatively rarely, because the modes of two samples can differ greatly even if the samples have very similar distributions. If one of the 3 participants who recalled 9 words recalled only 5 instead, the mode would have been 5 rather than 9. But the mode does have its uses. For example, a home builder might decide to include a two-car garage on a new house because 2 is the mode for the number of cars owned by American families; more people will be content with a two-car garage than with any other size.

The median and the mean differ most in the degree to which they are affected by extreme scores. If the highest score in our sample were changed from 11 to 111, the median would be unaffected, whereas the mean would jump from 8.0 to 18.0. Most people would find the median (which remains 8.5) a more compelling "average" than the mean in such a situation, since most of the scores in the distribution are close to the median but are not close to the mean (18.0). This is why medians are often preferred when the data become highly variable, even though the mean has computational advantages.

The advantages of the median become particularly clear with distributions of scores that contain a few extreme values. Such distributions are said to be *skewed*, and a classic example is income distribution, since there are only a few very high incomes but many low ones. Suppose we sample ten individuals from a neighborhood and find their yearly incomes (in thousands of dollars) to be

10, 12, 20, 20, 40, 40, 40, 80, 80, 4,000

The median income for this sample is 40 ($40,000), since both the fifth and sixth scores are 40. This value reflects the income of the typical individual. The mean income for this sample, however, is (10 + 12 + 20 + 20 + 40 + 40 + 40 + 80 + 80 + 4,000)/ 10 = 418, or $418,000. A politician who wants to demonstrate that her neighborhood has prospered might—quite accurately—use these data to claim that the average (mean) income is $418,000. If, on the other hand, she wished to plead for financial relief, she might say—with equal accuracy—that the average (median) income is only $40,000. There is no single "correct" way to find an "average" in this situation, but it is obviously important to know which average (that is, which measure of central tendency) is being used.

When deviations in either direction from the mean are equally frequent, the distribution is said to be *symmetrical*. In such distributions, the mean and the median are likely to be close to each other in actual value, and so either can be used in describing the data. Many psychological variables have symmetrical distributions, but for variables with skewed distributions, like income, measures of central tendency must be chosen with care.

MEASURES OF VARIABILITY

In reducing an entire frequency distribution to an average score, we have discarded a lot of very useful information. Suppose the National Weather Service measures the temperature every day for a year in various cities and calculates a mean for each city. This tells us something about the city's climate, but certainly does not tell us everything. This is shown by the fact that the mean temperature in both San Francisco and Albuquerque is 56 degrees Fahrenheit. But the climates of the two cities differ considerably, as indicated in Table A.2.

The weather displays much more variability in the course of a year in Albuquerque than in San Francisco, but, of course, this variability is not reflected in the mean. One way to measure this variability is the *range*, the highest score minus the lowest. The range of temperatures in San Francisco is 15, while in Albuquerque it is 42.

A shortcoming of the range as a measure of variability is that it reflects the values of only two scores in the entire sample. As an example, consider the following distributions of ages in two college classes:

Distribution *A*: 19, 19, 19, 19, 19, 20, 25

Distribution *B*: 17, 17, 17, 20, 23, 23, 23

Intuitively, distribution *A* has less variability, since all scores but one are very close to the mean. Yet the range of scores is the same (6) in both distributions. The problem arises because the range is determined by only two of the seven scores in each distribution.

A better measure of variability would incorporate every score in the distribution rather than just two. One might think that the variability could be measured by asking how far each individual score is away from the mean, and then taking the average of these distances. This would give us a measure that we could interpret (roughly) as "on average, all the data points are only two units from the mean" (or "... three units ..." or whatever it turned out to be). The most straightforward way to measure this would be to find the arithmetic difference (by subtraction) between each score and the mean (that is, computing [score − M] for each score), and then to take the average of these differences (that is, add up all of these differences, and divide by the number of observations):

$$\frac{\text{sum of }(\text{score} - M)}{N}$$

This hypothetical measure is unworkable, however, because some of the scores are greater than the mean and some are smaller, so that the numerator is a sum of both positive and negative terms. (In fact, it turns out that the sum of the positive terms equals

TABLE A.2	TEMPERATURE DATA FOR TWO CITIES (DEGREES FAHRENHEIT)			
CITY	LOWEST MONTH	MEAN	HIGHEST MONTH	RANGE
Albuquerque, New Mexico	35	56	77	42
San Francisco, California	48	56	63	15

the sum of the negative terms, so that the expression shown above always equals zero.) The solution to this problem is simply to square all the terms in the numerator, thus making them all positive.* The resulting measure of variability is called the *variance (V)*:

$$V = \frac{\text{sum of } (\text{score} - M)^2}{N} \tag{1}$$

The calculation of the variance for the control group in the word-imagery experiment is shown in Table A.3. As the table shows, the variance is obtained by subtracting the mean (M, which equals 8) from each score, squaring each result, adding all the squared terms, and dividing the resulting sum by the total number of scores (N, which equals 10), yielding a value of 4.4.

Because deviations from the mean are squared, the variance is expressed in units different from the scores themselves. If our dependent variable were a distance, measured in centimeters, the variance would be expressed in square centimeters. As we will see in the next section, it is convenient to have a measure of variability that can be added to or subtracted from the mean; such a measure ought to be expressed in the same units as the original scores. To accomplish this end, we employ another measure of variability, the *standard deviation*, or *SD*. The standard deviation is derived from the variance by taking the square root of the variance. Thus

$$SD = \sqrt{V}$$

In our example, the standard deviation is about 2.1, the square root of the variance which is 4.4.

---

* An alternative solution would be to sum the *absolute value* of these differences, that is, to consider only the magnitude of this difference for each score, not the sign. The resulting statistic, called the average deviation, is little used, however, primarily because absolute values are not easily dealt with in certain mathematical terms that underlie statistical theory. As a result, statisticians prefer to transform negative into positive numbers by squaring them.

TABLE A.3   CALCULATING VARIANCE

SCORE	SCORE − MEAN	(SCORE − MEAN)²
8	$8 - 8 = 0$	$0^2 = 0$
11	$11 - 8 = 3$	$3^2 = 9$
6	$6 - 8 = -2$	$(-2)^2 = 4$
7	$7 - 8 = -1$	$(-1)^2 = 1$
5	$5 - 8 = -3$	$(-3)^2 = 9$
9	$9 - 8 = 1$	$1^2 = 1$
5	$5 - 8 = -3$	$(-3)^2 = 9$
9	$9 - 8 = 1$	$1^2 = 1$
9	$9 - 8 = 1$	$1^2 = 1$
11	$11 - 8 = 3$	$3^2 = 9$
		sum = 44

$$V = \frac{\text{sum of } (\text{score} - \text{mean})^2}{N} = \frac{44}{10} = 4.4$$

CONVERTING SCORES TO COMPARE THEM

Suppose a person takes two tests. One measures his memory span—how many digits he can remember after one presentation. The other test measures his reading speed—how quickly he can read a 200-word essay. It turns out that he can remember 8 digits and needs 140 seconds for the essay. Is there any way to compare these two numbers, to decide whether he can remember digits as well (or worse or equally well) as he can read? On the face of it, the question seems absurd; it seems like comparing apples and oranges. But for some purposes, we would want to compare these numbers. For example, a first step toward identifying people with dyslexia is documenting that their reading ability is markedly lower than we would expect, based on their intellectual performance in other areas. For this purpose, a comparison much like the one just sketched might be useful. But how do we compare digits-remembered to number-of-seconds-needed-for-reading?

In fact, there is a way to make this comparison, starting with an assessment of how each of these two scores compares to the scores of other persons who have been given the same two tests.

PERCENTILE RANKS

One way of doing this is by transforming each of the two scores into a *percentile rank*. The percentile rank of a score indicates the percentage of all scores that lie below that given score. Let us assume that 8 digits is the 78th percentile. This means that 78 percent of the relevant comparison group remembers fewer digits. Let us further assume that a score of 140 seconds in the reading task is the 53rd percentile of the same comparison group. We can now answer the question with which we started. This person can remember digits more effectively than he can read. By converting into percentile ranks we have rendered incompatible scores compatible, allowing us to compare the two.

STANDARD SCORES

For many statistical purposes there is an even better method of comparing scores or of interpreting the meaning of individual scores. This is to express them by reference to the mean and standard deviation of the frequency distribution of which they are a part. This is done by converting the individual scores into *standard scores* (often called *z-scores*). The formula for calculating a *z*-score is:

$$z = \frac{(\text{score} - \text{M})}{\text{SD}} \tag{2}$$

Suppose you take a test that measures aptitude for accounting and are told your score is 36. In itself, this number cannot help you decide whether to pursue or avoid a career in accounting. To interpret your score you need to know both the average score and how variable the scores are. If the mean is 30, you know you are above average, but how far above average is 6 points? This might be an extreme score or one attained by many, depending on the variability of the distribution.

Let us suppose that the standard deviation of the distribution is 3. Your *z*-score on the accounting test is (36 - 30)/3 = +2. That is, your score is 2 SDs above the mean.

But how to use this information? Let us say that you are still unsure whether to become an accountant, and so you take a screen test to help you decide whether to become an actor instead. Here, your score is 100. This is a larger number than the 36 you scored on the earlier test, but it may not reveal much acting aptitude. Suppose the mean score on the screen test is 80, and the standard deviation is 20; then your *z*-score is (100 − 80)/20 = +1. In acting aptitude, you are 1 SD above the mean (that is, *z* = +1)—above average but not by much. In accounting aptitude, you are 2 SDs above the mean (that is, $z = +2$), and so the use of z-scores makes your relative abilities clear.

Percentile rank and a z-score give similar information, but, to convert one into the other, we need a bit more information.

THE NORMAL DISTRIBUTION

Frequency histograms can have a wide variety of shapes, but many variables that interest psychologists have a **normal distribution** (often called a **normal curve**), which is a symmetrical distribution of the shape shown in Figure A.3. (For more on normal curves, see Chapter 14.) The graph is smooth, unlike the histogram in Figure A.1, because it describes the distribution of scores from a very large sample. The normal curve is bell shaped, with most of its scores near the mean; the farther a score is from the mean, the less likely it is to occur. Among the many variables whose distributions are approximately normal are IQ, scholastic aptitude test (SAT) scores, and women's heights (see Table A.4).*

These three variables—IQ, SAT score, and height—obviously cannot literally have the same distribution, since their means and standard deviations are different (Table A.4 gives plausible values for them). In what sense, then, can they all be said to be normally distributed? The answer is that the shape of the distributions for all these variables is the same. For example, an IQ of 115 is 15 points, or 1 SD, above the IQ mean of 100; a height of 165 centimeters is 5 centimeters, or 1 SD, above the height mean of 160 centimeters. Both scores, therefore, have z-scores of 1. And crucially, the percentage of heights between 160 and 165 centimeters is the same as the percentage of IQ scores between 100 and 115, that is, 34 percent. This is true not just for these two variables, but in general: it is the percentage of scores that lie between the mean and 1 SD above the mean for any normally distributed variable.

THE PERCENTILE RANK OF A Z-SCORE

In fact, this point can be put more generally: each normal curve has its own mean and its own standard deviation. But all normal curves have the same shape, and, as a result, the percentage of scores that fall between the mean and +1 standard deviation (and so have z-scores between 0 and 1.0) is always the same: 34 percent. Likewise, for all normal curves, the percentage of the scores that fall between +1 standard deviation and +2

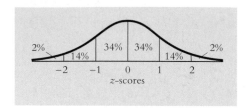

A.3   Normal distribution   *Values taken from any normally distributed variable (such as those presented in Table A.4) can be converted to z-scores by the formula z = (score – M)/(SD). The figure shows graphically the proportions that fall between various values of z.*

---

* Men's heights are also normally distributed, but the distribution of the heights of *all* adults is not. Such a distribution would have two peaks, one for the modal height of each sex, and would thus be shaped quite differently from the normal curve. Distributions with two modes are called *bimodal*.

TABLE A.4	NORMALLY DISTRIBUTED VARIABLES						
			VALUES CORRESPOINDING TO SPECIFIC Z-SCORES				
VARIABLE	MEAN	STANDARD DEVIATION	−2	−1	0	1	2
IQ	100	15	70	85	100	115	130
SAT	500	100	300	400	500	600	700
Height (women)	160 cm	5 cm	150	155	160	165	170

standard deviations (and so have z-scores between 1.0 and 2.0) is always the same: 14 percent. And, since normal curves are symmetrical, the same proportions hold for below the mean (and so 34 percent of the scores have z-scores between 0 and −1, and so on). These relationships are illustrated in Figure A.3.

These facts allow us to convert any z-score directly into a percentile rank. A z-score of 1 has a percentile rank of 84. That is, 84 percent of all the scores are below this particular score. (This is true because 34 percent of the scores lie between the mean and z = 1, and 50 percent of the scores lie blow the mean). Likewise, a z-score of −1 (1 SD below the mean) corresponds, in a normal distribution, to a percentile rank of 16: only 16 percent of the scores are lower. And so on.

HOW THE NORMAL CURVE ARISES

Why should variables such as height or IQ (and many others) form distributions that have this particular shape? Mathematicians have shown that whenever a given variable is the sum of many smaller variables, its distribution will be close to that of the normal curve. One example is lifetime earnings—obviously the sum of what one has earned on many prior occasions. A different example is height. Height can be thought of as the sum of the contributions of the many genes and the many environmental factors that influence this trait; it, therefore, satisfies the general condition. The basic idea is that the many different factors that influence a given measure (such as the genes for height) operate independently of the others, and, for each of these factors, it is a matter of chance whether the factor applies to a particular individual or not. Thus, if someone's father had a certain height-promoting gene on one chromosome but not on the other chromosome in the pair, then it would literally be a matter of chance whether the person inherited this gene or not (and likewise for each of the other genes—and surely there are many—that determine height). The person's height would also depend on accidents in his experience—for example, whether, just by bad luck, he happened to catch the flu at an age that interrupted what would have otherwise been a strong growth spurt.

In essence, then, we can think of each person's height as dependent on a succession of coin tosses, with each toss describing whether that person received the height-promoting factor or not—inherited the gene or not, got the flu at just the wrong time or not, and so on. Of course, each factor contributes its own increment to the person's height, and so his ultimate height depends on how many of these factors fell the right way. Thus, if we want to predict the person's height, we need to explore the (relatively simple) mathematics that describe how these chance events unfold.

Let us imagine that someone literally does toss a coin over and over, with each head corresponding to a factor that tends to increase height and each tail to a factor that tends to diminish it. Predicting the person's height, therefore, would be equivalent to predicting how many heads, in total, the person will obtain after a certain number of tosses. If the coin is tossed only once, then there will be either 0 heads or 1 head, and these are equally likely. The resulting distribution is shown in the top panel of Figure A.4.

If the number of tosses (which we will call N) is 2, then 0, 1, or 2 heads can arise. However, not all these outcomes are equally likely: 0 heads come up only if the sequence tail-tail (TT) occurs; 2 heads only if head-head (HH) occurs; but 1 head results from either HT or TH. The distribution of heads for N = 2 is shown in the second panel of Figure A.4. The area above 1 head has been subdivided into two equal parts, one for each possible sequence containing a single head.*

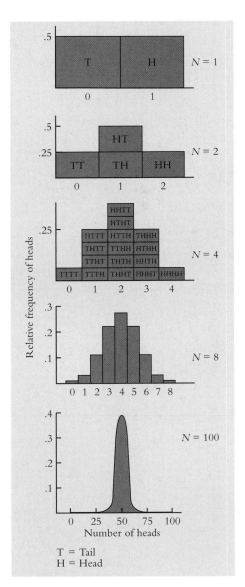

A.4 **Histograms showing expected number of heads in tossing a fair coin N times**   *In successive panels, N = 1, 2, 4, and 8. The bottom panel illustrates the case when N = 100 and shows a smoothed curve.*

---

* The distribution of the number of heads is called the *binomial distribution*, because of its relation to the binomial theorem: the number of head-tail sequences that can lead to k heads is the $(k + 1)$st coefficient of $(a + b)^N$.

As *N* increases, the distribution of the number of heads looks more and more like the normal distribution, as the subsequent panels of Figure A.4 show. When *N* becomes as large as the number of factors that determine height, the distribution of the number of heads is virtually identical to the normal distribution, and this gives us just the claim we were after: as we have described, this logic of coin tossing corresponds reasonably well to the logic of the factors governing height, and so, just as the distribution of coin tosses will (with enough tosses) be normally distributed, so will height. The same logic applies to many other measures of interest to psychologists—the distribution of people's intelligence or personality traits, the distribution of response times in an experimental procedure, the distribution of students' scores on a mid-term exam. These, too, are influenced by a succession of chance factors, and so, just like the coin tosses, they will be normally distributed.

DESCRIBING THE RELATION BETWEEN TWO VARIABLES: CORRELATION

So far, we have focused on how psychologists measure a single variable—what scales they use, how they measure the variable's average or its variability. In general, though, investigators want to do more than this—they want to ask how two (or more) variables are related to each other. Is there a relationship between the sex of a child (the independent variable) and how physically aggressive (the dependent variable) that child is? Is there a relationship between using visual imagery (the independent variable) and memory (the dependent variable)? One way to measure this relationship is by examining the *correlation* between the two variables.*

POSITIVE AND NEGATIVE CORRELATION

Imagine that a manager of a taxicab company wants to identify drivers who will earn relatively large amounts of money (for themselves and, of course, for the company). The manager makes the plausible guess that one relevant factor is the driver's knowledge of the local geography, so she devises an appropriate test of street names, routes from place to place, and so on, and administers the test to each driver. The question is whether this test score is related to the driver's job performance as measured by his weekly earnings. To decide, the manager has to find out whether there is a correlation between the test score and the earnings—that is, whether they tend to vary together.

In the taxicab example, the two variables will probably be positively correlated—as the independent variable (test score) increases, the dependent variable (earnings) will generally increase too. But other variables may be negatively correlated—when one increases, the other will tend to decrease. An example is a phenomenon called Zipf's law, which states that words that occur frequently in a language tend to be relatively short. The two variables—word length and word frequency—are negatively correlated, since one variable tends to increase as the other decreases.

---

* In Chapter 1, we contrasted experimental and correlational designs; correlational designs are those which exploit differences that exist independently of the investigator's manipulations. Thus a comparison between boys and girls is a correlational design (because the sex difference certainly exists independently of the investigator's procedures), and so is a comparison between, say, young children and old children. All of this is different from the *statistical technique* that computes correlations. The statistic is just a specific means of exploring the relationship between two variables. Correlational designs often use correlational statistics, but often do not.

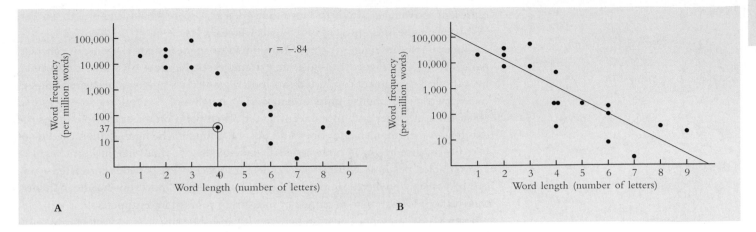

A.5 Scatter plot of a negative correlation between word length and word frequency

Correlational data are often displayed in a *scatter plot* (or *scatter diagram*) in which values of one variable are shown on the *x*-axis and variables of the other on the *y*-axis. Figure A.5A is a scatter plot of word frequency versus word length for the words in this sentence.* Each word is represented by a single point. An example is provided by the word *plot*, which is four letters long and occurs with a frequency of 37 times per million words of English text (and is represented by the circled dot). The points on the graph display a tendency to decrease on one variable as they increase on the other, although the relation is by no means perfect.

It is helpful to draw a line through the various points in a scatter plot that comes as close as possible to all of them (Figure A.5B). The line is called a *line of best fit*, and it indicates the general trend of the data. Here, the line slopes downward because the correlation between the variables is negative.

The three panels of Figure A.6 are scatter plots showing the relations between other pairs of variables. In Figure A.6A hypothetical data from the taxicab example show that there is a positive correlation between test score and earnings (since the line of best fit slopes upward). Test score is not a perfect predictor of on-the-job performance, however, since the points are fairly widely scattered around the line. Points above the line

A.6 Scatter plots of various correlations (A) The scatter plot and line of best fit show a positive correlation between a taxi-driving test and earnings. (B) A perfect positive correlation. The line of best fit passes through all the points. (C) A correlation of zero. The line of best fit is horizontal.

*There is no point for the "word" A.5A in this sentence. The frequencies of the other words are taken from H. Kucera and W. N. Francis, *Computational Analysis of Present-Day American English* (Providence, R. I.: Brown University Press, 1967).

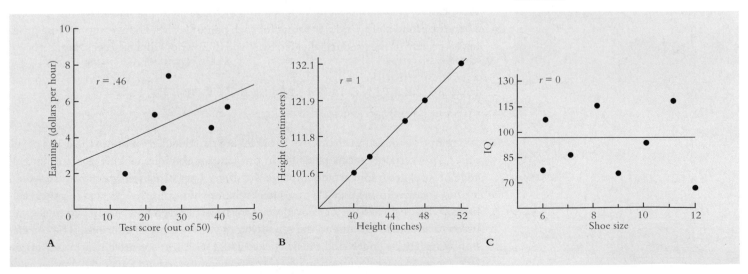

represent individuals who earn more than their test score would lead one to predict; points below the line represent individuals who earn less.

The examples in Figures A.5 and A.6A illustrate moderate correlations; in contrast, panels B and C of Figure A.6 illustrate extreme cases. Figure A.6B shows data from a hypothetical experiment conducted in a fourth-grade class to illustrate the relation between metric and English units of length. The heights of five children are measured twice, once in inches and once in centimeters; each point on the scatter plot gives the two height measurements for one child. All the points in the figure fall on the line of best fit, because height in centimeters always equals 2.54 times height in inches. The two variables, height in centimeters and height in inches, are perfectly correlated—one can be perfectly predicted from the other. Thus, once you know your height in inches, there is no information to be gained by measuring yourself in centimeters.

Figure A.6C presents a relation between IQ and shoe size. These variables are unrelated to each other; people with big feet have neither a higher nor a lower IQ than people with small feet. The line of best fit is therefore horizontal: The best guess of an individual's IQ is the same no matter what his or her shoe size—it is the mean IQ of the population.

THE CORRELATION COEFFICIENT

Correlations are usually described by a *correlation coefficient*, denoted *r*, a number that expresses the strength and the direction of the correlation. For positive correlations, *r* is positive; for negative correlations, it is negative; for variables that are completely uncorrelated, *r* equals 0. The largest positive value *r* can have is +1.00, which represents a perfect correlation (as in Figure A.6B); the largest possible negative value is −1.00, which is also a perfect correlation. The closer the points in a scatter plot come to falling on the line of best fit, the nearer *r* will be to +1.00 or −1.00 and the more confident we can be in predicting scores on one variable from scores on the other. The values of *r* for the scatter plots in Figures A.5 and A.6A are given on the figures.

The method for calculating *r* between two variables, *X* and *Y*, is shown in Table A.5 (on the next page). The formula is:

$$r = \frac{\text{sum}\,(z_x z_y)}{N} \tag{3}$$

The variable z_x is the z-score corresponding to *X*; z_y is the z-score corresponding to *Y*. To find *r*, each *X* and *Y* score must first be converted to a z-score by subtracting the mean for that variable and then dividing by the standard deviation for the variable. Then the product of z_x and z_y is found for each pair of scores. The average of these products (the sum of the products divided by *N*, the number of pairs of scores) is *r*.

INTERPRETING AND MISINTERPRETING CORRELATIONS

It is tempting to assume that if two variables are correlated, then one is the cause of the other. This certainly seems plausible in our taxicab example, in which greater knowledge of local geography would improve the driver's performance, which in turn would lead to greater earnings. Cause-and-effect relationships are also reflected in other real-life correlations. There is, for example, a correlation between how much loud music you listen to as an adolescent and the sensitivity of your hearing in later life. (The correlation is negative—more loud music is associated with less sensitive hearing.) And, in fact, there is a causal connection here, because listening to loud music can damage your

TABLE A.5   CALCULATION OF THE CORRELATION COEFFICIENT

1. Data (from Figure A.6A).

Test score (X)	Earnings (Y)
45	6
25	2
15	3
40	5
25	6
30	8

2. Find the mean and standard deviation for X and Y.

For X, mean $= 30$, standard deviation $= 10$
For Y, mean $= 5$, standard deviation $= 2$

3. Convert each X and each Y to a z-score, using $z = \dfrac{(\text{score} - M)}{SD}$

X	Y	z-score for X (z_x)	z-score for Y (z_y)	$z_x z_y$
45	6	1.5	0.5	0.75
25	2	−0.5	−1.5	0.75
15	3	−1.5	−1.0	1.50
40	5	1.0	0.0	0.00
25	6	−0.5	0.5	−0.25
30	8	0.0	1.5	0.00
				2.75

4. Find the product $z_x z_y$ for each pair of scores.

5. $r = \dfrac{\text{sum } (z_x z_y)}{N} = \dfrac{2.75}{6} = .46$

hearing. Similarly, there is a correlation between the vividness of your visual imagery while awake and how often you remember your dreams on awakening (Cory, Ormiston, Simmel, & Dainoff, 1975). This correlation is positive—greater vividness is associated with more frequent dream recall. And here, too, there may be a causal connection: vivid waking imagery creates a mental perspective similar to the nighttime experience of dreaming, and this similarity of perspective facilitates recall.

However, as we emphasized in Chapter 1 and again in many other contexts in this book, often a correlation does *not* indicate a cause-and-effect relationship, or, if it does, the direction of causation is ambiguous. For example, consider the negative correlation between obesity and life expectancy: people who are overweight tend to die younger than people who are not overweight. For many years, this was interpreted as a cause-and-effect relationship: being overweight caused early death. Newer evidence, however, suggests that this is incorrect. Instead, it turns out that obesity is often associated with inactivity, and inactivity is what causes the problems. Overweight people who are active actually have lower mortality rates than normal-weight people who are sedentary (Kampert, Blair, Barlow, & Kohl, 1996).

Thus, a correlation, by itself, cannot indicate a cause-and-effect relationship. Some correlations do indicate causation, but many do not. As a result, correlational results are important and instructive but must be interpreted with care.

INTERPRETING THE DATA

Any data collected in the real world contain variability, and data in psychology are no exception. In memory experiments, for example, different research participants recall different numbers of items, and the same participant is likely to perform differently if tested again later. But investigators nonetheless hope to draw general conclusions from data despite this variability. Nor is variability necessarily the enemy, because as we shall see, understanding the sources of variability in one's data can provide insights into the factors that influence the data.

Let us first consider how the pattern of variability can be used as a source of information concerning why the data are as they are. From this base, we will turn to the specific procedures that researchers use in implementing this logic, as they seek to ask whether their data are reliable or not and whether their data will support their conclusions or not. (Some readers may prefer to focus just on the procedures necessary for statistical analysis, rather than the underlying conceptualization; those readers can skip ahead to the heading, "Hypothesis testing.")

ACCOUNTING FOR VARIABILITY

As an example of how variability may be explained, consider a person shooting a pistol at a target. Although she always aims at the bull's-eye, the shots scatter around it (Figure A.7A). Assuming that the mean is the bull's-eye, the variance of these shots is the average squared deviation of the shots from the center. Suppose we find this variance to be 100; we next must explain it.

If the shooting was done outdoors, the wind may have increased the spread; moving the shooter to an indoor shooting range produces the tighter grouping shown in Figure A.7B. The new variance is 80, a reduction of 20 percent. This means that the wind accounts for 20 percent of the original variance.

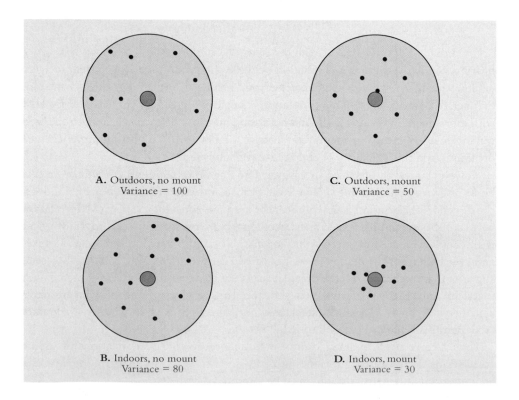

A. Outdoors, no mount
Variance = 100

C. Outdoors, mount
Variance = 50

B. Indoors, no mount
Variance = 80

D. Indoors, mount
Variance = 30

A.7 Results of target shooting under several conditions In each case, the bull's-eye is the mean, and the variance is the average squared deviation of the shots from the bull's-eye.

In addition, some of the initial variance may have resulted from the unsteady hand of the shooter, so we now mount the gun (although still leaving it outdoors). This yields a variance of 50 (Figure A.7C), a reduction of 50 percent. So 50 percent of the variance can be attributed to the shaky hand of the shooter. To find out how much of the variance can be explained by both the wind and the shaking, we mount the gun and move it indoors; now we may find a variance of only 30 (Figure A.7D). This means we have explained 70 percent of the variance, leaving 30 percent unaccounted for.*

But not all changes in the situation will reduce the variance. For example, if we find that providing the shooter with earmuffs leaves the variance unchanged, we know that none of the original variance was due to the noise of the pistol.

VARIANCE AND EXPERIMENTS

Figure A.8 shows how this approach can be applied to the experiment on visual imagery described earlier (see pp. A4–A5). Figure A.8A shows the distribution of scores for all twenty people in the experiment lumped together; the total variance of this overall distribution is 6.25. But as we saw, the ten members of the experimental group had been instructed to use visual imagery in memorizing, whereas the ten members of the control group were given no special instructions. How much of the overall variance can be explained by the difference in these instructions? In

*We are grateful to Paul Rozin for suggesting this example.

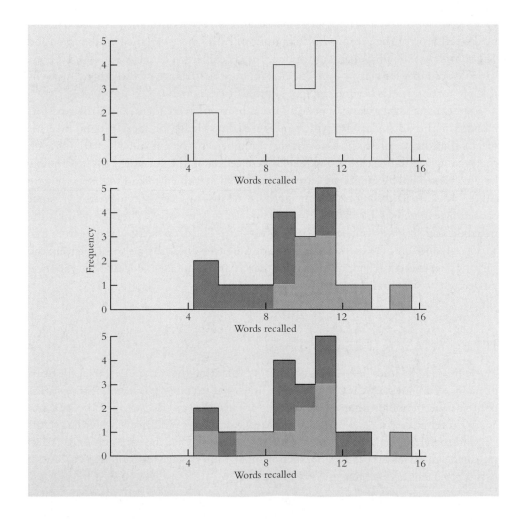

A.8 Accounting for variance in an experiment on memorizing   (A) The distribution of number of words recalled is shown for all twenty participants lumped together; the variance of this distribution is 6.25. (B) The distributions of the experimental and control groups are displayed separately. The number of words recalled by the group that received imagery instructions is shown in blue; the number recalled by the control group that received no special instructions is shown in red. Within each of these groups, the variance is about 4.00. (C) The distribution of words recalled is plotted separately for men and women regardless of how they were instructed. Blue indicates the number of words recalled by women, red the number recalled by men. The variance is 6.25.

Figure A.8B, the distributions are no longer lumped together. They are instead presented as two separate histograms; the people who received imagery instructions are shown in blue, while those who did not are indicated in red. As the figure shows, there is less variability within either the imagery group or the control group than within the overall distribution that lumped both kinds of participants together. While the variance in the overall distribution is 6.25, the variance within the two subgroups averages to only 4.0. We conclude that the difference between the two sets of instructions accounted for 36 percent of the variance and that 64 percent $(4 \div 6.25)$ still remains unexplained.

Figure A.8C shows a situation in which an independent variable (in this case, sex) accounts for little or none of the variance. In this figure, the participants' scores are again presented as two histograms—separately depicting the scores of the men and the women (regardless of whether they were instructed to use imagery or not). The men's scores are shown in red, the women's in blue. Now the variance of the two subgroups (that is, men versus women) averages to 6.25, a value identical to that found for the overall distribution. We conclude that the participant's sex accounts for none of the overall variance in recall.

VARIANCE AND CORRELATION

The technique of explaining the variance in one variable by attributing it to the effect of another variable can also be applied to correlational studies. Here, the values of one variable are explained (that is, accounted for) when the values of the other variable are known. Recall the taxicab example, in which a correlation of +.46 was found between taxi drivers' earnings and their scores on an aptitude test. Since the correlation is neither +1.00 nor 0, some but not all of the variance in job performance can be explained by the test scores. The greater the magnitude of r, the more variance is accounted for. The rule is that the proportion of variance that is explained equals r^2. If $r = +.46$, one variable accounts for $(.46)^2 = .21$ (21 percent) of the variance of the other. (Just why this proportion is r^2 is beyond the scope of this discussion.)

To put this another way, suppose all the cab drivers were identical in their performance on the aptitude test, which measured knowledge of local geography. This means that the variance on that variable would be zero. As a result, the variability on the second variable, earnings, would be reduced, and the formula tells us by how much. The original variance on earnings can be determined from the data in Figure A.6A. It is 4. Its correlation with the aptitude test is +.46. If we remove the variance caused by differences in how much the cab drivers know about local geography, the variability on earnings will be $4 - (.46)^2 \times 4 = 3.16$. The drop in the variance from 4 to 3.16 is a reduction of 21 percent. So the aptitude test does help us to predict taxicab earnings, for it accounts for 21 percent of the variance. But a good deal of the variance, 79 percent, is still unexplained.

HYPOTHESIS TESTING

The logic we have described—cast in terms of explaining the variance—lies at the heart of many techniques used for statistical analysis. For example, we saw that the participant's sex accounts for none of the overall variance in recall in our (hypothetical) imagery experiment; this is what tells us that we can reject the hypothesis that sex is relevant to performance in this task. Conversely, we saw that the variance is reduced if we divide the data according to experimental group (imagery group versus control group); this tells us that imagery is relevant here.

But how exactly is this logic put into practice? In this section, we tackle this question by means of some simple examples.*

Much behavioral research attempts to answer questions such as: Does the amount of food a person eats depend on the effort required to eat it? Can people learn while they are sleeping? Is drug *X* more effective than drug *Y*? Each of these questions suggests an experiment.

TESTING HYPOTHESES ABOUT SINGLE SCORES

We will begin by testing a hypothesis about single scores. Consider the problem in identifying people with dyslexia. As one step in identifying such people, we might give each person a test of reading comprehension. If the person's score was unusually low, this might be an indication of dyslexia (although several other tests would be needed to confirm this possibility). The question, though, is how low a score must be before it is "unusually low."

We know from the start that reading scores among nondyslexic readers vary—some read rather well, others read at some middle level, and some read rather poorly. As a result, it is possible that a poor reader is not dyslexic at all; he is simply at the low end of the normal range for reading skills. How can we evaluate this possibility?

Suppose we tested a large number of nondyslexic readers and found that the average reading score is 50, that the standard deviation of these scores is 10, and that the scores are normally distributed. We now look at the reading score from an individual we are concerned about. Let us say that her score is 40. How likely is it that she has dyslexia? This is equivalent to asking: How *un*likely is a score of 40 within the distribution of scores obtained by the general population (that is, a population of people who we believe are *not* dyslexic)? To answer these questions, we can convert her score to a *z*-score by computing its distance from the mean and dividing this difference by the standard deviation. The resulting *z*-score is $(40 - 50)/10$ or -1 SD. Since the distribution is normal, Figure A.3 tells us that 16 percent of the general population would score as low or even lower than this. Under the circumstances, it's plausible that a score of 40 does not indicate dyslexia; this score is common enough even among people without dyslexia. Our conclusion might be different, though, if the score were 30 or below. For then the *z*-score would be $(30 - 50)/10$ or -2, 2 SDs below the mean for the general population. Only 2 percent of the population obtain scores this low, and so we might now feel more comfortable concluding that a person with this particular score is likely not to be drawn from the general population. Instead, we might conclude that this score is likely to have been drawn from a *different* population—the population of people who do in fact suffer from dyslexia.

In this example we have to decide between two hypotheses about this individual's score. One hypothesis is that the score was drawn from the population of nondyslexic readers. True, a score of 40 or even 30 might seem atypical, but, on this view, this is

---

* The logic of explaining variance is crucial for most statistical procedures, but this logic turns out to be most visible with more complicated cases—for example, cases involving the comparison of two different groups (as in the example illustrated in Figure A.8), or the analysis of experiments in which two variables are manipulated. (For example, an experimenter might ask whether imagery instructions are as helpful for children as they are for adults; in this case, the experiment's design would have four groups: children and adults, and, then, within each of these groups, some participants given imagery instructions and some not). In the following pages, however, we have chosen to use simpler examples. This makes the underlying logic, in terms of explaining the variance, a bit less obvious, but it also makes the statistical procedures themselves much easier to grasp!

merely a reflection of the ordinary variability around the mean of the broader population. This is the ***null hypothesis***, the hypothesis that there really is no systematic difference between the particular observation we are interested in and other observations we have made on other occasions and with other individuals. The alternative hypothesis is that the null hypothesis is *false* and that the score now before us is far enough away from the other scores for us to conclude that it did not arise by chance and is instead in a different category (in our example, the category of scores obtained by people with dyslexia).

As we have already suggested, the choice between these two hypotheses turns out to be a matter of probabilities. In essence, we start by adopting the working assumption that the null hypothesis is correct, and ask, within this assumption, what the probability would be of obtaining the score we have before us. If this probability—computed from the z-score—is relatively high (that is, if this score would be observed relatively often if the null hypothesis were correct), we conclude that the score poses no challenge to the null hypothesis, and so we accept the null hypothesis as probably correct. If, on the other hand, we start by assuming the null hypothesis, but then calculate that the score would be extremely rare under the null hypothesis, then we have two choices: either we have just observed an extremely rare event or the null hypothesis is false. Since the first of these choices is, by definition, very unlikely, we opt for the second choice.

With this logic, all depends on the z-score associated with our observation, and so, in the context of hypothesis testing, the z-score is referred to as the ***critical ratio***. Behavioral scientists generally stipulate a critical ratio of 2 as the cutoff point. If it is 2 or more, they generally reject the null hypothesis and conclude that the test observation is systematically different from the control observations. Critical ratios of 2 or more are considered ***statistically reliable***, which is just another way of saying that the null hypothesis can be rejected. Critical ratios of less than 2 are considered too small to allow the rejection of the null hypothesis.*

This general procedure is not foolproof. It is certainly possible for an individual to have a reading score of 30 (a critical ratio of 2) or even lower without being dyslexic. According to Figure A.3, this will happen about 2 percent of the time. Raising the cutoff value to a critical ratio of 3 or 4 would make such errors less common but would not eliminate them entirely; furthermore, raising the critical value might mean failure to detect some individuals with dyslexia. One of the important consequences of the variability in psychological data can be seen here: the investigator who has to decide between two interpretations of the data (the null hypothesis and the alternative hypothesis) cannot be correct all the time. Using statistics, in other words, is a matter of playing the odds.

TESTING HYPOTHESES ABOUT MEANS

In the preceding discussion, our concern was with hypotheses about single scores. We now turn to the more commonly encountered problems in which the hypotheses involve means.

In many experiments, the investigator compares two or more groups—participants tested with or without a drug, with or without imagery instructions, and so on. Suppose we get a difference between the groups. How do we decide whether the difference is genuine rather than due merely to chance?

---

* Many authors use the term *statistically significant* instead of *statistically reliable*, and the decision process we are describing is sometimes referred to as *significance testing*. However, the term we are using, *reliability*, seems preferable for two reasons. First, what the statistics are measuring really is a matter of reliability—that is, whether the observation before us is likely to be an accident (and so probably would not reappear if we ran the test again), or whether it is reliable (and so would reappear if we retested). Second, the term *significance* implies that a result is important, consequential, worth publicizing. The statistical tests tell us none of those things, and so a "statistically significant" result might, in truth, be entirely insignificant in the eyes of the world! Hence the label of *statistical significance* seems a misnomer.

TABLE A.6 NUMBER OF ITEMS RECALLED WITH AND WITHOUT IMAGERY INSTRUCTION, FOR TEN PARTICIPANTS

SUBJECT	SCORE WITH IMAGERY	SCORE WITHOUT IMAGERY	IMPROVEMENT
Alphonse	11	5	6
Betsy	15	9	6
Cheryl	11	5	6
Davis	9	9	0
Earl	13	6	7
Fred	10	11	−1
Germaine	11	8	3
Hortense	10	11	−1
Imogene	8	7	1
Jerry	12	9	3
Mean	11	8	3

$$\text{Variance of improvement scores} = \frac{\text{sum of (score} - 3)^2}{10} = 8.8$$

$$\text{Standard deviation of improvement scores} = \sqrt{8.8} = 2.97$$

Let us return to the experiment in which memory for words was tested with and without instructions to imagine the items. To simplify, we will here consider a modified version of the experiment in which the same participants serve in both the imagery and the nonimagery conditions. Each participant memorizes a list of 20 words without instructions, then memorizes a second list of 20 words under instructions to visualize. What we want to know is whether the participants show any improvement with the imagery instructions. There is no separate control group in this experiment. Because each person's score while using imagery can be compared with his score without using imagery, each provides his own control.*

Table A.6 gives data for the ten participants in the experiment. For each one, the table lists the number of words recalled without imagery instructions, the number recalled with such instructions, and the improvement (the difference between the two scores). The mean improvement overall is 3 words, from a mean of 8 words recalled without imagery to a mean of 11 words with imagery. But note that this does not hold for all participants. For example, for Fred and Hortense, the "improvement" is negative: they both do better without imagery instructions. But is there an imagery facilitation effect overall? Put in other words, is the difference between the two conditions statistically reliable?

---

* This sort of design, in which participants serve in more than one condition, is called a *within-subjects design*, in contrast to a *between-subjects design* in which different people serve in the different conditions. Within-subjects designs have certain advantages; among them, we can obviously be certain that the participants in one group are identical to the participants in the other group. But within-subjects designs also introduce their own complications. For example, if the participants serve in one condition first, then in the other condition, then this creates a confound: any differences observed might be due to the effects of practice, which obviously benefits the second condition. For present purposes, we ignore these complications (and also the steps needed to control for this confound). For more on this issue, though, see Chapter 1. In any case, the logic of the statistics here is very similar to the logic relevant to between-subjects designs, and so we will use this (simpler) case as a way to convey this logic.

As one way to approach this question, note that, ultimately, we are not trying to draw conclusions about the specific ten people we ran in the experiment. Instead, we want to draw broader conclusions, about the population at large. One way to make sure our data justify such broad conclusions would be to test the entire population in our study—every adult in North America, justifying claims about North America, or every adult in Europe, justifying claims about Europe, and so on.

Of course, we could not run these huge studies—they would require absurd amounts of time and effort. What we do instead is test a sample of individuals, and so we observe a mean *for this sample*. But can we extrapolate from this sample? It is useful to keep in mind here that we might easily have run a different sample, and it would have produced its own mean, or some other sample, with its own mean, and on and on and on for the vast number of samples we could have tested. Each sample would produce a mean (called, for obvious reasons, a *sample mean*), and, if we did in fact run sample after sample, we would end up with a set of sample means. From that set—from the distribution of sample means—we could compute a mean of all the means, and this would tell us something about the broader population (and so this mean of means, averaging together all the samples we might gather, is called the *population mean*). We could also ask how variable this set is—by computing a standard deviation for the distribution of sample means.

What we really want to ask, therefore, is whether the sample mean we actually obtained (based on the data in Table A.6) is representative of the population mean—the average that we would observe if we ran sample after sample after sample and averaged them all together. The possibility that we hope for is that our sample mean *is* representative of this larger group, which is equivalent to claiming that we would get roughly the same result if we were to do the experiment a second, third, or fourth time. A different possibility, though, is that our sample mean is just a lucky accident—showing an apparent difference between the conditions that would not show up reliably if we performed the experiment again and again. This latter possibility is, in this context, the null hypothesis. As we mentioned, the null hypothesis is, in general, a claim that there is no systematic difference between the observations we are comparing. In the dyslexia case, this was a claim that the person we had tested was not systematically different from the broader population. In the present case, it is a claim that there is no systematic difference between memory with imagery and memory without. It is, therefore, the claim that, if we conducted the memory experiment again and again, we would not observe a difference, and therefore the difference that has emerged in our data is just a fluke.

We test the null hypothesis in the memory experiment in the same way that we did in our dyslexia example. In that example, we computed a critical ratio (that is, a *z*-score) based on the difference between the score we had actually observed and the mean that was predicted by the null hypothesis. The null hypothesis claimed that the individual we tested was not dyslexic, and so the relevant mean was the mean for the broad population of nondyslexics. In the present example, we follow the same logic. The null hypothesis claims that, if we run the test over and over, we will not observe a difference, and so the mean we should expect, on this hypothesis, is zero. (In other words, the null hypothesis claims that the population mean, in this case the mean difference between the imagery and control conditions, is zero.)

The formula we will use for the present case is the standard one:

$$Z = \frac{(\text{score} - \text{M})}{\text{SD}}$$

The score we will use in this calculation will be the sample mean we actually obtained—a value of 3 (see Table A.6). The mean (M) will be the mean assumed by the null hypothesis—in this case, zero. But what is the denominator? It is the standard deviation from the set of all the sample means, a measure of how variable the data would be as we move from one sample to another. This value—the standard deviation of a distribution of sample means—is called the *standard error (SE)* of the mean. Its value is determined by two factors: the standard deviation of the sample and the size of that sample. Specifically,

$$SE = \frac{SD}{\sqrt{N-1}} \tag{4}$$

Why this formula takes this particular form is beyond the scope of our discussion. Two elements of the formula should, however, seem sensible. First, in calculating the standard error, all we have to go on in most cases is information about the actual sample we have observed. We have no information about all those other samples that we might have tested (but actually did not!). Therefore, it is plausible that our estimate of how variable the data would be in general (and this is, of course, exactly what the standard error measures) depends heavily on how variable our original sample is (that is, what the standard deviation of the sample measures). It should, in other words, be no surprise that the standard error is proportional to the standard deviation.

Second, it should also seem right that the standard error goes down as the size of our particular sample goes up. If our sample included only two or three observations, then it is entirely likely that our sample mean has been drawn off by one or more atypical scores. If our sample was larger, then the impact of these atypical scores would be diluted within the larger data set. In that case, our sample would more likely be reflective of the population at large, and our estimate of the standard error is correspondingly lowered.

In any case, with the standard error now defined, we can conclude our analysis of the results of our memorization experiment. The critical ratio to be evaluated is

$$\text{Critical ratio} = \frac{\text{obtained sample mean} - \text{population mean}}{SE}$$

Since the population mean is assumed to be zero (by the null hypothesis), this expression becomes

$$\text{Critical ratio} = \frac{\text{obtained sample mean}}{SE} \tag{5}$$

To compute the standard error, we first find the standard deviation of the imagery scores; this turns out to be 2.97, as shown in Table A.6. Then equation (4) tells us

$$SE = \frac{SD}{\sqrt{N-1}} = \frac{2.97}{\sqrt{10-1}} = .99$$

The critical ratio is now the obtained mean difference divided by the standard error, or 3/.99 = 3.03. This is clearly larger than 2.0, so we conclude that the observed difference in memory between the imagery and control conditions probably should not be attributed to chance. Said differently, the sample we have run (which does show a difference between conditions) is probably representative of the data we would get if we ran the experiment again, with a new group of participants and a new set of stimuli. Thus the pattern is deemed reliable, and so we can conclude that giving visual imagery instructions does improve recall.*

CONFIDENCE INTERVALS

In using statistics to test hypotheses, we ask whether a certain sample mean could have been drawn by chance from a set of sample means distributed around some assumed population mean. (When testing the null hypothesis, this assumed population mean is zero.) But there is another way of phrasing the entire issue: given a sample of data with its own sample mean, can we extrapolate from this in a fashion that allows us to specify, with reasonable confidence, what the possible range of values might be for the population mean? If we know the standard error of the mean, the answer is yes. We have already seen that about 2 percent of the scores in a normal distribution are more than 2 SDs above the distribution's mean (see Figure A.3). Similarly, about 2 percent of the scores have values lower than 2 SDs below the mean. Since this is so, we can conclude that the chances are roughly 96 in 100 that the population mean is within an interval whose largest value is 2 SEs above the sample mean and whose lowest value is 2 SEs below. Because we can be fairly (96 percent) confident that the actual population mean will fall within this specified range, it is often called the *confidence interval*.

As an example, consider the prediction of elections. During election campaigns, polling organizations report the current standing of various candidates by statements such as the following: "In a poll of 1,000 registered voters, 57 percent favored candidate Smith; the margin of error was 3 percent." This margin of error is the confidence interval around the proportion (that is, ±3 percent).

To determine this confidence interval, the pollsters compute the standard error of the proportion they found (in this case, .57). This standard error is analogous to the standard error of a mean we discussed in the previous section. Given an N of 1,000,

---

* There are several simplifications in this account. One is that the critical ratio described here does not have an exactly normal distribution. When the sample size is large, this effect is unimportant, but for small samples (like the one in the example) they can be material. To deal with these and related problems, statisticians often use measures that refer to distributions other than the normal one. An example is the *t*-test, a kind of critical ratio based on what is called the *t*-distribution.

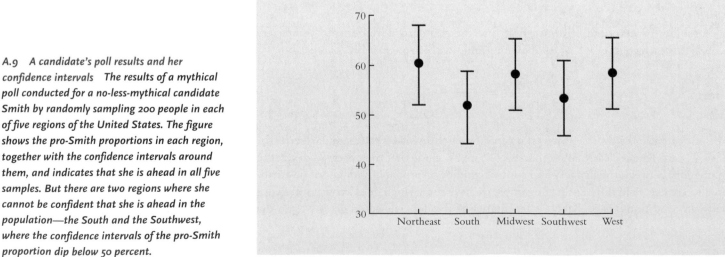

A.9 A candidate's poll results and her confidence intervals *The results of a mythical poll conducted for a no-less-mythical candidate Smith by randomly sampling 200 people in each of five regions of the United States. The figure shows the pro-Smith proportions in each region, together with the confidence intervals around them, and indicates that she is ahead in all five samples. But there are two regions where she cannot be confident that she is ahead in the population—the South and the Southwest, where the confidence intervals of the pro-Smith proportion dip below 50 percent.*

this standard error happens to be .015.* Since 2 × .015 is .03 or 3 percent, the appropriate confidence interval for our example is the interval from 54 to 60 percent. Under the circumstances, candidate Smith can be fairly confident that she has the support of at least 50 percent of the electorate, since 50 percent is well below the poll's confidence interval (see Figure A.9).

SOME IMPLICATIONS OF STATISTICAL INFERENCE

The methods of testing hypotheses and estimating confidence intervals that we just described are routinely employed in evaluating the results of psychological research. But they have several characteristics that necessarily affect the interpretation of all such results.

THE PROBABILISTIC NATURE OF HYPOTHESIS TESTING AND CONFIDENCE INTERVALS

As we have already noted, the nature of statistical testing always leaves the possibility of error. In our dyslexia case, we discussed the fact that it is unlikely that someone with a score 2 SDs below the population mean is, in truth, drawn from that population, but it is still possible. (In fact we know exactly how often this sort of unusual occurrence would occur: 2 percent of the time.) Likewise, if we use a confidence interval of ± 2 SEs, the chance that the population mean (or proportion, or whatever) falls outside of that interval is less than 4 or 5 in 100. This is a small chance for error, but it is still a chance.

Do we want to be more confident than this? If so, we might use a confidence interval of ± 3 SEs, where the equivalent chance is only 1 in 1,000. The same holds for critical ratios. If we want to be cautious, we might insist that the critical ratio be larger than the usually assumed value of 2—perhaps 3 (a chance factor of 1 in 2,000) or 4 (1 in 20,000), and so on. But the likelihood of these chance occurrences is never zero, and so, as long as there is some unexplained variance, there is some possibility of error.

The probabilistic nature of statistical reasoning has another consequence. Even if we can come to a correct conclusion about the mean of a population (or a proportion, as in polls), we cannot generalize to individuals. The variability within the population (or within our sample) simply prohibits us from applying claims, true for the population, to each individual within the population. Thus, a study which shows that men have higher scores than women on spatial relations tests does not preclude the existence of brilliant female artists or architects.

THE ROLE OF SAMPLE SIZE

A last point concerns the role of sample size in affecting how the results are interpreted. The larger the sample, the smaller the standard error and the smaller the confidence interval around the mean or the proportion. This can have major effects on hypothesis testing.

Suppose that, in the population, a certain independent variable produces a very small difference. As an example, suppose that the population difference between men and

---

* The standard error of a proportion (e.g., the proportion of polled voters who express pro-X sentiments) is analogous to the standard error of the mean and measures the precision with which our sample proportion estimates the population proportion. The formula for the standard error of a proportion p is:

$$SE_p = \sqrt{\frac{p \times (1 - p)}{N}}$$

In our example, $p = .57$ and $N = 1,000$, so $SE_p = .015$.

women on a certain test of spatial relations is 1 percent. We would probably be unable to reject the null hypothesis (that is, the hypothesis that there is no sex difference on the test) with samples of moderate size. But if the sample size were sufficiently large, we could reject the null hypothesis. For an N of such magnitude would lead to a decrease in the standard errors of the sample means, which in turn would lead to an increase in the critical ratio. Someone who read a report of this experiment would now learn that, by using thousands of participants, we discovered a reliable difference of 1 percent. A fair reaction to this bit of intelligence would be that the null hypothesis can indeed be rejected, but that the psychological significance of this finding is rather slight. The moral is simple: Statistical reliability does indicate a difference and, moreover, indicates that the difference is unlikely to be a fluke or chance occurrence. But statistical reliability, by itself, does not indicate whether the effect discovered is of psychological significance or of any practical importance.

SUMMARY

- Statistical methods concern the ways in which investigators describe, organize, and interpret collections of numerical data. A crucial concern of statistical endeavors is to interpret the *variability* that is encountered in all research.

- An early step in processing numerical data is *scaling*, a procedure for assigning numbers to psychological responses. Scales can be *categorical, ordinal, interval,* or *ratio scales.* These differ in the degree to which they can be subjected to arithmetical operations.

- An important step in organizing the data is to arrange them in a *frequency distribution,* often displayed in graphic form, as in a *histogram.* Frequency distributions are summarized by a *measure of central tendency.* The common measure of central tendency is the *mean* (M), though sometimes another measure, the *median,* may be preferable, as in cases when the distribution is *skewed.* Important measures of variability are the *variance* (V) and the *standard deviation* (SD).

- One way of comparing two scores drawn from different distributions is to convert both into *percentile ranks.* Another is to transform them into z-scores, which express the distance of a score from its mean in standard deviations. The percentile rank of a z-score can be computed if the shape of that score's distribution is known. An important example is the *normal distribution,* graphically displayed by the *normal curve,* which describes the distribution of many psychological variables and is basic to much of statistical reasoning.

- In some studies, the relation between variables is expressed in the form of a *correlation,* which may be positive or negative. It is measured by r, the correlation coefficient, a number that can vary from +1.00 to −1.00. Correlations reflect the extent to which two variables vary together, but they do not necessarily indicate that one of them causes the other.

- One of the main functions of statistical methods is to help test hypotheses about a population given information about the sample. An important example is the difference between mean scores obtained under two different conditions. Here, the investigator has to decide between the *null hypothesis,* which asserts that the difference was obtained by chance, and the *alternative hypothesis,* which asserts that the difference is genuine and exists in the population. The decision is made by dividing the obtained mean difference by the *standard error* (SE), a measure of the variability of that mean difference. If the resulting ratio, called the *critical ratio,* is large enough, the null hypothesis is rejected, the alternative hypothesis is accepted, and the difference is said to be *statistically reliable.* A related way of making statistical decisions is by using a *confidence interval,* or margin of error. This is based on the variability of the scores from a sample and determines the interval within which the population mean or proportion probably falls.

GLOSSARY

abnormal psychology   *See* psychopathology.

above-average effect   A data pattern, commonly observed in individualist cultures, in which people rate themselves as being above average on many dimensions, for example, a better driver than the average, more likeable than the average, and so on.

accommodation   (1) The process by which the lens is thickened or flattened to focus on an object. (2) In Piaget's theory of development, one of the twin processes that underlies cognitive development. Accommodation is the way the child changes his schemas as he continues to interact with the environment. *See* assimilation.

acetylcholine (Ach)   A neurotransmitter found in many parts of the nervous system. Among many other functions, it serves as an excitatory transmitter at the synaptic junctions between muscle fibers and motor neurons.

ACh   *See* acetylcholine.

achromatic colors   Colors, such as black, white, and the neutral grays, that do not have the property of hue.

acquisition   The initial step toward remembering in which new information is taken in.

action potential   A brief change in the electrical potential of an axon, which is the physical basis of the nervous impulse.

activity dependence   A property of neuronal plasticity such that changes in a neuron's functioning will occur only if that neuron is active (i.e., firing) at the same time as another neuron.

actor-observer difference   The difference in attributions made by actors who describe their own actions and observers who describe another person's. The former emphasizes external, situational causes; the latter, internal, dispositional factors. *See also* fundamental attribution error.

act-outcome representation   A type of association hypothesized by Edward Tolman to be the product of instrumental learning; an organism that has acquired this sort of association has acquired the knowledge that a certain type of act leads to a particular outcome.

acuity   The ability to distinguish between separate points projected on the retina. Acuity is greatest in the fovea, where the receptors are closely bunched together.

acute stress disorder   A reaction sometimes observed in individuals who have experienced a traumatic event, characterized by recurrent nightmares and waking flashbacks of the traumatic event.

adaptation   The process by which the sensitivity to a stimulus declines if the stimulus is continually presented.

addiction   The result of repeated use of some drugs. The consequences are increased tolerance and also withdrawal symptoms if the drug is unavailable, usually causing the addiction to be self-perpetuating.

adipose cells   The cells within the body that provide long-term storage of energy resources, usually in the form of fatty acids that can be converted to glucose when needed.

adrenal glands   Organs in the body, located at the top of the kidneys, that are part of the endocrine system. The adrenal glands release hormones directly into the bloodstream, including hormones crucial for regulating the body's response to stress.

affective disorders   A form of psychopathology for which the predominant disturbances lie in mood and motivation; these disorders include depression and bipolar disorder.

affective neuroscience   A field that employs methods drawn from cognitive neuroscience to study affective processes.

afferent nerves   Nerves that carry messages to the brain.

agency   A term referring to the view that a person has about the origins of her behaviors. People in individualist cultures often have a sense of agency in which the person herself is regarded as the source of the actions; people in collectivist cultures have a sense of agency that emphasizes the role of the situation.

aggression   Hostile action directed against another member of one's species, usually intended to do physical or social harm or, for hostile intent, to limit the target's actions. Aggression must be distinguished from the behaviors involved in predation.

aggressive-rejected   A status in some children who are not respected or liked by their peers (and thus: rejected), and who become aggressive as a result.

agnosia   A disturbance in the organization of sensory information produced by lesions in certain cortical areas. An example is visual agnosia in which the patient can see but often does not recognize what he sees.

agonists   Drugs that enhance the activity of a neurotransmitter, often by increasing the amount of transmitter substance available (e.g., by blocking reuptake or by increasing the availability of precursors).

agoraphobia   The fear of being alone and outside of the home, especially in a public place; often observed in those with panic disorder. *See also* phobia.

algorithm   In problem solving, a procedure in which all of the steps toward the solution are specified. *See also* heuristics.

all-or-none law   A law that describes the fact that all action potentials have the same amplitude regardless of the stimulus that triggered them.

alpha rhythm   A pattern of regular pulses, between eight and twelve per second, visible in the EEG waves of a person who is relaxed but awake, and typically with eyes closed.

Alzheimer's disease   A degenerative brain disorder characterized by memory loss followed by increasing disorientation and culminating in total physical and mental helplessness. One of the major sites of the destruction is a pathway of acetylcholine-releasing cells leading from the base of the forebrain to the cortex and hippocampus. *See also* acetylcholine.

American Sign Language (ASL)   The manual-visual language system of deaf persons in America.

amino acid   The building blocks of proteins.

amplitude   The height of a wave crest, used as a measure of intensity of a sound or light wave.

amygdala   An almond-shaped structure in the temporal lobe that plays a central role in emotion and in the evaluation of stimuli.

amyloid plaques   Large blobs of amyloid protein created in the development of Alzheimer's disease; these plaques seem to trigger an immune response in the brain, resulting in the death of many neurons.

anal character   An adult personality pattern allegedly produced (according to psychoanalysts) by a fixation on the anal stage. This character includes traits like orderliness and stinginess.

analgesic   A pain reliever.

analogical representation   A representation that shares some of the physical characteristics of an object; for example, a picture of a mouse is an analogical representation because it looks like the small rodent it represents.

anal stage   In psychoanalytic theory, the stage of psychosexual development during which the focus of pleasure is on activities related to elimination.

analytic intelligence   According to some investigators, the type of intelligence typically measured by intelligence tests and crucial for success in academic pursuits.

androgen   Any male sex hormone (e.g., testosterone).

androgenized females   Individuals who genetically are females (i.e., have the XX chromosome pattern) but who were exposed in utero to high levels of the male hormone, androgen.

anecdotal evidence   Evidence (usually just a few cases) collected informally, as in anecdotes told from one person to another.

anomia   A difficulty in finding words that is often experienced by people with brain injuries.

anorexia nervosa   An eating disorder that primarily afflicts young women and that is characterized by an exaggerated concern with being overweight and by compulsive dieting, sometimes to the point of self-starvation and death. *See also* bulimia.

A-not-B effect   The tendency of infants around nine months of age to search for a hidden object by reaching for place *A*, where it was previously hidden, rather than a new place *B*, where it was hidden most recently while the child was watching.

ANS   *See* autonomic nervous system.

antagonists   Drugs that impede the activity of a neurotransmitter, often by decreasing the amount available (e.g., by speeding reuptake and decreasing availability of precursors).

antecedents   In the context of emotion, antecedents are the precursors of emotion.

anterograde amnesia   A memory deficit suffered after some brain damage. It is an inability to learn and remember any information encountered after the injury, with little effect on memory for information acquired before the injury. *See also* retrograde amnesia.

antidepressants   Medications designed to counteract depression.

antimanics   Drugs that alleviate the symptoms of mania, the energetic phase of bipolar disorder.

antisocial personality disorder   Also called psychopathy or sociopathy. The term describes persons who get into continual trouble with society, are indifferent to others, are impulsive, and have little concern for the future or remorse about the past.

anxiety   A global apprehensiveness related to uncertainty.

anxiety disorders   *See* acute stress disorder, dissociative disorders, generalized anxiety disorder, obsessive-compulsive disorder, panic disorder, phobia, post-traumatic stress disorder (PTSD), social phobia.

anxiety hierarchy   *See* systematic desensitization.

anxiolytics   Drugs that alleviate the symptoms of anxiety.

anxious/avoidant   One of the types of mother-child attachment. Children who are anxious/avoidant are distant or aloof when their mothers are present, although they sometimes search for her in her absence.

anxious/resistant   One of the types of mother-child attachment. Children who are anxious/resistant do not explore, even in their mother's presence, but become quite upset when she leaves.

aphasia   A disorder of language produced by lesions in certain areas of the cortex. A lesion in Broca's area leads to nonfluent aphasia, one in Wernicke's area to fluent aphasia.

apparent movement   The perception of movement produced by stimuli that are stationary but flash on and off at appropriate positions and at appropriate time intervals.

appraisals   The conscious or unconscious interpretations of a situation which determine how a person will respond emotionally to that situation.

apraxia   A serious disturbance in the organization of voluntary action produced by lesions in certain cortical areas, often in the frontal lobes.

archetypes   According to Carl Jung, the stories and images that constitute our collective unconscious.

arousal   Activation in any of the body's systems (e.g., activation of the sympathetic nervous system or the cerebral cortex). Arousal as a general term has resisted definition, because sometimes one system is activated while another is not.

ASL   *See* American Sign Language.

ASQ   *See* attributional-style questionnaire.

assessment   The broad set of procedures used to gather information about an individual's psychological state; the assessment may in some cases lead to a diagnosis.

assimilation   In Piaget's theory, one of the twin processes by means of which cognitive development proceeds. Assimilation is the process whereby the environment is interpreted in terms of the schemas the child has at the time. *See* accomodation.

association   A linkage between two psychological processes or representations as a result of past experience in which the two have occurred together.

associative links   Connections in memory that tie one memory, or one concept, to another.

associative retrieval   A type of memory retrieval that seems swift and effortless: the sought-after information simply "pops" into mind.

attachment   The strong, enduring, emotional bond between a child and its caregivers, and said to be the basis for relationships in later life.

attention deficit/hyperactivity disorder (ADHD)   A form of psychopathology diagnosed in young children, and characterized by a range of behavioral problems; children with this disorder are impulsive and have difficulty keeping their attention focused on a task.

attitude   A fairly stable, evaluative disposition that makes a person think, feel, or behave positively or negatively about some person, group, or social issue.

attributional style   The way a person typically explains the things that happen in his or her life.

attributional-style questionnaire (ASQ)   A questionnaire designed to assess a person's habitual pattern of attributing events in a certain way (e.g., to internal forces or external ones, to forces that influence just that event or to broader forces).

atypical antidepressants A recently developed group of medications that work in varied ways on serotonin, norepinephrine, and dopamine systems to combat the symptoms of depression.

atypical antipsychotics Drugs (such as Clozaril, Risperdal, and Zyprexa) that operate by blocking receptors for both dopamine and serotonin; these drugs seem to be effective in treating schizophrenic patients' positive symptoms, such as thought disorders and hallucinations, as well as their negative symptoms, such as apathy and emotional blunting.

auditory canal The tube that carries sound from the outer ear to the eardrum.

auditory ossicles The three bones of the middle ear that transmit vibrations from the eardrum to the oval window.

authoritarian parents One of the four types of parents; authoritarian parents adhere to strict standards about how children should behave, and attempt to mold their children's behavior accordingly.

authoritarian personality A cluster of personal attributes (e.g., submission to persons above and harshness to those below) and social attitudes (e.g., prejudice against minority groups) that is sometimes held to constitute a distinct personality.

authoritative parents One of the four types of parents; authoritative parents exercise power over their children, but accept the reciprocal obligation to respond to their children's opinions and reasonable demands.

authoritative-reciprocal pattern A pattern of child rearing in which parents exercise considerable power but also respond to the child's point of view and reasonable demands. Parents following this pattern set rules of conduct and are fairly demanding but also encourage the child's independence and self-expression.

authority ranking relationship A type of relationship based on power and hierarchy, exemplified by many of the relationships in traditional companies, universities, and military organizations.

autism A form of psychopathology diagnosed in young children, and characterized by a wide range of developmental problems, including language and motor problems.

autocratic pattern A pattern of child rearing in which the parents control the child strictly, setting stern and usually unexplained rules whose infraction leads to severe, often physical, punishment.

automaticity The state that is achieved when an action has gone through the process of automatization.

autonomic division *See* autonomic nervous system.

autonomic nervous system (ANS) A part of the nervous system that controls the internal organs, usually not under voluntary control.

availability heuristic A rule of thumb often used to make probability estimates, which depends on the frequency with which certain events readily come to mind. This can lead to errors, since, for example, very vivid events will be remembered out of proportion to their actual frequency of occurrence.

aversion therapy A form of behavior therapy in which the undesirable response leads to an aversive stimulus (e.g., the patient shocks herself every time she reaches for a cigarette).

avoidance responses Responses that allow an organism to avoid contact with an aversive stimulus.

axon Part of a neuron that transmits impulses to other neurons or effectors.

axonal branches A structure in many neurons in which the axon forks into several branches, with the neuronal impulse propagated to all branches.

axon terminals The knoblike swellings on the ends of an axon. The terminals contain the synaptic vesicles that are filled with neurotransmitters.

basal ganglia In the extrapyramidal motor system, a set of subcortical structures in the cerebrum that send messages to the spinal cord through the midbrain to modulate various motor functions.

basal metabolic rate The speed at which organisms ordinarily "burn" food to maintain themselves; this rate is higher for endotherms than for ectotherms.

basic emotions According to some theorists, a small set of elemental, built-in emotions revealed by distinctive patterns of physiological reaction and facial expression.

basilar membrane *See* cochlea.

behavioral contrast A pattern of responding in which an organism seems to evaluate a reward relative to other rewards that are available or that have been available recently. For example, an animal might respond only weakly to a reward of two pellets if it recently received a reward of five pellets for some other response.

behavioral data Data about a person based on direct observation of that person.

belongingness in learning The fact that the ease with which associations are formed depends on the items to be associated. This holds for classical conditioning in which some conditioned stimulus-unconditioned stimulus combinations are more effective than others (e.g., learned taste aversions) and for instrumental conditioning in which some response-reinforcer combinations work more easily than others (e.g., specific defense reactions in avoidance conditioning of species). *See also* biological constraints, equipotentiality.

benzodiazepines A class of medications used to combat anxiety; the class includes Valium, Xanax, and Klonopin.

beta-blocker A medication intended to control autonomic arousal, and often used in the treatment of anxiety disorders.

beta rhythm A rhythmic pattern in the electrical activity of the brain, often observed when one is engaged in active thought.

between-subject comparisons Within an experiment, comparing one group of individuals to a different group; usually contrasted with within-subject comparisons.

Big Five A nickname often used to refer to five apparently crucial dimensions of personality: extroversion, neuroticism (or emotional instability), agreeableness, conscientiousness, and openness to experience. These five traits often emerge from factor analyses of trait terms.

binding problem The problem confronted by the brain of recombining the elements of a stimulus, once these elements have been separately analyzed by different neural systems.

binocular disparity An important cue for depth perception. Each eye obtains a different view of an object, the disparity becoming less pronounced the farther the object is from the observer.

biological constraints Principles governing what each species can learn easily and what it cannot learn at all. *See also* belongingness in learning.

biomedical model An approach to mental disorders that emphasizes somatogenic causes.

biopsychosocial viewpoint A perspective often taken in discussions of psychopathology, with the perspective including biological factors (e.g., genetics or hormonal influences), psychological factors (i.e., a style of thinking) and social factors (i.e., the presence of social support).

bipolar cells The intermediate neural cells in the eye that are stimulated by the receptors and excite the ganglion cells.

bipolar disorder A mood disorder in which the patient swings from one emotional extreme to another, experiencing both manic and depressive episodes. Formerly called manic-depressive psychosis.

bisexuality A sexual orientation in which a person has erotic and romantic feelings for both their own and the opposite sex.

blindsight The ability of a person with a lesion in the visual cortex to reach toward or guess at the orientation of objects projected on the part of the visual field that corresponds to this lesion, even though they report that they can see absolutely nothing in that part of their visual field.

blind spot The region of the retina that contains no visual receptors and therefore cannot produce visual sensations.

blocking effect An effect produced when two conditioned stimuli, *A* and *B*, are both presented together with the unconditioned stimulus (US). If stimulus *A* has previously been associated with the unconditioned stimulus while *B* has not, the formation of an association between stimulus *B* and the US will be impaired (i.e., blocked).

blood-brain barrier Specialized membranes that surround the blood vessels within the brain and that filter toxins and other harmful chemicals, ensuring brain cells a relatively pure blood supply.

Body Mass Index (BMI) The commonly-used measure of whether someone is at a healthy weight or not; BMI is calculated as weight (in kilograms) divided by the square of height (in meters); a BMI between 18.5 and 24.9 is considered normal.

bottom-up processes *See* top-down processes.

brightness A perceived dimension of visual stimuli—the extent to which they appear light or dark.

brightness constancy The capacity to perceive an object as having an unchanging brightness, despite the fact that changes in illumination cause a change in how much light reflects off the object and reaches the eye.

brightness contrast The perceiver's tendency to exaggerate the physical difference in the light intensities of two adjacent regions. As a result, a gray patch looks brighter on a black background, darker on a white background.

Broca's area A brain area in the frontal lobe crucial for language production. *See also* aphasia.

bulimia An eating disorder characterized by repeated binge-and-purge bouts. In contrast to anorexics, bulimics tend to be of roughly normal weight. *See also* anorexia nervosa.

bystander effect The phenomenon that underlies many examples of failing to help strangers in distress: the larger the group a person is in (or thinks he is in), the less likely he is to come to a stranger's assistance. One reason is diffusion of responsibility (no one thinks it is his responsibility to act).

California Psychological Inventory (CPI) A commonly used personality test, aimed especially at high-school and college students, that tests for traits such as dominance, sociability, responsibility, and so on.

cannabinoid (CB) receptors Receptors in the midbrain which are sensitive to endogenously produced substances that chemically resemble the active ingredient in marijuana.

Cannon-Bard theory of emotion A theory of emotion which holds that a stimulus elicits an emotion by triggering a particular response in the brain (in the thalamus) which then causes both the physiological changes associated with the emotion and the emotional experience itself.

case markers Indicators used by a language to relate a word and the "action" in the sentence, for example, whether the word identifies the source of the action, the receiver of the action, and so on. In most languages, case markers occur as function morphemes; very often they serve as suffixes at the ends of noun content morphemes.

case study An observational study in which one person is studied intensively. *See also* single-case experiment.

catatonic schizophrenia A subcategory of schizophrenia. Its main symptoms are peculiar motor patterns, such as periods in which the patient is immobile and maintains strange positions for hours on end.

catch trials Trials in a signal detection experiment in which no signal is presented. These trials ensure that the observer is taking the task seriously and truly trying to determine whether a signal is present or not.

categorical scale A scale that divides responses into categories that are not numerically related. *See also* interval scale, nominal scale, ordinal scale, ratio scale.

causal ambiguity A status in which there is no way to determine which of several causes actually produced an observation. In circumstances of causal ambiguity, no conclusions about causes can be drawn.

causal attribution A step of inferring or concluding what the cause of an observation was.

CB receptors *See* cannabinoid (CB) receptors.

CCK *See* cholecystokinin.

cell body The portion of the cell that contains the metabolic machinery which keeps the cell alive and able to function.

central fissure The anatomical "valley" that divides the frontal lobes on each side of the brain from the parietal lobes.

central nervous system (CNS) The brain and spinal cord.

central route to persuasion The processes involved in attitude change when someone cares about an issue and devotes resources to thinking about the issue. This route depends on evidence and good arguments, and is contrasted with the *peripheral route*.

central trait A trait that is associated with many other attributes of the person who is being judged. Warmth and coldness are central because they are important in determining overall impressions.

CER *See* conditioned emotional response.

cerebellum Two small hemispheres that form part of the hindbrain and control muscular coordination and equilibrium.

cerebral cortex The outermost layer of the gray matter of the cerebral hemispheres.

childhood amnesia The failure to remember the events of our very early childhood. This is sometimes ascribed to massive change in retrieval cues, sometimes to different ways of encoding memories in early childhood.

choice reaction time A measure of the speed of mental processing in which the subject has to choose between one of several responses depending on which stimulus is presented.

cholecystokinin (CCK) A hormone released by the duodenum that appears to send a "stop eating" message to the brain.

chromatic colors Colors that have a discernible hue. These are in contrast to the achromatic colors, which include black, the various shades of gray, and white.

chromosomes Structures in the nucleus of each cell that contain the genes, the units of hereditary transmission. A human cell has forty-six chromosomes, arranged in twenty-three pairs. One of these pairs consists of the sex chromosomes. In males, one member of the pair is an X chromosome, the other a Y chromosome. In females, both members are X chromosomes. *See also* gene, X chromosome.

chunking A process of reorganizing (or recoding) materials in memory that permits a number of items to be packed into a larger unit.

circadian rhythm A rhythm that spans about a twenty-four-hour day, such as that of the sleep-waking cycle. Circadian rhythms in humans originate from a clock circuit in the hypothalamus that is set by information from the optic nerve about whether it is day or night.

classical antipsychotics Drugs (such as Thorazine and Haldol) that operate by blocking receptors for dopamine; these drugs seem to be effective in treating many schizophrenic patients' positive symptoms, such as thought disorders and hallucinations. Also called major tranquillizers and neuroleptics.

classical conditioning A form of learning in which a previously neutral stimulus, the conditioned stimulus (CS), is paired with an unconditioned stimulus (US) regardless of what the animal does. In effect, what has to be learned is the relation between these two stimuli. *See also* instrumental conditioning.

classical psychoanalysis The method developed by Sigmund Freud which assumes that a patient's ills stem from unconscious defenses against unacceptable urges that date back to early childhood.

clinical observation   A source of data in which one observes patients with some biological or psychological problem and seeks to draw conclusions from this about normal brain or mental functioning.

CNS   *See* central nervous system.

cochlea   A coiled structure in the inner ear that contains the basilar membrane whose deformation by sound-produced pressure stimulates the auditory receptors.

cocktail-party effect   The effect one experiences in settings such as noisy parties, where one tunes in to the voice of the person one is talking to and filters out the other voices as background noise. This phenomenon is often taken as the model for studying selective attention.

cognitive dissonance   An inconsistency among some experiences, beliefs, attitudes, or feelings. According to dissonance theory, this sets up an unpleasant state that people try to reduce by reinterpreting some part of their experiences to make them consistent with the others.

cognitive map   A mental representation of spatial layout that indicates what is where, and what leads to what.

cognitive reappraisal A form of emotion regulation in which an individual changes her emotional response to a situation by altering her appraisal of that situation.

cognitive rehabilitation   Techniques involving new strategies that enable a person to function normally despite mental problems or biological damage.

cognitive science   A multidisciplinary attempt to address questions about the mind by integrating what we know from psychology, linguistics, philosophy, anthropology, and computer science.

cognitive therapy   An approach to therapy that tries to change some of the patient's habitual modes of thinking about herself, her situation, and her future. It is related to behavioral therapy because it regards such thought patterns as a form of behavior.

collective unconscious   A set of primordial stories and images, hypothesized by Carl Jung to be shared by all of humanity, and which he proposed underlie and shape our perceptions and desires.

collectivism   A cultural pattern in which people are considered to be fundamentally interdependent and obligations within one's family and immediate community are emphasized. Many of the societies of Latin America, and most of the cultures of Asia and Africa, are collectivist. *See also* individualism.

collectivistic cultures   *See* collectivism.

color circle   A means of representing the visible hues, arranged in a circle according to perceptual similarity.

color solid   A three-dimensional object allowing one to display all three dimensions of color: brightness, saturation, and hue. Brightness is represented by height (with black at the bottom and white at the top), saturation by radius (with achromatic colors at the center of the solid and fully saturated colors at the periphery), and hue by angular position around the solid.

commissures   The thick bundles of fibers that carry information back and forth between the left and right halves of the brain.

communal sharing relationship   A type of relationship in which the "self" is expanded to include the "other," so that each person in the relationship contributes to the common good.

comorbidity   The tendency for different forms of mental disorder to occur together, in the same individual.

companionate love   A state of emotion (usually contrasted with romantic love) characterized by the affection we feel for those whose lives are deeply intertwined with our own.

comparative approach   *See* comparative method.

comparative method   A research method in which one makes systematic comparisons among different species in order to gain insights into the function of a particular structure or behavior, or the evolutionary origins of that structure or behavior.

compensatory reaction   An internally produced response through which the body seeks to reduce the effects of some external influence by producing a reaction opposite in its characteristics to those of the external influence. For example, the body produces an increase in pain sensitivity in response to the decrease in pain sensitivity caused by morphine, thereby canceling out morphine's reaction and so producing drug tolerance.

complementary colors   Two colors that, when additively mixed with each other in the right proportions, produce the sensation of gray.

compliance   When people change their behavior because someone has asked them to.

compulsions   *See* obsessive-compulsive disorder.

computerized tomography scan   *See* CT scan.

concept   A class or category that subsumes a number of individual instances. An important way of relating concepts is through propositions, which make some assertion that relates a subject (e.g., *chickens*) and a predicate (e.g., *lay eggs*).

concordance   The probability that a person who stands in a particular familial relationship to a patient (e.g., an identical twin) has the same disorder as the patient.

concrete operations period   In Piaget's theory, the period from ages six or seven to about eleven. At this time, the child has acquired mental operations that allow him to abstract some essential attributes of reality, such as number and substance, but these operations are as yet applicable only to concrete events and cannot be considered entirely in the abstract.

conditional statements   Statements of the format "if…then…," such as "If he calls me, then we can go to the movies." Called conditional because the "if" clause states the condition under which the "then" clause is guaranteed to be true.

conditioned emotional response (CER)   A type of conditioned response that involves a complex set of behaviors characterizing fear. In many cases, the CER is measured by its capacity to interrupt other ongoing behaviors.

conditioned reflex   *See* conditioned response.

conditioned reinforcer   An initially neutral stimulus that acquires reinforcing properties through pairing with another stimulus that is already reinforcing.

conditioned response (CR)   A response elicited by some initially neutral stimulus, the conditioned stimulus (CS), as a result of pairings between that CS and an unconditioned stimulus (US). This CR is typically not identical with the unconditioned response though it often is similar to it. *See also* conditioned stimulus (CS), unconditioned response (UR), unconditioned stimulus (US).

conditioned stimulus (CS)   In classical conditioning, the stimulus which comes to elicit a new response by virtue of pairings with the unconditioned stimulus. *See also* conditioned response (CR), unconditioned response (UR), unconditioned stimulus (US).

cones   Visual receptors that respond to greater light intensities and give rise to chromatic (color) sensations.

confabulation   Sincere but false recollections, usually produced when one encounters a gap in the memory record and (unwittingly) tries to fill this gap.

confederate   Someone who appears to be a research participant but actually is part of the research team.

confidence interval   An interval around a sample mean within which the population mean is likely to fall. In common practice, the largest value of the interval is 2 standard errors above the mean and the smallest value is 2 standard errors below it.

confirmation bias   The tendency to seek evidence to support one's hypothesis rather than to look for evidence that will undermine the hypothesis.

confirmed hypothesis   A hypothesis that has been tested many times and each time has made successful predictions.

conformity   A change in behavior due to explicit or implicit social pressure.

confounds Variables within a study that might influence the pattern of results and thereby introduce ambiguity regarding why the results are as they are.

connectionist model A model of how information in memory is retrieved that relies on distributed representations. In a distributed representation, a concept is conveyed by a pattern of activation across an entire network, rather than by the activation of a single node. In such models, processing depends on having just the right links between concepts, at just the right strengths.

conscience The hypothesized set of beliefs and tendencies that produce a desire to act in a moral manner, and a feeling of guilt when one does not act morally.

conscious level Thoughts and feelings of which one is currently aware.

construal The way people make sense of the world around them.

content morphemes Morphemes that carry the main burden of meaning (e.g., *strange*). This is in contrast to function morphemes that add details to the meaning but also serve various grammatical purposes (e.g., the suffixes *s* and *er*, the connecting words *and*, *or*, *if*, and so on).

context reinstatement A step aimed at improving someone's ability to remember, by putting her back into the same mental and physical state that she was in during the initial learning.

contingency management A form of behavior therapy in which the environment is structured such that certain behaviors are reliably followed by well-defined consequences.

contralateral control The pattern in which movements on the right side of the body are controlled by the left half of the brain, while movements on the left side of the body are controlled by the right half of the brain. Contralateral control is seen in nearly all vertebrate nervous systems.

control group A group to which the experimental manipulation is not applied.

control system A mechanism that can change the operation of some process or machine in response to feedback.

convergent validity One of the assessments of whether a test measures what it is supposed to measure. The assessment seeks agreement between the test being evaluated and some other test designed to measure roughly the same thing.

conversion disorder Formerly called conversion hysteria. A condition in which there are physical symptoms that seem to have no physical basis. They instead appear to be linked to psychological factors and are often believed to serve as a means of reducing anxiety. *See also* hysteria.

convolutions The wrinkles visible in the cortex that allow the enormous surface area of the human cortex to be stuffed into the relatively small space of the skull.

cornea The eye's transparent outer coating.

corpus callosum A bundle of fibers that connects the two cerebral hemispheres.

correct negative One of the four possible outcomes in a detection task. If the signal is *not* present and the person says so, this is a correct negative. *See* miss.

correlation The tendency of two variables to vary together. If one goes up as the other goes up, the correlation is positive; if one goes up as the other goes down, the correlation is negative.

correlational studies Studies in which the investigator is seeking to observe the relationship among variables that were in place prior to the study (as opposed to factors that the investigator creates or manipulates).

correlation coefficient (*r*) A number that expresses both the size and the direction of a correlation, varying from +1.00 (perfect positive correlation) through 0.00 (absence of any correlation) to −1.00 (perfect negative correlation).

correlation matrix A data table reporting the correlations among multiple variables.

correspondence problem In a moving display, the difficulty in determining which aspects of the display now visible correspond to which aspects of the display visible a moment ago.

cortex The outermost layer of an organ in the body.

cortisol A substance secreted by the adrenal glands in response to stress.

counterbalance A procedural step through which an experiment is arranged so that possible confounds will have an equal effect on all conditions, and thus cannot influence the comparison between conditions.

courtship rituals Particular behaviors that announce an organism's reproductive availability and intentions.

covariation *See* correlation.

CPI *See* California Psychological Inventory.

cranial nerves The twelve pairs of nerves that enter and exit directly from the hindbrain. These nerves control movements of the head and neck, carry sensations from them including vision, olfaction, and audition, and regulate the various glandular secretions in the head.

creative intelligence The form of intelligence alleged by some authors as essential for devising new ideas or new strategies. Often contrasted with analytic intelligence or practical intelligence.

critical period A period in the development of an organism when it is particularly sensitive to certain environmental influences. Outside of this period, the same environmental influences have little effect (e.g., the period during which a duckling can be imprinted). After embryonic development, this phenomenon is rarely all-or-none. As a result, most developmental psychologists prefer the term *sensitive period*.

critical period hypothesis The proposal that certain skills must be gained or ideas acquired at a particular age or developmental stage. A related, but less rigid proposal is the *sensitive* period hypothesis, which suggests that the skills are just more likely to be gained during that stage.

critical ratio A score, usually a *z*-score, that determines whether an investigator will accept or reject the null hypothesis. If a test score exceeds the critical ratio, the null hypothesis is rejected.

crystallized intelligence The repertoire of information, cognitive skills, and strategies acquired by the application of fluid intelligence to various fields. This is said to increase with age, in some cases into old age. *See also* fluid intelligence.

CT (computerized tomography) scan A technique for examining brain structure in living humans by constructing a composite X-ray picture based on views from all different angles. Also called CAT (computerized axial tomography) scan.

cultural competence An understanding of how a patient's beliefs, values, and expectations for therapy are shaped by his or her cultural background.

cultural display rules Learned but deeply ingrained conventions that govern what facial expressions of emotion may or may not be shown in what contexts.

cupboard theory A hypothesis about the infant's attachment to the primary caregiver; according to this theory, the attachment is motivated largely by the fact that the mother is a source of nourishment (whether through breast or bottle).

DA *See* dopamine.

data driven A process determined by the input received (often, the sensory information) rather than being determined by pre-existing ideas or expectations.

death instincts A motive postulated by Freud to explain aggression, war, and suicide.

debriefing A step at the end of a procedure in which participants are told what the procedure involved and why it was designed as it was, and in which any manipulations to the participants' beliefs or state are undone.

decibels The logarithmic units used to describe sound intensity (or amplitude).

decision criteria An organism's rule for how much evidence it needs before making a response (including: how clearly a person must see a signal before announcing that, yes, they see it.).

declarative knowledge Knowing "that" (e.g., knowing someone's name), as contrasted with procedural knowledge, which is knowing "how" (e.g., knowing how to ride a bicycle).

deductive reasoning Reasoning in which one tries to determine whether some statement follows logically from certain premises, as in the analysis of syllogisms. This is in contrast with inductive reasoning in which one observes a number of particular instances and tries to determine a general rule that covers them all.

deep processing *See* depth-of-processing hypothesis.

defense mechanism In psychoanalytic theory, a collective term for a number of reactions that try to ward off or lessen anxiety by various unconscious means. *See also* displacement, projection, rationalization, reaction formation, repression.

deferred imitation A pattern in which someone recreates another person's behaviors after a delay—so that, for example, a child might perform a behavior that she saw someone else perform days earlier.

definitional theory of word meaning The theory that our mental representation of word meaning is made up of a small number of simpler concepts. The representation of bachelor, for example, is made up of "adult," "unmarried," and "male."

dehumanization of the victim Steps often taken to make a potential victim seem not human (labeling him as vermin, for example, or treating him as a mere number); these steps make aggression toward the victim more likely and less troubling to the aggressor.

deindividuation A weakened sense of personal identity in which self-awareness is diminished and one's own goals are merged in the collective goals of a group.

deinstitutionalization A movement intended to obtain better and less expensive care for chronically mentally ill patients in their own communities rather than at large, centralized hospitals.

delusions Systematized false beliefs, often of grandeur or persecution.

delusions of persecution A delusion in which the person believes that other people are seeking to harm him.

demand characteristics The cues that tell a research participant what the experimenter expects.

democratic leadership style A leadership style in which the leader encourages group members to make decisions in a democratic fashion.

dendrites A typically highly branched part of a neuron that receives impulses from receptors or other neurons and conducts them toward the cell body and axon.

dendritic spines Little knobs that are attached to the surface of the dendrites and serve as the "receiving stations" for most synapses.

deoxyribonucleic acid (DNA) The complex molecule that is the constituent of genes.

dependent variable The thing that is measured or recorded in an experiment, called the dependent variable because the experiment seeks to ask whether this variable *depends on* (is caused by or predicted by) another variable (the independent variable). Typically, experiments are done to find out if the independent variable does have an influence on the dependent variable.

depressants Drugs that have the effect of diminishing activity levels.

depressive stupor An extreme state of depression in which the person may become entirely unresponsive, rock back and forth, urinate or defecate on herself, and mutter incoherently.

depth cues Sources of information that signal the distance from the observer to the distal stimulus. Some depth cues are present in a single retinal image (the pictorial cues), some require a comparison of the information received from the two eyes (binocular cues), some involve the pattern of motion in the retinal image (parallax and optic flow), and some arise from the positions of the eyes in viewing (e.g., convergence angle).

depth-of-processing hypothesis A theory of memory that stresses the nature of encoding at the time of acquisition. It argues that deeper levels of processing (e.g., attending to a word's meaning) lead to better retention and retrieval than shallower levels of processing (e.g., attending to the word's sound). Thus, maintenance rehearsal leads to much poorer retrieval than elaborative rehearsal. *See also* elaborative rehearsal, maintenance rehearsal.

detection threshold The level of stimulus intensity that marks the weakest (dimmest, or softest, or least intense) stimulus a person can reliably detect.

diagnosis A practitioner's best opinion, based on a patient's signs and symptoms, as to the patient's specific disorder.

Diagnostic and Statistical Manual for Mental Disorders (DSM) *See* DSM-IV.

diathesis-stress model A conception of psychopathology that distinguishes factors that create a risk of illness (the diathesis) and then other factors that turn the risk into an actual problem (the stress).

dichotic presentation An experimental procedure in which the participant hears two simultaneous messages, one presented to each ear. Typically, one of these is to be attended to and the other ignored.

difference threshold The amount by which a given stimulus must be increased or decreased so that the research participant can perceive a just-noticeable difference (jnd).

diffusion of responsibility *See* bystander effect.

directed thinking Thinking that is aimed at the solution of a problem.

direction specific Responding to motion in just one direction.

disconfirmed hypothesis A hypothesis that has been tested but for which the data do not conform to the pattern it predicted.

discriminant validity One of the assessments of whether a test measures what it is supposed to measure. The assessment seeks a distinction between the test being evaluated and some other test designed to measure different capacities or behaviors.

discrimination A process of learning to respond to certain stimuli that are reinforced and not to others that are unreinforced.

discriminative stimuli In instrumental conditioning, the external stimuli that signal a particular relationship between the instrumental response and the reinforcer. For example, a green light is a positive discriminative stimulus when it signals to a pigeon that it will now get food if it hops on a treadle; the reverse is true of a red light, or the negative discriminative stimulus, which indicates that this action will not now lead to a food reward.

dishabituation An increase in responsiveness caused by the presentation of something novel, following a series of presentations of something familiar.

disorganized schizophrenia A subtype of schizophrenia in which the predominant symptoms are extreme incoherence of thought and marked inappropriateness of behavior and affect.

displacement In psychoanalytic theory, a redirection of an impulse from a channel that is blocked into another, more available outlet (e.g., displaced aggression, as in a child who hits a sibling when punished by her parents).

dispositional attributions Attributions which focus on factors that are internal to the person, such as a person's traits, preferences, and other internal qualities.

dissociation (1) A term used for symptoms when a patient is impaired in one function but relatively unaffected in another. (2) In post-traumatic stress disorder (PTSD), the period of numbness immediately after the trauma in which the sufferer feels estranged, socially unresponsive, and oddly unaffected by the traumatizing event. (3) A defense mechanism in which one seeks to create a sense of physical or psychological distance from the threatening event, person, or stimulus.

dissociative amnesia A form of memory loss in which an individual seems unable to remember some period of her life, or even her entire past, including her own identity. This memory loss is often understood as a means of coping with extraordinarily painful events.

dissociative disorders Disorders in which a whole set of mental events seems to be stored out of ordinary consciousness. These include dissociative amnesia, fugue states, and, very rarely, cases of dissociative identity disorder.

Dissociative Experiences Scale A self-report measure that asks people directly how often they have experienced various perceptions or behaviors characteristic of dissociation.

dissociative fugue A state in which the person wanders away from home, and then, days or even months later, suddenly realizes that he is in a strange place and does not know how he got there; this pattern is often understood as a means of coping with (and escaping from) extraordinarily painful events.

dissociative identity disorder Formerly multiple personality disorder. A dissociative disorder that results in a person developing two or more distinct personalities.

distal stimulus An object or event outside (e.g., a tree) as contrasted to the proximal stimulus (e.g., the retinal image of the tree), which is the pattern of physical energies that originates from the distal stimulus and impinges on a sense organ.

distance cues *See* depth cues.

distributed representations A model of cognitive organization, especially semantic memory, in which each concept is represented, not by a designated node or group of nodes, but by a widespread pattern of activation across the entire network. *See also* connectionist model, local representations, network model, node.

dizygotic (DZ) One of the two types of twins. *See also* fraternal twins.

doctrine of specific nerve energies The law formulated by Johannes Müller which holds that differences in sensory quality are not caused by differences in the stimuli themselves but by the different nervous structures that these stimuli excite. Thus, stimulating the retina will produce sensations of light, whether the retina is stimulated by a beam of light or pressure to the eyeball.

dodo bird verdict An expression often used to summarize the comparison of the effectiveness of different forms of psychotherapy. According to the dodo bird in *Alice in Wonderland*, "Everyone has won and all must have prizes." Regarding psychotherapy, this statement is understood to mean that all the major forms of psychotherapy are equally effective.

dominance hierarchy A social order developed by animals that live in groups by which certain individuals are understood to have a certain status or rank, and this determines their access to resources and how they exert power over others.

dominant A relationship among genes such that if the gene on one chromosome specifies one developmental path, and the corresponding gene on the other chromosome specifies a different path, a gene that is dominant will govern the outcome. If a gene is recessive, it will govern the outcome only if the corresponding gene on the other chromosome redundantly specifies the same (recessive) trait.

dopamine (DA) A neurotransmitter involved in various brain structures, including those that control motor action.

dopamine hypothesis Asserts that schizophrenics are oversensitive to the neurotransmitter dopamine. Evidence for this view comes from the fact that the classical antipsychotics, which alleviate positive schizophrenic symptoms, block dopamine transmission. *See also* classical antipsychotics.

dopamine-serotonin interaction hypothesis Asserts that schizophrenics are oversensitive to both dopamine and serotonin. Evidence for this view comes from the fact that atypical antipsychotics, which relieve both positive and negative symptoms, block receptors for both dopamine and serotonin. *See also* atypical antipsychotics.

double-blind design *See* double-blind technique.

double-blind technique A technique for evaluating a manipulation independent of the effects produced by the expectations of research participants (placebo

effects) or the experimenters. This is done by assigning participants to the experimental group or a placebo group with both the participants and the researchers in ignorance of who is assigned to which group. *See also* placebo effect.

double dissociation A pattern of evidence in which we show that we can manipulate one process without influencing another, and then can show the reverse—that we can manipulate the second process without influencing the first. This pattern of evidence provides powerful confirmation that the two processes are qualitatively distinct from each other.

downward drift The proposed process through which schizophrenics fall to the bottom of the socioeconomic ladder because they cannot hold down a job or sustain a personal relationship.

dream condensation The idea that events in a dream flash by in a very fast sequence, taking much less time than the dreamed-about events would ordinarily require.

drive A term used by Hull (among others) to refer to a state of internal bodily tension, such as hunger or thirst or the need for sleep.

drive-reduction theory A theory that claims that all built-in rewards are at bottom reductions of some noxious bodily state. The theory has difficulty in explaining motives in which one seeks stimulation, such as sex and curiosity.

DSM-IV The current diagnostic manual of the American Psychiatric Association (adopted in 1994), a substantial revision of its predecessor, *DSM-III-R*.

dual-center theory A hypothesis about the hypothalamic control of eating. One center (in the lateral hypothalamus) was hypothesized as the "on" center, the initiator of eating; another center (in the ventromedial region) was hypothesized as the "off" center, the terminator of eating. Current evidence indicates, however, that these brain regions, while crucial for eating, are only a part of the circuits controlling eating.

dual-process theory The proposal that thinking often relies on a fast, efficient, effortless set of strategies, but also sometimes relies on a slower, more laborious, but less risky set of strategies.

duplex theory of vision The theory that rods and cones handle different aspects of vision. The rods are the receptors for night vision; they operate at low light intensities and lead to achromatic (colorless) sensations. The cones are used in day vision; they respond at higher illumination levels, have greater acuity, and are responsible for sensations of color.

dynamic systems theory A proposal offered to describe many aspects of child development, and also some aspects of brain functioning. In this proposal, many forces act on a system simultaneously, and the resulting behavior can be understood as a sum of this set of forces.

dyslexia Any difficulty in reading not associated with obvious problems like bad eyesight.

eardrum The taut membrane that transmits vibrations caused by sound waves across the middle ear to the inner ear.

ECT *See* electroconvulsive therapy.

ectotherms Organisms that control their body temperature by using mechanisms that are mostly external (such as choosing a sunny or shady environment). Previously called *cold blooded*.

EEG *See* electroencephalography, electroencephalogram.

effectors Organs of action; in humans, muscles and glands.

efferent nerves Nerves that carry messages to the effectors.

ego In Freud's theory, a set of reactions that try to reconcile the id's blind pleasure strivings with the demands of reality. These lead to the emergence of various skills and capacities that eventually become a system that can look at itself—an "I." *See also* id and superego.

egocentrism In Piaget's theory, a characteristic of preoperational children, an inability to see another person's point of view.

ego psychology A school of psychodynamic thought that emphasizes the skills and adaptive capacities of the ego.

elaborative rehearsal Rehearsal in which material is actively reorganized and elaborated while in working memory. In contrast to maintenance rehearsal, this confers considerable benefit for subsequent memory. *See also* maintenance rehearsal.

Electra complex *See* Oedipus complex.

electrical synapses Synapses in which the electrical signal of one axon potential directly influences another axon, without the chemical intermediates involved at most other synapses.

electroconvulsive therapy (ECT) A somatic treatment, mostly used for cases of severe depression, in which a brief electric current is passed through the brain to produce a convulsive seizure.

electroencephalogram (EEG) A record of the summed activity of cortical cells picked up by wires placed on the skull.

electroencephalography The procedure through which one records an electroencephalogram.

embryo The earliest stage in a developing animal. In humans, up to about eight weeks after conception.

emotion regulation The ability to control, diminish, or change one's own feelings.

emotional intelligence The ability to understand one's own emotions and others', and also the ability to control one's own emotions.

emotions Affective responses (such as joy, sadness, pride, and anger), which are characterized by loosely linked changes in three domains: behavior (how we act), subjective experience (how we feel), and physiology (how various systems in our bodies respond).

empathy A direct emotional response to another person's emotions.

empiricism A school of thought that holds that all knowledge comes by way of empirical experience, that is, through the senses.

encoding specificity The hypothesis that retrieval is most likely if the context at the time of recall approximates that during the original encoding.

endocrine glands *See* endocrine system.

endocrine system The system of ductless glands whose secretions are released directly into the bloodstream and affect organs elsewhere in the body (e.g., adrenal gland, pancreas, pituitary gland).

endorphin A drug produced within the brain itself whose effects and chemical composition are similar to such pain-relieving opiates as morphine.

endotherms Organisms that control their body temperature by using mechanisms that are mostly internal or physiological. Previously called *warm blooded.*

engram In the brain, the actual representation of a memory; i.e., the trace left by an earlier (and now remembered) event.

entity theorists Individuals who believe some aspect of personality or intellectual functioning is fixed.

epinephrine (adrenaline) A neurotransmitter released into the bloodstream by the adrenal medulla as part of sympathetic activation leading to a diverse set of effects (e.g., racing heart).

episodic memory Memory for specific events, including events outside of the laboratory (e.g., the event of your tenth birthday) or inside (e.g., the event of memorizing a particular story). Often contrasted with generic or semantic memory.

equality matching relationship A type of relationship in which each partner gives something to the other and expects to receive something in return.

equipotentiality principle The claim (contradicted by much evidence) that organisms can learn to associate any response with any reward or to associate any pair of stimuli.

escape responses Responses that allow an organism to end an aversive state, for example, to gain warmth while cold, or to terminate an electric shock.

estrogen A female sex hormone that dominates the first half of the female cycle through ovulation.

estrus In mammals, the period in the cycle when the female is sexually receptive (in heat).

etiology The cause or origins of something, such as a disease.

evidence-based practice (EBP) The broad notion that each form of therapy must be based on solid research documenting the effectiveness of the therapy.

evolution via natural selection The biological process through which organisms change across the various generations. Organisms that have an advantage in survival and reproduction are more likely to transmit their genes to the next generation, and so the traits linked to those genes will be more frequent in the next generation.

evolutionary psychology A theoretical perspective that argues that many psychological questions can be illuminated by considering the selective pressures that have been in place for a species as it evolved.

exchange relationship A hypothesized type of social relationship in which the relationship depends on reciprocity; if goods (or esteem or loyalty) are given by one of the partners in the relationship, then the other must respond in kind.

excitation threshold The voltage difference between a neuron's interior and exterior that, if exceeded, causes the neuron to fire. This voltage is about −55 millivolts in mammals. If the voltage reaches this threshold (from a "resting" voltage of −70 millivolts), the neuron's membrane destabilizes, leading to an action potential.

excitation transfer The transfer of autonomic arousal from one situation to another, as when strenuous exercise leads to an increased arousal when presented with aggression-arousing or erotic stimuli.

experiential therapies A family of therapies that, in general, seek to create a genuinely empathic and accepting atmosphere in therapy, and also challenge the patient to deepen his experience.

experimental group The group within an experimental design that receives the (potential) effects of the independent variable.

experimental manipulation The thing that is deliberately altered in an experiment in order to learn about its effects. The experimental manipulation defines the *independent variable* (e.g., presence or absence of an instruction, or a happy or sad story).

explanatory style The characteristic manner in which a person explains good or bad fortunes that befall him. An explanatory style in which bad fortunes are generally attributed to internal, global, and stable causes may create a predisposition that makes a person vulnerable to depression.

explicit attitude An attitude that a person acknowledges having and can be expressed; often contrasted with an implicit attitude. *See also* implicit attitude.

explicit memory Memory retrieval in which there is awareness of remembering at the time of retrieval. *See also* implicit memory.

external validity The degree to which a study's participants, stimuli, and procedures adequately reflect the world as it actually is.

extinction In classical conditioning, the weakening of the tendency of the conditioned stimulus (CS) to elicit the conditioned response (CR) by unreinforced presentations of the CS. In instrumental conditioning, a decline in the tendency to perform the instrumental response brought about by unreinforced occurrences of that response.

eyewitness identification A selection, usually from a group of people or photographs, made by someone who observed a crime (or a simulation of a crime, in a research study), picking the person who was the perpetrator of that crime.

face validity One of the assessments of whether a test measures what it is supposed to mesure. This assessment asks broadly whether it makes sense, on reflection, that the test is measuring what it is designed to measure.

facial-feedback hypothesis   The hypothesis that our facial movements feed back to our emotional experience, so that changes in our facial responses lead to changes in our emotional experiences.

factor analysis   A statistical method for studying the interrelations among various tests, the object of which is to discover what the tests have in common and whether these communalities can be ascribed to one or several factors that run through all or some of these tests.

false alarm   A response indicating that a signal is present when it is not. Cases include hearing tones that are not presented, or concluding that a suspect is guilty when she is in fact innocent.

false consensus effect   The tendency to exaggerate support for one's own position.

familiarity   Usually, the subjective sense that a stimulus has been encountered before. In some circumstances, though, people show a different reaction to a previously encountered stimulus (in comparison to a novel stimulus), indicating an effect of familiarization, but they have no subjective sense that the stimulus is familiar.

family resemblance structure   Overlap of features among members of a category such that no members of the category have all of the features but all members have some of them.

feature detectors   Neurons in the retina or brain that respond to specific features of the stimulus, such as movement, orientation, and so on.

feature net   A model of pattern recognition in which there is a network of detectors, with feature detectors at the bottom.

Fechner's law   The assertion that the strength of a sensation is proportional to the logarithm of physical stimulus intensity.

feedback   A system in which an action produces some consequence that affects (feeds back on) the action. In negative feedback, the consequence stops or reverses the action (e.g., thermostat-controlled furnace). In positive feedback, the consequence strengthens the action (e.g., rocket that homes in on airplanes).

fetus   The stage in gestation following the embryonic stage. In humans, from about eight weeks until birth.

FI schedule   *See* fixed-interval (FI) schedule.

figure   The object focused on, with the rest of the stimulus input considered merely as "background" (*see* ground). By virtue of being focused on, the figure gains certain other attributes: it is seen as having distinct edges, for example, while the same edges merely mark places that the ground drops from view. *See* figure-ground organization.

figure-ground organization   The segregation of the visual field into a part (the figure) that stands out against the rest (the ground).

file-drawer problem   A tendency for disappointing or negative results not to be reported (and so merely dumped into a file drawer). This tendency can cause a bias in the pattern of evidence available.

fissures   Deep grooves in the brain, between convolutions, or in some cases marking the boundaries between large structures.

5HT   *See* serotonin.

5-hydroxy-tryptamine   *See* serotonin.

fixation   (1) In problem solving, the result of rigid mental sets that makes it difficult for people to approach a problem in new and different ways. (2) In Freud's theory of personality, the lingering attachment to an earlier stage of pleasure seeking, even after a new stage has been attained.

fixed-interval (FI) schedule   A pattern of rewards in which an organism can earn some reinforcement only after a certain time period (the interval) has elapsed. After that time period, the very next response will be rewarded. In a fixed-interval one-minute schedule, for example, any responses during the initial minute will not be rewarded. The very first response after the minute will be rewarded.

fixed-ratio (FR) schedule   A pattern of rewards in which an organism can earn some reinforcement only by producing a certain number of responses. In a fixed-ratio 5 schedule, for example, the animal must respond five times in order to be rewarded.

flashbulb memories   Vivid, detailed memories said to be produced by unexpected and emotionally important events.

fluent aphasias   A syndrome derived from a specific form of brain damage, in which the person seems able to produce speech but is unable to understand what is said to her. In most cases, the sentences produced by the person make little sense, consisting instead of "word salad."

fluid intelligence   The ability, which is said to decline with age, to deal with essentially new problems. *See also* crystallized intelligence.

Flynn effect   An effect observed worldwide over the last several decades in which IQ scores seem to be rising.

fMRI scan   *See* functional MRI (fMRI) scan.

follicles   Ova-containing sacs in the mammalian ovary.

foot-in-the-door technique   A technique of persuasion, initially used by door-to-door salespeople, in which one first obtains a small concession that then makes it easier to persuade the target to make a subsequent, larger concession.

forebrain   In mammals, the bulk of the brain. Its foremost region includes the cerebral hemispheres; its rear includes the thalamus and hypothalamus.

forgetting curve   A curve showing the inverse relationship between memory and the retention interval.

formal operations period   In Piaget's theory, the period from about age eleven on, when genuinely abstract mental operations (e.g., the ability to entertain hypothetical possibilities) can be undertaken.

fovea   The area of the retina on which an image falls when the viewer is looking directly at the source of the image. Acuity is greater when the image falls on the fovea than it is when it falls on any other portion of the retina.

fragment-completion task   A procedure sometimes used for testing implicit memory; the participant is given a fragment of a word (C__O__O__I__E) and has to fill in the missing letters to complete an actual word (CROCODILE). Success in this task is much more likely if the target word was encountered recently.

framing   A heuristic that affects the subjective desirability of an event by changing the standard of reference for judging the desirability (e.g., by comparing all outcomes to the worst-possible result, rather than comparing them to the best-possible result).

fraternal twins   Twins that arise from two different eggs that are (simultaneously) fertilized by different sperm cells. Their genetic similarity is no greater than that between ordinary siblings. *See also* identical twins.

free association   Method used in psychoanalytic therapy in which the patient is to say anything that comes to her mind, no matter how apparently trivial, unrelated, or embarrassing.

free recall   A test of memory that asks for as many items in a list as a research participant can recall regardless of order.

frequency   (1) In sound waves or light waves, the number of wave peaks per second. In sound, frequency governs the perceived pitch of the sound; in light, frequency governs the perceived hue of the light. (2) In statistical analysis, the number of occurrences of a particular observation.

frequency distribution   An arrangement in which scores are tabulated by how often they occur.

frequency estimates   A person's estimates of how often he has encountered a particular event or object.

frequency theory   The proposal that the perception of a tone's pitch is coded by the rate of firing of neurons in the auditory system. This proposal is probably correct for the perception of lower pitches, but certainly false for higher pitches.

frontal lobe   The lobe in each cerebral hemisphere that includes the prefrontal area and the motor projection areas.

FR schedule   *See* fixed-ration (FR) schedule.

functional MRI (fMRI) scan   An adaptation of the standard MRI procedures that can measure fast-changing physiology (mostly blood flow and oxygen use) within the brain.

function morphemes   Words or parts of words that help specify the relations among words. Examples include the *–s* morpheme in English used to mark plurals, the *–ed* morpheme which marks the past tense, or the word *will*, used to mark future tense. *See also* content morphemes.

fundamental attribution error   The tendency to attribute behaviors to dispositional qualities while underrating the role of the situation. *See also* actor-observer difference.

g   *See* general intelligence.

GABA (gamma-amino butyric acid)   The most widely distributed inhibitory transmitter of the central nervous system.

GAD   *See* generalized anxiety disorder.

gamma-amino butyric acid   *See* GABA.

gamma-band oscillation   A particular rhythm of about forty pulses per second; different neurons in different parts of the brain all fire at this rate and in synchrony when they are responding to (different aspects of) the same stimulus.

ganglion   A neural control center that integrates messages from different receptor cells and coordinates the activity of different muscle fibers; plural: ganglia.

ganglion cells   In the retina, one of the intermediate links between the receptor cells and the brain. The axons of the ganglion cells converge into a bundle of fibers that leave the eyeball as the optic nerve. *See also* bipolar cells.

garden path   A term used to describe sentences that initially lead the listener toward one interpretation but then demand a different interpretation, for example, "Fat people eat accumulates."

gender constancy   The recognition that being male or female is to all intents and purposes irrevocable.

gender identity   The inner sense of being male or female. *See also* gender role, sexual orientation.

gender role   The set of external behavior patterns a given culture deems appropriate for each sex. *See also* gender identity, sexual orientation.

gene   The unit of hereditary transmission, located at a particular place in a given chromosome. Both members of each chromosome pair have corresponding locations at which there are genes that carry instructions about the same characteristic (e.g., eye color). If one member of a gene pair is dominant and the other is recessive, the dominant gene will exert its effect regardless of what the recessive gene calls for. The characteristic called for by the recessive gene will only be expressed if the other member of the gene pair is also recessive. *See also* chromosomes.

general intelligence (*g*)   A mental attribute that is hypothesized as being called on in any intellectual task a person has to perform.

generalization gradient   The curve that shows the relationship between the tendency to respond to a new stimulus and its similarity to the original conditioned stimulus (CS).

generalized anxiety disorder (GAD)   A mental disorder whose primary characteristic is an all-pervasive, "free-floating" anxiety. A member of the diagnostic category "anxiety disorders," which also includes phobias and obsessive-compulsive disorders. *See also* anxiety disorders.

general paresis   A psychosis characterized by progressive decline in cognitive and motor function culminating in death, reflecting a deteriorating brain condition produced by syphilitic infection.

generic memory   Memory for items of knowledge as such (e.g., The capital of France is Paris), independent of the occasion on which they are learned.

genetic sex   A designation of an organism's sex based entirely on the genetic pattern, whether XY (male) or XX (female). Often contrasted with morphological sex, which is based on anatomical features.

geniculate nucleus   *See* lateral geniculate nucleus.

genital stage   In psychoanalytic theory, the stage of psychosexual development reached in adult sexuality in which sexual pleasure involves not only one's own gratification but also the social and bodily satisfaction brought to another person.

genome   The catalog of all of a species' genes.

genotype   The genetic blueprint of an organism which may or may not be overtly expressed by its phenotype. *See also* phenotype.

geons   Primitive geometric figures, such as cubes, cylinders, and pyramids, from which all other shapes are created through combination. In many models of pattern recognition, the organism must first determine which geons are present and then determine what the objects are.

Gestalt   An organized whole such as a visual form or a melody.

Gestalt psychology   A theoretical approach that emphasizes the role of organized wholes (Gestalten) in perception and other psychological processes.

glands   Bodily organs that produce hormones. *See also* endocrine system.

glial cells   Cells in the brain that act as guidewires for growing neurons, provide a supportive scaffolding for mature neurons, and form the myelin sheath and blood-brain barrier.

glove anesthesia   A condition sometimes seen in conversion disorders, in which there is an anesthesia of the entire hand with no loss of feeling above the wrist. This symptom makes no organic sense given the anatomical arrangement of the nerve trunks and indicates that the condition has a psychological basis.

glucoreceptors   Receptors in the brain (in the area of the hypothalamus) that detect the amount of glucose in the bloodstream.

glucose   The form of sugar that is the major source of energy for most bodily tissues. If plentiful, much of it is converted into glycogen and stored.

glutamate   The most critical neurotransmitter in the retina, it also appears to be important for long-term memory and the perception of pain.

glycogen   A stored form of metabolic energy derived from glucose. To be used, it must first be converted back into glucose.

goal neglect   A pattern of behavior in which someone fails to keep in mind what her goal is, so that (for example) she relies on habitual responses even if those responses will not move the person toward the goal.

goal state   The situation one is trying to reach or set up when solving a problem.

gonads   The body's primary sexual organs—ovaries in the female, testes in the male.

good continuation   A factor in visual grouping. Contours tend to be seen in such a way that their direction is altered as little as possible.

gray matter   That portion of the brain that appears gray. The color reflects the absence of myelination (which makes neural tissue appear white). The gray matter consists of the cell bodies, dendrites, and unmyelinated axons that comprise the nervous system's microcircuitry.

great-person theory   The notion that significant events in history are caused by specific and exceptional individuals, rather than being precipitated largely by surrounding events.

ground   The backdrop against which a figure is viewed. *See* figure-ground organization.

grouping   The step in perception in which one determines which elements of the display belong together, as parts of a larger unit, and which do not.

group polarization   A pattern often observed in group discussions in which the attitudes of each member of the group become more extreme as a result of the discussion, even though the discussion drew their attention to arguments on the other side of the issue, arguments that plausibly might have moderated their views.

groupthink   A pattern of thinking that occurs when a group works on a problem, especially if the group is highly cohesive, faced by some external threat, and closed to outside information or opinions.

H   *See* heritability ratio.

habituation   A decline in the tendency to respond to stimuli that have become familiar. While short-term habituation dissipates in a matter of minutes, long-term habituation may persist for days or weeks.

habituation procedure   A widely used method for studying infant perception. After some exposure to a visual stimulus, an infant becomes habituated and stops looking at it. The extent to which a new stimulus leads to renewed interest and resumption of looking is taken as a measure of the extent to which the infant regards this new stimulus as different from the old one to which he became habituated.

hair cells   The auditory receptors in the cochlea, lodged between the basilar membrane and other membranes above.

hallucinations   Perceived experiences that occur in the absence of actual sensory stimulation.

heritability ratio (*H*)   This refers to the relative importance of heredity and environment in determining the observed variation of a particular trait. More specifically, *H* is the proportion of the variance of the trait in a given population that is attributable to genetic factors.

hertz (Hz)   A measure of frequency in number of cycles per second.

heterosexuality   A sexual orientation leading to a choice of sexual partners of the opposite sex.

heuristics   In problem solving, a procedure that has often worked in the past and is likely, but not certain, to work again. Heuristics typically sacrifice accuracy or guarantee of success in order to gain efficiency. *See also* algorithm.

hierarchy of needs   According to Maslow and other adherents of the humanistic approach, human needs are arranged in a hierarchy with physiological needs such as hunger at the bottom, safety needs further up, the need for attachment and love still higher, and the desire for esteem yet higher. At the very top of the hierarchy is the striving for self-actualization. By and large, people will only strive for the higher-order needs when the lower ones are fulfilled. *See also* self-actualization.

higher-order invariants   Aspects of the stimulus input, usually involving ratios or relationships, that remain unchanged despite changes in viewing circumstances. For example, if a viewer walks toward a car, the retinal image cast by that car grows larger as the viewing distance shrinks. Even so, there is no change in the relationship between the car's image size and, say, the image size of the person standing next to the car. Some have hypothesized that by attending to this unchanging ratio, the viewer can gain a more accurate perception of the car's size.

hindbrain   The rearmost portion of the brain just above the spinal cord, which includes the pons, medulla, and cerebellum.

hippocampus   A subcortical brain structure located in the temporal lobe, and which plays a pivotal role in learning and memory. Damage to the hippocampus (and related structures) typically leads to anterograde amnesia.

histogram   A graphic rendering of a frequency distribution which depicts the distribution by a series of contiguous rectangles. *See also* frequency distribution.

hit   A response indicating that a signal is present when it is in fact present. *See* false alarm.

homeostasis   The body's tendency to maintain the conditions of its internal environment by various forms of self-regulation.

homogamy   The tendency of like to mate with like.

homosexuality   A sexual orientation leading to a choice of partners of the same sex.

hormone   A chemical released by one of the glands. Hormones travel through the bloodstream and control a number of bodily functions, including metabolic rate, arousal level, sugar output of the liver, and so on.

hue   A perceived dimension of visual stimuli whose meaning is close to the term color (e.g., red, blue).

humanistic approach   Asserts that what is most important about people is how they achieve their selfhood and actualize their potentialities. *See also* psychodynamic approach, situationism, sociocultural approach.

Huntington's disease   A progressive hereditary disorder that involves degeneration of the basal ganglia and that results in jerky limb movements, facial twitches, and uncontrolled writhing of the body.

hypnosis   A temporary, trancelike state that can be induced in normal persons. During hypnosis, various hypnotic or posthypnotic suggestions sometimes produce effects that resemble some of the symptoms of conversion disorders. *See also* conversion disorder.

hypochondriasis   A disorder in which the sufferer believes he has a specific disease and typically goes from doctor to doctor to be evaluated for it.

hypomania   A mild manic state in which the individual seems infectiously merry, extremely talkative, charming, and indefatigable.

hypothalamus   A small structure at the base of the forebrain that plays a vital role in the control of the autonomic nervous system, of the endocrine system, and of the major biological drives.

hysteria   An older term for a group of presumably psychogenic disorders including conversion disorders and dissociative disorders. Since DSM-III, it is no longer used as a diagnostic category, in part because of an erroneous implication that the condition is more prevalent in women (Greek *hystera*—womb). *See also* conversion disorder, dissociative disorders, glove anesthesia.

id   In Freud's theory, a term for the most primitive reactions of human personality, consisting of blind strivings for immediate biological satisfaction regardless of cost. *See also* ego, superego.

ideal self   The concept that each person holds describing how they ought to behave; in self theories, the self that one would ideally like to be.

ideas of reference   A characteristic of some mental disorders, notably schizophrenia, in which the patient begins to think that external events are specially related to her personally (e.g., "People walk by and follow me").

identical twins   Twins that originate from a single fertilized egg that then splits into two exact replicas that develop into two genetically identical individuals. *See also* fraternal twins.

identity crisis   A hypothesized period of adolescence in which the individual must discover who and what he really is.

ill-defined problems   Problems for which the goal state is defined only in general terms, and for which the available steps in reaching that goal state are not specified.

illusory conjunction   A pattern of errors found, for example, in visual search tasks, in which observers correctly perceive the features present (redness, greenness, roundness, angularity) but misperceive how these were combined in the display (and so they might see a green *O* and a red *X* when, in fact, a green *X* and red *O* were presented).

illusory correlation   A perception that two facts or observations tend to occur together, even though they do not, such as the erroneous belief that all accountants are introverted.

imitation   The surprisingly complex process through which an organism behaves in a fashion that is guided by (and, usually, copies) the actions of another organism.

implicit attitude An attitude that a person does not realize she holds, but which nonetheless influences her actions and other beliefs.

implicit measures of attitudes Attitudinal measures which do not involve explicit reports by the participant. Examples include measures of facial behavior and reaction times in response to various attitude-relevant stimuli.

implicit memory Memory retrieval in which there is no awareness of remembering at the time of retrieval. *See also* explicit memory.

implicit theories of personality Beliefs about the way in which different patterns of behavior of people hang together and why they do so.

impression management The steps that people take to influence or guide how other people perceive them.

imprinting A learned attachment that is formed at a particular period in life (the critical, or sensitive, period) and is difficult to reverse (e.g., the duckling's acquired tendency to follow whatever moving stimulus it encounters twelve to twenty-four hours after hatching).

impulsivity A tendency to act without reflecting on one's actions.

incidental learning Learning without trying to learn (e.g., as in a study in which participants judge a speaker's vocal quality when she recites a list of words and are later asked to produce as many of the words as they can recall).

incremental theorists Individuals who believe some aspect of personality or intellectual functioning is malleable.

incubation The hypothetical process of continuing to work on a problem unconsciously after one has ceased to work on that problem consciously. Most contemporary investigators are skeptical about whether such a process truly exists.

independent variable The variable used within a study as a possible basis for making predictions. In an actual experiment, the independent variable is manipulated by the experimenter; in a correlational study, the independent variable is observed and then used as a (potential) basis for predicting other data.

individualism A cultural pattern in which people are considered to be fundamentally independent and in which the emphasis is on the ways a person can stand out through achieving private goals. Individualist societies include the dominant cultures of the United States, Western Europe, Canada, and Australia. *See also* collectivism.

individualistic cultures *See* individualism.

induced motion Perceived movement of an objectively stationary stimulus that is enclosed by a moving framework.

induced motion of the self A pattern in which surrounding objects are in fact moving but are perceived as stationary, and in which the self is therefore (falsely) perceived as moving. An example occurs in traffic, when the next car rolls forward but is misperceived as stationary and one's own car is misperceived as rolling backward.

inductive reasoning Reasoning in which one observes a number of particular instances and tries to determine a general rule that covers them all.

informant data Data about a person derived from others who know the person well.

informational influence A source of conformity that derives from people's desire to make the correct decision or action.

information-processing approach A perspective that seeks to explain some aspect of behavior by referring to the underlying capacities to remember, pay attention, solve problems, and so on.

informed consent A procedural step, conducted before an experiment begins, in which the research participants are asked to give their agreement to participate, based on full information about what the experiment will involve.

in-group The social group that one is a member of, usually perceived as more homogeneous than other groups of which one is not a member.

in-group favoritism The tendency to favor one's own group.

inhibited temperament A personality style characterized by a fear of novelty that is evident early in life.

inhibitor A stimulus which signals that an event is not coming, and which thereby produces a response opposite to that ordinarily produced by the stimulus that is now signaled as not coming.

initial state The status a person is in at the start of her attempts toward solving a problem. In solving the problem she hopes to move from this initial state to the problem's goal state.

inner ear The portion of the ear in which the actual transduction of sound takes place.

inspection time The time someone needs to make a simple discrimination between two stimuli; inspection time turns out to be reasonably well correlated with standard measures of intelligence.

instrumental conditioning Also called operant conditioning. A form of learning in which a reinforcer (e.g., food) is given only if the animal performs the instrumental response (e.g., pressing a lever). In effect, what has to be learned is the relationship between the response and the reinforcer. *See also* classical conditioning.

internal working model A set of beliefs and expectations about how people behave in social relationships, and also guidelines for interpreting others' actions, and habitual responses to make in social settings.

intentional learning The placing of new information into memory that takes place when the person anticipates that their memory will be tested later, so that the person tries in some fashion to learn the material. (Often contrasted with incidental learning.)

internal validity The degree to which a study is successful at measuring what it purports to measure, with all confounds removed and the dependent variable sensibly measured.

International Classification of Disease System (ICD-10) One of the commonly used classification schemes for mental illness. (The ICD is often used in Europe; in the United States, the classification scheme is more commonly the one provided by the *Diagnostic and Statistical Manual of Mental Disorders*.

interneurons Neurons that carry information from one neuron to another (rather than to a gland or muscle fiber or from a sensory receptor).

interpersonal therapy (IPT) A mode of therapy originally intended as a brief method to counter depression, but now extended to other disorders. In this therapy, the focus is on the patient's gaining an understanding of how she interacts with others, and then learning new and more beneficial ways of interacting and communicating.

interposition A monocular depth cue in which objects that are farther away are blocked from view by any other opaque object obstructing their optical path to the eye.

interrater reliability A measure of the agreement among several independent observers of an event or stimulus.

intersexual A child who is not clearly male or female, in some cases because of genetic factors, in others because of morphology.

intersubjectivity The mutual understanding that people share during communication.

interval scale A scale in which equal differences between scores can be treated as equal so that the scores can be added or subtracted. *See also* categorical scale, nominal scale, ordinal scale, ratio scale.

intrinsic motivation Motivation that seems inherent in an activity itself, as when we engage in an activity for its own sake or merely because it is fun.

introspection The process of "looking within" through which a person might try to observe (and perhaps report) the contents of his own mind—his thoughts, beliefs, and feelings, and in some cases the processes through which he came to those current thoughts, beliefs, or feelings.

intrusion errors Memory mistakes in which someone remembers elements that did not actually occur as part of an earlier event (so that these other elements "intrude" into the memory).

in vivo desensitization A step used in treating phobias in which the person, at the end of therapy, is gradually exposed to instances of the phobic stimulus or situation in the real world.

ion channels Biochemical "windows" in a cell wall that allow ions to flow in or out of the cell.

ion pumps Biochemical mechanisms that use energy to move ions either into or out of the cell.

iris The smooth circular muscle in the eye that surrounds the pupil and contracts or dilates under reflex control in order to govern the amount of light entering.

ITP *See* interpersonal therapy.

James-Lange theory of emotions A theory that asserts that the subjective experience of emotion is the awareness of one's own bodily reactions in the presence of certain arousing stimuli.

jnd *See* just-noticeable difference.

just-noticeable difference (jnd) The smallest possible difference between two stimuli that an organism can reliably detect.

kinesthesis A general term for sensory information generated by receptors in the muscles, tendons, and joints which informs us of our skeletal movement.

kin-selection hypothesis The proposal that helpful or altruistic behavior is more likely among organisms that are genetically related to each other than it is among unrelated organisms; the logic of the proposal is that helpful behavior among related organisms promotes the survival of their shared genes.

knowledge-driven processes Processes that are influenced by the person's knowledge and prior beliefs; usually contrasted with data-driven processes.

Korsakoff's syndrome A brain disorder characterized by serious memory disturbances. The most common cause is extreme and chronic alcohol use.

latent content In psychoanalytic interpretation, the actual wishes and concerns that a dream or behavior is intended to express; usually contrasted with manifest content.

latent learning Learning that occurs without being manifested by performance.

lateral geniculate nucleus An important neural waystation on the path from the eye to the brain; ganglion neurons on the retina send their signals to the lateral geniculate nucleus; from there, other neurons carry the signal to the visual cortex in the occipital lobe.

lateral inhibition The tendency of adjacent neural elements of the visual system to inhibit each other; it underlies brightness contrast and the accentuation of contours. *See also* brightness contrast.

lateralization An asymmetry of function of the two cerebral hemispheres. In most right-handers, the left hemisphere is specialized for language functions, while the right hemisphere is better at various visual and spatial tasks.

law of effect A theory that the tendency of a stimulus to evoke a response is strengthened if the response is followed by reward and is weakened if the response is not followed by reward. Applied to instrumental learning, this theory states that as trials proceed, incorrect bonds will weaken while the correct bond will be strengthened.

learned helplessness A condition created by exposure to inescapable aversive events. This retards or prevents learning in subsequent situations in which escape or avoidance is possible.

learned helplessness theory The theory that depression is analogous to learned helplessness effects produced in the laboratory. *See also* learned helplessness.

learned taste aversion A specialized form of learning in which an organism learns to avoid a taste after just one pairing of that taste with illness. For example, an animal will avoid a food that on an earlier occasion made it sick.

learning curve A curve in which some index of learning (e.g., the number of drops of saliva in Pavlov's classical conditioning experiment) is plotted against trials or sessions.

learning model As defined in the text, a subcategory of the pathology model that (1) views mental disorders as the result of some form of faulty learning, and (2) believes that these should be treated by behavior therapists according to the laws of classical and instrumental conditioning or by cognitive therapists who try to affect faulty modes of thinking. *See also* cognitive therapy.

learning theorists A group of theorists who argued that most learning can be understood in terms of a small number of principles that apply to all organisms and all situations.

lens The portion of the eye that bends light rays and thus can focus an image on the retina.

leptin A chemical produced by the adipose cells that seems to signal that plenty of fat is stored and that no more fat is needed. This signal may diminish eating.

lesions The damage incurred by an area of the brain.

lexical decision task A task in which the participant must decide as quickly as possible whether a stimulus (*book, trup, filt*) is or is not a word.

lexical hypothesis This hypothesis holds that the words we use to describe people have been shaped by a kind of linguistic natural selection. Words that are useful descriptors have continued to be used across generations. Words that are not useful have stopped being used and become "extinct." This hypothesis has provided justification for using the dictionary as a source of trait terms.

life data Data about a person derived from public sources.

life instincts A motive postulated by Freud to explain eating, drinking, and sex.

life-span development The process of change and development that can be observed across the entire span of life, from prenatal development to death.

limbic system A group of interconnected subcortical structures crucial for many emotional and motivaton activities, and many aspects of learning and memory. The limbic system includes the hypothalamus, the amygdala, and other structures.

linear perspective A cue for distance that can be portrayed on a flat surface, exploiting the fact that objects appear smaller if viewed from a distance, and that parallel lines seem to converge as they recede into depth.

line of best fit A line drawn through the points in a scatter diagram. It yields the best prediction of one variable when given the value of the other variable.

lobes Rounded substructures within a larger organ. The brain, for example, contains four major lobes—the frontal, parietal, temporal, and occipital.

localization of function The process of determining what each region of the brain contributes to which aspects of thinking and behavior.

local representations A model of cognitive organization, especially semantic memory, in which each concept is represented by a single node or, more plausibly, a group of nodes. *See also* distributed representations, node.

lock-and-key model The theory that neurotransmitter molecules will only affect the postsynaptic membrane if their shape fits into that of certain synaptic receptor molecules.

locomotion The processes and abilities through which one moves around on one's own.

longitudinal fissure The front-to-back cleavage that divides the left and right hemispheres of the brain.

long-term memory Those parts of the memory system that are currently dormant and inactive, but have enormous storage capacity. *See also* stage theory of memory, working memory.

long-term potentiation (LTP) A form of cellular plasticity in which a postsynaptic neuron becomes more sensitive (potentiated) to the signal received from the presynaptic neuron. This potentiation is usually produced by a rapid and sustained burst of firing by the presynaptic neuron. The potentiation can then spread to other presynaptic neurons provided that they have fired in the past at the same time as the presynaptic cell that produced the potentiation in the first place. *See also* activity dependence.

loss aversion   A strong tendency to regard losses as considerably more important than gains of comparable magnitude, and, with this, a tendency to take steps to avoid possible loss.

LTP   *See* long-term potentiation.

Mach bands   The accentuated edges between two adjacent regions that differ in brightness. This sharpening is maximal at the borders where the distance between the two regions is smallest and the contrast most striking.

magic number   According to George Miller, the number (seven plus or minus two) that represents the holding capacity of the working memory system.

magnetic resonance imaging (MRI)   *See* MRI.

magno cells   Ganglion cells found largely in the periphery of the retina that, because of their sensitivity to brightness changes, are particularly suited to the perception of motion and depth. *See also* parvo cells.

maintenance rehearsal   Repetition to keep material in working memory for a while. In contrast to elaborative rehearsal, this confers little long-term benefit for longer-term retention. *See also* elaborative rehearsal.

major depression   A mood disorder in which patients are disabled by guilt or sadness (especially in Western cultures), experience a loss of energy, pleasure and motivation, and disturbances of sleep, diet, and other bodily functions.

major histocompatibility complex (MHC)   Part of the genome involved in the immune system's ability to target invading cells and leave one's own cells alone.

mania   A mood disorder characterized by racing thoughts, pressured speech, irritability or euphoria, and marked impairments in judgment. *See also* bipolar disorder.

manifest content   In psychoanalytic interpretation, the immediately visible, surface content of a dream or behavior. This content is hypothesized to be a means of representing the latent content in disguised form, to protect the person from the anxiety associated with the latent content.

manualized therapy   A form of therapy, often used in research, in which the sequence of therapy is explicitly described in a manual which indicates what steps to take in the therapy, what instructions to offer, and so on.

market pricing relationship   A type of relationship in which each participant is primarily concerned with making sure that what he is putting into the relationship is proportional to what he is getting out of it.

matching hypothesis   The hypothesis that persons seek romantic or sexual partners who possess a similar level of physical attractiveness.

mean (M)   *See* measure of central tendency.

means-end analysis   An important strategy for problem solving in which one's current position and resources are continually evaluated with respect to one's goal.

measure of central tendency   A single number intended to summarize an entire distribution of experimental results. Three commonly used measures of central tendency are: (1) the mode, or the score that occurs most frequently; (2) the median, or the point that divides the distribution into two equal halves; and (3) the mean, or the arithmetic average.

medial forebrain bundle (MFB)   A tract of fibers that runs through the base of the forebrain and parts of the hypothalamus. Electric stimulation of this bundle is usually experienced as rewarding.

median   *See* measure of central tendency.

medulla   Part of the hindbrain and the rearmost portion of the brain, just adjacent to the spinal cord. It is involved in the control of respiration, circulation, balance, and protective reflexes such as coughing and sneezing.

melatonin   A neurohormone secreted by the pineal gland that is involved in regulating the sleep-waking cycle.

memory acquisition   The processes of gaining new knowledge, that is, of establishing new memories in long-term storage.

memory consolidation   The biological process, taking place in the hours after an event is experienced, that creates a long-lasting representation of the event in memory.

memory encoding   The process of "translating" information into a format in which it can be stored for later use.

memory span   The number of items that can be recalled after a single presentation. *See also* magic number.

memory trace   The record in the nervous system that actually preserves a memory of a past experience.

menstrual flow   The discharge consisting of the sloughed-off uterine lining that was built up in preparation for a fertilized ovum, that signals the onset of menstruation.

mental disorders   A clinically-significant problem in thinking, behavior, or emotion that is associated with distress, disability, or significantly increased risk of suffering.

mental health parity   The policy position that insurance plans should reimburse for the costs of treating mental disorders on the same terms that they do for other medical disorders.

mental images   Analogical representations that reserve some of the characteristic attributes of our senses.

mental maps   A mental representation of the spatial layout of a scene, whether a small scene (so that the representation might show, say, the locations of various objects on a table top) or a larger scene (e.g., a representation of an entire city).

mental representations   Internal symbols that stand for something but are not equivalent to it, such as internalized actions, images, or words.

mental rotation   A task in which participants are presented with a rotated figure and must discern whether the figure is normal or, say, mirror-reversed. Participants apparently must visualize the figure rotated to an upright position before responding.

mental set   The predisposition to perceive, remember, or think of one thing rather than another.

meta-analysis   A statistical technique for combining the results of many studies even when the studies used different methods to collect the data. This technique has been useful in many areas, including studies on the outcome of psychotherapy.

metacognition   A general term for knowledge about knowledge, as in knowing that we do or do not remember something.

method of loci   A mnemonic technique that requires the learner to visualize each of the items she wants to remember in a different spatial location (locus). Recall requires that each location be mentally inspected for the item placed there.

MFB   *See* medial forebrain bundle.

MHC   *See* major histocompatibility complex.

microcircuitry   Networks of interneurons within which most of the brain's information processing occurs.

midbrain   The portion of the brain between hindbrain and forebrain that is involved in arousal, the sleep-waking cycle, and auditory and visual targeting.

middle ear   An antechamber to the inner ear which amplifies the sound-produced vibrations of the eardrum and transfers them to the cochlea. *See also* cochlea.

midlife transition   A period of time proposed by many authors in which individuals reappraise what they have done with their lives thus far and may reevaluate their marriage and career.

minimal groups paradigm   A small group interaction paradigm in which groups of individuals are formed on obviously arbitrary grounds.

Minnesota Multiphasic Personality Inventory (MMPI)   A structured (objective) test of personality; the most widely used personality test.

misinformation effect   The result of a procedure in which people experience an event, and then are later exposed to questioning or some overt suggestion that misrepresents the event (e.g., a person who has seen a red car may be told later that the car was blue). The misinformation effect refers to the fact that people often remember the misinformation, rather than the original information.

miss   One of the four possible outcomes in a detection task. If the signal is present and the person says it is not, this is a miss. *See* correct negative.

mixed states   A pattern sometimes observed with bipolar disorder in which the person displays a combination of mania and depression, for example, tearfulness and pessimism combined with grandiosity and racing thoughts.

MMPI   *See* Minnesota Multiphasic Personality Inventory.

mnemonics   Deliberate strategies for helping memory, many of which use imagery.

mode   *See* measure of central tendency.

monocular depth cues   Features of the visual stimulus (e.g., linear perspective and motion parallax) that indicate depth even when it is viewed with one eye.

monogamy   A mating pattern in which a reproductive partnership is based on a special, more or less permanent tie between one male and one female.

monozygotic (MZ)   One of the two types of twins. *See also* identical twins.

mood disorders   A group of disorders distinguished primarily by changes in mood and motivation; these include bipolar disorder and major depression. *See also* bipolar disorder, major depression, mania.

moods   Affective responses that are typically longer-lasting than emotions, and less likely to have a specific object.

morbid obesity   The level of obesity at which someone's health is genuinely at risk, usually defined as a BMI over 40.

morpheme   The smallest significant unit of meaning in a language (e.g., the word boys has two morphemes, *boy* and *s*). *See also* content morpheme, function morpheme.

morphological sex   Classification as male or female based on one's sex organs and bodily appearance (e.g., ovaries, vagina, and smooth facial skin versus testes, penis, and facial hair).

Motherese   A whimsical term for the singsong speech pattern that mothers and other adults generally employ when talking to infants.

motion detectors   Cells in the visual cortex that are sensitive to an image moving across the retina.

motion parallax   A depth cue provided by the fact that, as an observer moves, the images cast by nearby objects move more rapidly on the retina than the images cast by objects farther away.

motoneurons   Neurons whose cell bodies are in the brain or spinal cord and whose axons terminate on muscle fibers.

MRI (magnetic resonance imaging)   A noninvasive neurodiagnostic technique that relies on nuclear magnetic resonance. An MRI scan passes a high frequency alternating magnetic field through the brain to detect the different resonant frequencies of its nuclei. A computer then assembles this information to form a picture of brain structure. *See also* functional MRI (fMRI) scan.

MS   *See* multiple sclerosis.

multicausal models   A conception of a particular effect that emphasizes the role of many factors in leading to that effect.

multimodal therapy   A form of therapy that deliberately weaves together multiple types and multiple forms of therapy.

multiple intelligences   In Howard Gardner's theory, the six essential, independent mental capacities, some of which are outside the traditional academic notions of intelligence, i.e., linguistic, logical-mathematical, spatial, musical, bodily-kinesthetic, and personal intelligence.

multiple sclerosis (MS)   A progressive neurological disease wherein the immune system mistakenly destroys the myelin sheaths that comprise the brain's white matter, producing manifestations such as numbness, blindness, and paralysis.

myelin sheath   The series of fatty wrappers, formed by special glial cells, that surround the axons of those neurons that must communicate over long distances in the nervous system and that allow for fast propagation of action potentials along those axons. *See also* nodes of Ranvier.

national character   The idea that people in different cultures have different personalities.

nativism   The view that some important aspects of perception and of other cognitive processes are innate.

natural selection   The explanatory principle by which Darwin accounted for biological evolution. It refers to the greater likelihood of successful reproduction for those organisms possessing attributes that are advantageous in a given environment. If these attributes are hereditary, then they will be well represented in the next generation, and, if the process continues over many generations, it can result in wholesale changes in bodily form and behavior.

NE   *See* norepinephrine.

negative afterimage   In color vision, the persistence of an image that possesses the hue complementary to that of the stimulus (e.g., seeing a yellow afterimage after staring at a blue lamp), resulting from the operation of opponent processes.

negative cognitive schema   For Aaron Beck, the core cognitive component of depression, consisting of an individual's automatic negative interpretations concerning himself, his future, and the world. *See also* explanatory style.

negative feedback   *See* feedback.

negative symptoms of schizophrenia   Symptoms that involve deficits in normal functioning, such as apathy, impoverished speech, and emotional blunting. *See also* positive symptoms of schizophrenia.

neglect syndrome   The result of certain lesions of the right parietal lobe that leave a patient inattentive to stimuli to her left (e.g., not eating food on the left side of the plate) and result in her ignoring the left side of her body (e.g., putting makeup on only the right side of her face).

neocortex   The outermost, convoluted layer of the forebrain, often referred to merely as the cortex.

nerve growth factor   A neurochemical that promotes the sprouting of new neuronal connections.

nerve impulse   *See* action potential.

network models   Theories of cognitive organization, especially of semantic memory, which hold that items of information are represented by a system of nodes linked through associative connections. *See also* connectionist model, distributed representations, local representations, node.

neural correlates   The events in the nervous system that happen at the same time as (and are thus correlated with) the mental or behavioral events we hope to explain.

neural plasticity   The capacity for neurons to alter their functioning as a result of experience.

neural plate   A small thickening, running the length of the embryo, from which the neural tube and, eventually, the nervous system, develop.

neural stem cells   Cells within the fetus that are the developmental precursors of neurons.

neural tube   The tubular structure, formed by the fusion of the edges of the neural plate, from which the central nervous system (forebrain, midbrain, hindbrain, and spinal cord) develops.

neurodevelopmental disorder   A disorder that stems from early brain abnormalities. Many researchers believe that schizophrenia is one such disorder and may originate in abnormal fetal brain development.

neurofibrillary tangles   Stringy debris observed in the brain as a consequence of the neuron degeneration in Alzheimer's disease.

neurogenesis   The process through which the nervous system grows and develops, a process including cellular signaling, differentiation, migration and proliferation.

neuroimaging techniques   Methods that permit noninvasive study and depiction of brain structure or function. *See also* CT scan, MRI, functional MRI scan, and PET scan.

neuromuscular junction   The location where a motoneuron meets a muscle fiber; activation of this neuron causes the muscle fiber to contract.

neuron   A nerve cell.

neuronal workspace hypothesis   A broad hypothesis about the neural basis of consciousness. According to this hypothesis, the processing of specific aspects of a stimulus or task can be done by neurons.

neuropeptide Y (NPY)   A chemical found widely in the brain and periphery. In the brain, it acts as a neurotransmitter; when administered at sites in and near the hypothalamus, it is a potent elicitor of eating.

neuropsychologists   Investigators who draw claims about brain-behavior relationships, using evidence from cases of brain damage, plus close observation of the changes in function associated with that damage.

neuropsychology   The study of brain-damaged individuals with the aim of learning how brain function makes psychological processes and achievements possible.

neuroscience   A multidisciplinary project, drawing on psychology, biology, and chemistry, aimed at learning how the nervous system functions.

neurosis   A broad term once used for mental disorders whose primary symptoms are anxiety or what seem to be defenses against anxiety. Since the adoption of DSM-III, the term has been dropped as a broad diagnostic label, and what were once considered the various subcategories of neurosis (e.g., phobia, anxiety, conversion and dissociative disorders) are now classified as separate disorders.

neurotoxin   Any chemical poisonous to neurons.

neurotransmitters   The chief means of communication among neurons; neurotransmitters are chemicals released by one neuron (usually: the presynaptic neuron), which then can trigger a response in another neuron (usually: the postsynaptic neuron).

neurotrophic factors   Chemicals that influence developing neural cells.

NGF   *See* nerve growth factor.

node   A point in a network at which a number of connections converge.

nodes of Ranvier   The gaps occurring between the glial-cell wrappers that form the myelin sheath surrounding many kinds of axons. The nodes are crucial to the rapidity at which neural impulses travel along myelinated axons.

nominal scale   A scale in which responses are ordered only into different categories. *See also* categorical scale, interval scale, ordinal scale, ratio scale.

nonfluent aphasia   Speech disorder in which the main difficulty is in speech production, often involving damage to Broca's area in the frontal lobe.

norepinephrine (NE)   The neurotransmitter found in the nerves of the sympathetic branch of the autonomic nervous system. It is also one of the neurotransmitters involved in various arousal systems in the brain.

normal curve   A symmetrical, bell-shaped curve that describes the probability of obtaining various combinations of chance events. It depicts the normal distribution, the frequency distribution of many physical and psychological attributes of humans and animals.

normal distribution   A frequency distribution whose graphic representation has a symmetrical, bell-shaped form—the normal curve. Its characteristics are often referred to when investigators test statistical hypotheses and make inferences about the population from a given sample.

normative influence   A source of conformity that derives from people's desire to be liked (or not appear foolish).

norm of reciprocity   The norm that suggests that a favor must be repaid.

norms   In intelligence testing, the scores taken from a large sample of the population against which an individual's test scores are evaluated.

NPY   *See* neuropeptide Y.

nucleus accumbens   A dopamine-rich area in the forebrain that is critical in the physiology of reward.

null hypothesis   The hypothesis that an obtained difference is merely a chance fluctuation from a population in which the true mean difference is zero.

obedience   Behavior that conforms to an instruction or command from another person.

object permanence   The conviction that an object remains perceptually constant over time and exists even when it is out of sight. According to Piaget, this does not develop until infants are eight months old or more.

object relations   A school of psychodynamic thought that emphasizes the real (as opposed to fantasized) relations an individual has with others.

observational learning   A mechanism of socialization whereby a child observes another person who serves as a model and then proceeds to imitate what that model does.

observational study   A study in which the investigator does not manipulate any of the variables but simply observes their relationship as they occur naturally.

obsessive-compulsive disorder (OCD)   A disorder whose symptoms are obsessions (persistent and irrational thoughts or wishes) and compulsions (uncontrollable, repetitive acts), which seem to be defenses against anxiety. A member of a diagnostic category called anxiety disorders, which also includes generalized anxiety disorder and phobias.

occipital lobe   The rearmost lobe in each cerebral hemisphere, which includes the primary visual projection area.

OCD   *See* obsessive-compulsive disorder.

OCD spectrum disorders   A family of disorders believed to derive from the same genetic inheritance, and involving the basal ganglia and frontal lobes. All involve some form of obsessive and compulsive symptoms and may benefit from the same kinds of medications as OCD.

Oedipus complex   In psychoanalytic theory, a general term for the cluster of impulses and conflicts hypothesized to occur during the phallic phase, at around age five. In boys, a fantasized form of intense, possessive sexual love is directed at the mother, which is soon followed by hatred for and fear of the father. As the fear mounts, the sexual feelings are pushed underground and the boy identifies with the father. An equivalent process is hypothesized in girls and is called the Electra complex.

one-trial learning   In classical conditioning, the establishment of a conditioned response (CR) after only one pairing of conditioned stimulus (CS) and unconditioned stimulus (US).

ontogeny   The process of an individual's development during its lifespan (usually contrasted with phylogeny—the process of a species' development over the span of evolution).

operant In Skinner's system, an instrumental response, defined by the effect it has (the way it "operates") on the environment. *See also* instrumental conditioning.

operant conditioning *See* instrumental conditioning.

operation span An experimental procedure used to measure someone's working memory capacity. In this procedure, participants are asked to memorize one set of items while "operating on" a different task.

operations According to Piaget, the mental transformations and relationships that underlie logical thought.

opponent-process theory (1) A theory of color vision that proposes three pairs of color antagonists: red-green, blue-yellow, and white-black. Excitation of one member of a pair automatically inhibits the other member. (2) A theory of motivation that asserts that the nervous system tends to counteract any deviation from the neutral point on the pain-pleasure dimension. If the original stimulus is maintained, there is an attenuation of the emotional state one is in; if it is withdrawn, the opponent process reveals itself, and the emotional state swings sharply in the opposite direction.

optic flow The phenomenon wherein an object's retinal image enlarges as we approach the object and shrinks as we retreat from it. It is used as a depth cue by the visual system.

optic nerve The bundle of fibers that proceeds from each eyeball to the brain, made up of axons whose cell bodies are retinal ganglion cells.

oral character According to Freud, a personality type based on a fixation at the oral stage of development and whose manifestations can include passive dependency or "biting" hostility. *See also* oral stage.

oral stage In psychoanalytic theory, the earliest stage of psychosexual development during which the primary source of bodily pleasure is stimulation of the mouth and lips, as in sucking at the breast.

ordinal scale A scale in which responses are rank-ordered by relative magnitude but in which the intervals between successive ranks are not necessarily equal. *See also* categorical scale, interval scale, nominal scale, ratio scale.

orexins Hormones synthesized in the lateral hypothalamus that are potent elicitors of eating.

organic brain syndromes Mental disorders that are reliably associated with definitive brain damage (e.g., Alzheimer's disease).

orienting The tendency of an organism to shift its attention and sensory surfaces (e.g., by moving the eyes or turning the ears) to inspect a novel or unexpected stimulus.

ought self In self theories, the ought self is the self one thinks one should be.

outcome expectations A set of beliefs, drawn from experience, about what the consequences (rewards or punishments) of certain actions are likely to be.

outer ear The portion of the structures of the ear that includes the earflap, the auditory canal, and the outer surface of the eardrum.

out-group A social group with which one does not identify or to which one does not belong.

out-group homogeneity effect A phenomenon related to stereotyping in which a member of a group (the in-group) tends to view members of another group (the out-group) as more alike (less varied) than are members of his or her own group.

oval window The membrane separating the middle ear from the inner ear.

overregularization errors A pattern of mistakes in which a person treats irregular cases as though they followed the rules, for example, saying "goed" instead of "went," or "foots" instead of "feet."

overwrite A hypothesized process in which later arriving information about an event replaces (and so "overwrites") information that was originally in memory for that same event.

oxytocin A hormone manufactured mostly in the hypothalamus that plays an important role in regulating sexual activity, nesting, and breast-feeding.

pancreas An organ in the body, part of the endocrine system, that (among its other functions) secretes insulin.

PANDAS *See* pediatric autoimmune neuropsychiatric disorders associated with streptococcal infections.

panic attack A sudden episode consisting of terrifying bodily symptoms such as labored breathing, choking, dizziness, tingling in the hands and feet, sweating, trembling, heart palpitations, and chest pain. Panic attacks occur in a number of mental disorders and are common in phobias, panic disorder, and post-traumatic stress disorder (PTSD).

panic disorder An anxiety disorder characterized by repeated or disabling panic attacks. *See also* anxiety disorders, panic attack.

parallel distributed processing (PDP) Models of cognitive processing in which the relevant symbolic representations do not correspond to any one unit of the network but to the state of the network as a whole. *See also* connectionist model, distributed representation.

paranoid schizophrenia A subcategory of schizophrenia. Its dominant symptom is a set of delusions that are often elaborately systematized, usually of grandeur or persecution.

parasympathetic branch A division of the autonomic nervous system that serves vegetative functions and conserves bodily energies (e.g., slowing heart rate). Its action is often antagonistic to that of the sympathetic branch.

parietal lobe The lobe in each cerebral hemisphere that lies between the occipital and frontal lobes, and that includes the primary sensory projection area.

Parkinson's disease A degenerative neurological disorder characterized by various motor difficulties that include tremor, muscular rigidity, and slowed movement. This disease involves degeneration of dopamine-releasing neurons in the basal ganglia of the forebrain, which are crucial for motor control.

parsing The process through which a perceiver determines which parts of the figure belong with other parts (so that the parts are perceived as different aspects of a single object).

partial reinforcement A condition in which repeated responses are reinforced only some of the time.

parvo cells Ganglion cells found throughout the retina that, because of their sensitivity to differences in hue, are particularly suited to the perception of color and form. *See also* magno cells.

pattern recognition The process by which the perceptual system identifies the forms it encounters.

pattern theory The theory that a stimulus attribute is not coded by being sent along specific sensory fibers, but rather by a specific pattern of firing of all the relevant sensory fibers.

PDP *See* parallel distributed processing.

pediatric autoimmune neuropsychiatric disorders associated with streptococcal infections (PANDAS) A medical condition related to streptococcus, commonly producing one or more of the OCD spectrum disorders.

penis envy In psychoanalytic theory, the wish for a penis that is assumed to ensue normally in females as part of the Electra complex.

percentile rank The percentage of all the scores in a distribution that lie below a given score.

perceptual constancies Constant attributes of a distal object, such as its shape and size, that we are able to perceive despite vagaries of the proximal stimulus.

perceptual organization   A step of interpretation, provided by the perceiver, in which decisions are made about which elements of the display belong together, as parts of a larger whole, and which elements belong to different objects.

perceptual parsing   The process of grouping various visual elements of a scene appropriately, deciding which elements go together and which do not.

peripheral nervous system   The parts of the nervous system outside the central nervous system, including the cranial and spinal nerves that exit the skull and spinal column, respectively.

peripheral route to persuasion   The processes involved in attitude change when someone does not care particularly about an issue or devotes few resources to thinking about the issue. This route depends on superficial considerations, such as the appearance of the person giving the persuasive information, and is contrasted with the *central route*.

permastore   Near-permanent retention of some kinds of items in memory, mostly involving semantic or general knowledge (e.g., multiplication tables, names of family members).

permissive parents   One of the four types of parents; permissive parents set few explicit dos and don'ts for their children, and try not to assert their authority.

permissive pattern   A parental style in which parents try not to assert their authority and impose few restrictions or demands on their children.

perseveration   The tendency to repeat the same response inappropriately, typically accompanying the defects in strategy formation often observed with prefrontal lesions.

persona   The Latin word for the mask that Greek and Roman actors wore to indicate the character that they were playing. The word personality comes from *persona*.

personal space   The physical region all around us whose intrusion we guard against. This aspect of human behavior has been likened to territoriality in animals.

personality disorders   Problems in a person's day to day functioning that can create considerable distress both for the person and for others around her, usually diagnosed via Axis 2 of the *Diagnostic and Statistical Manual of Mental Disorders*.

personality paradox   The idea that people seem to behave much less consistently than a trait conception would predict.

persuasive communications   Messages that openly try to convince us to act a certain way or to hold a particular belief.

PET (positron emission tomography) scan   A technique for examining brain function by observing the degree of metabolic activity of different regions of the brain.

phallic stage   In psychoanalytic theory, the stage of psychosexual development during which the child begins to regard his or her genitals as a major source of gratification.

phenotype   The overt appearance and behavior of an organism, regardless of its genetic blueprint. *See also* genotype.

phenylalanine   An amino acid that cannot be transformed due to an enzyme deficiency in those with phenylketonuria (PKU). In an infant with PKU, phenylalanine is converted into a toxic agent that accumulates in an infant's bloodstream and damages the developing nervous system.

phenylketonuria (PKU)   A condition in which one lacks the gene that enables one to metabolize phenylalanine. If detected early enough, this condition can be treated by means of a special diet. If not detected early, this disorder can cause a severe form of retardation. *See also* phenylalanine.

phobia   An anxiety disorder that is characterized by an intense and, at least on the surface, irrational fear. *See also* anxiety disorders, social phobia.

phoneme   The smallest significant unit of sound in a language. In English, it corresponds roughly to a letter of the alphabet (e.g., apt, tap, and pat are all made up of the same phonemes).

photopigment   A chemical that changes its form in response to light. Photopigments in the eye are altered by incoming light, producing an electrical change that is the initial signal to the nervous system that light is present.

photoreceptor   One of the visual-pigment-filled light-sensitive cells at the back of the retina, whether rods or cones. These are the cells that transduce light energy into neural impulses, launching the processes of vision.

phrase   An organized sequence of words within a sentence that functions as a unit.

phrase structure description   A tree diagram that shows the hierarchical structure of a sentence. The descending branches of the tree correspond to smaller and smaller units of sentence structure.

phylogeny   The process of a species' development over the span of evolution (usually contrasted with ontogeny—the process of an individual's development during its lifespan).

physiological data   Data about a person derived from measurement of biological structures and processes.

pictorial cues   The monocular depth cues (such as interposition, linear perspective, and relative size) that the eye exploits as depth cues; these cues are an optical consequence of the projection of a three-dimensional world onto a flat surface.

pitch   The psychological dimension of sound that corresponds to frequency; as frequency increases, pitch appears to rise.

pituitary gland   An endocrine gland that is actually a functional extension of the hypothalamus. The pituitary gland is often called the master gland because many of its secretions trigger hormone secretions in other glands.

PKU   *See* phenylketonuria.

placebo   In medical practice, a term for a chemically inert substance that produces real medical benefits because the patient believes it will help her.

placebo effect   The medical or psychological benefits of a treatment produced simply because a patient believes the treatment has therapeutic powers.

place theory   A theory of pitch proposed by Hermann von Helmholtz which states that different regions of the basilar membrane respond to different sound frequencies. The nervous system interprets the excitation from different basilar regions as different pitches.

plasticity   The changeability of a trait or behavior with experience (e.g., eye color shows little plasticity, while hair color shows considerably more).

pleasure principle   One of two major principles that Freud held governed psychological life. The pleasure principle is thought to characterize the id, which seeks to reduce tensions generated by biological urges.

pluralistic ignorance   A situation in which individuals in a group don't know that there are others in the group who share their perception (and often, their confusion), and interpret the others' inaction as reflecting knowledge that in truth is not there.

polyandry   A type of mating system in which one female monopolizes the reproductive efforts of several males.

polygamy   Any mating system, including polyandry and polygymy, in which one member of a sex monopolizes the reproductive efforts of several members of the other sex.

polygenic inheritance   Inheritance of an attribute whose expression is controlled not by one but by many gene pairs.

polygyny   A type of polygamous mating system in which one male monopolizes the reproductive efforts of several females.

pons   The topmost portion of the hindbrain just above the medulla and in front of the cerebellum; it is involved in coordinating facial sensations and muscular actions, and in regulating sleep and arousal.

population   The entire group of research participants (or test trials) about which the investigator wants to draw conclusions. *See also* sample.

position constancy   The capacity to perceive an object as having an unchanging location in space, despite the fact that changes in the viewer's position cause a change in the spatial position of the retinal image cast by the object.

positive psychology   A movement within the field of psychology that seeks to emphasize in its research the factors that make people healthy, happy, able to cope, or well adjusted to their life circumstances.

positive symptoms of schizophrenia   Symptoms that involve behavior or thinking that is either less pronounced or nonexistent in normal individuals, such as hallucinations, delusions, or bizarre behavior. *See also* negative symptoms of schizophrenia.

positron emission tomography (PET) scan   *See* PET scan.

possible selves   Self-schemas for who one may be in the future.

postconventional reasoning   According to Lawrence Kohlberg, the fifth and sixth stages of moral reasoning, in which one's reasoning is concerned with ideals and broad moral principles.

postsynaptic membrane   The membrane of the receiving cell across the synaptic gap that contains specialized receptor sites.

postsynaptic neuron   The cell receiving a neural message at the synapse.

post-traumatic stress disorder (PTSD)   A chronic, sometimes lifelong disorder that has its onset some time after an especially stressful traumatic event. Symptoms include dissociation, recurrent nightmares, flashbacks, and sleep disturbances. *See also* acute stress disorder, anxiety disorders, dissociation.

potentiation   In motivation, the tendency to make some behaviors, perceptions, and feelings more probable than others. *See also* long-term potentiation.

power   The ability to control what happens either to oneself or to others.

practical intelligence   The intelligence required to solve everyday problems.

preconscious level   Mental processes that are not currently in focal awareness, but that could easily be brought to awareness.

preconventional reasoning   According to Lawrence Kohlberg, the first and second stages of moral reasoning, in which one's reasoning is concerned with getting rewards and avoiding punishments.

precursor   A substance required for the chemical manufacture of some other substance.

predicate   *See* concept.

predictive validity   An assessment of whether a test measures what it is intended to measure; the assessment hinges on the correlation between the test score and some external criterion (e.g., a correlation between a scholastic aptitude test score and college grades).

prefrontal area   The frontmost portion of the frontal lobes, which is involved in working memory, strategy formation, and response inhibition.

prefrontal lobotomy   A neurosurgical treatment that surgically cuts the connections between the prefrontal areas of the frontal lobes and the rest of the brain. Once used widely (and mostly unsuccessfully) for many mental disorders but now performed very rarely.

preoperational period   In Piaget's theory, the period from about ages two to six during which children come to represent actions and objects internally but cannot systematically manipulate these representations or relate them to each other. The child is therefore unable to conserve quantity across perceptual transformations and also is unable to take points of view other than his own.

preparedness theory of phobias   The theory that phobias grow out of a built-in predisposition (preparedness) to learn to fear certain stimuli (e.g., snakes and spiders) that may have posed serious dangers to our primate ancestors.

prescriptionism   The view that psychotherapeutic treatments for mental disorders may ultimately be like prescriptions for medications: tailored to both the disorder and the individual patient.

presynaptic facilitation   A process that underlies many kinds of learning, documented in studies of *Aplysia*. It occurs when learning results in the increased readiness of presynaptic neurons to fire.

presynaptic neuron   The cell that shoots a neurotransmitter across the synaptic gap.

prevalence   For a particular illness or condition, the number of active cases in a population at any point in time.

prevention focus   An orientation to avoid doing harm thought to arise when we compare our actual self to our ought self.

primacy effect   (1) In free recall, the tendency to recall the first items on a list more readily than those in the middle. (2) In forming an impression of another person, the tendency to give greater weight to attributes noted at the outset than to those noted later. *See also* recency effect.

primary attachment figure   The main person to whom an infant attaches psychologically.

primary messengers   The neurochemicals responsible for neuron-to-neuron communication in chemical synapses, i.e., neurotransmitters. Primary messengers are contrasted with second messengers, those neurochemicals responsible for communication within neurons.

primary motor projection area   A strip of cortex located at the back of the frontal lobe just ahead of the primary sensory projection area in the parietal lobe. This region is the primary projection area for muscular movements.

primary projection areas   Regions of the cortex that serve as receiving stations for sensory information or as dispatching stations for motor commands.

primary reinforcers   Stimuli that serve as reinforcers because they are of immediate biological signifiance; examples include food, water, or escape from the scent of a predator.

primary sensory projection area   Areas of the cortex that are the initial "receiving stations" for sensory information.

priming effect   Phenomenon wherein giving a participant advance knowledge about or exposure to a stimulus can increase the ease of its subsequent recall or recognition.

prisoner's dilemma   A particular arrangement of payoffs in a two-person situation in which each individual has to choose between two alternatives without knowing the other's choice. The payoff structure is arranged such that the optimal strategy for each person depends upon whether she can trust the other or not. If trust is possible, the payoffs for each will be considerably higher than if there is no trust.

probability of response   A common measure of the strength of conditioning, assessing the likelihood that a response will be produced.

procedural knowledge   *See* declarative knowledge.

progesterone   A female sex hormone that dominates the latter phase of the female cycle during which the uterine walls thicken to receive the embryo.

prognosis   The forecast of how a situation (including an illness) will improve or fail to improve in the future.

projection   In psychoanalytic theory, a mechanism of defense in which various forbidden thoughts and impulses are attributed to another person rather than the self, thus warding off some anxiety (e.g., "I hate you" becomes "You hate me").

projective techniques   Sometimes called unstructured personality tests. Methods of assessing personality that use relatively ambiguous stimuli in order to elicit responses that are unguarded and authentic. The most common projective techniques are the TAT and the Rorschach inkblot test.

promotion focus An orientation to actively pursue valued goals thought to arise when we compare our actual self to our ideal self.

propagation The spread of the action potential down an axon, caused by successive destabilizations of the neuronal membrane.

proposition *See* concept.

prosocial A description of behaviors that seek to help and comfort others.

prosopagnosia The inability to recognize faces, usually produced by lesions in the parietal lobes.

prototype The typical example of a category of (e.g., a robin is a prototypical bird for many Americans).

prototype theory The theory that concepts are formed around average or typical exemplars rather than lists of single attributes.

proximal stimulus The stimulus information that actually reaches the sensory receptors. *See also* distal stimulus.

proximity (1) In perception, the closeness of two figures. The closer together they are, the more they will tend to be grouped together perceptually. (2) The nearness of people, which is one of the most important determinants of attraction and liking.

pseudohermaphroditism The most common kind of intersexuality, in which individuals have ambiguous genitalia. *See also* intersexual.

psychoanalysis (1) A theory of both normal and abnormal human personality development, formulated by Freud, whose key assertions include unconscious conflict and early psychosexual development. (2) A method of therapy that draws heavily on this theory of personality. Its main aim is to have the patient gain insight into her own unconscious thoughts and feelings. Therapeutic tools employed toward this end include free association, interpretation, and the appropriate use of the transference relationship between patient and analyst. *See also* free association, transference.

psychodynamic approach An approach to personality originally derived from psychoanalytic theory that asserts that personality differences are based on unconscious (dynamic) conflicts within the individual. *See also* humanistic approach, situationism, sociocultural approach, trait approach.

psychodynamic model An approach to mental disorders which holds that they are the end-products of internal psychological conflicts that generally originate in one's childhood experiences. *See also* learning model.

psychogenic disorders Disorders whose origins are psychological rather than organic (e.g., phobias).

psychogenic symptoms Symptoms believed to result from some psychological cause rather than from actual tissue damage.

psychological intensity The magnitude of a stimulus as it is perceived, not in terms of its physical attributes.

psychometric approach to intelligence An attempt to understand the nature of intelligence by studying the pattern of results obtained on intelligence tests.

psychopathology (1) The study of mental disorders, or (2) the mental disorder itself.

psychophysics An approach to understanding perception that relates the characteristics of physical stimuli to attributes of the sensory experience they produce.

psychosis Loss of contact with reality (most often evidenced as delusions or hallucinations), as can occur in severe cases of many kinds of mental disorders such as mania, major depression, or schizophrenia.

psychosurgery Neurosurgery performed to alleviate manifestations of mental disorders that cannot be brought under control using psychotherapy, medication, or other standard treatments. Psychosurgery can be helpful in severe cases of, for example, obsessive-compulsive disorder.

psychotherapy As used here, a collective term for all forms of treatment that use psychological rather than somatic methods.

psychotropic drugs Medications that seem to control, or at least moderate, the manifestations of mental disorder.

PTSD *See* post-traumatic stress disorder.

punishment A way to suppress a response by having its occurrence followed by an aversive event.

puzzle box An apparatus used by Edward Thorndike to demonstrate trial-and-error learning in cats. Animals were required to perform a simple action in order to escape the puzzle box and obtain food.

r *See* correlation coefficient.

random assignment In experimental design, the random placement of participants in experimental versus control groups in order to insure that all groups are matched at the outset of the experiment.

random sample *See* sample.

random sampling A process of selecting stimuli or participants for a procedure in which there is an equal chance of selecting any member of the broader population; this helps ensure that the sample is representative of the population.

randomized clinical trial (RCT) A procedure for evaluating the outcome of therapy, usually involving randomized assignment of participants either to a treatment or no-treatment group, and often relying on manualized therapy.

range A measure of the variability contained in a set of scores, calculated by subtracting the lowest score from the highest.

rationalization In psychoanalytic theory, a mechanism of defense by means of which unacceptable thoughts or impulses are reinterpreted in more acceptable and, thus, less anxiety-arousing terms (e.g., the jilted lover who convinces herself that she never loved her fiancé anyway).

ratio scale An interval scale in which there is a true zero point, thus allowing statements about proportions (e.g., this sound is twice as loud as the other). *See also* categorical scale, interval scale, nominal scale, ordinal scale.

reaction formation In psychoanalytic theory, a mechanism of defense in which a forbidden impulse is turned into its opposite (e.g., hate toward a sibling becomes exaggerated love).

reality principle One of two major principles that Freud held governed psychological life. The reality principle is thought to characterize the ego, which gains pleasure pragmatically, by finding strategies that work in the real world.

reasoning The determination of the conclusions that can be drawn from certain premises.

reasoning schemas A series of rules, derived from ordinary practical experience, used to guide reasoning about problems involving conditions.

recall A task in which some item must be produced from memory. *See also* recognition.

recency effect In free recall, the tendency to recall items at the end of the list more readily than those in the middle. *See also* primacy effect (in free recall).

receptive field The retinal area in which visual stimulation affects a particular cell's firing rate.

recessive gene *See* gene.

reciprocal altruism A pattern of helpful behavior in which one organism does something for another, and so gains the benefit that the second organism will do something for the first.

reciprocal inhibition The arrangement by which excitation of some neural system is accompanied by inhibition of that system's antagonist (as in antagonistic muscles).

reciprocity principle   A basic rule of many social interactions that decrees that one must repay whatever one has been given.

recoding   Changing the form in which information is stored.

recognition   A task in which a participant must judge whether he has encountered a stimulus previously. *See also* recall.

recollection   Explicit remembering of an event, including the context in which the event took place. Often contrasted with familiarity, which may just be the broad sense that the event has happened before, but without any memory of the actual episode.

reconditioning   In classical conditioning, the presentation of further reinforced conditioning trials after a conditioned response (CR) has been extinguished.

reflex   A simple, stereotyped reaction in response to some stimulus (e.g., limb flexion in withdrawal from pain).

rehearsal   *See* elaborative rehearsal, maintenance rehearsal.

relational aggression   A strategy for attaining social advantage by manipulating others' social alliances. Females are apparently more relationally aggressive, whereas males are apparently more physically aggressive.

relational models theory   A theory of human relationships that describes four types of relationships: equality matching, market pricing, communal sharing, and authority ranking.

relative size   A monocular depth cue in which far-off objects produce a smaller retinal image than nearby objects of the same size.

reliability   The degree of consistency with which a test measures a trait or attribute. Assuming that a trait or attribute remains constant, a perfectly reliable test of that measure will produce the same score each time it is given.

reliability coefficient   The coefficient used in determining the consistency of mental tests, that is, the repeatability of their results. It is usually derived from test-retest correlations or from correlations between alternative forms of a test. *See also* test-retest method.

REM rebound   The tendency to spend more time in REM sleep if deprived of it on previous nights. REM rebound often occurs during withdrawal from medications that suppress REM sleep (e.g., barbiturates or alcohol).

REM sleep   The type of sleep characterized by rapid eye movements, an EEG indicative of high cortical arousal, speeded heart rate and respiration, near-paralysis of limb muscles, and recall of highly visual dreams.

repetition priming   An increase in the likelihood that an item will be identified, recognized, or recalled caused by recent exposure to that item, which may occur without explicit awareness.

replication   A repetition of an experiment that yields the same results.

report bias   A tendency to announce some outcomes more often than others. For example, gamblers might suffer from a report bias, boasting about their wins but keeping quiet about their losses.

representative heuristic   A rule of thumb by means of which we estimate the probability that an object (or event) belongs to a certain category based on how prototypical it is of that category, regardless of how common it actually is. *See also* prototype.

repressed memory   In psychoanalytic theory, a memory that is so anxiety-laden that it has been pushed out of consciousness where it may fester until it is "recovered."

repression   In psychoanalytic theory, a mechanism of defense by means of which thoughts, impulses, or memories that give rise to anxiety are pushed out of consciousness.

resistance   In psychoanalysis, a term describing the patient's failure to associate freely and say whatever enters her head.

response amplitude   The size of a response, used commonly as a sign of response strength in classical and operant conditioning.

response rate   The number of responses per unit of time. This is one measure of the strength of an operant response.

response suppression   The inhibition of a response by conditioned fear.

resting potential   The difference in voltage across a neuronal membrane when the neuron is not firing.

restructuring   A reorganization of a problem that can facilitate its solution; a characteristic of creative thought.

retention interval   In memory experiments, the time that elapses between the original learning and a later test.

retina   The tissue-thin structure at the back of the interior of the eye that contains the photoreceptors, several layers of intermediate neurons, and the cell bodies of the axons that form the optic nerve.

retinal image   The image of an object that is projected on the retina. Its size increases with the size of that object and decreases with the object's distance from the eye.

retrieval   The process of searching for some item in memory and of finding it. If retrieval fails, this may or may not mean that the relevant memory trace is missing. The trace may simply be inaccessible.

retrieval cue   A stimulus that helps one to recall a memory.

retrieval failure   The inability to access a memory, often due to poor encoding; an alternative to erasure as an explanation for forgetting.

retrieval paths   The mental connections, linking one idea to the next, that one uses in locating a bit of information in memory.

retrograde amnesia   A memory deficit, often suffered after a head injury, in which the patient loses memory of some period prior to the injury. *See also* anterograde amnesia.

reversible figures   Visual patterns that easily allow more than one interpretation, including figures that allow parsing such that what is initially figure becomes ground and vice versa.

rhodopsin   The photopigment used in the rods within the retina.

rhythm   The pattern of timing in the delivery of a stimulus, such as music or speech.

risk factors   Circumstances or variables that increase the danger that someone will develop an illness or disorder.

risky shift   A pattern in which a group appears more willing to take chances, or more willing to take an extreme stance, than the individual group members would have been on their own.

rods   Photoreceptors in the retina that respond to lower light intensities and give rise to achromatic (colorless) sensations. *See also* cones.

romantic love   A state of emotion characterized by idealization of the beloved, turbulent emotions, and obsessive thoughts. *See also* companionate love.

Romeo-and-Juliet effect   The intensification of romantic love that can occur with parental opposition.

rooting reflex   In the infant, the sucking elicited by stroking applied on or around the lips; aids breast-feeding.

Rorschach inkblot technique   A projective (unstructured) personality assessment that requires the examinee to look at a series of inkblots and report everything she sees in them.

rules of syntax   The regular principles governing how words can be assembled into sentences, and also describing the structure of those sentences.

SAD   *See* seasonal affective disorders.

sample   A subset of a population selected by the investigator for study. A random sample is constructed such that each member of the population has an equal chance of being picked. A stratified sample is constructed such that every relevant subgroup of the population is randomly sampled in proportion to its size. *See also* population.

sample mean   The mean for a particular group of observations; often contrasted with the population mean, which is the mean of every possible observation. The population mean can also be obtained by obtaining the sample mean for sample after sample after sample, and then taking the mean of these means.

saturation   A perceived dimension of visual stimuli that describes the "strength" of a color—the extent to which it appears rich or pale (e.g., light pink vs. hot pink).

savant syndrome   A syndrome in a mentally retarded person who has some remarkable talent that seems out of keeping with his low level of general intelligence. Previously idiot savant, a term now abandoned as derogatory.

scaling   A procedure for assigning numbers to a subject's responses. *See also* categorical scale, interval scale, nominal scale, ordinal scale, ratio scale.

scatter diagram   *See* scatter plot.

scatter plot   A graph depicting the relationship between two interval- or ratio-scale variables, with each axis representing one variable; often used to graph correlation data.

Schachter-Singer theory of emotion   A theory of emotion that holds that emotional experience results from the interpretation of bodily responses in the context of situational cues.

schedule of reinforcement   The pattern of occasions on which responses are to be reinforced. Commonly, reinforcement is scheduled after a stipulated number of responses occurs or when a response occurs after a preset time interval has elapsed. *See also* fixed-ratio schedule, fixed-interval schedule.

schema   (1) In theories of memory and thinking, a term that refers to a general cognitive structure in which information is organized. (2) In Piaget's theory of development, a mental pattern.

schizophrenia   A group of severe mental disorders characterized by at least some of the following: marked disturbance of thought, withdrawal, inappropriate or flat emotions, delusions, and hallucinations. See also catatonic schizophrenia, disorganized schizophrenia, negative symptoms of schizophrenia, paranoid schizophrenia, positive symptoms of schizophrenia.

SD   *See* standard deviation.

seasonal affective disorder (SAD)   A mood disorder that shows reliable fluctuations with the time of year. One example is a depression that ensues in the fall when the days become shorter and ends in the spring when the days lengthen.

second messengers   Neurochemicals within the neuron that regulate such mechanisms as the creation of receptor sites for specific neurotransmitters and the synthesis of the neuron's own neurotransmitter, thus determining the neuron's overall responsiveness. *See also* primary messengers.

second-order conditioning   A form of learning in which a stimulus is first made meaningful or consequential for an organism through an initial step of learning, and then that stimulus is used as a basis for learning about some new stimulus. For example, an animal might first learn to associate a bell with food (first-order conditioning), but then learn to associate a light with the bell (second-order conditioning).

secure base   According to John Bowlby, the relationship for a child in which the child feels safe and protected.

securely attached   One of the types of parent-child attachment, securely attached children explore and play with toys in their mother's presence, but show minor distress when she leaves.

selection task   A commonly used research task in which participants must decide which cards to turn over in order to determine if a rule has been followed or not.

selective serotonin reuptake inhibitors (SSRIs)   Medications such as Prozac, Zoloft, and Paxil that increase serotonin turnover in the brain and find wide use as treatments for depression, obsessive-compulsive disorder, panic disorder, and many other disorders.

self-actualization   According to Abraham Maslow and some other adherents of the humanistic approach to personality, the full realization of one's potential. *See also* hierarchy of needs.

self-concept   Generally, the sum of one's beliefs about and attitudes toward oneself. For Carl Rogers, the sense of oneself as both agent and object.

self-control   The ability to pursue a goal while adequately managing internal conflicts about it, or to delay pursuing a goal because of other considerations or constraints.

self-disclosure   The act of revealing personal information; usually occurs reciprocally and facilitates intimacy.

self-efficacy   The sense a person has about what things he can plausibly accomplish.

self-esteem   The relative balance of positive and negative judgments about oneself.

self-fulfilling prophecies   Beliefs about how a person will act which actually make that action more likely.

self-handicapping   A self-protective strategy in which one arranges for an obvious and nonthreatening obstacle to one's own performance, such that any failure can be attributed to the obstacle and not to one's own limitations.

Self-Monitoring Scale   A personality measure that seeks to determine the degree to which a person alters or adjusts their behavior in order to act appropriately in new circumstances.

self-organizing   A term used to describe a system that finds its own equilibrium state, its own balance among diverse forces. To find this equilibrium, the system is simultaneously pulled or pushed by many forces, and so naturally finds the position that represents the "balance point" among all of these forces.

self-perception theory   The theory that we know our own attitudes and feelings only indirectly, by observing our own behavior and then performing much the same processes of attribution that we employ when trying to understand others.

self-report data   Data supplied by the research participant describing herself (usually, ratings of attitudes or moods, or tallies of behavior), rather than that collected by the experimenter.

self-report measures   Measures derived by asking participants questions, usually in the form of questionnaires.

self-schema   An organized knowledge structure that refers to the self.

self-serving attributional bias   A bias toward explanations that make oneself seem better in some way. These often take the form of dispositional explanations for one's successes and situational explanations for one's failures

semantic feature   The smallest significant unit of meaning within a word (e.g., male, human, and adult are semantic features of the word man).

semantic memory   The component of generic memory that concerns the meaning of words and concepts.

semantic priming   The enhanced performance on verbal tasks that occurs when the items being considered have similar meanings.

semantic role   The part that each word plays in the "who did what to whom" drama described by a sentence; one word takes the role of being the cause of the action, another, the source of the action, and so on.

sensations   According to the empiricists, the primitive experiences that emanate from the senses (e.g., greenness, bitterness).

sensation seeking   A predisposition to seek novel experiences, look for thrills and adventure, and be highly susceptible to boredom.

sensitive period   *See* critical period.

sensitivity An organism's ability to detect a stimulus (or a difference among stimuli), measured separately from the organism's decision criterion.

sensorimotor intelligence In Piaget's theory, intelligence during the first two years of life, consisting mainly of sensations and motor impulses, with little in the way of internalized representations.

sensory coding The process through which the nervous system represents the qualities of the incoming stimulus—whether auditory or visual, for example, or whether a red light or a green one, a sour taste or a sweet taste.

sensory neurons Neurons that convey information from sense organs to other portions of the nervous system.

sensory quality A distinguishing attribute of a stimulus (e.g., brightness or hue or pitch).

sentence A sequence of words constructed in accord with the rules of syntax. "The boy hit the ball" is a sentence, but "Ball the hit boy the," is not. Sentences do not have to be meaningful: "The green idea tripped" is a sentence, although "Tripped idea green the" is not.

separation anxiety A pattern of emotions and behaviors that reflect a child's fear when her mother (or other caregiver) leaves the room; separation anxiety is usually observed in children 6 to 8 months of age.

serotonin (5HT) A neurotransmitter involved in many of the mechanisms of sleep, arousal, aggression, and mood.

set point A general term for the level at which negative feedback tries to maintain stability. An example is the setting of a thermostat.

sexual dimorphism The state of affairs, observed in many species, in which the sexes differ in form (such as deer antlers or peacock tail feathers) or size. Sexual dimorphism is minimal among monogamous animals and maximal among polygamous ones.

sexual orientation A person's predisposition to choose members of the same or the opposite sex as romantic and sexual partners. See also bisexuality, heterosexuality, and homosexuality.

shadowing The procedure, often used in dichotic presentations, in which a participant is asked to repeat aloud, word for word, only what she hears through one earphone.

shallow processing The encoding of a stimulus using its superficial characteristics, such as the way a word sounds or the typeface in which it is printed.

shape constancy The tendency to perceive objects as retaining their shapes despite changes in our angle of regard that produce changes in the image projected on the retina.

shaping An instrumental learning procedure in which an animal (or human) learns a rather difficult response through the reinforcement of successive approximations to that response. See also successive approximations.

short-term memory See stage theory of memory.

signal-detection theory The theory that the act of perceiving or not perceiving a stimulus is actually a judgment about whether a momentary sensory experience is due to background noise alone or to the background noise plus a signal. The theory also includes a procedure for measuring sensory sensitivity.

signs In psychopathology, what the diagnostician observes about a patient's physical or mental condition (e.g., tremor, inattentiveness). See also symptoms, syndrome.

similarity In perception, a principle by which we tend to group like figures, especially by color and orientation.

simple reaction time A measurement of the speed with which a research participant can respond to a stimulus.

simultaneous color contrast The effect produced by the fact that any region in the visual field tends to induce its complementary color in adjoining areas. For example, a gray patch will tend to look bluish if surrounded by yellow and yellowish if surrounded by blue.

simultaneous multiple-constraint satisfaction A process through which the nervous system (or a perceiver) seeks a response or an interpretation of the input that (a) fits with several requirements (the "multiple constraints"), but which seeks this response or interpretation by (b) being influenced by all the requirements at the same time ("simultaneous"), rather than considering them one by one.

sine waves Waves (e.g., sound waves or light waves) that correspond to the plot of the trigonometric sine function.

single-case experiment A study in which the investigator manipulates the values of some independent variable, just as she would in an experiment with many participants, and then assesses the effects of this variable by recording a single participant's responses. See also case study.

situational attributions Attributions that focus on factors that are external to a person, such as the weather, the difficulty of an exam, or other qualities of the situation.

situationism The view that human behavior is largely determined by the characteristics of the situation rather than personal predispositions. See also humanistic approach, psychodynamic approach, sociocultural perspective, trait approach.

size constancy The tendency to perceive objects as retaining their size, despite the increase or decrease in the size of the image projected on the retina caused by moving closer to or farther from the objects.

skewed A term used to describe distributions of experimental results that are asymmetrical (tending to have outlying values at one end).

skin senses The group of senses, including pressure, warmth, cold, and pain, through which an organism gains information about its immediate surround.

sleep paralysis The phenomenon of waking up unable to move for several seconds, due to the persistence of the loss of muscle tone that occurs during REM sleep. While sleep paralysis is sometimes frightening, it is harmless.

sleep-wake cycle A daily rhythm in which the body moves from alert vigilance to sleep and back again.

slow-wave sleep Type of sleep characterized by slow, rolling eye movements, an EEG indicative of low cortical arousal, slowed heart rate and respiration, and recall of "boring," mostly verbal dreams.

smooth muscles The nonstriated muscles controlled by the autonomic nervous system that constrict the blood vessels to help regulate blood pressure and that line many internal organs such as those that produce peristalsis in the digestive tract.

social cognition The way in which we interpret and try to comprehend social events.

social-cognitive approach A perspective on personality which argues that in explaining behavior, we should emphasize neither the person's traits by themselves nor the situation by itself. Instead, we should examine how people and situations change, moment by moment, in their interactions.

social comparison A process of reducing uncertainty about one's own beliefs and attitudes by comparing them to those of others.

social development A child's growth in his or her relations with other people.

social exchange A theory that asserts that each partner in a social relationship gives something to the other and expects to get something in return.

social facilitation The tendency to perform better in the presence of others than when alone. This facilitating effect works primarily for simple or well-practiced tasks.

social-identity theory A theory that holds that people derive their self-concepts and self-esteem in part from the status and accomplishments of the various groups to which they belong.

social impact theory The theory that the influence others exert on an individual increases with their number, their immediacy, and their strength (e.g., status).

social inhibition   When the presence of an audience impairs performance.

socialization   The process whereby the child acquires the patterns of behavior characteristic of his or her society.

social learning theory   A theoretical approach to socialization and personality that is midway between radical behaviorism and cognitive approaches to learning. It stresses learning by observing others who serve as models and who show the child whether a response he already knows should or should not be performed.

social loafing   An example of the diffusion of social impact in which people working collectively on a task generate less total effort than they would had they worked alone.

social phobia   A fear of embarrassment or humiliation that causes people to avoid situations that might expose them to public scrutiny. *See also* anxiety disorders, phobia.

social psychology   The study of how we think about, feel about, and behave toward other people (both real and imagined), as well as how the thoughts, feelings, and behaviors of other people influence us.

social referencing   A process of relying on the facial expressions of others as a cue about the situation.

sociocultural perspective   Within social psychology and personality psychology, the view that many psychological phenomena, some of which have been presumed to be universal, result from or are affected substantially by cultural norms. *See also* humanistic approach, psychodynamic approach, trait approach, situationism.

sociometric data   Data that describe group interactions.

sociopathy   *See* antisocial personality disorder.

soma   *See* cell body.

somatic division   A division of the peripheral nervous system primarily concerned with the control of the skeletal musculature and the transmission of information from the sense organs.

somatization disorder   A mental disorder in which the patient reports miscellaneous aches and pains in various bodily systems that do not add up to any known syndrome in physical medicine.

somatoform disorders   The generic term for mental disorders in which bodily symptoms predominate despite the absence of any known physical cause; included are conversion disorder, hypochondriasis, somatization disorder, and somatoform pain disorder.

somatoform pain disorder   A mental disorder in which the sufferer describes chronic pain for which there is no discernible physical basis.

somatogenic hypothesis   The hypothesis that mental disorders result from organic (bodily) causes.

somatosensory area   *See* primary sensory projection area.

sound waves   Successive pressure variations in the air that vary in amplitude and wavelength.

source confusion   A type of memory error in which information acquired in one context is remembered as having been encountered in another (e.g., a person's recalling that she had chocolate cake on her last birthday when she actually had it two birthdays ago).

spatial summation   The process whereby two or more stimuli that are individually below threshold will elicit a reflex if they occur simultaneously at different points on the body.

spatial thinking   The mental computations engaged in when we must locate objects and discern the spatial relationships among them.

specificity theory   An approach to sensory experience which asserts that different sensory qualities are signaled by different neurons. These neurons are somehow labeled with their quality, so that whenever they fire, the nervous system interprets their activation as that particular sensory quality.

specific language impairment   A syndrome in which individuals are very slow to learn language and throughout their lives have difficulty in understanding and producing many sentences, even though these individuals seem normal on most other measures, including measurements of intelligence.

specific phobias   Any of the disorders characterized by extreme and irrational fear of a particular object or situation.

spectral sensitivity   The pattern of a receptor's (or pigment's) reactions to different wavelengths of light.

spectral sensitivity curve   A graphical representation of a receptor's spectral sensitivity.

split-half reliability   An assessment of whether a test is consistent in what it measures, determined by asking whether performance on one half of the test is correlated with performance on the other half.

spontaneous recovery   The reappearance of a previously extinguished response after a time interval in which neither the conditioned stimulus (CS) nor the unconditioned stimulus (US) is presented.

SSRIs   *See* selective serotonin reuptake inhibitors.

stage theory of memory   An approach to memory that proposes several memory stores. One is short-term (or working) memory, which holds a small amount of information for fairly short intervals; another is long-term memory, which can hold vast amounts of information for extended periods. According to the theory, information can only be transferred to long-term memory if it has first been in short-term memory.

standard deviation (SD)   A measure of the variability of a frequency distribution, calculated as the square root of the variance $(V) - SD = \sqrt{V}$. *See also* variance (V).

standardization sample   The group of individuals to which a test is given to decide what "normal" performance on the test looks like.

standard score (z-score)   A score that is expressed as a deviation from the mean in standard deviations (SDs), which allows a comparison of scores drawn from different distributions; if M is the mean, then $z = (\text{score} - M)/SD$.

Stanford Prison Study   A social psychological study conducted at Stanford University by Philip Zimbardo. Its aim was to study the impact of roles on behavior. Participants were randomly assigned to play the role of either prisoner or guard. This study was terminated early because of the role-induced punitive behavior on the part of the "guards."

statistical reliability   The degree to which an observed difference in sample means reflects a real difference in population means and is not attributable to chance.

statistics   The process of quantitatively describing, analyzing, and making inferences about numerical data.

stereotypes   Schemas by which people try to categorize complex groups. Group stereotypes are often negative, especially when applied to minority groups. *See also* out-group homogeneity effect.

stereotype threat   A hypothesized mechanism through which a person's performance on a test (e.g., a test of intelligence) is influenced by her perception that the test results may confirm others' stereotypes about her.

stimulant   An influence (typically, a drug) that has activating or excitatory effects on brain or bodily functions (e.g., amphetamines, Ritalin, cocaine).

stimulus generalization   In classical conditioning, the tendency to respond to stimuli other than the original conditioned stimulus (CS). The greater the similarity between the CS and the new stimulus (CS+), the greater generalization will be. An analogous phenomenon in instrumental conditioning is a response to stimuli other than the original discriminative stimulus.

storage capacity   The amount of information that can be retained in memory. *See also* magic number.

Strange Situation   An experimental procedure used to assess attachment. In this procedure, the child is brought into an unfamiliar room that contains many toys, and is allowed to explore with the mother present. After a while, the mother leaves, and then, after a few more minutes, returns.

strategic retrieval   A deliberate effort to recall information by supplying one's own retrieval cues (e.g., "Let's *see*, the last time I remember seeing my wallet was …").

stratified sampling   An experimental procedure in which each subgroup of the population is sampled in proportion to its size.

stress   In psychopathology, the psychological or physical wear-and-tear that, together with a preexisting vulnerability, may lead to mental disorder.

stress-inoculation therapy   A type of cognitive therapy aimed at teaching the person responses that he can engage in during stressful times, such as "This will soon be over," or, "I know I can handle this."

strong situations   Situations that produce near uniformity in behavior.

Stroop effect   A marked decrease in the speed of naming the colors in which various color names (such as green, red, etc.) are printed when the colors and the names are different. An important example of automatization.

Structured Clinical Interview for DSM Diagnosis (SCID)   A common diagnostic or assessment procedure designed to ask questions directly pertinent to certain diagnostic categories.

structured interview   An assessment procedure in which specific questions are asked in a specific sequence, with attention to certain types of content.

structured personality test   A personality test (e.g., the MMPI or CPI) that asks specific questions and requires specific answers.

subcortical structures   Usually the forebrain structures, such as those comprising the limbic system and extrapyramidal motor system, that lie beneath the cortex.

subject   Usually the "actor" or "topic" specified in a sentence, with the rest of the sentence providing some information or comment about that actor or topic.

subjective contours   Perceived contours that do not exist physically. We tend to complete figures that have gaps in them by perceiving a contour as continuing along its original path.

subroutines   In a hierarchical organization, lower-level operations that function semiautonomously but are supervised by higher-level ones.

subsyndromal case   An instance of a mental disorder in which someone does show symptoms, but not at a level of intensity, frequency, or duration that would justify a formal diagnosis.

successive approximations   The process of shaping a response by rewarding closer and closer versions of the desired response. *See also* shaping.

sufficient condition   A requirement which, if satisfied, guarantees a certain outcome. For example, the combination of being adult, unmarried, human and male are sufficient for someone's being a bachelor.

superego   In Freud's theory, reaction patterns that emerge from within the ego, represent the internalized rules of society, and come to control the ego by punishment with guilt. *See also* ego, id.

syllables   A grouping of phonemes such that the phonemes can be pronounced as one unit.

syllogism   A logic problem containing two premises and a conclusion that may or may not follow from them.

symbolic representation   A type of mental representation that does not correspond to the physical characteristics of that which it represents. Thus, the word *mouse* does not resemble the small rodent it represents. *See also* analogical representation.

symmetrical distribution   A distribution of numerical data in which deviations in either direction from the mean are equally frequent.

sympathetic branch   The division of the autonomic nervous system that mobilizes the body's energies for physical activity (e.g., increasing heart rate, sweating, and respiration). Its action is typically antagonistic to that of the parasympathetic branch.

symptoms   In psychopathology, what the patient reports about his physical or mental condition (e.g., nervousness, hearing voices). *See also* signs, syndrome.

synapse   The juncture of two neurons, consisting of the presynaptic and postsynaptic membranes, and—in nonelectrical synapses—the synaptic gap between them.

synaptic gap   The space between two communicating neurons; neurotransmitters are released by the presynaptic neuron, cross the synaptic gap, and trigger a response in the postsynaptic neuron.

synaptic reuptake   The process through which neurotransmitters are reabsorbed by the presynaptic neuron, so that they can be released again, sending a new signal, the next time that axon fires.

synaptic vesicles   Tiny sacs within a presynaptic membrane that contain the neurotransmitter; when the presynaptic neuron fires, some of these vesicles burst and eject their contents into the synaptic gap.

syndrome   A pattern of signs and symptoms that tend to co-occur.

System 1   One of the terms used for the fast, automatic type of reasoning specified by dual-process models. Also referred to as intuition or association-driven thought.

System 2   One of the terms used for the slower, more effortful, but more accurate type of reasoning specified by dual-process models. Also referred to as reasoning or rule-driven thought.

systematic desensitization   A behavior therapy that tries to remove anxiety connected to various stimuli by gradually counterconditioning to them a response incompatible with fear, usually muscular relaxation. The stimuli are usually evoked as mental images according to an anxiety hierarchy, whereby relaxation is conditioned to the less frightening stimuli before the more frightening ones.

tabula rasa   The notion that each person is born as a "blank slate," that is, without innate knowledge, so that all knowledge must be gained from experience.

tacit knowledge   Practical "how to" knowledge that is unwittingly accumulated from everyday experience.

tape-recorder theory of memory   The erroneous view that the brain contains an indelible record of everything one experiences.

TAT   *See* Thematic Apperception Test.

tau protein   A protein that normally helps sustain the internal structure of the brain's axons. Its metabolism somehow goes awry, however, in the development of Alzheimer's disease.

taxonomy   A classification scheme.

technical eclecticism   *See* multimodal therapy.

temperament   In modern usage, a characteristic level of reactivity and energy, often thought to be constitutional.

temporal contiguity   Co-occurrence of stimuli. A condition Pavlov thought would be favorable for forming associations; actually forward pairing is most favorable.

temporal lobe   The lobe of the cortex lying below the temples in each cerebral hemisphere, which includes the primary auditory projection area, Wernicke's area, and subcortically, the amygdala and hippocampus.

temporal summation   The process whereby a stimulus that is below threshold will elicit a reflex if the stimulus occurs repeatedly.

territory   A term used by ethologists to describe a region a particular animal stakes out as its own. The territory holder is usually a male, but in some species the territory is held by a mating pair or by a group.

testable hypothesis   A hypothesis that has been formulated specifically enough so that it is clear what observations would confirm the hypothesis and what observations would challenge it.

testosterone The principal male sex hormone in mammals. *See also* androgen.

test profile A graphical indication of an individual's performance on several components of a test. This is often useful for guidance or clinical evaluation because it indicates that person's pattern of abilities or traits.

test-retest reliability An assessment of whether a test is consistent in what it measures, determined by asking whether the test results on one occasion are correlated with the results from the same test (or a close variant on it) on another occasion. *See also* reliability coefficient.

texture gradient A distance cue based on changes in surface texture that depend on how far away the observer is.

thalamus A part of the lower portion of the forebrain that serves as a major relay and integration center for sensory information.

that's-not-all technique A sales technique that relies on improving an initially modest deal, thereby pulling for reciprocation, which often takes the form of purchasing the item.

Thematic Apperception Test (TAT) A projective technique in which persons are shown a set of pictures and asked to make up a story about each one.

theory of mind A set of interrelated concepts used to try to make sense of our own mental processes and those of others, including the variation in beliefs and desires from one person to another.

thermoregulation The process by which organisms maintain a constant body temperature. For ectotherms, it is matter of external behavior such as seeking sun or shade, while for endotherms it also involves numerous internal adjustments such as sweating.

third-variable problem The major obstacle to discerning causation from correlation, because two variables may be correlated only because of the operation of a third variable. For example, sales of ice cream are correlated with rates of violent crime, but only because both increase during hot weather and decrease during cold weather.

timbre The quality of a sound separate from its pitch or loudness; it is timbre that distinguishes a clarinet from an oboe, or one person's voice from another.

tip-of-the-tongue phenomenon The condition in which one remains on the verge of retrieving a word or name but continues to be unsuccessful.

TMS *See* transcranial magnetic stimulation.

tolerance *See* opponent-process theory of motivation.

tone A difference in pitch used in some languages (such as Mandarin Chinese) to signal differences in meaning.

top-down processes Processes in form recognition that begin with larger units and then proceed to smaller units (e.g., from phrases to words to letters). This contrasts with bottom-up processes, which start with smaller component parts and gradually build up to the larger units (e.g., from letters to words to phrases). One demonstration of top-down processing is provided by context effects in which knowledge or expectations affect what one sees.

trace consolidation A hypothesis that newly acquired memory traces undergo a gradual change that makes them more and more resistant to any disturbance.

trait *See* trait approach.

trait approach The view that differences in personality are best characterized in terms of underlying, possibly innate, attributes (traits) that predispose one toward patterns of thinking and behavior that are essentially consistent over time and across situations. *See also* humanistic approach, psychodynamic approach, situationism, sociocultural perspective.

transcranial magnetic stimulation (TMS) A technique through which repeated magnetic stimulation at the surface of the skull is used (at some strengths) to stimulate a region of the brain or (at other strengths) to cause a temporary lesion of a region of the brain.

transduction The process by which a receptor reacts to some physical stimulus (e.g., light or pressure) and creates action potentials in another neuron.

transection Surgical cutting of a nerve tract or brain region, performed to isolate functionally the regions on either side.

transference In therapy, a patient's tendency to respond to the analyst in ways that re-create her responses to the major figures in her own life.

transfer of training tests Procedures used to ascertain whether skills learned in one setting generalize to other settings.

transposition The phenomenon whereby visual and auditory patterns (i.e., figures and melodies) remain essentially the same even though the parts of which they are composed change.

trichromatic color vision The principle underlying human color vision. Color vision occurs through the operation of three sets of cones, each maximally sensitive to a different wavelength of light.

true hermaphroditism Rare type of intersexuality in which an individual possesses reproductive tissue of both sexes (e.g., testes and ovaries).

ultimatum task A task commonly used to measure people's tendency toward fairness or selfishness in dividing some resource.

ultradian rhythm The 90- to 100-minute biological rhythm that characterizes the alternation of REM and slow-wave periods during sleep and attentiveness while awake. *See also* circadian rhythm.

unconditional positive regard For Carl Rogers, the belief that one is accepted and loved without reservation; an essential component of Rogerian psychotherapy.

unconditioned reflex *See* unconditioned response.

unconditioned response (UR) In classical conditioning, the response that is elicited without prior training by the unconditioned stimulus (US). *See also* conditioned response (CR), conditioned stimulus (CS), unconditioned stimulus (US).

unconditioned stimulus (US) In classical conditioning, the stimulus that elicits the unconditioned response (UR) and the presentation of which acts as reinforcement. See conditioned response (CR), conditioned stimulus (CS), unconditioned response (UR).

unconscious inference A process postulated by Hermann von Helmholtz to explain certain perceptual phenomena such as size constancy. For example, an object is perceived to be at a certain distance and this is unconsciously taken into account in assessing its retinal image size, with the result that size constancy is maintained. *See also* size constancy.

unconscious level Mental processes that are not—and cannot easily become—the object of focal awareness.

uninvolved parenting One of the four types of parents; uninvolved parents are so overwhelmed by their own concerns that they provide few rules and demands for the children, and are relatively insensitive to their children's needs.

unipolar depression *See* major depression.

unique blue The hue corresponding to a wavelength of 445 nanometers, which is perceived as containing no red or green.

unique green The hue corresponding to a wavelength of 500 nanometers, which is perceived as containing no blue or yellow.

unique yellow The hue corresponding to a wavelength of 570 nanometers, which is perceived as containing no red or green.

validity The extent to which a test measures what it is supposed to measure. *See also* predictive validity.

validity scales Scales used within a measure (e.g., a personality test) designed to assess whether the examinee is trying to disguise their traits or their attitudes.

variability The degree to which scores in a frequency distribution depart from the central value. See also central tendency, measure of central tendency, standard deviation (SD), variance (V).

variable-interval (VI) schedule A pattern of rewards similar to a fixed-interval schedule, but with the interval used varying from reward to reward. Thus, on a variable-interval 1 schedule, reward will be available *on average* after one minute has gone by, but for some rewards the actual interval might be shorter or longer.

variable-ratio (VR) schedule A pattern of rewards similar to a fixed-ratio schedule, but with the ratio used varying from reward to reward. Thus, on a variable-ratio 5 schedule, reward will be available *on average* after five responses, but for some rewards the number of required responses might be fewer, and for others more.

variance (V) A measure of the variability of a frequency distribution. It is computed by finding the difference between each score and the mean (M), squaring the result, adding all these squared deviations, and dividing the sum by the number of cases. If N is the number of scores, then $V = \text{sum of } (\text{score} - M)^2 / N$.

vasocongestion A contraction of the capillaries that squeezes blood away from that area. *See also* vasoconstriction.

vasoconstriction The constriction of blood vessels brought on by activation of the sympathetic branch of the autonomic nervous system. Vasoconstriction occurs in emergencies, when blood is diverted from the skin and internal organs to the muscles. It is also crucial in mammalian thermoregulation; in response to excessive cold, blood is diverted from the skin to reduce heat loss. *See also* vasodilatation.

vasodilatation The dilating of blood vessels brought on by activation of the parasympathetic division of the autonomic nervous system. Vasodilatation is one component of mammalian thermoregulation; in response to excessive heat, warm blood flows to the body's surface and results in heat loss by radiation. *See also* vasoconstriction.

vasovagal reaction A reaction from the parasympathetic branch of the nervous system in which the pulse slows, blood pressure drops, the muscles go slack, and the person can fall to the ground in a dead faint.

vegetative signs Physical manifestations that often accompany major depression, such as loss of appetite and weight loss, weakness, fatigue, poor bowel functioning, sleep disorders (most often early-morning awakenings), and loss of interest in sex.

ventral tegmental area (VTA) A region in the midbrain containing dopamine-releasing pathways thought to be involved in reward.

vestibular senses A set of receptors that provide information about the orientation and movements of the head, located in the semicircular canals and the vestibular sacs of the inner ear.

vicarious conditioning A form of learning in which a person (or, in some studies, a monkey) can acquire a conditioned response merely by observing some other person (or monkey) going through the conditioning procedure.

videorecorder theory A mistaken view of memory, the theory implies that memory operates just as a videorecorder does—with information initially "recorded" into memory, just as a camera records information onto a videotape or DVD, and where the information resides in dormant form until the moment of retrieval and "playback."

VI schedule *See* variable-interval (VI) schedule.

visible spectrum The range of wavelengths to which our visual system can respond, extending from about 400 (the wavelength usually perceived as the color violet) to 750 nanometers (the wavelength usually perceived as the color reddish orange).

visual imagery The capacity to form and use quasi-perceptual representations, often referred to as mental pictures, in the absence of the relevant visual input.

visual perspective A cue to distance that takes advantage of the fact that (because of the principles of optics) parallel lines appear to converge as they recede into the distance, and objects cast smaller images if they are further away from the viewer.

visual pigment The chemical inside a photoreceptor that, when exposed to light, changes form, thus releasing some energy and triggering a neural impulse. The chemical is then restored to its original form so that it becomes ready to respond to the next bit of incoming light.

visual search task A task in which observers are asked to hunt for a specified target within a field of stimuli. The identity of the target can be defined in various ways ("look for the red item," or "look for the green letter *H*"), and the background items can vary both in number and in identity.

visual segregation The step in perception that involves locating an object's boundary, so that the perceiver can discern where one object stops and the next begins.

VR schedule *See* variable-ratio (VR) schedule.

VTA *See* ventral tegmental area.

wavelength The distance between the crests of two successive waves and the major determinant of pitch (for sound) and hue (for light).

weak situations Situations that allow for a wide range of behaviors.

Weber fraction In Weber's law, the fraction given by the change in stimulus intensity (ΔI) divided by the standard intensity (I) required to produce a just-noticeable difference: $\Delta I / I = C$.

Weber's law The observation that the size of the difference threshold is proportional to the intensity of the standard stimulus.

well-defined problems Problems for which there is a clear-cut way of deciding whether a proposed solution is correct. This contrasts with ill-defined problems, for which it is unclear what a correct solution might be.

Wernicke's area A brain area adjacent to the auditory projection area, damage to which leads to deficits in understanding word meaning.

"what" system The system of visual circuits and pathways leading from the visual cortex to the temporal lobe, especially involved in object identification.

"where" system The system of visual circuits and pathways leading from the visual cortex to the parietal lobe, especially involved in the spatial localization of objects and in the coordination of movements.

white matter Whitish-appearing patches and paths in the brain composed of myelinated axons.

Whorfian hypothesis The proposal that the language one speaks determines both what and also how one thinks. In its strong form, this hypothesis indicates that people cannot think in ways not allowed or included within their language.

withdrawal symptoms A consequence of drug addiction that occurs when the drug is withheld. These effects tend to be the opposite of those produced by the drug itself.

withdrawn-rejected A status in some children who are not respected or liked by their peers (and thus: rejected) and who become anxious as a result

within-subject comparisons Within the same study, comparing each participant's behavior in one situation to the same participant's behavior in another situation; usually contrasted with between-subject comparisons.

working memory A part of the memory system that is currently activated but has relatively little cognitive capacity.

X chromosome One of the two sex chromosomes containing the genes that determine whether a given animal will be male or female. In mammalian females, both sex chromosomes are X chromosomes; in mammalian males, there is one X chromosome and one Y chromosome.

Y chromosome *See* X chromosome.

Young-Helmholtz theory   A theory of color vision which holds that each of the three receptor types (short-wave, medium-wave, and long-wave) gives rise to the experience of one basic color (blue, green, or red).

zone of proximal development   The range of accomplishments that are beyond what the child could do on his or her own, but are possible if the child is given help or guidance.

REFERENCES

ABRAHAM, K. (1927). The influence of oral eroticism on character formation. In K. Abraham, *Selected papers* (pp. 393–406). London: Hogarth Press.

ABRAMSON, L. Y., ALLOY, L. B., HANKIN, B. L., HAEFFEL, G. J., MACCOON, D. G., & GIBB, B. E. (2002). Cognitive vulnerability—stress models of depression in a self-regulatory and psychobiological context. In I. H. Gotlib & C. L. Hammen (Eds.), *Handbook of depression* (pp. 268–294). New York: Guilford Press.

ABRAMSON, L. Y., SELIGMAN, M. E. P., & TEASDALE, J. D. (1978). Learned helplessness in humans: Critique and reformulation. *Journal of Abnormal Psychology, 87*, 49–74.

ACKERMAN, P. L., & BEIER, M. E. (2005). Knowledge and intelligence. In O. Wilhelm & R. Engle (Eds.), *Handbook of understanding and measuring intelligence* (pp. 125–139). Thousand Oaks, CA: Sage.

ACKERMAN, P. L., BEIER, M. E., & BOYLE, M. O. (2002). Individual differences in working memory within a nomological network of cognitive and perceptual speed abilities. *Journal of Experimental Psychology: General, 131*, 567–589.

ACKERMAN, P. L., BEIER, M. E., & BOYLE, M. O. (2005). Working memory and intelligence: The same or different constructs? *Psychological Bulletin, 131*, 30–60.

ACSF INVESTIGATORS. (1992). AIDS and sexual behaviour in France. *Nature, 360*, 407–409.

ADAMS, D. B., GOLD, A. R., & BURT, A. D. (1978). Rise in female initiated sexual activity at ovulation and its suppression by oral contraceptives. *New England Journal of Medicine, 299*, 1145–1150.

ADAMSON, L., & FRICK, J. (2003). The still face: A history of a shared experimental paradigm. *Infancy, 4*, 451–473.

ADDIS, M. E., & KRASNOW, A. D. (2000). A national survey of practicing psychologists' attitudes towards psychotherapy treatment manuals. *Journal of Consulting and Clinical Psychology, 68*, 331–339.

ADLER, N. T. (1979). On the physiological organization of social behavior: Sex and aggression. In P. Marler & J. G. Vandenbergh (Eds.), *Handbook of behavioral neurobiology: Vol. 3. Social behavior and communication* (pp. 29–71). New York: Plenum.

ADOLPH, E. F. (1947). Urges to eat and drink in rats. *American Journal of Physiology, 151*, 110–125.

ADORNO, T. W., ADORNO, E. F.-B., LEVINSON, D. J., SANFORD, R. N., IN COLLABORATION WITH ARON, B., LEVINSON, M. H., & MORROW, W. (1950). *The authoritarian personality.* New York: Harper.

AHN, W.-K, & GRAHAM, L. M. (1999). The impact of necessity and sufficiency in the Wason four-card task. *Psychological Science, 10*, 237–242.

AINSWORTH, M. D. S., & BELL, S. M. (1970). Attachment, exploration, and separation: Illustrated by the behavior of one-year-olds in a strange situation. *Child Development, 41*, 49–67.

AINSWORTH, M. D. S., BLEHAR, M. C., WATERS, E., & WALL, S. (1978). *Patterns of attachment.* Hillsdale, NJ: Erlbaum.

ALBERT, M. S., JONES, K., SAVAGE, C. R., BERKMAN, L., SEEMAN, T., BLAZER, D., ET AL. (1995). Predictors of cognitive change in older persons: MacArthur studies of successful aging. *Psychology and Aging, 10*, 578–589.

ALDAG, R. J., & FULLER, S. R. (1993). Beyond fiasco: A reappraisal of the groupthink phenomenon and a new model of group decision processes. *Psychological Bulletin, 113*(3), 533–552.

ALEXANDER, F., & FRENCH, T. (1946). *Psychoanalytic theory.* New York: Ronald Press.

ALEXANDER, K. W., QUAS, J. A., GOODMAN, G. S., GHETTI, S., EDELSTEIN, R. S., REDLICH, A. D., ET AL. (2005). Traumatic impact predicts long-term memory for documented child sexual abuse. *Psychological Science, 16*, 33–40.

ALLDERIDGE, P. (1979). Hospitals, mad houses, and asylums: Cycles in the care of the insane. *British Journal of Psychiatry, 134*, 321–324.

ALLEN, J., & SEIDENBERG, M. S. (1999) The emergence of grammaticality in connectionist networks. In B. MacWhinney (Ed.), *The emergence of language* (pp. 115–151). Hillsdale, NJ: Erlbaum.

ALLEN, L. S., HINES, Z. M., SHRYNE, J. E., & GORSKI, R. A. (1989). Two sexually dimorphic cell groups in the human brain. *Journal of Neuroscience, 9*, 497–506.

ALLEN, V. L. (1975). Social support for non-conformity. In L. Berkowitz (Ed.), *Advances in experimental social psychology: Vol. 8.* New York: Academic Press.

ALLEN, V. L., & LEVINE, J. M. (1971). Social support and conformity: The role of independent assessment. *Journal of Experimental Social Psychology, 7*, 48–58.

ALLOY, L. B., ABRAMSOM, L. Y., & FRANCIS, E. L. (1999). Do negative cognitive styles confer vulnerability to depression? *Current Directions in Psychological Science, 8*, 128–132.

ALLPORT, F. H. (1920). The influence of the group upon association and thought. Journal of *Experimental Psychology, 3*, 159–182.

ALLPORT, G. W. (1937). *Personality: A psychological interpretation.* New York: Henry Holt.

ALLPORT, G. W. (1968). The historical background of modern social psychology. In G. Lindzey & E. Aronson (Eds.), *The handbook of social psychology* (2nd ed., Vol. 1, pp. 1–80). Reading, MA: Addison-Wesley.

ALLPORT, G. W., & ODBERT, H. S. (1936). Trait-names: A psychological study. *Psychological Monographs, 47*(Whole No. 211).

ALTMANN G., & STEEDMAN, M. (1988). Interaction with context during human sentence processing. *Cognition, 30*, 191–238.

ALTMANN, E. M., & GRAY, W. D. (2002). Forgetting to remember: The functional relationship of decay and interference. *Psychological Science, 13*, 27–33.

ALTMANN, G. T. M., & KAMIDE, Y. (1999). Incremental interpretation at verbs: Restricting the domain of subsequent reference. *Cognition, 73,* 247–264.

AMATO, P. R., & KEITH, B. (1991). Parental divorce and the well-being of children: A meta-analysis. *Psychological Bulletin, 110,* 26–46.

AMATO, P. R. (2001). Children of divorce in the 1990s: An update of the Amato and Keith (1991) meta-analysis. *Journal of Family Psychology, 15*(3), 355–370.

AMBADY, N., SHIH, M., KIM, A., & PITTINSKY, T. L. (2001). Stereotype susceptibility in children: Effects of identity activation on quantitative performance. *Psychological Science, 12,* 385–390.

AMERICAN PSYCHIATRIC ASSOCIATION. (1994). *Diagnostic and statistical manual of mental disorders* (4th ed.). Washington, DC: Author.

AMERICAN PSYCHOLOGICAL ASSOCIATION. (1981). Ethical principles of psychologists. *American Psychologist, 36,* 633–638.

AMERICAN PSYCHOLOGICAL ASSOCIATION. (1982). *Ethical principles in the conduct of research with human participants.* Washington, DC: Author.

AMERICAN PSYCHOLOGICAL ASSOCIATION PRESIDENTIAL TASK FORCE ON EVIDENCE-BASED PRACTICE. (2006). Evidence-based practice in psychology. *American Psychologist, 61,* 271–285.

ANDERSEN, E., DUNLEA, A., & KEKELIS, L. (1993). The impact of input: language acquisition in the visually impaired. *First Language, 13,* 23–49.

ANDERSON, C. A., & BUSHMAN, B. J. (2001). Effects of violent video games on aggressive behavior, aggressive cognition, aggressive affect, physiological arousal, and prosocial behavior: A meta-analytic review of the scientific literature. *Psychological Science, 12,* 353–360.

ANDERSON, C. A., & BUSHMAN, B. J. (2002). Human aggression. *Annual Review of Psychology, 53,* 27–51.

ANDERSON, J. (1993). *Rules of the mind.* Hillsdale, NJ: Erlbaum.

ANDERSON, J. R. (1990). *Cognitive psychology and its implications* (3rd ed.). San Francisco: Freeman.

ANDERSON, J. R. (1996). ACT: A simple theory of complex cognition. *American Psychologist, 51,* 355–365.

ANDERSON, M. C., OCHSNER, K. N., KUHL, B., COOPER, J., ROBERTSON, E. GABRIELI, ET AL. (2004). Neural systems underlying the suppression of unwanted memories. *Science, 303,* 232–235.

ANDERSSON, M. (1982). Female choice selects for extreme tail length in a widowbird. *Nature, 299,* 818–820.

ANDREASEN, N. C., ARNDT, S., ALLIGER, R., MILLER, D., & FLAUM, M. (1995). Symptoms of schizophrenia. *Archives of General Psychiatry, 52,* 341–351.

ANDREASEN, N. C., & BLACK, D. W. (1996). *Introductory textbook of psychiatry* (2nd ed.). Washington, DC: American Psychiatric Press.

ANDREASEN, N. C., NASRALLAH, H. A., DUNN, V., OLSEN, S. C., GROVE, W. M., EHRHARDT, J., ET AL. (1986). Structural abnormalities in the frontal system in schizophrenia: A magnetic resonance imaging study. *Archives of General Psychiatry, 43,* 136–144.

ANDREWS, G., & HARVEY, R. (1981). Does psychotherapy benefit neurotic patients? A reanalysis of the Smith, Glass, and Miller data. *Archives of General Psychiatry, 38,* 1203–1208.

ANGRIST, B., SATHANANTHAN, G., WILK, S., & GERSHON, S. (1974). Amphetamine psychosis: Behavioral and biochemical aspects. *Journal of Psychiatric Research, 11,* 13–24.

ANTHONY, L. (2000). Naturalizing radical translation. In A. Orenstein & P. Kotatko (Eds.), *Knowledge, language, and logic* (pp. 141–150). Dordrecht: Kluwer.

ARENDT, H. (1965). *Eichmann in Jerusalem: A report on the banality of evil.* New York: Viking Press.

ARIETI, S. (1959). Schizophrenia: The manifest symptomatology, the psychodynamic and formal mechanisms. In S. Arieti (Ed.), *American handbook of psychiatry: Vol. 1* (pp. 455–484). New York: Basic Books.

ARMITAGE, C. J., & CONNER, M. (2001). Efficacy of the theory of planned behaviour: A meta-analytic review. *British Journal of Social Psychology, 40,* 471–499.

ARMSTRONG, S. L., GLEITMAN, L. R., & GLEITMAN, H. (1983). What some concepts might not be. *Cognition, 13,* 263–308.

ARNDT, S., ANDREASEN, N. C., FLAUM, M., MILLER, D., & NOPOULOS, P. (1995). A longitudinal study of symptom dimensions in schizophrenia. Prediction and patterns of change. *Archives of General Psychiatry, 52,* 352–360.

ARNETT, J. (1995). The young and the reckless: Adolescent reckless behavior. *Current Directions in Psychological Science, 4*(3), 67–71.

ARNETT, J. J. (1999). Adolescent storm and stress, reconsidered. *American Psychologist, 54,* 317–326.

ARNOLD, M. (1960). *Emotion and personality* (2 vols.). New York: Columbia University Press.

ARO, H., & TAIPALE, V. (1987). The impact of timing of puberty on psychosomatic symptoms among fourteen- to sixteen-year-old Finnish girls. *Child Development, 58*(1), 261–268.

ARONSON, E., & MILLS, J. (1959). The effect of severity of initiation on liking for a group. *Journal of Abnormal and Social Psychology, 59,* 177–181.

ARONSON, E., & PATNOE, S. (1997). *Cooperation in the classroom: The jig-saw method.* New York: Longman.

ARONSON, E., TURNER, J. A., & CARLSMITH, J. M. (1963). Communicator credibility and communication discrepancy as determinants of opinion change. *Journal of Abnormal and Social Psychology, 67,* 31–36.

ARONSON, E., WILSON, T. D., & AKERT, R. (2005). *Social psychology* (5th. ed.) New York: Prentice-Hall.

ARRIGO, J. M., & PEZDEK, K. (1997). Lessons from the study of psychogenic amnesia. *Current Directions in Psychological Science, 6,* 148–152.

ASCH, S. E. (1951). Effects of group pressure upon the modification and distortion of judgments. In H. Guetzkow (Ed.), *Groups, leadership and men* (pp. 177–190). Pittsburgh: Carnegie Press.

ASCH, S. E. (1952). *Social psychology.* New York: Prentice-Hall.

ASCH, S. E. (1955, November). Opinions and social pressure. Scientific American, 193, 31–35.

ASCH, S. E. (1956). Studies of independence and conformity: A minority of one against a unanimous majority. *Psychological Monographs, 70*(9, Whole No. 416).

ASHER, E. J. (1935). The inadequacy of current intelligence tests for testing Kentucky Mountain children. *Journal of Genetic Psychology, 46,* 480–486.

ASLIN, R. N. (1987). Visual and auditory development in infancy. In J. D. Osofksy (Ed.), *Handbook of infant development* (2nd ed., pp. 5–97). New York: Wiley.

ASLIN, R. N., SAFFRAN, J. R., & NEWPORT, E. L. (1998). Computation of conditional probability statistics by 8-month-old infants. *Psychological Science, 9,* 321–324.

ASTRUP, A. (2000). Thermogenic drugs as a strategy for treatment of obesity. *Endocrine, 13,* 207-212.

ATKINS, C. M., SELCHER, J. C., PETRAITIS, J. J., TRZASKOS, J. M., & SWEATT, J. D. (1998). The MAPK cascade is required for mammalian associative learning. *Nature Neuroscience, 1,* 602–609.

ATKINSON, R. C., & SHIFFRIN, R. M. (1968). Human memory: A proposed system and its control. In K. W. Spence & J. T. Spence (Eds.), *The psychology of learning and motivation: Vol. 2* (pp. 89–105). New York: Academic Press.

ATRAN, S. (1998). Folk biology and the anthropology of science: Cognitive universals and cultural particular. *Behavior and Brain Sciences, 21,* 541–611.

AVERILL, J. R. (1975). A semantic atlas of emotional concepts. *JSAS Catalog of Selected Documents in Psychology, 5,* 330.

AVERILL, J. R. (1985). The social construction of emotion: With special reference to love. In K. J. Gergen & K. E. Davis (Eds.), *The social construction of the person* (pp. 89–109). New York: Springer-Verlag.

AVIEZER, O., SAGI, A., JOELS, T., & ZIV, Y. (1999). Emotional availability and attachment representations in kibbutz infants and their mothers. *Developmental Psychology, 35*(3), 811–821.

AWH, E., DHALIWAL, H., CHRISTENSEN, S., & MATSUKURA, M. (2001). Evidence for two components of object-based selection. *Psychological Science, 12*, 329–334.

AX, A. F. (1953). The physiological differentiation of fear and anger in humans. *Psychosomatic Medicine, 15*, 433–442.

AYLLON, T., & AZRIN, N. H. (1968). *The token economy: A motivational system for therapy and rehabilitation.* New York: Appleton-Century-Crofts.

AZRIN, N. H., & HOLZ, W. C. (1966). Punishment. In W. K. Honig (Ed.), *Operant behavior: Areas of research and application.* New York: Appleton-Century-Crofts.

BAARS, B. J. (1988). Momentary forgetting as a "resetting" of a conscious global workspace due to competition between incompatible contexts. In M. J. Horowitz (Ed.), *Psychodynamics and cognition* (pp. 269–293). Chicago: University of Chicago Press.

BAARS, B. J., & FRANKLIN, S. (2003). How conscious experience and working memory interact. *Trends in Cognitive Science, 7*, 166–172.

BACHTOLD, D. (2003). Drug safety: Conflict-of-interest allegations derail inquiry into antidepressant's "dark side." *Science, 300*, 33.

BADDELEY, A. D., & HITCH, G. J. (1977). Recency re-examined. In S. Dornic (Ed.), *Attention and performance* (Vol. 6, pp. 646–667). Hillsdale, New Jersey: Erlbaum.

BAER, L., RAUCH, S. L., BALLANTINE, H. T., MARTUZA, R., COSGROVE, R., CASSEM, E., ET AL. (1995). Cingulotomy for intractable obsessive-compulsive disorder. Prospective long-term follow-up of 18 patients. *Archives of General Psychiatry, 52*, 384–392.

BAGWELL, C. L., NEWCOMB, A. F., & BUKOWSKI, W. M. (1998). Preadolescent friendship and peer rejection as predictors of adult adjustment. *Child Development, 69*(1), 140–153.

BAHRICK, H. (1984). Semantic memory content in permastore: 50 years of memory for Spanish learned in school. *Journal of Experimental Psychology: General, 113*, 1–29.

BAHRICK, H., & HALL, L. (1991). Lifetime maintenance of high school mathematics content. *Journal of Experimental Psychology: General, 120*, 20–33.

BAHRICK, H., HALL, L., GOGGIN, J., BAHRICK, L., & BERGER, S. (1994). Fifty years of language maintenance and language dominance in bilingual Hispanic immigrants. *Journal of Experimental Psychology: General, 123*, 264–283.

BAILEY, C., & CHEN, M. (1989). Time course of structural changes at identified sensory neuron synapses during long-term sensitization in aplysia. *Journal of Neuroscience, 9*, 1774–1780.

BAILEY, J. M., & PILLARD, R. C. (1991). A genetic study of male sexual orientation. *Archives of General Psychiatry, 48*, 1089–1096.

BAILEY, J. M., PILLARD, R. C., NEALE, M. C., & AGYEI, Y. (1993). Heritable factors influence sexual orientation in women. *Archives of General Psychiatry, 50*, 217–223.

BAILEY, M., & ZUCKER, K. (1995). Childhood sex-typed behavior and sexual orientation: A conceptual analysis and quantitative review. *Developmental Psychology, 31*, 43–55.

BAILLARGEON, R. (1987). Object permanence in 3 1/2- and 4 1/2-month-old infants. *Developmental Psychology, 23*, 655–664.

BAILLARGEON, R. (1994). How do infants learn about the physical world? *Current Directions in Psychological Science, 3*(5), 133–140.

BAILLARGEON, R. (2004). Infants' physical world. *Current Directions in Psychological Science, 13*, 89–94.

BAILLARGEON, R., & GRABER, M. (1987). Where is the rabbit? 5 1/2-Month-old infants' representation of the height of hidden objects. *Cognitive Development, 2*, 375–392.

BAILLARGEON, R., & WANG, S.-H. (2002). Event categorization in infancy. *Trends in Cognitive Science, 6*, 85–93.

BAILLARGEON, R., SPELKE, E. S., & WASSERMAN, S. (1985). Object permanence in five-month-old infants. *Cognition, 20*, 191–208.

BAKER, M. (2001). The atoms of meaning: The mind's hidden rules of grammar. New York: Basic Books.

BAKER, M. (2005). Mapping the terrain of language learning. *Language Learning and Development, 1*(1), 65–93.

BALDWIN, D. A. (1991). Infants' contribution to the achievement of joint reference. *Child Development, 62*, 875–890.

BALTES, P. B., & STAUDINGER, U. M. (2000). Wisdom: A metaheuristic (pragmatic) to orchestrate mind and virtue toward excellence. *American Psychologist, 55*(1), 122–136.

BALTES, P. B., STAUDINGER, U. M., & LINDENBERGER, U. (1999). Lifespan psychology: Theory and application to intellectual functioning. *Annual Review of Psychology, 50*, 471–507.

BANCROFT, J. (1986). The roles of hormones in female sexuality. In Dennerstein & Fraser (Eds.), *Hormones and behavior* (pp. 551–560). Amsterdam: International Society of Psychosomatic Obstetrics and Gynecology, Elsevier.

BANDURA, A. (1969). *Principles of behavior modification.* New York: Holt, Rinehart & Winston.

BANDURA, A. (1977). *Social learning theory.* Englewood Cliffs, NJ: Prentice Hall.

BANDURA, A. (1986). *Social foundations of thought and action: A social cognitive theory.* Englewood Cliffs, NJ: Prentice Hall.

BANDURA, A. (1997). *Self-efficacy: The exercise of control.* New York: Freeman.

BANDURA, A. (2001). Social cognitive theory: An agentic perspective. *Annual Review of Psychology, 52*, 1–26.

BANTICK, R. A., DEAKIN, J. F., & GRASBY, P. M. (2001). The 5–HT1A receptor in schizophrenia: A promising target for novel atypical neuroleptics? *Journal of Psychopharmacology, 15*, 37–46.

BARBER, J. P., CONNOLLY, M. B., CRITS-CHRISTOPH, P., GLADIS, L., & SIQUELAND, L. (2000). Alliance predicts patients' outcome beyond in-treatment change in symptoms. *Journal of Consulting and Clinical Psychology, 68*, 1027–1032.

BARCH, D. M. (2003). Cognition in schizophrenia: Does working memory work? *Current Directions in Psychological Science, 12*, 146–150.

BARCKLAY, J. R., BRANSFORD, J. D., FRANKS, J. J., McCARRELL, N. S., & NITSCH, K. (1974). *Comprehension and semantic flexibility. Journal of Verbal Learning and Verbal Behavior, 13*, 471–481.

BARDO, M. T., DONOHEW, R. L., & HARRINGTON, N. G. (1996). Psychobiology of novelty seeking and drug seeking behavior. *Behavioural Brain Research, 77*, 23–43.

BARGH J. A., CHEN M., & BURROWS, L. (1996). Automaticity of social behavior: Direct effects of trait construct and stereotype activation on action. *Journal of Personality and Social Psychology, 71*, 230–244.

BARGH, J. A., & FERGUSON, M. J. (2000). Beyond behaviorism: On the automaticity of higher mental processes. *Psychological Bulletin, 126*(6), 925–945.

BARKLEY, R. A. (1997). *ADHD and the nature of self-control.* New York: Guilford Press. Barlow, D. H. (2002). *Anxiety and its disorders: The nature and treatment of anxiety and panic* (2nd ed.). New York: Guilford Press.

BARLOW, D. H. (1988). *Anxiety and its disorders.* New York: Guilford Press.

BARLOW, D. H. (2004). Psychological treatments. *American Psychologist, 59*, 869–879.

BARLOW, D. H., & HERSON, M. (1984). *Single case experimental designs: Strategies for studying behavior change* (2nd ed.). New York: Pergamon Press.

BARRETT, L. F. (1998). Discrete emotions or dimensions? The role of valence focus and arousal focus. *Cognition and Emotion, 12*, 579–599.

BARRETT, L. F. (2004). Feelings or words? Understanding the content in self-report ratings of emotional experience. *Journal of Personality and Social Psychology, 87*, 266–281.

BARRETT, L. F., & RUSSELL, J. A. (1999). The structure of current affect: Controversies and emerging consensus. *Current Directions in Psychological Science, 8*(1), 10–14.

BARRETT, L. F., & WAGER, T. D. (2006). The structure of emotion: Evidence from neuroimaging studies. *Current Directions in Psychological Science, 15*, 79–83.

BARRETT, L. F., MESQUITA, B., OCHSNER, K. N., & GROSS J. J. (2007). The experience of emotion. *Annual Review of Psychology*, in press.

BARRY, H., III, CHILD, I. L., & BACON, M. K. (1959). Relation of child training to subsistence economy. *American Anthropologist, 61*, 51–63.

BARSELOU, I. W. (1985). Ideals, central tendency and frequency of instantiation as determinants of graded structure in categories. *Journal of Experimental Psychology: Learning, Memory, and Cognition, 11*, 629–654.

BARTH, H., KANWISHER, N., & SPELKE, E. (2003). The construction of large number representations in adults. *Cognition, 86*, 201–221.

BARTHOLOMEW, K., & HOROWITZ, L. M. (1991). Attachment styles among young adults: A test of a four-category model. *Journal of Personality and Social Psychology, 61*, 226–244.

BARTLETT, F. C. (1932). *Remembering: A study in experimental and social psychology.* Cambridge: Cambridge University Press.

BARTOL, C. R., & COSTELLO, N. (1976). Extraversion as a function of temporal duration of electric shock: An exploratory study. *Perceptual and Motor Skills, 42*, 1174.

BASS, B. M. (1981). From leaderless group discussions to the cross-national assessment of managers. *Journal of Management, 7*, 63–76.

BASS, E., & DAVIS, L. (1988). *The courage to heal.* New York: Harper & Row.

BASSILI, J. N. (1993). Response latency versus certainty as indexes of the strength of voting intentions in a CATI survey. *Public Opinion Quarterly, 57*(1), 54–61.

BASSILI, J. N. (1995). Response latency and the accessibility of voting intentions: What contributes to accessibility and how it affects vote choice. *Personality and Social Psychology Bulletin, 21*(7), 686–695.

BATES, E. (1976). *Language and context: The acquisition of pragmatics.* New York: Academic Press.

BATES, E., CHEN, S., TZENG, O., LI, P. & OPIE, M. (1991). The noun-verb problem in Chinese aphasia. *Brain and Language, 41*, 203–233.

BATES, T. C., & SHIELES, A. (2003). Crystallized intelligence as a product of speed and drive for experience: The relationship of inspection time and openness to *g* and *Gc*. *Intelligence, 31*, 275–287.

BATESON, G. (1959). Cultural problems posed by a study of schizophrenic process. In A. Auerbach (Ed.), *Schizophrenia: An integrated approach* (pp. 125–148). New York: Ronald Press.

BATESON, G. (1960). Minimal requirements for a theory of schizophrenia. *Archives of General Psychiatry, 2*, 477–491.

BATSON, C. D., KOBRYNOWICZ, D., DINNERSTEIN, J. L., KAMPF, H. C., & WILSON, A. D. (1997). In a very different voice: Unmasking moral hypocrisy. *Journal of Personality and Social Psychology, 72*, 1335–1348.

BATSON, C. D., & THOMPSON, E. R. (2001). Why don't moral people act morally? Motivational considerations. *Current Directions in Psychological Science, 10*, 54–57.

BATSON, C. D., THOMPSON, E. R., & CHEN, H. (2002). Moral hypocrisy: Addressing some alternatives. *Journal of Personality and Social Psychology, 83*, 330–339.

BATSON, C. D., THOMPSON, E. R., SEUFERLING, G., WHITNEY, H., & STRONGMAN, J. A. (1999). Moral hypocrisy: Appearing moral to oneself without being so. *Journal of Personality and Social Psychology, 77*, 525–537.

BATTLE, Y. L., MARTIN, B. C., DORFMAN, J. H., & MILLER, L. S. (1999). Seasonality and infectious disease in schizophrenia: The birth hypothesis revisited. *Journal of Psychiatric Research, 33*, 501–509.

BAUER, P. J. (2005). Developments in declarative memory: Decreasing susceptibility to storage failure over the second year of life. *Psychological Science, 16*, 41–47.

BAUER, P. J., WIEBE, S. A., CARVER, L. J., WATERS, J. M., & NELSON, C. A. (2003). Developments in long-term explicit memory late in the first year of life. *Psychological Science, 14*, 629–635.

BAUM, A., & POSLUSZNY, D. M. (1999). Health psychology: Mapping biobehavioral contributions to health and illness. *Annual Review of Psychology, 50*, 137–163.

BAUMANN, B., & BOGERTS, B. (2001). Neuroanatomical studies on bipolar disorder [Suppl.]. *British Journal of Psychiatry, 41*, 142–147.

BAUMEISTER, R. F. (2001). Violent pride. *Scientific American, 284*, 96–101.

BAUMEISTER, R. F., CAMPBELL, J. D., KRUEGER, J. I., & VOHS, K. D. (2003). Does high self-esteem cause better performance, interpersonal success, happiness, or healthier lifestyles? *Psychological Science in the Public Interest, 4*(1), 1–44.

BAUMEISTER, R. F., CATANESE, K. R., & VOHS, K. D. (2001). Is there a gender difference in strength of sex drive? *Personality & Social Psychology Review, 5*, 242–273.

BAUMEISTER, R. F., & VOHS, K. D. (2004). Sexual economics: Sex as female resource for social exchange in heterosexual interactions. *Personality & Social Psychology Review, 8*(4), 339–363.

BAUMRIND, D. (1964). Some thoughts on the ethics of research: After reading Milgram's behavioral study of obedience. *American Psychologist, 19*, 421–423.

BAUMRIND, D. (1967). Child care practices anteceding three patterns of preschool behavior. *Genetic Psychology Monographs, 75*, 43–88.

BAUMRIND, D. (1971). Current patterns of parental authority. *Genetic Psychology Monographs, 1.*

BAUMRIND, D. (1977). Socialization determinants of personal agency. Paper presented at the biennial meetings of the Society for Research in Child Development, New Orleans. Cited in Maccoby, E. E. (1980). *Social development.* New York: Harcourt Brace Jovanovich.

BAUMRIND, D. (1986). Sex differences in moral reasoning: Response to Walker's (1984) conclusion that there are none. *Child Development, 57*, 511–521.

BAUMRIND, D. (1991). The influence of parenting style on adolescent competence and substance use. *Journal of Early Adolescence, 11*(1), 56–95.

BAYER, E. (1929). Beitrage zur Zweikomponententheorie des Hungers. *Zeitschrift der Psychologie, 112*, 1–54.

BAZERMAN, M. H. (1998). *Judgment in managerial decision making* (4th ed.). New York: Wiley.

BEAR, M. F., CONNORS, B. W., & PARADISO, M. A. (1996). *Neuroscience: Exploring the brain.* Baltimore: Williams & Wilkins.

BECHARA, A., DAMASIO, H., & DAMASIO, A. R. (2000). Emotion, decision making, and the orbitofrontal cortex. *Cerebral Cortex, 10*, 295–307.

BECK, A. T. (1967). *Depression: Causes and treatment.* Philadelphia: University of Pennsylvania Press.

BECK, A. T. (1976). *Cognitive therapy and the emotional disorders.* New York: International Universities Press.

BECK, A. T. (1985). Cognitive therapy. In H. I. Kaplan & J. Sadock (Eds.), *Comprehensive textbook of psychiatry* (4th ed.). Baltimore: Williams & Wilkins.

BECK, A. T., RUSH, A. J., SHAW, B. F., & EMERY, G. (1979). Cognitive therapy of depression. New York: Guilford Press.

BECKERS, T., MILLER, R. R., DE HOUWER, J., & URUSHIHARA, K. (2006). Reasoning rats: Forward blocking in Pavlovian animal conditioning is sensitive to constraints of causal inference. *Journal of Experimental Psychology: General, 135*(1), 92–102.

BÉDARD, J., & CHI, M. (1992). Expertise. *Current Directions in Psychological Science, 1*, 135–139.

BEER, R. D. (2000). Dynamical approaches to cognitive science. *Trends in Cognitive Science, 4*, 91–99.

BEGG, I., ANAS, A., & FARINACCI, S. (1992). Dissociation of processes in belief: Source recollection, statement familiarity, and the illusion of truth. *Journal of Experimental Psychology: General, 121*, 446–458.

BEHRMANN, M. (2000). The mind's eye mapped onto the brain's matter. *Current Directions in Psychological Science, 9,* 50–54.

BEITMAN, B. D., GOLDFRIED, M. R., & NORCROSS, J. C. (1989). The movement toward integrating the psychotherapies: An overview. *American Journal of Psychiatry, 146,* 138–147.

BÉKÉSY, G. VON. (1957). The ear. *Scientific American, 197,* 66–78. (Eds.), *Sex and gender: A theological and scientific inquiry* (pp. 235–245). St. Louis, MO: The Pope John Center.

BELL, A. P., WEINBERG, M. S., & HAMMERSMITH, S. K. (1981). *Sexual preference: Its development in men and women.* Bloomington: Indiana University Press.

BELLUGI, U. (1971). Simplification in children's language. In R. Huxley & E. Ingram (Eds.), *Language acquisition: Models and methods.* New York: Academic Press.

BELLUGI, U., MARKS, S., BIHRLE, A., & SABO, H. (1991). Dissociation between language and cognitive function in Williams syndrome. In D. Bishop & K. Mogford (Eds.), *Language development in exceptional circumstances.* Hillsdale, NJ: Erlbaum.

BELOFF, H. (1957). The structure and origin of the anal character. *Genetic Psychology Monographs, 55,* 141–172.

BEM, D. J. (1967). Self-perception: An alternative interpretation of cognitive dissonance phenomena. *Psychological Review, 74,* 183–200.

BEM, D. J. (1972). Self-perception theory. In L. Berkowitz (Ed.), *Advances in experimental social psychology: Vol. 6* (pp. 2–62). New York: Academic Press.

BENBOW, C. P. (1988). Sex differences in mathematical reasoning ability in intellectually talented preadolescents: Their nature, effects, and possible causes. *Behavior and Brain Sciences, 11,* 169–232.

BENBOW, C. P., LUBINSKI, D., SHEA, D. L., & EFTEKHARI-SANJANI, H. (2000). Sex differences in mathematical reasoning ability at age 13: Their status 20 years later. *Psychological Science, 11,* 474–480.

BENBOW, C. P., & STANLEY, J. C. (1983). Sex differences in mathematical reasoning: More facts. *Science, 222,* 1029–1031.

BENET-MARTÍNEZ, V. (1999). Exploring indigenous Spanish personality constructs with a combined emic-etic approach. In J. C. Lasry, J. G. Adair, & K. L. Dion (Eds.), *Latest contributions to cross-cultural psychology: Selected papers from the Thirteenth International Congress of the International Association for Cross-Cultural Psychology* (pp. 151–175). Lisse, The Netherlands: Swets & Zeitliner.

BENNETT, C., LINDSKOLD, S., & BENNETT, R. (1973). The effects of group size and discussion time on the risky shift. *Journal of Social Psychology, 91*(1), 137–147.

BENSON, H., & FRIEDMAN, R. (1996). Harnessing the power of the placebo effect and renaming it "remembered wellness." *Annual Review of Medicine, 47,* 193–199.

BERENBAUM, S. (2002). Prenatal androgen and sexual differentiation of behavior. In E. Eugster & O. Pescovitz (Eds.), *Developmental endocrinology: From research to clinical practice* (pp. 293–311). Totowa, NJ: Humana Press.

BERGER, P. L., & LUCKMANN, T. (1966). *The social construction of reality: A treatise in the sociology of knowledge.* Garden City, NY: Doubleday.

BERLIN, B., & KAY, P. (1969). *Basic color terms: Their universality and evolution.* Berkeley and Los Angeles: University of California Press.

BERMAN, D. E., & DUDAI, Y. (2001). Memory extinction, learning anew, and learning the new: Dissociations in the molecular machinery of learning in the cortex. *Science, 291,* 2417–2419.

BERMANT, G., & DAVIDSON, J. M. (1974). *Biological bases of sexual behavior.* New York: Harper & Row.

BERNARD, V. W., OTTENBERG, P., & REDL, F. (1965). Dehumanization: A composite psychological defense in relation to modern war. In M. Schwebel (Ed.), *Behavioral science and human survival* (pp. 64–82). Palo Alto, CA: Science and Behavior Books.

BERNDT, T. J. (1996). Friendship quality affects adolescents' self-esteem and social behavior. In W. Bukowski, A. Newcomb, & W. Hartup (Eds.), *The company they keep: Friendship during childhood and adolescence* (pp. 346–365). New York: Cambridge University Press.

BERNDT, T. J. (1999). Friends' influence on students' adjustment to school. *Educational Psychologist, 34*(1), 15–28.

BERNDT, T. J., & KEEFE, K. (1995). Friends' influence on adolescents' adjustment to school. *Child Development, 66,* 1312–1329.

BERNSTEIN, A. E., & LENHART, S. A. (1993). *The psychodynamic treatment of women.* Washington, DC: American Psychiatric Press.

BERSCHEID, E. (1985). Interpersonal attraction. In G. Lindzey & E. Aronson (Eds.), *The handbook of social psychology* (Vol. 2, pp. 413–484). New York: Random House.

BERSCHEID, E., DION, K., WALSTER, E., & WALSTER, G. W. (1971). Physical attractiveness and dating choice: A test of the matching hypothesis. *Journal of Experimental Social Psychology, 7,* 173–189.

BERSCHEID, E., & HATFIELD, E. (1978). *Interpersonal attraction* (2nd ed.). Reading, MA: Addison-Wesley.

BERSCHEID, E., & WALSTER, E. (1974). Physical attractiveness. In L. Berkowitz (Ed.), *Advances in experimental social psychology: Vol. 7.* New York: Academic Press.

BERSCHEID, E., & WALSTER, E. H. (1978). *Interpersonal attraction* (2nd ed.). Reading, MA: Addison-Wesley.

BESSENOFF, G. R., & SHERMAN, J. W. (2000). Automatic and controlled components of prejudice toward fat people: Evaluation versus stereotype activation. *Social Cognition, 18*(4), 329–353.

BEST, D., WILLIAMS, J., CLOUD, J., DAVIS, S., ROBERTSON, L. EDWARDS, J., ET AL. (1977). Development of sex-trait stereotypes among young children in the United States, England, and Ireland. *Child Development, 48,* 1375–1384.

BETTELHEIM, B. (1975). *The uses of enchantment: The meaning and importance of fairy tales.* New York: Random House.

BEVER, T. G. (1970). The cognitive basis for linguistic structures. In J. R. Hayes (Ed.), *Cognition and the development of language* (pp. 279–362). New York: Wiley.

BIEDERMAN, I. (1987). Recognition-by-components: A theory of human image understanding. *Psychological Review, 94,* 115–147.

BIEDERMAN, J., WILENS, T. E., MICK, E., MILBERGER, S., SPENCER, T. J., & FARAONE, S. V. (1995). Psychoactive substance use disorders in adults with attention deficit hyperactivity disorder (ADHD): Effects of ADHD and psychiatric comorbidity. *American Journal of Psychiatry, 152,* 1652–1658.

BIGELOW, A. (1987). Early words of blind children. *Journal of Child Language, 14*(1), 1–22.

BIGELOW, B., & LAGAIPA, J. (1975). Children's written descriptions of friendship: A multi-dimensional analysis. *Developmental Psychology, 41,* 857–858.

BINET, A. (1911). *Les idées modernes sur les enfants.* Paris: Flammarion. Republished by Flammarion in 1973 with a Preface by Jean Piaget. [Published in English as: *Modern Ideas about Children.* Menlo Park, CA: Suzanne Heisler, 1984.]

BIRMAHER, B., & BRENT, D. (1998). Practice parameters for the assessment and treatment of children and adolescents with depressive disorders. *Journal of the American Academy of Child and Adolescent Psychiatry, 37,* 63S–83S.

BJORKLUND, D. F., & SHACKELFORD, T. K. (1999). Differences in parental investment contribute to important differences between men and women. *Current Directions in Psychological Science, 8*(3), 86–89.

BLACK, D. W., & ANDREASEN, N. C. (1994). Schizophrenia, schizophreniform disorder, and delusional paranoid disorder. In J. A. Talbott, R. E. Hales, & S. C. Yudofsky (Eds.), *American Psychiatric Press textbook of psychiatry* (pp. 411–463). Washington, DC: American Psychiatric Press.

BLACK, D. W., & NOYES, R. (1990). Comorbidity in obsessive-compulsive disorder. In J. D. Maser & C. D. Cloninger (Eds.), *Comorbidity in anxiety and mood disorders* (pp. 305–316). Washington, DC: American Psychiatric Press.

BLAIR, I. V., & BANAJI, M. R. (1996). Automatic and controlled processes in stereotype priming. *Journal of Personality and Social Psychology, 70.*

BLAKEMORE, J. E. O. (2003). Children's beliefs about violating gender norms: Boys shouldn't look like girls, and girls shouldn't act like boys. *Sex Roles, 48*(9–10), 411–419.

BLANCHETTE, I., & DUNBAR, K. (2000). How analogies are generated: The roles of structural and superficial similarity. *Memory and Cognition, 28*(1), 108–124.

BLASCOVICH, J., SPENCER, S. J., QUINN, D., & STEELE, C. (2001). African Americans and high blood pressure: The role of stereotype threat. *Psychological Science, 12,* 225–229.

BLASS, T. (ED.). (2000). *Obedience to authority: Current perspectives on the Milgram paradigm.* Mahwah, NJ: Erlbaum.

BLEULER, E. (1911). *Dementia praecox, or the group of schizophrenias* (J. Zinkin & N. D. C. Lewis, Trans.). New York: International Universities Press, 1950.

BLIER, P., & ABBOTT, F. V. (2001). Putative mechanisms of action of antidepressant drugs in affective and anxiety disorders and pain. *Journal of Psychiatry and Neuroscience, 26,* 37–43.

BLISS, E. L. (1980). Multiple personalities: Report of fourteen cases with implications for schizophrenia and hysteria. *Archives of General Psychiatry, 37,* 1388–1397.

BLISS, T. V. P., & LOMO, T. (1973). Long-term potentiation of synaptic transmission in the dentate area of the anesthetized rabbit following stimulation of the perforant path. *Journal of Physiology, 232,* 331–356.

BLOCK, J., & BLOCK, J. H. (2006). Venturing a 30-year longitudinal study. *American Psychologist, 61,* 315–327.

BLOCK, N. (1997). Biology vs. computation in the study of consciousness. *Behavioral and Brain Sciences, 20,* 1.

BLOCK, N. (2001). Paradox and cross purposes in recent work on consciousness. *Cognition, 79,* 197–219.

BLOOM, F. E. (1993). Advancing a neurodevelopmental origin for schizophrenia. *Archives of General Psychiatry, 50,* 224–227.

BLOOM, L. (1993). *The transition from infancy to language: Acquiring the power of expression.* New York: Cambridge University Press.

BLOOM, P. (1996). Intention, history, and artifact concepts. *Cognition, 60,* 1–29.

BLOOM, P. (2000). *How children learn the meanings of words.* Cambridge, MA: MIT Press.

BLOOM, P. (2002). Mindreading, communication, and the learning of the names for things. *Mind and Language, 17,* 37–54.

BLURTON-JONES, N., & KONNER, M. J. (1976). !Kung knowledge of animal behavior. In B. Lee & I. DeVore (Eds.), *Kalahari hunter-gatherers.* Cambridge, MA: Harvard University Press.

BOGEN, J. E., FISHER, E. D., & VOGEL, P. J. (1965). Cerebral commissurotomy: A second case report. *Journal of the American Medical Association, 194,* 1328–1329.

BOLLES, R. C. (1970). Species-specific defense reactions and avoidance learning. *Psychological Review, 77,* 32–48.

BOLLES, R. C., & BEECHER, M. D. (EDS.). (1988). *Evolution and learning.* Hillsdale, NJ: Erlbaum.

BOLTON, P., & BETANCOURT, T. S. (2004). Mental health in postwar Afghanistan. *Journal of the American Medical Association, 292,* 626–628.

BOND, R., & SMITH, P. B. (1996). Culture and conformity: A meta-analysis of studies using Asch's (1952, 1956) line judgment task. *Psychological Bulletin, 119*(1), 111–137.

BOOK, A. S., STARZYK, K. B., & QUNISEY, V. L (2001). The relationship between testosterone and aggression: A meta-analysis. *Aggression and Violent Behavior, 6,* 579–599.

BOOTH, A. E., & WAXMAN, S. R. (2002). Word learning is "smart": evidence that conceptual information affects preschoolers' extension of novel words. *Cognition, 84,* B11–B22.

BORDEN, V. M. H., & LEVINGER, G. (1991). Interpersonal transformations in intimate relationships. In W. H. Jones & D. Perlman (Eds.), *Advances in personal relationships: Vol. 2* (pp. 35–56). London: Jessica Kingsley Publishers.

BORKENAU, P., RIEMANN, R., ANGLEITNER, A., & SPINATH, F. M. (2001). Genetic and environmental influences on observed personality: Evidence from the German Observational Study of Adult Twins. *Journal of Personality and Social Psychology, 80*(4), 655–668.

BORNSTEIN, M. H. (1973). Color vision and color naming: A psychophysiological hypothesis of cultural difference. *Psychological Bulletin, 80,* 257–285.

BORNSTEIN, M. H. (1985). Human infant color vision and color perception. *Infant Behavior and Development, 8*(1), 109–113.

BOTVINICK, M. M., COHEN, J. D., & CARTER, C. S. (2004). Conflict monitoring and anterior cingulate cortex: An update. *Trends in Cognitive Science, 8,* 539–546.

BOUCHARD, T. J., JR. (1984). Twins reared apart and together: What they tell us about human diversity. In S. Fox (Ed.), *The chemical and biological bases of individuality* (pp. 147–184). New York: Plenum.

BOUCHARD, T. J., JR., & MCGUE, M. (1981). Familial studies of intelligence: A review. *Science, 212,* 1055–1059.

BOUCHARD, T. J., JR., LYKKEN, D. T., MCGUE, M., SEGAL, N. L., & TELLEGEN, A. (1990). Sources of human psychological differences: The Minnesota study of twins reared apart. *Science, 250,* 223–250.

BOURET, S. G., DRAPER, S. J., & SIMERLY, R. B. (2004). Trophic action of leptic on hypothalamic neurons that regulate feeding. *Science, 304,* 108–110.

BOWER, G. H. (1970). Analysis of a mnemonic device. *American Scientist, 58,* 496–510.

BOWER, G. H. (1972). Analysis of a mnemonic device. In M. Coltheart (Ed.), *Readings in cognitive psychology.* Toronto: Holt, Rinehart & Winston.

BOWER, G. H., BLACK, J. B., & TURNER, T. J. (1979). Scripts in memory for text. *Cognitive Psychology, 11,* 177–220.

BOWER, G. H., MCLEAN, J., & MEACHEM, J. (1966). Value of knowing when reinforcement is due. *Journal of Comparative and Physiological Psychology, 62,* 184–192.

BOWER, J. M., & PARSONS, L. M. (2003). Rethinking the "lesser brain." *Scientific American, 289,* 50–57.

BOWERMAN, M. (1982). Reorganizational processes in language development. In E. Wanner & L. R. Gleitman (Eds.), *Language development: State of the art.* New York: Cambridge University Press.

BOWMAKER, J. K., & DARTNALL, H. J. A. (1980). Visual pigments and rods and cones in a human retina. *Journal of Physiology, 298,* 501–511.

BRABECK, M. (1983). Moral judgement: Theory and research on differences between males and females. *Developmental Review, 3,* 274–291.

BRACKETT, M. A., & MAYER, J. D. (2003). Convergent, discriminant, and incremental validity of competing measures of emotional intelligence. *Personality and Social Psychology Bulletin, 29,* 1147–1158.

BRADLEY, G. W. (1978). Self-serving biases in the attribution process: A reexamination of the fact or fiction question. *Journal of Personality and Social Psychology, 13,* 420–432.

BRADLEY, S. J., OLIVER, G. D., CHERNICK, A. B., & ZUCKER, K. J. (1998). Experiment of nurture: Ablatio penis at 2 months, sex reassignment at 7 months, and a psychosexual follow-up in young adulthood. *Pediatrics, 102,* e9 (electronic article available at http://www.pediatrics.org/cgi/content/full/102/1/e9).

BRADSHAW, J. L. (2001). *Developmental disorders of the frontostrial system: Neuropsychological, neuropsychiatric, and evolutionary perspectives.* Philadelphia: Psychology Press/Taylor & Francis.

BRAILOWSKY, S., & GARCIA, O. (1999). Ethanol, GABA and epilepsy. *Archives of Medical Research, 30,* 3–9.

BRANNON, E. (2003). Number knows no bounds. *Trends in Cognitive Science, 7,* 279–281.

BRANSFORD, J. D., & JOHNSON, M. K. (1972). Contextual prerequisites for understanding. *Journal of Verbal Learning and Verbal Behavior, 11,* 717–726.

BRAUER, M., JUDD, C. M., & GLINER, M. D. (1995). The effects of repeated expressions on attitude polarization during group discussions. *Journal of Personality and Social Psychology, 68*(6), 1014–1029.

BREMNER, J. D., SOUTHWICK, S. M., JOHNSON, D. R., YEHUDA, R., & CHARNEY, D. S. (1993). Childhood physical abuse and combat-related posttraumatic stress disorder in Vietnam veterans. *American Journal of Psychiatry, 150,* 235–239.

BRENDGEN, M., VITARO, F., & BUKOWSKI, W. (2000). Deviant friends and early adolescents' emotional and behavioral adjustment. *Journal of Research on Adolescence, 10,* 173–189.

BRENNAN, K. A., CLARK, C. L., & SHAVER, P. R. (1998). Self-report measurement of adult attachment: An integrative overview. In J. A. Simpson & W. S. Rholes (Eds.), *Attachment theory and close relationships* (pp. 46–76). New York: Guilford Press.

BRENNEN, T., BAGULEY, T., BRIGHT, J., & BRUCE, V. (1990). Resolving semantically induced tip-of-the-tongue states for proper nouns. *Memory & Cognition, 18,* 339–347.

BRENNER, C. (1982). *The mind in conflict.* New York: International Universities Press.

BRESLAU, N., CHILCOAT, H. D., KESSLER, R. C., & DAVIS, G. C. (1999). Previous exposure to trauma and PTSD effects of subsequent trauma: Results from the Detroit Area Survey of Trauma. *American Journal of Psychiatry, 156,* 902–907.

BRETHERTON, I. (1990). Open communication and internal working models: Their role in the development of attachment relationships. In R. A. Thompson (Ed.), *Socioemotional development: Vol. 36. Nebraska Symposium on Motivation* (pp. 57–113). Lincoln: University of Nebraska Press.

BREWER, J., ZHAO, Z., DESMOND, J., GLOVER, G., & GABRIELI, J. (1998). Making memories: Brain activity that predicts how well visual experience will be remembered. *Science, 281,* 1185–1187.

BREWER, W. F., & TREYENS, J. C. (1981). Role of schemata in memory for places. *Cognitive Psychology, 13,* 207–230.

BREWIN, C. R. (1998). Intrusive autobiographical memories in depression and post-traumatic stress disorder. *Applied Cognitive Psychology, 12,* 359–370.

BRICKMAN, J. C., & D'AMATO, B. (1975). Exposure effects in a free-choice situation. *Journal of Personality and Social Psychology, 32,* 415–420.

BRICKMAN, P., COATES, D., & JANOFF-BULLMAN, R. (1978). Lottery winners and accident victims: Is happiness relative? *Journal of Personality and Social Psychology, 36,* 917–927.

BRIDGEMAN, B., & LEWIS, C. (1996). Gender differences in college mathematics grades and SAT-M scores: A reanalysis of Wainer & Steinberg. *Journal of Educational Measurement, 33,* 257–270.

BRIDGEMAN, B., & STARK, L. (1991). Ocular proprioception and efference copy in registering visual direction. *Vision Research, 31,* 1903–1913.

BRIDGES, P. (1987). Psychosurgery for resistant depression. In J. Zohar & R. H. Belmaker, (Eds.), *Treating resistant depression* (pp. 397–411). New York: PMA Publishing.

BROADBENT, D. E. (1958). *Perception and communication.* London: Pergamon Press.

BRODY, G. H., & GE, X. (2001). Linking parenting processes and self-regulation to psychological functioning and alcohol use during early adolescence. *Journal of Family Psychology, 15*(1), 82–94.

BRODY, L., & HALL, J. (2000). Gender, emotion, and expression. In M. Lewis & J. Haviland-Jones (Eds.), *Handbook of emotions* (2nd ed., pp. 338–349). New York: Guilford Press.

BROWN, A. (1991). A review of the Tip-of-the-Tongue Experience. *Psychological Bulletin, 109,* 204–223.

BROWN, A. (2002). Consolidation theory and retrograde amnesia in humans. *Psychonomic Bulletin and Review, 9,* 403–425.

BROWN, A. S., COHEN, P., HARKAVY-FRIEDMAN, J., & BABULAS, V. (2001). Prenatal rubella, premorbid abnormalities, and adult schizophrenia. *Biological Psychiatry, 49,* 473–486.

BROWN, A., & MITCHELL, D. (1994). A reevaluation of semantic versus nonsemantic processing in implicit memory. *Memory and Cognition, 22,* 533–541.

BROWN, B. B. (1990). Peer groups and peer cultures. In S. S. Feldman & G. R. Elliott (Eds.), *At the threshold: The developing adolescent.* Cambridge, MA: Harvard University Press.

BROWN, B., CLASEN, D., & EICHER, S. (1986). Perception of peer pressure, peer conformity dispositions and self reported behavior among adolescents. *Developmental Psychology, 22,* 521–530.

BROWN, B., MORAY, M., & KINNEY, D. (1994). Casting adolescent crowds in a relational perspective: Caricature, channel and context. In R. Montemayor, G. Adams, & T. Gullotta (Eds.), *Personal relationships in adolescence: Vol. 6. Advances in adolescent development.* Thousand Oaks, CA: Sage.

BROWN, C. M., HAGOORT, P., & TER KEURS, M. (1999). Electrophysiological signatures of visual lexical processing of open- and closed-class words. *Journal of Cognitive Neuroscience, 11,* 261– 281.

BROWN, D. E. (1991). *Human universals.* New York: McGraw-Hill.

BROWN, E., DEFFENBACHER, K., & STURGILL, W. (1977). Memory for faces and the circumstances of encounter. *Journal of Applied Psychology, 62,* 311–318.

BROWN, G. W., & HARRIS, T. (1978). *Social origins of depression: A study of psychiatric disorder in women.* London: Tavistock.

BROWN, J. F. (1940). *The psychodynamics of abnormal behavior.* New York: McGraw-Hill.

BROWN, J., & DUNN, J. (1996). Continuities in emotion understanding from 3 to 6 years. *Child Development, 67,* 789–802.

BROWN, P., & DELL, G. L. (1987). Adapting production to comprehension: The explicit mention of instruments. *Cognitive Psychology, 19,* 441–472.

BROWN, R. (1957). Linguistic determinism and parts of speech. *Journal of Abnormal and Social Psychology, 55,* 1–5.

BROWN, R. (1958). *Words and things.* New York: Free Press, Macmillan.

BROWN, R. (1965). *Social psychology.* New York: Free Press, Macmillan.

BROWN, R. P., & JOSEPHS, R. A. (1999). A burden of proof: Stereotype relevance and gender differences in math performance. *Journal of Personality and Social Psychology, 76,* 246–257.

BROWN, R., & BELLUGI, U. (1964). Three processes in the child's acquisition of syntax. *Harvard Educational Review, 34,* 133–151.

BROWN, R., & KULIK, J. (1977). Flashbulb memories. *Cognition, 5,* 73–99.

BROWN, R., & MCNEILL, D. (1966). The tip of the tongue phenomenon. *Journal of Verbal Learning and Verbal Behavior, 5,* 325–327.

BRUCH, H. (1973). *Eating disorders.* New York: Basic Books.

BRUCH, H. (1978). *The golden cage.* Cambridge, MA: Harvard University Press.

BRUCK, M., & CECI, S. J. (1999). The suggestibility of children's memory. *Annual Review of Psychology, 50.*

BRUGGEMAN, E., & HART, K. (1996). Cheating, lying, and moral reasoning by religious and secular high school students. *Journal of Educational Research, 89,* 340–344.

BRUNER, J. S., & TAGIURI, R. (1954). The perception of people. In G. Lindzey (Ed.), *Handbook of social psychology: Vol. 2.* Reading, MA: Addison-Wesley.

BUCHANAN, G. M., & SELIGMAN, M. E. P. (EDS.). (1995). *Explanatory style.* Hillsdale, NJ: Erlbaum.

BUCHANAN, T. W., & ADOLPHS, R. (2003). The neuroanatomy of emotional memory in humans. In D. Reisberg & P. Hertel (Eds.), *Emotion and memory.* New York: Oxford University Press.

BUCHANAN, T. W., & ADOLPHS, R. (2004). The neuroanatomy of emotional memory in humans. In D. Reisberg & P. Hertel (Eds.), *Memory and emotion* (pp. 42–75). N.Y.: Oxford University Press.

BUGNYAR T, KOTRSCHAL K, (2002). Observational learning and the raiding of food caches in ravens, *Corvus corax*: is it 'tactical' deception? *Animal Behavior, 64*, 185–195.

BULLER, D. J. (2005). Evolutionary psychology: The emperor's new paradigm. *Trends in Cognitive Science, 9*, 277–283.

BULLER, D. J., FODOR, J., & CRUME, T. L. (2005). The emperor is still underdressed. *Trends in Cognitive Science, 9*, 508–510.

BULLOCK, T. H., BENNETT, M. V., JOHNSTON, D., JOSEPHSON, R., MARDER, E., & FIELDS, R. D. (2005). The Neuron Doctrine, redux. *Science, 310*, 791–793.

BULLOCK, W. A., & GILLILAND, K. (1993). Eysenck's arousal theory of introversion-extraversion: A covergent measures investigation. *Journal of Personality and Social Psychology, 64*, 113–123.

BURGER, J. M. (1986). Increasing compliance by improving the deal: The that's-not-all technique. *Journal of Personality and Social Psychology, 51*(2), 277–283.

BURGER, J. M., REED, M., DeCESARE, K., RAUNER, S., & ROZOLIS, J. (1999). The effects of initial request size on compliance: More about the that's-not-all technique. *Basic and Applied Social Psychology, 21*(3), 243–249.

BURGESS, E. W., & WALLIN, P. (1943). Homogamy in social characteristics. *American Journal of Sociology, 49*, 109–124.

BURKE, M. J., & PRESKHORN, S. H. (1995). Short-term treatment of mood disorders with standard antidepressants. In F. E. Bloom & D. Kupfer (Eds.), *Psychopharmacology: The fourth generation of progress* (pp. 1053–1065). New York: Raven.

BURNETT, S. A., LANE, D. M., & DRATT, L. M. (1979). Spatial differences and sex differences in quantitative ability. *Intelligence, 3*, 345–354.

BURNS, J. M. (1978). *Leadership*. New York: Harper & Row.

BURT, S. A., KRUEGER, R. F., McGUE, M., & IACONO, W. G. (2001). Sources of covariation among attention-deficit/hyperactivity disorder, oppositional defiant disorder, and conduct disorder: The importance of shared environment. *Journal of Abnormal Psychology, 110*, 516–525.

BUSEY, T. A., TUNNICLIFF, J., LOFTUS, G. R., & LOFTUS, E. F. (2000). Accounts of the confidence-accuracy relation in recognition memory. *Memory & Cognition, 7*, 26–48.

BUSHMAN, B. J., & BAUMEISTER, R. F. (2002). Does self-love or self-hate lead to violence? *Journal of Research in Personality, 36*(6), 543–545.

BUSS, A., & PLOMIN, R. (1984). *Temperament: Early developing personality traits*. Hillsdale, NJ: Erlbaum.

BUSS, A. H., & PLOMIN, R. (1984). *Temperament: Early developing personality traits*. Hillsdale, NJ: Erlbaum.

BUSS, D. M. (1989). Sex differences in human mate preferences: Evolutionary hypotheses tested in 37 cultures. *Behavioral and Brain Sciences, 12*, 1–50.

BUSS, D. M. (1992). Mate preference mechanisms: Consequences for partner choice and intrasexual competition. In J. H. Barkow, L. Cosmides, & J. Tooby (Eds.), *The adapted mind* (pp. 249–266). New York: Oxford University Press.

BUSS, D. M. (2004). *Evolutionary psychology: The new science of the mind*. Boston: Allyn and Bacon.

BUSS, D. M., & BARNES, M. F. (1986). Preferences in human mate selection. *Journal of Personality and Social Psychology, 50*, 559–570.

BUSS, D. M., & HASELTON, M. (2005). The evolution of jealousy. *Trends in Cognitive Science, 9*, 506–507.

BUSS, D. M., & SCHMITT, D. P. (1993). Sexual strategies theory: An evolutionary perspective on human mating. *Psychological Review, 100*(2), 204–232.

BUSS, D. M., LARSEN, R. J., WESTEN, D., & SEMMELROTH, J. (2001). Sex differences in jealousy: Evolution, physiology, and psychology. In W. Parrott (Ed.), *Emotions in social psychology:Essential readings*. Philadelphia:Psychology Press.

BUTCHER, J. N., DAHLSTROM, W. G., GRAHAM, J. R., TELLEGEN, A., & KAEMMER, B. (2001). *MMPI-2 (Minnesota Multiphasic Personality Inventory-2) manual for administration and scoring* (2nd ed.). Minneapolis: University of Minnesota Press.

BUTCHER, J. N., WILLIAMS, C. L., GRAHAM, J. R., ARCHER, R. P., TELLEGEN, A., BEN-PORATH, Y. S., ET AL. (1992). *MMPI-A (Minnesota Multiphasic Personality Inventory—Adolescent) manual for administration, scoring, and interpretation*. Minneapolis: University of Minnesota Press.

BUTLER, R. A. (1954). Incentive conditions which influence visual exploration. *Journal of Experimental Psychology, 48*, 19–23.

BUTTERWORTH, G., & COCHRAN, E. (1980). Towards a mechanism of joint visual attention in human infancy. *International Journal of Behavioral Development, 3*, 253–272.

BUTTERWORTH, G., & JARRETT, N. (1991). What minds have in common is space: Spatial mechanisms serving joint visual attention in infancy. Perspectives on the child's theory of mind [Special issue]. *British Journal of Developmental Psychology, 9*, 55–72.

BUZSÁKI, G., & DRAGUHN, A. (2004). Neuronal oscillations in cortical networks. *Science, 304*, 1926–1929.

BYRNE, R. W., & WHITEN, A. (EDS.). (1988). *Machiavellian intelligence: Social expertise and the evolution of intellect in monkeys, apes, and humans*. New York: Oxford University Press.

BYRNES, J. P. (2005). Gender differences in math: Cognitive processes in an expanded framework. In A. M. Gallagher & J. C. Kaufman (Eds.), *Gender differences in mathematics: An integrative psychological approach* (pp. 73–98). New York: Cambridge University Press.

CABEZA, R., & NYBERG, L. (2000). Imaging cognition II: An empirical review of 275 PET and fMRI studies. *Journal of Cognitive Neuroscience, 12*, 1–47.

CABRERA, N. J., TAMIS-LeMONDA, C. S., BRADLEY, R. H., HOFFERTH, S., & LAMB, M. E. (2000). Fatherhood in the twenty-first century. *Child Development, 71*, 127–136.

CACIOPPO, J. T., & PETTY, R. E. (1981). Electromyograms as measures of extent and affectivity of information processing. *American Psychologist, 36*, 441–456.

CACIOPPO, J. T., BERNTSON, G. G., & KLEIN, D. J. (1992). What is emotion? The role of somatovisceral afference, with special emphasis on somatovisceral "illusions." *Review of Personality and Social Psychology, 14*, 63–98.

CACIOPPO, J. T., BERNTSON, G. G., LARSEN, J. T., POEHLMANN, K. M., & ITO, T. A. (2000). The psychophysiology of emotion. In M. Lewis & J. Haviland-Jones (Eds.), *Handbook of emotions* (2nd ed., pp. 173–191). New York: Guilford Press.

CACIOPPO, J. T., MARSHALL-GOODELL, B. S., TASSINARY, L. G., & PETTY, R. E. (1992). Rudimentary determinants of attitudes: Classical conditioning is more effective when prior knowledge about the attitude stimulus is low than high. *Journal of Experimental Social Psychology, 28*, 207–233.

CAHILL, L., BABINSKY, R., MARKOWITSCH, H. J., & McGAUGH, J. L. (1996). The amygdala and emotional memory. *Nature, 377*, 295–296.

CALABRESE, J. R., & WOYSHVILLE, M. J. (1995). Lithium therapy: Limitations and alternatives in the treatment of bipolar disorders. *Annals of Clinical Psychiatry, 7*, 103–112.

CALLAGHAN, T., ROCHAT, P., LILLARD, A., CLAUX, M. L., ODDEN, H., ITAKURA, S., ET AL. (2005). Synchrony in the onset of mental-state reasoning: Evidence from five cultures. *Psychological Science, 16*, 378–384.

CAMPBELL, F. A., & RAMEY, C. T. (1994). Effects of early intervention on intellectual and academic achievement: A follow up study of children from low income families. *Child Development, 65*(2), 684–698.

CAMPBELL, J. B., & HAWLEY, C. W. (1982). Study habits and Eysenck's theory of extraversion-introversion. *Journal of Research in Personality, 16*, 139–146.

CAMPBELL, J. D., TESSER, A., & FAIREY, P. J. (1986). Conformity and attention to the stimulus: Some temporal and contextual dynamics. *Journal of Personality and Social Psychology, 51*, 315–324.

CAMPFIELD, L. A., & ROSENBAUM, M. (1992). Human hunger. Is there a role for blood glucose dynamics? *Appetite, 18*, 244.

CAMPFIELD, L. A., & SMITH, F. J. (1990a). Systemic factors in the control of food intake. In E. M. Stricker (Ed.), *Handbook of behavioral neurobiology: Vol. 10. Neurobiology of food and fluid intake* (pp. 183–206). New York: Plenum.

CAMPFIELD, L. A., & SMITH, F. J. (1990b). Transient declines in blood glucose signal meal initiation. *International Journal of Obesity, 14*, 15–33.

CAMPOS, J., ANDERSON, D. BARBU-ROTH, M., HUBBARD, E., HERTENSTEIN, M., & WITHERINGTON, D. (2000). Travel broadens the mind. *Infancy, 1*, 149–219.

CANLI, T., ZHAO, Z., BREWER, J., GABRIELI, J. D. E., & CAHILL, L. (2000). Event-related activation in the human amygdala associates with later memory for individual emotional response. *Journal of Neuroscience, 20*(19).

CANNON, T. D., MEDNICK, S. A., & PARNAS, J. (1990). Antecedents of predominantly negative- and predominantly positive-symptom schizophrenia in a high-risk population. *Archives of General Psychiatry, 47*, 622–632.

CANNON, T. D., ROSSO, I. M., HOLLISTER, J. M., BEARDEN, C. E., SANCHEZ, L. E., & HADLEY, T. (2000). A prospective cohort study of genetic and perinatal influences in schizophrenia. *Schizophrenia Bulletin, 26*, 351–366.

CANNON, W. B. (1927). The James-Lange theory of emotions: A critical examination and an alternative theory. *American Journal of Psychology, 39*, 106–124.

CANNON, W. B. (1929). *Bodily changes in pain, hunger, fear and rage* (rev. ed.). New York: Appleton-Century.

CANNON, W. B. (1932 and 1960). *The wisdom of the body* (revised and enlarged). New York: Norton.

CANTOR, J., & ENGLE, R. (1993). Working-memory capacity as long-term memory activation: An individual-differences approach. *Journal of Experimental Psychology: Learning, Memory and Cognition, 19*, 1101–1114.

CANTOR, N., & MISCHEL, W. (1979). Prototypes in person perception. In L. Berkowitz (Ed.), *Advances in experimental social psychology: Vol. 12*. New York: Academic Press.

CARAMAZZA, A., & HILLIS, A. (1991). Lexical organization of nouns and verbs in the brain. *Nature, 349*, 788–790.

CAREY, D. B. (2001). Do action systems resist visual illusions? *Trends in Cognitive Science, 5*, 109–113.

CAREY, S. (1978). The child as word learner. In M. Halle, J. Bresnan, & G. A. Miller (Eds.), *Linguistic theory and psychological reality* (pp. 264–293). Cambridge, MA: MIT Press.

CAREY, S. (1985). *Conceptual change in childhood*. Cambridge, MA: MIT Press.

CARLSON, E. B., & PUTNAM, E. W. (1993). An update on the Dissociative Experiences Scale. *Dissociation, 6*, 16–27.

CARLSON, G., & TANENHAUS, M. (1988). Thematic roles and language comprehension. In W. Wilkins (Ed.), *Syntax and semantics: Vol. 21. Thematic relations*. San Diego, CA: Academic Press.

CARLYLE, T. (1841). *On heroes, hero-worship, and the heroic in history*. Berkeley: University of California Press, 1992.

CARNAGEY, N. L., & ANDERSON, C. A. (2005). The effects of reward and punishment in violent video games on aggressive affect, cognition and behavior. *Psychological Science, 16*, 883–889.

CARPENTER, P. A., MIYAKE, A., & JUST, M. A. (1995). Language comprehension: Sentence and discourse processing. *Annual Review of Psychology, 46*, 91–120.

CARROLL, J. B. (1993). *Human cognitive abilities: A survey of factor-analytic studies*. New York: Cambridge University Press.

CARROLL, L. (1969). *Alice in wonderland*. Abridged by J. Frank and illustrated by M. M. Torrey. New York: Random House (originally published 1865).

CARTER, C. S., MINTUN, M., NICHOLS, T., & COHEN, J. D. (1997). Anterior cingulate gyrus dysfunction and selective attention deficits in schizophrenia: $^{15}OH_2O$ PET study during single-trial Stroop task performance. *American Journal of Psychiatry, 154*, 1670–1675.

CASE, R., & OKAMOTO, Y. (1996). The role of central conceptual structures in the development of children's thought. *Monographs of the Society for Research in Child Development, 61*(1–2), v-265.

CASELLI, M.-C., BATES, E., CASADIO, P., & FENSON, J. (1995). A cross-linguistic study of early lexical development. *Cognitive Development, 10*(2), 159–199.

CASPI, A., & HERBENER, E. (1990). Continuity and change: Assortative marriage and the consistency of personality in adulthood. *Journal of Personality and Social Psychology, 58*, 250–258.

CASPI, A., & MOFFITT, T. E. (1991). Individual differences are accentuated during periods of social change: The sample case of girls at puberty. *Journal of Personality and Social Psychology, 61*(1), 157–168.

CASPI, A., & MOFFITT, T. E. (1993). When do individual differences matter? A paradoxical theory of personality coherence. *Psychological Inquiry, 4*(4), 247–271.

CASPI, A., SUGDEN, K., MOFFITT, T. E., TAYLOR, A., CRAIG, I. W., HARRINGTON, H., ET AL. (2003). Influence of life stress on depression: Moderation in the 5–HTT gene. *Science, 301*, 386–389.

CASSIDY, J., & ASHER, S. R. (1992). Loneliness and peer relations in young children. *Child Development, 63*(2), 350–365.

CASTELLANOS, F. X., SONUGA-BARKE, E. J., MILHAM, M. P., & TANNOCK, R. (2006). Characterizing cognition in ADHD: Beyond executive dysfunction. *Trends in Cognitive Sciences, 10*, 117–123.

CASTLE, J., GROOTHUES, C., BREDENKAMP, D., BECKETT, C., O'CONNOR, T., RUTTER, M., ET AL. (1999). Effects of qualities of early institutional care on cognitive attainment. *American Journal of Orthopsychiatry, 69*, 424–437.

CASTONGUAY, L., REID, J., & HALPERIN, G. (IN PRESS). Reconciliation and integration in psychotherapy: A strategy to address the complexity of human change. In G. Stricker & T. Widiger, T. (Eds.), *Comprehensive handbook of psychology: Vol. 8. Clinical psychology*. New York: Wiley.

CATE, R. M., LEVIN, L. A., & RICHMOND, L. S. (2002). Premarital relationship stability: A review of recent research. *Journal of Social and Personal Relationships, 19*, 261–284.

CATRAMBONE, R. (1998). The subgoal learning model: Creating better examples so that students can solve novel problems. *Journal of Experimental Psychology: General, 127*(4), 355–376.

CATTELL, R. B. (1957). *Personality and motivation structure and measurement*. New York: Harcourt, Brace and World.

CATTELL, R. B. (1963). Theory of fluid and crystallized intelligence: A critical experiment. *Journal of Educational Psychology, 54*, 1–22.

CATTELL, R. B. (1966). *The scientific analysis of personality*. Chicago: Aldine.

CATTELL, R. B. (1971). *Abilities: Their structure, growth, and action*. Boston: Houghton Mifflin.

CECI, S., & BRUCK, M. (1995). *Jeopardy in the courtroom: A scientific analysis of children's testimony*. Washington, DC: American Psychological Association.

CECI, S., & LIKER, J. (1986). Academic and nonacademic intelligence: An experimental separation. In R. J. Sternberg & R. K. Wagner (Eds.), *Practical intelligence: Nature and origins of competence in everyday life* (pp. 119–142). New York: Cambridge University Press.

CECI, S., HUFFMAN, M., & SMITH, E. (1994). Repeatedly thinking about a non-event: Source misattributions among preschoolers. *Consciousness and Cognition, 3*, 388–407.

CECI, S. J., & WILLIAMS, W. M. (1997). Schooling, intelligence, and income. *American Psychologist, 52*, 1051–1058.

CENTERWALL, B. S. (1989). Exposure to television as a risk factor for violence. *American Journal of Epidemiology, 129*, 643–652.

CERVONE, D., & SHODA, Y. (1999). Beyond traits in the study of personality coherence. *Current Directions in Psychological Science, 8*, 27–32.

CESARIO, J., PLAKS, J., & HIGGINS, E. T. (2006). Automatic social behavior as motivated preparation to interact. *Journal of Personality and Social Psychology, 80*, 893–910.

CHAIKEN, S., LIBERMAN, A., & EAGLY, A. H. (1989). Heuristic and systematic information processing within and beyond the persuasion context. In J. S. Uleman & J. A. Bargh (Eds.), *Unintended thought* (pp. 212–252). New York: Guilford Press.

CHALMERS, D. (1995). Facing up to the problem of consciousness. *Journal of Consciousness Studies, 2,* 200–219.

CHAMBERS, D., & REISBERG, D. (1985). Can mental images be ambiguous? *Journal of Experimental Psychology: Human Perception and Performance, 11,* 317–328.

CHAMBLESS, D. L., BAKER, M. J., BAUCOM, D. H., BEUTLER, L. E., CALHOUN, K. S., CRITS-CHRISTOPH, P., ET AL. (1998). Update on empirically validated therapies, II. *Clinical Psychologist, 51,* 3–16.

CHANDLER, C. (1994). Studying related pictures can reduce accuracy, but increase confidence, in a modified recognition test. *Memory & Cognition, 22,* 273–280.

CHAPMAN, M., ZAHN-WAXLER, C., COOPERMAN, G., & IANNOTTI, R. (1987). Empathy and responsibility in the motivation of children's helping. *Developmental Psychology, 23,* 140–145.

CHARMAN, T., BARON-COHEN, S., SWETTENHAM, J., COX, A., BAIRD, G., & DREW, A. (1998). An experimental investigation of social-cognitive abilities in infants with autism: Clinical implications. *Infant Mental Health Journal, 19,* 260–275.

CHARTRAND, T., PINCKERT, S., & BURGER, J. M. (1999). When manipulation backfires: The effects of time delay and requester on the foot-in-the-door technique. *Journal of Applied Social Psychology, 29*(1), 211–221.

CHASE, W. G., & SIMON, H. A. (1973a). The mind's eye in chess. In W. G. Chase (Ed.), *Visual information processing.* New York: Academic Press.

CHASE, W. G., & SIMON, H. A. (1973b). Perception in chess. *Cognitive Psychology, 4,* 55–81.

CHEN, M., & BARGH, J. A. (1997). Nonconscious behavioral confirmation processes: The self-fulfilling consequences of automatic stereotype activation. *Journal of Experimental Social Psychology, 33*(5), 541–560.

CHENEY, D. L., & SEYFARTH, R. M. (1990). *How monkeys see the world.* Chicago: University of Chicago Press.

CHENG, P. W., & HOLYOAK, K. J. (1986). Pragmatic reasoning schemas. *Cognitive Psychology, 17,* 391–416.

CHENG, P. W., HOLYOAK, K. J., NISBETT, R. E., & OLIVER, L. M. (1985). Pragmatic versus syntactic approaches to training deductive reasoning. *Cognitive Psychology, 18,* 293–328.

CHERRIER, M. M., ASTHANA, S., PLYMATE, S., BAKER, L., MATSUMOTO, A. M., PESKIND, E., ET AL. (2001). Testosterone supplementation improves spatial and verbal memory in healthy older men. *Neurology, 57,* 80–88.

CHERRY, E. C. (1953). Some experiments upon the recognition of speech, with one and with two ears. *Journal of the Acoustical Society of America, 25,* 975–979.

CHERYAN, S., & BODENHAUSEN, G. V. (2000). When positive stereotypes threaten intellectual performance: The psychological hazards of "model minority" status. *Psychological Science, 11,* 399–402.

CHESS, S., & THOMAS, A. (1982). Infant bonding: Mystique and reality. *American Journal of Orthopsychiatry, 52,* 213–221.

CHEUNG, F. M., & LEUNG, K. (1998). Indigenous personality measures: Chinese examples. *Journal of Cross-Cultural Psychology, 29,* 233–248.

CHEVRIER, J., & DELORME, A. (1983). Depth perception in Pandora's box and size illusion: Evolution with age. *Perception, 12,* 177–185.

CHI, M. T., & KOESKE, R. D. (1983). Network representation of a child's dinosaur knowledge. *Developmental Psychology, 19*(1), 29–39.

CHI, M. T. H. (1978). Knowledge structures and memory development. In R. S. Siegler (Ed.), *Children's thinking: What develops?* (pp. 73–96). Hillsdale, NJ: Erlbaum.

CHI, M. T. H., FELTOVICH, P. J., & GLASER, R. (1981). Categorization and representation of physics problems by experts and novices. *Cognitive Science, 5,* 121–152.

CHOI, S., & BOWERMAN, M. (1991). Learning to express motion events in English and Korean: The influence of language-specific lexicalization patterns. *Cognition, 41,* 83–121.

CHOMSKY, N. (1959). Review of B. F. Skinner "Verbal Behavior." *Language, 35,* 26–58.

CHOMSKY, N. (1965). *Aspects of the theory of syntax.* Cambridge, MA: MIT Press.

CHOMSKY, N. (1981a). Knowledge of language: Its elements and origins. *Philosophical Transactions of the Royal Society of London, 295*(1077, Series B), 223–234.

CHOMSKY, N. (1981b). *Lectures on government and binding.* Dordrecht: Foris.

CHOMSKY, N. (1995). *The minimalist program.* Cambridge, MA: MIT Press.

CHOUINARD, C. (2004). Issues in the clinical use of benzodiazepines: Potency, withdrawal, and rebound. *Journal of Clinical Psychiatry, 65*(Suppl. 5), 7–12.

CHRISTIAN, K., BACHMAN, H. J., & MORRISON, F. J. (2000). Schooling and cognitive development. In R. J. Sternberg & R. L. Grigorenko (Eds.), *Environmental effects on cognitive abilities.* Mahwah, NJ: Erlbaum.

CHRISTIANSEN, M. H., & CHATER, N. (2001). Connectionist psycholinguistics: Capturing the empirical data. *Trends in Cognitive Science, 5*(2), 82–88.

CHRISTIANSEN, M. H., CHATER, N., & SEIDENBERG, M. S. (1999). Connectionist models of human language processing: Progress and prospects [Special issue]. *Cognitive Science, 23.*

CHRYSIKOU, E., & WEISBERG, R. W. (2005). Following the wrong footsteps: Fixation effects of pictorial examples in a design problem-solving task. *Journal of Experimental Psychology: Learning, Memory and Cognition, 31,* 1134–1148.

CHUA, S. E., & MCKENNA, P. J. (1995). Schizophrenia: A brain disease? *British Journal of Psychiatry, 166,* 563–582.

CHURCH, R. M. (1969). Response suppression. In B. A. Campbell & R. M. Church (Eds.), *Punishment and aversive behavior.* New York: Appleton-Century-Crofts.

CHURCHLAND, P. S., & SEJNOWSKI, T. J. (1992). *The computational brain.* Cambridge, MA: MIT Press.

CIALDINI, R. B. (1993). *Influence: Science and practice* (3rd ed.). New York: HarperCollins.

CIALDINI, R. B., & GOLDSTEIN, N. J. (2004). Social influence: Compliance and conformity. *Annual Review of Psychology, 55,* 591–621.

CIALDINI, R. B., PETTY, R. E., & CACIOPPO, J. T. (1981). Attitude and attitude change. In M. R. Rosenzweig & L. W. Porter (Eds.), *Annual Review of Psychology, 32,* 357–404.

CIALDINI, R. B., TROST, M. R., & NEWSOM, J. T. (1995). Preference for consistency: The development of a valid measure and the discovery of surprising behavioral implications. *Journal of Personality and Social Psychology, 69*(2), 318–328.

CIALDINI, R. R., VINCENT, J. E., LEWIS, S. K., CATALAN, J., WHEELER, D., & DARBY, L. (1975). Reciprocal concession procedure for inducing compliance: The door-in-the-face technique. *Journal of Personality and Social Psychology, 31,* 206–215.

CILLESSEN, A. H. N., & BUKOWSKI, W. M. (2000). Conceptualizing and measuring peer acceptance and rejection. In A. H. N. Cillessen & W. M. Bukowski (Eds.), *Recent advances in the measurement of acceptance and rejection in the peer system* (pp. 3–10). San Francisco: Jossey-Bass.

CIPOLOTTI, L. (2001). Long-term retrograde amnesia . . . The crucial role of the hippocampus. *Neuropsychologia, 39,* 151–172.

CLARK, D. A., & BECK, A. T. (WITH ALFORD, B.). (1999). *Scientific foundations of cognitive theory and therapy of depression.* New York: Wiley.

CLARK, D. M. (1986). A cognitive approach to panic. *Behavior Research and Therapy, 24,* 461–470.

CLARK, E. V. (1987). The principle of contrast: A constraint on acquisition. In B. MacWhinney (Ed.), *Mechanisms of language acquisition.* Hillsdale, NJ: Erlbaum.

CLARK, E. V., GELMAN, S. A., & LANE, N. M. (1985). Compound nouns and category structure in young children. *Child Development, 56,* 84–94.

CLARK, L. A., & HARRISON, J. A. (2001). Assessment instruments. In W. J. Livesley (Ed.), *Handbook of personality disorders* (pp. 277–306). New York: Guilford Press.

CLARK, M. S., & MILLS, J. (1979). Interpersonal attraction in exchange and communal relationships. *Journal of Personality and Social Psychology, 37,* 12–24.

CLARK, M. S., & MILLS, J. (1993). The difference between communal and exchange relationships: What it is and is not. *Personality and Social Psychology Bulletin, 19,* 684–691.

CLARK, M. S., MILLS, J., & POWELL, M. C. (1986). Keeping track of needs in communal and exchange relationships. *Journal of Personality and Social Psychology, 51*(2), 333–338.

CLARK, M. S., OUELLETTE, R., POWELL, M. C., & MILBERG, S. (1987). Recipient's mood, relationship type, and helping. *Journal of Personality and Social Psychology, 53*(1), 94–103.

CLARK, R. E., MANNS, J. R., & SQUIRE, L. R. (2003). Classical conditioning, awareness, and brain systems. *Trends in Cognitive Science, 6,* 524–531.

CLARKE, A. C. (1952). An examination of the operation of residual propinquity as a factor in mate selection. *American Sociological Review, 27,* 17–22.

CLARKE-STEWART, A. (1978). And daddy makes three: The father's impact on mother and young child. *Child Development, 49,* 466–478.

CLAUSEN, J. (1975). The social meaning of differential physical and sexual maturation. In S. Dragastin & J. Elder (Eds.), *Adolescence in the life cycle.* Washington, DC: Hemisphere Press.

CLAYTON, A. H. (2001). Recognition and assessment of sexual dysfunction associated with depression [Suppl.]. *Journal of Clinical Psychiatry, 62*(3), 5–9.

COBB, S. (1941). *Foundations of neuropsychiatry.* Baltimore: Williams & Wilkins.

COHEN, A., & RAFAL, R. D. (1991). Attention and feature integration: Illusory conjunctions in a patient with a parietal lobe lesion. *Psychological Science, 2,* 106–110.

COHEN, G., & BURKE, D. (EDS.). (1993). *Memory for proper names.* Hillsdale, NJ: Erlbaum.

COHEN, N. J., & SQUIRE, L. R. (1980). Preserved learning and retention of pattern-analyzing skill in amnesia: Dissociation of knowing how and knowing what. *Science, 210,* 207–210.

COHEN, Y. A. (1953). A study of interpersonal relations in a Jamaican community. Unpublished doctoral dissertation, Yale University.

COIE, J. D., & DODGE, K. A. (1983). Continuities and changes in children's social status: A five-year longitudinal study. *Merrill-Palmer Quarterly, 29*(3), 261–282.

COLAPINTO, J. (2000). *As nature made him: The boy who was raised as a girl.* New York: HarperCollins.

COLBY, A., & KOHLBERG, L. (1987). *The measurement of moral judgment, Vol. 1: Theoretical foundations and research validation; Vol. 2: Standard issue scoring manual.* New York: Cambridge University Press.

COLE, M., & COLE, S. R. (2001). *The development of children* (4th ed.). New York: Worth.

COLE, P. M. (1985). Display rules and the socialization of affective displays. In G. Zivin (Ed.), *The development of expressive behavior: Biology-environmental interactions* (pp. 269–290). New York: Academic Press.

COLLAER, M., & HINES, M. (1995). Human behavioral sex differences: A role for gonadal hormones during early development? *Psychological Bulletin, 118,* 55–107.

COLLINS, A. M., & LOFTUS, E. F. (1975). A spreading activation theory of semantic processing. *Psychological Review, 82,* 407–428.

COLLINS, W. A., MACCOBY, E. E., STEINBERG, L., HETHERINGTON, E. M., & BORNSTEIN, M. H. (2000). Contemporary research on parenting: The case for nature and nurture. *American Psychologist, 55*(2), 218–232.

COLOMBO, J. (2001). The development of visual attention in infancy. *Annual Review of Psychology, 52,* 337–367.

COLWILL, R. M., & RESCORLA, R. A. (1985). Postconditioning devaluation of a reinforcer affects instrumental responding. *Journal of Experimental Psychology: Animal Behavior Processes, 11,* 120–132.

CONEL, J. L. (1939). *The postnatal development of the human cortex: Vol. 1.* Cambridge, MA: Harvard University Press.

CONEL, J. L. (1947). *The postnatal development of the human cortex: Vol. 3.* Cambridge, MA: Harvard University Press.

CONEL, J. L. (1955). *The postnatal development of the human cortex: Vol. 5.* Cambridge, MA: Harvard University Press.

CONNORS, E., LUNDREGAN, T., MILLER, N., & MCEWAN, T. (1996). *Convicted by juries, exonerated by science: Case studies in the use of DNA evidence to establish innocence after trial.* Alexandria, VA: National Institute of Justice.

CONWAY, A. R. A., COWAN, N., & BUNTING, M. (2001). The cocktail party phenomenon revisited: The importance of working memory capacity. *Psychonomics Bulletin & Review, 8,* 331–335.

CONWAY, A. R., KANE, M. J., BUNTING, M. F., HAMBRICK, D. Z., WILHELM, O., & ENGLE, R. (2005). Working memory span tasks: A methodological review and user's guide. *Psychonomics Bulletin and Review, 12,* 769–786.

CONWAY, M. A. (ED.). (1997). *Recovered memories and false memories.* New York: Oxford University Press.

CONWAY, M. A., & FTHENAKI, K. (1999). Disruption and loss of autobiographical memory. In L. S. Cermak (Ed.), *Handbook of neuropsychology: Memory.* Amsterdam: Elsevier.

CONWAY, M. A., COHEN, G., & STANHOPE, N. (1991). On the very long-term retention of knowledge acquired through formal education: Twelve years of cognitive psychology. *Journal of Experimental Psychology (General), 120,* 395–409.

CONWAY, M., ANDERSON, S., LARSEN, S., DONNELLY, C., MCDANIEL, M., MCCLELLAND, A. G. R., ET AL. (1994). The formation of flashbulb memories. *Memory and Cognition, 22,* 326–343.

COOK, R. G., CAVOTO, K. K., & CAVOTO, B. R. (1995). Same-different texture discrimination and concept learning by pigeons. *Journal of Experimental Psychology: Animal Behavior Processes, 21*(3), 253–260.

COOLEY, C. H. (1902). *Human nature and the social order.* New York: Scribner's.

COONEY, J. W., & GAZZANIGA, M. S. (2003). Neurological disorders and the structure of human consciousness. *Trends in Cognitive Science, 7,* 161–165.

COOPER, J., ZANNA, M. P., & GOETHALS, G. R. (1974). Mistreatment of an esteemed other as a consequence affecting dissonance reduction. *Journal of Experimental Social Psychology, 10,* 224–233.

COOPER, L. A., & SHEPARD, R. N. (1973). The time required to prepare for a rotated stimulus. *Memory and Cognition, 1,* 246–250.

COOPER, Z., & FAIRBURN, C. G. (2001). A new cognitive behavioural approach to the treatment of obesity. *Behavior Research and Therapy, 39,* 499–511.

CORKIN, S. (1965). Tactually-guided maze-learning in man: Effects of unilateral cortical excisions and bilateral hippocampal lesions. *Neuropsychologia, 3,* 339–351.

CORKIN, S. (1984). Lasting consequences of bilateral medial temporal lobectomy: Clinical course and experimental findings in H.M. *Seminar in Neurology, 4,* 249–259.

CORY, T. L., ORMISTON, D. W., SIMMEL, E., & DAINOFF, M. (1975). Predicting the frequency of dream recall. *Journal of Abnormal Psychology, 84,* 261–266.

CORYELL, W. (1996). Psychotic depression. *Journal of Clinical Psychiatry, 57*[Suppl.](3), 27–31.

COSMIDES, L. (1989). The logic of social exchange: Has natural selection shaped how humans reason? Studies with the Wason selection task. *Cognition, 31,* 187–276.

COSMIDES, L., & TOOBY, J. (1992). Cognitive adaptations for social exchange. In J. H. Barkow, L. Cosmides, & J. Tooby (Eds.), *The adapted mind: Evolutionary psychology and the generation of culture* (pp. 163–228). New York: Oxford University Press.

COSMIDES, L., & TOOBY, J. (2005). Neurocognitive adaptations designed for social exchange. In D. M. Buss (Ed.), *The handbook of evolutionary psychology* (pp. 583–627). Hoboken, NJ: Wiley.

COSMIDES, L., TOOBY, J., FIDDICK, L., & BRYANT, G. A. (2005). Detecting cheaters. *Trends in Cognitive Science, 9,* 505–506.

COSTA, P. T., & MCCRAE, R. R. (1992). *Revised NEO Personality Inventory (NEO-PI-R) and NEO Five-Factor Inventory professional manual.* Odessa, FL: Psychological Assessment Resources.

COTMAN, C. W., & NEEPER, S. (1996). Activity-dependent plasticity and the aging brain. In E. L. Schneider & J. W. Rose (Eds.), *Handbook of the biology of aging* (4th ed.). San Diego, CA: Academic Press.

COURAGE, M., & HOWE, M. (2002). From infant to child: The dynamics of cognitive change in the second year of life. *Psychological Bulletin, 128*, 250–277.

COURCHESNE, E., TOWNSEND, J. P., & SAITOH, O. (1994). The brain in infantile autism: Posterior fossa structures are abnormal. *Neurology, 44*, 214–223.

COUSINS, S. D. (1989). Culture and self-perception in Japan and the United States. *Journal of Personality and Social Psychology, 56*, 124–131.

COUVILLON, P., & BITTERMAN, M. E. (1980). Some phenomena of associative conditioning in honeybees. *Journal of Comparative and Physiological Psychology, 94*, 878–885.

COUZIN, J. (2004). Volatile chemistry: Children and antidepressants. *Science, 305*, 468–470.

COUZIN, J. (2005). A heavyweight battle over CDC's obesity forecasts. *Science, 308*, 770–771.

COWEY, A., & STOERIG, P. (1992). Reflections on blindsight. In A. D. Milner & M. D. Rugg, (Eds.), *The neuropsychology of consciousness* (pp. 11–38). San Diego, CA: Academic Press.

CRAIGHEAD, L. W., CRAIGHEAD, W. E., KAZDIN, A. E., & MAHONEY, M. J. (EDS.). (1994). *Cognitive and behavioral interventions: An empirical approach to mental health problems.* Boston: Allyn and Bacon.

CRAIK, F., & JENNINGS, J. M. (1992). Human memory. In F. Craik & T. Salthouse (Eds.), *Handbook of aging and cognition* (pp. 51–110). Hillsdale, NJ: Erlbaum.

CRAIK, F. I. M., & BIALYSTOK, E. (2006). Cognition through the lifespan: Mechanisms of change. *Trends in Cognitive Science, 10*, 131–138.

CRAIK, F. I. M., & LOCKHART, R. S. (1972). Levels of processing. A framework for memory research. *Journal of Verbal Learning and Verbal Behavior, 11*, 671–684.

CRAIK, F. I. M., & SALTHOUSE, T. A. (EDS.). (2000). *The handbook of aging and cognition* (2nd ed.). Hillsdale, NJ: Erlbaum.

CRAIK, F. I. M., & TULVING, E. (1975). Depth of processing and the retention of words in episodic memory. *Journal of Experimental Psychology: General, 104*, 268–294.

CRAIK, F. I. M., & WATKINS, M. J. (1973). The role of rehearsal in short-term memory. *Journal of Verbal Learning and Verbal Behavior, 12*, 599–607.

CRAIN, S., & STEEDMAN, M. (1985). On not being led up the garden path: The use of context by the psychological syntax parser. In D. Dowty, L. Kartunnen, & A. Zwicky (Eds.), *Natural language parsing.* Cambridge: Cambridge University Press.

CRASKE, M. G. (1999). *Anxiety disorders: Psychological approaches to theory and treatment.* Boulder, CO: Westview Press.

CRAWFORD, M., & CHAFFIN, R. (1997). The meanings of difference: Cognition in social and cultural context. In P. J. Caplan, M. Crawford, J. S. Hyde, & J. T. E. Richardson (Eds.), *Gender differences in human cognition* (pp. 81–130). New York: Oxford University Press.

CRESPI, L. (1942). Quantitative variation in incentive and performance in the white rat. *American Journal of Psychology, 55*, 467–517.

CRICK, N. R. (1996). The role of overt aggression, relational aggression, and prosocial behavior in the prediction of children's future social adjustment. *Child Development, 67*(5), 2317–2327.

CRICK, N. R., & LADD, G. W. (1993). Children's perceptions of their peer experiences: Attributions, loneliness, social anxiety, and social avoidance. *Developmental Psychology, 29*(2), 244–254.

CRICK, R., & KOCH, C. (1995). Are we aware of neural activity in primary visual cortex? *Nature, 375*, 121–123.

CRITS-CHRISTOPH, P. (1997). Limitations of the "dodo bird" verdict and the role of clinical trials in psychotherapy research: Comment on Wampold et al. (1997). *Psychological Bulletin, 122*, 216–220

CROCKER, J., & LUHTANEN, R. (1990). Collective self-esteem and ingroup bias. *Journal of Personality and Social Psychology, 58*, 60–67.

CROFT, C., O'CONNOR, T. G., KEAVENEY, L., GROOTHUES, C., RUTTER, M., & ENGLISH AND ROMANIAN ADOPTION STUDY TEAM (2001). Longitudinal change in parenting associated with developmental delay and catch-up. *Journal of Child Psychology and Psychiatry and Allied Disciplines, 42*, 649–659.

CROOK, C. (1987). Taste and olfaction. In P. Salapateck & L. Cohen (Eds.), *Handbook of infant perception: From perception to cognition: Vol. 2* (pp. 237–264). Orlando, FL: Academic Press.

CROW, T. J. (1982). Two dimensions of pathology in schizophrenia: Dopaminergic and non-dopaminergic. *Psychopharmacology Bulletin, 18*, 22–29.

CROW, T. J. (1985). The two-syndrome concept: Origins and current status. *Schizophrenia Bulletin, 11*, 471–486.

CROWDER, R. G. (1976). *Principles of learning and memory.* Hillsdale, NJ: Erlbaum.

CROWLEY, K., CALLANAN, M. A., TENENBAUM, H. R., & ALLEN, E. (2001). Parents explain more often to boys than to girls during shared scientific thinking. *Psychological Science, 12*, 258–261.

CRUTCHFIELD, R. S. (1955). Conformity and character. *American Psychologist, 10*, 191–199.

CSIBRA, G., & GERGELY, G. (2005). Social learning and social cognition: The case for pedagogy. In M. H. Johnson & Y. Munakata (Eds.), *Processes of change in brain and cognitive development: Attention and performance XXI* (pp. 1–15). New York: Oxford University Press.

CSIBRA, G., DAVIS, G., SPRATLING, M. W., & JOHNSON, M. H. (2000). Gamma oscillations and object processing in the infant brain. *Science, 290*, 1582–1585.

CULBERTSON, F. (1997). Depression and gender. *American Psychologist, 52*, 25–31.

Cutting, J. (1995). Descriptive psychopathology. In S. Hirsch & D. Weinberger (Eds.), *Schizophrenia* (pp. 15–27). London: Blackwell Science.

CUMMINGS, E. M., & DAVIES, P. (1994). *Children and marital conflict: The impact of family dispute and resolution. Guilford series on social and emotional development.* New York: Guilford Press.

CUMMINS, D. (1992). Role of analogical reasoning in induction of problem categories. *Journal of Experimental Psychology: Learning, Memory and Cognition, 18*, 1103–1124.

CUMMINS, D. D., & ALLEN, C. (EDS.) (1998). *The evolution of mind.* New York: Oxford University Press.

CUNNINGHAM, M. R., ROBERTS, A. R., BARBEE, A. P., DRUEN, P. B., & WU, C.-H. (1998). "Their ideas of beauty are, on the whole, the same as ours": Consistency and variability in the cross-cultural perception of female physical attractiveness. *Journal of Personality and Social Psychology, 68*, 261–279.

CUNNINGHAM, W. A., PREACHER, K. J., & BANAJI, M. R. (2001). Implicit attitude measures: Consistency, stability, and convergent validity. *Psychological Science, 121*(2), 163–170.

CURTISS, S. (1977). *Genie: A linguistic study of a modern-day "wild child."* New York: Academic Press.

CUTLER, A. (1994). Segmentation problems, rhythmic solutions. In L. R. Gleitman & B. Landau (Eds.), Lexical acquisition [Special issue]. *Lingua, 92*, 81–104.

CUTLER, A., MEHLER, J., NORRIS, D., & SEGUI, J. (1986). The syllable's differing role in the segmentation of French and English. *Journal of Memory and Language, 25*.

CUTLER, A., & OTAKE, T. (1994). Mora or phoneme? Further evidence for language-specific listening. *Journal of Memory and Language, 33*, 824–844.

CUTTING, J. (1986). Outcome in schizophrenia: Overview. In T. A. Kerr & R. P. Snaith (Eds.), *Contemporary issues in schizophrenia* (pp. 436–440). Washington, DC: American Psychiatric Press.

DABBS, J. M. (1992). Testosterone measurements in social and clinical psychology. *Journal of Social and Clinical Psychology, 11*, 302–321.

DADDS, M. R. (1995). *Families, children, and the development of dysfunction.* Thousand Oaks, CA: Sage.

DALE, A. J. D. (1975). Organic brain syndromes associated with infections. In A. M. Freedman, H. I. Kaplan, & B. J. Sadock (Eds.), *Comprehensive textbook of psychiatry—II: Vol. 1* (pp. 1121–1130). Baltimore: Williams & Wilkins.

DALEY, T. C., WHALEY, S. E., SIGMAN, M. D., ESPINOSA, M. P., & NEUMANN, C. (2003). IQ on the rise: The Flynn effect in rural Kenyan children. *Psychological Science, 14*, 215–219.

DALY, M., & WILSON, M. (2005). The "Cinderella effect" is no fairy tale. *Trends in Cognitive Science, 9*, 507–508.

DAMASIO, A. R. (1994). *Descartes' error: Emotion, reason, and the human brain.* New York: G. P. Putnam.

DAMASIO, A. R., & DAMASIO, H. (1994). Cortical systems for retrieval of concrete knowledge: The convergence zone framework. In C. Koch & J. L. Davis (Eds.), *Large-scale neuronal theories of the brain* (pp. 61–74). Cambridge, MA: MIT Press.

DAMASIO, A. R., DAMASIO, H., & VAN HOESEN, G. W. (1982). Prosopagnosia: Anatomic basis and behavioral mechanisms. *Neurology, 32*, 331–341.

DAMASIO, A. R., TRANEL, D., & DAMASIO, H. (1989). Disorders of visual recognition. In H. Goodglass & A. R. Damasio (Eds.), *Handbook of neuropsychology: Vol. 2.* New York: Elsevier.

DANEMAN, M., & HANNON, B. (2001). Using working memory theory to investigate the construct validity of multiple-choice reading comprehension tests such as the SAT. *Journal of Experimental Psychology: General, 130*, 208–223.

DANTHIIR, V., ROBERTS, R. D., SCHULZE, R., & WILHELM, O. (2005). Mental speed: On frameworks, paradigms, and a platform for the future. In O. Wilhelm & R. W. Engle (Eds.), *Handbook of understanding and measuring intelligence* (pp. 27–46). Thousand Oaks, CA: Sage.

DARLEY, J. M., & BATSON, C. D. (1973). "From Jerusalem to Jericho": A study of situational and dispositional variables in helping behavior. *Journal of Personality and Social Psychology, 27*, 100–108.

DARLEY, J., & LATANÉ, B. (1968). Bystander intervention in emergencies: Diffusion of responsibility. *Journal of Personality and Social Psychology, 10*, 202–214.

DARNTON, R. (1984). The meaning of Mother Goose. *New York Review of Books, February 2*, 41–47.

DARWIN, C. (1871). *The descent of man, and selection in relation to sex.* London: Murray.

DARWIN, C. (1872a). *The origin of species.* New York: Macmillan, 6th ed., 1962.

DARWIN, C. (1872b). *The expression of the emotions in man and animals.* London: Appleton.

DARWIN, C. (1877). A biographical sketch of a young child. *Kosmos, 1*, 367–376. As cited in Bornstein, M.H. Chromatic vision in infancy. In H. Reese & L. Lipsitt (Eds.), *Advances in child development and behavior:* Vol. 12. New York: Academic Press.

DAVACHI, L., MARIL, A., & WAGNER, A. (2001). When keeping in mind supports later bringing to mind: Neural markers of phonological rehearsal predict subsequent remembering. *Journal of Cognitive Neuroscience, 13*, 1059–1070.

DAVACHI, L., MITCHELL, J., & WAGNER, A. (2003). Multiple routes to memory: Distinct medial temporal lobe processes build item and source memories. *Proceedings of the National Academy of Science, 100*, 2157–2162.

DAVIDSON, A. R., & JACCARD, J. J. (1979). Variables that moderate the attitude-behavior relation: Results of a longitudinal survey. *Journal of Personality and Social Psychology, 37*, 1364–1376.

DAVIDSON, J. M. (1969). Hormonal control of sexual behavior in adult rats. In G. Rasp (Ed.), *Advances in bioscience: Vol. 1* (pp. 119–169). New York: Pergamon.

DAVIDSON, J. M. (1986). Androgen replacement therapy in a wider context: Clinical and basic aspects. In L. Dennerstein & I. Fraser (Eds.), *Hormones and behavior* (pp. 433–440). Amsterdam: International Society of Psychosomatic Obstetrics and Gynecology, Elsevier.

DAVIDSON, R. J., & SUTTON, S. K. (1995). Affective neuroscience: The emergence of a discipline [Special issue]. *Current Opinion in Neurobiology, 5*, 217–224.

DAVIES, K. G., & WEEKS, R. D. (1993). Temporal lobectomy for intractable epilepsy: Experience with 58 cases over 21 years. *British Journal of Neurosurgery, 7*, 23–33.

DAVIES, P., & FORMAN, E. (2002). Children's patterns of preserving emotional security in the interparental subsystem. *Child Development, 73*, 1880–1903.

DAVIS, D. E. (1964). The physiological analysis of aggressive behavior. In W. Etkin (Ed.), *Social behavior and organization among vertebrates.* Chicago: University of Chicago Press.

DAVIS, H. P., & SQUIRE, L. R. (1984). Protein synthesis and memory: A review. *Psychological Bulletin, 96*, 518–559.

DAVIS, J. M. (1985a). Antipsychotic drugs. In H. I. Kaplan & J. Sadock (Eds.), *Comprehensive textbook of psychiatry* (4th ed., pp. 1481–1513). Baltimore: Williams & Wilkins.

DAVIS, J. O., & PHELPS, J. A. (1995). Twins with schizophrenia: Genes or germs? *Schizophrenia Bulletin, 21*, 13–18.

DAVIS, J. O., PHELPS, J. A., & BRACHA, H. S. (1995). Prenatal development of monozygotic twins and concordance for schizophrenia [erratum appears in Schizophrenia Bulletin (1995) 214:539]. *Schizophrenia Bulletin, 21*, 357–366.

DAVIS, K. (1947). Final note on a case of extreme social isolation. *American Journal of Sociology, 52*, 432–437.

DAVIS, P. H., & OSHERSON, A. (1977). The concurrent treatment of a multiple-personality woman and her son. *American Journal of Psychotherapy, 31*, 504–515.

DAWES, R. M. (1994). *House of cards: Psychology and psychotherapy built on myth.* New York: Free Press.

DE GROOT, A. D. (1965). *Thought and choice in chess.* The Hague: Mouton.

DE QUERVAIN, D. J., FISCHBACHER, U., TREYER, V., SCHELLHAMMER, M., SCHNYDER, U., BUCK, A., ET AL. (2004). The neural basis of altruistic punishment. *Science, 305*, 1254–1258.

DE RENZI, E. (2000). Prosopagnosia. In M. J. Farah & T. E. Feinberg, (Eds.), *Patient-based approaches to cognitive neuroscience* (pp. 85–95). Cambridge, MA: MIT Press.

DE RIDDER, D., SCHREURS, K., & BENSING, J. (2000). The relative benefits of being optimistic: Optimism as a coping resource in multiple sclerosis and Parkinson's disease. *British Journal of Health Psychology, 5*, 141–155.

DE ROUGEMONT, D. (1940). *Love in the western world.* New York: Harcourt Brace Jovanovich.

DE VALOIS, R. L. (1965). Behavioral and electrophysiological studies of primate vision. In W. D. Neff (Ed.), *Contributions of sensory physiology: Vol. 1.* New York: Academic Press.

DE WAAL, F. (1982). *Chimpanzee politics.* New York: Harper & Row.

DEARY, I. J. (2000). *Looking down on human intelligence: From psychometrics to the brain.* Oxford, England: Oxford University Press.

DEARY, I. J. (2001a). Human intelligence differences: A recent history. *Trends in Cognitive Science, 5*, 127–130.

DEARY, I. J. (2001b). Human intelligence differences: Toward a combined experimental-differential approach. *Trends in Cognitive Science, 5*, 164–170.

DEARY, I. J., & DERR, G. (2005). Reaction time explains IQ's association with death. *Psychological Science, 16*, 64–69.

DEARY, I. J., & STOUGH, C. (1996). Intelligence and inspection time: Achievements, prospects, and problems. *American Psychologist, 51*, 599–608.

DEARY, I. J., WHITEMAN, M. C., STARR, J. M., WHALLEY, L. J., & FOX, H. C. (2004). The impact of childhood intelligence on later life: Following up the Scottish Mental Surveys of 1932 and 1947. *Journal of Personality and Social Psychology, 86*, 130–147.

DECASPER, A. J., & FIFER, W. P. (1980). Of human bonding: Newborns prefer their mothers' voices. *Science, 208*, 1174–1176.

DECI, E. L., KOESTNER, R., & RYAN, R. M. (1999a). A meta-analytic review of experiments examining the effects of extrinsic reward. *Psychological Bulletin, 125*, 627–668.

DECI, E. L., KOESTNER, R., & RYAN, R. M. (1999b). The undermining effect is a reality after all—Extrinsic rewards, task interest, and self-determination: Reply to Eisenberger, Pierce, and Cameron (1999) and Lepper, Henderlong, and Gingras (1999). *Psychological Bulletin, 125*, 692–700.

DEECKE, L., SCHEID, P., & KORNHUBER, H. H. (1968). Distribution of readiness potential, pre-motion positivity, and motor potential of the human cerebral cortex preceding voluntary finger movements. *Experimental Brain Research, 7*, 158–168.

DEHAENE, S., IZARD, V., PICA, P., & SPELKE, E. (2006). Core knowledge of geometry in an Amazonian indigene group. *Science, 311*, 381–384.

DEHAENE, S., & NACCACHE, L. (2001). Toward a cognitive neuroscience of consciousness: Basic evidence and workspace framework. *Cognition, 79*, 1–37.

DEHAENE-LAMBERTZ, G., DEHAENE, S., & HERTZ-PANNIER, L. (2002). Functional neuroimaging of speech perception in infants. *Science, 298*, 2013–2015.

DELL, G. S., ET AL. (1999). Connectionist models of language production: Lexical access and grammatical encoding. *Cognitive Science, 23*, 517–542.

DEMONET, J. F., WISE, R., & FRACKOWIAK, R. S. J. (1993). Language functions explored in normal subjects by positron emission tomography: A critical review. *Human Brain Mapping, 1*, 39–47.

DEMULDER, E., DENHAM, S., SCHMIDT, M., & MITCHELL, J. (2000). Q-sort assessment of attachment security during the preschool years: Links from home to school. *Developmental Psychology, 36*, 274–282.

DESIMONE, R., ALBRIGHT, T. D., GROSS, C. G., & BRUCE, C. (1984). Stimulus-selective properties of inferior temporal neurons in the macaque. *Journal of Neuroscience, 4*, 2051–2062.

DESTENO, D., BARTLETT, M. Y., & SALOVEY, P. (2002). Sex differences in jealousy: Evolutionary mechanism or artifact of measurement. *Journal of Personality and Social Psychology, 83*, 1103–1116.

DEUTSCH, J. A., PUERTO, A., & WANG, M. L. (1978). The stomach signals satiety. *Science, 201*, 165–167.

DEVANE, W. A., DYSARZ, F. A., JOHNSON, M. R., MELVIN, L. S., & HOWLETT, A. C. (1988). Determination and characterization of a cannabinoid receptor in rat brain. *Molecular Pharmacology, 34*, 605–613.

DEVANE, W. A., HANUS, L., BREUER, A., PERTWEE, R. G., STEVENSON, L. A., GRIFFIN, G., ET AL. (1992). Isolation and structure of a brain constituent that binds the cannabinoid receptor. *Science, 258*, 1946–1949.

DHAWAN, N., ROSEMAN, I. J., NAIDU, R., & RETTEK, S. (1995). Self-concepts across two cultures: India and the United States. *Journal of Cross-Cultural Psychology, 26*, 606–621.

DI BLAS, L., FORZI, M., & PEABODY, D. (2000). Evaluative and descriptive dimensions from Italian personality factors. *European Journal of Personality, 14*, 279–290.

DIAMOND, A. (1988). The abilities and neural mechanisms underlying A-not-B performance. *Child Development, 59*, 523–527.

DIAMOND, A. (1989, May). Developmental progression in human infants and infant monkeys, and the neural bases of A-not-B and delayed response performance. Paper presented at a meeting on "The development and neural bases of higher cognitive functions," Philadelphia, PA.

DIAMOND, A., & GOLDMAN-RAKIC, P. S. (1989). Comparative development of human infants and rhesus monkeys on Piaget's A-not-B task: Evidence for dependence on dorsolateral prefrontal cortex. *Experimental Brain Research, 74*, 24–40.

DIAMOND, M., & SIGMUNDSON, K. (1997). Sex reassignment at birth: A long-term review and clinical implications. *Archives of Pediatric and Adolescent Medicine, 151*, 298–304.

DIAMOND, R., & ROZIN, P. (1984). Activation of existing memories in the amnesic syndrome. *Journal of Abnormal Psychology, 93*, 98–105.

DICKENS, W. T., & FLYNN, J. R. (2001). Heritability estimates versus large environmental effects: The IQ paradox resolved. *Psychological Review, 108*(2), 346–369.

DICKINSON, A. (1987). Animal conditioning and learning theory. In H. J. Eysenck & I. Martin (Eds.), *Theoretical foundations of behavior theory.* New York: Plenum.

DICKS, H. V. (1972). *Licensed mass murder: A sociopsychological study of some S. S. killers.* New York: Basic Books.

DIENER, E. (1979). Deindividuation: The absence of self-awareness and self-regulation in group members. In P. Paulus (Ed.), *The psychology of group influence* (pp. 209–242). Hillsdale, NJ: Erlbaum.

DIENER, E., SHIGEHIRO, O., & LUCAS, R. E., (2003). Personality, culture, and subjective well-being: Emotional and cognitive evaluations of life. *Annual Review of Psychology, 54*, 403–425.

DIENER, E., SMITH, H., & FUJITA, F. (1995). The personality structure of affect. *Journal of Personality and Social Psychology, 69*, 130–141.

DION, K., BERSCHEID, E., & WALSTER, E. (1972). What is beautiful is good. *Journal of Personality and Social Psychology, 24*, 285–290.

DION, K. K., & DION, K. L. (1996). Cultural perspectives on romantic love. *Personal Relationships, 3*, 5–17.

DITTMAN, R. W., KAPPES, M. W. E., & KAPPES, M. H. (1992). Sexual behavior in adolescent and adult females with congenital adrenal hyperplasia. *Psychoneuroendocrinology, 17*, 153–170.

DOBBINS, I., FOLEY, H., SCHACTER, D., & WAGNER, A. (2002). Executive control during episodic retrieval: Multiple prefrontal processes subserve source memory. *Neuron, 35*, 989–996.

DODGE, K. A., & PETTIT, G. S. (2003). A biopsychosocial model of the development of chronic conduct problems in adolescence. *Developmental Psychology, 39*(2), 349–371.

DOHRENWEND, B. P. (2000). The role of adversity and stress in psychopathology: Some evidence and its implications for theory and research. *Journal of Health and Social Behavior, 41*, 1–19.

DOHRENWEND, B. P., LEVAV, I., SHROUT, P. E., SCHWARTZ, S., NAVEH, G., LINK, B. G., ET AL. (1992). Socioeconomic status and psychiatric disorders: The causation-selection issue. *Science, 255*, 946–952.

DOI, T. (1973). *The anatomy of dependence.* Tokyo: Kodansha.

DOLCOS, F., LABAR, K. S., & CABEZA, R. (2006). The memory-enhancing effect of emotion: Functional neuroimaging evidence. In B. Uttl, N. Ohta, & A. L. Siegenthaler (Eds.), *Memory and emotion: Interdisciplinary perspectives* (pp. 107–134). Malden, MA: Blackwell Publishing.

DOMJAN, M. (1983). Biological constraints on instrumental and classical conditioning: Implications for general process theory. In G. H. Bower (Ed.), *The psychology of learning and motivation: Vol. 17.* New York: Academic Press.

DOMJAN, M. (2005). Pavlovian conditioning: A functional perspective. *Annual Review of Psychology, 56*, 179–206.

DOMJAN, M., CUSATO, B., & KRAUSE, M. (2004). Learning with arbitrary versus ecological conditioned stimuli: Evidence from sexual conditioning. *Psychonomics Bulletin & Review, 11*, 232–246.

DORNBUSCH, S. M., RITTER, P. L., LIEDERMAN, P. H., ROBERTS, D. F., & FRALEIGH, M. J. (1987). The relation of parenting style to adolescent school performance: Schools and development [Special issue]. *Child Development, 58*, 1244–1257.

DOUGHERTY, D. D., RAUCH, S. L., & JENIKE, M. A. (2002). Pharmacological treatments for obsessive compulsive disorder. In P. E. Nathan, & J. M. Gorman (Eds.), *A guide to treatments that work* (2nd ed., pp. 387–410). New York: Oxford University Press.

DUPAUL, G. J., & BARKLEY, R. A. (1998). Medication therapy. In R. A. Barkley (Ed.), *Attention-deficit hyperactivity disorder: A handbook for diagnosis and treatment.* New York: Guilford Press.

DOUVAN, E., & ADELSON, J. (1958). The psychodynamics of social mobility in adolescent boys. *Journal of Abnormal and Social Psychology, 56*, 31–44.

DOVIDIO, J. F., & GAERTNER, S. L. (1999). Reducing prejudice: Combating intergroup biases. *Current Directions in Psychological Science, 8*(4), 101–105.

DOWNEY, G., LEBOLT, A., RINCON, C & FREITAS, A. (1998). Rejection sensitivity and children's interpersonal difficulties. *Child Development, 69,* 1074–1091.

DRAGUNS, J. G., KRYLOVA, A. V., ORYOL, V. E., RUKAVISHNIKOV, A. A., & MARTIN, T. A. (2000). Personality characteristics of the Nentsy in the Russian Arctic: A comparison with ethnic Russians by means of NEO-PI-R and POI. *American Behavioral Scientist, 44,* 126–140.

DRISCOLL, R., DAVIS, K. E., & LIPETZ, M. E. (1972). Parental interference and romantic love: The Romeo and Juliet effect. *Journal of Personality and Social Psychology, 24,* 1–10.

DUDAI, Y. (2004). The neurobiology of consolidations, or, how stable is the engram. *Annual Review of Psychology, 55,* 51–86.

DUKE, P., CARLSMITH, J., JENNINGS, D., MARTIN, J., DORNBUSCH, S., GROSS, R., ET AL. (1982). Educational correlates of early and late sexual maturation in adolescence. *Journal of Pediatrics, 100,* 633–637.

DUKER, P. C, & SEYS, D. M. (1996). Long-term use of electrical aversion treatment with self-injurious behavior. *Research in Developmental Disabilities, 17,* 293–301.

DUNBAR, K., & BLANCHETTE, I. (2001). The in vivo/in vitro approach to cognition: The case of analogy. *Trends in Cognitive Science, 5,* 334–339.

DUNCAN, J. (1994). Attention, intelligence, and the frontal lobes. In M. Gazzaniga (Ed.), *The cognitive neurosciences.* Cambridge, MA: MIT Press.

DUNCAN, J. (1995). Attention, intelligence, and the frontal lobes. In M. S. Gazzaniga (Ed.), *The cognitive neurosciences* (pp. 721–733). Cambridge, MA: MIT Press.

DUNCAN, J., BUNDESEN, C., OLSON, A., HYMPHREYS, G., CHAVDA, S., & SHIBUYA, H. (1999). Systematic analysis of deficits in visual attention. *Journal of Experimental Psychology: General, 128,* 450–478.

DUNCAN, J., RUDIGER, J. S., KOLODNY, J., BOR, D., HERZOG, H., AHMED, A., ET AL. (2000). A neural basis for general intelligence. *Science, 289,* 457–460.

DUNCKER, K. (1945). On problem solving. *Psychological Monographs,* (Whole No. 270), 1–113.

DUNNING, D., & COHEN, G. L. (1992). Egocentric definitions of traits and abilities in social judgment. *Journal of Personality and Social Psychology, 63,* 341–355.

DUNNING, D., HEATH, C., & SULS, J. M. (2004). Flawed self-assessment: Implications for health, education, and the workplace. *Psychological Science in the Public Interest, 5,* 69–106.

DUNNING, D., MEYEROWITZ, J. A., & HOLZBERG, A. D. (1989). Ambiguity and self-evaluation: The role of idiosyncratic trait definitions in self-serving assessments of ability. *Journal of Personality and Social Psychology, 57,* 1082–1090.

DUNPHY, D. C. (1963). The social structure of urban adolescent peer groups. *Sociometry, 26,* 230–246.

DUPOUX, E., ET AL (1997). A distressing "deafness" in French? *Journal of Memory and Language, 36,* 406–421.

DUTTON, D. G., & ARON, A. P. (1974). Some evidence for heightened sexual attraction under conditions of high anxiety. *Journal of Personality and Social Psychology, 30,* 510–517.

DWECK, C. S., HONG, Y.-y., & CHIU, C. Y. (1993). Implicit theories and individual differences in the likelihood and meaning of dispositional inference. *Personality and Social Psychology Bulletin, 19,* 644–656.

DYKEMA, J., BERGBOWER, K., DOCTORA, J. D., & PETERSON, C. (1996). An attributional style questionnaire for general use. *Journal of Psychoeducational Assessment, 14,* 100–108.

EAGLE, M. N., & WOLITSKY, D. L. (1992). Psychoanalytic theories of psychotherapy. In D. K. Freedheim (Ed.), *History of psychotherapy.* Washington, DC: American Psychological Association.

EAGLY, A. H., & CHAIKEN, S. (1993). *The psychology of attitudes.* Fort Worth, TX: Harcourt Brace Jovanovich.

EAGLY, A. H., & CROWLEY, M. (1986). Gender and helping behavior: A meta-analytic review of the social psychological literature. *Psychological Bulletin, 100,* 283–308.

EAGLY, A. H., & WOOD, W. (1999). The origins of sex differences in human behavior: Evolved dispositions versus social roles. *American Psychologist, 54*(6), 408–423.

EAGLY, A. H., ASHMORE, R. D., MAKHIJANI, M. G., & LONGO, L. C. (1991). What is beautiful is good, but . . . : A meta-analytic review of research on the physical attractiveness stereotype. *Psychological Bulletin, 110,* 109–128.

EARLES, J. L., CONNOR, L. T., SMITH, A. D., & PARK, D. C. (1998). Interrelations of age, self-reported health, speed, and memory. *Psychology and Aging, 12,* 675–683.

EASTERBROOK, G. (2005, May 30). The end of war? Explaining fifteen years of diminishing violence. *The New Republic,* 18–21.

EATON, W. O., & YU, A. P. (1989). Are sex differences in child motor activity a function of sex differences in maturational status? *Child Development, 60,* 1005–1011.

EBBINGHAUS, H. (1885). *Memory.* New York: Teacher's College, Columbia University, 1913. Reprint edition, New York: Dover, 1964.

EDMONDS, J. M. (ED.). (1929). *The characters of Theophrastus.* Cambridge, MA: Harvard University Press.

EFRON, R. (1990). *The decline and fall of hemispheric specialization.* Hillsdale, NJ: Erlbaum.

EGETH, H., JONIDES, J., & WALL, S. (1972). Parallel processing of multielement displays. *Cognitive Psychology, 3,* 674–698.

EGLIN, M., ROBERTSON, L. C., & KNIGHT, R. T. (1989). Visual search performance in the neglect syndrome. *Journal of Cognitive Neuroscience, 1,* 372–385.

EHRHARDT, A., & BAKER, S. (1974). Fetal androgens, human central nervous system differentiation, and behavior sex differences. In R. C. Friedman, R. M. Richart, & R. L. van de Wiele (Eds.), *Sex differences in behavior* (pp. 33–52). New York: Wiley.

EHRHARDT, A., EPSTEIN, R., & MONEY, J. (1968). Fetal androgens and female gender identity in the early-treated adrenogenital syndrome. *Johns Hopkins Medical Journal, 122,* 165–167.

EIBL-EIBESFELDT, I. (1970). *Ethology: The biology of behavior.* New York: Holt, Rinehart & Winston.

EIMAS, P. D., SIQUELAND, E. R., JUSCZYK, P., & VIGORITO, J. (1971). Speech perception in infants. *Science, 171,* 303–306.

EISENBERG, A. R. (1999). Emotion talk among Mexican American and Anglo American mothers and children from two social classes. *Merrill-Palmer Quarterly, 45*(2), 267–284.

EISENBERG, N. (1986). *Altruistic emotion, cognition and behavior.* Hillsdale, NJ: Erlbaum.

EISENBERG, N. (2000). Emotion, regulation and moral development. In S. Fiske, D. Schacter, & Zahn-Waxler (Eds.), *Annual Review of Psychology, 51,* 665–697.

EISENBERG, N., & FABES, R. (1998). Prosocial development. In W. Damon (Ed.), *Handbook of child psychology* (5th Ed.): Vol. 3. *Social, emotional, and personality development* (N. Eisenberg, Vol. Ed.) (pp. 701–778). New York: Wiley.

EISENBERG, N., CUMBERLAND, A., & SPINRAD, T. L. (1998). Parental socialization of emotion. *Psychological Inquiry, 9*(4), 241–273.

EISENBERG, N., FABES, R. A., KARBON, M., MURPHY, B. C., & ET AL. (1996). The relations of children's dispositional prosocial behavior to emotionality, regulation, and social functioning. *Child Development, 67*(3), 974–992.

EISENBERG, N., FABES, R. A., MILLER, P., SHELL, R., SHEA, C., & MAY-PLUMLESS, T. (1990). Preschoolers' vicarioius motion responding and their situational and dispositional prosocial behavior. *Merrill-Palmer Quarterly, 36,* 507–529.

EISENBERG, N., FABES, R. A., SCHALLER, M., CARLO, G., & ET AL. (1991). The relations of parental characteristics and practices to children's vicarious emotional responding. *Child Development, 62*(6), 1393–1408.

EISENBERG, N., FABES, R., GUTHRIE, I., & REISER, M. (2000). Dispositional emotionality and regulation: Their role in predicting quality of social functioning. *Journal of Personality and Social Psychology, 78,* 136–157.

EISENBERG, N., FABES, R., SHEPARD, S., MURPHY, B., JONES, S., & GUTHRIE, I. (1998). Contemporaneous and longitudinal prediction of children's sympathy from dispositional regulation and emotionality. *Developmental Psychology, 34,* 910–924.

EISENBERG, N., GERSHOFF, E. T., FABES, R. A., SHEPARD, S. A., CUMBERLAND, A. J., LOSOYA, S. H., ET AL. (2001). Mother's emotional expressivity and children's behavior problems and social competence: Mediation through children's regulation. *Developmental Psychology, 37*(4), 475–490.

EISENBERGER, R., PIERCE, W. D., & CAMERON, J. (1999). Effects of reward on intrinsic motivation—negative, neutral, and positive: Comment on Deci, Koestner, and Ryan (1999). *Psychological Bulletin, 125,* 677–691.

EKMAN, P. (1972). Universals and cultural differences in facial expressions of emotion. In J. Cole (Ed.), *Nebraska Symposium on Motivation, 1971: Vol. 19* (pp. 207–283). Lincoln: University of Nebraska Press.

EKMAN, P. (1973). Cross-cultural studies of facial expression. In P. Ekman (Ed.), *Darwin and facial expression* (pp. 169–222). New York: Academic Press.

EKMAN, P. (1980). *The face of man: Expression of universal emotions in a New Guinea village.* New York: Garland STPM Press.

EKMAN, P. (1984). Expression and the nature of emotion. In P. Ekman & K. Scherer (Eds.), *Approaches to emotion* (pp. 319–343). Hillsdale, NJ: Erlbaum.

EKMAN, P. (1994). Strong evidence for universals in facial expression: A reply to Russell's mistaken critique. *Psychological Bulletin, 115,* 268–287.

EKMAN, P., & FRIESEN, W. V. (1969). Nonverbal leakage and clues to deception. *Psychiatry, 32,* 88–106.

EKMAN, P., & FRIESEN, W. V. (1975). *Unmasking the face.* Englewood Cliffs, NJ: Prentice-Hall.

EKMAN, P., FRIESEN, W. V., & O'SULLIVAN, M. (1988). Smiles when lying. *Journal of Personality and Social Psychology, 54,* 414–420.

EKMAN, P., & OSTER, H. (1979). Facial expression of emotion. *Annual Review of Psychology, 30,* 527–554.

ELBERT, T., PANTEV, C., WIENBRUCH, C., ROCKSTROH, B., & TAUB, E. (1995). Increased cortical representation of the fingers of the left hand in string players. *Science, 270,* 305–307.

ELFENBEIN, H. A., & AMBADY, N. (2002). On the universality of cultural specificity of emotion recognition: A meta-analysis. *Psychological Bulletin, 128,* 203–235.

ELKIN, I., SHEA, M. T., WATKINS, J. T., IMBER, S. D., SOTSKY, S. M., COLLINS, J. S., ET AL. (1989). National Institute of Mental Health treatment of depression collaborative research program: General effectiveness of treatments. *Archives of General Psychiatry, 46,* 971–982.

ELKIN, R. A., & LEIPPE, M. R. (1986). Physiological arousal, dissonance, and attitude change: Evidence for a dissonance-arousal link and a "don't remind me" effect. *Journal of Personality and Social Psychology, 51,* 55–65.

ELKINS, R. L. (1991). An appraisal of chemical aversion emetic therapy approaches to alcoholism treatment. *Behaviour Research and Therapy, 29,* 387–413.

ELLEMERS, N., SPEARS, R., & DOSSJE, B. (2002). Self and social identity. *Annual Review of Psychology, 53,* 161–186.

ELLENBERGER, H. F. (1970). *The discovery of the unconscious.* New York: Basic Books.

ELLIOT, M. A., & MÜLLER, H. J. (2000). Evidence for 40–Hz oscillatory short-term visual memory revealed by human reaction-time measurements. *Journal of Experimental Psychology: Learning, Memory, and Cognition, 26,* 7093–7718.

ELLIOTT, R., GREENBERG, L. S., & LIETAER, G. (2004). Research on experiential psychotherapies. In M. J. Lambert (Ed.), *Bergin and Garfield's handbook of psychotherapy and behavior change* (5th ed., pp. 493–540). New York: Wiley.

ELLIS, A. (1962). *Reason and emotion in psychotherapy.* Secaucus, NJ: Lyle Stuart.

ELLIS, L., & AMES, M. A. (1987). Neurohormonal functioning and sexual orientation: A theory of homosexuality-heterosexuality. *Psychological Bulletin, 101,* 233–258.

ELMAN, J. L. (1991). Distributed representation, simple recurrent networks, and grammatical structure. *Machine Learning, 7,* 195–225.

ELPHICK, M. R., & EGERTOVA, M. (2001). The neurobiology and evolution of cannabinoid signalling. *Philosophical Transactions: Biological Sciences, 356,* 381–408.

EMMELKAMP, P. M. G. (2004). Behavior therapy with adults. In M. J. Lambert (Ed.), *Bergin and Garfield's handbook of psychotherapy and behavior change* (5th ed., pp. 393–446). New York: Wiley.

EMMELKAMP, P. M. G., KRIJN, M., HULSBOSCH, A. M., DE VRIES, S., SCHUEMIE, M. J., & VAN DER MAST, C. A. P. G. (2002). Virtual reality treatment versus exposure in vivo: A comparative evaluation in acrophobia. *Behaviour Research and Therapy, 40,* 509–516.

EMMERICH, W. (1966). Continuity and stability in early social development, II. Teacher ratings. *Child Development, 37,* 17–27.

ENGEL, A. K., & SINGER, W. (2000). Temporal binding and the neural correlates of sensory awareness. *Trends in Cognitive Science, 5,* 16–25.

ENGLE, R. W., TUHOLSKI, S. W., LAUGHLIN, J. E., & CONWAY, A. R. A. (1999). Working memory, short-term memory, and general fluid intelligence: A latent variable approach. *Journal of Experimental Psychology: General, 128,* 309–331.

ENGLUND, M., LEVY, A., HYSON, D., & SROUFE, L. (2000). Adolescent social competence: Effectiveness in a group setting. *Child Development, 71,* 1049–1060.

ENNS, J. T. (2004). *The thinking eye, the seeing brain.* New York: Norton.

ENQUIST, M., & LEIMAR, O. (1990). The evolution of fatal fighting. *Animal Behaviour, 39,* 1–9.

EPSTEIN, H. T. (1978). Growth spurts during brain development: Implications for educational policy and practice. In J. S. Chard & A. F. Mirsky (Eds.), *Education and the brain.* Chicago: University of Chicago Press.

EPSTEIN, S. (1979) The stability of behavior: I. On predicting most of the people much of the time. *Journal of Personality and Social Psychology, 37,* 1097–1126.

EPSTEIN, W. (1961). The influence of syntactical structure on learning. *American Journal of Psychology, 74,* 80–85.

ERDELYI, M. H. (1985). *Psychoanalysis: Freud's cognitive psychology.* New York: Freeman.

ERIKSEN, C. W., & HOFFMAN, J. E. (1972). Temporal and spatial characteristics of selective encoding from multielement displays. *Perception and Psychophysics, 12,* 201–204.

ERIKSON, E. H. (1963). *Childhood and society.* New York: Norton.

ERIKSON, E. H., & COLES, R. (EDS.). (2000). *The Erik Erikson reader.* New York: Norton.

ERIKSSON, P. S., PERFILIEVA, E., BJÖRK-ERIKSSON, T., ALBORN, A., NORDBORG, C., PETERSON, D., ET AL. (1998). Neurogenesis in the adult human hippocampus. *Nature Medicine, 4,* 1313–1317.

ESSER, J. K. (1998). Alive and well after 25 years: A review of groupthink research. *Organizational Behavior and Human Decision Processes, 73*(2–3), 116–141.

ESSES, V. M., HADDOCK, G., & ZANNA, M. P. (1993). Values, stereotypes, and emotions as determinants of intergroup attitudes. In D. M. Mackie & D. L. Hamilton (Eds.), *Affect, cognition, and stereotyping: Interactive processes in group perception* (pp. 137–166). New York: Academic Press.

ESTES, W. K., & SKINNER, B. F. (1941). Some quantitative properties of anxiety. *Journal of Experimental Psychology, 29,* 390–400.

EVANS, J. S. B. T., & FEENEY, A. (2004). The role of prior belief in reasoning. In J. P. Leighton & R. J. Sternberg (Eds.), *The nature of reasoning* (pp. 78–102). New York: Cambridge University Press.

EVANS, J. S. B. T., NEWSTEAD, S. E., & BYRNE, R. M. J. (1993). *Human reasoning: The psychology of deduction.* London: Erlbaum.

EXNER, J. E. (1974). *The Rorschach system.* New York: Grune and Stratton.

EXNER, J. E. (1978). *A comprehensive system: Current research and advanced interpretation: Vol. 2.* New York: Wiley Interscience.

EXNER, J. E., JR. (1993). *The Rorschach: A comprehensive system: Vol. 1. Basic foundations* (3rd ed). New York: Wiley.

EYER, D. E. (1992). *Mother-infant bonding: A scientific fiction.* New Haven, CT: Yale University Press.

EYSENCK, H. J. (1961). The effects of psychotherapy. In H. J. Eysenck (Ed.), *Handbook of abnormal psychology* (pp. 697–725). New York: Basic Books.

EYSENCK, H. J. (1986). Toward a new model of intelligence. *Personality and Individual Differences, 7*(5), 731–736.

EYSENCK, H. J., VERSUS KAMIN, L. (1981). *The intelligence controversy.* New York: Wiley.

EYSENCK, M. W. (1987). Arousal and personality: The origins of a theory. In J. Strelau & H. J. Eysenck (Eds.), *Personality dimensions and arousal* (pp. 1–13). New York: Plenum.

FABES, R. A., EISENBERG, N., SMITH, M. C., & MURPHY, B. C. (1996). Getting angry at peers: Associations with liking of the provocateur. *Child Development, 67*(3), 942–956.

FAGOT, B. (1997). Attachment, parenting, and peer interactions of toddler children. *Developmental Psychology, 33,* 389–499.

FAGOT, B. I. (1995). Psychosocial and cognitive determinants of early gender-role development. *Annual Review of Sex Research, 6,* 1–31.

FAGOT, B. I., LEINBACH, M. D., & HAGEN, R. (1986). Gender labeling and adoption of same-sex behaviors. *Developmental Psychology, 22,* 440–443.

FAIRBURN, C. G., JONES, R., PEVELER, R., HOPE, R., & O'CONNOR, M. (1993). Psychotherapy and bulimia nervosa: Long-term effects of interpersonal psychotherapy, behavior therapy, and cognitive behavior therapy. *Archives of General Psychiatry, 50,* 419–428.

FALLON, A. E., & ROZIN, P. (1985). Sex differences in perceptions of desirable body shape. *Journal of Abnormal Psychology, 94,* 102–105.

FANSELOW, M. S., POULOS, A. M. (2005). The neuroscience of mammalian associative learning. *Annual Review of Psychology, 56,* 207–234.

FANT, L. G. (1972). *Ameslan: An introduction to American Sign Language.* Silver Springs, MD: National Association of the Deaf.

FANTZ, R. (1963). Pattern vision in newborn infants. *Science, 140,* 296–297.

FARAH, M. (1988). Is visual imagery really visual? Overlooked evidence from neuropsychology. *Psychological Review, 95,* 307–317.

FARAH, M. (1990). *Visual agnosia.* Cambridge, MA: MIT Press.

FARAH, M. J. (2004). *Visual agnosia* (2nd ed.). Cambridge, MA: MIT Press/Bradford Books.

FARAH, M. J., & FEINBERG, T. E. (2000). Disorders of perception and awareness. In M. J. FARAH & T. E. FEINBERG, (EDS.), *Patient-based approaches to cognitive neuroscience* (pp. 143–154). Cambridge, MA: MIT Press.

FARIS, R. E. L., & DUNHAM, H. W. (1939). *Mental disorders in urban areas.* Chicago: University of Chicago Press.

FAZIO, R. H. (1995). Attitudes as object-evaluation associations: Determinants, consequences, and correlates of attitude accessibility. In R. E. Petty & J. A. Krosnick (Eds.), *Attitude strength: Antecedents and consequences* (pp. 247–282). Mahwah, NJ: Erlbaum.

FAZIO, R. H., ZANNA, M. P., & COOPER, J. (1977). Dissonance and self-perception: An integrative view of each theory's proper domain of application. *Journal of Experimental Social Psychology, 13,* 464–479.

FEDER, H. H. (1984). Hormones and sexual behavior. *Annual Review of Psychology, 35,* 165–200.

FEDERAL BUREAU OF INVESTIGATION. (2004). Crime in the United States 2004: Uniform crime reports. Washington, DC: U. S. Government Printing Office.

FEENEY, B. C., & COLLINS, N. L. (2001). Predictors of caregiving in adult intimate relationships: An attachment theoretical perspective. *Journal of Personality and Social Psychology, 80*(6), 972–994.

FEIN, S., & SPENCER, S. J. (1997). Prejudice as self-image maintenance: Affirming the self through derogating others. *Journal of Personality and Social Psychology, 73,* 31–44.

FEINGOLD, A. (1988). Matching for attractiveness in romantic partners and same-sex friends: A meta-analysis and theoretical critique. *Psychological Bulletin, 104,* 226–232.

FEINGOLD, A. (1992). Good-looking people are not what we think. *Psychological Bulletin, 111,* 304–341.

FEINGOLD, A. (1994). Gender differences in personality: A meta-analysis. *Psychological Bulletin, 116,* 429–456.

FEINMAN, J. A., & DUNNER, D. L. (1996). The effect of alcohol and substance abuse on the course of bipolar affective disorder. *Journal of Affective Disorders, 37,* 43–49.

FELDMAN, H., GOLDIN-MEADOW, S., & GLEITMAN, L. R. (1978). Beyond Herodotus: The creation of language by linguistically deprived deaf children. In A. Lock (Ed.), *Action, gesture, and symbol: The emergence of language* (pp. 351–414). New York: Academic Press.

FERGUSON, J. M. (2001). The effects of antidepressants on sexual functioning in depressed patients: A review [Suppl.]. *Journal of Clinical Psychiatry, 62*(3), 22–34.

FERNALD, A. (1985). Four-month-old infants prefer to listen to motherese. *Infant Behavior and Development, 8,* 181–195.

FERNALD, A. (1992). Human maternal vocalizations to infants as biologically relevant signals: An evolutionary perspective. In J. H. Barkow, L. Cosmides, & J. Tooby (Eds.), *The adapted mind* (pp. 391–428). New York: Oxford.

FESTINGER, L. (1954). A theory of social comparison processes. *Human Relations, 7,* 117–140.

FESTINGER, L. (1957). *A theory of cognitive dissonance.* Stanford, CA: Stanford University Press.

FESTINGER, L. (1962, October). Cognitive dissonance. *Scientific American, 207,* 93–107.

FESTINGER, L., & CARLSMITH, J. M. (1959). Cognitive consequences of forced compliance. *Journal of Abnormal and Social Psychology, 58,* 203–210.

FESTINGER, L., PEPITONE, A., & NEWCOMB, T. (1952). Some consequences of deindividuation in a group. *Journal of Abnormal and Social Psychology, 47,* 387–389.

FIEDLER, F. E. (1978). Recent developments in research on the contingency model. In L. Berkowitz (Ed.), *Group processes.* New York: Academic Press.

FIGLEY, C. R. (1978). Symptoms of delayed combat stress among a college sample of Vietnam veterans. *Military Medicine, 143,* 107–110.

FILLMORE, C. (1968). The case for case. In E. Bach & R. Harms (Eds.), *Universals in linguistic theory.* New York: Holt, Rinehart and Winston.

FINK, B., & PENTON-VOAK, I. (2002). Evolutionary psychology of facial attractiveness. *Current Directions in Psychological Science, 11,* 154–158.

FINKE, R. (1993). Mental imagery and creative discovery. In B. Roskos-Ewoldsen, M. J. Intons-Peterson, & R. Anderson (Eds.), *Imagery, creativity, and discovery* (pp. 255–285). New York: North-Holland.

FINKE, R., WARD, T., & SMITH, S. (1992). *Creative cognition: Theory, research and applications.* Cambridge, MA: MIT Press.

FINUCANE, M. L., ALHAKAMI, A., SLOVIC, P., & JOHNSON, S. M. (2000). The affect heuristic in judgments of risks and benefits. *Journal of Behavioral Decision Making, 13,* 1–17.

FISHER, C., & GLEITMAN, L. R. (2002). Breaking the linguistic code: Current issues in early language learning. In C. R. Gallistel (Vol. Ed.), *Stevens' handbook of experimental psychology: Vol. 3. Learning, motivation, and emotion* (pp. 1–54). New York: Wiley.

FISHER, R. P., & CRAIK, F. I. M. (1977). The interaction between encoding and retrieval operations in cued recall. *Journal of Experimental Psychology: Human Learning and Memory, 3,* 701–711.

FISHER, S., & GREENBERG, R. P. (1977). *The scientific credibility of Freud's theory and therapy.* New York: Basic Books.

FISKE, A. P. (1992). The four elementary forms of sociality: Framework for a unified theory of social relations. *Psychological Review, 99,* 689–723.

FISKE, A. P. (2004). Relational models theory 2.0. In N. Haslam (Ed.), *Relational models theory: A contemporary overview* (pp. 3–25). Mahway, NJ: Erlbaum.

FISKE, A. P., & HASLAM, N. (2005). The four basic social bonds: Structures for coordinating interactions. In M. W. Baldwin (Ed.), *Interpersonal cognition* (pp. 267–298). New York: Guilford Press.

FISKE, A. P., KITAYAMA, S., MARKUS, H. R., & NISBETT, R. E. (1998). The cultural matrix of social psychology. In D. T. Gilbert, S. T. Fiske, & G. Lindzey (Eds.), *The handbook of social psychology* (4th ed., pp. 915–981). New York: McGraw-Hill.

FISKE, D. W. (1949). Consistency of the factorial structures of personality ratings from different sources. *Journal of Abnormal Social Psychology, 44,* 329–344.

FISKE, S. T. (1998). Stereotyping, prejudice, and discrimination. In D. T. Gilbert, S. T. Fiske, & G. Lindzey (Eds.), *The handbook of social psychology* (4th ed., pp. 357–411). New York: McGraw-Hill.

FIVUSH, R. (1993). Emotional content of parent-child conversations about the past. In C. Nelson (Ed.), *Memory and affect in development. Minnesota Symposia on Child Psychology,* Vol. 23 (pp. 39–77). Hillsdale, NJ: Erlbaum.

FIVUSH, R. (1998). The stories we tell: How language shapes autobiography. *Applied Cognitive Psychology, 12*(5), 483–487.

FIVUSH, R., BROTMAN, M. A., BUCKNER, J. P., & GOODMAN, S. H. (2000). Gender differences in parent-child emotion narratives. *Sex Roles, 42*(3–4), 233–253.

FIVUSH, R., & HADEN, C. (EDS.). (2003). *Autobiographical memory and the construction of a narrative self: Developmental and cultural perspectives.* Hillsdale, NJ: Erlbaum.

FIVUSH, R., & NELSON, K. (2004). Culture and language in the emergence of autobiographical memory. *Psychological Science, 15,* 573–577.

FLAVELL, J. H. (1985). *Cognitive development* (2nd ed.). Englewood Cliffs, NJ: Prentice-Hall.

FLAVELL, J. H., FLAVELL, E. R., & GREEN, F. L. (1983). Development of the appearance-reality distinction. *Cognitive Psychology, 15,* 95–120.

FLEESON, W. (2004). Moving personality beyond the person-situation debate: The challenge and the opportunity of within-person variability. *Current Directions in Psychological Science, 13,* 83–87.

FLODERUS-MYRHED, B., PEDERSEN, N., & RASMUSON, L. (1980). Assessment of heritability for personality, based on a short form of the Eysenck Personality Inventory: A study of 12,898 twin pairs. *Behavior Genetics, 10,* 153–162.

FLYNN, J. R. (1984). The mean IQ of Americans: Massive gains 1932 to 1978. *Psychological Bulletin, 95*(1), 29–51.

FLYNN, J. R. (1987). Massive IQ gains in 14 nations: What IQ tests really measure. *Psychological Bulletin, 101*(2), 171–191.

FLYNN, J. R. (1999). Searching for justice: The discovery of IQ gains over time. *American Psychologist, 54,* 5–20.

FOA, E., DANCU, C., HEMBREE, E., JAYCOX, L., MEADOWS, E., & STREET, G. (1999). A comparison of exposure therapy, stress inoculation training, and their combination for reducing posttraumatic stress disorder in female assault victims. *Journal of Consulting and Clinical Psychology, 67,* 194–200.

FOCH, T. T., & McCLEARN, G. E. (1980). Genetics, body weight, and obesity. In A. J. Stunkard (Ed.), *Obesity* (pp. 48–71). Philadelphia: Saunders.

FODOR, J. (1997). Connectionism and the problem of systematicity (continued): Why Smolensky's solution still doesn't work. *Cognition, 62*(1), 109–119.

FODOR, J. A. (1983). *The modularity of mind.* Cambridge, MA: MIT Press, Bradford Books.

FODOR, J. A., & PYLYSHYN, Z. W. (1988). Connectionism and cognitive architecture: A critical analysis. *Cognition, 28,* 3–71.

FOLLETTE, W., & GREENBERG, L. S. (2005). Technique factors in treating dysphoric disorders. In L. Castonguay & L. Beutler (Eds.), *Therapeutic principles of change that work* (pp. 83–110). New York: Oxford University Press.

FONG, G., & NISBETT, R. (1991). Immediate and delayed transfer of training effects in statistical reasoning. *Journal of Experimental Psychology: General, 120,* 34–45.

FONG, G., KRANTZ, D., & NISBETT, R. (1986). The effects of statistical training on thinking about everyday problems. *Cognitive Psychology, 18,* 253–292.

FORD, C. S., & BEACH, F. A. (1951). *Patterns of sexual behavior.* New York: Harper & Row.

FOSSHAGE, J. L. (1983). The psychological function of dreams: A revised psychoanalytic perspective. *Psychoanalysis and Contemporary Thought, 6,* 641–669.

FOUCAULT, M. (1965). *Madness and civilization.* New York: Random House.

FOX, N. A., HENDERSON, H. A., MARSHALL, P. J., NICHOLS, K. E., & GHERA, M. M. (2005). Behavioral inhibition: Linking biology and behavior within a developmental framework. *Annual Review of Psychology, 56,* 235–262.

FRALEY, R. (2002). Attachment stability from infancy to adulthood: Meta-analysis and dynamic modeling of developmental mechanisms. *Personality and Social Psychology Review, 6,* 123–151.

FRANK, E., & SPANIER, C. (1995). Interpersonal psychotherapy for depression: Overview, clinical efficacy, and future directions. *Clinical Psychology Science and Practice, 2,* 349–369.

FRANKEL, F. H. (1993). Adult reconstruction of childhood events in the multiple personality disorder literature. *American Journal of Psychiatry, 150,* 954–958.

FRASIER, L., & FODOR, J. D. (1978). The sausage machine: A new two-stage parsing model. *Cognition, 6,* 291–325.

FREDRICKSON, B. L. (1998). What good are positive emotions? *Review of General Psychology, 2,* 300–319.

FREDRICKSON, B. L., MAYNARD, K. E., HELMS, M. J., HANEY, T. L., SIEGLER, I. C., & BAREFOOT, J. C. (2000). Hostility predicts magnitude and duration of blood pressure response to anger. *Journal of Behavioral Medicine, 23,* 229–243. Freedman, D., & Freedman, N. (1969). Behavioural differences between Chinese-American and European-American newborns. *Nature, 224,* 1227.

FREEDMAN, J. L., & FRASER, S. C. (1966). Compliance without pressure: The foot-in-the-door technique. *Journal of Personality and Social Psychology, 4,* 195–202.

FREEMAN, D. (1983). *Margaret Mead and Samoa: The making and unmaking of an anthropological myth.* Cambridge, MA: Harvard University Press.

FREESE, J., & MELAND, S. (2002). Seven tenths incorrect: Heterogeneity and change in the waist-to-hip ratios of *Playboy* centerfold models and Miss America pageant winners—Statistical data included. *Journal of Sex Research, 39,* 133–138.

FREMOUW, W. J., PERCZEL, M., & ELLIS, T. E. (1990). *Suicide risk: Assessment and response guidelines.* Elmsford, NY: Pergamon.

FREUD, A. (1937). *The ego and the mechanisms of defence.* Oxford, England: Hogarth.

FREUD, A. (1946). *The ego and the mechanisms of defense.* London: Hogarth Press.

FREUD, S. (1900). The interpretation of dreams. In J. Strachey (Trans. and Ed.), *The complete psychological works: Vols. 4–5.* New York: Norton, 1976.

FREUD, S. (1901). *The psychopathology of everyday life* (A. Tyson, Trans.). New York: Norton, 1971.

FREUD, S. (1905). Three essays on the theory of sexuality. In J. Strachey (Trans. and Ed.), *The complete psychological works: Vol. 7.* New York: Norton, 1976.

FREUD, S. (1908). Character and anal eroticism. In P. Rieff (Ed.), *Collected papers of Sigmund Freud: Character and culture.* New York: Collier Books, 1963.

FREUD, S. (1911). Psychoanalytic notes upon an autobiographical account of a case of paranoia (dementia paranoides). In J. Strachey (Trans. and Ed.), *The complete psychological works: Vol. 12.* New York: Norton, 1976.

FREUD, S. (1917). *A general introduction to psychoanalysis* (J. Riviere, Trans.). New York: Washington Square Press, 1952.

FREUD, S. (1923). *The ego and the id* (J. Riviere, Trans.). New York: Norton, 1962.

FREUD, S. (1925). Some psychical consequences of the anatomical distinction between the sexes. In J. Strachey (Trans. and Ed.), *The complete psychological works: Vol. 19.* New York: Norton, 1976.

FREUD, S. (1933). Femininity. In J. Strachey (Trans. and Ed.), *The complete psychological works: Vol. 22* (pp. 112–115). New York: Norton, 1976.

FREUD, S. (1933/1964). *New introductory lectures on psychoanalysis.* New York: Norton.

FREUD, S., & BREUER, J. (1895). Studies on hysteria. In J. Strachey (Trans. and Ed.), *The complete psychological works: Vol. 2.* New York: Norton, 1976.

FREUND, A. M., & BALTES, P. B. (1998). Selection, optimization, and compensation as strategies of life management: Correlations with subjective indicators of successful aging. *Psychology and Aging, 13,* 531–543.

FREYD, J. (1996). *Betrayal trauma: The logic of forgetting childhood abuse.* Cambridge, MA: Harvard University Press.

FREYD, J. J. (1998). Science in the memory debate. *Ethics & Behavior, 8,* 101–113.

FRIDLUND, A. J. (1994). *Human facial expression: An evolutionary view.* San Diego, CA: Academic Press.

FRIDLUND, A. J., EKMAN, P., & OSTER, H. (1983). Facial expression of emotion: Review of literature, 1970–1983. In A. Siegman (Ed.), *Nonverbal behavior and communication.* Hillsdale, NJ: Erlbaum.

FRIEDERICI, A. D., & WESSELS, J. M. I. (1993). Phonotactic knowledge of word boundaries and its use in infant speech perception. *Perception and Psychophysics, 54,* 287–295.

FRIEDMAN, H. S., & MILLER-HERRINGER, T. (1991). Nonverbal displays of emotion in public and private: Self-monitoring, personality, and expressive cues. *Journal of Personality and Social Psychology, 61,* 766–775.

FRIEDMAN, J. (2003). A war on obesity, not the obese. *Science, 299,* 856–858.

FRIEDMAN, M. I. (1990a). Body fat and the metabolic control of food intake. *International Journal of Obesity, 14,* 53–67.

FRIEDMAN, M. I. (1990b). Making sense out of calories. In E. M. Stricker (Ed.), *Handbook of behavioral neurobiology: Vol. 10. Neurobiology of food and fluid intake* (pp. 513–529). New York: Plenum.

FRIEDMAN, M. I., & STRICKER, E. M. (1976). The physiological psychology of hunger: A physiological perspective. *Psychological Review, 83,* 409–431.

FRIEDMAN, M. J., & MARSELLA, A. J. (1996). Posttraumatic stress disorder: An overview of the concept. In A. J. Marsella, M. J. Friedman, E. T. Gerrity, & R. M. Scurfield (Eds.), *Ethnocultural aspects of posttraumatic stress disorder: Issues, research, and clinical applications* (pp. 11–32). Washington, DC: American Psychological Association.

FRIEDMAN, N., MIYAKE, A., CORLEY, R., YOUNG, S., DeFRIES, J., & HEWITT, J. (2006). Not all executive functions are related to intelligence. *Psychological Science, 17,* 172–179.

FRIES, P., REYNOLDS, J. H., RORIE, A. E., & DESIMONE, R. (2001). Modulation of oscillatory neural synchronization by selective visual attention. *Science, 291,* 1560–1563.

FRIESEN, W. V. (1972). *Cultural differences in facial expressions in a social situation: An experimental test of the concept of display rules.* Unpublished doctoral dissertation, University of California, San Francisco.

FRIJDA, N. H. (1986). *The emotions.* New York, NY; Paris, France: Cambridge University Press; Editions de la Maison des Sciences de l'Homme.

FRITH, C. D., & FRITH, U. (1999). Interacting minds—a biological basis. *Science, 286,* 1692–1695.

FROME, P. M., & ECCLES, J. S. (1998). Parents' influence on children's achievement-related perceptions. *Journal of Personality and Social Psychology, 74*(2), 435–452.

FROMKIN, V., KRASHEN, S., CURTISS, S., RIGLER, D., & RIGLER, M. (1974). The development of language in Genie: A case of language acquisition beyond the "critical period." *Brain and Language, 1,* 81–107.

FROST, P. (1994). Preference for darker faces in photographs at different phases of the menstrual cycle: Preliminary assessment of evidence for a hormonal relationship. *Perceptual and Motor Skills, 79*(1, Pt. 2), 507–514.

FRYE, D., ZELAZO, P. D., & BURACK, J. A. (1998). Cognitive complexity and control: I. Theory of mind in typical and atypical development. *Current Directions in Psychological Science, 7,* 116–120.

FUJIMOTO, W. Y., BERGSTROM, R. W., BOYKO, E. J., LEONETTI, D. L., NEWELL-MORRIS, L. L., & WAHL, P. W. (1995). Susceptibility to development of central adiposity among populations. *Obesity Research, 3*(suppl. 2), 179S–186S.

FULLER, R. K., & HILLER-STURMHOFEL, S. (1999). Alcoholism treatment in the United States. An overview. *Alcohol Research and Health, 23,* 69–77.

FURNHAM, A., TAN, T., & McMANUS, C. (1997). Waist-to-hip ratio preferences for body shape: A replication and extension. *Personality and Individual Differences, 22,* 539–549.

GABRIELI, J. D. E., FLEISCHMAN, D. A., KEANE, M. M., REMINGER, S. L., & MORRELL, F. (1995). Double dissociation between memory systems underlying explicit and implicit memory in the human brain. *Psychological Science, 6,* 76–82.

GALATI, D., SCHERER, K. R., & RICCI-BITTI, P. E. (1997). Voluntary facial expression of emotion: Comparing congenitally blind with normally sighted encoders. *Journal of Personality and Social Psychology, 73,* 1363–1379.

GALLAGHER, A. M., & KAUFMAN, J. C. (2005). Gender differences in mathematics: What we know and what we need to know. In A. M. Gallagher & J. C. Kaufman (Eds.), *Gender differences in mathematics: An integrative psychological approach* (pp. 316–331). New York: Cambridge University Press.

GALLAGHER, H. L., & FRITH, C. D. (2003). Functional imaging of "theory of mind." *Trends in Cognitive Science, 7,* 77–83.

GALLISTEL, C. R. (1990). *The organization of learning.* Cambridge, MA: MIT Press (Bradford).

GALLISTEL, C. R. (1994). Space and time. In N. J. Mackintosh (Ed.), *Animal learning and cognition* (pp. 221–253). New York: Academic Press.

GALLISTEL, C. R., & GELMAN, R. (2000). Non-verbal numerical cognition: From reals to integers. *Trends in Cognitive Science, 4,* 59–65.

GALLO, V., & CHITAJALLU, R. (2001). Unwrapping glial cells from the synapse: what lies inside? *Science, 292,* 872–873.

GALTON, F. (1883). *Inquiries into human faculty and its development.* London: Macmillan.

GANAWAY, G. K. (1989). Historical versus narrative truth: Clarifying the role of exogenous trauma in the etiology of MPD and its variants. *Dissociation, 2,* 205–220.

GANEV, K., ONCHEV, G., & IVANOV, P. (1998). A 16–year follow-up study of schizophrenia and related disorders in Sofia, Bulgaria. *Acta Psychiatrica Scandinavica, 98,* 200–207.

GANGESTAD, S., & SNYDER, M. (2000). Self-monitoring: Appraisal and reappraisal. *Psychological Bulletin, 126,* 530–555.

GARB, H. N., WOOD, J. M., LILIENFELD, S. O., & NEZWORSKI, M. T. (2002). Effective use of projective techniques in clinical practice: Let the data help with selection and interpretation. *Professional Psychology: Research & Practice, 33,* 454–463.

GARBER, J., & HOROWITZ, J. L. (2002). Depression in childhood. In I. H. Gotlib & C. L. Hammen (Eds.), *Handbook of depression* (pp. 510–540). New York: Guilford Press. Goff, D. C., & Coyle, J. T. (2001). The emerging role of glutamate in the pathophysiology and treatment of schizophrenia. *American Journal of Psychiatry, 158,* 1367–1377.

GARCIA, J., & KOELLING, R. A. (1966). The relation of cue to consequence in avoidance learning. *Psychonomic Science, 4,* 123–124.

GARDNER, H. (1983). *Frames of mind: The theory of multiple intelligences.* New York: Basic Books.

GATHERCOLE, S. E., & PICKERING, S. J. (2000a). Assessment of working memory in six- and seven-year-old children. *Journal of Educational Psychology, 92,* 377–390.

GATHERCOLE, S. E., & PICKERING, S. J. (2000b). Working memory deficits in children with low achievements in the national curriculum at seven years of age. *British Journal of Educational Psychology, 70,* 177–194.

GAUVAIN, M. (2001). Cultural tools, social interaction and the development of thinking. *Human Development, 44*(2–3), 126–143.

GAY, P. (1998). *Freud: A life for our time.* New York: Norton.

GAZZANIGA, M., IVRY, R., & MANGUN, G. (2002). *Cognitive neuroscience: The biology of the mind.* New York: Norton.

GEARY, D. C. (1998). *Male, female: The evolution of human sex differences.* Washington, DC: American Psychological Association.

GEARY, D. C. (2000). Evolution and proximate expression of human paternal investment. *Psychological Bulletin, 126,* 55–77.

GEARY, D. C. (2005). Evolution of life-history trade-offs in mate attractiveness and health: Comment on Weeden & Sabini (2005). *Psychological Bulletin, 131,* 654–657.

GEARY, D. C., & BJORKLUND, D. F. (2000). Evolutionary developmental psychology. *Child Development, 71,* 57–65.

GEEN, R. G. (2001). *Human aggression* (2nd ed.). London: Taylor & Francis.

GEKOSKI, M., ROVEE-COLLIER, C., & CARULLI-RABINOWITZ, V. (1983). A longitudinal analysis of inhibition of infant distress: The origins of social expectations? *Infant Behavior and Development, 6,* 339–351.

GELMAN, R. (1978). Cognitive development. *Annual Review of Psychology, 29,* 297–332.

GELMAN, R., & BAILLARGEON, R. (1983). A review of some Piagetian concepts. In P. Mussen (Ed.), E. M. Markman, & J. H. Flavell (Vol. Eds.), *Carmichael's manual of child psychology: Vol 3. Cognitive development* (pp. 167–230). New York: Wiley.

GELMAN, R., & GALLISTEL, R. C. (1978). *The child's understanding of number.* Cambridge, MA: Harvard University Press.

GELMAN, S., & RAMAN, L. (2002). Folk biology as a window onto cognitive development. *Human Development, 45,* 61–68.

GENTNER, D. (1983). Structure-mapping: A theoretical framework for analogy. *Cognitive Science 7,* 155–170.

GENTNER, D., & BORODITSKY, L. (2001). Individuation, relativity and early word learning. In M. Bowerman & S. C. Levinson (Eds.), *Language acquisition and conceptual development* (pp. 215–256). New York: Cambridge University Press.

GENTNER, D., & JEZIORSKI, M. (1989). Historical shifts in the use of analogy in science. In B. Gholson, W. Shadish, R. Neimeyer, & A. Houts (Eds.), *Psychology of science: Contributions to metascience.* Cambridge: Cambridge University Press.

GERARD, H. B., & MATHEWSON, G. C. (1966). The effects of severity of initiation on liking for a group: A replication. *Journal of Experimental Social Psychology, 2,* 278–287.

GERGELY, G., & WATSON, J. (1999). Early socio-emotional development: Contingency perception and the social-biofeedback model. In P. Rochat (Ed.), *Early social cognition* (pp. 101–136). Mahwah, NJ: Erlbaum.

GERHARDT, P. F., HOLMES, D. L., ALESSANDRI, M., & GOODMAN, M. (1991). Social policy on the use of aversive interventions: Empirical, ethical, and legal considerations. *Journal of Autism and Developmental Disorders, 21,* 265–277.

GERKEN, L. (1996). Prosody's role in language acquisition and adult parsing. *Journal of Psycholinguistic Research, 25*(2), 345–356.

GERKEN, L. (2006). Decisions, decisions: Infant language learning when multiple generalizations are possible. *Cognition,* B67–B74.

GERKEN, L., LANDAU, B., & REMEZ, R. (1990). Function morphemes in young children's speech perception and production. *Developmental Psychology, 26*(2), 204–216.

GERMAN, T. P., & BARRETT, H. C. (2005). Functional fixedness in a technologically sparse culture. *Psychological Science, 16,* 1–5.

GERSHOFF, E. (2002). Corporal punishment by parents and associated child behaviors and experiences: A meta-analysis. *Psychological Bulletin, 128,* 539–579.

GERSHON, A., DANNON, P., & GRUNHAUS, L. (2003). Transcranial magnetic stimulation in the treatment of depression. *American Journal of Psychiatry, 160,* 835–845.

GERSHON, E. S., NURNBERGER, J. I., JR., BERRETTINI, W. H., & GOLDIN, L. R. (1985). Affective disorders: Genetics. In H. I. Kaplan & J. Sadock (Eds.), *Modern synopsis of comprehensive textbook of psychiatry* (4th ed.). Baltimore: Williams & Wilkins.

GERSTNER, C., & DAY, D. V. (1994). Cross-cultural comparison of leadership prototypes. *Leadership Quarterly, 5,* 121–134.

GESCHWIND, N. (1970). The organization of language and the brain. *Science, 170,* 940–944.

GEWIRTZ, J. C., & DAVIS, M. (2000). Using Pavlovian higher-order conditioning paradigms to investigate the neural substrates of emotional learning and memory. *Learning & Memory, 7,* 257–266.

GHAZANFAR, A. A., & HAUSER, M. D. (1999). The neuroethology of primate vocal communication: Substrates for the evolution of speech. *Trends in Cognitive Sciences, 3*(10), 377–381.

GIBBS, W. W. (1996). Gaining on fat. *Scientific American, 275,* 88–94.

GIBSON, J. J. (1950). *The perception of the visual world.* Boston: Houghton Mifflin.

GIBSON, J. J. (1966). *The senses considered as perceptual systems.* Boston: Houghton Mifflin.

GIBSON, J. J. (1979). *The ecological approach to visual perception.* Boston: Houghton Mifflin.

GICK, M. L., & HOLYOAK, K. J. (1980). Analogical problem solving. *Cognitive Psychology, 12,* 306–355.

GICK, M. L., & HOLYOAK, K. J. (1983). Schema induction and analogical transfer. *Cognitive Psychology, 15,* 1–38.

GIGERENZER, G., & HOFFRAGE, U. (1995). How to improve Bayesian reasoning without instruction: Frequency formats. *Psychological Review, 102,* 684–704.

GIGERENZER, G., & HOFFRAGE, U. (1999). Overcoming difficulties in Bayesian reasoning: A reply to Lewis and Keren (1999) and Mellers and McGraw (1999). *Psychological Review, 106,* 425–430.

GIGERENZER, G., & HUG, K. (1992). Domain-specific reasoning: Social contracts, cheating and perspective change. *Cognition, 43,* 127–172.

GILBERT, D. T. (1989). Thinking lightly about others: Automatic components of the social inference process. In J. S. Uleman & J. A. Bargh (Eds.), *Unintended thought* (pp. 189–211). New York: Guilford Press.

GILBERT, S. J., & SHALLICE, T. (2002). Task switching: A PDP model. *Cognitive Psychology, 44*(3), 297–337.

GILES, J. W., GOPNIK, A., & HEYMAN, G. D. (2002). Source monitoring reduces the suggestibility of preschool children. *Psychological Science, 13,* 288–291.

GILHOOLY, K. (1988). *Thinking: Direct, undirected and creative* (2nd ed.). New York: Academic Press.

GILLIGAN, C. (1982). *In a different voice: Psychological theory and women's development.* Cambridge, MA: Harvard University Press.

GILLIGAN, C. (1986). Profile of Carol Gilligan. In S. Scarr, R. A. Weinberg, & A. Levine, *Understanding development* (pp. 488–491). New York: Harcourt Brace Jovanovich.

GILOVICH, T. (1991). *How we know what isn't so.* New York: Free Press.

GILOVICH, T., KELTNER, D., & NISBETT, R. E. (2006). Social psychology. New York: Norton.

GITLIN, M. J. (2001). Treatment-resistant bipolar disorder. *Bulletin of the Menninger Clinic, 65,* 26–40.

GIURFA, M., ZHANG, S., JENETT, A., MENZEL, R., & SRINIVASAN, M. V. (2001). The concepts of "sameness" and "difference" in an insect. *Nature, 410*(6831), 930–933.

GLADUE, B. A., GREEN, R., & HELLMAN, R. E. (1984). Neuroendocrine responses to estrogen and sexual orientation. *Science, 225,* 1496–1498.

GLEITMAN, H. (1963). Place-learning. *Scientific American, 209,* 116–122.

GLEITMAN, H. (1971). Forgetting of long-term memories in animals. In W. K. Honig & P. H. R. James (Eds.), *Animal memory* (pp. 2–46). New York: Academic Press.

GLEITMAN, H. (1985). Some trends in the study of cognition. In S. Koch, & D. E. Leary (Eds.), *A century of psychology as science* (pp. 420–436). New York: McGraw-Hill.

GLEITMAN, H. (1990). Some reflections on drama and the dramatic experience. In I. Rock (Ed.), *The legacy of Solomon Asch: Essays in cognition and social psychology.* Hillsdale, NJ: Erlbaum.

GLEITMAN, H., & JONIDES, J. (1976). The cost of categorization in visual search: Incomplete processing of targets and field items. *Perception and Psychophysics, 20*(4), 281–288.

GLEITMAN, L. R. (1986). Biological dispositions to learn language. In W. Demopolous & A. Marras (Eds.), *Language learning and concept acquisition.* Norwood, NJ: Ablex.

GLEITMAN, L. R. (1990). The structural sources of verb meanings. *Language Acquisition, 1,* 3–55.

GLEITMAN, L. R., & GLEITMAN, H. (1997), What is a language made out of? *Lingua, 100,* 29–55.

GLEITMAN, L. R., & WANNER, E. (1982). Language acquisition: The state of the state of the art. In E. Wanner & L. R. Gleitman (Eds.), *Language acquisition: State of the art* (pp. 3–48). New York: Cambridge University Press.

GLEITMAN, L. R., CASSIDY, K., PAPAFRAGOU, A., NAPPA, R., & TRUESWELL, J. T. (2005). Hard words. *Journal of Language Learning and Development, 1*(1), 23–64.

GLEITMAN, L. R., GLEITMAN, H., LANDAU, B., & WANNER, E. (1988). Where learning begins: Initial representations for language learning. In F. J. Newmeyer (Ed.), *Linguistics: The Cambridge survey: Vol. 3. Language: Psychological and biological aspects* (pp. 150–193). New York: Cambridge University Press.

GLEITMAN, L. R., GLEITMAN, H., & SHIPLEY, E. F. (1972). The emergence of the child as grammarian. *Cognition, 1*(2), 137–164.

GLEITMAN, L. R., LI, P., PAPAFRAGOU, A., GALLISTEL, C.R., & ABARBINELL, L. (2005). Spatial reasoning and cognition: cross-linguistic studies. Symposium conducted at annual meeting of the Cognitive Science Society, Stresa, Italy.

GLICK, I. D., MURRAY, S. R., VASUDEVAN, P., MARDER, S. R., & HU, R. J. (2001). Treatment with atypical antipsychotics: New indications and new populations. *Journal of Psychiatric Research, 35,* 187–191.

GLICK, J. (1975). Cognitive development in cross-cultural perspective. In F. G. Horowitz (Ed.), *Review of child development research: Vol. 4.* Chicago: University of Chicago Press.

GOBET, F., & SIMON, H. A. (1996a). Recall of random and distorted chess positions: Implications for the theory of expertise. *Memory and Cognition, 24,* 493–503.

GOBET, F., & SIMON, H. A. (1996b). The roles of recognition processes and look-ahead search in time-constrained expert problem solving: Evidence from grandmaster-level chess. *Psychological Science, 7,* 52–55.

GOBET, F., & SIMON, H. A. (2000). The relative contributions of recognition and search-evaluation processes to high-level chess performance: Reply to Lassiter. *Psychological Science, 11*(2), 174.

GOBET, F., LANE, P. C. R., CROKER, S., CHENG, P. C.-H., JONES, G., OLIVER, I., ET AL. (2001). Chunking mechanisms in human learning. Trends in *Cognitive Science, 5,* 236–243.

GOEBEL, R., KHORRAM-SEFAT, D., MUCKLIN, L., HACKER, H., & SINGER, W. (1998). The constructive nature of vision: Direct evidence from functional magnetic resonance imaging studies of apparent motion and motion imagery. *European Journal of Neuroscience, 10*(5), 1563–1573.

GOLDBERG, E. M., & MORRISON, S. L. (1963). Schizophrenia and social class. *British Journal of Psychiatry, 109,* 785–802.

GOLDBERG, L. R. (1982). From ace to zombie: Some explorations in the language of personality. In C. Spielberger & J. N. Butcher (Eds.), *Advances in personality assessment: Vol. 1.* Hillsdale, NJ: Erlbaum.

GOLDBERG, L. R. (2001). Analyses of Digman's child-personality data: Derivation of Big-Five factor scores from each of six samples. *Journal of Personality, 69,* 709–743.

GOLDEN, T. (1990, April 2). Ill, possibly violent, and no place to go. *New York Times,* pp. A1, B4.

GOLDFRIED, M. R., & DAVISON, G. C. (EDS.). (1994). *Clinical behavior therapy.* New York: Wiley.

GOLDIN-MEADOW, S. (2000). Learning with and without a helping hand. In B. Landau, J. Sabini, J. Jonides, & E. L. Newport (Eds.), *Perception, cognition, and language: Essays in honor of Henry and Lila Gleitman* (pp. 121–138). Cambridge, MA: MIT Press.

GOLDIN-MEADOW, S., & FELDMAN, H. (1977). The development of language-like communication without a language model. *Science, 197,* 401–403.

GOLDMAN-RAKIC, P. (1987). Development of cortical circuitry and cognitive function. *Child Development, 58,* 601–622.

GOLDMAN-RAKIC, P. (1998). The prefrontal landscape: Implications of functional architecture for understanding human mentation and the central executive. In A. C. Roberts & T. W. Robbins (Eds.), *The prefrontal cortex: Executive and cognitive functions* (pp. 87–102). New York: Oxford University Press.

GOLDSTEIN, E. B. (1989). *Sensation and perception* (3rd ed.). Belmont, CA: Wadsworth.

GOLDSTONE, R. L., LIPPA, Y., & SHIFFRIN, R. M. (2001). Altering object representations through category learning. *Cognition, 78,* 27–43.

GOLOMBOK, S., & TASKER, F. (1996). Do parents influence the sexual orientation of their children? Findings from a longitudinal study of lesbian families. *Developmental Psychology, 32*(1), 3–11.

GOMBRICH, E. H. (1961). *Art and illusion.* Princeton, NJ: Bollingen Series, Princeton University Press.

GOOD, G. E., & SHERROD, N. B. (2001). The psychology of men and masculinity: Research status and future directions. In R. K. Unger (Ed.), *Handbook of the psychology of women and gender* (pp. 201–214). New York: Wiley.

GOODALE, M. A. (1995). The cortical organization of visual perception and visuomotor control. In S. M. Kosslyn & D. Osherson (Eds.), *Visual cognition: An invitation to cognitive science* (2nd ed.). Cambridge, MA: MIT Press.

GOODALE, M. A., & MILNER, A. D. (2004). *Sight unseen.* New York: Oxford University Press.

GOODENOUGH, F. L. (1932). Expression of the emotions in a blind-deaf child. *Journal of Abnormal and Social Psychology, 27,* 328–333.

GOODMAN, G. S., GHETTI, S., QUAS, J. A., EDELSTEIN, R. S., ALEXANDER, K. W., REDLICH, A., D., ET AL. (2003). A prospective study of memory for child sexual abuse: New findings relevant to the repressed-memory controversy. *Psychological Science, 14,* 113–118.

GOODWIN, F. K., & JAMISON, K. R. (1990). *Manic depressive illness.* New York: Oxford University Press.

GOPNIK, A. (1999). Theory of mind. In R. A. Wilson & F. C. Keil (Eds.), *The MIT encyclopedia of the cognitive sciences* (pp. 838–841). Cambridge, MA: MIT Press.

GOPNIK, A., & MELTZOFF A. N. (1997). *Words, thoughts and theories.* Cambridge, MA: MIT Press.

GOPNIK, M., & CRAGO, M. B. (1990). Familial aggregation of a developmental language disorder. *Cognition, 39,* 1–50.

GORDON H. (1923). Mental and scholastic tests among retarded children. *Educational pamphlet,* no. 44. London: Board of Education.

GORDON, P. (2004). The origin of argument structure in infant event representations. In A. Brugos, L. Micciulla, & C. E. Smith (Eds.), *Proceedings of the 28th Annual Boston University Conference on Language Development,* Boston MA: November 2004 (pp. 189–198). Somerville MA: Cascadilla Press.

GORELICK, D. A., & BALSTER, R. L. (1995). Phencyclidine (PCP). In F. E. Bloom & D. J. Kupfer (Eds.), *Psychopharmacology: The fourth generation of progress* (pp. 1767–1776). New York: Raven Press.

GOREN, C. C., SARTY, M., & WU, P. Y. K. (1975). Visual following and pattern discrimination of face-like stimuli by newborn infants. *Pediatrics, 56,* 544–559.

GOSLING, S. D., & JOHN, O. P. (1999). Personality dimensions in nonhuman animals: A cross-species review. *Current Directions in Psychological Science, 8,* 69–75.

GOTTESMAN, I. I. (1991). *Schizophrenia genesis: The origins of madness.* New York: Freeman.

GOTTFREDSON, L. S. (1997). Mainstream science on intelligence: An editorial with 52 signatories, history, and bibliography. *Intelligence, 24,* 13–23.

GOTTFREDSON, L. S. (2004). Intelligence: Is it the epidemiologists' elusive "fundamental cause" of social class inequalities in health? *Journal of Personality and Social Psychology, 86,* 174–199.

GOULD, J. L. (1990). Honey bee cognition. *Cognition, 37,* 83–103.

GOULD, S. J. (1991). Exaptation: A crucial tool for evolutionary psychology. *Journal of Social Issues, 47,* 43–65.

GOULD, S. J., & LEWONTIN, R. C. (1979). The spandrels of San Marco and the Panglossian paradigm: A critique of the adaptationist programme. *Proceedings of the Royal Society of London, 205,* 581–598.

GOULDNER, A. W. (1960). The norm of reciprocity: A preliminary statement. *American Sociological Review, 25,* 161–179.

GRAAF, R. DE, BIJL, R. V., SMIT, F., VOLLEBERGH, W. A. M., & SPIJKER, J. (2002). Risk factors for 12–month comorbidity of mood, anxiety, and substance use disorders: Findings from the Netherlands Mental Health Survey and Incidence Study. *American Journal of Psychiatry, 159,* 620–629.

GRAF, P., & MANDLER, G. (1984). Activation makes words more accessible, but not necessarily more retrievable. *Journal of Verbal Learning and Verbal Behavior, 23,* 553–568.

GRAF, P., MANDLER, G., & HADEN, P. (1982). Simulating amnesic symptoms in normal subjects. *Science, 218,* 1243–1244.

GRAF, P., MANDLER, G., & SQUIRE, L. R. (1984). The information that amnesic patients don't forget. *Journal of Experimental Psychology: Learning, Memory, and Cognition, 10,* 164–178.

GRAHAM, C. H., & HSIA, Y. (1954). Luminosity curves for normal and dichromatic subjects including a case of unilateral color blindness. *Science, 120,* 780.

GRAHAM, P. J. (ED.). (1998). *Cognitive-behaviour therapy for children and families.* New York: Cambridge University Press.

GRAMMER, K., FINK, B., MOLLER, A. P., & MANNING, J. T. (2005). Physical attractiveness and health: Comment on Weeden & Sabini (2005). *Psychological Bulletin, 131,* 658–661.

GRAMMER, K., FINK, B., MOLLER, A., & THORNHILL, R. (2003). Darwinian aesthetics: Sexual selection and the biology of beauty. *Biological Reviews, 78,* 385–407.

GRANT, H. M., BREDAHL, L. C., CLAY, J., FERRIE, J., GROVES, J. E., McDORMAN, T. A., ET AL. (1998). Context-dependent memory for meaningful material: Information for students. *Applied Cognitive Psychology, 12,* 617–623.

GRANT, V. W. (1976). *Falling in love.* New York: Springer.

GRAY, C. M., KOENIG, P., ENGEL, A. K., & SINGER, W. (1989). Oscillatory responses in cat visual cortex exhibit inter-columnar synchronization which reflects global stimulus properties. *Nature, 338*(6213), 334–337.

GRAY, J. A. (1994). Three fundamental emotion systems. In P. Ekman & R. J. Davidson (Eds.), *The nature of emotion: Fundamental questions* (pp. 243–247). New York: Oxford University Press.

GRAY, J. R., CHABRIS, C. F., & BRAVER, T. S. (2003). Neural mechanisms of general fluid intelligence. *Nature Neuroscience, 6,* 316–322.

GREEN, D. M. (1976). *An introduction to hearing.* New York: Academic Press.

GREEN, G. D., & CLUNIS, D. M. (1988). Married lesbians. Lesbianism: Affirming nontraditional roles [Special issue]. *Women and Therapy, 8,* 41–49.

GREEN, M. F., KERN, R. S., BRAFF, D. L., & MINTZ, J. (2000). Neurocognitive deficits and functional outcome in schizophrenia: Are we measuring the "right stuff"? *Schizophrenia Bulletin, 26,* 119–136.

GREEN, R. (1979). Childhood cross-gender behavior and subsequent sexual preference. *American Journal of Psychiatry, 136,* 106–108.

GREEN, R. G. (1998). Aggression and antisocial behavior. In D. T. Gilbert, S. T. Fiske, & G. Lindzey, G. (Eds.), *The handbook of social psycology: Vol. 2* (4th ed., pp. 317–356). New York: McGraw Hill.

GREEN, R. L., HOFFMAN, L. T., MORSE, R., HAYES, M. E. B., & MORGAN, R. F. (1964). *The educational status of children in a district without public schools.* Cooperative Research Project No. 23211. Washington, DC: Office of Education. U.S. Department of Health, Education, and Welfare.

GREEN, S. (1975). Variation of vocal pattern with social situation in the Japanese monkey (Macaca fuscata): A field study. In L. A. Rosenblum (Ed.), *Primate behavior* (pp. 1 –102). New York: Academic Press.

GREEN, S. K., BUCHANAN, D. R., & HEUER, S. K. (1984). Winners, losers, and choosers: A field investigation of dating initiation. *Personality and Social Psychology Bulletin, 10,* 502–511.

GREENBERG, P., SISITSKY, T., KESSLER, R., FINKELSTEIN, S., BERNDT, E., DAVIDSON, J., ET AL. (1999). The economic burden of anxiety disorders in the 1990s. *Journal of Clinical Psychiatry, 60,* 427–435.

GREENE, J., & HAIDT, J. (2003). How (and where) does moral judgment work? *Trends in Cognitive Science, 6,* 517–523.

GREENFIELD, P. M. (1966). On culture and conservation. In J. R. Bruner, R. R. Olver, & P. M. Greenfield (Eds.), *Studies in cognitive growth.* New York: Wiley.

GREENFIELD, P. M. (1997). You can't take it with you: Why ability assessments don't cross cultures. *American Psychologist, 52,* 1115–1124.

GREENFIELD, P. M., KELLER, H., FULIGNI, A., & MAYNARD, A. (2003). Cultural pathways through universal development. *Annual Review of Psychology, 54,* 461–490.

GREENWALD, A., SPANGENBERG, E., PRATKANIS, A., & ESKENAZI, J. (1991). Double-blind tests of subliminal self-help audiotapes. *Psychological Science, 2,* 119–122.

GREENWALD, A. G., & NOSEK, B. A. (2001). Health of the Implicit Association Test at age 3. *Zeitschrift Fuer Experimentelle Psychologie, 48*(2), 85–93.

GREENWALD, A. G., BANAJI, M. R., RUDMAN, L. A., FARNHAM, S. D., NOSEK, B. A., & MELLOTT, D. S. (2002). A unified theory of implicit attitudes, stereotypes, self-esteem, and self-concept. *Psychological Review, 109*(1), 3–25.

GREENWALD, A. G., McGHEE, D. E., & SCHWARTZ, J. L. K. (1998). Measuring individual differences in implicit cognition: The implicit association test. *Journal of Personality and Social Psychology, 74*(6), 1464–1480.

GREENWALD, A. G., NOSEK, B. A., & BANAJI, M. R. (2003). Understanding and using the implicit association test: I. An improved scoring algorithm. *Journal of Personality and Social Psychology, 85,* 197–216.

GREWAL, D., & SALOVEY, P. (2005). Feeling smart: The science of emotional intelligence. *American Scientist, 93,* 330–339.

GRICE, H. P. (1975). Logic and conversation. In P. Cole & J. L. Morgan (Eds.), *Syntax and semantics 3: Speech acts.* New York: Academic Press.

GRIGGS, R. A., & COX, J. R. (1982). The elusive thematic-materials effect in Wason's selection task. *British Journal of Psychology, 73,* 407–420.

GRIMSHAW, J. (1990). *Argument structure.* Cambridge, MA: MIT Press.

GROOP, L. C., & TUOMI, T. (1997). Non-insulin-dependent diabetes mellitus—a collision between thrifty genes and an affluent society. *Annals of Medicine, 29,* 37–53.

GROSS, A. L., & BALLIF, B. (1991). Children's understanding of emotion from facial expressions and situations: A review. *Developmental Review, 11*(4), 368–398.

GROSS, J. J. (1998a). Antecedent- and response-focused emotion regulation: Divergent consequences for experience, expression, and physiology. *Journal of Personality and Social Psychology, 74,* 224–237.

GROSS, J. J. (1998b). The emerging field of emotion regulation: An integrative review. *Review of General Psychology, 2,* 271–299.

GROSS, J. J. (2001). Emotion regulation in adulthood: Timing is everything. *Current Directions in Psychological Science, 10,* 214–219.

GROSS, J. J. (ED.). (2007). *Handbook of emotion regulation*. New York: Guilford Press.

GROSS, J. J., & LEVENSON, R. W. (1997). Hiding feelings: The acute effects of inhibiting negative and positive emotion. *Journal of Abnormal Psychology, 106,* 95–103.

GROSS, J. J., FREDRICKSON, B. F., & LEVENSON, R. W. (1994). The psychophysiology of crying. *Psychophysiology, 31,* 460–468.

GROSS, J. J., RICHARDS, J. M., & JOHN, O. P. (2006). Emotion regulation in everyday life. In D. K. Snyder, J. A. Simpson, & J. N. Hughes (Eds.), *Emotion regulation in families: Pathways to dysfunction and health* (pp. 13–35). Washington, DC: American Psychological Association.

GROTZER, T. A., & PERKINS, D. N. (2000). Teaching intelligence: A performance conception. In R. J. Sternberg (Ed.), *Handbook of intelligence.* Cambridge: Cambridge University Press.

GRUBER-BALDINI, A. L., SCHAIE, K. W., & WILLIS, S. L. (1995). Similarity in married couples: A longitudinal study of mental abilities and rigidity-flexibility. *Journal of Personality and Social Psychology, 69,* 191–203.

GRUDNIK, J. L., & KRANZLER, J. H. (2001). Meta-analysis of the relationship between intelligence and inspection time. *Intelligence, 29,* 523–535.

GRÜNBAUM, A. (1996). Is psychoanalysis viable? In W. O'Donohue & R. F. Kitchener, (Eds.), *The philosophy of psychology* (pp. 281–290). London: Sage.

GUDYKUNST, W. B., YANG, S. M., & NISHIDA, T. (1987). Cultural differences in self-consciousness and self-monitoring. *Communication Research, 14,* 7–34.

GUESBECK, N. R., HICKEY, M. S., MacDONALD, K. G., PORIES, W. J., HARPER, I., RAVUSSIN, E., ET AL. (2001). Substrate utilization during exercise in formerly morbidly obese women. *Journal of Applied Physiology, 90,* 1007–1012.

GURSKY, J. T., & KRAHN, L. E. (2000). The effects of antidepressants on sleep: A review. *Harvard Review of Psychiatry, 8,* 298–306.

GUTH, W., SCHMITTBERGER, R., & SCHWARZE, B. (1982). An experimental analysis of ultimatum bargaining. *Journal of Economic Behavior and Organizations, 3,* 367–388.

GUTTMANN, N., & KALISH, H. I. (1956). Discriminability and stimulus generalization. *Journal of Experimental Psychology, 51,* 79–88.

HACKMANN, A., CLARK, D. M., & McMANUS, F. (2000). Recurrent images and early memories in social phobia. *Behaviour Research and Therapy, 38,* 601–610.

HADDAD, P. (1999). Do antidepressants have any potential to cause addiction? *Journal of Psychopharmacology, 13,* 300–307.

HADLEY, S. W., & STRUPP, H. H. (1976). Contemporary accounts of negative effects in psychotherapy: An integrated account. *Archives of General Psychiatry, 33,* 1291–1302.

HALBERSTADT, J., & RHODES, G. (2000). The attractiveness of nonface averages: Implications for an evolutionary explanation of the attractiveness of average faces. *Psychological Science, 11,* 285–289.

HALL, C. S. (1966). *The meaning of dreams.* New York: McGraw-Hill.

HALL, D. G., QUANTZ, D. H., PERSONAGE, K. A., ET AL. (2000). Preschoolers' use of form class cues in word learning. *Developmental Psychology, 36*(4), 449–462.

HALPERN, D. (1992). *Sex differences in cognitive abilities* (2nd ed.). Hillsdale, NJ: Erlbaum.

HALPERN, D. (2000). *Sex differences in cognitive abilities* (3rd ed.). Mahwah, NJ: Erlbaum.

HAMANN, S. (2001). Cognitive and neural mechanisms of emotional memory. *Trends in Cognitive Sciences, 5,* 394–400.

HAMBRICK, D. Z. (2005). The role of domain knowledge in higher-level cognition. In O. Wilhelm & R. Engle (Eds.), *Handbook of understanding and measuring intelligence* (pp. 361–372). Thousand Oaks, CA: Sage.

HAMBURG, D. A., MOOS, R. H., & YALOM, I. D. (1968). Studies of distress in the menstrual cycle and the postpartum period. In R. P. Michael (Ed.), *Endocrinology and human behavior* (pp. 94–116). London: Oxford University Press.

HAMILL, R., WILSON, T. D., & NISBETT, R. E. (1980). Insensitivity to sample bias: Generalizing from atypical cases. *Journal of Personality and Social Psychology, 39,* 578–589.

HAMILTON, C. (2000). Continuity and discontinuity of attachment from infancy through adolescence. *Child Development, 71,* 690–694.

HAMILTON, D. L., & ROSE, T. L. (1980). Illusory correlation and the maintenance of stereotypic beliefs. *Journal of Personality and Social Psychology, 39,* 832–845.

HANEY, C., & ZIMBARDO, P. (1998). The past and future of U.S. prison policy: Twenty-five years after the Stanford Prison Experiment. *American Psychologist, 53*(7), 709–727.

HANEY, C., BANKS, C., & ZIMBARDO, P. (1973). Interpersonal dynamics in a simulated prison. *International Journal of Criminology and Penology, 1*(1), 69–97.

HANNON, B., & DANEMAN, M. (2001). A new tool for measuring and understanding individual differences in the component processes of reading comprehension. *Journal of Educational Psychology, 93,* 103–128.

HAPPÉ, F., BROWNELL, H., & WINNER, E. (1999). Acquired "theory of mind" impairments following stroke. *Cognition, 70,* 211–240.

HARE, R. D., COOKE, D. J., & HART, S. D. (1999). Psychopathy and sadistic personality disorder. In T. B. P. Millon (Ed.), *Oxford textbook of psychopathology* (pp. 555–584). Oxford, England: Oxford University Press.

HAREVEN, T. K. (1978). The last stage: Historical adulthood and old age. In E. H. Erikson (Ed.), *Adulthood* (pp. 201–216). New York: Norton.

HARKINS, S. G., & SZYMANSKI, K. (1989). Social loafing and group evaluation. *Journal of Personality and Social Psychology, 56*(6), 934–941.

HARLEY, T. A., & BOWN, H. E. (1998). What causes a tip-of-the-tongue state? Evidence for lexical neighbourhood effects in speech production. *British Journal of Psychology, 89,* 151–174.

HARLOW, H. F. (1958). The nature of love. *American Psychologist, 13,* 673–685.

HARLOW, H. F. (1962). The heterosexual affectional system in monkeys. *American Psychologist, 17,* 1–9.

HARLOW, H. F., & HARLOW, M. K. (1972). The young monkeys. In *Readings in psychology today* (2nd ed.). Del Mar, CA: CRM Books.

HARLOW, H. F., & NOVAK, M. A. (1973). Psychopathological perspectives. *Perspectives in Biology and Medicine, 16,* 461–478.

HARMON-JONES, E., & MILLS, J. (1999). *Cognitive dissonance: Progress on a pivotal theory in social psychology.* Washington, DC: American Psychological Association.

HARRIS, C. R. (2002). Sexual and romantic jealousy in heterosexual and homosexual adults. *Psychological Science, 13,* 7–12.

HARRIS, G. W., & MICHAEL, R. P. (1964). The activation of sexual behavior by hypothalamic implants of estrogen. *Journal of Physiology, 171,* 275–301.

HARRIS, J. R. (1995). Where is the child's environment? A group socialization theory of development. *Psychological Review, 102,* 458–489.

HARRIS, J. R. (1998). *The nurture assumption: Why children turn out the way they do.* New York: Free Press.

HARRIS, J. R. (2000). Socialization, personality development and the child's environments: A comment on Vandell (2000). *Developmental Psychology, 36,* 711–723.

HARRIS, M. J., & ROSENTHAL, R. (1985). Mediation of interpersonal expectancy effects: 31 meta-analyses. *Psychological Bulletin, 97,* 363–386.

HARRIS, P. (1989). *Children and emotion.* Oxford: Blackwell.

HARRIS, P., GUZ, G., LIPIAN, M., & MAN-SHU, Z. (1985). Insight into the time course of emotion among Western and Chinese children. *Child Development, 56,* 972–988.

HARRIS, P. L. (1987). The development of search. In P. Salapatek & L. Cohen (Eds.), *Handbook of infant perception* (pp. 155–208). New York: Academic Press.

HARRIS, Z. (1951). *Methods in structural linguistics.* Chicago: Chicago University Press.

HART, C., NEWELL, L., & OLSEN, S. (2003). Parenting skills and social-communicative competence in childhood. In J.Green & B. Burleson (Eds.), *Handbook of communication and social interaction skills* (pp. 753–800). Mahwah, NJ: Erlbaum.

HART, D., & CHMIEL, S. (1992). Influence of defense mechanisms on moral judgment development: A longitudinal study. *Developmental Psychology, 28*(4), 722–730.

HART, D., & FEGLEY, S. (1995). Prosocial behavior and caring in adolescence: Relations to self-understanding and social judgment. *Child Development, 66*(5), 1346–1359.

HART, D., LUCCA-IRIZARRY, N., & DAMON, W. (1986). The development of self-understanding in Puerto Rico and the United States. *Journal of Early Adolescence, 6*, 293–304.

HARTER, S. (1990). Causes, correlates and the functional role of global self-worth: A life span perspective. In R. J. Sternberg & J. Kolligan (Eds.), *Competence considered* (pp. 67–97). New Haven, CT: Yale University Press.

HARTMANN, H. (1964). *Essays on ego psychology: Selected problems in psychoanalytic theory.* New York: International Universities Press.

HARTRUP, W. (1996). The company they keep: Friendships and their developmental significance. *Child Development, 67*, 1–13.

HARTSHORNE, H., & MAY, M. A. (1928). *Studies in the nature of character: Vol. 1.* New York: Macmillan.

HARVEY, L. O., JR., & LEIBOWITZ, H. (1967). Effects of exposure duration, cue reduction, and temporary monocularity on size matching at short distances. *Journal of the Optical Society of America, 57*, 249–253.

HASSELMO, M. E. (1999). Neuromodulation: Acetylcholine and memory consolidation. *Trends in Cognitive Science, 6*, 351–359.

HATFIELD, E. (1988). Passionate and companionate love. In R. J. Sternberg & M. L. Barnes (Eds.), *The psychology of love.* New Haven, CT: Yale University Press.

HAUSER, M. (1996). *The evolution of commmunication.* Cambridge, MA: MIT Press.

HAY, P., SACHDEV, P., CUMMING, S., SMITH, J. S., LEE, T., KITCHENER, P., ET AL. (1993). Treatment of obsessive-compulsive disorder by psychosurgery. *Acta Psychiatrica Scandinavica, 87*, 197–207.

HAYES, J. (1985). Three problems in teaching general skills. In S. Chipman, J. Segal, & R. Glaser (Eds.), *Thinking and learning skills* (pp. 391–406). Hillsdale, NJ: Erlbaum.

HAYWARD, W. G., & TARR, M. J. (1995). Spatial language and spatial representation. *Cognition, 55*, 39–84.

HEALY, A. F., & MILLER, G. A. (1970). The verb as the main determinant of sentence meaning. *Psychonomic Science, 20*, 372.

HECKERS S. (1997). Neuropathology of schizophrenia: Cortex, thalamus, basal ganglia, and neurotransmitter-specific projection systems. *Schizophrenia Bulletin, 23*, 403–421.

HEDGES, L. V., & NOWELL, A. (1995). Sex differences in mental test scores, variability, and numbers of high-scoring individuals. *Science, 269*, 41–45.

HEIDER, E. R. (1972). Universals in color naming and memory. *Journal of Experimental Psychology, 93*, 1–20.

HEIDER, F. (1958). *The psychology of interpersonal relationships.* New York: Wiley.

HEIM, C., OWENS, M. J., PLOTSKY, P. M., & NEMEROFF, C. B. (1997). Endocrine factors in the pathophysiology of mental disorders. *Psychopharmacology Bulletin, 33*, 185–192.

HEINE, S. J. (2005). Constructing good selves in Japan and North America. In R. M. Sorrentino, M. Richard, D. Cohen, J. M. Olson, & M. P. Zanna (Eds.), *Culture and social behavior: The Tenth Ontario Symposium* (pp. 115–143). Hillsdale, NJ: Erlbaum.

HEINE, S. J., & LEHMAN, D. R. (1997). The cultural construction of self-enhancement: An examination of group-serving biases. *Journal of Personality and Social Psychology, 72*, 1268–1283.

HELD, J. D., ALDERTON, D. L., FOLEY, P. P., & SEGALL, D. O. (1993). Arithmetic reasoning gender differences: Explanations found in the Armed Services Vocational Aptitude Battery (ASVAB). *Learning and Individual Differences, 5*, 171–186.

HELMHOLTZ, H. (1909). *Wissenschaftliche Abhandlungen, II* (pp. 764–843). Leipzig: Barth.

HEMPHILL, J. F., HARE, R. D., & WONG, S. (1998). Psychopathy and recidivism: A review. *Legal and Criminological Psychology, 3*, 139–170.

HENDERLONG, J., & LEPPER, M. R. (2002). The effects of praise on children's intrinsic motivation: A review and synthesis. *Psychological Bulletin, 128*(5), 774–795.

HENDRY, D. P. (ED.). (1969). *Conditioned reinforcement.* Homeward, IL: Dorsey Press.

HENRY, P. J., STERNBERG, R. J., & GRIGORENKO, E. (2005). Capturing successful intelligence through measures of analytic, creative, and practical skills. In O. Wilhelm & R. Engle (Eds.), *Understanding and measuring intelligence* (pp. 295–311). Thousand Oaks, CA: Sage.

HENSS, R. (2000). Waist-to-hip ratio and female attractiveness. Evidence from photographic stimuli and methodological considerations. *Personality and Individual Differences, 28*, 501–513.

HERBERT, A., GERRY, N. P., McQUEEN, M.HEID, I. M., PFEUFER, A., ILLIG, T., ET AL. (2006). A common genetic variant is associated with adult and childhood obesity. *Science 312*, 279–283.

HERDT, G., & McCLINTOCK, M. (2000). The magical age of 10. *Archives of Sexual Behavior, 29*(6), 587–606.

HERMAN, L., & UYEYAMA, R. (1999). The dolphin's grammatical competency: Comments on Kako (1999). *Animal Learning & Behavior, 27*, 18–23.

HERMANN, D., & YODER, C. (1998). The potential effects of the implanted memory paradigm on child subjects. *Applied Cognitive Psychology, 12*(3), 198–206.

HERR, S. S. (1990). The law on aversive and nonaversive behavioral intervention. In S. L. Harris & J. S. Handleman (Eds.), *Aversive and nonaversive interventions: Controlling life-threatening behavior by the developmentally disabled* (pp. 80–118). New York: Springer.

HERRNSTEIN, R. J. (1979). Acquisition, generalization, and discrimination reversal of a natural concept. *Journal of Experimental Psychology: Animal Behavior Processes, 5*, 118–129.

HERRNSTEIN, R. J., & MURRAY, C. A. (1994). *The bell curve: Intelligence and class structure in American life.* Cambridge, MA: Free Press.

HERRNSTEIN, R. J., LOVELAND, D. H., & CABLE, C. (1976). Natural concepts in pigeons. *Journal of Experimental Psychology: Animal Behavior Processes, 2*, 285–311.

HERRNSTEIN, R. J., NICKERSON, R. S., DE SANCHEZ, M., & SWETS, J. A. (1986). Teaching thinking skills. *American Psychologist, 41*, 1279–1289.

HESPOS, S. J., & BAILLARGEON, R. (2001a). Infants' knowledge about occlusion and containment events: A surprising discrepancy. *Psychological Science, 12*, 141–147.

HESPOS, S. J., & BAILLARGEON, R. (2001b). Reasoning about containment events in very young infants. *Cognition, 78*, 207–245.

HESS, E. H. (1959). Imprinting. *Science, 130*, 133–141.

HESS, E. H. (1973). *Imprinting: Early experience and the developmental psychobiology of attachment.* New York: Van Nostrand.

HETHERINGTON, E. M., BRIDGES, M., & INSABELLA, G. M. (1998). What matters? What does not? Five perspectives on the association between marital transitions and children's adjustment. *American Psychologist, 53*(2), 167–184.

HEWSTONE, M., RUBIN, M., & WILLIS, H. (2002). Intergroup bias. *Annual Review of Psychology, 53*, 575–604.

HIER, D. B., & CROWLEY, W. F. (1982). Spatial ability in androgen-deficient men. *New England Journal of Medicine, 306*, 1202–1205.

HIGBEE, K. L. (1977). *Your memory: How it works and how to improve it.* Englewood Cliffs, NJ: Prentice-Hall.

HIGGINS, E. T. (1997). Beyond pleasure and pain. *American Psychologist, 52,* 1280–1300.

HIGGINS, J., WILLIAMS, R., & McLAUGHLIN, T. (2001). The effects of a token economy employing instructional consequences for a third-grade student with learning disabilities: A data-based cast study. *Education and Treatment of Children, 24,* 99–106.

HIGGINS, R., SNYDER, C. R., & BERGLAS, S. (EDS.). (1990). *Self-handicapping: The paradox that isn't.* New York: Plenum Press.

HILGARD, E. R. (1986). *Divided consciousness: Multiple controls in human thought and action* (rev. ed.). New York: Wiley.

HILL, A. L. (1978). Savants: Mentally retarded individuals with specific skills. In N. R. Ellis (Ed.), *International review of research in mental retardation: Vol. 9.* New York: Academic Press.

HILL, C. T., RUBIN, L., & PEPLAU, L. A. (1976). Breakups before marriage: The end of 103 affairs. *Journal of Social Issues, 32,* 147–168.

HILTS, P. J. (1995). *Memory's ghost: The strange tale of Mr. M and the nature of memory.* New York: Simon and Schuster.

HINELINE, P. N., & RACHLIN, H. (1969). Escape and avoidance of shock by pigeons pecking a key. *Journal of the Experimental Analysis of Behavior, 12,* 533–538.

HINES, M. (1990). Gonadal hormones and human cognitive development. In J. Balthazar, (Ed.), *Hormones, brains, and behaviors in vertebrates 1. Sexual differentiation neuroanatomical aspects, neurotransmitters, and neuropeptides l.* Basel: Karger.

HINES, M. (2004). Androgen, estrogen, and gender: Contributions of the early hormone environment to gender-related behavior. In A. Eagly, A. Beall, & R. J. Sternberg (Eds), *The psychology of gender* (2nd ed., pp. 9–37). New York: Guilford Press.

HINES, M., BROOK, C., & CONWAY, G. (2004). Psychosexual development: Core gender identity, sexual orientation and recalled childhood gender role behavior in women and men with congenital adrenal hyperplasia (CAH). *Journal of Sex Research, 1,* 75–81.

HINTZMAN, D. L. (1990). Human learning and memory: Connections and dissociations. *Annual Review of Psychology, 41,* 109–139.

HIRSCHFELD, R. M. A., & GOODWIN, F. K. (1988). Mood disorders. In J. A. Talbott, R. E. Hales, & S. C. Yudofsky (Eds.), *The American Psychiatric Press textbook of psychiatry: Vol. 7.* Washington, DC: American Psychiatric Press.

HIRSH-PASEK, K., & GOLINKOFF, R. (1996). *The origins of grammar: Evidence from early language comprehension.* Cambridge, MA: MIT Press.

HIRSH-PASEK, K., GOLINKOFF, R., FLETCHER, A., DEGASPE-BEAUBIEN, F., & CAULEY, K. (1985, October). In the beginning: One-word speakers comprehend word order. Paper presented at Boston Child Language Conference, Boston, MA.

HODGES, E. V. E., MALONE, M. J., & PERRY, D. G. (1997). Individual risk and social risk as interacting determinants of victimization in the peer group. *Developmental Psychology, 33*(6), 1032–1039.

HOEBEL, B. G., & TEITELBAUM, P. (1976). Weight regulation in normal and hyperphagic rats. *Journal of Physiological and Comparative Psychology, 61,* 189–193.

HOFF-GINSBERG, E., & TARDIF, T. (1995). Socioeconomic status and parenting. In M. H. Bornstein (Ed.), *Handbook of parenting: Vol. 2. Biology and ecology of parenting* (pp. 161–188). Hillsdale, NJ: Erlbaum.

HOFFMAN, M. (2000). *Empathy and moral development: Implications for caring and justice.* New York: Cambridge University Press.

HOFFMAN, M. L. (1970). Moral development. In P. H. Mussen (Ed.), *Carmichael's manual of child psychology* (3rd. ed., vol. 2, pp. 457–558). New York: Wiley.

HOFFMAN, M. L. (1977a). Empathy, its development and prosocial implications. In C. B. Keasey (Ed.), *Nebraska Symposium on Motivation, 25,* 169–217.

HOFFMAN, M. L. (1977b). Sex differences in empathy and related behaviors. *Psychological Bulletin, 84,* 712–722.

HOFFMAN, M. L. (1979). Development of moral thought, feeling, and behavior. *American Psychologist, 34,* 295–318.

HOFFMAN, M. L. (1984). Empathy, its limitations, and its role in a comprehensive moral theory. In W. M. Kurtines & L. Gewirtz (Eds.), *Morality, moral behavior, and moral development* (pp. 283–302). New York: Wiley.

HOFSTEDE, G. (2001). *Culture's consequences: Comparing values, behaviors, institutions, and organizations across nations* (2nd ed.). Thousand Oaks, CA: Sage.

HOFSTEDE, G., & McCRAE, R. R. (2004). Personality and culture revisited: Linking traits and dimensions of culture. *Cross-Cultural Research: The Journal of Comparative Social Science, 38*(1), 52–88.

HOLDEN, C. (2003). Psychiatric drugs: Excited by glutamate. *Science, 300,* 1866–1868.

HOLLAND, J. H., HOLYOAK, K. F., NISBETT, R. E., & THAGARD, P. R. (1986). *Induction.* Cambridge, MA: MIT Press.

HOLLAND, P. (1984). Origins of behavior in Pavlovian conditioning. *Psychology of Learning and Motivation, 18,* 129–174.

HOLLANDER, E., & McCARLEY, A. (1992). Yohimbine treatment of sexual side effects induced by serotonin reuptake blockers. *Journal of Clinical Psychiatry, 53,* 197–199.

HOLLANDER, E. P. (1985.) Leadership and power. In G. Lindzey & E. Aronson (Eds.), *Handbook of social psychology: Vol 2* (3rd ed.). New York: Random House.

HOLLINGSHEAD, A. B., & REDLICH, F. C. (1958). *Social class and mental illness: A community study.* New York: Wiley.

HOLLIS, K. L. (1984). The biological function of Pavlovian conditioning: The best defense is a good offense. *Journal of Experimental Psychology: Animal Learning and Behavior, 10,* 413–425.

HOLLISTER, L. E., & CSERNANSKY, J. G. (1990). *Clinical pharmacology of psychotherapeutic drugs* (3rd. ed.). New York: Churchill-Livingstone.

HOLLON, S. D., & BECK, A. T. (2004). Cognitive and cognitive behavioral therapies. In M. J. Lambert (Ed.), *Garfield and Bergin's handbook of psychotherapy and behavior change: An empirical analysis* (5th ed., pp. 447–492). New York: Wiley.

HOLLON, S. D., & BECK, A. T. (IN PRESS).

HOLLON, S. D., & FAWCETT, J. (1995). Combined medication and psychotherapy. In G. O. Gabbard (Ed.), *Treatments of psychiatric disorders, Vol. 1* (2nd ed., pp. 1221–1236). Washington, DC: American Psychiatric Press.

HOLLON, S. D., STEWART, M. O., & STRUNK, D. (2006). Enduring effects for cognitive behavior therapy in the treatment of depression and anxiety. *Annual Review of Psychology, 57,* 285–315.

HOLLON, S. D., THASE, M. E., & MARKOWITZ, J. C. (2002). Treatment and prevention of depression. *Psychological Science in the Public Interest, 3,* 39–77.

HOLLOS, M., & RICHARDS, F. A. (1993). Gender-associated development of formal operations in Nigerian adolescents. *Ethos, 21*(1), 24–52.

HOLM, K. H., CICCHETTI, F., BJÖRKLUND, L., BOONMAN, Z., TANDON, P., COSTANTINI, L. C., ET AL. (2001). Enhanced axonal growth from fetal human bcl-2 transgenic mouse dopamine neurons transplanted to the adult rat striatum. *Neuroscience 104,* 397–405.

HOLMES, D. (1990). The evidence for repression: An examination of sixty years of research. In J. Singer (Ed.), *Repression and dissociation: Implications for personality theory, psychopathology, and health* (pp. 85–102). Chicago: University of Chicago Press.

HOLTZMAN, P. S., KRINGLEN, E., MALTHYSSE, S., FLANAGAN, S. D., LIPTON, R. B., CRAMER, G., ET AL. (1988). A single dominant gene can account for eye tracking dysfunctions and schizophrenia in offspring of discordant twins. *Archives of General Psychiatry, 45,* 641–647.

HOLWAY, A. F., & BORING, E. G. (1947). Determinants of apparent visual size with distance variant. *American Journal of Psychology, 54,* 21–37.

HÖNEKOPP, J. (2006). Once more: Is beauty in the eye of the beholder? Relative contributions of private and shared taste to judgments of facial attractiveness. *Journal of Experimental Psychology: Human Perception and Performance, 32,* 199–209.

Hong, Y.-y., Chiu, C. Y., & Dweck, C. S. (1997). Lay dispositionism and implicit theories of personality. *Journal of Personality and Social Psychology, 73,* 19–30.

Hong, Y.-y., Chiu, C. Y., Dweck, C. S., & Sacks, R. (1997). Implicit theories and evaluative processes in person cognition. *Journal of Experimental Social Psychology, 33,* 296–323.

Hook, S. (1955). *The hero in history.* Boston: Beacon Press.

Hooley, J. (2004). Do psychiatric patients do better clinically if they live with certain kinds of families? *Current Directions in Psychological Science, 13,* 202–205.

Hooley, J. M. (1985). Expressed emotion: A review of the critical literature. *Clinical Psychology Review, 5,* 119–139.

Horn, J. L. (1985). Remodeling old models of intelligence. In B. B. Wolman (Ed.), *Handbook of intelligence: Theories, measurements, and applications* (pp. 267–300). New York: Wiley.

Horn, J. L., & Noll, J. (1994). A system for understanding cognitive capabilities: A theory and the evidence on which it is based. In D. K. Detterman (Ed.), *Current topics in human intelligence: Vol. 4. Theories of intelligence.* Norwood, NJ: Ablex.

Horvath, A. O., & Luborsky, L. (1993). The role of the therapeutic alliance in psychotherapy. *Journal of Consulting and Clinical Psychology, 61,* 561–573.

Hoshino-Browne, E., Zanna, A. S., Spencer, S. J., & Zanna, M. P. (2004). Investigating attitudes cross-culturally: A case of cognitive dissonance among East Asians and North Americans. In G. R. Maio & G. Haddock (Eds.), *Contemporary perspectives on the psychology of attitudes: The Cardiff Symposium.* East Sussex, England: Psychology Press.

Hosken, D. J. (2001). Size and fluctuating asymmetry in sexually selected traits. *Animal Behaviour, 62,* 603–605.

Hovland, C. I., & Weiss, W. (1952). The influence of source credibility on communication effectiveness. *Public Opinion Quarterly, 15,* 635–650.

Howard, K. I., Krause, M. S., Saunders, S. M., & Kopta, S. M. (1997). Trials and tribulations in the meta-analysis of treatment differences: Comments on Wampold et al. (1997). *Psychological Bulletin, 122,* 221–225.

Howes, C. (1990). Can the age of entry into child care and the quality of child care predict adjustment in kindergarten? *Developmental Psychology, 26,* 292–303.

Howes, C. (1996). The earliest friendships. In W. Bukowsi, A. Newcomb, & W. Hartup, W. (Eds.), *The company they keep: Friendships in childhood and adolescence* (pp. 66–86). New York: Cambridge University Press.

Hrdy, S. B., & Williams, G. C. (1983). Behavioral biology and the double standard. In S. K. Wasser (Ed.), *The social behavior of female vertebrates* (pp. 3–17). New York: Academic Press.

Hrobjartsson, A., & Gotzsche, P. C. (2001). Is the placebo powerless? An analysis of clinical trials comparing placebo with no treatment. *New England Journal of Medicine, 344,* 1594–1602.

Huang, M. P., & Alessi, N. E. (1996). The Internet and the future of psychiatry. *American Journal of Psychiatry, 153,* 861–869.

Hubel, D. H., & Wiesel, T. N. (1959). Receptive fields of single neurons in the cat's visual cortex. *Journal of Physiology, 148,* 574–591.

Hubel, D. H., & Wiesel, T. N. (1968). Receptive fields and functional architecture of monkey striate cortex. *Journal of Physiology, 195,* 215–243.

Hudspeth, A. J. (1989). How the ear's works work. *Nature, 341,* 397–404.

Huesmann, L. R., & Miller, L. S. (1994). Long-term effects of repeated exposure to media violence in childhood. In L. R. Huesmann (Ed.), *Aggressive behavior: Current perspectives.* New York: Plenum.

Huesmann, L. R., Lagerspetz, K., & Eron, L. D. (1984). Intervening variables in the TV violence-aggression relation: Evidence from two countries. *Developmental Psychobiology, 20,* 1120–1134.

Hughes, C., & Cutting, A. L. (1999). Nature, nurture, and individual differences in early understanding of mind. *Psychological Science, 10*(5), 429–432.

Hughes, C., & Dunn, J. (1998). Understanding mind and emotion: Longitudinal associations with mental-state talk between young friends. *Developmental Psychology, 34,* 1026–1037.

Hughes, J., Smith, T. W., Kosterlitz, H., Fothergill, L., Morgan, B., & Morris, H. (1975). Identification of two related pentapeptides from the brain with potent opiate agonist activity. *Nature, 258,* 577–579.

Huguet, P., Galvaing, M. P., Monteil, J. M., & Dumas, F. (1999). Social presence effects in the Stroop task: Further evidence for an attentional view of social facilitation. *Personality and Social Psychology, 77*(5), 1011–1025.

Hume, D. (1739/1978). *A treatise on human nature.* Oxford: Clarendon.

Hunsley, J., & Bailey, J. M. (1999). The clinical utility of the Rorschach: Unfulfilled promises and an uncertain future. *Psychological Assessment, 11,* 266–277.

Hunt, E. (1976). Varieties of cognitive power. In L. B. Resnick (Ed.), *The nature of intelligence.* Hillsdale, NJ: Erlbaum.

Hunt, E. (1985a). The correlates of intelligence. In D. K. Detterman (Ed.), *Current topics in human intelligence: Vol. 1.* Norwood, NJ: Ablex.

Hunt, E. (1985b). Verbal ability. In R. J. Sternberg (Ed.), *Human abilities: An information processing approach* (pp. 31–58). New York: Freeman.

Hunt, E. (1995). *Will we be smart enough? A cognitive analysis of the coming workforce.* New York: Russell Sage Foundation.

Hunt, P. J., & Hillery, J. M. (1973). Social facilitation in a coaction setting: An examination of the effects over learning trials. *Journal of Experimental Social Psychology, 9,* 563–571.

Hurley, R. A., Black, D. N., Stip, E., & Taber, K. H. (2000). Surgical treatment of mental illness: Impact of imaging. *Journal of Neuropsychiatry and Clinical Neuroscience, 12,* 421–424.

Hurvich, L. M. (1981). *Color vision.* Sunderland, MA: Sinauer Assoc.

Hurvich, L. M., & Jameson, D. (1957). An opponent-process theory of color vision. *Psychological Review, 64,* 384–404.

Huston, T. L., Ruggiero, M., Conner, R., & Geis, G. (1981). Bystander intervention into crime: A study based on naturally occurring episodes. *Social Psychology Quarterly, 44,* 14–23.

Hutchinson, R. R., & Renfrew, J. W. (1966). Stalking attack and eating behaviors elicited from the same sites in the hypothalamus. *Journal of Comparative and Physiological Psychology, 61,* 360–367.

Huttenlocher, J. (1974). The origins of language comprehension. In R. L. Solso (Ed.), *Theories in cognitive psychology: The Loyola symposium* (pp. 331–368). Potomac, MD: Erlbaum.

Huttenlocher, J., Smiley, P., & Charney, R. (1983). Emergence of action categories in the child: Evidence from verb meanings. *Psychological Review, 90,* 72–93.

Huttenlocher, P. R. (1979). Synaptic density in human frontal cortex—developmental changes and effects of aging. *Brain Research, 163,* 195–205.

Hyde, D. M. (1959). An investigation of Piaget's theories of the development of the concept of number. Unpublished doctoral dissertation, University of London. Quoted in J. H. Flavell (Ed.), (1963). *The developmental psychology of Jean Piaget* (p. 383). New York: Van Nostrand Reinhold.

Hyde, J. S. (2005). The gender similarities hypothesis. *American Psychologist, 60,* 581–592.

Hyman, I., & Billings, F. J. (1998). Individual differences and the creation of false childhood memories. *Memory, 6,* 1–20.

Hyman, I., Husband, T., & Billings, F. (1995). False memories of childhood experiences. *Applied Cognitive Psychology, 9,* 181–198.

Hyman, S. E., & Fenton, W. S. (2003). What are the right targets for psychopharmacology? *Science, 299,* 350–351.

Hymel, S., Bowker, A., & Woody, E. (1993). Aggressive versus withdrawn unpopular children: Variations in peer and self-perceptions in multiple domains. *Child Development, 64*(3), 879–896.

INAGAKI, K., & HATANO, G. (2004). Vitalistic causality in young children's naive biology. *Trends in Cognitive Science, 8,* 356–362.

INTERNATIONAL HUMAN GENOME SEQUENCING COSORTIUM (IHGSC) (2001). Initial sequencing and analysis of the human genome. *Nature, 409,* 860–921.

IRVINE, J. T. (1978). Wolof "magical thinking": Culture and conservation revisited. *Journal of Crosscultural Psychology, 9,* 300–310.

ISACSON, O. (1999). The neurobiology and neurogenetics of stem cells. *Brain Pathology, 9,* 495–498.

ISHA, A., & SAGI, D. (1995). Common mechanisms of visual imagery and perception. *Science, 268,* 1772–1774.

IVY, G. O., MACLEOD, C. M., PETIT, T. L., & MARKUS, E. J. (1992). A physiological framework for perceptual and cognitive changes in aging. In F. I. M. Craik & T. A. Salthouse (Eds.), *The handbook of aging and cognition.* Hillsdale, NJ: Erlbaum.

IZARD, C. E. (1971). *The face of emotion.* New York: Appleton-Century-Crofts.

IZARD, C. E. (1977). *Human emotions.* New York: Plenum.

IZARD, C. E. (1994). Innate and universal facial expressions: Evidence from developmental cross-cultural research. *Psychological Bulletin, 115,* 288–299.

IZARD, C., FANTAUZZO, C., CASTLE, J., HAYNES, O., RAYIAS, M., & PUTNAM, P. (1995). The ontogeny and significance of infants' facial expressions in the first 9 months of life. *Developmental Psychology, 31,* 997–1013.

JABLENSKY, A., & COLE, S.W. (1997). Is the earlier age at onset of schizophrenia in males a confounded finding? *British Journal of Psychiatry, 170,* 234–240.

JACKENDOFF, R. (2002). *Foundations of language: Brain, meaning, grammar, evolution.* Oxford: Oxford University Press.

JACKSON, L. A., HUNTER, J. E., & HODGE, C. N. (1995). Physical attractiveness and intellectual competence: A meta-analytic review. *Social Psychology Quarterly, 58,* 108–122.

JACOBS, A. (1955). Formation of new associations to words selected on the basis of reaction-time-GSR combinations. *Journal of Abnormal and Social Psychology, 51,* 371–377.

JACOBS, B. L. (2004). Depression: The brain finally gets into the act. *Current Directions in Psychological Science, 13,* 103–106.

JACOBSEN, F. M. (1992). Fluoxetine-induced sexual dysfunction and an open trial of yohimbine. *Journal of Clinical Psychiatry, 53,* 119–122.

JACOBSEN, L. K., GIEDD, J. N., BERQUIN, P. C., KRAIN, A. L., HAMBURGER, S. D., KUMRA, S., ET AL. (1997). Quantitative morphology of the cerebellum and fourth ventricle in childhood-onset schizophrenia. *American Journal of Psychiatry, 154,* 1663–1669.

JACOBY, L. L. (1983). Perceptual enhancement: Persistent effects of an experience. *Journal of Experimental Psychology: Learning, Memory and Cognition, 9,* 21–38.

JACOBY, L. L., & DALLAS, M. (1981). On the relationship between autobiographical memory and perceptual learning. *Journal of Experimental Psychology: General, 3,* 306–340.

JACOBY, L. L., & WITHERSPOON, D. (1982). Remembering without awareness. *Canadian Journal of Psychology, 36,* 300–324.

JAMES, L. E., & BURKE, D. M. (2000). Phonological priming effects on word retrieval and tip-of-the-tongue experiences in young and older adults. *Journal of Experimental Psychology: Learning, Memory and Cognition, 26,* 1378–1391.

JAMES, W. (1890). *Principles of psychology.* New York: Henry Holt.

JAMISON, K. R. (1995). Manic-depressive illness and creativity. *Scientific American, 272,* 62–67.

JANG, K. L., LIVESLEY, W. J., & VERNON, P. A. (1996). Heritability of the big five personality dimensions and their facets: A twin study. *Journal of Personality, 64,* 577–591.

JANG, K. L., PARIS, J., ZWEIG-FRANK, H., & LIVESLEY, W. J. (1998). Twin study of dissociative experience. *Journal of Nervous and Mental Disease, 186,* 345–351.

JANICAK, P. G., DAVIS, J. M., GIBBONS, R. D., ERICKSEN, S., CHANG, S., & GALLAGHER, P. (1985). Efficacy of ECT: A meta-analysis. *American Journal of Psychiatry, 142,* 297–302.

JANIS, I. (1971). Groupthink. *Psychology Today, 5,* 43–76.

JANIS, I. (1982). *Groupthink: Psychological studies of policy decisions and fiascoes* (2nd ed.). Boston: Houghton Mifflin.

JANKOWIAK, W. R., & FISCHER, E. F. (1992). A cross-cultural perspective on romantic love. *Ethnology, 31,* 149–155.

JANOWSKY, J. S., OVIATT, S. K., & ORWOLL, E. S. (1994). Testosterone influences spatial cognition in older men. *Behavioral Neuroscience, 108,* 325–332.

JAVITT, D. C., & COYLE, J. T. (2004, January). Decoding schizophrenia. *Scientific American, 290,* 48–55.

JENIKE, M. A. (2001). An update on obsessive-compulsive disorder. *Bulletin of the Menninger Clinic, 65,* 4–25.

JENKINS, J. G., & DALLENBACH, K. M. (1924). Oblivescence during sleep and waking. *American Journal of Psychology, 35,* 605–612.

JENNINGS, E. E. (1972). *An anatomy of leadership: Princes, heroes, and supermen.* New York: McGraw-Hill.

JENSEN, A. R. (1985). The nature of the black-white difference on various psychometric tests: Spearman's hypothesis. *Behavioral and Brain Sciences, 8,* 193–263.

JENSEN, A. R. (1987). Individual differences in the Hick paradigm. In P. A. Vernon (Ed.), *Speed of information processing and intelligence.* Norwood, NJ: Ablex.

JETTEN, J., POSTMES, T., & MCAULIFFE, B. J. (2002). "We're all individuals": Group norms of individualism and collectivism, levels of identification and identity threat. *European Journal of Social Psychology, 32*(2), 189–207.

JOBE, J., TOURANGEAU, R., & SMITH, A. (1993). Contributions of survey research to the understanding of memory. *Applied Cognitive Psychology, 7,* 567–584.

JOCKIN, V., MCGUE, M., & LYKKEN, D. T. (1996). Personality and divorce: A genetic analysis. *Journal of Personality and Social Psychology, 71,* 288–299.

JOHN, O. P. (1990). The "Big Five" taxonomy: Dimensions of personality in the natural language and in questionnaires. In L. A. Pervin (Ed.), *Handbook of personality: Theory and research* (pp. 676–1000). New York: Guilford Press.

JOHN, O. P., DONAHUE, E. M., & KENTLE, R. L. (1991). *The Big Five Inventory—Versions 4a and 54.* Berkeley: University of California, Berkeley, Institute of Personality and Social Research.

JOHN, O. P., & SRIVASTAVA, S. (1999). The Big Five trait taxonomy: History, measurement, and theoretical perspectives. In L. A. Pervin & O. P. John (Eds.), *Handbook of personality: Theory and research* (2nd ed., pp. 139–153). New York: Guilford.

JOHNS, M., SCHMADER, T., & MARTENS, A. (2005). Knowing is half the battle: Teaching stereotype threat as a means of improving women's math performance. *Psychological Science, 16,* 175–179.

JOHNSON, A. M., WADSWORTH, J., WELLINGS, K., BRADSHAW, S., & FIELD, J. (1992). Sexual lifestyles and HIV risk. *Nature, 360,* 410–412.

JOHNSON, J., & NEWPORT, E. (1989). Critical period efforts in second-language learning: The influence of maturational state on the acquisition of English as a second language. *Cognitive Psychology, 21,* 60–99.

JOHNSON, M. H. (1993). Cortical maturation and the development of visual attention in early infancy. In M. H. Johnson (Ed.), *Brain development and cognition.* Cambridge, MA: Blackwell.

JOHNSON, R. D., & DOWNING, L. L. (1979). Deindividuation and valence of cues: Effects on prosocial and antisocial behavior. *Journal of Personality and Social Psychology, 37*(9), 1532–1538.

JOHNSON, R. E. (1979). *Juvenile delinquency and its origins.* New York: Cambridge University Press.

JOHNSON, S. P. (2004). Development of perceptual completion in infancy. *Psychological Science, 15,* 769–775.

JOHNSTON, V. S., HAGEL, R., FRANKLIN, M., FINK, B., & GRAMMER, K. (2001). Male facial attractiveness: Evidence for hormone mediated adaptive design. *Evolution and Human Behavior, 22,* 251–267.

JOINER, T. E., JR. (1997). Shyness and low social support as interactive diatheses, with loneliness as mediator: Testing an interpersonal-personality view of vulnerability to depressive symptoms. *Journal of Abnormal Psychology, 106,* 386–394.

JOINT STATEMENT ON THE IMPACT OF ENTERTAINMENT VIOLENCE ON CHILDREN: CONGRESSIONAL PUBLIC HEALTH SUMMIT. (2000. July 26). Retrieved October 22, 2002, from http://www.aap.org/advocacy/releases/jstmtevc.htm.

JOIREMAN, J., ANDERSON, J., & STRATHMAN, A. (2003). The aggression paradox: Understanding links among aggression, sensation seeking, and the consideration of future consequences. *Journal of Personality and Social Psychology, 84,* 1287–1302.

JONES, E. E., & BERGLAS, S. (1978). Control of attributions about the self through self handicapping strategies: The appeal of alcohol and the role of underachievement. *Personality and Social Psychology Bulletin, 4*(2), 200–206.

JONES, E. E., & NISBETT, R. E. (1972). The actor and the observer: Divergent perceptions of the cause of behavior. In E. E. Jones, D. E. Karouse, H. H. Kelley, R. E. Nisbett, S. Valins, & B. Weiner (Eds.), *Attribution perceiving the causes of behavior.* Morristown, NJ: General Learning Press.

JONES, E., & WESSELY, S. (2001). Psychiatric battle casualties: An intra- and inter-war comparison. *British Journal of Psychiatry, 178,* 242–247.

JONES, P. B., BEBBINGTON, P., FOERSTER, A., LEWIS, S. W., MURRAY, R. M., RUSSELL, A., ET AL. (1993). Premorbid social underachievement in schizophrenia: Results from the Camberwell Collaborative Psychosis Study. *British Journal of Psychiatry, 162,* 65–71.

JONES, R. E. (1983). Street people and psychiatry: An introduction. *Hospital Community Psychiatry, 34,* 807–811.

JONES, S. S. (1996). Imitation or exploration? Young infants' matching of adults' oral gestures. *Child Development, 67,* 1952–1969.

JONIDES, J. (1980). Toward a model of the mind's eye's movement. *Canadian Journal of Psychology, 34,* 103–112.

JONIDES, J. (1983). Further toward a model of the mind's eye's movement. *Bulletin of the Psychonomic Society, 21,* 247–250.

JONIDES, J. (2000). Mechanisms of verbal working memory revealed by neuroimaging studies. (2000). In B. Landau, J. Sabini, J. Jonides, and E. Newport (Eds), *Perception, cognition, and language: Essays in honor of Henry and Lila Gleitman* (pp. 87–104). Cambridge, MA: MIT Press.

JORGENSEN, B. W., & CERVONE, J. C. (1978). Affect enhancement in the pseudo recognition task. *Personality and Social Psychology Bulletin, 4,* 285–288.

JOSHI, A.K. (2002) Tree adjoining grammar. In R. Mitkov (Ed.), *Handbook of computational linguistics* (pp. 483–498). New York: Oxford University Press.

JOSLYN, S. L., & OAKES, M. A. (2005). Directed forgetting of autobiographical events. *Memory & Cognition, 33,* 577–587.

JOSSELSON, R. (1980). Ego development in adolescence. In J. Adelson (Ed.), *Handbook of adolescent psychology* (pp. 188–211). New York: Wiley.

JOST, J. T., GLASER, J., KRUGLANSKI, A. W., & SULLOWAY, F. J. (2003). Political conservatism as motivated social cognition. *Psychological Bulletin, 129*(3), 339–375.

JOY, L. A., KIMBALL, M. M., & ZABRACK, M. L. (1986). Television and aggressive behavior. In T. M. Williams (Ed.), *The impact of television: A natural experiment involving three towns.* New York: Academic Press.

JUDD, L. L., PAULUS, M. P., WELLS, K. B., & RAPAPORT, M. H. (1996). Socioeconomic burden of subsyndromal depressive symptoms and major depression in a sample of the general population. *American Journal of Psychiatry, 153,* 1411–1417.

JUDY, B., & NELSON, E. S. (2000). Relationship between parents, peers, morality, and theft in an adolescent sample. *High School Journal, 83*(3), 31–42.

JUNG, C. G. (1964). *Man and his symbols.* Garden City, NY: Doubleday.

JUSCZYK, P. W., CUTLER, A., & REDANZ, N. J. (1993). Infants' preference for the predominant stress patterns of English words. *Child Development, 64,* 675–687.

JUSCZYK, P. W., FRIEDERICI, A. D., WESSELS, J. M., SVENKERUD, V. Y., & JUSCZYK, A. M. (1993). Infants' sensitivity to the sound patterns of native language words. *Journal of Memory and Language, 32,* 402–420.

JUST, M. A., & CARPENTER, P. A. (1992). A capacity theory of comprehension: Individual differences in working memory. *Psychological Review, 99*(1), 122–149.

JUSTER, H. R., & HEIMBERG, R. G. (1995). Social phobia. Longitudinal course and long-term outcome of cognitive-behavioral treatment. *Psychiatric Clinics of North America, 18,* 821–842.

KAGAN, J. (1994). *Galen's prophecy: Temperament in human nature.* New York: Basic Books.

KAGAN, J. (2003). Biology, context, and developmetnal inquiry. *Annual Review of Psychology, 54,* 1–23.

KAGAN, J., & SNIDMAN, N. (1991). Temperamental factors in human development. *American Psychologist, 46,* 856–862.

KAHANA-KALMAN, R., & WALKER-ANDREWS, A. (2001). The role of person familiarity in young infants' perception of emotional expressions. *Child Development, 72,* 352–369.

KAHN, I., DAYACHI, L., & WAGNER, A. (2004). Functional-neuroanatomic correlates of recollection: Implications for models of recognition memory. *Journal of Neuroscience, 24,* 4171–4180.

KAHNEMAN, D. (2003). A perspective on judgment and choice: Mapping bounded rationality. *American Psychologist, 58,* 697–720.

KAHNEMAN, D., DIENER, E., & SCHWARZ, N. (EDS.). (1999). *Well-being: The foundations of hedonic psychology.* New York: Russell Sage Foundation.

KAHNEMAN, D., & TVERSKY, A. (1972). Subjective probability: A judgment of representativeness. *Cognitive Psychology, 3,* 430–454.

KAHNEMAN, D., & TVERSKY, A. (1973). On the psychology of prediction. *Psychological Review, 80,* 237–251.

KAHNEMAN, D., & TVERSKY, A. (1984). Choices, values and frames. *American Psychologist, 39,* 341–350.

KAHNEMAN, D., & TVERSKY, A. (1996). On the reality of cognitive illusions. *Psychological Review, 103,* 582–591.

KAISER, E., & TRUESWELL, J. C. (2002, March). A new "look" in the processing of non-canonical word orders. Paper presented at the 15th Annual CUNY Conference on Human Sentence Processing, New York, NY.

KAKO, E. (1999). Elements of syntax in the systems of three language-trained animals. *Animal Learning & Behavior, 27,* 1–14.

KALICK, S. M., ZEBROWITZ, L. A., LANGLOIS, J. H., & JOHNSON, R. M. (1998). Does human facial attractiveness honestly advertise health? Longitudinal data on an evolutional question. *Psychological Science, 9,* 8–13.

KAMIN, L. J. (1965). Temporal and intensity characteristics of the conditioned stimulus. In W. F. Prokasy (Ed.), *Classical conditioning.* New York: Appleton-Century-Crofts.

KAMIN, L. J. (1968). "Attention-like" processes in classical conditioning. In M. R. Jones (Ed.), *Miami symposium on the prediction of behavior: Aversive stimuli.* Miami: University of Miami Press.

KAMIN, L. J. (1974). *The science and politics of I.Q.* New York: Wiley.

KAMINSKY, H. (1984). Moral development in historical perspective. In W. M. Kurtines & J. L. Gerwitz (Eds.), *Morality, moral behavior, and moral development.* New York: Wiley.

KAMPERT, J. B., BLAIR, S. N., BARLOW, C. E., & KOHL, H. W., III. (1996). Physical activity, physical fitness, and all-cause and cancer mortality: A prospective study of men and women. *Annals of Epidemiology, 6,* 452–457.

KANAYA, T., SCULLIN, M. H., & CECI, S. (2003). The Flynn effect and U.S. policies: The impact of rising IQ scores on American society via mental retardation diagnoses. *American Psychologist, 58,* 778–790.

KANDEL, D. B. (1978). Similarity in real-life adolescent friendship pairs. *Journal of Personality and Social Psychology, 36,* 306–312.

KANDEL, E. R., & HAWKINS, R. D. (1992). The biological basis of learning and individuality. *Scientific American, 267,* 78–87.

KANE, M. J. (2005). Full frontal fluidity? Looking in on the neuroimaging of reasoning and intelligence. In O. Wilhelm & R. Engle (Eds.), *Handbook of understanding and measuring intelligence* (pp. 141–163). Thousand Oaks, CA: Sage.

KANE, M. J., & ENGLE, R. W. (2003). Working-memory capacity and the control of attention: The contributions of goal neglect, response competition, and task set to Stroop interference. *Journal of Experimental Psychology: General, 132,* 47–70.

KANE, M. J., HAMBRICK, D. Z., & CONWAY, A. R. (2005). Working memory capacity and fluid intelligence are strongly related constructs: Comment on Ackerman, Beier, and Boyle (2005). *Psychological Bulletin, 131,* 66–71.

KAPUR, N. (1999). Syndromes of retrograde amnesia. *Psychological Bulletin, 125,* 800–825.

KAPUR, S., & REMINGTON, G. (1996). Serotonin-dopamine interaction and its relevance to schizophrenia. *American Journal of Psychiatry, 153,* 466–476.

KARAU, S. J., & WILLIAMS, K. D. (1993). Social loafing: A meta-analytic review and theoretical integration. *Journal of Personality and Social Psychology, 65*(4), 681–706.

KASSER, T., & SHARMA, Y. S. (1999). Reproductive freedom, educational equality, and females' preference for resource-acquisition characteristics in mates. *Psychological Science, 10*(4), 374–377.

KATO, T., & KATO, N. (2000). Mitochondrial dysfunction in bipolar disorder. *Bipolar Disorders, 2*(3, Pt. 1), 180–190.

KATZ, J. J., & FODOR, J. A. (1963). The structure of a semantic theory. *Language, 39,* 170–210.

KAWAKAMI, K., DION, K. L., & DOVIDIO, J. F. (1998). Racial prejudice and stereotype activation. *Personality and Social Psychology Bulletin, 24*(4), 407–416.

KAY, P. (1996). Intra-speaker relativity. In J. J. Gumperz & S. C. Levinson (Eds.), *Rethinking linguistic relativity. Studies in the social and cultural foundations of language.* Cambridge: Cambridge University Press.

KAY, P., & REGIER, T. (2006). Language, thought, and color: Recent developments. *Trends in Cognitive Sciences, 10*(2), 51–54.

KAZDIN, A. E. (2003). Psychotherapy for children and adolescents. *Annual Review of Psychology, 54,* 253–276.

KAZDIN, A. E., & BENJET, C. (2003). Spanking children: Evidence and issues. *Current Directions in Psychological Science, 12*(3), 99–103.

KAZDIN, A. E., & WEISZ, J. R. (EDS.). (2003). *Evidence-based psychotherapies for children and adolescents.* New York: Guilford Press.

KEATING, D. (2004). Cognitive and brain development. In R. Lerner. & L. Steinberg (Eds.), *Handbook of adolescent psychology* (pp. 45–84). New York: Wiley.

KECK, P. E., JR., & MCELROY, S. L. (2002). Carbamazepine and valproate in the maintenance treatment of bipolar disorder. *Journal of Clinical Psychiatry, 63*(Suppl. 10), 13–17.

KEGL, J., SENGHAS, A. & COPPOLA, M. (1999). Creation through contact: Sign language emergence and sign language change in Nicaragua. In Degraff, M., (Ed.), *Language creation and language change: Creolization, diachrony, and development* (pp. 179–237). Cambridge, MA: MIT Press.

KEIL, F. L. (1989). *Concepts, kinds, and cognitive development.* Cambridge, MA: MIT Press.

KELLEY, H. H. (1967). Attribution theory in social psychology. In D. Levine (Ed.), *Nebraska Symposium on Motivation* (pp. 192–238). Lincoln: University of Nebraska Press.

KELLEY, H. H., & MICHELA, J. L. (1980). Attribution theory and research. *Annual Review of Psychology, 31,* 457–501.

KELLEY, S., & MIRER, T. W. (1974). The simple act of voting. *American Political Science Review, 68,* 572–591.

KELLMAN, P. J., & SHIPLEY, T. F. (1991). A theory of visual interpolation in object perception. *Cognitive Psychology, 23,* 141–221.

KELLMAN, P. J., & SPELKE, E. S. (1983). Perception of partially occluded objects in infancy. *Cognitive Psychology, 15,* 483–524.

KELLMAN, P. J., GARRIGAN, P., & SHIPLEY, T. F. (2005). Object interpolation in three dimensions. *Psychological Review, 112,* 586–609.

KELLMAN, P. J., SPELKE, E. S., & SHORT, K. R. (1986). Infant perception of object unity from translatory motion in depth and vertical translation. *Child Development, 57,* 72–86.

KELLY, G. A. (1955). *The psychology of personal constructs.* New York: Norton.

KELLY, M. H., & MARTIN, S. (1994). Domain-general abilities applied to domain-specific tasks: Sensitivity to probabilities in perception, cognition, and language. In L. R. Gleitman & B. Landau (Eds.), Lexical acquisition [Special issue]. *Lingua, 92,* 108–140.

KELSOE, J. R. (1997). The genetics of bipolar disorder. *Psychiatric Annals, 27,* 285–292.

KELTNER, D., & BUSWELL, B. N. (1997). Embarrassment: Its distinct form and appeasement functions. *Psychological Bulletin, 122,* 250–270.

KELTNER, D., GRUENFELD, D. H., & ANDERSON, C. (2003). Power, approach, and inhibition. *Psychological Review, 110,* 265–284.

KENDALL, P. C. (1990). Cognitive processes and procedures in behavior therapy. In C. M. Franks, G. T. Wilson, P. C. Kendall, & J. P. Foreyt (Eds.), *Review of behavior therapy: Theory and practice* (pp. 103–137). New York: Guilford Press.

KENDALL, P. C., & BRASWELL, L. (1985). *Cognitive-behavioral therapy for impulsive children.* New York: Guilford Press.

KENDALL-TACKETT, K. A., WILLIAMS, L. M., & FINKELHOR, D. (1993). Impact of sexual abuse on children: A review and synthesis of recent empirical studies. *Psychological Bulletin, 113,* 164–180.

KENDLER, K. S., & GRUENBERG, A. M. (1984). An independent analysis of the Danish adoption study of schizophrenia: VI. The relationship between psychiatric disorders as defined by DSM-III in the relatives and adoptees. *Archives of General Psychiatry, 41,* 555–564.

KENDLER, K. S., KARKOWSKI, L. M., & PRESCOTT, C. A. (1999). Fears and phobias: Reliability and heritability. *Psychological Medicine, 29,* 539–553.

KENNY, D., & ZACCARO, S. J. (1983). An estimate of variance due to traits in leadership. *Journal of Applied Psychology, 68,* 678–685.

KENRICK, D. T., & CIALDINI, R. B. (1977). Romantic attraction: Misattribution versus reinforcement explanations. *Journal of Personality and Social Psychology, 35,* 381–391.

KENRICK, D. T., CIALDINI, R. B., & LINDER, D. E. (1979). Misattribution under fear-producing circumstances: Four failures to replicate. *Personality and Social Psychology Bulletin, 5,* 329–334.

KERR, M. E., & BOWEN, M. (1988). *Family evaluation.* New York: Norton.

KERR, N., & BRAY, R. (2005). Simulation, realism, and the study of the jury. In N. Brewer & K. Williams (Eds.), *Psychology and law: An empirical perspective* (pp. 322–364). New York: Guilford Press.

KERR, N. L., & TINDALE, R. S. (2004). Group performance and decision making. *Annual Review of Psychology, 55,* 623–655.

KESSLER, R. C., AVENEVOLI, S., & RIES MERIKANGAS, K. (2001). Mood disorders in children and adolescents: An epidemiologic perspective. *Biological Psychiatry, 49,* 1002–1014.

KESSLER, R. C., BERGLUND, P., DEMLER, O., JIN, R., MERIKANGAS, K. R., & WALTERS, E. E. (2005). Lifetime prevalence and age-of-onset distributions of *DSM-IV* disorders in the National Comorbidity Survey Replication. *Archives of General Psychiatry, 62,* 593–602.

KESSLER, R. C., KELLER, M. B., & WITTCHEN, H.-U. (2001). The epidemiology of generalized anxiety disorder. *Psychiatric Clinics of North America, 24,* 19–39.

KESSLER, R. C., MCGONAGLE, K. A., ZHAO, S., NELSON, C. B., HUGHES, M., ESHLEMAN, S., ET AL. (1994). Lifetime and 12-month prevalence of *DSM-III-R* psychiatric disorders in the United States: Results from the National Comorbidity Survey. *Archives of General Psychiatry, 51,* 8–19.

KETY, S. S. (1988). Schizophrenic illness in the families of schizophrenic adoptees: Findings from the Danish National Sample. *Schizophrenia Bulletin, 14,* 217–222.

KHANNA, S. M., & LEONARD, D. G. B. (1982). Basilar membrane tuning in the cat cochlea. *Science, 215,* 305–306.

KIHLSTROM, J. F. (1993). The recovery of memory in the laboratory and the clinic. Paper presented at the 1993 conventions of the Rocky Mountain and the Western Psychological Associations, Phoenix, AZ.

KIHLSTROM, J. F. (1997). Suffering from reminiscences: Exhumed memory, implicit memory, and the return of the repressed. In M. Conway (Ed.), *Recovered memories and false memories* (pp. 100–117). New York: Oxford University Press.

KIHLSTROM, J. F. (2002). No need for repression. *Trends in Cognitive Sciences, 6*(12), 502.

KIHLSTROM, J. F., & CANTOR, N. (2000). Social intelligence. In R. J. Sternberg (Ed.), *Handbook of Intelligence* (2nd ed., pp. 359–379). Cambridge, England: Cambridge University Press.

KIHLSTROM, J. F., & SCHACTER, D. L. (2000). Functional amnesia. In F. Boller & J. Grafman (Eds.), *Handbook of neuropsychology* (2nd ed., Vol. 2, pp. 409–427). Amsterdam: Elsevier.

KILHAM, W., & MANN, L. (1974). Level of destructive obedience as a function of transmitter and executant roles in the Milgram obedience paradigm. *Journal of Personality and Social Psychology, 29,* 696–702.

KILPATRICK, L., & CAHILL, L. (2003) Amygdala modulation of parahippocampal and frontal regions during emotionally influenced memory storage. *Neuroimage, 20,* 2091–2099.

KIM, H., & MARKUS, H. R. (1999). Deviance or uniqueness, harmony or conformity? A cultural analysis. *Journal of Personality and Social Psychology, 77*(4), 785–800.

KIM, J. Y., & NAM, S. H. (1998). The concept and dynamics of face: Implications for organizational behavior in Asia. *Organization Science, 9*(4), 522–534.

KIMBERG, D. Y., D'ESPOSITO, M., & FARAH, M. J. (1998). Cognitive functions in the prefrontal cortex—working memory and executive control. *Current Directions in Psychological Science, 6,* 185–192.

KIMBLE, G. A. (1961). *Hilgard and Marquis' conditioning and learning.* New York: Appleton-Century-Crofts.

KIMURA, D., & WATSON, N. (1989). The relation between oral movement and speech. *Brain and Language, 37,* 565–590.

KINGSTONE, A., FRIESEN, C., & GAZZANIGA, M. (2000). Reflexive joint attention depends on lateralized cortical connections. *Psychological Science, 11,* 159–166.

KINSBOURNE, M. (2000). How is consciousness expressed in the cerebral activation manifold? *Brain and Mind, 2,* 265–274

KINSEY, A., POMEROY, W. B., & MARTIN, C. E. (1948). *Sexual behavior in the human male.* Philadelphia: Saunders.

KINSEY, A., POMEROY, W., MARTIN, C., & GEBHARD, P. (1953). *Sexual behavior in the human female.* Philadelphia: Saunders.

KITAYAMA, S., MARKUS, H. R., MATSUMOTO, H., & NORASAKKUNKIT, V. (1997). Individual and collective processes in the construction of the self: Self-enhancement in the United States and self-criticism in Japan. *Journal of Personality and Social Psychology, 72,* 1245–1267.

KITAYAMA, S., SNIBBE, A. C., MARKUS, H. R., & SUZUKI, T. (2004). Is there any "free" choice? Self and dissonance in two cultures. *Psychological Science, 15,* 527–533.

KITZINGER, C. (2001). Sexualities. In R. K. Unger (Ed.), *Handbook of the psychology of women and gender* (pp. 272–285). New York: Wiley.

KLAHR, D., & SIMON, H. A. (2001). What have psychologists (and others) discovered about the process of scientific discovery? *Current Directions in Psychological Science, 10,* 75–79.

KLAUER, K. C., MUSCH, J., & NAUMER, B. (2000). On belief bias in syllogistic reasoning. *Psychological Review, 107,* 852–884.

KLAUS, M. H., & KENNELL, J. H. (1976). *Maternal-infant bonding: The impact of early separation or loss on family development.* St. Louis, MO: Mosby.

KLAUS, M. H., KENNELL, J. H., PLUMB, N., & ZUEHLKE, S. (1970). Human maternal behavior at the first contact with her young. *Pediatrics, 46,* 187.

KLEINMAN, A. (1986). *Social origins of distress and disease: Neurasthenia, depression, and pain in modern China.* New Haven, CT: Yale University Press.

KLERMAN, G., & WEISSMAN, M. (1993). Interpersonal psychotherapy for depression: Background and concepts. In *New applications of interpersonal therapy.* Washington, DC: American Psychological Association Press.

KLIMA, E., & BELLUGI, U., WITH BATTISON, R., BOYES-BRAEM, P., FISCHER, S., FRISHBERG, N., ET AL. (1979). *The signs of language.* Cambridge, MA: Harvard University Press.

KLINE, P. (1995). A critical review of the measurement of personality and intelligence. In D. H. Saklofske & M. Zeidner (Eds.), *International handbook of personality and intelligence* (pp. 505–524). New York: Plenum.

KLOPFER, B., AINSWORTH, M., KLOPFER, W. G., & HOLT, R. R. (1954). *Developments in the Rorschach technique.* Yonkers, NY: World Book.

KLUFT, R. P. (1987). An update on multiple-personality disorder. *Journal of Hospital and Community Psychiatry, 38,* 363–373.

KNUTSON, B. (2004) Sweet revenge? *Science, 305,* 1246–1247.

KOCHANSKA, G. (1993). Toward a synthesis of parental socialization and child temperament in early development of conscience. *Child Development, 64,* 325–347.

KOCHANSKA, G. (1995). Children's temperament, mother's discipline, and security of attachment: Multiple pathways to emerging internalization. *Child Development, 66,* 597–615.

KOCHANSKA, G. (1997). Multiple pathways to conscience for children with different temperaments: From toddlerhood to age 5. *Developmental Psychology, 33,* 228–240.

KOCHANSKA, G. (2001). Emotional development in children with different attachment histories: The first three years. *Child Development, 72*(2), 474–490.

KOCHANSKA, G. (2002). Mutually responsive orientation between mothers and their young children: A context for the early development of conscience. *Current Directions in Psychological Science, 11*(6), 191–195.

KOCHANSKA, G., AKSAN, N., KNAACK, A., & RHINES, H. (2004). Maternal parenting and children's conscience: Early security as a moderator. *Child Development, 75,* 1229–1242.

KOEKOEK, S., HULSCHER, H., DORTLAND, B., HENBROEK, R., ELGERSMA, Y., RUIGROK, T., ET AL. (2003). Cerebellar LTD and learning-dependent timing of conditioned eyeline responses. *Science, 301,* 1736–1739.

KOHLBERG, L. (1969). Stage and sequence: The cognitive developmental approach to socialization. In D. A. Goslin (Ed.), *Handbook of socialization theory of research* (pp. 347–480). Chicago: Rand McNally.

KOHLBERG, L., LEVINE, C., & HEWER, A. (1984). Synopses and detailed replies to critics. In L. Kohlberg (Ed.), *The psychology of moral development: The nature and validity of moral stages* (pp. 320–386). San Francisco: Harper & Row.

KOHN, A. (1993). *Punished by rewards.* New York: Houghton Mifflin.

KOHN, M. L. (1968). Social class and schizophrenia: A critical review. In D. Rosenthal & S. S. Kety (Eds.), *The transmission of schizophrenia* (pp. 155–174). London: Pergamon.

KOLB, B., & WHISHAW, I. Q. (1996). *Fundamentals of human neuropsychology* (4th ed.). New York: Freeman.

KOLB, B., GIBB, R., & ROBINSON, T. E. (2003). Brain plasticity and behavior. *Current Directions in Psychological Science, 12,* 1–5.

KOLB, I., & WHISHAW, I. Q. (2001). *An introduction to brain and behavior.* New York: Worth.

KONDRO, W. (1998). New rules on human subjects could end debate in Canada. *Science, 280,* 1521.

KONDZIOLKA, D., WECHSLER, L., GOLDSTEIN, S., MELTZER, C., THULBORN, K. R., GEBEL, J., ET AL. (2000). Transplantation of cultured human neuronal cells for patients with stroke. *Neurology, 55*(4), 565–569.

KORN, J. H. (1997). *Illusions of reality: A history of deception in social psychology.* Albany: State University of New York Press.

KOSSLYN, S. M., & PASCUAL-LEONE, A., ET AL. (1999). The role of area 17 in visual imagery: Convergent evidence from PET and rTMS. *Science, 284,* 167–170.

KOSSLYN, S. M., BALL, T. M., & REISSER, B. J. (1978). Visual images preserve metric spatial information: Evidence from studies of image scanning. *Journal of Experimental Psychology: Human Perception and Performance, 4,* 1–20.

KRAMER, A. F., & WILLIS, S. L. (2002). Enhancing the cognitive vitality of older adults. *Current Directions in Psychological Science, 11,* 173–177.

KRAMER, P. D. (1993). *Listening to Prozac.* New York: Viking.

KRASNE, F. B., & GLANZMAN, D. L. (1995). What we can learn from invertebrate learning. *Annual Review of Psychology, 45,* 585–624.

KRAUS, S. J. (1995). Attitudes and the prediction of behavior: A meta analysis of the empirical literature. *Personality and Social Psychology Bulletin, 21*(1), 58–75.

KREBS, D. L., & DENTON, K. (2005). Toward a more pragmatic approach to morality: A critical evaluation of Kohlberg's model. *Psychological Review, 112*(3), 629–649.

KREBS, J. R. (1982). Territorial defence in the great tit (Parus Major L.). *Ecology, 52,* 2–22.

KRING, A. M., & GORDON, A. H. (1998). Sex differences in emotion: Expression, experience, and physiology. *Journal of Personality and Social Psychology, 74,* 686–703.

KRUGLANSKI, A. W., PIERRO, A., MANNETTI, L., & GRADA, E. D. (2006). Groups as epistemic providers: Need for closure and the unfolding of group-centrism. *Psychological Review, 113*(1), 84–100.

KRUPNICK, J. L., SOTSKY, S. M., SIMMENS, S., MOYER, J., ELKIN, I., WATKINS, J., ET AL. (1996). The role of the therapeutic alliance in psychotherapy and pharmacotherapy outcome: Findings in the National Institute of Mental Health Treatment of Depression Collaborative Research Program. *Journal of Consulting and Clinical Psychology, 64,* 532–539.

KRUSCHKE, J. K., & BLAIR, N. J. (2000). Blocking and backward blocking involve learned inattention. *Psychonomics Bulletin and Review, 7,* 636–645.

KUAN, D. Y., ROTH, K. A., FLAVELL, R. A., & RAKIC, P. (2000). Mechanisms of programmed cell death in the developing brain. *Trends in Neuroscience, 23,* 291–297.

KUHL, P., WILLIAMS, K., LACERDA, F., STEVENS, K., & LINDBLOM, B. (1992). Linguistic experience alters phonetic perception in infants by six months of age. *Science, 255,* 606–608.

KUHN, D. (2006). Do cognitive changes accompany developments in the adolescent brain? *Perspectives on Psychological Science, 1,* 59–67.

KUHN, D., NASH, S., & BRUCKEN, L. (1978). Sex-role concepts of two- and three-year-olds. *Child Development, 49,* 445–451.

KUMARI, V., FFYTCHE, D. H., WILLIAMS, S. C., & GRAY, J. A. (2004). Personality predicts brain responses to cognitive demands. *Journal of Neuroscience, 24,* 10636–10641.

KUNCEL, N. R., HEZLETT, S. A., & ONES, D. S. (2004). Academic performance, career potential, creativity, and job performance: Can one construct predict them all? *Journal of Personality and Social Psychology, 86,* 148–161.

KUNDA, Z. (1990). The case for motivated reasoning. *Psychological Bulletin, 108,* 480–498.

KUNDA, Z., FONG, G. T., SANITIOSO, R., & REBER, E. (1993). Directional questions direct self conceptions. *Journal of Experimental Social Psychology, 29*(1), 63–86.

KUNDA, Z., & NISBETT, R. E. (1986). The psychometrics of everyday life. *Cognitive Psychology, 18,* 195–224.

KURDEK, L. A. (2005). What do we know about gay and lesbian couples? *Current Directions in Psychological Science, 14,* 251–254.

KURTZ, S. N. (1991). Polysexualization: A new approach to Oedipus in the Trobriands. *Ethos, 19,* 68–101.

KURZBAN, R., & LEARY, M. R. (2001). Evolutionary origins of stigmatization: The functions of social exclusion. *Psychological Bulletin, 127,* 187–208.

KYLLONEN, P. C., & CHRISTAL, R. E. (1990). Reasoning ability is (little more than) working memory capacity? *Intelligence, 14*(4), 389–433.

LA ROSA, J., & DIAZ-LOVING, R. (1991). Evaluation of the self-concept: A multidimensional inventory/Evaluacion del autoconcepto: una escala multidimensional. Revista Latinoamericana de Psicologia. *Special Personality, 23,* 15–33.

LABORATORY OF COMPARATIVE HUMAN COGNITION. (1983). Culture and cognitive development. In P. Mussen (Ed.), *Handbook of child psychology: Vol. 1. History, theory and methods* (4th ed.). New York: Wiley.

LADD, G., KOCHENDERFER, B., & COLEMAN, C. (1996). Friendship quality as a predictor of young children's early school adjustment. *Child Development, 67,* 1103–1118.

LADD, G., & PRICE, J. (1987). Predicting children's social and school adjustment following the transition from preschool to kindergarten. *Child Development, 58,* 1168–1189.

LADEFOGED, P. (1975) *A course in phonetics.* New York: Harcourt, Brace Jovanovich.

LAFARGE, L. (1993). The early determinants of penis envy. In R. A. Glick & S. P. Roose, (Eds.), *Rage, power, and aggression. The role of affect in motivation, development, and adaptation: Vol. 2* (pp. 80–101). New Haven, CT: Yale University Press.

LAGATTUTA, K., WELLMAN, H., & FLAVELL, J. (1997). Preschoolers' understanding of the link between thinking and feeling: Cognitive cuing and emotional change. *Child Development, 68,* 1081–1104.

LAIBLE, D. (2004). Mother-child discourse surrounding a child's past behavior at 30 months: Links to emotional understanding and early conscience development at 36 months. *Merrill-Palmer Quarterly, 50,* 159–180.

LAIBLE, D., & THOMPSON, R. A. (1998). Attachment and emotional understanding in preschool children. *Developmental Psychology, 34,* 1038–1045.

LAIBLE, D., & THOMPSON, R. A. (2000). Mother-child discourse, attachment security, shared positive affect, and early conscience development. *Child Development, 71,* 1424–1440.

LAIBLE, D., & THOMPSON, R. A. (2002). Mother-child conflict in the toddler years: Lessons in emotion, morality, and relationships. *Child Development, 73,* 1187–1203.

LAIRD, R., JORDAN, K., DODGE, K., PETTIT, G., & BATES, J. (2001). Peer rejection in childhood, involvement with antisocial peers in early adolescence, and the development of externalizing problems. *Development and Psychopathology, 13,* 337–354.

LALONDE, J. K., HUDSON, J. I., GIGANTE, R. A., & POPE, H. G., JR. (2001). Canadian and American psychiatrists' attitudes toward dissociative disorders diagnoses. *Canadian Journal of Psychiatry, 46,* 407–412.

LALUMIERE, M., BLANCHARD, R., & ZUCKER, K. (2000). Sexual orientation and handedness in men and women: A meta-analysis. *Psychological Bulletin, 126,* 575–592.

LAMARINE, R. (1995). Child and adolescent depression. *Journal of School Health, 65,* 390–394.

LAMB, H. R. (1984). Deinstitutionalization and the homeless mentally ill. *Hospital Community Psychiatry, 35,* 899–907.

LAMB, H. R. (1998). Deinstitutionalization at the beginning of the new millennium. *Harvard Review of Psychiatry, 6,* 1–10.

LAMB, H. R., & BACHRACH, L. L. (2001). Some perspectives on deinstitutionalization. *Psychiatric Services, 52,* 1039–1045.

LAMB, M. E. (ED.). (1987). *The father's role: Cross-cultural perspectives.* Hillsdale, NJ: Erlbaum.

LAMB, M. E. (ED.). (1997). *The role of the father in child development* (3rd ed.). New York: Wiley.

LAMB, M., & MALKIN, C. (1986). The development of social expectations in distress-relief sequences: A longitudinal study. *International Journal of Behavioral Development, 9,* 235–249.

LAMBERT, M. J., & BERGIN, A. E. (1994). The effectiveness of psychotherapy. In A. E. Bergin & S. L. Garfield (Eds.), *Handbook of psychotherapy and behavior change* (4th ed., pp. 143–189). New York: Wiley.

LANDAU, B. (1982). Will the real grandmother please stand up? The psychological reality of dual meaning representations. *Journal of Psycholinguistic Research, 11,* 47–62.

LANDAU, B., & GLEITMAN, L. R. (1985). *Language and experience: Evidence from the blind child.* Cambridge, MA: Harvard University Press.

LANDAU, B., & MUNNICH, E. (1998). The representation of space of spatial language: Challenges for cognitive science. In P. Olivier & K. Gapp (Eds.), *Representation and processing of spatial expressions* (pp. 263–272). Mahwah, NJ: Erlbaum.

LANDAU, B., & STECKER, D. (1990). Objects and places: Geometric and syntactic representations in early lexical learning. *Cognitive Development, 5,* 287–312.

LANDAU, B., & ZUKOWSKI, A. (2002). Objects, motions, and paths: Spatial language of children with Williams Syndrome. Developmental Neuropsychology [Special issue, C. B. Mervis (Ed.)].

LANDAU, B., SMITH, L., & JONES, S. (1988). The importance of shape in early lexical learning. *Cognitive Development, 3,* 299–321.

LANDIS, C., & HUNT, W. A. (1932). Adrenalin and emotion. *Psychological Review, 39,* 467–485.

LANG, B., & PERNER, J. (2002). Understanding of intention and false belief and the development of self-control. *British Journal of Developmental Psychology, 20*(1), 67–76.

LANG, P. J., DAVIS, M., & OHMAN, A. (2000). Fear and anxiety: Animal models and human cognitive psychophysiology. *Journal of Affective Disorders, 61,* 137–159.

LANGER, E. J., & RODIN, J. (1976). The effects of choice and enhanced personal responsibility for the aged: A field experiment in an institutional setting. *Journal of Personality and Social Psychology, 34,* 191–198.

LANGLOIS, J. H., & DOWNS, A. C. (1980). Mothers, fathers, and peers as socialization agents of sex-typed play behaviors in young children. *Child Development, 51,* 1237–1347.

LANGLOIS, J. H., KALAKANIS, L., RUBENSTEIN, A. J., LARSON, A., HALLAM, M., & SMOOT, M. (2000). Maxims or myths of beauty? A meta-analytic and theoretical review. *Psychological Bulletin, 126*(3), 390–423.

LANGLOIS, J. H., ROGGMAN, L. A., CASEY, R. J., RITTER, J. M., RIESER-DANNER, L. A., & JENKINS, V. Y. (1987). Infant preferences for attractive faces: Rudiments of a stereotype. *Developmental Psychobiology, 23,* 363–369.

LANYON, R. I., & GOLDSTEIN, L. D. (1971). *Personality assessment.* New York: Wiley.

LAPIERE, R. (1934). Attitudes versus actions. *Social Forces, 13,* 230–237.

LARSEN, R. J., & DIENER, E. (1992). Promises and problems with the circumplex model of emotion. In M. S. Clark (Ed.), *Emotion: Review of personality and social psychology* (Vol. 13, pp. 25–59). Newbury Park, CA: Sage.

LARSEN, R. J., KASIMATIS, M., & FREY, K. (1992). Facilitating the furrowed brow: An unobtrusive test of the facial feedback hypothesis applied to unpleasant affect. *Cognition and Emotion, 6,* 321–338.

LASSITER, G. D. (2000). The relative contributions of recognition and search-evaluation processes to high-level chess performance: Comment on Gobet and Simon. *Psychological Science, 11*(2), 172–173.

LATANÉ, B. (1981). The psychology of social impact. *American Psychologist, 36,* 343–356.

LATANÉ, B., & NIDA, S. (1981). Group size and helping. *Psychological Bulletin, 89,* 308–324.

LATANÉ, B., NIDA, S. A., & WILSON, D. W. (1981). The effects of group size on helping behavior. In J. P. Rushton & R. M. Sorrentino (Eds.), *Altruism and helping behavior: Social, personality, and developmental perspectives.* Hillsdale, NJ: Erlbaum.

LATANÉ, B., WILLIAMS, K., & HARKINS, S. (1979). Many hands make light the work: The causes and consequences of social loafing. *Journal of Personality and Social Psychology, 37,* 822–332.

LATTAL, K. M., HONARVAR, S., & ABEL, T. (2004). Effects of post-session injections of anisomycin on the extinction of a spatial preference and on the acquisition of a spatial reversal preference. *Behavioural Brain Research, 153,* 327–339.

LAU, R. R., & RUSSELL, D. (1980). Attributions in the sports pages. *Journal of Personality and Social Psychology, 39,* 29–38.

LAURSEN, B., COY, K., & COLLINS, W. (1998). Reconsidering changes in parent-child conflict across adolescence: A meta-analysis. *Child Development, 69,* 817–832.

LAWRIE, S. M., & ABUKMEIL, S. S. (1998). Brain abnormality in schizophrenia: A systematic and quantitative review of volumetric magnetic resonance imaging studies. *British Journal of Psychiatry, 172,* 110–120.

LAYZER, D. (1972). Science or superstition: A physical scientist looks at the I.Q. controversy. *Cognition, 1,* 265–300.

LAZAREVA, O. F., FREIBURGER, K. L., & WASSERMAN, E. A. (2004). Pigeons concurrently categorize photographs at both basic and superordinate levels. *Psychonomic Bulletin & Review, 11*(6), 1111–1117.

LAZARUS, A. A. (1971). *Behavior therapy and beyond.* New York: McGraw-Hill.

LAZARUS, A. A. (1981). *The practice of multi-modal therapy.* New York: McGraw-Hill.

LAZARUS. R. S. (1991). *Emotion and adaptation.* Oxford, England: Oxford University Press.

LE BON, G. (1895). *The crowd.* New York: Viking Press, 1960.

LEA, S. E. G., & RYAN, C. M. E. (1990). Unnatural concepts and the theory of concept discrimination in birds. In M. L. Commons, R. J. Herrnstein, S. Kosslyn, & D. Mumford (Eds.), *Quantitative analysis of behavior, Vol. 8: Behavioral approaches to pattern recognition and concept formation* (pp. 165–185). Hillsdale, NJ: Erlbaum.

LEAPER, C., ANDERSON, K. J., & SANDERS, P. (1998). Moderators of gender effects on parents' talk to their children: A meta-analysis. *Developmental Psychology, 34*(1), 3–27.

LEARY, M. R., TAMBOR, E. S., TERDAL, S. K., & DOWNS, D. L. (1995). Self-esteem as an interpersonal monitor: The sociometer hypothesis. *Journal of Personality and Social Psychology, 68,* 518–530.

LECKMAN, J. F., ZHANG, H., ALSOBROOK, J. P., & PAULS, D. L. (2001). Symptom dimensions in obsessive-compulsive disorder: Toward quantitative phenotypes. *American Journal of Medical Genetics, 105,* 28–30.

LEDOUX, J. E. (1995). Emotion: Clues from the brain. *Annual Review of Psychology, 46,* 209–235.

LEE, A., HOBSON, R. P., & CHIAT, S. (1994). I, you, me, and autism: An experimental study. *Journal of Autism and Developmental Disorders, 24,* 155–176.

LEE, D., & YOUNG, K. (2001). Post-traumatic stress disorder: Diagnostic issues and epidemiology in adult survivors of traumatic events. *International Review of Psychiatry, 13,* 150–158.

LEHMAN, D., & NISBETT, R. (1990). A longitudinal study of the effects of undergraduate education on reasoning. *Developmental Psychology, 26,* 952–960.

LEHMAN, D., LEMPERT, R. O., & NISBETT, R. E. (1988). The effects of graduate training on reasoning: Formal discipline and thinking about everyday-life events. *American Psychologist, 43,* 431–442.

LEIBOWITZ, S. F. (1991). Brain neuropeptide Y: An integrator of endocrine, metabolic and behavioral processes. *Brain Research Bulletin, 27,* 333–337.

LENNEBERG, E. H. (1967). *Biological foundations of language.* New York: Wiley.

LÉPINE, R., BARROUILLET, P., & CAMOS, V. (2005). What makes working memory spans so predictive of high-level cognition? *Psychonomic Bulletin and Review, 12,* 165–170.

LEPPER, M. R., GREENE, D., & NISBETT, R. E. (1973). Undermining children's intrinsic interest with extrinsic rewards: A test of the "overjustification" hypothesis. *Journal of Personality and Social Psychology, 28,* 129–137.

LeROITH, D., SHILOACH, J., & ROTH, J. (1982). Is there an earlier phylogenetic precursor that is common to both the nervous and endocrine systems? *Peptides, 3,* 211–215.

LESLIE, A. M. (1992). Pretense, autism, and the theory of mind module. *Current Directions in Psychological Science, 1,* 18–21.

LETTVIN, J. Y., MATURAN, H. R., McCULLOCH, W. S., & PITTS, W. H. (1959). What the frog's eye tells the frog's brain. *Proceedings of the Institute of Radio Engineers, 47,* 1940–1951.

LEVAY, S. (1991). A difference in hypothalamic sctructure between heterosexual and homosexual men. *Science, 253,* 1034–1037.

LEVELT, W. (1970). A scaling approach to the study of syntactic relations. In G. Flores d'Arcais & W. Levelt (Eds.), *Advances in psycholinguistics* (pp. 109–121). Amsterdam: North-Holland.

LEVELT, W. J. M. (1989). Speaking: From intention to articulation. Cambridge, MA: MIT Press.

LEVENSON, R. W. (1992). Autonomic nervous system differences among emotions. *Psychological Science, 3,* 23–27.

LEVENSON, R. W. (1994). The search for autonomic specificity. In P. Ekman & R. J. Davidson (Eds.), *Human emotions: A functional view* (pp. 252–257). New York: Oxford University Press.

LEVENSON, R. W. (1999). The intrapersonal functions of emotion. *Cognition and Emotion, 13,* 481–504.

LEVENSON, R. W. (2003). Autonomic specificity and emotion. In R. J. Davidson, K. R. Scherer, & H. H. Goldsmith (Eds.), *Handbook of affective sciences* (pp. 212–224). New York: Oxford University Press.

LEVENSON, R. W., EKMAN, P., HEIDER, K., & FRIESEN, W. V. (1992). Emotion and autonomic nervous system activity in the Minangkabau of West Sumatra. *Journal of Personality and Social Psychology, 62,* 972–988.

LEVIN, I., & GAETH, G. (1988). How consumers are affected by the framing of attribute information before and after consuming the product. *Journal of Consumer Research, 15,* 374–378.

LEVINE, J. M., & MORELAND, R. L. (1998). Small groups. In D. Gilbert, S. Fiske, & G. Lindzey (Eds.), *The handbook of social psychology* (4th ed., pp. 415–469). Boston: McGraw-Hill.

LEVINE, L. J., & PIZARRO, D. A. (2004). Emotion and memory research: A grumpy overview. *Social Cognition, 22*(5), 530–554.

LEVINE, L., STEIN, N., & LIWAG, M. (1999). Remembering children's emotions: Sources of concordant and discordant accounts between parents and children. *Developmental Psychology, 35,* 790–801.

LEVINE, S. C., HUTTENLOCHER, J., TAYLOR, A., & LANGROCK, A. (1999). Early sex differences in spatial skill. *Developmental Psychology, 35,* 940–949.

LEVINSON, S. (2003). Space in language and cognition: Explorations in linguistic diversity. Cambridge: Cambridge University Press.

LEVY, G. D., TAYLOR, M. G., & GELMAN, S. A. (1995). Traditional and evaluative aspects of flexibility in gender roles, social conventions, moral rules, and physical laws. *Child Development, 66*(2), 515–531.

LEVY, J. (1985). Right brain, left brain: Facts and fiction. *Psychology Today, 19,* 38–44.

LEVY, W. B., & STEWARD, O. (1979). Synapses as associative memory elements in the hippocampal formation. *Brain Research, 175,* 233–245.

LEWIN, K. (1939). Field theory and experiment in social psychology: Concepts and methods. *American Journal of Sociology, 44,* 868–897.

LEWINSOHN, P. M., JOINER, T., & ROHDE, P. (2001). Evaluation of cognitive diathesis-stress models in predicting major depressive disorder in adolescents. *Journal of Abnormal Psychology, 110,* 203–215.

LEWIS, C., & KEREN, G. (1999). On the difficulties underlying Bayesian reasoning: A comment on Gigerenzer and Hoffrage. *Psychological Review, 106,* 411–416.

LEWIS, D. O., YEAGER, C. A., SWICA, Y., PINCUS, J. H., & LEWIS, M. (1997). Objective documentation of child abuse and dissociation in 12 murderers with dissociative identity disorder. *American Journal of Psychiatry, 154,* 1703–1710.

LEWIS, J. R., BATES, B. C., & LAWRENCE, S. (1994). Empirical studies of projection: A critical review. *Human Relations, 47*(11), 1295–1319.

LEWIS, M. D., & GRANIC, I. (2000). *Emotion, development, and self-organization: Dynamic systems approaches to emotional development.* New York: Cambridge University Press.

LEWIS, M., ALESSANDRI, S., & SULLIVAN, M. (1990). Violation of expectancy, loss of control, and anger expressions in young infants. *Developmental Psychology, 26,* 745–751.

LEWIS, M., STANGER, C., & SULLIVAN, M. W. (1989). Deception in 3-year-olds. *Developmental Psychology, 25*(3), 439–443.

LEWONTIN, R. C. (1976). Race and intelligence. In N. J. Block & G. Dworkin (Eds.), *The IQ controversy* (pp. 78–92). New York: Pantheon.

LI, P., & GLEITMAN, L. R. (2002). Turning the tables: Language and spatial reasoning. *Cognition, 83,* 265–294.

LIBERMAN, A. M., COOPER, F. S., SHANKWEILER, D. P., & STUDDERT-KENNEDY, M. (1967). Perception of the speech code. *Psychological Review, 74,* 431–461.

LICHTER, D. G., & CUMMINGS, J. L. (Eds.). (2001). *Frontal-subcortical circuits in psychiatric and neurological disorders.* New York: Guilford Press.

LIEBERMAN, J. A. (1995). Signs and symptoms. Commentary. *Archives of General Psychiatry, 52,* 361–363.

LIEBERMAN, M. D., OCHSNER, K. N., GILBERT, D. T., & SCHACTER, D. L. (2001). Attitude change in amnesia and under cognitive load. *Psychological Science, 12,* 135–140.

LIFF, Z. A. (1992). Psychoanalysis and dynamic techniques. In D. K. Freedheim (Ed.), *History of psychotherapy.* Washington, DC: American Psychological Association.

LILIENFELD, S. O., KIRSCH, I., SARBIN, T. R., LYNN, S. J., CHAVES, J. F., GANAWAY, G. K., ET AL. (1999). Dissociative identity disorder and the sociocognitive model: Recalling the lessons of the past. *Psychological Bulletin, 125,* 507–523.

LILLARD, A. (1998). Enthnopsychologies: Cultural variations in theories of mind. *Psychological Bulletin, 123,* 3–32.

LILLARD, A. S. (1997). Other folks' theories of mind and behavior. *Psychological Science, 8,* 268–274.

LINTON, M. (1978). Real world memory after six years: An in vivo study of very long term memory. In M. M. Gruneberg, P. E. Morris, & R. N. Sykes (Eds.), *Practical aspects of memory* (pp. 69–76). London: Academic Press.

LIPTON, J. S., & SPELKE, E. S. (2006). Preschool children master the logic of number word meanings. *Cognition, 98,* B57–B66.

LISMAN, J. (2003). Long-term potentiation: Outstanding questions and attempted synthesis. *Philosophical Transactions of the Royal Society London: B. Biological Science, 348,* 829–842.

LIVESLEY, W. J. (ED.). (2001). *Handbook of personality disorders: Theory, research, and treatment.* New York: Guilford Press.

LIVSON, N., & PESKIN, H. (1980). Perspectives on adolescence from longitudinal research. In J. Adelsen (Ed.), *Handbook of adolescent psychology.* New York: Wiley.

LOCKE, J. (1690). *An essay concerning human understanding.* A. D. Woozley (Ed.). Cleveland: Meridian Books, 1964.

LOCKRIDGE, C., & BRENNAN, S. (2002). Addressees' needs influence speakers' early syntactic choices. *Psychonomic Bulletin and Review, 9,* 550–557.

LOEHLIN, J. C. (1992). *Genes and environment in personality development.* Newbury Park, CA: Sage.

LOEHLIN, J. C., LINDZEY, G., & SPUHLER, J. N. (1975). *Race difference in intelligence.* San Francisco: Freeman.

LOFTUS, E. F. (1993). The reality of repressed memories. *American Psychologist, 48,* 518–537.

LOFTUS, E. F. (1997). Creating false memories. *Scientific American, 277*(3), 70–75.

LOFTUS, E. F. (2003). Make-believe memories. *American Psychologist, 58*(11), 867–873.

LOGUE, A. W. (1986). *The psychology of eating and drinking.* New York: Freeman.

LOHMAN, D. (2000). Complex information processing and intelligence. In R. J. Sternberg (Ed.), *Handbook of human intelligence* (2nd ed., pp. 285–340). Cambridge, MA: Cambridge University Press.

LONDON, P. (1970). The rescuers: Motivational hypotheses about Christians who saved Jews from the Nazis. In J. Macaulay & L. Berkowitz (Eds.), *Altruism and helping behavior* (pp. 241–250). New York: Academic Press.

LOPES, P. N., SALOVEY, P., CÔTÉ, S., & BEERS, M. (2005). Emotion regulation ability and the quality of social interaction. *Emotion, 5*, 113–118.

LORD, C. G., ROSS, L., & LEPPER, M. R. (1979). Biased assimilation and attitude polarization: The effects of prior theories on subsequently considered evidence. *Journal of Personality and Social Psychology, 37*(11), 2098–2109.

LORD, R. G., DeVADER, C. L., & ALLIGER, G. M. (1986). A meta-analysis of the relationship between personality traits and leadership perceptions: An application of validity generalization procedures. *Journal of Applied Psychology, 7*, 401–410.

LORENZ, K. (1935). Der Kumpan in der Umwelt des Vogels. Der Artgenosse als auslösendes Moment sozialer Verhaltensweisen. *Journal für Ornithologie, 83*, 137–215, 289–413.

LORENZ, K. Z. (1966). *On aggression.* London: Methuen.

LOVE, J., HARRISON, L., SAGI-SCHWARTZ, A., ET AL. (2003). Child care quality matters: How conclusions may vary with context. *Child Development, 74*, 1021–1033.

LUBINSKI, D. (2004). Introduction to the special section on cognitive abilities: 100 years after Spearman's (1904) "'General intelligence,' objectively determined and measured." *Journal of Personality and Social Psychology, 86*, 96–111.

LUBINSKI, D., & BENBOW, C. P. (2000). States of excellence. *American Psychologist, 55*(1), 137–150.

LUBORSKY, L. I., SINGER, B., & LUBORSKY, L. (1975). Comparative studies of psychotherapies. *Archives of General Psychiatry, 20*, 84–88.

LUCHINS, A. S. (1942). Mechanization in problem-solving: The effect of Einstellung. *Psychological Monographs, 54*(Whole No. 248).

LUGINBUHL, J. E. R., CROWE, D. H., & KAHAN, J. P. (1975). Causal attributions for success and failure. *Journal of Personality and Social Psychology, 31*, 86–93.

LUO, Y., & BAILLARGEON, R. (2005). Can a self-propelled box have a goal? Psychological reasoning in 5-month-old infants. *Psychological Science, 16*, 601–608.

LURIA, A. R. (1966). *Higher cortical functions in man.* New York: Basic Books.

LURIA, A. R. (1976). Cognitive development: Its cultural and social foundations. Cambridge, MA: Harvard University Press.

LUTZ, C. (1986). The domain of emotion words on Ifaluk. In R. Harr (Ed.), *The social construction of emotions* (pp. 267–288). Oxford: Blackwell.

LUTZ, C. (1988). *Unnatural emotions.* Chicago: University of Chicago Press.

LUZZATTI, C., RAGGI, R., ZONCA, G., PISTARINI C., CONTARDI A., & PINNA G. (2001). Verb-noun double dissociation in aphasic lexical impairments: The role of word frequency and imageability. *Brain and Language*, 1–13.

LYDIARD, R. B., BRAWMAN-MINTZER, O., & BALLENGER, J. C. (1996). Recent developments in the psychopharmacology of anxiety disorders. *Journal of Consulting and Clinical Psychology, 64*, 660–668.

LYNN, R. (1994). Sex differences in intelligence and brain size: A paradox resolved. *Personality and Individual Differences, 17*(2), 257–271.

LYNN, S. J., LOCK, T. G., MYERS, B., & PAYNE, D. G. (1997). Recalling the unrecallable: Should hypnosis be used to recover memories in psychotherapy? *Current Directions in Psychological Science, 6*, 79–83.

MAASS, A., KARASAWA, M., POLITI, F., & SUGA, S. (2006). Do verbs and adjectives play different roles in different cultures? A cross-linguistic analysis of person representation. *Journal of Personality and Social Psychology, 90*, 734–750.

MACCOBY, E. E. (2000). Parenting and its effects on children: On reading and misreading behavior genetics. *Annual Review of Psychology, 51*, 1–27.

MACCOBY, E. E., & JACKLIN, C. N. (1974). *The psychology of sex differences.* Stanford, CA: Stanford University Press.

MACCOBY, E. E., & JACKLIN, C. N. (1980). Sex differences in aggression: A rejoinder and reprise. *Child Development, 51*, 964–980.

MACCOBY, E. E., & MARTIN, J. A. (1983). Socialization in the context of the family: Parent-child interaction. In P. H. Mussen (Ed.) & M. E. Hetherington (Vol. Ed.), *Carmichael's manual of child psychology: Vol. 4. Socialization, personality and social development* (pp. 1–102). New York: Wiley.

MACDONALD, M. C., PEARLMUTTER, N. J., & SEIDENBERG, M. S. (1994). The lexical nature of syntactic ambiguity resolution. *Psychological Review, 101*(4), 676–703.

MACK, A. (2003). Inattentional blindness: Looking without seeing. *Current Directions in Psychological Science, 12*, 180–184.

MACK, A., & ROCK, I. (1998). *Inattentional blindness.* Cambridge, MA: MIT Press.

MACNAMARA, J. (1982). *Names for things.* Cambridge, MA: MIT Press.

MACNICHOL, E. F., JR. (1986). A unifying presentation of photopigment spectra. *Vision Research, 29*, 543–546.

MACPHAIL, E. M. (1996). Cognitive function in mammals: The evolutionary perspective. *Cognitive Brain Research, 3*, 279–290.

MADDUX, J. E. (1995). *Self-efficacy, adaptation, and adjustment: Theory, research, and application.* Englewood Cliffs, NJ: Prentice-Hall.

MAFFEI, M., HALAAS, J., RAVUSSIN, E., PRATLEY, R. E., LEE, G. H., ZHANG, Y., ET AL. (1995). Leptin levels in human and rodent: Measurement of plasma leptin and ob RNA in obese and weight-reduced subjects. *Nature Medicine, 1*, 1155–1161.

MAGNUSSON, D., & ENDLER, N. S. (1977). Interactional psychology: Present status and future prospects. In D. Magnusson & N. S. Endler (Eds.), *Personality at the crossroads* (pp. 3–31). New York: Wiley.

MAGOUN, H. W., HARRISON, F., BROBECK, J. R., & RANSON, S. W. (1938). Activation of heat loss mechanisms by local heating of the brain. *Journal of Neurophysiology, 1*, 101–114.

MAGUIRE, M. C., & DUNN, J. (1997). Friendships in early childhood, and social understanding. *International Journal of Behavioral Development, 21*(4), 669–686.

MAHER, B. A. (1966). *Principles of psychopathology.* New York: McGraw-Hill.

MAIN, M., & SOLOMON, J. (1990). Procedures for identifying infants as disorganized/disoriented during the Ainsworth Strange Situation. In M. T. Greenberg, D. Cicchetti & E. M. Cummings (Eds.), *Attachment in the preschool years: Theory, research, and intervention* (pp. 121–160). Chicago: University of Chicago Press.

MALDONADO, J. R., BUTLER, L. D., & SPIEGEL, D. (2002). Treatments for dissociative disorders. In P. Nathan and J. M. Gorman (Eds.), *A guide to treatments that work* (2nd ed., pp. 463–496). New York: Oxford University Press.

MALHI, G. S., & BARTLETT, J. R. (2000). Depression: A role for neurosurgery? *British Journal of Neurosurgery, 14*, 415–422.

MALHI, G. S., & BARTLETT, J. R. (2000). Depression: A role for neurosurgery? *British Journal of Neurosurgery, 14*, 415–422.

MALINOWSKI, B. (1926). *Crime and custom in savage society.* London: Paul, Trench, and Trubner.

MALINOWSKI, B. (1927). *Sex and repression in savage society.* New York: Meridian, 1955.

MANDLER, J. M. (2000). Perceptual and conceptual processes in infancy. *Journal of Cognition and Development, 1*, 3–36.

MANGELSDORF, S. C., SHAPIRO, J. R., & MARZOLF, D. (1995). Developmental and temperamental differences in emotional regulation in infancy. *Child Development, 66*(6), 1817–1828.

MANTELL, D. M., & PANZARELLA, R. (1976). Obedience and responsibility. *British Journal of Social and Child Psychology, 15*, 239–245.

MARAÑON, G. (1924). Review of Fr. *Endocrinology, 2*, 301.

MARCH, J. S., LEONARD, H. L., & SWEDO, S. E. (1995). Obsessive-compulsive disorder. In J. S. March (Ed.), *Anxiety disorders in children and adolescents* (pp. 251–275). New York: Guilford Press.

MARCUS, D. E., & OVERTON, W. F. (1978). The development of cognitive gender constancy and sex-role preferences. *Child Development, 49,* 434–444.

MARCUS, G. F., PINKER, S., ULLMAN, M., HOLLANDER, M., ROSEN, T. J., & XU, F. (1992). Overregularization in language acquisition. *Monographs of the Society for Research in Child Development, 57*(4, Serial No. 228).

MARCUS, G. F., VIJAYAN, S., BANDI RAO, S., & VISHTON, P. M. (1999) Rule learning by seven-month-old infants. *Science, 283,* 77–80.

MARCUS, J., HANS, S. L., AUERBACH, J. G., & AUERBACH, A. G. (1993). Children at risk for schizophrenia: The Jerusalem Infant Development Study. II. Neuro behavioral deficits at school age. *Archives of General Psychiatry, 50,* 797–809.

MARESCHAL, D. (2000). Object knowledge in infancy: Current controversies and approaches. *Trends in Cognitive Science, 4,* 408–416.

MARKMAN, E. (1989). *Categorization and naming in children: Problems of induction.* Cambridge, MA: MIT Press.

MARKMAN, E. M. (1994). Constraints children place on word meanings. In P. Bloom (Ed.), *Language acquisition: Core readings.* Cambridge, MA: MIT Press.

MARKMAN, E. M., & HUTCHINSON, J. E. (1984). Children's sensitivity to constraints on word meaning: Taxonomic vs. thematic relations. *Cognitive Psychology, 16,* 1–27.

MARKMAN, E. M., & WACHTEL, G. A. (1988). Children's use of mutual exclusivity to constrain the meaning of words. *Cognitive Psychology, 20,* 121–157.

MARKSON, I., & BLOOM, P. (1997) Evidence against a dedicated system for word learning in children. *Nature, 385,* 813–815.

MARKUS, H. R. (1977). Self-schemata and processing information about the self. *Journal of Personality and Social Psychology, 35,* 63–78.

MARKUS, H. R., & KITAYAMA, S. (1991). Culture and the self: Implications for cognition, emotion, and motivation. *Psychological Review, 98,* 224–253.

MARKUS, H. R., & NURIUS, P. (1986). Possible selves. *American Psychologist, 41,* 954–969.

MARLER, P. R. (1970). A comparative approach to vocal learning: Song development in white-crowned sparrows. *Journal of Comparative and Physiological Psychology Monographs, 71*(No. 2, Part 2), 1–25.

MARLOWE, F., & WETSMAN, A. (2001). Preferred waist-to-hip ratio and ecology. *Personality and Individual Differences, 30,* 481–489.

MARR, D. (1982). *Vision.* San Francisco: Freeman.

MARSELLA, A. J., DUBANOSKI, J., HAMADA, W. C., & MORSE, H. (2000). The measurement of personality across cultures: Historical conceptual, and methodological issues and considerations. *American Behavioral Scientist, 44,* 41–62.

MARSHALL, G. D., & ZIMBARDO, P. G. (1979). Affective consequences of inadequately explained physiological arousal. *Journal of Personality and Social Psychology, 37,* 970–988.

MARSHALL, M., & GURR, T. (2005). *Peace and conflict 2005: A global survey of armed conflicts, self-determination movements, and democracy.* College Park, MD: Center for International Development and Conflict Management.

MARSHALL, N. L. (2004). The quality of early child care and children's development. *Current Directions in Psychological Science, 13,* 165–168.

MARSLEN-WILSON, W. (1975). Sentence perception as an interactive parallel process. *Science, 189,* 226–228.

MARSLEN-WILSON, W. D., & TEUBER, H. L. (1975). Memory for remote events in anterograde amnesia: Recognition of public figures from news photographs. *Neurobiologia, 13,* 353–364.

MARTIN, D. J., GARSKE, J. P., & DAVIS, M. K. (2000). Relation of the therapeutic alliance with outcome and other variables: A meta-analytic review. *Journal of Consulting and Clinical Psychology, 68,* 438-450.

MARTIN, J. A., KING, D. R., MACCOBY, E. E., & JACKLIN, C. N. (1984). Secular trends and individual differences in toilet-training progress. *Journal of Pediatric Psychology, 9,* 457–467.

MARTIN, L. (1986). "Eskimo words for snow": A case study in the genesis and decay of an anthropological example. *American Anthropologist, 88,* 418–423.

MARTIN, P., & ALBERS, P. (1995). Cerebellum and schizophrenia: A review. *Schizophrenia Bulletin, 21,* 241–251.

MARTINEZ, J. L., & DERRICK, B. E. (1996). Long-term potentiation and learning. *Annual Review of Psychology, 47,* 173–203.

MARX, J. (2003). Cellular warriors at the battle of the bulge. *Science, 299,* 846–849.

MASLACH, C. (1979). Negative emotional biasing of unexplained physiological arousal. *Journal of Personality and Social Psychology, 37,* 953–969.

MASLOW, A. H. (1968). *Toward a psychology of being* (2nd ed.). Princeton, NJ: Van Nostrand.

MASLOW, A. H. (1970). *Motivation and personality* (2nd ed.). New York: Harper.

MASLOW, A. H. (1996). *Future visions: The unpublished papers of Abraham Maslow* (E. Hoffman, Ed.). Thousand Oaks, CA: Sage.

MASTERS, M. S., & SANDERS, B. (1993). Is the gender difference in mental rotation disappearing? *Behavior Genetics, 23,* 337–341.

MATARAZZO, J. D. (1983). The reliability of psychiatric and psychological diagnosis. *Clinical Psychology Review, 3,* 103–145.

MATIN, L., PICOULT, E., STEVENS, J., EDWARDS, M., & MACARTHUR, R. (1982). Ocuparalytic illusion: Visual-field dependent spatial mislocations by humans partially paralyzed with curare. *Science, 216,* 198–180.

MATSON, J. L., & SEVIN, J. A. (1994). Issues in the use of aversives: Factors associated with behavior modification for autistic and other developmentally disabled people. In E. Schopler & G. B. Mesibov (Eds.), *Behavioral issues in autism* (pp. 211–225). New York: Plenum.

MATSUMOTO, D., YOO, S. H., HIRAYAMA, S., & PETROVA, G. (2005). Development and validation of a measure of display rule knowledge: The Display Rule Assessment Inventory. *Emotion, 5,* 23–40.

MATTHEWS, G., ZEIDNER, M., & ROBERTS, R. D. (2003). *Emotional intelligence: Science and Myth.* Cambridge, MA: MIT Press.

MATTHEWS, G., ZEIDNER, M., & ROBERTS, R. D. (2005). Emotional intelligence: An elusive ability? In O. Wilhelm & R. Engle (Eds.), *Handbook of understanding and measuring intelligence* (pp. 79–99). Thousand Oaks, CA: Sage.

MATTHEWS, K. A., BATSON, C. D., HORN, J., & ROSENMAN, R. H. (1981). "Principles in his nature which interest him in the fortune of others . . .": The heritability of empathic concern for others. *Journal of Personality, 49*(3), 237–247.

MATTISON, A., & MCWHIRTER, D. (1987). Male couples: The beginning years. Intimate Relationships: Some Social Work Perspectives on Love [Special issue]. *Journal of Social Work and Human Sexuality, 5,* 67–78.

MAUSS, I. B., LEVENSON, R. W., MCCARTER, L., WILHELM, F. H., & GROSS, J. J. (2005). The tie that binds? Coherence among emotional experience, behavior, and autonomic physiology. *Emotion, 5,* 175–190.

MAYER, J. D., SALOVEY, P., CARUSO, D. R., & SITARENIOS, G. (2003). Measuring emotional intelligence with the MSCEIT V2.0. *Emotion, 3,* 97–105.

MAYES, A. R. (1988). *Human organic memory disorders.* New York: Cambridge University Press.

MAYHAN, W. G. (2001). Regulation of blood-brain barrier permeability. *Microcirculation, 8,* 89–104.

MCCLEARN, G. E., & DEFRIES, J. C. (1973). *Introduction to behavioral genetics.* San Francisco: Freeman.

MCCLELLAND, J. L., & PATTERSON, K. (2002). Rules or connections in past-tense inflections: What does the evidence rule out? *Trends in Cognitive Science, 6*(11), 465–472.

McClelland, J. L., & Rumelhart, D. E. (Eds.). (1986). *Parallel distributed processing: Explorations in the microstructure of cognition: Vol. 2. Psychological and biological models.* Cambridge, MA: MIT Press.

McClelland, J. L., & Seidenberg, M. S. (2000). Why do kids say goed and brang? *Science, 287,* 47–48.

McClelland, J. L., Rumelhart, D. E., & Hinton, G. E. (1986). The appeal of parallel distributed processing. In D. E. Rumelhart, J. L. McClelland, and the PDP Research Group (Eds.), *Parallel distributed processing: Vol. 1. Foundations* (pp. 3–44). Cambridge, MA: MIT Press.

McClintock, M. K., & Adler, N. T. (1978). The role of the female during copulation in wild and domestic Norway rats (*Rattus Norvegicus*). *Behaviour, 67,* 67–96.

McCloskey, M., Wible, C. G., & Cohen, N. J. (1988). Is there a special flashbulb-memory mechanism? *Journal of Experimental Psychology: General, 117,* 171–181.

McConnell, A. R., & Leibold, J. M. (2001). Relations among the Implicit Association Test, discriminatory behavior, and explicit measures of racial attitudes. *Journal of Experimental Social Psychology, 37*(5), 435–442.

McCrae, R. R., & Costa, P. T. (1987). Validation of the five-factor model of personality across instruments and observers. *Journal of Personality and Social Psychology, 52,* 81–90

McCrae, R. R., & Costa, P. T., Jr. (1997). Personality trait structure as a human universal. *American Psychologist, 52,* 509–516.

McCrae, R. R., & Costa, P. T., Jr. (2003). *Personality in adulthood: A five-factor theory perspective* (2nd ed.). New York: Guilford Press.

McCrae, R. R., & Terracciano, A. (2005). Universal features of personality traits from the observer's perspective: Data from 50 cultures. *Journal of Personality and Social Psychology, 88,* 547–561.

McCranie, E. W., Hyer, L. A., Boudewyns, P. A., & Woods, M. G. (1992). Negative parenting behavior, combat exposure and PTSD symptom severity. Test of a person-event interaction model. *Journal of Nervous and Mental Disease, 180,* 431–438.

McCreary, D. R. (1994). The male role and avoiding femininity. *Sex Roles, 31,* 517–531.

McCrink, K., & Wynn, K. (2004). Large-number addition and subtraction by 9-month-old infants. *Psychological Science, 15,* 776–781.

McEwen, B. S., Biegon, A., Davis, P. G., Krey, L. C., Luine, V. N., McGinnis, M., et al. (1982). Steroid hormones: Humoral signals which alter brain cell properties and functions. *Recent Progress in Brain Research, 38,* 41–83.

McFall, R. M., & Treat, T. A. (1999). Quantifying the information value of clinical assessments with signal detection theory. *Annual Review of Psychology, 50,* 215–242.

McGaugh, J. (2003). *Memory and emotion.* New York: Columbia University Press.

McGaugh, J. L. (2000). Memory—a century of consolidation. *Science, 287,* 248–251.

McGee, A. W., Yang, Y., Fischer, Q. S., Daw, N. W., & Strittmatter, S. M. (2005). Experience-driven plasticity of visual cortex limited by myelin and Nogo receptor. *Science, 5744,* 2222–2226.

McGeoch, J. A., & Irion, A. L. (1952). *The psychology of human learning* (2nd ed.). New York: Longmans, Green.

McGhie, A., & Chapman, J. (1961). Disorders of attention and perception in early schizophrenia. *British Journal of Medical Psychology, 34,* 103–116.

McGrath, J., Welham, J., & Pemberton, M. (1995). Month of birth, hemisphere of birth, and schizophrenia. *British Journal of Psychiatry, 167,* 783–785.

McGregor, G. P., Desaga, J. F., Ehlenz, K., Fischer, A., Heese, F., Hegele, A., et al. (1996). Radiommunological measurement of leptin in plasma of obese and diabetic human subjects. *Endocrinology, 137,* 1501–1504.

McGue, M., & Lykken, D. T. (1992). Genetic influence on risk of divorce. *Psychological Science, 3,* 368–372.

McGue, M., Bouchard, T. J., Jr., Iacono, W. G., & Lykken, D. T. (1993). Behavioral genetics of cognitive ability: A life span perspective. In R. Plomin & G. E. McClearn (Eds.), *Nature, nurture and psychology* (pp. 59–76). Washington, DC: American Psychological Association.

McGuire, W. J. (1985). The nature of attitude and attitude change. In G. Lindzey & E. Aronson (Eds.), *Handbook of social psychology: Vol. 2* (3rd ed.). New York: Random House.

McIntosh, A. R., Rajah, M. N., & Lobaugh, N. J. (1999). Interactions of prefrontal cortex in relation to awareness in sensory learning. *Science, 284,* 1531–1533.

McNally, R. J. (2003). *Remembering trauma.* Cambridge, MA: Harvard University Press.

McNally, R. J. (2003a). Progress and controversy in the study of posttraumatic stress disorder. *Annual Review of Psychology, 54,* 229–252.

McNaughton, B. L., Douglas, R. M., & Goddard, G. V. (1978). Synaptic enhancement in fascia dentata: Cooperativity among coactive afferents. *Brain Research, 157,* 277–293.

Mead, G. H. (1934). *Mind, self, and society from the standpoint of a social behaviorist* (C. W. Morris, Ed.). Chicago: University of Chicago Press.

Mead, M. (1928). *Coming of age in Samoa.* New York: William Morrow.

Mealey, L., Bridgstock, R., & Townsend, G. C. (1999). Symmetry and perceived facial attractiveness: A monozygotic co-twin comparison. *Journal of Personality and Social Psychology, 76,* 151–158.

Medin, D. I., Atran, S., Cox, D., Coley, J., & Proffitt, J. S. (2006). Folkbiology of freshwater fish, *Cognition, 99*(3), 237–273.

Medin, D. L., & Bazerman, M. H. (1999). Broadening behvioral decision research: Multiple levels of cognitive processing. *Psychonomic Bulletin & Review, 6,* 533–546.

Medin, D. L., Goldstone, R. L., & Gentner, D. (1993). Respects for similarity. *Psychological Review, 100*(2), 254–278.

Medin, D. L., Schwartz, H., Blok, S. V., & Birnbaum, L. A. (1999). The semantic side of decision making. *Psychonomics Bulletin and Review, 6,* 562–569.

Mednick, S. A., Huttunen, M. O., & Macho'n, R. A. (1994). Prenatal influenza infections and adult schizophrenia. *Schizophrenia Bulletin, 20,* 263–267.

Meeter, M., & Murre, J. M. J. (2004). Consolidation of long-term memory: Evidence and alternatives. *Psychological Bulletin, 130,* 843–857.

Mehler, J., et al. (1996) Coping with linguistic diversity: The infant's viewpoint. In J. L. Morgan & K. Demuth (Eds.), *Signal to syntax: Bootstrapping from speech to grammar in early acquisition* (pp. 101–116). Hillsdale, NJ: Erlbaum.

Mehler, J., Jusczyk, P., Lambertz, G., Halsted, N., Bertoncini, J., & Amiel-Tison, C. (1988). A precursor to language acquisition in young infants. *Cognition, 29,* 143–178.

Mehler, J., & Nespor, M. (2004). Linguistic rhythm and the development of language. In A. Belletti & L. Rizzi (Eds.) Structures and beyond: The cartography of syntactic structures. Oxford: Oxford University Press.

Meichenbaum, D. (1985). *Stress inoculation training.* New York: Pergamon.

Meichenbaum, D. (1993). Changing conceptions of cognitive behavior modification: Retrospect and prospect. *Journal of Consulting and Clinical Psychology, 61,* 202–204.

Meichenbaum, D. (1996). Stress inoculation training for coping with stressors. *Clinical Psychologist, 49,* 4–7. .

Mellers, B. A., & McGraw, A. P. (1999). How to improve Bayesian reasoning: Comment on Gigerenzer and Hoffrage. *Psychological Review, 106,* 417–424.

Mellers, B., Chang, S.-J., Birnbaum, M., & Ordóñez, L. (1992). Preferences, prices, and ratings in risky decision making. *Journal of Experimental Psychology: Human Perception and Performance, 18,* 347–361.

Mellers, B., Hertwig, R., & Kahneman, D. (2001). Do frequency representations eliminate conjunction effects? An exercise in advance collaboration. *Psychological Science, 12,* 269–275.

MELTZER, H. Y. (1986). Lithium mechanisms in bipolar illness and altered intracellular calcium functions. *Biological Psychiatry, 21,* 492–510.

MELTZER, H. Y. (1987). Biological studies in schizophrenia. *Schizophrenia Bulletin, 13,* 77–111.

MELTZOFF, A. N. (1995). Understanding the intentions of others: Re-enactment of intended acts by 18-month-old children. *Developmental Psychology, 31*(5), 838–850.

MELTZOFF, A. N., & MOORE, M. K. (1977). Imitation of facial and manual gestures by human neonates. *Science, 198,* 75–78.

MELTZOFF, A. N., & MOORE, M. K. (1998). Infant intersubjectivity: Broadening the dialogue to include imitation, identity and intention. In S. Braten (Ed.), *Intersubjective communication and emotion in early ontogeny.* Cambridge: Cambridge University Press.

MELTZOFF, A. N., GOPNIK, A., & REPACHOLI, B. M. (1999). Toddlers' understanding of intentions, desires and emotions: Explorations of the dark ages. In P. D. Zelazo & J. W. Astington (Eds.), *Developing theories of intention: Social understanding and self-control* (pp. 17–41). Mahwah, NJ: Erlbaum.

MENYUK, P. (1977). *Language and maturation.* Cambridge, MA: MIT Press.

MENZEL, E. W. (1973). Chimpanzee spatial memory organization. *Science, 182,* 943–945.

MENZEL, E. W. (1978). Cognitive maps in chimpanzees. In S. H. Hulse, H. Fowler, & W. K. Honig (Eds.), *Cognitive processes in animal behavior* (pp. 375–422). Hillsdale, NJ: Erlbaum.

MERVIS, C. B., & CRISAFI, M. (1978). Order acquisition of subordinate, basic, and superordinate level categories. *Child Development, 49,* 988–998.

METCALFE, J. (1986). Premonitions of insight predict impending error. *Journal of Experimental Psychology: Learning, Memory and Cognition, 12,* 623–634.

METCALFE, J., & WEIBE, D. (1987). Intuition in insight and noninsight problem solving. *Memory and Cognition, 15,* 238–246.

MEYER, D. E., & SCHVANEVELDT, R. W. (1971). Facilitation in recognizing pairs of words: Evidence of a dependence between retrieval operations. *Journal of Experimental Psychology, 90,* 227–234.

MEYER-BAHLBURG, H. F. L., GRUEN, R. S., NEW, M. I., BELL, J. J., MORISHIMA, A., SHIMSHI, M., ET AL. (1996). Gender change from female to male in classical congenital adrenal hyperplasia. *Hormones and Behavior, 30,* 319–332.

MEZZACAPPA, E. S., KATKIN, E. S., & PALMER, S. N. (1999). Epinephrine, arousal, and emotion: A new look at two-factor theory. *Cognition and Emotion, 13,* 181–199.

MICALLEF, J., & BLIN, O. (2001). Neurobiology and clinical pharmacology of obsessive-compulsive disorder. *Clinical Neuropharmacology, 24,* 191–207.

MICHAELS, J. W., BLOOMEL, J. M., BROCATO, R. M., LINKOUS, R. A., & ROWE, J. S. (1982). Social facilitation and inhibition in a natural setting. *Replications in Social Psychology, 2,* 21–24.

MIKULINCER, M., & SHAVER, P. R. (2005). Attachment theory and emotions in close relationships: Exploring the attachment-related dynamics of emotional reactions to relational events. *Personal Relationships, 12,* 149–168.

MILAM, J. E., RICHARDSON, J. L., MARKS, G., KEMPER, C. A., & McCUTCHAN, A. J. (2004). The roles of dispositional optimism and pessimism in HIV disease progression. *Psychology & Health, 19,* 167–181.

MILGRAM, S. (1963). Behavioral study of obedience. *Journal of Abnormal and Social Psychology, 67,* 371–378.

MILGRAM, S. (1965). Some conditions of obedience and disobedience to authority. *Human Relations, 18,* 57–76.

MILGRAM, S. (1974). *Obedience to authority.* New York: Harper & Row.

MILGRAM, S., & MURRAY, T. H. (1992). Can deception in research be justified? In B. Slife & J. Rubenstein (Eds.), *Taking sides: Clashing views on controversial psychological issues* (7th ed.). Guilford, CT: Dushkin Publishing Group.

MILLER, A. G. (1986). *The obedience experiments: A case study of controversy in social science.* New York: Praeger.

MILLER, D. T. (1976). Ego involvement and attribution for success and failure. *Journal of Personality and Social Psychology, 34,* 901–906.

MILLER, D. T. (1999). The norm of self-interest. *American Psychologist, 54*(12), 1053–1060.

MILLER, E. M. (1994). Intelligence and brain myelination: A hypothesis. *Personality and Individual Differences, 17,* 803–832.

MILLER, G. (2005a). The dark side of glia. *Science, 308,* 778–781.

MILLER, G. (2005b). Mutant mice reveal secrets of the brain's impressionable youth. *Science, 309,* 2145.

MILLER, G. (2006a). China: Healing the metaphorical heart. *Science, 311,* 462–463.

MILLER, G. (2006b). The unseen: Mental illness's global toll. *Science, 311,* 458–460. Mineka, S., & Ben Hamida, S. (1998). Observational and nonconscious learning. In W. O'Donohue (Ed.), *Learning and behavior therapy* (pp. 421–439). Needham Heights, MA: Allyn and Bacon.

MILLER, G. A. (1956). The magical number seven plus or minus two: Some limits in our capacity for processing information. *Psychological Review, 63,* 81–97.

MILLER, J. G. (1984). Culture and the development of everyday social explanation. *Journal of Personality and Social Psychology, 46,* 961–978.

MILLER, J. G., & BERSOFF, D. M. (1998). The role of liking in perceptions of the moral responsibility to help: A cultural perspective. *Journal of Experimental Social Psychology, 34*(5), 443–469.

MILLER, J. G., BERSOFF, D. M., & HARWOOD, R. L. (1990). Perceptions of social responsibilities in India and in the United States: Moral imperatives or personal decisions? *Journal of Personality and Social Psychology, 58*(1), 33–47.

MILLER, L. C., PUTCHA-BHAGAVATULA, A. D., & PEDERSEN, W. C. (2002). Men's and women's mating preferences: Distinct evolutionary mechanisms? *Current Directions in Psychological Science, 11,* 88–93.

MILLER, L. K. (1999). The Savant Syndrome: Intellectual impairment and exceptional skill. *Psychological Bulletin, 125,* 31–46.

MILLER, N. E., BAILEY, C. J., & STEVENSON, J. A. F. (1950). Decreased "hunger" but increased food intake resulting from hypothalamic lesions. *Science, 112,* 256–259.

MILLER, P. A., EISENBERG, N., FABES, R. A., & SHELL, R. (1989). Mothers' emotional arousal as a moderator in the socialization of children's empathy. *New Directions for Child Development, 44.*

MILLER, R. R., BARNET, R. C., & GRAHAME, N. J. (1995). Assessment of the Rescorla-Wagner model. *Psychological Bulletin, 117,* 363–387.

MILLS, J., & CLARK, M. S. (1994). Communal and exchange relationships: Controversies and research. In R. Erber & R. Gilmour (Eds.), *Theoretical frameworks for personal relationships* (pp. 29–42). Hillsdale, NJ: Erlbaum.

MILNER, B. (1966). Amnesia following operation on the temporal lobes. In C. W. M. Whitty & O. L. Zangwill (Eds.), *Amnesia* (pp. 109–133). London: Butterworth.

MILNER, B., & PETRIDES, M. (1984). Behavioural effects of frontal-lobe lesions in man. *Trends in Neurosciences, 7,* 403–407.

MINEKA, S., & ZINBARG, R. (2006). A contemporary learning theory perspective on the etiology of anxiety disorders: It's not what you thought it was. *American Psychologist, 61*(1), 10–26.

MINUCHIN, S. (1974). *Families and family therapy.* Cambridge, MA: Harvard University Press.

MISCHEL, W. (1968). *Personality and assessment.* New York: Wiley.

MISCHEL, W. (1973). Towards a cognitive social learning reconceptualization of personality. *Psychological Review, 80,* 252–283.

MISCHEL, W. (1974). Processes in delay of gratification. In L. Berkowitz (Ed.), *Advances in experimental social psychology: Vol. 7.* New York: Academic Press.

MISCHEL, W. (1984). Convergences and challenges in the search for consistency. *American Psychologist, 39,* 351–364.

MISCHEL, W. (2004). Toward an integrative science of the person. *Annual Review of Psychology, 55*, 1–22.

MISCHEL, W., & BAKER, N. (1975). Cognitive appraisals and transformations in delay behavior. *Journal of Personality and Social Psychology, 31*, 254–261.

MISCHEL, W., & MISCHEL, H. N. (1983). Development of children's knowledge of self-control strategies. *Child Development, 54*, 603–619.

MISCHEL, W., & MOORE, B. (1980). The role of ideation in voluntary delay for symbolically presented awards. *Cognitive Therapy and Research, 4*, 211–221.

MISCHEL, W., & SHODA, Y. (1995). A cognitive-affective system theory of personality: Reconceptualizing situations, dispositions, dynamics, and invariance in personality structure. *Psychological Review, 102*, 246–268.

MISCHEL, W., & SHODA, Y. (1998). Reconciling processing dynamics and personality dispositions. *Annual Review of Psychology, 49*, 229–258.

MISCHEL, W., & SHODA, Y. (2000). A cognitive-affective system theory of personality: Reconceptualizing situations, dispositions, dynamics, and invariance in personality structure. In E. T. Higgins & A. W. Kruglanski (Eds.), *Motivational science: Social and personality perspectives* (pp. 150–176). Philadelphia: Psychology Press/Taylor & Francis.

MISCHEL, W., SHODA, Y., & MENDOZA-DENTON, R. (2002). Situation-behavior profiles as a locus of consistency in personality. *Current Directions in Psychological Science, 11*, 50–54.

MISCHEL, W., SHODA, Y., & PEAKE, P. K. (1988). The nature of adolescent competencies predicted by preschool delay of gratification. *Journal of Personality and Social Psychology, 54*, 687–696.

MISCHEL, W., SHODA, Y., & RODRIGUEZ, M. L. (1992). Delay of gratification in children. In G. Loewenstein & J. Elster, (Eds), *Choice over time* (pp. 147–164). New York: Russell Sage Foundation.

MISELIS, R. R., & EPSTEIN, A. N. (1970). Feeding induced by 2-deoxy-D-glucose injections into the lateral ventrical of the rat. *Physiologist, 13*, 262.

MISHLER, E. G., & WAXLER, N. E. (1968). Family interaction and schizophrenia: Alternative frameworks of interpretation. In D. Rosenthal & S. S. Kety (Eds.), *The transmission of schizophrenia* (pp. 213–222). New York: Pergamon.

MITA, T. H., DERMER, M., & KNIGHT, J. (1977). Reversed facial images and the mere exposure hypothesis. *Journal of Personality and Social Psychology, 35*, 597–601.

MIYASHITA, Y. (1995). How the brain creates imagery: Projection to primary visual cortex. *Science, 268*, 1719–1720.

MOFFITT, T. E., CASPI, A., & RUTTER, M. (2006). Measured gene-environment interactions in psychopathology: Concepts, research strategies, and implications for research, intervention, and public understanding of genetics. *Perspectives on Psychological Sciences, 1*, 5–27.

MOFFITT, T. E., CASPI, A., HARKNESS, A. R., & SILVA, P. A. (1993). The natural history of change in intellectual performance: Who changes? How much? Is it meaningful? *Journal of Child Psychology and Psychiatry and Allied Disciplines, 34*(4), 455–506.

MOGHADDAM, F. (1998). *Social psychology: Exploring universals across cultures*. New York: Freeman.

MOLONEY, D. P., BOUCHARD, T. J., JR., & SEGAL, N. L. (1991). A genetic and environmental analysis of the vocational interests of monozygotic and dizygotic twins reared apart. *Journal of Vocational Behavior, 39*, 76–109.

MONEY, J. (1980). *Love and love sickness*. Baltimore: Johns Hopkins University Press.

MONEY, J., & EHRHARDT, A. A. (1972). *Man and woman, boy and girl*. Baltimore: Johns Hopkins University Press.

MONROE, S. M., & HADJIYANNAKIS, K. (2002). The social environment and depression: Focusing on severe life stress. In I. H. Gotlib and C. L. Hammen (Eds.), *Handbook of depression* (pp. 314–340). New York: Guilford Press.

MONTAGUE, D., & WALKER-ANDREWS, A. (2002). Mothers, fathers, and infants: The role of person familiarity and parental involvement in infants' perception of emotional expressions. *Child Development, 73*, 1339–1352.

MONTE, C. F., & SOLLOD, R. N. (2003). *Beneath the mask: An introduction to theories of personality* (7th ed.). Danvers, MA: Wiley.

MONTGOMERY, S. A. (1995). Selective serotonin reuptake inhibitors in the acute treatment of depression. In F. E. Bloom & D. Kupfer (Eds.), *Psychopharmacology: The fourth generation of progress* (pp. 1043–1051). New York: Raven.

MOONEY, C. (2005). The Republican war on science. New York: Basic Books.

MOORE, C., & DUNHAM, P. (EDS.). (2004). *Joint attention: Its origin and role in development*. Hillsdale, NJ: Erlbaum.

MOORHEAD, G., FERENCE, R., & NECK, C. P. (1991). Group decision fiascoes continue: Space shuttle Challenger and a revised groupthink framework. *Human Relations, 44*(6), 539–550.

MORA, F., ROLLS, E. T., & BURTON, M. J. (1976). Modulation during learning of the responses of neurons in the lateral hypothalamus to the sight of food. *Experimental Neurology, 53*, 508–519.

MORA, G. (1975). Historical and theoretical trends in psychiatry. In A. M. Freedman, H. I. Kaplan, & B. J. Sadock (Eds.), *Comprehensive textbook of psychiatry: Vol. 1* (pp. 1–75). Baltimore: Williams & Wilkins.

MORAY, N. (1959). Attention in dichotic listening: Affective cues and the influence of instructions. *Quarterly Journal of Experimental Psychology, 11*, 56–60.

MORELAND, R. L., & ZAJONC, R. B. (1982). Exposure effects in person perception: Familiarity, similarity, and attraction. *Journal of Experimental Social Psychology, 18*, 395–415.

MORELLI, G., ROGOFF, B., OPPENHEIM, D., & GOLDSMITH, D. (1992). Cultural variation in infants sleeping arrangements: Questions of independence. *Developmental Psychology, 28*, 604–613.

MORGAN, C. D., & MURRAY, H. A. (1935). A method for investigating fantasies: The Thematic Apperception Test. *Archives of Neurological Psychiatry, 34*, 289–306.

MORGAN, C. P., & ARAM, J. D. (1975). The preponderance of arguments in the risky shift phenomenon. *Journal of Experimental Social Psychology, 11*(1), 25–34.

MORGAN, J. L. (1996). A rhythmic bias in preverbal speech segmentation. *Journal of Memory and Language, 35*, 666–688.

MORRIS, M. W., & PENG, K. (1994). Culture and cause: American and Chinese attributions for social and physical events. *Journal of Personality and Social Psychology, 67*, 949–971.

MORSBACH, H., & TYLER, W. J. (1986). In R. Harr (Ed.), *The social construction of emotions* (pp. 289–307). Oxford: Blackwell.

MORSELLA, E. (2005). The function of phenomenal states: Supramodular interaction theory. *Psychological Review, 112*, 1000–1021.

MORSELLA, E., LEVINE, L. R., & BARGH, J. A. (2004). Nonconscious activation of action plans: A cascade model of automatic social behavior. Unpublished manuscript, Yale University.

MOSCOVICI, S., & ZAVALLONI, M. (1969). The group as a polarizer of attitudes. *Journal of Personality and Social Psychology, 12*(2), 125–135.

MOSER, M. B. (1999). Making more synapses: A way to store information? *Cellular and Molecular Life Sciences, 55*, 593–600.

MOUNTS, N. S., & STEINBERG, L. (1995). An ecological analysis of peer influence on adolescent grade point average and drug use. *Developmental Psychology, 31*(6), 915–922.

MULFORD, R. (1986). First words of the blind child. In M. Smith & J. Locke (Eds.), *The emergent lexicon: The child's development of a linguistic vocabulary*. New York: Academic Press.

MULICK, J. A. (1990). The ideology and science of punishment in mental retardation. *American Journal on Mental Retardation, 95*, 142–156.

MULLEN, M. K. (1994). Earliest recollections of childhood: A demographic analysis. *Cognition, 52*(1), 55–79.

MULLEN, M. K., & YI, S. (1995). The cultural context of talk about the past: Implications for the development of autobiographical memory. *Cognitive Development, 10*(3), 407–419.

MULROW, C. D., WILLIAMS, J. W., JR., CHIQUETTE, E., AGUILAR, C., HITCHCOCK-NOEL, P., LEE, S., ET AL. (2000). Efficacy of newer medications for treating depression in primary care patients. *American Journal of Medicine, 108,* 54–64.

MURPHY, F. C., NIMMO-SMITH, I., & LAWRENCE, A. D. (2003). Functional neuroanatomy of emotion: A meta-analysis. *Cognitive, Affective, and Behavioral Neuroscience, 3,* 207–233.

MURPHY, G. L. (2002). *The big book of concepts.* Cambridge, MA: MIT Press.

MURRAY, C. (1998). *Income inequality and IQ.* Washington, DC: American Enterprise Institute.

MURRAY, L., & TREVARTHEN, C. (1985). *Social perception in infants.* New York: Ablex.

MUSSELL, M., MITCHELL, J., CROSBY, R., FULKERSON, J., HOBERMAN, H., & ROMANO, J. (2000). Commitment to treatment goals in prediction of group cognitive-behavioral therapy treatment outcome for women with bulimia nervosa. *Journal of Consulting and Clinical Psychology, 68,* 432–437.

NADEL, L., & JACOBS, W. J. (1998). Traumatic memory is special. *Current Directions in Psychological Science, 7,* 154–157.

NADEL, L., & MOSCOVITCH, M. (2001). The hippocampal complex and long-term memory revisited. *Trends in Cognitive Science, 5,* 228–230.

NAIGLES, L. G. (1990). Children use syntax to learn verb meanings. *Journal of Child Language, 17,* 357–374.

NARROW, W. REGIER, D., RAE, D., MANDERSCHEID, R., & LOCKE, B. (1993). Use of services by persons with mental and addictive disorders: Findings from the National Institute of Mental Health Epidemiologic Catchment Area Program. *Archives of General Psychiatry, 50,* 95–107.

NATHAN, P. E., & GORMAN, J. M. (EDS.). (2002). *A guide to treatments that work* (2nd ed.). New York: Oxford University Press.

NATHAN, P. E., STUART, S. P., & DOLAN, S. L. (2000). Research on psychotherapy efficacy and effectiveness: Between Scylla and Charybdis? *Psychological Bulletin, 126,* 964–981.

NATIONAL RESEARCH COUNCIL AND INSTITUTE OF MEDICINE (2000). *From neurons to neighborhoods: The science of early childhood development.* Committee on Integrating the Science of Early Childhood Development. J. Shonkoff & D. Phillips (Eds.), Board on Children, Youth, and Families, Commission on Behavioral and Social Sciences and Education. Washington, DC: National Academy Press.

NAUTA, W. J. H., & FEIRTAG, M. (1986). *Fundamental neuroanatomy.* New York: Freeman.

NAVARRA, P., DELLO RUSSO, C., MANCUSO, C., PREZIOSI, P., & GROSSMAN, A. (2000). Gaseous neuromodulators in the control of neuroendocrine stress axis. *Annals of the New York Academy of Sciences, 917,* 638–646.

NAZZI, T., BERTONCINI, J., & MEHLER, J. (1998). Language discrimination by newborns: Toward an understanding of the role of rhythm. *Journal of Experimental Psychology: Human Perception and Performance, 24,* 756–766.

NEEDHAM, D., & BEGG, I. (1991). Problem-oriented training promotes spontaneous analogical transfer: Memory-oriented training promotes memory for training. *Memory and Cognition, 19,* 543–557.

NEIMEYER, G. J. (1984). Cognitive complexity and marital satisfaction. *Journal of Social and Clinical Psychology, 2,* 258–263.

NEISSER, U. (1982a). *Memory observed.* San Francisco: Freeman.

NEISSER, U. (1982b, January). On the trail of the tape-recorder fallacy. Paper presented at a symposium on "The influence of hypnosis and related states on memory: Forensic implications" at the meetings of the American Association for the Advancement of Science, Washington, DC.

NEISSER, U. (1986). Remembering Pearl Harbor: Reply to Thompson and Cowan. *Cognition, 23,* 285–286.

NEISSER, U. (1997). Rising scores on intelligence tests. *American Scientist, 85,* 440–447.

NEISSER, U. (ED.). (1998). *The rising curve: Long-term gains in IQ and related measures.* Washington, DC: American Psychological Association.

NEISSER, U., & BECKLEN, R. (1975). Selective looking: Attending to visually specified events. *Cognitive Psychology, 7*(4), 480–494.

NEISSER, U., BOODOO, G., BOUCHARD, T. J., JR., & BOYKIN, A. W. (1996). Intelligence: Knowns and unknowns. *American Psychologist, 51*(2), 77–101.

NELSON, K., & FIVUSH, R. (2000). Socialization of memory. In E. Tulving & F. I. M. Craik (Eds.), *The Oxford handbook of memory* (pp. 283–295). London: Oxford University Press.

NEMETH, C., & CHILES, C. (1988). Modeling courage: The role of dissent in fostering independence. *European Journal of Social Psychology, 18,* 275–280.

NETTELBECK, T., & YOUNG, R. (1996). Intelligence and the savant syndrome: Is the whole greater than the sum of the fragments? *Intelligence, 22,* 49–68.

NEUGEBAUER, R. (1979). Medieval and early modern theories of mental illness. *Archives of General Psychiatry, 36,* 477–484.

NEWCOMB, A. F., & BAGWELL, C. L. (1995). Children's friendship relations: A meta-analytic review. *Psychological Bulletin, 117*(2), 306–347.

NEWCOMB, A. F., BUKOWSKI, W. M., & PATTEE, L. (1993). Children's peer relations: A meta-analytic review of popular, rejected, neglected, controversial, and average sociometric status. *Psychological Bulletin, 113*(1), 99–128.

NEWCOMBE, F., RATCLIFF, G., & DAMASIO, H. (1987). Dissociable visual and spatial impairments following right posterior cerebral lesions: Clinical, neuropsychological and anatomical evidence. *Neuropsychologia, 25*(1 B), 149–161.

NEWCOMBE, N. S. (2002). The nativist-empiricst controversy in the context of recent research on spatial and quantitative development. *Psychological Science, 13,* 395–401.

NEWELL, A., & SIMON, H. A. (1972). *Human problem solving.* Englewood Cliffs, NJ: Prentice-Hall.

NEWMAN, E. A., & ZAHS, K. R. (1998). Modulation of neuronal activity by glial cells in the retina. *Journal of Neuroscience, 18,* 4022–4028.

NEWPORT, E. (1990). Maturational constraints on language learning. *Cognitive Science, 14,* 11–28.

NEWPORT, E. L. (1999). Reduced input in the acquisition of signed languages: Contributions to the study of creolization. In M. DeGraff (Ed.), *Language creation and language change: Creolization, diachrony, and development.* Cambridge, MA: MIT Press.

NEWPORT, E. L., & ASHBROOK, E. F. (1977). The emergence of semantic relations in American Sign Language. *Papers and Reports in Child Language Development, 13,* 16–21.

NICHD EARLY CHILD CARE RESEARCH NETWORK. (1997). The effects of infant child care on infant-mother attachment security: Results of the NICHD study of early child care. *Child Development, 68,* 860–879.

NICHD EARLY CHILD CARE RESEARCH NETWORK (2001). Child-care and family predictors of preschool attachment and stability from infancy. *Developmental Psychology, 37,* 847–862.

NICHD EARLY CHILD CARE RESEARCH NETWORK. (2003). Does quality of child care affect child outcomes at age 4 1/2? *Developmental Psychology, 39,* 451–469.

NICHD EARLY CHILD RESEARCH NETWORK (2006). Child-care effect sizes for the NICHD Study of Early Child Care and Youth Development. *American Psychologist, 61,* 99–116.

NICHOLSON, R. A., & BERMAN, J. S. (1983). Is follow-up necessary in evaluating psychotherapy? *Psychological Bulletin, 93,* 261–278.

NICKERSON, R. A., & ADAMS, M. J. (1979). Long-term memory for a common object. *Cognitive Psychology, 11,* 287–307.

NISBETT, R., & ROSS, L. (1980). *Human inference: Strategies and shortcomings of social judgment.* Englewood Cliffs, NJ: Prentice-Hall.

NISBETT, R. E. (1980). The trait construct in lay and professional psychology. In L. Festinger (Ed.), *Retrospections on social psychology* (pp. 109–130). New York: Oxford University Press.

NISBETT, R. E. (2003). *The geography of thought: Why we think the way we do.* New York: Free Press.

NISBETT, R. E., & COHEN, D. (1996). *Culture of honor: The psychology of violence in the South.* Boulder, CO: Westview Press.

NISBETT, R. E., KRANTZ, D. H., JEPSON, C., & KUNDA, Z. (1983). The use of statistical heuristics in everyday inductive reasoning. *Psychological Review, 90,* 339–363.

NISBETT, R. E., & MIYAMOTO, Y. (2005). The influence of culture: Holistic versus analytic perception. *Trends in Cognitive Science, 9,* 467–473.

NISBETT, R. E., PENG, K., CHOI, I., & NORENZAYAN, A. (2001). Culture and systems of thought: Holistic versus analytic cognition. *Psychological Review, 108*(2), 291–310.

NISBETT, R. E., & WILSON, T. D. (1977). Telling more than we can know: Verbal reports on mental processes. *Psychological Review, 84,* 231–259.

NOLEN-HOEKSMA, S. (1987). Sex differences in unipolar depression: Evidence and theory. *Psychological Bulletin, 101,* 259–282.

NOPOULOS, P., FLAUM, M., & ANDREASEN, N. C. (1997). Sex differences and brain morphology in schizophrenia. *American Journal of Psychiatry, 154,* 1648–1654.

NORCROSS, J. C., & FREEDHEIM, D. K. (1992). Into the future: Retrospect and prospect in psychotherapy. In D. K. Freedheim (Ed.), *History of psychotherapy.* Washington, DC: American Psychological Association.

NORMAN, W. T. (1963). Toward an adequate taxonomy of personality attributes: Replicated factor structure in peer nomination personality ratings. *Journal of Abnormal and Social Psychology, 66,* 574–583.

NUTT, D. J. (2001). Neurobiological mechanisms in generalized anxiety disorder [Suppl.]. *Journal of Clinical Psychiatry, 62*(11), 22–27.

NYITI, R. M. (1976). The development of conservation in the Meru children of Tanzania. *Child Development, 47*(4), 1122–1129.

O'CONNOR, T. G., RUTTER, M., BECKETT, C., KEAVENEY, L., KREPPNER, J. M., & ENGLISH AND ROMANIAN ADOPTION STUDY TEAM. (2000). The effects of global severe privation on cognitive competence: Extension and longitudinal follow-up. *Child Development, 71*(2), 376–390.

O'NEILL, D. K., ASTINGTON, J. W., & FLAVELL, J. H. (1992). Young children's understanding of the role that sensory experiences play in knowledge acquisition. *Child Development, 63*(2), 474–490.

OAKES, P. J., & TURNER, J. C. (1980). Social categorization and intergroup behavior: Does minimal intergroup discrimination make social identity more positive? *European Journal of Social Psychology, 10,* 295–301.

OBERAUER, K., SCHULZE, R., WILHELM, O., & SÜSS, H.-M. (2005). Working memory and intelligence: Their correlation and their relation: Comment on Ackerman, Beier, and Boyle (2005). *Psychological Bulletin, 131,* 61–65.

OCHSNER, K. N., KNIERIM, K., LUDLOW, D. H., HANELIN, J., RAMACHANDRAN, T., GLOVER, G., ET AL. (2004). Reflecting upon feelings: An fMRI study of neural systems supporting the attribution of emotion to self and other. *Journal of Cognitive Neuroscience, 16,* 1746–1772.

ODIORNE, J. M. (1957). Color changes. In M. E. Brown (Ed.), *The physiology of fishes: Vol. 2.* New York: Academic Press.

OESTERMAN, K., BJOERKQVIST, K., LAGERSPETZ, K. M. J., KAUKIAINEN, A., LANDAU, S. F., FRACZEK, A., ET AL. (1998). Cross-cultural evidence of female indirect aggression. *Aggressive Behavior, 24*(1), 1–8.

OFSHE, R. (1992). Inadvertent hypnosis during interrogation: False confession due to dissociative state; mis-identified multiple personality and the Satanic Cult Hypothesis. *International Journal of Clinical and Experimental Hypnosis, 40,* 125–136.

ÖHMAN, A., & MINEKA, S. (2001). Fears, phobias, and preparedness: Toward an evolved module of fear and fear learning. *Psychological Review, 108,* 483–522.

ÖHMAN, A., & MINEKA, S. (2003). The malicious serpent: Snakes as a prototypical stimulus for an evolved module of fear. *Current Directions in Psychological Science, 12,* 5–9.

ÖHMAN, A., & SOARES, J. J. (1993). On the automatic nature of phobic fear: Conditioned electrodermal responses to masked fear-relevant stimuli. *Journal of Abnormal Psychology, 102*(1), 121–132.

OKASHA, A., & OKASHA, T. (2000). Mental health in Cairo (Al-Qahira). *International Journal of Mental Health, 28,* 62 68.

OLFSON, M., & KLERMAN, G. L. (1993). Trends in the prescription of psychotropic medications. The role of physician specialty. *Medical Care, 31,* 559–564.

OLLENDICK, T., & KING, N. (EDS.). (1994). *International handbook of phobic and anxiety disorders in children and adolescents: Issues in clinical child psychology.* New York: Plenum.

OLSON, D. J. (1991). Species differences in spatial memory among Clark's nutcrackers, scrub jays, and pigeons. *Journal of Experimental Psychology: Animal Behavior Processes, 17*(4), 363–376.

OLSON, W. K. (1997). *The excuse factory: How employment law is paralyzing the American workplace.* New York: Free Press.

ONISHI, K., & BAILLARGEON, R. (2005). Do 15-month-old infants understand false belief? *Science, 308,* 255–258.

ÖHMAN, A. (2005). The role of the amygdala in human fear: Automatic detection of threat. *Psychoneuroendocrinology, 30,* 953–958.

ÖHMAN, A., & SOARES, J. J. F. (1994). "Unconscious anxiety": Phobic responses to masked stimuli. *Journal of Abnormal Psychology, 103,* 231–240.

OPPENHEIM, D., SAGI, A., & LAMB, M. (1988). Infant-adult attachments on the kibbutz and their relation to socioemotional development 4 years later. *Developmental Psychology, 24,* 427–433.

ORLANSKY, H. (1949). Infant care and personality. *Psychological Bulletin, 46,* 1–48.

ORNE, M. T. (1951). The mechanisms of hypnotic age regression: An experimental study. *Journal of Abnormal and Social Psychology, 58,* 277–299.

ORTONY, A., CLORE, G. L., & COLLINS, A. (1988). *The cognitive structure of emotions.* New York: Cambridge University Press.

OZER, E. J., & WEISS, D. S. (2004). Who develops posttraumatic stress disorder? *Current Directions in Psychological Science, 13,* 169–172.

PALLIER, C., CHRISTOPHE, A., & MEHLER, J. (1997). Language-specific listening. *Trends in Cognitive Science, 1*(4).

PALMER, S. E. (2002). Perceptual grouping: It's later than you think. *Current Directions in Psychological Science, 11*(3), 101–106.

PANKSEPP, J. (1991). Affective neuroscience: A conceptual framework for the neurobiological study of emotions. *International Review of Studies on Emotion, 1,* 59–99.

PANKSEPP, J. (1998). *Affective neuroscience: The foundations of human and animal emotions.* Oxford, England: Oxford University Press.

PAPAFRAGOU, A., MASSEY, C., & GLEITMAN, L. R. (2006). When English proposes what Greek presupposes, *Cognition, 98*(3), B75–B86.

PARKE, R. D. (1981). *Fathers.* Cambridge, MA: Harvard University Press.

PARKER, G., MAHENDRAN, R., KOH, E. S., & MACHIN, D. (2000). Season of birth in schizophrenia: No latitute at the equator. *British Journal of Psychiatry, 176,* 68–71.

PARKER, J., RUBIN, K., PRICE, J., & DEROSIER, M. (1995). Peer relationships, child development and adjustment: A developmental psychopathology. In Cicchetti, D. & Cohen, D. (Eds.), *Developmental Psychopathology.* NY: Wiley.

PARNAS, J., & JORGENSEN, A. (1989). Premorbid psychopathology in schizophrenia spectrum. *British Journal of Psychiatry, 155,* 623–627.

PARSONS, J. E., ADLER, T. F., & KACZALA, C. M. (1982). Socialization of achievement attitudes and beliefs: Parental influences. *Child Development, 53*(2), 310–321.

PASHLER, H., JOHNSTON, J. C., & RUTHRUFF, E. (2000). Attention and performance. *Annual Review of Psychology, 52,* 629–651.

PAVLOV, I. (1927). *Conditioned reflexes.* Oxford: Oxford University Press.

PAYNE, J. D., NADEL, L., BRITTON, W. B., & JACOBS, W. J. (2004). The biopsychology of trauma and memory. In D. Reisberg & P. Hertel (Eds.), *Memory and emotion* (pp. 76–128). New York: Oxford University Press.

PEARCE, J. M., & BOUTON, M. E. (2001). Theories of associative learning in animals. *Annual Review of Psychology, 52,* 111–139.

PEDERSEN, P. B., FUKUYAMA, M., & HEATH, A. (1989). Client, counselor, and contextual variables in multicultural counseling. In P. B. Pedersen, J. G. Draguns, W. J. Lonner, & J. E. Trimble (Eds.), *Counseling across cultures* (pp. 23–52). Honolulu: University of Hawaii.

PEDERSEN, W. C., MILLER, L. C., PUTCHA-BHAGAVATULA, A. D., & YANG, Y. (2002). Evolved sex differences in the number of partners desired? The long and the short of it. *Psychological Science, 13,* 157–161.

PEDERSON, E., DANZIGER, E., WILKINS, D., LEVINSON, S., KITA, S., & SENFT, G. (1998). Semantic typology and spatial conceptualization. *Language 74*(3), 557–589.

PEÑA, M., BONATTI, L., NESPOR, M., & MEHLER, J. (2002). Signal driven computations in speech processing. *Science, 298,* 604–607.

PEÑA, M., MAKI, A., KOVA, D., DEHAENE-LAMBERTZ, G., KOIZUMI, H., BOUQUET, F., ET AL. (2003). Sounds and silence: An optical topography study of language recognition at birth. *Proceedings of the National Academy of Sciences, 100*(20), 11702–11705.

PENDERGAST, M. (1995). *Victims of memory: Sex abuse accusations and shattered lives.* Hinesburg, VT: Upper Access.

PENFIELD, W., & RASMUSSEN, T. (1950). *The cerebral cortex of man.* New York: Macmillan.

PENNISI, E. (2005). Strong personalities can pose problems in the mating game. *Science, 309,* 694–695.

PENTON-VOAK, I. S., & PERRETT, D. I. (2000). Female preference for male faces changes cyclically: Further evidence. *Evolution and Human Behavior, 21*(1), 39–48.

PEPLAU, L. A. (2003). Human sexuality: How do men and women differ? *Current Directions in Psychological Science, 12,* 37–40.

PEPPERBERG, I. (1999). Rethinking syntax: A commentary on E. Kako's "Elements of syntax in the systems of three language-trained animals." *Animal Learning & Behavior, 27,* 15–17.

PERDUE, C. W., DOVIDIO, J. F., GURTMAN, M. B., & TYLER, R. B. (1990). Us and them: Social categorization and the process of intergroup bias. *Journal of Personality and Social Psychology, 59,* 475–486.

PERKINS, D. N., & GROTZER, T. A. (1997). Teaching intelligence. *American Psychologist, 52,* 1125–1133.

PERLS, F. S. (1967). Group vs. individual therapy. *ETC, 24,* 306–312.

PERLS, F. S. (1969). *Gestalt therapy verbatim.* Moab, UT: Real People Press.

PERNER, J., & LANG, B. (1999). Development of theory of mind and executive control. *Trends in Cognitive Science, 6,* 337–344.

PERNER, J., & RUFFMAN, T. (2005). Infants' insight into the mind: How deep? *Science, 308,* 214–216.

PERROTT, D. A., GENTNER, D., & BODENHAUSEN, G. V. (2005). Resistance is futile: The unwitting insertion of analogical inferences in memory. *Psychonomics Bulletin & Review, 12,* 696–702.

PETERSON, C. (1999). Personal control and well-being. In D. Kahneman, E. Diener, & N. Schwarz (Eds.), *Well-being: The foundations of hedonic psychology* (pp. 288–301). New York: Russell Sage Foundation.

PETERSON, C. T., & SELIGMAN, M. E. P. (2004). Character strengths and virtues: A handbook and classification. Washington, DC: APA Press and Oxford University Press.

PETERSON, C., & MCCABE, A. (1994). A social interactionist account of developing decontextualized narrative skill. *Developmental Psychology, 30*(6), 937–948.

PETERSON, C., & PARK, C. (1998). Learned helplessness and explanatory style. In D. F. Barone, M. Hersen, & V. Van Hasselt (Eds.), *Advanced personality* (pp. 287–310). New York: Plenum.

PETERSON, C., & SELIGMAN, M. E. P. (1984). Causal explanations as a risk factor for depression: Theory and evidence. *Psychological Review, 91,* 341–374.

PETERSON, C., SEMMEL, A., von BAEYER, C., ABRAMSON, L. Y., METALSKY, G. I., & SELIGMAN, M. E. P. (1982). The Attributional Style Questionnaire. *Cognitive Therapy and Research, 6,* 287–299.

PETERSON, C., & VAIDYA, R. S. (2001). Explanatory style, expectations, and depressive symptoms. *Personality and Individual Differences, 31,* 1217–1223.

PETERSON, M. A., & ENNS, J. T. (2005). The edge complex: Implicit memory for figure assignment in shape perception. *Perception & Psychophysics, 67,* 727–740.

PETERSON, R. S., & BEHFAR, K. J. (2005). Leadership as group regulation. In D. M. Messick & R. M. Kramer (Eds.), *The psychology of leadership: New perspectives and research* (pp. 143–162). Mahwah, NJ: Erlbaum.

PETERSON, S. E., FOX, P. T., POSNER, M. I., MINTUN, M., & RAICHLE, M. E. (1988). Positron emission tomographic studies of the processing of single words. *Journal of Cognitive Neuroscience, 1,* 153–170.

PETRILL, S. A., LUO, D., THOMPSON, L. A., & DETTERMAN, D. K. (2001). Inspection time and the relationship among elementary cognitive tasks, general intelligence, and specific cognitive abilities. *Intelligence, 29,* 487–496.

PETTIGREW, T. F. (1998). Intergroup contact theory. *Annual Review of Psychology, 49.*

PETTIGREW, T. F., & TROPP, L. R. (2006). A meta-analytic test of intergroup contact theory. *Journal of Personality and Social Psychology, 90,* 751–783.

PETTITO, L. (1988). "Language" in the prelinguistic child. In F. S. Kessel (Ed.), *The development of language and language researchers: Essays in honor of Roger Brown* (pp. 187–222). Hillsdale, NJ: Erlbaum.

PETTY, R. E, WEGENER, D. T., & FABRIGAR, L. R. (1997). Attitudes and attitude change. *Annual Review of Psychology, 48,* 609–647.

PETTY, R. E., & CACIOPPO, J. T. (1985). The elaboration likelihood model of persuasion. In L. Berkowitz (Ed.), *Advances in experimental social psychology: Vol. 19.* New York: Academic Press.

PHAN, K. L., WAGER, T. D., TAYLOR, S. F., & LIBERZON, I. (2002). Functional neuroanatomy of emotion: A meta-analysis of emotion activation studies in PET and fMRI. *Neuroimage, 16,* 331–348.

PHELPS, E. A. (2006). Emotion and cognition: Insights from studies of the human amygdala. *Annual Review of Psychology, 57,* 27–53.

PHILIPS, M. F., MATTIASSON, G., WIELOCH, T., BJÖRKLAND, A., JOHANSSON, B. B., & TOMASEVIC, G. (2001). Neuroprotective and behavioral efficacy of nerve growth factor-transfected hippocampal progenitor cell transplants after experimental traumatic brain injury. *Journal of Neurosurgery, 94,* 765–774.

PHILLIPS, A. T., WELLMAN, H. M., & SPELKE, E. S. (2002). Infants' ability to connect gaze and emotional expression to intentional action. *Cognition, 85,* 53–78.

PIAGET, J. (1952). *The origins of intelligence in children.* New York: International University Press.

PICCINELLI, M., PINI, S., BELLANTUONO, C., & WILKINSON, G. (1995). Efficacy of drug treatment in obsessive-compulsive disorder: A meta-analytic review. *British Journal of Psychiatry, 166,* 424–443.

PILIAVIN, J. A., & CALLERO, P. L. (1991). Giving blood: The development of an altruistic identity. Baltimore, MD: Johns Hopkins University Press.

PINCUS, H., ZARIN, D., TANIELIAN, T., JOHNSON, J., WEST, J., PETTIT, A., ET AL. (1999). Psychiatric patients and treatments in 1997: Findings from the American Psychiatric Association Practice Research Network. *Archives of General Psychiatry, 56,* 441–449.

PINKER, S. (1984). *Language learnability and language development.* Cambridge, MA: Harvard University Press.

PINKER, S. (1994). *The language instinct: How the mind creates language.* New York: HarperPerennial.

PINKER, S. (1995). Why the child holded the baby rabbits: A case study in language acquisition. In L. R. Gleitman & M. Liberman (Eds.), *Language: An invitation to cognitive science: Vol. 1* (2nd ed., pp. 107–133). Cambridge, MA: MIT Press.

PINKER, S. (1997). *How the mind works.* New York: Norton

PINKER, S. (1999a). *How the mind works.* New York.: Norton.

PINKER, S. (1999b). *Words and rules: The ingredients of language.* New York: Basic Books.

PINKER, S. (2002). *The blank slate.* New York: Viking.

PINKER, S., & ULLMAN, M. T. (2002). The past and future of the past tense. *Trends in Cognitive Sciences, 6*(11), 456–463.

PINTO, S., ROSEBERRY, A., LIU, H., DIANO, S., SHANABROUGH, M., CAI, X., ET AL. (2004). Rapid rewiring of arcuate nucleus feeding circuits by leptin. *Science, 304,* 110–115.

PIPP, S., EASTERBROOKS, M. A., & BROWN, S. R. (1993). Attachment status and complexity of infants' self- and other-knowledge when tested with mother and father. *Social Development, 2,* 1–14.

PITTENGER, C., & KANDEL, E. R. (2003). In search of general mechanisms for long-lasting plasticity: Aplysia and the hippocampus. *Philosophical Transactions of the Royal Society London: B. Biological Science, 358,* 757–763.

PLOMIN, R., & DANIELS, D. (1987). Why are children from the same family so different from one another? *Behavioral and Brain Sciences, 10,* 1–16.

PLOMIN, R., & DEFRIES, J. C. (1985). A parent-offspring adoption study of cognitive abilities in early childhood. *Intelligence, 9,* 341–356.

PLOMIN, R., & McGUFFIN, P. (2003). Psychopathology in the postgenomic era. *Annual Review of Psychology, 54,* 205–228.

PLOMIN, R., & SPINATH, F. M. (2004). Intelligence: Genetics, genes, and genomics. *Journal of Personality and Social Psychology, 86,* 112–129.

PLOMIN, R., CORLEY, R., DEFRIES, J. C., & FULKER, D. W. (1990). Individual differences in television viewing in early childhood: Nature as well as nurture. *Psychological Science, 1,* 371–377.

PLOMIN, R., FULKER, D. W., CORLEY, R., & DEFRIES, J. C. (1997). Nature, nurture, and cognitive development from 1 to 16 years: A parent-offspring adoption study. *Psychological Science, 8,* 442–447.

POLDRACK, A., & WAGNER, A. (2004). What can neuroimaging tell us about the mind? Insights from prefrontal cortex. *Current Directions in Psychological Science, 13,* 177–181.

POLEY, W. (1974). Dimensionality in the measurement of authoritarian and political attitudes. *Canadian Journal of Behavioral Science, 6,* 83–94.

POLLACK, M. H. (2001). Comorbidity, neurobiology, and pharmacotherapy of social anxiety disorder [Suppl.]. *Journal of Clinical Psychiatry, 62*(12), 24–29.

POPE, H. G., HUDSON, J. I., BODKIN, J. A., & OLIVA, P. (1998). Questionable validity of "dissociative amnesia" in trauma victims. *British Journal of Psychiatry, 172,* 210–215.

PORSOLT, R. D., LePICHON, M., & JALFRE, M. (1977). Depression: A new animal model sensitive to antidepressant treatments. *Nature, 266,* 730–732.

PORTER, S., BIRT, A. R., YUILLE, J. C., & LEHMAN, D. R. (2000). Negotiating false memories: Interviewer and rememberer characteristics relate to memory distortion. *Psychological Science, 11,* 507–510.

POSNER, M., SNYDER, C., & DAVIDSON, B. (1980). Attention and the detection of signals. *Journal of Experimental Psychology: General, 109,* 160–174.

POULOS, C. X., & CAPPELL, H. (1991). Homeostatic theory of drug tolerance: A general model of physiological adaptation. *Psychological Review, 98,* 390–408.

POVINELLI, D. J. (2000). *Folk physics for apes: Tthe chimpanzee's theory of how the world works.* Oxford: Oxford University Press.

POVINELLI, D. J., BERING, J. M., & GIAMBRONE S. (2000). Toward a science of other minds: Escaping the argument by analogy. *Cognitive Science, 24,* 509–542.

POWDERLY, W. G., LANDAY, A., & LEDERMAN, M. M. (1998). Recovery of the immune system with antiretroviral therapy: The end of opportunism? *Journal of the American Medical Association, 280,* 72–77.

POWELL, H. A. (1969). Genealogy, residence, and kinship in Kiriwina. *Man, 4,* 177–202.

PRASADA, S., & PINKER, S. (1993a). Generalizations of regular and irregular morphology. *Language and Cognitive Processes, 8,* 1–56.

PRASADA, S., & PINKER, S. (1993b). Similarity-based and rule-based generalizations in inflectional morphology. *Language and Cognitive Processes, 8,* 1–56.

PREMACK, A., & PREMACK, D. (1983). *The mind of an ape.* New York: Norton.

PREMACK, D. (1965). Reinforcement theory. In D. Levine (Ed.), *Nebraska Symposium on motivation.* Lincoln: University of Nebraska Press.

PREMACK, D. (1976). *Intelligence in ape and man.* Hillsdale, NJ: Erlbaum.

PREMACK, D. (1978). On the abstractness of human concepts: Why it would be difficult to talk to a pigeon. In S. H. Hulse, H. Fowler, & W. K. Honig (Eds.), *Cognitive processes in animal behavior.* Hillsdale, NJ: Erlbaum.

PREMACK, D., & WOODRUFF, G. (1978). Does the chimpanzee have a theory of mind? *Behavioral and Brain Sciences, 4,* 515–526.

PRINZ, J. J. (2002). *Furnishing the mind: Concepts and their perceptual basis.* Cambridge, MA: MIT Press.

PUTNAM, F. W., GUROFF, J. J., SILBERMAN, E. K., BARBAN, L., & POST, R. M. (1986). The clinical phenomenology of multiple personality disorder: Review of 100 recent cases. *Journal of Clinical Psychiatry, 47,* 285–293.

PUTNAM, K. E. (1979). Hypnosis and distortions in eye witness memory. *International Journal of Clinical and Experimental Hypnosis, 27,* 437–448.

PYSZCZYNSKI, T., GREENBERG, J., SOLOMON, S., ARNDT, J., & SCHIMEL, J. (2004). Why do people need self-esteem? A theoretical and empirical review. *Psychological Bulletin, 130,* 435–468.

QUINE, W. (1960). *Word and object.* New York: Wiley.

QUINLAN, P. T. (2003). Visual feature integration theory: Past, present and future. *Psychological Bulletin, 129,* 643–673.

RADANT, A., TSUANG, D., PESKIND, E. R., McFALL, M., & RASKIND, W. (2001). Biological markers and diagnostic accuracy in the genetics of posttraumatic stress disorder. *Psychiatry Research, 102,* 203–215.

RAE, C., DIGNEY, A. L., McEWAN, S. R., & BATES, T. C. (2003). Oral creatine monohydrate supplementation improves brain performance: A double-blind, placebo-controlled, cross-over trial. *Proceedings of the Royal Society of London, Series B: Biological Sciences, 270,* 2147–2150.

RAFAL, R., & ROBERTSON, L. (1995). The neurology of visual attention. In M. Gazzaniga, (Ed.), *The cognitive neurosciences* (pp. 625–648). Cambridge, MA: MIT Press.

RAJARAM, S. (1993). Remembering and knowing: Two means of access to the personal past. *Memory & Cognition, 21,* 89–102.

RAKIC, P. (1995). Corticogenesis in human and nonhuman primates. In M. Gazzaniga (Ed.), *The cognitive neurosciences* (pp. 127–145). Cambridge, MA: MIT Press.

RAMI-GONZALEZ, L., BERNARDO, M., BOGET, T., SALAMERO, M., GIL-VERONA, J. A., & JUNQUE, C. (2001). Subtypes of memory dysfunction associated with ECT: characteristics and neurobiological bases. *Journal of ECT, 17,* 129–135.

RAMÓN Y CAJAL, S. (1913). *Degeneration and regeneration of the nervous system* (R. M. Day, Trans., 1928). London: Oxford University Press.

RAMÓN Y CAJAL, S. (1937). *Recollections of my life* (E. Horne-Craigie, Trans.). Philadelphia: American Philosophical Society.

RAMUS, F., NESPOR, M., & MEHLER, J. (1999). Correlates of linguistic rhythm in the speech signal. *Cognition, 73,* 265–292.

RANGANATH, C., YONELINAS, A. P., COHEN, M. X., DY, C. J., TOM, S., & D'ESPOSITO, M. (2003). Dissociable correlates for familiarity and recollection within the medial temporal lobes. *Neuropsychologia, 42,* 2–13.

RAPAPORT, M. H., & JUDD, L. L. (1998). Minor depressive disorder and subsyndromal depressive symptoms: Functional impairment and response to treatment. *Journal of Affective Disorders, 48,* 227–232.

RAPAPORT, M. H., PANICCIA, G., & JUDD, L. L. (1995). A review of social phobia. *Psychopharmacology Bulletin, 31,* 125–129.

RAPPAPORT, Z. H. (1992). Psychosurgery in the modern era: Therapeutic and ethical aspects. *Medicine and Law, 11,* 449–453.

RASMUSSEN, S. A. (1993). Genetic studies of obsessive-compulsive disorder. *Annals of Clinical Psychiatry, 5,* 241–247.

RATEY, J., & JOHNSON, C. (1997). *Shadow syndromes.* New York: Pantheon.

RAUCH, S. L., & SAVAGE, C. R. (2000). Investigating cortico-striatal pathophysiology in obsessive-compulsive disorders: Procedural learning and imaging probes. In W. K. Goodman, M. J. Rudorfer, & J. D. Maser (Eds.), *Obsessive-compulsive disorder: Contemporary issues in treatment. Personality and clinical psychology series* (pp. 133–154). Mahwah, NJ: Erlbaum.

RAVEN, B. H., & RUBIN, J. Z. (1976). Social psychology: People in groups. England: Wiley.

RAVUSSIN, E. (1994). Effects of a traditional lifestyle on obesity in Pima Indians. *Diabetes Care, 17,* 1067–1074.

RAVUSSIN, E., & BOUCHARD, C. (2000). Human genomics and obesity: Finding appropriate drug targets. *European Journal of Pharmacology, 410,* 131–145.

RAYNER, K., CARLSON, M., & FRAZIER, L. (1983). The interaction of syntax and semantics during sentence processing: Eye movements in the analysis of semantically biased sentences. *Journal of Verbal Learning and Verbal Behavior, 22,* 358–374.

REBER, A. S. (1985). *The Penguin dictionary of psychology.* New York: Viking Penguin.

REBERG, D., & BLACK, A. H. (1969). Compound testing of individually conditioned stimuli as an index of excitatory and inhibitory properties. *Psychonomic Science, 17,* 3031.

RECANZONE, G., SCHREINER, C., & MERZENICH, M. (1993). Plasticity in the frequency representation of primary auditory cortex following discrimination training in adult owl monkeys. *Journal of Neuroscience, 13,* 87–103.

RECHT, D. R., & LESLIE, L. (1988). Effect of prior knowledge on good and poor readers' memory of text. *Journal of Educational Psychology, 80*(1), 16–20.

REED, M., & ROUNDTREE, P. (1997). Peer pressure and adolescent substance abuse. *Journal of Quantitative Criminology, 13,* 143–180.

REESE, E., & FIVUSH, R. (1993). Parental styles of talking about the past. *Developmental Psychology, 29*(3), 596–606.

REEVES, L., & WEISBERG, R. W. (1994). The role of content and abstract information in analogical transfer. *Psychological Bulletin, 115*(3), 381–400.

REGAN, P. C., & BERSCHEID, E. (1999). *Lust: What we know about human sexual desire.* Thousand Oaks, CA: Sage.

REGIER, T., KAY, P., & COOK, R. S. (2005). Focal colors are universal after all. *Proceedings of the National Academy of Sciences, 102*(23), 8386–8391.

REINER, W. (2004). Psychosexual development in genetic males assigned female: The cloacal exstrophy experience. *Child and Adolescent Psychiatric Clinics of North America, 13,* 657–674.

REISBERG, D. (2006). *Cognition: Exploring the science of the mind* (3rd ed.). New York: Norton.

REISBERG, D., & HERTEL, P. (EDS.). (2004). *Memory and emotion.* New York: Oxford University Press.

REISBERG, D., & HEUER, F. (2004). Memory for emotional events. In D. Reisberg & P. Hertel (Eds.), *Memory and emotion* (pp. 3–41). New York: Oxford University Press.

REISBERG, D., & HEUER, F. (2005). Visuospatial images. In P. Shah & A. Miyake (Eds.), *The Cambridge Handbook of Visuospatial Thinking* (pp. 35–80). New York: Cambridge University Press.

REISBERG, D., SMITH, J. D., BAXTER, D. A., & SONENSHINE, M. (1989). "Enacted" auditory images are ambiguous; "Pure" auditory images are not. *Quarterly Journal of Experimental Psychology, 41A,* 619–641.

REISENZEIN, R. (1983). The Schachter theory of emotions: Two decades later. *Psychological Bulletin, 94,* 239–264.

REISS, D., & MARINO, L. (2001). Mirror self-recognition in the bottlenose dolphin: A case of cognitive convergence. *Proceedings of the National Academy of Science, 98*(10), 5937–5942.

REISS, D., McCOWAN, B., & MARINO L. (1997). Communicative and other cognitive characteristics of bottlenose dolphins. *Trends in Cognitive Science, 1*(2), 140–145.

RENSINK, R. A. (2002). Change detection. *Annual Review of Psychology, 53,* 245–277.

REPACHOLI, B. M., & GOPNIK, A. (1997). Early reasoning about desires: Evidence from 14- and 18-month-olds. *Developmental Psychology, 33*(1), 12–21.

RESCORLA, R. A. (1967). Pavlovian conditioning and its proper control procedures. *Psychological Review, 74,* 71–80.

RESCORLA, R. A. (1988). Behavioral studies of Pavlovian conditioning. *Annual Review of Neuroscience, 11,* 329–352.

RESCORLA, R. A. (1991). Associative relations in instrumental learning: The eighteenth Bartlett Memorial lecture. *Quarterly Journal of Experimental Psychology, 43b,* 1–23.

RESCORLA, R. A. (1993a). Inhibitory associations between S and R extinction. *Animal Learning and Behavior, 21,* 327–336.

RESCORLA, R. A. (1993b). Preservation of response-outcome associations through extinction. *Animal Learning and Behavior, 21,* 238–245.

RESCORLA, R. A., & WAGNER, A. R. (1972). A theory of Pavlovian conditioning: Variations in the effectiveness of reinforcement and non-reinforcement. In A. H. Black & W. F. Prokasy (Eds.), *Classical conditioning II.* New York: Appleton-Century-Crofts.

REST, J., NARVAEZ, D., BEBEAU, M., & THOMAS, J. (1999). *Postconventional moral thinking: A neo-Kohlbergian approach.* Mahwah, NJ: Erlbaum.

REUTER-LORENZ, P. A. (2002). New visions of the aging mind and brain. *Trends in Cognitive Science, 6,* 394–400.

REVELEY, A. M., REVELEY, M. A., CLIFFORD, C. A., ET AL. (1982). Cerebral ventricular size in twins discordant for schizophrenia. *Lancet, 1,* 540–541.

REY, G. (1996). Concepts and stereotypes. In E. Margolis & S. Laurence (Eds.), *Concepts: Core readings* (pp. 278–299). Cambridge MA: MIT Press.

REYNOLDS, C. R., CHASTAIN, R. L., KAUFMAN, A. S., & McLEAN, J. E. (1987). Demographic characteristics and IQ among adults: Analysis of the WAIS—R standardization sample as a function of the stratification variables. *Journal of School Psychology, 25*(4), 323–342.

RHODES, G. (2006). The evolutionary psychology of facial beauty. *Annual Review of Psychology, 57,* 199–226.

RHODES, G., PROFFITT, F., GRADY, J. M., & SUMICH, A. (1998). Facial symmetry and the perception of beauty. *Psychonomics Bulletin and Review, 5,* 659–669.

RHODES, G., SUMICH, A., & BYATT, G. (1999). Are average facial configurations attractive only because of their symmetry? *Psychological Science, 10,* 52–59.

RIBOT, T. (1882). *Diseases of memory.* New York: Appleton.

RICHARDS, J. M., & GROSS, J. J. (2000). Emotion regulation and memory: The cognitive costs of keeping one's cool. *Journal of Personality and Social Psychology, 79,* 410–424.

RICHARDS, J. M., & GROSS, J. J. (2006). Personality and emotional memory: How regulating emotion impairs memory for emotional events. *Journal of Research in Personality.*

RICKELS, K., & RYNN, M. A. (2001). What is generalized anxiety disorder? [Suppl.] *Journal of Clinical Psychiatry, 62*(11), 4–12.

RIEFFE, C., TERWOGT, M. M., KOOPS, W., STEGGE, H., & OOMEN, A. (2001). Preschoolers' appreciation of uncommon desires and subsequent emotions. *British Journal of Developmental Psychology, 19,* 259–274.

RIGGIO, R. E., & MURPHY, S. E. (EDS.). (2002). *MULTIPLE INTELLIGENCES AND LEADERSHIP.* MAHWAH, NJ: ERLBAUM.

RINCK, M. (1999). Memory for everyday objects: Where are the digits on numerical keypads? *Applied Cognitive Psychology, 13,* 329–350.

RINGELMANN, M. (1913). Recherches sur les moteurs animés: Travail de l'homme. *Annales de l'institut National Agronomique* (Series 2), *12,* 1–40.

RIPS, L. (1990). Reasoning. *Annual Review of Psychology, 41,* 321–353.

ROBBIN, A. A. (1958). A controlled study of the effects of leucotomy. *Journal of Neurology, Neurosurgery and Psychiatry, 21,* 262–269.

ROBBINS, S. J. (1990). Mechanisms underlying spontaneous recovery in autoshaping. *Journal of Experimental Psychology: Animal Behavior Processes, 16,* 235–249.

ROBERSON, D., ET AL. (2005). Color categories: Evidence for the cultural relativity hypothesis. *Cognitive Psychology, 50,* 378–411.

ROBERTSON, I. H., & MANLY, T. (1999). Sustained attention deficits in time and space. In G. W. Humphreys & J. Duncan (Eds.), *Attention, space, and action: Studies in cognitive neuroscience* (pp. 297–310). New York: Oxford University Press.

ROBERTSON, L., TREISMAN, A., FRIEDMAN-HILL, S., & GRABOWECKY, M. (1997). The interaction of spatial and object pathways: Evidence from Balint's syndrome. *Journal of Cognitive Neuroscience, 9*(3), 295–317.

ROBINSON, L. A., BERMAN, J. S., & NEIMEYER, R. A. (1990). Psychotherapy for the treatment of depression: A comprehensive review of controlled outcome research. *Psychological Bulletin, 108,* 30–49.

RODIN, J. (1990). Control by any other name: Definitions, concepts, and processes. In J. Rodin, C. Schooler, & K. W. Schaie (Eds.), *Self-directedness: Cause and effects throughout the life course* (pp. 1–17). Hillsdale, NJ: Erlbaum.

RODIN, J., & LANGER, E. J. (1977). Long-term effects of a control-relevant intervention with the institutionalized aged. *Journal of Personality and Social Psychology, 35,* 897–902.

RODMAN, H. R., GROSS, C. G., & ALBRIGHT, T. D. (1989). Afferent basis of visual response properties in area MT of the macaque. I. Effects of striate cortex removal. *Journal of Neuroscience, 9,* 2033–2050.

RODRIGUEZ, M. L., MISCHEL, W., & SHODA, Y. (1989). Cognitive person variables in the delay of gratification of older children at risk. *Journal of Personality and Social Psychology, 57,* 358–367.

ROEDIGER, H. L., III. (1980). Memory metaphors in cognitive psychology. *Memory and Cognition, 8,* 231–246.

ROGERS, C. R. (1951). *Client-centered therapy: Its current practice, implications, and theory* (2nd eds.). Boston: Houghton Mifflin.

ROGERS, C. R. (1959). A theory of therapy, personality, and interpersonal relationships as developed in the client-centered framework. In S. Koch (Ed.), *Psychology: A study of a science: Vol. 3.* New York: McGraw-Hill.

ROGERS, C. R. (1961). *On becoming a person: A therapist's view of psychotherapy.* Boston: Houghton Mifflin.

ROGERS, T. B., KUIPER, N. A., & KIRKER, W. S. (1977). Self-reference and the encoding of personal information. *Journal of Personality and Social Psychology, 35,* 677–688.

ROGOFF, B. (1990). *Apprenticeship in thinking.* New York: Oxford University Press.

ROGOFF, B. (1998). Cognition as a collaborative process. In W. Damon (Ed.), *Handbook of child psychology, Vol. 2* (5th ed., pp. 679–744). New York: Wiley.

ROGOFF, B. (2000). *Culture and development.* New York: Oxford University Press.

ROGOFF, B., PARADISE, R., ARAUZ, R. M., CORREA-CHÁVEZ, M., & ANGELILLO, C. (2003). Firsthand learning through intent participation. *Annual Review of Psychology, 54,* 175–203.

ROLAND, P. E., LARSEN, B., LASSEN, N. A., & SKINHØJ, E. (1980). Supplementary motor area and other cortical areas in organization of voluntary movements in man. *Journal of Neurophysiology, 43,* 539–560.

ROLLS, E. J. (1978). Neurophysiology of feeding. *Trends in Neurosciences, 1,* 1–3.

ROMANES, G. J. (1882). *Animal intelligence.* London: Kegan Paul.

ROOPNARINE, J. L., JOHNSON, J. E., & HOOPER, F. H. (1994). *Children's play in diverse cultures.* Albany, NY: SUNY Press.

ROPER, T. J. (1983). Learning as a biological phenomenon. In T. R. Halliday & P. J. B. Slater (Eds.), *Genes, development and behavior: Vol. 3. Animal Behavior,* (pp. 178–212). Oxford: Blackwell.

RORSCHACH, H. (1921). *Psychodiagnostik.* Berne: Bircher.

ROSCH, E. H. (1973a). Natural categories. *Cognitive Psychology, 4,* 328–350.

ROSCH, E. H. (1973b). On the internal structure of perceptual and semantic categories. In T. E. Moore (Ed.), *Cognitive development and the acquisition of language.* New York: Academic Press.

ROSCH, E. H. (1978). Principles of categorization. In E. Rosch & B. Lloyd (Eds.), *Cognition and categorization.* Hillsdale, NJ: Erlbaum.

ROSCH, E. H., & MERVIS, C. B. (1975). Family resemblances: Studies in the internal structure of categories. *Cognitive Psychology, 7,* 573–605.

ROSEN, G. (1966). *Madness in society.* Chicago: University of Chicago Press.

ROSEN, W. D., ADAMSON, L. B., & BAKEMAN, R. (1992). An experimental investigation of infant social referencing: Mothers' messages and gender differences. *Developmental Psychology, 28*(6), 1172–1178.

ROSENFELD, P., GIACALONE, R. A., & TEDESCHI, J. T. (1984). Cognitive dissonance and impression management explanations for effort justification. *Personality and Social Psychology Bulletin, 10,* 394–401.

ROSENSTEIN, M. J., MILAZZO-SAYRE, L. J., & MANDERSCHEID, R. W. (1989). Care of persons with schizophrenia: A statistical profile. *Schizophrenia Bulletin, 15,* 45–58.

ROSENTHAL, A. M. (1964). *Thirty-eight witnesses.* New York: McGraw-Hill.

ROSENTHAL, D. (1970). *Genetic theory and abnormal behavior.* New York: McGraw-Hill.

ROSENTHAL, R. (1991). Teacher expectancy effects: A brief update 25 years after the Pygmalion experiment. *Journal of Research in Education, 1,* 3–12.

ROSENTHAL, R. (2002). Covert communication in classrooms, clinics, courtrooms, and cubicles. *American Psychologist, 57,* 839–849.

ROSENTHAL, R., & JACOBSON, L. (1968). *Pygmalion in the classroom: Teacher expectation and pupils' intellectual development.* New York: Holt, Rinehart & Winston.

ROSENZWEIG, M. R., LEIMAN, A. K., & BREEDLOVE, S. M. (1996). *Biological psychology.* Sunderland, MA: Sinauer.

ROSER, M., & GAZZANIGA, M. S. (2004). Automatic brains—interpretive minds. *Current Directions in Psychological Science, 13,* 56–59.

ROSS, C. A. (1997). *Dissociative identity disorder: Diagnosis, clinical features, and treatment of multiple personality.* New York: Wiley.

ROSS, C. A. (1999). Subpersonalities and multiple personalities: A dissociative continuum? In J. Rowan and M. Cooper (Eds.), *The plural self: Multiplicity in everyday life* (pp. 183–197). London: Sage.

ROSS, D. F., READ, J. D., & TOGLIA, M. P. (EDS.). (1994). *Adult eyewitness testimony: Current trends and developments.* New York: Cambridge University Press.

ROSS, H. S., & LOLLIS, S. P. (1989). A social relations analysis of toddler peer relationships. *Child Development, 60*(5), 1082–1091.

ROSS, J., & LAWRENCE, K. Q. (1968). Some observations on memory artifice. *Psychonomic Science, 13,* 107–108.

ROSS, L. (1977). The intuitive psychologist and his shortcomings: Distortions in the attribution process. In L. Berkowitz (Ed.), *Advances in experimental social psychology: Vol. 10.* New York: Academic Press.

Ross, L., Amabile, T. M., & Steinmetz, J. L. (1977). Social roles, social control, and biases in social perception processes. *Journal of Experimental Social Psychology, 35,* 817–829.

Roth, A., & Fonagy, P. (2004). *What works for whom? A critical review of psychotherapy research* (2nd ed.). New York: Guilford Press.

Rothbart, M. K., & Ahadi, S. A. (1994). Temperament and the development of personality. *Journal of Abnormal Psychology, 103,* 55–66.

Rothbart, M., & Bates, J. (1998). Temperament. In W. Damon & N. Eisenberg (Eds.), *Handbook of child psychology* (5th ed.): *Vol. 3. Social, emotional and personality development* (pp. 105–176). New York: Wiley.

Rothbaum, F., & Tsang, B. Y. P. (1998). Lovesongs in the United States and China: On the nature of romantic love. *Journal of Cross-Cultural Psychology, 29,* 306–319.

Rothbaum, F., Weisz, J., Pott, M., Miyake, K., & Morelli, G. (2000). Attachment and culture: Security in the United States and Japan. *American Psychologist, 55,* 1093–1104.

Rovee-Collier, C. (1999). The development of infant memory. *Current Directions in Psychological Science, 8*(3), 80–85.

Rovee-Collier, C. K. (1990). The "memory system" of prelinguistic infants. In A. Diamond (Ed.), *The development and neural bases of higher cognitive functions.* New York: New York Academy of Sciences.

Rovee-Collier, C. K., & Hayne, H. (1987). Reactivation of infant memory: Implications for cognitive development. In H. W. Reese (Ed.), *Advances in child development and behavior: Vol. 20.* New York: Academic Press.

Rovee-Collier, C., & Gerhardstein, P. (1997). The development of infant memory. In N. Cowan (Ed.), *The development of memory in childhood: Studies in developmental psychology.* Hove, England: Psychology Press.

Rowe, A. D., Bullock, P. R., Polkey, C. E., & Morris, R. G. (2001). "Theory of mind" impairments and their relationship to executive functioning following frontal lobe excisions. *Brain, 124,* 600–616.

Rozin, P. (1999). The process of moralization. *Psychological Science, 10,* 218–221.

Rozin, P., & Kalat, J. W. (1971). Specific hungers and poison avoidance as adaptive specializations of learning. *Psychological Review, 78,* 459–486.

Rozin, P., & Kalat, J. W. (1972). Learning as a situation-specific adaptation. In M. E. P. Seligman & J. L. Hager (Eds.), *Biological boundaries of learning* (pp. 66–96). New York: Appleton-Century-Crofts.

Rozin, P., & Schull, J. (1988). The adaptive-evolutionary point of view in experimental psychology. In R. C. Atkinson, R. J. Herrnstein, G. Lindzey, & R. D. Luce (Eds.), *Steven's handbook of experimental psychology: Vol. 1 Perception and motivation* (2nd ed., pp. 503–546). New York: Wiley.

Rozin, P., Dow, S., Moscovitch, M., & Rajaram, S. (1998). What causes humans to begin and end a meal? A role for memory for what has been eaten, as evidenced by a study of multiple meal eating in amnesic patients. *Psychological Science, 9,* 392–396.

Rozin, P., Markwith, M., & Stoess, C. (1997). Moralization and becoming a vegetarian: The transformation of preferences into values and the recruitment of disgust. *Psychological Science, 8,* 67–73.

Rubenstein, J. L., & Rakic, P. (1999). Genetic control of cortical development. *Cerebral Cortex, 9,* 521–523.

Rubin, H., Bukowski, W., & Parker, J. (1998). Peer interactions, relationships and groups. In W. Damon & N. Eisenberg (Eds.), *Handbook of child psychology* (5th ed.): *Vol. 3. Social, emotional and personality development* (pp.619–700). New York: Wiley.

Ruffman, T., Perner, J., & Parkin, L. (1999). How parenting style affects false belief understanding. *Social Development, 8,* 395–411.

Rumelhart, D. E. (1997). The architecture of mind: A connectionist approach. In J. Haugeland (Ed.), *Mind design 2: Philosophy, psychology, artificial intelligence* (2nd ed.). Cambridge, MA: MIT Press.

Rumelhart, D. E., & McClelland, J. L. (1986) On learning past tenses of English verbs. In J. L. McClelland & D. E. Rumelhart (Eds.), *Parallel distributed processing: Vol. 2* (pp. 216–271). Cambridge, MA: MIT Press.

Russek, M. (1971). Hepatic receptors and the neurophysiological mechanisms controlling feeding behavior. In S. Ehrenpreis (Ed.), *Neurosciences research: Vol. 4.* New York: Academic Press.

Russell, J. A. (1980). A circumplex model of affect. *Journal of Personality and Social Psychology, 39,* 1161–1178.

Russell, J. A. (1983). Pan-cultural aspects of human conceptual organization of emotions. *Journal of Personality and Social Psychology, 45,* 1281–1288.

Russell, J. A. (1994). Is there universal recognition of emotion from facial expressions? A review of the cross-cultural studies. *Psychological Bulletin, 115,* 102–141.

Rutter, M., & O'Connor, T., G. (2004). Are there biological programming effects for psychological development? Findings from a study of Romanian adoptees. *Developmental Psychology, 40,* 81–94.

Ryff, C. D., & Singer, B. (1998). The contours of positive human health. *Psychological Inquiry, 9,* 1–28.

Sabini, J., Siepmann, M., & Stein, J. (2001). The really fundamental attribution error in social psychological research. *Psychological Inquiry, 12,* 1–15.

Sackeim, H. A., Devanand, D. P., & Nobler, M. S. (1995). Electroconvulsive therapy. In F. E. Bloom & D. Kupfer (Eds.), *Psychopharmacology: The fourth generation of progress* (pp. 1123–1141). New York: Raven.

Sackeim, H. A., Prudic, J., Devanand, D. P., Kiersky, J. E., Fitzsimons, L., Moody, et al. (1993). Effects of stimulus intensity and electrode placement on the efficacy and cognitive effects of electroconvulsive therapy. *New England Journal of Medicine, 328,* 839–846.

Sackett, D. L., Straus, S. E., Richardson, W. S., Rosenberg, W., & Haynes, R. B. (2000). *Evidence-based medicine: How to practice and teach EBM* (2nd ed.). London: Churchill Livingstone.

Sadler, H., Davison, L., Carroll, C., & Kounts, S. L. (1971). The living, genetically unrelated, kidney donor. *Seminars in Psychiatry, 3,* 86–101.

Saffran, J. R., Aslin, R. N., & Newport, E. L. (1996). Statistical learning by 8-month-old infants. *Science, 274,* 1926–1928.

Saffran, J. R., Senghas, A., & Trueswell, J. C. (2001). The acquisition of language by children. PNAS, 98(23) 12874–12875.

Saghir, M. T., & Robins, E. (1973). *Male and female homosexuality.* Baltimore: Williams & Wilkins.

Sagi, A., & Hoffman, M. L. (1976). Empathic distress in the newborn. *Developmental Psychology, 12,* 175–176.

Salovey, P., & Mayer, J. D. (1990). Emotional intelligence. *Imagination, Cognition, and Personality, 9,* 185–211.

Salovey, P., Rothman, A. J., Detweiler, J. B., & Steward, W. T. (2000). Emotional states and physical health. *American Psychologist, 55*(1), 110–121.

Salthouse, T. A. (1991). *Theoretical perspectives on cognitive aging.* Hillsdale, NJ: Erlbaum.

Salthouse, T. A. (2000). Steps toward the explanation of adult age differences in cognition. In T. J. Perfect & E. A. Maylor (Eds.), *Models of cognitive aging.* New York: Oxford University Press.

Salthouse, T. A. (2004). What and when of cognitive aging. *Current Directions in Psychological Science, 13,* 140–144.

Sanfey, A. G., Rilling, J. K., Aronson, J. A., Nystrom, L. E., & Cohen, J. D. (2003). The neural basis of economic decision-making in the Ultimatum Game. *Science, 300,* 1755–1758.

Santarelli, L., Saxe, M., Gross, C., Surget, A., Battaglia, F., Dulawa, S., et al. (2003). Requirement of hippocampal neurogenesis for the behavioral effects of antidepressants. *Science, 301,* 805–809.

SANTINI, E., GE, H., REN, K., DEORTIZ, S., & QUIRK, G. (2004). Consolidation of fear extinction requires protein synthesis in the medial prefrontal cortex. *Journal of Neuroscience, 24,* 5704–5710.

SAPOLSKY, R. M. (1998). *The trouble with testosterone.* New York: Simon & Schuster.

SATIR, V. (1967). *Conjoint family therapy* (rev. ed.). Palo Alto, CA: Science and Behavior Books.

SAVAGE-RUMBAUGH, E. S., & FIELDS, W. (2000). Linguistic, cultural and cognitive capacities of bonoboas (*Pan paniscus*). *Culture & Psychology, 6,* 131–153.

SAVIN, H. B. (1973). Professors and psychological researchers: Conflicting values in conflicting roles. *Cognition, 2,* 147–149.

SAVIN-WILLIAMS, R. C. (2006). Who's gay? Does it matter? *Current Directions in Psychological Science, 15*(1), 40–44.

SAWA, A., & SNYDER, S. H. (2002). Schizophrenia: Diverse approaches to a complex disease. *Science, 296,* 692–695.

SAWAMOTO, K., NAKAO, N., KAKISHITA, K., OGAWA, Y., TOYAMA, Y., YAMAMOTO, A., ET AL. (2001). Generation of dopaminergic neurons in the adult brain from mesencephalic precursor cells labeled with a nestin-GFP transgene. *Journal of Neuroscience, 21,* 3895–3903.

SAXE, G. (1981). Body parts as numerals: A developmental analysis of numeration among the Oksapmin in Papua, New Guinea. *Child Development, 52,* 306–316.

SAXE, R., CAREY, S., & KANWISHER, N. (2004). Understanding other minds: Linking developmental psychology and functional neuroimaging. *Annual Review of Psychology, 55,* 87–124.

SAXENA, S., BRODY, A. L., MAIDMENT, K. M., DUNKIN, J. J., COLGAN, M., ALBORZIAN, S., ET AL. (1999). Localized orbitofrontal and subcortical metabolic changes and predictors of response to paroxetine treatment in obsessive-compulsive disorder *Neuropsychopharmacology, 21,* 683–693.

SAYWITZ, K. J., & GEISELMAN, E. (1998). Interviewing the child witness: Maximizing completeness and minimizing error. In S. Lynn & K. McConkey (Eds.), *Truth in memory* (pp. 190–223). New York: Guilford

SCAIFE, M., & BRUNER, J. S. (1975). The capacity for joint visual attention in the infant. *Nature, 253*(5489), 265–266.

SCARR, S. (1987). Distinctive environments depend upon genotypes. *Behavioral and Brain Sciences, 10,* 38–39.

SCARR, S. (1992). Developmental theories for the 1990s: Development and individual differences. *Child Development, 63,* 1–19.

SCARR, S. (1997). Why child care has little impact on most children's development. *Current Directions in Psychological Science, 6,* 143–148.

SCARR, S., & CARTER-SALTZMAN, L. (1982). Genetics and intelligence. In R. J. Sternberg (Ed.), *Handbook of human intelligence* (pp. 792–896). New York: Cambridge University Press.

SCARR, S., & WEINBERG, R. A. (1976). IQ test performance of black children adopted by white families. *American Psychologist, 31,* 726–739.

SCARR, S., & WEINBERG, R. A. (1983). The Minnesota adoption studies genetic differences and malleability. *Child Development, 54,* 260–267.

SCERIF, G., & KARMILOFF-SMITH, A. (2005). The dawn of cognitive genetics: Crucial developmental caveats. *Trends in Cognitive Science, 9,* 126–135.

SCHACHTER, S., & SINGER, J. (1962). Cognitive, social and physiological determinants of emotional state. *Psychological Review, 69,* 379–399.

SCHACHTER, S., & SINGER, J. E. (1979). Comments on the Maslach and Marshall-Zimbardo experiments. *Journal of Personality and Social Psychology, 37,* 989–995.

SCHACHTER. F. (1982). Sibling deidentification and split-parent identification: A family tetrad. In M. Lamb and B. Sutton-Smith (Eds.), *Sibling relationships: Their nature and significance over the lifespan.* Hillsdale, NJ: Erlbaum.

SCHACTER, D. L. (1996). *Searching for memory: The brain, the mind and the past.* New York: Basic Books.

SCHAFE, G., NADER, K., BLAIR, H., & LEDOUX, J. (2001). Memory consolidation of Pavlovian fear conditioning: A cellular and molecular perspective. *Trends in Neuroscience, 24,* 540–546.

SCHAIE, K. W. (1996). *Intellectual development in adulthood: The Seattle Longitudinal study.* New York: Cambridge University Press.

SCHAIE, K. W., & WILLIS, S. L. (1996). Psychometric intelligence and aging. In F. Blanchard Fields & T. M. Hess (Eds.), *Perspectives on cognitive change in adulthood and aging* (pp. 293–322). New York: McGraw-Hill.

SCHERER, K. R., SCHORR, A., & JOHNSTONE, T. (EDS.). (2001). *Appraisal processes in emotion: Theory, methods, research.* New York: Oxford University Press.

SCHILDKRAUT, J. J. (1965). The catecholamine hypothesis of affective disorders: A review of supporting evidence. *American Journal of Psychiatry, 122,* 509–522.

SCHMIDT, F. L., & HUNTER, J. (2004). General mental ability in the world of work: Occupational attainment and job performance. *Journal of Personality and Social Psychology, 86,* 162–173.

SCHMIDT, F. L., & HUNTER, J. E. (1998). The validity and utility of selection methods in personnel psychology: Practical and theoretical implications of 85 years of research findings. *Psychological Bulletin, 124*(2), 262–274.

SCHMITT, D. P., & BUSS, D. M. (2001). Human mate poaching: Tactics and temptations for infiltrating existing mateships. *Journal of Personality & Social Psychology, 80*(6), 894–917.

SCHNEIDER, B., & STEVENSON, D. (1999). *The ambitious generation: America's teenagers, motivated but directionless.* New Haven: Yale University Press.

SCHNEIDER, B., ATKINSON, L., & TARDIF, C. (2001). Child-parent attachment and children's peer relations: A quantitative review. *Developmental Psychology, 37,* 86–100.

SCHNEIDER, D. J. (1973). Implicit personality theory: A review. *Psychological Bulletin, 79,* 294–309.

SCHNEIDER, W., GRUBER, H., GOLD, A., & OPWIS, K. (1993). Chess expertise and memory for chess positions in children and adults. *Journal of Experimental Child Psychology, 56*(3), 328–349.

SCHOFIELD, W. (1964). *Psychotherapy: The purchase of friendship.* Englewood Cliffs, NJ: Prentice-Hall.

SCHRAW, G., DUNKLE, M., & BENDIXEN, L. (1995). Cognitive processes in well-defined and ill-defined problem solving. *Applied Cognitive Psychology, 9,* 523–538.

SCHROEDER, H. E. (1973). The risky shift as a general choice shift. *Journal of Personality and Social Psychology, 27*(2), 297–300.

SCHUL, Y., & VINOKUR, A. D. (2000). Projection in person perception among spouses as a function of the similarity in their shared experiences. *Personality and Social Psychology Bulletin, 26*(8), 987–1001.

SCHULZ-HARDT, S. FREY, D., LÜTHGENS, C., & MOSCOVICI, S. (2000). Biased information search in group decision making. *Journal of Personality and Social Psychology, 78,* 655–669.

SCHUNK, D. H. (1984). Self-efficacy perspective on achievement behavior. *Educational Psychologist, 19*(1), 48–58.

SCHUNK, D. H. (1985). Self-efficacy and classroom learning. *Psychology in the Schools, 22*(2), 208–223.

SCHWARTZ, B. L. (1999). Sparkling at the end of the tongue: The etiology of tip-of-the-tongue phenomenology. *Psychonomics Bulletin & Review, 5,* 379–393.

SCHWARTZ, B., WASSERMAN, E. A., & ROBBINS, S. (2002). Psychology of learning and behavior (5th ed.). New York: Norton.

SCHWARTZ, C. E., WRIGHT, C. I., SHIN, L. M., KAGAN, J., & RAUCH, S. L. (2003). Inhibited and uninhibited infants "grown up": Adult amygdalar response to novelty. *Science, 300,* 1952–1953.

SCHWARTZ, D., DODGE, K., PETTIT, G., BATES, J., & THE CONDUCT PROBLEMS PREVENTION RESEARCH GROUP. (2000). Friendshihp as a moderating factor in the pathway between early harsh home environment and later victimization in the peer group. *Developmental Psychology, 36,* 646–662.

SCHWARZ, N. (1999). Self-reports: How the questions shape the answers. *American Psychologist, 54*, 93–105.

SCHWARZER, R. (ED.) (1992). *Self-efficacy: Thought control of action.* Washington, DC: Hemisphere.

SCHWEDER, R. A. (1994). "You're not sick, you're just in love": Emotion as an interpretive system. In P. Ekman & R. J. Davidson (Eds.), *The nature of emotion* (pp. 32–47). New York: Oxford University Press.

SCHWEITZER, E., RICKELS, K., & UHLENHUTH, E. H. (1995). Issues in the long-term treatment of anxiety disorders. In F. E. Bloom & D. Kupfer (Eds.), *Psychopharmacology: The fourth generation of progress* (pp. 1349–1359). New York: Raven.

SCOTT, F. J., & BARON-COHEN, S. (1996). Imagining real and unreal things: Evidence of a dissociation in autism. *Journal of Cognitive Neuroscience, 8*, 371–382.

SCRIBNER, S. (1975). Recall of classical syllogisms: A cross-cultural investigation of error on logical problems. In R. J. Falmagne (Ed.), *Reasoning, representation and process in children and adults* (pp. 153–174). Hillsdale, NJ: Erlbaum.

SEEMAN, M. V. (1997). Psychopathology in women and men: Focus on female hormones. *American Journal of Psychiatry, 154*, 1641–1647.

SEGALL, M. H., DASEN, P. R., BERRY, J. W., & POORTINGA, Y. H. (1999). *Human behavior in global perspective: An introduction to cross-cultural psychology* (2nd ed.). New York: Pergamon Press.

SEGERSTROM, S. C. (2000). Personality and the immune system: Models, methods, and mechanisms. *Annals of Behavioral Medicine, 22*, 180–190.

SEIDENBERG, M. (2005). Connectionist models of word reading. *Current Directions in Psychological Science, 14*, 238–242.

SELFRIDGE, O. G. (1959). Pandemonium: A paradigm for learning. In D. V. Blake & A. M. Uttley (Eds.), *Proceedings of the Symposium on the Mechanisation of Thought Processes.* London: HM Stationary Office.

SELIGMAN, M. E. P. (1970). On the generality of the laws of learning. *Psychological Review, 77*, 406–418.

SELIGMAN, M. E. P. (1971). Phobias and preparedness. *Behavior Therapy, 2*, 307–320.

SELIGMAN, M. E. P. (1975). *Helplessness: On depression, development, and death.* San Francisco: Freeman.

SELIGMAN, M. E. P. (1995). The effectiveness of psychotherapy: The Consumer Reports study. *American Psychologist, 50*, 965–974.

SELIGMAN, M. E. P., & CSIKSZENTMIHALYI, M. (2000). Positive psychology: An introduction. *American Psychologist, 55*(1), 5–14.

SELIGMAN, M. E. P., & GILLHAM, J. (2000). *The science of optimism and hope: Research essays in honor of Martin E. P. Seligman.* Philadelphia: Templeton Foundation Press.

SELIGMAN, M. E. P., & HAGER, J. L. (EDS.). (1972). *Biological boundaries of learning.* New York: Appleton-Century-Crofts.

SELIGMAN, M. E. P., KLEIN, D. C., & MILLER, W. R. (1976). Depression. In H. Leitenberg (Ed.), *Handbook of behavior modification and behavior therapy.* Englewood Cliffs, NJ: Prentice-Hall.

SELIGMAN, M. E. P., & MAIER, S. F. (1967). Failure to escape traumatic shock. *Journal of Experimental Psychology, 74*, 1–9.

SELIGMAN, M. E. P., MAIER, S. F., & SOLOMON, R. L. (1971). Unpredictable and uncontrollable aversive events. In F. R. Brush (Ed.), *Aversive conditioning and learning.* New York: Academic Press.

SELIGMAN, M. E., NOLEN-HOEKSEMA, S., THORNTON, N., & THORNTON, K. M. (1990). Explanatory style as a mechanism of disappointing athletic performance. *Psychological Science, 1*, 143–146.

SELIGMAN, M. E. P., STEEN, T., PARK, N., & PETERSON, C. (2005). Positive psychology progress: Empirical validation of interventions. *American Psychologist, 60*, 410–421.

SELIGMAN, M. E., & SCHULMAN, P. (1986). Explanatory style as a predictor of productivity and quitting among life insurance sales agents. *Journal of Personality & Social Psychology, 50*, 832–838.

SELIGMAN, M. E., STEEN, T. A. PARK, N., & PETERSON, C. (2005). Positive psychology progress: Empirical validation of interventions. *American Psychologist, 60*, 410–421.

SENGHAS, A. (1995a). Conventionalization in the first generation: A community acquires a language. *Journal of Contemporary Legal Issues, 6*, 501–519.

SENGHAS, A. (1995b). The development of Nicaraguan Sign Language via the language acquisition process. In D. MacLaughlin & S. McEwen (Eds.), *Proceedings of the Boston University Conference on Language Development, 19*, 543–552.

SERENO, A. B., & MAUNSELL, J. H. R. (1998). Shape selectivity in primate lateral intraparietal cortex. *Nature, 395*, 500–503.

SERPELL, R. (2000). Intelligence and culture. In R. J. Sternberg (Ed.), *Handbook of intelligence* (2nd ed., pp. 549–580). New York: Cambridge University Press.

SERVIN, A., NORDENSTROM, A., LARSSON, A., & BOHLIN, G. (2003). Prenatal androgens and gender-typed behavior: A study of girls with mild and severe forms of congenital adrenal hyperplasia. *Developmental Psychology, 39*(3), 440–450.

SETHI, A., MISCHEL, W., ABER, J. L., SHODA, Y., & RODRIGUEZ, M. L. (2000). The role of strategic attention deployment in development of self-regulation: Predicting preschoolers' delay of gratification from mother-toddler interactions. *Developmental Psychology, 36*, 767–777.

SHADER, R. I., & GREENBLATT, D. J. (1995). The pharmacotherapy of acute anxiety. In F. E. Bloom & D. Kupfer (Eds.), *Psychopharmacology: The fourth generation of progress* (pp. 1341–1348). New York: Raven.

SHADISH, W. R., MATT, G. E., NAVARRO, A. M., SIEGLE, G., CRITS-CHRISTOPH, P., HAZELRIGG, M., ET AL. (1997). Evidence that therapy works in clinically representative conditions. *Journal of Consulting and Clinical Psychology, 65*, 355–365.

SHAFFER, D. (2004). *Social and personality development* (5th ed.). New York: Wadsworth.

SHAM, P. V. C., O'CALLAGHAN, E., TAKEI, N., MURRAY, G. K., HARE, E. H., & MURRAY, R. M. (1992). Schizophrenia following pre-natal exposure to influenza epidemics between 1939 and 1960. *British Journal of Psychiatry, 160*, 461–466.

SHANAB, M. E., & YAHYA, K. A. (1977). A behavioral study of obedience in children. *Journal of Personality and Social Psychology, 35*, 530–536.

SHAVER, P., & CLARK, C. (1994). The psychodynamics of adult romantic attachment. In J. Masling & R. Bornstein (Eds.), *Empirical perspectives on object relations theory. Empirical studies of psychoanalytic theories: Vol. 5* (pp. 105–156). Washington, DC: American Psychological Association.

SHAVER, P., SCHWARTZ, J., KIRSON, D., & O'CONNOR, C. (1987). Emotion knowledge: Further exploration of a prototype approach. *Journal of Personality and Social Psychology, 52*, 1061–1086.

SHAVITT, S., SWAN, S., LOWREY, T. M., & WANKE, M. (1994). The interaction of endorser attractiveness and involvement in persuasion depends on the goal that guides message processing. *Journal of Consumer Psychology, 3*(2), 137–162.

SHEA, M. (1995). Interrelationships among categories of personality disorders. In W. J. Livesley (Ed.), *The DSM-IV personality disorders* (pp. 397–406). New York: Guilford Press.

SHEAR, M. K., PILKONIS, P. A., CLOITRE, M., & LEON, A. C. (1994). Cognitive behavioral treatment compared with nonprescriptive treatment of panic disorder. *Archives of General Psychiatry, 51*, 395–401.

SHELLEY, P. B. (1821). To a skylark. As published in A. T. Quiller-Couch (Ed.), *The Oxford book of English verse* (1900). Oxford: Clarendon.

SHEPARD, R. N., & COOPER, L. A. (1982). Mental images and their transformations. Cambridge, MA: MIT Press.

SHEPHERD, G. M. (1994). Discrimination of molecular signals by the olfactory receptor neuron. *Neuron, 13*, 771–790.

SHERIF, M. (1937). An experimental approach to the study of attitudes. *Sociometry, 1*, 90–98.

SHERIF, M. (1966). *The common predicament: Social psychology of intergroup conflict and cooperation.* Boston: Houghton Mifflin.

SHERIF, M., HARVEY, O. J., WHITE, B. J., HOOD W. R., & SHERIF, C. W. (1961). *Intergroup conflict and competition: The Robbers Cave experiment.* Norman: University of Oklahoma Book Exchange.

SHERRINGTON, C. (1906). *The integrative action of the nervous system.* New Haven, CT: Yale University Press.

SHETTLEWORTH, S. J. (1972). Constraints on learning. In D. S. Lehrman, R. A. Hinde, & E. Shaw (Eds.), *Advances in the study of behavior: Vol. 4.* New York: Academic Press.

SHETTLEWORTH, S. J. (1983). Memory in food-hoarding birds. *Scientific American, 248,* 102–110.

SHETTLEWORTH, S. J. (1984). Learning and behavioral ecology. In J. R. Krebs & N. B. Davies (Eds.), *Behavioral ecology* (2nd ed., pp. 170–194). Oxford: Blackwell.

SHETTLEWORTH, S. J. (1990). Spatial memory in food-storing birds. *Philosophical Transactions of the Royal Society, Series B, 329,* 143–151.

SHI, R., MORGAN, J. L., & ALLOPENNA, P. (1998). Phonological and acoustic bases for earliest grammatical category assignment: A cross-linguistic perspective. *Journal of Child Language, 25,* 169–201.

SHIAH, I. S., & YATHAM, L. N. (2000). Serotonin in mania and in the mechanism of action of mood stabilizers: A review of clinical studies. *Bipolar Disorders, 2,* 77–92.

SHIPLEY, E. F., KUHN, I. F., & MADDEN, E. C. (1983). Mothers' use of superordinate category terms. *Journal of Child Language, 10,* 571–588.

SHOBE, K. K., & KIHLSTROM, J. F. (1997). Is traumatic memory special? *Current Directions in Psychological Science, 6,* 70–74.

SHODA, Y., MISCHEL, W., & PEAKE, P. K. (1990). Predicting adolescent cognitive and self-regulatory competencies from preschool delay of gratification: Identifying diagnostic conditions. *Developmental Psychology, 26,* 978–986.

SHULMAN, S., ELICKER, J., & SROUFE, L. A. (1994). Stages of friendship growth in preadolescence as related to attachment history. *Journal of Social and Personal Relationships, 11*(3), 341–361.

SICOLY, F., & ROSS, M. (1977). Facilitation of ego-biased attributions by means of self-serving observer feedback. *Journal of Personality and Social Psychology, 35,* 734–741.

SIEGAL, M. (1997). *Knowing children: Experiments in conversation and cognition* (2nd ed.). New York: Psychology Press.

SIEGEL, A., & DEMETRIKOPOULOS, M. K. (1993). Hormones and aggression. In J. Schulkin (Ed.), *Hormonally induced changes in mind and brain* (pp. 99–127). San Diego, CA: Academic Press.

SIEGEL, S. (1977). Morphine tolerance acquisition as an associative process. *Journal of Experimental Psychology: Animal Behavior Processes, 3,* 1–13.

SIEGEL, S. (1983). Classical conditioning, drug tolerance, and drug dependence. In Y. Israel, F. B. Slower, H. Kalant, R. E. Popham, W. Schmidt, & R. G. Smart (Eds.), *Research advances in alcohol and drug abuse: Vol. 7* (pp. 207–246). New York: Plenum.

SIEGEL, S., & ALLAN, L. G. (1998). Learning and homeostasis: Drug addiction and the McCollough effect. *Pyschological Bulletin, 124,* 230–239.

SIEGEL, S., KIM, J. A. & SOKOLWSKA, M. (2003). Situational-specificity of caffeine tolerance. *Circulation, 108,* E38.

SIEGLER, R. S. (1996). *Emerging minds: The process of change in children's thinking.* New York: Oxford University Press.

SIGELMAN, C. K., MILLER, T. E., & WHITWORTH, L. A. (1986). The early development of stigmatizing reactions to physical differences. *Journal of Applied Developmental Psychology, 7*(1), 17–32.

SILK, J. B. (1986). Social behavior in evolutionary perspective. In B. B. Smuts, D. L. Cheney, R. M. Seyfarth, R. W. Wrangham, & T. T. Struhsaker (Eds.), *Primate societies.* Chicago: University of Chicago Press.

SIMCOCK, G., & HAYNE, H. (2002). Breaking the barrier? Children fail to translate their preverbal memories in language. *Psychological Science, 13,* 225–231.

SIMNER, M. L. (1971). Newborn's response to the cry of another infant. *Developmental Psychology, 5,* 136–150.

SIMONS, D. J. (2000). Attentional capture and inattentional blindness. *Trends in Cognitive Science, 4,* 147–155.

SIMONS, D. J., & CHABRIS, C. F. (1999). Gorillas in our midst: Sustained inattentional blindness for dynamic events. *Perception, 28*(9), 1059–1074.

SIMONTON, D. K. (2000). Creativity: Cognitive, personal, developmental, and social aspects. *American Psychologist, 55*(1), 151–158.

SIMONTON, D. K. (2003). Scientific creativity as constrained stochastic behavior: The integration of product, person, and process perspectives. *Psychological Bulletin, 129,* 475–494.

SIMPSON, E. L. (1974). Moral development research: A case of scientific cultural bias. *Human Development, 17,* 81–106.

SIMS, E. A. (1986). Energy balance in human beings: The problems of plentitude. *Vitamins and Hormones: Research and Applications, 43,* 1–101.

SINGER, W. (1996). Neuronal synchronization: A solution to the binding problem? In R. R. Llinas, & P. S. Churchland (Eds.), *The mind-brain continuum: Sensory processes* (pp. 101–130). Cambridge, MA: MIT Press.

SINGH, D. (1993). Adaptive significance of female physical attractiveness: Role of waist-to-hip ratio. *Journal of Personality and Social Psychology, 65,* 293–307.

SINGH, D. (1994). Waist-to-hip ratio and judgment of attractiveness and healthiness of female figures by male and female physicians. *International Journal of Obesity and Related Metabolic Disorders, 18,* 731–737.

SINGH, D., & LUIS, S. (1995). Ethnic and gender consensus for the effect of waist-to-hip ratio on judgment of women's attractiveness. *Human Nature, 6,* 51–65.

SINHA, D. (1983). Human assessment in the Indian context. In S. H. Irvine & J. W. Berry, (Eds.), *Human assessment and cultural factors* (pp. 17–34). New York: Plenum.

SKINNER, B. F. (1938). *The behavior of organisms.* New York: Appleton-Century-Crofts.

SLOANE, R. B., STAPLES, F. R., CRISTOL, A. H., YORKSTON, N. J., & WHIPPLE, K. (1975). *Psychotherapy vs. behavior therapy.* Cambridge, MA: Harvard University Press.

SLOMAN, S. A. (1996). The empirical case for two systems of reasoning. *Psychological Bulletin, 119,* 3–22.

SLOVIC, P., FISCHOFF, B., & LICHTENSTEIN, S. (1982). Facts versus fears: Understanding perceived risk. In D. Kahneman, P. Slovic, & A. Tversky (Eds.), *Judgment under uncertainty: Heuristics and biases.* New York: Cambridge University Press.

SMITH, C. (1996). Women, weight and body image. In J. C. Chrisler, C. Golden, & P. D. Rozee (Eds.), *Lectures on the psychology of women.* New York: McGraw Hill.

SMITH, C., & LLOYD, B. (1978). Maternal behavior and perceived sex of infant: Revisited. *Child Development, 49,* 1263–1265.

SMITH, E. E., & MEDIN, D. L. (1981). *Categories and concepts.* Cambridge, MA: Harvard University Press.

SMITH, E. E., OSHERSON, D. N., RIPS, L. J., & KEAN, M. (1988). Combining prototypes: A selective modification model. *Cognitive Science, 12,* 485–527.

SMITH, L. (2005). Psychotherapy, classism, and the poor: Conspicuous by their absence. *American Psychologist, 60,* 687–696.

SMITH, L. B., & THELEN, D. (1993). *A dynamic systems approach to development: Applications.* Cambridge, MA: MIT Press.

SMITH, L. B., THELEN, E., TITZER, R., & MCLIN, D. (1999). Knowing in the context of acting: The task dynamics of the A-Not-B error. *Psychological Review, 106,* 235–260.

SMITH, L. B., & THELEN, E. (2003). Development as a dynamic system. *Trends in Cognitive Science, 7,* 343–348.

SMITH, M. (1983). Hypnotic memory enhancement of witnesses: Does it work? *Psychological Bulletin, 94,* 387–407.

SMITH, M. B. (1950). The phenomenological approach in personality theory: Some critical remarks. *Journal of Abnormal and Social Psychology, 45,* 516–522.

SMITH, M. L., GLASS, G. V., & MILLER, R. L. (1980). *The benefits of psychotherapy.* Baltimore: Johns Hopkins Press.

SMITH, P. B., & BOND, M. B. (1993). *Social psychology across cultures.* New York: Harvester Wheatsheaf.

SMITH, P. B., MISUMI, J., TAYEB, M., PETERSON, M., & BOND, M. (1989). On the generality of leadership style measures across cultures. *Journal of Occupational Psychology, 62*(2), 97–109.

SMITH, P., & DALISH, L. (1977). Sex differences in parent and infant behavior in the home. *Child Development, 48,* 1250–1254.

SMITH, S. M. (1979). Remembering in and out of context. *Journal of Experimental Psychology: Human Learning and Memory, 5,* 460–471.

SMITH, S. M., & BLANKENSHIP, S. E. (1989). Incubation effects. *Bulletin of the Psychonomic Society, 27*(4), 311–314.

SMITH, S. M., & VELA, E. (2001). Environmental context-dependent memory: A review and meta-analysis. *Psychonomics Bulletin and Review, 8,* 203–220.

SMOLENSKY, P. (1999). Grammar-based connectionist approaches to language. *Cognitive Science, 23,* 589–613.

SNEDEKER, J., & GLEITMAN, L. (2004). Why it is hard to label our concepts. In S. Waxman & G. Hall (Eds.), *Weaving a lexicon* (pp. 207– 294). New York: Cambridge University Press.

SNEDEKER, J., & GLEITMAN, L. (2004). Why it is hard to label our concepts. G. Hall & S. Waxman (Eds.), *Weaving a lexicon.* New York: Cambridge University Press.

SNIBBE, A., & MARKUS, H. R. (2005). You can't always get what you want: Social class, agency, and choice. *Journal of Personality and Social Psychology, 88,* 703–720.

SNOW, C., & HOEFNAGEL-HOHLE, M. (1978). The critical period for language acquisition: Evidence from second language learning. *Child Development, 49,* 1114–1128.

SNOW, R. E. (1994). Abilities in academic tasks. In R. J. Sternberg & R. K. Wagner (Eds.), *Mind in context: Interactionist perspectives on human intelligence* (pp. 3–37). Cambridge, England: Cambridge University Press.

SNOW, R. E. (1996). Aptitude development and education. *Psychology, Public Policy, and Law, 2,* 536–560.

SNYDER, D. K., CASTELLANI, A. M., & WHISMAN, M. A. (2006). Current status and future directions in couple therapy. *Annual Review of Psychology, 57,* 317–344.

SNYDER, M. (1987). *Public appearances/private realities.* New York: Freeman.

SNYDER, M. (1995). Self-monitoring: Public appearances versus private realities. In G. G. Brannigan & M. R. Merrens (Eds.), *The social psychologists: Research adventures* (pp. 35–50). New York: McGraw-Hill.

SNYDER, M., & OMOTO, A. M. (1992). Who helps and why? The psychology of aids volunteerism. In S. Spacapan & S. Oskamp (Eds). *Helping and being helped: Naturalistic studies* (pp. 213–239). Thousand Oaks, CA: Sage.

SNYDER, M., TANKE, E. D., & BERSCHEID, E. (1977). Social perception and interpersonal behavior: On the self-fulfilling nature of social stereotypes. *Journal of Personality and Social Psychology, 44,* 510–517.

SNYDER, M. L., STEPHAN, W. G., & ROSENFIELD, D. (1976). Egotism and attribution. *Journal of Personality and Social Psychology, 33,* 435–441.

SNYDER, S. H. (1976). The dopamine hypothesis of schizophrenia. *American Journal of Psychiatry, 133,* 197–202.

SOJA, N. N., CAREY, S., & SPELKE, E. S. (1991). Ontological categories guide young children's inductions of word meaning: Object terms and substance terms. *Cognition, 38,* 179–211.

SOKOLOWSKA, M., SIEGEL, S., & KIM, J. A. (2002). Intraadministration associations: Conditional hyperalgesia elicited by morphine onset cues. *Journal of Experimental Psychology: Animal Behavior Processes, 28*(3), 309–320.

SOX, H. C., JR., & WOOLF, S. H. (1993). Evidence-based practice guidelines from the U.S. Preventive Services Task Force. *Journal of the American Medical Association, 269,* 2678.

SPANOS, N. P. (1996). *Multiple identities and false memories: A sociocognitive perspective.* Washington, DC: American Psychological Association.

SPANOS, N. P., BURGESS, C. A., BURGESS, M. F., SAMUELS, C., & BLOIS, W. O. (1999). Creating false memories of infancy with hypnotic and nonhypnotic procedures. *Applied Cognitive Psychology, 13,* 201–218.

SPEAR, L. P. (2000). The adolescent brain and age-related behvioral manifestations. *Neuroscience and Biobehavioral Reviews, 24,* 417–463.

SPEARMAN, C. (1927). *The abilities of man.* London: Macmillan.

SPELKE, E. (2003). Core knowledge. In N. Kanwisher & J. Duncan (Eds.), *Attention and performance: Vol. 20. Functional neuroimaging of visual cognition.* New York: Oxford University Press.

SPELKE, E. S. (1994). Initial knowledge: Six suggestions. *Cognition, 50*(1–3), 431–445.

SPELKE, E. S. (2005). Sex differences in intrinsic aptitude for mathematics and science?: A critical review. *American Psychologist, 60*(9), 950–958.

SPELKE, E. S., & NEWPORT, E. (1998). Nativism, empiricism, and the development of knowledge. In R. Lerner (Ed), *Handbook of child psychology: Vol. 1. Theoretical models of human development* (5th ed.). New York: Wiley.

SPEMANN, H. (1967). *Embryonic development and induction.* New York: Hafner.

SPERBER, D., & WILSON, D. (1986). *Relevance: Communication and cognition.* Oxford: Blackwell.

SPERLING, G. (1960). The information available in brief visual presentations. *Psychological Monographs, 74*(Whole No. 11).

SPIRO, M. (1982). *Oedipus in the Trobriands.* Chicago: University of Chicago Press.

SPIRO, M. E. (1992). Oedipus redux. *Ethos, 20,* 358–376.

SPITZ, C. J., GOLD, A. R., & ADAMS, D. B. (1975). Cognitive and hormonal factors affecting coital frequency. *Archives of Sexual Behavior, 4,* 249–264.

SPRINGER, S. P., & DEUTSCH, G. (1998). *Left brain, right brain: Perspectives from cognitive neuroscience* (5th ed.). New York: Freeman.

SQUIRE, L. R. (1977). ECT and memory loss. *American Journal of Psychiatry, 134,* 997–1001.

SQUIRE, L. R. (1986). Mechanisms of memory. *Science, 232,* 1612–1619.

SQUIRE, L. R. (1987). *Memory and brain.* New York: Oxford University.

SQUIRE, L. R., & COHEN, N. J. (1979). Memory and amnesia: Resistance to disruption develops for years after learning. *Behavioral Biology and Neurology, 25,* 115–125.

SQUIRE, L. R., & COHEN, N. J. (1982). Remote memory, retrograde amnesia, and the neuropsychology of memory. In L. S. Cermak (Ed.), *Human memory and amnesia* (pp. 275–304). Hillsdale, NJ: Erlbaum.

SQUIRE, L. R., & COHEN, N. J. (1984). Human memory and amnesia. In J. McGaugh, G. Lynch, & N. Weinberger (Eds.), *Neurobiology of learning and memory.* New York: Guilford.

SRIVASTAVA, S., & BEER, J. S. (2005). How self-evaluations relate to being liked by others: Integrating sociometer and attachment perspectives. *Journal of Personality and Social Psychology, 89,* 966–977.

SROUFE, L. A., EGELAND, B., CARLSON, E., & COLLINS, W. A. (2005). *The Development of the person: The Minnesota Study of Risk and Adaptation from Birth to Adulthood.* New York: Guilford Publications.

STANLEY, B. G., MAGDALIN, W., & LEIBOWITZ, S. F. (1989). A critical site for neuropeptide Y-induced eating lies in the caudolateral paraventricular/perifornical region of the hypothalamus. *Society for Neuroscience Abstracts, 15,* 894.

STANLEY, J. (1993). Boys and girls who reason well mathematically. In G. R. Beck & K. Ackrill (Eds.), *The origins and development of high ability.* Chichester, England: Wiley.

STANOVCH, K. E., & WEST, R. F. (1998). Who uses base rates and P(D|~H)? An analysis of individual differences. *Memory & Cognition*, 26, 161–179.

STANOVICH, K. E., & WEST, R. F. (2000). Individual differences in reasoning: Implications for the rationality debate. *Behavioral and Brain Sciences*, 23, 645–665.

STARKEY, P., SPELKE, E. S., & GELMAN, R. (1983). Detection of intermodal numerical correspondences by human infants. *Science*, 222, 179–181.

STARKEY, P., SPELKE, E. S., & GELMAN, R. (1990). Numerical abstraction by human infants. *Cognition*, 36, 97–127.

STEELE, C. M. (1998). Stereotyping and its threat are real. *American Psychologist*, 53, 680–681.

STEELE, C. M., & ARONSON, J. (1995). Stereotype threat and the intellectual test performance of African Americans. *Journal of Personality and Social Psychology*, 69(5), 797–811.

STEINBERG, L., ELKMAN, J. D., & MOUNTS, N. S. (1989). Authoritative parenting, psychosocial maturity, and academic success among adolescents. *Child Development*, 60(6), 1424–1436.

STERN, P. C., & CARSTENSEN, L. L. (2000). *The aging mind*. Washington, DC: National Academy Press.

STERNBERG, R. J. (1977). *Intelligence, information processing, and analogical reasoning: The componential analysis of human abilities*. Hillsdale, NJ: Erlbaum.

STERNBERG, R. J. (1985). General intellectual ability. In R. Sternberg, *Human abilities: An information processing approach*. New York: Freeman.

STERNBERG, R. J. (1986). A triangular theory of love. *Psychological Review*, 93, 119–135.

STERNBERG, R. J. (1988). Triangulating love. In R. J. Sternberg & M. L. Barnes (Eds.), *The psychology of love* (pp. 119–138). New Haven, CT: Yale University Press.

STERNBERG, R. J. (1990). *Metaphors of mind*. New York: Cambridge University Press.

STERNBERG, R. J. (2000). The Holey Grail of general intelligence. *Science*, 289, 399–401.

STERNBERG, R. J. (2004). Culture and intelligence. *American Psychologist*, 59, 325–338.

STERNBERG, R. J., & DAVIDSON, J. E. (1983). Insight in the gifted. *Educational Psychologist*, 18, 51–57.

STERNBERG, R. J., & KAUFMAN, J. C. (1998). Human abilities. *Annual Review of Psychology*, 49, 479–502.

STERNBERG, R. J., & WAGNER, R. K. (1993). The egocentric view of intelligence and job performance is wrong. *Current Directions in Psychological Science*, 2, 1–5.

STERNBERG, R. J., WAGNER, R. K., WILLIAMS, W. M., & HORVATH, J. A. (1995). Testing common sense. *American Psychologist*, 50, 912–927.

STEVENS, A., & COUPE, P. (1978). Distortions in judged spatial relations. *Cognitive Psychology*, 10, 422–437.

STEVENS, L., & JONES, E. E. (1976). Defensive attributions and the Kelley cube. *Journal of Personality and Social Psychology*, 34, 809–820.

STEVENS, S. S. (1955). The measurement of loudness. *Journal of the Acoustical Society of America*, 27, 815–819.

STEWART, T. D. (1957). Stone age surgery: A general review, with emphasis on the New World. *Annual Review of the Smithsonian Institution*. Washington, DC: Smithsonian Institution.

STOKOE, W. C., JR. (1960). Sign language structure: An outline of the visual communication systems. *Studies in Linguistics*, Occasional Papers 8.

STOLZ, J. A., & BESNER, D. (1999). On the myth of automatic semantic activation in reading. *Current Directions in Psychological Science*, 8(2), 61–65.

STOOLMILLER, M. (2001). Synergistic interaction of child manageability problems and parent-discipline tactics in predicting future growth in externalizing behavior for boys. *Developmental Psychology*, 37(6), 814–825.

STORMS, M. D. (1973). Videotape and the attribution process: Reversing actors' and observers' points of view. *Journal of Personality and Social Psychology*, 27, 165–175.

STOWE, L. (1987). Thematic structures and sentence comprehension. In G. Carlson & M. Tanenhaus (Eds.), *Linguistic structure in language processing*. Dordrecht: Reidel.

STRACK, F., MARTIN, L. L., & STEPPER, S. (1988). Inhibiting and facilitating conditions of the human smile: A nonobtrusive test of the facial feedback hypothesis. *Journal of Personality and Social Psychology*, 54, 768–777.

STRIANO, T., & ROCHAT, P. (2000). Emergence of selective social referencing in infancy. *Infancy*, 1(2), 253–264.

STRICKER, E. M., & ZIGMOND, M. J. (1976). Recovery of function after damage to catecholamine-containing neurons: A neurochemical model for the lateral hypothalamic syndrome. In J. M. Sprague & A. N. Epstein (Eds.), *Progress in psychobiology and physiological psychology: Vol. 6* (pp. 121–188). New York: Academic Press.

STROOP, J. R. (1935). Studies of interference in serial verbal reactions. *Journal of Experimental Psychology*, 18, 643–662.

STUMPF, H., & STANLEY, J. C. (1998). Stability and change in gender-related differences on the College Board Advanced Placement and Achievement tests. *Current Directions in Psychological Science*, 7, 192–198.

STUSS, D. T., & LEVINE, B. (2002). Adult clinical neuropsychology: Lessons from studies of the frontal lobes. *Annual Review of Psychology*, 53, 401–433.

STYRON, W. (1990). *Darkness visible: A memoir of madness*. New York: Random House.

SUE S. (1998). In search of cultural competence in psychotherapy and counseling. *American Psychologist*, 53, 440–448.

SUE, D. W., & KIRK, B. A. (1973). Psychological characteristics of Chinese-American college students. *Journal of Counseling Psychology*, 19, 142–148.

SULLIVAN, P. F., NEALE, M. C., & KENDLER, K. S. (2000). Genetic epidemiology of major depression: Review and meta-analysis. *American Journal of Psychiatry*, 157, 1552–1562.

SULLOWAY, F. (1996). *Born to rebel*. New York: Pantheon Books.

SULLOWAY, F. J. (1979). *Freud, biologist of the mind: Beyond the psychoanalytic legend*. Cambridge, MA: Harvard University Press.

SULS, J. M. (1972). A two-stage model for the appreciation of jokes and cartoons: An information processing analysis. In J. H. Goldstein & P. E. McGhee (Eds.), *The psychology of humor* (pp. 81–100). New York: Academic Press.

SULS, J. M. (1983). Cognitive processes in humor appreciation. In P. E. McGhee & J. H. Goldstein (Eds.), *Handbook of humor research: Vol. 1* (pp. 39–58). New York: Springer.

SULS, J. M., & MILLER, R. L. (EDS.). (1977). *Social comparison processes: Theoretical and empirical perspectives*. New York: Washington Hemisphere.

SUPALLA, I., & NEWPORT, E. L. (1978). How many seats in a chair? The derivation of nouns and verbs in American Sign Language. In P. Siple (Ed.), *Understanding language through sign language research*. New York: Academic Press.

SUR, M., & RUBENSTEIN, J. L. R. (2005). Patterning and plasticity of the cerebral cortex. *Science*, 310, 805–810.

SUROWIECKI, J. (2004). *The wisdom of crowds*. New York: Doubleday.

SUTKER, P. B., ALLAIN, A. N., JR., & WINSTEAD, D. K. (1993). Psychopathology and psychiatric diagnoses of World War II Pacific Theater prisoner of war survivors and combat veterans. *American Journal of Psychiatry*, 150, 240–245.

SWEDO, S. E., PIETRINI, P., LEONARD, H. L., SCHAPIRO, M. B., RETTEW, D. C., GOLDBERGER, E. L., ET AL. (1992). Cerebral glucose metabolism in childhood-onset obsessive-compulsive disorder. Revisualization during pharmacotherapy. *Archives of General Psychiatry*, 49, 690–694.

SWETS, J. A., DAWES, R. M., & MONAHAN, J. (2000). Psychological Science can improve diagnostic decisions. *Psychological Science in the Public Interest*, 1, 1–26.

SWINGLEY, D., & FERNALD, A., (2002) Recognition of words referring to present and absent objects by 24–month-olds. *Journal of Memory and Language, 46,* 39–56.

SYMONS, D. (1979). *The evolution of human sexuality.* New York: Oxford University Press.

TAJFEL, H., & BILLIG, M. (1974). Familiarity and categorization in intergroup behavior. *Journal of Experimental Social Psychology, 10,* 159–170.

TAJFEL, H., BILLIG, M., BUNDY, R., & FLAMENT, C. (1971). Social categorization and intergroup behaviour. *European Journal of Social Psychology, 1,* 149–178.

TAKAHASHI, K. (1986). Examining the Strange-Situation procedure with Japanese mothers and 12–month-old infants. *Developmental Psychology, 22,* 265–270.

TAKATA, T. (1987). Self-deprecative tendencies in self-evaluation through social comparison. *Japanese Journal of Experimental Social Psychology, 27,* 27–36.

TANDON, R., & KANE, J. M. (1993). Neuropharmacologic basis for clozapine's unique profile [Letter]. *Archives of General Psychiatry, 50,* 158–159.

TANENHAUS, M. K., SPIVEY-KNOWLTON, M. J., EBERHARD, K. M., & SEDIVY, J. C. (1995). Integration of visual and linguistic information in spoken language comprehension. *Science, 268*(5217), 1632–1634.

TANNER, J. M. (1990). *Fetus into man: Physical growth from conception to maturity* (rev. ed.). Cambridge, MA: Harvard University Press.

TANNOCK, R. (1998). Attention deficit hyperactivity disorder: Advances in cognitive, neurobiological and genetic research. *Journal of Child Psychology and Psychiatry, 39,* 65–99.

TARR, M. J. (1995). Rotating objects to recognize them: A case study on the role of viewpoint dependency in the recognition of three-dimensional objects. *Psychonomic Bulletin & Review, 2,* 55–82.

TAYLOR, M., ESBENSEN, B. M., & BENNETT, R. T. (1994). Children's understanding of knowledge acquisition: The tendency for children to report that they have always known what they have just learned. *Child Development, 65*(6), 1581–1604.

TAYLOR, S. E., & FISKE, S. T. (1975). Point of view and perceptions of causality. *Journal of Personality and Social Psychology, 32,* 439–445.

TAYLOR, W. S., & MARTIN, M. F. (1944). Multiple personality. *Journal of Abnormal and Social Psychology, 39,* 281–300.

TEITELBAUM, P., & EPSTEIN, A. N. (1962). The lateral hypothalamic syndrome: Recovery of feeding and drinking after lateral hypothalamic lesions. *Psychological Review, 69,* 74–90.

TELLEGEN, A., LYKKEN, D. T., BOUCHARD, T. J., WILCOX, K. J., SEGAL, N. L., & RICH, S. (1988). Personality of twins reared apart and together. *Journal of Personality and Social Psychology, 54,* 1031–1039.

TERR, L. C. (1991). Acute responses to external events and posttraumatic stress disorders. In M. Lewis (Ed.), *Child and adolescent psychiatry: A comprehensive textbook* (pp. 755–763). Baltimore: Williams & Wilkins.

TERR, L. C. (1994). *Unchained memories: True stories of traumatic memories, lost and found.* New York: Basic.

TERRY, R., & COIE, J. D. (1991). A comparison of methods for defining sociometric status among children. *Developmental Psychology, 27*(5), 867–880.

TERVOORT, B. T. (1961). Esoteric symbolism in the communication behavior of young deaf children. *American Annals of the Deaf, 106,* 436–480.

TESSER, A., CAMPBELL, J., & SMITH, M. (1984). Friendship choice and performance: Self-evaluation maintenance in children. *Journal of Personality and Social Psychology, 46,* 561–574.

TETLOCK, P. E., PETERSON, R. S., McGUIRE, C., CHANG, S.-J., & ET AL. (1992). Assessing political group dynamics: A test of the groupthink model. *Journal of Personality and Social Psychology, 63*(3), 403–425.

THAPAR, A., & GREENE, R. (1994). Effects of level of processing on implicit and explicit tasks. *Journal of Experimental Psychology: Learning, Memory and Cognition, 20,* 671–679.

THARA, R. (2004). Twenty-year course of schizophrenia: The Madras Longitudinal Study. *Canadian Journal of Psychiatry, 49,* 564–569.

THELEN, E., SCHÖNER, G., SCHIER, C., & SMITH, L. B. (2001). The dynamics of embodiment: A field theory of infant perseverative reaching. *Behavioral & Brain Sciences, 24,* 34–86.

THOMAS, A., & CHESS, S. (1977). *Temperament and development.* New York: Brunner/Mazel.

THOMAS, A., & CHESS, S. (1984). Genesis and evaluation of behavioral disorders: From infancy to early adult life. *American Journal of Psychiatry, 141,* 1–9.

THOMPSON, C. P., & COWAN, T. (1986). Flashbulb memories: A nicer recollection of a Neisser recollection. *Cognition, 22,* 199–200.

THOMPSON, M. M., ZANNA, M. P., & GRIFFIN, D. W. (1995). Let's not be indifferent about (attitudinal) ambivalence. In R. E. Petty & J. A. Krosnick (Eds.), *Attitude strength: Antecedents and consequences: Vol. 4* (pp. 361–386). Mahwah, NJ: Erlbaum.

THOMPSON, R. A. (1994). Emotion regulation: A theme in search of definition. In N. Fox (Ed.), *The development of emotion regulation and dysregulation: Biological and behavioral aspects. Monographs of the Society for Research in Child Development, 59*(240), 25–52.

THOMPSON, R. A. (1998). Early sociopersonality development. In W. Damon (Ed.), *Handbook of child psychology* (5th ed.): *Vol. 3. Social, emotional, and personality development* (N. Eisenberg, Vol. Ed.) (pp. 25–104). New York: Wiley.

THOMPSON, R. A. (1999). Early attachment and later development. In J. Cassidy & P. Shaver (Eds.), *Handbook of attachment* (pp. 265–286). New York: Guilford.

THOMPSON, R. A. (2000). The legacy of early attachments. *Child Development, 71,* 145–152.

THOMPSON, R. A. (2006). The development of the person: Social understanding, relationships, self, conscience. In W. Damon & R. M. Lerner (Eds.), *Handbook of child psychology* (6th ed.): *Vol. 3. Social, emotional, and personality development* (N. Eisenberg, Vol. Ed.). New York: Wiley.

THOMPSON, R. A., LAIBLE, D., & ONTAI, L. (2003). Early understanding of emotion, morality, and the self: Developing a working model. In R. Kail (Ed.), *Advances in Child Development and Behavior: Vol. 31* (pp.137–171). San Diego: Academic.

THOMPSON, W. L., & KOSSLYN, S. M. (2000). Neural systems activated during visual mental imagery: A review and meta-analyses. In J. Mazziotta & A. Toga (Eds.), *Brain mapping II: The applications.* New York: Academic Press.

THORNHILL, R., & GANGESTAD, S. G. (1999). Facial attractiveness. *Trends in Cognitive Science, 3,* 452–460.

TIERNEY, A. J. (2000). Egas Moniz and the origins of psychosurgery: A review commemorating the 50th anniversary of Moniz's Nobel Prize. *Journal of the History of Neuroscience, 9,* 22–36.

TIETJEN, A. M., & WALKER, L. J. (1985). Moral reasoning and leadership among men in a Papua New Guinea society. *Developmental Psychology, 21,* 982–989.

TIMBERLAKE, W. (1995). Reconceptualizing reinforcement: A causal system approach to reinforcement and behavior change. In W. O'Donohue & L. Krasner (Eds.), *Theories in behavior therapy* (pp. 59–96). Washington, DC: APA Books.

TIMBERLAKE, W., & ALLISON, J. (1974). Response deprivation: An empirical approach to instrumental performance. *Psychological Review, 81,* 146–164.

TODOROV, A., MANDISODZA, A., GOREN, A., & HALL, C. (2005). Inferences of competence from faces predict election outcomes. *Science, 308,* 1623–1626.

TOLMAN, E. C. (1932). *Purposive behavior in animals and men.* New York: Appleton-Century-Crofts.

TOLMAN, E. C. (1948). Cognitive maps in rats and men. *Psychological Review, 55,* 189–208.

TOLMAN, E. C., & HONZIK, C. H. (1930). Introduction and removal of reward, and maze performance in rats. *University of California Publications in Psychology, 4,* 257–275.

TOLSTOY, L. (1868). *War and peace* (second epilogue). H. Gifford (Ed.), L. Maude & A. Maude (Trans.). New York: Oxford University Press, 1922.

Tomasello, M. (1994). Can an ape understand a sentence? A review of *Language comprehension in ape and child* by E. S. Savage-Rumbaugh et al. *Language & Communication, 14,* 377–390.

Tomasello, M. (2000). *The cultural origins of human cognition.* Cambridge, MA: Harvard University Press.

Tomasello, M. (2001). Perceiving intentions and learning words in the second year of life. In M. Bowerman & S. Levinson (Eds.), *Language acquisition and conceptual development.* Cambridge University Press.

Tomasello, M. (2002). The social bases of language acquisition. *Social Development, 1*(1), 67–87.

Tomasello, M. (2003). *Constructing a language.* Cambridge, MA: Harvard University Press.

Tomasello, M., Kruger, A., & Ratner, H. (1993). Cultural learning. *Behavioral and Brain Sciences, 16,* 495–552.

Tomasello, M., Strosberg R., & Akhtar, N. (1996). Eighteen month old children learn words in non-ostensive contexts. *Journal of Child Language, 23,* 157–176.

Tomkins, S. S. (1962). *Affect, imagery, consciousness: The positive affects* (Vol. 1). New York: Springer.

Tomkins, S. S. (1963). *Affect, imagery, consciousness: Vol. 2. The negative affects.* New York: Springer.

Tong, F., Nakayama, K., Vaughan, J. T., & Kanwisher, N. (1998). Binocular rivalry and visual awareness in human extrastriate cortex. *Neuron, 21,* 753–759.

Tooby, J., & Cosmides, L. (1990). The past explains the present: Emotional adaptations and the structure of ancestral environments. *Ethology and Sociobiology, 11,* 375–424.

Torgersen, S. (1986). Genetic factors in moderately severe and mild affective disorders. *Archives of General Psychiatry, 43,* 222–226.

Torrey, E. F. (1983). *Surviving schizophrenia: A family manual.* New York: Harper & Row.

Torrey, E. F. (1992). *Freudian fraud: The malignant effect of Freud's theory on American thought and culture.* New York: HarperCollins.

Tourangeau, R., & Ellsworth, P. C. (1979). The role of facial response in the experience of emotion. *Journal of Personality and Social Psychology, 37,* 1519–1531.

Treisman, A. M. (1986a). Features and objects in visual processing. *Scientific American, 255,* 114–125.

Treisman, A. M. (1986b). Properties, parts, and objects. In K. R. Boff, L. Kaufman, & J. P. Thomas (Eds.), *Handbook of perception and human performance: Vol. II* (Chapter 35). New York: Wiley.

Treisman, A. M. (1988). Features and objects: The Fourteenth Barlett Memorial Lecture. *Quarterly Journal of Experimental Psychology, 40A,* 201–237.

Treisman, A. M., & Gelade, G. (1980). A feature-integration theory of attention. *Cognitive Psychology, 12,* 97–136.

Treisman, A. M., & Souther, J. (1985). Search assymetry: A diagnostic for preattentive processing of separable features. *Journal of Experimental Psychology: General, 114,* 285–310.

Triandis, H. (1994). Major cultural syndromes and emotion. In S. Kitayama & H. R. Markus (Eds.), *Emotion and culture* (pp. 285–306). Washington, DC: American Psychological Association.

Triandis, H. C. (1989). Cross-cultural studies of individualism and collectivism. *Nebraska Symposium on Motivation, 37,* 41–134. Lincoln: University of Nebraska Press.

Triandis, H. C., & Suh, E. M. (2002). Cultural influences on personality. *Annual Review of Psychology, 53*(1), 133–160.

Triplett, N. (1898). The dynamogenic factors in pacemaking and competition. *American Journal of Psychology, 9,* 507–533.

Trivers, R. L. (1972). Parental investment and sexual selection. In B. Campbell (Ed.), *Sexual selection and the descent of man* (pp. 139–179). Chicago: Aldine.

Tropp, L. R., & Pettigrew, T. F. (2005). Relationships between intergroup contact and prejudice among minority and majority status groups. *Psychological Science, 16,* 951–957.

True, W. R., Rise, J., Eisen, S., Heath, A. C., Goldberg, J., Lyons, M., et al. (1993). A twin study of genetic and environmental contributions to liability for posttraumatic stress symptoms. *Archives of General Psychiatry, 50,* 257 264.

Trueswell, J. C., Sekerina, I., Hill, N. M., & Logrip, M. L. (1999). The kindergarten-path effect: Studying on-line sentence processing in young children. *Cognition, 73,* 89–134.

Trueswell, J. C., & Tanenhaus, M. K. (1994). Toward a lexicalist framework of constraint-based syntactic ambiguity resolution. In C. Clifton, Jr., & L. Frazier (Eds.), *Perspectives on sentence processing* (pp. 155–179). Hillsdale, NJ: Erlbaum.

Trueswell, J. C., Tanenhaus, M. K., & Garnsey, S. M. (1994). Semantic influences on parsing: Use of thematic role information in syntactic ambiguity resolution. *Journal of Memory and Language, 33,* 285–318.

Tsai, J. L., & Chentsova-Dutton, Y. (2002). Different models of cultural orientation in American- and overseas-born Asian Americans. In K. Kurasaki, S. Okazaki, & S. Sue (Eds.), *Asian American mental health: Assessment theories and methods* (pp. 95–106). New York: Kluwer Academic/Plenum.

Tsuang, M. T., Gilbertson, M. W., & Faraone, S. V. (1991). The genetics of schizophrenia. *Schizophrenia Research, 4,* 157–171.

Tucker, M., & Ellis, R. (2001). The potentiation of grasp types during visual object categorization. *Visual Cognition, 8,* 769–800.

Tucker, M., & Ellis, R. (2004). Action priming by briefly presented objects. *Acta Psychologica, 116,* 185–203.

Tulving, E. (1985). How many memory systems are there? *American Psychologist, 40,* 385–398.

Tulving, E., & Osler, S. (1968). Effectiveness of retrieved cues in memory for words. *Journal of Experimental Psychology, 77,* 593–606.

Tulving, E., Schacter, D. L., & Stark, H. A. (1982). Priming effects in word-fragment completion are independent of recognition memory. *Journal of Experimental Psychology: Learning, Memory, and Cognition, 8,* 336–342.

Tulving, E., Schacter, D. L., McLachlan, D. R., & Moscovitch, M. (1988). Priming of semantic autobiographical knowledge: A case study of retrograde amnesia. *Brain and Cognition, 8,* 3–20.

Tulving, E., & Thomson, D. M. (1973). Encoding specificity and retrieval processes in episodic memory. *Psychological Review, 80,* 352–373.

Tupes, E. C., & Christal, R. E. (1961, May). *Recurrent personality factors based on trait ratings (ASD-TR-61–97).* Lackland Air Force Base, TX: Aeronautical Systems Division, Personnel Laboratory.

Turati, C. (2004). Why faces are not special to newborns: An alternative account of the face preference. *Current Directions in Psychological Science, 13,* 5–8.

Turkheimer, E., Haley, A., Waldron, M., D'Onofrio, B., & Gottesman, I. I. (2003). Socioeconomic status modifies heritability of IQ in young children. *Psychological Science, 14,* 623–628.

Turkheimer, E., & Waldron, M. (2000). Nonshared environment: A theoretical, methodological, and quantitative review. *Psychological Bulletin, 126*(1), 78–108.

Turner, J., Brown, R., & Tajfel, H. (1979). Social comparison and group interest in ingroup favouritism. *European Journal of Social Psychology, 9,* 187–204.

Tversky, A. (1977). Features of similarity. *Psychological Review, 84*(4), 327–352.

Tversky, A., & Kahneman, D. (1973). Availability: A heuristic for judging frequency and probability. *Cognitive Psychology, 5,* 207–232.

Tweney, R. D., Doherty, M. E., & Mynatt, C. R. (1981). *On scientific thinking.* New York: Columbia University Press.

U.S. Department of Health and Human Services. (2001). *Mental health: Culture, race, and ethnicity—A supplement to mental health: A report of the Surgeon General.* Rockville, MD: U.S. Department of Health and Human Services, Public Health Service, Office of the Surgeon General.

U.S. DEPARTMENT OF LABOR. (1995). *Marital and family characteristics of the labor force from the March 1994 Current Population Survey.* Washington, DC: Bureau of Labor Statistics.

UNGERLEIDER, L. G., & HAXBY, J. V. (1994). "What" and "where" in the human brain. *Current Opinions in Neurobiology, 4,* 157–165.

UNGERLEIDER, L. G., & MISHKIN, M. (1982). Two cortical visual systems. In D. J. Ingle, M. A. Goodale, & R. J. W. Mansfield (Eds.), *Analysis of visual behavior* (pp. 549–586). Cambridge, MA: MIT Press.

URBERG, K. A., DEGIRMENCIOGLU, S. M., & PILGRIM, C. (1997). Close friend and group influence on adolescent cigarette smoking and alcohol use. *Developmental Psychology, 33*(5), 834–844.

URWIN, C. (1983). Dialogue and cognitive functioning in the early language development of three blind children. In A. E. Mills (Ed.), *Language acquisition in the blind child.* London: Croom Helm.

VAILLANT, G. E. (1974). Natural history of male psychological health. II. Some antecedents of healthy adult adjustment. *Archives of General Psychiatry, 31,* 15–22.

VAILLANT, G. E. (1976). Natural history of male psychological health. V: Relation of choice of ego mechanisms of defense to adult adjustment. *Archives of General Psychiatry, 33,* 535–545.

VAILLANT, G. E. (1977). *Adaptation to life.* Boston: Little, Brown.

VAILLANT, G. E. (1994). "Successful aging" and psychosocial well-being: Evidence from a 45-year study. In E. H. Thompson (Ed.), *Older men's lives: Vol. 6. Research on men and masculinities* (pp. 2–41). Thousand Oaks, CA: Sage.

VAILLANT, G. E., BOND, M., & VAILLANT, C. O. (1986). An empirically validated hierarchy of defense mechanisms. *Archives of General Psychiatry, 43,* 786–794.

VALENSTEIN, E. S. (1986). *Great and desperate cures.* New York: Basic Books.

VALENZUELA, M. (1990). Attachment in chronically underweight young children. *Child Development, 61,* 1984–1996.

VALENZUELA, M. (1997). Maternal sensitivity in a developing society: The context of urban poverty and infant chronic undernutrition. *Developmental Psychology, 33,* 845–855.

VAN DE VLIERT, E. (2006). Autocratic leadership around the globe: Do climate and wealth drive leadership culture? *Journal of Cross-Cultural Psychology, 37*(1), 42–59.

VAN DER LELY, H. K., & CHRISTIAN, V. (2000). Lexical word formation in Grammatical SLI children: A grammar-specific or input processing deficit? *Cognition, 75,* 33–63.

VAN ESSEN, D. C., & DEYOE, E. A. (1995). Concurrent processing in the primate visual cortex. In M. S. Gazzaniga (Ed.), The cognitive neurosciences (pp. 383–400). Cambridge, MA: MIT Press.

VAN GEERT, P. (2002). Developmental dynamics, intentional action, and fuzzy sets. In N. Granott & J. Parziale (Eds.), *Microdevelopment: Transition processes in development and learning.* New York: Cambridge University Press.

VAN IJZENDOORN, M. (1997). Attachment, emergent morality and aggression: Toward a developmental socioemotional model of antisocial behaviour. *International Journal of Behavioral Development, 21,* 703–727.

VAN IJZENDOORN, M., SCHUENGEL, C., & BAKERMANS-KRANENBURG, M. (1999). Disorganized attachment in early childhood: Meta-analysis of precursors, concomitants, and sequelae. *Development and Psychopathology, 11,* 225–249.

VAN SICKLE, M., DUNCAN, M., KINGSLEY, P., MOUIHATE, A., URBANI, P., MACKIE, K., ET AL. (2005). Identification and functional characterization of brainstem cannabinoid CB2 receptors. *Science, 310,* 329–332.

VANDELL, D. L. (2000). Parents, peer groups, and other socializing influences. *Developmental Psychology, 36*(6), 699–710.

VANDELL, D. L., HENDERSON, V. K., & WILSON, K. S. (1988). A longitudinal study of children with day care experiences of varying quality. *Child Development, 59,* 1286–1292.

VAUGHN, B. E., EGELAND, B. R., SROUFE, L. A., & WATERS, E. (1979). Individual differences in infant-mother attachment at twelve and eighteen months: Stability and change in families under stress. *Child Development, 50,* 971–975.

VAULTIN, R. G., & BERKELEY, M. A. (1977). Responses of single cells in cat visual cortex to prolonged stimulus movement: Neural correlates of visual aftereffects. *Journal of Neurophysiology, 40,* 1051–1065.

VEIZOVIC, T., BEECH, J. S., STROEMER, R. P., WATSON, W. P., & HODGES, H. (2001). Resolution of stroke deficits following contralateral grafts of conditionally immortal neuroepithelial stem cells. *Stroke, 32,* 1012–1019.

VENTER, J. C., ADAMS, M. D., MYERS, E. W., LI, P. W., MURAL, R. J., SUTTON, G. G., ET AL. (2001). The sequence of the human genome. *Science, 291,* 1304–1351.

VERHAEGHEN, P., & SALTHOUSE, T. A. (1997). Meta-analyses of age-cognition relations in adulthood: Estimates of linear and nonlinear age effects and structural models. *Psychological Bulletin, 122*(3), 231–249.

VERKHRATSKY, A. (1998). Calcium signalling in glial cells. *Journal of Physiology, 506,* 15.

VERNON, P. A. (ED.). (1987). *Speed of information processing and intelligence.* Canada: Ablex.

VICKERS, J. C., DICKSON, T. C., ADLARD, P. A., & SAUNDERS, H. L. (2000). The causes of neural degeneration in Alzheimer's disease. *Neurobiology, 60,* 139–165.

VITEVITCH, M. S. (2003). Change deafness: The inability to detect changes between two voices. *Journal of Experimental Psychology: Human Perception and Performance, 29,* 333–342.

VOLKMAR, F. R., SZATMARI, P., & SPARROW, S. S. (1993). Sex differences in pervasive developmental disorders. *Journal of Autism and Developmental Disorders, 23,* 579–591.

VONDRA, J., SHAW, D., SWEARINGEN, L., COHEN, M., & OWENS, E. (2001). Attachment stability and emotional and behavioral regulation from infancy to preschool age. *Development and Psychopathology, 13,* 13–33.

VRIJ, A. (2002). Deception in children: A literature review and implications for children's testimony. In H. Westcott, G. Davies, & R. Bull (Eds.), *Children's testimony: A handbook of psychological research and forensic practice* (pp. 175–194). New York: Wiley.

VUONG, Q. C., & TARR, M. J. (2004). Rotation direction affects object recognition. *Vision Research, 44,* 1717–1730.

VYGOTSKY, L. S. (1978). *Mind in society.* Cambridge, MA: Harvard University Press.

WACHTEL, P. L. (1977). *Psychoanalysis and behavior therapy: Toward an integration.* New York: Basic Books.

WACHTEL, P. L. (1982). What can dynamic therapies contribute to behavior therapy? *Behavior Therapy, 13,* 594–609.

WADDINGTON, J. L., TORREY, E. F., CROW, T. J., & HIRSCH, S. R. (1991). Schizophrenia, neurodevelopment, and disease. *Archives of General Psychiatry, 48,* 271–273.

WAGNER, A. D., KOUTSTAAL, W., & SCHACTER, D. L. (1999). When encoding yields remembering: Insights from event-related neuroimaging. *Philosophical Transactions of the Royal Society of London, Biology, 354,* 1307–1324.

WAGNER, A. D., SCHACTER, D. L., ROTTE, M., KOUTSTAAL, W., MARIL, A., DALE, A., ET AL. (1998). Building memories: Remembering and forgetting of verbal experiences as predicted by brain activity. *Science, 281,* 1188–1191.

WAGNER, A. D., SHANNON, B. J., KAHN, I., & BUCKNER, R. (2005). Parietal lobe contributions to episodic memory retrieval. *Trends in Cognitive Science, 9,* 445–453.

WAGNER, R. K. (1987). Tacit knowledge in everyday intelligent behavior. *Journal of Personality and Social Psychology, 52,* 1236–1247.

WAGNER, R. K. (2000). Practical intelligence. In R. J. Sternberg (Ed.), *Handbook of human intelligence* (pp. 380–395). New York: Cambridge University Press.

WAGNER, R. K., & STERNBERG, R. J. (1987). Tacit knowledge in managerial success. *Journal of Business and Psychology, 1,* 301–312.

WAKEFIELD, J. C. (1992). The concept of mental disorder: On the boundary between biological facts and social values. *American Psychologist, 47*(3), 373–388.

WALKER, E., GRIMES, K. E., DAVIS, D. M., & SMITH, A. J. (1993). Childhood precursors of schizophrenia: Facial expressions of emotion. *American Journal of Psychiatry, 150,* 1654–1660.

WALKER, E., KESTLER, L., BOLLINI, A., & HOCHMAN, K. (2004). Schizophrenia: Etiology and course. *Annual Review of Psychology, 55,* 401–430.

WALKER, E., SAVOIE, T., & DAVIS, D. (1994). Neuromotor precursors of schizophrenia. *Schizophrenia Bulletin, 20,* 441–452.

WALKER, L. J. (1984). Sex differences in the development of moral reasoning: A critical review. *Child Development, 55,* 677–691.

WALKER, L. J. (1989). Sex differences in the development of moral reasoning: A reply to Baumrind. *Child Development, 57,* 522–526.

WALKER, L. J. (1995). Sexism in Kohlberg's moral psychology. In W. M. Kurtines & J. L. Gewirtz (Eds.), *Moral development: An introduction.* Boston: Allyn and Bacon.

WALKER, L. J., & MORAN, T. J. (1991). Moral reasoning in a communist Chinese society. *Journal of Moral Education, 20,* 139–155.

WALLACE, J., SCHNEIDER, T., & McGUFFIN, P. (2002). Genetics of depression. In I. Gotlib & C. Hammen (Eds.), *Handbook of depression* (pp. 169–191). New York: Guilford Press.

WALLAS, G. (1926). *The art of thought.* New York: Harcourt, Brace.

WALLER, N. G., & ROSS, C. A. (1997). The prevalence and biometric structure of pathological dissociation in the general population: Taxometric and behavior genetic findings. *Journal of Abnormal Psychology, 106,* 499–510.

WALSTER, E., ARONSON, E., & ABRAHAMS, D. (1966). On increasing the persuasiveness of a low prestige communicator. *Journal of Experimental Social Psychology, 2,* 325–342.

WALSTER, E., ARONSON, E., ABRAHAMS, D., & ROTTMAN, L. (1966). The importance of physical attractiveness in dating behavior. *Journal of Personality and Social Psychology, 4,* 508–516.

WAMPOLD, B. E., MONDIN, G. W., MOODY, M., STICH, F., BENSON, K., & AHN, H. (1997). A meta-analysis of outcome studies comparing bona fide psychotherapies: Empirically, "all must have prizes." *Psychological Bulletin, 122,* 203–216.

WAPNER, W. T., JUDD, T., & GARDNER, H. (1978). Visual agnosia in an artist. *Cortex, 14,* 343–364.

WARREN, S. L., HUSTON, L., EGELAND, B., & SROUFE, L. A. (1997). Child and adolescent anxiety disorders and early attachment. *Journal of the American Academy of Child & Adolescent Psychiatry, 36,* 637–644.

WARRINGTON, E. K., & WEISKRANTZ, L. (1978). Further analysis of the prior learning effect in amnesic patients. *Neuropsychologia, 16,* 169–176.

WASON, P. C. (1960). On the failure to eliminate hypotheses in a conceptual task. *Quarterly Journal of Experimental Psychology, 12,* 129–140.

WASON, P. C. (1966). Reasoning. In Foss, B. (Ed.), *New horizons in psychology* (pp. 135–151). Middlesex, England: Penguin.

WASON, P. C. (1968). On the failure to eliminate hypotheses—A second look. In P. C. Wason & P. N. Johnson-Laird (Eds.), *Thinking and reasoning.* Harmondsworth, England: Penguin.

WASSERMAN, E. A., HUGART, J. A., & KIRKPATRICK-STEGER, K. (1995). Pigeons show same-different conceptualization after training with complex visual stimuli. *Journal of Experimental Psychology: Animal Behavior Processes, 21,* 248–252.

WATERS, E., & CUMMINGS, E. M. (2000). A secure base from which to explore close relationships. *Child Development, 71*(1), 164–172.

WATERS, E., MERRICK, S., TREBOUX, D., CROWELL, J., & ALBERSHEIM, L. (2000). Attachment security in infancy and early adulthood: A twenty-year longitudinal study. *Child Development, 71,* 684–689.

WATERS, E., WIPPMAN, J., & SROUFE, L. A. (1979). Attachment, positive affect, and competence in the peer group: Two studies in construct validation. *Child Development, 50,* 821–829.

WATSON, D., & CLARK, L. A. (1992). Affects separable and inseparable: On the hierarchical arrangement of the negative affects. *Journal of Personality and Social Psychology, 62,* 489–505.

WATSON, J. B. (1925). *Behaviorism.* New York: Norton.

WATSON, J. S. (1967). Memory and "contingency analysis" in infant learning. *Merrill-Palmer Quarterly, 13,* 55–76.

WAUGH, N. C., & NORMAN, D. A. (1965). Primary memory. *Psychological Review, 72,* 89–104.

WECHSLER, D. (1958). *The measurement and appraisal of adult intelligence* (4th ed.). Baltimore: Williams & Wilkins.

WEEDEN, J., & SABINI, J. (2005). Physical attractiveness and health in Western societies: A review. *Psychological Bulletin, 131,* 635–653.

WEINFIELD, N., SROUFE, L., & EGELAND, B. (2000). Attachment from infancy to early adulthood in a high-risk sample: Continuity, discontinuity, and their correlates. *Child Development, 71,* 695–702.

WEINGARTNER, H., & PARKER, E. S. (Eds.) (1984). *Memory consolidation: Psychobiology of cognition.* Hillsdale, NJ: Erlbaum.

WEISBERG, R. (1986). *Creativity: Genius and other myths.* New York: Freeman.

WEISKRANTZ, L. (1986). *Blindsight: A case study and implications.* Oxford: Clarendon Press.

WEISKRANTZ, L., & WARRINGTON, E. K. (1979). Conditioning in amnesic patients. *Neuropsychologia, 18,* 177–184.

WEISS, A., KING, J. E., & FIGUEREDO, A. J. (2000). The heritability of personality factors in chimpanzees (Pan troglodytes). *Behavior Genetics, 30,* 213–221.

WEISS, L. H., & SCHWARZ, J. C. (1996). The relationship between parenting types and older adolescents' personality, academic achievement, adjustment, and substance use. *Child Development, 67,* 2101–2114.

WEISSMAN, M. M., & MARKOWITZ, J. C. (1994). Interpersonal psychotherapy. Current status. *Archives of General Psychiatry, 51,* 599–606.

WEISZ, J. R., DOSS, A., & HAWLEY, K. (2005). Youth psychotherapy outcome research: A review and critique of the evidence base. *Annual Review of Psychology, 56,* 337–364.

WEISZ, J. R., HAWLEY, K., & DOSS, A. (2004). Empirically tested psychotherapies for youth internalizing and externalizing problems and disorders. *Child and Adolescent Psychiatric Clinics of North America, 13,* 729–815.

WELLMAN, H., CROSS, D., & WATSON, J. (2001). Meta-analysis of theory-of-mind development: The truth about false belief. *Child Development, 72,* 655–684.

WELLMAN, H., & GELMAN, S. (1992). Cognitive development: Foundational theories of core domains. *Annual Review of Psychology, 43,* 337–375.

WELLMAN, H., & LAGATUTTA, K. H. (2000). In S. Baron-Cohen, H. Tager-Flusberg, & D. J. Cohen (Eds.), *Understanding other minds* (pp. 21–49). New York: Oxford University Press.

WELLMAN, H. M. (1990). *The child's theory of mind.* Cambridge, MA: MIT Press.

WELLMAN, H. M., & BARTSCH, K. (1988). Young children's reasoning about beliefs. *Cognition, 30,* 239–277.

WELLMAN, H. M., & WOOLEY, J. D. (1990). From simple desires to ordinary beliefs: The early development of everyday psychology. *Cognition, 35,* 245–275.

WELLS, G., & OLSON, E. (2002). Eyewitness identification. *Annual Review of Psychology, 54,* 277–295.

WELLS, G. L., OLSON, E. A., & CHARMAN, S. D. (2002). The confidence of eyewitnesses in their identifications from lineups. *Current Directions in Psychological Science, 11,* 151–154.

WENDER, P. H., KETY, S. S., ROSENTHAL, D., SCHULSINGER, F., & ORTMANN, J. (1986). Psychiatric disorders in the biological relatives of adopted individuals with affective disorders. *Archives of General Psychiatry, 43,* 923–929.

WEREBE, M. G., & BAUDONNIERE, P.-M. (1991). Social pretend play among friends and familiar preschoolers. *International Journal of Behavioral Development, 14*(4), 411–428.

WERKER, J. (1991). The ontogeny of speech perception. In I. G. Mattingly & M. Studdert-Kennedy (Eds.), *Modularity and the motor theory of speech perception: Proceedings of a conference to honor Alvin M. Liberman* (pp. 91–109). Hillsdale, NJ: Erlbaum.

WERKER, J. F. (1995). Exploring developmental changes in cross-language speech perception. In L. R. Gleitman & M. Liberman (Eds.), *An invitation to cognitive science: Vol. 1* (pp. 87–106). Cambridge, MA: MIT Press.

WERKER, J. F., & TEES, R. C. (1984). Cross-language speech perception: Evidence for perceptual reorganization during the first year of life. *Infant Behavior and Development, 7,* 49–63.

WERTHEIMER, M. (1912). Experimentelle Studien über das Gesehen von Bewegung. *Zeitschrift frPsychologie, 61,* 161–265.

WERTHEIMER, M. (1923). Untersuchungen zur Lehre von der Gestalt, II. *Psychologische Forschung, 4,* 301–350.

WEST, S. G., WHITNEY, G., & SCHNEDLER, R. (1975). Helping a motorist in distress: The effects of sex, race, and neighborhood. *Journal of Personality and Social Psychology, 31,* 691–698.

WESTEN, D. (1998). The scientific legacy of Sigmund Freud: Toward a psychodynamically informed psychological science. *Psychological Bulletin, 124,* 333–371.

WESTEN, D., & BRADLEY, R. (2005). Empirically supported complexity: Rethinking evidence-based practice in psychotherapy. *Current Directions in Psychological Science, 14,* 266–271.

WESTEN, D., NOVOTNY, C., & THOMPSON-BRENNER, H. (2004). The empirical status of empirically supported psychotherapies: Assumptions, findings, and reporting in controlled clinical trials. *Psychological Bulletin, 130,* 631–663.

WESTERMEYER, J. (1987). Public health and chronic mental illness. *American Journal of Public Health, 77,* 667–668.

WETHINGTON, E. (2000). Expecting stress: Americans and the "midlife crisis." *Motivation & Emotion, 24,* 85–103.

WHEELER, L. R. (1942). A comparative study of the intelligence of East Tennessee mountain children. *Journal of Educational Psychology, 33,* 321–334.

WHITE, D. J., & GALEF, B. G. (1998) Social influence on avoidance of dangerous stimuli by rats. *Animal Learning and Behavior, 26*(4): 433–438

WHITE, G. L. (1980). Physical attractiveness and courtship progress. *Journal of Personality and Social Psychology, 39,* 660–668.

WHORF, B. (1956). *Language, thought, and reality: Selected writings of Benjamin Lee Whorf.* New York: Wiley.

WICKELGREN, W. A. (1974). *How to solve problems.* San Francisco: Freeman.

WIDIGER, T. A., & CLARK, L. A. (2000). Toward *DSM-V* and the classification of psychopathology. *Psychological Bulletin, 126,* 946–963.

WIDIGER, T. A., & SANDERSON, C. J. (1995). Toward a dimensional mode of personality disorders. In W. J. Livesley (Ed.), *The DSM-IV personality disorders* (pp. 433–458). New York: Guilford Press.

WIENS, A. N., & MENUSTIK, C. E. (1983). Treatment outcome and patient characteristics in an aversion therapy program for alcoholism. *American Psychologist, 38,* 1089–1096.

WIESENTHAL, D. L., ENDLER, N. S., COWARD, T. R., & EDWARDS, J. (1976). Reversibility of relative competence as a determinant of conformity across different perceptual tasks. *Representative Research in Social Psychology, 7,* 319–342.

WILCOXIN, H. C., DRAGOIN, W. B., & KRAL, P. A. (1971). Illness-induced aversions in rat and quail: Relative salience of visual and gustatory cues. *Science, 171,* 826–828.

WILHELM, F. H., TRABERT, W., & ROTH, W. T. (2001). Physiologic instability in panic disorder and generalized anxiety disorder. *Biological Psychiatry, 49,* 596–605.

WILLIAMS, G. C. (1966). *Adaptation and natural selection.* Princeton, NJ: Princeton University Press.

WILLIAMS, J. E., SATTERWHITE, R. C., & BEST, D. L. (1999). Pancultural gender stereotypes reivisited: The five factor model. *Sex Roles, 40*(7–8), 513–525.

WILLIAMS, L. (1994). Recall of childhood trauma: A prospective study of women's memories of child sexual abuse. *Journal of Consulting and Clinical Psychology, 62,* 1167–1176.

WILLIS, S. L., & REID, J. D. (EDS.). (1999). *Life in the middle: Psychological and social development in middle age.* San Diego: Academic Press.

WILSON, D. H., REEVES, A. G., GAZZANIGA, M. S., & CULVER, C. (1977). Cerebral commissurotomy for the control of intractable seizures. *Neurology, 27,* 708–715.

WILSON, G. T. (1991). Chemical aversion conditioning in the treatment of alcoholism: Further comments. *Behaviour Research and Therapy, 29,* 415–419.

WILSON, G. T. (1998). Manual-based treatment and clinical practice. *Clinical Psychology: Science and Practice, 5,* 363–375.

WILSON, G. T., & FAIRBURN, C. G. (2002). Treatments for eating disorders. In P. E. Nathan & J. M. Gorman (Eds.), *A guide to treatments that work* (2nd ed., pp. 559–592). New York: Oxford University Press.

WILSON, J. Q. (1997). *Moral judgment: Does the abuse excuse threaten our legal system?* New York: Basic Books.

WIMMER, H., & PERNER, J. (1983). Beliefs about beliefs: Representation and constraining function of wrong beliefs in young children's understanding of deception. *Cognition, 13,* 103–128.

WINNER, E. (2000). The origins and ends of giftedness. *American Psychologist, 55*(1), 159–169.

WINOGRAD, E., & NEISSER, U. (EDS.). (1993). *Affect and accuracy in recall: Studies of "flashbulb" memories.* New York: Cambridge University Press.

WIRSHING, W. C., MARDER, S. R., VAN PUTTEN, T., & AMES, D. (1995). Acute treatment of schizophrenia. In F. E. Bloom & D. Kupfer (Eds.), *Psychopharmacology: The fourth generation of progress* (pp. 1259–1266). New York: Raven.

WITHERINGTON, D. C., CAMPOS, J. J., & HERTENSTEIN, M. J. (2001). Principles of emotion and its development in infancy. In G. Bremner & A. Fogel (Eds.), *Blackwell handbook of infant development* (pp. 427–464). Malden, MA: Blackwell Publishing.

WITTENBRINK, B., JUDD, C. M., & PARK, B. (1997). Evidence for racial prejudice at the implicit level and its relationship with questionnaire measures. *Journal of Personality and Social Psychology, 72*(2), 262–274.

WITTGENSTEIN, L. (1953). *Philosophical investigations.* G. E. M. Anscombe (Trans.) Oxford: Blackwell.

WIXTED, J. T. (2004). The psychology and neuroscience of forgetting. *Annual Review of Psychology, 55,* 235–269.

WOHL, J. (1989). Cross-cultural psychotherapy. In P. B. Pedersen, J. G. Draguns, W. J. Lonner, & J. E. Trimble (Eds.), *Counseling across cultures* (pp. 79–113). Honolulu: University of Hawaii.

WOICIECHOWSKY, C., VOGEL, S., MEYER, B. U., & LEHMANN, R. (1997). Neuropsychological and neurophysiological consequences of partial callosotomy. *Journal of Neurosurgical Science, 41,* 75–80.

WOLF, M. E., & MOSNAIM, A. D. (1990). *Post-traumatic stress disorder: Etiology, phenomenology, and treatment.* Washington, DC: American Psychiatric Press.

WOLFE, J. M. (2003). Moving towards solutions to some enduring controversies in visual search. *Trends in Cognitive Science, 7,* 70–76.

WOLLEN, K. A., WEBER, A., & LOWRY, D. (1972). Bizarreness versus interaction of mental images as determinants of learning. *Cognitive Psychology, 3,* 518–523.

WOLPE, J. (1958). *Psychotherapy by reciprocal inhibition.* Stanford, CA: Stanford University Press.

WOLPE, J. (1996). *The practice of behavior therapy* (4th ed.). New York: Pergamon Press.

WOLPE, J., & LAZARUS, A. A. (1966). *Behavior therapy techniques: A guide to the treatment of neuroses.* Elmsford, NY: Pergamon.

WOLPE, J., & PLAUD, J. J. (1997). Pavlov's contributions to behavior therapy: The obvious and the not so obvious. *American Psychologist, 52,* 966–972.

WOOD, A. J., & GOODWIN, G. M. (1987). A review of the biochemical and neuropharmacological actions of lithium. *Psychological Medicine, 17,* 579–600.

WOOD, N., & COWAN, N. (1995). The cocktail party phenomenon revisited: How frequent are attention shifts to one's name in an irrelevant auditory channel? *Journal of Experimental Psychology: Learning, Memory and Cognition, 21*, 255–260.

WOOD, W. (2000). Attitude change: Persuasion and social influence. *Annual Review of Psychology, 51*, 539–570.

WOOD, W., & EAGLY, A. H. (2002). A cross-cultural analysis of the behavior of women and men: Implications for the origins of sex differences. *Psychological Bulletin., 128*(5), 699–727.

WOODRUFF, P. W. R., WRIGHT, I. C., BULLMORE, E. T., BRAMMER, M., HOWARD, R. J., WILLIAMS, S. C. R., ET AL. (1997). Auditory hallucinations and the temporal cortical response to speech in schizophrenia: A functional magnetic resonance imaging study. *American Journal of Psychiatry, 154*, 1676–1682.

WOODS, S. C., & RAMSAY, D. S. (2000). Pavlovian influences over food and drug intake. *Behavior and Brain Research, 10*, 175–182.

WOODWARD, A. L. (1998). Infants selectively encode the goal object of an actor's reach. *Cognition, 69*, 1–34.

WOOLF, N. J. (1998). A structural basis for memory storage in mammals. *Progress in Neurobiology, 55*, 59–77.

WU, X., HART, C., DRAPER, T., & OLSEN, J. (2001). Peer and teaching sociometrics for preschool children: Cross-informant concordance, temporal stability, and reliability. *Merrill-Palmer Quarterly, 47*, 416–443.

WYNN, K. (1992). Addition and subtraction by human infants. *Nature, 358*, 749–750.

WYNN, K. (1995). Infants possess a system of numerical knowledge. *Current Directions in Psychological Science, 4*, 172–176.

XU, F. (2002). The role of language in acquiring object concepts in infancy. *Cognition, 85*, 223–250.

YAMAGATA, S., SUZUKI, A., ANDO, J., ONO, Y., KIJIMA, N., YOSHIMURA, K., ET AL. (2006). Is the genetic structure of human personality universal? A cross-cultural twin study from North America, Europe, and Asia. *Journal of Personality and Social Psychology, 80*, 987–998.

YAN, L, DAVIGLUS, M., LIU, K., STAMLER, J., WANG, R. PIRZADA, A., ET AL. (2006). Midlife Body Mass Index and hospitalization and mortality in older age. *Journal of the American Medical Association, 295*, 190–198.

YANG, S.-Y., & STERNBERG, R. J. (1997). Taiwanese Chinese people's conceptions of intelligence. *Intelligence, 25*, 21–36.

YARMEY, A. (1973). I recognize your face but I can't remember your name: Further evidence on the tip-of-the-tongue phenomenon. *Memory & Cognition, 1*, 287–290.

YEHUDA, R. (1997). Sensitization of the hypothalamic-pituitary-adrenal axis in posttraumatic stress disorder. In R. Yehuda & A. C. McFarlane (Eds.), Psychobiology of posttraumatic stress disorder. *Annals of the New York Academy of Sciences, 821*, 57–75.

YU, D., & SHEPARD, G. (1998). Is beauty in the eye of the beholder? *Nature, 396*, 321–322.

YUSSEN, S. R., & LEVY, V. M. (1975). Developmental changes in predicting one's own span of memory. *Journal of Experimental Child Psychology, 19*, 502–508.

ZAIDEL, E. (1976). Auditory vocabulary of the right hemisphere following brain bisection or hemidecortication. *Cortex, 12*, 191–211.

ZAIDEL, E. (1983). A response to Gazzaniga. Language in the right hemisphere, convergent perspectives. *American Psychologist, 38*(5), 542–546.

ZAIDI, L. Y., & FOY, D. W. (1994). Childhood abuse experiences and combat-related PTSD. *Journal of Traumatic Stress, 7*, 33–42.

ZAJONC, R. B. (1965). Social facilitation. *Science, 149*, 269–274.

ZAJONC, R. B. (1968). Attitudinal effects of mere exposure. *Journal of Personality and Social Psychology, 9*(Monograph suppl.), 1–27.

ZAJONC, R. B. (1980). Feeling and thinking: Preferences need no inferences. *American Psychologist, 35*, 151–175.

ZAJONC, R. B. (1984). On the primacy of affect. *American Psychologist, 39*, 117–123.

Zajonc, R. B., & McIntosh, D. N. (1992). Emotions research: Some promising questions and some questionable promises. *Psychological Science, 3*, 70–74.

ZAJONC, R. B., ADELMANN, P. K., MURPHY, S. T., & NIEDENTHAL, P. M. (1987). Convergence in the physical appearance of spouses. *Motivation and Emotion, 11*, 335–346.

ZAJONC, R. B., HEINGARTNER, A., & HERMAN, E. M. (1969). Social enhancement and impairment of performance in the cockroach. *Journal of Personality and Social Psychology, 13*, 83–92.

ZAKRISKI, A., & COIE, J. (1996). A comparison of aggressive-rejected and non-aggressive-rejected children's interpretations of self-directed and other-directed aggression. *Child Development, 67*, 1048–1070.

ZARAGOZA, M. S., & MITCHELL, K. J. (1996). Repeated exposure to suggestion and the creation of false memories. *Psychological Science, 7*, 294–300.

ZARKIN, G. A., GRABOWSKI, H. G., MAUSKOPF, J., BANNERMAN, H. A., & WEISLER, R. H. (1995). Economic evaluation of drug treatment for psychiatric disorders. In F. E. Bloom & D. Kupfer (Eds.), *Psychopharmacology: The fourth generation of progress* (pp. 1897–1905). New York: Raven.

ZELAZO, P. D., & FRYE, D. (1998). Cognitive complexity and control: II. The development of executive function in childhood. *Current Directions in Psychological Science, 7*, 121–125.

ZENTALL, T. R. (2000). Symbolic representation by pigeons. *Current Directions in Psychological Science, 9*, 118–123.

ZIGLER, E. F., & CHILD, I. L. (1973). *Socialization and personality development.* Reading, MA: Addison-Wesley.

ZIGLER, E., & CHILD, I. L. (1969). Socialization. In G. Lindzey & E. Aronson (Eds.), *The handbook of social psychology: Vol. 3* (pp. 450–589). Reading, MA: Addison-Wesley.

ZILBOORG, G., & HENRY, G. W. (1941). *A history of medical psychology.* New York: Norton.

ZIMBARDO, P. G. (1969). The human choice: Individuation, reason, and order versus deindividuation, impulse and chaos. In W. J. Arnold & E. Levine (Eds.), *Nebraska Symposium on Motivation* (pp. 237–308). Lincoln, NE: University of Nebraska Press.

ZIMBARDO, P. G. (1970). The human choice: Individuation, reason and order versus deindividuation, impulse and chaos. In W. J. Arnold & D. Levine, (Eds.), *Nebraska Symposium on Motivation: Vol 18.* Lincoln, NE: University of Nebraska Press.

ZIMBARDO, P. G. (1973). On the ethics of intervention in human psychological research: With special reference to the Stanford prison experiment. *Cognition, 2*(2), 243–256.

ZIMBARDO, P. G. (2005). Abu Ghraib: The evil of inaction, and the heroes who acted. *The Western Psychologist, 18*(1), 4–5.

ZIMMERMAN, M., MATTIA, J. I., & POSTERNACK, M. A. (2002). Are subjects in pharmacological treatment trials of depression representative of patients in routine clinical practice? *American Journal of Psychiatry, 159*, 469–473.

ZORILLA, L.T. E., & CANNON, T. D. (1995). Structural brain abnormalities in schizophrenia: Distribution, etiology, and implications. In S. A. Mednick (Ed.), *Neural development in schizophrenia: Theory and research.* New York: Plenum Press.

ZUBIN, J., & SPRING, B. (1977). Vulnerability: A new view of schizophrenia. *Journal of Abnormal Psychology, 86*, 103–126.

ZUCKER, K. J. (2001). Biological influences on psychosexual differentiation. In R. K. Unger (Ed.), *Handbook of the psychology of women and gender.* New York: Wiley.

ZUCKER, K. J., BRADLEY, S. J., OLIVER, G., BLAKE, J., FLEMING, S., & HOOD, J. (1996). Psychosexual development of women with congenital adrenal hyperplasia. *Hormones and Behavior, 30*, 300–318.

ZUCKERMAN, M. (1979). *Sensation seeking: Beyond the optimum level of arousal.* Hillsdale, NJ: Erlbaum.

ZUCKERMAN, M. (1983). A biological theory of sensation seeking. In M. Zuckerman (Ed.), *Biological bases of sensation seeking, impulsivity, and anxiety.* Hillsdale, NJ: Erlbaum.

ZUCKERMAN, M. (1987a). All parents are environmentalists until they have their second child. Peer commentary on Plomin, R., & Daniels, D. Why are children from the same family so different from one another? *Behavioral and Brain Sciences, 10,* 38–39.

ZUCKERMAN, M. (1987b). A critical look at three arousal constructs in personality theories: Optimal levels of arousal, strength of the nervous system, and sensitivities to signals of reward and punishment. In J. Strelau & H. J. Eysenck (Eds.), *Personality dimensions and arousal: Perspectives on individual differences* (pp. 217–230). New York: Plenum.

ZUCKERMAN, M. (1990). The psychophysiology of sensation seeking [Special issue]. Biological foundations of personality: Evolution, behavioral genetics, and psychophysiology. *Journal of Personality, 58,* 313–345.

ZUCKERMAN, M. (1994). *Behavioral expressions and biosocial bases of sensation seeking.* New York: Cambridge University Press.

ZUGER, B. (1984). Early effeminate behavior in boys. *Journal of Nervous and Mental Disease, 172,* 90–96.

ZUMBAHLEN, M., & CRAWLEY, A. (1997). Infants' early referential behavior in prohibition contexts: The emergence of social referencing. *Infant Behavior and Development, 19*(1), 243–243.

ACKNOWLEDMENTS AND CREDITS

NUMBERED ART AND PHOTOS

Chapter 1: **1.1(A)** Photograph by Robert Estall/Corbis; **1.1(B)** Photograph by Wolfgang Kaehler/Corbis. **1.2(A)** Photograph by George H. Harrison/Grant Heilman; **1.2(B)** Photograph by Peter Hendrie/The Image Bank.

Chapter 2: **2.1** From *Bodily Changes in Pain, Hunger, Fear and Rage* by W. B. Cannon. **2.5** From Bouchard, Tremblay, et.al, The response to long-term overfeeding in identical twins. *New England Journal of Medicine* 322: pp. 1477–1482. **2.7** Photograph by Walter Chandoha. **2.8(top)** Yann Arthus-Bertrand/Corbis; **2.8(bottom)** Caroline Penn/Corbis. **2.9(A)** Photograph by Rod Williams, © Bruce Coleman, Inc., 1988; **2.9(B)** Kevin Schafer, Corbis. **2.10** Layne Kennedy/Corbis. **2.12** Garry D. McMichael/Photo Researchers, Inc. **2.13** Photograph © Rudie H. Kuiter, Oxford Scientific Films.

Chapter 3: **3.1** From Descartes, R. (1662). *Trait de l'homme*, Haldane, E.S. and Ross, G.R.T. (trans.) Cambridge University Press. **3.2** David Becker/SPL/Photo Researchers, Inc.. **3.3(A)** Courtesy Warren Museum, Harvard Medical School; **3.3(B)** Damasio, H., Grabowski, T., Frank, R., Galaburda, A.M., & Damasio, A.R. (1994), *The return of Phineas Gage: Clues about the brain from the skull of a famous patient*, Science, 264; courtesy Hanna Damasio. **3.4** Photograph © Paul Shambroom. **3.5** Zephyr/SPL/Photo Researchers, Inc. **3.11** Children's Hospital & Medical Center/Corbis. **3.16** From *Higher Cortical Functions in Man*, 2nd ed, by A.R. Luria. Copyright © 1979 by Consultants Bureau Enterprises, Inc. and Basic Books, Inc. Reprinted by permission of Basic Books, a member of Perseus Books, L.L.C.; Luria, A.R.: "Drawings by a patient with visual agnosia" from Higher Cortical Functions in Man. Copyright © 1976. Reprinted by permission of publisher, Kluwer Academic/Plenum Publishers. **3.17** *Physiological Psychology*, 2nd ed., by Mark Rosenzweig and Arnold Leiman. **3.19** Adapted from *Brain: A Scientific American Book*, edited by Scientific American. **3.21** Nancy Kedersha/SPL/Photo Researchers, Inc. **3.24** Adapted from *Biology: The Unity and Diversity of Life* 6th edition by Starr/Taffart. **3.26** Eccles, J.C., *The Understanding of the Brain*, Copyright © The McGraw-Hill Companies. Reproduced with the permission of The McGraw-Hill Companies. **3.28** Adapted from Bloom, Peripheral nervous system, synaptic transmission and limbic system. Reprinted with the permission of Thirteen/WNET New York. **3.29** © Lewis and Everhart and Zeevi/Visuals Unlimited. **3.30** Rosenzweig, Leiman, "Lock and Key Model of Synaptic transmission" from *Physiological Psychology*. Copyright © 1989 M.R. Rosenzweig and A.L. Leiman. Reprinted with the permission of the authors.

Chapter 4: **4.2** Pushkin Museum, Moscow, Russia. Photo: Bridgeman Art Library. **4.4** Gibson, James J. "The Senses Considered As Perceptual Systems." Copyright © 1966 by Houghton Mifflin Company. Reprinted by permission. **4.5** Thompson, Richard, "Sine Waves of Hertz Tones" from *Introduction to Biopsychology*. Reprinted by permission of author. **4.9(A)** Adapted from Lindsay P. H., and Norman, D. A., *Human Information Processing*, 2nd edition, p. 136. New York: Academic Press, 1977; **4.9(B)** "Motion Parallax" Coren, Porac, Ward from *Sensation and Perception*. Copyright © John Wiley & Sons, Inc. Reprinted by permission of John Wiley & Sons, Inc. **4.13** Adapted from *Sensation and Perception*, Third Edition, by Stanley Coren and Lawrence M. Ward. 1989. Harcourt Brace & Company. **4.17** Hering, E., "The effect of distance between contrasting regions" from *Outlines of a Theory of the Light Sense*, p. 150–51. Copyright © Springer-Verlag. Reprinted by permission of the publisher. **4.18** Vasarely, Victor, "Contrast" Smithsonian Institution from *Arcturus II*, Hirshorn Museum & Sculpture Garden. Copyright © 1966. Reprinted with the permission of Michele Vasarely. **4.19** "Mach Bands," Coren, Porac, Ward from *Sensation and Perception*. Copyright © John Wiley & Sons, Inc. Reprinted by permission of John Wiley & Sons, Inc. **4.23** Hurvich, L. M., *Color Vision*. Sunderland, Mass.: Sinauer Associates, 1981. **4.27** Photographs by Fritz Goro/Life Magazine, © Time Warner, Inc. **4.28** Hurvich, L. M., and Jameson, D., An Opponent-Process Theory of Color Vision, *Psychological Review* 64 (1957): 384–404. Reprinted by permission of Leo Hurvich. **4.29** DeValois, R. L., and DeValois, K. K., Neural Coding of Color, in Carterette, E. C., and Friedman, M. P., (Eds.), *Handbook of Perception*, vol. 5. New York: Academic Press, 1975. **4.31** Adapted from Figure 11.28 from Schiffman, H. *Sensation and Perception* 2/e. 1982. John Wiley & Sons, Inc. **4.32** Adapted from Kuffler, S. W., Discharge pattern and functional organization of mammalian retina, *Journal of Neurophysiology* 16 (1953): 37–68. **4.33** Hubel, D. H., The visual cortex of the brain, *Scientific American* 209 (November 1963): 54–58.

Chapter 5: **5.1** *Perception*, 2/e by Hochberg, J. © Reprinted by permission of Pearson Education, Inc. Upper Saddle River, NJ. **5.6(A)** © Stephen J. Krasemann/Allstock; **5.6(B)** Lee Snider/Corbis. **5.7** Gibson, James J. "The Perception of the Visual World" Copyright © 1950 by Houghton Mifflin Company. Reprinted with permission. **5.12** Duncker, K., Uber induzierte Bewegung, Psychologische Forschung 12 (1929), 180–259. Copyright © 1929 by Springer-Verlag, Inc. Adapted by permission of Springer-Verlag, Inc. **5.19** Kanizsa, G. "Subjective Contours" from *Scientific American* 234. Copyright © 1976 Reprinted by permission of Jerome Kuhl. **5.20(A):** Photograph by Jeffery Grosscup. **5.24** Figure 10 from *Gestalt Psychology* by Dr. Wolfgang Kohler. 1947. Liveright Publishing Corporation. **5.25** Photographs by Michael & Patricia Fogden/Corbis. **5.30** Selfridge, Oliver, "Context influences perception (pattern recognition)" from *Proceedings of the Western Computer Conference*. Copyright © 1955. Reprinted with the permission of the author. **5.31** Gibson, James J. "The Perception of the Visual World" Copyright © 1950 by Houghton Mifflin Company. Reprinted with permission. **5.39** Biederman, I., Recognition-by-components: A theory of human image understanding, *Psychological Review* 94 (1987):115–47. **5.40** From Martha Farah, *Visual Agnosia. Disorders of Object Recognition*, Cambridge, MA, The MIT Press, 1990. **5.44** Penrose, L. S. & Penrose, R. "Impossible objects: A special type of visual illusion" from *British Journal of Psychology* 49, 31–33. Reproduced with permission from the British Journal of Psychology. **5.45** Courtesy of The Metropolitan Museum of Art.

Chapter 6: **6.4** Pavlov, I.P. *Lectures on Conditioned Reflexes*, Vol. I. Reprinted by permission of the publisher, International Publishers Company, Inc. **6.5** Stimulus control by Moore, John W. in *Classical Conditioning II: Research and Theory* edited by Black/Prokasy. 1972. Prentice-Hall, Inc., Upper Saddle River, NJ. **6.6** Spooner, A., and Kellogg, W. N., The backward conditioning curve, *American Journal of Psychology* 60 (1947): 321–34. 1947. The University of Illinois Press. **6.12(A)** Photograph by Mike Salisbury; **6.12(B)** Photograph by Susan M. Hogue. **6.13** From *A Primer of Operant Conditioning* by G. S. Reynolds. (Scott, Foresman & Co.). **6.14** Richard Vogel/AP Photo. **6.15** Colwill, R. M., and Rescorla, R. A., Postconditioning devaluation of a reinforcer affects instrumental responding, *Journal of Experimental Psychology: Animal Behavior Processes* 11 (1985): 120–32.

Chapter 7: 7.1 From *Psychological Review, Primary memory* by N. C. Waugh and D. A. Norman, Vol. 72: pp. 89–108. 7.2 Adapted from Murdock, B., The serial position effect of free recall, *Journal of Experimental Psychology* 64 (1962): 482–88. 7.3 Glanzer, M., and Cunitz, A., Two storage mechanisms in free recall, *Journal of Verbal Learning and Verbal Behavior* 5 (1966): 351–60. 7.7 Photograph by Ronald James. 7.8 Adapted from Bower, G. H. "Analysis of mnemonic device" from *American Scientist* 58. Reprinted by American Scientist 1970. 7.9 Baddeley, Alan. "Context-dependent memory in two environments: On land and underwater" from *British Journal of Psychology* 66. Copyright © 1975. Reprinted by permission of publisher. 7.13 Orne, M. T., The mechanisms of hypnotic age regression: An experimental study, *Journal of Abnormal and Social Psychology* 58 (1951): 277–99. 7.14 From Scientific American "The Anatomy of Memory" by M. Mishkin and T. Appenzeller, vol. 256, pp. 80–89; 7.15(A) From *Fundamentals of Human Neuropsychology*, 2nd ed., by B. Kolb and I. Q. Whishaw, Figure 20-5, p. 485. San Francisco: W. H. Freeman and Company; 7.15(B) Milner, B., Corkin, S., and Teuber, H. L., Further analysis of the hippocampal amnesic syndrome: Fourteen-year follow-up of H.M., *Psychologia* 6 (1968): 215–34.

Chapter 8: 8.2 *Science*, Mental rotation of 3-D objects by R. N. Shepard and J. Metzler, vol. 171, pp. 701–703. 1971 American Association for the Advancement of Science. 8.3 Adapted from Kosslyn, S. M., Ball, T. M., and Reisser, V. J., Visual images preserve metric spatial information: Evidence from studies of image scanning, *Journal of Experimental Psychology: Human Perception and Performance* 4 (1978): 47–60. 8.8 and Answers Scheerer, M. (1963). Problem solving. *Scientific American*, 208, 118–128. 8.11 R. Bootzin, *Psychology Today: An Introduction*. Copyright The McGraw-Hill Companies. Reproduced with the permission of The McGraw-Hill Companies. 8.14 and Answer Scheerer, M., Goldstein, K., and Boring, E. G., A Demonstration of Insight: The Horse-Rider Puzzle from *American Journal of Psychology* 54. Copyright © 1941 by the Board of Trustees of the University of Illinois. Used with permission of the University of Illinois Press. 8.17 Engraving by Walter H. Ruff; courtesy The Granger Collection. 8.18 Suls, Jerry, "A Two-stage model of the appreciation of jokes and cartoons" from *The Psychology of Humor*. Copyright Jerry Suls. Reprinted with the permission of the author.

Chapter 9: 9.2 After *On the Origins of Language*, by P. L. Lieberman, 1975, New York: Macmillan. 9.6 By permission. From Merriam-Webster's Collegiate © Dictionary 10th Edition © 2002, by Merriam-Webster's, Incorporated. 9.7 Courtesy Sharon Armstrong. 9.8 "Towards a Descriptive Framework for Spatial Deixis," by C. Fillmore, 1982, in R. J. Jarvella & W. Klein (Eds.), *Speech, Place, and Action: Studies in Deixis and Related Topics*, Chichester, England: Wiley. 9.11 Reprinted from *Cognition*, Vol. 73, Altmann Gerry, "Incremental interpretation at verbs restricting the domain of subsequent reference" pp 247–264 Copyright © 1999 with permission of Elsevier Science. 9.13(A) Photograph by Philip Morse, University of Wisconsin; 9.13(B) Eimas et al. Reprinted "Speech Perception in Infants" from *Science* 171:303 with permission from American Association for the Advancement of Science. Copyright © 1971 AAAS. 9.16 Adapted from Roberta Golinkoff. 9.18 Roger Brown, Courtney Cazden, and Ursula Bellugi-Klima, "The Child's Grammar from I to III", in Hill, J. P. (Ed.), *Minnesota Symposia on Child Psychology, Volume 2*. Copyright © 1969 by The University of Minnesota Press. Reprinted by permission of the publisher. 9.19 AP Photos. 9.20 Frishberg, N., *Arbitrariness and iconicity: Historical change in American Sign Language*, Language 51 (1975): 696–719. Photographs of and by Ted Supalla. 9.21 Yovovich, Noel, "Self-made signs in a deaf boy never exposed to sign language. Copyright © 1982. Reprinted with the permission of the illustrator, Noel Yovovich. 9.22 Drawings courtesy Robert Thacker. 9.23 P. R. Marler, "A Comparative approach to vocal learning" from *Journal of Comparative and Physiological Psychology Monograph* 71. Copyright © 1970 by the American Psychological Association. Reprinted with permission. 9.24 Reprinted from *Cognitive Psychology*, Johnson & Newport, Vol. 21, "Critical period effects in second language learning", pp 60–99, copyright © 1989, with permission of Elsevier Science. 9.25 Elissa L. Newport, "Maturational constraints on language learning" from *Cognitive Science*. Reprinted with the permission of the author.

Chapter 10: 10.1 Conel, J.L., *The Postnatal Development of the Human Cortex*, vols. 1, 3, 5. Cambridge, MA: Harvard University Press, 1939, 1947, 1955. 10.2 Tanner, J.M. "Physical growth" from *Carmichael's Manual of Child Psychology* 3/e. Reprinted by permission of John Wiley & Sons, Inc. 10.3 Photograph courtesy of M. M. Grumbach. 10.6 Geri Enberg Photography. 10.7 Geri Enberg Photography. 10.8 Geri Enberg Photography. 10.10 Kellman,

Philip, "Perception of partially occluded objects in infancy" from *Cognitive Psychology*. Copyright © 1983 Reprinted by permission of author, Philip Kellman. 10.11 Adapted from Baillargeon, R., Object permanence in 3½- and 4½-month-old infants, *Developmental Psychology* 23 (1987): 655–64. 10.13 Courtesy Adele Diamond. 10.15 Johnson & Morton "Rudimentary face recognition in newborns" from *Biology of Cognitive Development: The Case of Face Recognition*. Reprinted by permission of publisher, Blackwell Publishers. 10.16 From A.N. Meltzoff & M.K. Moore, "Imitation of facial and manual gestures by human neonates." Science, 1977, 198, 75–78. 10.18 Linda B. Smith, Department of Psychology, Program in Cognitive Sciences, Indiana University, Bloomington.

Chapter 11: 11.1 Photograph by Martin Rogers/Stock Boston. 11.2 Robert Marvin. Estate of Mary Ainsworth. 11.3 Nina Leen/Time Pix/Getty Images. 11.5 Courtesy Harry Harlow, University of Wisconsin Primate Laboratory. 11.8 Kohlberg, L., Development of children's orientation towards a moral order in sequence in the development of moral thought, *Vita Humana* 6 (1963): 11–36. 11.9 © Reuters Newsmedia Inc./Corbis. 11.10(left) Courtesy Dan Reisberg; 11.10(middle) © Bill Gillette/Stock Boston; 11.10(right) Stone/Getty Images. 11.11(left) © Spencer Grant/The Picture Cube; 11.11(middle) Ole Graf/zeta/Corbis; 11.11(right) Erik Freeland/Corbis.

Chapter 12: 12.7 Paul Ekman, "Attempts to porta emotion by New Guinea tribesman" from *Unmasking the Face*. Copyright 1980. Reprinted with the permission of the author, Paul Ekman.

Chapter 13: 13.1 Asch, S. E., Studies of independence and conformity: A minority of one against a unanimous majority, *Psychological Monographs* 70 (9, Whole No. 416), 1956. 13.2 © by Stanley Milgram. From the film *Obedience*, distributed by Penn State Audio-Visual Services. 13.3 © by Stanley Milgram. From the film *Obedience*, distributed by Penn State Audio-Visual Services. 13.5 Latané, B., & Rodin, J. (1969). A lady in distress: Inhibiting effects of friends and strangers on bystander intervention. *Journal of Experimental Social Psychology*, 5, 189–202. 13.6 David Turnley/Corbis Sygma. 13.7 Leonardo da Vinci. *La Jaconde (Mona Lisa)*, Louvre, Paris; photograph courtesy of Service Photographique de la Réunion des Musées Nationaux.

Chapter 14: 14.6 *Wechsler Adult Intelligence Scale®*. Copyright © 1997 by Harcourt Assessment, Inc. Reproduced with permission. All rights reserved. 14.7 Lewis, H.K. "A sample item from the Progressive Matrices Test" from *Standard Progressive Matrices*. Copyright © J. C. Raven Ltd. 14.9 Dunne, Tom, Figure 8: Emotional Intelligence Test in "Feeling Smart" from *American Scientist*, volume 93, p. 336. Reprinted by permission of Tom Dunne. 14.10 Selfe, S. Nadia: *A Case of Extraordinary Drawing Ability in an Autistic Child*. New York: Academic Press, 1977. Reproduced by permission of Academic Press and Lorna Selfe. 14.11 Courtesy Photofest.

Chapter 15: 15.3 Lewis J. Merrim/Photo Researchers, Inc. 15.4 Photograph by Mimi Forsyth/Monkmeyer; 15.6 *Motivation and Personality* by Maslow © Reprinted by permission of Pearson Education, Inc. Upper Saddle River, NJ.

Chapter 16: 16.1 Negative #31568. Courtesy Department of Library Services, The American Museum of Natural History. 6.2 William Hogarth, *The Madhouse*, 1735/1763/. Photo: Bettmann/Corbis. 16.3 © Stock Montage, Inc. 16.4 Lanyon, R. I., & Goldstein, L. D. (1971). *Personality assessment*. New York: Wiley. 16.5 Photograph by Bill Bridges/Globe Photos. 16.6 Data from Faris, R. E. L., and Dunham, H. W., *Mental Disorders in Urban Areas*. Chicago: University of Chicago Press, 1939.

Chapter 17: 17.1(A) Courtesy Historical Pictures Service. 17.1(B) Courtesy National Library of Medicine. 17.1(C) Culver Pictures. 17.4 Will McIntyre/Photo Researchers, Inc.

TABLES

Table 4.1 From *Fundamentals of Psychology*, by F. A. Geldard, 1962, New York: Wiley. Table 4.4 From *The Human Senses*, by F. A. Geldard, 1972, New York: Wiley. Table 11.1 Adapted from Kohlberg, L., Classification of moral judgment into levels and stages of development, in Sizer, Theodore R., *Religion and Public Education*, pp. 171–73. 1967. Houghton Mifflin Company. Table 11.2 Erikson, E. H., *Childhood and Society*. New York: W. W. Norton & Company, Inc., 1963. Table 14.4 Wechsler, D., *The Measurement and Appraisal of Adult*

Intelligence, 4th ed. Baltimore, Md.: The Williams & Wilkins Co., 1958. Table adapted from the Manual for the Wechsler Adult Intelligence Scale.

Unnumbered Photos and Art

2 Musée Picasso, Paris, France. Photo: Réunion des Musées Nationaux/Art Resource, NY. 5(top) Flying Colours Ltd/ Royalty-Free/Getty Images. 7(top) Reuters/Corbis; 7(bottom) Photograph by Jane Carter. 8(top) Courtesy Neal E. Miller, Rockefeller University; 8(bottom left) Courtesy Museo del Prado; 8(bottom right) AFP/Getty Images. 10(left) Photofusion Picture Library/Alamy; 10(right) Wood (RSR)/Rex USA. 12 Rosenstein, D., & Oster H. (1988). *Differential facial responses to four basic tastes in newborns*. Child Development, 59, 1555–1568. 14(bottom) Courtesy of Sidney Harris, ScienceCartoonsPlus.com. 15(top) © 2002 The New Yorker Collection from cartoonbank.com. All rights reserved; 15(bottom) Courtesy of American Media, Inc. 16: Courtesy of Clarence Brown. 18 Juergen Hasenkopf/ Alamy. 19(top) Corbis; 19(bottom) Courtesy of John Chase http://members.aol.com/ chasetoons. 22 David R Frazier Photolibrary, Inc./Alamy. 23 Paramount Classics/Photofest © Paramount Classics. 25(top) Dimitri Lindt; TempSport/Corbis. 27 Archives Jean Piaget/Université De Genève. 29(top) Bettmann/Corbis; 29(bottom) Bill Luster/Corbis. 36 David C./Corbis. 38 Oeffentliche Kunstsammlung, Basel, Switzerland. Photo: Art Resource, NY. 41(top) Daniel J. Cox/Corbis; 41(bottom) The National Portrait Gallery, London. 42 Grant, Peter R., *Darwin's Finches, Ecology and evolution of Darwin's finches*. Copyright © 1986 by Princeton University Press. Reprinted by permission of Princeton University Press. 43 Leonard Lessin/Photo Researchers, Inc. 44 Bettmann/Corbis. 46 Donna Day/ Getty Images. 50 Peter Brueghel the Elder, *The Peasants' Wedding*, 1568, Kunsthistorisches Museum. Photograph © Erich Lessing/Art Resource, NY. 51(bottom) AP/Rockefeller University. 58 William Manning/Corbis. 59 Left Lane Productions/Corbis. 61(top) Mike Cassese/Reuters/Corbis; 61(bottom) Jérome Sesini/In Visu/Corbis. 62 Warner Bros./Photofest. 68 From G. Rhodes, A. Sumich, and G. Byatt. *Are Average Facial Configurations Attractive Only Because of Their Symmetry?* Psychological Science. Vol 10, No. 1, January 1999. 69 Grant Wood, *American Gothic*, 1920, oil on beaver board, 76 x 63.3 cm. Art Institute of Chicago, Friends of American Art Collection; photograph © 1990, The Art Institute of Chicago. All Rights Reserved. 71(bottom) Phil McCarten/Reuters/Corbis. 73 David Appleby/ Paramount Pictures/Bureau L.A. Collections/Corbis. 74 Sony Pictures/ZUMA/Corbis. 78 Albright-Knox Art Gallery/Corbis. 80(top) Courtesy National Library of Medicine. 84(bottom) AJ Photo/Hop Americain/Science Photo Library/Photo Researchers, Inc. 93(top) Courtesy The Natural History Museum, London. 101(A) SPL/Photo Researchers, Inc.; 101(B) CNRI/SPL/Photo Researchers, Inc.; 101(C) Guigoz/Dr. A. Privat/Petit Format/Science Source/Photo Researchers, Inc. 107(top) Courtesy National Library of Medicine. 113 Copyright Dennis Kunkel Microscopy, Inc. 118 Private Collection. © 2003 C. Herscovici, Brussels/Artists Rights Society (ARS), New York. Photo: Giraudon/Art Resource, NY. 120(top) Courtesy National Portrait Gallery, London; 120(bottom) Detail from *The Bermuda Group* by John Smibert. Courtesy Yale University Art Gallery, gift of Isaac Lothrop of Plymouth, Massachusetts. 122 Culver Pictures, Inc., New York. 126 Jim Pickerell/cgstock. 134 Courtesy National Library of Medicine. 147(bottom) Photographs courtesy of Department of Psychology, University of Pennsylvania. 154 From Al Seckel, *The Great Book of Optical Illusion* (Firefly Books, 2002). Reprinted with permission. 156 Claude Monet, *Terrace at Sainte-Adresse*, oil on canvas, $38^5/_8 \times 51^1/_8$", reproduced by permission of The Metropolitan Museum of Art, New York, purchased with special contributions and purchase funds given or bequeathed by friends of the Museum, 1967.210. 157(bottom) Index Stock/Alamy. 159(top) Alexander Walter/Stone/Getty Images. 162(bottom) © Globus Studios/The Stock Market. 164 Photograph by Paul Haller. 171(top) Courtesy E. J. Gibson. 184 From Tarbus et al. *Eye-movements and Vision*. Copyright © 1967, Plenum Publishing Corp. Reprinted with the permission of the publisher. 187 Courtesy of Daniel Simons. 188 Anton Vengo/SuperStock. 192 Mary-Anne Martin/Fine Arts. 194 Kunsthistorisches Museum, Vienna. Photo: Erich Lessing/Art Resource, NY. 199(top) Bettmann/Corbis. 209 David Hills/Alamy. 212(top) Nina Leen/Time Pix/Getty Images. 215 Philip Brittan/Alamy. 217(top) Brownie Harris/Corbis; 217(bottom right) Royalty-Free/Corbis; 217(bottom left) Marc Romanelli/Getty Images. 219 Courtesy Psychology Department, University of California, Berkeley. 224 Hamburger Kunsthalle, Hamburg, Germany. Photo: Bildarchiv Preussischer Kulturbesitz/Art Resource, NY. 225 W. Perry Conway/Corbis. 226 LWA-Dann Tardif/Corbis. 232 Jacob Lawrence. *The Libraries are Appreciated*, 1943. © Gwendolyn Knight Lawrence. Photo: Philadelphia Museum of Art/Corbis. 234 Geri Enberg Photography. 238 Richard Lewisohn/Royalty-Free/Getty Images. 239 David Butow/Corbis. 242 © Sidney Harris. 243 Tate Gallery, London, Great

Britain. Photo: Tate Gallery, London/Art Resource, NY. 245 David Leeson/Dallas Morning News/Corbis Sygma. 248 Cartoon by Abner Dean. 251(left) Tom Stewart/Corbis; 251(right) Amos Nachoum/Corbis. 252 John Marshall Mantel/AP Photos. 263(top) AP Photos; 263(bottom) Chris Collins/Corbis. 270 *Chess Player #2* by Jodi Bonassi. Reproduced with permission of the artist. 272 *Saint Jerome* by Guido Reni. Photo: Alinari/Art Resource, NY. 273(left) Photograph by Lee Miller, Lee Miller Archives, Chiddingly, England; 273(right) Giraudon/Art Resource, NY. 289 John Caldwell. 291(top) © 1998 Sidney Harris. 293 Illustration by Henry Gleitman. 297 Kobal Collection/20th Century Fox. 312 Jim Frazier/Getty Images. 314(top) William Blake, *Adam Naming the Beasts*; Stirling Maxwell Collection, Pollok House, Glasgow Museums & Art Galleries. 315(bottom) Photographs George Keoki Stender/CoralReefNetwork.com. 317(top) Courtesy Leigh Rubin, Creators Syndicate, Inc. © Leigh Rubin. 320 Reproduced from Lewis Carroll's *Alice in Wonderland*, original illustrations by John Tenniel; in color for this edition by Martina Selvay, Secaucus, N.J.: Castle Books. 321(bottom left to right) Photographs by Tim Wright, Wolfgang Kaehler, Kevin Schafer/Corbis, Mark Jones/Minden Pictures. 322(bottom) © The New Yorker Collection 1977 Kaufman from Cartoonbank.com. All rights reserved. 323(right) Rune Hellestad/Corbis; 323(left) Alfeo Dixon/ZUMA/Corbis. 324 Reproduced from Lewis Carroll's *Alice in Wonderland*, original drawings by John Tenniel; in color for this edition by Martina Selway, Secaucus, N.J.: Castle Books. 325(top) Reproduced from Lewis Carroll's *Alice in Wonderland*, original drawings by John Tenniel; in color for this edition by Martina Selway. Secaucus, N.J.: Castle Books. 330 Jose Luis Pelaez Inc./Getty Images; Getty Images. 331 Jack Liu. 342(top) Courtesy Ann Senghas, 2004. 346 Anna Clopet/Corbis. 347 Lewis Carroll, *Through the Looking Glass*, illustration by John Tenniel, courtesy of General Research Division, The New York Public Library, Astor, Lenox, and Tilden Foundations. 350(bottom) Courtesy Lila Gleitman. 354 Illustration Works/Getty Images. 356 Kirsten Soderlind/Corbis. 358 From *Biological Science*, Sixth edition by James Gould and William T. Keeton. W.W. Norton & Company, Inc. 360(top) Photograph by Kenneth Garrett 1984/Woodfin Camp; 360(bottom) R. M., Poulos, R.W., and Strauss, G. D., *Developmental Psychology*, Fig. III-10, p. 81. Englewood Cliffs, N.J.: Prentice-Hall, Inc., 1974. Originally adapted from H.M. Halverston, printed by The Journal Press, 1931. 362 © The New Yorker Collection 1989 Shanahan from TheCartoonbank.com. All rights reserved. 363 Detail from Michelangelo's *Creation of Eve*, Sistine Chapel; courtesy Scala/Art Resource, NY. 364 Photograph by Yves Debraine/Black Star. 365(bottom) Photograph by Steve Skloot/Photo Researchers, Inc. 375(top) Courtesy Antoine Le Metayer; 375(bottom) Courtesy Antoine Le Metayer. 379 Meg Takamura/Getty Images. 382 Peter Johnson/Corbis. 383 Anders Ryman/Corbis. 384(top) Chev Wilkinson/Getty Images; 384(bottom) From: *Parallel Paths to Constructivism: Jean Piaget and Lev Vygotsky*, by Susan Pass. Courtesy Information Age Publishing, Inc. 385 Sven Hagolani/zefa/Corbis. 386 Don Mason/Corbis. 387 Benainous, © Gamma. 390 Tom Stewart Photography/Corbis. 396 Deidre Scherer, *GIFTS*, 1996. From the collection of St. Mary's Foundation, Rochester, NY. © Deidre Scherer. Reproduced with permission of the artist. 398 Royalty-free/Corbis. 399(top) Royalty-free/Corbis; 399(bottom) Mel Yates/Getty Images. 401(top) Photograph by J. Blyenberg/Leo de Wys. 402(top) Larry Williams/Corbis; 402(bottom) Robert Marvin. Esate of Mary Ainsworth. 405 Photograph courtesy of Photo Researchers, Inc. 406 Photograph © 1993 Stephen Shames/Matrix. 408 Gideon Mendel/Corbis. 409 © Spencer Grant/Stock Boston. 410(top) Peter Johnson/Corbis; 410(bottom) © The New Yorker Collection © 1971 Frascino from Cartoonbank.com. All rights reserved. 412 Ed Bock/Corbis. 415(top) Pat Doyle/Corbis; 415(bottom) Paul Barton/Corbis. 416(bottom) The Everett Collection. 420(top) © 2001 Blaine Harrington; 420(bottom) Photograph by Janet Kelly/Reading Eagle-Times, © Reading Eagle Company. 422(top) Kevin Fleming/Corbis; 422(bottom) Royalty-Free/Corbis. 426(bottom) Frederic Larson/San Francisco Chronicle/Corbis. 427(top) Mural from the Tomb of the Diver (c. 480 B.C.–470 B.C.), courtesy National Archaeological Museum, Paestrum, Italy; 427(bottom) Frederic Larson/San Francisco Chronicle/Corbis. 429 © Oliver Pierce/Black Star. 430(top) Edward Munch, *Puberty*, 1894–95; © The Munch Museum/The Munch-Ellingsen Group/ARS 1994. 431(top) Mark Gamba/Corbis. 433 Ronnie Kaufman/Corbis. 436 Graham Dean/Corbis. 438 (top) © The New Yorker Collection 1975 Chas. Addams from Cartoonbank.com. All rights reserved; 438(bottom) Stockbyte Platinum/Alamy. 439(top left) Titan Sports/Corbis; 439(top right) AFP/Getty Images; 439(bottom) Owaki-Kulla/Corbis. 440 Robert Garvey/Corbis. 441 Everett Collection. 445(top) Walter Hodges/Corbis; 445(bottom) Larry Williams/Corbis. 446(top) Jose Luis Pelaez, Inc./Corbis; 446(bottom) Archives of the History of American Psychology, University of Akron; The Carolyn and Muzafer Sherif Papers. 447 Walker Art Gallery, National Museums, Liverpool. Photo: Bridgeman Art Library. 448 © Mike Twohy, 2007. Cartoonbank.com. All rights reserved. 451 Ariel Skelley/Corbis. 452(top) Wally McNamee/Corbis; 452(bottom) Photograph © Mark

Name Index

Page numbers in *italics* refer to illustrations.

SUBJECT INDEX

Page numbers in *italics* refer to illustrations, tables and charts.

Freud, Sigmund, *580*, 632, 652–53
  on adolescence, 571–73, 592
  analytic couch of, 576–77, *576*
  Anna Freud and, 577–78, *578*
  case studies of, 27
  on dreams, 573–74, 577, 592
  on hysteria, 599
  on mythology, 574, *574*
  psychoanalysis and, 567–81, *567*, 592, 643–44, *646*
  psychopathology of everyday life and, 573
  on slips of the tongue, 573, *573*, 577
  on stages of psychosexual development, 571–73, 576, 592
  on the unconscious, 304
Freudian slips, 573, *573*, 577
friendships, 412–14, 435
Fromm, Erich, 578
frontal lobe, 92, 96, 611, 612, 625
functional MRI (fMRI), *4*, 84, *85*
function morphemes, 316–17, 326, 352
fundamental attribution error, 440–42, *441*, 475
fusiform face area (FFA), 306, *306*

g (general intelligence), 528–30, *529*, 533, 549
GABA (gamma-amino butyric acid), 109, 624, 640
Gage, Phineas, 27, 82, *82*, 86, 96, 302
Galapagos Islands, 41, *42*
Galileo Galilei, 80, 81
Galton, Francis, 497, 520–22
gamma-amino butyric acid (GABA), 109, 640
gamma-band oscillation, 183
ganglia, 97–98, 138, *139*, 180
ganglion cells, 180
  see also magno cells; parvo cells
gangs, 61, *61*
garden path, 326–27, 352
Gardner, Howard, on multiple intelligences, 536–37, 549
Gates, Bill, 490, *490*
gender:
  autism and, 629
  culture and, 421, 435
  depression and, 600, 619
  development of, 421–26, 435
  emotions and, 469
  genetic determination of, 43, *43*, 360, *361*
  moral reasoning and, 417–18, 435
  personality and, 566
  physical development and, 362, 393
  suicide and, 615
  see also sex, sexuality
gender constancy, 425
gender identity, 421, 425–26, 435
gender roles, 421–23, *422*, 435
  ability differences in, 423–25, 435
  aggression and, 58–59, *59*
  intellectual aptitude and, 423–25, 435
  sex differences in, 422–23
Gene (patient), 259
gene-environment interactions, 360–63
general intelligence (g), 528–30, *529*, 533, 549
generalization gradient, 202, *202*, 209, 213
generalized anxiety disorder, 623–24, 640
general paresis, 598, 637
generic knowledge and memory, 253–54, 258–59, 268
generic memory, 258–59, 268, 278
genes, genetics, 43–44
  attention deficit/hyperactivity disorder (ADHA) and, 629

cognitive capacities and, 361, *361*, 393
creation of nervous system and, 98–99
depression and, 600
dominant vs. recessive, 43–44
environment vs., 360–63, 539–42, 545–48, 561–62, 564–66
gender determination and, 43, *43*, 360, *361*
human genome, 43
intelligence and, 539–42, *541*, 545–48, 550
International Human Genome Sequencing Consortium, and, 43
IQ and, 540–42
learn capacity and, 542
mental disorders and, 608, *608*, 616, 619, 624, 633
personality traits and, 560–61
sexual orientation and, 427–28
"thrifty gene" hypothesis, 54–55
genetic predisposition:
  for anorexia, 11
  for homosexuality, 427–28
  for obesity, 54
genetic sex, 421
genetic survival, 44–45, 72
genetic transmission, 43–44, 360, 393
geniculate nucleus, 138
Genie, 340
genital stage, 571, 592
genitalia:
  ambiguous, 423, 425
genome, human, 43
genotype, 44, 76, 539–40
Genovese, Kitty, 498, *498*
geons, 179, *179*, 190
Gestalt psychology, 166
gestalt therapy, 645–46
gestural language, 340–42, *340*, *341*
ghost sickness, Native American, 605
Gibson, James J., 171–72, *171*
Gilligan, Carol, on moral reasoning, 417–18
glial cells, 102, *102*, 105, 114, 117
glove anesthesia, 567, *567*
glucoreceptors, 51, *52*, 76
glucose, 7, 50–51, *51*
glutamates, 637
  schizophrenia and transmission dysfunction of, 611, 632
glycogen, 7, 50–51, *51*
goal neglect, 302, 309
goal state, in problem solving, 281, 309
gonads, 362
good continuation, 168, *168*
Good Samaritan, 500
Good Samaritan, The (Bassano), 500
Government Bureau (Tooker), *645*
Graham, Martha, 288
grasp reflex, 359, *360*, 393
gratification, delay of, 589–90, *589*, 592
great-person theory, 489–90
ground:
  in form perception, 168–69, *168*, 190
group dynamics, 492–501, 512
  deindividuation, 494–96, 512
  mere presence effects and, 492–93, *492*, 512
group inhibition, *500*
group polarization, 496–97, 512
group therapy, 653–54, *654*, 667
groupthink, 497, *497*, 512
growth, developmental, 358–60, *359*, 393

guilt, 470–71
  cognitive dissonance from, 461
  survival, 625

habituation, 197–98, 229
habituation procedures, 368, 393
hair cells, as auditory receptors, 134, *134*
Haldol, 637
hallucinations, 606, 632
  depression and, 614
halo effect, 67
Hamlet (Shakespeare), 33, *615*
handicappers, IQ and, 534–35, *534*
Harlow, Harry, 399–400, 407
Hartmann, Heinz, 578
Harvard College, 579
Hawn, Goldie, 323
Head Start, 539
hearing (audition), 129–36
  frequency theory in, 134–35
  language in absence of, 340–41, *340*, *341*
  nervous system and, 136
  place theory in, 134
  sound as stimulus for, 129–36, *130*
  tonotopic map and, 136, *136*
  transduction in, 133–35
  Weber fraction for, *124*
hebephrenia, 607
Helmholtz, Hermann von, 134–35, *134*, 145–46, 162
  on unconscious inference, 173
helping, 497–501, *499*, *501*, 512
  costs of, 500
helplessness:
  hopelessness and depression and, 617–18, 633
  learned helplessness, 220–21, *221*, 230
  learned helplessness and depression and, 221, 633
  learned helplessness theory, 617, 633
Hering, Ewald, 147
heritability, intelligence and, 544, *544*
heritability ratio, 544, 550
heroin, 111
Herrnstein, R. J, 539
hertz, 132, *132*
Hertz, Heinrich, 132
heterosexuality, 426–27, 435
heuristics, 293–96, 309
hierarchical conception, of intelligence, 529–30, *529*, 549
hierarchy, relationship, 503
hierarchy of needs, 581–83, *582*
Higgins, E. Tory, 448
higher-order invariants, 171–72
hindbrain, 87–89, *87*, *88*, 116
hippocampus, 89, 114, *261*
Hitler, Adolf, 585
H.M., 27, 261–62, *261*, *262*
Hogarth, William, *598*
homelessness, 607, 638, *638*
homeostasis, 46–49, 55, 76
  internal, 208
Homer, 243
Homer Reciting his Poems (Thomas), *243*
homogamy, 507, 513
homosexuality, 426–28, *426*, *427*, 435
  origins of, 427–28, 435
Horemhab offering wine to Annubis, 189
hormones:
  aggression and, 59
  androgens, 362